Welcome to
EXPLORING CORPORATE STRATEGY

Strategy is a fascinating subject. It's about the overall direction of all kinds of organisations, from multinationals to entrepreneurial start-ups, from charities to government agencies, and many more. **Strategy raises the big questions** about these organisations – how they grow, how they innovate and how they change. As a manager of today or of tomorrow, **you will be involved** in influencing, implementing or communicating these strategies.

Our aim in writing *Exploring Corporate Strategy* is to give you a **comprehensive understanding** of the issues and techniques of strategy, and to **help you get a great final result** in your course. Here's how you might make the most of the text:

- Explore hot topics in **new chapters** on innovation and entrepreneurship, international strategy, and the practice of strategy to **put you at the cutting edge** of the field.

- Read the **key debates** and the different **strategy 'lenses'** to give you new perspectives and set you on your way to **better grades in your assignments and exams.**

- Follow up on the **recommended readings** at the end of each chapter. They're specially selected as accessible and valuable sources that will enhance your learning and **give you an extra edge** in your course work.

Also, look out for the Key Concepts and Audio Summary icons in the text, which direct you to the website at **www.pearsoned.co.uk/ecs*** where you can

- Check and reinforce your understanding of key concepts using **self-assessment questions, audio summaries** and **interactive exercises**, and

- Revise key terms using **electronic flashcards** and a **glossary** in 6 languages.

We want *Exploring Corporate Strategy* to give you what you need: a comprehensive view of the subject, an ambition to put that into practice, and – of course – success in your studies. We also hope you'll be just as intrigued by the key issues of strategy as we are!

So, read on and good luck!

Gerry Johnson
Kevan Scholes
Richard Whittington

* P.S. In order **to log in to the website**, you'll need to **register with the access code** included with all new copies of the book.

Gerry Johnson BA, PhD (left) is Professor of Strategic Management at Lancaster University Management School and a Senior Fellow of the UK Advanced Institute of Management (AIM) Research. He is the author of numerous books, has published papers in many of the foremost management research journals in the world and is a regular speaker at the major academic conferences throughout the world. He also serves on the editorial boards of the *Academy of Management Journal*, the *Strategic Management Journal* and the *Journal of Management Studies*. His research is into strategic management practice, processes of strategy development and strategic change in organisations. As a consultant he works with senior management teams on issues of strategy development and strategic change where he applies many of the concepts from *Exploring Corporate Strategy* to help them challenge, question and develop the strategies of their organisations.

Kevan Scholes MA, PhD, DMS, CIMgt, FRSA (centre) is Principal Partner of Scholes Associates – specialising in strategic management. He is also Visiting Professor of Strategic Management and formerly Director of the Sheffield Business School, UK. He has extensive experience of teaching strategy to both undergraduate and postgraduate students at several universities. In addition his corporate management development work includes organisations in manufacturing, many service sectors and a wide range of public service organisations. He has regular commitments outside the UK – including Ireland, Australia and New Zealand. He has also been an advisor on management development to a number of national bodies and is a Companion of The Chartered Management Institute.

Richard Whittington MA, MBA, PhD (right) is Professor of Strategic Management at the Saïd Business School and Millman Fellow at New College, University of Oxford. He is author or co-author of eight books and has published many journal articles. He is a senior editor of *Organization Studies* and serves on the editorial boards of *Organization Science*, the *Strategic Management Journal* and *Long Range Planning*, amongst others. He has had full or visiting positions at the Harvard Business School, HEC Paris, Imperial College London, the University of Toulouse and the University of Warwick. He is active in executive education and consulting, working with organisations from across Europe, the USA and Asia. His current research is focused on strategy practice and international management.

8TH EDITION

EXPLORING CORPORATE STRATEGY

TEXT & CASES

Gerry Johnson

Lancaster University Management School

Kevan Scholes

Sheffield Hallam University

Richard Whittington

Saïd Business School, University of Oxford

An imprint of **Pearson Education**

Harlow, England • London • New York • Boston • San Francisco • Toronto
Sydney • Tokyo • Singapore • Hong Kong • Seoul • Taipei • New Delhi
Cape Town • Madrid • Mexico City • Amsterdam • Munich • Paris • Milan

Pearson Education Limited
Edinburgh Gate
Harlow
Essex CM20 2JE
England

and Associated Companies throughout the world

Visit us on the World Wide Web at:
www.pearsoned.co.uk

Fifth edition published under the Prentice Hall imprint 1998
Sixth edition published under the Financial Times Prentice Hall imprint 2002
Seventh edition 2005
Eighth edition published 2008

ISBN: 978-0-273-71191-9 (text only)
ISBN: 978-0-273-71192-6 (text and cases)

British Library Cataloguing-in-Publication Data
A catalogue record for this book is available from the British Library

10 9 8 7 6 5 4 3
11 10 09

Typeset in 9.5/13pt Linoletter by 35
Printed and bound by Rotolito Lombarda, Italy

The publisher's policy is to use paper manufactured from sustainable forests.

Brief Contents

Visit the *Exploring Corporate Strategy, eighth edition* Companion Website at **www.pearsoned.co.uk/ecs**. Register to create your own personal account using the access code supplied with this book to find valuable **student** learning material including:

- **Key concepts: audio downloads, animations** and **quick tests** to reinforce your understanding
- **Chapter audio summaries** that you can download or listen to online
- **Self assessment questions** and a **personal gradebook** so you can test your learning and track your progress
- **Revision flashcards** to help you prepare for your exams
- A **multi-lingual online glossary** to explain key concepts
- Guidance on **how to analyse a case study**
- **Links** to relevant sites on the web so you can explore more about the organisations featured in the case examples and case studies

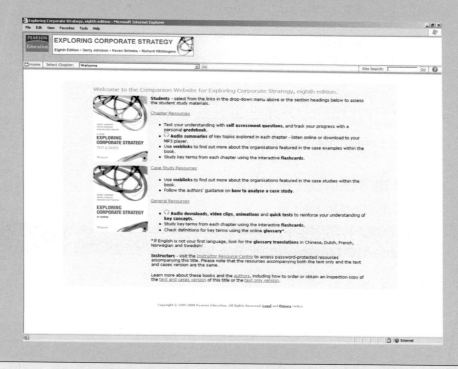

Detailed Contents

Part I THE STRATEGIC POSITION

Part III STRATEGY IN ACTION

CASE STUDIES

Supporting resources

Visit the *Exploring Corporate Strategy, eighth edition* Companion Website at **www.pearsoned.co.uk/ecs**.

Register to create your own personal account using the access code supplied with the copy of the book. Access the following teaching and learning resources:

Resources for students

- **Key concepts: audio downloads, animations** and **quick tests** to reinforce your understanding
- **Chapter audio summaries** that you can download or listen to online
- **Self assessment questions** and a **personal gradebook** so you can test your learning and track your progress
- **Revision flashcards** to help you prepare for your exams
- A **multi-lingual online glossary** to explain key concepts
- Guidance on **how to analyse a case study**
- **Links** to relevant sites on the web so you can explore more about the organisations featured in the case examples and case studies

Also: The student Companion Website with Grade Tracker provides the following features:

- Enables students to save their scores from self assessment questions, and lecturers to monitor the scores of their class
- Search tool to help locate specific items of content
- Online help and support to assist with website usage and troubleshooting

Resources for instructors

- **Instructor's manual**, including extensive teaching notes for cases and suggested teaching plans
- Media-rich downloadable **PowerPoint slides**, including animations, video clips and key exhibits from the book
- **Classic cases** – over 30 case studies from previous editions of the book
- Secure **testbank** containing over 600 questions

Also: the following instructor resources are available off-line:

- Instructor's manual in hard copy, with CD containing PowerPoint slides and classic cases
- Video resources on DVD

For more information please contact your local Pearson Education sales representative or visit **www.pearsoned.co.uk/ecs**

List of Illustrations

List of Exhibits

Preface

About *Exploring Corporate Strategy*

We are delighted to offer this eighth edition of *Exploring Corporate Strategy*. With sales of previous editions approaching 800,000, we know that we have many loyal readers. At the same time, the strategy field is constantly changing. For this edition, therefore, we have consulted our users to introduce several new features, while taking care to retain features that have been well-proven with many students and tutors from all over the world. Here we will highlight the key innovations of this edition, and then recap some of the classic features of the book.

The principal innovation of the eighth edition is to reorganise existing materials and introduce new materials to create four new chapters. These new chapters reflect advances in academic research, changes in practice and course developments in many universities around the world. These chapters are:

- **Chapter 5: Culture and Strategy**, incorporating a strong historical theme, with the growing appreciation of phenomena such as path-dependency and institutionalised patterns of behaviour

- **Chapter 8: International Strategy**, reflecting of course the growing internationalisation of business, but also the international ambitions of students in many universities

- **Chapter 9: Innovation and Entrepreneurship**, responding to the increasing pace of innovation in many industries and the growing interest amongst many students in establishing their own enterprises

- **Chapter 15: The Practice of Strategy**, emerging in part from a new research domain in which two of the authors are active, but also the need for students to have insight into the practical details of who gets involved in strategy, what they do and the methodologies they use.

While adding these chapters, we have been very aware of the need to offer students manageable amounts of reading. Accordingly we have slimmed down the text, so that students now have more, but shorter chapters than in previous editions. Overall, the eighth edition is shorter than the seventh.

A second significant development for this edition is the extension of the Strategy Lenses from three to four. We believe strongly that a strategy textbook should not encourage a narrow orthodoxy with regard to strategic issues. The Strategy Lenses are one of the ways in which we try to help students see strategy in different ways. As well as the analytically-orientated Design Lens, the gradualist style of the Experience Lens and the innovative Ideas Lens, we introduce a Discourse Lens. This Discourse Lens reflects both the growth of academic research on the role of language in strategy and the practical importance of mastering this language in the 'strategic conversation' of organisations. At the same time as adding this fourth lens, we have adopted a new format for the Lens-inspired 'commentaries' that follow each of the three Parts of the book. This format is designed to be concise and user-friendly.

As well as these innovations, the eighth edition builds on established strengths of the book which are outlined in the following section on to how to get the most from all the features and learning materials of *Exploring Corporate Strategy*.

We hope that you will benefit from and enjoy using this eighth edition of *Exploring Corporate Strategy*. We are always happy to receive your feedback; you can contact us at the email addresses given below.

Authors' Acknowledgements

Many people have helped us with the development of this new edition. In addition to the Advisory Board, acknowledged on the following page, many other adopters of the book provide more informal advice and suggestions - many of whom we have had the pleasure of meeting at our annual teachers' workshops. This kind of feedback is invaluable. Also, our students and clients at Sheffield, Strathclyde, Lancaster and Oxford and the many other places where we teach. They are a constant source of ideas and challenge and it would be impossible to write a book of this type without this direct feedback. Our own work and contacts have expanded considerably as a result of our book and we now all have important links across the world who have been a source of stimulation to us. Our contacts in Ireland, Holland, Denmark, Sweden, France, Canada, Australia, New Zealand, Singapore and the USA are especially valued.

We would like to thank those who have contributed directly to the book by providing case studies, and those organisations that have been brave enough to be written up as case studies. The growing popularity of *Exploring Corporate Strategy* has often presented these case study companies with practical problems in coping with direct enquiries from tutors and students. We hope that those using the book will respect the wishes of the case study companies and *not* contact them directly for further information. There are many colleagues that we need to thank for assisting us in improving our understanding of particular aspects of the subject or related area. Strategy is such a vast domain this assistance is essential if the book is to remain up-to-date. So thank you to, Julia Balogun, John Barbour, George Burt, Stéphane Girod, Mark Gilmartin, Royston Greenwood, Paula Jarzabkowski, Phyl Johnson, Aidan McQuade, Michael Mayer, Jill Shepherd, Angela Sutherland, Thomas Powell and Basak Yakis. Special thanks are due to all those who provided and helped develop illustrations and cases - their assistance is acknowledged at the foot of those illustrations - thank you to all these contributors. Thanks are also due to Christine Reid and Scott McGowan at Strathclyde for their valuable assistance with references. Our thanks are also due to those who have had a part in preparing the manuscript for the book, in particular, Lorna Carlaw at Strathclyde and Kate Goodman at Oxford.

Gerry Johnson (gerry.johnson@lancaster.ac.uk)
Kevan Scholes (KScholes@scholes.u-net.com)
Richard Whittington (richard.whittington@sbs.ox.ac.uk)

November 2007

Exploring Corporate Strategy Advisory Board

Special thanks are due to the following members of the Advisory Board for their valued, insightful and constructive comments, which have helped shape the contents of this eighth edition:

Anders Soderholm	Umea Universiteit
Antony Beckett	University Of West England
Bruce Millett	University of Southern Queensland
Erik Dirksen	Universiteit Van Amsterdam
Frederic Frery	ESCP-EAP, Paris
Ian McKeown	University of Wolverhampton
James Cunningham	National University of Ireland, Galway
Jamie Weatherston	University Of Northumbria
Jesper Norus	Copenhagen Business School (F)
Jill Shepherd	Simon Fraser University
John Toth	Leeds Metropolitan University
Keld Harbo	Aarhus School of Business
Mary Klemm	Bradford University
Mike Danilovic	Jonkoping Business School
Hans Roosendaal	University of Twente
Rehan Ul Haq	University Of Birmingham
Robert Morgan	Cardiff University
Ron Livingstone	Glasgow Caledonian University
Sarah Dixon	Kingston University
Tina McGuiness	Sheffield University

It is with sadness that we have learned of the death of Jesper Norus in the summer of 2006. We take this opportunity to express our sincere condolences to his family and friends, colleagues and students by whom he will be much missed.

Getting the Most from
Exploring Corporate Strategy

This eighth edition of *Exploring Corporate Strategy* builds on the established strengths of the book, proven over seven best-selling editions. A range of in-text features and supplementary resources have been developed to enable you and your students to gain maximum added value to the teaching and learning of strategy.

- **Outstanding pedagogical features**. Each chapter has clear learning outcomes, definitions of key concepts in the margins, practical questions associated with real-life Illustrations, and concise end-of-chapter case examples through which students can easily apply what they have learnt.

- **Flexibility of use**. You can choose to use either the Text & Cases version of the book, or – if you don't use longer cases (or have your own) – the Text only version. The provision of Key Debates, Commentaries and strategy 'Lenses' allow you to dig deeper into the tensions and complexity of strategy.

  The two versions (Text & Cases and Text only) will be complemented by a brand new concise version of the text, *Fundamentals of Strategy*, in December 2008.

- **Up-to-date materials**. As well as the new chapters, we have thoroughly revised the other chapters, updating the references so that you can easily access the latest research. We have also incorporated new theoretical perspectives, such as complexity theory, discourse theory and strategy-as-practice.

- **Encouraging critical thinking**. As well as the four Strategy Lenses, we encourage critical thinking by ending each chapter with a 'key debate', introducing students to research evidence and theory on key issues of the chapter and encouraging them to take a view.

  Our 'three circles' model - depicting the overlapping issues of strategic position, strategic choices and strategy-in-action - challenges a simple linear, sequential view of the strategy process.

- **Case and examples**. A wide range of Illustrations, Case Examples and (in the text and cases version) longer Case Studies are fresh and engage with student interests and day-to-day experience. The majority of these are entirely new to this edition; the remainder are fully revised. Finally, we draw these examples from all over the world, with no bias to North America, and use examples from the public and voluntary sectors as well as the private.

- **Attractive text layout and design**. We make careful use of colour and photography to improve clarity and ease of 'navigation' through the text. Reading the text should be an enjoyable and straight forward process.

- **Teaching and learning support**. You and your students can access a wealth of resources at www.pearsoned.co.uk/ecs, including the following:

For students

- audio material to explain Key Concepts
- self-assessment questions to measure progress and understanding
- flashcards, a multilingual glossary, and weblinks for revision and research

For instructors

- an Instructor's Manual which provides a comprehensive set of teaching support, including guidance on the use of case studies and assignments, and advice on how to plan a programme using the text
- Powerpoint slides
- a test-bank of assessment questions
- Classic Cases from previous editions of the book

In addition to the website, a printed copy of the Instructor's Manual is also available.

- **Video resources on DVD**. A DVD has been specially created for in-class use and contains briefings on selected topics from the authors, and material to support some of the case studies in the book:

  1. 'With the Experts' (the authors explain key concepts)
     Strategy in Different Contexts
     Porter's Five Forces
     Core Competences
     Strategic Drift and the Cultural Web
  2. Case Study organisations
     SAB Miller – international development
     eBay – success and sustainability
     Amazon.com – business level strategy
     Eurotunnel – a clash of national cultures
     Manchester United – football club or business?
     easyJet – competitive strategy
     Marks & Spencer – two CEOs on managing turnaround

  You can order and find out more about these resources from your local Pearson Education representative (**www.pearsoned.co.uk/replocator**).

- **Teachers' Workshop**. We run an annual workshop to facilitate discussion of key challenges and solutions in the teaching of strategic management. Details of forthcoming workshops can be found at **www.pearsoned.co.uk/ecsworkshop**.

- **Complementary textbooks**. Four further textbooks, written in collaboration with Gerry Johnson and Kevan Scholes, build on key themes of Exploring Corporate Strategy and examine these in more depth. These are all available from Pearson Education:

  Exploring Strategic Change (3rd edition, 2008); J. Balogun and V. Hope Hailey
  *Exploring Public Sector Strategy (*2001); G. Johnson and K. Scholes (editors)
  Exploring Techniques of Analysis and Evaluation in Strategic Management (1998); V. Ambrosini
  *Exploring Strategic Financial Management (*1998); T. Grundy

Guided Tour

→ Navigation and setting the scene

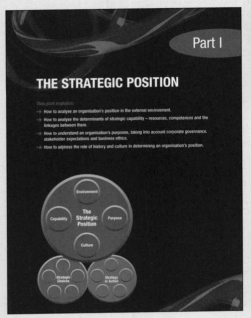

Learning outcomes enable you to check that you have understood all the major areas by the end of the chapter.

Part opening page identifies the chapters and topics covered within each part.

The **'three circles' navigational diagram** shows where you are in the three-part structure that underpins the book.

→ Strategy in context

Illustrations showcase the application of specific strategic issues in the real world so you can identify and relate theory and practice.

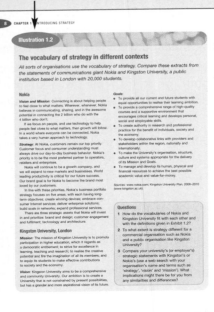

The **Case example** at the end of each chapter provides a broad view of the topic of the chapter in the context of a wide range of global organisations and in a variety of sectors.

→ Critical thinking and further study

Key debate – the final illustration in each chapter invites you to reflect on topical and contentious questions of strategy.

Work assignments are organised into two levels of difficulty, and provide interesting and stimulating questions to test your learning of key concepts and applications.

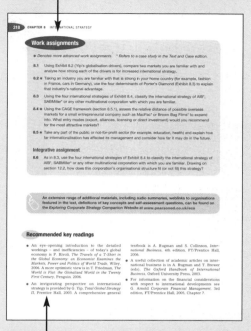

Recommended key readings direct you to other relevant sources so that you can read and research further into the key topics discussed in the chapter.

Commentaries appear at the end of each Part, presenting a view of strategy through four different 'lenses' to help you to see strategy in different ways and widen your perspectives.

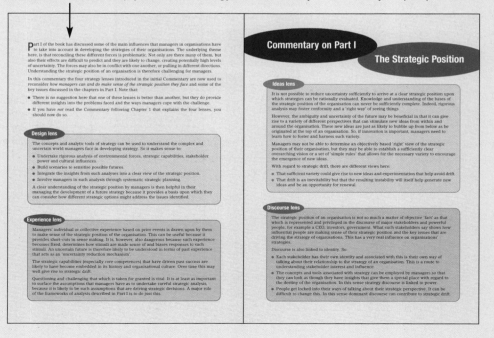

→ Checking your understanding

Key concept icons in the text direct you to audio and other resources on the companion website where you can check and reinforce your understanding of key concepts.

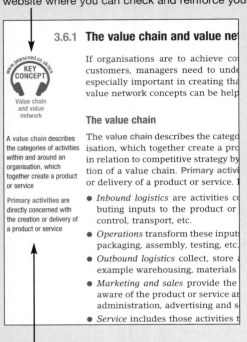

3.6.1 The value chain and value ne[twork]

If organisations are to achieve co[mpetitive advantage?] customers, managers need to und[erstand] especially important in creating tha[t] value network concepts can be help[ful]

The value chain

The value chain describes the catego[ries] isation, which together create a pr[oduct] in relation to competitive strategy by[...] tion of a value chain. **Primary activi[ties]** or delivery of a product or service. [...]

- *Inbound logistics* are activities c[on]buting inputs to the product or [...] control, transport, etc.
- *Operations* transform these input[s] packaging, assembly, testing, etc.
- *Outbound logistics* collect, store [...] example warehousing, materials [...]
- *Marketing and sales* provide the [...] aware of the product or service a[nd] administration, advertising and s[...]
- *Service* includes those activities t[...]

A value chain describes the categories of activities within and around an organisation, which together create a product or service

Primary activities are directly concerned with the creation or delivery of a product or service

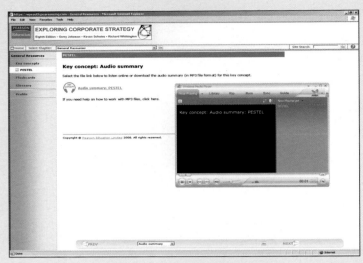

Key terms are highlighted in the text with a brief explanation in the margin when they first appear. These terms are also included in the **Glossary** at the end of the book and on the companion website where you can find them in six languages.

You can test your understanding of these key terms using **flashcards** on the website.

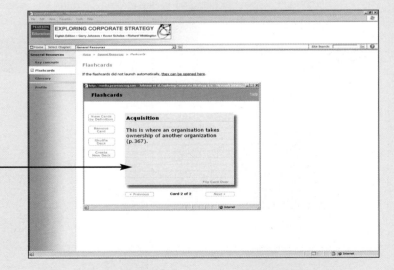

→ **Checking your understanding** (continued)

Use the **Self-assessment questions** on the companion website to test your knowledge.
Save your score in a personal gradebook and track your progress.

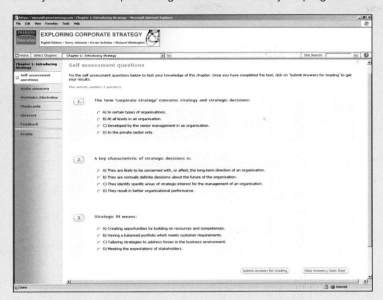

Chapter summaries recap and reinforce the key points to take away from the chapter.
Download or listen online to the **audio summaries** on the companion website.

Explore more on the companion website at **www.pearsoned.co.uk/ecs**

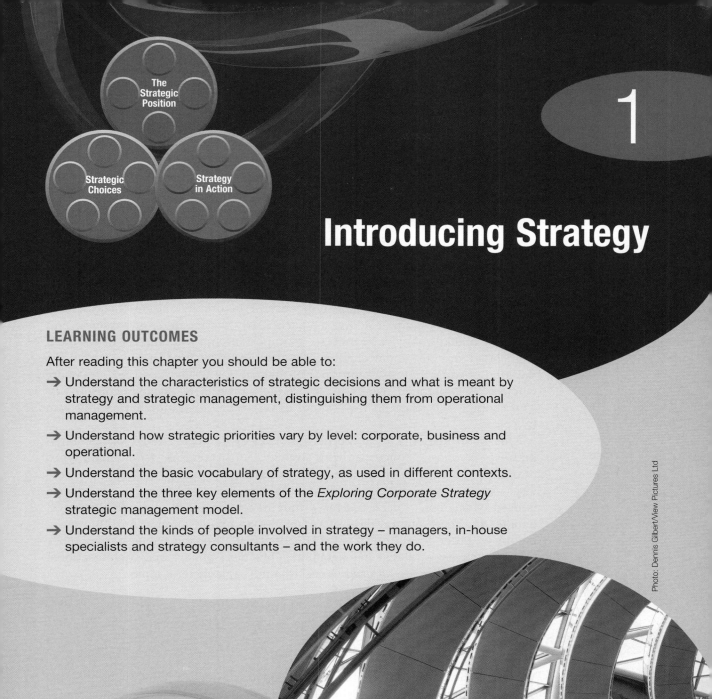

The Strategic Position

Strategic Choices

Strategy in Action

1

Introducing Strategy

LEARNING OUTCOMES

After reading this chapter you should be able to:

→ Understand the characteristics of strategic decisions and what is meant by strategy and strategic management, distinguishing them from operational management.

→ Understand how strategic priorities vary by level: corporate, business and operational.

→ Understand the basic vocabulary of strategy, as used in different contexts.

→ Understand the three key elements of the *Exploring Corporate Strategy* strategic management model.

→ Understand the kinds of people involved in strategy – managers, in-house specialists and strategy consultants – and the work they do.

Photo: Dennis Gilbert/View Pictures Ltd

1.1 INTRODUCTION

In November 2006 Yahoo! manager Brad Garlinghouse issued a memo that directly challenged the senior management of the Internet giant. Leaked to the media as 'The Peanut Butter Manifesto', his memo accused Yahoo!'s leadership of lacking strategic direction. Growth had slowed, Google had overtaken Yahoo! in terms of online advertising revenues, and the share price had fallen by nearly a third since the start of the year. According to Brad Garlinghouse, Yahoo! was spread too thin, like peanut butter. It was time for strategic change.

All organisations are faced with the challenges of strategic direction: some from a desire to grasp new opportunities, others to overcome significant problems, as at Yahoo!. This book deals with why changes in strategic direction take place in organisations, why they are important, how such decisions are taken, and the concepts that can be useful in understanding these issues. This introductory chapter addresses particularly the meaning of 'strategy' and 'strategic management', why they are so important and what distinguishes them from other organisational challenges, tasks and decisions. It also introduces the kind of work that different types of managers involved in strategy may do, whether as general managers, in-house specialists or as strategy consultants. The chapter will draw on the Yahoo! example in Illustration 1.1 to illustrate its points.

This book uses the term 'corporate' strategy for two main reasons. First, because the book is concerned with strategy and strategic decisions in all types of organisation – small and large, commercial enterprises as well as public services – and the word 'corporate' embraces them all. Second, because, as the term is used in this book (discussed more fully in section 1.2.2), 'corporate strategy' denotes the most general level of strategy in an organisation and in this sense embraces other levels of strategy. Readers will probably come across other terms, such as 'strategic management', 'business policy' and 'organisational strategy', but these are all used to describe the same general topic.

1.2 WHAT IS STRATEGY?

KEY CONCEPT

Strategy

Why were the issues facing Yahoo! described as 'strategic'?[1] What types of issues are strategic and what distinguishes them from operational issues in organisations?

1.2.1 The characteristics of strategic decisions

The words 'strategy' and 'strategic decisions' are typically associated with issues like these:

● *The long-term direction* of an organisation. Brad Garlinghouse explicitly recognised that strategic change in Yahoo! would require a 'marathon and not a sprint'. Strategy at Yahoo! involved long-term decisions about what sort of company it should be, and realising these decisions would take plenty of time.

- *The scope of an organisation's activities*. For example, should the organisation concentrate on one area of activity, or should it have many? Brad Garlinghouse believed that Yahoo! was spread too thinly over too many different activities.

- *Advantage* for the organisation over competition. The problem at Yahoo! was that it was losing its advantage to faster-growing companies such as Google. Advantage may be achieved in different ways and may also mean different things. For example, in the public sector, strategic advantage could be thought of as providing better value services than other providers, thus attracting support and funding from government.

- *Strategic fit with the business environment*. Organisations need appropriate *positioning* in their environment, for example in terms of the extent to which products or services meet clearly identified market needs. This might take the form of a small business trying to find a particular niche in a market, or a multinational corporation seeking to buy up businesses that have already found successful market positions. According to Brad Garlinghouse, Yahoo! was trying to succeed in too many environments.

- *The organisation's resources and competences*.[2] Following 'the resource-based view' of strategy, strategy is about exploiting the strategic capability of an organisation, in terms of its resources and competences, to provide competitive advantage and/or yield new opportunities. For example, an organisation might try to leverage resources such as technology skills or strong brands. Yahoo! claims a brand 'synonymous with the Internet', theoretically giving it clear advantage in that environment.

- *The values and expectations* of powerful actors in and around the organisation. These actors – individuals, groups or even other organisations – can drive fundamental issues such as whether an organisation is expansionist or more concerned with consolidation, or where the boundaries are drawn for the organisation's activities. At Yahoo!, the senior managers may have pursued growth in too many directions and been too reluctant to hold themselves accountable. But lower-level managers, ordinary employees, suppliers, customers and Internet users all have a stake in the future of Yahoo! too. The beliefs and values of these *stakeholders* will have a greater or lesser influence on the strategy development of an organisation, depending on the power of each. Certainly, Brad Garlinghouse was making a bold bid for influence over what seemed to be a failing strategy.

Overall, the most basic definition of strategy might be 'the long-term direction of an organisation'. However, the characteristics described above can provide the basis for a fuller definition:

Strategy is the margin note: Strategy is the *direction* and *scope* of an organisation over the *long term*, which achieves *advantage* in a changing *environment* through its configuration of *resources and competences* with the aim of fulfilling *stakeholder* expectations

Strategy is the *direction* and *scope* of an organisation over the *long term*, which achieves *advantage* in a changing *environment* through its configuration of *resources and competences* with the aim of fulfilling *stakeholder* expectations.

Exhibit 1.1 summarises these characteristics of strategic decisions and also highlights some of the implications:

- *Complexity* is a defining feature of strategy and strategic decisions and is especially so in organisations with wide geographical scope, such as multinational

Yahoo!'s peanut butter manifesto

Strategy can involve hard decisions about the scope of the business, its management and its organisation structure.

In November 2006, Brad Garlinghouse, MBA graduate and a Yahoo! senior vice president, wrote a memo to his top managers arguing that Yahoo!, the diversified Internet company, was spreading its resources too thinly, like peanut butter on a slice of bread. Edited extracts from the memo follow:

Three and half years ago, I enthusiastically joined Yahoo!. The magnitude of the opportunity was only matched by the magnitude of the assets. And an amazing team has been responsible for rebuilding Yahoo!. . . .

But all is not well. . . .

I imagine there's much discussion amongst the Company's senior-most leadership around the challenges we face. At the risk of being redundant, I wanted to share my take on our current situation and offer a recommended path forward, an attempt to be part of the solution rather than part of the problem.

RECOGNIZING OUR PROBLEMS

We lack a focused, cohesive vision for our company. We want to do everything and be everything – to everyone. We've known this for years, talk about it incessantly, but do nothing to fundamentally address it. We are scared to be left out. We are reactive instead of charting an unwavering course. We are separated into silos that far too frequently don't talk to each other. And when we do talk, it isn't to collaborate on a clearly focused strategy, but rather to argue and fight about ownership, strategies and tactics. . . .

I've heard our strategy described as spreading peanut butter across the myriad opportunities that continue to evolve in the online world. The result: a thin layer of investment spread across everything we do and thus we focus on nothing in particular.

I hate peanut butter. We all should.

We lack clarity of ownership and accountability. The most painful manifestation of this is the massive redundancy that exists throughout the organization. We now operate in an organizational structure – admittedly created with the best of intentions – that has become overly bureaucratic. For far too many employees, there is another person with dramatically similar and overlapping responsibilities. This slows us down and burdens the company with unnecessary costs.

There's a reason why a centerfielder and a left fielder have clear areas of ownership. Pursuing the same ball repeatedly results in either collisions or dropped balls. Knowing that someone else is pursuing the ball and hoping to avoid that collision – we have become timid in our pursuit. Again, the ball drops.

We lack decisiveness. Combine a lack of focus with unclear ownership, and the result is that decisions are either not made or are made when it is already too late. Without a clear and focused vision, and without complete clarity of ownership, we lack a macro perspective to guide our decisions and visibility into who should make those decisions. We are repeatedly stymied by challenging and hairy decisions. We are held hostage by our analysis paralysis.

We end up with competing (or redundant) initiatives and synergistic opportunities living in the different silos of our company. . . .

SOLVING OUR PROBLEMS

We have awesome assets. Nearly every media and communications company is painfully jealous of our

firms, or wide ranges of products or services. For example, Yahoo! faces the complexity both of a fast-moving market environment and poorly organised internal businesses.

- *Uncertainty* is inherent in strategy, because nobody can be sure about the future. For Yahoo!, the Internet environment is one of constant and unforeseeable innovation.

position. We have the largest audience, they are highly engaged and our brand is synonymous with the Internet.

If we get back up, embrace dramatic change, we will win.

I don't pretend there is only one path forward available to us. However, at a minimum, I want to be part of the solution and thus have outlined a plan here that I believe can work. It is my strong belief that we need to act very quickly or risk going further down a slippery slope. The plan here is not perfect; it is, however, FAR better than no action at all.

There are three pillars to my plan:

1 Focus the vision.
2 Restore accountability and clarity of ownership.
3 Execute a radical reorganization.

1 Focus the vision
a) We need to boldly and definitively declare what we are and what we are not.
b) We need to exit (sell?) non core businesses and eliminate duplicative projects and businesses.

My belief is that the smoothly spread peanut butter needs to turn into a deliberately sculpted strategy – that is narrowly focused. . . .

2 Restore accountability and clarity of ownership
a) Existing business owners must be held accountable for where we find ourselves today – heads must roll,
b) We must thoughtfully create senior roles that have holistic accountability for a particular line of business. . . .
c) We must redesign our performance and incentive systems.

I believe there are too many BU [Business Unit] leaders who have gotten away with unacceptable results and worse – unacceptable leadership. Too often they (we!) are the worst offenders of the problems outlined here. We must signal to both the employees and to our shareholders that we will hold these leaders (ourselves) accountable and implement change. . . .

3 Execute a radical reorganization
a) The current business unit structure must go away.
b) We must dramatically decentralize and eliminate as much of the matrix as possible.
c) We must reduce our headcount by 15–20%.

I emphatically believe we simply must eliminate the redundancies we have created and the first step in doing this is by restructuring our organization. We can be more efficient with fewer people and we can get more done, more quickly. We need to return more decision making to a new set of business units and their leadership. But we can't achieve this with baby step changes. We need to fundamentally rethink how we organize to win. . . .

I love Yahoo!. I'm proud to admit that I bleed purple and yellow. I'm proud to admit that I shaved a Y in the back of my head.

My motivation for this memo is the adamant belief that, as before, we have a tremendous opportunity ahead. I don't pretend that I have the only available answers, but we need to get the discussion going; change is needed and it is needed soon. We can be a stronger and faster company – a company with a clearer vision and clearer ownership and clearer accountability.

We may have fallen down, but the race is a marathon and not a sprint. I don't pretend that this will be easy. It will take courage, conviction, insight and tremendous commitment. I very much look forward to the challenge.

So let's get back up.

Catch the balls.

And stop eating peanut butter.

Source: Extracts from Brad Garlinghouse's memo to Yahoo! managers, November 2006. Reprinted in *Wall Street Journal*, 16 November 2006.

Questions

1 Why were the issues facing Yahoo! described as strategic? Refer to Exhibit 1.1.

2 Identify examples of issues that fit each of the circles of the model in Exhibit 1.3.

● *Operational decisions* are linked to strategy. For example, any attempt to co-ordinate Yahoo!'s business units more closely will have knock-on effects on web-page designs and links, career development and advertiser relationships. This link between overall strategy and operational aspects of the organisation is important for two other reasons. First, if the operational aspects of the organisation are not in line with the strategy, then, no matter how well

Exhibit 1.1 **Strategic decisions**

Strategic decisions are about:

- The **long-term** direction of an organisation
- The **scope** of an organisation's activities
- Gaining **advantage** over competitors
- Addressing changes in the **business environment**
- Building on resources and competences (**capability**)
- **Values and expectations** of stakeholders

Therefore they are likely to:

- Be **complex** in nature
- Be made in situations of **uncertainty**
- Affect **operational** decisions
- Require an **integrated** approach (both inside and outside an organisation)
- Involve considerable **change**

considered the strategy is, it will not succeed. Second, it is at the operational level that real strategic advantage can be achieved. Indeed, competence in particular operational activities might determine which strategic developments might make most sense.

- *Integration* is required for effective strategy. Managers have to cross functional and operational boundaries to deal with strategic problems and come to agreements with other managers who, inevitably, have different interests and perhaps different priorities. Yahoo! for example needs an integrated approach to powerful advertisers such as Sony and Vodafone from across all its businesses.

- *Relationships and networks* outside the organisation are important in strategy, for example with suppliers, distributors and customers. For Yahoo!, advertisers and users are crucial sets of relationships.

- *Change* is typically a crucial component of strategy. Change is often difficult because of the heritage of resources and because of organisational culture. According to Brad Garlinghouse at least, Yahoo!'s barriers to change seem to include a top management that is afraid of taking hard decisions and a lack of clear accountability amongst lower-level management.

1.2.2 Levels of strategy

Strategies exist at a number of levels in an organisation. Taking Yahoo! again as an example, it is possible to distinguish at least three different levels of strategy. The top level is **corporate-level strategy**, concerned with the overall scope of an organisation and how value will be added to the different parts (business units) of the organisation. This could include issues of geographical coverage, diversity of products/services or business units, and how resources are to be allocated between the different parts of the organisation. For Yahoo!, whether to sell some of its existing businesses is clearly a crucial corporate-level decision. In general, corporate-level strategy is also likely to be concerned with the expectations of owners – the shareholders and the stock market. It may well take form in an explicit or implicit statement of 'mission' that reflects such expectations. Being clear about corporate-level strategy is important: determining the range of business to include is the *basis* of other strategic decisions.

> **Corporate-level strategy** is concerned with the overall purpose and scope of an organisation and how value will be added to the different parts (business units) of the organisation

The second level is **business-level strategy**, which is about how the various businesses included in the corporate strategy should compete in their particular markets (for this reason, business-level strategy is sometimes called 'competitive strategy'). In the public sector, the equivalent of business-level strategy is decisions about how units should provide best value services. This typically concerns issues such as pricing strategy, innovation or differentiation, for instance by better quality or a distinctive distribution channel. So, whereas corporate-level strategy involves decisions about the organisation as a whole, strategic decisions relate to particular strategic business units (SBUs) within the overall organisation. A **strategic business unit** is a part of an organisation for which there is a distinct external market for goods or services that is different from another SBU. Yahoo!'s strategic business units include businesses such as Yahoo! Photos and Yahoo! Music.

> **Business-level strategy** is about how to compete successfully in particular markets

> **A strategic business unit** is a part of an organisation for which there is a distinct external market for goods or services that is different from another SBU

Of course, in very simple organisations with only one business, the corporate strategy and the business-level strategy are nearly identical. None the less, even here, it is useful to distinguish a corporate-level strategy, because this provides the framework for whether and under what conditions other business opportunities might be added or rejected. Where the corporate strategy does include several businesses, there should be a clear link between strategies at an SBU level and the corporate level. In the case of Yahoo!, relationships with online advertisers stretch across different business units, and using, protecting and enhancing the Yahoo! brand is vital for all. The corporate strategy with regard to the brand should support the SBUs, but at the same time the SBUs have to make sure their business-level strategies do not damage the corporate whole or other SBUs in the group.

The third level of strategy is at the operating end of an organisation. Here there are **operational strategies**, which are concerned with how the component parts of an organisation deliver effectively the corporate- and business-level strategies in terms of resources, processes and people. For example, Yahoo! has web-page designers in each of its businesses, for whom there are appropriate operational strategies in terms of design, layout and renewal. Indeed, in most businesses, successful business strategies depend to a large extent on decisions that are taken, or activities that occur, at the operational level. The integration of operational decisions and strategy is therefore of great importance, as mentioned earlier.

> **Operational strategies** are concerned with how the component parts of an organisation deliver effectively the corporate- and business-level strategies in terms of resources, processes and people

Illustration 1.2

The vocabulary of strategy in different contexts

All sorts of organisations use the vocabulary of strategy. Compare these extracts from the statements of communications giant Nokia and Kingston University, a public institution based in London with 20,000 students.

Nokia

Vision and Mission: Connecting is about helping people to feel close to what matters. Wherever, whenever, Nokia believes in communicating, sharing, and in the awesome potential in connecting the 2 billion who do with the 4 billion who don't.

If we focus on people, and use technology to help people feel close to what matters, then growth will follow. In a world where everyone can be connected, Nokia takes a very human approach to technology.

Strategy: At Nokia, customers remain our top priority. Customer focus and consumer understanding must always drive our day-to-day business behavior. Nokia's priority is to be the most preferred partner to operators, retailers and enterprises.

Nokia will continue to be a growth company, and we will expand to new markets and businesses. World leading productivity is critical for our future success. Our brand goal is for Nokia to become the brand most loved by our customers.

In line with these priorities, Nokia's business portfolio strategy focuses on five areas, with each having long-term objectives: create winning devices; embrace consumer Internet services; deliver enterprise solutions; build scale in networks; expand professional services.

There are three strategic assets that Nokia will invest in and prioritize: brand and design; customer engagement and fulfilment; technology and architecture.

Kingston University, London

Mission: The mission of Kingston University is to promote participation in higher education, which it regards as a democratic entitlement; to strive for excellence in learning, teaching and research; to realise the creative potential and fire the imagination of all its members; and to equip its students to make effective contributions to society and the economy.

Vision: Kingston University aims to be a comprehensive and community University. Our ambition is to create a University that is not constrained by present possibilities, but has a grander and more aspirational vision of its future.

Goals:

- To provide all our current and future students with equal opportunities to realise their learning ambition.
- To provide a comprehensive range of high-quality courses and a supportive environment that encourages critical learning and develops personal, social and employable skills.
- To create authority in research and professional practice for the benefit of individuals, society and the economy.
- To develop collaborative links with providers and stakeholders within the region, nationally and internationally.
- To make the University's organisation, structure, culture and systems appropriate for the delivery of its Mission and Goals.
- To manage and develop its human, physical and financial resources to achieve the best possible academic value and value-for-money.

Sources: www.nokia.com; Kingston University Plan, 2006–2010 (www.kingston.ac.uk).

Questions

1 How do the vocabularies of Nokia and Kingston University fit with each other and with the definitions given in Exhibit 1.2?

2 To what extent is strategy different for a commercial organisation such as Nokia and a public organisation like Kingston University?

3 Compare your university's (or employer's) strategic statements with Kingston's or Nokia's (use a web search with your organisation's name and terms such as 'strategy', 'vision' and 'mission'). What implications might there be for you from any similarities and differences?

1.2.3 The vocabulary of strategy

Although a definition of strategy was given at the end of section 1.2.1, in practice you will encounter many different definitions from different authors. You will also find a variety of terms used in relation to strategy, so it is worth devoting a little space to clarifying some of these. Exhibit 1.2 and Illustration 1.2 employ some of the terms that you will come across in this and other books on strategy and in everyday business usage. Exhibit 1.2 explains these in relation to a personal strategy readers may have followed themselves – improving physical fitness.

Exhibit 1.2	The vocabulary of strategy	
Term	**Definition**	**A personal example**
Mission	Overriding purpose in line with the values or expectations of stakeholders	Be healthy and fit
Vision or strategic intent	Desired future state: the aspiration of the organisation	To run the London Marathon
Goal	General statement of aim or purpose	Lose weight and strengthen muscles
Objective	Quantification (if possible) or more precise statement of the goal	Lose 5 kilos by 1 September and run the marathon next year
Strategic capability	Resources, activities and processes. Some will be unique and provide 'competitive advantage'	Proximity to a fitness centre, a successful diet
Strategies	Long-term direction	Exercise regularly, compete in marathons locally, stick to appropriate diet
Business model	How product, service and information 'flow' between participating parties	Associate with a collaborative network (e.g. join running club)
Control	The monitoring of action steps to: <ul><li>assess effectiveness of strategies and actions</li><li>modify as necessary strategies and/or actions</li></ul>	Monitor weight, kilometres run and measure times: if progress satisfactory, do nothing; if not, consider other strategies and actions

Not all these terms are always used in organisations or in strategy books: indeed, in this book the word 'goal' is rarely used. It will also be seen, through the many examples in this book, that terminology is not used consistently across organisations (see also Illustration 1.2). Managers and students of strategy need to be aware of this. Moreover, it may or may not be that mission, goals, objectives, strategies and so on are written down precisely. In some organisations this is done very formally; in others a mission or strategy might be implicit and, therefore, must be deduced from what an organisation is doing. However, as a general guideline the following terms are often used:

- A *mission* is a general expression of the overall purpose of the organisation, which, ideally, is in line with the values and expectations of major stake-holders and concerned with the scope and boundaries of the organisation. It is sometimes referred to in terms of the apparently simple but challenging question: *'What business are we in?'*

- A *vision* or *strategic intent* is the desired future state of the organisation. It is an aspiration around which a strategist, perhaps a chief executive, might seek to focus the attention and energies of members of the organisation.

- If the word *goal* is used, it usually means a general aim in line with the mission. It may well be qualitative in nature.

- On the other hand, an *objective* is more likely to be quantified, or at least to be a more precise aim in line with the goal. In this book the word 'objective' is used whether or not there is quantification.

- *Strategic capability* is concerned with the *resources and competences* that an organisation can use to provide value to customers or clients. *Unique resources* and *core competences* are the bases upon which an organisation achieves strategic advantage and is distinguished from competitors.

- The concept of *strategy* has already been defined. It is the long-term direction of the organisation. It is likely to be expressed in broad statements both about the direction that the organisation should be taking and the types of action required to achieve objectives. For example, it may be stated in terms of market entry, new products or services, or ways of operating.

- A *business model* describes the structure of product, service and information flows and the roles of the participating parties. For example, a traditional model for manufactured products is a linear flow of product from component manufacturers to product manufacturers to distributor to retailers to consumers. But information may flow directly between the product manufacturer and the final consumer (advertising and market research).

- *Strategic control* involves monitoring the extent to which the strategy is achieving the objectives and suggesting corrective action (or a reconsideration of the objectives).

As the book develops, many other terms will be introduced and explained. These are the basics with which to begin.

Illustration 1.2 compares strategy vocabulary from two organisations operating in very different *contexts*. Nokia is a private sector communications giant, competing against global corporations such as Motorola and Samsung. Profit is vital to Nokia, but still it sees its vision and mission in terms of connecting more people around the world. Kingston University, on the other hand, is a public university, with a commitment to increasing participation in higher education. But it too must earn revenues, and needs to make a surplus in order to be able to invest in the future. Kingston University is also competing for students and research funds, going head to head with similar universities in the United Kingdom and around the world. Corporate-level and business-level strategies are no less important for a public body such as Kingston University as a commercial one like Nokia.

Strategy vocabulary, therefore, is relevant to a wide range of contexts. A small entrepreneurial start-up will need a strategy statement to persuade investors and lenders of its viability. Public sector organisations need strategy statements not only to know what to do, but also to reassure their funders and regulators that what they do is what they should be doing. Voluntary organisations need to communicate exciting strategies in order to inspire volunteers and donors. If they are to prosper within the larger organisation, SBU managers need to propose clear strategies that are consistent with the objectives of their corporate owners and with the needs of other SBUs within the corporate whole. Even privately held organisations need persuasive strategy statements to motivate their employees and to build long-term relationships with their key customers or suppliers. Strategy vocabulary, therefore, is used in many different contexts, for many different purposes. Strategy is part of the everyday language of work.

1.3 STRATEGIC MANAGEMENT

The term *strategic management* underlines the importance of managers with regard to strategy. Strategies do not happen just by themselves. Strategy involves people, especially the managers who decide and implement strategy. Thus this book uses strategic management to emphasise the human element of strategy.

The strategic management role is different in nature from other aspects of management. An operational manager is most often required to deal with problems of operational control, such as the efficient production of goods, the management of a salesforce, the monitoring of financial performance or the design of some new system that will improve the level of customer service. These are all very important tasks, but they are essentially concerned with effectively managing resources already deployed, often in a limited part of the organisation within the context of an existing strategy. Operational control is what managers are involved in for most of their time. It is vital to the success of strategy, but it is not the same as strategic management.

For managers, strategic management involves a greater scope than that of any one area of operational management. Strategic management is concerned with complexity arising out of ambiguous and non-routine situations with organisation-wide rather than operation-specific implications. This is a major challenge for managers who are used to managing on a day-to-day basis the resources they control. It can be a particular problem because of the background of managers who may typically have been trained, perhaps over many years, to undertake operational tasks and to take operational responsibility. Accountants find that they still tend to see problems in financial terms, IT managers in IT terms, marketing managers in marketing terms, and so on. Of course, each of these aspects is important, but none is adequate alone. The manager who aspires to manage or influence strategy needs to develop a capability to take an overview, to conceive of the whole rather than just the parts of the situation facing an organisation. This is often referred to as the 'helicopter view'.

Because strategic management is characterised by its complexity, it is also necessary to make decisions and judgements based on the *conceptualisation* of difficult issues. Yet the early training and experience of managers is often about taking action, or about detailed *planning* or *analysis*. This book explains many analytical approaches to strategy, and it is concerned too with action related to the management of strategy. However, the major emphasis is on the importance of understanding the *strategic concepts* which inform this analysis and action.

Strategic management can be thought of as having three main elements within it, and it is these that provide the framework for the book. **Strategic management** includes understanding *the strategic position* of an organisation, making *strategic choices* for the future and managing *strategy in action*. Exhibit 1.3 shows these elements and defines the broad coverage of this book. The next sections of this chapter discuss each of these three elements of strategic management and identify the main issues that make up each element. But first it is important to understand why the exhibit has been drawn in this particular way.

Exhibit 1.3 could have shown the three elements in a linear sequence – first understanding the strategic position, then strategic choices and finally turning

Strategic management includes understanding *the strategic position* of an organisation, *strategic choices* for the future and managing *strategy in action*

| Exhibit 1.3 | The *Exploring Corporate Strategy* model |

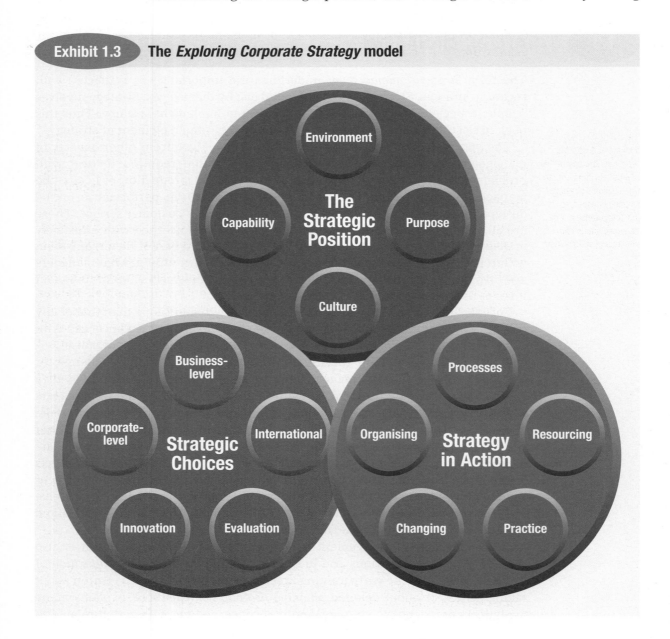

strategy into action. Indeed, many texts on the subject do just this. However, in practice, the elements of strategic management do not follow this linear sequence – they are interlinked and feed back on each other. For example, in some circumstances an understanding of the strategic position may best be built up from the experience of trying a strategy out in practice. Test marketing a prototype would be a good example. Here strategy in action informs understanding of the strategic position.

The interconnected circles of Exhibit 1.3 are designed to emphasise this non-linear nature of strategy. Position, choices and action should be seen as closely related, and in practice none has priority over another. It is only for structural convenience that the subject has been divided into sections in this book; the book's sequence is not meant to suggest that the process of strategic management must follow a neat and tidy path. Indeed, the evidence provided in Chapter 15 on how strategic management happens in practice suggests that it usually does not occur in tidy ways.

1.3.1 The strategic position

The **strategic position** is concerned with the impact on strategy of the external environment, an organisation's strategic capability (resources and competences) and the expectations and influence of stakeholders

www.pearsoned.co.uk/ecs

KEY CONCEPT

Strategic position

Understanding the **strategic position** is concerned with identifying the impact on strategy of the external environment, an organisation's strategic capability (resources and competences) and the expectations and influence of stakeholders. The sorts of questions this raises are central to future strategies and these issues are covered in the four chapters of Part I of this book:

● The *environment*. The organisation exists in the context of a complex political, economic, social, technological, environmental (i.e. green) and legal world. This environment changes and is more complex for some organisations than for others. How this affects the organisation could include an understanding of historical and environmental effects, as well as expected or potential changes in environmental variables. Many of those variables will give rise to *opportunities* and others will exert *threats* on the organisation – or both. A problem that has to be faced is that the range of variables is likely to be so great that it may not be possible or realistic to identify and understand each one. Therefore it is necessary to distil out of this complexity a view of the key environmental impacts on the organisation. Chapter 2 examines how this might be possible.

● The *strategic capability* of the organisation – made up of *resources and competences*. One way of thinking about the strategic capability of an organisation is to consider its *strengths* and *weaknesses* (for example, where it is at a competitive advantage or disadvantage). The aim is to form a view of the internal influences – and constraints – on strategic choices for the future. It is usually a combination of resources and high levels of competence in particular activities (in this book referred to as *core competences*) that provide advantages which competitors find difficult to imitate. Chapter 3 examines strategic capability in detail.

● Chapter 4 explores the major influences of *stakeholder expectations* on an organisation's *purposes*. Purpose is encapsulated in an organisation's *vision*, *mission* and *values*. Here the issue of *corporate governance* is important: who *should* the organisation primarily serve and how should managers be held responsible for this? This raises issues of *corporate social responsibility* and *ethics*. The chapter explores how both variations in international corporate governance systems and the *power* configurations within particular organisations can influence purpose.

● Chapter 5 examines how *cultural and historical influences* can also influence strategy. Cultural influences can be *organisational*, *sectoral* or *national*. Historical influences can create *lock-in* on particular strategic trajectories. The impact of these influences can be *strategic drift*, a failure to create necessary change. The chapter demonstrates how managers can analyse and challenge these historical and cultural influences on strategy.

These positioning issues were all important for Yahoo! as it faced its crisis in 2006. The external environment offered the threat of growing competition from Google. Its strong Internet brand and existing audience were key resources for defending its position. The company was struggling with its purposes, with top management apparently indecisive. The company none the less had inherited a strong culture, powerful enough to make Brad Garlinghouse shave a Y on his head and believe that his blood bled in the corporate colours of his employer.

1.3.2 Strategic choices

Strategic choices involve understanding the underlying bases for future strategy at both the business unit and corporate levels and the options for developing strategy in terms of both the directions and methods of development

Strategic choices involve the options for strategy in terms of both the directions in which strategy might move and the methods by which strategy might be pursued. For instance, an organisation might have to choose between alternative diversification moves, for example entering into new products and markets. As it diversifies, it has different methods available to it, for example developing a new product itself or acquiring an organisation already active in the area. Typical options and methods are covered in the five chapters that make up Part II of this book, as follows:

● There are strategic choices in terms of how the organisation seeks to compete at the *business level*. Typically these involve pricing and differentiation strategies, and decisions about how to compete or collaborate with competitors. These issues of business-level strategies will be discussed in Chapter 6.

● At the highest level in an organisation there are issues of *corporate-level strategy*, which are concerned with the scope, or breadth, of an organisation. These include *diversification* decisions about the portfolio of products and the spread of markets. For Yahoo!, being spread over too many businesses seems to be the major strategic problem. Corporate-level strategy is also concerned with the relationship between the separate parts of the business and how the corporate 'parent' adds value to these various parts. At Yahoo!, it is not clear how much the corporate parent is adding value to its constituent parts. These issues about the role of the centre and how it adds value are *parenting* issues and will be discussed in Chapter 7.

● *International strategy* is a form of diversification, into new geographical markets. It is often at least as challenging as diversification. Chapter 8 examines choices organisations have to make about which geographical markets to prioritise and how to enter them, by export, licensing, direct investment or acquisition.

● At the start of every organisation is an act of *entrepreneurship*. Most organisations have to *innovate* constantly simply to survive. Chapter 9 considers choices about innovation and entrepreneurship. Innovation choices involve issues such as being first-mover into a market, or simply a follower, and how much to listen to customers in developing new products or services. Entrepreneurship choices are many, but include choices of funding, building key external relationships, and timing of exit.

● Organisations have to make choices about the *methods* by which they pursue their strategies. Many organisations prefer to grow 'organically', in other words by building new businesses with their own resources. Other organisations might develop by mergers/acquisitions and/or strategic alliances with other organisations. These alternative methods are discussed in Chapter 10. Chapter 10 concludes with a discussion of the *success criteria* according to which different strategic choices can be evaluated.

1.3.3 Strategy in action

Strategy in action is concerned with ensuring that strategies are working in practice

Organising **strategy in action** is concerned with ensuring that chosen strategies are actually put into action. These issues are covered in the five chapters of Part III, and include the following:

● First of all, it is important to consider the *strategy development processes* of an organisation. The strategies that an organisation actually pursues are typically a mixture of the *intended* and the *emergent*. Intended strategies are the product of formal strategic planning and decision making, but the strategy that is actually pursued is typically somewhat emergent, including bottom-up initiatives, rapid responses to unanticipated opportunities and threats, and sheer chance. Chapter 11 considers the respective roles of intention and emergence in the overall strategy development of organisations.

● *Structuring* an organisation to support successful performance. This includes organisational *structures*, *processes* and *relationships* (and the interaction between these elements). According to Brad Garlinghouse, structural silos, matrix organisation and bureaucracy were all big problems for Yahoo!. These kinds of issue will be discussed in Chapter 12.

● *Resourcing* strategies in the separate resource areas (people, information, finance and technology) of an organisation in order to support overall strategies. The reverse is also important to success, that is the extent to which new strategies are built on the particular resource and competence strengths of an organisation. Chapter 13 considers this two-way relationship.

● Managing strategy very often involves *strategic change*, and Chapter 14 looks at the various issues involved in managing change. This will include the need to understand how the context of an organisation should influence the approach to change and the different types of *roles* for people in managing change. It also looks at the *styles* that can be adopted for managing change and the levers by which change can be effected.

● The final chapter of the book considers the actual *practice of strategy*. Thus Chapter 15 gets inside the overall processes of strategy development and change to look at the detailed activities involved – the *people* included in strategy, the *activities* they have to do and the kinds of *methodologies* they use to do it. These kinds of practicalities are a fitting end to the book and essential equipment for those who will have to go out and do strategy themselves.

1.4 STRATEGY AS A SUBJECT OF STUDY

Strategy as a subject of study has come a long way in the fifty or so years it has existed. In the beginning, strategy was to do with the *task of the general manager* and, perhaps most obviously, took form in the *business policy* courses run at universities such as Harvard going back to the 1960s. The continual question posed here was 'what would you do if you took over as chief executive of such and such an organisation?' The approach was based on the common-sense experience of executives and not so much on theory or research. Teaching was dominated by attempts to replicate real business situations in the classroom by the exposure of students to many case studies of strategic problems.[2]

In parallel there developed in the 1960s and 1970s the influence of books on *corporate planning*.[3] Here the emphasis was on trying to analyse the various influences on an organisation's well-being in such a way as to identify opportunities or threats to future development. It took the form of highly systematised approaches to planning – incorporating the mathematical techniques of operational research and economics. This analytic approach is a dominant legacy in the study of the subject. It assumes that managers can make optimal decisions for their organisations based on finding out all they possibly can about their organisational world and then making a rational analysis of alternatives. This was a highly influential approach and, for example, gave rise to specialist corporate planning departments in organisations in the private and public sectors, especially in the 1970s.

Both of these approaches came in for considerable criticism in the last decades of the twentieth century.[4] First, although the case study method is still a very important means of bringing 'real life' into the classroom, on its own the old business policy approach lacked a substantial research basis. There was little evidence to back up the common sense, and few theoretical frameworks to generalise beyond individual cases. Second, the analytical approach of specialised corporate planning departments proved poorly able to cope with the apparently more dynamic and competitive business world that emerged from the late 1970s. Three- or five-year strategic plans soon got overtaken by events. The response has been twofold.

On the one hand, academics have developed a growing body of research addressing the implications of different strategies for the financial performance of organisations. This body of research is known as the *content approach*, focused on the content (or nature) of different strategic options – such as innovation, diversification or internationalisation. For content researchers, the typical question is what sort of strategy performs best under what conditions. They argue that managers can benefit from lessons drawn from such research in order to make wiser strategic decisions. Strategic analysis and planning are more effective if underpinned by rigorous research evidence. The main academic discipline which inspires this research is economics, with the work of Michael Porter on industry structure in the 1980s and the resource-based theories of the 1990s particularly exemplary in this respect.[5]

On the other hand, a very different stream of research, led by such figures as Henry Mintzberg and Andrew Pettigrew, drew on sociology and psychology to argue that people were too imperfect and the world too complex for heavy reliance on analysis and planning, however rigorous the economics research.[6] From the 1970s, they and their followers developed a *process approach* to strategy, studying the realities of strategic decision making and strategic change processes.[7] These process researchers have shown again and again the real-world messiness of strategy formulation and implementation. The implication is that it is impossible to analyse everything up front and predict the future, and that the search for economically optimal decisions is futile. It is better to work with, rather than against, the messiness of organisations. This means accepting that managers make decisions which are as much to do with organisational politics and the history and culture of the organisation as they are to do with the economics of strategy, and that strategies will often get derailed in implementation. In this view, recognising imperfections and complexities is actually more effective than ignoring them, as in some purely economics approaches.

The twenty-first century has seen the emergence and growing acceptance of new streams of research that offer still more promising means of coping with organisational reality. This book highlights three:

● *Complexity theory*, drawn from the physical sciences, can be used to help manage the messy world of organisations. According to researchers such as Ralph Stacey and Kathy Eisenhardt, complexity theory principles can be used to achieve order and progress in the social world just as stable patterns of behaviour and well-adapted species seem to emerge in the natural world.[8] The hands-off methods of complexity theory, rather than the heavy-handed approaches of traditional management, are the best way to cope with real-world organisations. Complexity theory is one of the inspirations in the strategy as ideas lens (see section 1.6).

● *Discourse* researchers such as David Knights have drawn on sociological theories of language to point to how discourse – the way in which we talk about organisations – shapes what actually goes on.[9] The discourse perspective in particular highlights how mastery of strategy language and jargon can be a 'resource' for managers through which they gain influence and power and establish their legitimacy and identity as strategists. In this view, knowing how to 'talk strategy' is a key skill in organisational life. The insights of this view are encapsulated in the strategy as discourse lens (see below).

● *Strategy-as-practice* researchers have built on sociological and psychological traditions to examine more closely the actual practice of managers in strategy, developing a detailed understanding of the activities and techniques involved.[10] In some ways, these researchers are returning to the real case approach of the Harvard general manager perspective, but this time seeking to underpin it with systematic research. The promise of strategy-as-practice research is an enhanced capacity to design more practical strategy processes and train more skilled and reflective practitioners, allowing for the real complexities and unintended consequences of organisational life. Chapter 15 particularly draws on this new strategy-as-practice perspective.

Thus half a century of strategy research has produced many ways of approaching strategy. All can provide valuable insights and this book draws on them extensively. For example, while Chapters 2 and 3 rely heavily on economic approaches to analysing environments and resources, Chapters 4 and 5 adopt a strongly sociological and psychological sensitivity to organisational complexity and cultures. Subsequent chapters draw equally on economic, sociological and psychological perspectives. A strong theme in this book is that managers work best if open to different perspectives on the same problem, thereby enlarging their set of possible solutions. The importance of different perspectives is pursued through the strategy lenses (see section 1.6).

1.5 STRATEGY AS A JOB

Most readers of this book will have to engage with strategy to some extent or another. Strategy is not just the preserve of top management. Middle and lower-level managers have to work within their organisation's strategy, meeting the objectives set by the strategy and observing the constraints. Managers have to communicate strategy to their teams, and will achieve greater performance from them the more convincing they are in interpreting it. Indeed, middle and lower-level managers can increasingly play a part in shaping strategy. Brad Garlinghouse's attempt to influence strategy at Yahoo! is an extreme case, but involvement in strategy 'away-days' and various strategy consultation procedures is now a common experience for middle managers in many organisations (see Chapter 15). Being able to participate in an organisation's 'strategic conversation' – engaging with senior managers on the big issues facing them – is often part of what it takes to win promotion.[11]

Strategy, then, is part of many managers' ordinary jobs. However, there are specialist strategists as well, in both private and public sectors. Despite the disappointed hopes in analytical corporate planning of the 1960s and 1970s, there are many in-house strategic planning jobs available. Typically requiring a formal business education of some sort, strategic planning is a potential career route for many readers, especially after some operational experience. Strategy consulting has been a growth industry in the last decades, with the original leading firms such as McKinsey & Co., the Boston Consulting Group and Bain joined now by more generalist consultants such as Accenture, IBM Consulting and PwC, each with its own strategy consulting arm.[12] Again, business graduates are in demand for strategy consulting roles.[13]

The interviews in Illustration 1.3 give some insights into the different kinds of strategy work that managers and strategy specialists can do. Galina, the manager of an international subsidiary, Masoud, working in a governmental strategy unit, and Chantal, a strategy consultant, all have different experiences of strategy, but there are some common themes also. All find strategy work stimulating and rewarding. The two specialists, Masoud and Chantal, talk more than Galina of the analytical tools. Galina discovered directly the possible limits of a strategic plan, with the changes that were imposed in the first few years in the United Kingdom. She emphasises the importance of flexibility in strategy and the value of getting her managers to see the 'whole picture' through involving them in strategy making. But Masoud and Chantal too are concerned for much more than analysis. Chantal emphasises the importance of gaining 'traction' with clients, building consensus in order to ensure implementation. Masoud likewise does not take implementation for granted, continuing to work with departments after the delivery of recommendations. He sees strategy and delivery as intimately connected, with people involved in delivery needing an understanding of strategy to be effective, and strategists needing to understand delivery. For him, strategy is a valuable stepping stone in a career, something that will underpin his possible next move into a more operational role.

Strategy, then, is not just about abstract organisations: it is a job that people do. The task of this book is partly to equip readers to do this job better, and to work with others who have to do strategy too. Chapters 11 and 15 specifically discuss the various roles of middle and senior managers, strategic planners and strategy consultants in strategy work.

1.6 THE STRATEGY LENSES

The **strategy lenses** are four different ways of looking at the issues of strategy development for an organisation

This chapter has already highlighted the different perspectives on strategy that have emerged from strategy research. The practical value of different perspectives is explored in this book through the four **strategy lenses**. These lenses are introduced more fully immediately after this chapter and will provide the framework for separate *commentaries* on each of the three parts of this book. The important point of these lenses is to avoid approaching strategic problems from a single perspective. Looking at problems in different ways will raise new issues and new solutions. Thus, although the lenses are drawn from academic research on strategy, they should also be highly practical in the job of doing strategy.

In brief the four lenses see strategy as follows:

● *Strategy as design*. This takes the view that strategy development can be a logical process in which the forces and constraints on the organisation are weighed carefully through analytic and evaluative techniques to establish clear strategic direction. This creates conditions in which carefully planned strategy implementation should occur. The design lens usually grants top management the leadership role in strategy, with middle and lower management given supporting roles in implementation. This view is perhaps the most commonly held one about how strategy should be developed and what managing strategy is about. It is the traditional 'textbook' view.

● *Strategy as experience*. Here the view is that future strategies of organisations are heavily influenced by the experience of managers and others in the organisation based on their previous strategies. Strategies are driven not so much by clear-cut analysis as by the taken-for-granted assumptions and ways of doing things embedded in the culture of organisations. Insofar as different views and expectations within the organisation exist, they will be resolved not just through rational processes, as in the design lens, but through processes of

Illustration 1.3

Strategists

For Galina, Masoud and Chantal, strategy is a large part of their jobs.

Galina

After a start in marketing, Galina became managing director of the British subsidiary of a Russian information technology company at the age of 33. As well as developing the strategy for her local business, she has to interact regularly with the Moscow headquarters:

Moscow is interested in the big picture, not just the details. They are interested in the future of the business.

The original strategic plans for the subsidiary had had to be adapted heavily:

When we first came here, we had some ideas about strategy, but soon found the reality was very different to the plans. The strategy was not completely wrong, but in the second stage we had to change it a lot: we had to change techniques and adapt to the market. Now we are in the third stage, where we have the basics and need to focus on trends, to get ahead and be in the right place at the right time.

Galina works closely with her management team on strategy, taking them on an annual 'strategy away-day' (see Chapter 15):

Getting people together helps them see the whole picture, rather than just the bits they are responsible for. It is good to put all their separate realities together.

Galina is enthusiastic about working on strategy:

I like strategy work, definitely. The most exciting thing is to think about where we have come from and where we might be going. We started in a pub five years ago and we have somehow implemented what we were hoping for then. Strategy gives you a measure of success. It tells you how well you have done.

Her advice is:

Always have a strategy – have an ultimate idea in mind. But take feedback from the market and from your colleagues. Be ready to adjust the strategy: the adjustment is the most important.

Masoud

Aged 27, Masoud is a policy advisor in a central government strategy unit in the United Kingdom. He provides analysis and advice for ministers, often on a cross-departmental basis. He typically works on projects for several months at a time, continuing to work with responsible service departments after the delivery of recommendations. Projects involve talking to experts inside and outside government, statistical analysis, scenario analyses (see Chapter 2), sensitivity analyses (see Chapter 10), hypothesis testing (see Chapter 15) and writing reports and making presentations. As he has progressed, Masoud has become increasingly involved in the management of strategy projects, rather than the basic analysis itself.

Masoud explains what he likes most about strategy work in government:

bargaining and negotiation. Here, then, the view is that there is a tendency for the strategy to build on and continue what has gone on before.

● *Strategy as ideas.* Neither of the above lenses is especially helpful in explaining innovation. Design approaches risk being too rigid and top down; experience builds too much on the past. How then do new ideas come about? The ideas lens emphasises the importance of promoting diversity in and around organisations, which can potentially generate genuinely new ideas. Here strategy is seen as not so much planned from the top as emergent from within

I like most the challenge. It's working on issues that really matter, and often it's what you are reading about in the newspapers. They are really tough issues; these are problems facing the whole of society.

He thinks people should get involved in strategy:

I would encourage people to do strategy, because it gets to the heart of problems. In all organisations, having some experience of working on strategy is very valuable, even if it is not what you want to major on your whole career.

Masoud is considering moving into service delivery as the next step of his career, because he sees knowledge of strategy and knowledge of operations as so interconnected:

Part of doing strategy is you have to understand what can be delivered; and part of doing delivery is you have to understand the strategy.

Chantal

Chantal is in her early thirties and has worked in Paris for one of the top three international strategy consultancies since graduating in business. Consulting was attractive to her originally because she liked the idea of helping organisations improve. She chose her particular consultancy because

I had fun in the interview rounds and the people were inspiring. I pictured myself working with these kinds of topics and with these kinds of people.

She enjoys strategy consulting:

What I like is solving problems. It's a bit like working on a mystery case: you have a problem and then you have to find a solution to fit the company, and help it grow and to be better.

The work is intellectually challenging:

Time horizons are short. You have to solve your case in two to three months. There's lots of pressure. It pushes you and helps you to learn yourself. There are just three to four in a team, so you will make a significant contribution to the project even as a junior. You have a lot of autonomy and you're making a contribution right from the start, and at quite a high level.

The work can involve financial and market modelling (see Chapters 2 and 10), interviewing clients and customers, and working closely with the client's own teams. Chantal explains:

As a consultant, you spend a lot of time in building solid fact-based arguments that will help clients make business decisions. But as well as the facts, you have to have the ability to get traction. People have to agree, so you have to build consensus, to make sure that recommendations are supported and acted on.

Chantal summarises the appeal of strategy consulting:

I enjoy the learning, at a very high speed. There's the opportunity to increase your skills. One year in consulting is like two years in a normal business.

Source: interviews (interviewees anonymised).

Questions

1 Which of these strategy roles appeals to you most – manager of a business unit in a multinational, in-house strategy specialist or strategy consultant? Why?

2 What would you have to do to get such a role?

and around organisations as people respond to an uncertain and changing environment with a variety of initiatives. New ideas will emerge, but they are likely to have to battle for survival against other ideas and against the forces for conformity to past strategies (as the experience lens explains).

● *Strategy as discourse.* This lens sees strategy in terms of language. Managers spend most of their time communicating. Therefore command of strategy language becomes a resource for managers by which to shape 'objective' strategic analyses to their personal views and to gain influence, power and legitimacy. Approaching strategy as a discourse makes managers very attentive to the language in which they frame strategic problems, make strategy proposals, debate issues and then finally communicate strategic decisions. The language of strategy, and the concepts that underpin that language, can shape the strategy agenda in terms of what is discussed and how. Strategy 'talk' matters.

SUMMARY

- Strategy is the *direction* and *scope* of an organisation over the *long term*, which achieves *advantage* in a changing *environment* through its configuration of *resources and competences* with the aim of fulfilling *stakeholder* expectations.

- Strategic decisions are made at a number of levels in organisations. *Corporate-level strategy* is concerned with an organisation's overall purpose and scope; *business-level (or competitive) strategy* with how to compete successfully in a market; and *operational strategies* with how resources, processes and people can effectively deliver corporate- and business-level strategies. Strategic management is distinguished from day-to-day operational management by the complexity of influences on decisions, the organisation-wide implications and their long-term implications.

- Strategic management has three major elements: understanding the *strategic position*, making *strategic choices* for the future and managing *strategy in action*. The strategic position of an organisation is influenced by the external environment, internal strategic capability and the expectations and influence of stakeholders. Strategic choices include the underlying bases of strategy at both the corporate and business levels and the directions and methods of development. Strategic management is also concerned with understanding which choices are likely to succeed or fail. Managing strategy in action is concerned with issues of structuring, resourcing to enable future strategies and managing change.

- The study of strategy has moved on from the original business policy and strategic planning traditions, to develop two main streams: strategy *content*, concerned with the nature of different strategic options; and strategy process, concerned with *processes* such as strategic decision making and strategic change. More approaches are currently developing, such as complexity theory, strategy discourse and strategy-as-practice.

- Strategy is also a kind of job. It is done full time by *strategic planners* and *strategy consultants*. Strategy is also an important part of the responsibilities of many managers: not just senior managers and managers responsible for strategic business units, but also those managers needing to influence their organisation's overall strategic direction.

- Organisations' strategic issues are best seen from a variety of perspectives, as suggested by the four *strategy lenses*. A *design* lens sees strategy in logical analytical ways. An *experience* lens sees strategy as the product of individual experience and organisational culture. The *ideas* lens sees strategy as emerging from new ideas within and around an organisation. The *discourse* lens highlights the role of strategy language in shaping understandings within organisations, and points to the importance of being able to talk this language effectively.

Work assignments

*✱ Denotes more advanced work assignments.   * Refers to a case study in the Text and Cases edition.*

1.1   Drawing on Exhibit 1.2 and Illustration 1.2 as guides, note down and explain examples of the vocabulary of strategy used in the annual report or website of an organisation of your choice (for example, your university).

1.2   Using the *Exploring Corporate Strategy* model of Exhibit 1.3, map key issues relating to strategic position, strategic choices and strategy into action for either the Ministry of Sound* or an organisation with which you are familiar with (for example, your university).

1.3 ✱ Using annual reports, press articles and the Internet, write a brief case study (similar to that of Electrolux or Ministry of Sound*) that shows the strategic development and current strategic position of an organisation of your choice.

1.4 ✱ Using Exhibit 1.3 as a guide, show how the elements of strategic management differ in:

(a) a small business (e.g. MacPac*, Ekomate* or Brown Bag Films*)
(b) a large multinational business (e.g. Electrolux, SABMiller*, AIB*)
(c) a non-profit organisation (e.g. NHS Direct* or the Salvation Army*).

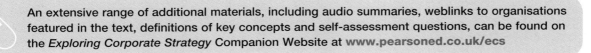

An extensive range of additional materials, including audio summaries, weblinks to organisations featured in the text, definitions of key concepts and self-assessment questions, can be found on the *Exploring Corporate Strategy* Companion Website at **www.pearsoned.co.uk/ecs**

Recommended key readings

It is always useful to read around a topic. As well as the specific references below, we particularly highlight:

- For general overviews of the evolving nature of the strategy discipline, R. Whittington, *What is strategy – and does it matter?*, 2nd edition, International Thompson, 2000; and H. Mintzberg, B. Ahlstrand and J. Lampel, *Strategy Safari: a Guided Tour through the Wilds of Strategic Management*, Simon & Schuster, 2000.

- Two classic and accessible articles on what strategy is, and might not be, are M. Porter, 'What is strategy?', *Harvard Business Review*, November–

December (1996), pp. 61–78; and D. Hambrick and J. Fredrickson, 'Are you sure you have a strategy?', *Academy of Management Executive*, vol. 19, no. 4 (2005), pp. 51–62.

- For contemporary developments in strategy practice, business newspapers such as the *Financial Times*, *Les Echos* and the *Wall Street Journal* and business magazines such as *Business Week*, *The Economist*, *L'Expansion* and *Manager-Magazin*. See also the websites of the leading strategy consulting firms: www.mckinsey.com; www.bcg.com; www.bain.com.

References

1. The question 'What is strategy?' has been discussed in R. Whittington, *What is strategy – and does it matter?*, International Thomson, 1993/2000; M. Porter, 'What is strategy?', *Harvard Business Review*, November–December, 1996, pp. 61–78; and F. Fréry, 'The fundamental dimensions of strategy', *MIT Sloan Management Review*, vol. 48, no. 1 (2006), pp. 71–75.

2. The Harvard 'business policy' tradition is discussed in L. Greiner, A. Bhambri and T. Cummings, 'Searching for a strategy to teach strategy', *Academy of Management Learning and Education*, vol. 2, no. 4 (2003), pp. 401–420.

3. The classic book is H.I. Ansoff, *Corporate Strategy*, Penguin, 1965. For a summary of his work, see 'Obituary: Igor Ansoff, the father of strategic management', *Strategic Change*, vol. 11 (2002), pp. 437–438.

4. For reviews of the contemporary state of strategy as a discipline, see H. Volberda, 'Crisis in strategy: fragmentation, integration or synthesis', *European Management Review*, vol. 1, no. 1 (2004), pp. 35–42; and J. Mahoney and A. McGahan, 'The field of strategic management within the evolving science of strategic organization', *Strategic Organization*, vol. 5, no. 1 (2007), 79–99.

5. The classic statement of the industry structure view is M. Porter, *Competitive Strategy: Techniques for Analysing Industries and Firms*, Free Press, 1980. The classic statement of the resource-based view is J. Barney, 'Firm resources and sustained competitive advantage', *Journal of Management*, vol. 17, no. 1 (1991), pp. 91–120.

6. Henry Mintzberg's classic articles are collected in H. Mintzberg, *Mintzberg on Management: Inside our Strange World of Organizations*, Free Press, 1989. See also A. Pettigrew and R. Whipp, *Managing Change for Competitive Success*, Blackwell, 1991.

7. Two recent collections in the strategy process tradition are G. Szulanski, J. Porac and Y. Doz (eds), *Strategy Process: Advances in Strategic Management*, JAI Press, 2005; and S. Floyd, J. Roos, C. Jacobs and F. Kellermans (eds), *Innovating Strategy Process*, Blackwell, 2005.

8. See R. Stacey, *Managing Chaos: Dynamic business strategies in an unpredictable world*, Kogan Page, 1992; and S. Brown and K. Eisenhardt, *Competing on the Edge: Strategy as structured chaos*, HBR Press, 1998.

9. D. Knights, 'Changing spaces: the disruptive impact of a new epistemological location for the study of management', *Academy of Management Review*, vol. 17, no. 4 (1992), pp. 514–536; and R. Suddaby and R. Greenwood, 'Rhetorical strategies of legitimacy', *Administrative Science Quarterly*, vol. 50 (2005), pp. 35–67.

10. For recent samples of practice research, see G. Johnson, A. Langley, L. Melin and R. Whittington, *Strategy as Practice: Research Directions and Resources*, Cambridge University Press, 2007; and the special issue of P. Jarzabkowski, J. Balogun and D. Seidl, 'Strategizing: the challenge of a practice perspective', *Human Relations*, vol. 60, no. 1 (2007), pp. 5–27.

11. F. Westley, 'Middle managers and strategy: microdynamics of inclusion', *Strategic Management Journal*, vol. 11, no. 5 (1990), 337–351.

12. The major strategy consulting firms have a wealth of information on strategy careers and strategy in general: see www.mckinsey.com; www.bcg.com; www.bain.com.

13. University careers advisers can provide good advice on strategy consulting and strategic planning opportunities. See also www.vault.com.

Electrolux

By 2005 Sweden's Electrolux was the world's largest producer of domestic and professional appliances for the kitchen, cleaning and outdoor use. Its products included cookers, vacuum cleaners, washing machines, fridges, lawn mowers, chain saws and also tools for the construction and stone industries. It employed about 70,000 people and sold about 40 million products annually in about 150 countries. Its annual sales in 2005 were 129 billion Swedish krona (~€14bn; ~£10bn) and profits about 3.9bn krona (~€420m). But 2005 saw two changes that would push the company into second place in the industry – behind the US company *Whirlpool*. First, Whirlpool completed its acquisition of *Maytag* – which gave it about 47 per cent market share in the USA and global sales of some $US19bn (~€15bn). Second, Electrolux announced that it was to demerge its outdoor products division (mowers, chain saws, etc.) as *Husqvarna.* This left Electrolux to focus on the indoor products for both the home and professional cooking and cleaning organisations. So the 'new Electrolux' would have 57,000 employees and global sales of some SEK 104bn (~€11bn).

Photo: Electrolux

History

This was just the latest shift in strategy at Electrolux whose impressive growth and development started under the leadership of Alex Wenner-Gren in 1920s' Sweden. The early growth was built around an expertise in industrial design creating the leading products in refrigeration and vacuum cleaning. By the mid-1930s the company had also established production outside Sweden in Germany, UK, France, USA and Australia.

The period following the Second World War saw a major growth in demand for domestic appliances and Electrolux expanded its range into washing machines and dishwashers. In 1967 Hans Werthén took over as president and embarked on a series of acquisitions

that restructured the industry in Europe: 59 acquisitions were made in the 1970s alone followed by major acquisitions of Zanussi (Italy), White Consolidated Products (USA), the appliance division of Thorn EMI (UK) the outdoor products company Poulan/Weed Eater (USA) and AEG Hausgeräte (Germany). But the biggest acquisition of the 1980s was the Swedish Granges Group (this was a diversification into a metals conglomerate).

As a result of all these acquisitions, by 1990 75 per cent of Electrolux's sales were outside Sweden and this increased in the 1990s as Leif Johansson expanded into Eastern Europe, Asia (India and Thailand) and Central and South America (Mexico and Brazil). He then disposed of many of the 'non-core' industrial activities (particularly Granges). A major restructuring in the late 1990s created the shape of the group for the early 2000s – with about 85 per cent of sales in consumer durables and 15 per cent in related products for professional users (such as professional food service and laundry equipment).

The market

The 2005 annual report highlighted three critically important aspects of the company's markets that their strategies had to address:

Globalisation

'Electrolux operates in an industry with strong global competition. . . . Productivity within the industry has risen over the years, and consumers are offered increasingly better products at lower prices. More and more manufacturers are establishing plants in countries where production costs are considerably lower . . . and also purchasing more components there. In time, production costs for the major producers will essentially be at the same level. This will stimulate a shift of competitive focus to product development, marketing and brand-building.'

Market polarisation

'The combination of changing consumer preferences, the growth of global retail chains and greater global competition is leading to polarisation of the market. More consumers are demanding basic products. Companies that can improve efficiency in production and distribution will be able to achieve profitable growth in this segment. At the same time, demand for higher-price products is increasing.'

Consolidation of retailers

'The dealer structure in the household-appliances market [particularly in the USA] is being consolidated. Traditional dealers are losing market shares to large retail chains. The big chains benefit from high purchasing volumes and wide geographical coverage. This gives them greater opportunities to keep prices low. [But in turn, producers'] costs of serving large retailers is often lower than for traditional outlets, thanks to large volumes and efficient logistics.'

These three factors were also connected. For example, the rapid penetration of Asian producers (for example, LG and Samsung) into the US market was through securing big contracts with major US retailers (The Home Depot and Lowe's respectively).

Electrolux strategies

In the 2005 annual report the Chief Executive (Hans Stråberg) reflected on his first four years with the company and the challenges for the future:

Four years ago I took over as President and CEO of Electrolux. My goal was to accelerate the development of Electrolux as a market-driven company, based on greater understanding of customer needs. . . . We [said that we] would achieve [our goals] by:

- Continuing to cut costs and drive out complexity in all aspects of operations
- Increasing the rate of product renewal based on consumer insight
- Increasing our investment in marketing, and building the Electrolux brand as the global leader in our industry.

He continued by describing the major changes in strategy that had occurred over those four years whilst looking forward to the continuing and new challenges after the demerger in 2006:

Managing under-performers

We have divested or changed the business model for units that could be considered as non-core operations or in which profitability was too low. [For example], instead of continuing production of air-conditioners in the US, which was not profitable, we out-sourced these products to a manufacturer in China. Our operations in motors and compressors have been divested.

Moving production to low-cost countries

Maintaining competitive production costs is a prerequisite for survival in our markets. We will work on improving profitability either by divesting specific units or by changing the business model. It is also important to continue relocating production from high-cost to low-cost countries. . . . We have shut down plants where costs were much too high, and built new ones in countries with competitive cost levels. For example, we moved production of refrigerators from Greenville in the US to Juarez in Mexico. This has enabled us to cut costs and at the same time open a state-of-the-art production unit for serving the entire North American market. The goal is for these activities to be largely completed by late 2008.

More efficient production and logistics

We have put a good deal of time and effort into making production and logistics more efficient. This has involved reducing the number of product platforms, increasing productivity, reducing inventory levels and increasing delivery accuracy.

More efficient purchasing

Purchasing is another area where we have implemented changes in order to improve our cost position, mainly through better coordination at the global level. We have launched a project designed to drastically reduce the number of suppliers. We have also intensified our cooperation with suppliers in order to cut the costs of components. [But] there is a good deal still to be done. Among other things, we are increasing the share of purchases from low-cost countries.

Intensified product renewal

Our future depends on how well we can combine a continued focus on costs with intensified product renewal and systematic development of both our brands and our personnel. . . . Our process for product development based on consumer insight reduces the risk of incorrect investment decisions. Achieving better impact in development of new products has involved making global coordination more efficient, which has given us a number of new global products. The result of our investments in product development over the past years is clearly reflected in the number of product launches for core appliances, which rose from about 200 in 2002 to about 370 in 2005. . . . Investment in product development has risen by SEK 500 million (~€77m) over the past three years. Our goal is to invest at least 2% of sales in product development. We will continue to launch new products at a high rate.

Access to competence

Over the past years we have established [talent management] processes and tools that ensure the Group of access to competence in the future. Active leadership development, international career opportunities and a result-oriented corporate culture enable us to successfully develop our human resources. In order to lead development in our industry, we will have to act fast and dare to do things differently. [We will also need] a strong environmental commitment and good relations with our suppliers.

Starting to build a strong global brand

When I took over as President and CEO in 2002 I stressed that we had to prioritise building of the Electrolux brand, both globally and across all product categories. A strong brand enables a significant price premium in the market, which leads to a sustainable long-term increase in margin. Work on building a strong brand has been very comprehensive. The share of products sold under the Electrolux brand has risen from 16% of sales in 2002 to almost 50% in 2005. We will continue to work on building the Electrolux brand as the global leader in our industry. Our goal is for our investment in brand-building to correspond to at least 2% of sales.

Looking ahead to the near future

Hans Stråberg concluded his review of the business by a look forward to the following year:

We expect the Group to report higher profitability again in 2006. . . . In both North America and Europe we are going to launch a number of important new products. Professional Indoor Products will improve its position in the North American market in 2006 by developing new distribution channels for food-service equipment. The success of our floor-care operation in the higher price segments will continue, among other things on the basis of higher volumes for cyclone vacuum cleaners.

There will be no change in the rate of relocation of production to low-cost countries. During the second half of 2006 we will see the full effect of the cost-savings generated by moving production from Greenville in the US to Juarez in Mexico. We expect that sales will be adversely affected by the strike at our appliance plant in Nuremberg, Germany [planned to close in 2007]. Continued reduction of purchasing costs is a very important factor for increasing our profitability in 2006.

The strategy that has been effectively implemented in recent years by everyone in our organisation is paying off. In 2006 we will continue this important work on strengthening the Electrolux brand, launching new products and reducing costs.

Sources: Company website (www.electrolux.com); annual report 2005.

Questions

1 Refer to section 1.2.1 and explain why the issues facing Electrolux were strategic. Try to find examples of all of the items cited in that section.

2 What levels of strategy can you identify at Electrolux? (Refer to section 1.2.2.)

3 Identify the main factors about the strategic position of Electrolux. List these separately under environment, capability and expectations (see section 1.3.1). In your opinion which are the most important factors?

4 Think about strategic choices for the company in relation to the issues raised in section 1.3.2.

5 What are the main issues about strategy into action that might determine the success or failure of Electrolux's strategies? (Refer to section 1.3.3.)

Commentary

The Strategy Lenses

KEY CONCEPT
www.pearsoned.co.uk/ecs

Strategy
lenses

Chapter 1 showed that the way strategy has been taught and researched has changed over the years. As this has happened different perspectives on the subject have arisen. The argument here is that these different perspectives are helpful in at least three ways:

- They provide *different insights* on strategy and the management of strategy. Think of everyday discussions you have. It is not unusual for people to say: 'But if you look at it this way. . . .' Taking one view can lead to a partial and perhaps biased understanding. A fuller picture, giving different insights, can be gained from multiple perspectives.

- These different insights can also prompt thinking about different *options or solutions* to strategic problems.

- They also flag up the *limitations and possible dangers* of one approach over another.

There is, therefore, both conceptual and practical value in taking a multi-perspective approach to strategy.

This commentary builds on the historically different perspectives on strategy to develop four *lenses* through which strategy in organisations can be viewed. They are:

- *Strategy as design.* The view that strategy development can be a logical process in which the forces and constraints on the organisation are weighed carefully through analytic and evaluative techniques to establish clear strategic direction and a basis for the carefully planned implementation of strategy. This is the most commonly held view about how strategy is developed and what managing strategy is about.

- *Strategy as experience.* The view that the strategies of organisations are substantially influenced by the experience of people (not least managers), taken-for-granted assumptions and ways of doing things in organisations. It is a perspective that helps account for the tendency for strategies to develop incrementally on the basis of the past and for them to be difficult to change. It also flags up the importance of understanding and challenging that which is taken for granted in organisations.

- *Strategy as ideas.* Emphasises the importance of variety and diversity in and around organisations that potentially helps generate new ideas. This perspective suggests that managing strategy is about creating the organisational context to foster the emergence of these ideas and developing them as they emerge. There is much less emphasis here on planned direction from the top.

- *Strategy as discourse*. Highlights the central importance of the language of strategy as a 'resource' for managers. Not only is this language the basis for communicating and explaining strategy, but also it is a basis for gaining influence and power and establishing the legitimacy and identity of the strategist.

The rest of this commentary explains the lenses in more detail. In so doing, the discussion addresses some key dimensions of strategic management. Amongst these are:

- *Rationality*. The extent to which the development of strategy is a rationally managed act. Of course the design lens assumes this is the case, but the other lenses raise questions about it.

- *Innovation* and change. The extent to which the management of strategy is likely to develop innovatory, change-oriented organisations; or conversely, consolidate strategies rooted in past experience and ways of doing things.

- *Legitimacy*. How strategy and the involvement in the management of strategy provide an identity for people – usually managers – of power, authority and influence in their organisations.

The lenses are then used in commentaries (on mauve pages) to interpret the content of the main chapters at the end of each part of the book and to encourage readers to reflect on the issues that have been raised in preceding chapters.

Strategy as design

The design lens views strategy development as a logical process in which the forces and constraints on the organisation are analysed and evaluated to establish clear strategic direction and a basis for the planned implementation of strategy

The design lens builds on two main principles. The first is that managers are, or should be, rational decision makers. The second is that they should be taking decisions about how to optimise economic performance of their organisations. Most managers would probably agree that that is what they are there to do. The principles of economics and the guidelines provided by the decision sciences support and feed the notion that this is what strategic management is all about.

Rational choice is based on the consideration of the consequences and therefore the 'anticipations of the future effects of possible actions'.[1] The implication is that managers can and should be able to weigh the benefits and disbenefits of different strategic options on the basis of evidence that informs them of likely outcomes of decisions they make. There are strong parallels here with the way strategic management is often explained in textbooks, by tutors and indeed by managers. Stated more fully, the assumptions typically underpinning a *design* view of strategy are as follows. First, in terms of *how strategic decisions are made*:

- *Systematic analysis*. Although the range of influences on an organisation's performance are many, careful analysis can identify those most likely to influence the organisation significantly. It may be possible to forecast, predict or build scenarios about future impacts so that managers can think through the conditions in which their organisation is likely to operate.

- *Strategic positioning*. This analysis provides a basis for the matching of organisational strengths and resources with changes in the environment so as to take advantage of opportunities and overcome or circumvent threats.

Arguably the strongest influence in providing ways of doing this has been the writings of Michael Porter[2] in the early 1980s (see Chapter 2).

- *Analytic thinking precedes and governs action.* Strategy making is often seen as a *linear process.* Decisions about what the strategy should be in terms of its content come first and are cascaded down through the organisation to those who have to make things happen. Decisions about what the strategy should be are therefore separate from and precede its implementation.

- *Objectives* are clear and explicit and the basis upon which *options are evaluated.* Given a thorough analysis of the factors internal and external to the organisation to inform management about the strategic position of the organisation, a range of options for future strategic direction are then considered and evaluated in terms of the objectives and that analysis. A strategic decision is then made on the basis of what is considered to be optimal, given all these considerations.

The design lens also makes assumptions about the *form and nature of organisations*:

- *Organisations are hierarchies.* It is the responsibility of top management to plan the destiny of the organisation. They make important decisions, and lower levels of management, and eventually the population of an organisation, carry out these decisions and implement the strategy decided at the top.

- *Organisations are rational systems.* Since the complexity organisations face can be understood analytically such that logical conclusions are reached, the associated assumption is that people in the organisation will adopt and accept such logic. The system can be controlled rationally too. *Control systems* (for example, budgets, targets, appraisals) provide the means by which top management can measure whether or not others in the organisation are meeting expected objectives and behaving in line with the strategy so that managers further up in the hierarchy can take corrective action.

- *Organisations are mechanisms* by which strategy can be put into effect. They are analogous to engineered systems or, perhaps, machines. So how an organisation is structured and controlled (see Chapter 12) needs to be suited to the strategy. There need to be internal mechanisms to ensure that strategy is, indeed, being considered rationally and dispassionately. For example, issues of corporate governance are largely concerned with the self-interest or wrongdoing of senior executives. However, the measures taken to address this problem have tended to focus on structured solutions, such as attempts to set up regulating committees and how boards of directors should be structured. The assumption has been that structures will, or should, affect behaviour.

Implications for management

Managers often talk as if strategy comes about in their organisations – or *should* come about – much as the design lens suggests: it is seen as valuable by managers. Arguably there are six reasons for this:

- *Dealing with complexity and uncertainty.* The design lens provides a means of coping with and talking about complex and uncertain issues in a rational, logical and structured way. Indeed there are *concepts*, *tools* and *techniques* that enable managers to help with this.

- Important *stakeholders may expect and value such an approach*. For example, banks, financial analysts, investors and employees, so it is an important means of gaining their support and confidence.

- *Management power and legitimacy*. Managers, particularly CEOs, face complex and often challenging situations. The assumptions, tools and techniques of design provide them with ways in which they can feel in control and exercise control in such circumstances.

- Rationality is *deeply rooted* in our way of thinking and in our systems of education. In this sense the design lens is embedded in our human psyche. For example, even when managers admit that strategy is not actually developed in ways the design lens suggests, they often think it should be.

- *A rational world*. Increasingly there seems to be evidence of an all-embracing rationality in our world. We live in a time of computer technology, global communication, space exploration, advanced medicine and so on: a world in which science and reasoned solutions to the problems we face seem to surround us and provide so many benefits.

- *The language of strategy*. In many respects the design lens, especially in its emphasis on analysis and control, is the orthodox approach to strategy development most commonly written about in books, taught at business schools and verbalised by management when they discuss the strategy of their organisations. So it is a useful language to know (see the discourse lens below).

Managers who see their role like this may be highly analytical and seen as credible, influential (and therefore legitimate) strategists, as Exhibit I.i shows. The associated assumption is that change and innovation can, or at least should be able to, be achieved through such rational and mechanistic approaches, though as the exhibit suggests, this may be less clearly so.

Exhibit I.i　**Design lens**

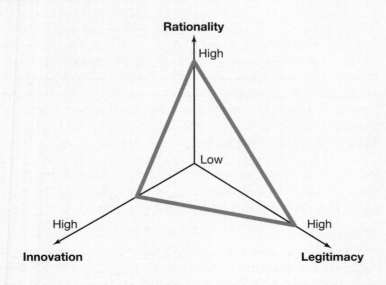

In summary, the design lens is useful in *thinking through and planning strategy* and as a way of managers positioning themselves as *credible strategists*. The question is whether this is an accurate or sufficient portrayal of strategic management. This book argues that the design lens is indeed useful but not sufficient. Other explanations help a fuller understanding of the practice of strategic management and provide insights into how the management of strategy can be approached.

Strategy as experience

Much of the evidence from research on how strategies actually develop gives a different picture than that seen through the design lens. As early as the 1950s, Herbert Simon and Charles Lindblom[3] pointed out that rational decision-making models were unrealistic. It is not possible to obtain the information necessary to achieve the sort of exhaustive analysis required; it is not possible to predict an uncertain future; there are limits in terms of cost and time in undertaking such analysis; organisations and environments are changing continually, so it is not possible for managers to take long-term decisions at a point in time. There are also psychological limitations on managers themselves which mean that they cannot be expected to weigh the consequences of all options or be the objective analysts such rationality would expect – a point which is discussed more fully below. The best that can be expected is what Simon termed 'bounded rationality' which results in managers *satisficing* rather than optimising: they do the best they can within the limits of their circumstances, knowledge and experience. The emphasis of the experience lens is, then, on the influence on strategy development of people's *individual and collective experience* and their *taken-for-granted assumptions*.

The experience lens views strategy development as the outcome of individual and collective experience of individuals and their taken-for-granted assumptions

Individual experience and bias

Human beings function effectively not least because they have the cognitive capability to make sense of problems or issues they encounter. They recognise and make sense of these on the basis of past experience and what they come to believe to be true about the world. More formally, individual experience can be explained in terms of the mental (or cognitive) models people build over time to help make sense of their situation. Managers are no exception to this. When they face a problem they make sense of it in terms of the mental models that are the basis of their experience. This has major advantages. They are able to relate such problems to prior events and therefore have comparisons to draw upon. They can interpret one issue in the light of another. They therefore have bases for making decisions built on prior experience. If they did not have such mental models they could not function effectively; they would meet each situation as though they were experiencing it for the first time.

There are, however, downsides. Mental models simplify complexity. It is not possible for managers to operate in terms of 'perfect knowledge'. Understanding the effects of such *simplification processes* is important. Even if managers have a very rich understanding of their environment, they will not bring that complex understanding to bear for all situations and decisions. They will access part of that knowledge.[4] This is called *selective attention*: selecting from total understanding the parts of knowledge that seem most relevant. Managers also use *exemplars* and *prototypes*. For example, commonly competitors become prototypical. Television company executives came to see other television companies – even specific channels – as their competitors. They therefore readily accepted that satellite broadcasting could introduce new competition because it would introduce new television channels. However, they failed to see that the Internet and sites such as YouTube would become an alternative to watching television. There is also the risk that the 'chunk' of information most often used becomes the only information used and that stimuli from the environment are selected out to fit these dominant representations of reality. Information that squares with other television channels being the competitors is taken on board, whilst information counter to that is not. Sometimes this distortion can lead to severe errors as managers miss crucial indicators because they are, in effect, scanning the environment for issues and events that are familiar or readily recognisable.[5]

Whilst managers tend to see threats rather than opportunities in their environment,[6] they also often exaggerate and overestimate benefits[7] (known as 'attribution error'); for example, when it comes to investment decisions, forecasting the outcomes of risky projects and their own (or their organisation's) influence over events. They also tend to discount luck and inflate the capabilities of their organisation, whilst discounting or reducing the potential of competitors. As we all do, managers also typically make sense of new issues in the context of past issues; so when it comes to strategic decisions they are also likely to resolve a problem in much the same way as they dealt with a previous one seen as similar. Moreover, again, they are likely to search for evidence that supports those inclinations.

In summary, there are three important points:

- *Cognitive bias is inevitable*. The interpretation of events and issues in terms of prior experience is bound to occur. The idea that managers approach problems and issues of a strategic nature entirely dispassionately and objectively is unrealistic.

- *The future is likely to be made sense of in terms of the past*. Such interpretation and bias arise from experience of the past, not least in terms of what is seen to have worked or given rise to problems in the past. This is one explanation of why strategies tend to develop incrementally from prior strategy (see section 5.2.1).

- None the less, *experience may confer legitimacy and power*. Managers with extensive experience may well be seen as experts or have significant influence in an organisation.

There now exists a good deal of research that seeks to understand the strategy of organisations and the management of strategy in cognitive and sense-making terms, more fully explained by Gerard Hodgkinson and Paul Sparrow,[8] for example.

However, managers do not operate purely as individuals; they work and interact with others in organisations, and at this collective level there are also reasons to expect similar tendencies.

Collective experience and organisational culture

Meaning is not just a matter of individual cognition, but has a collective aspect to it. In this context cultural influences are important: indeed culture was defined by the anthropologist Clifford Geertz as 'socially established structures of meaning'.[9] It is an emphasis that Mats Alvesson, writing about organisational culture, agrees with.[10] How people, managers included, respond to and deal with issues is culturally informed. Central to the concept of culture is the importance of what is 'taken for granted' in terms of assumptions and in terms of activities or practices – 'the way we do things around here'. In everyday life, for example, there are assumptions such as the role of the family. However, these assumptions and associated ways of behaving differ between societies in different parts of the world. In organisational life, an equivalent example might be the different assumptions about the role of top managers in Western firms as compared with Japanese firms and the behaviours associated with such assumptions. However, taken-for-granted aspects of culture also exist at different levels: for example, within a managerial function such as marketing or finance; an organisational unit such as a business; or more widely a professional grouping, such as accountants, an industry sector or even a national culture. The links between culture and strategy are therefore important. They are discussed more fully in Chapter 5, but are also explored in the commentary sections in the book.

Implications for management

Viewed through the experience lens, strategies are seen to develop as managers try to relate their experience to the strategic issues that they face. There are four main implications:

- *Bargaining and negotiation* may take place between managers on the basis of different interpretations of events according to their past experience. This is the more likely, since managers' personal reputation and standing are likely to be based partly on such experience. This perspective is reflected in discussions of strategy development as political process (Chapters 4 and 14).

- There is a risk of *strategic drift* if managers are 'captured' by their own and their colleagues' experience. In such circumstances the strategy of the organisation gradually drifts away from the realities of its environment and towards an internally determined view of the world. This can lead to significant performance downturn and, potentially, the demise of the organisation (see section 5.2).

- *Strategic change* or *innovation is likely to be problematic*. It should not be assumed that the drawing up of a strategic plan laying out the logic of a strategic direction will of itself change that which is taken for granted. The notion that reasoned argument necessarily changes deeply embedded assumptions or ways of doing things is flawed; readers need only think of their own experience in trying to persuade others to rethink their religious beliefs or, indeed, allegiances to sports teams to realise this.

- *Surfacing, questioning and challenging* taken-for-granted experience and assumptions can therefore be of key importance in strategic management.

Exhibit I.ii   **Experience lens**

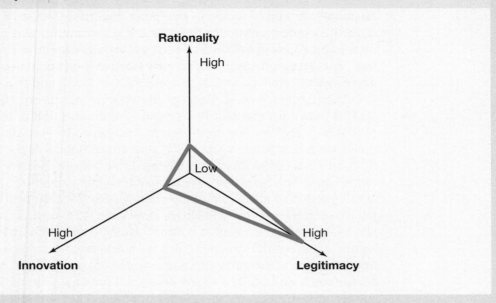

This may be achieved by using the strategy tools and techniques, but can also be seen as part of the political process of organizations.

Exhibit I.ii summarises the discussion in relation to the three dimensions of strategy. The experience lens suggests that it is much more difficult to make strategic changes than the design lens might imply. And rationality, in the sense of the careful weighing of options in a search for optimal solutions, is not the emphasis, but rather people's individual and collective experience. Managers' experience may, however, be seen by colleagues as relevant and important and therefore bestow a degree of legitimacy.

Strategy as ideas

The extent to which the two lenses described so far explain innovation and the generation of new ideas is rather limited. The experience lens rather emphasises the tendency for organisations to conform to past ways of doing things. Notionally a design approach could promote innovation, but in fact tends to so emphasise control that it is also likely to result in conformity rather than innovation. So how to account for innovative strategies, processes and products? Moreover, how do organisations faced with fast-changing environments and short decision horizons, such as those in high-technology businesses or the fashion industries, cope with the speed of change and innovation required?

The **ideas lens** sees strategy as emergent from the ideas that bubble up from the variety and diversity in and around organisations

The **ideas lens** builds on complexity theory[11] and evolutionary theory[12] which, as Shona Brown and Kathy Eisenhardt[13] have shown, are helpful when it comes to explaining the sources of and conditions that help generate innovation. The basic tenets of evolutionary theory – variation, selection and retention – provide an understanding of how organisational context is important in relation to the generation of new ideas and how managers may help shape that context. The emphasis of complexity theory on how systems cope with uncertainty in non-linear ways adds to that understanding. Viewed through the ideas lens, top-down design and direction of strategy is de-emphasised. Rather, strategies are seen as emerging from ideas that bubble up from the variety and diversity in and around organisations.

The importance of variety

New ideas are generated in conditions of variety and diversity, whereas conditions of uniformity give rise to fewer new ideas. Whether the concern is with species, as in the natural world, people in societies or indeed ideas in organisations,[14] uniformity is not the norm; there exists *variety*. There is an ever-changing environment, different types of businesses, a variety of groups and individuals, a variety of their experience and ideas, and there are deviations from routine ways of doing things.[15] Evolution helps explain how any living system, including an organisation, evolves through natural selection acting upon such variation.

Variety is likely to be greatest where the environment is changing fastest. For example, in our biological world there has been the rapid development of new strains of viruses given the advances in modern medicine to fight them. There are parallels with regard to organisations. Organisations in industry sectors that are developing and fragmented tend to be more innovative than those in mature and concentrated industries,[16] because of the diversity of ideas that exist in such dynamic conditions. Take the example of the microelectronics industry. It is a fast-changing industry. This has spawned many different types of businesses, from hardware manufacturers through to software boutiques and firms engaged in applications of such technology. Within these organisations, in turn, there develop new ideas as people interpret opportunities and potential applications differently.

A good deal of this variety occurs naturally and quite likely outside managers' direct control. Since sensing of its environment takes place throughout an organisation, new ideas quite likely come from low down in an organisation, not just from the top.[17] Such ideas may not be well formed and will be more or less well informed and, at the individual level at least, they may be very diverse. Bill McKelvey refers to this as the 'distributed intelligence' of an organisation.[18] Moreover, innovation in large organisations often comes from outside their boundaries, perhaps from smaller businesses.[19]

People in organisations may seek to generate such variety and some of the ways they do this are discussed below. Variation may not, however, always be intentional. In the natural world, change and newness come about because of *imperfections* – a mutation of a gene, for example – that may provide the basis for a 'fitter' organism in a changing environment. In organisations, ideas are also copied imperfectly between individuals, groups or organisations. Some of these will give rise to innovations better suited to the changing environment. A research chemist's idea may be taken up by a marketing executive but interpreted differently from the original idea. Managers in one organisation may seek to copy the strategy of another, but will not do things in exactly the same way. Some of these imperfect copies will not be successful; but others may be. One famous example is Post-It, which originated in an 'imperfect' glue being applied to paper, but which resulted in a semi-adhesive for which the researcher saw market potential. There may also be surprises and unforeseen circumstances in the environment, the unexpected skills or views introduced by new appointees or unintended consequences arising from management initiatives.

Complexity theorists also point to the fact that all this differs markedly from the essentially linear view of the design lens. They refer to 'non-linearity' and show how, in such circumstances, apparently insignificant initial events can lead to major outcomes.

Of course, whilst organisations have the potential for huge variety, there may be intentional or non-intentional suppression of such variety. People's mental models and the culture of an organisation act as filters of ideas that do not 'fit'. Formal processes of control, planning and evaluation act to regularise what ideas will and will not go forward. The self-interest of powerful managers may block ideas counter to their own. So pressures for conformity may see off the potential novelty. Getting the appropriate balance between the need for sufficient control and a context that will stimulate new ideas becomes crucial.

Selection and retention

The implication of the design lens is that the selection of a strategy is a matter of deliberate choice to optimise some sort of outcome, for example competitive advantage leading to enhanced profits. Whilst deliberate acts of managers are not denied here, the ideas lens and evolutionary theory in particular suggest that selection is 'blind'[20] in the sense that outcomes cannot be known. Managers may exercise judgement and choice, but the strategies that develop are also the result of other processes of selection and retention. These include:

- *Functional benefit.* An idea may meet the needs of environmental and market forces. However many of these (from climate changes to competitor responses) can at best be partially known. There may, however, be other functions such as serving the *interests of individuals* within the organisation, for example in furthering career aspirations.
- *Alignment.* An idea is likely to be more successful if it *aligns with other successful ideas*, for example because it is what other organisations are doing or it fits the culture and experience of the organisation itself.
- *Attraction.* Some strategic ideas, by their very nature, are more or less attractive than others.[21] For example, ideas that are altruistic tend to spread and get adopted most.[22] In line with this, complexity theory emphasises the need for sufficient support or 'positive feedback', and some ideas are likely to attract this than others. For example, a new product idea in a science-based company received support because it addressed 'green' issues and its potential benefits interested colleagues in other divisions, friends and families of the managers developing it. The new product idea persisted despite strong evidence of its lack of commercial viability.

● *Retention*. As well as processes of selection, there are processes of retention. '*Retention* occurs when selected variations are preserved, duplicated or other-wise reproduced'[23] leading to their future repetition. One key factor here is the extent to which ideas become routinised and thus retained. Routinisation varies from formal procedures (for example, job descriptions), accounting and control systems, management information systems, training, organisation structuring, to the formal or informal standardisation of work routines and the eventual embedding of such routines in the culture of the organisation.

The important point here is that managers cannot know the future and therefore cannot predict or control outcomes. None the less the internal and external context of the organisation will have a key impact on what new ideas are generated, selected and retained.

Implications for management[24]

A key message from the ideas lens is that managers need to be wary of assuming they can control the generation and adoption of new ideas. However, managers can foster new ideas and innovation by *creating the context* and conditions where they are more likely to emerge. First, they can do this by considering what the appropriate *boundaries* are for the organisation:

● The more the *boundaries between the organisation and its environment* are reduced, the more innovation is likely to occur. For some high-technology businesses it is difficult to see quite what their boundaries are. They are net-works, intimately linked to their wider environment. As that environment changes, so do the ideas in the network. For example, in Formula One motor racing the different teams are intimately linked with the wider motor industry as well as other areas of advanced technology. As a result of this networking new ideas get imitated (but changed) very rapidly. In contrast an organisation where people are insulated from the environment, perhaps by relying on particular ways of doing things, as in a highly rule-based bureaucracy, will generate less variety of ideas and less innovation.

● *Interaction and cooperation* within organisations encourages variety and the spread of ideas.[25] However, there may be limits to this. Too many 'connections' may lead to an over-complex system.[26] There is also a danger that organ-isational structures become too established such that people's relationships become too predictable and ordered; rather, ideas tend to be generated more where there are 'weak ties' based on less established relationships.[27] All this may help explain why so much effort is spent by managers in changing organ-isational structures in the search for the most appropriate working environ-ment (see Chapter 12).

Second, by promoting appropriate *behaviour* in an organisation. For example:

● *Questioning and challenge* is important. There are many organisations that have processes and procedures to foster new ideas. For example, large organ-isations often move executives across businesses or divisions with the specific intention of encouraging new ideas and challenging prevailing views.

Exhibit I.iii **Adaptive tensions**

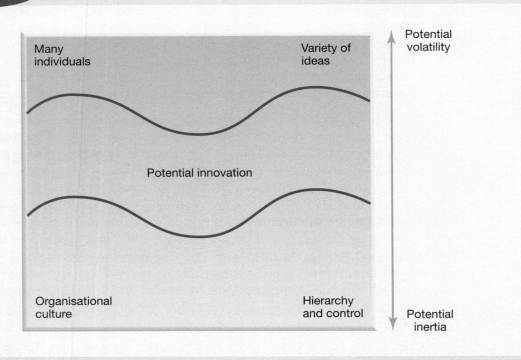

- *Experimentation* is important. This may take different forms. Some organisations have formal incentive programmes to encourage such experimentation. Others have established it as part of their culture. For example, Google gives staff 20 per cent of their time to pursue their own projects. Strategic experiments at an organisational level,[28] such as alliances and joint ventures, are also ways in which organisations may try out possible strategy developments and generate new ideas without overcommitment.

- Through *adaptive tension*. Since high levels of control and strict hierarchy are likely to encourage conformity and reduce variety, establishing appropriate levels of control therefore becomes crucial. Some complexity theorists argue that innovation and creativity emerge when there is sufficient order to make things happen but not when there is such rigidity of control as to prevent such innovation. This is the idea of 'adaptive tension' or 'edge of chaos'.[29] Innovation occurs most readily when the organisation never quite settles down into a steady state or equilibrium and volatility arising from variation is given sufficient rein (see Exhibit I.iii), though of course not to the extent that the organisation cannot function.

- *Order-generating rules*. There is no need for elaborate control to create sufficient order for an organisation to work effectively. Complexity theory suggests that ordered patterns of behaviour can come about through just a few 'order-generating rules'. Richard Pascale gives an example from the cement industry in Mexico. Cemex has done away with tight, planned scheduling for distributing its cement, because it has realised that the construction projects it is delivering to hardly ever proceed as scheduled:

> Cemex loads its fleets of cement trucks each morning and dispatches them with no preordained destination. The trick lies in how they make their rounds. Like ants scavenging a territory, they are guided to their destination by simple rules. . . . Cemex uses an algorithm based on *greed* (deliver as much cement as rapidly as possible to as many customers as possible) and *repulsion* (avoid duplication of effort by staying as far away from the other cement trucks as possible).[30]

● *Pattern recognition.* Ideas within the organisation are more likely to be developed by a reliance on 'pattern recognition' than formal analysis and planning. Strategy development is more about being able to discern promising ideas, monitor how they 'function' and 'fit' (see above) as they develop by being highly sensitive to their outcome and impact and mould the most promising into coherent strategies. Managers need to develop the competences to do this rather than being over-reliant on the formal tools and techniques of the design lens. In addition, since new ideas are unlikely to emerge fully formed – indeed they may be the result of 'imperfect copying', managers have to learn to tolerate such imperfection and allow for failures if they want innovation.

The ideas lens helps an understanding of where innovative strategies come from and how organisations cope with dynamic environments. It therefore de-emphasises the directive role of managers, their rationality and their power and therefore poses questions about whether or not top management really have control over strategic direction to the extent the design lens suggests. Exhibit I.iv summarises this.

Exhibit I.iv   **Ideas lens**

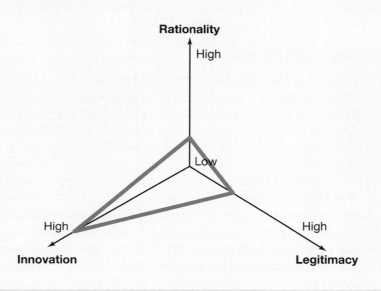

Strategy as discourse[31]

In many ways management is about discourse. Managers spend 75 per cent of their time communicating with others[32] in gathering information, persuading others of a course of action or following up decisions. In particular the management of strategy has a high discursive component. Managers and consultants talk about strategy and strategy is written as formal plans and mission statements, explained in annual reports and in newspaper releases. Efforts to get employees and other stakeholders to buy into strategy are also fundamentally discursive. Discourse is the language resource by which strategy is communicated, sustained and perpetuated. The ability to use discursive resources effectively can, then, be a distinct advantage and competence for an individual (see Chapter 15 on strategy practice which discusses strategy 'conversations'). Looking at strategy development in terms of **strategy as discourse** can also provide valuable insights. There are a number of linked concepts that help here.

Strategy as discourse sees strategy development in terms of language as a 'resource' for managers by which strategy is communicated, explained and sustained and through which managers gain influence, power and establish their legitimacy and identity as strategists.

Discourse and rationality

As discussion of the design lens pointed out, rationality is a central component of the orthodox language of strategy. From a management point of view, then, appearing rational is key to making strategy: 'To be rational is to make persuasive sense.'[33] Strategic management must seem more than just hunch and intuition; it is more like science and the models are like scientific models. As such, managers familiar with such logic can call on it and employ it to justify the 'rightness' of their arguments and views. Indeed David Knights[34] points out that even when managers find themselves unable to achieve the goals of strategy – unable, for example, to achieve competitive advantage – they do not deny the logic of the strategy, merely the ability of the organisation to achieve it. They may employ this language because they are themselves persuaded of the logic of a strategy, because they believe that by doing so their arguments will carry more weight with others, because it is the typical way in which strategy is communicated or because, by so doing, it positions themselves as an authority on the subject.

Discourse and influence

The language of strategy certainly seems to be convincing to others. David Barry and Michael Elmes[35] point out that strategy discourse has the characteristics to make it so. Strategy is not only written about in impressive documents – strategic plans or annual reports, for example – but also written about important phenomena such as markets, competitors and customers. It is often associated with 'heroic' chief executives or successful firms. Strategy discussions take place in important places such as boardrooms or strategy away-days. There is also evidence that the employment of strategy discourse works. Managers consciously employ the vocabulary and concepts of strategy to effect change,[36] to justify and legitimise strategies that are to be followed,[37] or to ensure conformity to the right ways to manage strategy.[38] In other words, managers draw on the concepts of strategy and the apparent 'rightness' of strategy concepts to convince others to comply.

Discourse, identity and legitimacy

How managers talk about strategy also positions them in relation to others, either by their own deliberate choice or as a result of how they are perceived. Discourse is therefore also related to the identity and legitimacy of managers. The common use of the language of rationality has been highlighted above. At other times or in other circumstances managers may also employ different discourse. For example, in trying to get a strategy implemented down the line drawing on the manager's previous experience as a 'hands-on worker' doing the job at an operational level might be useful. In other circumstances reference to prior experience in turning around an organisation may matter. In other contexts the language of the 'visionary leader' or the innovative entrepreneur may be employed.

As David Knights and Glenn Morgan[39] suggest, strategy discourse may be consciously or unconsciously employed by managers – particularly top managers – to provide for themselves certain benefits. It helps legitimise a manager as a knowledgeable strategist, employing the right concepts, using the right logic, doing the right thing and being at the forefront of management thinking. It also provides the sense of centrality, of 'making a difference' to the most centrally important aspects of organisational survival. Since over time different strategy discourses have been more or less the fashion, some elements of discourse are likely to be more effective than others at different times. In the 1960s and 1970s it was the language of corporate or strategic planning; in the 1980s there came to be more of an emphasis on organisational culture; and latterly strategy has become discussed and communicated more in terms of competences.

Discourse as power

In turn the discourse of strategy is linked to power and control[40]. By understanding the concepts of strategy, or being seen to do so, it is top managers or strategy specialists who are positioned as having the knowledge about how to deal with the really difficult problems the organisation faces. The possession of such knowledge gives them power over others who do not have it. It 'allows managers to imagine themselves as controllers of . . . economic life'.[41]

Thus the discourse of strategy can also operate as social control. Groups may adopt particular ways of thinking, behaving and speaking about strategy. For example, some organisations, especially consultants, have developed their own discourse on strategy. Non-adherence to such approaches can bring about sanctions, as many strategy consultants have found! Or there may develop ways of approaching strategic issues that are embedded in particular discourse, for example a push to cut costs. In one sense the need to cut costs is indisputable. However, it can foster a mindset in which cutting becomes the norm and it is difficult to propose expansion or experimentation which would not lead to reduced costs. Indeed, such discourse may become part of a culture: taken for granted, difficult to recognise, difficult to question or change and therefore a powerful influence on behaviour. In this sense discourse is associated with power when it attracts followers and is self-reproducing and self-reinforcing.

Discourse and a critical perspective

A more extreme extension of these perspectives on strategy discourse is that the concepts and models of strategy are less to do with substance and more to do with image, identity and power: that the concepts of strategy are employed, developed and sustained as a basis for sustaining top management control and authority in league with a consultancy profession and academic profession that feeds it; that strategy is a convenient management myth.

Implications for managers

The fundamental lesson for managers is that the language of strategy they employ matters. The discourse lens provides a way of considering how this is so and, in turn, concepts and cues by which managers can manage more effectively:

- *Discourse and context*. It should be clear from the preceding discussion that different strategy discourses are likely to be more or less effective in different contexts and circumstances. How a strategy is explained and justified to a potential investor may call for a major emphasis on logic and reason underpinning a financial case. A similarly rational approach may be needed to persuade fellow managers, but perhaps with an additional component related to the benefits in terms of their own interests, future influence and standing. A similar explanation to the workforce of an organisation will have to address the implications for job security, but perhaps also needs to be expressed in ways that reinforce confidence in management. A press release on strategy will likely need to give thought to the main headlines or 'sound bites'. Careful thought needs to go into how strategy is explained and justified to whom.

- *Discourse and the management of strategic change*. Strategy discourse plays an especially important role in the diffusion of innovations, new management practices and the management of change.[42] In particular, different forms of language may be more or less useful in achieving the adoption and retention of new practices.[43] Language that appeals to emotion and self-interest may help adoption, but a reliance on this may lead to the early rejection of new practices. A more rational approach may mean that it takes longer to achieve adoption but will be less likely to result in early rejection. Language that appeals to or relates to accepted ways of doing things may, however, help ensure retention.

- *Common discourse*. It may be beneficial to seek to develop a common language of strategy in an organisation. This is a common reason for management development programmes in relation to strategy. The argued benefit is that managers can then communicate on the basis of a common set of generally understood concepts, terms and tools of strategy which makes strategy debate more effective. It is also a role management educators provide in the diffusion of strategy concepts and language of course.

- *A critical perspective for managers*. A less extreme and perhaps more constructive view of a critical perspective on strategy is that the discourse lens should prompt managers and students alike to question just how substantial concepts and models to do with strategy really are. Are they really based on sound evidence and theory; do they really make a difference; or are they just

Exhibit I.v   **Discourse lens**

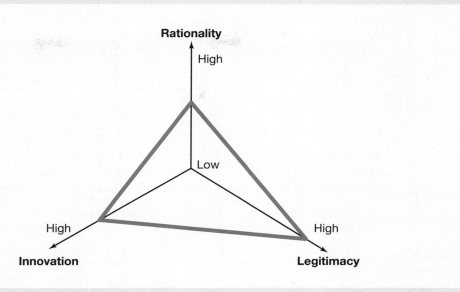

useful devices for managers to gain power and influence? In this sense, seeing strategy as discourse can prompt the healthy questioning of concepts, ideas and assumptions that might otherwise be taken for granted.

In summary, as shown in Exhibit I.v, the discourse lens emphasises that managers may well see the strategy arena as where power, identity, recognition (and therefore legitimacy) are sought. It raises the question of the extent to which managers rely on the appearance, if not the reality, of rational argument. The extent to which such discourse promotes change will depend on the motivations of the managers and the nature of the language used. However there is certainly evidence that language can play an important role in the management of change.

Conclusion

The core assumptions and underpinning theories of the four lenses of design, experience, ideas and discourse are summarised in Exhibit I.vi. They are not offered here as an exhaustive list. They are an attempt to encapsulate different approaches and insights into the complex concept of strategy. The suggestion is that you may usefully extend your exploration of different lenses yourself. It should be apparent in what you have read so far that the lenses presented here in fact each include several perspectives themselves. For example, the experience lens builds on explanations from cognition, sociology and cultural anthropology and the ideas lens builds on both evolutionary theory and complexity theory. So, within these lenses there are finer-grained insights that can be gained and the references and key readings should help with that. In addition there are whole books written that provide multiple perspectives on strategy, from the four that Richard Whittington[44] offers to the ten of Henry Mintzberg and his co-authors.[45]

| Exhibit I.vi | A summary of the strategy lenses |

Strategy as:

	Design	Experience	Ideas	Discourse
Overview/ summary	Deliberate positioning through rational processes to optimise economic performance	Incremental development as the outcome of individual and collective experience and the taken for granted	Emergence of order and innovation through variety, in and around the organisation	The language and concepts of strategy used as a basis for establishing identity and gaining influence, power and legitimacy
Assumptions about organisations	Mechanistic, hierarchical, rational systems	Cultures based on experience, legitimacy and past success	Complex and potentially diverse organic systems	Arenas of power and influence
Role of top management	Strategic decision makers	Enactors of their experience	'Coaches', creators of context and pattern recognisers	Exercising or gaining power and influence over others
Underpinning theories	Economics; decision sciences	Institutional theory; theories of culture; psychology	Complexity and evolutionary theories	Discourse theory; critical management theory

However, there are two overarching messages that come through consistently. The first is the one with which this commentary began: in considering a topic like strategy, it helps to take more than one perspective. The second is that, in so doing, there is a need to question the conventional wisdom of strategy encapsulated in the design lens. In particular the central tenet of managers at the top planning and directing strategy through machine-like organisations is too limited a view of what strategic management is about.

In the rest of the book the four lenses are employed in commentaries at the end of Parts I, II and III in particular to examine critically the coverage of each part and consider the management implications.

References

1. A useful review of the principles of rational decision making can be found in J.G. March, *A Primer on Decision Making: How Decisions Happen*, Simon & Schuster, 1994, Chapter 1, Limited Liability, pp. 1–35.
2. See M.E. Porter, *Competitive Strategy*, Free Press/Collier Macmillan, 1980, and *Competitive Advantage*, Free Press/Collier Macmillan, 1985.
3. See H.A. Simon, *The New Science of Management Decision*, Prentice Hall, 1960; and C.E. Lindblom, 'The science of muddling through', *Public Administration Review*, vol. 19 (1959), pp. 79–88.
4. For a review of these points see the introduction to J. Dutton, E. Walton and E. Abrahamson, 'Important dimensions of strategic issues: separating the wheat from the chaff', *Journal of Management Studies*, vol. 26, no. 4 (1989), pp. 380–395.

5. See A. Tversky and D. Kahnemann, 'Judgements under uncertainty: heuristics and biases', *Science*, vol. 185 (1975), pp. 1124–1131.

6. See J.E. Dutton and S.E. Jackson, 'Categorizing strategic issues: links to organizational action', *Academy of Management Review*, vol. 12 (1987), pp. 76–90. Also M.H. Anderson and M.L. Nicols, 'Information gathering and changes in threat and opportunity perceptions', *Journal of Management Studies*, vol. 44, no. 3 (2007), pp. 367–387.

7. See D. Lovallo and D. Kahneman, 'Delusions of success', *Harvard Business Review*, vol. 81, no. 7 (2003), pp. 56–64.

8. For a thorough explanation of the role of psychological processes in strategy see G.P. Hodgkinson and P.R. Sparrow, *The Competent Organization*, Open University Press, 2002.

9. See C. Geertz, *The Interpretation of Culture*, Basic Books, 1973, p. 12.

10. See M. Alvesson, *Understanding Organizational Culture*, Sage, 2002, p. 3.

11. For a fuller discussion of complexity theory in relation to strategy see R.D. Stacey, *Strategic Management and Organisational Dynamics: The Challenge of Complexity*, 3rd edition, Pearson Education, 2000.

12. For a systematic discussion of the implications of evolutionary theory on management see H. Aldrich, *Organizations Evolving*, Sage, 1999.

13. See S.L. Brown and K.M. Eisenhardt, *Competing on the Edge*, Harvard Business School Press, 1998.

14. An excellent discussion of the development of ideas (or what the authors refer to as 'memes') and the relationship of this to the role and nature of organisations can be found in J. Weeks and C. Galunic, 'A theory of the cultural evolution of the firm: the intra-organizational ecology of memes', *Organization Studies*, vol. 24, no. 8 (2003), pp. 1309–1352.

15. M.S. Feldman and B.T. Pentland, 'Reconceptualizing organizational routines as a source of flexibility and change', *Administrative Science Quarterly*, vol. 48, (2003), 94–118, show how 'performative' variations from standardised (they call them ostensive) routines may create variation which creates organisational change.

16. See Z.J. Acs and D.B. Audretsch, 'Innovation in large and small firms – an empirical analysis', *American Economic Review*, vol. 78, September (1988), pp. 678–690.

17. See G. Johnson and A.S. Huff, 'Everyday innovation/everyday strategy', in G. Hamel, G.K. Prahalad, H. Thomas and D. O'Neal (eds), *Strategic Flexibility – Managing in a Turbulent Environment*, Wiley, 1998, pp. 13–27. Patrick Regner also shows how new strategic directions can grow from the periphery of organisations in the face of opposition from the centre; see 'Strategy creation in the periphery: inductive versus deductive strategy making', *Journal of Management Studies*, vol. 40, no. 1 (2003), pp. 57–82.

18. Bill McKelvey, a complexity theorist, argues that the variety within this distributed intelligence is increased because individual managers seek to become better informed about their environment: see B. McKelvey, 'Simple rules for improving corporate IQ: basic lessons from complexity science', in P. Andriani and G. Passiante (eds), *Complexity, Theory and the Management of Networks*, Imperial College Press, 2004.

19. See E. von Hippel, *The Sources of Innovation*, Oxford University Press, 1988.

20. The concept of blind selection is explained more fully in the chapter by D. Barron on evolutionary theory in the *Oxford Handbook of Strategy*, ed. D. Faulkner and A. Campbell, Oxford University Press, 2003.

21. See Weeks and Galunic, reference 14.

22. The role of altruism and other bases of attraction is discussed by Susan Blackmore in *The Meme machine*, Oxford University Press, 1999.

23. See Aldrich, reference 12, p. 30.

24. For other imlications see some of the references above. In particular Brown and Eisenhardt, reference 13, McKelvey, reference 18 and Stacey, reference 11.

25. See M.S. Granovetter, 'The strength of weak ties', *American Journal of Sociology*, vol. 78, no. 6 (1973), pp. 1360–1380.

26. See McKelvey, reference 18.

27. M.S. Granovetter, (1973) 'The strength of weak ties', *American journal of Sociology*, vol. 78, no. 6, pp. 1360–1380.

28. Brown and Eisenhardt, reference 13, refer to 'low cost probes' as ways in which organisations carry out such experimentation.

29. This is the term used by Brown and Eisenhardt, reference 13, amongst others.

30. See R.T. Pascale, M. Millermann and L. Gioja, *Surfing the Edge of Chaos: The Laws of Nature and the New Laws of Business*, Texere, 2000, pp. 8–9.

31. We are grateful for the help of Nic Beech in the drafting of this section.

32. H. Mintzberg, *The Nature of Managerial Work*, Harper & Row, 1973.

33. This quote is from S.E. Green Jr, 'A Rhetorical theory of diffusion', *Academy of Management Review*, vol. 29, no. 4 (2004), pp. 653–669.

34. See D. Knights, 'Changing spaces: the disruptive impact of a new epistemological location for the study of management', *Academy of Management Review*, vol. 17, no. 3 (1992), pp. 514–536.

35. D. Barry and M. Elmes, 'Strategy retold: toward a narrative view of strategic discourse', *Academy of Management Review*, vol. 22, no. 2 (1997).

36. For example see C. Hardy, I. Palmer and N. Philips, 'Discourse as a strategic resource', *Human Relations*, vol. 53, no. 9 (2000); and L. Heracleous and M. Barrett, 'Organizational change as discourse: communicative actions and deep structures in the context of information technology implementation', *Academy of Management Journal*, vol. 44, no. 4 (2001), pp. 755–778.

37. See R. Suddaby and R. Greenwood, 'Rhetorical strategies of legitimacy', *Administrative Science Quarterly*, vol. 50 (2005), pp. 35–67. Also J. Sillence and F. Mueller, 'Switching strategic perspective: the reframing of accounts of responsibility', *Organization Studies*, vol. 28, no. 2 (2007), pp. 175–176.

38. See L. Oakes, B. Townley and D.J. Cooper, 'Business planning as pedagogy: language and institutions in a changing institutional field', *Administrative Science Quarterly*, vol. 43, no. 2 (1998), pp. 257–292.

39. D. Knights and G. Morgan 'Corporate strategy, organizations and subjectivity', *Organization Studies*, vol. 12, no. 2 (1991), pp. 251–273.

40. For example see Strategy Discourse in a Global Retailer: a Supplement to Rationalist and Interpretive Accounts, by Mahmoud Ezzamel and Hugh Willmott, *Organization Studies*, vol. 29, no. 2 (2008), pp. 191–217.

41. A. Spicer, 'Book review of *Recreating Strategy*', *Organization Studies*, vol. 25, no. 7 (2004), p. 1256.

42. See reference 36.

43. See references 37 and 38.

44. R. Whittington, *What is Strategy – and Does it Matter*?, 2nd edition, Thomson, 2000.

45. H. Mintzberg, B. Ahlstrand and J. Lampel, *Strategy Safari*, Prentice Hall, 1998.

Part I

THE STRATEGIC POSITION

This part explains:

→ How to analyse an organisation's position in the external environment.

→ How to analyse the determinants of strategic capability – resources, competences and the linkages between them.

→ How to understand an organisation's purposes, taking into account corporate governance, stakeholder expectations and business ethics.

→ How to address the role of history and culture in determining an organisation's position.

Introduction to Part I

This part of the book is concerned with understanding the strategic position of the organisation. By this is meant the factors that have to be taken into account at the outset of strategy development. There are two basic views here: one stresses external factors in the organisation's strategic position; the other emphasises internal factors. On the external side, many argue that environmental factors are what matters most to success: strategy development should be primarily about seeking attractive opportunities in the marketplace. Those favouring a more internal approach, on the other hand, argue that an organisation's specific strategic capabilities, resources or cultures should drive strategy. It is from these internal characteristics that distinctive strategies and superior performance can be built. In this view, organisations should focus on those environmental opportunities for which they start with a distinctive advantage in terms of internal characteristics.

It is important not to take too static or unified a view of either the environment or the organisation's inherited internal position. Environments change, and internal capabilities and resources need to develop, or 'stretch', in order to match such change.* Also, organisations are rarely simple, homogeneous units. There are different stakeholders, different cultures and different kinds of purpose within most organisations. These various internal drivers and constraints need to be understood as part of the internal position of an organisation.

Accordingly, Part I has four chapters, starting with analysis of the external position, and then developing an internal perspective incorporating dynamics and differences within the organisation:

- The overall theme of Chapter 2 is how managers can analyse the uncertain and increasingly complex world around them. This is addressed by considering various layers of influence from macro-environmental issues to specific forces affecting the competitive position. However, simply identifying particular influences is not sufficient. The challenge for a strategist is to understand the interaction of these different forces and how these impact on the organisation.

- Chapter 3 is concerned with understanding an organisation's strategic capability and how this underpins the competitive advantage of the organisation or sustains excellence in providing value-for-money products or services. This is explained by considering four main issues: what is meant by 'strategic

---

* The notion of strategy as 'stretch', rather than a static 'fit' to the environment, was introduced by G. Hamel and C.K. Prahalad, *Competing for the Future*, Harvard Business School Press, 1994. See also D.J. Teece, G. Pisano and A. Shuen, 'Dynamic capabilities and strategic management', *Strategic Management Journal*, vol. 18, no. 3 (1997), pp. 509–534.

capability'; how this might provide competitive advantage for organisations; how managers might analyse capabilities; and how they might manage the development of such capabilities.

- Chapter 4 is about how expectations 'shape' organisational purposes and strategies. This is considered within four main themes. Corporate governance is concerned with understanding whom the organisation is there to serve. Stakeholder influence raises the important issue of power relationships in organisations. A discussion of corporate social responsibility raises the question of what organisations should and should not be doing strategically, with implications for individuals' ethics. All of this is brought together in considering how strategists might express and explain the strategic purpose of their organisations.

- Chapter 5 takes an historical and cultural perspective on strategy. The business environment, the capabilities of an organisation and the expectations of stakeholders have historical roots. The theme of the chapter is that understanding history and culture helps managers develop the future strategy of their organisations. The chapter begins by explaining the phenomenon of strategic drift that highlights the importance of history and culture in relation to strategy development and the challenges of managing strategic change. The chapter then examines the influence of the history of an organisation on its current and future strategy and goes on to consider how that history can be analysed. It then explains how cultural influences at the national, institutional and organisational levels influence current and future strategy. It then explains the cultural web as a means of analysing culture and its influence on strategy.

Although this part of the book addresses the various topics in separate chapters, it should be stressed that there are strong links between these different influences on strategy. In practice, the external and internal views need to be reconciled. Environmental pressures for change will be constrained by the capabilities available to make changes, or by organisational cultures which may lead to resistance to change. Internal capabilities will be valuable only if the environment offers profitable opportunities to use them. Also, placing the analysis of position in a separate part, distinct from Parts II and III considering strategic choices and putting strategy into action, does not mean that these are distinct issues in practice. As the overlapping circles of Exhibit 1.3 in Chapter 1 underline, strategy is not a sequential process and strategic choices and strategic action feed back directly into both the understanding and the reality of strategic position.

Nevertheless, by providing for an analysis of the starting position, Part I is the foundation for approaching the kinds of strategic choices that an organisation typically has to make. For example, the nature of the environment and capabilities it has together help shape how an organisation should compete and the range of products and services it should offer. Similarly they inform the methods managers can choose between in order to pursue strategies, whether by building on internal resources, or by acquiring other organisations, or by partnering with others. These choices are pursued further in Part II.

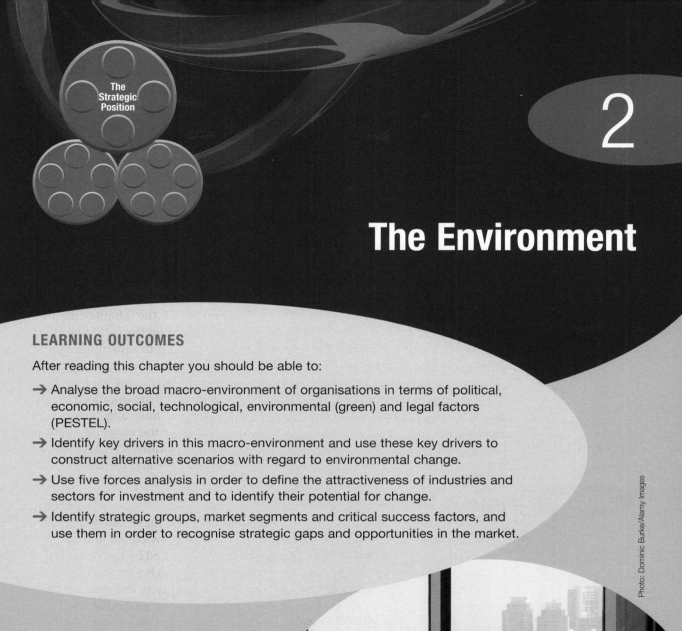

2

The Environment

LEARNING OUTCOMES

After reading this chapter you should be able to:

→ Analyse the broad macro-environment of organisations in terms of political, economic, social, technological, environmental (green) and legal factors (PESTEL).

→ Identify key drivers in this macro-environment and use these key drivers to construct alternative scenarios with regard to environmental change.

→ Use five forces analysis in order to define the attractiveness of industries and sectors for investment and to identify their potential for change.

→ Identify strategic groups, market segments and critical success factors, and use them in order to recognise strategic gaps and opportunities in the market.

Photo: Dominic Burke/Alamy Images

2.1 INTRODUCTION

The environment is what gives organisations their means of survival. In the private sector, satisfied customers are what keep an organisation in business; in the public sector, it is government, clients, patients or students that typically play the same role. However, the environment is also the source of threats: for example, hostile shifts in market demand, new regulatory requirements, revolutionary technologies or the entry of new competitors. Environmental change can be fatal for organisations. To take one example, after 200 years of prosperity, print publisher Encyclopedia Britannica was nearly swept out of existence by the rise of electronic information sources, such as Microsoft's Encarta and the online Wikipedia. It is vital that managers analyse their environments carefully in order to anticipate and – if possible – influence environmental change.

This chapter therefore provides frameworks for analysing changing and complex environments. These frameworks are organised in a series of 'layers' briefly introduced here and summarised in Exhibit 2.1:

● *The macro-environment* is the highest-level layer. This consists of broad environmental factors that impact to a greater or lesser extent on almost all organisations. Here, the PESTEL framework can be used to identify how future trends in the *political, economic, social, technological, environmental ('green') and legal* environments might impinge on organisations. This PESTEL analysis provides the broad 'data' from which to identify *key drivers of change*. These

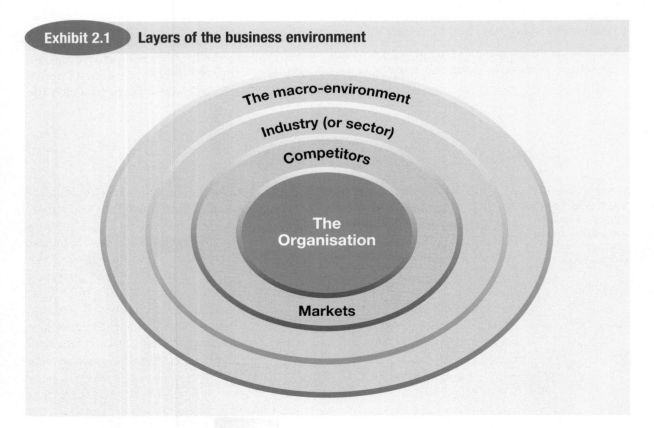

Exhibit 2.1 **Layers of the business environment**

key drivers can be used to construct *scenarios* of possible futures. Scenarios consider how strategies might need to change depending on the different ways in which the business environment *might* change.

- *Industry*, or *sector*, forms the next layer with this broad general environment. This is made up of organisations producing the same products or services. Here the *five forces* framework is particularly useful in understanding the attractiveness of particular industries or sectors and potential threats from outside the present set of competitors. This chapter's key debate (Illustration 2.6) addresses the importance of industry factors, rather than business-specific factors, in determining success.

- *Competitors and markets* are the most immediate layer surrounding organisations. Within most industries or sectors there will be many different organisations with different characteristics and competing on different bases, some closer to a particular organisation, some more remote. The concept of *strategic groups* can help identify close and more remote competitors. Similarly, in the marketplace, customers' expectations are not all the same. They have a range of different requirements the importance of which can be understood through the concepts of *market segments* and *critical success factors*.

This chapter works through these three layers in turn, starting with the macro-environment.

2.2 THE MACRO-ENVIRONMENT

The three concepts in this section – PESTEL, key drivers and scenarios – are interrelated tools for analysing the broad macro-environment of an organisation. PESTEL provides a wide overview; key drivers help focus on what is most important; and scenarios build on key drivers to explore different ways in which the macro-environment might change.

2.2.1 The PESTEL framework

The PESTEL framework categorises environmental influences into six main types: political, economic, social, technological, environmental and legal

www.pearsoned.co.uk/ecs

KEY CONCEPT

PESTEL

The **PESTEL framework** (Illustration 2.1) provides a comprehensive list of influences on the possible success or failure of particular strategies. PESTEL stands for Political, Economic, Social, Technological, Environmental and Legal.[1] Politics highlights the role of governments; Economics refers to macro-economic factors such as exchange rates, business cycles and differential economic growth rates around the world; Social influences include changing cultures and demographics, for example ageing populations in many Western societies; Technological influences refer to innovations such as the Internet, nanotechnology or the rise of new composite materials; Environmental stands specifically for 'green' issues, such as pollution and waste; and finally Legal embraces legislative constraints or changes, such as health and safety legislation or restrictions on company mergers and acquisitions.

For managers, it is important to analyse how these factors are changing now and how they are likely to change in the future, drawing out implications for the

Illustration 2.1

PESTEL analysis of the airline industry

Environmental influences on organisations can be summarised within six categories. For the airline industry, an initial list of influences under the six PESTEL analysis categories might include the following:

Political

- Government support for national carriers
- Security controls
- Restrictions on migration

Economic

- National growth rates
- Fuel prices

Social

- Rise in travel by elderly
- Student international study exchanges

Technological

- Fuel-efficient engines and airframes
- Security check technologies
- Teleconferencing for business

Environmental

- Noise pollution controls
- Energy consumption controls
- Land for growing airports

Legal

- Restrictions on mergers
- Preferential airport rights for some carriers

Questions

1 What additional environmental influences would you add to this initial list for the airline industry?

2 From your more comprehensive list, which of these influences would you highlight as likely to be the 'key drivers for change' for airlines in the coming five years?

organisation. Many of these factors are linked together. For example, technology developments may simultaneously change economic factors (for example, creating new jobs), social factors (facilitating more leisure) and environmental factors (reducing pollution). As can be imagined, analysing these factors and their interrelationships can produce long and complex lists.

Rather than getting overwhelmed by a multitude of details, therefore, it is necessary to step back eventually to identify the **key drivers for change**. Key drivers for change are the high-impact factors likely to affect significantly the success or failure of strategy. Typical key drivers will vary by industry or sector. For example, a clothing retailer may be primarily concerned with social changes driving customer tastes and behaviour, for example forces encouraging out-of-town shopping. A computer manufacturer is likely to be concerned with technological

The **key drivers for change** are environmental factors that are likely to have a high impact on the success or failure of strategy change, for example increases in microprocessor speeds. Public sector managers are likely to be especially concerned with social change (for example, an ageing population), political change (changing government funding and policies) and legislative change (introducing new requirements). Identifying key drivers for change helps managers to focus on the PESTEL factors that are most important and which must be addressed as the highest priority. Many other changes will depend on these key drivers anyway (for example, an ageing population will drive changes in public policy and funding). Without a clear sense of the key drivers for change, managers will not be able to take the decisions that allow for effective action.

2.2.2 Building scenarios

When the business environment has high levels of uncertainty arising from either complexity or rapid change (or both), it is impossible to develop a single view of how environment influences might affect an organisation's strategies and indeed it would be dangerous to do so. Scenario analyses are carried out to allow for different possibilities and help prevent managers from closing their minds to alternatives. Thus **scenarios** offer plausible alternative views of how the business environment of an organisation might develop in the future.[2] They typically build on PESTEL analyses and the key drivers for change, but do not offer a single forecast of how the environment will change.

Scenarios are detailed and plausible views of how the business environment of an organisation might develop in the future based on key drivers for change about which there is a high level of uncertainty

Scenarios typically start from the key drivers with the greatest uncertainty. Such key drivers could create radically different views of the future according to how they turn out. For example, in the oil business, key drivers might be technological change, oil reserves, economic growth and international political stability. It might be assumed that technological change and oil reserves are relatively certain, while economic growth and political stability are not. Scenarios could be constructed around different views about future political stability and economic growth. These key drivers are of course interrelated: high political instability and low economic growth are likely to go together. Constructing plausible alternative views of how the business environment might develop in the future therefore depends on knitting together interrelated drivers into internally consistent scenarios. In this analysis so far, therefore, two internally consistent and plausible scenarios could be proposed: one based on low growth and high instability, the other based on high growth and low instability.

Note that scenario planning does not attempt to predict the unpredictable: the point is to consider plausible alternative futures. Sharing and debating alternative scenarios improves organisational learning by making managers more perceptive about the forces in the business environment and what is really important. Managers should also evaluate and develop strategies (or contingency plans) for each scenario. They should then monitor the environment to see how it is actually unfolding and adjust strategies accordingly.

Because debating and learning are so valuable in the scenario building process, and scenarios deal with such high uncertainty, some scenario experts advise managers to avoid producing just three scenarios. Three scenarios tend to fall into a range of 'optimistic', 'middling' and 'pessimistic'. Managers naturally focus on the middling scenario and neglect the other two, reducing the amount

Illustration 2.2

Scenarios for the biosciences in 2020

Nobody knows the future, but they can prepare for possible alternatives.

In 2006, researchers at the Wharton Business School collaborated with leading companies such as Hewlett Packard, Johnson & Johnson and Procter & Gamble to produce four scenarios for the future of biosciences in 2020. Biosciences include exciting high-tech industries such as genomics, stem cell therapy, cloning and regenerative medicine. The aim was to provide a broad framework for governments, business, researchers and doctors to work within as they considered the future for their particular specialities. The Wharton team were mindful that previous high-tech domains had failed to deliver on their initial promise: nuclear power for example fell radically out of favour from the late 1970s. The future for the biosciences is far from certain.

The Wharton team identified two fundamental but uncertain drivers for change: technological advance and public acceptance. On the first, the uncertainty was about the success of the technologies: after all, nuclear power had not deliverd the cheap energy originally hoped for. With regard to the second, public opinion regarding the biosciences is in the balance, with many calling for an end to stem cell research and cloning. The possibilities of technological success or failure, and public acceptance or rejection, define a matrix with four basic scenarios.

Where's the beef proposes a world in which large corporate and government research initiatives has failed to deliver hoped-for cures for diseases such as Alzheimer's and AIDS, but the public still has high expectations. Companies would be under fire and at risk of political intervention. The *Much ado about nothing* scenario is a world in which the public becomes sceptical after many technological disappointments. The result is that government funding for company and university research dries up. *The Biosciences held hostage* scenario is a very different one, in which technological successes actually frighten the public into a reaction against technology, ethical and safety concerns driving tight restrictions on research, testing and marketing. Finally, the *New age of medicine* offers the prospect of both success and acceptance, a world in which private corporations and university research labs would prosper together as they delivered breakthrough innovations to a grateful public.

The point of the four scenarios is not to say that one is more likely than the others. The Wharton team show that all four scenarios are perfectly possible. Whereas bioscience companies might easily become too focused on the positive *New age* scenario, they need to bear in mind the other possibilities. The implication is that they should be cautious in their expectations of technological breakthroughs and manage public opinion skillfully, otherwise biosciences could become the nuclear industry of the twenty-first century.

Source: http://mackcenter.wharton.upenn.edu/biosciences.

	Technology fails	Technology succeeds
Public acceptance	Where's the beef?	New age of medicine
Public rejection	Much ado about nothing	Biosciences held hostage

Source: Adapted from P.J.H. Schoemaker and M.S. Tomczyk (eds) *The Future of Biosciences*, The Mack Center, 2006.

Question

Over which of the two drivers – technological advance and public acceptance – do companies have the most influence? How should they exercise this influence?

of organisational learning and contingency planning. It is therefore typically better to have two or four scenarios, avoiding an easy mid-point. It does not matter if the scenarios do not come to pass: the value lies in the process of exploration and contingency planning that the scenarios set off.

Illustration 2.2 shows an example of scenario planning for the biosciences to 2020. Rather than incorporating a multitude of factors, the authors focus on two key drivers which (i) have high potential impact and (ii) are uncertain: technological advance and public acceptance. Both of these drivers may have different futures, which can be combined to create four internally consistent scenarios of the future. These four scenarios are each given memorable titles, to facilitate communication and debate. The authors do not predict that one will prevail over the others, nor do they allocate relative probabilities. Prediction would close down debate and learning, while probabilities would imply a spurious kind of accuracy.

Scenarios are especially useful where there are a limited number of key drivers influencing the success of strategy; where there is a high level of uncertainty about such influences; where outcomes could be radically different; and where organisations have to make substantial commitments into the future that may be highly inflexible and hard to reverse in adverse circumstances. The oil industry, where companies must invest in exploring oilfields which may have lives of 20 years or more, has traditionally been a leader in the use of scenarios because it faces a combination of all four of these conditions.[3]

2.3   INDUSTRIES AND SECTORS

An **industry** is a group of firms producing the same principal product or service

The previous section looked at how forces in the macro-environment might influence the success or failure of an organisation's strategies. But the impact of these general factors tends to surface in the more immediate environment through changes in the competitive forces surrounding organisations. An important aspect of this for most organisations will be competition within their industry or sector. Economic theory defines an **industry** as 'a group of firms producing the same principal product'[4] or, more broadly, 'a group of firms producing products that are close substitutes for each other'.[5] This concept of an industry can be extended into the public services through the idea of a *sector*. Social services, health care or education also have many producers of the same kinds of services, which are effectively competing for resources. From a strategic management perspective it is useful for managers in any organisation to understand the competitive forces in their industry or sector since these will determine the attractiveness of that industry and the likely success or failure of particular organisations within it.

The **five forces framework** helps identify the attractiveness of an industry or sector in terms of competitive forces

This section looks first at Michael Porter's *five forces framework* for industry analysis and then introduces techniques for analysing the *dynamics* of industries or sectors.

2.3.1   Competitive forces – the five forces framework

Porter's **five forces framework**[6] was originally developed as a way of assessing the attractiveness (profit potential) of different industries. The five forces constitute

| Exhibit 2.2 | **The five forces framework** |

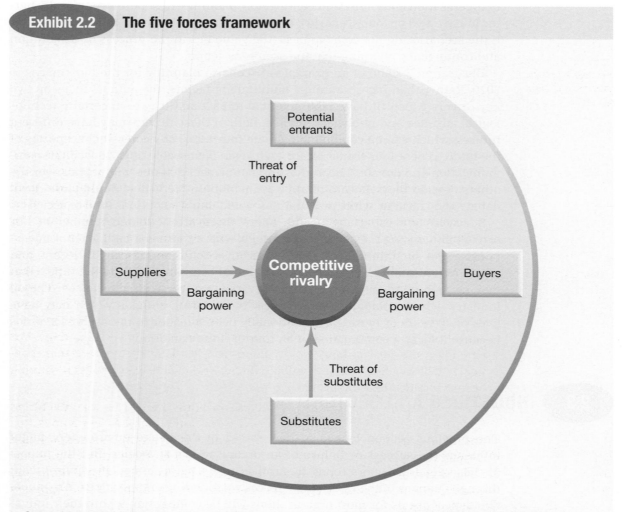

KEY CONCEPT

Porter's five forces

an industry's 'structure' (see Exhibit 2.2). Although initially developed with businesses in mind, industry structure analysis with the five forces framework is of value to most organisations. It can provide a useful starting point for strategic analysis even where profit criteria may not apply: in most parts of the public sector, each of the five forces has its equivalents. As well as assessing the attractiveness of an industry or sector, the five forces can help set an agenda for action on the various 'pinch-points' that they identify.

The five forces are: the *threat of entry* into an industry; the *threat of substitutes* to the industry's products or services; the *power of buyers* of the industry's products or services; the *power of suppliers* into the industry; and the *extent of rivalry* between competitors in the industry. Porter's essential message is that where these five forces are high, then industries are not attractive to compete in. There will be too much competition, and too much pressure, to allow reasonable profits. The rest of this section will introduce each of the five forces in more detail.

The threat of entry

Barriers to entry are factors that need to be overcome by new entrants if they are to compete successfully

How easy it is to enter the industry obviously influences the degree of competition. Threat of entry depends on the extent and height of **barriers to entry**. Barriers are the factors that need to be overcome by new entrants if they are to compete successfully. High barriers to entry are good for incumbents (existing competitors), because they protect them from new competitors coming in. Typical barriers are as follows:

- *Scale and experience*. In some industries, *economies of scale* are extremely important: for example, in the production of automobiles or the advertising of fast-moving consumer goods. Once incumbents have reached large-scale production, it will be very expensive for new entrants to match them and until they reach a similar volume they will have higher unit costs. This scale effect is accentuated where there are high *investment requirements* for entry, for example research costs in pharmaceuticals or capital equipment costs in automobiles. Barriers to entry also come from *experience curve* effects that give incumbents a cost advantage because they have learnt how to do things more efficiently than an inexperienced new entrant could possibly do (see Chapter 3). Until the new entrant has built up equivalent experience over time, it will tend to produce at higher cost. Of course, changing 'business models' can alter scale effects or make certain kinds of experience redundant. For example, Internet banking requires only 10,000 customers to be viable (particularly if they are from a profitable niche) and makes experience in running branches much less important.

- *Access to supply or distribution channels*. In many industries manufacturers have had control over supply and/or distribution channels. Sometimes this has been through direct ownership (vertical integration), sometimes just through customer or supplier loyalty. In some industries this barrier has been overcome by new entrants who have bypassed retail distributors and sold directly to consumers through e-commerce (for example, Dell Computers and Amazon).

- *Expected retaliation*. If an organisation considering entering an industry believes that the retaliation of an existing firm will be so great as to prevent entry, or mean that entry would be too costly, this is also a barrier. Retaliation could take the form of a price war or a marketing blitz. Just the knowledge that incumbents are prepared to retaliate is often sufficiently discouraging to act as a barrier. This dynamic interaction between incumbents and potential new entrants will be discussed more fully in section 2.3.2 In global markets this retaliation can take place at many different 'points' or locations (see Chapter 8).

- *Legislation or government action*. Legal restraints on new entry vary from patent protection (for example, pharmaceuticals), to regulation of markets (for example, pension selling), through to direct government action (for example, tariffs). Of course, organisations are vulnerable to new entrants if governments remove such protection, as has happened with deregulation of the airline industry.

- *Differentiation*. Differentiation means providing a product or service with higher perceived value than the competition; its importance will be discussed more fully in Chapter 6. Cars are differentiated, for example, by quality and branding. Steel, by contrast, is by and large a commodity, undifferentiated and therefore sold by the tonne. Steel buyers will simply buy the cheapest. Differentiation reduces the threat of entry because it increases customer loyalty.

The threat of substitutes

Substitutes can reduce demand for a particular 'class' of products as customers switch to the alternatives

Substitutes are products or services that offer a similar benefit to an industry's products or services, but by a different process. For example, aluminium is a substitute for steel in automobiles; trains are a substitute for cars; films and theatre are substitutes for each other. Managers often focus on their competitors in their own industry, and neglect the threat posed by substitutes. Substitutes can reduce demand for a particular 'class' of products as customers switch to alternatives – even to the extent that this class of products or services becomes obsolete. However, there does not have to be much actual switching for the substitute threat to have an effect. The simple risk of substitution puts a cap on the prices that can be charged in an industry. Thus, although Eurostar has no direct competitors in terms of train services from Paris to London, the prices it can charge are ultimately limited by the cost of flights between the two cities.

There are two important points to bear in mind about substitutes:

● *The price/performance ratio* is critical to substitution threats. A substitute is still an effective threat even if more expensive, so long as it offers performance advantages that customers value. Thus aluminium is more expensive than steel, but its relative lightness and its resistance to corrosion give it an advantage in some automobile manufacturing applications. It is the ratio of price to performance that matters, rather than simple price.

● *Extra-industry effects* are the core of the substitution concept. Substitutes come from outside the incumbents' industry and should not be confused with competitors' threats from within the industry. The value of the substitution concept is to force managers to look outside their own industry to consider more distant threats and constraints. The more threats of substitution there are, the less attractive the industry is likely to be.

The power of buyers

Buyers are the organisation's immediate customers, not necessarily the ultimate consumers

Customers, of course, are essential for the survival of any business. But sometimes customers – here **buyers** – can have such high bargaining power that their suppliers are hard pressed to make any profits at all.

Buyer power is likely to be high when some of the following conditions prevail:

● *Concentrated buyers.* Where a few large customers account for the majority of sales, buyer power is increased. This is the case on items such as milk in the grocery sector in many European countries, where just a few retailers dominate the market. If a product or service accounts for a high percentage of the buyers' total purchases their power is also likely to increase as they are more likely to 'shop around' to get the best price and therefore 'squeeze' suppliers than they would for more trivial purchases.

- *Low switching costs*. Where buyers can easily switch between one supplier or another, they have a strong negotiating position and can squeeze suppliers who are desperate for their business. Switching costs are typically low for weakly differentiated commodities such as steel.

- *Buyer competition threat*. If the buyer has some facilities to supply itself, or if it has the possibility of acquiring such facilities, it tends to be powerful. In negotiation with its suppliers, it can raise the threat of doing the suppliers' job themselves. This is called *backward vertical integration*, moving back to sources of supply, and might occur if satisfactory prices or quality from suppliers cannot be obtained. For example, glass manufacturers have lost power against their buyers as some large window manufacturers have decided to produce some of their own glass.

It is very important that *buyers* are distinguished from *ultimate consumers*. Thus for companies like Nestlé or Unilever, their buyers are retailers such as Carrefour or Tesco, not ordinary consumers (see discussion of the 'strategic customer' in section 2.4.3). Carrefour and Tesco have much more negotiating power than an ordinary consumer would have. The high buying power of such supermarkets has become a major source of pressure for the companies supplying them.

The power of suppliers

Suppliers supply the organisation with what is required to produce the product or service, and include labour and sources of finance

Suppliers are those who supply the organisation with what it needs to produce the product or service. As well as fuel, raw materials and equipment, this can include labour and sources of finance. The factors increasing supplier power are the converse to those for buyer power. Thus *supplier power* is likely to be high where there are:

- *Concentrated suppliers*. Where just a few producers dominate supply, suppliers have more power over buyers. The iron ore industry is now concentrated in the hands of three main producers, leaving the steel companies, relatively fragmented, in a very weak negotiating position for this essential raw material.

- *High switching cost*. If it is expensive or disruptive to move from one supplier to another, then the buyer becomes relatively dependent and correspondingly weak. Microsoft is a powerful supplier because of the high switching costs of moving from one operating system to another. Buyers are prepared to pay a premium to avoid the trouble, and Microsoft knows it.

- *Supplier competition threat*. Suppliers have increased power where they are able to cut out buyers who are acting as intermediaries. Thus airlines have been able to negotiate tough contracts with travel agencies as the rise of online booking has allowed them to create a direct route to customers. This is called *forward vertical integration*, moving up closer to the ultimate customer.

Most organisations have many suppliers, so it is necessary to concentrate the analysis on the most important ones or types. If their power is high, suppliers can capture all their buyers' own potential profits simply by raising their prices. Star football players have succeeded in raising their rewards to astronomical levels, while even the leading football clubs – their 'buyers' – struggle to make money.

Competitive rivalry

These wider competitive forces (the four arrows in the model) all impinge on the direct competitive rivalry between an organisation and its most immediate rivals. Thus low barriers to entry increase the number of rivals; powerful buyers with low switching costs force their suppliers to high rivalry in order to offer the best deals. The more competitive rivalry there is, the worse it is for incumbents within the industry.

Competitive rivals are organisations with similar products and services aimed at the same customer group (that is, not substitutes). In the European transport industry, Air France and British Airways are rivals; trains are a substitute. As well as the influence of the four previous forces, there are a number of additional factors directly affecting the degree of competitive rivalry in an industry or sector:

Competitive rivals are organisations with similar products and services aimed at the same customer group

- *Competitor balance*. Where competitors are of roughly equal size there is the danger of intense competition as one competitor attempts to gain dominance over others. Conversely, less rivalrous industries tend to have one or two dominant organisations, with the smaller players reluctant to challenge the larger ones directly (for example, by focusing on niches to avoid the 'attention' of the dominant companies).

- *Industry growth rate*. In situations of strong growth, an organisation can grow with the market, but in situations of low growth or decline, any growth is likely to be at the expense of a rival, and meet with fierce resistance. Low-growth markets are therefore often associated with price competition and low profitability. The *industry life cycle* influences growth rates, and hence competitive conditions: see section 2.3.2.

- *High fixed costs*. Industries with high fixed costs, perhaps because they require high investments in capital equipment or initial research, tend to be highly rivalrous. Companies will seek to reduce unit costs by increasing their volumes: to do so, they typically cut their prices, prompting competitors to do the same and thereby triggering price wars in which everyone in the industry suffers. Similarly, if extra capacity can only be added in large increments (as in many manufacturing sectors, for example a chemical or glass factory), the competitor making such an addition is likely to create short-term overcapacity in the industry, leading to increased competition to use capacity.

- *High exit barriers*. The existence of high barriers to exit – in other words, closure or disinvestment – tends to increase rivalry, especially in declining industries. Excess capacity persists and consequently incumbents fight to maintain market share. Exit barriers might be high for a variety of reasons: for example, high redundancy costs or high investment in specific assets such as plant and equipment that others would not buy.

- *Low differentiation*. In a commodity market, where products or services are poorly differentiated, rivalry is increased because there is little to stop customers switching between competitors and the only way to compete is on price.

Implications of five forces analysis

The five forces framework provides useful insights into the forces at work in the industry or sector environment of an organisation. Illustration 2.3 describes the

Illustration 2.3

The consolidating steel industry

Five forces analysis helps understand the changing attractiveness of an industry.

For a long time, the steel industry was seen as a static and unprofitable one. Producers were nationally based, often state owned and frequently unprofitable – between the late 1990s and 2003, more than 50 independent steel producers went into bankruptcy in the USA. The twenty-first century has seen a revolution. For example, during 2006, Mittal Steel paid $35bn (£19.6bn; €28bn) to buy European steel giant Arcelor, creating the world's largest steel company. The following year, Indian conglomerate Tata bought Anglo-Dutch steel company Corus for $13bn. These high prices indicated considerable confidence in being able to turn the industry round.

New entrants

In the last 10 years, two powerful groups have entered world steel markets. First, after a period of privatisation and reorganisation, large Russian producers such as Severstal and Evraz entered export markets, exporting 30 million tonnes of steel by 2005. At the same time, Chinese producers have been investing in new production facilities, in the period 2003–2005 increasing capacity at a rate of 30 per cent a year. Since the 1990s, Chinese share of world capacity has increased more than two times, to 25 per cent in 2006, and Chinese producers have become the world's third largest exporter just behind Japan and Russia.

Substitutes

Steel is a nineteenth-century technology, increasingly substituted for by other materials such as aluminium in cars, plastics and aluminium in packaging and ceramics and composites in many high-tech applications. Steel's own technological advances sometimes work to reduce need: thus steel cans have become about one-third thinner over the last few decades.

Buyer power

Key buyers for steel include the global car manufacturers, such as Ford, Toyota and Volkswagen, and leading can producers such as Crown Holdings, which makes one-third of all food cans produced in North America and Europe. Such companies buy in volume, coordinating purchases around the world. Car manufacturers are sophisticated users, often leading in the technological development of their materials.

Supplier power

The key raw material for steel producers is iron ore. The big three ore producers – CVRD, Rio Tinto and BHP Billiton – control 70 per cent of the international market. In 2005, iron ore producers exploited surging demand by increasing prices by 72 per cent; in 2006 they increased prices by 19 per cent.

Competitive rivalry

The industry has traditionally been very fragmented: in 2000, the world's top five producers accounted for only 14 per cent of production. Most steel is sold on a commodity basis, by the tonne. Prices are highly cyclical, as stocks do not deteriorate and tend to flood the market when demand slows. In the late twentieth century demand growth averaged a moderate 2 per cent per annum. The start of the twenty-first century saw a boom in demand, driven particularly by Chinese growth. Between 2003 and 2005, prices of sheet steel for cars and fridges trebled to $600 (£336; €480) a tonne. Companies such as Nucor in the USA, Thyssen-Krupp in Germany as well as Mittal and Tata responded by buying up weaker players internationally. New steel giant Mittal accounted for about 10 per cent of world production in 2007. Mittal actually reduced capacity in some of its Western production centres.

Questions

1 In recent years, which of the five forces has become more positive for steel producers, which less so?

2 Explain the acquisition strategies of players such as Mittal, Tata and Nucor.

3 In the future, what might change to make the steel industry less attractive or more attractive?

five forces in the changing steel industry. It is important, however, to use the framework for more than simply listing the forces. The bottom line is an assessment of the attractiveness of the industry. The analysis should conclude with a judgement about whether the industry is a good one to compete in or not.

The analysis should next prompt investigation of the *implications* of these forces. For example:

- *Which industries to enter (or leave)?* The fundamental purpose of the five forces model is to identify the relative attractiveness of different industries: industries are attractive when the forces are weak. Managers should invest in industries where the five forces work in their favour and avoid or disinvest from markets where they are strongly against.

- *What influence can be exerted?* Industry structures are not necessarily fixed, but can be influenced by deliberate managerial strategies. For example, organisations can build barriers to entry by increasing advertising spend to improve customer loyalty. They can buy up competitors to reduce rivalry and increase power over suppliers or buyers. Influencing industry structure involves many issues relating to *competitive strategy* and will be a major concern of Chapter 6.

- *How are competitors differently affected?* Not all competitors will be affected equally by changes in industry structure, deliberate or spontaneous. If barriers are rising because of increased R&D or advertising spending, smaller players in the industry may not be able to keep up with the larger players, and be squeezed out. Similarly, growing buyer power is likely to hurt small competitors most. Strategic group analysis is helpful here (see section 2.4.1).

Although originating in the private sector, five forces analysis can have important implications for organisations in the public sector too. For example, the forces can be used to adjust the service offer or focus on key issues. Thus it might be worth switching managerial initiative from an arena with many crowded and overlapping services (for example, social work, probation services and education) to one that is less rivalrous and where the organisation can do something more distinctive. Similarly, strategies could be launched to reduce dependence on particularly powerful and expensive suppliers, for example energy sources or high-shortage skills.

Key issues in using the five forces framework

The five forces framework has to be used carefully and is not necessarily complete, even at the industry level. When using this framework, it is important to bear the following three issues in mind:

- *Defining the 'right' industry.* Most industries can be analysed at different levels. For example, the airline industry has several different segments such as domestic and long haul and different customer groups such as leisure, business and freight (see section 2.4.2 below). The competitive forces are likely to be different for each of these segments and can be analysed separately. It is often useful to conduct industry analysis at a disaggregated level, for each distinct segment. The overall picture for the industry as a whole can then be assembled.

- *Converging industries*. Industry definition is often difficult too because industry boundaries are continuously changing. For example, many industries, especially in high-tech arenas, are undergoing **convergence**, where previously separate industries begin to overlap or merge in terms of activities, technologies, products and customers.[7] Technological change has brought convergence between the telephone and photographic industries, for example, as mobile phones increasingly include camera and video functions. For a camera company like Kodak, phones are increasingly a substitute and the prospect of facing Nokia or Samsung as direct competitors is not remote.

Convergence is where previously separate industries begin to overlap in terms of activities, technologies, products and customers

- *Complementary products*. Some analysts argue for a 'sixth force', organisations supplying complementary products or services. These **complementors** are players from whom customers buy complementary products that are worth more together than separately. Thus Dell and Microsoft are complementors insofar as computers and software are complementary products for buyers. Microsoft needs Dell to produce powerful machines to run its latest-generation software. Dell needs Microsoft to work its machines. Likewise, television programme makers and television guide producers are complements. Complementors raise two issues. The first is that complementors have opportunities for *cooperation*. It makes sense for Dell and Microsoft to keep each other in touch with their technological developments, for example. This implies a significant shift in perspective. While Porter's five forces sees organisations as battling against each other for share of industry value, complementors may cooperate to increase the value of the whole cake.[8] The second issue, however, is the potential for some complementors to demand a high share of the available value for themselves. Microsoft has been much more profitable than the manufacturers of complementary computer products and its high margins may have depressed the sales and margins available to companies like Dell. The potential for cooperation or antagonism with such a complementary 'sixth force' needs to be included in industry analyses.[9]

Complementors are products or services for which customers are prepared to pay more if together than if they stand alone

2.3.2 The dynamics of industry structure

Industry structure analysis can easily become too static: after all, structure implies stability.[10] However, the previous sections have raised the issue of how competitive forces change *over time*. The key drivers for change are likely to alter industry structures and scenario analyses can be used to understand possible impacts. This section examines three additional approaches to understanding change in industry structure: the *industry life-cycle* concept; the notion of *hypercompetitive cycles of competition*; and *comparative five forces analyses*.

The industry life cycle

The power of the five forces typically varies with the stages of the industry life cycle. The industry life-cycle concept proposes that industries start small in their development stage, then go through a period of rapid growth (the equivalent to 'adolescence' in the human life cycle), culminating in a period of 'shake-out'. The final two stages are first a period of slow or even zero growth ('maturity'), before the final stage of decline ('old age'). Each of these stages has implications for the five forces.[11]

The *development stage* is an experimental one, typically with few players exercising little direct rivalry and highly differentiated products. The five forces are likely to be weak, therefore, though profits may actually be scarce because of high investment requirements. The next stage is one of high growth, with rivalry low as there is plenty of market opportunity for everybody. Buyers may be keen to secure supplies and lack sophistication about what they are buying, so diminishing their power. One downside of the growth stage is that barriers to entry may be low, as existing competitors have not built up much scale, experience or customer loyalty. Another potential downside is the power of suppliers if there is a shortage of components or materials that fast-growing businesses need for expansion. The *shake-out stage* begins as the growth rate starts to decline, so that increased rivalry forces the weakest of the new entrants out of the business. In the *maturity stage*, barriers to entry tend to increase, as control over distribution is established and economies of scale and experience curve benefits come into play. Products or service tend to standardise. Buyers may become more powerful as they become less avid for the industry's products or services and more confident in switching between suppliers. For major players, market share is typically key to survival, providing leverage against buyers and competitive advantage in terms of cost. Finally, the *decline stage* can be a period of extreme rivalry, especially where there are high exit barriers, as falling sales force remaining competitors into dog-eat-dog competition. Exhibit 2.3 summarises some of the conditions that can be expected at different stages in the life cycle.

It is important to avoid putting too much faith in the inevitability of life-cycle stages. One stage does not follow predictably after another: industries vary widely in the length of their growth stages, and others can rapidly 'de-mature' through radical innovation. The telephony industry, based for nearly a century on fixed-line telephones, de-matured rapidly with the introduction of mobile and

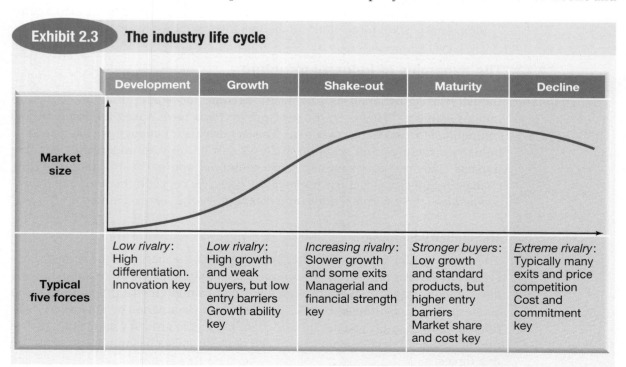

Exhibit 2.3 **The industry life cycle**

	Development	Growth	Shake-out	Maturity	Decline
Market size					
Typical five forces	*Low rivalry:* High differentiation. Innovation key	*Low rivalry:* High growth and weak buyers, but low entry barriers Growth ability key	*Increasing rivalry:* Slower growth and some exits Managerial and financial strength key	*Stronger buyers:* Low growth and standard products, but higher entry barriers Market share and cost key	*Extreme rivalry:* Typically many exits and price competition Cost and commitment key

Internet telephony. Anita McGahan warns of the 'maturity mindset', which can leave many managers complacent and slow to respond to new competition.[12] Managing in mature industries is not necessarily just about waiting for decline. Although steady progress through the stages is not inevitable, the life-cycle concept does none the less remind managers that conditions will change over time. Especially in fast-moving industries, five forces analyses need to be reviewed quite regularly.

Hypercompetition and competitive cycles[13]

Competitors constantly interact in terms of competitive moves: price cuts are matched and innovations imitated. These sequences of move and counter-move are called *cycles of competition*. In some industries, these interactions become so intense and fast that industry structures are constantly undermined. Such industries are *hypercompetitive* (intensely competitive), trapped by the aggressive interactions of competitors into negative downward cycles for all concerned. Competitors attack and counter-attack each other in a way that precludes stability and makes sustainable profits impossible. The cycle of competition concept underlines the fact that industry structures are not 'natural', but are often created and reshaped by the deliberate strategies of competitors. Exhibit 2.4 shows a theoretical cycle of competition, and an empirical example is given in Illustration 2.4.

Exhibit 2.4 **Cycles of competition**

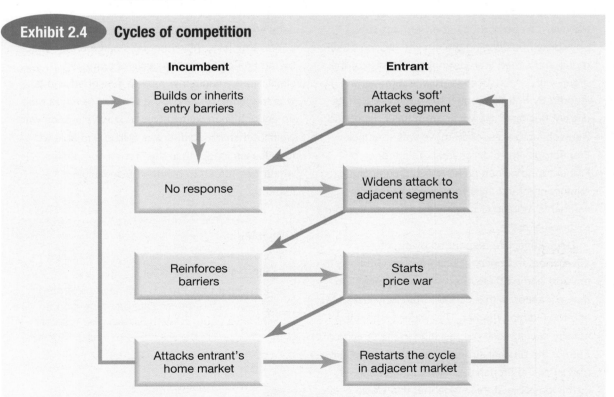

Illustration 2.4

Cycles of competition

Changes in the business environment and moves by competitors erode the competitive position of organisations which, in turn, respond by counter-moves. Competition moves through cycles and any competitive advantage is temporary.

Consider the interactions between Francotop, the highly profitable dominant player in a French consumer goods niche, and Deutschespitze, a German company with a similar product that was wishing to become a significant European-wide player.

Deutschespitze's first competitive move was to target a consumer age group where consumption and brand awareness in France were both low. Francotop had limited its marketing efforts to the over-25 age groups – the Germans saw a possibility of extending the market into the 18–25 group and aimed their promotional efforts at the group with some success. This first move was ignored by Francotop as it did not impact on its current business. However, from this bridgehead Deutschespitze's second move was to attack Francotop's key older market. This triggered Francotop to launch an advertising campaign reinforcing brand awareness in its traditional segments, hoping to confine the German company to its initial niche.

Deutschespitze responded by counter-advertising and price reductions – undermining the margins earned by its French rival. Competition then escalated with a counter-attack by Francotop into the German market. This wider competitive activity played itself out resulting in the erosion of both of the original strongholds and a progressive merger of the French and German markets.

It is possible at this stage that this whole cycle of competition could have repeated itself in an adjacent market, such as the UK. However, what happened was that Deutschespitze saw an opportunity to move away from this *cost/quality* basis of competition by adapting the product for use by businesses. Its core competences in R&D allowed it to get the adapted product to market faster than its French rival. It then consolidated these first-mover advantages by building and defending barriers. For example, it appointed key account salespeople and gave special offers for early adoption and three-year contracts.

Nevertheless, this stronghold came under attack by the French firm and a cycle of competition similar to the consumer market described above was triggered. However, the German firm had built up enough financial reserves to survive a price war, which it then initiated. It was willing and able to fund losses longer than the French competitor – which was forced to exit the business user market.

> ### Questions
> 1 Could the French firm have slowed down the cycle of competition?
> 2 How could the French firm have prevented the German firm escalating competition, to its advantage, in the business user market?

Exhibit 2.4 shows a cycle of competition involving various moves and counter-moves between competitors over time. The starting point is a new entrant attacking an incumbent's established market, apparently protected by inherited entry barriers. The new entrant sensibly attacks a particularly 'soft' (unprotected) segment of the overall market. If receiving no strong competitive response from the incumbent (that is, no retaliation), the new entrant widens its attack to adjacent segments of the incumbent's market. There is a danger of increased industry rivalry and rapidly falling industry profits. In Exhibit 2.4, the incumbent finally responds by increasing entry barriers, perhaps by reinforcing customers' loyalty through increased differentiation. The new entrant counters with a price war. The final resort of the incumbent is to attack the new entrant's home market, hoping to do enough damage there to persuade the new entrant to back off. Thus rivalry increases in that home industry as well. The incumbent meanwhile does its best to raise its barriers to entry.

Illustration 2.4 demonstrates a similar cycle of competition in an international context. Here moves and counter-moves by organisations and their competitors take place simultaneously in several locations. So a competitive move in one arena, the German company's aggressive move into France, did not trigger off a counter-move in that arena (France), but in its competitor's home territory (Germany).

The competitive dynamics between organisations competing in different product or geographical markets (as in Illustration 2.4) is known as *multi-point competition*, in other words competition at multiple points in a business's portfolio of businesses. The possibility of multi-point competition does not necessarily increase competitive rivalry. Indeed, it can reduce competitive rivalry by raising the costs and risks of aggressive moves and counter-moves.[14] For an incumbent, having a small presence in the main market of a potential competitor can discourage any aggressive move by the competitor, because the competitor knows it risks prompt retaliation in its own most valuable market, where it will hurt most.

Hypercompetition occurs where the frequency, boldness and aggressiveness of competitor interactions accelerate to create a condition of constant disequilibrium and change.[15] Industry structures are permanently unstable and no industry can be judged securely attractive for any substantial period of time. In hypercompetitive conditions, it may not be worth investing heavily in building up barriers to entry or trying to reduce rivalry, perhaps by acquisition of competitor companies. Competitor moves will inevitably undermine attractive industry structures. The sustainability of competitive advantage is discussed further in Chapter 3, with competitive moves under conditions of hypercompetition returned to in Chapter 6. Some analysts claim that industries in general are becoming more hypercompetitive, because of international competition or technological change. However, the research evidence is divided on the trend to hypercompetition and it is wise not to be panicked into unduly hypercompetitive behaviour.[16] Aggressive cycles have a reinforcing character that are hard to stop once begun.

Hypercompetition occurs where the frequency, boldness and aggressiveness of dynamic movements by competitors accelerate to create a condition of constant disequilibrium and change

Comparative industry structure analyses

The industry life cycle and cycles of competition notions underline the need to make industry structure analysis dynamic. One effective means of doing this is to compare the five forces over time in a simple 'radar plot'.

| Exhibit 2.5 | Comparative industry structure analysis |

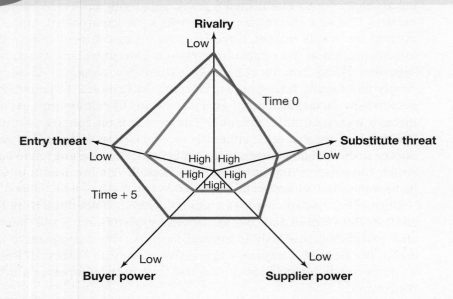

Source: Adapted from V. Lerville-Anger, F. Fréry, A. Gazengel and A. Ollivier, *Conduire le diagnostic global d'une unité industrielle*, Editions d'Organisation, Paris, 2001.

Exhibit 2.5 provides a framework for summarising the power of each of the five forces on five axes. Power diminishes as the axes go outwards. Where the forces are low, the total area enclosed by the lines between the axes is large; where the forces are high, the total area enclosed by the lines is small. The larger the enclosed area, therefore, the greater is the profit potential. In Exhibit 2.5, the industry at Time 0 (represented by the bright blue lines) has relatively low rivalry (just a few competitors) and faces low substitution threats. The threat of entry is moderate, but both buyer power and supplier power are relatively high. Overall, this looks like only a moderately attractive industry to invest in.

However, given the dynamic nature of industries, managers need to look forward: here five years represented by the dark blue lines in Exhibit 2.5. Managers are predicting in this case some rise in the threat of substitutes (perhaps new technologies will be developed). On the other hand, they predict a falling entry threat, while both buyer power and supplier power will be easing. Rivalry will reduce still further. This looks like a classic case of an industry in which a few players emerge with overall dominance. The area enclosed by the dark blue lines is large, suggesting a relatively attractive industry. For a firm confident of becoming one of the dominant players, this might be an industry well worth investing in.

Comparing the five forces over time on a radar plot thus helps to give industry structure analysis a dynamic aspect. Similar plots can be made to aid diversification decisions (see Chapter 7), where possible new industries to enter can be compared in terms of attractiveness. The lines are only approximate, of course, because they aggregate the many individual elements that make up each of the forces into a simple composite measure. Notice too that if one of the forces is very adverse, then this might nullify positive assessments on the other four axes: for example, an industry with low rivalry, low substitution, low entry barriers and low supplier power might still be unattractive if powerful buyers were able to demand highly discounted prices. With these warnings in mind, such radar plots can none the less be both a useful device for initial analysis and an effective summary of a final, more refined analysis.

2.4 COMPETITORS AND MARKETS

An industry or sector may be too high a level to provide for a detailed under-standing of competition. The five forces can impact differently on different kinds of players. For example, Ford and Porsche may be in the same broad industry (automobiles), but they are positioned differently: they face different kinds of buyer power and supplier power at the very least. It is often useful to disaggregate. Many industries contain a range of companies, each of which has different cap-abilities and competes on different bases. These competitor differences are cap-tured by the concept of *strategic groups*. Customers too can differ significantly. Such customer differences can be captured by distinguishing between *strategic customers* and ultimate consumers and between different *market segments*. Under-pinning strategic groups and market segments is recognition of what *customers value* and *critical success factors*. These various concepts will now be discussed.

2.4.1 Strategic groups[17]

Strategic groups are organisations within an industry with similar strategic characteristics, following similar strategies or competing on similar bases

www.pearsoned.co.uk/ecs
KEY CONCEPT
Strategic groups

Strategic groups are organisations within an industry or sector with similar strategic characteristics, following similar strategies or competing on similar bases. These characteristics are different from those in other strategic groups in the same industry or sector. For example, in the grocery retailing industry, super-markets, convenience stores and corner shops each form different strategic groups. There are many different characteristics that distinguish between stra-tegic groups but these can be grouped into two major categories (see Exhibit 2.6):[18] first, the *scope* of an organisation's activities (such as product range, geograph-ical coverage and range of distribution channels used); second, the *resource commitment* (such as brands, marketing spend and extent of vertical integration). Which of these characteristics are especially relevant in terms of a given industry needs to be understood in terms of the history and development of that industry and the forces at work in the environment.

Strategic groups can be mapped onto two-dimensional charts – for example, one axis might be the extent of product range and the other axis the size of marketing spend. One method for establishing key dimensions by which to map strategic groups is to identify top performers (by growth or profitability) in an industry and to compare them with low performers. Characteristics that are shared by top performers, but not by low performers, are likely to be particularly relevant for mapping strategic groups. For example, the most profitable firms in an industry might all be narrow in terms of product range and lavish in terms of marketing spend, while the less profitable firms might be more widely spread in terms of products and restrained in their marketing. Here the two dimen-sions for mapping would be product range and marketing spend. A potential recommendation for the less profitable firms would be to cut back their product range and boost their marketing. In Illustration 2.5, Figure 1 shows a strategic group map of the major providers of MBAs in The Netherlands in 2007.

Illustration 2.5

Strategic groups in Dutch MBA education

Mapping of strategic groups can provide insights into the competitive structures of industries or sectors and the opportunities and constraints for development.

In the mid-2000s there were three kinds of institutions offering MBA courses in The Netherlands: traditional universities, for-profit business schools (FPBSs) and polytechnics:

- Traditional universities offered a wide range of subjects, carried out research, and attracted students both nationally and internationally. Their programmes were more academic than vocational. A university degree was generally valued more highly than that of a polytechnic.

- FPBSs were relatively new, and provided MBA degrees only. Some of the FPBS now offer a DBA course as well. Usually they were located close to the centre or capital of the country. MBA education at FPBSs was generally more of the action learning type, which made it attractive for practising managers. Many students already had diplomas from a university or polytechnic. Several of these schools received accreditation from the Dutch Validation Council. In 2005 the Dutch minister of education and culture recognised NIMBAS, an FPBS, as an official 'universiteit'. NIMBAS later merged with TIAS, the business school of Universiteit Tilburg.

- Polytechnics (in The Netherlands named HogeScholen) often attracted students from the region and provided education aimed more at application of theory than at developing conceptual thinking. Some of the polytechnics provided MBA degrees, in some cases in cooperation with universities in the UK.

Figure 1 gives an indication of how these three types of institution were positioned in terms of geographical coverage and 'orientation'. Figure 2 shows the barriers confronting organisations who wished to move from one group to another (they show the barriers *into* a group). For example, if the FPBSs tried to 'enter' the strategic group of traditional universities they would need to build up a reputation in research or innovation. They may not be interested in doing research, since there would be high costs and little pay-off for their effort. In reverse, for traditional universities to move in the direction of the FPBSs may be difficult since the faculty may not have skills in action learning and may be inexperienced at working with older students.

Figure 3 shows where 'strategic space' might exist. These spaces are created by changes in the macro-

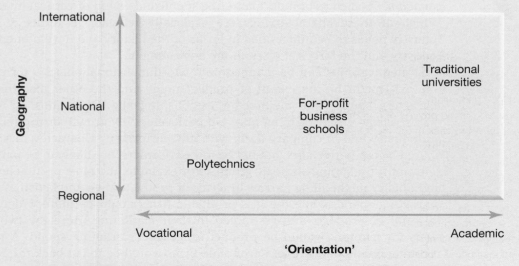

Figure 1 Strategic groups in MBA education in The Netherlands

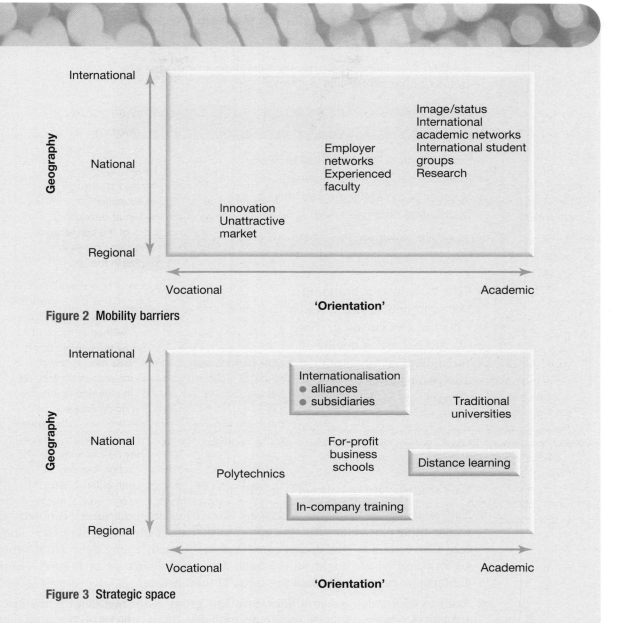

Figure 2 Mobility barriers

Figure 3 Strategic space

environment – particularly globalisation and information technology. This could provide opportunities for Dutch business schools to seek more international business. However, the reverse threat of international competitors entering the Dutch market was a major concern. Information and communication technology helps students study at their own place of work or at home, and also enables them to tap into an international network. So an American or British school could provide content over the Internet and local student support through partnerships with Dutch institutions. Indeed the University of Phoenix had already made efforts to do just this.

Source: This is an updated version of D.J. Eppink and S. de Waal, 'Global influences on the public sector', in G. Johnson and K. Scholes (eds), *Exploring Public Sector Strategy*, FT/Prentice Hall, 2001, chapter 3.

Question

How might this analysis influence the next strategic moves by each of the three types of institution?

Exhibit 2.6 **Some characteristics for identifying strategic groups**

It is useful to consider the extent to which organisations *differ* in terms of **characteristics** such as:

Scope of activities

- Extent of product (or service) diversity
- Extent of geographical coverage
- Number of market segments served
- Distribution channels used

Resource commitment

- Extent (number) of **branding**
- **Marketing effort** (e.g. advertising spread, size of salesforce)
- Extent of **vertical integration**
- Product or service **quality**
- **Technological leadership** (a leader or follower)
- **Size** of organisation

Sources: Based on M.E. Porter, *Competitive Strategy*, Free Press, 1980; and J. McGee and H. Thomas, 'Strategic groups: theory, research and taxonomy', *Strategic Management Journal*, vol. 7, no. 2 (1986), pp. 141–160.

This strategic group concept is useful in at least three ways:

- *Understanding competition.* Managers can focus on their direct competitors within their particular strategic group, rather than the whole industry. They can also establish the dimensions that distinguish them most from other groups, and which might be the basis for relative success or failure. These dimensions can then become the focus of their action.

- *Analysis of strategic opportunities.* Strategic group maps can identify the most attractive 'strategic spaces' within an industry. Some spaces on the map may be 'white spaces', relatively under-occupied. In the Dutch MBA market, for instance, examples are vocational degrees for the international market and semi-academic education for the regional in-company training market. Such white spaces might be unexploited opportunities. On the other hand, they could turn out to be 'black holes', impossible to exploit and likely to damage any entrant. A strategic group map is only the first stage of the analysis. White spaces need to tested carefully; not all are true strategic spaces.

- *Analysis of mobility barriers.* Of course, moving across the map to take advantage of opportunities is not costless. Often it will require difficult decisions and rare resources. Strategic groups are therefore characterised by 'mobility barriers', obstacles to movement from one strategic group to another. These are similar to barriers to entry in five forces analysis. In Illustration 2.5, Figure 2 shows examples of mobility barriers for the groupings identified in the industry. These may be substantial: to enter the international academic strategic group, a regional, vocational competitor would have to establish the appropriate image, mobilise networks, change its teaching methods and improve its remuneration levels. As with barriers to entry, it is good to be in a successful strategic group for which there are strong mobility barriers, to impede imitation.

2.4.2 Market segments

The concept of strategic groups discussed above helps with understanding the similarities and differences in the characteristics of 'producers' – those organisations that are actual or potential competitors. The concept of market segment focuses attention on differences in customer needs. A **market segment**[19] is a group of customers who have similar needs that are different from customer needs in other parts of the market. It will be seen in Chapter 3 that this understanding of what customers (and other stakeholders) value and how an organisation and its competitors are positioned to meet these needs are critical to understanding strategic capability.

A **market segment** is a group of customers who have similar needs that are different from customer needs in other parts of the market

The concept of market segments should remind managers of several important issues:

● *Customer needs* may vary for a whole variety of reasons – some of which are identified in Exhibit 2.7. Theoretically, any of these factors could be used to identify market segments. However, in practical terms it is important to consider which bases of segmentation are most important in any particular

Exhibit 2.7   Some bases of market segmentation

Type of factor	Consumer markets	Industrial/ organisational markets
Characteristics of people/ organisations	Age, sex, race Income Family size Life-cycle stage Location Lifestyle	Industry Location Size Technology Profitability Management
Purchase/use situation	Size of purchase Brand loyalty Purpose of use Purchasing behaviour Importance of purchase Choice criteria	Application Importance of purchase Volume Frequency of purchase Purchasing procedure Choice criteria Distribution channel
Users' needs and preferences for product characteristics	Product similarity Price preference Brand preferences Desired features Quality	Performance requirements Assistance from suppliers Brand preferences Desired features Quality Service requirements

market. For example, in industrial markets, segmentation is often thought of in terms of industrial classification of buyers – such as 'we sell to the domestic appliance industry'. However, it may be that this is not the most relevant basis of segmentation when thinking about the future. Segmentation by buyer behaviour (for example, direct buying versus those users who buy through third parties such as contractors) or purchase value (for example, high-value bulk purchasers versus frequent low-value purchasers) might be more appropriate in some markets. Indeed, it is often useful to consider different bases of segmentation in the same market to help understand the dynamics of that market and how these are changing.

- *Relative market share* (that is, share in relation to that of competitors) within a market segment is an important consideration. Organisations that have built up most experience in servicing a particular market segment should not only have lower costs in so doing, but also have built relationships which may be difficult for others to break down. What customers value will vary by market segment and therefore 'producers' are likely to achieve advantage in segments that are especially suited to their particular strengths. They may find it very difficult to compete on a broader basis. For example, a small local brewery competing against the big brands on the basis of its low prices underpinned by low costs of distribution and marketing is confined to that segment of the local market that values low price.

- How market segments can be *identified and 'serviced'*[20] is influenced by a number of trends in the business environment already discussed in this chapter. For example, the wide availability of consumer data and the ability to process it electronically combined with increased flexibility of companies' operations allow segmentation to be undertaken at a micro-level – even down to individual consumers (so-called 'markets of one'). So Internet shopping selectively targets consumers with special offers based on their past purchasing patterns. The emergence of more affluent, mobile consumers means that geographical segmentation may be much less effective than lifestyle segmentation (across national boundaries).

2.4.3 Identifying the strategic customer

Bringing goods and services to market usually involves a range of organisations performing different roles. In Chapter 3 this will be discussed in more detail through the concept of the value network. For example, most consumers purchase goods through retail outlets. So the manufacturers must attend to two sorts of customers – the shops, their direct customers, and the shops' customers, the ultimate consumers of the product. Although both customers influence demand, usually one of these will be more influential than the others – this is the strategic customer. The **strategic customer** is the person(s) at whom the strategy is primarily addressed because they have the most influence over which goods or services are purchased. Unless there is clarity on who the strategic customer is, managers can end up analysing and targeting the wrong people. It is the desires of the strategic customer that provide the starting point for strategy. The requirements of the other customers are not unimportant – they have to be met – but the requirements of the strategic customer are paramount. Returning to the

The **strategic customer** is the person(s) at whom the strategy is primarily addressed because they have the most influence over which goods or services are purchased

example, it should be clear that for many consumer goods the retail outlet is the strategic customer as the way it displays, promotes and supports products in store is hugely influential on the final consumer preferences. In the public sector the strategic customer is very often the 'body' which controls the funds or authorises use rather than the user of the service. So family doctors are the strategic customers of pharmaceutical companies and so on.

2.4.4 Understanding what customers value – critical success factors

Although the concept of market segments is useful, managers may fail to be realistic about how markets are segmented and the strategic implications of that segmentation. It will be seen in the next chapter that an understanding of customer needs and how they differ between segments is crucial to developing the appropriate strategic capability in an organisation. However, customers will value many product/service features to a greater or lesser degree. From the potential providers' viewpoint it is valuable to understand which features are of particular importance to a group of customers (market segment). These are known as the critical success factors. **Critical success factors** (CSFs) are those product features that are particularly valued by a group of customers and, therefore, where the organisation must excel to outperform competition.

> **Critical success factors** (CSFs) are those product features that are particularly valued by a group of customers and, therefore, where the organisation must excel to outperform competition

The extent to which the offerings of different providers address the factors valued by customers can be visualised by creating a strategy canvas[21] (see Exhibit 2.8). The canvas is a simple but useful way of comparing competitors' positions in a market and potential in different segments. The exhibit relates to the electrical engineering equipment market and illustrates the following:

- Five *critical success factors* are identified in Exhibit 2.8 as particularly important to customers on average (in rank order, the producer's reputation, after-sales service, delivery reliability, testing facilities and technical quality). These are *average* ranks for the five factors determining customer choices, given similar prices; note that individual customers vary.

- Three *competitor profiles* are drawn on the canvas against these factors. It is clear that the relative strengths that company A possesses are not the factors *most* valued by the average customer, whereas company B's strengths appear to have a better match. But nobody is doing particularly well with regard to testing and technical quality, which may be very important to same customers.

- *Segment choice* is the next issue. Company A could try to improve on the highest average rank factors. But companies B and C are already strong there, and their customers are highly satisfied. An alternative for company A is to focus on a particular market segment, those for whom testing and quality happen to be much more important than for the average customer. There is less competition there and greater room for improvement. This segment might be relatively small, but targeting this specifically could be much more profitable than tackling companies B and C head on in their areas of strength. Company A might focus on raising its profile at the right-hand end of the canvas.

The key messages from this example are that it is important to see value through the eyes of the customer and to be clear about *relative* strengths.

| Exhibit 2.8 | A strategy canvas – perceived value by customers in the electrical engineering equipment market |

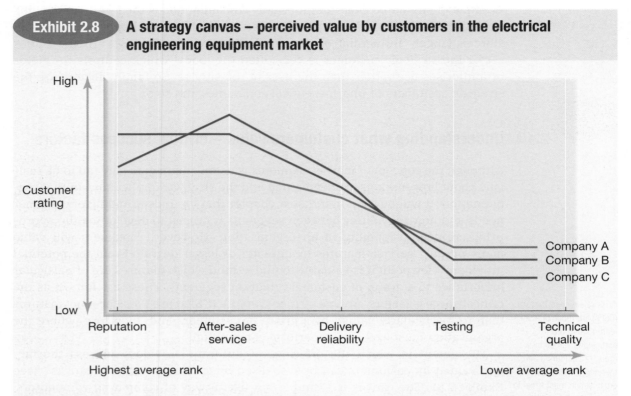

Although this might appear self-evident, a customer viewpoint and clarity about strengths may not be easy to achieve for several reasons:

● *Sense making*. Managers may not be able to *make sense* of the complex and varied behaviours they experience in their markets. Often they will have vast amounts of raw data about customer preferences and competitor moves, but they lack the capability to draw useful conclusions from these data (for example, to spot trends or connections). Market researchers and marketing consultants may be able to supply a clearer view from outside.

● *Distance from the ultimate customer*. Component and raw material suppliers, for example, may be distanced from the final users by several intermediaries – other manufacturers and distributors. Although these direct customers may be the strategic customers there is a danger that what value means to the final consumer is not understood. In other words, companies may be out of touch with what is ultimately driving demand for their product or service.

● *Internal biases*. Managers are prone to assume that their particular strengths are valued by customers, and that somehow their competitors are necessarily inferior. For example, professional groups in many public services have tended to assume that what they think best for the client automatically is the best, while being sceptical of private sector providers' ability to look after the 'true' needs of clients.

● *Changes over time*. Customers' values typically evolve, either because they become more experienced (through repeat purchase) or because competitive offerings become available which offer better value. Managers, however, are often trapped by their historical experience of the market (see Chapter 5).

2.5   OPPORTUNITIES AND THREATS

The concepts and frameworks discussed above should be helpful in understanding the factors in the macro-, industry and competitor/market environments of an organisation (Illustration 2.6 outlines a key debate: just how much do such industry and market factors affect successful strategic outcomes?). However, the critical issue is the *implications* that are drawn from this understanding in guiding strategic decisions and choices. The crucial next stage, therefore, is to draw from the environmental analysis specific strategic opportunities and threats for the organisation. Identifying these opportunities and threats is extremely valuable when thinking about strategic choices for the future (the subject of Chapters 6 to 9). Opportunities and threats forms one half of the strengths, weaknesses, opportunities and threats (SWOT) analyses that shape many companies' strategy formulation (see Chapter 3).[22] In responding strategically to the environment, the goal is to reduce identified threats and take advantage of the best opportunities.

A **strategic gap** is an opportunity in the competitive environment that is not being fully exploited by competitors

Taking advantage of a **strategic gap** is an effective way of managing threats and opportunities. W. Chan Kim and Renée Mauborgne have argued that if organisations simply concentrate on competing head to head with competitive rivals this will lead to competitive convergence where all 'players' find the environment tough and threatening.[23] They describe this as a 'red ocean' strategy – red because of the bloodiness of the competition and the red ink caused by financial losses. They urge instead that managers attempt 'blue ocean' strategies – searching for, or creating, wide open spaces, free from existing competition. Blue oceans are strategic gaps in the market, opportunities that are not being fully exploited by competitors. One such blue ocean strategy was the creation by Australian wine producers of fun, easy-to-understand and easy-to-drink wines. A red ocean strategy would have been to compete against the established French producers with fancy labels, wine jargon and complex tastes.

Strategic gaps can be identified with the help of the techniques in this chapter. In terms of Porter's five forces, strategic gaps are where rivalry is low. In terms of strategic group maps, gaps typically lie in the under-occupied 'white spaces'. In terms of the strategy canvas, potential strategic gaps are where a big difference can be established with the position of most companies on the various factors valued by customers.

With the concept of strategic gaps, six types of opportunity are particularly important, as follows.

Opportunities in substitute industries

Organisations face competition from industries that are producing substitutes, as discussed in section 2.3.1. But substitution also provides opportunities. In order to identify gaps a *realistic* assessment has to be made of the relative merits of the products/technologies (incumbent and potential substitutes) *in the eyes of the customer*. An example would be software companies substituting electronic versions of reference books and atlases for the traditional paper versions. From the customers' point of view, electronic versions have easier search facilities and are more likely to be up to date.

Opportunities in other strategic groups or strategic spaces

It is also possible to identify opportunities by looking across strategic groups – particularly if changes in the macro-environment make new market spaces economically viable. For example, deregulation of markets (say in electricity generation and distribution) and advances in IT (say with educational study programmes) could both create new market gaps. In the first case, the locally based smaller-scale generation of electricity becomes viable – possibly linked to waste incineration plants. In the latter case, geography can be 'shrunk' and educational programmes delivered across continents through the Internet and teleconferencing (together with local tutorial support). New strategic groups emerge in these industries/sectors.

Opportunities in targeting buyers

Sections 2.4.3 and 2.4.4 emphasised that the nature of the buyers can be complex, with the strategic customer critically important. It was also noted that there may be several people involved in the overall purchase decision. There may be opportunities in targeting neglected strategic customers or neglected influencers of purchasing decisions. It might, for instance, be worth targeting health and safety executives at a customer organisation: they might be willing to pay more for a safe product or service than the usual buyers in the purchasing department, typically more focused on cost.

Opportunities for complementary products and services

This involves a consideration of the potential value of complementary products and services. For example, in book retailing the overall 'book-buying experience' requires much more than just stocking the right books. It also includes providing an ambience conducive to browsing; the provision of a coffee bar might be seen as a complementary service.

Opportunities in new market segments

Looking for new market segments may provide opportunities but product/service features may need to change. If the emphasis is on selling emotional appeal, the alternative may be to provide a no-frills model that costs less and would appeal to another potential market. For example, the Body Shop, operating in the highly emotional cosmetics industry, challenged the accepted viewpoint. This was achieved by the production of purely functional products, noted for their lack of elaborate packaging or heavy advertising. This created new market space by attracting the consumer who wanted quality skin-care products without the added frills.

Opportunities over time

When predicting the impact of changes in the macro- or competitive environments it is important to consider how they are going to affect the consumer. Organisations can gain first-mover advantages that way. Cisco Systems realised that the future was going to create a significant need for high-speed data exchange and was at the forefront of producing equipment to address this future need. It identified new market space because no one else had assessed the likely implications of the Internet boom. This meant that it could offer specially designed products well ahead of its rivals, giving it an important competitive edge.

SUMMARY

- Environmental influences can be thought of as layers around an organisation, with the outer layer making up the *macro-environment*, the middle layer making up the *industry or sector* and the inner layer *strategic groups* and *market segments*.

- The macro-environment can be analysed in terms of the *PESTEL factors*, from which *key drivers of change* can be identified. Alternative *scenarios* about the future can be constructed according to how the key drivers develop.

- Industries and sectors can be analysed in terms of *Porter's Five Forces* – barriers to entry, substitutes, buyer power, supplier power and rivalry. Together, these determine industry or sector attractiveness, and can be influential for overall performance (see Key Debate, Illustration 2.6).

- Industries and sectors are dynamic, and their changes can be analysed in terms of the *industry life cycle, hypercompetitive cycles of competition* and *comparative five forces radar plots*.

- In the inner layer of the environment, *strategic group* analysis, *market segment* analysis and the *strategy canvas* can help identify strategic gaps or opportunities.

- *Blue ocean* strategies characterised by low rivalry are likely to be better opportunities than *red ocean* strategies with many rivals.

Illustration 2.6   **key debate**

How much does industry matter?

A good start in strategy must be to choose a profitable industry to compete in. But does simply being in the right industry matter more than having the right kinds of skills and resources?

This chapter has focused on the role of the environment in strategy making, with particular regard to industries. But the importance of industries in determining organisational performance has been challenged in recent years. This has led to a debate about whether strategy making should be externally orientated, starting with the environment, or internally orientated, starting with the organisation's own skills and resources (the focus of Chapter 3).[1]

Managers favouring an external approach look primarily *outside* the organisation, for example building market share in their industries through mergers and acquisitions or aggressive marketing. Managers favouring an internal approach concentrate their attention *inside* the organisation, fostering the skills of their people or nurturing technologies, for example. Because managerial time is limited, there is a real trade-off to be made between external and internal approaches.

The chief advocate of the external approach is Michael Porter, Professor at Harvard Business School and founder of the Monitor Consulting Group. An influential sceptic of this approach is Richard Rumelt, a student at Harvard Business School but now at University of California Los Angeles. Porter, Rumelt and others have done a series of empirical studies examining the relative importance of industries in explaining organisations' performance.

Typically, these studies take a large sample of firms and compare the extent to which variance in profitability is due to firms or industries (controlling for other effects such as size). If firms within the same industry tend to bunch together in terms of profitability, it is industry that is accounting for the greater proportion of profitability: an external approach to strategy is supported. If firms within the same industry vary widely in terms of profitability, it is the specific skills and resources of the firms that matter most: an internal approach is most appropriate.

The two most important studies in fact find that more of the variance in profitability is due to firms rather than industries – firms account for 47 per cent in Rumelt's study of manufacturing (see the figure).[2] However, when Porter and McGahan included service industries as well as manufacturing, they found a larger industry effect (19 per cent).[3]

The implication from this work is that firm-specific factors generally influence profitability more than industry factors. Firms need to attend carefully to their

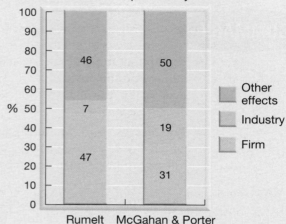

Per cent of variance in profitability due to:

own skills and resources. However, the greater industry effect found in Porter and McGahan's study of both manufacturing and services suggests that industry's importance varies strongly by industry. External influences can matter more in some industries than others.

Notes

1. E.H. Bowman and C.E. Helfat, 'Does corporate strategy matter?', *Strategic Management Journal*, vol. 22, no. 1 (2001), pp. 1–14.
2. R.P. Rumelt, 'How much does industry matter?', *Strategic Management Journal*, vol. 12, no. 2 (1991), pp. 167–185.
3. M.E. Porter and A.M. McGahan, 'How much does industry matter really?', *Strategic Management Journal*, vol. 18, Summer Special Issue (1997), pp. 15–30; M.E. Porter and A.M. McGahan, 'The emergence and sustainability of abnormal profits', *Strategic Organization*, vol. 1, no. 1 (2003), pp. 79–108.

Question

Porter and McGahan's study suggests that some industries influence member firms' profitabilities more than others: in other words, their profitabilities bunch together. Why might some industries have a larger influence on their members' profitability than others?

Work assignments

*Denotes more advanced work assignments.   * Refers to a case study in the Text and Cases edition.*

2.1   For an organisation of your choice, and using Illustration 2.1 as a model, carry out a PESTEL analysis and identify key drivers for change.

2.2 ✱ For the same organisation as in 2.1, and using Illustration 2.2 as a model, construct four scenarios for the evolution of its environment. What implications are there for the organisation's strategy?

2.3   Drawing on section 2.3, carry out a five forces analysis of the pharmaceutical industry* or the hifi industry*. What do you conclude about that industry's attractiveness?

2.4 ✱ Drawing on section 2.3, and particularly using the radar plot technique of Exhibit 2.5, choose two industries or sectors and compare their attractiveness in terms of the five forces (a) today; (b) in approximately three to five years' time. Justify your assessment of each of the five forces' strength. Which industry or sector would you invest in?

2.5   With regard to section 2.4.1 and Illustration 2.5, identify an industry (for example, the motor industry or clothing retailers) and, by comparing competitors, map out the main strategic groups in the industry according to key strategic dimensions. Try more than one set of key strategic dimensions to map the industry. Do the resulting maps identify any under-exploited opportunities in the industry?

2.6 ✱ Drawing on section 2.4.4, and particularly on Exhibit 2.8, identify critical success factors for an industry with which you and your peers are familiar (for example, clothing retailers or mobile phone companies). Using your own estimates (or those of your peers), construct a strategy canvas comparing the main competitors, as in Exhibit 2.8. What implications does your strategy canvas have for the strategies of these competitors?

2.7   To what extent are the models discussed in this chapter appropriate for analysing the environments of a public sector or not-for-profit organisation? Give examples to support your arguments.

Integrative assignment

2.8   Carry out a full analysis of an industry or sector of your choice (using for example PESTEL, Scenarios, Five Forces and Strategic Groups). Consider explicitly how the industry or sector is affected by globalisation (see Chapter 8, particularly Exhibit 8.2 on drivers) and innovation (see Chapter 9, particularly Exhibit 9.2 on product and process innovation).

An extensive range of additional materials, including audio summaries, weblinks to organisations featured in the text, definitions of key concepts and self-assessment questions, can be found on the *Exploring Corporate Strategy* Companion Website at **www.pearsoned.co.uk/ecs**

Recommended key readings

- The classic book on the analysis of industries is M.E. Porter, *Competitive Strategy*, Free Press, 1980. An updated view is available in M.E. Porter, 'Strategy and the Internet', *Harvard Business Review*, March (2001), pp. 2–19. An influential adaptation of Porter's basic ideas is W.C. Kim and R. Mauborgne, *Blue Ocean Strategy: How to Create Uncontested Market Space and Make Competition Irrelevant*, Harvard Business School Press, 2005.

- For approaches to how environments change, see K. van der Heijden, *Scenarios: the art of strategic conversation*, 2nd edition, Wiley, 2005, and the work of Michael Porter's colleague, A. McGahan, *How Industries Evolve*, Harvard Business School Press, 2004.

- A collection of academic articles on the latest views on PEST, scenarios and similar is the special issue of *International Studies of Management and Organization*, vol. 36, no. 3 (2006), edited by Peter McKiernan.

References

1. PESTEL is an extension of PEST (Politics, Economics, Social and Technology) analysis, taking more account of environmental ('green') and legal issues. For an application of PEST analysis to the world of business schools, relevant also to PESTEL, see H. Thomas, 'An analysis of the environment and competitive dynamics of management education', *Journal of Management Development*, vol. 26, no. 1 (2007), pp. 9–21.

2. For a discussion of scenario planning in practice, see K. van der Heijden, *Scenarios: the art of strategic conversation*, 2nd edition, Wiley, 2005. For how scenario planning fits with other forms of environmental analysis such as PESTEL, see P. Walsh, 'Dealing with the uncertainties of environmental change by adding scenario planning to the strategy reformulation equation', *Management Decision*, vol. 1, no. 43 (2005), pp. 113–122; and G. Burt, G. Wright, R. Bradfield and K. van der Heijden, 'The role of scenario planning in exploring the environment in view of the limitations of PEST and its derivatives', *International Studies of Management and Organization*, vol. 36, no. 3 (2006), pp. 50–76. For an extension of scenario analysis using causal fields, with a case study on the Iraq War, see B. MacKay and P. McKiernan, 'Back to the future: history and the diagnosis of environmental context', *International Studies of Management and Organization*, vol. 36, no. 3 (2006), pp. 93–110.

3. For the evolution of scenario practice at the Shell oil company, one of the most influential practitioners, see P. Cornelius, A. van de Putte and M. Romani, 'Three decades of scenario planning in Shell', *California Management Review*, vol. 49, no. 1 (2005), pp. 92–109.

4. D. Rutherford, *Routledge Dictionary of Economics*, 2nd edition, Routledge, 1995.

5. See M.E. Porter, *Competitive Strategy: Techniques for analysing industries and competitors*, Free Press, 1980, p. 5.

6. Porter, reference 5, chapter 1. C. Christensen, 'The past and future of competitive advantage', *Sloan Management Review*, vol. 42, no. 2 (2001), pp. 105–109 provides an interesting critique and update of some of the factors underlying Porter's five forces.

7. See L. Van den Berghe and K. Verweire, 'Convergence in the financial services industry', *Geneva Papers on Risk and Insurance*, vol. 25, no. 2 (2000), pp. 262–272; and A. Malhotra and A. Gupta, 'An investigation of firms' responses to industry convergence', *Academy of Management Proceedings*, 2001, pp. G1–6.

8. For discussions of the need for a collaborative as well as Porterian competitive approach to industry analysis, see J. Burton, 'Composite strategy: the combination of collaboration and competition', *Journal of General Management*, vol. 21, no. 1 (1995), pp. 3–28; and R. ul-Haq, *Alliances and Co-evolution: Insights from the Banking Sector*, Palgrave Macmillan, 2005.

9. The classic discussion is A. Brandenburger and B. Nalebuff, 'The right game: use game theory to shape strategy', *Harvard Business Review*, vol. 73, no. 4 (1995), pp. 57–71. On the dangers of 'complementors', see D. Yoffie and M. Kwak, 'With friends like these', *Harvard Business Review*, vol. 84, no. 9 (2006), pp. 88–98.

10. There is a good discussion of the static nature of the Porter model, and other limitations, in M. Grundy, 'Rethinking and reinventing Michael Porter's five forces model', *Strategic Change*, vol. 15 (2006), pp. 213–229.

11. A classic academic overview of the industry life cycle is S. Klepper, 'Industry life cycles', *Industrial and Corporate Change*, vol. 6, no. 1 (1996), pp. 119–143. See also A. McGahan, 'How industries evolve', *Business Strategy Review*, vol. 11, no. 3 (2000), pp. 1–16.

12. A. McGahan, 'How industries evolve', *Business Strategy Review*, vol. 11, no. 3 (2000), pp. 1–16.

13. For a full discussion of the dynamics of competition see R. D'Aveni (with R. Gunther), *Hypercompetitive Rivalries*, Free Press, 1995. For a critical overview of various recent perspectives on hypercompetition and turbulence, plus cases, see J. Slesky, J. Goes and O. Babüroglu, 'Contrasting perspectives of strategy making: applications in hyper environments', *Organization Studies*, vol. 28, no. 1 (2007), pp. 71–94.

14. J. Gimeno and C. Woo, 'Hypercompetition in a multi-market environment: the role of strategic similarity and

multi-market contact on competition de-escalation', *Organisation Science*, vol. 7, no. 3 (1996), pp. 323–341.

15. This definition is from D'Aveni, reference 12, p. 2. In his later book, R. D'Aveni, *Strategic Supremacy: How industry leaders create spheres of influence*, Simon & Schuster International, 2002, he gives examples of strategies that can help defend a strong position in conditions of hyper-competition.

16. G. McNamara, P. Vaaler and C. Devers, 'Same as ever it was: the search for evidence of increasing hypercom-petition', *Strategic Management Journal*, vol. 24 (2003), pp. 261–268; and R. Wiggins and T. Ruefli, 'Schumpeter's ghost: is hypercompetition making the best of times shorter?', *Strategic Management Journal*, vol. 26, no. 10 (2005), pp. 887–911.

17. For a review of the research on strategic groups see J. McGee, H. Thomas and M. Pruett, 'Strategic groups and the analysis of market structure and industry dynamics', *British Journal of Management*, vol. 6, no. 4 (1995), pp. 257–270. For an example of the use of strategic group analysis see C. Flavian, A. Haberberg and Y. Polo, 'Subtle strategic insights from strategic group analysis', *Journal of Strategic Marketing*, vol. 7, no. 2 (1999), pp. 89–106. A recent example is J. Pandian, J. Rajendran, H. Thomas and O. Furrer, 'Performance differences across strategic groups: an examination of financial market-based per-formance measures', *Strategic Change*, vol. 15, nos 7/8 (2006), pp. 373–383.

18. These characteristics are based on Porter, reference 5.

19. A useful discussion of segmentation in relation to competitive strategy is provided in M.E. Porter, *Com-petitive Advantage*, Free Press, 1985, chapter 7. See also the discussion on market segmentation in P. Kotler, G. Armstrong, J. Saunders and V. Wong, *Principles of Marketing*, 3rd European edition, FT/Prentice Hall, 2002, chapter 9. For a more detailed review of segmenta-tion methods see M. Wedel and W. Kamakura, *Market Segmentation: Conceptual and methodological foundations*, 2nd edition, Kluwer Academic, 1999.

20. M. Wedel, 'Is segmentation history?', *Marketing Research*, vol. 13, no. 4 (2001), pp. 26–29.

21. The term 'strategy canvas' was introduced by C. Kim and R. Maubourgne, 'Charting your company's future', *Harvard Business Review*, vol. 80, no. 6 (2002), pp. 76–82. There is similar discussion in G. Johnson, C. Bowman and P. Rudd's chapter, 'Competitor analysis', in V. Ambrosini with G. Johnson and K. Scholes (eds), *Exploring Techniques of Analysis and Evaluation in Strategic Management*, Prentice Hall, 1998.

22. The idea of SWOT as a common-sense checklist has been used for many years: for example, S. Tilles, 'Making strategy explicit', in I. Ansoff (ed.), *Business Strategy*, Penguin, 1968. See also T. Jacobs, J. Shepherd and G. Johnson's chapter on SWOT analysis in V. Ambrosini with G. Johnson and K. Scholes (see reference 21); and E. Valentin, 'SWOT analysis from a resource-based view', *Journal of Marketing Theory and Practice*, vol. 9, no. 2 (2001), pp. 54–69. SWOT will be discussed more fully in section 3.6.4 and Illustration 3.5.

23. W.C. Kim and R. Mauborgne, 'Value innovation: a leap into the blue ocean', *Journal of Business Strategy*, vol. 26, no. 4 (2005), pp. 22–28; and W.C. Kim and R. Mauborgne, *Blue Ocean Strategy: How to Create Uncontested Market Space and Make Competition Irrelevant*, Harvard Business School Press, 2005.

Global forces and the European brewing industry

Mike Blee and Richard Whittington

This case is centred on the European brewing industry and examines how the increasingly competitive pressure of operating within global markets is causing consolidation through acquisitions, alliances and closures within the industry. This has resulted in the growth of the brewers' reliance upon super brands.

In the first decade of the twenty-first century, European brewers faced a surprising paradox. The traditional centre of the beer industry worldwide, and still the largest regional market, Europe, was turning off beer. Beer consumption was falling in the largest markets of Germany and the United Kingdom, while burgeoning in emerging markets around the world. China, with 7 per cent annual growth, had become the largest single market by volume, while Brazilian volumes had overtaken Germany in 2005 (Euromonitor, 2006).

Table 1 details the overall decline of European beer consumption. Decline in traditional key markets is due to several factors. Governments are campaigning strongly against drunken driving, affecting the propensity to drink beer in restaurants, pubs and bars. There is increasing awareness of the effects of alcohol on health and fitness. Particularly In the United Kingdom, there is growing hostility towards so-called 'binge drinking', excessive alcohol consumption in pubs and clubs. Wines have also become increasingly popular in Northern European markets. However, beer consumption per capita varies widely between countries, being four times higher in Germany than in Italy, for example. Some traditionally low-consumption European markets have been showing good growth.

The drive against drunken driving and binge drinking has helped shift sales from the 'on-trade' (beer consumed on the premises, as in pubs or restaurants) to the off-trade (retail). Worldwide, the off-trade increased from 63 per cent of volume in 2000 to 66 per cent in 2005. The off-trade is increasingly dominated by large supermarket chains

Photo: Picturesbyrob/Alamy

such as Tesco or Carrefour, which often use cut-price offers on beer in order to lure people into their shops. More than one-fifth of beer volume is now sold through supermarkets. German retailers such as Aldi and Lidl have had considerable success with their own 'private-label' (rather than brewery-branded) beers. However, although on-trade volumes are falling in Europe, the sales values are rising, as brewers introduce higher-priced premium products such as extra-cold lagers or fruit-flavoured beers. On the other hand, a good deal of this increasing demand for premium products is being satisfied by the import of apparently exotic beers from overseas (see Table 2).

Brewers' main purchasing costs are packaging (accounting for around half of non-labour costs), raw material such as barley, and energy. The European packaging industry is highly concentrated, dominated by international companies such as Crown in cans and Owens-Illinois in glass bottles. During 2006, Dutch brewer Heineken complained of an 11 per cent rise in packaging costs.

Table 1 European beer consumption by country and year (000 hectolitres)

Country	1980	2000	2001	2002	2003	2004	2005
Austria	7651	8762	8627	8734	8979	8881	8970
Belgium	12945	10064	9986	9901	9935	9703	N/A
Denmark	6698	5452	5282	5202	5181	4862	N/A
Finland	2738	4024	4085	4136	4179	4370	N/A
France	23745	21420	21331	20629	21168	20200	N/A
Germany†	89820	103105	100904	100385	97107	95639	94994
Greece	N/A	4288	4181	4247	3905	N/A	N/A
Ireland	4174	5594	5625	5536	5315	5206	N/A
Italy	9539	16289	16694	16340	17452	17194	17340
Luxembourg	417	472	445	440	373	N/A	N/A
Netherlands	12213	13129	12922	11985	12771	12687	12747
Norway*	7651	2327	2290	2420	2270	2490	N/A
Portugal	3534	6453	6276	5948	6008	6266	6224
Spain	20065	29151	31126	30715	33451	N/A	N/A
Sweden	3935	5011	4932	4998	4969	4635	4566
Switzerland*	4433	4194	4141	4127	4334	4262	N/A
UK	65490	57007	58234	59384	60302	59195	N/A

* Non-EU countries; †1980 excludes GDR. Figures adjusted.

Source: www.Brewersofeurope.org.

Table 2 Imports of beer by country

Country	Imports 2002 (% of consumption or production*)	Imports 2004 (% of consumption or production)
Austria	5.1	6.4
Belgium	4.74	10.2
Denmark	2.6	N/A
Finland	2.3	7.3
France	23	31
Germany	3.1	4
Greece	4.1	N/A
Ireland	N/A	N/A
Italy	27.15	37
Luxembourg	N/A	38.4
Netherlands	3.2	14.4
Norway	5.4	N/A
Portugal	1.1	N/A
Spain	11.7	N/A
Sweden	N/A	18
Switzerland	15.4	15.6
UK	10.9	12.3

* Import figures do not include beers brewed under licence in home country; countries vary in measuring % of production or consumption.

Source: www.brewersofeurope.org.

Acquisition, licensing and strategic alliances have all occurred as the leading brewers battle to control the market. There are global pressures for consolidation due to overcapacity within the industry, the need to contain costs and benefits of leveraging strong brands. For example, Belgian brewer Interbrew purchased parts of the old Bass Empire, Becks and Whitbread in 2001 and in 2004 announced a merger with Am Bev, the Brazilian brewery group, to create the largest brewer in the world, InBev. The second largest brewer, the American Anheuser-Busch, has been investing in China, Mexico and Europe. In 2002, South African Breweries acquired the Miller Group (USA) and Pilsner Urquell in the Czech Republic, becoming SABMiller. Smaller players in fast-growing Chinese and South American markets are being snapped up by the large international brewers too. Medium-sized Australian brewer Fosters is withdrawing from direct participation in many international markets, for example selling its European brand-rights to Scottish & Newcastle. Table 3 lists the world's top 10 brewing companies, which accounted for around half of world beer volumes. There remain many small specialist and regional

Table 3 The world's top 10 brewery companies by volume: 2005

Company	Share global volume (%)	Country of origin
InBev	10.8	Brazil–Belgium
Anheuser-Busch	9.4	USA
SABMiller	7.3	South Africa (relocated to UK)
Heineken	5.7	Netherlands
Morelo	2.9	Mexico
Carlsberg	2.9	Denmark
Coors	2.6	USA
TsingTao	2.4	China
Baltic Brewery Holdings	2.2	Denmark/UK
Asahi	2.1	Japan

Source: Euromonitor International, *The World Brewing Industry*.

brewers, such as the Dutch company Grolsch (see below) or the British Cobra Beer, originating in the Indian restaurant market.

Four brewing companies

Heineken (The Netherlands)

Heineken is the biggest of the European brewery businesses, and has three-quarters of its sales in the region. Total sales in 2006 were €11.8bn (£8bn). About 5 per cent of sales are in Asia–Pacific and 17 per cent of sales are in the Americas. The company's biggest brands are Heineken itself and Amstel. The company remains a family-controlled business, which it claims gives it the stability and independence to pursue steady growth internationally.

Heineken's strategy overseas is to use locally acquired companies as a means of introducing the Heineken brand to new markets. It aims to strengthen local companies by transferring expertise and technology. The result is to create economies of scale for both the local beers and Heineken. Heineken's four priorities for action are to accelerate revenue growth, to improve efficiency and cost reduction, to speed up strategy implementation and to focus on those markets where the company believes it can win.

Grolsch (The Netherlands)

Royal Grolsch NV is a medium-size international brewing group, established in 1615. With overall

sales in 2005 of €313m, it is less than a twentieth of the size of Heineken. Its key products include Grolsch premium lager and new flavoured beers (Grolsch lemon and Grolsch pink grapefruit). In The Netherlands Grolsch holds the rights for the sale and distribution of the valued US Miller brand. About half its sales are obtained overseas, either through export or licensing of production: the United Kingdom is its second largest market. In 2005, Grolsch centralised its own production on a single new Dutch brewery to increase efficiency and volume, and opened a small additional 'trial' brewery in order to support innovation.

Innovation and branding are core to the company's strategy. The company believes that its strong and distinctive beers can succeed in a market of increased homogenisation. Its brand is reinforced by its striking green bottles and its unique swing-tops.

InBev (Belgium/Brazil)

InBev was created in 2004 from the merger of Belgian InterBrew and Brazilian AmBev. With a turnover of €13.3bn in 2006, it is the largest brewer in the world, holding number one or number two positions in 20 different countries. Its well-known international brands include Beck's and Stella Artois. Through a series of acquisitions, InBev has become the second largest brewer in China.

The company is frank about its strategy: to transform itself from the biggest brewing company in the world to the best. It aims to do this by building strong global brands and increasing efficiency. Efficiency gains will come from more central coordination of purchasing, including media and IT; from the optimisation of its inherited network of breweries; and from the sharing of best practice across sites internationally. Although acquisitions continue, InBev is now emphasising organic growth and improved margins from its existing businesses.

Scottish and Newcastle (UK)

Scottish and Newcastle is a European-focused brewing group based in Edinburgh. In 2005, its turnover was £3.9bn (€5.5bn). Its key brands include John Smiths, Kronenbourg, Kanterbrau, Baltika and (in Europe) Fosters. It is the fourth largest brewer in Europe in volume terms, and market leader in the UK, France and Russia. The company has made many acquisitions in the UK (including Bulmer's cider), France, Greece and Finland. The group's 50 per cent investment in Baltic Beverages has given it exposure to the fast-growing markets of Russia, Ukraine and the Baltic countries. In China, Scottish and Newcastle has a 20 per cent stake in CBC, the country's fifth largest brewery. In India, the company's United Breweries is the country's largest brewer, with the Kingfisher brand. In the USA, Scottish and Newcastle is the second largest importer of foreign beers. The company emphasises the development of innovative and premium beers, and is closing down its more inefficient breweries.

Questions

1 Using the data from the case (and any other sources available), carry out for the European brewing industry (i) a PESTEL analysis and (ii) a five forces analysis. What do you conclude?

2 For the four breweries outlined above (or breweries of your own choice) explain:
   (a) how these trends will impact differently on these different companies; and
   (b) the relative strengths and weaknesses of each company.

3

Strategic Capability

LEARNING OUTCOMES

After reading this chapter you should be able to:

→ Distinguish elements of strategic capability in organisations: resources, competences, core competences and dynamic capabilities.

→ Recognise the role of continual improvement in cost efficiency as a strategic capability.

→ Analyse how strategic capabilities might provide sustainable competitive advantage on the basis of their value, rarity, inimitability and non-substitutability.

→ Diagnose strategic capability by means of value chain analysis, activity mapping, benchmarking and SWOT analysis.

→ Consider how managers can develop strategic capabilities of organisations.

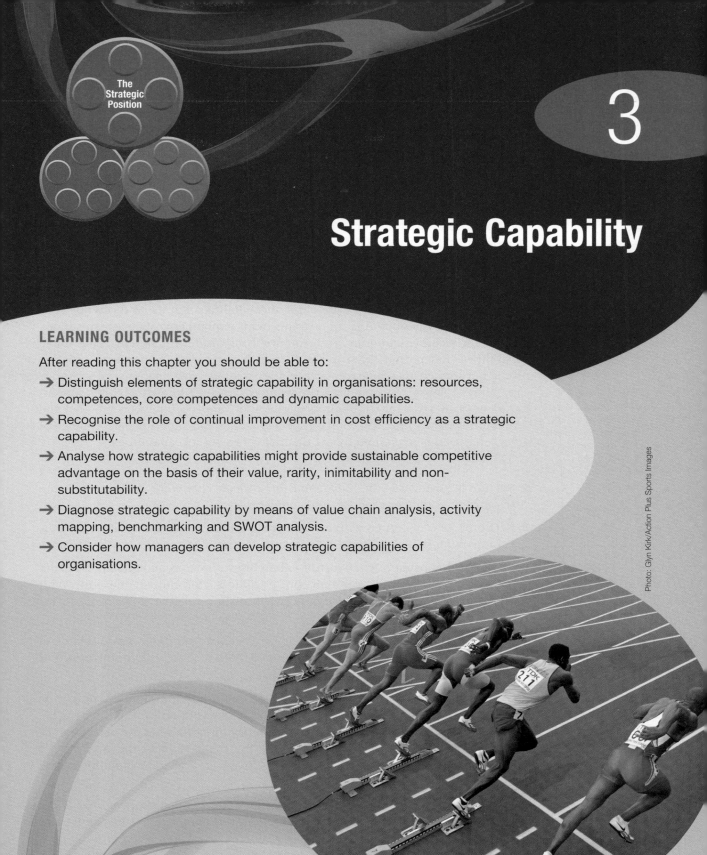

Photo: Glyn Kirk/Action Plus Sports Images

3.1 INTRODUCTION

Chapter 2 outlined how the external environment of an organisation can create both strategic opportunities and threats. However, Tesco, Sainsbury's and Asda all compete in the same environment, yet Tesco is a superior performer. It is not the environment that distinguishes between them but their internal *strategic capabilities*. The importance of strategic capability is the focus of this chapter. There are three key concepts that underpin the discussion. The first is that organisations are not identical, but have different capabilities; they are 'heterogeneous' in this respect. The second is that it can be difficult for one organisation to obtain or copy the capabilities of another. For example, Sainsbury's cannot readily obtain the whole of Tesco's retail sites, its management or its experience. The third arises from these: if an organisation is to achieve competitive advantage, it will do so on the basis of capabilities that its rivals do not have or have difficulty in obtaining. In turn this helps explain how some organisations are able to achieve superior performance compared with others. They have capabilities that permit them to produce at lower cost or generate a superior product or service at standard cost in relation to other organisations with inferior capabilities.[1] These concepts underlie what has become known as the **resource-based view** of strategy[2] (though it might more appropriately be labelled the 'capabilities view'): that the competitive advantage and superior performance of an organisation is explained by the distinctiveness of its capabilities.

> The **resource-based view** of strategy: the competitive advantage and superior performance of an organisation is explained by the distinctiveness of its capabilities

The chapter has six sections:

- Section 3.2 discusses the *foundations of strategic capability* and considers the distinction between *resources* and *competences*.

- Section 3.3 is concerned with a vital basis of strategic capability of any organisation, namely the ability to achieve and continually improve *cost efficiency*.

- Section 3.4 considers what sort of capabilities allow organisations to *sustain* competitive advantage over time (in a public sector context the equivalent concern might be how some organisations sustain relative superior performance over time).

- Section 3.5 discusses how the concept of *organisational knowledge* relates to strategic capability and how it might contribute to competitive advantage of organisations.

- Section 3.6 moves on to consider different ways strategic capability might be analysed. These include *value chain* and *value network* analyses, *activity mapping* and *benchmarking*. The section concludes by explaining the use of *SWOT* analysis as a basis for pulling together the insights from the analyses of the environment (explained in Chapter 2) and of strategic capability in this chapter.

- Finally section 3.7 discusses how managers can *develop strategic capability* through internal and external development, the management of people and the building of dynamic capabilities.

3.2   FOUNDATIONS OF STRATEGIC CAPABILITY

Strategic capability
is the resources and
competences of an
organisation needed for
it to survive and prosper

Different writers, managers and consultants use different terms and concepts in explaining the importance of strategic capability. Given such differences, it is important to understand how the terms are used here. Overall, **strategic capability** can be defined as the resources and competences of an organisation needed for it to survive and prosper. Exhibit 3.1 shows the elements of strategic capability that are employed in the chapter to explain the concept.

Exhibit 3.1   **Strategic capabilities and competitive advantage**

	Resources	Competences
Threshold capabilities	**Threshold resources** ● Tangible ● Intangible	**Threshold competences**
Capabilities for competitive advantage	**Unique resources** ● Tangible ● Intangible	**Core competences**

3.2.1   Resources and competences

Tangible resources are
the physical assets of an
organisation such as
plant, labour and finance

Intangible resources are
non-physical assets such
as information, reputation
and knowledge

Perhaps the most basic concept is that of *resources*. **Tangible resources** are the physical assets of an organisation such as plant, people and finance. **Intangible resources**[3] are non-physical assets such as information, reputation and knowledge. Typically, an organisation's resources can be considered under the following four broad categories:

● *Physical resources* – such as the machines, buildings or the production capacity of the organisation. The nature of these resources, such as the age, condition, capacity and location of each resource, will determine the usefulness of such resources.

● *Financial resources* – such as capital, cash, debtors and creditors, and suppliers of money (shareholders, bankers, etc.).

● *Human resources* – including the mix (for example, demographic profile), skills and knowledge of employees and other people in an organisation's networks.

● *Intellectual capital* – as an intangible resource – includes patents, brands, business systems and customer databases. An indication of the value of these is that when businesses are sold, part of the value is 'goodwill'. In a knowledge-based economy intellectual capital is likely to be a major asset of many organisations.

Such resources are certainly important, but what an organisation does – how it employs and deploys these resources – matters at least as much as what resources it has. There would be no point in having state-of-the-art equipment or valuable knowledge or a valuable brand if they were not used effectively. The efficiency and effectiveness of physical or financial resources, or the people in an organisation, depends on not just their existence but how they are managed, the cooperation between people, their adaptability, their innovatory capacity, the relationship with customers and suppliers, and the experience and learning about what works well and what does not. The term **competences** is used to mean the skills and abilities by which resources are deployed effectively through an organisation's activities and processes.

Competences are the skills and abilities by which resources are deployed effectively through an organisation's activities and processes

Within these broad definitions, other terms are commonly used. As the explanation proceeds, it might be useful to refer to the two examples provided in Exhibit 3.2, one relating the concepts to a business and the other to sport.

3.2.2 Threshold capabilities

A distinction needs to be made between capabilities (resources or competences) that are at a threshold level and those that might help the organisation achieve

Exhibit 3.2	Strategic capability: the terminology	
Term	**Definition**	**Example (athletics)**
Strategic capability	The ability to perform at the level required to survive and prosper. It is underpinned by the resources and competences of the organisation	Equipment and athletic ability suited to a chosen event
Threshold resources	The resources needed to meet customers' minimum requirements and therefore to continue to exist	A healthy body (for individuals) Medical facilities and practitioners Training venues and equipment Food supplements
Threshold competences	Activities and processes needed to meet customers' minimum requirements and therefore to continue to exist	Individual training regimes Physiotherapy/injury management Diet planning
Unique resources	Resources that underpin competitive advantage and are difficult for competitors to imitate or obtain	Exceptional heart and lungs Height or weight World-class coach
Core competences	Activities that underpin competitive advantage and are difficult for competitors to imitate or obtain	A combination of dedication, tenacity, time to train, demanding levels of competition and a will to win

Threshold capabilities are those capabilities needed for an organisation to meet the necessary requirements to compete in a given market

competitive advantage and superior performance. **Threshold capabilities** are those needed for an organisation to meet the necessary requirements to compete in a given market. These could be *threshold resources* required to meet minimum customer requirements: for example, the increasing demands by modern multiple retailers of their suppliers mean that those suppliers have to possess a quite sophisticated IT infrastructure simply to stand a chance of meeting retailer requirements. Or they could be the *threshold competences* required to deploy resources so as to meet customers' requirements and support particular strategies. Retailers do not simply expect suppliers to have the required IT infrastructure, but to be able to use it effectively so as to guarantee the required level of service.

Identifying and managing threshold capabilities raises at least two significant challenges:

● *Threshold levels of capability will change* as critical success factors change (see section 2.4.4) or through the activities of competitors and new entrants. To continue the example, suppliers to major retailers did not require the same level of IT and logistics support a decade ago. But the retailers' drive to reduce costs, improve efficiency and ensure availability of merchandise to their customers means that their expectations of their suppliers have increased markedly in that time and continue to do so. So there is a need for those suppliers continuously to review and improve their logistics resource and competence base just to stay in business.

● *Trade-offs* may need to be made to achieve the threshold capability required for different sorts of customers. For example, businesses have found it difficult to compete in market segments that require large quantities of standard product as well as market segments that require added value specialist products. Typically, the first requires high-capacity, fast-throughput plant, standardised highly efficient systems and a low-cost labour force; the second a skilled labour force, flexible plant and a more innovative capacity. The danger is that an organisation fails to achieve the threshold capabilities required for either segment.

KEY CONCEPT

Core competences **3.2.3 Unique resources and core competences**

Unique resources are those resources that critically underpin competitive advantage and that others cannot easily imitate or obtain

Core competences are the skills and abilities by which resources are deployed through an organisation's activities and processes such as to achieve competitive advantage in ways that others cannot imitate or obtain

While threshold capabilities are important, they do not of themselves create competitive advantage or the basis of superior performance. These are dependent on an organisation having distinctive or unique capabilities that competitors will find difficult to imitate. This could be because the organisation has **unique resources** that critically underpin competitive advantage and that others cannot imitate or obtain – a long-established brand, for example. It is, however, more likely that an organisation achieves competitive advantage because it has distinctive, or core, competences. The concept of core competences was developed, most notably, by Gary Hamel and C.K. Prahalad. While various definitions exist, here **core competences**[4] are taken to mean the skills and abilities by which resources are deployed through an organisation's activities and processes such as to achieve competitive advantage in ways that others cannot imitate or obtain. For example, a supplier that achieves competitive advantage in a retail market

Illustration 3.1

Strategic capabilities

Executives emphasise different strategic capabilities in different organisations.

Freeport-McMoRan Copper and Gold, Inc. is an international mining company in North America. It claims a leading position in the mining industry on the basis of 'large, long lived, geographically diverse assets and significant proven and probable reserves of copper, gold and molybdenum'. More specifically, in terms of its Indonesian operation it points to a 'principal asset' as the 'world class Grasberg mine discovered in 1988' which has 'the world's largest single copper reserve and world's largest single gold reserve'.

Source: Annual Report 2006.

Daniel Bouton, Chairman and CEO of **Société Générale**, in response to the question: *How do you maintain your competitive advantage in equity derivatives?*

The barrier to entry is high, because of two significant costs. The first is IT. The systems you need to perform well cost at least €200 million a year, and it's not something you can buy from Dell or SAP. The second is the sheer number of people you need to work on managing your risk. Before you launch a product, you need to have the front office guys that propose, calculate and write the first model. Then you need the IT guy that creates the IT system in order to be able to calculate risks every 10 seconds. And you need a good validating team in order to verify all the hypotheses. After that, you need high-quality middle and back office people.

Source: Interviewed by Clive Horwood in *Euromoney*, vol. 27, no. 447 (July 2006), pp. 84–89.

Tony Hall, Chief Executive of the **Royal Opera House**:

'world-class' is neither an idle nor boastful claim. In the context of the Royal Opera House the term refers to the quality of our people, the standards of our productions and the diversity of our work and initiatives. Unique? Unashamedly so. We shy away from labels such as 'elite', because of the obvious negative connotations of exclusiveness. But I want people to take away from here the fact that we are elite in the sense that we have the best singers, dancers, directors, designers, orchestra, chorus, backstage crew and administrative staff. We are also amongst the best in our ability to reach out to as wide and diverse a community as possible.

Source: Annual Review 2005/6, p. 11.

Dave Swift, President of **Whirlpool** North America:

Executing our strategy requires a unique toolkit of competencies that we continue to build for our people globally. The starting point of building new competencies is what we call 'Customer Excellence' – our ability to proactively understand and anticipate the needs of customers. Customer Excellence is a collection of tools that allows our people to analytically assess and prioritize the needs and desires of customers along all aspects of the purchase cycle – from when they first might investigate an appliance on a web site, to the in-store experience on a retailer's floor, to the features and aesthetics of the product, to the installation and service experience, and ultimately to their need to repeat this cycle. With these consumer insights in-hand, we then turn them into customer solutions through our innovation tools. As a result, our innovation capability has produced a robust pipeline of products, achieving a steady-state estimated value of over $3 billion. . . . Our knowledge of customers, coupled with our innovative customer solutions, is driving the attractiveness of our brands and creating greater value for our shareholders.

Source: Whirlpool Corporation 2005 Annual Report.

Questions

1 Categorise the range of capabilities highlighted by the executives in terms of section 3.2 and Exhibit 3.2.

2 With reference to section 3.4, which of the capabilities might be especially important in terms of achieving competitive advantage and why?

3 For an organisation of your choice undertake the same exercise as in questions 1 and 2 above.

might have done so on the basis of a unique resource such as a powerful brand, or by finding ways of providing service or building relationships with that retailer in ways that its competitors find difficult to imitate – a core competence. Section 3.4 of this chapter discusses in more depth the role played by unique resources and core competences in contributing to long-term competitive advantage.

Putting these concepts together, the summary argument is this. To survive and prosper an organisation needs to address the challenges of the environment that it faces, discussed in Chapter 2. In particular it must be capable of performing in terms of the critical success factors that arise from demands and needs of its customers, discussed in section 2.4.4. The strategic capability to do so is dependent on the resources and the competences it has. These must reach a threshold level in order for the organisation to survive. The further challenge is to achieve competitive advantage. This requires it to have strategic capabilities that its competitors find difficult to imitate or obtain. These could be unique resources but are more likely to be the core competences of the organisation. Illustration 3.1 shows how executives of different organisations describe the strategic capabilities of their organisations.

3.3 COST EFFICIENCY

Managers often refer to the management of costs as a key strategic capability. So it is. Moreover, understanding the management of cost efficiency as a strategic capability illustrates some of the points made in section 3.2.

Customers can benefit from cost efficiencies in terms of lower prices or more product features for the same price. The management of the cost base of an organisation could also be a basis for achieving competitive advantage (see sections 6.3.1 and 6.4.1). However, for many organisations the management of costs is becoming a threshold strategic capability for two reasons:

- *Customers do not value product features at any price*. If the price rises too high they will sacrifice value and opt for lower price. So the challenge is to ensure that an appropriate level of value is offered at an acceptable price. This means that everyone is forced to keep costs as low as possible, consistent with the value to be provided. Not to do so invites customers to switch products or invites competition.

- *Competitive rivalry* will continually require the driving down of costs because competitors will be trying to reduce their cost so as to underprice their rivals while offering similar value.

If cost is to be managed effectively, attention has to be paid to key *cost drivers* (see Exhibit 3.3), as follows:

- *Economies of scale* may be especially important in manufacturing organisations, since the high capital costs of plant need to be recovered over a high volume of output. Traditionally manufacturing sectors where this has been especially important have been motor vehicles, chemicals and metals. In other industries, such as drinks and tobacco and food, scale economies are important in distribution or marketing.[5]

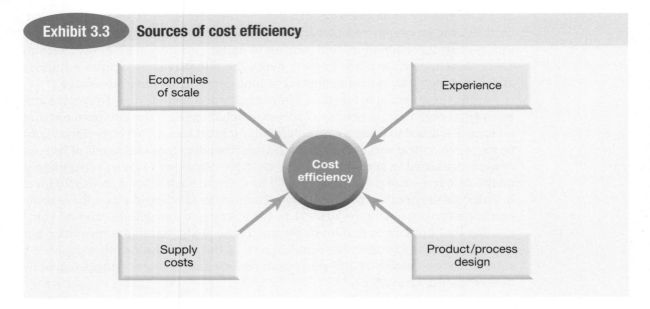

Exhibit 3.3   **Sources of cost efficiency**

- *Supply costs* can be important. Location may influence supply costs, which is why, historically, steel and glass manufacturing were close to raw material or energy sources. In some instances, ownership of raw materials was a unique resource, giving cost advantage. Supply costs are of particular importance to organisations that act as intermediaries, where the value added through their own activities is low and the need to identify and manage input costs is critically important to success. For example, retailers pay a great deal of attention to trying to achieve lower costs of supply than their competitors.

- *Product/process design* also influences cost. Efficiency gains in production processes have been achieved by many organisations through improvements in *capacity-fill*, *labour productivity*, *yield* (from materials) or *working capital* utilisation. Understanding the relative importance of each of these to maintaining a competitive position is important. For example, in terms of managing capacity-fill: an unfilled seat in a plane, train or theatre cannot be 'stocked' for later sale. So marketing special offers (while protecting the core business) and having the IT systems to analyse and optimise revenue are important capabilities. Product design will also influence costs in other parts of the value system – for example, in distribution or after-sales service. In the photocopier market, for example, Canon eroded Xerox's advantage (which was built on service and a support network) by designing a copier that needed far less servicing.

- *Experience*[6] can be a key source of cost efficiency and there is evidence it may provide competitive advantage in particular in terms of the relationship between the cumulative experience gained by an organisation and its unit costs – described as the *experience curve*. See Exhibit 3.4. The experience curve suggests that an organisation undertaking any activity develops competences in this activity over time and therefore does it more efficiently. Since companies with higher market share have more 'cumulative experience' – simply because high share gives them greater volumes of production or service – it follows that it is important to gain and hold market share, as discussed in Chapter 2. It is important to remember that it is the *relative market share* in

Exhibit 3.4   **The experience curve**

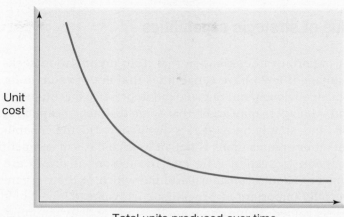

definable market segments that matters. There are important implications of the experience curve concept that could influence an organisation's competitive position.

● *Growth is not optional* in many markets. If an organisation chooses to grow more slowly than the competition, it should expect the competitors to gain cost advantage in the longer term – through experience.

● *Unit costs should decline year on year* as a result of cumulative experience. In high-growth industries this will happen quickly, but even in mature industries this decline in costs should occur. Organisations that fail to achieve this are likely to suffer at the hands of competitors who do. The implication of this is that *continual reduction in costs is a necessity* for organisations in competitive markets. Even if it is not able to provide competitive advantage, it is a threshold competence for survival.

● *First-mover advantage* can be important. The organisation that moves down the experience curve by getting into a market first should be able to reduce its cost base because of the accumulated experience it builds up over its rivals by being first.

3.4   CAPABILITIES FOR ACHIEVING AND SUSTAINING COMPETITIVE ADVANTAGE

The lessons of sections 3.2 and 3.3 are these: if the capabilities of an organisation do not meet customer needs, at least to a threshold level, the organisation cannot survive; and if managers do not manage costs efficiently and continue to improve on this, it will be vulnerable to those who can. However, if the aim is to achieve *competitive advantage* then the further question is: what strategic capabilities might provide competitive advantage in ways that can be sustained over time? If this is to be achieved, then other criteria are important.[7]

3.4.1 Value of strategic capabilities

It is important to emphasise that if an organisation seeks to build competitive advantage it must have capabilities that are of value to its customers. This may seem an obvious point to make but in practice it is often ignored or poorly understood. Managers may argue that some distinctive capability of their organisation is of value simply because it is distinctive. Having capabilities that are different from other organisations is not, of itself, a basis of competitive advantage. So the discussion in section 2.4.4 and the lessons it draws are important here too. Managers should consider carefully which of their organisation's activities are especially important in providing such value. They should also consider which are less valued. Value chain analysis and activity mapping explained in sections 3.6.1 and 3.6.2 can help here.

3.4.2 Rarity of strategic capabilities

Competitive advantage might be achieved if a competitor possesses a unique or rare capability. This could take the form of *unique resources*. For example, some libraries have unique collections of books unavailable elsewhere; a company may have a powerful brand; retail stores may have prime locations. Some organisations have patented products or services that give them advantage – resources that may need to be defended by a willingness to bring litigation against illegal imitators. For service organisations unique resources may be intellectual capital – particularly talented individuals.

Competitive advantage could also be based on rare competences: for example, unique skills developed over time. However, there are three important points to bear in mind about the extent to which rarity of competences might provide sustainable competitive advantage:

- *Ease of transferability*. Rarity may depend on who owns the competence and how easily transferable it is. For example, the competitive advantage of some professional service organisations is built around the competence of specific individuals – such as a doctor in 'leading-edge' medicine, individual fund managers, the manager of a top sports team or the CEO of a business. But since these individuals may leave or join competitors, this resource may be a fragile basis of advantage. More durable advantage *may* be found in competences that exist for recruiting, training, motivating and rewarding such individuals or be embedded in the culture that attracts them to the organisation – so ensuring that they do not defect to 'competitors'.

- *Sustainability*. It may be dangerous to assume that competences that are rare will remain so. *Rarity could be temporary*. If an organisation is successful on the basis of a unique set of competences, then competitors will seek to imitate or obtain those competences. So it may be necessary to consider other bases of sustainability.

● *Core rigidities*. There is another danger of redundancy. Rare capabilities may come to be what Dorothy Leonard-Barton refers to as '*core rigidities*',[8] difficult to change and therefore damaging to the organisation. Managers may be so wedded to these bases of success that they perceive them as strengths of the organisation and 'invent' customer values around them.

3.4.3 Inimitable strategic capabilities[9]

It should be clear by now that the search for strategic capability that provides sustainable competitive advantage is not straightforward. It involves identifying capabilities that are likely to be durable and which competitors find difficult to imitate or obtain.

At the risk of overgeneralisation, it is unusual for competitive advantage to be explainable by differences in the tangible resources of organisations, since over time these can usually be imitated or traded. Advantage is more likely to be determined by the way in which resources are deployed to create competences in the organisation's activities. For example, as suggested earlier, an IT system itself will not improve an organisation's competitive standing: it is how it is used that matters. Indeed, what will probably make most difference is how the system is used to bring together customer needs with activities and knowledge both inside and outside the organisation. It is therefore to do with linking sets of competences. So, extending the earlier definition, *core competences* are likely to be the skills and abilities to *link* activities or processes through which resources are deployed so as to achieve competitive advantage. In order to achieve this advantage, core competences therefore need to fulfil the following criteria:

● They must relate to an activity or process that underpins the value in the product or service features – as seen through the eyes of the customer (or other powerful stakeholder). This is the value criterion discussed earlier.

● The competences must lead to levels of performance that are significantly better than competitors (or similar organisations in the public sector).

● The competences must be difficult for competitors to imitate – or inimitable.

With regard to this third requirement of inimitability, Exhibit 3.5 summarises how this might be achieved and Illustration 3.2 also gives an example. The three main reasons are:

Complexity[10]

The core competences of an organisation may be difficult to imitate because they are complex. This may be for two main reasons.

● *Internal linkages*. It may be the ability to link activities and processes that, together, deliver customer value. The managers in Plasco (see Illustration 3.2) talked about 'flexibility' and 'innovation', but 'flexibility' or 'innovation' are themselves made up of and dependent on sets of related activities as Illustration 3.2 shows. Section 3.6.2 and Exhibit 3.8 below show how such linked sets of activities might be mapped so that they can be better understood. However, even if a competitor possessed such a map, it is unlikely that it would be able to replicate the sort of complexity it represents.

Illustration 3.2

Strategic capability for Plasco

Strategic capability underpinning competitive success may be based on complex linkages rooted in the history and culture of an organisation.

Plasco, a manufacturer of plastics goods, had won several major retail accounts from competitors. Managers were keen to understand the bases of these successes as a way of understanding strategic capabilities better. To do this they undertook an analysis of customer value (as explained in section 2.4.4). From this they identified that the major retailers with whom it had been successful particularly valued a powerful brand, a good product range, innovation, good service and reliable delivery. In particular, Plasco was outperforming competitors when it came to delivery, service and product range.

They then undertook an activity mapping exercise, as explained in section 3.6.2 (see Exhibit 3.8). Some of what emerged from this the senior management knew about; but they were not aware of some of the other explanations for success that emerged.

When they analysed the bases of reliable delivery, they could not find reasons why they were outperforming competitors. The logistics of the company were no different from other companies. They were essential but not unique – threshold resources and competences.

When they examined the activities that gave rise to the good service they provided, however, they found other explanations. They were readily able to identify that much was down to their having a more flexible approach than their competitors, the main one of which was a major US multinational. But the explanations for this flexibility were less obvious. The flexibility took form, for example, in the ability to amend the requirements of the retailers' orders at short notice; or when the buyers in the retailers had made an error, to 'bale them out' by taking back stock that had been delivered. What was much less obvious were the activities underpinning this flexibility. The mapping surfaced some explanations:

- The junior manager and staff within the firm were 'bending the rules' to take back goods from the major retailers when, strictly speaking, the policies and systems of the business did not allow it.

- Plant utilisation was relatively lower and less automated than competitors, so it was easier to change production runs at short notice. Company policy, on the other hand, was to improve productivity through increased utilisation and to begin to automate the plans. Lower levels of production management were not anxious to do this, knowing that if they did, it would reduce the flexibility and therefore diminish their ability to provide the service customers wanted.

Much of this was down to the knowledge of quite junior managers, sales representatives and staff in the factory as to 'how to work the system' and how to work together to solve the retailers' problems. This was not a matter of company policy or formal training, but custom and practice that had built up over the years. The result was a relationship between sales personnel and retail buyers in which buyers were encouraged to 'ask the impossible' of the company when difficulties arose.

Sound logistics and good-quality products were vital, but the core competences which underpinned their success were the result of linked sets of activities built up over the years which it was difficult, not only for competitors but also for people in the organisation, to identify clearly.

Questions

1 Why might it be difficult for a large, automated US plastics manufacturer to deal with retailers in the same way as Plasco?

2 How should Plasco senior managers respond to the explanations of strategic capability surfaced by the mapping?

3 What could erode the bases of competitive advantage that Plasco has?

Exhibit 3.5	**Criteria for inimitability of strategic capabilities**

● *External interconnectedness*. Organisations can make it difficult for others to imitate or obtain their bases of competitive advantage by developing activities together with the customer on which the customer is dependent on them. This is sometimes referred to as *co-specialisation*. For example, an industrial lubricants business moved away from just selling its products to customers by coming to agreements with them to manage the applications of lubricants within the customers' sites against agreed targets on cost savings. The more efficient the use of lubricants, the more both parties benefited. Similarly software businesses can achieve advantage by developing computer programs that are distinctively beneficial to specific customer needs.

Culture and history

Core competences may become embedded in an organisation's culture. Indeed, managers within an organisation may not understand them *explicitly* themselves. So coordination between various activities occurs 'naturally' because people know their part in the wider picture or it is simply 'taken for granted' that activities are done in particular ways. For example, in Plasco the experience in rapid changes in production runs and the close links between sales personnel, production and despatch were not planned or formalised: they were the way the firm had come to operate over the years.

Linked to this cultural embeddedness, therefore, is the likelihood that such competences have developed over time and in a particular way. The origins and history by which competences have developed over time are referred to as *path dependency,*[11] are specific to the organisation and cannot be imitated (also see section 5.3.1). Again, however, it should be noted that there is a danger that culturally embedded competences built up over time become so embedded that they are difficult to change: they become core rigidities.

Causal ambiguity[12]

Another reason why competences might be difficult to imitate is that competitors find it difficult to discern the causes and effects underpinning an organisation's advantage. This is called *causal ambiguity*. This could relate to any or all of the aspects of strategic capability discussed in the preceding sections of this chapter. Causal ambiguity may exist in two different forms:[13]

● *Characteristic ambiguity* – where the significance of the characteristic itself is difficult to discern or comprehend, perhaps because it is based on tacit knowledge or rooted in the organisation's culture. For example, it is quite possible that the 'rule bending' in Plasco would have been counter-cultural for its US rival and therefore not readily identified or seen as relevant or significant.

● *Linkage ambiguity* – where competitors cannot discern which activities and processes are dependent on which others to form linkages that create core competences. It would be difficult for competitors to understand the cause and effect linkages in Plasco given that the management of Plasco did not fully comprehend them themselves.

3.4.4 Non-substitutability of strategic capabilities[14]

Providing value to customers and possessing competences that are complex, culturally embedded and causally ambiguous may mean that it is very difficult for organisations to copy them. However, the organisation may still be at risk from substitution. Substitution could take two different forms:

● *Product or service substitution.* As already discussed in Chapter 2 in relation to the five forces model of competition, a product or service as a whole might be a victim of substitution. For example, increasingly e-mail systems have substituted for postal systems. No matter how complex and culturally embedded were the competences of the postal service, it could not avoid this sort of substitution.

● *Competence substitution.* Substitution might, however, not be at the product or service level but at the competence level. For example, task-based industries have often suffered because of an over-reliance on the competences of skilled craftworkers that have been replaced by expert systems and mechanisation.

In summary and from a resource-based view of organisations, managers need to consider whether their organisation has strategic capabilities to achieve and sustain competitive advantage. To do so they need to consider how and to what extent it has capabilities which are (i) valuable to buyers, (ii) rare, (iii) inimitable and (iv) non-substitutable. If such capabilities for competitive advantage do not exist, then managers need to consider if they can be developed. How this might be done is considered in section 3.7 below.

3.4.5 Dynamic capabilities

The discussion so far has tended to assume that strategic capabilities can provide sustainable competitive advantage over time: that they are durable. However, managers often claim that hypercompetitive conditions (see section 2.3.2) are becoming increasingly prevalent. Technology is giving rise to innovation at a faster rate and therefore greater capacity for imitation and substitution of existing products and services. None the less, even in such circumstances, some firms do achieve competitive advantage over others. To explain this, more emphasis has to be placed on the organisation's capability to change, innovate, to be flexible and to learn how to adapt to a rapidly changing environment.

> **Dynamic capabilities are** an organisation's abilities to renew and recreate its strategic capabilities to meet the needs of a changing environment

David Teece[15] argued that the strategic capabilities that achieve competitive advantage in such dynamic conditions are **dynamic capabilities**, by which he means an organisation's ability to *renew and recreate its strategic capabilities* to meet the needs of a changing environment.[16] Dynamic capabilities may be relatively formal, such as systems for new product development or procedures for agreement for capital expenditure. They may take the form of major strategic moves, such as acquisitions or alliances by which new skills are learned by the organisation. Or they may be more informal, such as the way in which decisions get taken faster than usual when a fast response is needed. They could also take the form of embedded 'organisational knowledge' (see section 3.5 below) about how to deal with particular circumstances the organisation faces, or how to innovate. Indeed, dynamic capabilities are likely to have both formal and informal, visible and invisible, characteristics associated with them. For example, Kathy Eisenhardt[17] has shown that successful acquisition processes that bring in new knowledge to organisations depend on high-quality pre- and post-acquisition analysis of how the acquisition can be integrated into the new organisation so as to capture synergies and bases of learning from that acquisition. However, hand in hand with these formal procedures will be more informal ways of doing things in the acquisition process built on informal personal relationships and the exchange of knowledge in more informal ways.

In summary, whereas in more stable conditions competitive advantage might be achieved by building capabilities that may be durable over time, in more dynamic conditions competitive advantage requires the building of capacity to change, innovate and learn – to build dynamic capabilities. Illustration 3.3 provides an example.

3.5 ORGANISATIONAL KNOWLEDGE[18]

> **Organisational knowledge** is the collective experience accumulated through systems, routines and activities of sharing across the organisation

As interest in strategic capabilities has grown, writers have come to emphasise the importance of organisational knowledge. **Organisational knowledge** is the collective experience accumulated through systems, routines and activities of sharing across the organisation. As such it is closely related to what has so far been discussed as the competences of an organisation.

There are several reasons why organisational knowledge has been highlighted as important. First, as organisations become more complex and larger, the need to share what people know becomes more of a challenge. Second, information systems have started to provide more sophisticated ways of doing this.[19] And

Illustration 3.3

Building dynamic capabilities in a new venture

Networks and partnerships can be a source of dynamic capabilities and learning for firms and for managers.

HMD Clinical is an Edinburgh-based clinical technological new venture that seeks to make large-scale clinical trials more efficient for drug development companies. HMD initially provided bespoke services using telephony technology (for example, interactive voice recognition) to monitor clinical trials. However, this was problematic, principally due to human error. HMD therefore sought to develop a product based on another technology – radiofrequency identification. HMD felt this would also offer the prospect of market diversification, especially through international expansion. However, making changes to the company's product market domain called for capabilities to expand or modify HMD's current configuration of resources and capabilities – in other words, for dynamic capabilities.

HMD decided to partner with a large established firm, which HMD saw as a potential source of legitimacy, resources and opportunities: Sun Microsystems, a multinational corporation with a significant presence in Scotland. Co-founder Ian Davison commented, 'There's a certain cache in being associated with a big company.' Sun was interested in HMD's product idea and within months there was progress in establishing the alliance. Davison believes that considerable benefit was derived by HMD: 'We got what we wanted out of the relationship because we managed to build a prototype using the Sun technology.' HMD's experience also illustrates the building of dynamic capabilities at various levels.

Opportunities arose for mutual learning. From HMD's perspective, the venture benefited from exposure to new technological ideas. Of particular advantage was Sun's ability to tap into its widespread resources and capabilities elsewhere in the UK and beyond (for example, Western Europe). Also, Sun's reputation opened doors for HMD. When the prototype was built, HMD made a joint sales call with Sun to a prospective international customer and a demonstration was subsequently held on Sun's Scottish premises. Such activities facilitated experiential learning about processes such as product development and sales.

There were also further benefits for HMD:

- *Product development*. In developing a prototype with Sun, HMD engaged in integrating resources and capabilities to achieve synergies; for example, its own customer-centric technological knowledge in the clinical trials domain was combined with Sun's hardware technology architecture.

- *Alliancing*. Through inputs from a public sector intermediary, HMD gained vital knowledge about formal aspects of alliancing, such as the legalities of sharing intellectual property; equally, HMD came to appreciate the utility of informal social networking in ensuring the smooth progress of joint activity.

- *Strategic decision making*. HMD was able to build new thinking within the firm in terms of, for example, the identification of external knowledge sources as evident from subsequent decisions to expand the alliance to include a third partner.

At the individual level within HMD managers also learned 'new tricks' by engaging in informal routines such as brainstorming sessions and everyday activities such as negotiating. Managers claimed that such learning would help HMD approach its next alliance by replicating certain aspects while modifying others. Davison commented: 'In future we would approach this sort of relationship in a broadly similar manner [but] I think we would attempt to set some clearer company goals and boundaries at the outset.'

Prepared by Shameen Prashantham, Department of Management, University of Glasgow.

Questions

1 At what levels could dynamic capabilities benefit organisations?

2 How do network relationships, such as strategic partnerships, potentially contribute to dynamic capability development?

3 What other joint activity within, and across, organisations could give rise to dynamic capabilities? How?

4 Can dynamic capability development be deliberately planned? How?

third, as explained already in this chapter, it is less likely that organisations will achieve competitive advantage through their physical resources and more likely that it will be achieved through the way they do things and their accumulated experience. So knowledge about how to do things that draws on that experience becomes crucially important.

Two points should be highlighted here:

- *Explicit and tacit organisational knowledge.* Organisational knowledge may take different forms. Nonaka and Takeuchi[20] distinguish between two types of knowledge. *Explicit knowledge* is codified, and 'objective' knowledge is transmitted in formal systematic ways. It may, indeed, take the form of a codified information resource such as a systems manual. In contrast, *tacit knowledge* is personal, context specific and therefore hard to formalise and communicate. As for individuals, organisational competence usually requires both kinds of knowledge. For example, a learner driver uses explicit knowledge, probably taught by an instructor, to develop knowledge on how to drive a car. The tacit knowledge required is, however, achieved through practical experience of driving. Arguably, the more formal and systematic the system of knowledge, the greater is the *danger of imitation*, and therefore the less valuable the knowledge becomes in competitive strategy terms. If knowledge can be codified, then there is more of a chance of it being copied. Non-imitatable competitive advantage is much more likely to exist where knowledge is lodged in the experience of groups of individuals.

- *Communities of practice.* The sharing of knowledge and experience in organisations is an essentially social and cultural process relying on *communities of practice*[21] developing and sharing information because it is mutually beneficial. This may happen through formal systems such as the Internet but it is also highly dependent on social contact and trust. Indeed, exchange of knowledge is more likely to occur in *cultures of trust* without strong hierarchical or functional boundaries. For example, organisations have tried to improve the sharing of knowledge by setting up IT-based systems to do it. However, there has been an increasing realisation that, while some of this knowledge can be codified and built into computer-based systems, it is very difficult to codify knowledge where its value is especially dependent on knowledge sharing.

These observations in turn flag up the links between organisational knowledge and other concepts discussed in this book. Organisational knowledge may be beneficial but needs to develop as the environment changes. As such, organisational knowledge and learning are closely linked concepts. In turn both need to be thought of in terms of the *dynamic capabilities* to adapt to changing conditions referred to in section 3.4.5 above. The links between knowledge, experience and social interaction also need to be considered in relation to cultural aspects of strategy addressed further in Chapter 5.

3.6 DIAGNOSING STRATEGIC CAPABILITY

So far this chapter has been concerned with explaining strategic capability and associated concepts. This section now provides some ways in which strategic capabilities can be diagnosed.

3.6.1 The value chain and value network

If organisations are to achieve competitive advantage by delivering value to customers, managers need to understand which activities they undertake are especially important in creating that value and which are not. Value chain and value network concepts can be helpful in understanding this.

The value chain

A **value chain** describes the categories of activities within and around an organisation, which together create a product or service

Primary activities are directly concerned with the creation or delivery of a product or service

The **value chain** describes the categories of activities within and around an organisation, which together create a product or service. The concept was developed in relation to competitive strategy by Michael Porter.[22] Exhibit 3.6 is a representation of a value chain. **Primary activities** are *directly* concerned with the creation or delivery of a product or service. For example, for a manufacturing business:

- *Inbound logistics* are activities concerned with receiving, storing and distributing inputs to the product or service including materials handling, stock control, transport, etc.
- *Operations* transform these inputs into the final product or service: machining, packaging, assembly, testing, etc.
- *Outbound logistics* collect, store and distribute the product to customers, for example warehousing, materials handling, distribution, etc.
- *Marketing and sales* provide the means whereby consumers/users are made aware of the product or service and are able to purchase it. This includes sales administration, advertising and selling.
- *Service* includes those activities that enhance or maintain the value of a product or service, such as installation, repair, training and spares.

Exhibit 3.6 **The value chain within an organisation**

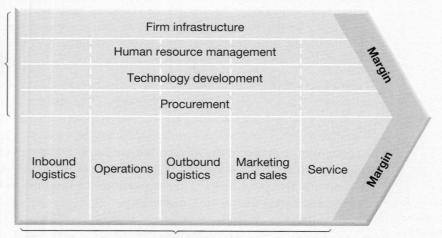

Source: Adapted with the permission of The Free Press, a Division of Simon & Schuster Adult Publishing Group, from *Competitive Advantage: Creating and Sustaining Superior Performance* by Michael E. Porter. Copyright © 1985, 1998 by Michael E. Porter. All rights reserved.

Each of these groups of primary activities is linked to support activities.
Support activities help to improve the effectiveness or efficiency of primary
activities:

Support activities help to improve the effectiveness or efficiency of primary activities

- *Procurement.* The *processes* that occur in many parts of the organisation for acquiring the various resource inputs to the primary activities.

- *Technology development.* All value activities have a 'technology', even if it is just know-how. Technologies may be concerned directly with a product (for example, R&D, product design) or with processes (for example, process development) or with a particular resource (for example, raw materials improvements).

- *Human resource management.* This transcends all primary activities. It is concerned with those activities involved in recruiting, managing, training, developing and rewarding people within the organisation.

- *Infrastructure.* The formal systems of planning, finance, quality control, information management, and the structures and routines that are part of an organisation's culture (see section 5.4).

The value chain can help with the analysis of the strategic position of an organisation in two different ways.

- As *generic descriptions of activities* that can help managers understand if there is a cluster of activities providing benefit to customers located within particular areas of the value chain. Perhaps a business is especially good at outbound logistics linked to its marketing and sales operation and supported by its technology development. It might be less good in terms of its operations and its inbound logistics. The value chain also prompts managers to think about the role different activities play. For example, in a local family-run sandwich bar, is sandwich making best thought of as 'operations' or as 'marketing and sales', given that its reputation and appeal may rely on the social relations and banter between customers and sandwich makers? Arguably it is 'operations' if done badly but 'marketing and sales' if done well.

- In terms of the *cost and value of activities*.[23] Illustration 3.4 shows this in relation to fish farming. Value chain analysis was used by Ugandan fish farmers as a way of identifying what they should focus on in developing a more profitable business model.

The value network

A single organisation rarely undertakes in-house all of the value activities from design through to delivery of the final product or service to the final consumer. There is usually specialisation of role so any one organisation is part of a wider *value network*. The **value network**[24] is the set of interorganisational links and relationships that are necessary to create a product or service (see Exhibit 3.7). So an organisation needs to be clear about what activities it ought to undertake itself and which it should not and, perhaps, should outsource. However, since much of the cost and value creation will occur in the supply and distribution chains, managers need to understand this whole process and how they can manage these linkages and relationships to improve customer value. It is not sufficient to look within the organisation alone. For example, the quality of a cooker or a

The value network is the set of interorganisational links and relationships that are necessary to create a product or service

Illustration 3.4

A value chain for Ugandan chilled fish fillet exports

Even small enterprises can be part of an international value chain. Analysing it can provide strategic benefits.

A fish factory in Uganda barely made any profit. Fish were caught from small motorboats owned by poor fishermen from local villages. Just before they set out they would collect ice and plastic fish boxes from the agents who bought the catch on their return. The boxes were imported, along with tackle and boat parts. All supplies had to be paid for in cash in advance by the agents. Sometimes ice and supplies were not available in time. Fish landed with insufficient ice achieved half of the price of iced fish, and sometimes could not be sold to the agents at all. The fish factory had always processed the fillets in the same way – disposing of the waste back into the lake. Once a week, some foreign traders would come and buy the better fillets; they didn't say who they sold them to, and sometimes they didn't buy very much.

By mapping the value chain it was clear that there were opportunities for capturing more value along the chain and reducing losses. Together with outside specialists, the fish factory and the fishing community developed a strategy to improve their capabilities, as indicated in the figure, until they became a flourishing international business, The Lake Victoria Fish Company, with regular air-freight exports around the world. You can see more of their current operations at http://www.ufpea.co.ug/, and find out more about the type of analytical process applied at www.justreturn.ch.

(The approximate costs and prices given represent the situation before improvements were implemented.)

> **Questions**
>
> 1 Draw up a value chain for another business in terms of the activities within its component parts.
>
> 2 Estimate the relative costs and/or assets associated with these activities.
>
> 3 What are the strategic implications of your analysis?

television when it reaches the final purchaser is influenced not only by the activities undertaken within the manufacturing company itself, but also by the quality of components from suppliers and the performance of the distributors.

It is therefore important that managers understand the bases of their organisation's strategic capabilities in relation to the wider value network. Four key issues are:

- *Which activities are centrally important* to an organisation's strategic capability and which less central? A firm in a highly competitive market may have to cut costs in key areas and decide it can only do so by outsourcing to lower-cost producers. Another firm may decide that it is important to retain direct control of centrally important capabilities, especially if they relate to activities and processes that it believes are central to its achieving competitive advantage. For example, diamond cutting businesses have traditionally had to source rough diamonds from the giant De Beers. However, in a revolutionary move

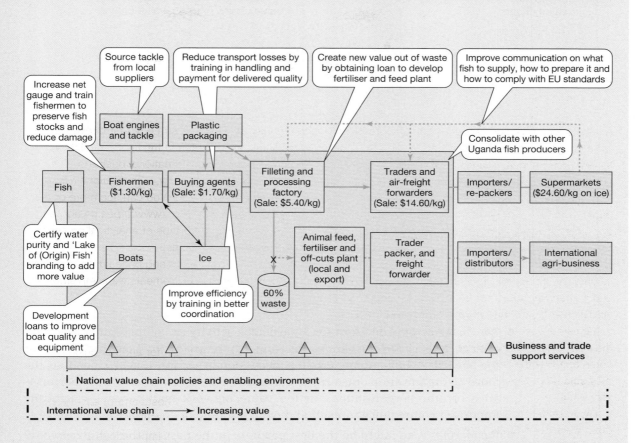

Source: Ian Sayers, Senior Adviser for the Private Sector, Division of Trade Support Services, International Trade Centre, Geneva. E-mail: sayers@intracen.org.

Profit pools refer to the different levels of profit available at different parts of the value network

the Lev Leviev Group decided to invest in its own diamond mining operations, arguing: 'Nothing is stable unless you own your own mine.'[25]

● *Where are the profit pools?*[26] **Profit pools** refer to the different levels of profit available at different parts of the value network. Some parts of a value network may be inherently more profitable than others because of the differences in competitive intensity. For example, in the computer industry microprocessors and software have historically been more profitable than hardware manufacture. The strategic question becomes whether it is possible to focus on the areas of greatest profit potential. Care has to be exercised here. It is one thing to identify such potential; it is another to be successful in it given the capabilities the organisation has. For example, in the 1990s many car manufacturers recognised that greater profit potential lay in services such as car hire and financing rather than manufacturing but they did not have the relevant competences to succeed in such sectors.

Exhibit 3.7 **The value network**

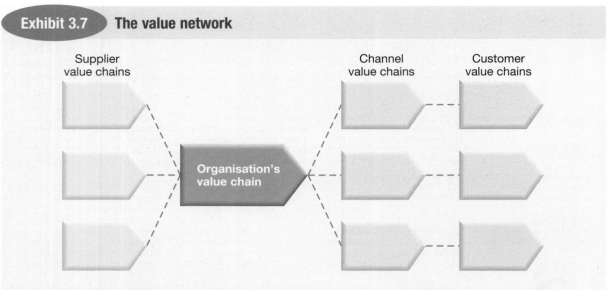

● *The 'make or buy'* decision for a particular activity or component is therefore critical. This is the *outsourcing* decision. There are businesses that now offer the benefits of outsourcing (see the discussion in section 12.4.2). Of course, the more an organisation outsources, the more its ability to influence the performance of other organisations in the value network may become a critically important competence in itself and even a source of competitive advantage.

● *Partnering*. Who might be the best partners in the parts of the value network? And what kind of *relationships* are important to develop with each partner? For example, should they be regarded as suppliers or should they be regarded as alliance partners (see section 10.2.3)? Some businesses have benefited from closer relationships with suppliers such that they increasingly cooperate on such things as market intelligence, product design and R&D.

3.6.2 Activity maps

Managers often find it difficult to identify with any clarity the strategic capability of their organisation. Too often they highlight capabilities not valued by customers but seen as important within the organisation, perhaps because they were valuable in the past. Or they highlight what are, in fact, critical success factors (product features particularly valued by customers) like 'good service' or 'reliable delivery', whereas strategic capability is about the resources, processes and activities that underpin the ability to meet such critical success factors. Or they identify capabilities at too generic a level. This is not surprising given that strategic capability is likely to be rooted in a complex, causally ambiguous set of linked activities (see section 3.4.3). But if they are to be managed proactively, finding a way of identifying and understanding capabilities and the linkages that are likely to characterise competences is important.

One way of undertaking such diagnosis is by means of an activity map that tries to show how the different activities of an organisation are linked together. Illustration 3.2 described the search by Plasco's management for the company's strategic capabilities using activity mapping. There are computer programs in existence that can be used,[27] or such analysis may be done more basically, for example by drawing network diagrams, as shown in Exhibit 3.8.[28] This map was generated by groups of managers from within the organisation, working with a facilitator, mapping the activities of their organisation on a large blank wall initially by using Post-Its.[29]

Exhibit 3.8 An activity system map*

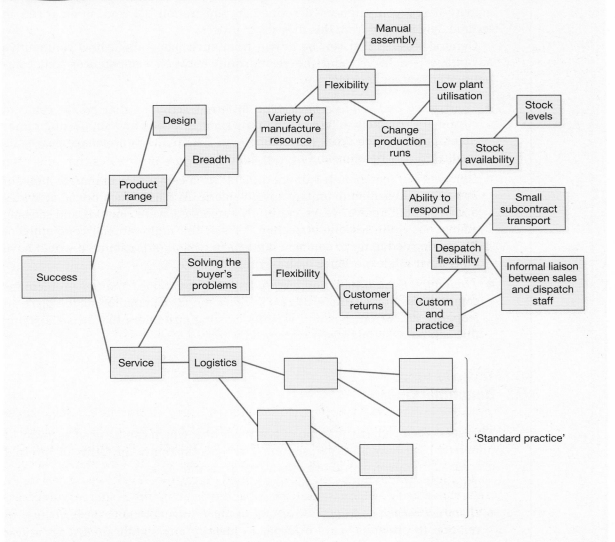

* This is an extract from an activity map.

They began by undertaking a competitor analysis as explained in section 2.4.4. The aim here was to identify (i) the critical success factors in relation to their customers and (ii) on which of these their business outperformed competitors. They identified the critical success factors of brand reputation, product range, innovation, excellence of service and reliability of delivery and that Plasco was seen as particularly successful in relation to competitors in terms of its level of service and its product range. Managers were relatively easily able to identify what Porter refers to as *higher order strategic themes*:[30] that the main benefits offered were to do with flexibility and rapid response. But the reasons why Plasco outperformed competitors did not emerge until these themes themselves were 'unpacked' by identifying the resources and competences that underpinned them. To do this managers kept asking themselves more and more specifically what activities 'delivered' the customer benefits. Exhibit 3.8 is only a selection of these activities. The eventual map consisted of hundreds of Post-Its, each representing an activity in some way contributing to strategic capability. The activity-based competences described in Illustration 3.2 and summarised in Exhibit 3.8 emerged from this diagnostic process.

General lessons that can be drawn from such maps about how competitive advantage is achieved and the relationship between competences and competitive advantage include:

- *Consistency and reinforcement*. The different activities that create value to customers are likely to be pulling in the same direction and supporting rather than opposing each other (for example, in Plasco an open management style facilitated rule bending and in turn flexibility).

- *Difficulties of imitation*. It is more difficult for a competitor to imitate a mix of linked activities than to imitate any given one. In Plasco such linked activities had been built up over years, culturally embedded, were complex and causally ambiguous – the lessons of section 3.4.3. If the multinational competitor of Plasco decided to try to compete on the same basis of flexibility it would have no comparable experience to draw on to do this.

- *Trade-offs*. Even if imitation were possible it could pose another problem for competitors. For example, Plasco's international competitor might place in jeopardy its current position with its existing customers that it is satisfying through more standardised mass production.

3.6.3 Benchmarking[31]

This section considers the value of *benchmarking*, which can be used as a way of understanding how an organisation's strategic capability, in terms of internal processes, compare with those of other organisations.

There are different approaches to benchmarking:

- *Historical benchmarking*. Organisations may consider their performance in relation to previous years in order to identify any significant changes. The danger is that this can lead to complacency since it is the rate of improvement compared with that of competitors that is really important.

- *Industry/sector benchmarking.* Insights about performance standards can be gleaned by looking at the comparative performance of other organisations in the same industry sector or between similar service providers against a set of performance indicators. Some public sector organisations have, in effect, acknowledged the existence of strategic groups by benchmarking against similar organisations rather than against everybody: for example, local government services and police treat 'urban' differently from 'rural' in their benchmarking and league tables. An overriding danger of industry norm comparisons (whether in the private or public sector) is, however, that the whole industry may be performing badly and losing out competitively to other industries that can satisfy customers' needs in different ways. Another danger with benchmarking within an industry is that the boundaries of industries are blurring through competitive activity and industry convergence. For example, supermarkets are (incrementally) entering retail banking and their benchmarking needs to reflect this (as does the benchmarking of the traditional retail banks).

- *Best-in-class benchmarking.* Best-in-class benchmarking compares an organisation's performance against 'best-in-class' performance – wherever that is found – and therefore seeks to overcome the limitations of other approaches. It may also help challenge managers' mindsets that acceptable improvements in performance will result from incremental changes in resources or competences. It can therefore encourage a more fundamental reconsideration of how to improve organisational competences. For example, British Airways improved aircraft maintenance, refuelling and turnround time by studying the processes surrounding Formula One Grand Prix motor racing pit stops.[32] A police force wishing to improve the way in which it responded to emergency telephone calls studied call centre operations in the banking and IT sectors.

The importance of benchmarking is, then, not so much in the detailed 'mechanics' of comparison but in the impact that these comparisons might have on behaviours. It can be usefully regarded as a process for gaining momentum for improvement and change. But it has dangers too:

- *Measurement distortion.* Benchmarking can lead to a situation where *you get what you measure* and this may not be what is intended strategically. It can therefore result in changes in behaviour that are unintended or dysfunctional. For example, the university sector in the UK has been subjected to rankings in league tables on research output, teaching quality and the success of graduating students in terms of employment and starting salaries. This has resulted in academics being 'forced' to orientate their published research to certain types of academic journals that may have little to do directly with the quality of the education in universities.

- *Surface comparisons.* Benchmarking compares inputs (resources), outputs or outcomes; it does not identify the reasons for the good or poor performance of organisations since the process does not compare competences directly. For example, it may demonstrate that one organisation is poorer at customer service than another but not show the underlying reasons. However, if well directed it could encourage managers to seek out these reasons and hence understand how competences could be improved.

Illustration 3.5

SWOT analysis of Pharmcare

A SWOT analysis explores the relationship between the environmental influences and the strategic capabilities of an organisation compared with its competitors.

(a) SWOT analysis for Pharmcare

	Environmental change (opportunities and threats)					
	Health care rationing	Complex and changing buying structures	Increased integration of health care	Informed patients	+	−
Strengths						
Flexible salesforce	+3	+5	+2	+2	12	0
Economies of scale	0	0	+3	+3	+6	0
Strong brand name	+2	+1	0	−1	3	−1
Health care education department	+4	+3	+4	+5	+16	0
Weaknesses						
Limited competences in biotechnology and genetics	0	0	−4	−3	0	−7
Ever lower R&D productivity	−3	−2	−1	−2	0	−8
Weak ICT competences	−2	−2	−5	−5	0	−14
Over-reliance on leading product	−1	−1	−3	−1	0	−6
Environmental impact scores	+9	+9	+9	+10		
	−6	−5	−14	−12		

(b) Competitor SWOT analyses

	Environmental change (opportunities and threats)				
	Health care rationing	Complex and changing buying structures	Increased integration of health care	Informed and passionate patients	Overall impact
Pharmcare *Big global player suffering fall in share price, low research productivity and post mega-merger bureaucracy*	−3 Struggling to prove cost-effectiveness of new drugs to new regulators of health care rationing	+6 Well-known brand, a flexible salesforce combined with a new health care education department creates positive synergy	−3 Weak ICT and lack of integration following mergers means sales, research and admin. are all underperforming	−2 Have yet to get into the groove of patient power fuelled by the Internet	−2 Declining performance over time worsened after merger
Company W *Big pharma with patchy response to change, losing ground in new areas of competition*	−4 Focus is on old-style promotional selling rather than helping doctors control costs through drugs	−4 Traditional salesforce not helped by marketing which can be unaccommodating of national differences	+0 Alliances with equipment manufacturers but little work done across alliance to show dual use of drugs and new surgical techniques	+4 New recruits in the ICT department have worked cross-functionally to involve patients like never before	−4 Needs to modernise across the whole company
Organisation X *Partnership between a charity managed by people with venture capital experience and top hospital geneticists*	+3 Potentially able to deliver rapid advances in genetic-based illnesses	+2 Able possibly to bypass these with innovative cost effective drug(s)	+2 Innovative drugs can help integrate health care through enabling patients to stay at home	+3 Patients will fight for advances in treatment areas where little recent progress has been made	+10 Could be the basis of a new business model for drug discovery – but all to prove as yet
Company Y *Only develops drugs for less common diseases*	+3 Partnering with big pharma allows the development of drugs discovered by big pharma but not economical for them to develop	0 Focus on small market segments so not as vulnerable to overall market structure, but innovative approach might be risky	+2 Innovative use of web to show why products still worthwhile developing even for less common illnesses	+1 Toll-free call centres for sufferers of less common illnesses Company, like patients, is passionate about its mission	+6 Novel approach can be considered either risky or a winner, or both!

Questions

1 What does the SWOT analysis tell us about the competitive position of Pharmcare with the industry as a whole?

2 How readily do you think executives of Pharmacare identify the strengths and weaknesses of competitors?

3 Identify the benefits and dangers (other than those identified in the text) of a SWOT analysis such as that in the illustration.

Prepared by Jill Shepherd, Segal Graduate School of Business, Simon Fraser University, Vancouver, Canada.

3.6.4 SWOT[33]

KEY CONCEPT

SWOT

The key 'strategic messages' from both the business environment (Chapter 2) and this chapter can be summarised in the form of an analysis of strengths, weaknesses, opportunities and threats (SWOT). **SWOT** summarises the key issues from the business environment and the strategic capability of an organisation that are most likely to impact on strategy development. This can also be useful as a basis against which to generate strategic options and assess future courses of action.

The aim is to identify the extent to which strengths and weaknesses are relevant to, or capable of dealing with, the changes taking place in the business environment. However, in the context of this chapter, if the strategic capability of an organisation is to be understood, it must be remembered that it is not absolute but relative to its competitors. So SWOT analysis is really only useful if it is comparative – if it examines strengths, weaknesses, opportunities and threats in relation to competitors. Illustration 3.5 takes the example of a pharmaceuticals firm (Pharmcare).[34] It assumes that key environmental impacts have been identified from analyses explained in Chapter 2 and that major strengths and weaknesses have been identified using the analytic tools explained in this chapter. A scoring mechanism (plus 5 to minus 5) is used as a means of getting managers to assess the interrelationship between the environmental impacts and the strengths and weaknesses of the firm. A positive (+) denotes that the strength of the company would help it take advantage of, or counteract, a problem arising from an environmental change or that a weakness would be offset by that change. A negative (–) score denotes that the strength would be reduced or that a weakness would prevent the organisation from overcoming problems associated with that change.

Pharmcare's share price had been declining because investors were concerned that its strong market position was under threat. This had not been improved by a merger that was proving problematic. The pharmaceutical market was changing with new ways of doing business, driven by new technology, the quest to provide medicines at lower cost and politicians seeking ways to cope with soaring health care costs and an evermore informed patient. But was Pharmcare keeping pace? The strategic review of the firm's position (Illustration 3.5a) confirmed its strengths of a flexible salesforce, well-known brand name and new health care department. However, there were major weakness, namely relative failure on low-cost drugs, competence in information and communication technology (ICT) and a failure to get to grips with increasingly well-informed users. When the impact of environmental forces on competitors was analysed (Illustration 3.5b), it showed that Pharmcare was still outperforming its traditional competitor (Company W), but potentially vulnerable to changing dynamics in the general industry structure courtesy of niche players (X and Y).

A SWOT analysis should help focus discussion on future choices and the extent to which an organisation is capable of supporting these strategies. There are, however, two main dangers:

● A SWOT exercise can generate very *long lists* of apparent strengths, weaknesses, opportunities and threats, whereas what matters is to be clear about what is really important and what is less important.

● There is a danger of *overgeneralisation*. Remember the lessons of sections 3.6.1 and 3.6.2. Identifying a very general explanation of strategic capability does not explain the underlying reasons for that capability. SWOT analysis is not a substitute for more rigorous, insightful analysis, for example by using the techniques and concepts explained in Chapters 2 and 3.

3.7 MANAGING STRATEGIC CAPABILITY

The previous section has been concerned with diagnosing strategic capability. This section considers what managers might do, other than such diagnosis, to manage and improve the strategic capability of their organisation.

3.7.1 Limitations in managing strategic capabilities

One lesson that emerges from an understanding of strategic capabilities is that the most valuable bases of strategic capability may lie in aspects of the organisation that are difficult to discern or be specific about. So, how is it possible to manage that which it is not always easy to be clear about? For example, in the Plasco illustration, some of the capabilities of that organisation were lodged in activities that the top management were not directly managing. It is important to understand what managers might be able to do and what they cannot do in terms of how much they understand and how much they value bases of strategic capability.[35] There may be different circumstances:

● *Competences are valued but not understood.* Managers may know that there are activities in their organisation that have a positive impact and may value them, but may not understand just how such positive impact arises. For example, the delivery of value may be dependent on highly specialised skills as in a cutting-edge hi-tech firm, or on complex linkages far down in the organisation. The lesson here is that managers may have to be careful about disturbing the bases of such capabilities while ensuring that they *monitor the outputs and benefits* created for customers.

● *Competences are not valued.* Managers may know that activities and processes exist in the organisation but not recognise their positive impact or value such activities. There are dangers here that managers take the wrong course of action. For example, they may cut out areas of activity that create actual or potential competitive advantage, perhaps because they are intent on cutting costs. Plasco managers might, for example, have sought to improve production efficiency so that they could have reduced flexibility. It would be wise to understand the value-creating capabilities more clearly using value chain analysis or activity mapping before as Plasco managers did before taking such decisions.

● *Competences are recognised, valued and understood.* This might be the outcome of the sort of analysis done by Plasco. Here managers may be able to nurture and further develop such competences, for example by ensuring that overall company policies support and enhance them. The danger can be that top management may seek to preserve such capabilities by over-formalising or codifying them such that they become 'set in stone'.

3.7.2 Developing strategic capabilities[36]

There are different ways in which managers might develop strategic capabilities:

- *Adding and changing capabilities*. Could capabilities be added, or changed so that they become more reinforcing of outcomes that deliver against critical success factors? For example, in Plasco, could even faster internal ways of responding to customer needs be found?

- *Extending capabilities*. Managers might identify strategic capabilities in one area of the business, perhaps customer service in one geographic business unit of a multinational, that are not present in other business units. They might then seek to extend this throughout all the business units. Whilst this seems straightforward, studies[37] find it is not. The capabilities of one part of an organisation might not be easily transferred to another because of the problems of managing change (see Chapter 14).

- *Stretching capabilities*. Managers may see the opportunity to build new products or services out of existing capabilities. Indeed, building new businesses in this way is the basis of related diversification, as explained in section 7.3.1.[38]

- *Entrepreneurial bricolage*. There is evidence[39] that strategic capabilities may be built by exploiting resources, skills and knowledge that have been ignored or rejected by others; indeed that this is often what entrepreneurs who develop new business models do. For example, the development of Danish wind turbines was based on improvising around available 'modest resources' and the skills of a 'constellation of different players';[40] social networks ignored by others have been used for building technology businesses and information systems designers experiment with different configurations to create new systems drawing from their and others' experience.

- *Ceasing activities*. Could current activities not central to the delivery of value to customers be done away with, outsourced or reduced in cost? This is what new industry entrants, such as Ryanair or easyJet in the airline industry, did to create new business models for low-cost airlines.

- *External capability development*. There may be ways of developing capabilities by looking externally. For example, managers may seek to develop or learn new capabilities by acquisition or by entering into alliances and joint ventures (see section 10.2.3).

3.7.3 Managing people for capability development

One of the lessons of this chapter is that strategic capability often lies in the day-to-day activities that people undertake in organisations, so developing the ability of people to recognise the relevance of what they do in terms of the strategic capability of the organisation is important. More specifically:

- *Targeted training and development* may be possible. Often companies design training and development programmes that are very general. For strategic purposes it may be important to target the development of competences which can provide competitive advantage. For example, an engineering business, whilst acknowledging the abilities its personnel had in the technical aspects of engineering products, recognised that these were attributes that competitors had too, and that there was a need to develop people's abilities to innovate more around value-adding customer service. The business therefore changed its training and development programmes to emphasise these requirements.

- *Staffing policies* might be employed to develop particular competences. For example, an oil company that sought to build its competitive advantage around the building of close customer relationships in markets for industrial oils did so by ensuring that senior field managers with an aptitude for this were promoted and sent to different parts of the world that needed to be developed in such ways.

- *Organisational learning* may be recognised as central, particularly in fast-changing conditions. Here successful firms may be those that have grown the *dynamic capabilities* (see section 3.4.5) to readjust required competences continually. In effect their competence becomes that of learning and development. In this context the characteristics of what has become known as a 'learning organisation' may become especially important (see section 11.5.2). Since this may require the acceptance that different, even conflicting ideas and views are valuable and that experimentation is the norm, managers need to consider how to protect and foster such behaviour. For example, it may be that those within the organisation who show most ability to contribute to such learning are the least powerful, perhaps quite junior in the hierarchy. They may need the protection of more powerful people.

- *Develop people's awareness* that what they do in their jobs can matter at the strategic level. It is a common complaint in organisations that 'no one values what I do'. Helping people see how their work relates to the bigger strategic picture can both enhance the likelihood that they will, indeed, contribute positively to helping achieve competitive success and increase their motivation to do so.

Illustration 3.6 summarises a key debate that writers on the strategic capabilities are pursuing.

SUMMARY

- *Strategic capability* is concerned with the adequacy and suitability of resources and competences required for an organisation to survive and prosper. Strategic capabilities comprise resources and competences, which are the way such resources are used and deployed.

- If organisations are to achieve *competitive advantage*, they require resources and competences which are both valuable to customers and difficult for competitors to imitate (such competences are known as *core competences*).

- The continual improvement of *cost efficiency* is a vital strategic capability if an organisation is to continue to prosper.

- The sustainability of competitive advantage is likely to depend on strategic capabilities being of *value to customers, rare, inimitable* or *non-substitutable*.

- In dynamic conditions, it is unlikely that such strategic capabilities will remain stable. In such circumstances *dynamic capabilities* are important, that is the ability to change strategic capabilities continually.

- Ways of *diagnosing organisational capabilities* include:
  - Analysing an organisation's *value chain and value network* as a basis of understanding how value to a customer is created and can be developed.
  - *Activity mapping* as a means of identifying more detailed activities which underpin strategic capabilities.
  - *Benchmarking* as means of understanding the relative performance of organisations and challenging the assumptions managers have about the performance of their organisation.
  - *SWOT analysis* as a way of drawing together an understanding of strengths, weaknesses, opportunities and threats an organisation faces.

- Managers need to think about how and to what extent they can manage the *development of the strategic capabilities* of their organisation by stretching and adding to such capabilities and by the way they manage people in their organisation.

Illustration 3.6   key debate

The resource-based view of competitive advantage: is it useful to managers?

The view that the management of strategic capability is central for achieving competitive advantage has been questioned.

Since the early 1990s, the resource-based view (RBV) of strategy has become highly influential. Much academic research is carried out on it and managers readily talk about the importance of building on core competences to gain competitive advantage. However, two US academics, Richard Priem and John Butler, have raised questions about the value of RBV.[1]

The critique

In the context of this chapter, two of Priem and Butler's observations are especially significant:

1 *The risk of tautology*. The underlying explanation of RBV is that the resource characteristics (or capabilities) that lead to competitive advantage are those that are valuable and rare. Since competitive advantage is defined in terms of value and rarity, they argue that this verges on tautology. To say that a business performs better than another because it has superior resources or is better at some things than other businesses is not helpful unless it is possible to be specific about what capabilities are important, why and how they can be managed.

2 *The lack of specificity*. However, there is typically little specific in what is written about RBV. And some would say the same is true when managers talk about capabilities or competences. 'Top management skills' or 'innovatory capacity' mean little without being specific about the activities and processes that comprise them. And there is relatively little research that identifies such specifics or how they can be managed. Priem and Butler suggest this is particularly so with regard to the argued importance of tacit knowledge in bestowing competitive advantage: 'This may be descriptively correct, but it is likely to be quite difficult for practitioners to effectively manipulate that which is inherently unknowable.' (The problem raised at the beginning of section 3.6.2.)

The response

Jay Barney,[2] one of the main proponents of RBV, accepts that there is a need to understand more about how resources are used and how people behave in bestowing competitive advantage. However, he defends the managerial relevance of RBV because he believes it highlights that managers need to identify and develop the most critical capabilities of a firm.

In his earlier writing[3] Barney had argued that an organisation's culture could be a source of sustainable advantage provided it was valuable, rare and difficult to imitate. In such circumstances he suggested managers should 'nurture these cultures'. However, he went on to argue that:

If one firm is able to modify its culture, then it is likely that others can as well. In this case the advantages associated with the culture are imitable and thus only a source of normal economic performance. Only when it is not possible to manage a firm's culture in a planned way does that culture have the potential of generating expected sustained superior financial performance.

In other words, he argues that valuable sources of competitive advantage are the intangible assets and resources or competences embedded in a culture in such a way that not only can competitors not imitate them, but managers cannot manage them.

Priem and Butler would no doubt argue that this makes their point: that RBV is not very helpful in providing practical help to managers.

Notes

1. R. Priem and J.E. Butler, 'Is the resource based view a useful perspective for strategic management research?', *Academy of Management Review*, vol. 26, no. 1 (2001), pp. 22–40.
2. J.B. Barney, 'Is the resource based view a useful perspective for strategic management research? Yes', *Academy of Management Review*, vol. 26, no. 1 (2001), pp. 41–56.
3. J.B. Barney, 'Organizational culture: can it be a source of sustained competitive advantage?', *Academy of Management Review*, vol. 11, no. 3 (1986), pp. 656–665.

Questions

1 How specific would the identification of strategic capabilities need to be to permit them to be managed to achieve competitive advantage?

2 Do you agree that if it were possible to identify and manage such capabilities they would be imitated?

3 Is the RBV useful?

Work assignments

Denotes more advanced work assignments. * Refers to a case study in the Text and Cases edition.

3.1 Using Exhibits 3.1 and 3.2 identify the resources and competences of an organisation with which you are familiar. You can answer this in relation to Amazon* or Formula One* if you so wish.

3.2 ✳ Undertake an analysis of the strategic capability of an organisation with which you are familiar in order to identify which capabilities, if any, meet the criteria of (a) value, (b) rarity, (c) robustness and (d) inimitability (see section 3.4). You can answer this in relation to Amazon* or Formula One* if you so wish.

3.3 ✳ For an industry or public service consider how the strategic capabilities that have been the basis of competitive advantage (or best value in the public sector) have changed over time. Why have these changes occurred? How did the relative strengths of different companies or service providers change over this period? Why?

3.4 Map out a value chain/network analysis for an organisation of your choice (referring to Illustration 3.4 could be helpful). You can answer this in relation to a case study in the book such as eBay, Tesco, Tui* or Ryanair* if you wish.

3.5 ✳ For a benchmarking exercise which you have access to, make a critical assessment of the benefits and dangers of the approach that was taken.

Integrative assignment

3.6 Prepare a SWOT analysis for an organisation of your choice and in relation to competitors (see Illustration 3.5). Explain why you have chosen each of the factors you have included in the analysis, in particular their relationship to other analyses you have undertaken in Chapters 2 and 3. What are the conclusions you arrive at from your analysis?

 An extensive range of additional materials, including audio summaries, weblinks to organisations featured in the text, definitions of key concepts and self-assessment questions, can be found on the *Exploring Corporate Strategy* Companion Website at **www.pearsoned.co.uk/ecs**

Recommended key readings

● For an understanding of the resource-based view of the firm, an early and much cited paper is by Jay Barney, 'Firm resources and sustained competitive advantage', *Journal of Management*, vol. 17 (1991), pp. 99–120. Also see the introductory paper by D. Hoopes, T. Madsen and G. Walker, 'Why is there a resource based view', in the special issue of the *Strategic Management Journal*, vol. 24, no. 10 (2003), pp. 889–902.

● The concept of dynamic capabilities is reviewed in C.L. Wang and P.K. Ahmed, 'Dynamic capabilities: a review and research agenda', *International Journal of Management Reviews*, vol. 9, no. 1 (2007), pp. 31–52.

● Michael Porter explains how mapping what he calls 'activity systems' can be important in considering competitive strategy in his article 'What is strategy?', *Harvard Business Review*, November–December (1996).

- For a critical discussion of the use and misuse of SWOT analysis see T. Hill and R. Westbrook, 'SWOT analysis: its time for a product recall', *Long Range Planning*, vol. 30, no. 1 (1997), pp. 46–52.

- For an understanding of the challenges of managing capability development see C. Bowman and N. Collier, 'A contingency approach to resource-

creation processes', *International Journal of Management Reviews*, vol. 8, no. 4 (2006), pp. 191–211. Also T. Baker and R.E. Nelson, 'Creating something from nothing: resource construction through entrepreneurial bricolage', *Administrative Science Quarterly*, vol. 50, no. 3 (2005), pp. 329–366.

References

1. Extraordinary profits as defined here are also sometimes referred to by economists as rents. For an explanation related to strategy, see R. Perman and J. Scoular, *Business Economics*, Oxford University Press, 1999, pp. 67–73.

2. The concept of resource-based strategies was introduced by B. Wernerfelt, 'A resource-based view of the firm', *Strategic Management Journal*, vol. 5, no. 2 (1984), pp. 171–180. A much cited paper is by J. Barney, 'Firm resources and sustained competitive advantage', *Journal of Management*, vol. 17, no. 1 (1991), pp. 99–120. There are now many books and papers that explain and summarise the approach. See for example the beginning of D.J. Teece, G. Pisano and A. Shuen, 'Dynamic capabilities and strategic management', *Strategic Management Journal*, vol. 18, no. 7 (1997), pp. 509–534; and the introductory paper by D. Hoopes, T. Madsen and G. Walker, 'Why is there a resource based view?', to the special issue of the *Strategic Management Journal*, vol. 24, no. 10 (2003), pp. 889–902.

3. Intangible resources have become increasingly recognised as being of strategic importance. See T. Clarke and S. Clegg, *Changing Paradigms: The transformation of management knowledge for the 21st century*, Harper Collins, 2000, p. 342 (this outlines Arthur Andersen's classification of intangible assets); R. Hall, 'The strategic analysis of intangible resources', *Strategic Management Journal*, vol. 13, no. 2, (1992), pp. 135–144; and also 'A framework linking intangible resources and capabilities to sustainable competitive advantage', *Strategic Management Journal*, vol. 14, no. 8 (1993), pp. 607–618.

4. Gary Hamel and C.K. Prahalad were the academics who promoted the idea of core competences. For example, G. Hamel and C.K. Prahalad, 'The core competence of the corporation', *Harvard Business Review*, vol. 68, no. 3 (1990), pp. 79–91. The idea of driving strategy development from the resources and competences of an organisation is discussed in G. Hamel and C.K. Prahalad, 'Strategic intent', *Harvard Business Review*, vol. 67, no. 3 (1989), pp. 63–76; and G. Hamel and C.K. Prahalad, 'Strategy as stretch and leverage', *Harvard Business Review*, vol. 71, no. 2 (1993), pp. 75–84. Also see G. Hamel and A. Heene (eds), *Competence-based Competition*, Wiley, 1994.

5. Perman and Scoular discuss economies of scale and differences between industry sectors in pages 91–100 of their book (see reference 1).

6. P. Conley, *Experience Curves as a Planning Tool*, available as a pamphlet from the Boston Consulting Group. See also A.C. Hax and N.S. Majluf, in R.G. Dyson (ed.), *Strategic Planning: Models and analytical techniques*, Wiley, 1990.

7. The headings used in this chapter are those used most commonly by writers in academic papers on RBV. These are sometimes referred to as VRIN, which stands for Valuable, Rare, difficult to Imitate and non-Substitutable, and were first identified by J. Barney, 'Firm resources and sustained competitive advantage', *Journal of Management*, vol. 17, no. 1 (1991), pp. 99–120.

8. For a full explanation of 'core rigidities' see D. Leonard-Barton, 'Core capabilities and core rigidities: a paradox in managing new product development', *Strategic Management Journal*, vol. 13 (Summer 1992), pp. 111–125.

9. See reference 7.

10. We use the word 'complexity'. Others use the word 'interconnectedness'. See for example K. Cool, L.A. Costa and I. Dierickx, 'Constructing competitive advantage', in A. Pettigrew, H. Thomas and R. Whittington (eds), *Handbook of Strategy and Management*, pp. 55–71, Sage, 2002.

11. For a fuller discussion of path dependency in the context of strategic capabilities, see the paper by Teece *et al.* (reference 2) and D. Holbrook, W. Cohen, D. Hounshell and S. Klepper, 'The nature, sources and consequences of firm differences in the early history of the semiconductor industry', *Strategic Management Journal*, vol. 21, nos 10–11 (2000), pp. 1017–1042.

12. The seminal paper on causal ambiguity is S. Lippman and R. Rumelt, 'Uncertain imitability: an analysis of interfirm differences in efficiency under competition', *Bell Journal of Economics*, vol. 13 (1982), pp. 418–438.

13. The distinction between and importance of characteristic and linkage ambiguity is explained in detail by A.W. King and C.P. Zeithaml, 'Competencies and firm performance: examining the causal ambiguity paradox', *Strategic Management Journal*, vol. 22, no. 1 (2001), pp. 75–99.

14. The importance of non-substitutability and ways of identifying possible bases of substitution are discussed in M.A. Peteraf and M.E. Bergen, 'Scanning dynamic competitive landscapes: a market and resource based framework', *Strategic Management Journal*, vol. 24, no. 10 (2003), pp. 1027–1042.

15. David Teece has written about dynamic capabilities in the paper referred to in reference 2. Also see C. Helfat, S. Finkelstein, W. Mitchell, M. Peteraf, H. Singh, D. Teece and S. Winter, *Dynamic Capabilities: Understanding strategic change in organizations*, Blackwell Publishing, 2007. Different writers have different views on what dynamic capabilities are but tend to emphasise relatively formal organisational processes such as product development, alliances and particular ways of taking decisions in firms: for example, K.M. Eisenhardt and J.A. Martin,

'Dynamic capabilities: what are they?', *Strategic Management Journal*, vol. 21, nos 10/11 (2000), pp. 1105–1121; M. Zollo and S. Winter, 'Deliberate learning and the evolution of dynamic capabilities', *Organization Science*, vol. 13, no. 3 (2002), pp. 339–351. A different view is that dynamic capabilities are about organisational learning (see the Commentary to Part I) which places more emphasis on the way the organisation is run, on the capacity of its culture to allow for or facilitate learning and adaptation.

16. For a summary paper on dynamic capabilities see C.L. Wang and P.K. Ahmed, 'Dynamic capabilities: a review and research agenda', *International Journal of Management Reviews*, vol. 9, no. 1 (2007), pp. 31–52.

17. See Eisenhardt and Martin, reference 15.

18. The importance of analysing and understanding knowledge is discussed in I. Nonaka and H. Takeuchi, *The Knowledge Creating Company*, Oxford University Press, 1995; and V. von Krogh, K. Ichijo and I. Nonaka, *Enabling Knowledge Creation: How to unlock the mystery of tacit knowledge and release the power of innovation*, Oxford University Press, 2000. There are also collections of articles on organisational knowledge: for example, the special issue of the *Strategic Management Journal*, ed. R. Grant and J.-C. Spender, vol. 17 (1996); and the *Harvard Business Review on Knowledge Management*, HBR Press, 1998.

19. Indeed Peter Drucker (see *Management Challenges for the 21st Century*, Butterworth–Heinemann, 1999) and others have referred to the growth of a 'knowledge-based economy'.

20. See reference 18.

21. E.C. Wenger and W.M. Snyder, 'Communities of practice: the organizational frontier', *Harvard Business Review*, vol. 73, no. 3 (2000), pp. 201–207; and E. Wenger, *Communities of Practice: Learning, Meaning and Identity*, Cambridge University Press, 1999.

22. An extensive discussion of the value chain concept and its application can be found in M.E. Porter, *Competitive Advantage*, Free Press, 1985.

23. For an extended example of value chain analysis see A. Shepherd, 'Understanding and using value chain analysis', in Veronique Ambrosini (ed.), *Exploring Techniques of Analysis and Evaluation in Strategic Management*, Prentice Hall, 1998.

24. P. Timmers, *Electronic Commerce*, Wiley, 2000, pp. 182–193, provides an interesting discussion of how value networks are being created and changed by IT.

25. This quote is attributed to Lev Leviev in the *Financial Times*, 14 December (2006), p. 10.

26. The importance of profit pools is discussed by O. Gadiesh and J.L. Gilbert, 'Profit pools: a fresh look at strategy', *Harvard Business Review*, vol. 76, no. 3 (1998), pp. 139–147.

27. A good example of such computer-based systems for analysing organisational capabilities can be found in a paper by C. Eden and F. Ackermann, 'Mapping distinctive competencies: a systemic approach', *Journal of the Operational Research Society*, vol. 51, no. 1 (2000), pp. 12–20.

28. For a more comprehensive account of the use of such network mapping, see V. Ambrosini, *Tacit and Ambiguous Resources as Sources of Competitive Advantage*, Palgrave Macmillan, 2003. Also see F. Ackermann and C. Eden with I. Brown, *Making Strategy*, Sage, 2005, chapter 6.

29. The paper by P. and G. Johnson, 'Facilitating group cognitive mapping of core competencies' (in *Mapping Strategic Knowledge*, ed. Anne Huff and Mark Jenkins, Sage, 2002), explains some of the problems of undertaking such mapping.

30. Michael Porter explains how mapping what he calls 'activity systems' can be important in considering competitive strategy in his article 'What is strategy?' (*Harvard Business Review*, vol. 74, no. 6 (1996), pp. 61–78).

31. Benchmarking is used extensively in both private and public sectors. S. Codling, *Benchmarking Basics*, Gower, 1998, is a practical guide to benchmarking. Also see J. Holloway, *Identifying Best Practices in Benchmarking*, Chartered Institute of Management Accountants, 1999. And for a review of the use of benchmarking in the public sector see M. Wisniewski, 'Measuring up to the best: a manager's guide to benchmarking', in G. Johnson and K. Scholes (eds), *Exploring Public Sector Strategy*, Financial Times/Prentice Hall, 2001, chapter 5.

32. See A. Murdoch, 'Lateral benchmarking, or what Formula One taught an airline', *Management Today*, November (1997), pp. 64–67. See also the Formula One case study in the case study section of this book (Text and Cases version only).

33. The idea of SWOT as a common-sense checklist has been used for many years: for example, S. Tilles, 'Making strategy explicit', in I. Ansoff (ed.), *Business Strategy*, Penguin, 1968. See also T. Jacobs, J. Shepherd and G. Johnson's chapter on SWOT analysis in V. Ambrosini (ed.), *Exploring Techniques of Strategy Analysis and Evaluation*, Prentice Hall, 1998. For a critical discussion of the (mis)use of SWOT, see T. Hill and R. Westbrook, 'SWOT analysis: it's time for a product recall', *Long Range Planning*, vol. 30, no. 1 (1997), pp. 46–52.

34. For background reading on the pharmaceutical industry see, for example, 'The drug industry – from bench to bedside', *The Economist*, 4 November (2006), and G. Pisano, *Science Business*, Harvard Business School Press, 2006.

35. This section draws on the work of Veronique Ambrosini; see reference 28.

36. For a fuller discussion of how managers may manage strategic capabilities, see C. Bowman and N. Collier, 'A contingency approach to resource-creation processes', *International Journal of Management Reviews*, vol. 8, no. 4 (2006), pp. 191–211.

37. See C.A. Maritan and T.H. Brush, 'Heterogeneity and transferring practices: implementing flow practices in multiple plants', *Strategic Management Journal*, vol. 24, no. 10 (2003), pp. 945–960.

38. In their 1990 paper, Hamel and Prahalad (see reference 4) discuss the stretching of competences as the basis of related diversification.

39. See T. Baker and R.E. Nelson, 'Creating something from nothing: resource construction through entrepreneurial bricolage', *Administrative Science Quarterly*, vol. 50, no. 3 (2005), pp. 329–366.

40. These quotes are from a study by R. Garud and P. Karnoe, 'Bricolage versus breakthrough: distributed and embedded agency in technological entrepreneurship', *Research Policy*, vol. 32, no. 2 (2003), pp. 277–300.

Making eBay work

Jill Shepherd, Segal Graduate School of Business
Simon Fraser University, Canada

In 2006, there were over 200 million eBayers worldwide. For around 750,000 people, eBay (http://www.ebay.com/) was their primary source of income. A survivor of the dot.com bust of the late 1990s, eBay represents a new business model courtesy of the Internet. Whatever statistics you choose – from most expensive item sold to number of auctions in any one day – the numbers amaze. 'This is a whole new way of doing business,' says Meg Whitman, the CEO and President since 1998. 'We're creating something that didn't exist before.'

Photo: Claro Cortes IV/Reuters/Corbis

eBay's business model

Value in eBay is created by providing a virtual worldwide market for buyers and sellers and collecting a tax on transactions as they happen. The business model of eBay relies on its customers being the organisation's product development team, sales- and marketing force, merchandising department and the security department. It is arguably the first web 2.0 company.

According to eBay managers, of key importance is listening to customers: keeping up with what they want to sell, buy and how they want to do it. If customers speak, eBay listens. Technology allows every move of every potential customer to be traced, yielding rich information. Conventional companies might spend big money on getting to know their customers and persuading them to provide feedback; for eBay such feedback is often free and offered without the need for enticement. Even so some of the company's most effective ways of getting user input do not rely on the net and do not come free. eBay organises Voice of the Customer groups which involve flying in a new group of about 10 sellers and buyers from around the country to its offices every few months to discuss the company in depth. Teleconferences are held for new features and policies, however small a change they involve.

Even so workshops and classes are held to teach people how to make the most of the site. Participants tend to double their selling activity on eBay after taking a class. Others run their own websites offering advice on how to sell on eBay. Rumours have it that buyers have devised computer programs that place bids in the last moment. Sellers that leave the site unable to compete any more are known to write blogs on what went wrong to help others.

The company is governed from both outside and within. The eBay system has a source of automatic control in the form of buyers and sellers rating each other on each transaction, creating rules and norms. Both buyers and sellers build up reputations which are valuable, in turn encouraging further good behaviour in themselves and others. Sales of illegal products are dealt with by withdrawing what is on sale and invariably banning the seller.

eBay's management

Meg Whitman's style and past have heavily influenced the management of eBay. When she joined the company in 1998, it was more of a collection of geeks, handpicked by the pony-tailed founder Pierre Omidyar, than a blue-chip, something which underpinned Omidyar's recruitment of Meg. Meg, an ex-consultant, filled many of the senior management roles including the head of the US business, head of international operations and vice president of consumer marketing with consultants. The result: eBay has become data and metric driven. 'If you can't measure it, you can't control it', Meg says. Whereas in the early days you could touch and feel the way the organisation worked, its current size means it needs to be measured. Category managers, reminiscent of Meg's days in Procter and Gamble, are expected to spend their days measuring and acting upon data within their fiefdom.

However, unlike their counterparts in Procter and Gamble, category managers in eBay can only indirectly control their products. They have no stock to reorder once levels of toothpaste or washing-up liquid run low on the supermarket shelves. They provide tools to buy and sell more effectively:

What they can do is endlessly try to eke out small wins in their categories – say, a slight jump in scrap-metal listings or new bidders for comic books. To get there, they use marketing and merchandising schemes such as enhancing the presentation of their users' products and giving them tools to buy and sell better.

Over and above this unusual existence, the work environment can be tough and ultra competitive, say ex-eBayers. Changes often come only after PowerPoint slides are exchanged and refined at a low level, eventually presented at a senior level and after the change has been approved in a sign-off procedure which includes every department.

In time eBay has upgraded its ability to ensure the technology does not rule. Until the late 1990s, the site was plagued with outages, including one in 1999 which shut the site down for 22 hours courtesy of software problems and no backup systems. Former Gateway Inc. Chief Information Officer Maynard Webb, who joined as president of eBay's technology unit, quickly took action to upgrade systems. Its use of technology is upgraded constantly. In 2005, Chris Corrado was appointed Senior Vice President and Chief Technology Officer. In eBay's press release COO Maynard Webb said:

Chris is one of the leading technology platform experts in the corporate world, and we are thrilled that he is joining us. It is testament to the tremendous reputation of the eBay technology organization that we were able to bring Chris to the team.

Meg is a leader who buys into the company in more ways than one. Having auctioned some $35,000 (€28,000; £19,500) worth of furnishings in her ski condo in Colorado to understand the selling experience, she became a top seller among the company's employees and ensured that her learning from the experience was listened to by fellow top execs. Meg is also known for listening carefully to her employees and expects her managers to do the same. As the business is as much, if not more, its customers, any false move can cause revolts within the community that is eBay.

Most of all, eBay tries to stay aware and flexible. Nearly all of its fastest-growing new categories emerged from registering seller activity in the area and quietly giving it a nudge at the right moment. For example, after noticing a few car sales, eBay created a separate site called eBay Motors in 1999, with special features such as vehicle inspections and shipping. Some four years later, eBay expects to gross some $1 billion worth of autos and parts, many of which are sold by professional dealers.

The democratic underpinning of eBay, whilst easily embraced by customers, can, however, take some getting used too. New managers take time to understand the ethos. 'Some of the terms you learn in business school – drive, force, commit – don't apply,' says former PepsiCo Inc. exec William C. Cobb, now President eBay North America, with a background in restaurants and PepsiCo, 'We're over here listening, adapting, enabling.'

Competition and cooperation

As the Internet has become a more competitive arena eBay has not stood still. In 2005 it bought Skype, the Internet telephony organisation (http://www.skype.com/), surrounded by much debate in the press as to the logic of the $2.6bn deal. With Skype, eBay argues it can create an unparalleled e-commerce engine, pointing to the 2002 purchase of online payment system PayPal (http://www.paypal.com/) that spurred on the business at that time. All three benefit from so-called network effects – the more members, the more valuable the company – and eBay has to be a world leader in managing network effects.

In 2006 it also announced a deal with Google. eBay is one of Google's biggest advert customers. Google in turn is attracted to eBay's Skype customers for click-to-call adverts. This deal was after eBay signed an advertising deal with Yahoo! which made some think eBay was teaming up with Yahoo! against Google's dominance. But in the interconnected world of the Internet, defining competition and cooperation is a new game. eBay also formed a partnership between Baidu Inc., a Chinese web portal bought by eBay in 2002, and eBay EachNet. Baidu promotes PayPal Beibao as the preferred payment method on Baidu whilst EachNet uses Baidu as its exclusive search provider. The development of a co-branded toolbar is set to cement the partnership. So whilst in the West Yahoo! and eBay are partnering against Google, in the East Yahoo! is a rival.

Despite eBay being the Internet auction phenomenon, it does not do as well in the East as the West. It pulled out of Japan, is suffering in Taiwan and lags behind a rival in China. In Korea, GMarket, partly owned by Yahoo!, is more or less equal in size to eBay's Internet Auction. GMarket offers less emphasis on open auctions than eBay, although eBay now does have eBay Express where new products from multiple sellers can be purchased in one transaction backed as ever by customer support including live chat.

Innovative marketing that makes the experience fun for shoppers and helps sellers improve their performance is perhaps another way GMarket differentiates itself from eBay. GMarket has itself attracted imitators.

Once a web 2.0 company always a web 2.0 company? Although the news did not produce much reaction when announced during an eBay Live! Session, in 2006 eBay created eBay Wiki (http://www.ebaywiki.com/), hosted by Jotspot, allowing people to contribute their knowledge of eBay to others, along with eBay blogs (http://blogs.ebay.com/). But eBay has always been about community so perhaps they will catch on in time.

Questions

1 Analyse eBay's strategic capability using an analytical framework(s) from the chapter.

2 What are the capabilities that have provided eBay with competitive advantage and why?

3 Using the concepts of sustainability and dynamic capabilities, how would you manage this capability (create new resources and competences, invest/divest in others, extend others), given:
   (a) New entrants in the marketplace?
   (b) The changing nature of eBay?

The Strategic Position

4

Strategic Purpose

LEARNING OUTCOMES

After reading this chapter you should be able to:

→ Identify the components of the governance chain of an organisation.

→ Understand differences in governance structures across the world and the advantages and disadvantages of these.

→ Identify differences in the corporate social responsibility stances taken by organisations and how ethical issues relate to strategic purpose.

→ Undertake stakeholder analysis as a means of identifying the influence of different stakeholder groups in terms of their power and interest.

→ Consider appropriate ways to express the strategic purpose of an organisation in terms of statements of values, vision, mission or objectives.

4.1 INTRODUCTION

The previous two chapters have looked respectively at the influence of the environment and capabilities on an organisation's strategic position. However, a fundamental decision that has to be taken concerns the *purpose* of the strategy that is to be followed. This is the focus of this chapter, together with the influences on such purpose by the expectations of *stakeholders* of an organisation. **Stakeholders** are those individuals or groups who depend on an organisation to fulfil their own goals and on whom, in turn, the organisation depends. An underlying issue raised by this chapter is whether the strategic purpose of the organisation should be determined in response to a particular stakeholder, for example shareholders in the case of a commercial enterprise, or to broader stakeholder interests – at the extreme society and the social good. This theme is considered in relation to a number of key issues.

> **Stakeholders** are those individuals or groups who depend on an organisation to fulfil their own goals and on whom, in turn, the organisation depends

- Section 4.2 considers *corporate governance* and the *regulatory framework* within which organisations operate. Here the concern is with the way in which formally constituted bodies such as investors or boards influence strategic purpose through the formalised processes of supervising executive decisions and actions. In turn this raises issues of *accountability*: who are strategists accountable to? There are significant differences in the approach to corporate governance internationally, broadly relating to either shareholder or wider stakeholder orientations, and these are also discussed.

- Section 4.3 is concerned with issues of *social responsibility and ethics*. Here the question is which purposes an organisation *should* fulfil. How should managers respond to the expectations society has of their organisations, both

Exhibit 4.1 Influences on strategic purpose

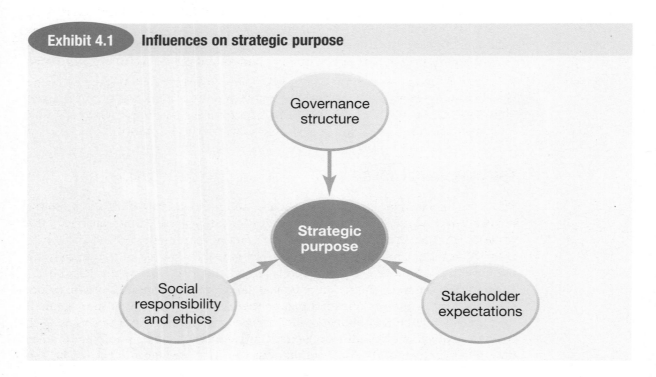

in terms of *corporate social responsibility* and in terms of the *behaviour of individuals* within organisations, including themselves?

● In all this it is, then, important to understand *different stakeholder expectations* and their relative influence on strategic purpose. This requires an understanding of both the *power* and *interest* of different stakeholder groups. This is addressed through *stakeholder analysis.*

● The chapter concludes by considering different ways in which organisations *express strategic purpose.* This may include statements of *values, vision, mission* or *objectives.*

Exhibit 4.1 summarises these different influences on strategic purpose discussed in the chapter.

4.2 CORPORATE GOVERNANCE[1]

Corporate governance is concerned with the structures and systems of control by which managers are held accountable to those who have a legitimate stake in an organisation

Corporate governance is concerned with the structures and systems of control by which managers are held accountable to those who have a legitimate stake in an organisation.[2] It has become an increasingly important issue for organisations for three main reasons.

● *The separation of ownership and management control* of organisations (which is now the norm except with very small businesses) means that most organisations operate within a hierarchy, or chain, of governance. This chain represents those groups that influence an organisation through their involvement in either ownership or management of an organisation.

● *Corporate scandals* since the late 1990s have increased public debate about how different parties in the governance chain should interact and influence each other. Most notable here is the relationship between shareholders and the boards of businesses, but an equivalent issue in the public sector is the relationship between government or public funding bodies and public sector organisations.

● *Increased accountability to wider stakeholder interests* has also come to be increasingly advocated; in particular the argument that corporations need to be more visibly accountable and/or responsive, not only to 'owners' and 'managers' in the governance chain but to wider social interest.

4.2.1 The governance chain

KEY CONCEPT
www.pearsoned.co.uk/ecs

Governance chain

The governance chain illuminates the roles and relationships of different groups involved in the governance of an organisation. In a small family business, the governance chain is quite simple: there are family shareholders; there is a board, with some family members; and there are managers, some of whom may be family too. Here there are just three layers in the chain. However, Exhibit 4.2 shows a governance chain for a typical large, publicly quoted organisation. Here the size of the organisation means there are extra layers of management internally, while being publicly quoted introduces more investor layers as well. Individual investors (the ultimate beneficiaries) often invest in public companies through collective funds, for example unit trusts or pension funds, which then

Exhibit 4.2	The chain of corporate governance: typical reporting structures

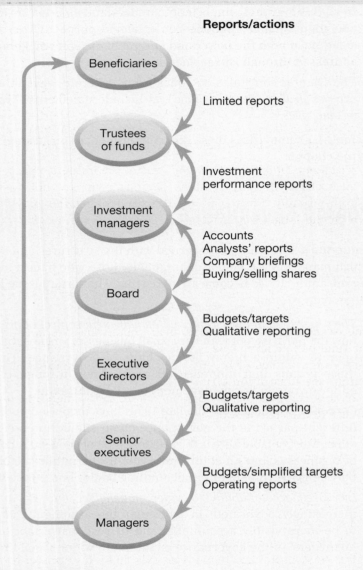

Source: Adapted from David Pitt-Watson, Hermes.

invest in a range of companies on their behalf. Such funds are of growing importance. In 2006, they owned 50 per cent of the equity of US corporations (19 per cent in 1970) and over 70 per cent in the UK (25 per cent in 1963), with similar growth elsewhere in Europe. Funds are typically controlled by trustees, with day-to-day investment activity undertaken by investment managers. So the ultimate beneficiaries may not even know which companies they have a financial stake in and have little power to influence the companies' boards directly.

The relationships in such governance chains can be understood in terms of the *principal–agent model*[3]. Here 'principals' pay 'agents' to act on their behalf, just as home-owners employ estate agents to sell their homes. In Exhibit 4.2, the beneficiaries are the ultimate principals and fund trustees are their agents in terms of achieving good returns on their investments. Further down the chain, company boards are principals too, with senior executives their agents in managing the company. There are many layers of agents between ultimate principals and the managers at the bottom, with the reporting mechanisms between each layer liable to be imperfect.

Principal–agent theory assumes that agents will not work diligently for principals unless incentives are carefully and appropriately aligned. However, it can be seen from Exhibit 4.2 that in large companies board members and other managers driving strategy are likely to be very remote from the ultimate beneficiaries of the company's performance. In such circumstances, the danger is twofold:

- *Misalignment of incentives and control.* As influence passes down the governance chain, the expectations of one group are not passed on to the next appropriately. For example, ultimate beneficiaries may be mainly concerned with the long-term security of their pension fund, but the investment managers and analysts or the boards with whom they interact may place a greater emphasis on short-term growth.

- *Self-interest.* Any agent in the chain may act out of self-interest. Managers will be striving for promotion and/or increased earnings, investment managers will be seeking to increase their bonuses, and so on.

The result may be that decisions are taken that are not in the best interests of the final beneficiary. This is just what has happened in the case of many of the corporate scandals of recent years, the most notorious of which was probably Enron (see Illustration 4.1).

In this context, the governance chain helps highlight important issues that affect the management of strategy:

- *Responsibility to whom?* A fundamental question in large corporations is whether executives should regard themselves as *solely* responsible to shareholders, or as 'trustees of the assets of the corporation' acting on behalf of a wider range of stakeholders?[4] (See the key debate, Illustration 4.6.) Even in terms of formal governance structures this varies across the world, as section 4.2.3 shows.

- *Who are the shareholders?* If managers do see themselves as primarily responsible to shareholders, what does this mean in terms of the governance chain? As explained above, the final beneficiaries are far removed from the managers, so for many managers responsibility to them is notional. In practical terms, directors of a firm are likely to engage most frequently with institutional representatives of those shareholders – an investment manager or analyst from a pension fund or insurance company perhaps. The principal–agent problem arises here too. The final beneficiaries are also distant for investment managers and analysts, who may also be pursuing their own self-interest. Strategists within a firm therefore face a difficult choice, even if they espouse primary responsibility to shareholders. Do they develop strategies they believe to be in the best interest of a highly fragmented group of unknown shareholders? Or to meet the needs and aspirations of the investment managers? A similar problem exists for public sector managers. They may see themselves as developing strategies in the public good, but they may face direct scrutiny

Illustration 4.1

The Enron corporate scandal

Executive decisions may not always be in the interest of shareholders; sometimes disastrously so.

Enron was one of the world's leading electricity, natural gas, pulp, paper and communications companies, based in Houston, Texas. It employed around 21,000 people with claimed revenues of $101bn (€80bn) in 2000. However at the end of 2001 it was revealed that its reported financial condition was sustained mostly by systematic and creative accounting fraud. When Enron sought Chapter 11 protection in the USA in late 2001, it was the biggest bankruptcy in US history and cost 4,000 employees their jobs. The scandal also caused the dissolution of Arthur Andersen, a Big Five accounting firm.

Many of Enron's recorded assets and profits were inflated, fraudulent and non-existent. Enron had put debts and losses into 'offshore' companies not included in the company's financial statements and used sophisticated financial transactions with related companies known as 'special purposes entities' (SPEs) to take unprofitable transactions off the company's books. Later investigations revealed that some executives at Enron knew about the offshore accounts that were hiding losses for the company. Chief Financial Officer Andrew Fastow led the team which created the off-books companies and manipulated the deals to provide himself, his family and friends with hundreds of millions of dollars in guaranteed revenue, at the expense of the stockholders. As the scandal unfolded, Enron shares dropped from over $90.00 to $0.30.

US Congressional hearings revealed that a group of Enron employees had been expressing concerns as early as 1998. Growing apprehension led to an all-employee meeting in mid-2001, where other related issues were discussed. Following the meeting, Sherron Watkins, Vice President, met with the then CEO, the late Ken Lay, handing him a memo detailing her concerns. She especially highlighted the roles of Vinson & Elkins, LLP, a large and reputable US law firm, and Arthur Andersen, LLP, as complicit with dubious deals. Top management asked Vinson & Elkins to investigate the concerns. However, the law firm reported that apart from some 'bad cosmetics',

and 'aggressive and creative accounting', they found no problem with the SPEs. Arthur Andersen in turn confirmed that it was comfortable with the accounting.

Late in October 2002, the Securities and Exchange Commission opened a formal inquiry into Enron, which also started a devastating trail of events at Arthur Andersen. By the time Andersen received notice from the SEC in mid-November, a large number of Enron-related audit documents had been destroyed. This subsequently led to Andersen's indictment in June 2002. The trial of Arthur Andersen also exposed its accounting fraud at WorldCom, setting off a wave of other accounting scandals.

J.P. Morgan Chase, Citigroup, Merrill Lynch, Credit Suisse First Boston, Canadian Imperial Bank of Commerce (CIBC), Bank America, Barclays Bank, Deutsche Bank; and Lehman Brothers were also named as players in the series of fraudulent transactions that ultimately cost shareholders more than $25bn. Two law firms were identified as involved in the fraud: Vinson & Elkins and Chicago-based Kirkland & Ellis, which Enron used to represent a number of SPEs.

By mid-2006, 16 of Enron's top executives, including Ken Lay, Jeff Skilling (CEO), David Delainey (Head of Enron's Energy Trading Unit), Richard Causey (Chief Accounting Officer), Andrew Fastow (Chief Financial Officer) and Mark Koenig (Head of Investor Relations), pleaded guilty or were convicted and in the process of being sentenced.

Prepared by Rajshree Prakash, University of Lancaster Management School.

Questions

1 What mechanisms in the governance chain should (or could) have prevented what happened at Enron?

2 What changes in corporate governance are required to prevent similar occurrences?

from an agency acting on behalf of the government. Is the strategy to be designed for the general public good, or to meet the scrutiny of the agency? For example, managers and doctors in the UK health service are dedicated to the well-being of their patients. But increasingly how they manage their services is governed by the targets placed upon them by a government department, which presumably also believes it is acting in the public good.

- *The role of institutional investors.* The role of institutional investors with regard to the strategy of firms differs according to governance structures around the world (see section 4.2.3). However, a common issue is the extent to which they do or should actively seek to influence strategy. Historically, in economies like those of the UK or USA investors have exerted their influence on firms simply through the buying and selling of shares rather than through an in-depth engagement with the company on strategic issues. The stock market becomes the judge of their actions through share price movements. There are signs, however, that investors are becoming more actively involved in the strategies of the firms in which they invest.[5] Such involvement varies a good deal[6] but has grown, and there is evidence that institutional investors that seek to work proactively with boards to develop strategy do better for beneficiaries than those who do not.[7]

- *Scrutiny and control.* Given the concerns about governance that have grown in the last decade, there have been increasing attempts to build means of scrutinising and controlling the activities of 'agents' in the chain to safeguard the interests of the final beneficiaries. Exhibit 4.2 indicates the information typically available to each 'player' in the chain to judge the performance of others in that chain. There are increasing statutory requirements as well as voluntary codes placed upon boards to disclose information publicly and regulate their activities. None the less managers are still left with a great deal of discretion as to what information to provide to whom and, indeed, what information to require of those who report to them. For example, what information should be presented to investment analysts who will influence a firm's share price? How specific should a chief executive be in explaining future strategy to shareholders in public statements such as annual reports? There are also issues of internal reporting that have to be resolved. What are the appropriate targets and measures to incentivise and control management within a firm? Should these primarily be concerned with the achievement of shareholder value? Or is a more balanced scorecard approach appropriate to meet the needs of various stakeholders (see section 12.3.5)? Are the typical accountancy methods (such as return on capital employed) the most appropriate measures or should measures be specifically designed to fit the needs of particular strategies or particular stakeholder/shareholder expectations? There are no categoric answers to these questions. How managers answer them will depend on what they decide the strategic purpose of the organisation is, which itself will be influenced by their view on whom they see themselves responsible to.

The governance chain, then, typically operates imperfectly for at least five reasons: (i) a lack of clarity on who the end beneficiaries are; (ii) unequal division of power between the different 'players' in the chain; (iii) with different levels of access to information available to them; (iv) potentially agents in the chain pursuing their own self-interest; and (v) using measures and targets reflecting their own interests rather than those of end beneficiaries. In such circumstances it is not surprising that there are attempts to reform corporate governance and that governance structures are changing around the world.

4.2.2   Corporate governance reforms

Many governments have been proactive in reforming aspects of corporate governance. The most notable has been the Sarbanes–Oxley Act in the USA that was one outcome of the Enron scandal. This tightened accounting standards and increased auditor independence from management.[8] Other governments have sponsored committees to advise on specific issues of corporate governance.[9] Initially these concentrated on internal financial controls and external disclosure of information.[10] Later committees focused on the broadening of internal control requirements beyond simply financial controls and looked at the role and effectiveness of non-executive directors.[11] The public sector picked up a similar agenda; in the UK there was particular interest in *risk management* of public sector organisations' strategies – a traditionally weak area.[12] These reforms have had significant impacts. For example, accountancy firms have been forced to separate their audit function from their advisory services and, indeed, sell off their managing consulting services as a result of the Sarbanes–Oxley Act, so the strategy of accounting firms was directly affected, as was the source of consultancy services for firms.

Surveys have also found that finance directors have switched their attention more to stewardship roles than to strategy roles,[13] and more emphasis has been placed on the role of independent non-executive directors to scrutinise the behaviour of firms. However, some executives have voiced concerns: for example, the managing director of the Bank of Queensland in Australia: 'Over regulation can and will kill the entrepreneurial spirit, it will crush innovation as more and more resources are shifted towards compliance and away from staying ahead of the pack.'[14] There is also a concern that, although changes in the structure of board committees might be needed, the really important issue is the behaviour of boards of directors. The implication for policy makers (in government) is that there is a need to find ways of sponsoring governance changes that will demonstrably encourage or require directors and managers (as 'agents') to behave in ways and pursue strategies that are in the interests of 'principals' in their governance chain as discussed above. Promoting such changes is a major challenge, given the concerns voiced about top executives' focus on building empires, climbing up through the hierarchy and increasing their personal financial rewards without due regard to the consequences on the final beneficiaries.

4.2.3   Different governance structures

The governing body of an organisation is typically a board of directors. The primary statutory responsibility of a board is to ensure that an organisation fulfils the wishes and purposes of the primary stakeholders. However, who these stakeholders are varies. In the private sector in some parts of the world it is shareholders, but in other parts of the world it is a broader or different stakeholder base. In the public sector, the governing body is accountable to the political arm of government – possibly through some intermediate 'agency' such as a funding body. These differences lead to differences in the way firms operate, how the purposes of an organisation are shaped and how strategies are developed as well as the role and composition of boards.[15]

At the most general level there are two governance structures: the shareholder model and the stakeholder model.[16] These are more or less common in different parts of the world.

A shareholder model of governance

Here shareholders have the legitimate primacy in relation to the wealth generated by the corporations, though proponents argue that maximising shareholder value benefits other stakeholders too. There is dispersed shareholding, though a large proportion of shares is held by financial institutions. At least in principle, the trading of shares provides a regulatory mechanism for maximising shareholder value, given that dissatisfied shareholders may sell their shares, the result being a drop in share price and the threat of takeovers for underperforming firms.

The shareholder model is epitomised by the economies of the USA and UK. Firms in the USA usually have a single-tier board structure, with a majority of non-executive directors. This emphasis on outside directors is intended to bring greater independence to the primary role of the board, that of oversight on behalf of shareholders. However, this is not without its problems. Typically the CEO plays a major role in selecting non-executives, which raises questions about their independence. There are also concerns that outside directors may not have sufficient time, or the requisite knowledge of firms' problems.[17]

The UK also has a single-tier board structure and increasingly a separation of the chair and the CEO, with the chair often non-executive. The proportion of the executive directors on the board of large companies is typically between one-third and one-half of the total board membership. The board has an executive role of driving the company forward as well as an oversight role on behalf of shareholders.

There are arguments for and against the shareholder model. The *argued advantages* include:

- *Benefits for investors*. Relative to the stakeholder model the investor gets a higher rate of return. Shareholders can also reduce risk through diversifying their holdings in an equity market where shares can be readily traded.

- *Benefits to the economy*. Since the system facilitates higher risk taking by investors, there is a higher likelihood of the encouragement of economic growth and of entrepreneurship. It is also argued that one reason why the UK gets more than its 'fair share' of inward investment to the EU is because the ownership structures are more open to new investors than elsewhere.

- *Benefits for management*. Arguably the separation of ownership and management makes strategic decisions more objectively related to the potentially different demands and constraints of financial, labour and customer markets. A diversified shareholding also means that no one shareholder is likely to control management decisions, provided the firm performs well.

The *argued disadvantages* include:

● *Disadvantages for investors*. Dispersed shareholdings prevent close monitoring of the management. This may result in the managers sacrificing shareholder value to pursue their own agendas. For example, CEOs may further their own egos at the expense of the shareholders with mergers that add no value.

● *Disadvantages for the economy: the risk of short-termism*. Lack of control of management may lead to them taking decisions to benefit their own careers (for example, to gain promotion). This, combined with the threat of takeovers, may encourage managers to focus on short-term gains at the expense of long-term projects.[18]

● *Corporate reputation and top management greed*. The lack of management control allows for the huge compensations the managers reward themselves in the form of salary, bonuses and stock options. In the USA CEOs have 531 times more compensation than their employees in comparison with Japan where the comparable figure is closer to a multiple of 10.[19]

The stakeholder model of governance

An alternative model of governance pursued in various forms is the stakeholder model. This is founded on the principle that wealth is created, captured and distributed by a variety of stakeholders. This may include shareholders but could include other investors, such as banks, as well as employees or their union representatives. As such, management need to be responsive to multiple stakeholders who, themselves, may be formally represented on boards.

However, stakeholder models are also sometimes known as the *block holder system of governance*.[20] One or two large group of investors come to dominate ownership. For example, in Germany just less than three-quarters of all the German listed companies have a majority owner. In addition, in countries like Germany and Sweden banks play a dominant role and Japanese banks tend to have shareholdings in organisations, as against simply providing loan capital. There is also likely to be a complex web of cross-shareholdings between companies.

Germany and Japan are often cited as examples of the stakeholder model. In Germany there is a two-tier board system. The supervisory board (*Aufsichtsrat*), mandatory for companies having more than 500 employees, and the management board (*Vorstand*). The supervisory board is a forum where the interest of various groups is represented, including shareholders and employees but also typically bankers, lawyers and stock exchange experts. Strategic planning and operational control are vested with the management board, but major decisions like mergers and acquisitions require approval of the supervisory board. In other European countries, notably The Netherlands and France, two-tier boards also exist.

In Japan, profit maximisation or shareholder value is not viewed as the ultimate goal of business enterprises so much as long-term growth and security of the company. There is concentrated ownership of firms, with a small group of shareholders owning a large percentage of the company, and a system of cross-shareholding, where large companies own shares of other companies and banks finance the same subgroup. Japanese firms have a single-tier board system. Directors are appointed from the executive managers of the company, so the board consists almost entirely of insiders.[21] A prerequisite of a good director has traditionally been someone who promotes the interests of employees.

There are *argued advantages* for the stakeholder model of governance:

- *Advantages for stakeholders*. Apart from the argument that the wider interests of stakeholders are taken into account, it is also argued that employee influence in particular is a deterrent to high-risk decisions and investments.

- *Advantages for investors*. Perhaps ironically it is argued that it is block investments that provide economic benefits in several ways. There may be a closer level of monitoring of management, with investors having greater access to information from within the firm. Given that power may reside with relatively few block investors, intervention may also be easier in case of management failure.

- *Long-term horizons*. It is argued that the major investors – banks or other companies, for example – are likely to regard their investments as long term, thus reducing the pressure for short-term results[22] as against longer-term performance.

There are also *argued disadvantages* of the stakeholder model of governance:

- *Disadvantages for management*. Close monitoring could lead to interference, slowing down of decision processes and the loss of management objectivity when critical decisions have to be made.

- *Disadvantages for investors*. Due to lack of pressure from shareholders, long-term investments are made on projects where the returns may be below market expectations.

- *Disadvantage for the economy*. There are fewer alternatives for raising finance, thus limiting the possibilities of growth and entrepreneurial activity.

These argued advantages and disadvantages are summarised in Exhibit 4.3.

It is also worth noting that there are implications with regard to the financing of businesses. In the shareholder model, equity is the dominant form of long-term finance and commercial banks provide debt capital, so relationships with bankers are essentially contractual. There are significant implications. Managers need to limit gearing to a prudent level, so more equity is needed for major strategy developments. It also means that the company itself has a higher degree of influence over strategic decisions since the banks are not seeking a strategic involvement with the company. However, if strategies start to fail, the organisation can become increasingly dependent on the bank as a key stakeholder. This often happens in family-owned small businesses. In the extreme banks may exercise their power through *exit* (that is, withdrawing funds), even if this liquidates the company. In contrast, in some stakeholder systems (notably Japan and to a lesser extent Germany), banks often have significant equity stakes or are part of the same parent company. They are less likely to adopt an arm's-length relationship and more likely to seek active strategic involvement.

Governance structures in transition

There are pressures for change to traditional governance models. Some of these have already been discussed in relation to the governance chain in section 4.2.1.

Exhibit 4.3   **Benefits and disadvantages of governance systems**

	Shareholder model	Stakeholder model
Benefits	For investors: ● Higher rate of return ● Reduced risk For the economy: ● Encourages entrepreneurship ● Encourages inward investment For management: ● Independence	For investors: ● Closer monitoring of management ● Longer-term decision horizons For stakeholders: ● Deterrent to high-risk decisions
Disadvantages	For investors: ● Difficult to monitor management For the economy: ● The risk of short-termism And top management greed	For management: ● Potential interference ● Slower decision making ● Reduced independence For the economy: ● Reduced financing opportunities for growth

There are, none the less, suggestions that there is a convergence around the world on the shareholder model of governance. This is because of many of the advantages explained above, in particular the view that there is mutual advantage to both shareholders and wider stakeholders. It is also because of the increasing role of institutional investors acting on behalf of a growing mass shareholder class and increasing globalisation and cross-country mergers and acquisitions.[23]

So, for example, in Japan, institutional and foreign investors are gaining influence, and deregulation and liberalisation are increasing the pressure to change governance structures. In Germany, too, there are pressures for change. In mid-2006, for example, Jürgen Thumann of the BDI industry federation argued that if German companies were to remain globally competitive, the employee representation on boards needed to be reviewed: not least because this would help reduce costs and speed decision making.

Similarly elsewhere, governance systems are in transition. In Sweden historically firms were privately owned or in the hands of family-controlled foundations, holding companies and investment companies. By 2005, however, less than 15 per cent of the market capitalisation was held by individual owners as institutional ownership increased.[24] Sweden's entry into the EU has also reduced restrictions on capital inflow and increasingly companies are becoming foreign owned. However, most companies still have a majority owner that gives them a controlling position akin to the stakeholder model.

In India there was a high level of state protectionism till the 1980s, with major industries like airlines and banks nationalised and restrictions on inward foreign investment. However, since 1991 there has been radical change. Import licensing has been abolished and import tariffs reduced. Restrictions on foreign equity have been relaxed in certain industries, some public sector enterprises have been disinvested and firms allowed to register on the international stock exchanges.[25] India is still characterised by family firms, but with increasing separation of ownership and management. The codes of governance being proposed indicate a move towards a shareholder model of governance with a single board and between 30 and 50 per cent non-executive directors.

In China the major stakeholders in firms are the state or quasi-state institutions. China has a two-tier board model. The supervisory board has a minimum of one-third of employees as members, but with limited influence on organisational activities, which is the responsibility of operating boards. Boards are required to have non-executive directors who have recently been required to be independent. The appointment of top management was tightly controlled by government but this has diminished over the years. Senior managers have, however, usually started their careers in government positions.[26]

Public services have a wide variety of arrangements for governing bodies, but there are some commonalities. Governing bodies are often 'representational' of key stakeholders, in practice even if not by regulation. This particularly applies to the place of employees and unions on governing bodies. There has been a move in many countries to increase the proportion of (so-called) independent members on governing bodies. These independent members are the nearest equivalent of the non-executive director in the private sector.

4.2.4 How governing bodies influence strategy

A common issue increasingly debated is, then, the role of boards of directors and of directors themselves. Since boards have the ultimate responsibility for the success or failure of an organisation as well as the benefits received by shareholders or wider stakeholders, they must be concerned with strategy. However, there are two broad choices on how they do this:

- Strategic management can be entirely *delegated to management* – with the board receiving and approving plans/decisions. Here the 'stewardship' role of the board requires processes that ensure that the purpose of the organisation and its strategies are not 'captured' by management at the expense of other stakeholders – particularly the owners. The Enron case is an extreme example of how this can happen.

- The board can *engage with management* in the strategic management process. But this has many practical problems concerning the time and knowledge level of (particularly) non-executive directors to perform their role this way. This problem can be especially pronounced in organisations such as charities or public bodies with governing boards or trustees of people committed to the mission of the organisation, keen to become involved but with limited operational understanding of it.

In the guidelines increasingly issued by governments[27] or advocated by commentators to try to ensure that boards act in the interests of their shareholders and beneficiaries, there are some common themes:

- Boards must be seen to *operate 'independently' of the management* of the company. So the role of non-executive directors is heightened.

- Boards must be *competent to scrutinise the activities of managers*. So the collective experience of the board, its training and the information at its disposal are crucially important.

- Directors must have the *time* to do their job properly. So limitations on the number of directorships that an individual can hold are also an important consideration.

- However, it is the *behaviour of boards* and their members that is likely to be most significant[28] whatever structural arrangements are put in place. For example, respect, trust, 'constructive friction' between board members, fluidity of roles, individual as well as collective responsibility, and the evaluation of individual director and collective board performance.

4.2.5 Ownership choices

Within the broad governance structures that exist, different forms of ownership will have an effect on the purposes of an organisation and the strategies pursued. There may in turn be issues as to whether the form of ownership is appropriate to the strategic purposes of an organisation.

- *Private or public ownership of equity* is an issue for commercial organisations. As they develop and grow, many organisations – for example, family businesses – move from private ownership to a publicly quoted corporation. Such a decision might be made because the owners decide that increased equity is required to finance the growth of the business. The family members who own the business need to recognise that their role will change. They become answerable to a much wider group of shareholders and to institutions acting for those shareholders.

- *Sale of all or part of the company* may be a choice faced by the board of directors of a business which has a responsibility to provide shareholders with a return on their investment. A board may arrive at the view that a different corporate parent would better achieve this primary purpose. Or a business may become the *target for an acquisition* and a board might decide that such an offer is more attractive to shareholders than the returns it can promise in the future.

- *Acquisition of another business* may also be considered. Acquiring other businesses may raise significant issues about the purpose of the corporate entity as Chapter 7 (section 7.4) shows. However, questions have been raised as to whether acquisitions are in the best interests of shareholders. Many fail to deliver the promised benefits to shareholders; at least in the short/medium term, they are likely to lead to loss of shareholder value. The concern centres on the principal–agent issue and the potential *conflict of interest* between a board of directors and the best interests of shareholders. Directors may pursue such acquisitions because they enlarge their empire, improve their financial rewards or because they feel that investment analysts expect acquisitive growth. Mergers and acquisitions are discussed more fully in Chapter 10 (section 10.2.2).

- *Mutual ownership and partnerships* have been the tradition in some sectors. Insurance companies and building societies were traditionally owned by their customers rather than by shareholders. In theory, such an arrangement might seem to bring together the principal beneficiaries of shareholders and customers and facilitate strategy being developed in the interest of both. However, ownership can remain highly fragmented under such a structure, leading to the same principal–agent problems discussed earlier. Indeed, many UK building societies have become banks and changed their form of ownership by de-mutualising, thus changing governance arrangements to be more similar to companies. There are also signs that law firms and accountancy firms, so long wedded to partnership structures, are also moving to more corporate models of ownership.

- *Privatisation* of public sector bodies has occurred in many countries. Historically, most public sector bodies were tightly controlled by central or local government. Governments took decisions to privatise in order to require organisations to face up to market forces, become more aware of customer needs and competitive pressures, and so as to provide access to private sector capital. In turn, managers found more latitude in terms of strategic choice – what they could provide in terms of product or services; the ability to diversify, raise capital for expansion, and so on.

4.3 BUSINESS ETHICS AND SOCIAL RESPONSIBILITY[29]

Underlying the discussion of corporate governance is the issue highlighted in the Introduction. Is the purpose of an organisation and its strategy for the benefit of a primary stakeholder such as the shareholders of a company, or is it there for the benefit of a wider group of stakeholders? In turn this raises the question of societal expectations placed on organisations and how these impact on an organisation's purposes. Governments have increasingly taken the view that these expectations cannot be achieved through regulation alone. This is the province of *business ethics* and it exists at two levels:

- At the *macro* level, there are issues about the role of businesses and other organisations in society. Expectations range from laissez-faire free enterprise at one extreme to shapers of society at the other. The broad ethical stance of an organisation is a matter of *corporate social responsibility*.

- At the *individual* level, business ethics is about the behaviour and actions of people in organisations. This is clearly an important issue for the management of organisations in general, but it is discussed here in terms of the role of managers in the strategic management process.

4.3.1 Corporate social responsibility

The regulatory environment and the corporate governance arrangements for an organisation determine its minimum obligations towards its stakeholders.

Corporate social responsibility (CSR) is concerned with the ways in which an organisation exceeds its minimum obligations to stakeholders specified through regulation. However, the legal and regulatory frameworks under which businesses operate pay uneven attention to the rights of different stakeholders. For example, *contractual stakeholders* – such as customers, suppliers or employees – have a legal relationship with an organisation, and *community stakeholders* – such as local communities, consumers (in general) and pressure groups – do not have the protection of the law.[30] CSR policies of companies will be particularly important to these community stakeholders.

Different organisations take very different stances on social responsibility. These different stances will also be reflected in how they manage such responsibilities. Exhibit 4.4 outlines four stereotypes to illustrate these differences. They represent a progressively more inclusive 'list' of stakeholder interests and a greater breadth of criteria against which strategies and performance will be judged. The discussion that follows also explains what such stances typically involve in terms of the ways companies act.[31]

The laissez-faire view (literally 'let do' in French) represents an extreme stance where organisations take the view that the only responsibility of business is the short-term interests of shareholders and to 'make a profit, pay taxes and provide jobs'.[32] It is for government to prescribe, through legislation and regulation, the

Exhibit 4.4	Corporate social responsibility stances

	Laissez-faire	Enlightened self-interest	Forum for stakeholder interaction	Shaper of society
Rationale	Legal compliance: make a profit, pay taxes and provide jobs	Sound business sense	Sustainability or triple bottom line	Social and market change
Leadership	Peripheral	Supportive	Champion	Visionary
Management	Middle management responsibility	Systems to ensure good practice	Board-level issue; organisation-wide monitoring	Individual responsibility throughout the organisation
Mode	Defensive to outside pressures	Reactive to outside pressures	Proactive	Defining
Stakeholder relationships	Unilateral	Interactive	Partnership	Multi-organisation alliances

constraints which society chooses to impose on businesses in their pursuit of economic efficiency. The organisation will meet these minimum obligations but no more. Expecting companies to exercise social duties beyond this can, in extreme cases, undermine the authority of government.

This stance may be taken by executives who are persuaded of it ideologically or by smaller businesses that do not have the resources to do other than minimally comply with regulations. Insofar as social good is pursued, this is justified in terms of improving profitability.[33] This might occur, for example, if social obligations were imposed as a requirement for gaining contracts (for example, if equal opportunities employment practices were required from suppliers to public sector customers) or to defend their reputation. Responsibility for such actions is likely to be with middle managers or functional heads rather than with the chief executive who is unlikely to see this role as part of his or her brief. Relationships with stakeholders are likely to be largely unilateral and one way rather than interactive. The danger here is, of course, that this may not be how society expects organisations to act. Indeed, it seems that society increasingly expects more than this from large organisations and the evidence is that chief executives themselves are aware of this and agree organisations should play a more proactive role.[34]

Enlightened self-interest is tempered with recognition of the *long-term financial benefit to the shareholder* of well-managed relationships with other stakeholders. The justification for social action is that it makes good business sense. An organisation's *reputation*[35] is important to its long-term financial success and there is a business case to be made for a more proactive stance on social issues in order to recruit and retain staff, for example. So corporate philanthropy[36] or welfare provision might be regarded as sensible expenditure like any other form of investment or promotion expenditure. The sponsorship of major sporting or arts events by companies is an example. The avoidance of 'shady' marketing practices is also necessary to prevent the need for yet more legislation in that area. Managers here would take the view that organisations not only have responsibility to their shareholders but also a responsibility for *relationships with* other stakeholders (as against *responsibilities to* other stakeholders) and communication with stakeholder groups is likely to be more interactive than for laissez-faire-type organisations. They may well also set up systems and policies to ensure compliance with best practice (for example, ISO 14000 certification, the protection of human rights in overseas operations, etc.) and begin to monitor their social responsibility performance. Top management may also play more of a part, at least insofar as they support the firm taking a more proactive social role.

A *forum for stakeholder interaction*[37] explicitly incorporates multiple stakeholder interests and expectations rather than just shareholders as influences on organisational purposes and strategies. Here the argument is that the performance of an organisation should be measured in a more pluralistic way than just through the financial bottom line. Companies in this category might retain uneconomic units to preserve jobs, avoid manufacturing or selling 'anti-social' products, and be prepared to bear reductions in profitability for the social good. Some financial service organisations have also chosen to offer socially responsible investment (SRI) 'products' to investors. These only include holdings in organisations that meet high standards of social responsibility in their activities.

However, here there are difficult issues of balance between the interests of different stakeholders. For example, many public sector organisations are, rightly, positioned within this group as they are subject to a wide diversity of expectations, and unitary measures of performance are often inadequate in reflecting this diversity. There are also many family-owned small firms that are in this category through the way that they operate. They will balance their own self-interest with that of their employees and local communities even where this might constrain the strategic choices they make (for example, overseas sourcing vs. local production). Organisations in this category inevitably take longer over the development of new strategies as they are committed to wide consultation with stakeholders and with managing the difficult political trade-offs between conflicting stakeholders' expectations as discussed in section 4.3.

BP claims to have embraced the logic of 'multi-stakeholder capitalism', believing that its long-term survival is not just dependent on its economic performance but on its social and environmental performance. Organisations such as BP may elevate CSR to board-level appointments and set up structures for monitoring social performance across its global operations. Targets, often through balanced scorecards, may be built into operational aspects of business and issues of social responsibility managed proactively and in a coordinated fashion. The expectation is that such a corporate stance will, in turn, be reflected in the ethical behaviour of individuals within the firm. Organisations that take this position do, of course, suffer if they are not seen to be meeting the standards of performance they espouse (see Illustration 4.2). Indeed, BP found this in 2006 when it suffered both in the US courts and worldwide in the press for its shortcomings in health and safety procedures that led to a fatal explosion at its refinery in Texas City.

Shapers of society regard financial considerations as of secondary importance or a constraint. These are activists, seeking to change society and social norms. The firm may have been founded for this purpose, as in the case of the Body Shop. The social role is, then, the *raison d'être* of the business. They may see their strategic purpose as 'changing the rules of the game' through which they may benefit but by which they wish to assure that society benefits. In this role it is unlikely that they will be operating on their own: rather they are likely to be partnering with other organisations, commercial and otherwise, to achieve their purposes.

The extent to which this is a viable ethical stance depends upon issues of regulation, corporate governance and accountability. It is easier for a privately owned organisation to operate in this way, since it is not accountable to external shareholders. Some would argue that the great historical achievements of the public services in transforming the quality of life for millions of people were largely because they were 'mission driven' in this way, supported by a political framework in which they operated. However, in many countries there have been challenges to the legitimacy of this mission-driven stance of public services and demands for citizens (as taxpayers) to expect demonstrable best value from them. Charitable organisations face similar dilemmas. It is fundamental to their existence that they have zeal to improve the interests of particular groups in society, but they also need to remain financially viable, which can lead to them being seen as over-commercial and spending too much on administration or promotional activities.

Illustration 4.2

BP, 'Beyond Petroleum' and the Texas City disaster

Companies have increasingly been explicit about their stance on social responsibility. But in so doing they can increase their vulnerability when things go wrong.

The global energy company BP under the leadership of John Browne has been applauded for developing an explicit code of social responsibility emphasising efficient and sustainable energy, energy diversity, concern for climate change, local development where it operates and high levels of safety. This stance was publicised in an advertising campaign promoting the slogan 'Beyond Petroleum'. Further, as John Browne stated (*Business Strategy Review*, vol. 17, no. 3 (2006), pp. 53–56), 'Our commitment to responsibility has to be expressed not in words, but in the actions of the business, day in and day out, in every piece of activity and every aspect of behaviour.'

It was, therefore, a major disaster, not only to the local community and its families, but also to BP when, in 2005, an explosion at BP's Texas City oil refinery killed 15 workers. In September 2005 BP was given a £12m (€17m) fine by the US Department of Labor for 300 safety violations at the Texas City plant.

The press were unremitting in their criticism. The disaster had happened in the same year as BP profits soared and Browne, himself, was given pay and share remuneration in 2005 estimated at £6.5m. BPs top management were aware of 'significant safety problems' not only at the Texas City refinery but at 34 other locations around the world. They emphasised cost cutting over safety. They didn't listen to people lower down in the organisation; they reported a staff survey that rated 'making money' as the top priority and 'people' as the lowest. Too many jobs have been outsourced to cheaper contractors, and so it went on.

In January 2007 John Browne announced that he would be quitting BP 18 months early to be succeeded by Tony Haywood who had been in charge of BP's exploration and production division.

Passed over was John Manzoni, the board director in charge of refining, with the responsibility of refineries.

In 2005 BP had asked James Baker, former US Secretary of State, to undertake an independent investigation. In January 2007, Baker reported:

BP has not provided effective process safety leadership and has not adequately established process safety as a core value across all its five U.S. refineries. . . . BP tended to have a short-term focus and its decentralized management system and entrepreneurial culture have delegated substantial discretion to U.S. refinery plant managers without clearly defining process safety expectations, responsibilities or accountabilities. . . . The company did not always insure that adequate resources were effectively allocated to support or sustain a high level of process safety performance.

The company relied excessively on monitoring injury rates which 'significantly hindered its perception of process risk'. Incidents and near misses were probably under-reported and, when spotted, root causes often not identified correctly.

BP responded that it planned 'significant external recruitment . . . to increase underlying capability in operations and engineering' and that modern process control systems would be installed at its refineries. But the company's social responsibility stance had taken a battering.

Questions

1 How would you categorize BP's stance on social responsibility in terms of Exhibit 4.4?

2 Can top management effectively manage social responsibility at local level? How?

3 Will the negative publicity around the Texas City disaster affect BP's strategy?

On the face of it, shapers of society represent the other end of the spectrum from laissez-faire firms. However, it is worth noting that some large firms that espouse a laissez-faire approach, arguably such as NewsCorp or Haliburton, are actively engaged in trying to shape society, albeit towards their view of the social role of business.

Increasingly there is a view by managers themselves that the laissez-faire position is not acceptable;[38] that businesses need to take a socially responsible position. This is not solely for ethical reasons but because there is a belief that there are advantages to businesses in so doing and dangers if they do not. Being socially responsible reduces the risk of negative stakeholder (not least customer) reactions and can help retain loyal, motivated employees. Social responsibility is therefore justified in terms of the 'triple bottom line' – social and environmental benefits as well as increased profits. Indeed it is argued that socially responsible strategies should be followed because they can provide a basis of gaining competitive advantage. The need is to seek 'win–win' situations to optimise the economic return on environmental investments:[39] 'The essential test . . . is not whether a cause is worthy but whether it presents an opportunity to create shared value – that is meaningful benefit for society that is also valuable to the business.'[40] Fighting the AIDS pandemic in Africa is not just a matter of 'good works' for a pharmaceutical company or an African mining company, it is central to their own interests. Similarly helping reduce carbon emissions provides a business opportunity for a car manufacturer.[41] The lobby for more eco-friendly packaging in Sweden prompted Ecolean to produce packaging that is not only environmentally friendly but costs 25 per cent less than its competitors.[42]

However, it is less clear whether there really are economic pay-offs. Arguably, if the competitive advantage case is to be taken seriously, then this should be evident in terms of enhanced profits. The evidence is equivocal. There is a claim for the links of an enlightened self-interest approach to superior financial performance.[43] For example, researchers have sought to establish if ethical investment funds outperform other funds because they invest in socially responsible firms? Some claim such funds perform no better or worse than others and argue that the case for CSR cannot be based on profit performance.[44] Others argue that there is evidence for higher performance if the abilities of such investors to spot the best investments is taken into account.[45] In short, the jury is out on this.

Exhibit 4.5 provides some questions against which an organisation's actions on CSR can be assessed. *Social auditing*[46] is a way of ensuring that issues of CSR are systematically reviewed and has been championed by a number of progressive organisations. This takes several forms, ranging from social audits undertaken by independent external bodies, through aspects of the social agenda that are now mandatory in company reporting (for example, some environmental issues) to voluntary social accounting by organisations themselves.

4.3.2 The role of individuals and managers

Ethical issues have to be faced at the individual as well as corporate level and can pose difficult dilemmas for individuals and managers. Some examples are shown in Illustration 4.3. These raise questions about the responsibility of an individual who believes that the strategy of his or her organisation is unethical (for

Exhibit 4.5 **Some questions of corporate social responsibility**

Should organisations be responsible for . . .

INTERNAL ASPECTS

Exployee welfare
. . . providing medical care, assistance with housing finance, extended sick leave, assistance for dependants, etc.?

Working conditions
. . . job security, enhancing working surroundings, social and sporting clubs, above-minimum safety standards, training and development, etc.?

Job design
. . . designing jobs to the increased satisfaction of workers rather than just for economic efficiency? This would include issues of work/life balance?

Intellectual property
. . . respecting the private knowledge of individuals and not claiming corporate ownership?

EXTERNAL ASPECTS

Environmental issues
. . . reducing pollution to below legal standards if competitors are not doing so?
. . . energy conservation?

Products
. . . dangers arising from the careless use of products by consumers?

Markets and marketing
. . . deciding not to sell in some markets?
. . . advertising standards?

Suppliers
. . . 'fair' terms of trade?
. . . blacklisting suppliers?

Employment
. . . positive discrimination in favour of minorities?
. . . maintaining jobs?

Community activity
. . . sponsoring local events and supporting local good works?

Human rights
. . . respecting human rights in relation to: child labour, workers' and union rights, oppressive political regimes? Both directly and in the choice of markets, suppliers and partners?

example, its trading practices) or is not adequately representing the legitimate interests of one or more stakeholder groups. Should that person leave the company on the grounds of a mismatch of values; or is *whistleblowing*[47] appropriate, such as divulging information to outside bodies, for example regulatory bodies or the press?

Given that strategy development can be an intensely political process with implications for the personal careers of those concerned, managers can find difficulties establishing and maintaining a position of integrity. There is also

Illustration 4.3

Ethical dilemmas

Managers face a range of different ethical dilemmas that need to be resolved.

Conflicting objectives

You are a Dutch manager in charge of the mining operations of your multinational company in Namibia. You employ mainly local workers on very low wages. Your operation provides livelihood for 1,000 families and is the mainstay of the local economy. There is no other local work other than subsistence farming. You have discovered many safety problems with the mine but the company engineer has advised that the cost of upgrading facilities would make the mine uneconomic. Closing the mine would cause a major political stir and harm the parent company's reputation. But keeping it open risks the chance of a major disaster.

Performance data

You are the recently appointed head teacher of a school that is now improving following a period of very poor performance under your predecessor. It has been made clear that one important performance indicator is pupil attendance levels – that must be brought up to the national average (95 per cent). You have now collected all the data for your regular statistical return and notice to your disappointment that your attendance record has fallen just below your required target. On discussing this with your deputy she asks if you would like her to 're-examine and correct' the attendance data before submission.

Bribery

You are the newly appointed manager in charge of a new sales office in New York set up following extensive market research by your British company. After a few months you discover that none of the company's products can be sold in New York without code approval from an obscure New York authority that is controlled by Local 4 of the electricians' union. Further investigation reveals that Local 4 had Mafia connections.

Shortly afterwards you are visited by Local 4 representatives who offer you a deal. If the company pays an annual 'consultative fee' of $12,000 (€10,000) (with escalation clauses as sales grew) you will secure approval in six months. The alternative is to attempt to secure approval alone, which informed sources say is unlikely to succeed.

Company policy is opposed to bribery. But the project is a make-or-break one for the company's ventures in the USA and your own career. Given the potential gains $12,000 is a small amount and would probably be approved if presented 'appropriately'.

Rationing

Rationing is one of the most important issues in many public sector organisations. You are a Swedish doctor working on secondment in charge of a local hospital in rural Nigeria. It receives financial support from the Nigerian government and a European medical charity. However, the medical facilities are poor, particularly supplies of medicines and blood. A bus leaving town has collided with a tourist vehicle. Apart from several fatalities there are four seriously injured survivors. Two are local children (one aged 2, the other 10), one is an elderly leader of a local tribe and the fourth is a German tourist. Unless they have urgent blood transfusions they are likely to die. There is only enough blood for two patients.

Questions

You are the 'player' faced with each of these dilemmas:

1 What choices of action do you have?

2 List the pros and cons of each choice to your organisation, the external parties and yourself.

3 Explain what you would do and justify your actions from an ethical point of view.

| Exhibit 4.6 | Ethical guidelines (based on Texas Instruments' approach to business ethics) |

Questions	Appropriate responses
Is action legal?	If no, stop immediately
Does it comply with our values?	If it does not, stop
If you do it, will you feel bad?	Ask your own conscience if you can live with it
How would this look in the newspaper?	Ask, if this goes public tomorrow would you do it today?
If you know it is wrong . . .	Don't do it
If you are not sure . . .	Ask
	And keep asking till you get an answer

Source: Angela Sutherland, Glasgow Caledonian University.

potential conflict between what strategies are in managers' own best interest and what strategies are in the longer-term interests of their organisation and the shareholders. Some organisations, such as Texas Instruments, set down explicit guidelines they expect their employees to follow (see Exhibit 4.6). Perhaps the biggest challenge for managers is to develop a high level of self-awareness of their own behaviour in relation to the issues raised above.[48] This can be difficult because it requires them to stand apart from often deep-rooted and taken-for-granted assumptions that are part of the culture of their organisation – a key theme of the next chapter.

4.4 STAKEHOLDER EXPECTATIONS[49]

www.pearsoned.co.uk/ecs
KEY CONCEPT

Stakeholders

It should be clear from the preceding sections that the decisions managers have to make about the purpose and strategy of their organisation are influenced by the expectations of stakeholders. This poses a challenge because there are likely to be many stakeholders, especially for a large organisation (see Exhibit 4.7), with different, perhaps conflicting, expectations. This means that managers need to take a view on (i) which stakeholders will have the greatest influence, therefore (ii) which expectations they need to pay most attention to and (iii) to what extent the expectations and influence of different stakeholders vary.

Exhibit 4.7	Stakeholders of a large organisation

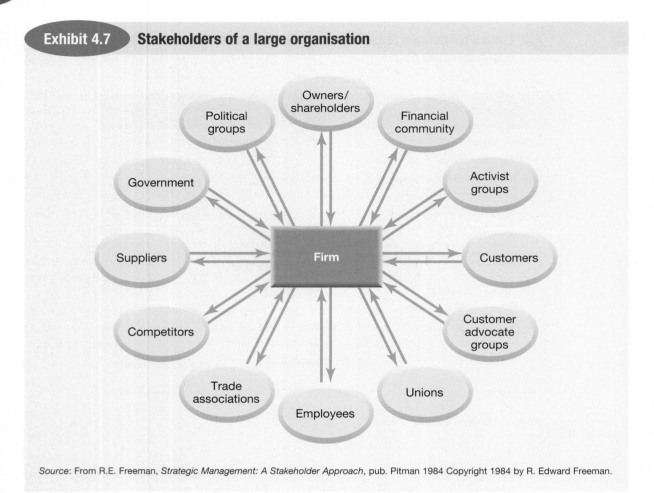

Source: From R.E. Freeman, *Strategic Management: A Stakeholder Approach*, pub. Pitman 1984 Copyright 1984 by R. Edward Freeman.

External stakeholders can be usefully divided into three types in terms of the nature of their relationship with the organisation and, therefore, how they might affect the success or failure of a strategy:[50]

● *Economic stakeholders*, including suppliers, competitors, distributors (whose influence can be identified using the five-forces framework from Chapter 2 (Exhibit 2.2) and shareholders (whose influence can be considered in terms of the governance chain discussed in section 4.2.1).

● *Socio/political stakeholders*, such as policy makers, regulators and government agencies who will influence the 'social legitimacy' of the strategy.

● *Technological stakeholders*, such as key adopters, standards agencies and owners of competitive technologies who will influence the diffusion of new technologies and the adoption of industry standards.

The influence of these different types of stakeholders is likely to vary in different situations. For example, the 'technological group' will be crucial for strategies of new product introduction whilst the 'social/political' group is usually particularly influential in the public sector context.

There are also stakeholder groups internal to an organisation, which may be departments, geographical locations or different levels in the hierarchy. Individuals may belong to more than one stakeholder group, and such groups may 'line up' differently depending on the issue or strategy in hand. Of course, external stakeholders may seek to influence an organisation's strategy through their links with internal stakeholders. For example, customers may exert pressure on sales managers to represent their interests within the company.

Since the expectations of stakeholder groups will differ, it is normal for conflict to exist regarding the importance or desirability of many aspects of strategy. In most situations, a compromise will need to be reached. Exhibit 4.8 shows some of the typical stakeholder expectations that exist and how they might conflict. Global organisations may have added complications as they are operating in multiple arenas. For example, an overseas division is part of the parent company, with all that implies in terms of expectations about behaviour and performance, but is also part of a local community, which has different expectations. These two 'worlds' may not sit comfortably alongside each other.[51]

For these reasons, the stakeholder concept is valuable when trying to understand the political context within which strategic developments take place. Indeed, taking stakeholder expectations and influence into account is an important aspect of strategic choice, as will be seen in Chapter 10.

Exhibit 4.8   ## Some common conflicts of expectations

- In order to grow, short-term profitability, cash flow and pay levels may need to be sacrificed.

- 'Short-termism' may suit managerial career aspirations but preclude investment in long-term projects.

- When family businesses grow, the owners may lose control if they need to appoint professional managers.

- New developments may require additional funding through share issue or loans. In either case, financial independence may be sacrificed.

- Public ownership of shares will require more openness and accountability from the management.

- Cost efficiency through capital investment can mean job losses.

- Extending into mass markets may require a decline in quality standards.

- In public services, a common conflict is between mass provision and specialist services (e.g. preventative dentistry or heart transplants).

- In large multinational organisations, conflict can result because of a division's responsibilities to the company and also to its host country.

4.4.1 Stakeholder mapping[52]

Stakeholder mapping identifies stakeholder expectations and power and helps in understanding political priorities

There are different ways in which stakeholder mapping can be used to gain an understanding of stakeholder influence.[53] The approach to **stakeholder mapping** here identifies stakeholder expectations and power and helps in understanding political priorities. It underlines the importance of two issues:

● How *interested* each stakeholder group is in impressing its expectations on the organisation's purposes and choice of strategies.

● Whether stakeholders have the *power* to do so (see section 4.4.3).

Power/interest matrix

The power/interest matrix can be seen in Exhibit 4.9. It describes the context within which a strategy might be pursued by classifying stakeholders in relation to the power they hold and the extent to which they are likely to show interest in supporting or opposing a particular strategy. The matrix helps in thinking through stakeholder influences on the development of strategy. However, it must be emphasised that how managers handle relationships will depend on the governance structures under which they operate (see section 4.2) and the stance taken on corporate responsibility (section 4.3.1). For example, in some countries unions may be very weak but in others they may be represented on supervisory boards; banks may take an 'arm's-length' relationship with regard to strategy in some countries, but be part of the governance structures in others. A laissez-faire type of business may take the view that it will only pay attention to stakeholders with the most powerful economic influence (for example, investors), whereas shapers of society might go out of their way to engage with

---

Exhibit 4.9 **Stakeholder mapping: the power/interest matrix**

Level of interest

Low — High

	Low interest	High interest
Low power	**A** Minimal effort	**B** Keep informed
High power	**C** Keep satisfied	**D** Key players

Power

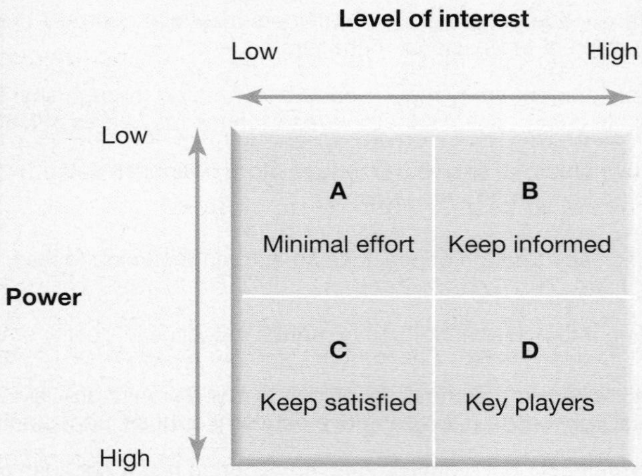

Source: Adapted from A. Mendelow, *Proceedings of the Second International Conference on Information Systems*, Cambridge, MA, 1991.

and influence the expectations and involvement of stakeholders who would not typically see themselves as influential.

In order to show the way in which the matrix may be used, the discussion here takes the perspective of a business where managers see themselves as formulating strategy by trying to ensure the compliance of stakeholders to their own assessment of strategic imperatives. In this context the matrix indicates the type of relationship that such an organisation might typically establish with stakeholder groups in the different quadrants. Clearly, the acceptability of strategies to *key players* (segment D) is of major importance. It could be that these are major investors, but it could also be particular individuals or agencies with a lot of power – for example, a major shareholder in a family firm or a government funding agency in a public sector organisation. Often the most difficult issues relate to stakeholders in segment C. Although these might, in general, be relatively passive, a disastrous situation can arise when their level of interest is underrated and they suddenly *reposition* to segment D and frustrate the adoption of a new strategy. Institutional shareholders such as pension funds or insurance firms can fall into this category. They may show little interest unless share prices start to dip, but may then demand to be heard by senior management.

Similarly, organisations might address the expectations of stakeholders in segment B, for example community groups, through information provision. It may be important not to alienate such stakeholders because they can be crucially important 'allies' in influencing the attitudes of more powerful stakeholders: for example, through *lobbying*.

Stakeholder mapping might help in understanding better some of the following issues:

● In *determining purpose and strategy*, which stakeholder expectations need to be most considered?

● Whether the *actual levels of interest and power* of stakeholders properly reflect the corporate governance framework within which the organisation is operating, as in the examples above (institutional investors, community groups).

● Who the key *blockers* and *facilitators* of a strategy are likely to be and how this could be responded to – for example, in terms of education or persuasion.

● Whether *repositioning* of certain stakeholders is desirable and/or feasible. This could be to lessen the influence of a key player or, in certain instances, to ensure that there are more key players who will champion the strategy (this is often critical in the public sector context).

● *Maintaining* the level of interest or power of some key stakeholders may be essential. For example, public 'endorsement' by powerful suppliers or customers may be critical to the success of a strategy. Equally, it may be necessary to discourage some stakeholders from repositioning themselves. This is what is meant by *keep satisfied* in relation to stakeholders in segment C, and to a lesser extent *keep informed* for those in segment B. The use of *side payments* to stakeholders as a means of securing the acceptance of new strategies can be a key maintenance activity. For example, a 'deal' may be done with another department to support them on one of *their* strategies if they agree not to oppose *this* strategy.

Illustration 4.4a

Stakeholder mapping at Tallman GmbH

Stakeholder mapping can be a useful tool for determining the political priorities for specific strategic developments or changes.

Tallman GmbH was a German bank providing both retail and corporate banking services throughout Germany, Benelux and France. There were concerns about its loss in market share in the corporate sector which was serviced from two centres – Frankfurt (for Germany and Benelux) and Toulouse (for France). It was considering closing the Toulouse operation and servicing all corporate clients from Frankfurt. This would result in significant job losses in Toulouse, some of which would be replaced in Frankfurt alongside vastly improved IT systems.

Two power/interest maps were drawn up by the company officials to establish likely stakeholder reactions to the proposed closure of the Toulouse operation. Map A represents the likely situation and

map B the preferred situation – where support for the proposal would be sufficient to proceed.

Referring to map A, it can be seen that, with the exception of customer X and IT supplier A, the stakeholders in box B are currently opposed to the closure of the Toulouse operation. If Tallman was to have any chance of convincing these stakeholders to change their stance to a more supportive one, the company must address their questions and, where possible, alleviate their fears. If such fears were overcome, these people might become important allies in influencing the more powerful stakeholders in boxes C and D. The supportive attitude of customer X could be usefully harnessed in this quest. Customer X was a multinational with

Map A: The likely situation

A	Shareholder M (–) Toulouse office (–) Customer X (+) French minister (–) Marketing (–) IT supplier A (+) **B**
Customer Z German minister **C**	Customer Y (+) Frankfurt office (+) Corporate finance (+) **D**

Map B: The preferred situation

French minister **A**	Shareholder M (–) Toulouse office (–) Marketing (–) IT supplier A (+) **B**
Customer Z German minister **C**	Customer X (+) Customer Y (+) Frankfurt office (+) Corporate finance (+) **D**

These questions can raise difficult ethical issues for managers in deciding the role they should play in the political activity surrounding stakeholder management. This takes the debate back to the considerations of governance and ethics discussed earlier in the chapter. For example, are managers really the honest brokers who weigh the conflicting expectations of stakeholder groups? Or should they be answerable to one stakeholder – such as shareholders – and hence is their role to ensure the acceptability of their strategies to other

operations throughout Europe. It had shown dissatisfaction with the inconsistent treatment that it received from Frankfurt and Toulouse.

The relationships Tallman had with the stakeholders in box C were the most difficult to manage since, whilst they were considered to be relatively passive, largely due to their indifference to the proposed strategy, a disastrous situation could arise if their level of interest was underrated. For example, if the German minister were replaced, her successor might be opposed to the strategy and actively seek to stop the changes. In this case they would shift to box D.

The acceptability of the proposed strategy to the current players in box D was a key consideration. Of particular concern was customer Y (a major French manufacturer who operated only in France – accounting for 20 per cent of Toulouse corporate banking income). Customer Y was opposed to the closure of the Toulouse operation and could have the power to prevent it from happening, for example by the withdrawal of its business. The company clearly needed to have open discussions with this stakeholder.

By comparing the position of stakeholders in map A and map B, and identifying any changes and mismatches, Tallman could establish a number of tactics to change the stance of certain stakeholders to a more positive one and to increase the power of certain stakeholders. For example, customer X could be encouraged to champion the proposed strategy and assist Tallman by providing media access, or even convincing customer Y that the change could be beneficial.

Tallman could also seek to dissuade or prevent powerful stakeholders from changing their stance to a negative one: for example, unless direct action were taken, lobbying from her French counterpart may well raise the German minister's level of interest. This has implications for how the company handles the situation in France. Time could be spent talking the strategy through with the French minister and also customer Y to try to shift them away from opposition at least to neutrality, if not support.

> ### Question
>
> To ensure that you are clear about how to undertake stakeholder mapping, produce your own complete analysis for Tallman GmbH against a different strategy, that is *to service all corporate clients from Toulouse*. Ensure that you go through the following steps:
>
> 1 Plot the most likely situation (map A) – remembering to be careful to *reassess* interest and power for each stakeholder in relation to this *new* strategy.
>
> 2 Map the preferred situation (map B).
>
> 3 Identify the mismatches – and hence the political priorities. Remember to include the need to *maintain* a stakeholder in its 'opening' position (if relevant).
>
> 4 Finish off by listing the actions you would propose to take and give a final view of the degree of political risk in pursuing this new strategy.

stakeholders? Or are they, as many authors suggest, the real power themselves, constructing strategies to suit their own purposes and managing stakeholder expectations to ensure acceptance of these strategies?

Illustration 4.4a shows some of the practical issues of using stakeholder mapping to understand the political context surrounding a new strategy and to establish political priorities. The example relates to a German bank with head-quarters in Frankfurt (Germany) and providing corporate banking services from

demonstrably fails to live them out in practice (see Illustration 4.2). It is also important to distinguish between the *core values* expressing the way the organisation *is*, as distinct from those to which the organisation wishes to *aspire*. Unless this distinction is clear there is room for considerable misunderstanding and cynicism about statements of corporate values. In either case such statements may be concerned with aspects of corporate social responsibility as discussed in section 4.3.

4.5.2 Mission and vision statements

A **mission statement** aims to provide employees and stakeholders with clarity about the overall purpose and *raison d'être* of the organisation.

A **vision statement** is concerned with what the organisation aspires to be

KEY CONCEPT

Mission and vision

Whereas corporate values may be a backcloth and set boundaries within which strategies are developed, a **mission statement** and a **vision statement** are typically more explicitly concerned with the purpose of an organisation in terms of its strategic direction. In practice the distinction between mission and vision statements can be hazy but they are intended to be different as follows:

● *A mission statement* aims to provide employees and stakeholders with clarity about the overall purpose and *raison d'être* of the organisation. It is therefore to do with building understanding and confidence about how the strategy of the organisation relates to that purpose.

● *A vision statement* is concerned with what the organisation aspires to be. Its purpose is to set out a view of the future so as to enthuse, gain commitment and stretch performance.

Although both mission and vision statements became widely adopted by the early 2000s, many critics regard them as bland and wide ranging.[57] However, arguably if there is substantial disagreement within the organisation or with stakeholders as to its mission (or vision), it may well give rise to real problems in resolving the strategic direction of the organisation. So, given the political nature of strategic management, they can be a useful means of focusing debate on the fundamentals of the organisation. Illustration 4.5 shows examples of mission, vision and value statements.

4.5.3 Objectives

Objectives are statements of specific outcomes that are to be achieved

Objectives are statements of specific outcomes that are to be achieved. Objectives – both at the corporate and at the business unit level – are often expressed in financial terms. They could be the expression of desired sales or profit levels, rates of growth, dividend levels or share valuations.[58] However, organisations may also have market-based objectives, many of which are quantified as targets – such as market share, customer service, repeat business and so on.

There are three related issues that managers need to consider with regard to setting objectives.

● *Objectives and measurement.* Objectives are typically quantified. Indeed, some argue[59] that objectives are not helpful unless their achievement can be measured. However, this does raise the question as to how many objectives

Illustration 4.5

Mission, vision and values statements

Can well-crafted statements of mission, vision or values be an important means of motivating an organisation's stakeholders?

Tata Steel

Mission 2007

Consistent with the vision and values of the founder Jamsetji Tata, Tata Steel strives to strengthen India's industrial base through the effective utilisation of staff and materials. The means envisaged to achieve this are high technology and productivity, consistent with modern management practices.

Tata Steel recognises that while honesty and integrity are the essential ingredients of a strong and stable enterprise, profitability provides the main spark for economic activity.

Overall, the company seeks to scale the heights of excellence in all that it does in an atmosphere free from fear, and thereby reaffirms its faith in democratic values.

Vision 2007

To seize the opportunities of tomorrow and create a future that will make us an EVA positive company.

To continue to improve the quality of life of our employees and the communities we serve.

To revitalise the core business for a sustainable future.

To venture into new businesses that will own a share of our future.

To uphold the spirit and values of Tatas towards nation building.

The Metropolitan Police

Mission and values

Our mission: Working together for a safer London.

Our values: Working together with all our citizens, all our partners, all our colleagues:

We will have pride in delivering quality policing. There is no greater priority.

We will build trust by listening and responding.

We will respect and support each other and work as a team.

We will learn from experience and find ways to be even better.

We are one team – we all have a duty to play our part in making London safer.

Villeroy & Boch

Company vision

To be the leading European lifestyle brand with high competence and trend-setting style for high-end design and living.

Five values – one philosophy

I. *Customers*. Our success is measured by the enthusiasm our customers show for our products and services. A constant challenge is to satisfy the high expectations architects, retailers, the trade and end consumers have of the 'Villeroy & Boch' brand. We convince them with competence and experience.

II. *Employees*. In the long run a strong market position can only be achieved by having innovative and committed employees. Our priority task is to motivate them and cultivate their team spirit, encouraging them to achieve personal and joint goals.

III: *Innovation*. If we lay claim to a leading position on the international markets it is not enough to follow trends. Those who want to secure their competitive edge worldwide must recognise and shape trends early on.

IV: *Earning power*. An important concern for us is to maintain the independence of the company and achieve long-term success. The fundamentals for this are a balanced portfolio, earnings-oriented growth, high and constant rates of return and appropriate dividends.

V: *Responsibility*. Not many companies have made regional economic history as well as European cultural and social history. Villeroy & Boch is one of them, and thus bears many responsibilities. We feel obligated not only to our employees, shareholders and customers, but also to the environment and society.

Questions

1 Which of these statements do you think are likely to motivate which stakeholders? Why?

2 Could any of them have been improved? How?

3 Identify other statements of mission, vision, purpose or values that you think are especially well crafted and explain why.

expressed in such ways are useful. Certainly there are times when specific quantified objectives are required, for example when urgent action is needed and it becomes essential for management to focus attention on a limited number of priority requirements – as in a *turnaround* situation (see section 14.5.1). If the choice is between going out of business and surviving, there is no room for latitude through vaguely stated requirements. However, it may be that in other circumstances – for example, in trying to raise the aspirations of people in the organisation – more attention needs to be paid to qualitative statements of purpose such as mission or vision statements.

● *Objectives and control.* A recurring problem with objectives is that managers and employees 'lower down' in the hierarchy are unclear as to how their day-to-day work contributes to the achievement of higher level of objectives. This could, in principle, be addressed by a 'cascade' of objectives – defining a set of detailed objectives at each level in the hierarchy. Many organisations attempt to do this to some extent. Here consideration needs to be given to a trade-off: how to achieve required levels of clarity on strategy without being over-restrictive in terms of the latitude people have. There is evidence, for

Exhibit 4.11   Simple rules

Turbulent markets require strategic flexibility to seize opportunities – but flexibility can be disciplined. Different types of simple rules help.

Type	Purpose	Example
How-to rules	Spell out key features of how a process is executed – 'What makes our process unique?'	Dell focus on focused customer segments. So a Dell business must be split in two when its revenue hits $1 billion.
Boundary rules	Focus managers on which opportunities can be pursued and which should not	In Miramax movie-picking process, every movie must: i) revolve around a central human condition, such as love; ii) have a main character appealing but deeply flawed; iii) have a clear story line.
Priority rules	Help managers rank the accepted opportunities	Intel's rule for allocating manufacturing capacity: allocation is based on a product's gross margin. (See Chapter 11 case example.)
Timing rules	Synchronise managers with the pace of emerging opportunities and other parts of the company	Nortel's product development time must be less than 18 months, which forces it to move quickly into new opportunities.
Exit rules	Help managers decide when to pull out of yesterday's opportunities	In Oticon, the Danish hearing aid company, if a key team member – manager or not – chooses to leave a project for another within the company, the project is killed.

Source: Reprinted by permission of *Harvard Business Review*. Exhibit adapted from 'Strategy as simple rules' by K.M. Eisenhardt and D.N. Sull, January 2001. Copyright © 2001 by the Havard Business School Publishing Corporation; all rights reserved.

example, that innovation is stymied by over-restrictive target setting and measurement.[60]

● *Simple rules.* Especially in organisations in which innovation and flexibility are important, there is evidence that managers need to be very clear about the very few overarching objectives that have to be met, sometimes known as 'simple rules', but then allow flexibility and latitude in how they are achieved. Research by Kathy Eisenhardt and her colleagues has begun to establish the nature of these simple rules.[61] Exhibit 4.11 summarises the types of rules they identify as important in organisations facing fast-changing environments; and gives some examples of how they take form and their effects. The suggestion is that the number of rules does not need to be many to result in consistent patterns of behaviour. In this respect the proposal builds on the arguments advanced by complexity theorists and explained in the Commentary on the lenses (see pages 36–41).

An underlying theme in this chapter has been that strategists have to consider the overall strategic purpose of their organisations. However, a central question that arises is what stakeholder expectations they should respond to in so doing. The key debate in Illustration 4.6 provides three views on this in the context of publicly quoted large commercial organisations.

SUMMARY

● The purpose of an organisation will be influenced by the expectations of its *stakeholders*.

● The influence of some key stakeholders will be represented formally within the *governance structure* of an organisation. This can be represented in terms of a *governance chain*, showing the links between ultimate beneficiaries and the managers of an organisation.

● There are two generic governance structures systems: the *shareholder model* and the *stakeholder model*. There are variations of these internationally, but some signs that there is convergence towards a shareholder model.

● There are also ethical dimensions to the purpose of an organisation. At an organisational level, this takes the form of its stance on *corporate social responsibility*. However, individual managers may also be faced with ethical dilemmas relating to the purpose of their organisation or the actions it takes.

● Different stakeholders exercise different influence on organisational purpose and strategy, dependent on the extent of their power and interest. Managers can assess the influence of different stakeholder groups through *stakeholder analysis*.

● An important managerial task is to decide how the organisation should express its strategic purpose through statements of *values*, *vision*, *mission* or *objectives*.

Illustration 4.6

key debate

Three views on the purpose of a business

Since there is no one categoric view of the overarching purpose of a business, stakeholders, including managers, have to decide.

Milton Friedman and profit maximisation

Milton Friedman, the renowned economist, wrote:[1]

In a free enterprise, private property system, a corporate executive is an employee of the owners of the business. He has direct responsibility to his employers. That responsibility is to conduct the business in accordance with their desires, which generally will be to make as much money as possible while conforming to the basic rules of society. . . . What does it mean to say that the corporate executive has a 'social responsibility'? . . . If the statement is not pure rhetoric, it must mean that he is to act in some way that is not in the interests of his employers. . . . Insofar as his actions in accord with his 'social responsibility' reduce returns to stockholders, he is spending their money. Insofar as his actions raise the price to customers, he is spending the customers' money. Insofar as his actions lower the wages of some employees he is spending their money.

Milton Friedman's maxim was that 'the business of business is business', that the 'only social responsibility of business is to increase its profit'. Market mechanisms are then adequate in themselves. If customers are not satisfied, they take their business elsewhere. If employees are not satisfied they work elsewhere. It is the job of government to ensure that there is a free market to allow those conditions to take effect.

Charles Handy's stakeholder view

Citing the corporate scandals of the last decade, Charles Handy[2] argues that the driving for shareholder value linked to stock options for executives, especially in the USA, has resulted in the system 'creating value where none existed'. He accepts

that there is, first, a clear and important need to meet the expectations of a company's theoretical owners: the shareholders. It would, however, be more accurate to call them investors, perhaps even gamblers. They have none of the pride or responsibility of ownership and are . . . only there for the money. . . . But to turn shareholders' needs into a purpose is to be guilty of a logical confusion. To mistake a necessary condition for a sufficient one. We need to eat to live; food is a necessary condition of life. But if we lived mainly to eat, making food a sufficient or sole purpose of life, we would become gross. The purpose of a business, in other words, is not to make a profit. It is to make a profit so that the business that can do something more or better. That 'something' becomes the real justification for the business.

The new capitalists' argument: 'Society and share owners are becoming one and the same'[3]

In their book *The New Capitalists*, the authors also recognise that 'a corporation is the property of its stock owners and should serve their interests'. However, it is the 'millions of pension holders and other savers . . . [who] . . . own the world's giant corporations'. These 'new capitalists are likely to be highly diversified in their investments'. Investment funds, such as pension funds, are their representatives and 'hold a tiny share in hundreds, perhaps even thousands, of companies around the world'. They then argue:

Imagine that all your savings were invested in one company. The success of that company alone would be your only interest. You would want it to survive, prosper and grow, even if that did damage to the economic system as a whole. But your perspective would change if you had investments in lots of companies. [Then] it is to your disadvantage that any business should seek to behave socially irresponsibly towards other businesses, the customers, employees or society generally. By so doing they will damage the interests of other firms in which you have an interest. The new capitalist has an interest in all the firms in which he or she is investing behaving responsibly: 'in creating rules that lead to the success of the economic system as a whole, even if, in particular circumstances, those rules may tie the hands of an individual company'. . . . managers of a business should quite properly 'concentrate single mindedly on the success of their own organisations . . . however they will not be serving their share owners interest if they undertake activities that may be good for them individually, but damaging to the larger economic system.

Notes

1. M. Friedman 'The social responsibility of business is to increase its profits', *New York Times. Magazine*, 13 September (1970).
2. C. Handy, 'What's a business for?', *Harvard Business Review*, December (2002), pp. 49–55.
3. S. Davies, J. Lukommik and D. Pitt-Watson, *The New Capitalists*, Harvard Business School Press, 2006.

Questions

1 Which view do you hold:
   (a) As a manager? (b) As a shareholder?

2 What are the implications of the different views for managers' development of organisational strategy?

Work assignments

*Denotes more advanced work assignments.   * Refers to a case study in the Text and Cases edition.*

4.1 ✳ For an organisation of your choice, map out a governance chain that identifies the key players through to the beneficiaries of the organisation's good (or poor) performance. To what extent do you think managers are:

  (a) knowledgeable about the expectations of beneficiaries;
  (b) actively pursuing their interests;
  (c) keeping them informed?

4.2 ✳ It is argued that many economies are shifting from a stakeholder to a shareholder model of governance. What are your own views of the strengths and weaknesses of these systems? Consider this in relation to an economy that is in transition in terms of governance.

4.3 For an organisation of your choice, use Exhibit 4.4 to establish the *overall stance* of the organisation on corporate social responsibility.

4.4 ✳ Identify the key corporate social responsibility issues which are of major concern in an industry or public service of your choice (refer to Exhibit 4.5). Compare the approach of two or more organisations in that industry, and explain how this relates to their competitive standing.

4.5 Using Illustration 4.4 as a worked example, identify and map out the stakeholders for Manchester United*, Direct and Care* or an organisation of your choice in relation to:

  (a) current strategies;
  (b) different future strategies of your choice.

  What are the implications of your analysis for the management?

4.6 Write mission and vision statements for an organisation of your choice and suggest what strategic objectives managers might set. Explain why you think these are appropriate.

Integrative assignment

4.7 Using specific examples explain how changes in corporate governance and in expectations about corporate social responsibility are requiring organisations to develop new competences (Chapter 3) and also creating dilemmas in the pursuit of shareholder value and managing people in organisations (see Chapter 13).

An extensive range of additional materials, including audio summaries, weblinks to organisations featured in the text, definitions of key concepts and self-assessment questions, can be found on the *Exploring Corporate Strategy* Companion Website at **www.pearsoned.co.uk/ecs**

Recommended key readings

- For books providing a fuller explanation of corporate governance: R. Monks and N. Minow (eds), *Corporate Governance*, 3rd edition, Blackwell, 2003; and J. Solomon, *Corporate Governance and Accountability*, 2nd edition, Wiley, 2007. For a provocative critique and proposals for the future of corporate governance linked to issues of social responsibility see S. Davies, J. Lukomnik and D. Pitt-Watson, *The New Capitalists*, Harvard Business School Press, 2006.

- For a review of different stances on corporate social responsibility see P. Mirvis and B. Googins, 'Stages of corporate citizenship', *California Management Review*, vol. 48, no. 2 (2006), pp. 104–126. Also D.A. Whetten, G. Rands and P. Godfrey, 'What are the responsibilities of business to society?', in A. Petigrew, H. Thomas and R. Whittington (eds), *Handbook of Strategy and Management*, Sage, 2002.

- For more about the stakeholder concept and analysis see K. Scholes' chapter in V. Ambrosini with G. Johnson and K. Scholes (eds), *Exploring Techniques of Analysis and Evaluation in Strategic Management*, Prentice Hall, 1998. For a case example of stakeholder analysis see J. Bryson, G. Cunningham and K. Lokkesmoe, 'What to do when stakeholders matter: the case of problem formulation for the African American men project of Hennepin County, Minnesota', *Public Administration Review*, vol. 62, no. 5 (2002), pp. 568–584.

- The case for the importance of clarity of strategic values and vision is especially strongly made by J. Collins and J. Porras, *Built to Last: Successful habits of visionary companies*, Harper Business, 2002 (in particular see chapter 11).

References

1. Useful general references on corporate governance are: R. Monks and N. Minow (eds), *Corporate Governance*, 3rd edition, Blackwell, 2003; and J. Solomon, *Corporate Governance and Accountability*, 2nd edition, Wiley, 2007. Those interested in an annual research update can find this in 'Corporate governance digest', *Business Horizons* (usually the May issue).

2. This definition is based on, but adapted from, that in S. Jacoby, 'Corporate governance and society', *Challenge*, vol. 48, no. 4 (2005), pp. 69–87.

3. The principal–agent model is part of agency theory which developed within organisational economics but is now widely used in the management field as described here. Two useful references are: K. Eisenhardt, 'Agency theory: an assessment and review', *Academy of Management Review*, vol. 14, no. 1 (1989), pp. 57–74; J.-J. Laffont and D. Martimort, *The Theory of Incentives: The Principal–Agent Model*, Princeton University Press, 2002.

4. The issue of to whom corporate managers should be accountable is discussed by J. Kay, 'The stakeholder corporation', in G. Kelly, D. Kelly and A. Gamble, *Stakeholder Capitalism*, Macmillan, 1997.

5. For a strong advocacy of this position see S. Davies, J. Lukomnik and D. Pitt-Watson, *The New Capitalists*, Harvard Business School Press, 2006.

6. For a typology and examples of ways in which investors engage with firms, see N. Amos and W. Oulton, 'Approaching and engaging with CR', *Corporate Responsibility Management*, vol. 2, no. 3 (2006), pp 34–37.

7. See M. Becht, J. Franks, C. Mayer and S. Rossi, *Returns to Shareholder Activism: Evidence from a clinical study of the Hermes UK Focus Fund*, European Corporate Governance Institute: http://www.ecgi.org/activism/index.php.

8. Sarbanes–Oxley Act of 2002, PL 107–204, 116 Stat 745 (30 July 2002).

9. The contribution of each of these reports is neatly summarised by G. Vinten, 'Corporate governance: the need to know', *Industrial and Commercial Training*, vol. 32, no. 5 (2000), pp. 173–178.

10. The Treadway (1987) and COSO (1992) Reports in the USA and the Cadbury Reports (1992 and 1996) in the UK.

11. For example, in the UK the Hampel (1998), Turnbull (1999) and Higgs (2003) Reports.

12. The importance of risk management in the public sector was addressed in 'Supporting innovation: managing risk in government departments', *Report by the Comptroller and Auditor General*, The Stationery Office, July 2000.

13. Role of CFOs in J. Weber, M. Arndt, E. Thornton, A. Barrett and D. Frost, 'CFOs in the hot seat', *Business Week*, 17 March (2003), pp. 65–68.

14. S. Wiesenthal, 'CFOs caught up in red tape', *Australian Financial Review*, 2003, p. 16.

15. These differences between countries are discussed in the general books (reference 1) and also in T. Clarke and S. Clegg, *Changing Paradigms: The transformation of management knowledge in the 21st century*, HarperCollins, 2000, chapter 5.

16. Within this broad classification there are other models. The market-oriented system, long-term investor system (A. Murphy and K. Topyan, 'Corporate governance: a critical survey of key concepts, issues, and recent reforms in the US', *Employee Responsibility and Rights Journal*, vol. 17, no. 2 (2005), pp. 75–89) is similar to the shareholder model as it advocates views like dispersed shareholdings and takeovers as a mechanism for corporate control. The long-term investor model and the Rhine model (M. Albert, *Capitalism against Capitalism*, Whurr Publishers, 1992) resemble the stakeholder model with a philosophy of a consensal approach towards group success with characteristics like stakeholder representation

on the boards and labour unions sharing power with the management.

17. From a Korn/Ferry International Survey cited by K. Keasey, S. Thompson and M. Wright, *Corporate Governance: Accountability, Enterprise and International Comparisons*, Wiley, 2005.

18. See Keasey *et al.* (reference 17) and also J.A. McCahery, P. Moerland, T. Raijmakers and L. Renneboog, *Corporate Governance Regimes: Convergence and diversity*, Oxford University Press, 2002.

19. See S. Jacoby (2005) (see reference 2).

20. J. Zwiebel, 'Block investment and partial corporate control', *Review of Economic Studies*, vol. 62, no. 211 (1995), p. 161.

21. See C.A. Mallin, *Corporate Governance*, Oxford University Press, 2004; and S.F. Copp, 'The institutional architecture of UK corporate governance reform: an evaluation', *Journal of Banking Regulation*, vol. 7, nos 1/2 (2006), pp. 41–63.

22. Short-termism as an issue in the Anglo-American tradition is contrasted with the 'Rhine model' more typical of Germany, Switzerland, Benelux and Northern European countries by M. Albert, 'The Rhine model of capitalism: an investigation', in W. Nicoll, D. Norburn and R. Schoenberg (eds), *Perspectives on European Business*, Whurr Publishers, 1995.

23. For further discussion on convergence, see H. Hansmann, and R. Kraakman, 'Toward a single model of corporate law?', in J.A. McCahery, P. Moerland, T. Raijmakers and L. Renneboog (eds), *Corporate Governance Regimes: Convergence and diversity*, Oxford University Press, 2002.

24. See R. Skog, 'A remarkable decade: the awakening of Swedish institutional investors', *European Business Law Review*, vol. 16, no. 5 (2005), pp. 1017–1031.

25. See V. Gupta and K. Gollakota, 'History, ownership forms and corporate governance in India', *Journal of Management History*, vol. 12, no. 2 (2006), pp. 185–197.

26. For further explanations of developments in China, see G.S. Liu and P. Sun, 'The class of shareholdings and its impacts on corporate performance: a case of state shareholdings in Chinese public corporations', *Corporate Governance*, vol. 13, no. 1 (2005), pp. 46–59; and G. Chen, M. Firth, D. Gao and O.M. Rui, 'Ownership structure, corporate governance, and fraud: evidence from China', *Journal of Corporate Finance*, vol. 12, no. 3 (2006), pp. 424–448.

27. In the USA: the Sarbanes–Oxley Act (2002). In the UK: D. Higgs, 'Review of the role and effectiveness of non-executive directors', UK Department of Trade and Industry, 2003.

28. See D. Norburn, B. Boyd, M. Fox and M. Muth, 'International corporate governance reform', *European Business Journal*, vol. 12, no. 3 (2000), pp. 116–133; J. Sonnenfeld, 'What makes great boards great', *Harvard Business Review*, vol. 80, no. 9 (2002), pp. 106–113.

29. There is a prolific flow of literature on business ethics. Readers can gain some useful insights into the field by reading P. Werhane and R.E. Freeman, 'Business ethics: the state of the art', *International Journal of Management Research*, vol. 1, no. 1 (1999), pp. 1–16. This is a useful summary of the recent publications on business ethics. Practising managers might wish to consult B. Kelley, *Ethics at Work*, Gower, 1999, which covers many of the

issues in this section and includes the Institute of Management guidelines on ethical management. Also see M.T. Brown, *Corporate Integrity: Rethinking organizational ethics and leadership*, Cambridge University Press, 2005.

30. J. Charkham, 'Corporate governance lessons from abroad', *European Business Journal*, vol. 4, no. 2 (1992), pp. 8–16.

31. Based on research undertaken at the Center for Corporate Citizenship at the Boston College, reported in P. Mirvis and B. Googins, 'Stages of corporate citizenship', *California Management Review*, vol. 48, no. 2 (2006), pp. 104–126.

32. Often quoted as a summary of Milton Friedman's argument is M. Friedman: 'The social responsibility of business is to increase its profits', *New York Times Magazine*, 13 September (1970).

33. See A. McWilliams and D. Seigel, 'Corporate social responsibility: a theory of the firm perspective', *Academy of Management Review*, vol. 26 (2001), pp. 117–127.

34. See *The State of Corporate Citizenship in the US: A view from inside, 2003–2004*, Center for Corporate Citizenship, Boston College; also reported in Mirvis and Googins, reference 31.

35. See S. Macleod, 'Why worry about CSR?', *Strategic Communication Management*, Aug/Sept (2001), pp. 8–9.

36. See M. Porter and M. Kramer, 'The competitive advantage of corporate philanthropy', *Harvard Business Review*, vol. 80, no. 12 (2002), pp. 56–68.

37. H. Hummels, 'Organizing ethics: a stakeholder debate', *Journal of Business Ethics*, vol. 17, no. 13 (1998), pp. 1403–1419.

38. D. Vogel, 'Is there a market for virtue? The business case for corporate social responsibility', *California Management Review*, vol. 47, no. 4 (2005), pp. 19–45.

39. S.A. Waddock and C. Bodwell, 'Managing responsibility: what can be learned from the quality movement', *California Management Review*, vol. 47, no. 1 (2004), pp. 25–37; and R. Orsato, 'Competitive environmental strategies: when does it pay to be green?', *California Management Review*, vol. 48, no. 2 (2006), pp. 127–143.

40. This quote is from Porter and Kramer, reference 36, p. 80.

41. These examples are given by Porter and Kramer, reference 36.

42. From Orsato, reference 39.

43. K. Schnietz and M. Epstein, 'Does a reputation for corporate social responsibility pay off?', *Social Issues in Management Conference Papers*, Academy of Management Proceedings, 2002. This paper shows that the Fortune 500 firms that were also in the Domini Social Index outperformed the others in terms of stock return.

44. See D. Vogel, reference 38.

45. M.L. Barnett and R.M. Salomon ('Beyond dichotomy: the curvilinear relationship between social responsibility and financial performance', *Strategic Management Journal*, vol. 27, no. 11 (2006), pp. 1101–1122) argue that research such as that by Vogel does not take sufficient account of the screening programmes of the investors. The more such screening takes place and depending on the type of screening, so performance may increase.

46. For a discussion of the range of performance measures being used in relation to CSR and their effectiveness, see A. Chatterji and D. Levine, 'Breaking down the wall of codes: evaluating non-financial performance measures',

California Management Review, vol. 48, no. 2 (2006), pp. 29–51.

47. See: T.D. Miethe, *Tough Choices in Exposing Fraud, Waste and Abuse on the Job*, Westview Press, 1999; G. Vinten, *Whistleblowing: Subversion or corporate citizenship?*, Paul Chapman, 1994; R. Larmer, 'Whistleblowing and employee loyalty', *Journal of Business Ethics*, vol. 11, no. 2 (1992), pp. 125–128.

48. M.R. Banaji, M.H. Bazerman and D. Chugh, 'How (UN)ethical are you?', *Harvard Business Review*, vol. 81, no. 12 (2003), pp. 56–64.

49. The early writings about stakeholders are still worthy of note. For example, the seminal work by R.M. Cyert and J.G. March, *A Behavioural Theory of the Firm*, Prentice Hall, 1964; I.I. Mitroff, *Stakeholder of the Organisational Mind*, Jossey Bass, 1983; R.E. Freeman, *Strategic Management: A stakeholder approach*, Pitman, 1984. Also see J. Bryson, 'What to do when stakeholders matter: stakeholder identification and analysis techniques', *Public Management Review*, vol. 6, no. 1 (2004), pp. 21–53.

50. Details of how these three groups interact with organisations can be found in J. Cummings and J. Doh, 'Identifying who matters: mapping key players in multiple environments', *California Management Review*, vol. 42, no. 2 (2000), pp. 83–104.

51. T. Kostova and S. Zaheer, 'Organisational legitimacy under conditions of complexity: the case of the multinational enterprise', *Academy of Management Review*, vol. 24, no. 1 (1999), pp. 64–81.

52. This approach to stakeholder mapping has been adapted from A. Mendelow, *Proceedings of the 2nd International Conference on Information Systems*, Cambridge, MA, 1991. See also K. Scholes' chapter, 'Stakeholder analysis', in V. Ambrosini with G. Johnson and K. Scholes (eds), *Exploring Techniques of Analysis and Evaluation in Strategic Management*, Prentice Hall, 1998. For a public sector explanation, see K. Scholes, 'Stakeholder mapping: a practical tool for public sector managers', in G. Johnson and K. Scholes (eds), *Exploring Public Sector Strategy*, Financial Times/Prentice Hall, 2001, chapter 9; and

J. Bryson, G. Cunningham and K. Lokkesmoe, 'What to do when stakeholders matter: the case of problem formulation for the African American men project of Hennepin County, Minnesota', *Public Administration Review*, vol. 62, no. 5 (2002), pp. 568–584.

53. For example, see J. Bryson *et al.* reference 52. Also see Kalle Pajunen, 'Stakeholder influences in organizational survival', *Journal of Management Studies*, vol. 43, no. 6 (2006), pp. 1261–1288.

54. D. Buchanan and R. Badham, *Power, Politics and Organisational Change: Winning the turf game*, Sage, 1999, provide a useful analysis of the relationship between power and strategy. See also S. Clegg, D. Courpasson and N. Phillips, *Power and Organizations*, Sage, 2006.

55. P. Lencioni, 'Make your values mean something', *Harvard Business Review*, vol. 80, no. 7 (2002), pp. 113–117.

56. See J. Collins and J. Porras, *Built to Last: Successful habits of visionary companies*, Harper Business, 2002.

57. For example, see B. Bartkus, M. Glassman and B. McAfee, 'Mission statements: are they smoke and mirrors?', *Business Horizons*, vol. 43, no. 6 (2000), pp. 23–28; and B. Bartkus, M. Glassman and B. McAfee, 'Mission statement quality and financial performance', *European Management Journal*, vol. 24, no. 1 (2006), pp. 86–94.

58. Communicating effectively with the investing community is essential, as discussed by A. Hutton, 'Four rules', *Harvard Business Review*, vol. 79, no. 5 (2001), pp. 125–132.

59. For example, I. Ansoff, *Corporate Strategy*, Penguin, 1968, p. 44, argued that objectives should be precise and measurable.

60. See A. Neely, 'Measuring performance in innovative firms', in R. Delbridge, L. Grattan and G. Johnson (eds), *The Exceptional Manager*, Oxford University Press, 2006, chapter 6.

61. This discussion is based on research by K.M. Eisenhardt and D.N. Sull, reported in 'Strategy as simple rules', *Harvard Business Review*, vol. 79, no. 1 (2001), pp. 107–116.

CASE EXAMPLE

(PRODUCT) RED and Gap

(RED) was created by Bono and Bobby Shriver, Chairman of DATA, to raise awareness and money for The Global Fund by teaming up with the world's most iconic brands to produce (PRODUCT) RED-branded products. A percentage of each (PRODUCT) RED product sold is given to The Global Fund. The money helps women and children with HIV/AIDS in Africa.[1]

The (RED) initiative was set up in early 2006, with Rwanda selected as the initial country to benefit from sales of the (RED) products. The first products launched in the UK were the (PRODUCT) RED American Express card and a (PRODUCT) RED vintage T-shirt from Gap launched in March 2006. Other companies joining the scheme included Motorola, Converse, Apple (introducing a (PRODUCT) RED iPod) and Emporio Armani. There was also a special (PRODUCT) RED edition of the *Independent*, guest edited by Bono.

Support for the (RED) campaign has come from Bill Gates, interviewed in *Advertising Age*: 'Red is about saving lives . . . if there's not enough money to buy drugs, people die, and so we can say, "Hey, let's just let that happen," or we can take all the avenues available to us.' He acknowledged that this included governments being more generous, but also believed that consumers wanted 'to associate themselves with saving lives' and that what Gap or Armani were doing through (PRODUCT) RED provided this opportunity.

Other commentators were not so positive. Another article in *Advertising Age*[2] claimed that the campaign had raised only $18m (€15m; £10m) in a year despite a marketing outlay by companies involved in the scheme (including Gap) of $100m. Gap was the biggest spender here with an advertising budget of $7.8m. A spokeswoman for (RED) claimed that the

Source: http://www.joinred.com/manifesto.asp.

Ad Age figure of 100 million was merely a 'phantom number pulled out of thin air'.

An article in the *Independent* went on to do its own mathematics, concluding that the figure raised was $25 million in six months and that, on an advertising investment of $40 million, this was a 'staggeringly good rate of return'.

They went on to argue:[3]

what the RED initiative has set out to do – and with some success if $25 million in six months is half the profits RED products would have made – is create a stream of revenue for the fight against AIDS in Africa which will far exceed one-off payments from corporate philanthropy budgets. It looks set to create a major source of cash for the global fund, and one which is sustainable. It is an entirely new model for fund raising.

But wouldn't it be better if people simply gave the money that they spend on the products directly to charity? 'If only that were the choice. But most people wouldn't give the cost of a new ipod to the global fund.' They continued:

The money RED has raised means that some 160,000 Africans will be put on life saving anti-retrovirals in the coming months, orphans are being fed and kept in school in Swaziland and a national HIV treatment and prevention programme has begun in Rwanda.

(RED) Gap

On their website Gap's Senior Vice President for Social Responsibility, Dan Henkle, explained Gap's commitment in relation to its work in Lesotho. Lesotho has a population of 1.8 million, with almost one-third HIV positive. Gap has invested significantly in the manufacture of T-shirts in that country, as well as in community initiatives, for example in HIV testing and treatment to garment workers. It has also promoted forums to encourage the growth of the garment industry in that country.

The British pressure group, Labour Behind the Label, which campaigns to improve the working conditions of garment workers around the world, expressed its support for efforts being made by Gap to move towards more responsible sourcing of products. By deciding to manufacture the (PRODUCT) RED T-shirts in Lesotho, Gap had helped to safeguard workers' likelihoods there at a time when other companies were increasingly sourcing garments from China and India:

While GAP, like all clothing companies, is a long way from resolving all workers' rights issues in its supply chain, it has come further than many. Whilst we would like to see initiatives like RED being more comprehensive in their attitude towards combining charity and political change, so far indications suggest that the way the RED T-shirt has been put together could be a positive step for the African garment industry as well as for the fight against AIDS.[4]

Others were less supportive. A parodying website, mirroring the Gap advertising, was set up by protesters in San Francisco. It urged people to support causes directly, rather than via shopping. Its message: 'Shopping is not a solution. Buy (Less). Give More. Join us in rejecting the ti(red) notion that shopping is a reasonable response to human suffering.'

And in October 2006 there was a lengthy critique in *The Times*:[5]

GAP, America's still-trendy mass-market clothing retailer, is winning plaudits over here for its new campaign . . .

designed to generate awareness and money to alleviate suffering in Africa. . . . It is pledging to give half of the profits from its iconic red T-shirts and leather jackets to Aids/HIV relief. The campaign was launched here last week, with the always crucial imprimatur of Hollywood. It features stars such as Steven Spielberg and Penelope Cruz in red T-shirts with one-word messages that say, with a modesty that doesn't fit quite as well as the clothes, INSPI(RED) and ADMI(RED). The message is that, by buying these products, ordinary mortals such as you and I (well, all right, you) can look like Hollywood stars and save lives in Africa too. You can almost taste the pity and charity oozing from Ms Cruz's pouted lips, the love pouring from Mr Spielberg's dewy eyes.

Sorry to play the curmudgeon here. But this latest concession to the galloping forces of corporate social responsibility, far from helping the benighted of the world, is actually going to make things worse. I am sick and TI(RED) of companies trying to demonstrate to me how seriously they take their supposed duty to bring joy to and remove pain from the world. They can take their charge card (S, CREWnecks and mobile phones and ask THEMSELVES) whether this is really the sort of thing they should be doing with their shareholders' money.

Now I don't here intend to demean the charitable spirit or the work of good people such as Bono or Bob Geldof, nor the perfectly decent motivation of millions in the wealthy world who genuinely want to help to improve the wretched lives of those less fortunate than themselves. Don't get me

Bono and Oprah promoting Gap

wrong; charity remains one of the finest of virtues and should, in almost all instances, be encouraged.

Nor am I going to point out the nauseating conspicuousness of the consumption represented by the RED campaign ('Look,' it says, 'I not only look good. I AM good!'). Nor am I even going to dwell on the fact, though I could, that for all the aid Africa has received over the past 50 years, the continent remains poorer than ever, and certainly poorer than parts of the world that have received little in the way of charity in that time.

My problem here is with what this does for the very idea of capitalism, for companies pursuing their real and entirely wholesome responsibility of making money. Free market capitalism, untrammelled by marketing people in alliance with special interest groups on a mission to save the world, has done more to alleviate poverty than any well-intentioned anti-poverty campaign in the history of the globe.

By concentrating on selling quality, low-priced goods, some of them made with labour that would otherwise lie idle (and dying) in the developing world, Gap saves lives. By helping to keep prices down and generating profits, Gap ploughs money back into the pockets of people in the US, the UK and elsewhere. Which creates the demand for imports of products from the developing world. Which keeps the poor of those countries from suffering even more than they do now.

In a complex world, we all operate in a division of labour. Companies make profits. It is what they are designed to do. It is what they do best. When they depart from that mission, they lead their employees and their shareholders down a long, slow route to perdition.

You think that is over the top? What is most troubling about campaigns such as Product Red is that they represent an accommodation with groups who think the business of capitalism is fundamentally evil. By appeasing people who regard globalisation as a process of exploitation, companies such as Gap are making the world much worse for all of us. They are implicitly acknowledging that their main business – selling things that people want for a profit – is inherently immoral and needs to be expiated by an occasional show of real goodness.

Rather than resisting it, they are nurturing and feeding an anti-business sentiment that will impoverish us all. What's more, this encroachment by companies is fundamentally undemocratic. Companies should not collude with interest groups and non-governmental organisations to decide on public priorities. That is for free people, through their elected governments, to do.

None of this is to say companies – or the people who run them – should not behave morally. They should observe not only the law, but the highest ethical standards, which means honesty, straight dealing and openness. It might even at times be in their corporate interests (ie, longer-term profitability) to contribute to political or charitable causes – in those cases shareholders can and should vote on the appropriation of funds for such purposes.

But shareholders – all of us – should be concerned when managements decide, for whatever reason, to make common cause with those who oppose the very principals on which their business is conducted. That represents a case of misguided corporate BULLS(HIT)TING the wrong target.

Notes

1. *Source*: (PRODUCT) RED website http://joinred.blogspot.com/.
2. M. Frazier, 'Costly Red Campaign reaps meager $18m', *Advertising Age*, vol. 78, no. 10 (5 March 2007).
3. P. Vallely, 'The Big Question: Does the RED campaign help big Western brands more than Africa', *Independent*, p. 50, 9 March (2007). Copyright The Independent, 9.3.07.
4. *Source*: http://www.labourbehindthelabel.org/content/view/67/51/.
5. Gerard Baker, 'Mind the Gap – with this attack on globalisation', *The Times*, 24 October (2006). © Gerard Baker. N.I. Syndication Limited, 24.10.06.

Questions

1 Drawing on the three perspectives in the key debate (Illustration 4.6) or the four stances in Exhibit 4.4, what is the rationale of:
   (a) The founders of (PRODUCT) RED?
   (b) Dan Henkle and Gap?
   (c) The author of the article in *The Times*?

2 What views might shareholders of Gap have of its involvement in (PRODUCT) RED?

3 In your view is (PRODUCT) RED an appropriate corporate activity?

4 If you were a shareholder of a company and wished to persuade top management to join the (PRODUCT) RED initiative, how might you do this? (Use stakeholder analysis as a means of considering this.)

The Strategic Position

5

Culture and Strategy

LEARNING OUTCOMES

After reading this chapter you should be able to:

→ Identify organisations that have experienced strategic drift and the symptoms of strategic drift.

→ Analyse how history influences the strategic position of organisations.

→ Analyse the influence of an organisation's culture on its strategy using the cultural web.

→ Recognise the importance of strategists questioning the taken-for-granted aspects of a culture.

Photo: Grant Pritchard/Britain on View

5.1 INTRODUCTION

Chapters 2, 3 and 4 have considered the important influences of the environment, organisational capabilities and stakeholder expectations on the development of strategy. Vital as these are to understand, there is a danger that managers only take into account relatively recent phenomena without understanding how those phenomena have come about or how the past influences current and future strategy. Many organisations have long histories. The large Japanese Mitsui Group was founded in the seventeenth century; Daimler-Chrysler was founded in the nineteenth century and there has been evident continuity in its values and design principles; managers in the UK retailer Sainsbury's still refer to the founding principles of the Sainsbury family in the nineteenth century; many public sector organisations – government departments, the police, universities, for example – are strongly influenced by their historical legacies that have become embedded in their cultures.

Historical and cultural perspectives can help an understanding of both opportunities and constraints that organisations face, many of which are also discussed in other chapters of this book. The business environment (Chapter 2) cannot be understood without considering how it has developed over time. The capabilities of an organisation (Chapter 3), especially those that provide organisations with competitive advantage, may have historical roots and have built up over time in

Exhibit 5.1 **Chapter structure**

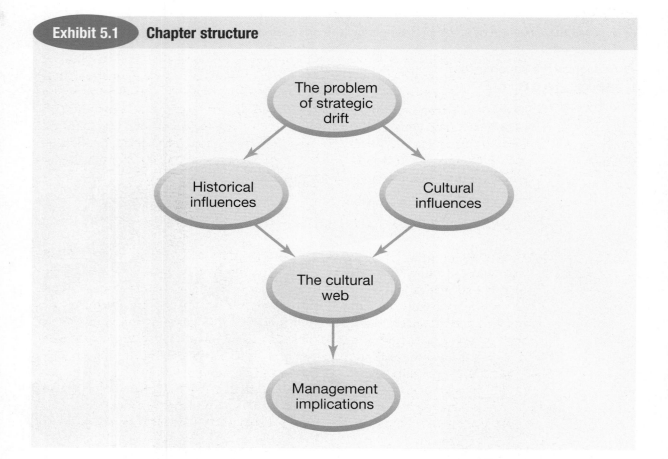

ways unique to that organisation. In so doing such capabilities may become part of the culture of an organisation – the taken-for-granted way of doing things – therefore difficult for other organisations to copy. However, they may also be difficult to change. So understanding the historical and cultural bases of such capabilities also informs the challenges of strategic change (Chapter 14). The powers and influence of different stakeholders are also likely to have historical origins that are important to understand. The theme of this chapter is, then, that the strategic position of an organisation has historical and cultural roots and that understanding those roots helps managers develop the future strategy of their organisations.

The chapter begins by explaining the phenomenon of strategic drift that highlights the importance of history and culture in relation to strategy development and identifies important challenges managers face in managing that development. The chapter then considers the two important and linked perspectives of history and culture. Section 5.3 examines the influence of the history of an organisation on its current and future strategy and goes on to consider how that history can be analysed. Section 5.4 then explains what is meant by culture and how cultural influences at the national, institutional and organisational levels influence current and future strategy. It then suggests how a culture can be analysed and its influence on strategy understood. Exhibit 5.1 summarises the chapter structure.

5.2 STRATEGIC DRIFT

Strategic drift is the tendency for strategies to develop incrementally on the basis of historical and cultural influences but fail to keep pace with a changing environment

Historical studies of organisations have shown a pattern that is represented in Exhibit 5.2. **Strategic drift**[1] is the tendency for strategies to develop incrementally on the basis of historical and cultural influences, but fail to keep pace with a changing environment. An example of strategic drift is given in Illustration 5.1. The reasons and consequences of strategic drift are important to understand, not only because it is common, but because it helps explain why organisations often 'run out of steam'. It also highlights some significant challenges for managers which, in turn, point to some important lessons.

5.2.1 Strategies change incrementally

KEY CONCEPT

Strategic drift

Strategies of organisations tend to change gradually. This is discussed more fully in Chapter 11. Here it is sufficient to summarise by explaining that there is a tendency for strategies to develop on the basis of what the organisation has done in the past – especially if that has been successful.[2] For example, Sainsbury's was one of the most successful retailers in the world for decades till the early 1990s, with its formula of selling food of a higher quality than competitors at reasonable prices. Always under the patriarchal guidance of a Sainsbury family chief executive, it gradually extended its product lines, enlarged its stores and its geographical coverage, but it did not deviate from its tried and tested ways of doing business. This is shown in phase 1 of the exhibit. In most successful businesses there are usually long periods of relative *continuity* during which established

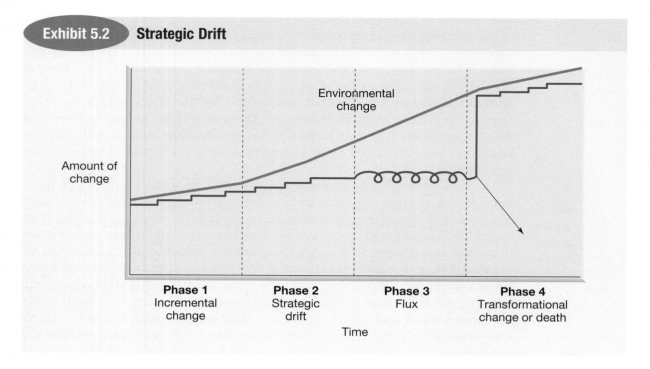

Exhibit 5.2   **Strategic Drift**

Amount of change

Environmental change

Phase 1	**Phase 2**	**Phase 3**	**Phase 4**
Incremental change	Strategic drift	Flux	Transformational change or death

Time

strategy remains largely unchanged or changes very *incrementally*. There are three main reasons for this:

● *Alignment with environmental change*. It could well be that the environment, particularly the market, is changing gradually and the organisation is keeping in line with those changes by such incremental change. It would make no sense for the strategy to change dramatically when the market is not doing so.

● *The success of the past*. There may be a natural unwillingness by managers to change a strategy significantly if it has been successful in the past, especially if it is built on capabilities that have been shown to be the basis of competitive advantage (see Chapters 3 and 6) or of innovation (see section 5.3.1 and Chapter 7).

● *Experimentation around a theme*. Indeed managers may have learned how to build variations around their successful formula, in effect experimenting without moving too far from their capability base. (This is akin to what some writers have referred to as 'logical incrementalism'; see section 11.3.1).

This poses challenges for managers, however. For how long and to what extent can they rely on incremental change building on the past being sufficient? When should they make more fundamental strategic changes? How are they to detect when this is necessary?

5.2.2   The tendency towards strategic drift

Whilst an organisation's strategy may continue to change incrementally, it may not change in line with the environment. This does not necessarily mean that there has to be dramatic environmental changes; phase 2 of Exhibit 5.2 shows environmental change accelerating, but it is not sudden. For Sainsbury's there

Illustration 5.1

Motorola: an analogue history facing a digital revolution

The bases of a firm's success may in turn be a cause of strategic drift.

In 1994 Motorola had 60 per cent of the US mobile telephone market. Founded in 1928, it was known for its technological innovation. It introduced the two-way walkie-talkie radio device commonly used in the Second World War, it marketed the first television to sell for under $200 in 1948. By the 1950s it had developed capabilities in printed circuit, ceramic substrate technology and electronic system design. By the 1970s it was a leading producer of microprocessors and was regarded as a world leader in technology.

However, even in the early days it was evident that the emphasis was on technology, rather than the market. Critics suggested that the firm put technology before consumers.

Mobile phones had been developed by Bell Labs in the 1970s. By the mid-1980s Motorola was the leading producer of cell phones using analogue technology, but none the less a logical progression from its military walkie-talkie systems using the post-war technology it had developed. However, these devices were bulky and expensive, targeted at business managers who were on the move and could not use landlines. The phones were not widely known or available.

By the mid-1990s Motorola was highly successful. From 1992 to 1995 sales revenue grew at an average of 27 per cent a year to reach $27bn (€22bn) and net income 58 per cent a year to reach $1.8bn.

However, by the mid-1990s digital technology for mobile phones was being developed through what was known as the Personal Communication System (PCS). This technology overcame some of the shortcomings of analogue technology. It reduced interference, allowed security codes to be encrypted and could deal with more subscribers than analogue. It was a technology that supported mass market development. The demand for digital phones grew rapidly, not amongst business people alone, but amongst a wider consumer market.

These consumers were much less concerned about functionality and much more concerned about ease of use and aesthetic appeal.

According to a Motorola chief executive of the time, Robert Galvin, the company 'was at the forefront of the development of digital technology'. However, it chose to stay with analogue technology for many years, licensing its digital to Nokia and Ericsson through which it earned increasing royalties. Indeed Motorola launched a new analogue phone, Star-TAC, and embarked on an aggressive marketing campaign to promote it.

Not only was it clear from the growing royalties that digital phones were taking off, wireless carrier customers were lobbying Motorola to develop digital phones: 'They told us we didn't know what we were talking about. . . . These were not friendly conversations. But Motorola didn't do it. Instead we launched with Ericsson, then Nokia.'

By 1998 Motorola's market share had dropped to 34 per cent and it was forced to lay off 20,000 people.

Source: Adapted from S. Finkelstein, 'Why smart executives fail: four case histories of how people learn the wrong lessons from history', *Business History*, vol. 48, no. 2 (2006), pp. 153–170.

Questions

1 Identify on a timeline between 1928 and 1998 the major events identified here. What does this analysis tell you about the reasons for the resistance of Motorola to new technology?

2 Given that Motorola had the technology and knew that the digital market was developing, give reasons as to why it persisted with analogue technology. (See Chapter 11 and the Commentaries as well as this chapter to help with this question.)

was the growing share of its rival, Tesco, accompanied by the growth of larger-size stores, with wider ranges of goods (for example, non-food) and changes in distribution logistics of competitors. These changes, however, had been taking place for many years. The problem that gives rise to strategic drift is that, as with many organisations, Sainsbury's strategy was not keeping pace with these changes. There are at least five reasons for this:

- *The problem of hindsight.* Chapter 2 has provided ways to analyse the environment and such analyses may yield insights. But how are managers to be sure of the direction and significance of such changes? Or changes may be seen as temporary. Managers may be understandably wary of changing what they are likely to see as a winning strategy on the basis of what might only be a fad in the market, or a temporary downturn in demand. It may be easy to see major changes with hindsight, but it may not be so easy to see their significance as they are happening.

- *Building on the familiar.* Managers may see changes in the environment about which they are uncertain or which they do not entirely understand. In these circumstances they may try to minimise the extent to which they are faced with such uncertainty by looking for answers that are familiar, which they understand and which have served them well in the past. This will lead to a bias towards continued incremental strategic change. For example, Sainsbury's managers clung to the belief that they had loyal customers who valued the superior quality of Sainsbury's goods. Tesco had been a cheaper retailer with what they saw as inferior goods. Surely the superior quality of Sainsbury's would continue to be recognised.

- *Core rigidities.* As Chapter 3 explains, success in the past may well have been based on capabilities that are unique to an organisation and difficult for others to copy. However, the capabilities that have been bases of advantage can become difficult to change, in effect *core rigidities*.[3] There are two reasons. First, over time, the ways of doing things that have delivered past success may become taken for granted. This may well have been an advantage in the past because it was difficult for competitors to imitate them. However, taken-for-granted core competences rarely get questioned and therefore tend to persist beyond their usefulness. Second, ways of doing things develop over time and become more and more embedded in organisational routines that reinforce and rely on each other and are difficult to unravel; this is discussed further in section 5.3.1.

- *Relationships become shackles.*[4] Success has probably been built on the basis of excellent relationships with customers, suppliers and employees. Maintaining these may very likely be seen as fundamental to the long-term health of the organisation. Yet these relationships may make it difficult to make fundamental changes to strategy that could entail changing routes to market or the customer base, developing products requiring different suppliers or changing the skill base of the organisation with the risk of disrupting relationships with the workforce.

- *Lagged performance effects.* The effects of such drift may not be easy to see in terms of the performance of the organisation. Financial performance may continue to hold up in the early stages of strategic drift. Customers may be loyal and the organisation, by becoming more efficient, cutting costs or simply trying harder, may continue to hold up its performance. So there may not be internal signals of the need for change or pressures from managers, or indeed external observers to make major changes.

However, over time, if strategic drift continues, there will be symptoms that become evident: a downturn in financial performance; a loss in market share to competitors perhaps; a decline in the share price. Indeed such a downturn may happen quite rapidly once external observers, not least competitors and financial analysts, have identified that such drift has occurred. Even the most successful companies may drift in this way. Indeed, there is a tendency – which Danny Miller has called the Icarus Paradox[5] – for businesses to become victims of the very success of their past. They become captured by the formula that has delivered that success.

5.2.3 A period of flux

The next phase (phase 3) may be a period of *flux* triggered by the downturn in performance. Strategies may change but in no very clear direction. There may also be management changes, often at the very top as the organisation comes under pressure to make changes from its stakeholders, not least shareholders in the case of a public company. There may be internal rivalry as to which strategy to follow, quite likely based on differences of opinion as to whether future strategy should be based on historic capabilities or whether those capabilities are becoming redundant. Indeed, there have been highly publicised boardroom rows when this has happened. All this may result in a further deterioration of confidence in the organisation: perhaps a further drop in performance or share price, a difficulty in recruiting high-quality management, or a further loss of customers' loyalty.

5.2.4 Transformational change or death

As things get worse it is likely that the outcome (phase 4) will be one of three possibilities: (i) the organisation may die (in the case of a commercial organis-ation it may go into receivership, for example); (ii) it may get taken over by another organisation; or (iii) it may go through a period of *transformational change*. Such change could take form in multiple changes related to the organ-isation's strategy: for example, a change in products, markets or market focus, changes of capabilities on which the strategy is based, changes in the top man-agement of the organisation and perhaps the way the organisation is structured.

Transformational change does not take place frequently in organisations and is usually the result of a major downturn in performance. Often it is transforma-tional changes that are heralded as the success stories of top executives; this is where they most visibly make a difference. The problem is that, from the point of view of market position, shareholder wealth and jobs, it may be rather too late. Competitive position may have been lost, shareholder value has probably already been destroyed and, very likely, many jobs will have been lost too. The time when 'making a difference' really matters most is in phase 2 in Exhibit 5.2, when the organisation is beginning to drift. However, a study of 215 major UK firms identified just 8 that had effected major transformational change without performance decline.[6] The problem is that, very likely, such drift is not easy to see before performance suffers. So in understanding the strategic position of an organisation so as to avoid the damaging effects of strategic drift, it is vital to take seriously the extent to which historical tendencies in strategy development tend to persist in the cultural fabric of organisations. The rest of this chapter focuses on this. The challenge is, then, how to manage change in such circumstances and this challenge is taken up in Chapter 11 on managing strategic change.

5.3 WHY IS HISTORY IMPORTANT?

If the tendency for strategic drift is to be understood, the history of organisations needs to be taken seriously by strategists. There are also other reasons why understanding history can help in understanding the strategic position of an organisation and in the management of strategy:

- *Managers' organisational experience*. Managers may have spent many years in an organisation or in an industry. The experience on which they base their decisions may be heavily influenced by that history (see the discussion on the 'experience lens' in the Commentary). It is helpful if managers can 'stand apart' from that history so as to understand the influence it has on themselves and their colleagues.

- *Avoiding recency bias*. Managers can give too much weight to recent events or performance, forgetting past patterns, resulting in either undue optimism or undue pessimism. Understanding the current situation in terms of the past can provide useful lessons. For example, have there been historical trends that may repeat themselves? How have competitors responded to strategic moves in the past? A historical perspective may also help managers see what gave rise to events that were seen as surprises in the past and learn from how their organisation dealt with them.

- *Misattribution of success?* Is it clear where current bases of success originate, how they developed and how this might inform future strategy development? The danger is that there may be a misattribution of causes of success, which may lie elsewhere than thought or even be the result of luck. Such misattribution could in turn lead to the reinforcement of wrong behaviours. For example, the future strategy of an engineering firm stressed the importance of proactively managing innovation of new products and services. This was because managers saw that its current growth was coming from just such an innovation, whilst the rest of its offering was showing no growth. However, a study of the origins of innovatory products in the firm showed that the limited extent to which they occurred was largely due to what appeared to be happenchance, or as a result of technologies inherited from acquisitions happening to be relevant to the business's core activities. Historically there was no evidence of innovation being internally planned or proactively managed. This historical perspective raised important questions about what the firm saw as its capabilities for managing future innovation.

- *'What if' questions*. History can also encourage managers to ask the 'what if' question. It can encourage them to imagine what might have happened had there been other influences in the environment, different responses from customers or competitors, or different initiatives or leadership within their organisation. It makes the present more evidently a product of circumstances and thus less fixed. So potentially it opens up the possibilities for changes in the future.

- *Detecting and avoiding strategic drift*. If managers sensitise themselves to the influence of the history of their organisation they stand a better chance of seeing current strategy as part of what Henry Mintzberg describes strategy as: 'a pattern in a stream of decisions'.[7] As such, managers are more likely to be able to question the extent to which the strategy they are seeking to develop is usefully informed by that history as distinct from being driven or captured by it. The discussion on the influence of organisational culture in section 5.4 is especially relevant here.

5.3.1 Path dependency

Path dependency is where early events and decisions establish policy paths that have lasting effects on subsequent events and decisions

A useful way of thinking of the role and influence of history is through the concept of *path dependency* and the associated notion of historical *lock-in*. **Path dependency** is where early events and decisions establish 'policy paths' that have lasting effects on subsequent events and decisions.[8] It has already been discussed in Chapter 3 in relation to the potential bases of competitive advantage and path-dependent capabilities (see section 3.4.3). Its origins, its impact and how it can be understood are therefore important.

Examples often relate to technology. There are many instances where the technology we employ is better explained by path dependency than by the optimisation of such technology. A famous one is the layout used for typewriter keyboards in many countries: QWERTY. This was originated in the nineteenth century for two main reasons. First, it is a layout that reduced the problem of the keys on mechanical typewriters getting tangled when typing fast. The second was to help salespeople at that time demonstrate the machine at maximum speed by putting all the letters of the word 'typewriter' on the top line. There are more optimal layouts, but QWERTY has remained with us in most countries for over 150 years despite the elimination of mechanical keys and the eventual development of personal computers.[9] There are countless other examples ranging from technologies in nuclear power stations through to VCR systems. Early decisions and commitments become 'locked in' over time, through widespread repeated usage by networks of suppliers and users who, in turn, build their own support systems around such technology.

Path dependency is not just about technology. It also relates to any form of behaviour that has its origins in the past and becomes entrenched. In an organisational and strategic context this is likely to take form over time in the development of behavioural routines supported by hardware and technology that make up systems of selling, marketing, recruiting, accounting, and so on.[10] Such routines also often become more widely 'institutionalised' than the organisation. Take the example of accounting systems. The lock-in of these has occurred at multiple levels involving networks comprising what people do, those with whom

Exhibit 5.3   **Path dependency and lock-in**

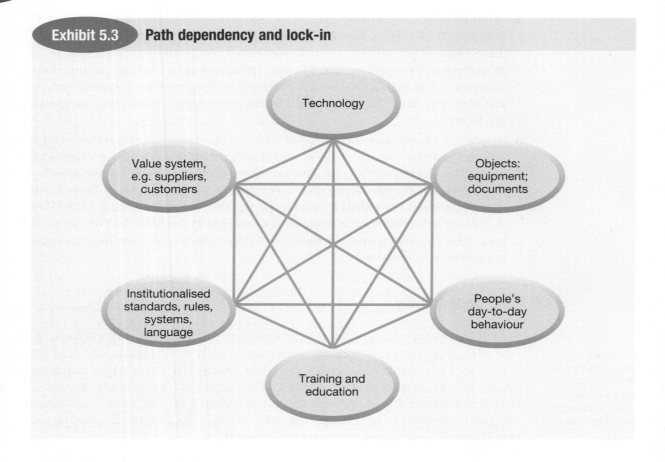

they interact within and outside their organisation, the standards and systems in which they are trained, and the objects and technologies they generate or use. All these have developed over time and mutually reinforce each other as Exhibit 5.3 illustrates. Rather like QWERTY, the 'rightness' or at least inevitability of such systems tends to be taken for granted. They also strongly influence decision making, not least in relation to strategic analysis and strategic choice. Historic accounting systems also persist despite increasing numbers of experts, both in the accountancy profession and elsewhere,[11] who point to fundamental weaknesses in such systems, not least the failure of accounting systems to provide measures for many of the factors that account for the market value of firms.

Path dependency is, then, a way of thinking about how historical events and decisions, within and around an organisation, have an effect on that organisation for good or ill. These include:

● *Building strategy around the path-dependent capabilities* that may have developed within an organisation. This is at the root of much of the arguments put forward for the building of competitive advantage discussed in Chapter 3 and further developed in Chapter 6. Indeed there is evidence that this is so. Path dependency has been shown to explain organisational strategies.[12] Firms tend to enter markets, focus on market segments and diversify in line with the previous path-dependent capabilities they have developed. In so doing they tend to focus on types of customers that they have serviced or capabilities on which their success has been based. This may be a basis for success but can also be dangerous as the Motorola example in Illustration 5.1 shows.

- The concept of *path creation* is, however, also relevant here. This suggests that some managers may actively seek to amend and deviate from path-dependent ways of doing things to the benefit of their organisations. They may be sensitive enough to history to recognise what they can and cannot change. Going too far may be risky (see the discussion on 'legitimacy' in section 5.4.2), but setting in motion changes that are accepted as appropriate and beneficial by others in the network may be a way of achieving advantage. Arguably this is what new players in the insurance market such as Tesco have done. They have not tried to change basic principles of insurance provision; they have significantly changed the way in which insurance is sold and distributed.

- *Innovation based on historic capabilities*. In the BMW museum in Munich there is a quote: 'Anyone who wants to design for the future has to leaf through the past.'[13] The museum may be about the history of BMW, but it is also about how the lessons of the past can give rise to new ideas and innovation. Indeed the Innovation and Technology Division of BMW is sited next to the museum and the archives of BMW. Innovation may build on historic capabilities in at least two ways. First, as technologies change, firms with experience and skills built over time that are most appropriate to those changes tend to innovate more than those that do not.[14] Or it could be that there are new combinations of knowledge as capabilities built up in adjacent technologies are adapted in innovative ways to new technological opportunities. For example, the development of lighting systems was derived from the way gas was distributed.[15] Similarly successful firms that created the TV industry were previously radio manufacturers and it was they that exhibited greater innovation as the industry developed than the non-radio producers.[16]

In relation to both path creation and innovation managers need to see the past in relation to the future and in so doing challenge the one with the other: ask what is relevant from the past that can help with the future and what does the future demand but also not require from the past? In doing this they also need to ask themselves the extent to which the environment is changing in such a way that their path-dependent capabilities will be relevant. In other words, if strategy is to evolve on the back of such capabilities, it can only do so if simultaneously the changes in markets, technologies and other aspects of the environment discussed in Chapter 2 are potentially converging with those capabilities. They need to develop a sensitivity, not only to the historic capabilities that matter, but also to the relationship of these to an evolving environment.

- *Management style* may also have its roots in history. This may be not only in terms of the values of the founder, which indeed may have a strong influence, but also in the interplay between past ways of doing things and the lessons learned from the organisation's evolving environment.[17] To take Tesco as an example again, it is now one of the most successful international retailers. In its early days it was a family firm run by Jack Cohen renowned for his blunt and authoritative style. This gave rise to internal conflicts within the firm and between suppliers and Tesco. Things are different in Tesco now, but the historic conflict has evolved into productive challenge and rivalry between managers and different parts of the firm that, arguably, have substantially contributed to its innovation and success.[18]

However, again there is another side to these potential benefits. The evolution of management style may not be in line with the needs of a changing environment, but over-influenced and bound by the legacy of the past. Similarly capabilities that are path dependent and rooted in history may become highly entrenched. Path dependency has sometimes been described as like the 'furrows in a road' that become deeper and deeper as more and more traffic goes along. Once that happens the traffic has no option but to go along those furrows. Hence capabilities, once the bases of competitive advantage and success, become core rigidities leading to the phenomenon of strategic drift explained in section 5.2.

5.3.2 Historical analysis

How then might managers undertake a historical strategic analysis of their organisation? There are a number of ways this may be done:[19]

- *Chronological analysis.* At the most basic level this involves setting down a chronology of key events showing changes in the organisation's environment – especially its markets – how the organisation's strategy itself has changed and with what consequences – not least financial. Some firms have done this much more extensively by commissioning extensive corporate histories. These may sometimes be little more than public relations exercises, but the better ones are serious exercises in documenting the history.[20] At the very least this historical understanding can help sensitise managers to the sort of questions raised above.

- *Cyclical influences.* Is there evidence of cyclical influences? Certainly these have been shown to exist in terms of economic cycles, but also in terms of cycles of industry activity, such as periods of high acquisition activity or indeed divestment activity. Understanding when these cycles might occur and how industry and market forces might change during such cycles can inform decisions on whether to build strategy in line with those cycles or in a counter-cyclical fashion.

- *Anchor points.* History may be regarded as continuous but historical events can also be significant for an organisation at particular points in time, sometimes known as 'anchor points'. These could be particularly significant events, either in terms of industry change or organisational strategic decisions. Or they might be policies laid down by a founder or by powerful senior executives; or major successes or failures or defining periods of time that have informed received wisdom or which managers have come to see as especially important. Such anchor points may be traced to many years ago in the organisation's history, yet may have profound effects on current organisational strategy, strategic thinking or exercise significant constraints on future strategy. This could, of course, be for the good: they may provide a very clear overall direction strategically that contributes to the sort of vision discussed in the previous chapter. They could, on the other hand, be a major barrier to challenging existing strategies or changing strategic direction. A famous example is Henry Ford's maxim 'You can have any colour provided it's black', which set a trajectory for mass production and low variety in the car industry for decades. Currently government (and political opposition) health policy in the UK is constrained by the historical mantra that health provision should be 'free at point of delivery' when it clearly is not. Apple's 1984 advertising campaign marked its clear positioning against IBM: the peak time TV ad featured a young female athlete hurling a sledgehammer at a sinister TV image of *Big Brother*, clearly referring to the then dominant IBM .

● *Historical narratives*. How do people in the organisation talk about and explain the history of their organisation? In trying to understand the foundations of the strategy of an organisation a new chief executive or an external consultant will typically spend a good deal of time talking with people to try to gain insights from their personal accounts of history.[21] What do they have to say about the way they see their organisation and its past, not least in terms of anchor points and origins of success? In turn, what are the implications for future strategy development? Does what they say suggest an organisation with the historic capabilities of relevance to particular markets and customers, one capable of innovation and change or one so rooted in past ways of doing things that there are risks of strategic drift?

History, then, is important in terms of how it influences current strategy for better or worse. As suggested here, there are ways in which history can be analysed. It is not always easy, however, to trace the links to the organisation as it currently exists. It is here that understanding the organisation's culture becomes important. The current culture of an organisation is, to a great extent, the legacy of its history; history becomes 'encapsulated in culture'.[22] So understanding an organisation's culture is one way of understanding the historical influences that, as we have seen, can be very powerful. The next section goes on to explain what culture is and how it can be analysed.

5.4 WHAT IS CULTURE AND WHY IS IT IMPORTANT?

There are many definitions of culture. Earlier in the book (see page xx) it was defined as 'socially established structures of meaning'.[23] Edgar Schein defines **organisational culture** more specifically as the 'basic *assumptions and beliefs* that are shared by members of an organisation, that operate unconsciously and define in a basic taken-for-granted fashion an organisation's view of itself and its environment'.[24] Related to this are taken-for-granted ways of doing things, the routines, that accumulate over time. In other words, culture is about that which is taken for granted but none the less contributes to how groups of people respond and behave in relation to issues they face. It therefore has important influences on the development and change of organisational strategy.

In fact cultural influences exist at multiple levels as Exhibit 5.4 shows. The sections that follow will identify the important factors and issues in terms of different cultural frames of reference and then show how organisational culture can be analysed and characterised as a means of understanding the influences of culture on both current and future organisational purposes and strategies.

Organisational culture is the 'basic *assumptions and beliefs* that are shared by members of an organisation, that operate unconsciously and define in a basic taken-for-granted fashion an organisation's view of itself and its environment'

www.pearsoned.co.uk/ecs
KEY CONCEPT

Organisational culture

Exhibit 5.4   **Cultural frames of reference**

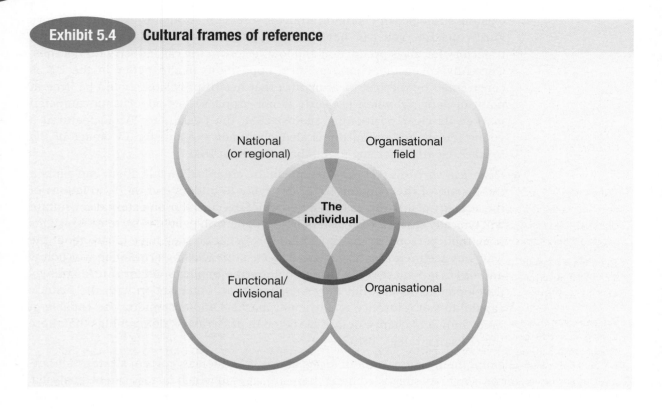

5.4.1 National and regional cultures

Many writers, perhaps the most well known of which is Geert Hofstede,[25] have shown how attitudes to work, authority, equality and other important factors differ from one country to another. Such differences have been shaped by powerful cultural forces concerned with history, religion and even climate over many centuries. Organisations that operate internationally need to understand and cope with such differences that can manifest themselves in terms of different standards, values and expectations in the various countries in which they operate.[26] For example, Euro Disney's attempt to replicate the success of the Disney theme parks in the USA was termed 'cultural imperialism' in the French media and has experienced difficulties. There was a decline in visitors of 0.3 per cent a year between 1999 and 2005. Illustration 5.2 also shows how cultural differences can pose challenges for managers seeking to develop markets in China.

Although they are not shown separately in Exhibit 5.4 (for reasons of simplification), it may also be important to understand *subnational* (usually regional) cultures. For example, attitudes to some aspects of employment and supplier relationships may differ at a regional level even in a relatively small and cohesive country like the UK, and quite markedly elsewhere in Europe (for example, between northern and southern Italy). There may also be differences between urban and rural locations.

Illustration 5.2

When in China . . .

As Western firms move into China, understanding Chinese ways of doing business becomes crucial.

David Hands has operated in Beijing for real estate firm Jones Lang Lasalle (JLL), where he had to develop the business in China. *Management Today* reported an interview with him:

There are a huge number of opportunities in China but it's crucial to sort the wheat from the chaff and you need to work on efficiency to do that. For example, we had problems with time management in the early stages. Imagine trying to set up a meeting where everybody is turning up at different times, and where nobody has thought to specify an agenda for the meeting. Or there will be three multi-hour meetings for a client who barely gives us any business. It was tough to make people understand the importance of breaking down costs versus benefits.

It took time to get the Chinese to value the advice that JLL could provide because, whilst they are accustomed to paying for goods, paying for services came as a culture shock:

You have to learn to go step by step and give a little. You can't turn up at someone's office and say: 'Pay me a large amount of money in advance'. And you have to really show them where you can add value to their operations.

There are also problems of understanding hierarchy:

You may think you are dealing with the top guy and he is asking you for a discount. You give him one. But then you meet up with another five managers in gradually ascending order and they all ask for discounts. So beware!

The symbols of hierarchy are not the same either. Unlike in some Western countries where status symbols such as car and clothing brands may signify status, in China senior management are likely to dress 'more drably':

Cheap clothing is important in a culture plagued by corruption: dressing down diverts attention from any ill-gotten gains, but the head honcho still wants to assert his authority and one way he does that is by having an entourage of flunkies. . . . I learnt early on that if I didn't reciprocate by going to meetings with one or more assistants, people would just take me less seriously.

To the Westerner there may also seem to be a lack of courtesy: 'They basically think they own you, in the same way as they own a car or luxury watch after they have paid for them.'

Staff relationships to the boss are also more important than staff relationships to the company: 'That's why you'll find staff cleaning their boss' cars on the weekend. We have to teach staff that this will not earn them promotion . . .'.

Another interviewee had experience of Chinese bureaucracy:

When you are negotiating with the government you need to find somebody who feels you can help him personally benefit from the deal. Once your interests are aligned, he can then guide you through the maze. . . . It's not a matter of getting somebody's name card and going out for a drink. In China you have to earn that person's gratitude and trust and you do that by doing them favours. The bigger the favour, the more they will help you professionally as well as privately.

Source: D. Slater, 'When in China . . .', *Management Today*, May (2006). Reproduced from *Management Today* magazine with the permission of the copyright owner, Haymarket Publications Limited.

Questions

1 On the evidence of these interviews identify how the cultural norms and taken-for-granted assumptions of Chinese managers differ from those of Western managers.

2 If you are seeking to operate in a country with a very different culture, other than talking with people experienced in that market, how else would you set about trying to understand the culture and its underlying assumptions?

5.4.2 **The organisational field**[27]

An **organisational field** is a community of organisations that interact more frequently with one another than with those outside the field and that have developed a shared meaning system

A **recipe** is a set of assumptions, norms and routines held in common within an organisational field about organisational purposes and a 'shared wisdom' on how to manage organisations

Legitimacy is concerned with meeting the expectations within an organisational field in terms of assumptions, behaviours and strategies

The culture of an organisation is also shaped by 'work-based' groupings such as an industry (or sector), a profession or what is sometimes known as an **organisational field**, which is a community of organisations that interact more frequently with one another than with those outside the field and that have developed a shared meaning system.[28] Such organisations may share a common technology, set of regulations or education and training. In turn this can mean that they tend to cohere around a **recipe**:[29] a set of assumptions, norms and routines held in common within an organisational field about organisational purposes and a 'shared wisdom' on how to manage organisations. For example, there are many organisations in the organisational field of 'justice', such as lawyers, police, courts, prisons and probation services. The roles of each are different and their detailed prescriptions as to how justice should be achieved differ. However, they are all committed to the principle that justice is a good thing which is worth striving for, they interact frequently on this issue, have developed shared ways of understanding and debating issues that arise and operate common routines or readily accommodate the routines of others in the field. Similar coherence around a recipe is common in other organisational fields, for example professional services such as accountancy (see Illustration 5.3) and many industries.

This links to the concept of path dependency discussed above. The different parties in an organisational field form a self-reinforcing network built on such assumptions and behaviours that, very likely, will lead to behavioural lock-in. Indeed professions, or trade associations, often attempt to formalise an organisational field where the membership is exclusive and the behaviour of members is regulated. Such cultural influences can be advantageous – say to customers – in maintaining standards and consistency between individual providers. Managers can, however, become 'institutionalised' such that they do not see the opportunities or indeed threats from outside their organisational field and their recipes are also likely to be very difficult to change.

Just as previous chapters have shown the importance of environmental forces (Chapter 2), strategic capabilities (Chapter 3) and stakeholder expectations (Chapter 4), within an organisational field *legitimacy* is an important influence. **Legitimacy** is concerned with meeting the expectations within an organisational field in terms of assumptions, behaviours and strategies. Strategies can be shaped by the need for legitimacy in several ways. For example, through *regulation* (for example, standards and codes of behaviour specified, perhaps by a professional body), *normative expectations* (what is socially expected), or simply that which is taken for granted as being appropriate (for example, the *recipe*). Over time, there tends to develop a consensus within an organisational field about strategies that will be successful or acceptable – so strategies themselves become legitimised. By conforming to such norms, organisations may secure approval, support and public endorsement, thus increasing their legitimacy. Stepping outside that strategy may be risky because important stakeholders (such as customers or bankers) may not see such a move as legitimate. Therefore, organisations tend to mimic each other's strategies. There may be differences in strategies between organisations but within bounds of legitimacy.[30] This is shown in the discussion of strategy in Illustration 5.3. Of course, some fringe players may actually represent successful future strategies (for example,

Illustration 5.3

Strategy debate in an accounting firm

The perceived legitimacy of a strategy may have different roots.

Edward Gray, the managing partner of QDG, one of the larger accountancy firms in the world, is discussing its global development with two of his senior partners. Global development had been the main issue at the firm's international committee in the USA the previous week. Like most accountancy firms, QDG is organised along national lines. Its origins were in auditing but it now offers tax and financial advice, corporate recovery and information systems services. International cooperation is based on personal contacts of partners across the world. However, large clients are beginning to demand a 'seamless global service'. At the meeting is Alan Clark, with 20 years' experience as a partner and a high reputation in the accountancy profession, and Michael Jones: new to QDG and unlike the others not an accountant, he heads up the information systems arm of QDG, having been recruited from a consultancy firm.

Gray:

Unless we move towards a more global form of business, QDG could lose its position as one of the leading accountancy firms in the world. Our competitors are moving this way, so we have to. The issue is how?

Clark was sympathetic but cautionary. He pointed out that clients were entering growing economies such as China:

Governments there will insist on international standards of practice, but they have difficulties. For example, in China there is often no real concept of profit, let alone how to measure it. If there is to be a market economy, the need for the services we provide is high. There are however major problems, not least, the enormous number of people required. It is not possible to churn out experienced accountants overnight. Our professional standards would be compromised. The firm cannot be driven by market opportunity at the expense of standards. There is another issue. Our business is based on personal relationships and trust; this must not be compromised in the name of 'global integration'.

Jones suggested that the problem was more challenging:

All our competitors are going global. They will be pitching for the same clients, offering the same services and the same standard of service. Where is the difference? To achieve any competitive advantage we need to do things differently and think beyond the obvious. For example why not a two-tier partnership, where smaller countries are non-equity partners? That would allow us to make decisions more quickly, allow us to enforce standards and give formal authority to senior partners looking after our major international clients.

Clark had expected this:

This is not an opportunity to make money; it's about the development of proper systems for the economies of previously closed countries. We need to co-operate with other firms to make sure that there are compatible standards. This cannot be helped by changing a partnership structure that has served well for a hundred years.

Gray:

The view of at last week's meeting was certainly that there is a need for a more internationally co-ordinated firm, with a more effective client management system, less reliance on who knows whom and more on drawing on the best of our people when we need them.

Clark:

I could equally argue that we have an unparalleled network of personal relationships throughout the world which we have been building for decades. That what we have to do is strengthen this using modern technology and modern communications.

Gray reconciled himself to a lengthy discussion.

Source: Adapted from the case study in G. Johnson and R. Greenwood, 'Institutional theory and strategic management', in Mark Jenkins and V. Ambrosini (eds), *Strategic Management: A Multiple-Perspective Approach*, Palgrave, 2007.

Questions

1 What are the underlying assumptions of the arguments being advanced by the three partners?

2 What may be the origins of these assumptions?

3 How do the different views correspond to the discussions of strategic capabilities (Chapter 3) and competitive strategy (Chapter 6)?

Internet providers of downloadable music), but *initially* this may not be seen – customers may remain loyal to established investors, bankers may be reluctant to fund such ventures and existing players in the market may dismiss what they see as aberrations.

Because the recipe varies from one field to another, the transition of managers between sectors can also prove difficult. For example, private sector managers have been encouraged to join public services in an attempt to inject new ways of doing things into the public sector. Many have expressed difficulties in gaining acceptance of their ways of working and in adjusting their management style to the different traditions and expectations of their new organisation, for example in issues like consensus building as part of the decision-making process. Or, to take the example in Illustration 5.3, Michael Jones's different career background means he has some quite different views on strategy from his accountant colleagues.

5.4.3 Organisational culture

The culture of an organisation is often conceived as consisting of four layers[31] (see Exhibit 5.5):

● *Values* may be easy to identify in an organisation, and are often written down as statements about an organisation's mission, objectives or strategies (see section 4.5). However, they can be vague, such as 'service to the community' or 'honouring equal employment opportunities'.

Exhibit 5.5   **Culture in four layers**

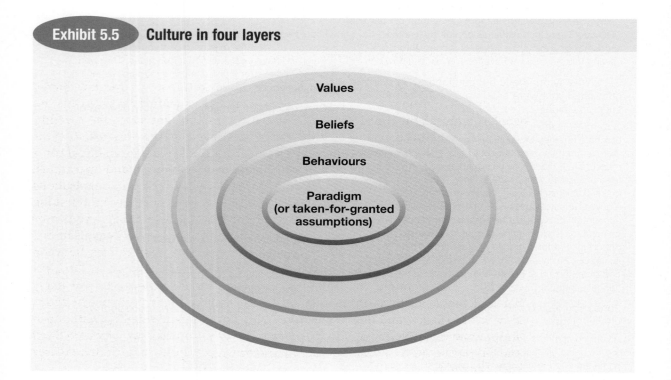

Values

Beliefs

Behaviours

Paradigm
(or taken-for-granted
assumptions)

- *Beliefs* are more specific, but again they can typically be discerned in how people talk about issues the organisation faces; for example, a belief that the company should not trade with particular countries, or that professional staff should not have their professional actions appraised by managers.

With regard to both values and beliefs it is important to remember that in relation to culture, the concern is with the collective rather than individuals' values and beliefs. Indeed it may be that individuals in organisations have values and beliefs that at times run counter to their organisation's, which can give rise to the sort of ethical tensions and problems discussed in section 4.3.2.

- *Behaviours* are the day-to-day way in which an organisation operates and can be seen by people both inside and outside the organisation. This includes the work routines, how the organisation is structured and controlled and 'softer' issues around symbolic behaviours.

- *Taken-for-granted assumptions* are the core of an organisation's culture. They are the aspects of organisational life which people find difficult to identify and explain. Here they are referred to as the organisational paradigm. The **paradigm** is the set of assumptions held in common and taken for granted in an organisation. For an organisation to operate effectively there is bound to be such a generally accepted set of assumptions. As mentioned above, these assumptions represent *collective experience* without which people would have to 'reinvent their world' for different circumstances that they face. The paradigm can underpin successful strategies by providing a basis of common understanding in an organisation, but can also be a major problem, for example when major strategic change is needed (see Chapter 14), or when organisations try to merge and find they are incompatible. The importance of the paradigm is discussed further in section 5.4.6.

A **paradigm** is the set of assumptions held relatively in common and taken for granted in an organisation

5.4.4 Organisational subcultures

In seeking to understand the relationship between culture and an organisation's strategies, it may be possible to identify some aspects of culture that pervade the whole organisation. However, there may also be important *subcultures* within organisations. These may relate directly to the structure of the organisation: for example, the differences between geographical divisions in a multinational company, or between functional groups such as finance, marketing and operations. Differences between divisions may be particularly evident in organisations that have grown through acquisition. Also different divisions may be pursuing different types of strategy and these different market positionings require or foster different cultures. Indeed, aligning strategic positioning and organisational culture is a critical feature of successful organisations. Differences between business functions also can relate to the different nature of work in different functions. For example, in a company like Shell or BP differences are likely between those functions engaged in 'upstream' exploration, where time horizons may be in decades, and those concerned with 'downstream' retailing, with much shorter market-driven time horizons. Arguably, this is one reason why both Shell and BP pay so much attention to trying to forge a corporate culture that crosses such functions.

5.4.5 Culture's influence on strategy

The taken-for-granted nature of culture is what makes it centrally important in relation to strategy and the management of strategy. There are two primary reasons for this:

● *Managing culture*. Because it is difficult to observe, identify and control that which is taken for granted, it is difficult to manage (see the key debate in Illustration 5.5 at the end of the chapter). This is why having a way to analyse culture so as to make it more evident is important – the subject of the next section.

● *Culture as a driver of strategy*. Organisations can be 'captured' by their culture and find it very difficult to change their strategy outside the bounds of that culture. Managers, faced with a changing business environment, are more likely to attempt to deal with the situation by searching for what they can understand and cope with in terms of the existing culture. The result is likely to be incremental strategic change with the risk of eventual strategic drift explained in section 5.2. Culture is, in effect, an unintended driver of strategy.

The effect of culture on strategy is shown in Exhibit 5.6.[32] Faced with a stimulus for action, such as declining performance, managers first try to improve the implementation of existing strategy. This might be through trying to lower cost,

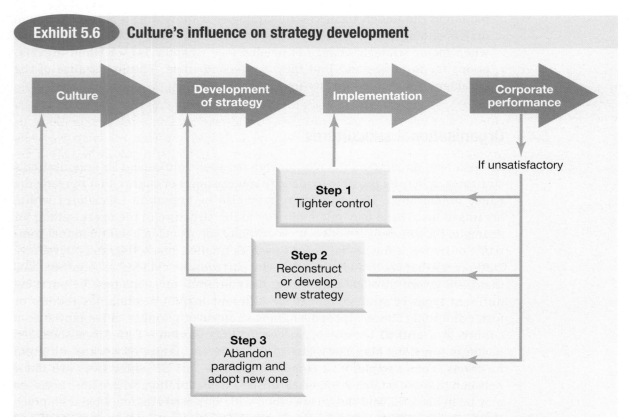

Exhibit 5.6   **Culture's influence on strategy development**

Source: Adapted from P. Grinyer and J.-C. Spender, *Turnaround: Managerial Recipes for Strategic Success*, Associated Business Press, 1979, p. 203.

improve efficiency, tighten controls or improve accepted ways of doing things. If this is not effective, a change of strategy may occur, but a change in line with the existing culture. For example, managers may seek to extend the market for their business, but assume that it will be similar to their existing market, and therefore set about managing the new venture in much the same way as they have been used to. Alternatively, even where managers know intellectually that they need to change, indeed know technologically how to do so, they find themselves constrained by path-dependent organisational routines and assumptions or political processes, as seems likely in Illustration 5.1. This often happens, for example, when there are attempts to change highly bureaucratic organisations to be customer oriented. Even if people who accept intellectually the need to change a culture's emphasis on the importance of conforming to established rules, routines and reporting relationships, they do not readily do so. The notion that reasoned argument necessarily changes deeply embedded assumptions rooted in collective experience built up over long periods of time is flawed. Readers need only think of their own experience in trying to persuade others to rethink their religious beliefs, or indeed allegiances to sports teams, to realise this. What occurs is the predominant application of the familiar and the attempt to avoid or reduce uncertainty or ambiguity. This is likely to continue until there is, perhaps, dramatic evidence of the redundancy of the culture, quite likely as the result of the organisation entering phases 3 or 4 of strategic drift (see Exhibit 5.2).

5.4.6 Analysing culture: the cultural web

The **cultural web** shows the behavioural, physical and symbolic manifestations of a culture that inform and are informed by the taken-for-granted assumptions, or paradigm

KEY CONCEPT
www.pearsoned.co.uk/ecs

Cultural web

In order to understand both the existing culture and its effects it is important to be able to analyse culture. The **cultural web**[33] is a means of doing this. The cultural web shows the behavioural, physical and symbolic manifestations of a culture that inform and are informed by the taken-for-granted assumptions, or paradigm, of an organisation (see Exhibit 5.7). It is in effect the inner two ovals in Exhibit 5.5. The cultural web can be used to understand culture in any of the frames of reference discussed above but is most often used at the organisational and/or functional levels in Exhibit 5.4.[34] The elements of the cultural web are as follows:

● The *paradigm* is at the core of Exhibit 5.5. In effect, the taken-for-granted assumptions and beliefs of the paradigm are the *collective experience* applied to a situation to make sense of it and inform a likely course of action. The assumptions of the paradigm may be very basic. For example, it may seem self-evident that a newspaper business's core assumptions are about the centrality of news coverage and reporting. However, from a strategic point of view, increasingly newspapers' revenues are reliant on advertising income and the strategy may need to be directed to this. The paradigm of a charity may be about doing good works for the needy: but this cannot be achieved if it is not run effectively for the purpose of raising money. So understanding what the paradigm is and how it informs debate on strategy matters. The problem is that, since it is unlikely to be talked about, trying to identify it can be difficult, especially if you are part of that organisation. Outside observers may find it relatively easy to identify simply by listening to what people say

Exhibit 5.7 The cultural web of an organisation

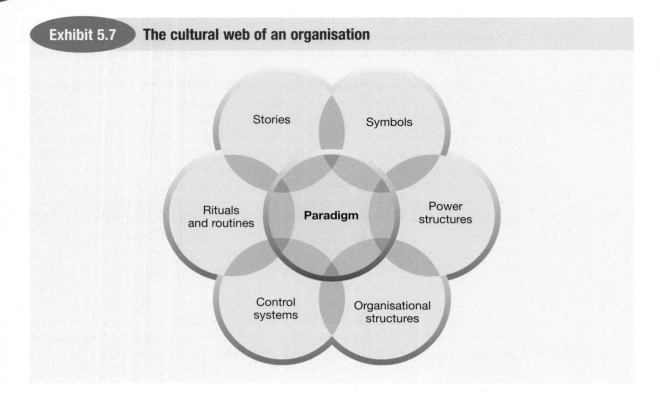

and watching what they do and emphasise, but this may not be so easy for insiders who are part of the culture. One way of 'insiders' getting to see the assumptions they take for granted is to focus initially on other aspects of the cultural web because these are to do with more visible manifestations of culture. Moreover, these other aspects are likely to act to reinforce the assumptions within that paradigm.

Routines are 'the way we do things around here on a day-to-day basis'.

- **Routines** are 'the way we do things around here' on a day-to-day basis. These may have a long history and may well be common across organisations (see section 5.3). At their best, these lubricate the working of the organisation, and may provide a distinctive organisational competence. However, they can also represent a taken-for-grantedness about how things should happen which, again, can be difficult to change.

Rituals are activities or events that emphasise, highlight or reinforce what is especially important in the culture.

- The **rituals** of organisational life are activities or events that emphasise, high-light or reinforce what is especially important in the culture. Examples include training programmes, interview panels, promotion and assessment proce-dures, sales conferences, and so on. An extreme example, of course, is the ritualistic training of army recruits to prepare them for the discipline required in conflict. However, rituals can also be informal activities such as drinks in the pub after work or gossiping around photocopying machines. A checklist of rituals is provided in Chapter 14 (see Exhibit 14.6).

- The *stories*[35] told by members of an organisation to each other, to outsiders, to new recruits, and so on, may act to embed the present in its organisational history and also flag up important events and personalities. They typically have to do with successes, disasters, heroes, villains and mavericks (who deviate from the norm). They can be a way of letting people know what is important in an organisation.

Symbols are objects, events, acts or people that convey, maintain or create meaning over and above their functional purpose

● **Symbols**[36] are objects, events, acts or people that convey, maintain or create meaning over and above their functional purpose. For example, offices and office layout, cars and titles have a functional purpose but are also typically signals about status and hierarchy. Particular people may come to represent specially important aspects of an organisation or historic turning points. The form of language used in an organisation can also be particularly revealing, especially with regard to customers or clients. For example, the head of a consumer protection agency in Australia described his clients as 'complainers'. In a major teaching hospital in the UK, consultants described patients as 'clinical material'. Whilst such examples might be amusing, they reveal an underlying assumption about customers (or patients) that might play a significant role in influencing the strategy of an organisation. Although symbols are shown separately in the cultural web, it should be remembered that many elements of the web are symbolic. So, routines, control and reward systems and structures are not only functional but also symbolic.

● *Power structures*. The most powerful groupings within an organisation are likely to be closely associated with the core assumptions and beliefs. For example, in firms that experience strategic drift, it is not unusual to find powerful executives who have long association with long-established ways of doing things. In analysing power the guidance given in Chapter 4 (section 4.4.2) is useful.

● *Organisational structure* is likely to reflect power and show important roles and relationships. Formal hierarchical, mechanistic structures may emphasise that strategy is the province of top managers and everyone else is 'working to orders'. Highly devolved structures (as discussed in Chapter 12) may signify that collaboration is less important than competition and so on.

● *Control systems*, measurements and reward systems emphasise what is important to monitor in the organisation. For example, public service organisations have often been accused of being concerned more with stewardship of funds than with quality of service. This is reflected in their procedures, which are more about accounting for spending rather than with quality of service. Individually based bonus schemes related to volume are likely to signal a culture of individuality, internal competition and an emphasis on sales volume rather than teamwork and an emphasis on quality.

Illustration 5.4 shows a cultural web drawn up by managers and staff in the Forestry Commission of the UK as part of a strategy development programme, together with a commentary on the significance of its elements. The key point to emerge was that at a time when this public body was charged with changing strategy towards opening up forests to the public, the staff saw themselves as technical experts and the public as a nuisance. Similar problems can often emerge through such an analysis. A cultural web analysis for an accountancy firm espousing closeness to clients as central to its strategy revealed a culture of 'partner care and centrality', rather than clients. Perhaps most significant, politicians and managers of the British Labour Party undertook a cultural web

Illustration 5.4

The cultural web of the UK Forestry Commission

The cultural web can be used to identify the behaviours and taken-for-granted assumptions of an organisation.

This is an adapted version of a cultural web produced by managers and staff of the UK Forestry Commission. The Forestry Commission (FC) was a public sector organisation charged with managing the forests of the UK.

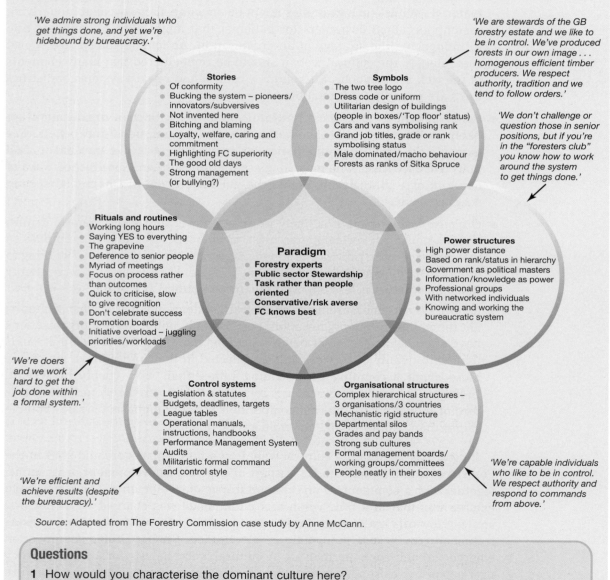

'We admire strong individuals who get things done, and yet we're hidebound by bureaucracy.'

'We are stewards of the GB forestry estate and we like to be in control. We've produced forests in our own image . . . homogenous efficient timber producers. We respect authority, tradition and we tend to follow orders.'

'We don't challenge or question those in senior positions, but if you're in the "foresters club" you know how to work around the system to get things done.'

Stories
- Of conformity
- Bucking the system – pioneers/innovators/subversives
- Not invented here
- Bitching and blaming
- Loyalty, welfare, caring and commitment
- Highlighting FC superiority
- The good old days
- Strong management (or bullying?)

Symbols
- The two tree logo
- Dress code or uniform
- Utilitarian design of buildings (people in boxes/'Top floor' status)
- Cars and vans symbolising rank
- Grand job titles, grade or rank symbolising status
- Male dominated/macho behaviour
- Forests as ranks of Sitka Spruce

Rituals and routines
- Working long hours
- Saying YES to everything
- The grapevine
- Deference to senior people
- Myriad of meetings
- Focus on process rather than outcomes
- Quick to criticise, slow to give recognition
- Don't celebrate success
- Promotion boards
- Initiative overload – juggling priorities/workloads

Paradigm
- **Forestry experts**
- **Public sector Stewardship**
- **Task rather than people oriented**
- **Conservative/risk averse**
- **FC knows best**

Power structures
- High power distance
- Based on rank/status in hierarchy
- Government as political masters
- Information/knowledge as power
- Professional groups
- With networked individuals
- Knowing and working the bureaucratic system

'We're doers and we work hard to get the job done within a formal system.'

Control systems
- Legislation & statutes
- Budgets, deadlines, targets
- League tables
- Operational manuals, instructions, handbooks
- Performance Management System
- Audits
- Militaristic formal command and control style

Organisational structures
- Complex hierarchical structures – 3 organisations/3 countries
- Mechanistic rigid structure
- Departmental silos
- Grades and pay bands
- Strong sub cultures
- Formal management boards/working groups/committees
- People neatly in their boxes

'We're efficient and achieve results (despite the bureaucracy).'

'We're capable individuals who like to be in control. We respect authority and respond to commands from above.'

Source: Adapted from The Forestry Commission case study by Anne McCann.

Questions

1 How would you characterise the dominant culture here?

2 What are the strategic implications?

analysis in the mid-1990s prior to their election victory of 1997. It revealed a party culturally 'built to oppose', as it had done with every government in power through its history – including Labour governments! Not surprisingly, Tony Blair, who became Prime Minister, saw culture change of the party as a major necessity.

5.4.7 Undertaking cultural analysis

If an analysis of the culture of an organisation is to be undertaken, there are some important issues to bear in mind:

- *The questions to ask.* Exhibit 5.8 outlines some of the questions that might help build up an understanding of culture using the cultural web.

- *Statements of cultural values.* As organisations increasingly make visible often carefully considered public statements of their values, beliefs and purposes – for example, in annual reports, mission or values statements and business plans – there is a danger that these are seen as useful and accurate descriptions of the organisational culture. But this is likely to be at best only partially true, and at worst misleading. This is not to suggest that there is any organised deception. It is simply that the statements of values and beliefs are often statements of the aspirations of a particular stakeholder (such as the CEO) rather than accurate descriptions of the actual culture. For example, an outside observer of a police force might conclude from its public statements of purpose and priorities that it had a balanced approach to the various aspects of police work – catching criminals, crime prevention, community relations. However, a deeper probing might quickly reveal that (in cultural terms) there is the 'real' police work (catching criminals) and the 'lesser work' (crime prevention, community relations).

- *Pulling it together.* The detailed 'map' produced by the cultural web is a rich source of information about an organisation's culture, but it is useful to be able to characterise the culture that the information conveys. Sometimes this is possible by means of graphic descriptors. For example, the managers who undertook a cultural analysis in the UK National Health Service (NHS) summed up their culture as 'The National Sickness Service'. Although this approach is rather crude and unscientific, it can be powerful in terms of organisational members seeing the organisation as it really is – which may not be immediately apparent from all of the detailed points in the cultural web. It can also help people to understand that culture drives strategies; for example, a 'national sickness service' would clearly prioritise strategies that are about spectacular developments in curing sick people above strategies of health promotion and prevention. So those favouring health promotion strategies need to understand that they are facing the need to change a culture and that in doing so they may not be able to assume that rational processes like planning and resource allocation will be enough (see Chapter 14).

The cultural analysis suggested in this chapter is also valuable in ways that relate to other parts of this book and the management of strategy:

- *Strategic capabilities.* As Chapter 3 makes clear, historically embedded capabilities are, very likely, part of the culture of the organisation. The cultural

Exhibit 5.8   **The cultural web: some useful questions**

Stories
- What core beliefs do stories reflect?
- How pervasive are these beliefs (through levels)?
- Do stories relate to:
  - strengths or weaknesses?
  - successes or failures?
  - conformity or mavericks?
- Who are the heroes and villains?
- What norms do the mavericks deviate from?

Symbols
- Are there particular symbols which denote the organisation?
- What status symbols are there?
- What does the language and jargon signify?
- What aspects of strategy are highlighted in publicity?

Routines and rituals
- Which routines are emphasised?
- Which are embedded in history?
- What behaviour do routines encourage?
- What are the key rituals?
- What core beliefs do they reflect?
- What do training programmes emphasise?
- How easy are rituals/routines to change?

Stories   Symbols

Routines and rituals   **Paradigm**   Power structures

Control systems   Organisational structures

Power structures
- How is power distributed in the organisation?
- What are the core assumptions and beliefs of the leadership?
- How strongly held are these beliefs (idealists or pragmatists)?
- Where are the main power blockages to change?

Control systems
- What is most closely monitored/controlled?
- Is emphasis on reward or punishment?
- Are controls related to history or current strategies?
- Are there many/few controls?

Organisational structures
- How mechanistic/organic are the structures?
- How flat/hierarchical are the structures?
- How formal/informal are the structures?
- Do structures encourage collaboration or competition?
- What types of power structure do they support?

Overall
- What do the answers to these questions suggest are the (four) fundemental assumptions that are the paradigm?
- How would you characterise the dominant culture?
- How easy is this to change?

analysis of the organisation therefore provides a complementary basis of analysis to an examination of strategic capabilities (see Chapter 3). In effect, such an analysis of capabilities should end up digging into the culture of the organisation, especially in terms of its routines, control systems and the everyday way in which the organisation runs, very likely on a 'taken-for-granted' basis.

- *Strategy development*. An understanding of organisational culture sensitises managers to the way in which historical and cultural influences will likely affect future strategy for good or ill. It therefore relates to the discussion on strategy development in Chapter 11.

- *Managing strategic change*. An analysis of the culture also provides a basis for the management of strategic change, since it provides a picture of the existing culture that can be set against a desired strategy so as to give insights as to what may constrain the development of that strategy or what needs to be changed in order to achieve it. This is discussed more extensively in Chapter 14.

- *Culture and experience*. There have been repeated references in this section to the role culture plays as a vehicle by which meaning is created in organisations. This was discussed more fully in the Commentary on the experience lens and provides a useful way in which many aspects of strategy can be considered (see the commentaries throughout the book).

5.5 MANAGING IN AN HISTORIC AND CULTURAL CONTEXT

History and culture are, then, important influences on the strategy of organisations. This leaves the challenging question of what managers can do about managing history and managing culture. Arguably there is little to be done about managing history; it has happened. There are, however, many examples in history of governments that have set about rewriting history and some would argue that corporations attempt to do much the same in their public relations. There is, however, a good deal written about the need to create or 'manage culture' (and it is a theme taken up in the context of managing strategic change in Chapter 14). This raises the question – or the challenge for managers – of just how realistic it is to be able to manage that which is taken for granted and historically based. This is the subject of the key debate in Illustration 5.5.

What is evident is that, if managers are to become path creators in strategy development, they need to be able to challenge, question and potentially change path dependent capabilities rooted in history and culture. To do this managers have, at the very least, to learn to be questioning of the very history that they have, perhaps, been part of or that has led to their existing positions. It should, therefore, be evident that one of the major requirements of a manager of strategy is to be able to encourage the questioning of that which is taken for granted. This may be possible through the sort of analytical tools covered in this chapter and in this book. However, it is also likely to require a management style – indeed a culture – that allows and encourages such questioning. If, on the other hand, the culture is such as to discourage such questioning, it is very unlikely that the lessons of history will be learned and much more likely that the dictates of history will be followed.

Illustration 5.5   **key debate**

Path dependency

Is history a powerful constraint on managers or an excuse for managerial inertia?

Brian Arthur, the Stanford economist, argued that when technologies compete for adoption, 'insignificant events may by chance give one of them an initial advantage in adoptions'. Such a technology may be technically inferior to alternatives but may then improve more than the others, so it may appeal to a wider proportion of potential adopters. It may therefore become further adopted and further improved. Thus it may happen that a technology that by chance gains an early lead in adoption may eventually 'corner the market' of potential adopters.

This has become known as 'path dependency', defined by Paul David as where 'important influences upon the eventual outcome can be exerted by temporally remote events, including happenings dominated by chance'. The result can be the unplanned 'lock-in' of that technology and the 'lock-out' of others.

Examples given of this include the QWERTY typewriter keyboard (see section 5.3.1), petrol cars over steam cars and the VHS video system over Betamax. All came to dominate, though the alternative systems were initially considered technically superior. The concept of path dependency has also come to be applied to strategy. Just as it may to be too expensive or too complex for managers to see it as worthwhile to change course to a potentially superior technology, so it may be for a strategy.

Others have argued that the notion of path dependency is exaggerated. Stephen Margolis and S.J. Liebowitz raise questions about the extent to which 'inferior technologies', persisting through path dependence, were really that inferior. For example, in typing contests typists using the QWERTY system were victorious over those who did not. And there were features of the VHS system preferred over Betamax when they were in competition.

In relation to public policy Adrian Kay also has reservations about the concept of path dependence. He likens it more to policies becoming institutionalised, taken for granted or just more complex: all creating problems for managing change, but none the less amenable to it. For example, there are many reasons why it is difficult to change the UK state pensions provision, not least the large sunk costs in the scheme and the shear complexity surrounding it. However, his studies show both policy stability and policy change and 'the notion of path dependency is only useful for accounting for the former'. Management can create the latter.

Luis Araujo and Debbie Harrison also argue that managers are not captured by history to the extent that path dependency suggests. Managers are able to make choices and overcome potential forces for inertia by having 'one foot in the past, the present and the future.' They are capable of reflecting on the benefits and disbenefits of history and doing something about it.

Sources:

L. Araujo and D. Harrison, 'Path dependence, agency and technological evolution', *Technology Analysis and Strategic Management*, vol. 14, no. 1 (2007), pp. 5–19.

W.B. Arthur, 'Competing technologies, increasing returns and lock in by historical events', *Economic Journal*, vol. 99 (1989), pp. 116–131.

P.A. David, 'Clio and the economics of QWERTY', *American Economic Review*, vol. 75 (1985), pp. 332–337.

A. Kay, 'A critique of the use of path dependency in policy studies', *Public Administration*, vol. 83, no. 3 (2005), pp. 553–571.

S.E. Margolis and S.J. Liebowitz, *Path Dependence: the New Palgrave of Economics and the Law*, 1998.

Questions

1 Summarise the arguments above in terms of the extent to which the authors believe that managers are locked into path-dependent histories.

2 Drawing on your own experience, and the arguments in this chapter and in the Commentaries, summarise the path dependency, institutional and cultural forces on managers.

3 What are your views about the extent to which such forces are a powerful constraining influences or an excuse for fatalism and management inertia?

SUMMARY

- The *history* and *culture* of an organisation may contribute to its strategic capabilities, but may also give rise to *strategic drift* as its strategy develops incrementally on the basis of such influences and fails to keep pace with a changing environment.

- Historical, *path-dependent* processes play a significant part in the success or failure of an organisation and need to be understood by managers. There are historical analyses that can be conducted to help uncover these influences.

- *Cultural* and *institutional influences* both inform and constrain the strategic development of organisations.

- Organisational culture is the basic assumptions and beliefs that are shared by members of an organisation, operate unconsciously and define in a basic taken-for-granted fashion an organisation's view of itself and its environment.

- An understanding of the culture of an organisation and its relationship to organisational strategy can be gained by using the *cultural web*.

Work assignments

*✶ Denotes more advanced work assignments.   * Refers to a case study in the Text and Cases edition.*

5.1 Identify four organisations that, in your view, are in the different phases of strategic drift (see Exhibit 5.2). Justify your selection.

5.2 ✶ In the context of section 5.3, undertake an historical analysis of the strategy development of an organisation and consider the question: 'Does history matter in managing strategy?'

5.3 Map out an organisational field (see section 5.4.2) within which an organisation of your choice operates. (As a basis for this you could for example use accountancy, a public sector organisation such as Direct and Care* or Formula One*.)

5.4 Identify (a) an organisation where its publicly stated values correspond with your experience of it and (b) one where they do not. Explain why (a) and (b) might be so.

5.5 Use the questions in Exhibit 5.8 to plot out a cultural web for Marks & Spencer A or an organisation of your choice.

5.6 ✶ By using a number of the examples from above, critically appraise the assertion that 'culture can only really be usefully analysed by the symptoms displayed in the way the organisation operates'. (You may wish to refer to Schein's book in the recommended key readings to assist you with this task.)

Integrative assignment

5.7 ✶ What is the relationship between strategic capabilities, competitive advantage, organisation culture, strategy development and the challenge of managing strategic change? (Refer to Chapters 3, 5, 6, 11 and 14.) Consider this in relation to a major change in strategy such as the development or adoption of a different basis of competitive strategy (see section 6.3) or the change to an e-business model.

An extensive range of additional materials, including audio summaries, weblinks to organisations featured in the text, definitions of key concepts and self-assessment questions, can be found on the *Exploring Corporate Strategy* Companion Website at **www.pearsoned.co.uk/ecs**

Recommended key readings

- For a more thorough explanation of the phenomenon of strategic drift see Gerry Johnson, 'Rethinking incrementalism', *Strategic Management Journal*, vol. 9 (1988), pp. 75–91; and 'Managing strategic change – strategy, culture and action', *Long Range Planning*, vol. 25, no. 1 (1992), pp. 28–36. (These papers also explain the cultural web.) Also see Donald S. Sull, 'Why good companies go bad', *Harvard Business Review*, July/August (1999), pp. 42–52.

- For an historical perspective on strategy see I. Greener, 'Theorizing path dependency: how does history come to matter in organizations?', *Management Decision*, vol. 40, no. 6 (2002), pp. 614–619; and

D.J. Jeremy, 'Business history and strategy', in A. Pettigrew, H. Thomas and A. Pettigrew (eds), *Handbook of Strategy and Management*, Sage, 2002, pp. 436–460.

- For a summary and illustrated explanation of institutional theory see Gerry Johnson and Royston Greenwood, 'Institutional theory and strategy', in Mark Jenkins and V. Ambrosini (eds), *Strategic Management: A Multiple-Perspective Approach*, Palgrave, 2007.

- For a comprehensive and critical explanation of organisational culture see Mats Alvesson, *Understanding Organizational Culture*, Sage, 2002.

References

1. For an explanation of strategic drift see G. Johnson, 'Rethinking incrementalism', *Strategic Management Journal*, vol. 9 (1988), pp. 75–91; and 'Managing strategic change – strategy, culture and action', *Long Range Planning*, vol. 25, no. 1 (1992), pp. 28–36. Also see E. Romanelli and M.L. Tushman, 'Organizational transformation as punctuated equilibrium: an empirical test', *Academy of Management Journal*, vol. 7, no. 5 (1994), pp. 1141–1166. They explain the tendency of strategies to develop very incrementally with periodic transformational change.

2. See D. Miller and P. Friesen, 'Momentum and revolution in organisational adaptation', *Academy of Management Journal*, vol. 23, no. 4 (1980), pp. 591–614.

3. See D. Leonard–Barton, 'Core capabilities and core rigidities: a paradox in managing new product development', *Strategic Management Journal*, vol. 13 (1992), pp. 111–125.

4. This is a term used by Donald S. Sull in accounting for the decline of high performing firms (see 'Why good companies go bad', *Harvard Business Review*, July/August (1999), pp. 42–52).

5. In the *Icarus Paradox* (D. Miller, Harper Collins, 1990) Danny Miller makes a convincing case that organisations' success leads to a number of potentially pathological tendencies, not least of which are the tendencies to inflate the durability of bases of success and to build future strategies relatively uncritically.

6. This research, known as the Successful Strategic Transformers (SST) Project, was in progress at the time of writing, a part of the UK Advanced Institute of Management Research initiative. The research was being undertaken

by Timothy Devinney, Gerry Johnson, George Yip and Manuel Hensmans.

7. The phrase 'Strategy as a pattern in a stream of decisions' is taken from H. Mintzberg, 'Patterns in strategy formation', *Management Science*, May (1978), pp. 934–948.

8. W.B. Arthur, 'Competing technologies, increasing returns and lock in by historical events', *Economic Journal*, vol. 99 (1989), 116–131.

9. P.A. David, 'Clio and the economics of QWERTY', *Economic History*, vol. 75, no. 2 (1985), pp. 332–337.

10. See I. Greener, 'Theorizing path dependency: how does history come to matter in organizations?', *Management Decision*, vol. 40, no. 6 (2002), pp. 614–619.

11. The world's biggest accounting firms have called for radical reform: 'Big four in call for real time accounts', *Financial Times*, 8 November (2006), p. 1.

12. From D. Holbrook, W. Cohen, D. Hounshell and S. Klepper, 'The nature, sources and consequences of firm differences in the early history of the semiconductor industry', *Strategic Management Journal*, vol. 21, nos 10–11 (2000), pp. 1017–1042.

13. This quote by André Malraux and the story of the BMW museum was provided by Mary Rose

14. See Holbrook *et al.*, reference 12.

15. Private correspondence with Mary Rose, the business historian, who suggests that: 'it links to Schumpeter and his notion of boundary crossing which may be between sectors, between technologies or informing the development and application of old technology with new knowledge'.

16. S. Klepper and K.L. Simons, 'Dominance by birthright: entry of prior radio producers and competitive ramifications in the US television receiver industry', *Strategic Management Journal*, vol. 21, nos 10–11 (2000), pp. 987–1016.

17. See J.R. Kimberley and H. Bouchikhi, 'The dynamics of organizational development and change: how the past shapes the present and constrains the future', *Organization Science*, vol. 6, no. 1 (1995), pp. 9–18.

18. This example is also taken from the SST research project referred to in reference 6.

19. Also see D.J. Jeremy, 'Business history and strategy', in A. Pettigrew, H. Thomas and R. Whittington (eds), *Handbook of Strategy and Management*, Sage, 2002, pp. 436–460.

20. For good examples of corporate histories see G. Jones, *Renewing Unilever: Transformation and Tradition*, Oxford University Press, 2005; R. Fitzgerald, *Rowntrees and the Marketing Revolution, 1862–1969*, Cambridge University Press, 1995; T.R. Gourvish, *British Railways 1948–73*, Cambridge University Press, 1986.

21. Walsh and Ungson make the point that 'Organisational memory' is stored in a number of ways but these include shared interpretations and individual recollections. See J.P. Walsh and G.R. Ungson, 'Organizational memory', *Academy of Management Review*, vol. 16, no. 1 (1991), pp. 57–91.

22. This quote is from S. Finkelstein, 'Why smart executives fail: four case histories of how people learn the wrong lessons from history', *Business History*, vol. 48, no. 2 (2006), pp. 153–170.

23. See C. Geertz, *The Interpretation of Culture*, Basic Books, 1973, p. 12; and M. Alvesson, *Understanding Organizational Culture*, Sage, 2002, p. 3.

24. This definition of culture is taken from E. Schein, *Organisational Culture and Leadership*, 2nd edition, Jossey-Bass, 1997, p. 6.

25. See G. Hofstede, *Culture's Consequences*, 2nd edition, Sage, 2001. For a critique of Hofstede's work see B. McSweeney, 'Hofstede's model of national cultural differences and their consequences: a triumph of faith – a failure of analysis', *Human Relations*, vol. 55, no. 1 (2002), pp. 89–118.

26. On cross-cultural management also see R. Lewis, *When Cultures Collide: Managing successfully across cultures*, 2nd edition, Brealey, 2000, a practical guide for managers. It offers an insight into different national cultures, business conventions and leadership styles. Also S. Schneider and J.-L. Barsoux, *Managing Across Cultures*, 2nd edition, Financial Times/Prentice Hall, 2003. T. Jackson, 'Management ethics and corporate policy: a cross-cultural comparison', *Journal of Management Studies*, vol. 37, no. 3 (2000), pp. 349–370, looks at how national culture influences management ethics and provides a useful link to section 4.4 of this book.

27. A useful review of research on this topic is T. Dacin, J. Goodstein and R. Scott, 'Institutional theory and institutional change: introduction to the special research forum', *Academy of Management Journal*, vol. 45, no. 1 (2002), pp. 45–57. For a more general review see G. Johnson and R. Greenwood, 'Institutional theory and strategy', in Mark Jenkins and V. Ambrosini (eds), *Strategic Management: A Multiple-Perspective Approach*, Palgrave, 2007.

28. This definition is taken from W. Scott, *Institutions and Organizations*, Sage, 1995.

29. The term 'recipe' was introduced to refer to *industries* by J. Spender, *Industry Recipes: The nature and sources of management judgement*, Blackwell, 1989. We have broadened its use by applying it to *organisational fields*. The fundamental idea that behaviours are driven by a collective set of norms and values remains unchanged.

30. D. Deephouse, 'To be different or to be the same? It's a question (and theory) of strategic balance', *Strategic Management Journal*, vol. 20, no. 2 (1999), pp. 147–166.

31. E. Schein, *Organisation Culture and Leadership*, 2nd edition, Jossey-Bass, 1997, and A. Brown, *Organisational Culture*, FT/Prentice Hall, 1998, are useful in understanding the relationship between organisational culture and strategy. For a useful critique of the concept of organisational culture see M. Alvesson, *Understanding Organizational Culture*, Sage, 2002.

32. Exhibit 5.4 is adapted from the original in P. Grinyer and J.C. Spender, *Turnaround: Managerial Recipes for Strategic Success*, Associated British Press, (1979) p. 203.

33. A fuller explanation of the cultural web can be found in G. Johnson, *Strategic Change and the Management Process*, Blackwell, 1987, and 'Managing strategic change: strategy, culture and action', *Long Range Planning*, vol. 25, no. 1 (1992), pp. 28–36. Also forthcoming at the time of writing is G. Johnson and A. McCann, *Changing Strategy: Changing Culture*, FT Publications.

34. A practical explanation of cultural web mapping can be found in G. Johnson, 'Mapping and re-mapping organisational culture', in V. Ambrosini with G. Johnson and K. Scholes (eds), *Exploring Techniques of Analysis and Evaluation in Strategic Management*, Prentice Hall, 1998.

35. See A.L. Wilkins, 'Organisational stories as symbols which control the organisation', in L.R. Pondy, P.J. Frost, G. Morgan and T.C. Dandridge (eds), *Organisational Symbolism*, JAI Press, 1983.

36. The significance of organisational symbolism is explained in G. Johnson, 'Managing strategic change: the role of symbolic action', *British Journal of Management*, vol. 1, no. 4 (1990), pp. 183–200.

Marks & Spencer (A)

Nardine Collier

The M&S formula for success

Michael Marks began his penny bazaars in the late 1880s. He soon decided he needed a partner to help run the growing firm and Tom Spencer, a cashier of Marks' supplier, was recommended. From this partnership Marks & Spencer (M&S) steadily grew. Simon Marks took over the running of M&S from his father, turning the penny bazaars into stores, establishing a simple pricing policy and introducing the 'St Michael' logo as a sign of quality. There was a feeling of camaraderie and a close-knit family atmosphere within the stores, with staff employed whom the managers believed would 'fit in' and become part of that family. The staff were also treated better and paid more than in other companies. The family nature of this firm dominated top management too: until the late 1970s the board was made up of family members only.

Marks was renowned for his personal, top-down, autocratic management style and his attention to detail. This also manifested itself in the way he dealt with suppliers. He always used the same UK-based suppliers and meticulously ensured that goods were exactly to specification, a relationship designed to build reliance of the suppliers and ensure high and consistent quality.

Until the late 1990s M&S was hugely successful in terms of profit and market share, running its operations according to a set of fundamental principles; namely to:

- offer customers high-quality, well-designed and attractive merchandise at reasonable prices under the brand name St Michael;

Photo: Charles Hewitt/Picture Post/Getty Images

- encourage suppliers to use the most modern and efficient production techniques;
- work with suppliers to ensure the highest standards of quality control;
- provide friendly, helpful service and greater shopping comfort and convenience to customers;
- improve the efficiency of the business, by simplifying operating procedures;
- foster good human relations with customers, suppliers and staff and in the communities in which M&S trade.

Its specialist buyers operated from a central buying office from which goods were allocated to the stores. The store managers followed central direction on merchandising, layout, store design and training. Every M&S store was identical in the procedures it followed, leading to a consistency of image and a guarantee of M&S standards. However, it also meant store managers were severely restricted in how they could respond to the local needs of customers.

During M&S's growth there were few changes to its methods of operation or strategies. Its reputation for good-quality clothing was built on basics, the essentials which every customer needed and would outlast the current fashion and trends seen in other high street retailers. As it did not have fitting rooms till the 1990s, all assistants carried tape measures and M&S would give a 'no quibble' refund to any customer who was unhappy with the product he or she had purchased. As its products remained in the stores all year round for most of its history it never held sales.

The success of M&S continued into the 1990s. Richard Greenbury, the CEO from 1991, explained this success:

we followed absolutely and totally the principles of the business with which I was embued. . . . I ran the business with the aid of my colleagues based upon the very long standing, and proven ways of running it. (Radio 4, August 2000)

Successive chief executives were renowned for their attention to detail in terms of supplier control, merchandise and store layout; and it seemed to work. M&S's success under Marks was often attributed to his understanding of customer preferences and trends. However, because of this, it could also mean that buyers tended to select merchandise which they knew chief executives would approve of. For example, since it was known Greenbury did not want M&S to be at the cutting edge of fashion, buyers concentrated on the types of product they knew he would like – 'classic, wearable fashions'.

There were other problems of centralised authority. On one occasion Greenbury had decided that to control costs there would be less full-time sales assistants. Although this led to an inability in stores to meet the service levels required by M&S, when Greenbury visited, all available employees were brought in so that it appeared the stores were giving levels of service that, at other times, they were not. It also meant there was little disagreement with directives from the top, so policies and decisions remained unchallenged even when executives or store managers were concerned about negative effects. Customer satisfaction surveys that showed decreasing satisfaction throughout the late 1990s

were kept from Greenbury by senior executives who felt he might be annoyed by the results.

A hitch in the formula

M&S's problems began to hit the headlines in October 1998 when it halted its expansion programme in Europe and America and in November announced a 23 per cent decline in first-half profits, causing its shares to fall drastically. Greenbury blamed a turbulent competitive environment, saying that M&S had lost sales and market share to its competitors from both the top and bottom ends of the retail market. Competitors at the top end of the market, such as the Gap, Oasis and Next, offered similarly priced goods, but more design focused with up-to-date fashions. At the bottom end, Matalan and supermarkets ranges such as the 'George' range at Asda offered basic clothing at significantly lower prices. Moreover, Tesco and Sainsbury's were now offering added value foods which had been pioneered by M&S.

Commentators suggested that M&S no longer understood or reacted to its customers' needs. It misread its target market, and could not understand that customers who purchased food or underwear might not want products from its home furnishings range. It had continued too long with its traditional formula and ignored changes in the marketplace. Greenbury was too focused on the day-to-day operations of the firm rather than long-term strategy. M&S was tied to a generalised view of the market, instead of trying to understand and tailor offerings to the various market segments. It had no loyalty card at a time when almost every other retailer did. Although a large proportion of M&S customers were women and much of the merchandise was womenswear, top management were dominated by men. Almost all managers and executives were promoted internally, starting at the bottom of the organisation and becoming immersed in its routines and traditions. It had an inward-looking culture strongly reinforced by Greenbury and his autocratic approach.

In November 1998, Greenbury announced that he would be stepping down. There followed a series of heavily publicised arguments between Keith Oates, Greenbury's deputy, and Peter Salsbury, another director, whom the media suggested was Greenbury's favoured successor. It was Salsbury who was eventually appointed as CEO. Oates elected to take early retirement. Analysts commented that, as Salsbury had only worked in womenswear, one of the worst-performing units in M&S, it might have been wiser to bring in an outsider.

During this period of boardroom scuffles, M&S's problems were compounded by its £192m (€270m) purchase of 19 Littlewoods department stores. These required refurbishment at a cost of £100m at the same time as existing M&S stores were being refurbished. The disruption had a far worse effect on customers than M&S had expected, leading Greenbury to describe the clothing section as a 'bloodbath'. In January 1999 M&S announced its second profits warning. It had been a bad Christmas trading period made worse by M&S overestimating sales and buying £250m worth of stock that then had to be heavily discounted.

New tactics . . . but more problems

In an attempt to regain confidence, Salsbury implemented a restructuring strategy, splitting the company into three: UK retail business, overseas business and financial services. He also established a company-wide marketing department to break down the power of the traditional buying fiefdoms established around product lines. The marketing department would adopt a customer-focused approach, rather than allowing buyers to dictate what the stores should stock. There were new clothing and food ranges, reinforced by a large-scale promotional campaign, to attempt to restore its image as an innovative retailer offering unique, quality products. Explaining that he wanted to move away from a bureaucratic culture by creating a decision-making environment that was unencumbered by hierarchy, Salsbury stripped away of layers of hierarchy and established a property division so that rents were charged to stores to make store managers more accountable for branch performance.

In June Greenbury retired a year early, a decision which came just before the board entered a three-day meeting to discuss 'a few hundred pages of its new strategy'. Salsbury commented:

What we are doing has moved away from his [Greenbury's] methodology and thought processes . . . decisions were reached without him being able to have an input. (*Financial Times*, 23 June 1999)

In September M&S stated that it was in the process of overseas sourcing while severing links with some UK suppliers, streamlining international operations, diversifying into home and Internet shopping, and creating a department dedicated to identifying new business opportunities. However, customers continued to voice their concerns regarding the clothing range:

There are so many items here to find and they don't tend to segregate it out, so there's something I might like next to something my granny might like. (*Financial Times*, 28 September 1999)

By November M&S had more bad news for its shareholders when it revealed its shares had fallen to the lowest price since 1991. There followed reports of Tesco, American pension fund companies and Philip Green, the retail entrepreneur, being interested in acquiring M&S. To counteract these rumours M&S implemented another management restructuring to become more customer focused, establishing seven business units: lingerie, womenswear, menswear, childrenswear, food, home, and beauty. Executives were appointed at just below board level to head the units, reporting directly to Salsbury who believed the flatter structure allowed M&S to be more responsive to market changes and customer needs.

A new horizon

In January 2000 Luc Vandevelde was appointed chairman. Belgian-born Vandevelde had left his managing director role at Promodés, the French food retailer, where he had achieved a sixfold increase in stock value. This was the first time anyone from outside M&S had been appointed to the position of chairman.

In the next two years there followed more changes. He unveiled an exclusive clothes collection from haute couture designers. Purchasing of the clothing range was shifted to almost 100 per cent Asian sources. M&S stopped using its famous green carrier bags, and relegated the St Michael logo to inside clothing. Stores were grouped on the basis of demographic characteristics and lifestyle patterns, instead of operating with the old system which allocated merchandise dependent on floor space. Still the fortunes of the company declined. In May 2000 M&S announced a fall in profit of £71.2m.

There was another restructuring into five operating divisions: UK retail; international retail; financial services; property; and ventures. Within the UK retail division seven customer business units were established, and to ensure customer focus each unit would have dedicated buying and selling teams. There was further store modernisation; more customer advisers on the shop floor; and the opening of three prototype stores where all new initiatives and concepts would be tested. M&S disclosed plans to offer clothes at a discounted price in factory outlet malls. Early in 2001 it announced its plans to withdraw from its stores in Europe and Brooks Brothers in America and franchise those in Hong Kong. In the midst of this, in September 2000, Salsbury retired.

Discussing the still disappointing end-of-year results, Vandevelde scaled back on the promises he had made on his arrival for recovery within two years. However, he was confident that he had the right recipe for recovery, it was just a matter of time.

There followed the decision to move out of its headquarters in Baker Street, London, and into a new building in Paddington. For those who had worked in M&S's headquarters, the grey and imposing building symbolised much that had gone wrong with the retailer. Its endless corridors were described as Kremlin-like, and the small individual offices reflected the status of the occupant by the thickness of the carpet. Former managers described the building as 'oppressive', with facilities that were not conducive to modern working practices, few casual meeting rooms, and a highly structured hierarchy for the 4,000 employees who worked there. Commentators were delighted with the move; they felt it showed M&S was at last tackling the problems at its core, not just altering merchandise and store layout.

It was not till the end of November 2001 that there were signs of an upturn in trading performance. This followed the arrival of Yasmin Yousef, a new creative designer, and the much heralded collaboration with George Davies, founder of Next and the creator of the 'George' clothing range at Asda. Davies introduced the Per Uno women's range targeted at 25–35 fashion-conscious customers to compete with brands like Mango and Kookai. Davies had secured a deal whereby he owned Per Una, and retained the profits from supplying M&S. To operate so autonomously he had invested £21m of his own money. He was therefore designing, manufacturing and distributing the clothes independently of M&S.

In 2001 Vandevelde also head-hunted Roger Holmes to be Head of UK Retailing. Holmes started his career as a consultant for McKinsey, moving to become Financial Director of DIY chain B&Q, Managing Director of retailers Woolworths, and finally Chief of Electricals for the Kingfisher group. Was a new era for M&S beginning?

Sources:

BBC2, 'Sparks at Marks', *The Money Programme*, 1 November (2000).

BBC2, 'Marks and Spencer', *Trouble at the Top*, 6 December (2001).

G. Beaver, 'Competitive advantage and corporate governance: shop soiled and needing attention, the case of Marks and Spencer plc', *Strategic Change*, vol. 8 (1999), pp. 325–334.

J. Bevan, *The rise and fall of Marks and Spencer*, Profile Books, (2001).

Channel 4, 'Inside Marks and Spencer', 25 February (2001).

Radio 4, Interview with Sir Richard Greenbury, 22 August (2000).

G. Rees, *St Michael: A history of Marks and Spencer*, Weidenfeld and Nicolson, (1969).

K. Tse, *Marks and Spencer: Anatomy of Britain's most efficiently managed company*, Pergamon, (1985).

Questions

1 Analyse the organisational culture of M&S in the 1990s.

2 Why was M&S so successful for so long?

3 Why did it suffer the downturn in the 1990s?

4 Why did the changes made from 1998 to 2001 fail to overcome the problems?

Part I of the book has discussed some of the main influences that managers in organisations have to take into account in developing the strategies of their organisations. The underlying theme here is that reconciling these different forces is problematic. Not only are there many of them, but also their effects are difficult to predict and they are likely to change, creating potentially high levels of uncertainty. The forces may also be in conflict with one another, or pulling in different directions. Understanding the strategic position of an organisation is therefore challenging for managers.

In this commentary the four strategy lenses introduced in the initial Commentary are now used to reconsider *how managers can and do make sense of the strategic position they face* and some of the key issues discussed in the chapters in Part I. Note that:

- There is no suggestion here that one of these lenses is better than another, but they do provide different insights into the problems faced and the ways managers cope with the challenge.
- If you have *not* read the Commentary following Chapter 1 that explains the four lenses, you should now do so.

Design lens

The concepts and analytic tools of strategy can be used to understand the complex and uncertain world managers face in developing strategy. So it makes sense to:

- Undertake rigorous analysis of environmental forces, strategic capabilities, stakeholder power and cultural influences.
- Build scenarios to sensitise possible futures.
- Integrate the insights from such analyses into a clear view of the strategic position.
- Involve managers in such analysis through systematic strategic planning.

A clear understanding of the strategic position by managers is then helpful in their managing the development of a future strategy because it provides a basis upon which they can consider how different strategic options might address the issues identified.

Experience lens

Managers' individual or collective experience based on prior events is drawn upon by them to make sense of the strategic position of the organisation. This can be useful because it provides short-cuts in sense making. It is, however, also dangerous because such experience becomes fixed, determines how stimuli are made sense of and biases responses to such stimuli. An uncertain future is therefore likely to be understood in terms of past experience that acts as an 'uncertainty reduction mechanism'.

The strategic capabilities (especially core competences) that have driven past success are likely to have become embedded in its history and organisational culture. Over time this may well give rise to strategic drift.

Questioning and challenging that which is taken for granted is vital. It is at least as important to surface the assumptions that managers have as to undertake careful strategic analysis, because it is likely to be such assumptions that are driving strategic decisions. A major role of the frameworks of analysis described in Part I is to do just this.

Commentary on Part I

The Strategic Position

Ideas lens

It is not possible to reduce uncertainty sufficiently to arrive at a clear strategic position upon which strategies can be rationally evaluated. Knowledge and understanding of the bases of the strategic position of the organisation can never be sufficiently complete. Indeed, rigorous analysis may foster conformity and a 'right way' of seeing things.

However, the ambiguity and uncertainty of the future may be beneficial in that it can give rise to a variety of different perspectives that can stimulate new ideas from within and around the organisation. These new ideas are just as likely to bubble up from below as be originated at the top of an organisation. So, if innovation is important, managers need to learn how to foster and harness such variety.

Managers may not be able to determine an objectively based 'right' view of the strategic position of their organisation, but they may be able to establish a sufficiently clear overarching vision or a set of 'simple rules' that allows for the necessary variety to encourage the emergence of new ideas.

With regard to strategic drift, there are different views here:

- That sufficient variety could give rise to new ideas and experimentation that help avoid drift.
- That drift is an inevitability but that the resulting instability will itself help generate new ideas and be an opportunity for renewal.

Discourse lens

The strategic position of an organisation is not so much a matter of objective 'fact' as that which is represented and privileged in the discourse of major stakeholders and powerful people, for example a CEO, investors, government. What such stakeholders say shows how influential people are making sense of their strategic position and the key issues that are driving the strategy of organisations. This has a very real influence on organisations' strategies.

Discourse is also linked to identity. So:

- Each stakeholder has their own identity and associated with this is their own way of talking about their relationship to the strategy of an organisation. This is a route to understanding stakeholder interest and influence.
- The concepts and tools associated with strategy can be employed by managers so that they can look as though they have insights that give them a special place with regard to the destiny of the organisation. In this sense strategy discourse is linked to power.
- People get locked into their ways of talking about their strategic perspective. It can be difficult to change this. In this sense dominant discourse can contribute to strategic drift.

STRATEGIC CHOICES

This part explains strategic choices in terms of:

→ How an organisation positions itself in relation to competitors in terms of its overall competitive strategy.

→ The scope and diversity of an organisation's products and therefore the nature of its corporate portfolio and how that portfolio is managed.

→ The geographic scope of the organisation and the bases of its international strategy.

→ The extent to which and how it seeks to foster innovation and entrepreneurial endeavour.

→ Ways in which it might pursue strategic options in terms of organic development, acquisitions or joint ventures.

→ The criteria and tools by which these choices might be evaluated.

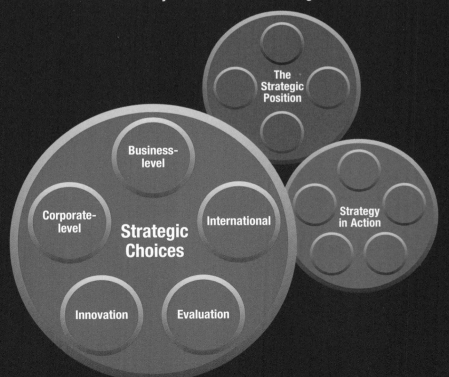

Introduction to Part II

Strategic choices are concerned with decisions about an organisation's future and the way in which it needs to respond to the many pressures and influences discussed in Part I of the book. In turn, the consideration of future strategies must be mindful of the realities of translating strategy into action which, in turn, can be significant constraints on strategic choice.

There are three overarching choices to be made as shown in Exhibit II.i. These are:

- The choices as to *how an organisation positions itself in relation to competitors*. This is a matter of deciding the overall basis of how to compete in a market. For example, if the aim is to pursue a strategy that provides lasting superior financial performance, is this to be achieved by competitive advantage on the basis of price or differentiation? Or is competitive advantage possible through being more flexible and fleeter of foot than competitors? Or is a more cooperative approach to competitors appropriate? These questions are addressed in Chapter 6.

- The choices of *products and markets for an organisation*. Should the organisation be very focused on just a few products and markets? Or should it be much broader in scope, perhaps very diversified in terms of both products (or services) and markets? This raises questions of corporate strategy addressed

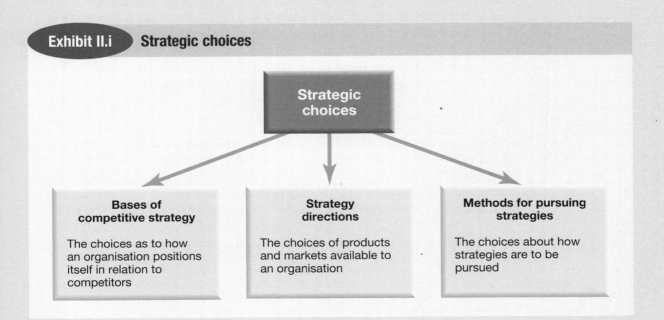

| Exhibit II.i | Strategic choices |

Strategic choices

Bases of competitive strategy	Strategy directions	Methods for pursuing strategies
The choices as to how an organisation positions itself in relation to competitors	The choices of products and markets available to an organisation	The choices about how strategies are to be pursued

in Chapter 7, international strategy in Chapter 8 and the extent of innovative and entrepreneurial endeavour in the organisation, which is discussed in Chapter 9.

● The choices about *how strategies are to be pursued.* For any of these choices, should they be pursued by organic development, acquisitions or through joint ventures with other organisations? This is the theme of the first part of Chapter 10.

This part of the book also asks:

● *How are these choices to be evaluated?* What are the criteria that might be used and the tools that are useful for this? This is the theme of the second part of Chapter 10.

The discussion in these chapters provides explanations and rationales for a wide range of strategic options. However, a word of warning: there is a potentially misleading distinction between undertaking the sort of strategy analysis that was explained in Part I of the book and considering the choices discussed in Part II. In two respects, they are not separate and disconnected:

1 *Key strategic issues.* The choices described here have to be considered in the context of the understanding of an organisation's strategic position. Here it is important that there is clarity on the *key strategic issues.* This means that strategists should be able to identify the really important issues that a strategy has to address from the very many other issues that, no doubt, will have arisen in their analysis. Too often the outcome of such analysis is a very long list of observations without any clarity of what such key issues are. There is no 'strategy tool' for this. This is a matter of informed judgement and, because managers usually work in groups, of debate. The analytic tools provided can help inform, but are not a substitute for judgement.

2 *Strategic analysis generates strategic options.* Part I of the book has provided ways in which strategists can identify forces at work in the business environment (Chapter 2), identify and build on strategic capabilities (Chapter 3), meet stakeholder expectations (Chapter 4) and build on the benefits, as well as be aware of the constraints of their organisation's historical and cultural context (Chapter 5). In understanding these different forces the strategist will have also begun to generate ideas and raise questions that generate strategic options. Identifying strategic options is therefore not restricted to the concepts in the chapters of Part II.

Another way of thinking about the link between Parts I and II of the book is by means of one of the most commonly used tools of strategy development. It is quite likely that the output of a strategic analysis may be pulled together in the form of a SWOT analysis (see section 3.6.4 and Illustration 3.5). This can also be used as a way of generating strategic options by using the TOWS matrix* as shown in Exhibit II.ii. This builds directly on the information in a SWOT analysis. Each box of the TOWS matrix can be used to identify options that address a

---

* See H . Weihrich 'The TOWS matrix – a tool for situational analysis', *Long Range Planning*, April (1982), pp. 54–66.

Exhibit II.ii   The TOWS matrix

		Internal factors	
		Strengths (S)	**Weaknesses (W)**
External factors	**Opportunities (O)**	**SO Strategic options** Generate options here that use strengths to take advantage of opportunities	**WO Strategic options** Generate options here that take advantage of opportunities by overcoming weaknesses
	Threats (T)	**ST Strategic options** Generate options here that use strengths to avoid threats	**WT Strategic options** Generate options here that minimise weaknesses and avoid threats

different combination of the internal factors (strengths and weaknesses) and the external factors (opportunities and threats). For example, the top left-hand box prompts a consideration of options that use the strengths of the organisation to take advantage of opportunities in the business environment. An example might be the extension of sales into an adjacent geographical market where demand is expected to grow quickly. The bottom right-hand box prompts options that minimise weaknesses and also avoid threats; for example, the avoidance of major competitors by focusing activities on specialist niches that the organisation is capable of servicing successfully.

6

Business-Level Strategy

LEARNING OUTCOMES

After reading this chapter you should be able to:

→ Identify strategic business units (SBUs) in organisations.

→ Explain bases of achieving competitive advantage in terms of 'routes' on the strategy clock.

→ Assess the extent to which these are likely to provide sustainable competitive advantage.

→ Identify strategies suited to hypercompetitive conditions.

→ Explain the relationship between competition and collaboration.

→ Employ principles of game theory in relation to competitive strategy.

6.1 INTRODUCTION

This chapter is about a fundamental strategic choice: what competitive strategy to adopt in order to gain competitive advantage in a market at the business unit level. For example, faced with increasing competition from low-price airlines, should British Airways seek to compete on price or maintain and improve its strategy of differentiation? Exhibit 6.1 shows the main themes that provide the structure for the rest of the chapter:

- First, *strategic business units (SBUs)* are explained. Most organisations have a number of SBUs, because they compete in different markets or market segments. These SBUs may or may not be organisationally separate but it may be necessary to consider if different competitive strategies are required for them. So it helps to identify the SBUs of an organisation.
- Next, *bases of competitive strategy* available to SBUs are considered. These include price-based strategies, differentiation strategies, hybrid and focus strategies.
- The later sections consider *ways of achieving competitive advantage*. This starts in section 6.4 by explaining bases for the *sustainability of competitive strategy* over time.
- However, in a fast-changing and uncertain world the sustainability of competitive advantage can be problematic, so other ways of competing successfully are discussed. The idea of *hypercompetition* (introduced in section 2.3.2) is revisited in section 6.5 to consider lessons for strategic choices.
- The potential benefits of *cooperative* strategies with competitors are then discussed in section 6.6.
- Finally *game theory* is introduced as a way of achieving advantage through an understanding of the interdependence of competitors' actions (section 6.7).

Exhibit 6.1 Business-level strategies

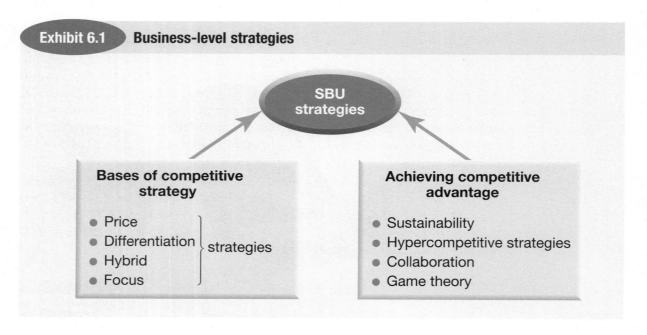

6.2   IDENTIFYING STRATEGIC BUSINESS UNITS

A strategic business unit (SBU) is a part of an organisation for which there is a distinct external market for goods or services that is different from another SBU

KEY CONCEPT

SBU

A **strategic business unit (SBU)** is a part of an organisation for which there is a distinct external market for goods or services that is different from another SBU. The identification of an organisation's SBUs helps the development of business-level strategies since these may need to vary from one SBU to another. In the sections that follow in the rest of this chapter the concepts discussed therefore relate to the SBUs that have been identified. The identification of SBUs does, however, raise three other issues considered briefly here but also elsewhere in the book:

- *A confusion of SBUs.* Since bases of competitive strategy may need to differ by markets (or market segment) the SBUs considered need to reflect this. However, potentially, managers may subdivide markets into many segments based on different criteria (see Exhibit 2.7). The result could be unmanageable in terms of identifying compatible bases of competitive strategy. So sensible judgements need to be made about which SBUs are most useful for strategy-making purposes.

- *Corporate complexity.* Similarly, too many SBUs can create excessive complexity in developing corporate-level strategy (see Chapter 7).

- *Organisational structure.* An SBU is an organisational unit for strategy-making purposes. An organisation may not actually be structured on the basis of SBUs, so consideration needs to be given to the relationship of SBUs and organisational design (see Chapter 13).[1] In the public sector the frequent 'repackaging' of activities within ministries in central government shows how difficult these judgements can be. For example, in the UK over the last few decades 'Education' has been partnered with 'Science', then 'Employment' and then with 'Skills'

There are external and internal criteria that can help in identifying appropriate SBUs:

- *Market-based criteria.* Different parts of an organisation might be regarded as the same SBU if they are targeting the same *customer types*, through the same sorts of *channels* and facing similar *competitors*. For example, a 'unit' tailoring products or services to specific local needs is a different SBU from one that offers standardised products or services globally. So are units that offer the same products to a customer group through significantly different channels (for example, retailing to consumers versus direct selling via the Internet).

- *Capabilities-based criteria.* Parts of an organisation should only be regarded as the same SBU if they have similar strategic capabilities. So for a food manufacturer branded goods should probably be considered a different SBU from retail 'own-brand' goods even though they are selling to the same end customers through the same channels.

6.3   BASES OF COMPETITIVE ADVANTAGE: THE 'STRATEGY CLOCK'

Competitive strategy is concerned with the basis on which a business unit might achieve competitive advantage in its market

KEY CONCEPT

Strategy clock

This section reviews different ways of thinking about **competitive strategy**, the bases on which a business unit might achieve competitive advantage in its market. For public service organisations, the equivalent concern is the bases on which the organisation chooses to achieve superior quality of services in competition with others for funding; that is, how it provides 'best value'.

Michael Porter[2] proposed three different 'generic' strategies by which an organisation could achieve competitive advantage: 'overall cost leadership', 'differentiation' and 'focus'. There is much debate as to exactly what each of these categories means. In particular many confuse Porter's 'cost leadership' with 'low price'. To remove such confusions this book employs 'market-facing' generic strategies similar to those used by Cliff Bowman and Richard D'Aveni.[3] These are based on the principle that competitive advantage is achieved by providing customers with what they want, or need, better or more effectively than competitors. Building on this proposition, the strategy clock (Exhibit 6.2) enshrines Porter's categories of differentiation and focus alongside price – as discussed in the sections below.

In a competitive situation, customers make choices on the basis of their perception of value for money, the combination of price and perceived product/service benefits. The 'strategy clock' represents different positions in a market where customers (or potential customers) have different 'requirements' in terms of value for money. These positions also represent a set of generic strategies for achieving competitive advantage. Illustration 6.1 shows examples of different competitive strategies followed by firms in terms of these different positions on the strategy clock. The discussion of each of these strategies that follows also acknowledges the importance of an organisation's costs – particularly relative to competitors. But it will be seen that cost is a strategic consideration for all strategies on the clock – not just those where the lead edge is low price.

Since these strategies are 'market facing' it is important to understand the critical success factors for each position on the clock. Customers at positions 1 and 2 are primarily concerned with price, but only if the product/service benefits meet their threshold requirements as discussed in Chapter 2 (section 2.4.3). This usually means that customers emphasise functionality over service or aspects such as design or packaging. In contrast, customers at position 5 require a customised product or service for which they are prepared to pay a price premium. The volume of demand in a market is unlikely to be evenly spread across the positions on the clock. In commodity-like markets demand is substantially weighted towards positions 1 and 2. Many public services are of this type too. Other markets have significant demand in positions 4 and 5. Historically professional services were of this type. However, markets change over time. Commodity-like markets develop value-added niches which grow as disposable incomes rise. For example, this has occurred in the drinks market with premium and speciality beers. And customised markets may become more commodity-like particularly where IT can demystify and routinise the professional content of the product – as in financial services.

So the strategy clock can help managers understand the changing requirements of their markets and the choices they can make about positioning and competitive advantage. Each position on the clock will now be discussed.

Exhibit 6.2   **The strategy clock: competitive strategy options**

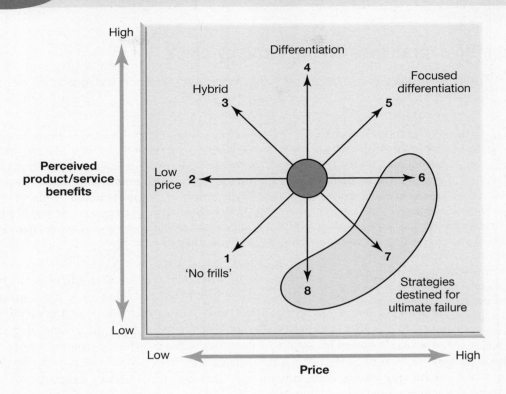

		Needs/risks
1	'No frills'	Likely to be segment specific
2	Low price	Risk of price war and low margins; need to be cost leader
3	Hybrid	Low cost base and reinvestment in low price and differentiation
4	Differentiation (a) Without price premium	Perceived added value by user, yielding market share benefits
	(b) With price premium	Perceive added value sufficient to bear price premium
5	Focused differentiation	Perceived added value to a particular segment, warranting price premium
6	Increased price/standard value	Higher margins if competitors do not follow; risk of losing market share
7	Increased price/low value	Only feasible in monopoly situation
8	Low value/standard price	Loss of market share

Items 3, 4, 5 bracketed as: **Differentiation**

Items 6, 7, 8 bracketed as: **Likely failure**

Note: The strategy clock is adapted from the work of Cliff Bowman (see D. Faulkner and C. Bowman, *The Essence of Competitive Strategy*, Prentice Hall, 1995). However, Bowman uses the dimension 'Perceived Use Value'.

Illustration 6.1

Competitive strategies on the strategy clock

The competitive strategies of UK grocery retailers have shifted in the last three decades.

The supermarket retail revolution in the UK began in the late 1960s and 1970s as, initially, Sainsbury's began to open up supermarkets. Since the dominant form of retailing at that time was the corner grocery shop, Sainsbury's supermarkets were, in effect, a hybrid strategy: very clearly differentiated in terms of the physical layout and size of the stores as well as the quality of the merchandise, but also lower priced than many of the corner shop competitors.

As more and more retailers opened up supermarkets a pattern emerged. Sainsbury's was the dominant differentiated supermarket retailer. Tesco grew as a 'pile it high, sell it cheap' no frills operator. Competing in between as lower priced, but also lower quality than Sainsbury's, were a number of other supermarket retailers.

The mid-1990s saw a major change. Under the leadership of Ian Maclaurin, Tesco made a dramatic shift in strategy. It significantly increased the size and number of its stores, dropped the 'pile it high, sell cheap' stance and began offering a much wider range of merchandise. Still not perceived as equal to Sainsbury's on quality, it none the less grew its market share at the expense of the other retailers and began to challenge Sainsbury's dominance. However the big breakthrough came for Tesco when it also shifted to higher-quality merchandise but still at perceived lower prices than Sainsbury's. In effect it was now adopting a hybrid strategy. In so doing it gained massive market share. By early 2007 this stood at over 30 per cent of the retail grocery market in the UK. In turn Sainsbury's had seen its share eroded to just 16 per cent, as it sought to find a way to resurrect its differentiated image of quality in the face of this competition.

In the meantime, other competitive strategy positions had consolidated. The low-price strategy was being followed by Asda (Wal-Mart) which also had a 16 per cent share of the market and Morrison's (with 11 per cent). In the no-frills segment was Netto, Lidl and Aldi, all retail formats that arrived in the 1990s from European neighbours and with a combined share of around 6 per cent.

The strategy of differentiation no longer really existed in a pure form. The closest was Waitrose (almost 4 per cent) emphasising a higher-quality image, but targeting a more select, upper-middle-class, market in selected locations. The focused differentiated stance remained the domain of the specialists: delicatessens and, of course in a London context, Harrods Food Hall.

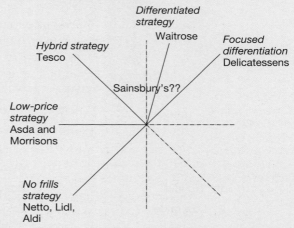

Questions

1 Who is 'stuck in the middle' here? Why?

2 Is a differentiated strategy or a low-price strategy defensible if there is a successful hybrid strategy, similar to that being followed by Tesco?

3 What might prevent other competitors following the Tesco strategy and competing successfully with them? (That is, does Tesco have strategic capabilities that provide sustainable competitive advantage?)

4 For another market of your choice, map out the strategic positions of the competitors in that market in terms of the strategy clock.

(Tesco is the case example in Chapter 10.)

6.3.1 Price-based strategies (routes 1 and 2)

A **'no frills' strategy** combines a low price, low perceived product/service benefits and a focus on a price-sensitive market segment

Route 1 is the **'no frills' strategy**, which combines a low price with low perceived product/service benefits and a focus on a price-sensitive market segment. These segments might exist because of the following:

- The existence of *commodity markets*. These are markets where customers do not value or discern differences in the offering of different suppliers, so price becomes the key competitive issue. Basic foodstuffs – particularly in developing economies – are an example.

- There may be *price-sensitive customers*, who cannot afford, or choose not, to buy better-quality goods. This market segment may be unattractive to major providers but offers an opportunity to others (Aldi, Lidl and Netto in Illustration 6.1, for example). In the public services funders with tight budgets may decide to support only basic-level provision (for example, in subsidised spectacles or dentistry).

- Buyers have *high power and/or low switching costs* so there is little choice – for example, in situations of tendering for government contracts.

- The strategy offers an opportunity to *avoid major competitors*. Where major providers compete on other bases, a low-price segment may be an opportunity for smaller players or a new entrant to carve out a niche or to use route 1 as a bridgehead to build volume before moving on to other strategies.

A **low-price strategy** seeks to achieve a lower price than competitors whilst trying to maintain similar perceived product or service benefits to those offered by competitors

Route 2, the **low-price strategy**, seeks to achieve a lower price than competitors whilst maintaining similar perceived product or service benefits to those offered by competitors. Increasingly this has been the competitive strategy chosen by Asda (owned by Wal-Mart) and Morrisons in the UK supermarket sector (see Illustration 6.1). In the public sector, since the 'price' of a service to the provider of funds (usually government) is the unit costs of the organisation receiving the budget, the equivalent is year-on-year efficiency gains achieved without loss of perceived benefits.

Competitive advantage through a low-price strategy might be achieved by focusing on a market segment that is unattractive to competitors and so avoiding competitive pressures eroding price. However, a more common and more challenging situation is where there is competition on the basis of price, for example in the public sector and in commodity-like markets. There are two pitfalls when competing on price:

- *Margin reductions for all*. Although tactical advantage might be gained by reducing price this is likely to be followed by competitors, squeezing profit margins for everyone.

- An *inability to reinvest*. Low margins reduce the resources available to develop products or services and result in a loss of perceived benefit of the product.

So, in the long run, both a 'no frills' strategy and a low-price strategy cannot be pursued without a *low-cost base*. However, low cost in itself is not a basis for advantage. Managers often pursue low cost that does not give them competitive advantage. The challenge is how costs can be reduced in ways which others cannot match such that a low-price strategy might give sustainable advantage. This is difficult but possible ways are discussed in section 6.4.1. Illustration 6.2 also shows how easyJet has sought to reduce costs to pursue its 'no frills' strategy.

Illustration 6.2

easyJet's 'no frills' strategy

Multiple bases for keeping costs down can provide a basis for a successful 'no frills' strategy.

Launched in 1995, easyJet was seen as the brash young upstart of the European airline industry and widely tipped to fail. But by the mid-2000s this Luton-based airline had done more than survive. From a starting point of six hired aircraft working one route, by 2006 it had 122 aircraft flying 262 routes to 74 airports and carrying over 33 million passengers per annum and impressive financial results: £129m profit on £1,619m revenue (≈ €187m on ≈ €2,348m).

The principles of its strategy and its business model were laid down in annual reports year by year. For example, in 2006:

● The internet is used to reduce distribution costs . . . now over 95% of all seats are sold online, making Easy Jet one of Europe's biggest internet retailers;
● Maximizing the utilization of substantial assets. We fly our aircraft intensively, with swift turnaround times each time we land. This gives us a very low unit cost;
● Ticket-less travel. Passengers receive booking details via an email rather than paper. This helps to significantly reduce the cost of issuing, distributing, processing and reconciling millions of transactions each year;
● No 'free lunch'. We eliminate unnecessary services, which are complex to manage such as free catering, pre-assigned seats, interline connections and cargo services. This allows us to keep our total costs of production low;
● Efficient use of airports. Easy Jet flies to main destination airports throughout Europe, but gains efficiencies compared to traditional carriers with rapid turnaround times, and progressive landing charge agreements with airports. [It might have added here that since it does not operate a hub system, passengers have to check in and offload their luggage at each stage. This means that aircraft are not held up whilst luggage is transferred between flights.]

It might also have added that other factors contributed to low costs:

● A focus on the Airbus A319 aircraft, and the retirement of 'old generation' Boeing 737 aircraft, meant 'a young fleet of modern aircraft secured at very competitive rates' benefiting maintenance costs. And, since an increasing proportion of these were owned by easyJet, financing costs were being reduced.
● A persistent focus on reducing ground handling costs.
● In the face of rising fuel costs, hedging on future buying of fuel.

In addition to all the factors above the 2006 annual report stated that easyJet's customer proposition is defined by

low cost with care and convenience. . . . We fly to main European destinations from convenient local airports and provide friendly onboard service. People are a key point of difference at Easy Jet and are integral to our success. This allows us to attract the widest range of customers to use our services – both business and leisure.

Source: easyJet annual report 2006.

Questions

1 Read sections 6.3.1 and 6.4.1 and identify the bases of easyJet's 'no frills' strategy.
2 How easy would it be for larger airlines such as BA to imitate the strategy?
3 On what bases could other low-price airlines compete with easyJet?

6.3.2 (Broad) Differentiation strategies (route 4)

A **differentiation strategy** seeks to provide products or services that offer benefits that are different from those of competitors and that are widely valued by buyers

The next option is a broad **differentiation strategy** providing products or services that offer benefits different from those of competitors and that are widely valued by buyers.[4] The aim is to achieve competitive advantage by offering better products or services at the same price or enhancing margins by pricing slightly higher. In public services, the equivalent is the achievement of a 'centre of excellence' status, attracting higher funding from government (for example, universities try to show that they are better at research or teaching than other universities).

The success of a differentiation approach is likely to be dependent on two key factors:

- *Identifying and understanding the strategic customer*. The concept of the strategic customer is helpful because it focuses consideration on who the strategy is targeting. However, this is not always straightforward, as discussed in section 2.4.3. For example, for a newspaper business, is the customer the reader of the newspaper, the advertiser, or both? They are likely to have different needs and be looking for different benefits. For a branded food manufacturer is it the end consumer or the retailer? It may be important that public sector organisations offer perceived benefits, but to whom? Is it the service user or the provider of funds? However, *what is valued* by the strategic customer can also be dangerously taken for granted by managers, a reminder of the importance of identifying critical success factors (section 2.4.2).

- *Identifying key competitors*. Who is the organisation competing against? For example, in the brewing industry there are now just a few major global competitors, but there are also many local or regional brewers. Players in each strategic group (see section 2.4.1) need to decide who they regard as competitors and, given that, which bases of differentiation might be considered. Heineken appears to have decided that it is the other global competitors – Carlsberg and Anheuser-Busch, for example. SABMiller built its global reach on the basis of acquiring and developing national brands and competing on the basis of local tastes and traditions, but has more recently also acquired Miller to compete globally.

The competitor analysis explained in section 2.4.4 (and Exhibit 2.8) can help in both of these regards:

- The *difficulty of imitation*. The success of a strategy of differentiation must depend on how easily it can be imitated by competitors. This highlights the importance of non-imitable strategic capabilities discussed in section 3.4.3.

- The extent of *vulnerability to price-based competition*. In some markets customers are more price sensitive than others. So it may be that bases of differentiation are just not sufficient in the face of lower prices. Managers often complain, for example, that customers do not seem to value the superior levels of service they offer. Or, to take the example of UK grocery retailing (see Illustration 6.1), Sainsbury's could once claim to be the broad differentiator on the basis of quality but customers now perceive that Tesco is comparable and seen to offer lower prices.

6.3.3 **The hybrid strategy (route 3)**

A **hybrid strategy** seeks simultaneously to achieve differentiation and a price lower than that of competitors

A **hybrid strategy** seeks simultaneously to achieve differentiation and low price relative to competitors. The success of this strategy depends on the ability to deliver enhanced benefits to customers together with low prices whilst achieving sufficient margins for reinvestment to maintain and develop bases of differentiation. It is, in effect, the strategy Tesco is seeking to follow. It might be argued that, if differentiation can be achieved, there should be no need to have a lower price, since it should be possible to obtain prices at least equal to the competition, if not higher. Indeed, there is a good deal of debate as to whether a hybrid strategy can be a successful competitive strategy rather than a suboptimal compromise between low price and differentiation.[5] If it is the latter, very likely it will be ineffective. However, the hybrid strategy could be advantageous when:

● Much *greater volumes* can be achieved than competitors so that margins may still be better because of a low-cost base, much as Tesco is achieving given its market share in the UK.

● *Cost reductions are available outside its differentiated activities*. For example, IKEA concentrates on building differentiation on the basis of its marketing, product range, logistics and store operations, but low customer expectations on service levels allow cost reduction because customers are prepared to transport and build its products.

● Used as an *entry strategy* in a market with established competitors. For example, in developing a global strategy a business may target a poorly run operation in a competitor's portfolio of businesses in a geographical area of the world[6] and enter that market with a superior product at a lower price to establish a foothold from which it can move further.

6.3.4 **Focused differentiation (route 5)**

A **focused differentiation** strategy seeks to provide high perceived product/service benefits justifying a substantial price premium, usually to a selected market segment (niche)

A **focused differentiation** strategy provides high perceived product/service benefits, typically justifying a substantial price premium, usually to a selected market segment (or niche). These could be premium products and heavily branded, for example. Manufacturers of premium beers, single malt whiskies and wines from particular chateaux all seek to convince customers who value or see themselves as discerning of quality that their product is sufficiently differentiated from competitors' products to justify significantly higher prices. In the public services, centres of excellence (such as a specialist museum) achieve levels of funding significantly higher than more generalist providers. However, focused differentiation raises some important issues:

● A *choice* may have to be made between a focus strategy (position 5) and broad differentiation (position 4). A firm following a strategy of international growth may have to choose between building competitive advantage on the basis of a common global product and brand (route 4) or tailoring its offering to specific markets (route 5) – an issue taken up again in Chapter 8 (section 8.4).

● *Tensions between a focus strategy and other strategies*. For example, broad-based car manufacturers, such as Ford, acquired premier marques, such as

Jaguar and Aston Martin, but learned that trying to manage these in the same way as mass market cars was not possible. By 2007 Ford had divested Aston Martin and was seeking to divest others. Such tensions limit the degree of diversity of strategic positioning that an organisation can sustain, an important issue for corporate-level strategy discussed in Chapter 7.

● *Possible conflict with stakeholder expectations.* For example, a public library service might be more cost efficient if it concentrated its development efforts on IT-based online information services. However, this would very likely conflict with its purpose of social inclusion since it would exclude people who were not IT literate.

● *Dynamics of growth for new ventures.* New ventures often start in very focused ways – offering innovative products or services to meet particular needs. It may, however, be difficult to find ways to grow such new ventures. Moving from route 5 to route 4 means a lowering of price and therefore cost, whilst maintaining differentiation features.

● *Market changes may erode differences between segments,* leaving the organisation open to much wider competition. Customers may become unwilling to pay a price premium as the features of 'regular' offerings improve. Or the market may be further segmented by even more differentiated offerings from competitors. For example, 'up-market' restaurants have been hit by rising standards elsewhere and by the advent of 'niche' restaurants that specialise in particular types of food.

6.3.5 Failure strategies (routes 6, 7 and 8)

A failure strategy is one that does not provide perceived value for money in terms of product features, price or both

A **failure strategy** is one which does not provide perceived value for money in terms of product features, price or both. So the strategies suggested by routes 6, 7 and 8 are probably destined for failure. Route 6 suggests increasing price without increasing product/service benefits to the customer, the strategy that monopoly organisations are accused of following. Unless the organisation is protected by legislation, or high economic barriers to entry, competitors are likely to erode market share. Route 7 is an even more disastrous extension of route 6, involving the reduction in product/service benefits whilst increasing relative price. Route 8, reduction in benefits whilst maintaining price, is also dangerous, though firms have tried to follow it. There is a high risk that competitors will increase their share substantially. There is also another basis of failure, which is for a business to be unclear as to its fundamental generic strategy such that it ends up being 'stuck in the middle' – a recipe for failure.

6.4 SUSTAINING COMPETITIVE ADVANTAGE

Organisations that try to achieve competitive advantage hope to preserve it over time and much of what is written about competitive strategy takes the need for sustainability as a central expectation. This section builds on the discussion in Chapter 3 (section 3.3.2) relating to strategic capability to consider how sustainability might be possible. However, increasingly, questions have been raised as to whether sustainability of competitive advantage is possible, so section 6.5 looks at competitive strategy in circumstances where sustainability is not possible or very difficult.

6.4.1 Sustaining price-based advantage

An organisation pursuing competitive advantage through low prices might be able to sustain this in a number of ways (see Exhibit 6.3):

● *Operating with lower margins* may be possible for a firm either because it has much greater sales volume than competitors or because it can cross-subsidise a business unit from elsewhere in its portfolio (see Chapter 7).

● *A unique cost structure.* Some firms may have unique access to low-cost distribution channels, be able to obtain raw materials at lower prices than competitors or be located in an area where labour cost is low.

● *Organisationally specific capabilities* may exist for a firm such that it is able to drive down cost throughout its value chain. Indeed Michael Porter defines cost leadership as '*the* low-cost producer in its industry . . . [who] must find and exploit all sources of cost advantage'[7] (see section 3.3 and Exhibit 3.3).

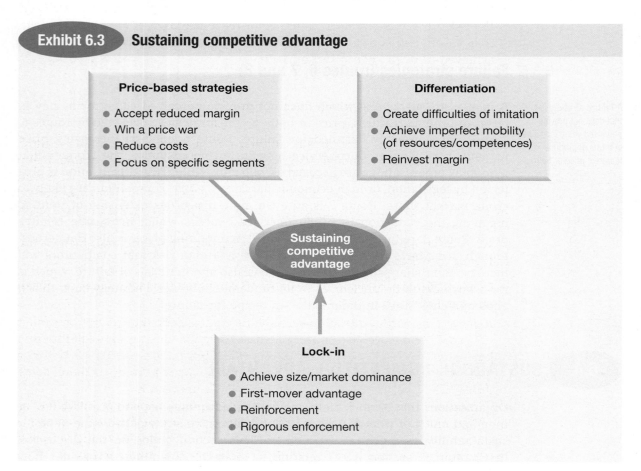

Exhibit 6.3 Sustaining competitive advantage

Price-based strategies
● Accept reduced margin
● Win a price war
● Reduce costs
● Focus on specific segments

Differentiation
● Create difficulties of imitation
● Achieve imperfect mobility (of resources/competences)
● Reinvest margin

Sustaining competitive advantage

Lock-in
● Achieve size/market dominance
● First-mover advantage
● Reinforcement
● Rigorous enforcement

Of course, if either of these last two approaches is to be followed it matters that the operational areas of low cost do truly deliver cost advantages to support real price advantages over competition. It is also important that competitors find these advantages difficult to imitate, as discussed in Chapter 3. This requires a mindset where innovation in cost reduction is regarded as essential to survival. An example of this is Ryanair in the low-price (no frills) airline sector which, in 2006, declared its ambition to be able to eventually offer passengers flights for free.

● *Focusing on market segments* where low price is particularly valued by customers but other features are not. An example is the success of dedicated producers of own-brand grocery products for supermarkets. They can hold prices low because they avoid the high overhead and marketing costs of major branded manufacturers. However, they can only do so provided they focus on that product and market segment.

There are, however, dangers with trying to pursue low-price strategies:

● *Competitors may be able to do the same*. There is no point in trying to achieve advantage through low price on the basis of cost reduction if competitors can do it too.

● Customers start to *associate low price with low product/service benefits* and an intended route 2 strategy slips to route 1 by default.

● Cost reductions may result in an *inability to pursue a differentiation strategy*. For example, outsourcing IT systems for reasons of cost efficiency may mean that no one takes a strategic view of how competitive advantage might be achieved through IT (see section 12.3).

6.4.2 Sustaining differentiation-based advantage

There is little point in striving to be different if competitors can imitate readily; there is a need for sustainability of the basis of advantage. For example, many firms that try to gain advantage through launching new products or services find them copied rapidly by competitors. Illustration 6.3 shows how wine producers in France and Australia have been seeking bases of differentiation over each other over the years.

Ways of attempting to sustain advantage through differentiation include the following (see Exhibit 6.3):

● *Create difficulties of imitation*. Section 3.3 discussed the factors that can make strategies difficult to imitate.

● *Imperfect mobility* such that the capabilities that sustain differentiation cannot be *traded*. For example, a pharmaceutical firm may gain great benefits from having top research scientists, or a football club from its star players, but they may be poached by competitors: they are tradable. On the other hand, some bases of advantage are very difficult to trade. For example:
  – *Intangible assets* such as brand, image or reputation that are intangible or competences rooted in an organisation's culture are difficult for a competitor to imitate or obtain. Indeed even if the competitor acquires the company to gain these, they may not readily transfer given new ownership.

Illustration 6.3

The strategy battle in the wine industry: Australia vs. France

The benefits of successful differentiation may be difficult to sustain.

For centuries French wines were regarded as superior. Building on the Appellation d'Origine Contrôlée (AOC) system, with its separate label requirements and controls for nearly 450 wine-growing regions, the emphasis was on the distinct regionality of the wines and the chateau-based branding. In the AOC system the individual wine-grower is a custodian of the *terroir* and its traditions. The quality of the wines and the distinct local differences are down to the differences in soil and climate as well as the skills of the growers, often on the basis of decades of local experience.

However, by 2001 the traditional dominance of French wines in the UK seemed to have ended, with sales of Australian wine outstripping them for the first time. This went hand in hand with huge growth in wine consumption as it became more widely available in supermarkets, where Australian wine was especially succesful. The success of Australian wines with retailers was for several reasons. The quality was consistent, compared with French wines that could differ by year and location. Whilst the French had always highlighted the importance of the local area of origin of the wine, in effect Australia 'branded' the country as a wine region and then concentrated on the variety of grape – a Shiraz or a Chardonnay, for example. This avoided the confusing details of the location of vineyards and the names of chateaux that many customers found difficult about French wines. The New World approach to the production of wine in terms of style, quality and taste was also based around consumer demand, not local production conditions. Grapes were sourced from wherever necessary to create a reliable product. French wines could be unpredictable – charming to the connoisseur, but infuriating to the dinner-party host, who expects to get what he or she paid for.

Between 1994 and 2003 France lost 84,000 growers. There was so much concern that in 2001, the French government appointed a committee to study the problem. The committee's proposals were that France should both improve the quality of its appellation wine and also create an entirely new range of quality, generic wines, so-called 'vins de cepage' (wines based on a grape variety). A company called

OVS planned to market the Chamarré brand – French for 'bursting with colours', to sell between £5 and £7 (€7.25 and €10.15), the price range where New World wines have made the biggest inroads. OVS President Pascal Renaudat, who has had 20 years in the wine business, explained:

We have to simplify our product and reject an arrogant approach that was perhaps natural to us. It is important to produce wine that corresponds to what people want to drink and at a good price. . . . This is not wine for connoisseurs. It is for pleasure.

'It's time to get rid of the stuffy pretentiousness that surrounds French wine,' said Renaud Rosari, Chamarré's master wine-maker. 'Chamarré is about bringing our wines to life for the consumers – the brand is lively, uncomplicated and approachable and means consistently high quality wines, with the fresh easy drinking style customers are looking for.'

There was qualified optimism: Jamie Goode of wineanorak.com saw it as a brave commercial decision. However: 'The trouble is that everybody is doing it. . . . Access to market is key. You need to get into the supermarkets, but you need to have a strong brand with which to negotiate or else they will savage you on price.'

Sources: Adapted from *Financial Times*, 11 February and 3/4 March (2001); *Independent*, 4 August (2003); *Sunday Times*, 5 February (2006); Guardian Unlimited, 7 February (2006).

Questions

1 Explain the high and distinct reputation of French wines of the past in terms of the bases of sustainable differentiation explained in sections 6.4.2 and 3.4.

2 What were the reasons for the success of Australian wines? Are these as sustainable?

3 What competitive strategy is Chamarré adopting to respond to the challenge of Australian (and other 'New World') wines?

- There may be *switching costs*. The actual or perceived cost for a buyer of changing the source of supply of a product or service may be high. Or the buyer might be dependent on the supplier for particular components, services or skills. Or the benefits of switching may simply not be worth the cost or risk.

- *Co-specialisation*, if one organisation's resources or competences are intimately linked with the buyers' operations. For example, a whole element of the value chain for one organisation, perhaps distribution or manufacturing, may be undertaken by another.

● A *lower-cost position* than competitors can allow an organisation to sustain better margins that can be reinvested to achieve and maintain differentiation. For example, Kellogg's or Mars may well be the lowest cost in their markets, but they reinvest their profits into branding and product and service differentiation, not low prices.

6.4.3 Strategic lock-in

Strategic lock-in is where an organisation achieves a proprietary position in its industry; it becomes an industry standard

Another approach to sustainability, whether for price-based or differentiation strategies, is the creation of **strategic lock-in**.[8] This is where an organisation achieves a proprietary position in its industry; it becomes an industry standard. For example, Microsoft became an industry standard. Many argue that technically the Apple Macintosh had a better operating system, but Microsoft Windows became the industry standard by working to ensure that the 'architecture' of the industry was built around it. Other businesses had to conform or relate to that standard in order to prosper.

The achievement of lock-in is likely to be dependent on (see Exhibit 6.3):

● *Size or market dominance*. It is unlikely that others will seek to conform to such standards unless they perceive the organisation that promotes it as dominant in its market.

● *First-mover dominance*. Such standards are likely to be set *early in life cycles of markets*. In the volatility of growth markets it is more likely that the single-minded pursuit of lock-in by the *first-movers* will be successful than when the market is mature. For example, Sky, with the financial support of News Corporation, was able to undercut competitors and invest heavily in technology and fast market share growth, sustaining substantial losses over many years, in order to achieve dominance.

● *Self-reinforcing commitment*. When one or more firms support the standard, more come on board, then others are obliged to, and so on.

● *Insistence on the preservation* of the lock-in position. Insistence on conformity to the standard is strict so rivals will be seen off fiercely. This can of course lead to problems, as Microsoft found in the US courts when it was deemed to be operating against the interests of the market.

6.4.4 **Responding to competitive threat**[9]

The preservation of competitive advantage in the face of competitors who attack by targeting customers on the basis of a different competitive strategy can be a serious threat. One of the most common is low-price competitors entering markets dominated by firms that have built a strong position through differentiation. For example, low-price airlines have taken substantial share from most of the leading airlines throughout the world. An equivalent situation in the public sector arises given the insistence by funding providers on year-on-year 'efficiency gains'. It is an opportunity for new entrants to undercut existing service providers, or indeed it may be that those providers find themselves being forced to undercut themselves.

Exhibit 6.4 suggests the series of questions that might be asked and the appropriate responses; there are also some general guidelines. First, *if a strategy of differentiation is retained* as the basis of retaliation (or in the public sector if the decision is to maintain a 'centre of excellence' status):

● *Build multiple bases of differentiation*. There is more likelihood of highlighting relative benefits if they are multiple; for example, Bang and Olufson's design of hi-fi systems linked to product innovation and its relationships with retailers to ensure they present its products distinctly in stores.

● *Ensure a meaningful basis of differentiation*. Customers need to be able to discern a meaningful benefit. For example, Gillette has found it difficult to persuade customers of the benefit of long-life Duracell batteries not only because low-price competitors offer multi-packs of cheap batteries to compete, but also because the demand for batteries has diminished.

● *Minimise price differences* for superior products or services. This is one reason why a hybrid strategy can be so effective of course.

● *Focus on less price-sensitive market segments*. For example, British Airways has switched its strategic focus to long-haul flights with a particular emphasis on business travellers.

Second, if differentiators decide to *set up a low-price business*:

● *Establish a separate brand* for the low-price business to avoid customer confusion.

● *Run the business separately* and *ensure it is well resourced*. The danger is that the low-price alternative is regarded as 'second class' or is over-constrained by the procedures and culture of the traditional business.

● *Ensure benefits to the differentiated offering* from the low-price alternative. For example, some banks offer lower charges through Internet banking subsidiaries. These lower-priced alternatives reach customers that the traditional banks might not reach and raise funds they would otherwise not have.

● *Allow the businesses to compete*. Launching the low-price business purely defensively is unlikely to be effective. It has to be allowed to compete as a viable separate SBU; as such, quite likely there will be substitution of one offering with another. Managers need to build this into their strategic plans and financial projections.

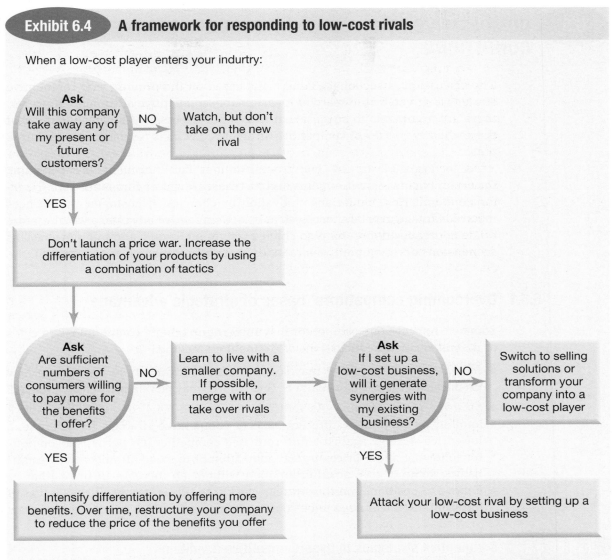

Exhibit 6.4   A framework for responding to low-cost rivals

When a low-cost player enters your indurtry:

Ask Will this company take away any of my present or future customers? — NO → Watch, but don't take on the new rival

YES ↓

Don't launch a price war. Increase the differentiation of your products by using a combination of tactics

Ask Are sufficient numbers of consumers willing to pay more for the benefits I offer? — NO → Learn to live with a smaller company. If possible, merge with or take over rivals → **Ask** If I set up a low-cost business, will it generate synergies with my existing business? — NO → Switch to selling solutions or transform your company into a low-cost player

YES ↓ (left)   YES ↓ (right)

Intensify differentiation by offering more benefits. Over time, restructure your company to reduce the price of the benefits you offer

Attack your low-cost rival by setting up a low-cost business

A third possibility is that differentiated businesses may *change their own business model*. For example:

● *Become solutions providers*. Low-price entrants are likely to focus on basic products or services so it may be possible to reconstruct the business model to focus on higher-value services. Many engineering firms have realised, for example, the higher-value potential of design and consultancy services rather than labour-based engineering operations that are easily undercut in price.

● *Become a low-price provider*. The most radical response would be to abandon the reliance on differentiation and learn to compete head-on with the low-price competitor.[10] Perhaps not surprisingly, there is not much evidence of the success of such a response, not least because it would mean competing on the basis of competences better understood by the incumbent.

6.5 COMPETITIVE STRATEGY IN HYPERCOMPETITIVE CONDITIONS

The discussion in sections 6.3 and 6.4 is based on the premise that competitive strategy is driven by the search for sustainable competitive advantage. However, there are arguments to suggest that this is not necessarily achievable and that there are other bases of competitive strategies. Sections 6.5, 6.6 and 6.7 address these.

As section 2.3.2 argued, many organisations face turbulent, fast-changing, uncertain business environments and increasing levels of competition, or *hyper-competition*.[11] Here imitation, innovation or changes of customer preferences mean advantage may be short-lived at best. Competitive advantage will therefore relate to organisations' ability to change fast, to be flexible and to innovate. This section considers competitive strategies in such conditions (see Exhibit 6.5).

6.5.1 Overcoming competitors' bases of strategic advantage

Some of the ways one competitor may undermine others' competitive strategies or defend against the incursions of competitors include:

- *Imitation*. One competitor may seek to achieve advantage by developing new products or entering new markets. Such moves may be relatively easily imitated.

- *Strategic (re)positioning*. As indicated in section 6.4.4, one firm may attack another by adopting a different basis of competitive strategy; for example, a low-price strategy against a differentiated competitor. Or perhaps a competitor following a low-price strategy may attempt to stave off another by establishing some degree of differentiation without an increase in price (that is, a move to position 3 on the strategy clock). As this is imitated new sources of differentiation will need to be sought. So innovation and agility are essential.

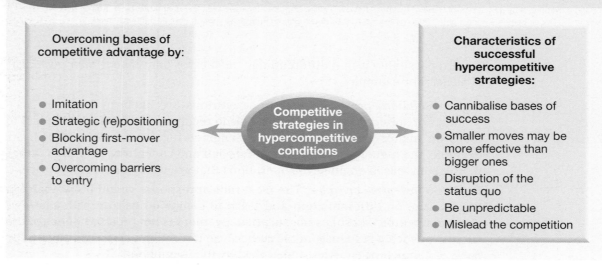

Exhibit 6.5   Competitive strategies in hypercompetitive conditions

Overcoming bases of competitive advantage by:

- Imitation
- Strategic (re)positioning
- Blocking first-mover advantage
- Overcoming barriers to entry

Competitive strategies in hypercompetitive conditions

Characteristics of successful hypercompetitive strategies:

- Cannibalise bases of success
- Smaller moves may be more effective than bigger ones
- Disruption of the status quo
- Be unpredictable
- Mislead the competition

- *Blocking first-mover advantages.* One competitor may try to achieve advantage as a *first-mover*. The key lesson here is not to allow that competitor to establish a dominant position before a response is made. Further, instead of launching an imitation product, the response might be a product with enhanced features, seeking to leapfrog or outflank the first-mover.

- *Overcoming barriers to entry.* Attempts to build barriers to entry may take different forms, but may be overcome. For example:
  - *Undermining competitors' strongholds.* Competitors may try to dominate a geographic area or market segment. However, these can be undermined. For example, in globalising markets the benefits of economies of scale built up in one area can be undermined by a competitor using the economies of scale from its own home territory to enter a market. Or in education, established institutions have become vulnerable to IT/Internet-based training offered by competitors who have written off the costs of materials development through sales in their home markets. Or where an organisation has built strongholds by tying up distribution channels, entrants may be able to use different distribution channels (for example, online retailing).
  - *Countering deep pockets.* Some competitors may have substantial surplus resources (sometimes called 'deep pockets') by which they try to withstand an intensive competitive war (see section 6.4.1). Such advantages may be overcome, for example by competitors *merging or building alliances* so they can compete from a stronger base.

6.5.2 Characteristics of successful hypercompetitive strategies

The radical argument put forward by Richard D'Aveni[12] is not only that managers need to rethink their approach to business-level strategy because it may no longer be possible to plan for sustainable positions of competitive advantage, but also that planning for long-term sustainability may actually destroy competitive advantage by slowing down response. Managers have to learn to be better at doing things faster than competitors. He provides some guidelines:

- *Cannibalise bases of success.* Sustaining old advantages distracts from developing new advantages. An organisation has to be willing to cannibalise the basis of its own success.

- *Attacking competitors' weaknesses can be unwise* as they learn about how their strengths and weaknesses are perceived and build their strategies accordingly.

- A series of *smaller moves may be more effective than bigger ones* because the longer-term direction is not as easily discernible by competitors and smaller moves create more flexibility and give a series *of temporary advantages*.

- *Disruption of the status quo* is strategic behaviour, not mischief. The ability constantly to 'break the mould' could be a core competence.

- *Be unpredictable.* If competitors can see a pattern they can predict the next competitive moves and quickly learn how to imitate or outflank an organisation. So surprise, unpredictability, even apparent irrationality can be important. Managers must learn ways of appearing to be unpredictable to the external world whilst, internally, thinking strategies through.

● *Mislead the competition.* Drawing on the lessons of game theory (see section 6.7), the strategist may signal moves competitors expect but which are not the moves that actually occur. Or the strategist might disguise its own success in a market.[13]

6.6 COMPETITION AND COLLABORATION[14]

So far the emphasis has been on competition and competitive advantage. However, advantage may not always be achieved by competing. Collaboration between organisations may be a way of achieving advantage or avoiding competition. Collaboration between potential competitors or between buyers and sellers is likely to be advantageous when the combined costs of purchase and buying transactions (such as negotiating and contracting) are lower through collaboration than the cost of operating alone. Collaboration also helps build switching costs. This can be shown by returning to the five forces framework from section 2.3.1 (also see Exhibit 6.6):

● *Collaboration to increase selling power.* In the aerospace industry component manufacturers might seek to build close links with customers. Achieving accredited supplier status can be tough, but may significantly increase seller power once achieved. It may also help in research and development activities, in reducing stock and in joint planning to design new products.

● *Collaboration to increase buying power.* Historically, the power and profitability of pharmaceutical companies were aided by the fragmented nature of their buyers – individual doctors and hospitals. But many governments have promoted, or required, collaboration between buyers of pharmaceuticals and centralised government drug-specifying agencies, the result of which has been more coordinated buying power.

● *Collaboration to build barriers to entry or avoid substitution.* Faced with threatened entry or substitute products, firms in an industry may collaborate to invest in research and development or marketing. Trade associations may promote an industry's generic features such as safety standards or technical specifications to speed up innovation and pre-empt the possibility of substitution.

● *Collaboration to gain entry and competitive power.* Organisations seeking to develop beyond their traditional boundaries (for example, geographical expansion) may collaborate with others to gain entry into new arenas. Gaining local market knowledge may also require collaboration with local operators. Indeed, in some parts of the world, governments require entrants to collaborate in such ways. Collaboration may also help in developing required infrastructure such as distribution channels, information systems or research and development activities. It may also be needed because buyers may prefer to do business with local rather than expatriate managers. Especially in hi-tech and hypercompetitive situations there is increasing disintegration (or 'unbundling') of value chains because there is innovatory competition at each stage of that chain. In such circumstances there also is likely to be increasing need for cooperative strategies between such competitors to offer coherent solutions for customers.[15]

Exhibit 6.6 **Competition and collaboration**

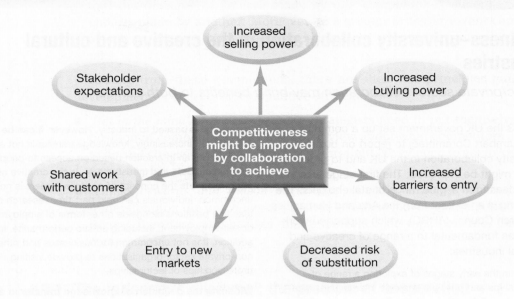

Collaboration to share work with customers. An important trend in public services is *co-production* with clients,[16] for example self-assessment of income tax. The motives include cost efficiency, quality/reliability improvement or increased 'ownership/responsibility' from the clients. Websites also facilitate customers' self-service (the virtual shopping basket is an example) or allow them to design or customise a product or service to their own specification (for example, when ordering a new computer).

In the public sector *gaining more leverage from public investment* may require collaboration to raise the overall standards of the sector or to address social issues that cross several professional fields (such as drugs or community safety). One difference from the private sector is that sharing of knowledge and dissemination of best practice is regarded as a duty or a requirement.

However, collaborating with competitors is not as easy as it sounds. Illustration 6.4 is an example of public/private sector collaboration in one sector.

6.7 **GAME THEORY**[17]

Game theory is concerned with the interrelationships between the competitive moves of a set of competitors

Game theory is concerned with the interrelationships between the competitive moves of a set of competitors. It is helpful in understanding the competitive dynamics of markets and in considering appropriate strategies in this light. There are two key assumptions in relation to understanding competitive dynamics in terms of game theory:

- *Rationality*. Competitors will behave rationally in trying to win to their own benefit.

www.pearsoned.co.uk/ecs
KEY CONCEPT
Game theory

trying to achieve a dominant position in the new market and the other does not, they would achieve even higher returns (represented in the top right and bottom left quadrants) so may be tempted to do this, or may fear that their rival will be tempted to do so if they do not. They each may also fear that, if they collaborate, after the early joint investment, the other may begin to dominate the market and benefit at the disproportionality. Or they may simply not trust each other. It is therefore quite likely that both parties will decide to go it alone to ensure that the other competitor does not get an advantage. This may mean that the returns from the investment needed to develop the market would be much lower for both than if they decided to cooperate – as shown in the top left quadrant.

A dominant strategy is one that outperforms other strategies whatever rivals choose

This is an example of what game theorists refer to as a **dominant strategy**: one that outperforms other strategies whatever rivals choose. In the prisoner's

---

Illustration 6.5

Innova and Dolla play a sequential game

The principles of game theory can provide insights into competitive strategy.

Innova and Dolla, competitors in the market for computer games, face a decision on investment in research and development. Innova has highly innovative designers but is short of the finance required to invest heavily in rapid development of products. Dolla is strong financially but relatively weak in terms of its research and design.

In terms of the crucial choice of investing in research and design or not, they both know that investing heavily would shorten the development time but would incur considerable costs. Indeed high levels of investment by both is the worst outcome: for Innova because its financial position is weak and it could be a risky route to follow; for Dolla because, if it can raise the finance, Innova has better chances of winning given its design capabilities.

Innova has a dominant strategy; to keep its investment low. If Dolla were to invest low, Innova would get a better pay-off because of its innovative capabilities. Indeed Dolla probably expects that Innova will keep levels of investment down. It also knows that if it goes for a low level of investment, it

has no advantage over Innova's superior innovative capabilities. For Dolla a low level of investment is a *dominated strategy* so the likelihood is that it will go for high levels of investment.

However, this can be reconsidered sequentially (see Figure 1). If Innova decides to invest low, it knows that Dolla is likely to respond high and gain the advantage (pay-off C). However, if Innova moves first and invests high, it places Dolla in a difficult position. If Dolla also invests high, it ends up with a low pay-off as does Innova (pay-off A). In these circumstances – provided that Dolla's strategist is a game theorist – Dolla might well reject that strategy and choose to invest low (with pay-off B).

Working through these different game logics, Innova should realise that if it waits for Dolla to make a move, it is bound to lose, but if it moves first and invests high, it stands a chance of winning. Of course there are risks here for Innova, not least financial. Also that Dolla may not believe that Innova will really invest high, so Innova has to be credible in its move. If it appears to waver, or not make a

dilemma example it would be better for there to be cooperation between the competitors. However, the fact is that if either of the competitors breaks rank the other one will suffer badly. So the dominant strategy is to go it alone. A general principle is that if there is a dominant strategy it makes sense to use it. It may well be that the end result is a lesser pay-off than could optimally be achieved, but it is better than losing out to the competitor.

In practice this 'lose–lose' outcome is not likely if there is a limited number of competitors interacting over time, because they learn to understand and accommodate each other. But something similar often occurs when there are many competitors jostling for position in a fragmented market. For example, whilst it might be logical for all competitors to hold prices at a relatively high level in such circumstances, no one expects anyone else to do so, and price wars result.

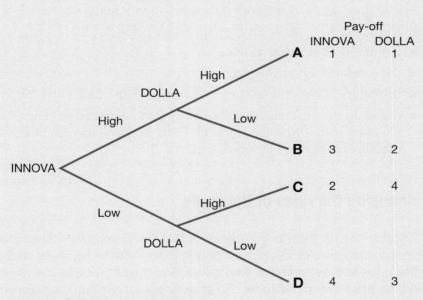

Figure 1 A sequential move game

Source: From *Thinking Strategically: The Competitive Edge in Business, Politics and Everyday Life* by Avinash K. Dixit and Barry J. Nalebuff. Copyright © 1991 by Avinash K. Dixit and Barry J. Natebuff. Used by permission of W.W. Norton & Company, Inc.

substantial enough investment, Dolla may invest high too and both lose out (pay-off A). Of course, if there is some way of Innova appearing to be credible in a decision to invest high whilst actually investing low, thus persuading Dolla to invest low too, then Innova achieves its *dominant strategy* (pay-off D).

Questions

1 Suggest other situations where game theory approaches might be useful and explain why.

2 What might prevent strategic decisions being made in this way?

6.7.2 Sequential games

The prisoner's dilemma is a simultaneous game, where competitors make decisions or strategic moves at the same time. This is not usually the case. A series of strategic decisions will typically be sequential, one party making a move, followed by the other. Here the guiding principle of 'think forwards and reason backwards' becomes especially important. The strategist needs to consider (i) what that competitor desires as the outcome, (ii) the sequence of moves that competitor might make based on that desired outcome and therefore (iii) the most advantageous strategy for itself. In doing this, it needs to be borne in mind that competitors will have different strategic capabilities and, linked to this, their own dominant strategies – for example, easyJet or Ryanair clearly have a dominant strategy of low price in the airline industry.

Illustration 6.5 shows how game theory reasoning might play out given these more complex conditions. If the situation is considered in terms of a sequential game, as in section 6.7.1, the best Innova can do is to follow its dominant strategy of investing low, which results in the least worst pay-off. Given that Innova will not be happy with this outcome, the illustration shows how considering the problem as a sequential game might help Innova gain advantage over its rival.

The illustration also shows how game theory helps strategists consider some important strategic lessons, in particular the importance of:

- the timing of strategic moves;
- the careful weighing of risk;
- the potential benefits of bluff and counter-bluff; and
- linked to this, establishing credibility and commitment. For example, in the illustration Innova could not achieve its desired outcome unless it had a reputation for sticking to its decisions.

6.7.3 Changing the rules of the game

Another lesson from game theory is that, by thinking through the logic of the game, a competitor might find that it is not able to compete effectively within the rules as they exist. For example, a firm might find that it is always battling it out on price but that with its cost structure it cannot hope to compete effectively. Or, as with the examples given here, that competition is always played out on the basis of a particular capability, such as heavy investment in research and development; this is a battle it cannot win. In such circumstances it may make sense to try to change the rules of the game. For example, in a market dominated by price-based strategies, a competitor might try to shift the rules of the game towards:

- *Clearer differentiation* based on what customers really value (see section 6.3.2).
- *More transparent pricing*, for example by trying to get published price lists established as the norm. On the face of it, this may not seem to avoid price competition, but the evidence is that greater transparency in this respect removes a significant basis for trying to achieve tactical advantage and therefore encourage more cooperative behaviour amongst competitors.

● *More incentives for customer loyalty*. The growth of loyalty cards in retailing is a good example. The principles of differentiation suggest that this is a weak strategy because competitors will imitate it. However, the pressure on competition through price can be reduced for all competitors.

Game theory does of course rely heavily on the principle of rationality, and it may well be that competitors do not always behave rationally. However, it does provide a way of thinking through the logic of interactive competitive markets and, in particular, when it makes sense to compete, on what bases, and when it makes sense to cooperate. At the very least it is important for managers to consider how competitors will respond to their preferred strategy.

An underlying theme in this chapter is the search for competitive advantage and the need for distinctiveness and strategies of differentiation to achieve this. The key debate in Illustration 6.6 reconsiders this theme and questions the extent to which differentiation does provide competitive advantage.

SUMMARY

● Competitive strategy is concerned with seeking competitive advantage in markets at the business level or, in the public services, providing best value services.

● Competitive strategy needs to be considered and defined in terms of strategic business units (SBUs).

● Different bases of competitive strategy include:
  – A *'no frills'* strategy, combining low price and low perceived added value.
  – A *low-price* strategy providing lower price than competitors at similar added value of product or service to competitors.
  – A *differentiation* strategy, which seeks to provide products or services which are unique or different from competitors.
  – A *hybrid* strategy, which seeks simultaneously to achieve differentiation and prices lower than competitors.
  – A *focused differentiation* strategy, which seeks to provide high perceived value justifying a substantial price premium.

● Managers need to consider the bases upon which price-based or differentiation strategies can be sustained based on strategic capabilities, developing durable relationships with customers or the ability to achieve a 'lock-in' position so becoming the 'industry standard' recognised by suppliers and buyers.

● In hypercompetitive conditions sustainable competitive advantage is difficult to achieve. Speed, flexibility, innovation and the willingness to change successful strategies are then important bases of competitive success.

● Strategies of collaboration may offer alternatives to competitive strategies or may run in parallel.

● Game theory provides a basis for thinking through competitors' strategic moves in such a way as to pre-empt or counter them.

Illustration 6.6 **key debate**

To be different or the same?

Can differentiation strategies rebound, making an organisation seem dangerously eccentric rather than delivering competitive advantage?

This chapter has introduced the potential value of differentiation strategies, in which the organisation emphasises its uniqueness. This is consistent also with the argument of the resource-based view (Chapter 3) in favour of the distinctiveness and inimitability of an organisation's resources. But how far should an organisation push its uniqueness, especially if there is a danger of it beginning to be seen as simply eccentric?

McKinsey & Co. consultant Philipp Natterman makes a strong case for differentiation.[1] He tracks the relationship between profitability and differentiation (in terms of pricing and product features) over long periods in both the personal computer and mobile phone industries. He finds that as differentiation falls over time, so too do industry profit margins. Natterman blames management techniques such as benchmarking (Chapter 3), which tend to encourage convergence on industry 'best practices'. The trouble with best practices is that they easily become standard practices. There is no competitive advantage in following the herd.

However, 'institutional theorists' such as Paul DiMaggio and Walter Powell point to some advantages in herd-like behaviour.[2] They think of industries as 'organisational fields' in which all sorts of actors must interact – customers, suppliers, employees and regulators. The ability of these actors to interact effectively depends upon being legitimate in the eyes of other actors in the field. Over time, industries develop institutionalised norms of legitimate behaviour, which it makes sense for everybody to follow. It is easier for customers and suppliers to do business with organisations that are more or less the same as the others in the industry. It is reassuring to potential employees and industry regulators if organisations do not seem highly eccentric. Especially when there is high uncertainty about what drives performance – for example, in knowledge-based industries – it can be a lot better to be legitimate than different. To the extent that customers, suppliers, employees and regulators value conformity, then it is valuable in itself. Being a 'misfit' can be costly.

This institutionalist appreciation of conformity makes sense of a lot of strategic behaviour. For example, merger waves in some industries seem to be driven by bandwagons, in which organisations become panicked into making acquisitions simply for fear of being left behind. Likewise, many management initiatives, such as business process re-engineering, e-business or outsourcing, are the product of fads and fashions as much as hard objective analysis. The insight from institutionalist theory, however, is that following the fashion is not necessarily a bad thing.

Thus institutional theory and the resource-based view appear to have opposing perspectives on the value of differentiation. David Deephouse has investigated this apparent trade-off between differentiation and conformity in the American banking industry and found a curvilinear relationship between differentiation and financial performance.[3] Strong conformity led to inferior performance; moderate differentiation was associated with improved performance; extreme differentiation appeared to damage performance.

Deephouse concludes in favour of 'balance' between differentiation and conformity. He also suggests that the value of differentiation depends on the extent to which key actors in the industry – customers, suppliers, employees, and so on – have converged on institutionalised norms of appropriate strategy. It seems that strategies can be too differentiated, but that how much 'too differentiated' is depends on the kind of industry that one is in.

Sources:
1. P.M. Natterman, 'Best practice does not equal best strategy', *McKinsey Quarterly*, no. 2 (2000), pp. 22–31.
2. P. DiMaggio and W. Powell, 'The iron cage revisited: institutional isomorphism and collective rationality in organizational fields', *American Sociological Review*, vol. 48 (1983), pp. 147–160.
3. D. Deephouse, 'To be different or to be the same? It's a question (and theory) of strategic balance', *Strategic Management Journal*, vol. 20 (1999), pp. 147–166.

Questions

1 To what extent do (a) universities and (b) car manufacturers compete by being different or the same?

2 Considering the nature of their industries, and key players within them, why might these organisations adopt these approaches to conformity or differentiation?

Work assignments

*Denotes more advanced work assignments.   * Refers to a case study in the Text and Case edition.*

6.1   Using Exhibit 6.2, the strategy clock, identify examples of organisations following strategic routes 1 to 5. If you find it difficult to be clear about which route is being followed, note down the reasons for this, and consider if the organisations have a clear competitive strategy.

6.2   You have been appointed personal assistant to the chief executive of a major manufacturing firm, who has asked you to explain what is meant by 'differentiation' and why it is important. Write a brief report addressing these questions.

6.3 ✲ How appropriate are bases of competitive advantage explained in section 6.3 for considering the strategies of public sector organisations? Illustrate your argument by reference to a public sector organisation of your choice.

6.4   Applying the lessons from section 6.4, consider how sustainable are the strategies of any of:

(a) Tesco
(b) Ryanair*
(c) an organisation of your choice.

6.5 ✲ Choose an industry or sector which is becoming more and more competitive (for example, financial services or fashion retailing). How might the principles of hypercompetitive strategies apply to that industry?

6.6   Drawing on sections 6.6 (on collaborative strategies) write a report for the chief executive of a business in a competitive market (for example, pharmaceuticals* or Formula One*) explaining when and in what ways cooperation rather than direct competition might make sense.

Integrative assignment

6.7 ✲ Refer to section 6.4.3 and Exhibit 6.3. If the achievement of 'lock-in' were to be the basis of an international strategy (Chapter 8) explain how this might influence the choices around both the direction and methods of strategy development (Chapter 10).

An extensive range of additional materials, including audio summaries, weblinks to organisations featured in the text, definitions of key concepts and self-assessment questions, can be found on the *Exploring Corporate Strategy* Companion Website at **www.pearsoned.co.uk/ecs**

Recommended key readings

- The foundations of the discussions of generic competitive strategies are to be found in the writings of Michael Porter, which include *Competitive Strategy* (1980) and *Competitive Advantage* (1985), both published by Free Press. Both are recommended for readers who wish to understand the background to discussions in sections 6.3 and 6.4 on competitive strategy and competitive advantage.

- Hypercompetition, and the strategies associated with its conditions, are explained in Richard D'Aveni, *Hypercompetitive Rivalries: Competing in highly dynamic environments*, Free Press, 1995. There is a lively debate about whether sustainable competitive advantage is possible. Two papers offering different evidence on this are: R.W. Wiggins and T.W. Ruefli, 'Schumpeter's ghost:

is hypercompetition making the best of times shorter?', *Strategic Management Journal*, vol. 26 (2005), pp. 887–911, which argues there is no evidence for sustainable competitive advantage; and G. Mcnamara, P.M. Vaaler and C. Devers, 'Same as it ever was: the search for evidence of increasing hypercompetition', *Strategic Management Journal*, vol. 24 (2003), pp. 261–278, which argues that it is.

- There is much written on game theory but a good deal of it can be rather inaccessible to the lay reader. An exception is the book by A.K. Dixit and B.J. Nalebuff, *Thinking Strategically*, W.W. Norton, 1991. R. McCain, *Game Theory: A Non-Technical Introduction to the Analysis of Strategy*, South Western, 2003, considers business strategy in game theory terms.

References

1. For a detailed discussion as to how organisational structures might 'address' an organisation's mix of SBUs see M. Goold and A. Campbell, *Designing Effective Organisations: How to create structured networks*, Jossey Bass, 2002. Also K. Eisenhardt and S. Brown, 'Patching', *Harvard Business Review*, vol. 77, no. 3 (1999), p. 72.
2. M. Porter, *Competitive Advantage*, Free Press, 1985.
3. See D. Faulkner and C. Bowman, *The Essence of Competitive Strategy*, Prentice Hall, 1995. A similar framework is also used by Richard D'Aveni, *Hypercompetitive Rivalries: Competing in highly dynamic environments*, Free Press, 1995.
4. B. Sharp and J. Dawes, 'What is differentiation and how does it work?', *Journal of Marketing Management*, vol. 17, nos 7/8 (2001), pp. 739–759, reviews the relationship between differentiation and profitability.
5. See, for example, D. Miller, 'The generic strategy trap', *Journal of Business Strategy*, vol. 13, no. 1 (1992), pp. 37–42; C.W.L. Hill, 'Differentiation versus low cost or differentiation and low cost: a contingency framework', *Academy of Management Review*, vol. 13, no. 3 (1998), pp. 401–412; and S. Thornhill and R. White, 'Strategic purity: a multi-industry evaluation of pure vs hybrid business strategies', *Strategic Management Journal*, vol. 28, no. 5 (2007), pp. 553–561.
6. See G. Hamel and C.K. Prahalad, 'Do you really have a global strategy?', *Harvard Business Review*, vol. 63, no. 4 (1985), pp. 139–148.
7. These quotes concerning Porter's three competitive strategies are taken from his book *Competitive Advantage*, Free Press, 1985, pp. 12–15.
8. The Delta Model is explained and illustrated more fully in A.C. Hax and D.L. Wilde II, 'The Delta Model', *Sloan Management Review*, vol. 40, no. 2 (1999), pp. 11–28.
9. This section is based on research by N. Kumar, 'Strategies to fight low cost rivals', *Harvard Business Review*, vol. 84, no. 12 (2006), pp. 104–113.
10. For a discussion of how to compete in such circumstances, see A. Rao, M. Bergen and S. Davis, 'How to fight a price war', *Harvard Business Review*, vol. 78, no. 2 (2000), pp. 107–115.

11. The extent to which hypercompetitive conditions exist is a matter of debate. There is evidence in support: see R.W. Wiggins and T.W. Ruefli, 'Schumpeter's ghost: is hypercompetition making the best of times shorter?', *Strategic Management Journal*, vol. 26 (2005), pp. 887–911. But there is also evidence against: see G. Mcnamara, P.M. Vaaler and C. Devers, 'Same as it was: the search for evidence of increasing hypercompetition', *Strategic Management Journal*, vol. 24 (2003), pp. 261–278.
12. See D'Aveni, reference 3.
13. For other examples of misleading signals see G. Stalk Jr, 'Curveball: strategies to fool the competition', *Harvard Business Review*, September (2006), pp. 115–122.
14. Useful books on collaborative strategies are Y. Doz and G. Hamel, *Alliance Advantage: The art of creating value through partnering*, Harvard Business School Press, 1998; *Creating Collaborative Advantage*, ed. Chris Huxham, Sage, 1996; and D. Faulkner, *Strategic Alliances: Co-operating to compete*, McGraw-Hill, 1995.
15. This case for cooperation in hi-tech industries is argued and illustrated by V. Kapur, J. Peters and S. Berman: 'High tech 2005: the horizontal, hypercompetitive future', *Strategy and Leadership*, vol. 31, no. 2 (2003), pp. 34–47.
16. See J. Brudney and R. England, 'Towards a definition of the co-production concept', *Public Administration Review*, vol. 43, no. 10 (1983), pp. 59–65; and J. Alford, 'A public management road less travelled: clients as co-producers of public services', *Australian Journal of Public Administration*, vol. 57, no. 4 (1998), pp. 128–137.
17. For readings on game theory see A.K. Dixit and B.J. Nalebuff, *Thinking Strategically*, W.W. Norton, 1991; A. Brandenburger and B. Nalebuff, *Co-opetition*, Profile Books, 1997; R. McCain, *Game Theory: A Non-Technical Introduction to the Analysis of Strategy*, South Western, 2003; and, for a summary, S. Regan, 'Game theory perspective', In M. Jenkins and V. Ambrosini (eds), *Advanced Strategic Management: A Multi-Perspective Approach*, 2nd edition, Palgrave Macmillan, 2007, pp. 83–101.
18. A. Brandenburger and B.J. Nalebuff, *Co-opetition*, Profile Books, 1997.

Madonna: still the reigning queen of pop?

Phyl Johnson, Strathclyde University Business School

The music industry has always been the backdrop
for one-hit wonders and brief careers. Pop stars who
have remained at the top for decades are very few.
Madonna is one such phenomenon; the question is,
after over 25 years at the top, how much longer can
it last?

Described by *Billboard Magazine* as the smartest
business woman in show business, Madonna, Louise
Ciccone, began her music career in 1983 with the hit
single 'Holiday' and in 2005–2006 once again enjoyed
chart success for her album 'Confessions on a Dance
Floor'. In the meantime she had consistent chart
success with her singles and albums, multiple sell-out
world tours, major roles in six films, picked up 18
music awards, been the style icon behind a range of
products from Pepsi and Max Factor to the Gap and
H&M, and became a worldwide best-selling children's
author.

The foundation of Madonna's business success
was her ability to sustain her reign as the 'queen
of pop' since 1983. Along with many others, Phil
Quattro, the President of Warner Brothers, has argued
that 'she always manages to land on the cusp of what
we call contemporary music, every established artist
faces the dilemma of maintaining their importance
and relevance, Madonna never fails to be relevant.'
Madonna's chameleon-like ability to change persona,
change her music genre with it and yet still achieve
major record sales has been the hallmark of her
success.

Madonna's early poppy style was targeted at
young 'wannabe' girls. The image that she portrayed
through hits such as 'Holiday' and 'Lucky Star' in
1983 was picked up by Macy's, the US-based
department store. It produced a range of *Madonna
lookalike* clothes that mothers were happy to
purchase for their daughters. One year later in 1984,
Madonna then underwent her first image change and,
in doing so, offered the first hint of the smart cookie
behind the media image. In the video for her hit

Photo: DPA/PA Photos

'Material Girl', she deliberately mirrored the glamour-
based, sexual pussycat image of Marilyn Monroe
whilst simultaneously mocking both the growing
materialism of the late 1980s and the men fawning
after her. Media analysts Sam and Diana Kirschner
commented that with this kind of packaging,
Madonna allowed the record companies to keep hold
of a saleable 'Marilyn image' for a new cohort of fans,
but also allowed her original fan base of now growing
up wannabe girls to take the more critical message
from the music. The theme of courting controversy
but staying marketable enough has been recurrent

throughout her career, if not slightly toned down in later years.

Madonna's subsequent image changes were more dramatic. First she took on the Catholic Church in her 1989 video 'Like a Prayer' where, as a red-dressed 'sinner', she kissed a black saint easily interpreted as a Jesus figure. Her image had become increasingly sexual whilst also holding on to a critical social theme: for example, her pointed illustration of white-only imagery in the Catholic Church. At this point in her career, Madonna took full control of her image in the $60m (€48m; £33m) deal with Time-Warner that created her record company Maverick. In 1991, she published a coffee-table soft-porn book entitled *Sex* that exclusively featured pictures of herself in erotic poses. Her image and music also reflected this erotic theme. In her 'Girlie' tour, her singles 'Erotica' and 'Justify my Love' and her fly-on-the-wall movie 'In bed with Madonna' she played out scenes of sadomasochistic and lesbian fantasies. Although allegedly a period of her career she would rather forget, Madonna more than survived it. In fact, she gained a whole new demography of fans who not only respected her artistic courage, but also did not miss the fact that Madonna was consistent in her message: her sexuality was her own and not in need of a male gaze. She used the media's love affair with her, and the *cause célèbre* status gained from having MTV ban the video for 'Justify my Love', to promote the message that women's sexuality and freedom is just as important and acceptable as men's.

Changing gear in 1996, Madonna finally took centre stage in the lead role in the film *Evita* that she had chased for over five years. She beat other heavyweight contenders for the role including Meryl Streep and Elaine Page, both with more acceptable pasts than Madonna. Yet she achieved the image transition from erotica to saint-like persona of Eva Peron and won critical acclaim to boot. Another vote of confidence from the 'establishment' came from Max Factor, who in 1999 signed her up to front its relaunch campaign that was crafted around a glamour theme. Procter and Gamble (owners of the Max Factor make-up range) argued that they saw Madonna as 'the closest thing the 90s has to an old-style Hollywood star . . . she is a real woman'.

With many pre-release leaks, Madonna's keenly awaited album 'Ray of Light' was released in 1998. Radio stations worldwide were desperate to get hold

of the album being billed as her most successful musical voyage to date. In a smart move, Madonna had teamed up with techno pioneer William Orbit to write and produce the album. It was a huge success, taking Madonna into the super-trendy techno sphere, not the natural environment for a pop star from the early 1980s. Madonna took up an 'earth mother/ spiritual' image and spawned a trend for all things Eastern in fashion and music. This phase may have produced more than just an image as it is the time in Madonna's life which locates the beginning of her continued faith in the Kabbalah tradition of Eastern spiritual worship.

By 2001, her next persona was unveiled with the release of her album 'Music'. Here her style had moved on again to 'acid rock'. With her marriage to British movie director Guy Ritchie, the ultimate 'American Pie' had become a fully fledged Brit babe earning the endearing nick name of 'Madge' in the British press.

By 2003 some commentators were suggesting that an interesting turn of events hinted that perhaps 'the cutting-edge' Madonna, 'the fearless', was starting to think about *being part of* rather than *beating* the establishment when she launched her new Che-Guevara-inspired image. Instead of maximising the potential of this image in terms of its political and social symbolism during the Second Gulf War, in April 2003 she withdrew her militaristic image and video for the album 'American Life'. That action timed with the publication of her children's book *The English Roses*, based on the themes of compassion and friendship, which sparked questions in the press around the theme 'has Madonna gone soft?'

By late 2003 she had wiped the military image from the West's collective memory with a glitzy high-profile ad campaign for the Gap, the clothing retailer in which she danced around accompanied by rapper Missy Elliot to a retrospective remix of her 1980s' track 'Get into the Groove'. Here Madonna was keeping the 'thirty-somethings', who remembered the track from first time around, happy. They could purchase jeans for themselves and their newly teenage daughters whilst also purchasing the re-released CD (on sale in store) for them to share and a copy of *The English Roses* (also promoted in the Gap stores) for perhaps the youngest member of the family.

Late 2005 saw the release of the 'Confessions on a Dance Floor' album that was marketed as her

Releases	Year	Image	Target audience
Lucky Star	1982	Trashy pop	Young wannabe girls, dovetailing from fading disco to emerging 'club scene'
Like a Virgin *Like a Prayer*	1984	Originally a Marilyn glamour image, then became a saint and sinner	More grown-up rebellious fan base, more critical female audience and male worshippers
Vogue *Erotica* *Bedtime Stories*	1990 1992 1994	Erotic porn star, sadomasochistic, sexual control, more Minelli in *Cabaret* than Monroe	Peculiar mix of target audiences: gay club scene, 1990s' women taking control of their own lives, also pure male titillation
Something to Remember Evita	1995	Softer image, ballads preparing for glamour image of *Evita* film role	Broadest audience target, picking up potential film audiences as well as regular fan base. Most conventional image. Max Factor later used this mixture of Marilyn and Eva Peron to market its glamour image
Ray of Light	1998	Earth mother, Eastern mysticism, dance music fusion	Clubbing generation of the 1990s, new cohort of fans plus original fan base of now 30-somethings desperately staying trendy
Music	2000	Acid rock, tongue in cheek Miss USA/cow girl, cool Britannia	Managing to hit the changing club scene and 30-something Brits
American Life	2003	Militaristic image Che Guevara Anti-consumerism of American dream	Unclear audience reliant on existing base
Confessions on a Dance Floor	2005	Retro-1980s' disco imagery, high-motion dance–pop sound	Strong gay–icon audience, pop–disco audience, dance-based audience

comeback album after her lowest-selling 'American Life'. It and the linked tour achieved one of the highest-selling peaks of her career. The album broke a world record for solo-female artists when it debuted at number one in 41 countries. By February 2007 it had sold 8 million copies. Here Madonna focused on the high-selling principal of *remix*, choosing samples of the gay–iconic disco favourites of Abba and Giorgio Moroder to be at the heart of her symbolic reinvention of herself from artist to DJ. By cross-marketing the album image with Dolce & Gabbana in its men's fashion shows, Madonna cashed in on her regaining the dance–pop crown. Will this, her latest album, stand the musical test of time? Who knows? But for now it seems to have more than met the moment.

Sources: 'Bennett takes the reins at Maverick', *Billboard Magazine*, 7 August (1999); 'Warner Bros expects Madonna to light up international markets', *Billboard Magazine*, 21 February (1998); 'Maverick builds on early success', *Billboard Magazine*, 12 November (1994); A., Jardine 'Max Factor strikes gold with Madonna', *Marketing*, vol. 29, (1999), pp. 14–15; S. Kirschner and D. Kirschner, 'MTV, adolescence and Madonna: a discourse analysis', in *Perspectives on Psychology & the Media*, American Psychological Association, Washington, DC, 1997; 'Warner to buy out maverick co-founder', *Los Angeles Times*, 2 March (1999); 'Why Madonna is back in Vogue', *New Statesman*, 18 September (2000); 'Madonna & Microsoft', *Financial Times*, 28 November (2000).

Questions

1 Describe and explain the strategy being followed by Madonna in terms of the explanation of competitive strategy given in Chapter 6.

2 Why has she experienced sustained success over the past two decades?

3 What might threaten the sustainability of her success?

Strategic Choices

7

Strategic Directions and Corporate-Level Strategy

LEARNING OUTCOMES

After reading this chapter you should be able to:

→ Identify alternative directions for strategy, including market penetration or consolidation, product development, market development and diversification.

→ Recognise when diversification is an effective strategy for growth.

→ Distinguish between different diversification strategies (related and unrelated) and identify conditions under which they work best.

→ Analyse the ways in which a corporate parent can add or destroy value for its portfolio of business units.

→ Analyse portfolios of business units and judge which to invest in and which to divest.

7.1 INTRODUCTION

Chapter 6 was concerned with choices at the level of single business or organisational units, for instance through pricing strategies or differentiation. This chapter is about choices of *products and markets* for an organisation to enter or exit (see Exhibit II.i in the Part Introduction). Should the organisation be very focused on just a few products and markets? Or should it be much broader in scope, perhaps very diversified in terms of both products (or services) and markets? Many organisations do choose to enter many new product and market areas. For example, the Virgin Group started out in the music business, but is now highly diverse, operating in the holiday, cinema, retail, air travel and rail markets. Sony began by making small radios, but now produces games, music and movies, as well as a host of electronic products. As organisations add new units, their strategies are no longer concerned just with the business-level but with the corporate-level choices involved in having many different businesses or markets.

The chapter begins by introducing Ansoff's matrix, which generates an initial set of alternative strategic directions. The four basic directions are *increased penetration* of existing markets; *market development*, which includes building new markets, perhaps overseas or in new customer segments; *product development*, referring to product improvement and innovation; and *diversification*, involving a significant broadening of an organisation's scope in terms of both markets and products. This chapter takes a particularly hard look at the diversification option, proposing good reasons for doing so and warning of less good reasons. Diversification does not always pay. Chapter 8 takes up internationalisation as one form of market development; Chapter 9 addresses product development in the form of innovation and entrepreneurship.

Diversification raises the other themes of the chapter. The first theme here is the role of the 'corporate-level' executives that perform a **corporate parent** role with regard to the individual business units that make up diversified organisations' portfolios. Given their detachment from the actual marketplace, how can corporate-level activities, decisions and resources add value to the actual businesses? As will be seen in this chapter's key debate (Illustration 7.6), there is considerable scepticism about the role of corporate-level strategy. The second theme is how to achieve a good mix of businesses within the corporate portfolio. Which businesses should corporate parents cultivate and which should they divest? Here various portfolio matrices help structure corporate-level choices.

The chapter is not just about large commercial businesses. Even small businesses may consist of a number of business units. For example, a local builder may be undertaking contract work for local government, work for industrial buyers and for local homeowners. Not only are these different market segments, but the mode of operation and capabilities required for competitive success are also likely to be different. Moreover, the owner of that business has to take decisions about the extent of investment and activity in each segment. Public sector organisations such as local government or health services also provide different services, which correspond to business units in commercial organisations. Corporate-level strategy is highly relevant to the appropriate drawing of organisational boundaries in the public sector, and privatisation and outsourcing

The **corporate parent** *refers to the levels of management above that of the business units, and therefore without direct interaction with buyers and competitors*

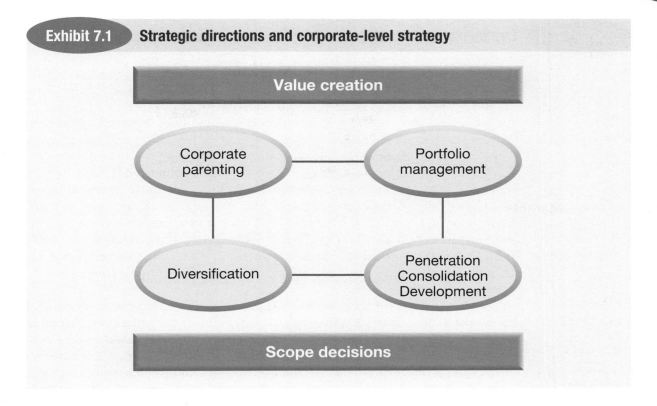

Exhibit 7.1 | Strategic directions and corporate-level strategy

decisions can be considered as responses to the failure of public sector organisations to add sufficient value by their parenting.

Exhibit 7.1 summarises the key themes of this chapter. After reviewing Ansoff's strategic directions, the chapter focuses specifically on diversification. Diversification in turn raises the two related topics of the role of the corporate parent and the use of business portfolio matrices.

7.2 STRATEGIC DIRECTIONS

www.pearsoned.co.uk/ecs

KEY CONCEPT

Strategic directions

The Ansoff product/market growth matrix[1] provides a simple way of generating four basic alternative directions for strategic development: see Exhibit 7.2. An organisation typically starts in box A, the top left-hand one, with its existing products and existing markets. According to the matrix, the organisation basically has a choice between *penetrating* still further within its existing sphere (staying in box A); moving rightwards by *developing new products* for its existing markets (box B); moving downwards by bringing its *existing products into new markets* (box C); or taking the most radical step of full *diversification*, with altogether new markets and new products (box D).

The Ansoff matrix explicitly considers growth options. Growth is rarely a good end in itself. Public sector organisations are often accused of growing out-of-control bureaucracies; similarly, some private sector managers are accused of empire building at the expense of shareholders. This chapter therefore adds

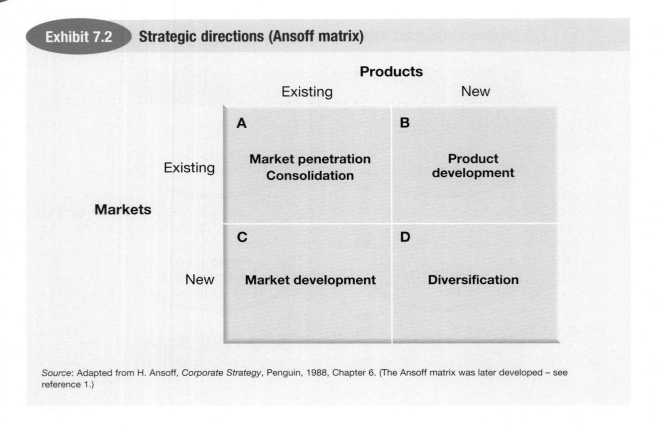

Exhibit 7.2   **Strategic directions (Ansoff matrix)**

Source: Adapted from H. Ansoff, *Corporate Strategy*, Penguin, 1988, Chapter 6. (The Ansoff matrix was later developed – see reference 1.)

consolidation as a fifth option. Consolidation involves protecting existing products and existing markets and therefore belongs in box A. The rest of this section considers the five strategic directions in more detail. See Illustration 7.1 for an application of the Ansoff matrix to Springer publishers.

7.2.1 Market penetration

> Market penetration is where an organisation gains market share

Further **market penetration**, by which the organisation takes increased share of its existing markets with its existing product range, is on the face of it the most obvious strategic direction. It builds on existing strategic capabilities and does not require the organisation to venture into uncharted territory. The organisation's scope is exactly the same. Moreover, greater market share implies increased power vis-à-vis buyers and suppliers (in terms of the five forces), greater economies of scale and experience curve benefits.

However, organisations seeking greater market penetration may face two constraints:

● *Retaliation from competitors.* In terms of the five forces (section 2.2), increasing market penetration is likely to exacerbate industry rivalry as other competitors in the market defend their share. Increased rivalry might involve price wars or expensive marketing battles, which may cost more than any market share gains are actually worth. The dangers of provoking fierce retaliation are greater in low-growth markets, as any gains in volume will be much more

Illustration 7.1

Strategic directions for Axel Springer

This German publishing company has many opportunities, and the money to pursue them.

In 2007, Mathias Döpfner, Chairman and Chief Executive of Axel Springer publishers, had about €2bn (£1.5bn) to invest in new opportunities. The previous year, the competition authorities had prohibited his full takeover of Germany's largest television broadcaster, ProSiebenSat.1. Now Döpfner was looking for alternative directions.

Founded in 1946 by Axel Springer himself, the company was in 2007 already Germany's largest publisher of newspapers and magazines, with more than 10,000 employees and over 150 titles. Famous print titles included *Die Welt*, the *Berliner Morgenpost*, *Bild* and *Hörzu*. Outside Germany, Axel Springer was strongest in Eastern Europe. The company also had a scattering of mostly small investments in German radio and television companies, most notably a continuing 12 per cent stake in ProSieben Sat.1. Axel Springer described its strategic objectives as market leadership in the German-language core business, internationalisaton and digitalisation of the core business.

Further digitalisation of the core newspaper and magazine business was clearly important and would require substantial funding. There were also opportunities for the launch of new print magazine titles in the German market. But Döpfner was considering acquisition opportunities: 'it goes without saying,' he told the *Financial Times*, 'that whenever a large international media company comes on to the market (i.e. is up for sale), we will examine it very closely – whether in print, TV or the online sector'.

Döpfner mentioned several specific kinds of acquisition opportunity. For example, he was still interested in buying a large European television broadcaster, even if it would probably have to be outside Germany. He was also attracted by the possibility of buying undervalued assets in the old media (namely, print), and turning them around in the style of a private equity investor: 'I would love to buy businesses in need of restructuring, where we can add value by introducing our management and sector expertise'. However, Döpfner reassured his shareholders by affirming that he felt no need 'to do a big thing in order to do a big thing'. He was also considering what to do with the 12 per cent minority stake in ProSiebenSat.1.

Main source: Financial Times Deutschland, 2 April (2007).

Questions

1 Referring to Exhibit 7.1, classify the various strategic directions considered by Mattias Döpfner for Axel Springer.

2 Using the Ansoff matrix, what other options could Döpfner pursue?

at the expense of other players. Where retaliation is a danger, organisations seeking market penetration need strategic capabilities that give a clear competitive advantage. In low-growth or declining markets, it can be more effective simply to acquire competitors. Some companies have grown quickly in this way. For example, in the steel industry the Indian company LNM (Mittal) moved rapidly in the 2000s to become the largest steel producer in the world by acquiring struggling steel companies around the world. Acquisitions can actually reduce rivalry, by taking out independent players and consolidating them under one umbrella: see also the consolidation strategy in section 7.2.2.

- *Legal constraints*. Greater market penetration can raise concerns from official competition regulators concerning excessive market power. Most countries have regulators with the powers to restrain powerful companies or prevent mergers and acquisitions that would create such excessive power. In the United Kingdom, the Competition Commission can investigate any merger or acquisition that would account for more than 25 per cent of the national market, and either halt the deal or propose measures that would reduce market power. The European Commission has an overview of the whole European market and can similarly intervene. For example, when Gaz de France and Suez, two utility companies with dominant positions in France and Belgium, decided to merge in 2006, the European Commission insisted that the two companies reduce their power by divesting some of their subsidiaries and opening up their networks to competition.[2]

7.2.2 Consolidation

Consolidation is where organisations focus defensively on their current markets with current products

Consolidation is where organisations focus defensively on their current markets with current products. Formally, this strategy occupies the same box in the Ansoff matrix as market penetration, but is not orientated to growth. Consolidation can take two forms:

- *Defending market share*. When facing aggressive competitors bent on increasing their market share, organisations have to work hard and often creatively to protect what they already have. Although market share should rarely be an end in itself, it is important to ensure that it is sufficient to sustain the business in the long term. For example, turnover has to be high enough to spread essential fixed costs such as R&D. In defending market share, differentiation strategies in order to build customer loyalty and switching costs are often effective.

- *Downsizing or divestment*. Especially when the size of the market as a whole is declining, reducing the size of the business through closing capacity is often unavoidable. An alternative is divesting (selling) some activities to other businesses. Sometimes downsizing can be dictated by the needs of shareholders, for instance an entrepreneur wishing to simplify his or her business on approaching retirement. Divesting or closing peripheral businesses can also make it easier to sell the core business to a potential purchaser.

The term 'consolidation' is sometimes also used to describe strategies of *buying up rivals* in a fragmented industry, particularly one in decline. By acquiring weaker competitors, and closing capacity, the consolidating company can gain market power and increase overall efficiency. As this form of consolidation increases market share, it could be seen as a kind of market penetration, but here the motivation is essentially defensive.

Although both consolidation and market penetration strategies are by no means static ones, their limitations often propel managers to consider alternative strategic directions.

7.2.3 **Product development**

Product development is
where organisations
deliver modified or new
products to existing
markets

Product development is where organisations deliver modified or new products (or services) to existing markets. This is a limited extension of organisational scope. In practice, even market penetration will probably require some product development, but here product development implies greater degrees of innovation. For Sony, such product development would include moving the Walkman portable music system from audio tapes, through CDs to MP3-based systems. Effectively the same markets are involved, but the technologies are radically different. In the case of the Walkman, Sony probably had little choice but to make these significant product developments. However, product development can be an expensive and high-risk activity for at least two reasons:

- *New strategic capabilities*. Product development typically involves mastering new technologies that may be unfamiliar to the organisation. For example, many banks entered online banking at the beginning of this century, but suffered many setbacks with technologies so radically different to their traditional high street branch means of delivering banking services. Success frequently depended on a willingness to acquire new technological and marketing capabilities, often with the help of specialised IT and e-commerce consultancy firms.[3] Thus product development typically involves heavy investments and high risk of project failures.

- *Project management risk*. Even within fairly familiar domains, product development projects are typically subject to the risk of delays and increased costs due to project complexity and changing project specifications over time. A famous recent case was the €11bn (£7.6bn) Airbus A380 double-decker airline project, which suffered two years of delays in the mid-2000s because of wiring problems. Airbus had managed several new aircraft developments before, but the high degrees of customisation required by each airline customer, and incompatibilities in computer-aided design software, led to greater complexity than the company's project management staff could handle.

Strategies for product development are considered further in Chapter 9.

7.2.4 **Market development**

Market development is
where existing products
are offered in new
markets

If product development is risky and expensive, an alternative strategy is market development. **Market development** involves offering existing products to new markets. Again, the extension of scope is limited. Typically, of course, this may entail some product development as well, if only in terms of packaging or service. Market development might take three forms:

- *New segments*. For example, in the public services, a college might offer its educational services to older students than its traditional intake, perhaps via evening courses.

- *New users*. Here an example would be aluminium, whose original users in packaging and cutlery manufacture are now supplemented by users in aerospace and automobiles.

● *New geographies*. The prime example of this is internationalisation, but the spread of a small retailer into new towns would also be a case.

In all cases, it is essential that market development strategies are based on products or services that meet the *critical success factors* of the new market (see section 2.4.4).

Strategies based on simply offloading traditional products or services in new markets are likely to fail. Moreover, market development faces similar problems as product development. In terms of strategic capabilities, market developers often lack the right marketing skills and brands to make progress in a market with unfamiliar customers. On the management side, the challenge is coordinating between different segments, users and geographies, which might all have different needs. International market development strategy is considered in Chapter 8.

7.2.5 Diversification

Diversification is defined as a strategy that takes an organisation away from both its existing markets and its existing products

Diversification is strictly a strategy that takes the organisation away from both its existing markets and its existing products (box D in Exhibit 7.1). In this sense, it radically increases the organisation's scope. In fact, much diversification is not as extreme as implied by the closed boxes of the Ansoff growth matrix. Box D tends to imply unrelated or conglomerate diversification (see section 7.3.2), but a good deal of diversification in practice involves building on relationships with existing markets or products. Frequently too, market penetration and product development entail some diversifying adjustment of products or markets. Diversification is a matter of degree.

None the less, the Ansoff matrix does make clear that the further the organisation moves from its starting point of existing products and existing markets, the more the organisation has to learn to do. Diversification is just one direction for developing the organisation, and needs to be considered alongside its alternatives. The drivers of diversification, its various forms and the ways it is managed are the main topics of this chapter.

7.3 REASONS FOR DIVERSIFICATION

In terms of the Ansoff matrix, diversification is the most radical strategic direction.[4] Diversification might be chosen for a variety of reasons, some more value creating than others. Three potentially value-creating reasons for diversification are as follows.

● *Efficiency gains* can be made by applying the organisation's existing resources or capabilities to new markets and products or services. These are often described as *economies of scope*, by contrast to economies of scale.[5] If an organisation has underutilised resources or competences that it cannot effectively close or sell to other potential users, it can make sense to use these resources or competences by diversification into a new activity. In other words, there are economies to be gained by extending the scope of the organisation's activities. For example, many universities have large resources in terms of halls of residence, which they must have for their students but which are underutilised out of term-time. These halls of residence are more efficiently used if the universities expand the scope of their activities into conferencing and tourism during vacation periods. Economies of scope may apply to both *tangible* resources, such as halls of residence, and *intangible* resources and competences, such as brands or staff skills. Sometimes these scope advantages are referred to as the benefits of **synergy**,[6] by which is meant that activities or assets are more effective together than apart (the famous $2 + 2 = 5$ equation). Thus a film company and a music publisher would be synergistic if they were worth more together than separately. Illustration 7.2 shows how a French company, Zodiac, has diversified following this approach.

> **Synergy** refers to the benefits that are gained where activities or assets complement each other so that their combined effect is greater than the sum of the parts

- *Stretching corporate parenting capabilities* into new markets and products or services can be another source of gain. In a sense, this extends the point above about applying existing competences in new areas. However, this point highlights corporate parenting skills that can otherwise easily be neglected. At the corporate parent level, managers may develop a competence at managing a range of different products and services which can be applied even to businesses which do not share resources at the operational unit level. C.K. Prahalad and R. Bettis have described this set of corporate parenting skills as the 'dominant general management logic', or 'dominant logic' for short.[7] Thus the French conglomerate LVMH includes a wide range of businesses – from champagne, through fashion and perfumes, to financial media – that share very few operational resources or competences. LVMH creates value for these specialised companies by adding parenting skills – for instance, the support of classic brands and the nurturing of highly creative people – that are relevant to all these individual businesses (see section 7.4.1).

- *Increasing market power* can result from having a diverse range of businesses. With many businesses, an organisation can afford to cross-subsidise one business from the surpluses earned by another, in a way that competitors may not be able to. This can give an organisation a competitive advantage for the subsidised business, and the long-run effect may be to drive out other competitors, leaving the organisation with a monopoly from which good profits can then be earned. This was the fear behind the European Commission's refusal to allow General Electric's \$43bn (£24bn; €37bn) bid for electronic controls company Honeywell in 2001. General Electric might have bundled its jet engines with Honeywell's aviation electronics in a cheaper package than rival jet engine manufacturers could possibly match. As aircraft manufacturers and airlines increasingly chose the cheaper overall package, rivals could have been driven out of business. General Electric would then have the market power to put up its prices without threat from competition.

There are several other reasons that are often given for diversification, but which are less obviously value creating and sometimes serve managerial interests more than shareholders' interests:

- *Responding to market decline* is one common but doubtful reason for diversification. It is arguable that Microsoft's diversification into electronic games such as the Xbox – whose launch cost \$500m (£280m; €415m) in marketing

Illustration 7.2

Zodiac: inflatable diversifications

An organisation may seek the benefits of synergies by building a portfolio of businesses through related diversification.

The Zodiac company was founded near Paris, France, in 1896 by Maurice Mallet just after his first hot-air balloon ascent. For 40 years, Zodiac manufactured only dirigible airships. In 1937, the German Zeppelin *Hindenburg* crashed near New York, which abruptly stopped the development of the market for airships. Because of the extinction of its traditional activity, Zodiac decided to leverage its technical expertise and moved from dirigibles to inflatable boats. This diversification proved to be very successful: in 2004, with over 1 million units sold in 50 years, the Zodiac rubber dinghy (priced at approximately €10,000 (£7,000)) was extremely popular worldwide.

However, because of increasing competition, especially from Italian manufacturers, Zodiac diversified its business interests. In 1978, it took over Aerazur, a company specialising in parachutes, but also in life vests and inflatable life rafts. These products had strong market and technical synergies with rubber boats and their main customers were aircraft manufacturers. Zodiac confirmed this move to a new market in 1987 by the takeover of Air Cruisers, a manufacturer of inflatable escape slides for aircraft. As a consequence, Zodiac became a key supplier to Boeing, McDonnell Douglas and Airbus. Zodiac strengthened this position through the takeover of the two leading manufacturers of aircraft seats: Sicma Aero Seats from France and Weber Aircraft from the USA. In 1997, Zodiac also took over, for €150m, MAG Aerospace, the world leader for aircraft vacuum waste systems. Finally, in 1999, Zodiac took over Intertechnique, a leading player in active components for aircraft (fuel circulation, hydraulics, oxygen and life support, electrical power, flight-deck controls and displays, systems monitoring, etc.). By combining these competences with its traditional expertise in inflatable products, Zodiac launched a new business unit: airbags for the automobile industry.

In parallel to these diversifications, Zodiac strengthened its position in inflatable boats by

the takeover of several competitors: Bombard-L'Angevinière in 1980, Sevylor in 1981, Hurricane and Metzeler in 1987.

Finally, Zodiac developed a swimming-pool business. The first product line, back in 1981, was based on inflatable structure technology, and Zodiac later moved – again through takeovers – to rigid above-ground pools, modular in-ground pools, pool cleaners and water purification systems, inflatable beach gear and air mattresses.

In 2003, total sales of the Zodiac group reached €1.48bn with a net profit of €115m. Zodiac was a very international company, with a strong presence in the USA. It was listed on the Paris Stock Exchange and rumours of takeovers from powerful US groups were frequent. However, the family of the founder, institutional investors, the management and the employees together held 55 per cent of the stocks.

Far above the marine and the leisure businesses, aircraft products accounted for almost 75 per cent of the total turnover of the group. Zodiac held a 40 per cent market share of the world market for some airline equipment: for instance, the electrical power systems of the new Airbus A380 were Zodiac products. In 2004, Zodiac even reached Mars: NASA Mars probes *Spirit* and *Opportunity* were equipped with Zodiac equipment, developed by its US subsidiary Pioneer Aerospace.

Prepared by Frédéric Fréry, ESCP-EAP European School of Management.

Questions

1 What were the bases of the synergies underlying each of Zodiac's diversifications?

2 What are the advantages and potential dangers of such a basis of diversification?

alone – is a response to slowing growth in its core software businesses. Share-holders might have preferred the Xbox money to have been handed back to shareholders, leaving Sony and Nintendo to make games, while Microsoft gracefully declined. Microsoft itself defends its various diversifications as a necessary response to convergence in electronic and computer media.

● *Spreading risk* across a range of businesses is another common justification for diversification. However, conventional finance theory is very sceptical about risk spreading by business diversification. It argues that investors can diver-sify more effectively themselves by investing in a diverse portfolio of quite dif-ferent companies. Whilst managers might like the security of a diverse range of businesses, investors do not need each of the companies they invest in to be diversified as well – they would prefer managers to concentrate on managing their core business as well as they can. On the other hand, for private busi-nesses, where the owners have a large proportion of their assets tied up in the business, it can make sense to diversify risk across a number of distinct activ-ities, so that if one part is in trouble, the whole business is not pulled down.

● *The expectations of powerful stakeholders*, including top managers, can some-times drive inappropriate diversification. Under pressure from Wall Street analysts to deliver continued revenue growth, in the late 1990s the US energy company Enron diversified beyond its original interest in energy trading into trading commodities such as petrochemicals, aluminium and even band-width.[8] By satisfying the analysts in the short term, this strategy boosted the share price and allowed top management to stay in place. However, it soon transpired that very little of this diversification had been profitable, and in 2001 Enron collapsed in the largest bankruptcy in history.

In order to decide whether or not such reasons make sense and help organ-isational performance, it is important to be clear about different forms of diversification, in particular the degree of relatedness (or unrelatedness) of business units in a portfolio. The next sections consider related and unrelated diversification.

7.3.1 Related diversification

Related diversification is corporate development beyond current products and markets, but within the capabilities or value network of the organisation

Vertical integration is backward or forward integration into adjacent activities in the value network

Backward integration is development into activities concerned with the inputs into the company's current business

Related diversification can be defined as corporate development beyond current products and markets, but within the capabilities or the value network of the organisation (see sections 3.4 and 3.8.1). For example, Procter and Gamble and Unilever are diversified corporations, but virtually all of their interests are in fast-moving consumer goods distributed through retailers. Their various busi-nesses benefit therefore from shared capabilities in R&D, consumer marketing, building relationships with powerful retailers and global brand development.

The value network provides one way of thinking about different forms of related diversification as shown in Exhibit 7.3:

● **Vertical integration** describes either backward or forward integration into adja-cent activities in the value network. **Backward integration** refers to develop-ment into activities concerned with the inputs into the company's current business (that is, they are further back in the value network). For example, the acquisition by a car manufacturer of a component supplier would be related

Exhibit 7.3   Related diversification options for a manufacturer

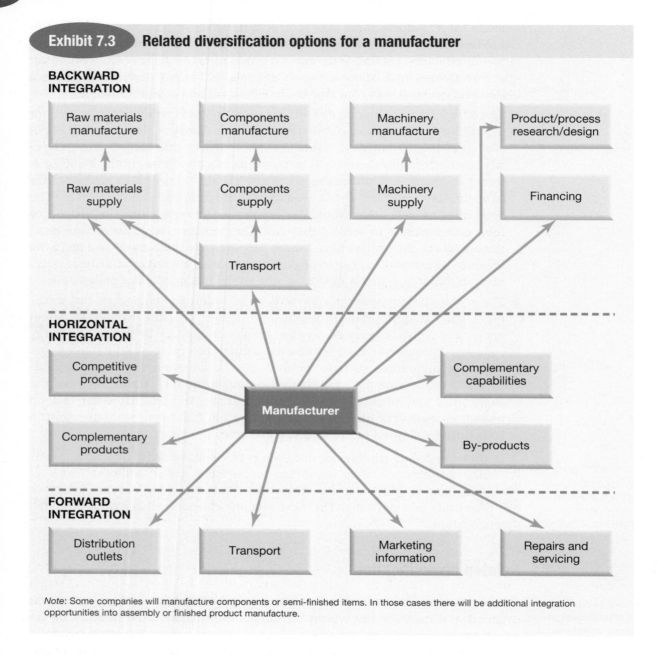

Note: Some companies will manufacture components or semi-finished items. In those cases there will be additional integration opportunities into assembly or finished product manufacture.

diversification through backward integration. **Forward integration** refers to development into activities which are concerned with a company's outputs (that is, are further forward in the value system): for a car manufacturer, this might be distribution, repairs and servicing.

● **Horizontal integration** is development into activities which are complementary or adjacent to present activities. For example, the Internet search company Google has spread horizontally into news, images and maps, amongst other services (another example is Zodiac – see Illustration 7.2).

It is important to recognise that capabilities and value links are distinct. A link through the value network does not necessarily imply the existence of capabilities. For example, in the late 1990s some car manufacturers began to integrate forward into repairs and servicing following a value network logic. The car manufacturers thought they could create value by using forward links to ensure a better overall customer experience with their cars. However, the manufacturers rapidly realised that these new businesses involved quite different capabilities: not manufacturing in large factories, but service in many scattered small units. In the end, the absence of relevant capabilities outweighed the potential from the value network links, and the car manufacturers generally withdrew from these forward integration initiatives. Synergies are often harder to identify and more costly to extract in practice than managers like to admit.[9]

It is also important to recognise that relationships have potential disadvantages. Related diversification can be problematic for at least two reasons:

- *corporate-level time and cost* as top managers try to ensure that the benefits of relatedness are achieved through sharing or transfer across business units;

- *business unit complexity*, as business unit managers attend to the needs of other business units, perhaps sharing resources or adjusting marketing strategies, rather than focusing exclusively on the needs of their own unit.

In summary, a simple statement such as 'relatedness matters' has to be questioned.[10] Whilst there is evidence that it may have positive effects on performance (see section 7.3.3), each individual diversification decision needs careful thought about just what relatedness means and what gives rise to performance benefits.

7.3.2 Unrelated diversification

Unrelated diversification is the development of products or services beyond the current capabilities and value network

If related diversification involves development within current capabilities or the current value network, **unrelated diversification** is the development of products or services beyond the current capabilities or value network. Unrelated diversification is often described as a *conglomerate* strategy. Because there are no obvious economies of scope between the different businesses, but there is an obvious cost of the headquarters, unrelated diversified companies' share prices often suffer from what is called the 'conglomerate discount' – in other words, a lower valuation than the individual constituent businesses would have if they stood alone. In 2003, the French conglomerate Vivendi-Universal, with interests spreading from utilities to mobile telephony and media, was trading at an estimated discount of 15–20 per cent. Naturally, shareholders were pressurising management to break the conglomerate up into its more highly valued parts.

However, the case against conglomerates can be exaggerated and there are certainly potential advantages to unrelated diversification in some conditions:

- *Exploiting dominant logics*, rather than concrete operational relationships, can be a source of conglomerate value creation. As at Berkshire Hathaway, a skilled investor such as Warren Buffett, the so-called Oracle of Omaha and one of the richest men in the world, may be able to add value to diverse businesses within his dominant logic.[11] Berkshire Hathaway includes businesses in different areas of manufacturing, insurance, distribution and retailing, but Buffet focuses on mature businesses that he can understand and whose managers he can trust. During the e-business boom of the late 1990s, Buffet deliberately avoided buying high-technology businesses because he knew they were outside his dominant logic. (See Illustration 7.3.)

Illustration 7.3

Berkshire Hathaway Inc.

A portfolio manager may seek to manage a highly diverse set of business units on behalf of its shareholders.

Berkshire Hathaway's Chairman is Warren Buffett, one of the world's richest men, and Charles Munger is Vice Chairman. The businesses in the portfolio are highly diverse. There are insurance businesses, including GEICO, the sixth largest automobile insurer in the USA, manufacturers of carpets, building products, clothing and footwear. There are service businesses (the training of aircraft and ship operators), retailers of home furnishings and fine jewellery, a daily and Sunday newspaper and the largest direct seller of housewear products in the USA.

The annual report of Berkshire Hathaway (2002) provides an insight into its rationale and management. Warren Buffett explains how he and his vice chairman run the business.

Charlie Munger and I think of our shareholders as owner-partners and of ourselves as managing partners. (Because of the size of our shareholdings we are also, for better or worse, controlling partners.) We do not view the company itself as the ultimate owner of our business assets but instead view the company as a conduit through which our shareholders own the assets. . . . Our long term economic goal . . . is to maximise Berkshire's average annual rate of gain in intrinsic business value on a per-share basis. We do not measure the economic significance or performance of Berkshire by its size; we measure by per-share progress.

Our preference would be to reach our goal by directly owning a diversified group of businesses that generate cash and consistently earn above average returns on capital. Our second choice is to own parts of similar businesses, attained primarily through purchases of marketable common stocks by our insurance subsidiaries. . . . Charlie and I are interested only in acquisitions that we believe will raise the per-share intrinsic value of Berkshire's stock.

Regardless of price we have no interest at all in selling any good businesses that Berkshire owns. We are also very reluctant to sell sub-par businesses as long as we expect them to generate at least some cash and as long as we feel good about their managers and labour relations. . . . Gin rummy managerial behaviour (discard your least promising business at each turn) is not our style. We would rather have our overall results penalised a bit than engaged in that kind of behaviour.

Buffett then explains how they manage their subsidiary businesses:

. . . we delegate almost to the point of abdication: though Berkshire has about 45,000 employees, only 12 of these are at headquarters. . . . Charlie and I mainly attend to capital allocation and the care and feeding of our key managers. Most of these managers are happiest when they are left alone to run their businesses and that is customarily just how we leave them. That puts them in charge of all operating decisions and of despatching the excess cash they generate to headquarters. By sending it to us, they don't get diverted by the various enticements that would come their way were they responsible for deploying the cash their businesses throw off. Further more, Charlie and I are exposed to a much wider range of possibilities for investing these funds than any of our managers could find in his/her own industry.

Questions

1 In what ways does Berkshire Hathaway conform (and not conform) to the archetypal portfolio manager described in section 7.4.2?

2 Using the checklist explained in section 7.4, suggest how and in what ways Berkshire Hathaway may or may not add value to its shareholders.

● *Countries with underdeveloped markets* can be fertile ground for conglomerates. Where external capital and labour markets do not yet work well, conglomerates offer a substitute mechanism for allocating and developing capital or managerial talent within their own organisational boundaries. For example, Korean conglomerates (the chaebol) were successful in the rapid growth phase of the Korean economy partly because they were able to mobilise investment and develop managers in a way that standalone companies in South Korea traditionally were unable to. Also, the strong cultural cohesion amongst managers in these chaebol reduced the coordination and monitoring costs that would be necessary in a Western conglomerate, where managers would be trusted less.[12] The same may be true today in other fast-growing economies that still have underdeveloped capital and labour markets.

It is important also to recognise that the distinction between related and unrelated diversification is often a matter of degree. As in the case of Berkshire Hathaway, although there are very few operational relationships between the constituent businesses, there is a relationship in terms of similar parenting requirements (see section 7.4.4). As in the case of the car manufacturers diversifying forwards into apparently related businesses such as repairs and servicing, operational relationships can turn out to be much less valuable than they appear at first. The blurred boundary between related and unrelated diversification is important for considering the performance consequences of diversification.

7.3.3 Diversification and performance

Because most large corporations today are diversified, but also because diversification can sometimes be in management's self-interest, many scholars and policy makers have been concerned to establish whether diversified companies really perform better than undiversified companies. After all, it would be deeply troubling if large corporations were diversifying simply to spread risk for managers, to save managerial jobs in declining businesses or to preserve the image of growth, as in the case of Enron.

Research studies of diversification have generally found some performance benefits, with *related diversifiers* outperforming both firms that remain *specialised* and those which have *unrelated* diversified strategies.[13] In other words, the diversification–performance relationship tends to follow an inverted (or upside down) U-shape, as in Exhibit 7.4. The implication is that some diversification is good – but not too much.

However, these performance studies produce statistical averages. Some related diversification strategies fail – as in the case of the vertically integrating car manufacturers – while some conglomerates succeed – as in the case of Berkshire Hathaway. The case against unrelated diversification is not solid, and effective dominant logics or particular national contexts can play in its favour. The conclusion from the performance studies is that, although on average related diversification pays better than unrelated, any diversification strategy needs rigorous questioning on its particular merits.

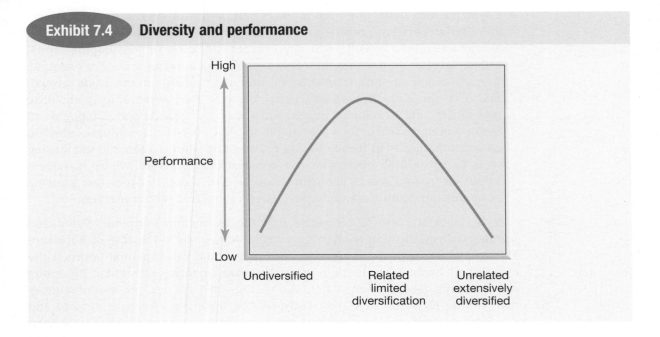

Exhibit 7.4 Diversity and performance

7.4 VALUE CREATION AND THE CORPORATE PARENT

Given the doubtful benefits of conglomerate diversification strategies, it is clear that some corporate parents do not add value. During 2006, two large US conglomerates, Tyco and Cendant, decided to break themselves up voluntarily, recognising that their subsidiary business units would be more valuable apart than together under their parenting. In the public sector too, units such as schools or hospitals are increasingly being given freedom from parenting authorities, because independence is seen as more effective. Some theorists even challenge the notion of corporate-level strategy altogether, the subject of the key debate in Illustration 7.6. This section examines how corporate parents can both add and destroy value, and considers three different parenting approaches that can be effective.

7.4.1 Value-adding and value-destroying activities of corporate parents[14]

Any corporate parent needs to demonstrate that it creates more value than it costs. This applies to both commercial and public sector organisations. For public sector organisations, privatisation or outsourcing is likely to be the consequence of failure to demonstrate value. Companies whose shares are traded freely on the stock markets face a further challenge. They must demonstrate that they create more value than any other rival corporate parent could create. Failure to do so is likely to lead to a hostile takeover or break-up (see Illustration 7.4 for a possible break-up of Cadbury Schweppes). Rival companies that think they can create

Illustration 7.4

A sweet deal for Nelson Peltz?

Financiers can make money out of over-diversified corporations, and managers have to respond.

Figure 1 Cadbury Schweppes share price, 2006–2007

Source: www.bigcharts.com. Marketwatch.Online by BigCharts.com. Copyright 2007 by Dow Jones & Company, Inc. Reproduced with permission of Dow Jones & Company, Inc. in format Textbook via Copyright Clearance Center.

In March 2007, American financier Nelson Peltz used his hedge fund Trian Fund Management LP to take a 3 per cent stake in Cadbury Schweppes PLC. Peltz was known as an activist shareholder, keen to extract maximum shareholder value through pressuring management or breaking up underperforming groups. Over the next few days, the Cadbury Schweppes share price rose by 15 per cent (see Figure 1).

Since 1969, Cadbury Schweppes had combined the chocolate and confectionary businesses of the original Cadbury company (founded 1824) with the carbonated drinks business of Schweppes (founded 1790). Cadbury's major confectionary brands included Dairy Milk, Creme Eggs and Dentyne gum. The company was the largest confectionery producer in the world, with 10 per cent market share, just ahead of Mars and Nestlé. The Schweppes business owned 7 Up and Dr Pepper, as well as the original Schweppes drinks. However, in its main market of the USA, it was still a distant number three to Coca-Cola and PepsiCo, who together accounted for 75 per cent of the carbonated drinks market. Cadbury Schweppes management were investing substantially in the drinks business, having bought up major bottling facilities during 2006. Todd Stitzer, the Cadbury Schweppes Chief Executive, had played a leading role in acquiring Dr Pepper and 7 Up back in 1995.

Two days after the announcement of Peltz's stake, Cadbury Schweppes stated it was actively considering the demerger of its drinks business. Options that were being examined for the drinks business included: making it a stand-alone company; selling the business outright to another company or private equity house; and floating a minority stake in the business and, over time, selling the remaining shares.

Soon after, rumours began to emerge of a possible merger between Cadbury Schweppes and Hershey, the American confectioner with over 5 per cent of the world confectionery market. Such a deal would give the merged company a commanding lead over competitors and substantial leverage over powerful retailers. Cadbury was weak in the US confectionary market, while Hershey was weak in Europe.

Sources: *Wall Street Journal* and *Financial Times*, various dates.

Questions

1 Why has the Cadbury Schweppes share price behaved in the way it has?

2 Why do you think Cadbury Schweppes had not acted earlier on the demerger option?

more value out of the business units can bid for the company's shares, on the expectation of either running the businesses better or selling them off to other potential parents. If the rival's bid is more attractive and credible than what the current parent can promise, shareholders will back it at the expense of incumbent management.

In this sense, competition takes place between different corporate parents for the right to own and control businesses. In the competitive market for the control of businesses, corporate parents must show that they have 'parenting advantage', on the same principle that business units must demonstrate competitive advantage. They must demonstrate that they are the best possible parents for the businesses they control. Parents therefore must have a very clear approach to how they create value. In practice, however, many of their activities can be value destroying as well as value creating.

Value-adding activities[15]

There are four main types of activity by which a corporate parent can add value.

- *Envisioning*. The corporate parent can provide a clear overall vision or *strategic intent* for its business units.[16] This vision should guide and motivate the business unit managers in order to maximise corporate-wide performance through commitment to a common purpose. The vision should also provide stakeholders with a *clear external image* about what the organisation as a whole is about: this can reassure shareholders about the rationale for having a diversified strategy in the first place. Finally, a clear vision provides a *discipline* on the corporate parent to stop it wandering into inappropriate activities or taking on unnecessary costs.

- *Coaching and facilitating*. The corporate parent can help business unit managers *develop strategic capabilities*, by coaching them to improve their skills and confidence. It can also facilitate cooperation and sharing across the business units, so improving the *synergies* from being within the same corporate organisation. Corporate-wide management courses are one effective means of achieving these objectives, as bringing managers across the business to learn management skills also provides an opportunity for them to build relationships between each other and see opportunities for cooperation.

- *Providing central services and resources*. The centre is obviously a provider of capital for *investment*. The centre can also provide central services such as treasury, tax and human resource advice, which if centralised can have *sufficient scale* to be efficient and to build up *relevant expertise*. Centralised services often have greater *leverage*: for example, combining the purchases of separate business units increases their bargaining power for shared inputs such as energy. This leverage can be helpful in *brokering* with external bodies, such as government regulators, or other companies in negotiating alliances. Finally, the centre can have an important role in managing expertise within the corporate whole, for instance by *transferring managers* across the business units or by creating shared *knowledge management* systems.

- *Intervening*. Finally, the corporate parent can also intervene within its business units in order to ensure appropriate performance. The corporate parent should be able closely to *monitor* business unit performance and *improve performance* either by replacing weak managers or by assisting them in turning around their businesses. The parent can also *challenge and develop* the strategic ambitions of business units, so that satisfactorily performing businesses are encouraged to perform even better.

Value-destroying activities

However, there are also three broad ways in which the corporate parent can inadvertently destroy value:

- *Adding management costs*. Most simply, the staff and facilities of the corporate centre are expensive. The corporate centre typically has the best-paid managers and the most luxurious offices. It is the actual businesses that have to generate the revenues that pay for them. If their costs are greater than the value they create, then the corporate centre's managers are net value destroying.

- *Adding bureaucratic complexity*. As well as these direct financial costs, there is the 'bureaucratic fog' created by an additional layer of management and the need to coordinate with sister businesses. These typically slow down managers' responses to issues and lead to compromises between the interests of individual businesses.

- *Obscuring financial performance*. One danger in a large diversified company is that the underperformance of weak businesses can be obscured. Weak businesses might be cross-subsidised by the stronger ones. Internally, the possibility of hiding weak performance diminishes the incentives for business unit managers to strive as hard as they can for their businesses: they have a parental safety net. Externally, shareholders and financial analysts cannot easily judge the performance of individual units within the corporate whole. Diversified companies' share prices are often marked down, because shareholders prefer the 'pure plays' of stand-alone units, where weak performance cannot be hidden.

These dangers suggest clear paths for corporate parents that wish to avoid value destruction. They should keep a close eye on centre costs, both financial and bureaucratic, ensuring that they are no more than required by their corporate strategy. They should also do all they can to promote financial transparency, so that business units remain under pressure to perform and shareholders are confident that there are no hidden disasters.

Overall, there are many ways in which corporate parents can add value. It is, of course, difficult to pursue them all and some are hard to mix with others. For example, a corporate parent that does a great deal of top-down intervening is less likely to be seen by its managers as a helpful coach and facilitator. Business unit managers will concentrate on maximising their own individual performance rather than looking out for ways to cooperate with other business unit managers for the greater good of the whole. For this reason, corporate parenting roles tend to fall into three main types, each coherent within itself but distinct from the others.[17] These three types of corporate parenting role are summarised in Exhibit 7.5.

Exhibit 7.5 **Portfolio managers, synergy managers and parental developers**

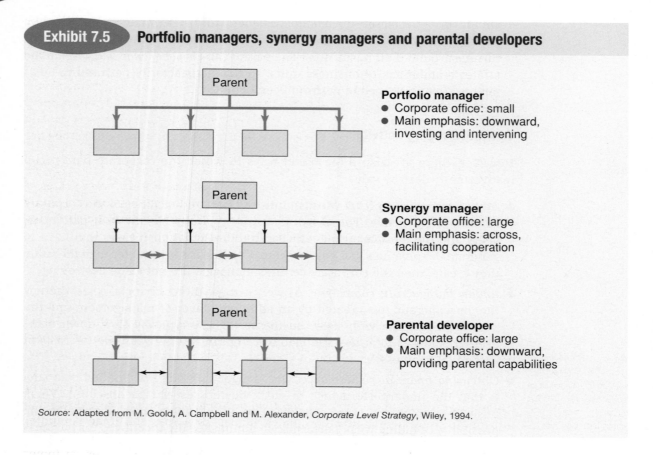

Source: Adapted from M. Goold, A. Campbell and M. Alexander, *Corporate Level Strategy*, Wiley, 1994.

7.4.2 The portfolio manager

A portfolio manager is a corporate parent acting as an agent on behalf of financial markets and shareholders

The **portfolio manager** operates as an active investor in a way that shareholders in the stock market are either too dispersed or too inexpert to be able to do. In effect, the portfolio manager is acting as an agent on behalf of financial markets and shareholders with a view to extracting more value from the various businesses than they could achieve themselves. Its role is to identify and acquire undervalued assets or businesses and improve them. The portfolio manager might do this, for example, by acquiring another corporation, divesting low-performing businesses within it and intervening to improve the performance of those with potential. Such corporations may not be much concerned about the relatedness (see sections 7.2.1 and 7.2.2) of the business units in their portfolio, typically adopting a conglomerate strategy. Their role is not to get closely involved in the routine management of the businesses, only to act over short periods of time to improve performance. In terms of the value-creating activities identified earlier, the portfolio manager concentrates on intervening and the provision (or withdrawal) of investment.

Portfolio managers seek to keep the cost of the centre low, for example by having a small corporate staff with few central services, leaving the business units alone so that their chief executives have a high degree of autonomy. They set clear financial targets for those chief executives, offering high rewards if they achieve them and likely loss of position if they do not. Such corporate parents can, of course, manage quite a large number of such businesses because they are not directly managing the everyday strategies of those businesses. Rather they are acting from above, setting financial targets, making central evaluations about the well-being and future prospects of such businesses, and investing, intervening or divesting accordingly.

Some argue that the days of the portfolio manager are gone. Improving financial markets mean that the scope for finding and investing cheaply in underperforming companies is much reduced. However, some portfolio managers remain and are successful. Private equity firms such as Apax Partners or Blackstone are a new way of operating a portfolio management style, typically investing in, improving and then divesting companies in loosely knit portfolios. For example, in 2006, Apax had investments in 360 separate businesses at different stages of development, ranging from Philips' former semiconductor division to Tommy Hilfiger clothing. Illustration 7.3 includes a description of the portfolio parenting approach of Warren Buffett at Berkshire Hathaway.

7.4.3 The synergy manager

The **synergy manager** is a corporate parent seeking to enhance value across business units by managing synergies across business units

Obtaining synergy is often seen as the prime *raison d'être* of the corporate parent.[18] Synergies are likely to be particularly rich in the case of related diversification. In terms of value-creating activities, the focus of a **synergy manager** is threefold: envisioning to build a common purpose; facilitating co-operation across businesses; and providing central services and resources. For example, at Apple, Steve Jobs' vision of his personal computers being the digital hub of the new digital lifestyle guides managers across the iMac computer business, iTunes and iPod to ensure seamless connections between the fast-developing offerings. The result is enhanced value through better customer experience. American giant GE facilitates cooperation by investing heavily in its management training activities, making it easier for managers to pass value-creating knowledge between businesses. A metals company diversified into both steel and aluminium might centralise its energy procurement, gaining synergy benefits through increased bargaining power over suppliers.

However, the problems in achieving such synergistic benefits are similar to those in achieving the benefits of relatedness (see section 7.3.1). Three problems are worth highlighting here:

- *Excessive costs.* The benefits in sharing and cooperation need to outweigh the costs of undertaking such integration, both direct financial costs and opportunity costs. Managing synergistic relationships tends to involve expensive investments in management time.

- *Overcoming self-interest.* Managers in the business units have to want to co-operate. Especially where managers are rewarded largely according to the performance of their own particular business unit, they are likely to be unwilling to sacrifice their time and resources for the common good.

- *Illusory synergies.* It is easy to overestimate the value of skills or resources to other businesses. This is particularly common when the corporate centre needs to justify a new venture or the acquisition of a new company. Claimed synergies often prove illusory when managers actually have to put them into practice.

The failure of many companies to extract expected synergies from their businesses has led to growing scepticism about the notion of synergy. Synergistic benefits are not as easy to achieve as would appear. It has proven very hard for Daimler Chrysler to find the promised synergies between its luxury Mercedes car business and mass market manufacturer Chrysler. However, synergy continues to be a common theme in corporate-level strategy, as Illustration 7.2 on Zodiac exemplifies.

7.4.4 The parental developer[19]

The parental developer is a corporate parent seeking to employ its own competences as a parent to add value to its businesses and build parenting skills that are appropriate for its portfolio of business units

The **parental developer** seeks to employ its own capabilities as a parent to add value to its businesses. This is not so much about how the parent can develop benefits *across* business units or transfer capabilities between business units, as in the case of managing synergy. Rather parental developers focus on the resources or capabilities they have as parents which they can transfer *downwards* to enhance the potential of business units. For example, a parent could have a valuable brand (as in the case of Virgin), or specialist skills in financial management or product development. If such parenting capabilities exist, corporate managers then need to identify a *parenting opportunity*: a business which is not fulfilling its potential but which could be improved by applying the parenting capability, such as branding or product development. Such parenting opportunities are therefore more common in the case of related rather than unrelated diversified strategies and are likely to involve exchanges of managers and other resources across the businesses. Key value-creating activities for the parent will be the provision of central services and resources.

The capabilities that parents have will vary. Royal Dutch Shell would argue that it is not just its huge financial muscle that matters but also that it is adept at negotiating with governments, as well as developing high-calibre internationally mobile executives who can work almost anywhere in the world within a Shell corporate framework. These capabilities are especially valuable in allowing it to develop businesses globally. 3M is single-mindedly concerned with inculcating a focus on innovation in its businesses. It tries to ensure a corporate culture based on this, set clear innovation targets for its businesses and elevate the standing of technical personnel concerned with innovation. Unilever has increasingly sought to focus on developing its core expertise in global branding and marketing in the fast-moving consumer goods market, with state-of-the-art R&D facilities to back it up. It would argue that this is where it can add greatest value to its businesses, and this belief has guided its investments and divestments over the years.

Managing an organisation on this basis does, however, pose at least four challenges:

● *Identifying parental capabilities*. A big challenge for the corporate parent is being sure about just how it can add value to business units. If the value-adding capabilities of the parent are wrongly identified then its contribution will be only counter-productive. There needs to be some hard evidence of such value-adding capabilities.

● *Parental focus*. If the corporate parent identifies that it has value-adding capabilities in particular and limited ways, the implication is that it should not be providing services in other ways, or if it does they should be provided at minimal cost. Corporate executives should focus their energy and time on activities where they really do add value. Some central services could be outsourced to specialist companies who can do it better.

● *The 'crown jewel' problem.* Some diversified companies have business units in their portfolios which are performing well but to which the parent adds little value. These can become 'crown jewels', to which corporate parents become excessively attached. The logic of the parental development approach is if the centre cannot add value, it is just a cost and therefore destroying value. Parental developers should divest businesses they do not add value to, even profitable ones. Funds raised by selling a profitable business can be reinvested in businesses where the parent can add value.

● *Sufficient 'feel'.* If the logic of the parental developer is to be followed then the executives of the corporate parent must also have 'sufficient feel' or understanding of the businesses within the portfolio to know where they can

---

Exhibit 7.6 **Value-adding potential of corporate rationales**

Value-adding activities (see section 7.4.1)	Portfolio manager	Synergy manager	Parental developer
Envisioning			
Developing strategic intent/mission		●	●
Clear external image		●	●
Setting disciplinary expectations	●		
Coaching and training			
Developing strategic capabilities		●	
Achieving synergies		●	
Central services and resources			
Investment	●	●	●
Scale advantages		●	
Transferring capabilities and knowledge		●	
Specialist expertise			●
Leverage and brokering		●	
Intervening			
Monitoring performance	●		
Improving business and performance			●
Challenging/developing strategy		●	●

add value and where they cannot: this is an issue taken up in section 7.5.3 in relation to the logic of portfolios.

The three roles of the parent can be considered in terms of the possible value-adding roles of corporate parents suggested in section 7.4.1. Exhibit 7.6 identifies how the main value-adding roles of corporate parents might differ in line with the discussion in sections 7.4.2–7.4.4.

7.5 PORTFOLIO MATRICES

The discussion in section 7.4 was about the rationales that corporate parents might adopt for the management of a multi-business organisation. This section introduces models by which managers can manage the various parts of their portfolio differently, or add and subtract business units within the portfolio. Each model gives more or less attention to the following three criteria:

● the *balance* of the portfolio, for example in relation to its markets and the needs of the corporation;

● the *attractiveness* of the business units in terms of how strong they are individually and how profitable their markets or industries are likely to be; and

● the *fit* that the business units have with each other in terms of potential synergies or the extent to which the corporate parent will be good at looking after them.

7.5.1 The growth/share (or BCG) matrix[20]

KEY CONCEPT

BCG and portfolio matrices

One of the most common and long-standing ways of conceiving of the balance of a portfolio of businesses is the Boston Consulting Group (BCG) matrix (see Exhibit 7.7). Here market share and market growth are critical variables for determining attractiveness and balance. High market share and high growth are, of course, attractive. However, the BCG matrix also warns that high growth demands heavy investment, for instance to expand capacity or develop brands. There needs to be a balance within the portfolio, so that there are some low-growth businesses that are making sufficient surplus to fund the investment needs of higher growth businesses.

The growth/share axes of the BCG matrix define four sorts of business:

A **star** is a business unit which has a high market share in a growing market

● A **star** is a business unit which has a high market share in a growing market. The business unit may be spending heavily to keep up with growth, but high market share should yield sufficient profits to make it more or less self-sufficient in terms of investment needs.

A **question mark** (or problem child) is a business unit in a growing market, but without a high market share

● A **question mark** (or problem child) is a business unit in a growing market, but not yet with high market share. Developing question marks into stars, with high market share, takes heavy investment. Many question marks fail to develop, so the BCG advises corporate parents to nurture several at a time. It is important to make sure that some question marks develop into stars, as existing stars eventually become cash cows and cash cows may decline into dogs.

| Exhibit 7.7 | The growth share (or BCG) matrix |

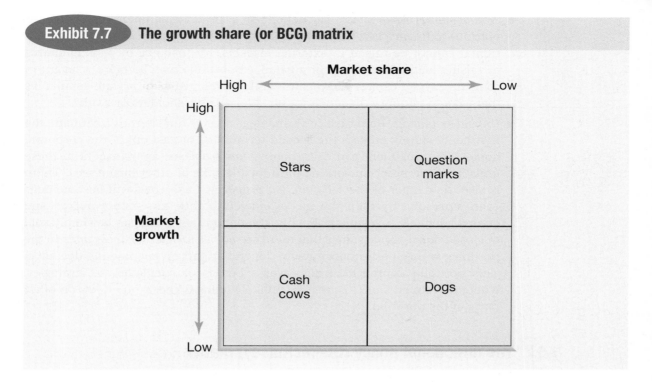

Market share diagram. Horizontal axis labelled "Market share" with arrow from High (left) to Low (right). Vertical axis labelled "Market growth" with arrow from Low (bottom) to High (top). Four quadrants: top-left "Stars", top-right "Question marks", bottom-left "Cash cows", bottom-right "Dogs".

A **cash cow** is a business unit with a high market share in a mature market

- A **cash cow** is a business unit with a high market share in a mature market. However, because growth is low, investment needs are less, while high market share means that the business unit should be profitable. The cash cow should then be a cash provider, helping to fund investments in question marks.

Dogs are business units with a low share in static or declining markets

- **Dogs** are business units with a low share in static or declining markets and are thus the worst of all combinations. They may be a cash drain and use up a disproportionate amount of company time and resources. The BCG usually recommends divestment or closure.

The BCG matrix has several advantages. It provides a good way of visualising the different needs and potential of all the diverse businesses within the corporate portfolio. It warns corporate parents of the financial demands of what might otherwise look like a desirable portfolio of high-growth businesses. It also reminds corporate parents that stars are likely eventually to wane. Finally, it provides a useful discipline to business unit managers, underlining the fact that the corporate parent ultimately owns the surplus resources they generate and can allocate them according to what is best for the corporate whole. Cash cows should not hoard their profits. Incidentally, surplus resources may not only be investment funds: the corporate parent can also reallocate business unit managers who are not fully utilised by low-growth cash cows or dogs.

However, there are at least three potential problems with the BCG matrix:

- *Definitional vagueness*. It can be hard to decide what high and low growth or share mean in particular situations. Managers are often keen to define themselves as 'high share' by defining their market in a particularly narrow way (for example, ignoring relevant international markets).

● *Capital market assumptions*. The notion that a corporate parent needs a balanced portfolio to finance investment from internal sources (cash cows) assumes that capital cannot be raised in external markets, for instance by issuing shares or raising loans. The notion of a balanced portfolio may be more relevant in countries where capital markets are underdeveloped or in private companies that wish to minimise dependence on external shareholders or banks.

● *Unkind to animals*. Both cash cows and dogs receive ungenerous treatment, the first being simply milked, the second terminated or cast out of the corporate home. This treatment can cause *motivation problems*, as managers in these units see little point in working hard for the sake of other businesses. There is also the danger of the *self-fulfilling prophecy*. Cash cows will become dogs even more quickly than the model expects if they are simply milked and denied adequate investment. Finally, the notion that a dog can be simply sold or closed down also assumes that there are *no ties to other business units* in the portfolio, whose performance might depend in part on keeping the dog alive. This portfolio approach to dogs works better for conglomerate strategies, where divestments or closures are unlikely to have knock-on effects on other parts of the portfolio.

7.5.2 The directional policy (GE–McKinsey) matrix

Another way to consider a portfolio of businesses is by means of the *directional policy matrix*[21] which categorises business units into those with good prospects and those with less good prospects. The matrix was originally developed by McKinsey & Co. consultants in order to help the American conglomerate General Electric manage its portfolio of business units. Specifically, the **directional policy matrix** positions business units according to (i) how attractive the relevant market is in which they are operating, and (ii) the competitive strength of the SBU in that market. Attractiveness can be identified by PESTEL or five forces analyses; business unit strength can be defined by competitor analysis (for instance, the strategy canvas): see Chapter 2. Some analysts also choose to show graphically how large the market is for a given business unit's activity, and even the market share of that business unit, as shown in Exhibit 7.8. For example, managers in a firm with the portfolio shown in Exhibit 7.8 will be concerned that they have relatively low shares in the largest and most attractive market, whereas their greatest strength is in a market with only medium attractiveness and smaller markets with little long-term attractiveness.

> The directional policy matrix positions SBUs according to (i) how attractive the relevant market is in which they are operating, and (ii) the competitive strength of the SBU in that market

The matrix also provides a way of considering appropriate corporate-level strategies given the positioning of the business units, as shown in Exhibit 7.9. It suggests that the businesses with the highest growth potential and the greatest strength are those in which to invest for growth. Those that are the weakest and in the least attractive markets should be divested or 'harvested' (that is, used to yield as much cash as possible before divesting).

The directional policy matrix is more complex than the BCG matrix. However, it can have two advantages. First, unlike the simpler four-box BCG matrix, the nine cells of the directional policy matrix acknowledge the possibility of a difficult middle ground. Here managers have to be carefully selective. In this sense, the directional policy matrix is less mechanistic than the BCG matrix,

Exhibit 7.8 **Directional policy (GE–McKinsey) matrix**

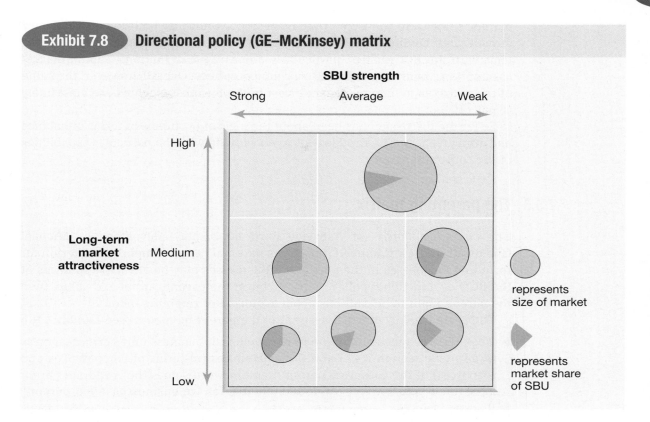

encouraging open debate on less clear-cut cases. Second, the two axes of the directional policy matrix are not based on single measures (that is, market share and market growth). Business strength can derive from many other factors than

Exhibit 7.9 **Strategy guidelines based on the directional policy matrix**

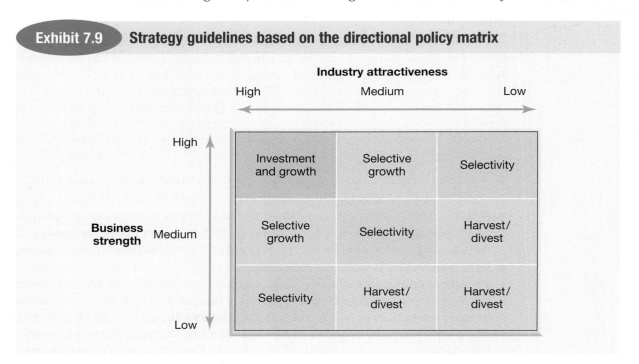

market share, and industry attractiveness does not just boil down to industry growth rates. On the other hand, the directional policy matrix shares some problems with the BCG matrix, particularly about vague definitions, capital market assumptions, motivation and self-fulfilling prophecy. Overall, however, the value of the matrix is to help managers invest in the businesses which are most likely to pay off.

So far the discussion has been about the logic of portfolios in terms of balance and attractiveness. The third logic is to do with 'fit' with the particular capabilities of the corporate parent.

7.5.3 The parenting matrix

The *parenting matrix* (or Ashridge Portfolio Display) developed by Michael Goold and Andrew Campbell introduces parental fit as an important criterion for including businesses in the portfolio.[22] Businesses may be attractive in terms of the BCG or directional policy matrices, but if the parent cannot add value, then the parent ought to be cautious about acquiring or retaining them.

There are two key dimensions of fit in the parenting matrix (see Exhibit 7.10):

- *'Feel'*. This is a measure of the fit between each business unit's *critical success factors* (see section 2.4.4) and the capabilities (in terms of competences and resources) of the corporate parent. In other words, does the corporate parent have the necessary 'feel', or understanding, for the businesses it will parent?

- *'Benefit'*. This measures the fit between the *parenting opportunities*, or needs, of business units and the capabilities of the parent. Parenting opportunities are about the upside, areas in which good parenting can benefit the business (for instance, by bringing marketing expertise). For the benefit to be realised, of course, the parent must have the right capabilities to match the parenting opportunities.

The power of using these two dimensions of fit is as follows. It is easy to see that a corporate parent should avoid running businesses that it has no *feel* for. What is less clear is that parenting should be avoided if there is no *benefit*. This challenges the corporate parenting of even businesses for which the parent has high feel. Businesses for which a corporate parent has high feel but can add little benefit should either be run with a very light touch or be divested.

Exhibit 7.10 shows four kinds of business along these two dimensions of feel and benefit:

- *Heartland* business units are ones which the parent understands well and can continue to add value to. They should be at the core of future strategy.

- *Ballast* business units are ones the parent understands well but can do little for. They would probably be at least as successful as independent companies. If not divested, they should be spared as much corporate bureaucracy as possible.

- *Value trap* business units are dangerous. They appear attractive because there are opportunities to add value (for instance, marketing could be improved), but they are deceptively attractive, because the parent's lack of feel will result in more harm than good (that is, the parent lacks the right marketing skills). The parent will need to acquire new capabilities if it is to be able to move value trap businesses into the heartland. It might be easier to divest to another corporate parent who could add value, and will pay well for the chance.

Illustration 7.5

Splitting the Home Office

After 225 years of combining justice and national security responsibilities, the British 'Home Office' was declared no longer 'fit for purpose'.

Since the eighteenth century, the British Home Office (roughly equivalent to many countries' Interior Ministry) had been an unusual combination of both justice and national security functions. By 2007, it had 70,000 civil servants responsible for running the justice system (courts and so on), the police, the prisons, the probation service, counter-terrorism, intelligence, drug control, passports, identity cards, border controls, the asylum system, anti-social behaviour policy and equality and diversity policy (concerned with race, gender, the disabled, etc.).

But the Home Office was seen as a failed organisation. During 2006, the Home Office had been involved in many apparent fiascos. It was revealed that records had not been kept on British citizens committing crimes abroad, that there was no tally on escaped convicts, that foreign criminals were not being deported, that there was a backlog for the consideration of asylum seekers running to many thousands, that convicted criminals were being kept long term in police cells because of a lack of suitable prison accommodation, and so on. A former Home Office adviser commented:

This department has become too big to manage. Its left hand does not know what its right is doing. The government can no longer avoid confronting the hard question of whether it is safe to leave it intact. It has turned into a dinosaur with a brain too small to co-ordinate its gigantic body.

Charles Clarke, Home Secretary (Home Office Minister), was forced to resign. His successor,

John Reid, declared the Home Office as 'unfit for purpose'. The Home Office was split. A new Ministry for Justice took charge of running the criminal justice system, with responsibilities for criminal law, sentencing and the prison and probation services. The Home Office meanwhile took on additional tasks in counter-terrorism, while retaining its other existing responsibilities such as the police, crime reduction, immigration and asylum, and identity and passports. The change was widely summarised as 'separating catching criminals from sentencing them'.

Ousted minister Charles Clarke commented on the changes to his old department: 'I think the problem with the department is a lack of coordination between its various elements. Dividing the Home Office will make those problems far worse.'

Sources: *Guardian*, 5 February (2007); *The Economist*, 31 March (2007).

Questions

1 How could the old Home Office 'add value' to its constituent parts? How might it 'destroy value'?

2 What corporate parenting style is appropriate for the new Home Office (portfolio management, synergy management or parental developer)?

| Exhibit 7.10 | The parenting matrix: the Ashridge Portfolio Display |

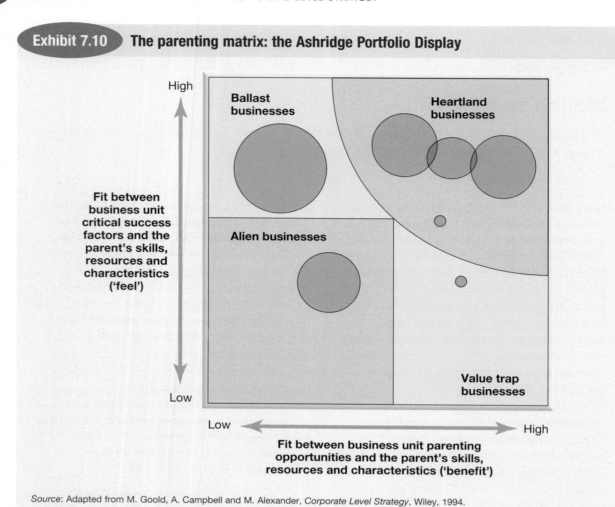

Source: Adapted from M. Goold, A. Campbell and M. Alexander, *Corporate Level Strategy*, Wiley, 1994.

● *Alien* business units are clear misfits. They offer little opportunity to add value and the parent does not understand them anyway. Exit is definitely the best strategy.

This approach to considering corporate portfolios places the emphasis firmly on how the parent benefits the business units. It requires careful analysis of both parenting capabilities and business unit parenting needs. The parenting matrix can therefore assist hard decisions where either high feel or high parenting opportunities tempt the corporate parent to acquire or retain businesses. Parents should concentrate on actual or potential heartland businesses, where there is both high feel and high benefit.

The concept of fit has equal relevance in the public sector (see Illustration 7.5). The implication is that public sector managers should control directly only those services and activities for which they have special managerial expertise. Other services should be outsourced or set up as independent agencies. Whilst outsourcing, privatising and setting up independent agencies are often driven as much by political dogma as by corporate-level strategy analysis (see Illustration 7.6), the trend in many countries recently has been in this direction.

Illustration 7.6

Why have corporate-level strategies anyway?

Do we really need diversified corporations?

The notion of corporate strategy assumes that corporations should own and control businesses in a range of markets or products. But 'transaction cost' economist Oliver Williamson believes that diversified corporations should only exist in the presence of 'market failures'.[1] If markets worked well, there would be no need for business units to be coordinated through managerial structures. Business units could be independent, coordinating where necessary by simple transactions in the marketplace. The 'invisible hand' of the market could replace the 'visible hand' of managers at corporate headquarters. There would be no 'corporate strategy'.

Market failures favouring the diversified corporation occur for two reasons:

- *'Bounded rationality'*. People cannot know everything that is going on in the market, so perfectly rational market transactions are impossible. Information, for instance on quality and costs, can sometimes be better inside the corporate fold.

- *'Opportunism'*. Independent businesses trading between each other may behave opportunistically, for example by cheating on delivery or quality promises. Cheating can sometimes be policed and punished more easily within a corporate hierarchy.

According to Williamson, activities should only be brought into the corporation when the 'transaction costs' of coping with bounded rationality (gaining information) and opportunism (guarding against cheats) are lower inside the corporate hierarchy than they would be if simply relying on transactions in the marketplace.

This comparison of the transaction costs of markets and hierarchies has powerful implications for trends in product diversification:

- Improving capital markets may reduce the relative information advantages of conglomerates in managing a set of unrelated businesses. As markets get better at capturing information there will be less need for conglomerates, something that may account for the recent decline in conglomerates in many economies.

- Improving protection of intellectual property rights may increase the incentives for corporations to license out their technologies to companies, rather than trying to do everything themselves. If the prospect of collecting royalties improves, there is less advantage for corporations keeping everything in-house.

Thus fewer market failures also mean narrower product scope.

Williamson's 'transaction cost' view puts a heavy burden on corporations to justify themselves. Two defences are possible. First, knowledge is hard to trade in the market. Buyers can only know the value of new knowledge once they have already bought it. Because they can trust each other, colleagues in sister business units within the same corporation are better at transferring knowledge than independent companies are in the open market.[2] Second, corporations are not just about minimising the costs of information and cheating, but also about maximising the value of the combined resources. Bringing creative people together in a collective enterprise enhances knowledge exchange, innovation and motivation. Corporations are value creators as well as cost minimisers.[3]

Sources:
1. O.E. Williamson, 'Strategy research: governance and competence perspectives', *Strategic Management Journal*, vol. 12 (1998), pp. 75–94.
2. B. Kogut and U. Zander, 'What firms do? Coordination, identity and learning', *Organization Science*, vol. 7, no. 5 (1996), pp. 502–519.
3. S. Ghoshal, C. Bartlett and P. Moran, 'A new manifesto for management', *Sloan Management Review*, Spring (1999), pp. 9–20.

Question

Consider a diversified corporation such as Cadbury Schweppes or Unilever: what kinds of hard-to-trade knowledge might it be able to transfer between product and country subsidiaries and is such knowledge likely to be of increasing or decreasing importance?

SUMMARY

- Many corporations comprise several, sometimes many, business units. Decisions above the level of business units are the concern of what in this chapter is called the *corporate parent*.

- Corporate strategy is concerned with decisions of the corporate parent about (i) the *product* and *market scope*, and (ii) how it seeks to *add value* to that created by its business units.

- Product diversity is often considered in terms of *related* and *unrelated* diversification.

- Performance tends to suffer if organisations become very diverse, or unrelated, in their business units.

- Corporate parents may seek to add value by adopting different *parenting roles*: the portfolio manager, the synergy manager or the parental developer.

- Corporate parents can destroy value as well as create it, and should be ready to *divest* units for which they cannot create value.

- There are several *portfolio models* to help corporate parents manage their businesses, of which the most common are: the BCG matrix, the directional matrix and the parenting matrix.

Work assignments

✳ *Denotes more advanced work assignments.*   * *Refers to a case study in the Text and Cases edition.*

7.1   Using the Ansoff matrix (Exhibit 7.2), identify and explain possible strategic directions for any one of these case organisations: CRH*, Numico*, News Corporation*.

7.2   Go to the website of any large multi-business organisation (for example, Google, Tata Group, Siemens) and assess the degree to which its corporate-level strategy is characterised by (a) related or unrelated diversification and (b) a coherent 'dominant logic' (see section 7.3.1).

7.3   For any large multi-business corporation (as in 7.2), explain how the corporate parent should best create value for its component businesses (as portfolio manager, synergy manager or parental developer: see section 7.4). Would all the businesses fit equally well?

7.4 ✳   For any large multi-business corporation (as in 7.2), plot the business units on a portfolio matrix (for example, the BCG matrix: section 7.5). Justify any assumptions about the relative positions of businesses on the relevant axes of the matrix. What managerial conclusions do you draw from this analysis?

7.5   For any large multi-business organisation (see 7.2), map the business units on the Ashridge parenting matrix (Exhibit 7.10).

Integrative assignment

7.6   Take a case of a recent merger or acquisition (see Chapter 10), and assess the extent to which it involved related or unrelated diversification (if either) and how far it was consistent with the company's existing dominant logic. Using share price information (see www.bigcharts.com or similar), assess shareholders' reaction to the merger or acquisition. How do you explain this reaction?

An extensive range of additional materials, including audio summaries, weblinks to organisations featured in the text, definitions of key concepts and self-assessment questions, can be found on the *Exploring Corporate Strategy* Companion Website at **www.pearsoned.co.uk/ecs**

Recommended key readings

- An accessible discussion of strategic directions is provided by A. Campbell and R. Park, *The Growth Gamble: When leaders should bet on big new businesses*, Nicholas Brealey, 2005.
- M. Goold and K. Luchs, 'Why diversify: four decades of management thinking', in D. Faulkner and A. Campbell (eds), *The Oxford Handbook of Strategy*, vol. 2, Oxford University Press, pp. 18–42,

provides an authoritative overview of the diversification option over time.
- A summary of different portfolio analyses is provided in D. Faulkner, 'Portfolio matrices', in V. Ambrosini (ed.), *Exploring Techniques of Analysis and Evaluation in Strategic Management*, Prentice Hall, 1998.

References

1. This figure is an extension of the product/market matrix: see I. Ansoff, *Corporate Strategy*, Penguin, 1988, chapter 6. The Ansoff matrix was later developed into the one show below.

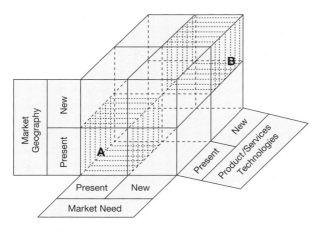

Source: H. Ansoff, *The New Corporate Strategy*, Wiley, 1988.

2. For the European Commission competition authority, see http://ec.europa.eu/comm/competition; for the UK Competition Commission, see http://www.competition-commission.org.uk/.
3. See, for example, J. Huang, M. Enesi and R. Galliers, 'Opportunities to learn from failure with electronic commerce: a case study of electronic banking', *Journal of Information Technology*, vol. 18, no. 1 (2003), pp. 17–27.
4. For discussions of the challenge of sustained growth and diversification, see A. Campbell and R. Parks, *The Growth*

Gamble, Nicholas Brearly, 2005, and D. Laurie, Y. Doz and C. Sheer, 'Creating new growth platforms', *Harvard Business Review*, vol. 84, no. 5 (2006), pp. 80–90.
5. On economies of scope, see D.J. Teece, 'Towards an economic theory of the multi-product firm', *Journal of Economic Behavior and Organization*, vol. 3 (1982), pp. 39–63.
6. M. Goold and A. Campbell, 'Desperately seeking synergy', *Harvard Business Review*, vol. 76, no. 2 (1998), pp. 131–145.
7. See C.K. Prahalad and R. Bettis, 'The dominant logic: a new link between diversity and performance', *Strategic Management Journal*, vol. 6, no. 1 (1986), pp. 485–501; and R. Bettis and C.K. Prahalad, 'The dominant logic: retrospective and extension', *Strategic Management Journal*, vol. 16, no. 1 (1995), pp. 5–15.
8. For a theoretical discussion and empirical study of management interests and diversification, see M. Goranova, T. Alessandri, P. Brandes and R. Dharwadkar, 'Managerial ownership and corporate diversification: a longitudinal view', *Strategic Management Journal*, vol. 28, no. 3 (2007), pp. 211–226.
9. A. Pehrson, 'Business relatedness and performance: a study of managerial perceptions', *Strategic Management Journal*, vol. 27, no. 3 (2006), pp. 265–282.
10. A. Campbell and K. Luchs, *Strategic Synergy*, Butterworth –Heinemann, 1992.
11. See Prahalad and Bettis, reference 7.
12. See C. Markides, 'Corporate strategy: the role of the centre', in A. Pettigrew, H. Thomas and R. Whittington (eds), *Handbook of Strategy and Management*, Sage, 2002. For a discussion of recent chaebol changes, see J. Chang and H.-H. Shin, 'Governance system effectiveness following the crisis: the case of Korean business group headquarters', *Corporate Governance: an International Review*, vol. 14, no. 2 (2006), pp. 85–97.

13. L.E. Palich, L.B. Cardinal and C. Miller, 'Curvilinearity in the diversification-performance linkage: an examination of over three decades of research', *Strategic Management Journal*, vol. 21 (2000), pp. 155–174. The inverted-U relationship is the research consensus, but studies often disagree, particularly finding variations over time and across countries. For recent context sensitive studies, see M. Mayer and R. Whittington, 'Diversification in context: a cross national and cross temporal extension', *Strategic Management Journal*, vol. 24 (2003), pp. 773–781; and A. Chakrabarti, K. Singh and I. Mahmood, 'Diversification and performance: evidence from East Asian firms', *Strategic Management Journal*, vol. 28 (2007), pp. 101–120.

14. For a good discussion of corporate parenting roles, see Markides in reference 11. A recent empirical study of corporate headquarters is D. Collis, D. Young and M. Goold, 'The size, structure and performance of corporate headquarters', *Strategic Management Journal*, vol. 28, no. 4 (2007), pp. 383–406.

15. M. Goold, A. Campbell and M. Alexander, *Corporate Level Strategy*, Wiley, 1994, is concerned with both the value-adding and value-destroying capacity of corporate parents.

16. For a discussion of the role of a clarity of mission, see A. Campbell, M. Devine and D. Young, *A Sense of Mission*, Hutchinson Business, 1990. However, G. Hamel and C.K. Prahalad argue in chapter 6 of their book, *Competing for the Future*, Harvard Business School Press, 1994, that mission statements have insufficient impact for the competence of a clarity of 'strategic intent'. This is more likely to be a brief but clear statement which focuses more on clarity of strategic direction (they use the word 'destiny') than on how that strategic direction will be achieved. See also Hamel and Prahalad on strategic intent in the *Harvard Business Review*, vol. 67, no. 3 (1989), pp. 63–76.

17. The first two rationales discussed here are based on a paper by M. Porter, 'From competitive advantage to corporate strategy', *Harvard Business Review*, vol. 65, no. 3 (1987), pp. 43–59.

18. See A. Campbell and K. Luchs, *Strategic Synergy*, Butterworth–Heinemann, 1992.

19. The logic of parental development is explained extensively in Goold *et al.*, reference 15.

20. For a more extensive discussion of the use of the growth/share matrix see A.C. Hax and N.S Majluf, 'The use of the growth-share matrix in strategic planning', *Interfaces*, vol. 13, no. 1 (1992), pp. 40–46; and D. Faulkner, 'Portfolio matrices', in V. Ambrosini (ed.), *Exploring Techniques of Analysis and Evaluation in Strategic Management*, Prentice Hall, 1998; for source explanations of the BCG matrix see B.D. Henderson, *Henderson on Corporate Strategy*, Abt Books, 1979.

21. A. Hax and N. Majluf, 'The use of the industry attractiveness-business strength matrix in strategic planning', in R. Dyson (ed.), *Strategic Planning: Models and analytical techniques*, Wiley, 1990.

22. The discussion in this section draws on M. Goold, A. Campbell and M. Alexander, *Corporate Level Strategy*, Wiley, 1994, which provides an excellent basis for understanding issues of parenting.

The Virgin Group

Aidan McQuade

Introduction

The Virgin Group is one of the UK's largest private companies. The group included, in 2006, 63 businesses as diverse as airlines, health clubs, music stores and trains. The group included Virgin Galactic, which promised to take paying passengers into sub-orbital space.

The personal image and personality of the founder, Richard Branson, were highly bound up with those of the company. Branson's taste for publicity has led him to stunts as diverse as appearing as a cockney street trader in the US comedy *Friends*, to attempting a non-stop balloon flight around the world. This has certainly contributed to the definition and recognisability of the brand. Research has showed that the Virgin name was associated with words such as 'fun', 'innovative', 'daring' and 'successful'.

In 2006 Branson announced plans to invest $3bn (€2.4bn; £1.7bn) in renewable energy. Virgin, through its partnership with a cable company NTL, also undertook an expansion into media challenging publicly the way NewsCorp operated in the UK and the effects on British democracy. The nature and scale of both these initiatives suggests that Branson's taste for his brand of business remains undimmed.

Origins and activities

Virgin was founded in 1970 as a mail order record business and developed as a private company in music publishing and retailing. In 1986 the company was floated on the stock exchange with a turnover of £250m (€362.5m). However, Branson became tired of the public listing obligations: he resented making presentations in the City to people whom, he believed, did not understand the business. The pressure to create short-term profit, especially as the share price began to fall, was the final straw: Branson decided to take the business back into private ownership and the

Photo: Steve Bell/Rex Features

shares were bought back at the original offer price.

The name Virgin was chosen to represent the idea of the company being a virgin in every business it entered. Branson has said that: 'The brand is the single most important asset that we have; our ultimate objective is to establish it as a major global name.' This does not mean that Virgin underestimates the importance of understanding the *businesses* that it is branding. Referring to his intent to set up a 'green' energy company producing ethanol and cellulosic ethanol fuels in competition with the oil industry, he said, 'We're a slightly unusual company in that we go into industries we know nothing about and immerse ourselves.'

Virgin's expansion had often been through joint ventures whereby Virgin provided the brand and its partner provided the majority of capital. For example, the Virgin Group's move into clothing and cosmetics required an initial outlay of only £1,000, whilst its partner, Victory Corporation, invested £20m. With Virgin Mobile, Virgin built a business by forming partnerships with existing wireless operators to sell services under the Virgin brand name. The carriers' competences lay in network management. Virgin set out to differentiate itself by offering innovative

This case was updated and revised by Aidan McQuade, University of Strathclyde Graduate School of Business, based upon work by Urmilla Lawson.

services. Although it did not operate its own network, Virgin won an award for the best wireless operator in the UK.

Virgin Fuels appears to be somewhat different in that Virgin is putting up the capital and using the Virgin brand to attract attention to the issues and possibilities that the technology offers.

In 2005 Virgin announced the establishment of a 'quadruple play' media company providing television, broadband, fixed-line and mobile communications through the merger of Branson's UK mobile interests with the UK's two cable companies. This Virgin company would have 9 million direct customers, 1.5 million more than BSkyB, and so have the financial capacity to compete with BSkyB for premium content such as sports and movies.[1] Virgin tried to expand this business further by making an offer for ITV. This was rejected as undervaluing the company and then undermined further with the purchase of an 18 per cent share of ITV by BSkyB. This prompted Branson to call on regulators to force BSkyB to reduce or dispose of its stake citing concerns that BSkyB would have material influence over the free-to-air broadcaster.[2]

Virgin has been described as a 'keiretsu' organisation – a structure of loosely linked, autonomous units run by self-managed teams that use a common brand name. Branson argued that, as he expanded, he would rather sacrifice short-term profits for long-term growth of the various businesses.

Some commentators have argued that Virgin had become an endorsement brand that could not always offer real expertise to the businesses with which it was associated. However, Will Whitehorn, Director of Corporate Affairs for Virgin, stated, 'At Virgin we know what the brand means and when we put our brand name on something we are making a promise.'

Branson saw Virgin adding value in three main ways, aside from the brand. These were their public relations and marketing skills; its experience with greenfield start-ups; and Virgin's understanding of the opportunities presented by 'institutionalised' markets. Virgin saw an 'institutionalised' market as one dominated by few competitors, not giving good value to customers because they had become either inefficient or preoccupied with each other. Virgin believed it did well when it identified such complacency and offered more for less. The entry into fuel and media industries certainly conforms to the model of trying to shake up 'institutionalised' markets.

Corporate rationale

In 2006 Virgin still lacked the trappings of a typical multinational. Branson described the Virgin Group as 'a branded venture capital house'.[3] There was no 'group' as such; financial results were not consolidated either for external examination or, so Virgin claimed, for internal use. Its website described Virgin as a family rather than a hierarchy. Its financial operations were managed from Geneva.

In 2006 Branson explained the basis upon which he considered opportunities: they have to be global in scope, enhance the brand, be worth doing and have an expectation of a reasonable return on investment.[4] Each business was 'ring-fenced', so that lenders to one company had no rights over the assets of another. The ring-fencing seems also to relate not just to provision of financial protection, but also to a business ethics aspect. In an interview in 2006 Branson cricitised supermarkets for selling cheap CDs. His criticism centred on the supermarkets' use of loss leading on CDs damaging music retailers rather than fundamentally challenging the way music retailers do business. Branson has made it a central feature of Virgin that it shakes up institutionalised markets by being innovative. Loss leading is not an innovative approach.

Virgin has evolved from being almost wholly comprised of private companies to a group where some of the companies are publicly listed.

Virgin and Branson

Historically, the Virgin Group had been controlled mainly by Branson and his trusted lieutenants, many of whom had stayed with him for more than 20 years. The increasing conformity between personal interest and business initiatives could be discerned in the establishment of Virgin Fuels. In discussing his efforts to establish a 'green' fuel company in competition with the oil industry Branson made the geopolitical observation that non-oil-based fuels could 'avoid another Middle East war one day'; Branson's opposition to the Second Gulf War is well publicised.[5] In some instances the relationship between personal conviction and business interests is less clear cut. Branson's comments on the threat to British democracy posed by NewsCorp's ownership of such a large percentage of the British media could be depicted as either genuine concern from a public figure or sour grapes from a business rival just been beaten out of purchasing ITV.

More recently Branson has been reported as talking about withdrawing from the business 'which more or less ran itself now',[6] and hoping that his son Sam might become more of a Virgin figurehead.[7] However, while he was publicly contemplating this withdrawal from business, Branson was also launching his initiatives in media and fuel. Perhaps Branson's idea of early retirement is somewhat more active than most.

Corporate performance

By 2006 Virgin had, with mixed results, taken on one established industry after another in an effort to shake up 'fat and complacent business sectors'. It had further set its sights on the British media sector and the global oil industry.

Airlines clearly were an enthusiasm of Branson's. According to Branson, Virgin Atlantic, which was 49 per cent owned by Singapore Airways, was a company that he would not sell outright: 'There are some businesses you preserve, which wouldn't ever be sold, and that's one.' Despite some analysts' worries that airline success could not be sustained given the 'cyclical' nature of the business, Branson maintained a strong interest in the industry, and included airline businesses such as Virgin Express (European), Virgin Blue (Australia) and Virgin Nigeria in the group. Branson's engagement with the search for 'greener' fuels and reducing global warming had not led him to ground his fleets. but rather to prompt a debate on measures to reduce carbon emissions from aeroplanes.

At the beginning of the twenty-first century the most public problem faced by Branson was Virgin Trains, whose Cross Country and West Coast lines were ranked 23rd and 24th out of 25 train-operating franchises according to the Strategic Rail Authority's Review in 2000. By 2002 Virgin Trains was reporting profits and paid its first premium to the British government.

The future

The beginning of the twenty-first century also saw further expansion by Virgin, from airlines, spa finance and mobile telecoms in Africa, into telecoms in Europe, and into the USA. The public flotation of individual businesses rather than the group as a whole has become an intrinsic part of the 'juggling' of finances that underpins Virgin's expansion.

Some commentators have identified a risk with Virgin's approach: 'The greatest threat [is] that . . . Virgin brand . . . may become associated with failure.'[8] This point was emphasised by a commentator[9] who noted that 'a customer who has a bad enough

experience with any one of the product lines may shun all the others'. However, Virgin argues that its brand research indicates that people who have had a bad experience will blame that particular Virgin company or product but will be willing to use other Virgin products or services, due to the very diversity of the brand. Such brand confidence helps explain why Virgin should even contemplate such risky and protracted turnaround challenges as its rail company.

Sarah Sands recounts that Branson's mother 'once proudly boasted that her son would become Prime Minster'. Sands futher commented that she thought his mother underestimated his ambition.[10] With Virgin's entry into fuel and media and Branson's declarations that he is taking on the oil corporations and NewsCorp, Sands may ultimately prove to have been precient in her comment.

Notes

1. *Sunday Telegraph*, 4 December (2005).
2. *Independent*, 22 November (2006).
3. Hawkins (2001a, b).
4. PR Newswire Europe, 16 October (2006).
5. *Fortune*, 6 February (2006).
6. *Independent on Sunday*, 26 November (2006).
7. Ibid.
8. *The Times* 1998, quoted in Vignali (2001).
9. Wells (2000).
10. *Independent on Sunday*, 26 November (2006).

Sources: *The Economist*, 'Cross his heart', 5 October (2002); 'Virgin on the ridiculous', 29 May (2003); 'Virgin Rail: tilting too far', 12 July (2001). P. McCosker, 'Stretching the brand: a review of the Virgin Group', *European Case Clearing House*, 2000. *The Times*, 'Virgin push to open up US aviation market', 5 June (2002); 'Branson plans $1bn US expansion', 30 April (2002). *Observer*, 'Branson eyes 31bn float for Virgin Mobile', 18 January (2004). *Strategic Direction*, 'Virgin Flies High with Brand Extensions', vol. 18, no. 10, (October 2002). R. Hawkins, 'Executive of Virgin Group outlines corporate strategy' *Knight Ridder/Tribune Business News*, July 29 (2001a). R. Hawkins, 'Branson in new dash for cash', *Sunday Business*, 29 July (2001b); *South China Morning Post*, 'Virgin shapes kangaroo strategy aid liberalisation talks between Hong Kong and Australia will determine carrier's game-plan', 28 June (2002). C. Vignali, 'Virgin Cola', *British Food Journal*, vol. 103, no. 2 (2001), pp. 131–139. M. Wells, 'Red Baron', *Forbes Magazine*, vol. 166, no. 1, 7 March (2000).

Questions

1 What is the corporate rationale of Virgin as a group of companies?

2 Are there any relationships of a strategic nature between businesses within the Virgin portfolio?

3 How does the Virgin Group, as a corporate parent, add value to its businesses?

4 What were the main issues facing the Virgin Group at the end of the case and how should they be tackled?

International Strategy

LEARNING OUTCOMES

After reading this chapter you should be able to:

→ Assess the internationalisation potential of different markets, sensitive to variations over time.

→ Identify sources of competitive advantage in international strategy, both through global sourcing and exploitation of local factors embodied in Porter's Diamond.

→ Distinguish between four main types of international strategy.

→ Rank markets for entry or expansion, taking into account attractiveness, cultural and other forms of distance and competitor retaliation threats.

→ Assess the relative merits of different market entry modes, including joint ventures, licensing and foreign direct investment.

Photo: (FREELENS Pool) Tack/STILL Pictures
The Whole Earth Photo Library

8.1 INTRODUCTION

The last chapter introduced market development as a strategy, in relation to the Ansoff matrix. This chapter focuses on a specific but important kind of market development, operating in different geographical markets. This kind of internationalisation raises choices about which countries to compete in, how far to modify the organisation's range of products or services and how to manage across borders. These kinds of questions are relevant to a wide range of organisations nowadays. There are of course the large traditional multinationals such as Nestlé, Toyota and McDonald's, but increasingly new small firms are also 'born global', building international relationships right from the start. Public sector organisations too are having to make choices about collaboration, outsourcing and even competition with overseas organisations. European Union legislation requires public service organisations to accept tenders from non-national providers.

Exhibit 8.1 places international strategy as the core theme of the chapter. International strategy, however, depends ultimately on both the external environment (as in Chapter 2) and organisational capabilities (as in Chapter 3). On the environmental side, Exhibit 8.1 highlights internationalisation drivers; on the capabilities side, it emphasises international and national sources of advantage. The choice of international strategy in turn tends to shape the selection of country markets and the modes of market entry.

This chapter examines key issues in international strategy as follows. The next section introduces the *drivers of internationalisation*. The chapter then considers international and national sources of competitive advantage, particularly those located in *global sourcing* and those in the nationally specific factors embodied

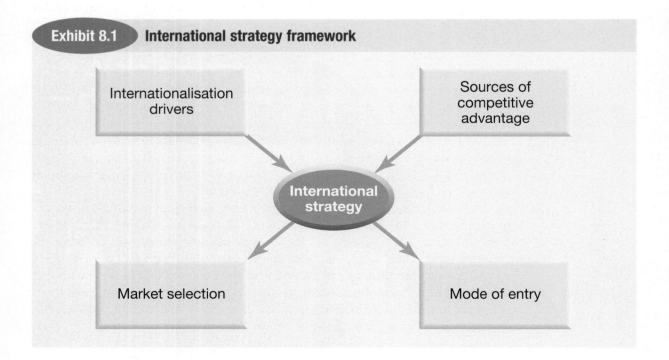

Exhibit 8.1   International strategy framework

Internationalisation drivers

Sources of competitive advantage

International strategy

Market selection

Mode of entry

in Michael Porter's *Diamond framework*. In the light of these drivers and sources of competitive advantage, the chapter describes different *types of international strategy*. As different geographical markets tend to demand significant product or service modifications, some international strategies take the organisation from simple market development to increasingly diversified strategies.[1] From here, the chapter moves on to analyse market selection and market entry. Here, the chapter stresses the interdependence of market attractiveness with *various kinds of distance* and the threat of *competitor retaliation*. The relative advantages of different *entry modes* are then considered, including joint ventures, foreign direct investment and licensing. *Entry sequences* are discussed, including those for new firms and emerging market multinationals. The final two sections examine parallel issues to those addressed with regard to diversification in Chapter 7: internationalisation and *performance* and *portfolio* management.

8.2   INTERNATIONALISATION DRIVERS

Yip's internationalisation drivers

There are many general pressures increasing internationalisation. Barriers to international trade, investment and migration are all now much lower than they were a couple of decades ago. International regulation and governance have improved, so that investing and trading overseas is less risky. Improvements in communications – from cheaper air travel to the Internet – make movement and the spread of ideas much easier around the world. Not least, the success of new economic powerhouses such as the so-called BRICs – Brazil, Russia, India and China – is generating new opportunities and challenges for business internationally.[2]

However, not all these internationalisation trends are one way. Nor do they hold for all industries. For example, migration is now becoming more difficult between some countries. The Internet and cheap air travel are making it easier for expatriate communities to stick with home cultures, rather than merging into a single global 'melting pot' of tastes and ideas. Many so-called multinationals are concentrated in quite particular markets, for example North America and Western Europe, or have a very limited set of international links, for example supply or outsourcing arrangements with just one or two countries overseas. Markets vary widely in the extent to which consumer needs are standardising – compare computer operating systems to tastes in chocolate. In short, managers need to beware 'global baloney', by which economic integration into a single homogenised and competitive world is wildly exaggerated (see the key debate, Illustration 8.6). As in the Chinese retail market (Illustration 8.1), international drivers are usually a lot more complicated than that.

Given internationalisation's complexity, international strategy should be underpinned by a careful diagnosis of the strength and direction of trends in particular markets. George Yip's 'drivers of globalisation' framework provides a basis for such a diagnosis (see Exhibit 8.2).[3] Note though that, while this framework refers to the need for a *global strategy*, with all parts of the business carefully coordinated around the world, most of these drivers also apply to broader *international strategies*, allowing for more limited overseas operations and looser coordination between them (see section 8.4). Accordingly, Yip's drivers can be thought of simply as 'internationalisation drivers'. The four drivers are as follows:

Illustration 8.1

Chinese retail: global or local?

Internationalisation is not a simple process, as supermarket chains Carrefour and Wal-Mart have found in China.

At the start of the twenty-first century, China is a magnet for ambitious Western supermarket chains. Growing at 13 per cent a year, the Chinese market is predicted by Euromonitor to reach $747bn. (£418bn; €380bn) by 2010. Some 520 million people are expected to join the Chinese upper middle class by 2025. With the local industry fragmented and focused on particular regions, large Western companies might have an advantage.

In 1995, after six years' experience in neighbouring Taiwan, French supermarket chain Carrefour was the first to enter the Chinese market in a substantial fashion. By 2006, Carrefour was the sixth largest retailer in China, though the market being what it is, this meant only 0.6 per cent overall market share. The world's largest retailer, the American Wal-Mart, was close behind, especially with its acquisition in 2006 of a Taiwanese chain with outlets on the mainland. These two rivals are pursuing very different strategies. Wal-Mart is pursuing its standard centralised purchasing and distribution strategy, supplying as much as it can from its new, state-of-the-art distribution centre in Shenzen. Carrefour is following a decentralised strategy: except in Shanghai, where it has several stores, Carrefour allows its local store managers, scattered across the many different regions of China, to make their own purchasing and supply decisions.

The growth of companies such as Carrefour and Wal-Mart, as well as local chains, demonstrates that already there is a substantial market for the Western supermarket experience. Carrefour, for example, was a pioneer of 'private label' goods in China, while Wal-Mart brings logistical expertise. Growing wealth and exposure to foreign ideas will no doubt increase Chinese receptiveness. None the less, progress has been slow. Wal-Mart has yet to make a profit in China; Carrefour finally is, but its 2–3 per cent margins are significantly below the nearly 5 per cent margins it enjoys in France.

One early discovery for Wal-Mart was that Chinese consumers prefer frequent shopping trips, buying small quantities each time. While Wal-Mart assumed that Chinese consumers would drive to out-of-town stores and fill their cars with large frozen multi-packs on a once-a-week shop, much like Americans, in fact Chinese customers would break open the multi-packs to take just the smaller quantities they required. Now Wal-Mart supplies more of its frozen foods loose, offering customers a scoop so they can take exactly the amount they want. In 2006, moreover, Wal-Mart allowed trade unions into its stores, in marked contrast to its policy in the rest of the world.

Another discovery for Western retailers is the amount of regional variation in this vast and multi-ethnic country. In the north of China, soya sauces are important; in central China, chilli pepper sauces are required; in the South, it is oyster sauces that matter. For fruit, northerners must have dates; southerners want lychees. In the north, the cold means more demand for red meat and, because customers are wearing layers of clothing, wider store aisles. Northerners do not have much access to hot water, so they wash their hair less frequently, meaning that small sachets of shampoo sell better than large bottles.

Sources: Financial Times, Wall Street Journal and Euromonitor (various dates).

Questions

1 What are the pros and cons of the different China strategies pursued by Carrefour and Wal-Mart?

2 What might be the dangers for a large Western retailer in staying out of the Chinese market?

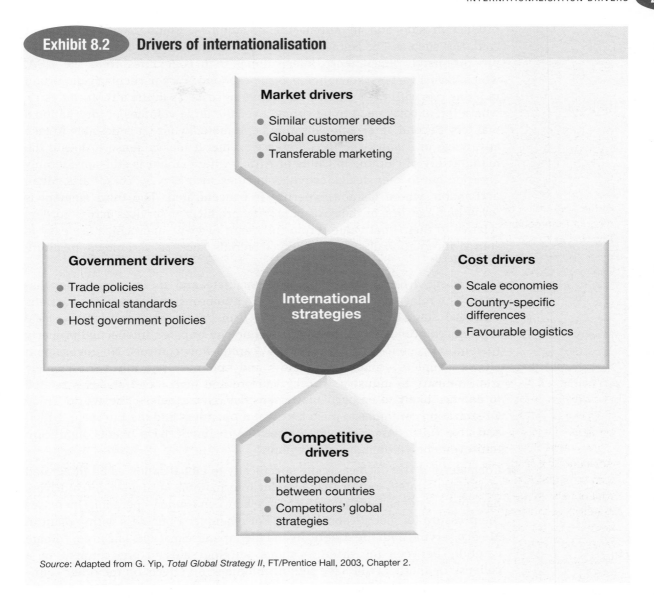

Exhibit 8.2   **Drivers of internationalisation**

Market drivers

- Similar customer needs
- Global customers
- Transferable marketing

Government drivers

- Trade policies
- Technical standards
- Host government policies

International strategies

Cost drivers

- Scale economies
- Country-specific differences
- Favourable logistics

Competitive drivers

- Interdependence between countries
- Competitors' global strategies

Source: Adapted from G. Yip, *Total Global Strategy II*, FT/Prentice Hall, 2003, Chapter 2.

- *Market drivers*. A critical facilitator of internationalisation is some standard-isation of markets. There are three components underlying this driver. First, the presence of *similar customer needs and tastes*: the fact that in most societies consumers have similar needs for easy credit has promoted the worldwide spread of a handful of credit card companies such as Visa. Second, the presence of *global customers*: for example, car component companies have become more international as their customers, such as Toyota or Ford, have internationalised, and required standardised components for all their factories around the world. Finally, *transferable marketing* promotes market globalis-ation: brands such as Coca-Cola are still successfully marketed in very similar ways across the world.

- *Cost drivers*. Costs can be reduced by operating internationally. Again, there are three main elements to cost drivers. First, increasing volume beyond what a national market might support can give *scale economies*, both on the production side and in purchasing of supplies. Companies from smaller countries such as The Netherlands and Switzerland tend therefore to become proportionately much more international than companies from the USA, which have a vast market at home. Scale economies are particularly important in industries with high product development costs, as in the aircraft industry, where initial costs need to be spread over the large volumes of international markets. Second, internationalisation is promoted where it is possible to take advantage of *country-specific differences*. Thus it makes sense to locate the manufacture of clothing in China or Africa, where labour is still considerably cheaper, but to keep design activities in cities such as New York, Paris, Milan or London, where fashion expertise is concentrated. The third element is *favourable logistics*, or the costs of moving products or services across borders relative to their final value. From this point of view, microchips are easy to source internationally, while bulky materials such as assembled furniture are harder.

- *Government drivers*. These can both facilitate and inhibit internationalisation. The relevant elements of policy are numerous, including tariff barriers, technical standards, subsidies to local firms, ownership restrictions, local content requirements, controls over technology transfer, intellectual property (patenting) regimes and currency and capital flow controls. No government allows complete economic openness and openness typically varies widely from industry to industry, with agriculture and high-tech industries related to defence likely to be particularly sensitive. Nevertheless, the World Trade Organization continues to push for greater openness and the European Union and the North American Free Trade Agreement have made significant improvements in their specific regions.[4]

- *Competitive drivers*. These relate specifically to globalisation as an integrated worldwide strategy rather than simpler international strategies. Such drivers have two elements. First, *interdependence* between country operations increases the pressure for global coordination. For example, a business with a plant in Mexico serving both the American and the Japanese markets has to coordinate carefully between the three locations: surging sales in one country, or a collapse in another, will have significant knock-on effects on the other countries. The second element relates directly to competitor strategy. The presence of *globalised competitors* increases the pressure to adopt a global strategy in response because competitors may use one country's profits to cross-subsidise their operations in another. A company with a loosely coordinated international strategy is vulnerable to globalised competitors, because it is unable to support country subsidiaries under attack from targeted, subsidised competition. The danger is of piecemeal withdrawal from countries under attack, and the gradual undermining of any overall economies of scale that the international player may have started with.[5]

The key insight from Yip's drivers framework is that the internationalisation potential of industries is variable. There are many different factors that can support or inhibit it, and an important step in determining an internationalisation strategy is a realistic assessment of the true scope for internationalisation in the particular industry. Illustration 8.2 explains some of the reasons for Deutsche Post's increasing international diversity since the late 1990s.

Illustration 8.2

Deutsche Post's increasing international diversity

Globalising markets and political and regulatory change are amongst the reasons for an organisation's increasing international diversity.

The internationalisation of Deutsche Post is closely linked to the opportunities and pressures resulting from the deregulation of national and international markets and the associated globalisation of the transport and logistics industries. The foundation was laid by the 'big bang' reform of the German postal system in 1990. The 'Law concerning the Structure of Posts and Telecommunication' retained Deutsche Post as a state-owned company but aimed to prepare the company for gradual privatisation (the firm went public in 2000 with an initial sale of 29 per cent of share capital). In the following years the company went through a period of consolidation and restructuring which saw the integration of the former East German Post. By 1997, a year which saw a liberalisation of the German postal market, the company had put into place the groundwork for a period of rapid international expansion.

The subsequent globalisation of Deutsche Post's activities was largely driven by the demands of a growing number of business customers for a single provider of integrated national and international shipping and logistics services. Over the next five years Deutsche Post responded by acquiring key players in the international transport and logistics market, notably Danzas and DHL, with the aim of 'becoming the leading global provider of express and logistics services'. This international expansion enabled Deutsche Post – renamed Deutsche Post World Net (DPWN) in order to highlight its global ambitions – to gain, for example, a major contract with fellow German company BMW for the transport, storage and delivery of cars to its Asian dealerships. As part of its so-called 'START' programme, DPWN initiated, in 2003, a programme aimed at harmonising its products and sales structures, creating integrated networks and implementing group-wide process management in order to

realise the benefits of the economies of scale resulting from its global operations. At the same time DPWN implemented its 'One brand – One face to the customer' motto by making the DHL brand its global 'public face' with the expectation that this 'familiar and trusted brand name will aid us as we continue to develop globalised services'.

Deregulation and wider political changes, reflected in the elimination of trade restrictions, continued to drive international expansion. China's entry into the World Trade Organization enhanced the potential for growth in its international postal market. Accordingly, DPWN strengthened its commitment to this increasingly important market and was rewarded with a 35 per cent growth rate over the period from 2002 to 2004 and, through a joint venture with Sinotrans, gained a 40 per cent market share of Chinese cross-border express services. DPWN aimed to exploit regulatory changes closer to home as well. With its subsidiary Deutsche Post Global Mail (UK) gaining a long-term licence for unlimited bulk mail delivery from the British regulator 'Postcomm', DPWN saw further opportunity for growth in the UK and continued to expand its presence in the British postal market through the acquisition of postal operator Speedmail.

Sources: www.dpwn.de/enrde/press/news; DPWN Annual Report 2002.

Prepared by Michael Mayer, Bath University.

Questions

1 What were the internationalisation drivers associated with DPWN's strategy?

2 Evaluate the pros and cons of both a multidomestic strategy and a global strategy for DPWN.

8.3 NATIONAL AND INTERNATIONAL SOURCES OF ADVANTAGE

As is clear from the earlier discussion of cost drivers in international strategy, the location of activities is a crucial source of potential advantage and one of the distinguishing features of international strategy relative to other diversification strategies. As Bruce Kogut has explained, an organisation can improve the configuration of its *value chain and network*[6] by taking advantage of country-specific differences (see section 3.6.1). There are two principal opportunities available: the exploitation of particular *national advantages*, often in the company's home country, and sourcing advantages overseas via an *international value network*.

8.3.1 Porter's Diamond[7]

KEY CONCEPT

Porter's diamond

As for any strategy, internationalisation needs to be based on possession of some sustainable competitive advantage (see Chapter 3). This competitive advantage has usually to be substantial. After all, a competitor entering a market from overseas typically starts with considerable *dis*advantages relative to existing home competitors, which will usually have superior market knowledge, established relationships with local customers, strong supply chains and the like. A foreign entrant must have significant competitive advantages to overcome such disadvantages. The example of the American giant retailer Wal-Mart provides an illustration: Wal-Mart has been successful in many Asian markets with relatively underdeveloped retail markets, but was forced to withdraw from Germany's maturer market after nearly a decade of failure in 2006. In Germany, unlike in most Asian markets, Wal-Mart had no significant competitive advantage over domestic retailers.

Chapter 3 addresses competitive advantage in general, but the international context raises specifically national sources of advantage that can be substantial and hard to imitate. Countries, and regions within them, often become associated with specific types of enduring competitive advantage: for example, the Swiss in private banking, the north Italians in leather and fur fashion goods, and the Taiwanese in computer laptops. Michael **Porter's Diamond** helps explain why some nations tend to produce firms with sustained competitive advantages in some industries more than others (see Exhibit 8.3). The degree of national advantage varies from industry to industry.

Porter's Diamond suggests that there are inherent reasons why some nations are more competitive than others, and why some industries within nations are more competitive than others

Porter's Diamond suggests there are four interacting determinants of national, or home base, advantage in particular industries (these four determinants together make up a diamond-shaped figure). The home base determinants are:

- *Factor conditions*. These refer to the 'factors of production' that go into making a product or service (that is, raw materials, land and labour). Factor condition advantages at a national level can translate into general competitive advantages for national firms in international markets. For example, the linguistic ability of the Swiss has provided a significant advantage to their banking industry. Cheap energy has traditionally provided an advantage for the North American aluminium industry.

Exhibit 8.3   **Porter's Diamond – the determinants of national advantages**

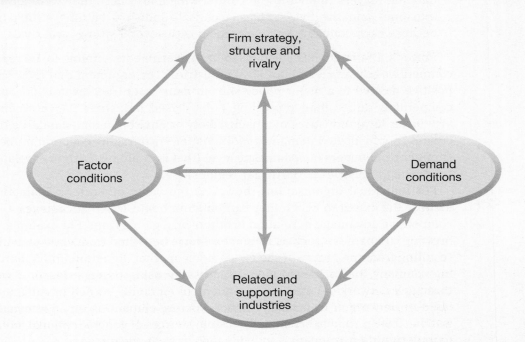

- *Home demand conditions*. The nature of the domestic customers can become a source of competitive advantage. Dealing with sophisticated and demanding customers at home helps train a company to be effective overseas. For example, Japanese customers' high expectations of electrical and electronic equipment provided an impetus for those industries in Japan leading to global dominance of those sectors. Sophisticated local customers in France and Italy have helped keep their local fashion industries at the leading edge for many decades.

- *Related and supporting industries*. Local 'clusters' of related and mutually supporting industries can be an important source of competitive advantage. These are often regionally based, making personal interaction easier. In northern Italy, for example, the leather footwear industry, the leather working machinery industry, and the design services which underpin them, group together in the same regional cluster to each other's mutual benefit. Silicon Valley forms a cluster of hardware, software, research and venture capital organisations which together create a virtuous circle of high-technology enterprise.

- *Firm strategy, industry structure and rivalry*. The characteristic strategies, industry structures and rivalries in different countries can also be bases of advantage. German companies' strategy of investing in technical excellence gives them a characteristic advantage in engineering industries and creates large pools of expertise. A competitive local industry structure is also helpful: if too dominant in their home territory, local organisations can become complacent and lose advantage overseas. Some domestic rivalry can actually be an advantage, therefore. For example, the long-run success of the Japanese car companies is partly based on government policy sustaining several national players (unlike in the United Kingdom, where they were all merged into one) and the Swiss pharmaceuticals industry became strong in part because each company had to compete with several strong local rivals.

Porter's Diamond has been used by governments aiming to increase the competitive advantage of their local industries. The argument that rivalry can be positive has led to a major policy shift in many countries towards encouraging competition rather than protecting home-based industries. Governments can also foster local industries by raising safety or environmental standards (that is, creating sophisticated demand conditions) or encouraging cooperation between suppliers and buyers on a domestic level (that is, building clusters of related and supporting industries in particular regions).

For individual organisations, however, the value of Porter's Diamond is to identify the extent to which they can build on home-based advantages to create competitive advantage in relation to others on a global front. For example, Dutch brewing companies – such as Heineken – have benefited from early globalisation resulting from the nature of the Dutch home market. Benetton, the Italian clothing company, has achieved global success by using its experience of working through a network of largely independent, often family-owned manufacturers to build its network of franchised retailers. Before embarking on an internationalisation strategy, managers should seek out sources of general national advantage to underpin their company's individual sources of advantage.

8.3.2 The international value network

Global sourcing:
purchasing services and
components from the
most appropriate
suppliers around the
world regardless of
their location

However, the sources of advantage need not be purely domestic. For international companies, advantage can be drawn from the international configuration of their *value network*. Here the different skills, resources and costs of countries around the world can be systematically exploited in order to locate each element of the value chain in that country or region where it can be conducted most effectively and efficiently. This may be achieved both through foreign direct investments and joint ventures but also through **global sourcing**, that is by purchasing services and components from the most appropriate suppliers around the world, regardless of their location. For example, in the UK, the National Health Service has been sourcing medical personnel from overseas to offset a shortfall in domestic skills and capacity.

Different locational advantages can be identified:

● *Cost advantages* include labour costs, transportation and communications costs and taxation and investment incentives. Labour costs are important. American and European firms, for example, are increasingly moving software programming tasks to India where a computer programmer costs an American firm about one-quarter of what it would pay for a worker with comparable skills in the USA. As wages in India have risen, Indian IT firms have already begun moving work to even more low-cost locations such as China with some predicting that subsidiaries of Indian firms will come to control as much as 40 per cent of China's IT service exports.

Illustration 8.3

Boeing's global R&D network

Organisations may seek to exploit locational advantages worldwide.

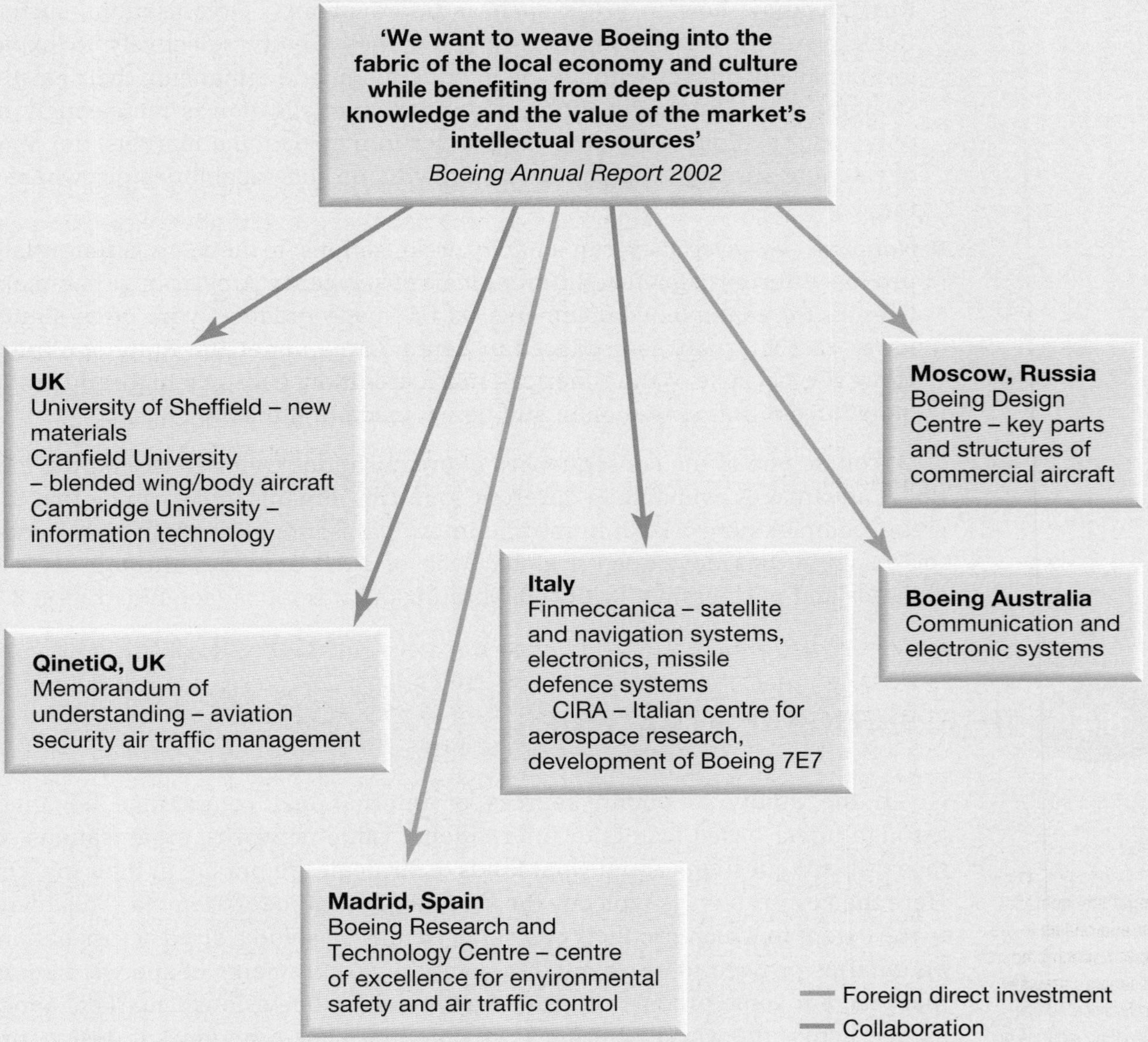

'We want to weave Boeing into the fabric of the local economy and culture while benefiting from deep customer knowledge and the value of the market's intellectual resources'
Boeing Annual Report 2002

UK
University of Sheffield – new materials
Cranfield University – blended wing/body aircraft
Cambridge University – information technology

QinetiQ, UK
Memorandum of understanding – aviation security air traffic management

Italy
Finmeccanica – satellite and navigation systems, electronics, missile defence systems
CIRA – Italian centre for aerospace research, development of Boeing 7E7

Madrid, Spain
Boeing Research and Technology Centre – centre of excellence for environmental safety and air traffic control

Moscow, Russia
Boeing Design Centre – key parts and structures of commercial aircraft

Boeing Australia
Communication and electronic systems

— Foreign direct investment
— Collaboration

Sources: Boeing.com, Boeing Annual Report 2002, Aviation International News Online.
Prepared by Michael Mayer, Bath University.

Questions

1 What reasons might be driving the internationalisation of Boeing's R&D activities?
2 What challenges might Boeing face as it internationalises its R&D activities?

- *Unique capabilities* may allow an organisation to enhance its competitive advantage. A reason for Accenture to locate a rapidly expanding software development office in the Chinese city of Dalian was that communication with potential Japanese and Korean multinational firms operating in the region was easier than if an equivalent location in India or the Philippines had been chosen. Organisations may also seek to exploit advantages related to specific technological and scientific capabilities. Boeing, for example, located its largest engineering centre outside of the USA in Moscow to help it access Russian know-how in areas such as aerodynamics. Organisations such as Boeing are thus increasingly leveraging their ability selectively to exploit locational advantages with a view to building on and enhancing their existing strategic capabilities. Put differently, internationalisation is increasingly not only about exploiting existing capabilities in new national markets, but about developing strategic capabilities by drawing on the capabilities elsewhere in the world.

- *National characteristics* can enable organisations to develop differentiated product offerings aimed at different market segments. American guitar-maker Gibson, for example, complements its US-made products with often similar, lower-cost alternatives produced in South Korea under the Epiphone brand. However, because of the American music tradition, Gibson's high-end guitars benefit from the reputation of still being 'made in the USA'.

Of course one of the consequences of organisations trying to exploit the locational advantages available in different countries' organisations can be that they create complex networks of intra- and interorganisational relationships. Boeing, for example, has developed a global web of R&D activities through its subsidiaries and partnerships with collaborating organisations (see Illustration 8.3).

8.4 INTERNATIONAL STRATEGIES

The **global–local dilemma** relates to the extent to which products and services may be standardised across national boundaries or need to be adapted to meet the requirements of specific national markets

Given the ability to obtain sources of international competitive advantage through home-based factors or international value networks, organisations still face difficult questions about what kinds of strategies to pursue in their markets. Here the key problem is typically the so-called **global–local dilemma**. This relates to the extent to which products and services may be standardised across national boundaries or need to be adapted to meet the requirements of specific national markets. For some products and services – such as televisions – markets appear similar across the world, offering huge potential scale economies if design, production and delivery can be centralised. For other products and services – such as television programming – tastes still seem highly nationally specific, drawing companies to decentralise operations and control as near as possible to the local market. This global–local dilemma can evoke a number of responses from companies pursuing international strategies, ranging from decentralisation to centralisation, with positions in between.

This section introduces four different kinds of international strategy, based on choices about the international *configuration* of the various activities an organisation has to carry out and the degree to which these activities are then *coordinated*

Exhibit 8.4   **Four international strategies**

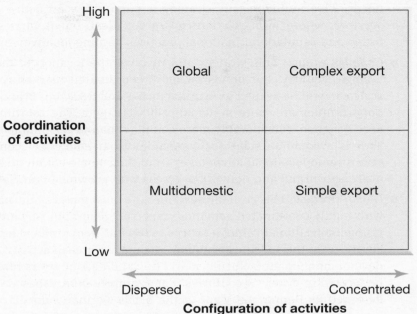

Source: Adapted from M.E. Porter, 'Changing patterns of international competition'. Copyright © 1986, by The Regents of the University of California. Reprinted from the *California Management Review*, vol. 28, no. 2. By permission of The Regents. 'NB Porter's strategies are relabelled for consistency with the rest of this book.

KEY CONCEPT

Four international strategies

internationally (see Exhibit 8.4). More precisely, configuration refers to the geographical dispersion or concentration of activities such as manufacturing and R&D, while coordination refers to the extent to which operations in different countries are managed in a decentralised way or a centrally coordinated way. The four basic international strategies are:[8]

- *Simple export*. This strategy involves a concentration of activities (particularly manufacturing) in one country, typically the country of the organisation's origin. At the same time, marketing of the exported product is very loosely coordinated overseas, perhaps handled by independent sales agents in different markets. Pricing, packaging, distribution and even branding policies may be determined locally. This strategy is typically chosen by organisations with a strong locational advantage – as determined by the Porter Diamond, for example – but where either the organisation has insufficient managerial capabilities to coordinate marketing internationally or where coordinated marketing would add little value, for example in agricultural or raw material commodities.

- *Multidomestic*. This strategy is similarly loosely coordinated internationally, but involves a dispersion overseas of various activities, including manufacturing and sometimes product development. Instead of export, therefore, goods and services are produced locally in each national market. Each market is treated independently, with the needs of each local domestic market given priority – hence 'multidomestic'. Local adaptations can make the overall corporate portfolio increasingly diversified. This strategy is appropriate where there are few economies of scale and strong benefits to adapting to local needs. This multidomestic strategy is particularly attractive in professional services, where local relationships are critical, but it carries risks towards brand and reputation if national practices become too diverse.

- *Complex export*. This strategy still involves the location of most activities in a single country, but builds on more coordinated marketing. Economies of scale can still be reaped in manufacturing and R&D, but branding and pricing opportunities are more systematically managed. The coordination demands are, of course, considerably more complex than in the simple export strategy. This is a common stage for companies from emerging economies, as they retain some locational advantages from their home country, but seek to build a stronger brand and network overseas with growing organisational maturity.

- *Global strategy*. This strategy describes the most mature international strategy, with highly coordinated activities dispersed geographically around the world. Using international value networks to the full, geographical location is chosen according to the specific locational advantage for each activity, so that product development, manufacturing, marketing and headquarters functions might all be located in different countries. For example, Detroit-based General Motors designed its Pontiac Le Mans at the firm's German subsidiary Opel, with its high engineering skills; developed its advertising via a British agency with the creativity strengths of London; produced many of the more complex components in Japan, exploiting its sophisticated manufacturing and technological capabilities; and assembled the car in South Korea, a location where a lower-cost, yet skilled, labour force was available. All this, of course, required high investments and skill in coordination (see also the discussion of the transnational structure in Chapter 12).

In practice, these four international strategies are not absolutely distinct. Managerial coordination and geographical concentration are matters of degree rather than sharp distinctions. Companies may often oscillate within and between the four strategies. Their choices, moreover, will be influenced by changes in the internationalisation drivers introduced earlier. Where, for example, tastes are highly standardised, companies will tend to favour complex export or global strategies. Where economies of scale are few, the logic is more in favour of multidomestic strategies.

8.5   MARKET SELECTION AND ENTRY

Having decided on an international strategy built on significant sources of competitive advantage and supported by strong internationalisation drivers, managers need next to decide which countries to enter. Not all countries are equally attractive. To an extent, however, countries can initially be compared using the standard environmental analysis techniques, for example along the dimensions identified in the PESTEL framework (see section 2.2.1) or according to the industry five forces (section 2.3). However, there are specific determinants of market attractiveness that need to be considered in internationalisation strategy, and they can be analysed under two main headings: the intrinsic characteristics of the market and the nature of the competition. A key point here is how initial estimates of country attractiveness can be modified by various measures of *distance* and the likelihood of competitor *retaliation*. The section concludes by considering different *entry modes* into national markets.

8.5.1 Market characteristics

At least four elements of the PESTEL framework are particularly important in comparing countries for entry:

- *Political*. Political environments vary widely between countries and can alter rapidly. Russia since the fall of communism has seen frequent swings for and against private foreign enterprise. Governments can of course create significant opportunities for organisations. For example, the official regional development agency Scottish Enterprise provided a subsidy in order to attract the 2003 MTV music awards to the Scottish capital Edinburgh, while political and regulatory changes can create opportunities for international expansion as with Deutsche Post (see Illustration 8.2). It is important, however, to determine the level of *political risk* before entering a country.

- *Economic*. Key comparators in deciding entry are levels of gross domestic product and disposable income which help in estimating the potential size of the market. Fast-growth economies obviously provide opportunities, and in developing economies such as China growth is translating into an even faster creation of a high-consumption middle class. However, companies must also be aware of the stability of a country's currency which may affect its income stream. There can be considerable *currency risk*.

- *Social*. Social factors will clearly be important, for example the availability of a well-trained workforce or the size of demographic market segments – old or young – relevant to the strategy. Cultural variations need to be considered, for instance in defining tastes in the marketplace.

- *Legal*. Countries vary widely in their legal regime, determining the extent to which businesses can enforce contracts, protect intellectual property or avoid corruption. Similarly, policing will be important for the security of employees, a factor that in the past has deterred business in some South American countries.

It is quite common to rank country markets against each other on criteria such as these and then to choose the countries for entry that offer the highest relative scores. However, Pankaj Ghemawat has pointed out that what matters is not just the attractiveness of different countries relative to each other, but also the compatibility of the possible countries with the internationalising firm itself.[9] The argument is that, for firms coming from any particular country, some countries are more 'distant' – or incompatible – than others. In other words, companies with different nationalities would not fit equally well in all the top-ranked countries. A South American market might rank the same as an East African market in terms of attractiveness, but a Spanish company would probably be more at home in the first than the second. As well as a relative ranking of countries, therefore, each company has to add its assessment of countries according to their 'closeness'.

In arguing that 'distance still matters', Ghemawat offers a 'CAGE framework', with each letter of the acronym highlighting different dimensions of distance:

- *Cultural distance*. The distance dimension here relates to differences in language, ethnicity, religion and social norms. Cultural distance is not just a matter of similarity in consumer tastes, but extends to important compatibilities in terms of managerial behaviours. Here, for example, American firms might be closer to Canada than to Mexico, which Spanish firms might find relatively compatible.

- *Administrative and political distance*. Here distance is in terms of incompatible administrative, political or legal traditions. Colonial ties can diminish difference, so that the shared heritage of France and its former West African colonies creates certain understandings that go beyond linguistic advantages. Institutional weaknesses – for example, slow or corrupt administration – can open up distance between countries. So too can political differences: Chinese companies are increasingly able to operate in parts of the world that American companies are finding harder, for example parts of the Middle East and Africa.

- *Geographical distance*. This is not just a matter of the kilometres separating one country from another, but involves other geographical characteristics of the country such as size, sea access and the quality of communications infrastructure. For example, Wal-Mart's difficulties in Europe relate to the fact that its logistics systems were developed in the geographically enormous space of North America, and proved much less suitable for the smaller and more dense countries of Europe. Transport infrastructure can shrink or exaggerate physical distance. France is much closer to large parts of Continental Europe than to the UK, because of the barrier presented by the English Channel and the UK's relatively poor road and rail infrastructure.

- *Economic*. The final element of the CAGE framework refers particularly to wealth distances. Here, instead of simply assuming that a wealthy market is a good one to enter, and a poor market a bad one, the framework points to the differing capabilities of companies from different countries. Multinationals from rich countries are typically weak at serving consumers in poorer markets (see Illustration 8.4 for how Unilever approaches this problem). In developing countries, rich-country multinationals often end up focusing on economic elites. In reverse, it often takes a long time for companies from developing countries to learn all the requirements that the middle classes from wealthy countries routinely expect.[10]

8.5.2 Competitive characteristics

Assessing the relative attractiveness of markets by PESTEL and CAGE analyses is only the first step. The second element relates to competition. Here, of course, Porter's five forces framework can help (see section 2.3). For example, country markets with many existing competitors, powerful buyers (perhaps large retail chains such as in much of North America and Northern Europe) and low barriers to further new entrants from overseas would typically be unattractive.

Illustration 8.4

Strategic innovation at Hindustan Lever Ltd

Large multinational corporations may still need to tailor their products and services to local market needs.

Unilever is one of the world's biggest consumer products companies. It seeks to establish its brands on a global basis and support them with state-of-the-art research and development. However, it is acutely aware that markets differ and that, if it is to be global, it has to be prepared to adapt to local market conditions. It also recognises that if it is to have global reach, it has to be able to market its goods in poorer areas as well as richer areas. Indeed it estimates that by 2010 half of its sales will come from the developing world – an increase of over 30 per cent from the equivalent figure in 2000.

In the rural areas of India Hindustan Lever is setting about marketing Unilever's branded goods in ways suited to local conditions.

Much of the effort goes into marketing branded goods in local 'haats' or market places, where Unilever representatives sell the products from the back of trucks using loudspeakers to explain the brand proposition. Local executives argue that, poor as people are, they 'aren't naturally inclined to settle for throwaway versions of the real deal – if the companies that make the real deal bother to explain the difference'.

To help develop the skills to do this Lever management trainees in India begin their careers by spending weeks living in rural villages where they eat, sleep and talk with the locals: 'Once you have spent time with consumers, you realise that they want the same things you want. They want a good quality of life.'

The same executives have innovated further in the way goods are marketed. They have developed direct sales models where women, belonging to self-help groups that run micro credit operations, sell Lever products so as to make their collectives' savings grow. Where television viewing is uncommon, Hindustan Lever marketing executives have also mounted thousands of live shows at cattle and trade markets, employing rural folklore. The aim here is not just to push the Lever brands, it is to explain the importance of more frequent washing and better hygiene. Indeed sales personnel attend religious festivals and use ultraviolet light wands on people's hands to show the dangers of germs and dirt.

But it is not just the way the goods are marketed that is tailored to rural India. Product development is also different. For example, Indian women are very proud of the care of their hair and regard hair grooming as a luxury. However, they tend to use the same soap for body washing as for washing their hair. So Lever has dedicated research and development efforts into finding a low-cost soap that can be used for the body and for the hair and which is targeted to smaller towns and rural areas.

As Keki Dadiseth, a director of Hindustan Lever, puts it: 'Everyone wants brands. And there are a lot more poor people in the world than rich people. To be a global business . . . you have to participate in all segments.'

Source: Rekha Balu, 'Strategic innovation: Hindustan Lever Ltd', *FastCompany.com* (www.fastcompany.com/magazine), issue 47, June (2001).

Questions

1 What are the challenges a multinational such as Unilever faces in developing global brands whilst encouraging local responsiveness?

2 What other examples of local tailoring of global brands can you think of?

3 Multinationals have been criticised for marketing more expensive branded goods in poorer areas of developing countries. What are your views of the ethical dimensions to Hindustan Lever's activities?

| Exhibit 8.5 | International competitor retaliation |

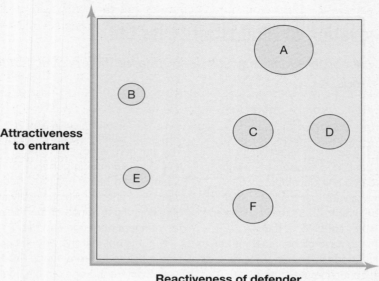

Attractiveness to entrant

Reactiveness of defender

However, an additional consideration is the likelihood of retaliation from other competitors.

In the five forces framework, retaliation potential relates to rivalry, but managers can extend this by using insights directly from 'game theory' (see section 6.7). Here the likelihood and ferocity of potential competitor reactions are added to the simple calculation of relative country market attractiveness. As in Exhibit 8.5, country markets are aligned against two axes.[11] The first is *market attractiveness* to the new entrant, based on PESTEL, CAGE and five forces analyses, for example. In the exhibit, countries A and B are the most attractive to the entrant. The second is the *defender's reactiveness*, likely to be influenced by the market's attractiveness to the defender but also by the extent to which the defender is working with a globally integrated, rather than multidomestic, strategy. A defender will be more reactive if the markets are important to it and it has the managerial capabilities to coordinate its response. Here, the defender is highly reactive in countries A and D. The third element is the *clout* (that is, power) that the defender is able to muster in order to fight back. Clout is typically a function of share in the particular market, but might be influenced by connections to other powerful local players, such as retailers or government. In Exhibit 8.5, clout is represented by the size of the bubbles, with the defender having most clout in countries A, C, D and F.

Choice of country to enter can be significantly modified by adding reactiveness and clout to calculations of attractiveness. Relying only on attractiveness, the top-ranked country to enter in Exhibit 8.5 is country A. Unfortunately, it is also one in which the defender is highly reactive, and the one in which it has most clout. Country B becomes a better international move than A. In turn, country C is a better prospect than country D, because, even though they are equally attractive, the defender is less reactive. One surprising result of taking defender reactiveness and clout into account is the re-evaluation of country E: although ranked fifth on simple attractiveness, it might rank second overall if competitor retaliation is allowed for.

This sort of analysis is particularly fruitful for considering the international moves of two interdependent competitors, such as Unilever and Procter and Gamble or British Airways and Singapore Airlines. In these cases the analysis is relevant to any aggressive strategic move, for instance the expansion of existing operations in a country as well as initial entry. Especially in the case of globally integrated competitors, moreover, the overall clout of the defender must be taken into account. The defender may choose to retaliate in other markets than the targeted one, counter-attacking wherever it has the clout to do damage to the aggressor. Naturally, too, this kind of analysis can be applied to interactions between diversified competitors as well as international ones: each bubble could represent different products or services.

8.5.3 Entry modes

Once a particular national market has been selected for entry, an organisation needs to choose how to enter that market. Entry modes differ in the degree of resource commitment to a particular market and the extent to which an organisation is operationally involved in a particular location. The key entry mode types are: exporting; contractual arrangement through licensing and franchising; joint ventures and alliances; and foreign direct investment, which in turn may involve the acquisition of established companies or 'greenfield' investments, the development of facilities 'from scratch'. These alternative methods of strategy development are explained further in section 10.3, but the specific advantages and disadvantages for international market entry are summarised in Exhibit 8.6.

Entry modes are often selected according to stages of organisational development. Internationalisation brings organisations into new and often unknown territory, requiring managers to learn new ways of doing business.[12] Internationalisation is therefore traditionally seen as a sequential process whereby companies gradually increase their commitment to newly entered markets, accumulating knowledge and increasing their capabilities along the way. This

Staged international expansion: firms initially use entry modes that allow them to maximise knowledge acquisition whilst minimising the exposure of their assets

strategy of **staged international expansion** means that firms begin by using entry modes such as licensing and exporting that allow them to acquire local knowledge whilst minimising the exposure of their assets. Once firms have sufficient knowledge and confidence, they can then sequentially increase their exposure, perhaps first by a joint venture and finally by direct foreign investment. An example is the entry of automobile manufacturer BMW into the American market. After a lengthy period of exporting from Germany to the USA, BMW set up a manufacturing plant in Spartanburg, South Carolina, in order to strengthen its competitive position in the strategically important American market.

In contrast to the gradual internationalisation followed originally by many large and established firms, some small firms are now internationalising rapidly at early stages in their development using multiple modes of entry to several countries. These are the so-called 'born global' firms.[13] GNI, the mini-multinational

Exhibit 8.6 **Market entry modes: advantages and disadvantages**

Exporting

Advantages

- No operational facilities needed in the host country
- Economies of scale can be exploited
- By using Internet, small/inexperienced firms can gain access to international markets

Disadvantages

- Does not allow the firm to benefit from the locational advantages of the host nation
- Limits opportunities to gain knowledge of local markets and competitors
- May create dependence on export intermediaries
- Exposure to trade barriers such as import duties
- Incurs transportation costs
- May limit the ability to respond quickly to customer demands

Joint ventures and alliances

Advantages

- Investment risk shared with partner
- Combining of complementary resources and know-how
- May be a governmental condition for market entry

Disadvantages

- Difficulty of identifying appropriate partner and agreeing appropriate contractual terms
- Managing the relationship with the foreign partner
- Loss of competitive advantage through imitation
- Limits ability to integrate and coordinate activities across national boundaries

Licensing

Advantages

- Contractually agreed income through sale of production and marketing rights
- Limits economic and financial exposure

Disadvantages

- Difficulty of identifying appropriate partner and agreeing contractual terms
- Loss of competitive advantage through imitation
- Limits benefits from the locational advantages of host nation

Foreign direct investment

Advantages

- Full control of resources and capabilities
- Facilitates integration and coordination of activities across national boundaries
- Acquisitions allow rapid market entry
- Greenfield investments allow development of state-of-the-art facilities and can attract financial support from the host government

Disadvantages

- Substantial investment in and commitment to host country leading to economic and financial exposure
- Acquisition may lead to problems of integration and coordination
- Greenfield entry time consuming and less predictable in terms of cost

in Illustration 8.5, illustrates this born global process. In achieving this rapid internationalisation, born global firms need to manage simultaneously the process of internationalisation and develop their wider strategy and infrastructure, whilst often lacking the usually expected experiential knowledge to do so.

Emerging country multinationals too are often moving quickly through entry modes. Prominent examples are the Chinese white goods multinational Haier, the Indian pharmaceuticals company Ranbaxy Laboratories and Mexico's Cemex cement company. These companies' international strategies are not simply

---

Illustration 8.5

The mini-multinational

GNI, a biotechnology start-up, has fewer than 100 employees, but operates in five countries in four continents.

Christopher Savoie is an American entrepreneur who originally studied medicine in Japan, becoming fluent in Japanese and adopting Japanese citizenship. In 2001, he founded GNI, a biotechnology company that by 2006 had raised 3bn yen (€20m) in investment funds, including a stake from famed global investment bank Goldman Sachs. The company already has operations in Tokyo and Fukuoka, Japan; in Shanghai, China; in Cambridge and London, UK; and in San Jose in California. There is also collaboration with a laboratory in Auckland, New Zealand. Savoie comments: 'We take the best in each country and put them together.'

GNI's strategy is to focus on Asian ailments that have been neglected by big Western pharmaceutical companies, for example stomach cancer and hepatitis. According to Savoie: 'Asia has been getting the short end of the stick. As a small company, we had to choose a niche, and we thought that half of humanity was an acceptable place to start.'

GNI's scientists work on umbilical cords, providing genetic tissue that has been virtually unaffected by the environment. However, Japanese parents traditionally keep their children's umbilical cords. GNI therefore works with the Rosie Maternity Hospital in Cambridge to source its basic genetic materials. On the other hand, GNI in Japan has ready access to supercomputers, and Japanese scientists have worked out the algorithms required to analyse the genetic codes. Japan also has been the main source of investment funds, where regulations on start-ups are relaxed. China comes in as an effective place to test treatments on patients. Regulatory advantages mean that trials can be carried out more quickly in China, moreover for one-tenth of the cost in Japan. In 2005, GNI merged with Shanghai Genomics, a start-up run by two US-educated entrepreneurs. Meanwhile, in San Jose, there is a business development office seeking out relationships with the big American pharmaceutical giants.

Savoie describes the business model as essentially simple:

We have a Chinese cost structure, Japanese supercomputers and, in Cambridge, access to ethical materials (umbilical cords) and top clinical scientists. This is a network we can use to take high-level science and turn it into molecules to compete with the big boys.

Sources: D. Pilling, 'March of the mini-multinational', *Financial Times*, 4 May (2006); www.gene-networks.com.

Questions

1 Analyse GNI's value network in terms of cost advantages, unique capabilities and national characteristics.

2 What managerial challenges will GNI face as it grows?

export and cost based.[14] Typically they develop *unique capabilities* in their home market, in areas neglected by established multinationals. They then move on to establish outposts in more developed markets. For example, because of the needs of the Chinese market, Haier became skilled at very efficient production of simple white goods, providing a cost advantage that is transferable outside a Chinese manufacturing base. In 1999, Haier set up a manufacturing operation in South Carolina in the USA, competing head-on with Western giant multi-nationals such as General Electric and Whirlpool on their home territory.

8.6 INTERNATIONALISATION AND PERFORMANCE

Just as for product and service diversity discussed in section 7.2.3 the relationship between internationalisation and performance has been extensively researched.[15] Some of the main findings from such research are these:

- *An inverted-U curve*. While the potential performance benefits of internationalisation are substantial, in that it allows firms to realise economies of scale and scope and benefit from the locational advantages available in countries around the globe, the combination of diverse locations and diverse business units also gives rise to high levels of organisational complexity. After a point, the costs of organisational complexity may exceed the benefits of internationalisation. Accordingly, theory and the balance of evidence suggest an inverted-U-shaped relationship between internationalisation and performance (similar to the findings on product/service diversification shown in Exhibit 7.4 and reported in section 7.2.3), with moderate levels of internationalisation leading to the best results. However, Yip's recent research on large British companies suggests that managers may be getting better at internationalisation, with substantially internationalized firms actually seeing performance improving at the point where international sales are above about 40 per cent of total sales.[16] Experience and commitment to internationalisation may be able deliver strong performance for highly internationalised firms.

- *Service sector disadvantages*. A number of studies have suggested that, in contrast to firms in the manufacturing sector, internationalisation may not lead to improved performance for service sector firms. There are three possible reasons for such an effect. First, the operations of foreign service firms in some sectors (such as accountants or banks) remain tightly regulated and restricted in many countries; second, due to the intangible nature of services, they are often more sensitive to cultural differences and require greater adaptation than manufactured products which may lead to higher initial learning costs; third, services typically require a significant local presence and reduce the scope for the exploitation of economies of scale in production compared with manufacturing firms.[17]

- *Internationalisation and product diversity*. An important question to consider is the interaction between internationalisation and product/service diversification. Compared with single-business firms it has been suggested that product-diversified firms are likely to do better from international expansion because they have already developed the necessary skills and structures for managing internal diversity. At the other end of the spectrum there is general consensus that firms that are highly diversified in terms of both product and international markets are likely to face excessive costs of coordination and control leading to poor performance. As many firms have not yet reached levels of internationalisation where negative effects outweigh possible gains, and because of current scepticism with regard to the benefits of high levels of product diversification, many companies currently opt for reducing their product diversity while building their international scope. Unilever, for example, has been combining a strategy of growing internationalisation with de-diversification.

8.7 ROLES IN AN INTERNATIONAL PORTFOLIO

Just as for product diversification, international strategies imply different relationships between subsidiary operations and the corporate centre. The complexity of the strategies followed by organisations such as General Motors or Unilever can result in highly differentiated networks of subsidiaries with a range of distinct strategic roles. Subsidiaries may play different roles according to the level of local resources and capabilities available to them and the strategic importance of their local environment (see Exhibit 8.7):[18]

Exhibit 8.7   Subsidiary roles in multinational firms

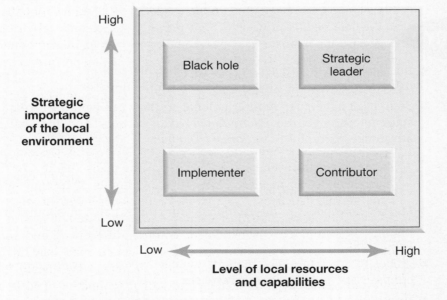

Strategic leaders (in the context of international strategy) are subsidiaries that not only hold valuable resources and capabilities but are also located in countries that are crucial for competitive success

Contributors are subsidiaries with valuable internal resources but located in countries of lesser strategic significance, which none the less play key roles in a multinational organisation's competitive success

Implementers simply execute strategies developed elsewhere and may generate surplus financial resources to help fund initiatives elsewhere

Black holes are subsidiaries located in countries that are crucial for competitive success but with low-level resources or capabilities

● **Strategic leaders** are subsidiaries that not only hold valuable resources and capabilities but are also located in countries that are crucial for competitive success because of, for example, the size of the local market or the accessibility of key technologies. Japanese and European subsidiaries in the USA often play this role.

● **Contributors**, subsidiaries with valuable internal resources but located in countries of lesser strategic significance, can nevertheless play key roles in a multinational organisation's competitive success. The Australian subsidiary of the Swedish telecommunications firm Ericsson played such a role in developing specialized systems for the firm's mobile phone business.

● **Implementers**, though not contributing substantially to the enhancement of a firm's competitive advantage, are important in the sense that they help generate vital financial resources. In this sense, they are similar to the 'cash cows' of the BCG matrix. The danger is that they turn into the equivalent of 'dogs'.

● **Black holes** are subsidiaries located in countries that are crucial for competitive success but with low-level resources or capabilities. This is a position many subsidiaries of American and European firms found themselves in over long periods in Japan. They have some of the characteristics of 'question marks' in the BCG matrix, requiring heavy investment (like an astrophysicist's black hole, sucking matter in). Possibilities for overcoming this unattractive position include the development of alliances and the selective and targeted development of key resources and capabilities.[19]

Again this does, of course, in turn relate to how these subsidiaries are controlled and managed and this is discussed in Chapter 12. See also the key debate in Illustration 8.6.

SUMMARY

● *Internationalisation potential* in any particular market is determined by four drivers: market, cost, government and competitors' strategies.

● Sources of advantage in international strategy can be drawn from both global sourcing through the *international value network* and national sources of advantage, as captured in *Porter's Diamond*.

● There are four main types of international strategy, varying according to extent of *coordination* and *geographical configuration*: simple export, complex export, multidomestic and global.

● Market selection for international entry or expansion should be based on *attractiveness*, multidimensional measures of *distance* and expectations of competitor *retaliation*.

● Modes of entry into new markets include *export*, *licensing*, *joint ventures* and *alliances* and *foreign direct investment*.

● Internationalisation has an uncertain relationship to financial performance, with an *inverted-U curve* warning against over-internationalisation.

● Subsidiaries in an international firm can be managed by portfolio methods just as businesses in a diversified firm.

Illustration 8.6

Global, local or regional?

Debate rages over whether companies are really becoming more global, or whether local or indeed regional pressures remain strong.

Ted Levitt, Harvard Business School professor and former non-executive director of the international advertising firm Saatchi & Saatchi, has provocatively made the case for deep commitment to global strategies in all kinds of markets. He argues that modern communications technologies are creating homogeneous market needs, while manufacturing technologies are increasing the benefits of scale. Given the cost advantages of scale, and the diminishing importance of consumer differences, companies that commit to truly global strategies will be able to use low prices to sweep out all competitors still focused on local needs. He argues: 'The global company will seek to standardize its offering everywhere. . . . Companies that do not adopt to the new global realities will become victims of those that do.' He cites Coca-Cola, Rolex, Sony and McDonald's as exemplars of the trend. Companies should not hanker over detailed differences left over from the past, but recognise the big picture of coming globalisation.

Levitt's sweeping argument brought a spirited response from American academics Gerry Wind and Susan Douglas, warning of 'the Myth of Globalisation'. They challenge both the trend to homogenisation and the growing role of scale economies. Even apparently global companies adapt to country needs: for example, Coca-Cola sells local products in Japan alongside its classic Coke, and its Dasani bottled water is a success in the USA, but a failure in Europe. As to scale, new flexible automation technologies may even be reducing economic order sizes, allowing short production runs adapted to local needs. Besides, as the world gets richer, consumers will be less price sensitive and more ready to spend on indulging their local tastes. Wind and Douglas warn that blind confidence in the inevitability of globalisation will surely lead to business disappointment.

Between the two poles of global and local there is a third position: regional. Pankaj Ghemawat points out that most international trade is intra-regional. European countries trade predominantly with each other. The trend towards intra-regional trade is actually growing, from about 40 per cent of all trade 40 years ago to 55 per cent at the beginning of the twenty-first century. This is reflected in the nature of multinational companies as well. Alan Rugman calculates that in the early years of the twenty-first century over 300 out of the world's largest corporations still have more than half their sales in their home region. An apparently global company like McDonald's is effectively bi-regional, with 80 per cent of its sales concentrated in North America and Europe. Established multinationals such as General Electric and Procter and Gamble have 60 per cent and 55 per cent of their sales respectively back home in North America.

Ted Levitt might be impatient with these empirical details. The essential issue for him is: where are things going in the future? Certainly there are still local differences in taste, but are these declining overall? Maybe there is a growth of intra-regional trade, but is this just the result of transitional events such as the creation of the North American Free Trade Agreement or the sucking-in of imports by China? We should not be distracted by temporary blips on the grand highway to global integration.

Sources: T. Levitt, 'The globalization of markets', *Harvard Business Review*, May–June (1983), pp. 92–102; S. Douglas and G. Wind, 'The myth of globalization', *California Journal of World Business*, vol. 22, no. 4 (1987), pp. 19–30; P. Ghemawat, 'Regional strategies for global leadership', *Harvard Business Review*, December (2005), pp. 98–108; A. Rugman, *The regional multinationals*, Cambridge University Press, 2005.

Questions

1 Make a list of products and services which are getting more 'global' over time; then make a list of products and services which are getting less 'global'.

2 How many countries in the world have you visited in your lifetime? How many countries had your parents visited by the same age?

Work assignments

* Denotes more advanced work assignments.   * Refers to a case study in the Text and Case edition.

8.1 Using Exhibit 8.2 (Yip's globalisation drivers), compare two markets you are familiar with and analyse how strong each of the drivers is for increased international strategy.

8.2 * Taking an industry you are familiar with that is strong in your home country (for example, fashion in France, cars in Germany), use the four determinants of Porter's Diamond (Exhibit 8.3) to explain that industry's national advantage.

8.3 Using the four international strategies of Exhibit 8.4, classify the international strategy of AIB*, SABMiller* or any other multinational corporation with which you are familiar.

8.4 * Using the CAGE framework (section 8.5.1), assess the relative distance of possible overseas markets for a small entrepreneurial company such as MacPac* or Brown Bag Films* to expand into. What entry modes (export, alliances, licensing or direct investment) would you recommend for the most attractive markets?

8.5 * Take any part of the public or not-for-profit sector (for example, education, health) and explain how far internationalisation has affected its management and consider how far it may do in the future.

Integrative assignment

8.6 As in 8.3, use the four international strategies of Exhibit 8.4 to classify the international strategy of AIB*, SABMiller* or any other multinational corporation with which you are familiar. Drawing on section 12.2, how does this corporation's organisational structure fit (or not fit) this strategy?

 An extensive range of additional materials, including audio summaries, weblinks to organisations featured in the text, definitions of key concepts and self-assessment questions, can be found on the *Exploring Corporate Strategy* Companion Website at **www.pearsoned.co.uk/ecs**

Recommended key readings

- An eye-opening introduction to the detailed workings – and inefficiencies – of today's global economy is P. Rivoli, *The Travels of a T-Shirt in the Global Economy: an Economist Examines the Markets, Power and Politics of World Trade*, Wiley, 2006. A more optimistic view is in T. Friedman, *The World is Flat: the Globalized World in the Twenty First Century*, Penguin, 2006.

- An invigorating perspective on international strategy is provided by G. Yip, *Total Global Strategy II*, Prentice Hall, 2003. A comprehensive general

textbook is A. Rugman and S. Collinson, *International Business*, 4th edition, FT/Prentice Hall, 2006.

- A useful collection of academic articles on international business is in A. Rugman and T. Brewer (eds), *The Oxford Handbook of International Business*, Oxford University Press, 2003.

- For information on the financial considerations with respect to international developments see G. Arnold *Corporate Financial Management*, 3rd edition, FT/Prentice Hall, 2005, Chapter 7.

References

1. Indeed, many authors refer to internationalisation simply as 'international diversification': see N. Capar and M. Kotabe, 'The relationship between international diversification and performance in service firms', *Journal of International Business Studies*, vol. 34 (2003), pp. 345–355.

2. T. Friedman, *The World is Flat: the Globalized World in the Twenty First Century*, Penguin, 2006; and P. Rivoli, *The Travels of a T-Shirt in the Global Economy: an Economist Examines the Markets, Power and Politics of World Trade*, Wiley, 2006.

3. G. Yip, *Total Global Strategy II*, Prentice Hall, 2003.

4. Useful industry-specific data on trends in openness to trade and investment can be found at the World Trade Organization's site, www.wto.org.

5. G. Hamel and C.K. Prahalad, 'Do you really have a global strategy?', *Harvard Business Review*, vol. 63, no. 4 (1985), pp. 139–148.

6. B. Kogut, 'Designing global strategies: comparative and competitive value added changes', *Sloan Management Review*, vol. 27 (1985), pp. 15–28.

7. M. Porter, *The Competitive Advantage of Nations*, Macmillan, 1990.

8. This typology builds on the basic framework of M. Porter, 'Changing patterns of international competition', *California Management Review*, vol. 28, no. 2 (1987), pp. 9–39, but adapts its terms for the four strategies into more readily understandable terms: note particularly that here 'global' strategy is transposed to refer to the top left box, and the top right box is described as 'complex export'.

9. P. Ghemawat, 'Distance still matters', *Harvard Business Review*, September (2001), pp. 137–147.

10. For a good analysis of developing country companies and their opportunities, see T. Khanna and K. Palepu, 'Emerging giants: building world-class companies in developing countries', *Harvard Business Review*, October (2006), pp. 60–69.

11. This framework is introduced in I. Macmillan, A. van Putten and R. McGrath, 'Global gamesmanship', *Harvard Business Review*, vol. 81, no. 5 (2003), pp. 62–71.

12. For detailed discussions about the role of learning and experience in market entry see M.F. Guillén, 'Experience, imitation, and the sequence of foreign entry: wholly owned and joint-venture manufacturing by South Korean firms and business groups in China, 1987–1995', *Journal of International Business Studies*, vol. 83 (2003), pp. 185–198; and M.K. Erramilli, 'The experience factor in foreign market entry modes by service firms', *Journal of International Business Studies*, vol. 22, no. 3 (1991), pp. 479–501.

13. G. Knights and T. Cavusil, 'A taxonomy of born-global firms', *Management International Review*, vol. 45, no. 3 (2005), pp. 15–35.

14. For analyses of emerging country multinationals, see T. Khanna and K. Palepu, 'Emerging giants: building world-class companies in developing countries', *Harvard Business Review*, October (2006), pp. 60–69; and J. Sinha, 'Global champions from emerging markets', *McKinsey Quarterly*, no. 2 (2005), pp. 26–35.

15. A useful review of the international dimension is M. Hitt and R.E. Hoskisson, 'International diversification: effects on innovation and firm performance in product-diversified firms', *Academy of Management Journal*, vol. 40, no. 4 (1997), pp. 767–798.

16. For detailed results on British companies, see G. Yip, A. Rugman and A. Kudina, 'International success of British companies', *Long Range Planning*, vol. 39, no. 1 (2006), pp. 241–264.

17. See N. Capar and M. Kotabe, 'The relationship between international diversification and performance in service firms', *Journal of International Business Studies*, vol. 34 (2003), pp. 345–355; and F.J. Contractor, S.K. Kundu and C. Hsu, 'A three-stage theory of international expansion: the link between multinationality and performance in the service sector', *Journal of International Business Studies*, vol. 34 (2003), pp. 5–18.

18. C.A. Bartlett and S. Ghosal, *Managing Across Borders: The Transnational Solution*, The Harvard Business School Press, 1989, pp. 105–111; A.M. Rugman and A. Verbeke, 'Extending the theory of the multinational enterprise: internalization and strategic management perspectives', *Journal of International Business Studies*, vol. 34 (2003), pp. 125–137.

19. For a more far-reaching exploration of the role of subsidiaries in multinational corporations see J. Birkinshaw, *Entrepreneurship and the Global Firm*, Sage, 2000.

Lenovo computers: East meets West

Introduction

In May 2005, the world's thirteenth largest personal computer company, Lenovo, took over the world's third largest personal computer business, IBM's PC division. Lenovo, at that time based wholly in China, was paying $1.75bn (€1.4bn, £1bn) to control a business that operated all over the world and had effectively invented the personal computer industry back in 1981. Michael Dell, the creator of the world's largest PC company, commented simply: 'it won't work'.

Lenovo had been founded back in 1984 by Liu Chuanzhi, a 40-year-old researcher working for the Computer Institute of the Chinese Academy of Sciences. His early career had included disassembling captured American radar systems during the Vietnam War and planting rice during the Chinese Cultural Revolution. Liu Chuanzhi had started with $25,000 capital from the Computer Institute and promised his boss that he would build a business with revenues of $250,000. Working in the Computer Institute's old guardhouse, and borrowing its office facilities, one of Liu's first initiatives was reselling colour televisions. But real success started to come in 1987, when Lenovo was one of the first to package Chinese-character software with imported PCs.

Lenovo began to take off, with Liu using the support of his father, well placed in the Chinese government, to help import PCs cheaply through Hong Kong. During 1988, Lenovo placed its first job advertisement, and recruited 58 young people to join the company. Whilst the founding generation of Lenovo staff were in their forties, the new recruits were all in their twenties, as the Cultural Revolution had prevented any university graduates for a period of 10 years in China. Amongst the new recruits was Yang Yuanqing, who would be running Lenovo's PC business before he was 30, and later become Chairman of the new Lenovo–IBM venture at the age of 41. It was this new team which helped launch the

Lenovo's Chairman, Yang Yuanqing

production of the first Lenovo PC in 1990, and drove the company to a 30 per cent market share within China by 2005. The company had partially floated on the Hong Kong Stock Exchange in 1994.

The deal

Work on the IBM PC deal had begun in 2004, with Lenovo assisted by management consultancy McKinsey & Co. and investment banker Goldman Sachs. IBM wanted to dispose of its PC business, which had only 4 per cent market share in the USA and suffered low margins in a competitive market dominated by Dell and Hewlett Packard. Higher margin services and mainframe computers would be IBM's future. As well as Lenovo, IBM had private equity firm Texas Pacific Group in the bidding. Lenovo offered the best price, but Texas Pacific was persuaded enough to take a stake in the new group, while IBM took 13 per cent ownership. The government-owned Chinese Academy of Sciences still owned 27 per cent of the stock, the largest single shareholder.

The new Chairman, Yang Yuanqing, had a clear vision of what the company was to achieve, while recognising some of the challenges:

In five years, I want this (Lenovo) to be a very famous PC brand, with maybe double the growth of the industry. I want to have a very healthy profit margin, and maybe some other businesses beyond PCs, worldwide. We are at the beginnings of this new company, so we can define some fundamentals about the culture. The three words I use to describe this are trust, respect, compromise.

He continued:

As a global company maybe we have to sacrifice some speed, especially during our first phase. We need more communication. We need to take time to understand each other. But speed was in the genes of the old Lenovo. I hope it will be in the genes of the new Lenovo.

IBM was not leaving its old business to sink or swim entirely on its own. Lenovo had the right to use the IBM brand for PCs for five years, including the valuable ThinkPad name. IBM's salesforce would be offered incentives to sell Lenovo PCs, just as they had with IBM's own-brand machines. IBM Global Services was contracted to provide maintenance and support. IBM would have two non-voting observers on the Lenovo board. Moreover, Stephen Ward, the 51-year-old former head of IBM's PC division, was to become Lenovo's Chief Executive Officer.

Managing the new giant

Having an IBM CEO was not entirely a surprise. After all, the $13bn business was nearly 80 per cent ex-IBM and customers and employees had to be reassured of continuity. But there were some significant challenges for the new company to manage none the less.

Things had not started well. When the Chinese team first flew to New York to meet the IBM team, they had not been met at the airport as they had expected and was normal polite practice in China. Yang and Ward had disagreed about the location of the new headquarters, Yang wishing it to be shared between Beijing and near New York. Ward had prevailed, and Yang moved his family to the USA. The new organisation structure kept the old IBM business and the original Lenovo business as separate divisions. But still the new company needed considerable liaison with China, a 13-hour flight away, across 12 time zones. Teleconferencing between the East Coast and China became a way of life, with the Americans calling typically at either 6.00 in the morning or 11.00 at night to catch their Chinese colleagues. Calls were always in English, with many Chinese less than fluent and body language impossible to observe.

The Chinese nature of the company was an issue for some constituencies. IBM had had a lot of government business, and populist members of the US Congress whipped up a scare campaign about Chinese computers entering sensitive domains. In Germany, labour laws allowed a voluntary transition of IBM employees to Lenovo, and many German workers chose not to transfer, leaving the company short staffed. There was some discomfort amongst former IBM employees in Japan about Chinese ownership. Between the two dominant cultures, American and Chinese, there were considerable differences. Qiao Jian, Vice President for Human Resources, commented:

Americans like to talk; Chinese people like to listen. At first we wondered why they kept talking when they had nothing to say. But we have learnt to be more direct when we have a problem, and the Americans are learning to listen.

Cultural differences were not just national. Lenovo was a new and relatively simple company – basically one country, one product. Multinational giant IBM Corporation, founded in 1924, was far more complex. The Lenovo management team, mostly in their thirties, were much younger than IBM's, and the average age of the company as a whole was just 28. IBM was famous for its management processes and routines. Qiao Jian commented: 'IBM people set a time for a conference call and stick to it every week. But why have the call if there is nothing to report?' On the other hand, IBM people had a tendency for being late for meetings, something that was strictly discouraged within Lenovo.

Some results

At first, the response to the new Lenovo was positive. IBM customers stayed loyal and the stock price began to climb (see Figure 1). Remaining IBM executives recognised that at least they were part of a business committed to PCs, rather than the Cinderella in a much larger IBM empire. The fact that a Lenovo PC manufactured in China had a labour cost of just $3.00 offered a lot of opportunity.

However, market leader Dell responded to the new company with heavy price cuts, offering $100 savings

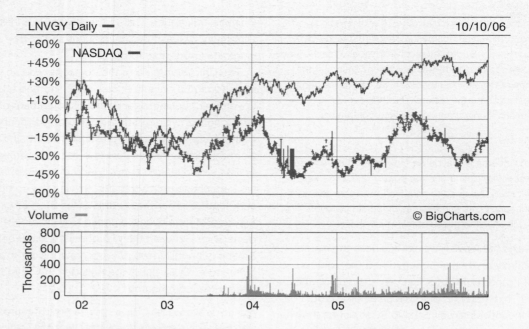

Figure 1 Lenovo Group's stock price, 2001–2006, compared with NASDAQ index

Source: www.bigcharts.com (11 October 2006). Marketwatch.Online by BigCharts.com. Copyright 2006 by Dow Jones & Company, Inc. Reproduced with permission of Dow Jones & Company, Inc. in the format Textbook via Copyright Clearance Center.

on the average machine. With market share in the crucial American market beginning to slip, ex-IBM CEO Stephen Ward was replaced in December 2005 by William Amelio. This was a coup for Lenovo, as Amelio had been running Dell's Asia–Pacific region. As well as knowing Lenovo's competitor from the inside, Amelio, based for several years in Singapore, had a good understanding of Asian business:

In the five years I have been in Asia, one thing I have learned . . . is to have a lot more patience. I have to be someone who has a high sense of urgency and drive, but I have also learned how to temper that in the various cultures that I have dealt with in order to be more effective.

Amelio started by addressing costs, removing 1,000 positions, or 10 per cent, from Lenovo's non-China workforce. He integrated the IBM business and the old Lenovo business into a single structure. The company launched a new range of Lenovo-branded PCs for small and medium-sized American business, a market traditionally ignored by IBM. To improve its reach in this segment, Lenovo expanded sales to big American retailers such as Office Depot. US market share began to recover, pushing beyond 4 per cent again. Lenovo began to consider entry into the Indian market.

Amelio's actions seemed to pay off. After a precipitous slide during the first half of 2006, the stock price turned up. But there was no disguising that the stock price in the autumn of 2006 was still below where it was five years earlier, and that it continued to trail the hi-tech American NASDAQ index.

Sources: L. Zhijun, *The Lenovo Affair*, Wiley, Singapore, 2006; *Business Week*, 7 August (2006), 20 April (2006), 22 December (2005) and 9 May (2005); *Financial Times*, 8 November (2005), 9 November (2005) and 10 November (2005).

Questions

1 What national sources of competitive advantage might Lenovo draw from its Chinese base? What disadvantages derive from its Chinese base?

2 In the light of the CAGE framework and the MacMillan *et al.* Competitor Retaliation framework (Exhibit 8.5), comment on Lenovo's entry into the American market.

3 Now that Lenovo is international, what type of generic international strategy should it pursue – simple export, multidomestic, complex export or global?

9

Innovation and Entrepreneurship

LEARNING OUTCOMES

After reading this chapter you should be able to:

→ Identify and respond to key innovation dilemmas, such as the relative emphases to place on technologies or markets, product or process innovations, and the broad business model.

→ Anticipate and to some extent influence the diffusion (or spread) of innovations.

→ Decide when being a first-mover or a follower is most appropriate in innovation, and how an incumbent organisation should respond to innovative challengers.

→ Anticipate key issues facing entrepreneurs as they go through the stages of growth, from start-up to exit.

→ Evaluate opportunities and choices facing social entrepreneurs as they create new ventures to address social problems.

Photo: Tracey Fahy/Alamy Images

9.1 INTRODUCTION

Innovation and entrepreneurship are fundamental drivers in today's economy. Steve Jobs is a technological innovator, whose creativity in computers, electronics and film led to Apple Computers and built Pixar into one of the world's leading animation companies. Sir Stelios Haji-Ioannou is a business model innovator, whose introduction of online ticketing and simplified airline routing has been at the heart of the easyJet airline. Nobel Prize winner Muhammad Yunus is a social entrepreneur and innovator, pioneer of microcredit – small loans to entrepreneurs too poor to be considered by ordinary banks – and founder of the Grameen Bank in Bangladesh.

This chapter centres on innovation, both as driven by independent entrepreneurs and as generated by people inside established organisations. Innovation is a key aspect of business-level strategy as introduced in Chapter 6, with implications for quality, price and sustainability. It is also one of the directions of growth highlighted in Chapter 7. Entrepreneurship is at the origins of all businesses. Innovation and entrepreneurship are linked by a common concern for the creation of new phenomena, whether new organisations or new products, services or processes. For private sector organisations operating in increasingly competitive markets, innovation is often a condition of simple survival. For public sector organisations too, ceaseless cost pressures and increasing public demands are compelling constant innovation and even new kinds of entrepreneurship.

Two themes run through this chapter. The first is timing. Critical timing decisions include when to be *first-mover* or *fast second* in innovation; when, and if, an innovation will reach its *tipping point*, the point where demand takes off; and, for an entrepreneurial new venture, when to bring in external managers or finally to exit. The other theme is relationships. Creating innovations or new organisations is very rarely done alone. Successful innovation and entrepreneurship are typically done through relationships. These relationships come in many forms: sometimes relationships between organisations and their customers; sometimes relationships between big business and small start-ups; sometimes between business and 'social entrepreneurs'. Exhibit 9.1 summarises the links between timing, relationships and both innovation and entrepreneurship.

Within this broad framework, this chapter will examine first innovation, then entrepreneurship:

- Section 9.2 starts with three *fundamental dilemmas* with regard to which managers must decide their focus: technology push as against market pull; product innovation rather than process innovation; and finally technological as opposed to broader business model innovation. None of these are absolute 'either–or' dilemmas, but managers must choose where to concentrate their limited resources.

- Section 9.3 considers issues surrounding the *diffusion*, or spread, of innovations in the marketplace. Diffusion can be accelerated or inhibited by managerial choices on both the supply side, for example product design, and the demand side, for example marketing. Diffusion processes often follow *S-curve patterns*, raising further typical issues for decision, particularly with regard to tipping points and tripping points.

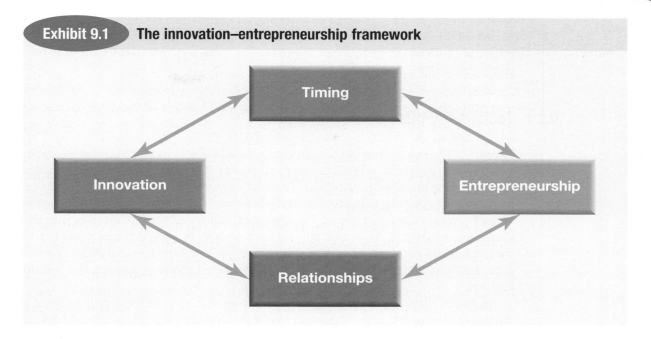

Exhibit 9.1 **The innovation–entrepreneurship framework**

- Section 9.4 completes the discussion of innovation by considering choices with regard to timing. This includes *first-mover* advantages and disadvantages, the opportunities of being *fast second* into a market, and the issue of how established incumbents should respond to innovative challengers.

- Section 9.5 addresses *entrepreneurship*. The section discusses typical choices facing entrepreneurs as their ventures progress through the uncertain *stages of growth*, from start-up to exit. It also examines the kinds of *relationships* that entrepreneurs may have to form, particularly with larger firms practising 'open innovation'.

- Section 9.6 finally introduces *social entrepreneurship*, by which individuals and small groups can launch innovative and flexible new initiatives that larger public agencies are often unable to pursue. Again, social entrepreneurs face choices with regard to relationships, particularly with big business.

The key debate of the chapter (Illustration 9.6) brings entrepreneurship and innovation together again by considering the issue of whether small or large firms are better at innovation.

> **Innovation** involves the conversion of new knowledge into a new product, process or service and the putting of this new product, process or service into use, either via the marketplace or by other processes of delivery

9.2   INNOVATION DILEMMAS

www.pearsoned.co.uk/ecs
KEY CONCEPT

Innovation dilemmas

Innovation raises fundamental strategic dilemmas for strategists. Innovation is more complex than just invention. Invention involves the conversion of new knowledge into a new product, process or service. **Innovation** adds the critical extra step of putting this new product, process or service into use, in the private sector typically via the marketplace and in the public sector through service delivery.[1] The strategic dilemmas stem from this more complex and extended process. Strategists have to make choices with regard to three fundamental issues:

how far to follow technological opportunity as against market demand; how much to invest in product innovation rather than process innovation; and finally whether to focus on technological innovation rather than extending innovation to their whole business model.[2]

9.2.1 Technology push or market pull

People often see innovation as driven by technology. In this *technology push*[2] view, technologists or scientists carry out research in their laboratories in order to create new knowledge. This new knowledge forms the basis for new products, processes or services that are then 'handed over' to the rest of the organisation to make, market and distribute. Technological advances push what goes into the marketplace. According to this perspective, managers should listen primarily to their scientists and technologists, let them follow their hunches and support them with ample resources. Generous R&D budgets are crucial to making innovation happen.

An alternative approach to innovation is *market pull*. Market pull reflects a view of innovation that goes beyond invention and sees the importance of actual use. The role of market pull has been promoted since Eric von Hippel's discovery that in many sectors users, not producers, are common sources of important innovations.[3] In designing their innovation strategies, therefore, organisations should listen in the first place to users rather than their own scientists and technologists. Von Hippel refines this focus on users to point out that in many markets it is not ordinary users that are the source of innovation, but *lead-users*. In medical surgery, top surgeons often adapt existing surgical instruments in order to carry out new types of operation. In extreme sports such as snowboarding or windsurfing, it is leading sportspeople who make the improvements necessary to greater performance. In this view, then, it is the pull of users in the market that is responsible for innovation. Managers need to build close relationships with lead-users such as the best surgeons or sporting champions. Marketing and sales functions identify the lead-users of a field and then scientists and technologists translate their inventive ideas into commercial products, processes or services that the wider market can use.

There are merits to both the technology push and market pull views. Relying heavily on existing users can make companies too conservative, and vulnerable to disruptive technologies that uncover needs unforeseen by existing markets (see section 9.4.3). On the other hand, history is littered with examples of companies that have blindly pursued technological excellence without regard to real market needs. Technology push and market pull are best seen as extreme views, therefore, helping to focus attention on a fundamental choice: relatively how much to rely on science and technology as sources of innovation, rather than what people are actually doing in the market. In practice, most organisations find a compromise between the two views, with the balance varying between industries and often over time. As at the skateboarding company Sole Technology, users may be key at start-up, but internally led innovation can become more important with growth (see Illustration 9.1). The key issue for managers is to be aware of the dilemma and to review their organisation's balance between the two extremes consciously rather than relying on habit or prejudice.

Illustration 9.1

Shoes for skateboarders

Innovation at Sole Technologies is driven by both users and technology.

After taking a degree in industrial software, Pierre André Senizergues started his career as a professional skateboarder in France. In less than 20 years, he created an action shoe and apparel business with $200m (£112m; €160m) sales, and seven brands, including Etnies with its famous upside-down 'E' and the big snowboarding boot brand ThirtyTwo. He also created the first skateboard shoe research laboratory in the world.

Things had not started out so promisingly for Senizergues. In 1988 he signed to ride for the skateboard brand of a new French venture. The very next year he was forced to retire from professional skateboarding with back problems. Although he spoke poor English and had little business experience, he persuaded his employer to grant him the licence to sell its Etnies shoes in the USA. The first five years were very hard, but Senizergues introduced his own designs and from the mid-1990s Etnies began to take off. In 1996, Senizergues bought the Etnies brand from the French venture and incorporated it and other brands – including éS, Emerica and ThirtyTwo – under the Sole Technology umbrella. Growth over the next 10 years ran at double digits per annum.

From the first, Senizergues had been able to use his expertise as a professional skateboarder in his designs. He told the *Financial Times*: 'In this market, you have to be authentic, you have to come from skateboarding.' For example, in the 1990s he had noticed that skateboarders were buying unsuitable low-top shoes for their looks, rather than high-top shoes with the proper performance characteristics. Senizergues responded by designing low-top shoes that had the necessary durability. His company has stayed close to its sports, sponsoring more than 100 athletes around the world. It listens closely to customers. The company's website has a design-your-own shoe facility and it often releases potential specifications for its new products through blogs, in order to solicit feedback and ideas. The average age of Sole Technology's 400 employees is 28, with many still involved in action sports.

However, Senizergues has also built the world's first skateboarding research facility, the Sole Technology Institute. With 10,000 square feet (930m^2), it reproduces typical skateboarding obstacles such as rails, stairs and ledges. Senizergues believes that it is time for skateboarding to do its own biomechanical research, instead of borrowing technologies developed in other sports. One of the outputs of the Sole Technology Institute has been the G202 gel-and-air bag technology. As the trend for girls' shoes moved towards slim silhouettes during 2006, this gel-and-air technology has allowed Sole Technology to keep right abreast of fashion.

Sources: *Financial Times*, 23 August (2006); *Footwear News*, 20 February (2006); www.soletechnology.com.

Questions

1 For what reasons is it important to be 'authentic' in the skateboarding shoe market?

2 If a big company like Nike or Adidas was looking to grow in this market, what would you advise it to do?

9.2.2 Product or process innovation

Just as managers must find a balance between technological push and market pull, so must they determine the relative emphasis to place on product or process innovation. *Product innovation* relates to the final product (or service) to be sold, especially with regard to its features; *process innovation* relates to the way in which this product is produced and distributed, especially with regard to improvements in cost or reliability. Some firms specialise more in product innovation, others more in process innovation. For example, in computers, Apple has generally pioneered in terms of product features (for instance, the iMac), while Dell has innovated in terms of efficient processes, for instance direct sales, modularity and build to order.

Industries often follow technological trajectories according to which the relative importance of product innovation and process innovation change over time. Periods of product innovation based on new features are often followed by periods of process innovation based on efficiency in production and delivery. William Abernathy, for example, has shown how the early history of the automobile was dominated by competition in product design, as pioneers competed as to whether cars should be fuelled by steam, electricity or petrol, place their engines at the front or at the rear, and have three wheels or four.[3] Once Henry Ford introduced the Model T, the industry settled on a *dominant design*: cars would generally be petrol driven, with their engines at the front and four wheels. As soon as this dominant design was established, the rate of product innovation fell as competition shifted to producing this basic type of car as efficiently as possible. Establishing the dominant design thus promoted a surge of process innovation. Here Ford pioneered again, with the epochal process innovation of the automated assembly line allowing mass production.

This sequence of product innovation leading to the establishment of a dominant design, after which competition shifts to process innovation, is a common one across many industries.[4] Exhibit 9.2 provides a general model of the relationship between product and process innovation. The model has several strategic implications:

- *New developing industries* typically favour product innovation, as competition is still around defining the basic features of the product or service.

- *Maturing industries* typically favour process innovation, as competition shifts towards efficient production of a dominant design of product or service.

- *Small new entrants* typically have the greatest opportunity in the early stages of an industry, competing with new features. Before the Model T, there were more than 100 competitors in the American automobile industry.

- *Large incumbent firms* typically have the advantage later as the dominant design is established and scale economies and the ability to roll out process innovations matter most. By the 1930s, there were just four large American automobile manufacturers, Ford, General Motors, Chrysler and American Motors, all producing very similar kinds of cars.

This sequence of product to process innovation is not always a neat one. In practice, product and process innovation are often pursued in tandem.[5] For example, each new generation of microprocessor also requires simultaneous process

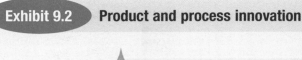

Exhibit 9.2 **Product and process innovation**

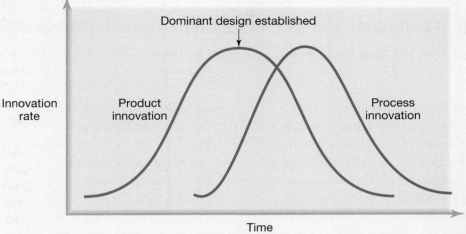

Source: Adapted from W.J. Abernathy and J.M. Utterback, 'A dynamic model of process and product innovation', *Omega*, vol. 3, no. 6 (1975), pp. 639–656.

innovation in order to manufacture the new microprocessor with increasing precision. However, the model does help managers confront the issue of where to focus, whether more on product features or more on process efficiency. It also points to whether competitive advantage is likely to be with small new entrants or large incumbent firms.

9.2.3 Technological or business model innovation

A key question for innovators is the importance of new knowledge in the form of scientific or technological advances. Many successful innovations do not rely simply upon new science or technology, but the reorganisation of all the elements of business into new combinations. Here innovators are creating whole new *business models*, bringing customers, producers and suppliers together in new ways, with or without new technologies. To return to easyJet, the entrepreneurial airline's business model cut out travel agents by using direct sales through the Internet, bringing customers and the airline together in a new way, while also using cheap secondary airports. Simplification of service and choice of airports were much more important than technological innovation. The Internet technology itself was not easyJet's creation and it had the same aircraft as most of its competitors.

Gary Hamel defines a business model as essentially a 'way of doing business'.[6] More formally, a **business model** describes the structure of product, service and information flows and the role of participating parties. The crucial elements of a business model can be seen in terms of two halves of the value chain framework, introduced in section 3.6.1:[7]

A **business model** describes the structure of product, service and information flows and the role of participating parties

Illustration 9.2

A Russian computer games entrepreneur's new business model

An upstart from the East takes on the best from the West.

In April 2006, 10 years after founding Nival Interactive, Sergey Orlovskiy announced a radical change of business model. From being a Russian-based developer of PC games, the company was shifting its headquarters to Los Angeles, taking on new management and targeting both PC and console markets. The games line-up already included 'Blitzkrieg', 'Heroes of Might and Magic', 'Night Watch' and 'Hammer and Sickle'. Orlovskiy explained: 'Normally our revenue increases from 20 to 50 per cent a year. Now we are going to increase it by 100 per cent, because we're changing the business model.'

Orlovskiy, then a 23-year-old IT student, originally founded the company as a PC games specialist. The first product sold 100,000 copies worldwide, a strong start for a PC game. Nival continued to design new PC games, with 'Blitzkrieg', a Second World War strategy game, launched in 2003, selling 1.5 million copies, three times the norm for a reasonably successful PC game. That same year, Nival partnered with French games publisher Ubisoft on the fifth edition of 'Heroes of Might and Magic', a top-selling fantasy strategy game. Nival had a significant cost advantage: Russian programmers cost four or five times less than American programmers.

But the PC games market is limited. PC games sales were less than $1bn (£560m; €800m) in 2005, while console games such as for the Xbox and PlayStation were five times that. In 2005, American venture capital fund Ener1 Group acquired 70 per cent of Nival for an undisclosed amount estimated to be around $10m. Ener1 proposed the change of model: a shift of leadership to the USA, an injection of capital and an expansion into console games, alongside the continued exploitation of programming cost advantages.

Sergey Orlovskiy became President of Nival, while the company took on new talent at the top. The new CEO was Kevin Bachus, one of the original four creators of the Xbox. Other new American managers had held senior positions at companies such as Atari, Electronic Arts, Sega and Sony. This management team were ready to launch the new business model. Described as 'reverse outsourcing', the model was not about a Western company outsourcing production to cheap locations in developing countries, but a low-cost company acquiring the very best American creativity and management. With its new talents and new capital, Nival expected its low-cost development teams – not just in Russia, but potentially in China or anywhere else around the world – to offer an unbeatable combination of economy and innovation.

Sources: Business Week, 3 March (2006) and www.nival.com. See also case example in Chapter 13.

Questions

1 In what respects would you describe Nival's recent transformation as a change in business model rather than a change in strategy?

2 What advantages and what problems might Orlovskiy personally find in this new set-up?

- *The product*. A business model may involve a particular way of defining what the product or service is and how it is produced. In terms of the value chain, this concerns technology development, procurement, inbound logistics, operations and procurement. Thus the business model for Linux open-source operating systems is based on a network of thousands of volunteer programmers, both freelancers and dedicated employees at companies such as IBM and Hewlett Packard. This is very different to Microsoft, for instance, whose business model is based on performing technology development in-house with its own employees.

- *The selling*. A business model may involve a particular way of selling or diffusing a product or service. In terms of the value chain, this concerns outbound logistics, marketing and sales and service. Thus Linux software is free to users, not sold as Microsoft software is. IBM and Hewlett Packard preload the free operating systems on their machines, benefiting through not having to pay a license fee to Microsoft. Linux distributors such as Red Hat earn their money by packaging Linux with user manuals, regular updates and service, and then charging customers annual subscription fees for support.

The business model concept overlaps strongly with the concept of business-level strategy.[8] However, the two concepts have useful differences in emphasis:

- *Radical versus incremental*. Business model change involves radical strategic transformation. On the other hand, many strategic initiatives are essentially incremental, making small adjustments within an existing business model: for example, investment in extra capacity or entry into new geographical markets. The business model concept can help managers confront the limitations of incremental adjustments and address the need sometimes for radical transformation.

- *Standard versus competitive*. In many industries, especially mature ones, business models are effectively standardised, with little difference in basic structure. Business-level strategy is more focused on how to obtain and sustain differentiation and advantage vis-à-vis competitors in the same industry. Business-level strategy thus keeps managers focused on how to position themselves against their competition.

Finally, the business model concept is valuable in helping managers to consider new scientific and technological knowledge as just one part of the whole package that contributes to innovation. Innovation can be drawn from all parts of the value chain, not just technology development (see Illustration 9.2).

9.3 INNOVATION DIFFUSION

Diffusion is the process by which innovations spread amongst users, varying in pace and extent

So far, this chapter has been concerned with sources and types of innovation, for example technology push or market pull. This section moves on to the **diffusion** of innovations after they have been introduced.[9] Since innovation is typically expensive, its commercial attractiveness can hinge on the pace – extent and speed – at which the market adopts new products and services. This pace of diffusion is something managers can influence from both the supply and demand sides, and which they can also model using the S-curve.

9.3.1 The pace of diffusion

The pace of diffusion can vary widely according to the nature of the products concerned. It took 20 years for personal computers to reach 60 per cent of American households. It took 10 years for the Internet to achieve equivalent usage. The pace of diffusion is influenced by a combination of supply-side and demand-side factors, over which managers have considerable control. On the *supply side*, pace is determined by product features such as the following:

- *Degree of improvement* in performance above current products (from a customer's perspective) that provides incentive to change. For example, 3G mobile phones did not provide sufficient performance improvement to prompt rapid switch in many markets.

- *Compatibility* with other factors, for example digital TV becomes more attractive as the broadcasting networks change more of their programmes to that format.

- *Complexity*, either in the product itself or in the marketing methods being used to commercialise the product: unduly complex pricing structures, as with many financial service products such as pensions, discourage consumer adoption.

- *Experimentation* – the ability to test products before commitment to a final decision – either directly or through the availability of information about the experience of other customers. This is why new product marketing often features satisfied customers and/or endorsements from suitable role models such as sports or pop celebrities.

- *Relationship management*, in other words how easy it is to get information, place orders and receive support. This relates to the choice of business model as described in section 9.2.3 above.

On the *demand side*, key factors driving the pace of diffusion are as follows:

- *Market awareness*. Many potentially successful products have failed through lack of consumer awareness – particularly when the promotional effort of the manufacturer has been confined to 'push' promotion to its intermediaries (for example, distributors).

- *Observability* (to potential adopters) of the benefits of the product or service in use. This is an important determinant in spreading adoption – for example, through creating a 'band wagon' effect. For some products this can be difficult if the benefits are intangible or do not accrue immediately (for example, financial investments). Intermediaries (such as distributors) also need to observe that there is benefit to them too. This could be observed if they see *their* competitors gaining commercial advantage from the new product.

- *Customer innovativeness*. The distribution of potential customers from early adopter groups (keen to adopt first) through to laggards (typically indifferent to innovations). Innovations are often targeted initially at early adopter groups – typically the young and the wealthy – in order to build the critical mass that will encourage more laggardly groups – the poorer and older – to join the bandwagon. Innovations targeted at laggardly groups will take off more slowly.

The various factors listed above provide a checklist against which innovation strategies can be assessed. For example, a manager writing a 'business case' to secure funds for improving particular product features would need to address many of the issues listed above. The business case should start by showing why the improved features might be *valued by customers* sufficiently to switch purchase or upgrade. It should also address issues of *compatibility* with other equipment that the consumer or distributor uses in conjunction with the product. In other words, at a minimum it is essential that the product or service matches the threshold requirements of both consumers and intermediaries. This may entail considerable effort to allay some of their concerns about switching to the new product. Adoption would be more likely if the product matches the *critical success factors (CSFs)* of consumers and intermediaries (see section 2.4.3). The marketing plan should address how these attributes would be *communicated* and who would be the initial *target audiences*. It should address how initial adoptions would then be *rolled out* into wider uptake in the market.[10]

9.3.2 The diffusion S-curve

The pace of diffusion is typically not steady. Successful innovations often diffuse according to an *S-curve* pattern.[11] The shape of the S-curve reflects a process of slow adoption in the early stages, followed by a rapid acceleration in diffusion, and ending with a plateau representing the limit to demand (Exhibit 9.3). The height of the S-curve shows the extent of diffusion; the shape of the S-curve shows the speed.

Exhibit 9.3 **The diffusion S-curve**

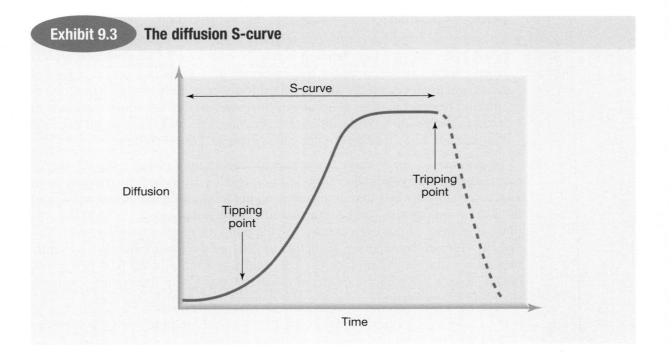

Diffusion rarely follows exactly this pattern, but none the less the S-curve can help managers anticipate upcoming issues. In particular, the S-curve points to four likely decision points:

A **tipping point** is where demand for a product or service suddenly takes off, with explosive growth

- *Timing of the 'tipping point'.* Demand for a new product and service may initially be slow but then reach a **tipping point** when it explodes onto a rapid upwards path of growth.[12] Tipping points are particularly explosive where there are strong *network effects*: in other words, where the value of a product or service is increased the more people in a network use them. Text messaging exploded in this way, because once some members of a social circle began to text each other, it became very worthwhile for all the other members to learn to do the same. Being aware of a possible tipping point ahead can help managers plan investment in capacity and distribution. Companies can easily underestimate demand. In the mid-1980s, American companies predicted that by 2000 there would be 900,000 mobile phones worldwide. That year came, and 900,000 phones were sold every 19 hours. The Finnish company Nokia was able to seize worldwide leadership.[13] Failing to anticipate a tipping point leads to missed sales and easy opportunities for competitors.

- *Timing of the plateau.* The S-curve also alerts managers to a likely eventual slow-down in demand growth. Again, it is tempting to extrapolate existing growth rates forwards, especially when they are highly satisfactory. But heavy investment immediately before growth turns down is likely to leave firms with overcapacity and carrying extra costs in a period of industry shake-out.

- *Extent of diffusion.* The S-curve does not necessarily lead to 100 per cent diffusion amongst potential users. Most innovations fail to displace previous-generation products and services altogether. For example, in music, traditional turntables and LP discs are still preferred over CD and MP3 players by many disc jockeys and music connoisseurs. A critical issue for managers then is to estimate the final ceiling on diffusion, being careful not to assume that tipping point growth will necessarily take over the whole market.

- *Timing of the 'tripping point'.* The tripping point is the opposite of the tipping point, referring to when demand suddenly collapses.[14] The presence of network effects can mean that a few customer defections can set off a market landslide. Such landslides are very hard to reverse. This is what happened to Internet browser pioneer Netscape as Microsoft started to counter-attack with its Explorer product. The tripping point concept warns managers all the time that a small dip in quarterly sales could presage a rapid collapse.

To summarise, the S-curve is a useful concept to help managers avoid simply extrapolating next year's sales from last year's sales. However, the tripping point also underlines the fact that innovations do not follow an inevitable process, and their diffusion patterns can be interrupted or reversed at any point. Most innovations, of course, do not even reach a tipping point, let alone a tripping point. The Segway Human Transporter, launched in 2001 as the environmentally-friendly technology that would replace the car, sold 6,000 units in its first two years, despite launch production capacity of nearly 500,000 a year. Illustration 9.3 shows the rapid but uneven progress of social networking site MySpace.com.

Illustration 9.3

The MySpace snowball

How long can the explosive growth of the social networking site MySpace continue?

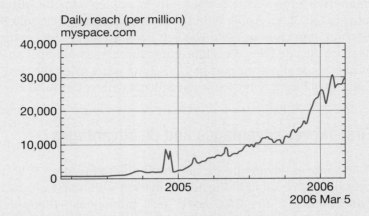

Figure 1 The traffic data is based on the set of Alexa toolbar uses, which may not be a representative sample of the global Internet population

Source: Alexa.com. © 2006 Alexa.

MySpace began in 2003 as a networking site for independent musicians in Los Angeles. By 2006 it was the most popular website in the USA, and had easily overtaken rival social networking sites such as Friendster and Facebook to claim nearly 80 per cent of online networking site visits. The site became highly attractive to advertisers such as Coca-Cola and Procter and Gamble, seeking access to the youth market. The Alexa market research company monitored MySpace's explosive growth in daily 'reach' from less than 1,000 in every million Internet users in 2004 to around 30,000 in early 2006: see Figure 1. Rupert Murdoch, owner of the multinational media conglomerate News Corporation, was so impressed that he bought the two-year-old company in 2005 for $580m (£324m; €259m).

Acquisition by News Corporation gave MySpace the capital to fund rapid innovation. During 2006, the company had 20 new products in development, including VoIP telephony, plus 11 new international sites. But there were many threats to continued growth. The sheer volume and chaos of user-controlled postings was creating capacity and reliability problems. There was mounting controversy about online predators and malicious gossip. New competitors were entering the market, such as YouTube with its popular video service. Ownership by the News Corporation was beginning to impose constraints in terms of content and style. Finally, there was the fear that as MySpace matured, it would no longer be so cool.

Sources: *Business Week*, 13 June (2005); www.wikipedia.org.

Questions

1 How should potential advertisers on MySpace have interpreted the upwards blip in its daily reach in late 2004 and the downwards blip in early 2006?

2 How would you forecast future demand for MySpace?

9.4 INNOVATORS AND FOLLOWERS

A key choice for managers is whether to lead or to follow in innovation. The S-curve concept seems to promote leadership in innovation. First-movers get the easy sales of early fast growth and can establish a dominant position. There are plenty of examples of first-movers who have built enduring positions on the basis of innovation leadership: Coca-Cola in drinks and Hoover in vacuum cleaners are powerful century-old examples. On the other hand, many first-movers fail. Even Apple failed with its pioneering Personal Digital Assistant, the Newton, launched in 1993. Hewlett Packard and Palm captured the PDA market nearly a decade later. This late-entry success is not unusual. Amazon entered the online bookselling market in 1995, four years after the real online pioneer, the Computer Literacy bookstore of Silicon Valley, California.

9.4.1 First-mover advantages and disadvantages

A first-mover advantage exists where an organisation is better off than its competitors as a result of being first to market with a new product, process or service

KEY CONCEPT

First mover advantages

A **first-mover advantage** exists where an organisation is better off than its competitors as a result of being first to market with a new product, process or service. Fundamentally, the first-mover is a monopolist, theoretically able to charge customers high prices without fear of immediate undercutting by competitors. In practice, however, innovators often prefer to sacrifice profit margins for sales growth and, besides, monopoly is usually temporary. There are five potentially more robust first-mover advantages:[15]

● *Experience curve benefits* accrue to first-movers, as their rapid accumulation of experience with the innovation gives them greater expertise than late entrants still relatively unfamiliar with the new product, process or service (see Exhibit 3.4).

● *Scale benefits* are typically enjoyed by first-movers, as they establish earlier than competitors the volumes necessary for mass production and bulk purchasing, for example.

● *Pre-emption of scarce resources* is an opportunity for first-movers, as late-movers will not have the same access to key raw materials, skilled labour or components, and will have to pay dearly for them.

● *Reputation* can be enhanced by being first, especially since consumers have little 'mind-space' to recognise new brands once a dominant brand has been established in the market.

● *Buyer switching costs* can be exploited by first-movers, by locking in their customers with privileged or sticky relationships that later challengers can only break with difficulty. Switching costs can be increased by establishing and exploiting a *technological standard* (see Chapter 6).

Experience curve benefits, economies of scale and the pre-emption of scarce resources all confer cost advantages on first-movers. It is possible for them to retaliate against challengers with a price war. Superior reputation and customer lock-in provide a marketing advantage, allowing first-movers to charge high prices, which can then be reinvested in order to consolidate their position against late-entry competitors.

But the experience of Apple with its Newton shows that first-mover advantages are not necessarily overwhelming. Late-movers have two principal potential advantages:[16]

- *Free-riding*. Late-movers can imitate technological and other innovation at less expense than originally incurred by the pioneers. Research suggests that the costs of imitation are typically only 65 per cent of the cost of innovation.

- *Learning*. Late-movers can observe what worked well and what did not work well for innovators. They may not make so many mistakes and be able to get it right first time.

9.4.2 First or second?

Given the potential advantages of late-movers, managers face a hard choice between striving to be first or coming in later. They should assess the likely value of first-mover and late-mover advantages in their particular case. In addition, there are three contextual factors managers should consider that might swing the balance between moving first or not:

- *Capacity for profit capture*. David Teece emphasises the importance of innovators being able to capture for themselves the profits of their innovations.[17] This depends on the ease with which followers can imitate. The likelihood of imitation depends on two primary factors. First, imitation is likely if the innovation is in itself *easy to replicate*: for example, if there is little tacit knowledge involved or if it is embedded in a product that is sold in the external marketplace (unlike many process technologies) and is therefore easy to 'reverse-engineer'. Second, imitation is facilitated if *intellectual property rights* are weak, for example where patents are hard to define or impractical to defend.[18] It is unwise for companies to invest in being first-movers if imitators are likely to be able quickly to seize their share of innovation profits.

- *Complementary assets*. Possession of the assets or resources necessary to scale up the production and marketing of the innovation is often critical.[19] Many small European biotech start-up companies face this constraint in the pharmaceuticals industry, where marketing and distribution in the USA, the world's largest market, are essential complementary assets, but are controlled by the big established pharmaceutical companies. Small European start-ups can find themselves obliged either to sell out to a larger company with the complementary marketing and distribution assets, or to license their innovation to it on disadvantageous terms. For organisations wishing to remain independent and to exploit their innovations themselves, there is little point in investing heavily to be first-mover in the absence of the necessary complementary assets.

- *Fast-moving arenas*. Where markets or technologies are moving very fast, and especially where both are highly dynamic, first-movers are unlikely to establish a durable advantage. The American electronics company Magnavox was the first to launch an electronic video game console in 1972, the Odyssey. But both the market and the technologies were evolving quickly. Magnavox only survived into the second generation of video game consoles, finally exiting in 1984. The seventh generation is now firmly dominated by Microsoft (entered in 2001), Sony (entered in 1994) and Nintendo (entered in 1983). In slower-moving markets and technologies, such as Coca-Cola's drinks arena, durable first-mover advantages are more probable. Managers need, therefore, to assess future market and technological dynamism in calculating the likely value of first-mover advantage.

For large established companies, Costas Markides and Paul Geroski argue, the most appropriate response to innovation, especially radical innovation, is often not to be a first-mover, but to be a 'fast second'.[20] Established companies typically do not have the cultures and systems to create new markets from scratch. What they do have are the financial, manufacturing, marketing and distribution assets that allow them to dominate a market once it has begun to emerge. The goal of a 'fast-second' organisation is to consolidate the early experiments of first-movers into a durable business model (see section 9.2.3). Fast-second companies may not be literally the second company into the market, but they dominate the second generation of competitors. For example, the established mainframe computer company IBM followed smaller innovative companies like Osborne and Apple into personal computers. The established Apple in turn followed pioneers such as Napster into online music. But, as the next section shows, even being 'fast second' can be challenging for incumbents.

9.4.3 The incumbents' response

For established companies in a market, innovation is often not so much an opportunity as a threat. Kodak's dominance of the photographic film market was made nearly worthless by the sudden rise of digital photography. As Clay Christensen has shown, the problem is that relationships between incumbent organisations and their customers can become too close.[21] Customers typically prefer incremental improvements to existing technologies, and are unable to imagine completely new technologies. Even lead-users typically adapt what they already have. Incumbents become used to making incremental innovations that meet, and even modestly surpass, existing customers' expectations. As in Exhibit 9.4, incumbents can usually improve their existing technology along a steady upwards trajectory, here Technology 1. Innovations on this trajectory are termed 'sustaining innovations', because they keep the existing basic technology up to date.

The challenge for incumbents, however, is switching from the existing trajectory of sustaining innovations for Technology 1 to the trajectory offered by the **disruptive innovation** represented by Technology 2. With a disruptive innovation, the new technology, even if initially inferior to the performance of existing technologies, has the potential quickly to become markedly superior. This superior performance can produce spectacular growth, either by creating new sets of customers or by undercutting the cost base of rival existing business models. Disruptive innovations are hard for incumbents to respond to because their initial poor performance is likely to upset existing customer relationships and because they typically involve changing their whole business model (see also Illustration 9.4). For example, in the music industry, the major record companies were long content to keep on selling traditional CDs through retailers, marketing them through promotions and radio-plugging. They responded to MP3 online music simply by prosecuting operators such as Napster for breach of copyright and highlighting the relatively poor sound quality of peer-to-peer file sharing.

A disruptive innovation creates substantial growth by offering a new performance trajectory that, even if initially inferior to the performance of existing technologies, has the potential to become markedly superior

| Exhibit 9.4 | Disruptive Innovation |

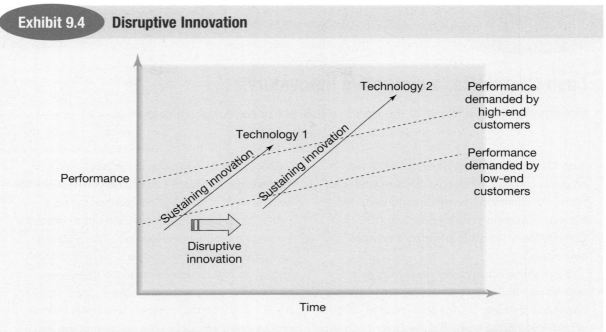

However, the British band Arctic Monkeys, and their small independent record company Domino, radically disrupted the majors' marketing model by giving away MP3 tracks free over the Internet in order to create an independent fan base. In 2006, the Arctic Monkeys' debut CD ended up selling nearly 400,000 copies in its first week, a record for the top 20 British album chart.

Incumbents can follow two policies to help keep them responsive to potentially disruptive innovations:

● *Develop a portfolio of real options*. Companies that are most challenged by disruptive innovations tend to be those built upon a single business model and with one main product or service. Rita McGrath and Ian MacMillan recommend that companies build portfolios of *real options* in order to maintain organisational dynamism.[22] Real options are limited investments that keep opportunities open for the future (for a more technical discussion, see Chapter 10). Establishing an R&D team in a speculative new technology or acquiring a small start-up in a nascent market would both be examples of real options, each giving the potential to scale up fast should the opportunity turn out to be substantial. McGrath and MacMillan's portfolio identifies three different kinds of options (Exhibit 9.5). Options where the market is broadly known, but the technologies are still uncertain, are *positioning options*: a company might want several of these, to ensure some position in an important market, by one technology or another. On the other hand, a company might have a strong technology, but be very uncertain about appropriate markets, in which case it would want to bet on several *scouting options* to explore which markets are actually best. Finally, a company would want some *stepping stone* options, very unlikely in themselves to work, but possibly leading to something more promising in the future. Even if they do not turn a profit,

Illustration 9.4

Lush Cosmetics, a disruptive innovator?

Continuous innovation is at the heart of this entrepreneurial venture

Lush Cosmetics is a fast-growing British bath products company, making distinctive (and even plain odd) shampoos, soaps, moisturisers and the like. The motto of its founder and CEO Mark Constantine is 'Innovate like mad, then start over again.'

Constantine's first career break was as a cosmetician at the Body Shop. By the late 1980s, products conceived by him accounted for 80 per cent of Body Shop sales. But the Body Shop was becoming conservative and rejected his concept of the 'bath bomb', a fizzing aromatic ball that dissolves in water. Constantine and a small team of fellow-believers left. After failure with a catalogues business, Cosmetics to Go, Constantine and his team set up Lush with one store in the small south coast town of Poole in 1994. In just over 10 years, Constantine built a €100m (£69m) business, with 320 stores in 35 countries. Bath bombs made up 40 per cent of the business, with up to 60,000 sold a day. The Body Shop meanwhile lost momentum and was sold to the French multinational L'Oréal in 2006.

Not willing to repeat the Body Shop's mistake, Constantine is committed to constant renewal of his range. The rule is that one-third of Lush products should be discontinued each year. An annual 'mafia meeting' of senior managers ruthlessly enforces the rule, despite frequent protests from loyal customers (on one occasion, customers threatened to parade naked through London's Trafalgar Square to keep a product). But the consequence of the rule is a commitment to introduce at least 100 new products a year to replace the old ones. Innovation is built into the Lush system.

One driver of innovation is the customers themselves. The name Lush came from a customer as a result of a company competition to find a name. Since then, customers have been constantly involved in product development. The eccentric and ethical style of the company generates fierce loyalty, so that customers describe themselves as 'Lushies' and participate in lively discussions in the chatroom on the company's website. Lushies propose new products, vote on alternatives and send in evocative names such as 'whoosh', 'aurora' and 'smitten' to inspire the company's cosmeticians to create new products. Lushies also post photographs of themselves, their pets and even their collections of Lush products, described as 'Lush porn'.

The company also works hard at generating new ideas itself. Constantine continues personally to work at new products, but he also hires new product designers with a brief to push the boundaries. Thus Japanese designer Noriko Miura has experimented with flavours for toothpaste such as green apple, salt and charcoal. Lush is determined not to meet the same fate as its failed progenitor, the Body Shop.

Sources: *Fast Company*, July (2005); www.lush.co.uk.

Questions

1 What are the advantages and disadvantages of a fixed rule such as discontinuing one-third of a product range annually?

2 What are the limits and dangers of customer-driven innovation as at Lush?

Exhibit 9.5   **Portfolio of innovation options**

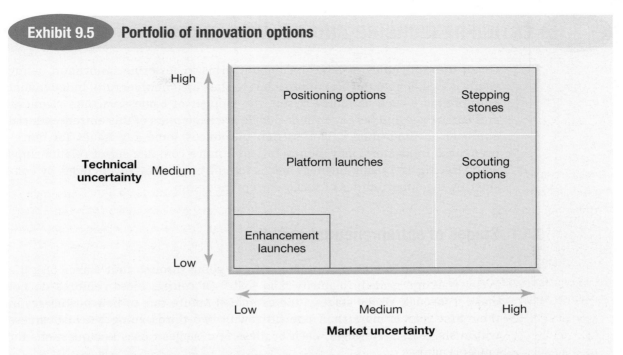

stepping stones should provide valuable learning opportunities. An important principle for options is: 'Fail fast, fail cheap, try again.'

- *Develop independent business units.* New ventures, especially when undertaken from a real options perspective, may need protection from the usual systems and disciplines of a core business. It would make no sense to hold the managers of a real option strictly accountable for sales growth and profit margin: their primary objective is preparation and learning. For this reason, large incumbent organisations often set up innovative businesses as independent business units, sometimes called *new venture divisions*, typically with managers hired specially from outside.[23] For example, in 2003 Delta Airlines, the American international airline dating from the 1920s, responded to the threat of low-cost airlines in its domestic markets by establishing Song Airlines as a stand-alone competitor. Song adopted the low-cost airline business model but also innovated with free personal entertainment systems at every seat, including audio MP3 selections, trivia games that could be played against other passengers and satellite television. In-flight safety instructions would be sung in different musical styles, by request. The risks of such independent business units are twofold.[24] First, the new units may be denied resources that the core business could easily supply, such as branding or management information systems. Second, innovation becomes isolated from the core business: for the core organisation, innovation is something that somebody else does. Delta responded to the second risk by reabsorbing Song into its main operations, at the same time incorporating several of Song's innovations such as satellite television.

9.5   ENTREPRENEURSHIP AND RELATIONSHIPS

Given the difficulties of large incumbent firms in fostering innovation, many would conclude that the best approach is to start up a new venture. Independent entrepreneurs such as James Dyson, the pioneer of bagless vacuum cleaners, and Larry Page and Sergey Brin of Google are exemplars of this entrepreneurial approach to innovation.[25] This section introduces some key issues for entrepreneurial innovators, and then points to a more complex set of relationships with large firms, raising further choices for entrepreneurs. It concludes by considering the opportunities of social entrepreneurship.

9.5.1   Stages of entrepreneurial growth

Entrepreneurial ventures are often seen as going through four stages of a life cycle: start-up; growth; maturity; and exit.[26] Of course, most ventures do not make it through all the stages – the estimated failure rate of new businesses in their first year is more than one-fifth, with two-thirds going out of business within six years.[27] However, each of these four stages raises key questions for entrepreneurs:

- *Start-up*. There are many challenges at this stage, but one key question with implications for both survival and growth is sources of capital. Loans from family and friends are common sources of funds, but these are typically limited and, given the new business failure rate, likely to lead to embarrassment. Bank loans and credit cards can provide funding too, but often they are too rigid in their requirement for interest and repayment to fit the irregular revenue streams of a start-up. *Venture capitalists* are specialised investors in new ventures. They usually insist on a seat on the venture's board of directors and may install their preferred managers. Venture capitalist backing has been shown to increase significantly the chances of a venture's success, but venture capitalists typically accept only about 1 in 400 propositions put to them.[28]

- *Growth*. A key challenge for growth ventures is management. Entrepreneurs have to be ready to move from doing to managing. Typically this transition occurs as the venture grows beyond about 20 employees. Many entrepreneurs make poor managers: if they had wanted to be managers, they would probably be working in a large corporation in the first place. The choice entrepreneurs have to make is whether to rely on their own managerial skills or to bring in professional managers. In 2001, the youthful founders of Google, Larry Page and Sergey Brin, responded to pressure from their venture capitalists by recruiting 46-year-old Eric Schmidt, former Chief Executive of the large software company Novell, to run their company.

- *Maturity*. The challenge for entrepreneurs at this stage is retaining their enthusiasm and commitment and generating new growth. This is a period when entrepreneurship changes to *intrapreneurship*, the generation of new ventures from inside the organisation. An important option is usually *diversification* into new business areas, a topic dealt with in Chapter 7. The move of the Russian computer games company Nival into console games is a typical example. When generating new ventures at this stage, it is critical to

Exhibit 9.6   **Stages of entrepreneurial growth and typical challenges**

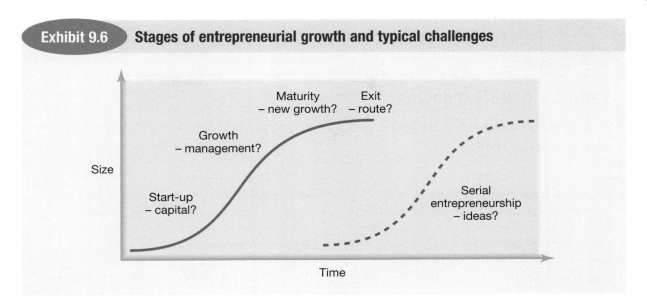

recall the odds on success. Research suggests that many small high-tech firms fail to manage the transition to a second generation of technology, and that it is often better at this point simply to look for exit.[29]

● *Exit.* This refers to departure from the venture, either by the founding entrepreneurs or by the original investors, or both. At the point of exit, entrepreneurs and venture capitalists will seek to release capital as a reward for their input and risk taking. Entrepreneurs may consider three prime routes to exit. A simple *trade sale* of the venture to another company is a common route. Thus MySpace was bought by NewsCorp just two years after foundation: see Illustration 9.3. Some entrepreneurs may sell to their own managers, in the form of a *management buy-out* (MBO). Another exit route for highly successful enterprises is an *Initial Public Offering* (IPO), the sale of shares to the public, for instance on the American NASDAQ exchange. IPOs usually involve just a portion of the total shares available, and may thus allow entrepreneurs to continue in the business and provide funds for further growth. Google raised $1.67bn (£0.93bn; €1.36bn) with its 2004 IPO, selling only 7 per cent of its shares. It is often said that good entrepreneurs plan for their exit right from start-up, and certainly venture capitalists will insist on this.

Entrepreneurs who have successfully exited a first venture often become *serial entrepreneurs*. Serial entrepreneurs are people who set up a succession of enterprises, investing the capital raised on exit from earlier ventures into new growing ventures. For serial entrepreneurs, the challenge often is no longer so much funding but good ideas.

9.5.2 Entrepreneurial relationships

For many, entrepreneurship is about independence, working for oneself. This pride in independence is reinforced by a common stereotype of entrepreneurs as heroic individuals, starting their businesses at night in a university laboratory (see Illustration 9.5), or in the spare room at home or in a local lock-up garage.

Illustration 9.5

Fatima's dignified gowns

A business administration degree is just the starting point for this entrepreneurial venture.

Fatima Ba-Alawi graduated in business administration from the University of Portsmouth in 2005. Less than one year later, seven National Health Service hospitals were trialling her innovative hospital gowns, with interest from private sector hospital operator Bupa too. Her new company, DCS Designs (Dignity, Comfort and Safety), had got off to a flying start.

Ba-Alawi had arrived in the United Kingdom in 1998, as a refugee from Somalia speaking no English. After studying for English GCSEs and A-levels, she says: 'I applied to the University of Portsmouth to read business administration because the idea of going into business always appealed to me'. She was keen to have her own business after finding it 'deeply unpleasant working for somebody else at a fast food outlet as a teenager'.

It was while working in a local hospital as a care assistant that her business idea came to her. Conventional hospital gowns were undignified for wearers and awkward for carers. Ba-Alawi designed a new type of gown which provided extra coverage for the back, gave better access points for medical drips and used easy press-stud buttoning. Her design was more dignified, more comfortable and more safe.

While still studying, Ba-Alawi approached the University of Portsmouth's Centre for Enterprise for support. She won £500 (€725) in the University's Enterprise Challenge competition, which she used to fund an initial prototype and carry out some market research. The University's enterprise mentoring service provided her with one-to-one coaching, which helped her develop her business plan. This business plan won a further University

prize, worth £2,000, which she used to fund a patent application and register her company, DCS Designs Ltd. She next put in a bid to the University's Student SEED Fund, gaining more support plus an office in the University's Centre for Enterprise and access to virtual office facilities. The SEED Fund allowed Ba-Alawi to manufacture sample gowns and distribute them to hospitals, at the same time as launching the DCS Designs website, which had a facility for user feedback. The local Enterprise Hub also provided access to a local patent attorney to help protect her intellectual property. Ba-Alawi commented on the University's role:

Having had the support of the University has made all the difference. It's much better to have a real business presence than to try to run this from my room at home! The University has not just given me the start up funds, but it has also given me the confidence and support I needed to take my idea off the ground and make it happen.

Sources: *Financial Times*, 12 April (2006); *Evening Standard*, 13 September (2005); www.port.ac.uk.

Questions

1 What challenges would you anticipate for Ba-Alawi's DCS Designs company if it takes off? How should she deal with them?

2 Does your experience of work and organisations give you any ideas for new ventures?

3 What does your university or college do to support student entrepreneurship?

William Hewlett and David Packard, founders of the famous computing and printer company, and Steve Jobs of Apple, are oft-quoted examples of the garage stereotype. But digging beneath the stereotype soon reveals a more complex story, in which relationships with large companies can be important right from the start. Typically entrepreneurs have worked for large companies beforehand, and continue to use relationships afterwards.[30,31] While Hewlett came fairly directly out of Stanford University's laboratories, Packard worked at General Electric and Litton Industries. The Hewlett Packard company used Litton Industries' foundries early on, and later used relationships at General Electric to recruit experienced managers. Steve Jobs worked for William Hewlett for a summer job aged 12, and later was the 40th employee at video games company Atari.

Entrepreneurship often involves close relationships with other companies, especially big companies. Entrepreneurs need to decide how to exploit their relationships, in particular with those powerful organisations that are driving innovation in their markets. Fortunately, the entrepreneurial need for relationships fits with the growing needs of large organisations themselves. These powerful organisations are increasingly shifting to what Henry Chesbrough calls a new 'open' model of innovation. In this *open innovation* model, even big organisations cease to rely on their own internal resources but draw increasingly on independent new ventures and external partners such as universities, suppliers and customers. Two concepts are currently particularly influential here:

- *Corporate venturing*. Many large corporations, such as Intel, Nokia and Shell, have developed corporate venture units that invest externally in new ventures as safeguards against disruptive innovations and potential drivers of future growth.[32] Large corporations gain by increasing the range of ideas they are exposed to, by protecting early stage ventures from internal bureaucracy and by spreading their risk. Entrepreneurs gain by accessing not just capital but also knowledge of large-company thinking in their domain and contacts with other members of the large company's network. It is crucial that both entrepreneurs and corporate venture capitalists continuously monitor the set of expectations behind the investment: is the investment more profit driven in terms of expecting good financial returns or is it more strategic, in the sense of being about technological or market development? Shifting expectations on the part of the corporate venture capitalist can lead to the disruption of longer-term plans by the entrepreneurial new venture. In recent years, companies such as Siemens and Nokia have sold or diluted their stakes in some of their corporate venture units, and companies such as Ericsson and Diageo have had to close them down entirely.

- *Ecosystems*. High-technology companies such as Cisco, IBM and Intel often foster 'ecosystems' of smaller companies: IBM had 1,398 alliances in the late 1990s, most with small firms. These ecosystems are communities of connected suppliers, agents, distributors, franchisees, technology entrepreneurs and makers of complementary products.[33] Apple for example has created an ecosystem around its iPod, in which more than a hundred companies manufacture accessories and peripherals such as cases, speakers and docking units. Large firms get the benefits of increased customer satisfaction through the provision of complementary products. Ecosystem members get the benefit of a large and often lucrative market: iPod accessories get plenty of retail shelf space and superior margins. However, large firms must manage their ecosystems actively for their advantage. These firms take up *platform leadership*, in which they consciously nurture independent companies through successive waves of innovation around their basic technological 'platform'.[34] Platform examples include the Palm Pilot PDA, which needs a continuously evolving range of software and connecting devices to maximise its value, and DoCoMo's i-mode 'always-on' Internet phones, whose launch required a host of web content providers to rewrite their websites in a compatible programming language. For entrepreneurial members of a business ecosystem, each new generation of a technology platform imposes a crucial choice about whether and how much to bet on a platform whose leadership they typically cannot influence.

9.5.3 Social entrepreneurship

Social entrepreneurship involves individuals and groups who create independent organisations to mobilise ideas and resources to address social problems, typically earning revenues but on a not-for-profit basis

Entrepreneurship is not just a matter for the private sector. The public sector has seen increasing calls for a more entrepreneurial approach to service creation and delivery.[35] Recently too the notion of social entrepreneurship has become common. **Social entrepreneurship** involves individuals and groups who create independent organisations to mobilise ideas and resources to address social problems, typically earning revenues but on a not-for-profit basis.[36] Independence and revenues generated in the market give social entrepreneurs the flexibility and dynamism to pursue social problems that pure public sector organisations are often too bureaucratic, or too politically constrained, to tackle. Social entrepreneurs have pursued a wide range of initiatives, including small loans ('microcredit') to peasants by the Grameen Bank in Bangladesh, employment creation by the Mondragon cooperative in the Basque region of Spain, and fair trade by Traidcraft in the United Kingdom. This wide range of initiatives raises at least three key choices for social entrepreneurs:

● *Social mission.* For social entrepreneurs, the social mission is primary. The social mission can embrace two elements: end objectives and operational processes. For example, the Grameen Bank has the end objective of reducing rural poverty, especially for women. The process is empowering poor people's own business initiatives by providing microcredit at a scale and to people that conventional banks would ignore.

● *Organisational form.* Many social enterprises take on cooperative forms, involving their employees and other stakeholders on a democratic basis and thus building commitment and channels for ideas. This form of organisation raises the issue of which stakeholders to include, and which to exclude. Cooperatives can also be slow to take hard decisions. Social enterprises therefore sometimes take more hierarchical charity or company forms of organisation. Cafédirect, the fair-trade beverages company, even became a publicly listed company, paying its first dividend to shareholders in 2006.

● *Business model.* Social enterprises typically rely to a large extent on revenues earned in the marketplace, not just government subsidy or charitable donations. Housing associations collect rents, microcredit organisations charge interest and fair-trade organisations sell produce. Social entrepreneurs are no different to other entrepreneurs, therefore, in having to design an efficient and effective business model. This business model might involve innovative

Illustration 9.6

key debate

Are large firms better innovators than small firms?

Just how much more innovative are small firms really?

The famous Austrian economist Joseph Schumpeter proposed that large firms are proportionately more innovative than small firms. This proposition is a controversial one. If true, it would discourage laboratory scientists and engineers from leaving their large-firm employers to set up their own ventures. It would encourage large firms like Google and Cisco to keep on buying up small innovative firms and absorbing them into their own corporate strategies. It would make government policy makers more tolerant of huge, domineering firms like Microsoft which claim that their large scale is important to continued innovation in computer software.

Schumpeter's proposition for the advantages of large firms in innovation has several points in its favour:

- Large firms have greater and more diverse resources, helping them to bring together all the various necessary elements for innovation.

- Large firms may have a greater propensity for innovation risk, knowing that they can absorb the costs of innovation failure.

- Large firms have better incentives to innovate, because they are more likely to be able to capitalise on innovation, having all the required complementary assets (distribution channels and so on) to roll it out fast and under their control.

On the other hand, there are good reasons why small firms might be more innovative:

- Small firms are typically more cohesive, so that knowledge is more easily shared.

- Small firms are typically more flexible and less bureaucratic, so that they can innovate faster and more boldly.

- Small firms are more motivated to innovate simply to survive, while large firms can simply defend and exploit their dominance of existing markets.

There has been plenty of research on whether small or large firms are proportionately more innovative. Some researchers have focused on the input side, for example measuring whether large firms are more research intensive in terms of R&D expenditure as a percentage of sales. Other researchers have focused on the output side, for example counting whether large firms have proportionately greater numbers of patents for innovations. There is no final consensus on the overall patterns of innovation. However, recent research findings suggest that in general:

- Large firms are relatively less research intensive in high-technology industries, for example electronics and software.

- Large firms are relatively more innovative in service industries than in manufacturing industries.

It seems that the research so far cannot provide any definite rules about whether large or small firms are better innovators in general. However, research scientists, acquisitive large firms and government policy makers need to consider carefully the specifics of particular industries.

Sources:
C. Camisón-Zornosa, R. Lapiedra-Alcani, M. Segarra-Ciprés and M. Boronat-Navarro, 'A meta-analysis of innovation and organizational size', *Organization Studies*, vol. 25, no. 3 (2004), pp. 331–361.

C.-Y. Lee and T. Sung, 'Schumpeter's legacy: a new perspective on the relationship between firm size and R&D', *Research Policy*, vol. 34 (2005), pp. 914–931.

Question

What kinds of managerial action might you consider if you were trying to increase the innovativeness of a large firm in a high-technology manufacturing industry?

changes in the value chain. Thus fair-trade organisations have often become much more closely involved with their suppliers than commercial organisations, for example advising farmers on agriculture and providing education and infrastructure support to their communities.

Social entrepreneurs, just like other entrepreneurs, often have to forge relationships with large commercial companies (see also Illustration 9.6). For example, a new social enterprise called Ten Senses established Bulgaria's first fair-trade shop with assistance from the multinational bank Citigroup and the oil company Royal Dutch Shell. Rosabeth Moss Kanter points out that the benefits to business of involvement with social enterprise can go beyond a feelgood factor and attractive publicity.[37] She shows that involvement in social enterprise can help develop new technologies and services, access new pools of potential employees, and create relationships with government and other agencies that can eventually turn into new markets. Kanter concludes that large corporations should develop clear strategies with regard to social entrepreneurship, not treat it as ad hoc charity.

SUMMARY

- Strategists face three fundamental dilemmas in innovation, concerning: the relative emphasis to put on *technology push* or *market pull*; whether to focus on *product* or *process innovation*; and finally how far to concentrate on *technological* innovation as opposed to broader *business model* innovation.

- Innovations often diffuse into the marketplace according to an *S-curve model* in which slow start-up is followed by accelerating growth (the *tipping point*) and finally a flattening of demand. Managers can influence this process by a combination of supply-side and demand-side initiatives. They should not assume that innovations will necessarily follow a smooth S-curve and should watch out for 'tripping points'.

- Managers have a choice between being *first into the marketplace* and entering later. There are advantages and disadvantages to both. Being first into the market without the required complementary assets and capacity to capture profits can simply be a waste of effort. *'Fast-second'* strategies are often more attractive.

- Established incumbents' businesses can easily become too *locked into* existing customer relationships and should beware *disruptive innovations* that uncover entirely new market needs. Incumbents can help protect themselves from conservatism by developing portfolios of *real options* and by organising independent *new venture units*.

- Entrepreneurs face characteristic dilemmas as their businesses go through the entrepreneurial life cycle of *start-up*, *growth*, *maturity* and *exit*. Entrepreneurs also have to choose how they relate to large firms, particularly as they may become involved in their *ecosystems* or strategies for *open innovation*. There is not conclusive evidence that entrepreneurial small firms are more innovative than large firms (see Key Debate, Illustration 9.6).

- *Social entrepreneurship* offers a flexible way of addressing social problems, raising dilemmas over appropriate missions, organisational forms and business models. Social entrepreneurs and large businesses also frequently have to choose how to relate to each other through mutually beneficial partnerships.

Work assignments

*✲ Denotes more advanced work assignments.   * Refers to a case study in the Text and Cases edition.*

9.1 ✲ For a new product or service that you have recently experienced and enjoyed, investigate the strategy of the company responsible. With reference to the dilemmas of section 9.2, explain whether the innovation was more technology push or market pull, product or process driven, or technological or more broadly business model based.

9.2 Go to a web traffic site (such as alexa.com) and compare over time trends in terms of 'page views' or 'reach' for older sites (such as Amazon.com) and newer sites (such as youtube.com, or any that has more recently emerged). With reference to section 9.3, how do you explain these trends and how would you project them forward?

9.3 ✲ With regard to a new product or service that you have recently experienced and enjoyed (as in 9.1), investigate the strategic responses of 'incumbents' to this innovation. To what extent is the innovation disruptive for them (see section 9.4.3)?

9.4 With reference to the entrepreneurial life cycle, identify the position of either MacPac*, Ekomate*, Brown Bag Film* or ACME*. What managerial issues might this case company anticipate in the coming years?

9.5 Use the Internet to identify a social entrepreneurial venture that interests you (via www.skollfoundation.org, for example), and, with regard to section 9.5.3, identify its social mission, its organisational form and its business model.

Integrative assignment

9.6 Consider a for-profit or social entrepreneurial idea that you or your friends or colleagues might have. Drawing on section 15.4.4, outline the elements of a strategic plan for this possible venture. What more information do you need to get?

An extensive range of additional materials, including audio summaries, weblinks to organisations featured in the text, definitions of key concepts and self-assessment questions, can be found on the *Exploring Corporate Strategy* Companion Website at **www.pearsoned.co.uk/ecs**

Recommended key readings

- P. Trott, *Innovation Management and New Product Development*, 3rd edition, FT/Prentice Hall, 2005, provides a comprehensive overview of innovation strategy issues. A lively and accessible survey of many innovation issues, together with a wealth of examples, is C. Markides and P. Geroski, *Fast second: how smart companies bypass radical innovation to enter and dominate new markets*, Josey-Bass, 2005.

- A good collection of accessible articles on specialised innovation topics by leading academics is J. Fagerberg, D. Mowery and R. Nelson (eds), *The Oxford Handbook of Innovation*, Oxford University Press, 2005. An equivalent collection on entrepreneurship is M. Casson, B. Yeung, A. Basu and N. Wadeson (eds), *The Oxford Handbook of Entrepreneurship*, Oxford University Press, 2006.

- P.A. Wickham, *Strategic Entrepreneurship*, 3rd edition, 2004, is becoming the standard European text with regard to entrepreneurial strategy.

- Social entrepreneurship is discussed usefully in A. Nicholls (ed.), *Social Entrepreneurship: New paradigms of sustainable social change*, Oxford University Press, 2006.

- For an overview of the associated financial considerations for new business start ups/proposals see G. Arnold, *Corporate Financial Management*, 3rd edition, FT/Prentice Hall, 2005, Chapter 2.

References

1. This definition adapts, in order to include the public sector, the definition in P. Trott, *Innovation Management and New Product Development*, 3rd edition, FT/Prentice Hall, 2005.

2. A good discussion of the academic models that underpin these dilemmas is in R. Rothwell, 'Successful industrial innovation: critical factors for the 1990s', *R&D Management*, vol. 22, no. 3 (1992), pp. 221–239.

3. W.J. Abernathy and J.M. Utterback, 'A dynamic model of process and product innovation', *Omega*, vol. 3, no. 6 (1975), pp. 142–160.

4. P. Anderson and M.L. Tushman, 'Technological discontinuities and dominant designs: a cyclical model of technological change', *Administrative Science Quarterly*, vol. 35 (1990), pp. 604–633.

5. J. Tang, 'Competition and innovation behaviour', *Research Policy*, vol. 35 (2006), pp. 68–82.

6. G. Hamel, *Leading the Revolution*, Harvard Business School Press, 2000.

7. J. Magretta, 'Why business models matter', *Harvard Business Review*, vol. 80, no. 5 (2002), pp. 86–92

8. Good discussions of business models and their relationship to business-level strategy can be found in G. Yip, 'Using strategy to change your business model', *Business Strategy Review*, vol. 15, no. 2 (2004), pp. 17–24; and G.M. Mansfield and L. Fourie, 'Strategy and business models – strange bedfellows? A case for convergence and its evolution into strategic architecture', *South African Business Management Journal*, vol. 15, no. 1 (2004), pp. 35–44.

9. Innovation diffusion is discussed in the classic E. Rogers, *Diffusion of Innovations*, Free Press, 1995; C. Kim and R. Maubourgne, 'Knowing a winning idea when you see one', *Harvard Business Review*, vol. 78, no. 5 (2000), pp. 129–138; and J. Cummings and J. Doh, 'Identifying who matters: mapping key players in multiple environments', *California Management Review*, vol. 42, no. 2 (2000), pp. 83–104 (see especially pp. 91–97).

10. J. Cummings and J. Doh, 'Identifying who matters: mapping key players in multiple environments', *California Management Review*, vol. 42, no, 2 (2000), pp. 83–104.

11. J. Nichols and S. Roslow, 'The S-curve: an aid to strategic marketing', *Journal of Consumer Marketing*, vol. 3, no. 2 (1986), pp 53–64; and F. Suarez and G. Lanzolla, 'The half-truth of first-mover advantage', *Harvard Business Review*, vol. 83 no. 4 (2005), pp. 121–127. This S-curve refers to innovation diffusion. However, the S-curve effect sometimes also refers to the diminishing performance increases available from a maturing technology: A. Sood and G. Tellis, 'Technological evolution and radical innovation', *Journal of Marketing*, vol. 69, no. 3 (2005), pp. 152–168.

12. M. Gladwell, *The Tipping Point*, Abacus, 2000. Tipping points are also important in public policy and can help anticipate emerging problems, for example crime waves and epidemics.

13. www.bbcnews.com, 12 January (2007).

14. S. Brown, 'The tripping point', *Marketing Research*, vol. 17, no. 1 (2005), pp. 8–13.

15. C. Markides and P. Geroski, *Fast second: how smart companies bypass radical innovation to enter and dominate new markets*, Josey-Bass, 2005; R. Kerin, P. Varadarajan and R. Peterson, 'First-mover advantage: a synthesis, conceptual framework and research propositions', *Journal of Marketing*, vol. 56, no. 4 (1992), pp. 33–52; and P.F. Suarez and G. Lanzolla, 'The half-truth of first-mover advantage', *Harvard Business Review*, vol. 83, no. 4 (2005), pp. 121–127

16. F. Suarez and G. Lanzolla, 'The half-truth of first-mover advantage', *Harvard Business Review*, vol. 83, no. 4 (2005), pp. 121–127. See also S. Min, U. Manohar and W. Robinson, 'Market pioneer and early follower survival risks: a contingency analysis of really new versus incrementally new product-markets', *Journal of Marketing*, vol. 70, no. 1 (2006), pp. 15–33.

17. David Teece, the academic authority in this area, refers to the capacity to capture profits the 'appropriability regime': see D. Teece, *Managing Intellectual Capital*, Oxford University Press, 2000.

18. An excellent survey of intellectual property rights is in *The Economist Magazine*, Survey: Patents and Technology, October 25 (2005).

19. D. Teece, *Managing Intellectual Capital*, Oxford University Press, 2000.

20. C. Markides and P. Geroski, *Fast second: how smart companies bypass radical innovation to enter and dominate new markets*, Jossey-Bass, 2005.

21. See J. Bower and C. Christensen, 'Disruptive technologies: catching the wave', *Harvard Business Review*, vol. 73, no. 1 (1995), pp. 43–53; and C. Christensen and M.E. Raynor, *The Innovator's Solution*, Harvard Business School Press, 2003.

22. R.G. McGrath and I. MacMillan, *The Entrepreneurial Mindset*, Harvard Business School Press, 2000.

23. C. Christensen and M.E. Raynor, *The Innovator's Solution*, Harvard Business School Press, 2003.

24. V. Govindarajan and C. Trimble, 'Organizational DNA for strategic innovation', *California Management Review*, vol. 43, no. 3 (2005), pp. 47–75.

25. Excellent textbooks on strategic entrepreneurship include J.A. Timmons, *New Venture Creation: Entrepreneurship in the 21st Century*, 6th edition, Irwin, 2004; and P.A. Wickham, *Strategic Entrepreneurship*, 3rd edition, FT/Prentice Hall, 2004.

26. Life-cycle models of entrepreneurship are discussed in S. Hanks, C. Watson, E. Jansen and G. Chandler, 'Tightening the life-cycle construct: a taxonomic study of growth stage configurations in high-technology organizations', *Entrepreneurship Theory and Practice*, Winter (1993), pp. 5–28; and D. Flynn and A. Forman, 'Life cycles of new venture organizations: different factors affecting performance', *Journal of Developmental Entrepreneurship*, vol. 6, no. 1 (2001), pp. 41–58.

27. D. Flynn and A. Forman, 'Life cycles of new venture organizations: different factors affecting performance', *Journal of Developmental Entrepreneurship*, vol. 6, no. 1 (2001), pp. 41–58.

28. D. Flynn and A. Forman, 'Life cycles of new venture organizations: different factors affecting performance', *Journal of Developmental Entrepreneurship*, vol. 6, no. 1 (2001), pp. 41–58.

29. R. Kaplinksy, 'Firm size and technical change', *Journal of Industrial Economics*, vol. 32, no. 1 (1983), pp. 39–59. For a detailed account of Cisco's policy of taking over high-technology firms, see D. Mayer and M. Kenney, 'Economic action does not take place in a vacuum: understanding Cisco's acquisition and development strategy', *Industry and Innovation*, vol. 11, no. 4 (2004), pp. 293–325.

30. P. Audia and C. Rider, 'A garage and an idea: what more does an entrepreneur need?', *California Management Review*, vol. 40, no. 1 (2005), pp. 6–28.

31. H. Chesbrough, *Open Innovation: the New Imperatives for Creating and Profiting from Technology*, Harvard Business School Press, 2003. The Research Director of Intel describes his company's 'open' approach in D. Tennenhouse, 'Intel's open-collaborative model of industry-university research', *Research and Technology Management*, July–August (2004), pp. 19–26.

32. H. Chesbrough, 'Making sense of corporate venture capital', *Harvard Business Review*, vol. 80, no. 3 (2002), pp. 4–11; A. Campbell, J. Birkinshaw, A. Morrison and R. van Basten Batenburg, 'The Future of corporate venturing', *MIT Sloan Management Review*, vol. 45, no. 1 (2003), pp. 33–41.

33. IBM's director of research describes ecosystems in P.M. Horn, 'The changing nature of innovation', *Research and Technology Management*, November–December (2005), pp. 28–33; see also B. Iyer, C.-H. Lee and N. Venkatraman, 'Managing in a "Small World Ecosystem"', *California Management Review*, vol. 48, no. 3 (2006), pp. 28–47.

34. A. Gawer and M. Cusumano, *Platform Leadership: how Intel, Microsoft and Cisco drive industry innovation*, Harvard Business School Press, 2002.

35. P. DuGay, 'Against enterprise', *Organization*, vol. 11, no. 1 (2004), pp. 37–48.

36. S. Alvord, L. Brown and C. Letts, 'Social entrepreneurship and societal transformation: an exploratory study', *Journal of Applied Behavioral Science*, vol. 43, no. 3 (2004), pp. 260–282; A. Nichols (ed.) *Social Entrepreneurship: New paradigms of sustainable social change*, Oxford University Press, 2006; J. Austin, H. Stevenson and J. Wei-Skillern, 'Social and commercial entrepreneurship: same, different, or both?', *Entrepreneurship Theory and Practice*, vol. 30, no. 1 (2006), pp. 1–22.

37. R. Moss Kanter, 'From spare change to real change', *Harvard Business Review*, May–June (1999), pp. 122–133.

Skype: innovators and entrepreneurs

Introduction

Niklas Zennström and Janus Friis are a golden pair in the Internet business. For a period during the early 2000s, their Kazaa peer-to-peer file sharing business was the world's largest music sharing site. After selling that business to Sharman Networks, they moved quickly to establish Skype in 2003, which quickly became the dominant player in the world's VoIP (Voice over Internet Protocol) telephone market. Skype's free Internet-based VoIP service was an attractive alternative to the expensive traditional landline and mobile telephone services, gaining 60 million users by 2005. That same year, they sold Skype to eBay for $2.6bn (£1.5bn; €2.1bn) – an impressive figure for a business whose total revenues were just $60m and had still not turned a profit.

Key issues for Zennström and Friis in 2006 were the long-term sustainability of their business model and their future under the ownership of eBay.

Two entrepreneurs

Zennström is the older of the two, aged 40 at the sale to eBay. He took a first degree in business and then an MSc in engineering and computer science from Uppsala University in Sweden. He then entered the telecommunications industry, spending nine years in Tele2, a fast-expanding European telecoms group. He met Friis in 1997, hiring him to manage a help-desk. Friis, a Dane, is 11 years younger and failed even to graduate from high school. But from the late 1990s the two worked closely together on a series of new ventures: as well as Kazaa and Skype, these included Altnet, claimed to be the world's first secure peer-to-peer wholesale network, Joltid, a company in traffic optimisation technologies, and the portal everyday.com.

Zennström has a modest personal style. In his London office, he shares a long desk with half a

Co-founders of Skype – Niklas Zennström (left) and Janus Friis (right)

dozen colleagues and he flies economy class, despite his height of 6ft 4in (1.93m). But he is absolutely committed to the idea of disruptive innovation. He told the *Financial Times*: 'It's everyone's obligation to fight against monopolies and also companies that provide bad services.' Of the traditional landline and mobile telephone companies, he declares: 'They deserve to be challenged. They provide bad and expensive service.'

About his partner Friis, he observes: 'I think he benefited from not having formal schooling. His thought process is much freer. He doesn't think conventionally.' However, he rejects the notion that Friis is the vision guy and he is simply the execution guy. 'We are very complementary with each other. It is a very creative process and it's easier to be creative with two people. You need to try things out and challenge each other.'

The Skype business model

Skype's software allows people to use the Internet to make free calls to other Skype users all over the world. Given the cost of traditional international calls, this was an exciting idea. Initial funding, however, was not easy to find as the music industry was still pursuing a lawsuit against the two founders regarding the illegal filesharing their earlier Kazaa venture appeared to facilitate. For fear of legal action, Zennström and Friis dared not even enter the USA. Most traditional venture capitalists gave the new venture a wide berth. Moreover, it was not easy to see how to make money out of free calls.

The business model is more complicated than that, of course. Most users have free calls, certainly. However, Skype has very low costs, as customers download the software off the Internet and it is the customers' computers and Internet connections that make the network. It costs nothing to keep connections open continuously. Marketing is cheap, because customers naturally invite others to join. Skype has no telephone help-desk, citing the overwhelming number of customers and the effectiveness of its standard Internet queries services. Skype makes its money from its ancillary services, such as SkypeOut, which allows customers to call traditional landline or mobile numbers for a fee, often very small. Zennström explains the model: 'We want to make as little money as possible per user. We don't have any cost per user, but we want a lot of them.'

This overturns the traditional landline and mobile phone business model. Traditional telephone companies of both types face high costs of both marketing and capacity building. Customers are typically charged according to distance and by the minute. The traditional principle is to maximise revenues per customer, completely the opposite to Skype. Zennström summarised to *Business Week*:

When you're a phone company, you have marketing and customer-acquisition costs. When you have a customer, you have an operational cost of running the network. Then you have a cost for billing systems. That's an operator business model.

The business model of Skype is completely different. Skype has a software business model. We don't have any distribution or marketing costs for each user – our software is spread virally. And when we have a new user, we have zero cost for serving that user because they're using P2P (peer-to-peer) software and their own bandwidth. So we have zero costs of getting new users and zero costs of running traffic. Our costs are only business development and software development.

Comparing the positions of the two types of companies, he added: 'Something that is a great business model for us is probably a terrible model for them.'

As shown in Figure 1, Skype's service was immensely attractive. With a tipping point in 2004, user numbers surged ahead. Of course, this success

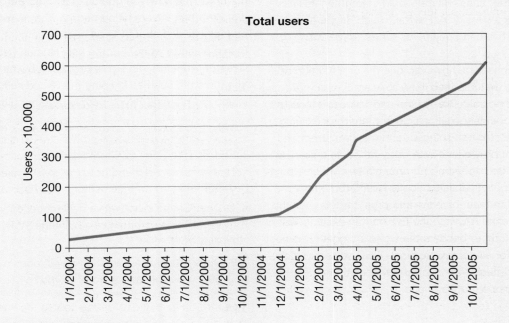

Figure 1 Skype's users

Source: www.wikipedia.com. This material is licensed under the GNU Free Documentation Licence. It uses material from the Wikipedia article 'Skype'.

raised an awkward paradox. If Skype became near universal, who would be left for people to call using the paid service of SkypeOut to access traditional phones?

eBay's move

Skype was always likely to be for sale. Zennström and Friis had sold Kazaa quickly and their initial funders would want a profitable early exit too. It was not surprising that rumours started during 2005 of possible acquisition from technology giants such as Google, Microsoft and Yahoo!. In the end, however, it was online auctioneer eBay who did the deal, slightly surprisingly as it was not seen as a communications company.

There are similarities in the underlying business models of the two companies. Both benefit from 'network effects', where value rises disproportionately fast with increasing members of the network. One more precise rationale from eBay's point of view was that Skype connections could be placed directly on the eBay site, allowing customers potentially to phone sellers with a single click of the button. Also, sellers could place voice links directly on their eBay sites, so that customers could click directly to a message, paying eBay a fee every time they did. On the other hand, Skype would strengthen its links with eBay's subsidiary PayPal, which Skype already used for managing payments for its SkypeOut service.

For Zennström, however, one major attraction of eBay was that it looked likely to leave Skype more alone. Companies like Yahoo! and Microsoft tend to integrate their acquisitions closely into their existing operations, extinguishing autonomy. Zennström and Friis might be working with eBay for some time. The deal included an 'earn-out' arrangement which would push Skype's final sale price to over $4bn if they managed to meet revenue and profit targets over the coming years. Anyway, the two had an exciting vision for the future: to become the world's biggest and best platform for all communication – text, voice or video – from any Internet-connected device, whether a computer or a mobile phone.

eBay's role

eBay had a lot to offer an ambitious company like Skype. Founded only in 1995, it had reached revenues of $4.55bn and 11,600 employees in the space of 10 years. Zennström commented of Meg Whitman, eBay's Chief Executive since 1998: 'I think I can learn a lot of things from Meg. We want to see things through, but we also have some other ideas.' Skype would still have its own strategy, budgets, culture and brands. Zennström insisted to the *Financial Times*:

One of the important things for us, but also one of the great things with eBay, is that we wanted to make sure that we could merge with a bigger company, but that Skype stays as one company. Meg said: 'Take advantage of the resources we have, but we are not going to tell you what to do because you're the best in the world to run your own business'.

The managerial demands of rapid growth were considerable. Staff quadrupled to 300 between 2005 and 2006, and included 30 nationalities scattered all over the world. eBay introduced five of its own senior managers to help, including a new president responsible for day-to-day operations, a chief financial officer and a new human resource director. But Skype was keen to preserve its own culture. According to Zennström, still the CEO, Skype's passionate, pioneering culture had to be both protected and nurtured: 'It's how you operate, how you behave. It starts when we are hiring people. They need to be really thrilled about Skype as a movement, rather than a place to work.' For the new Human Resources Director, Annemie van Rensburg, her job was about 'the fun stuff, such as keeping the Skype culture intact and bringing Skype people together globally'.

Sources: 'Phone Service the "Zero Cost" Way', *Business Week online*, 7 January (2004); www.wikipedia.org; *The Economist*, 15 September (2005); *Financial Times*, 17 and 19 April (2006).

Questions

1 Does Skype's innovative new model offer a sustainable competitive advantage? Why? Why not?

2 Does eBay have parenting advantages over other possible acquirers of Skype?

Strategy Methods and Evaluation

LEARNING OUTCOMES

After reading this chapter you should be able to:

→ Identify the *methods* by which strategies can be pursued: *organic development*, *mergers and acquisitions* and *strategic alliances*.

→ Employ three *success criteria* for evaluating strategic options: *suitability*, *acceptability* and *feasibility*.

→ Use a range of different *techniques for evaluating strategic options*.

Photo: John Crum/Alamy Images

,000

0,000

10.1   INTRODUCTION

This chapter rounds off Part II of the book, the whole of which has been concerned with strategic choices available to organisations, as outlined in Exhibit II.i. Chapter 6 offered a range of choices about how to position the organisation in relation to competitors. Within this generalised choice about the basis of competitive strategy, there are more specific choices to be made about the strategic direction of the organisation; in particular, which markets and which products are most appropriate. These choices were set out in Chapter 7 and developed further in Chapters 8 and 9 in the context of international strategy and strategy innovation. However, there is a third level of choice concerned with the *methods by which competitive strategy and strategic direction can be pursued*. This is the theme of section 10.2, the first half of this chapter.

Bearing in mind that the use of the concepts and tools introduced in Part I of the book will also have generated ideas about strategies that might be followed, the strategist may well need to consider many possible options. The second half of this chapter therefore discusses the *success criteria* by which they can be assessed and, building on these criteria, explains some of the *techniques for evaluating strategic options*.

Exhibit 10.1 summarises the overall structure of the chapter.

Exhibit 10.1   **Strategy methods and evaluation: chapter structure**

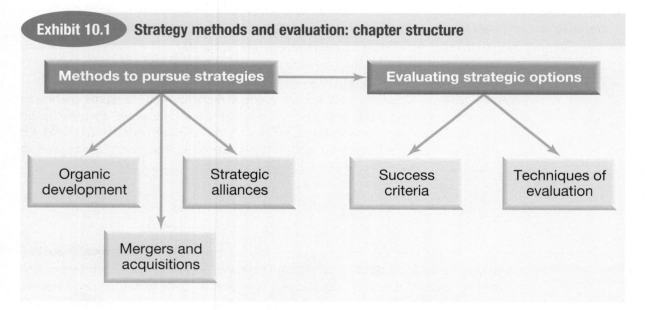

10.2   METHODS OF PURSUING STRATEGIES

A **strategic method** is the *means* by which a strategy can be pursued

Any of the strategy directions discussed in Chapters 6 to 9 may be undertaken in a different way or by a different **strategic method**: the *means* by which a strategy can be pursued. These methods can be divided into three types: organic development, acquisition (or disposal) and alliances.

10.2.1 Organic development[1]

Organic development
is where strategies are
developed by building
on and developing an
organisation's own
capabilities

Organic development (or internal development) is where strategies are developed by building on and developing an organisation's own capabilities. For many organisations organic development has been the primary method of strategy development, and there are some compelling reasons why this should be so:

- *Highly technical products* in terms of design or method of manufacture lend themselves to organic development since the process of development may be the best way of acquiring the necessary capabilities to compete successfully. These competences may of course in turn spawn new products and create new market opportunities.

- *Knowledge and capability development* may be enhanced by organic development. For example, a business may feel that the direct involvement gained from having its own salesforce rather than using sales agents gains greater market knowledge and therefore competitive advantage over other rivals more distant from their customers.

- *Spreading investment over time*. The final cost of developing new activities internally may be greater than that of acquiring other companies. However, spreading these costs over time may be a more favourable option than major expenditure at a point in time required for an acquisition. This is a strong motive for organic development in small companies or many public services that may not have the resources for major one-off investments.

- *Minimising disruption*. The slower rate of change of organic development may also minimise the disruption to other activities and avoid the political and cultural problems of acquisition integration that can occur (see section 10.2.2).

- *The nature of markets* may dictate organic development. In many instances organisations breaking new ground may not be in a position to develop by acquisition or joint development, since they are the only ones in the field. Or there may be few opportunities for acquisitions, as, for example, for foreign companies attempting to enter Japan.

10.2.2 Mergers and acquisitions[2]

An **acquisition** is where
an organisation takes
ownership of another
organisation

A **merger** is a mutually
agreed decision for joint
ownership between
organisations

KEY
CONCEPT

Mergers and
acquisitions

An **acquisition** is where an organisation takes ownership of another organisation, whereas a **merger** implies a mutually agreed decision for joint ownership between organisations. In practice, few acquisitions are hostile and few mergers are the joining of equals. So both acquisitions and mergers typically involve the managers of one organisation exerting strategic influence over the other. Worldwide merger and acquisition activity takes place on a major scale but tends to go in waves.[3] Globally the number of completed acquisitions tripled between 1991 and 2001. There was then a decline after 2000 but they still stood at $1.2 trillion ($\approx$ €1 trillion; £690bn) in 2002. Since then it has risen again and stood at almost $3.8 trillion in 2006[4] (see Exhibit 10.2). Global activity in mergers is dominated by North America and Western Europe whereas it is much less common in other economies, for example Japan. This reflects the influence of the differences in governance systems that exist (see section 4.2).

Exhibit 10.2	Worldwide mergers and acquisition by value ($bn)

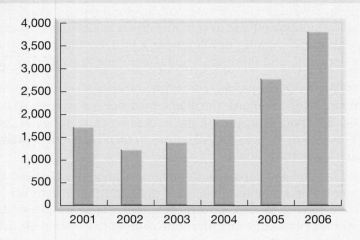

Source: 'All aboard the M&A express', *Sunday Times Business Focus*, 31 December (2006), p. 5. © NI Syndication Limited, 3.12.06.

Motives for acquisitions and mergers

There are different motives for developing through acquisition or merger. A major reason can be the need to keep up with a changing *environment*:

- *Speed of entry*. Products or markets may be changing so rapidly that acquisition becomes the only way of successfully entering the market, since the process of internal development is too slow.

- The *competitive situation* may influence a company to prefer acquisition. In static markets and where market shares of companies are steady it can be difficult for a new company to enter the market, since its presence may create excess capacity. If entry is by acquisition the risk of competitive reaction may be reduced.

- *Consolidation opportunities*. Where there are low levels of industry concentration, there may be an opportunity for improving the balance between supply and demand by acquiring companies and shutting down excess capacity. In many countries, *deregulation* of public utilities has also created a level of fragmentation that was regarded as suboptimal. This was then an opportunity for acquisitive organisations to rationalise provision and/or seek to gain other benefits, for example through the creation of 'multi-utility' companies offering electricity, gas, telecommunications and other services to customers.

- *Financial markets* may provide conditions that motivate acquisitions. If the share value or price/earnings (P/E) ratio of a company is high, it may see the opportunity to acquire a firm with a low share value or P/E ratio. Indeed, this is a major stimulus for the more opportunistic acquisitive companies. An extreme example is asset stripping, where the main motive is short-term gain by buying up undervalued assets and disposing of them piecemeal.

There may also be *capability considerations*:

● *Exploitation of strategic capabilities* can motivate acquisitions, for example through buying companies overseas in order to leverage marketing or R&D skills internationally.

● *Cost efficiency* is a commonly stated reason for acquisitions typically by merging units so as to rationalise resources (for example, head office services or production facilities) or gain scale advantages.

● *Obtaining new capabilities* may also be achieved through acquisitions, or at least be a motive for acquisition. For example, a company may be acquired for its R&D expertise, or its knowledge of particular business processes or markets.

Acquisition can also be driven by the *stakeholder expectations*:

● *Institutional shareholder expectations* may be for continuing growth and acquisitions may be a quick way to deliver this growth. There are considerable dangers, however, that acquisitive growth may result in value destruction rather than creation – for some of the reasons discussed in Chapter 7. For example, the 'parent' may not have sufficient feel for the acquired businesses and thus destroy value.

● *Managerial ambition* may motivate acquisitions because they speed the growth of the company. In turn, this might enhance managers' self-importance, provide better career paths and greater monetary rewards.

● *Speculative motives* of some stakeholders may stimulate acquisitions that bring a short-term boost to share value. Other stakeholders are usually wary of such speculation since their short-term gain can destroy longer-term prospects.

The key debate at the end of the chapter (Illustration 10.7) highlights the debate about the extent to which acquisitions are beneficial to different organisational stakeholders.

Acquisitions and financial performance

Acquisitions are not an easy or guaranteed route to improving financial performance.[5] As many as 70 per cent of acquisitions end up with lower returns to shareholders of both organisations. The most common mistake is in paying too much for a company – possibly through lack of experience in acquisitions, or poor financial advice (for example, from the investment bank involved). In addition the managers of the acquiring company may be over-optimistic about the benefits of the acquisition. An acquisition will probably include poor resources and competences as well as those which were the reason for the purchase. Or it may be that the capabilities of the merging organisations are not compatible. So much was the case, for example, in the 2004 acquisition in the UK of the Safeway supermarket chain by its competitor Morrisons. Amongst the problems was that Morrisons spent a year trying to integrate the IT systems of the two companies before abandoning the attempt. Indeed for this reason acquirers may attempt to buy products or processes rather than whole companies if possible. At the very best it may take the acquiring company considerable time to gain financial benefit from acquisitions.

Making acquisitions work[6]

The implementation agenda following an acquisition or merger will vary depending on its purpose.[7] None the less there are four frequently occurring issues that account for success or failure of an acquisition/merger:

- *Adding value*. The acquirer may find difficulty in adding value to the acquired business (the parenting issue as discussed in section 7.4).

- *Gaining the commitment of middle managers* responsible for the operations and customer relations in the acquired business is important in order to avoid internal uncertainties and maintain customer confidence. Linked to this, deciding which executives to retain in the acquired business needs to be done quickly.

- *Expected synergies may not be realised*, either because they do not exist to the extent expected or because it proves difficult to integrate the activities of the acquired business. For example, where the motive was the transfer of competences or knowledge it may be difficult to identify what these are (see sections 3.4.3 and 3.6.2).

- *Problems of cultural fit*. This can arise because the acquiring business finds that 'everyday' but embedded aspects of culture (for example, organisation routines) differ in ways that prove difficult to overcome but are not readily identifiable before the acquisition. This can be particularly problematic with cross-country acquisitions.[8]

10.2.3 Strategic alliances[9]

A strategic alliance is where two or more organisations share resources and activities to pursue a strategy

Strategic alliances

A **strategic alliance** is where two or more organisations share resources and activities to pursue a strategy.[10] They vary from simple two-partner alliances co-producing a product to one with multiple partners providing complex products and solutions. By the turn of the century the top 500 global companies had an average of 60 alliances each.[11] This kind of joint development of new strategies has become increasingly popular. This is because organisations cannot always cope with increasingly complex environments or strategies (such as globalisation)[12] from internal resources and competences alone. They may need to obtain materials, skills, innovation, finance or access to markets but recognise that these may be as readily available through cooperation as through ownership. The choice of acquisition or alliance is therefore one that many organisations face, as Illustration 10.1 shows. However, about half of all alliances fail.[13]

Motives for alliances[14]

A frequent reason for alliances is to obtain resources that an organisation needs but does not itself possess. For example, banks need to gain access to the payment systems that allow credit cards to be used in retail outlets (for example, Visa or MasterCard) and to the automated teller machines (ATMs) to allow cash withdrawals. These resources do not, however, confer competitive advantage on members of the alliance; nor are they intended to so: they are threshold requirements for modern banking. Such arrangements are *infrastructure alliances* that

Illustration 10.1

How law firms are going global

Organisations may have to decide between the benefits and risks of acquisition or alliances.

Both major UK and US law firms are extending their operations globally. However, this has taken different forms. 'Leading U.S. law firms harvest the world's largest legal market at home and plough cautiously elsewhere, while many of the biggest British based firms have placed a huge bet on building extensive international networks and a global presence.' As yet, it is unclear which choices will work best in terms of the preferences of their multinational clients: whether they will 'prefer to be served by one stop shop multi-national law firms, or by cherry picking different legal practices in different countries'.

Most of the largest law firms by revenue are from the USA. But the biggest are the 'magic circle' London-based law firms. In the 1990s these firms, with their relatively limited home market,

decided to move beyond their informal relationships with firms in other countries and either put in place formal partnerships or full mergers or open their own offices. . . . Three quarters of the top 25 British based firms have at least one wholly owned office in China, up from one third in 2004.

By 2007 the results were impressive: 'The biggest four magic circle firms out performed even the trend of globally rising profitability last year.'

There were problems, however. One was the differences between the legal systems in different countries. In the face of this 'English lawyers and the law society, their professional body, are keen to promote English law as a jurisdiction of choice for international business' and 'Britain's government and legal profession have begun an openly aggressive effort to persuade other countries to remove restrictions on how it's lawyers can operate'.

US firms have tended to focus at home where they have the benefit of most of the world's largest multinationals – even if they are concerned that more and more of them are choosing to register outside the USA as a result of the Sarbanes–Oxley rules on financial disclosure.

Their approach is that they can 'keep their profitability high by working their home market, running offices in a few key foreign centres and building links with local firms in countries where they have no presence'. This cuts running costs and insulates US firms from the risk of overcommitment to potentially risky markets. Indeed this is an approach that London-based law firm Slaughter and May has also adopted successfully 'shunning international expansion in favour of establishing a network of "best friends" firms in economically significant countries'.

Supporters of this approach also point to survey evidence that has found that the international capability of law firms does not feature in the top 10 requirements by their clients. They also argue that markets outside Europe are much less profitable.

In addition to all this, there is evidence of different overall approaches to mergers and acquisitions between US and UK firms: 'Big British firms are on the prowl almost permanently – if mostly fruitlessly – for merger partners (in the U.S.) that will give them the bigger toehold they want.' Contrast that with the partner at one of the biggest US law firms who says of mergers: 'That's not our way. We have never merged, we have never acquired and we are never going to.'

Source: 'Reach versus risk', *Financial Times*, 14 December (2006), p. 15.

Questions

1 Explain the different rationales for acquisition or alliance building for law firms in terms of the reasons given in sections 10.2.2 and 10.2.3 of the chapter.

2 What are the risks of each approach?

involve the sharing or pooling of resources and mechanism of cooperation, but which are not seeking to gain competitive advantage.[15] Here, however, we are concerned with *strategic alliances* that do seek to gain such advantage.

Motives for such alliances are of three main types:

● The need for *critical mass*, which alliances can achieve by forming partnerships with either competitors or providers of complementary products. This can lead to cost reduction and improved customer offering.

● *Co-specialisation* – allowing each partner to concentrate on activities that best match its capabilities: for example, to enter new geographical markets where an organisation needs local knowledge and expertise in distribution, marketing and customer support. Similarly alliances with organisations in other parts of the value chain (for example, suppliers or distributors) are common.

● *Learning* from partners and developing competences that may be more widely exploited elsewhere. For example, first steps into e-business may be achieved with a partner that has expertise in website development. However, the longer-term intention might be to bring those activities in-house. Organisations may also enter alliances as a means of *experimentation* since it allows them to break out of a sole reliance on the exploitation of their own resources and capabilities. Indeed they may use alliances as a basis for developing strategic options different from those being developed in house organically[16] (see the discussion on real options in section 10.3.2).

Types of alliance

There are different types of strategic alliance. Some may be formalised inter-organisational relationships. At the other extreme, there are loose arrangements of cooperation and informal networking between organisations, with no shareholding or ownership involved:

● *Joint ventures* are relatively formalised alliances and may take different forms themselves. Here organisations remain independent but set up a newly created organisation jointly owned by the parents. Joint ventures are a favoured means of collaborative ventures in China, for example. Local firms provide labour and entry to markets; Western companies provide technology, management expertise and finance.

● *Consortia* may involve two or more organisations in a joint venture arrangement typically more focused on a particular venture or project. Examples include large civil engineering projects, or major aerospace undertakings, such as the European Airbus. They might also exist between public sector organisations where services (such as public transport) cross administrative boundaries.

● *Networks* are less formal arrangements where organisations gain mutual advantage by working in collaboration without relying on cross-ownership arrangements and formal contracts. Carlos Jarillo suggests that characteristic of such network arrangements are a reliance on coordination through mutual adaptation of working relationships, mutual trust (see below) and, typically, a 'hub organisation' that may have promoted the network and maintains a proactive attitude to it.[17] Such networked arrangements may exist between competitors in highly competitive industries where some form of sharing is none the less beneficial. For example, in the Formula One industry,[18] where state-of-the-art know-how tends to flow between firms.

Other alliance arrangements exist usually of a contractual nature and unlikely to involve ownership:

- *Franchising* involves the franchise holder undertaking specific activities such as manufacturing, distribution or selling, whilst the franchiser is responsible for the brand name, marketing and probably training. Perhaps the best-known examples are Coca-Cola and McDonald's.

- *Licensing* is common in science-based industries where, for example, the right to manufacture a patented product is granted for a fee.

- With *subcontracting*, a company chooses to subcontract particular services or part of a process: for example, increasingly in public services responsibility for waste removal, cleaning and IT services may be subcontracted (or 'out-sourced') to private companies.

Exhibit 10.3 shows three important factors that can influence types of alliance:

- *Speed of market change* will require strategic moves to be made quickly. So less formal and flexible network arrangements may be more appropriate than a joint venture, which could take too long to establish.

- *The management of resources and capabilities*. If a strategy requires separate, dedicated, resources then a joint venture will be appropriate. In contrast, if the strategic purpose and operations of the alliance can be supported by the current resources of the partners this favours a looser contractual relationship or network.

Exhibit 10.3 Types of strategic alliance

INFLUENCING FACTORS	FORM OF RELATIONSHIP		
	Loose (Market) • Networks • Opportunistic alliances	**Contractual** • Licensing • Franchising • Subcontracting	**Ownership** • Consortia • Joint ventures
The Market • Speed of market change	Fast change	⟶	Slow change
Resources • Asset management	Managed separately by each partner	⟶	Managed together
• Partner's assets	Draws on 'parent's' assets	⟶	Dedicated assets for alliance
• Risk of losing assets to partner	High risk	⟶	Low risk
Expectations • Spreading financial risk	Maintains risk	⟶	Dilutes risk
• Political climate	Unfavourable climate	⟶	Favourable climate

● The *expectations and motives* of alliance partners will play a part. For example, if alliance partners see the alliance as a means of spreading their financial risk, this will favour more formal arrangements such as joint ventures.

Ingredients of successful alliances[19]

Although organisations may establish an alliance for one or more of the reasons outlined above, the benefits of alliances tend to evolve. It may, for example, be established to address a particularly complex technological opportunity, but yield new and unexpected opportunities. The success of alliances is therefore dependent on how they are managed and the way in which the partners foster the evolving nature of the partnership. Given this, success factors fall under three broad headings:

● *Strategic purpose*. A clear strategic purpose is likely to be helpful at the outset of an alliance. However, alliance members will, quite likely, have differing if compatible reasons for being part of the alliance. As an alliance develops it is likely that their expectations and perceived benefits will evolve – not least because they are often built to cope with dynamic or complex environments. If the expectations of alliance members start to diverge the alliance may eventually disintegrate. If the evolving expectations remain compatible or converge then it is likely the alliance will continue. It is also possible that convergence could give rise to more formalised ownership arrangements such as a merger of the alliance partners.[20]

● *Alliance expectations and benefits*. Similarly, given that the expectations of alliance partners may vary, managing those expectations as the alliance evolves is vital. At the most basic level, expectations cannot be met without a willingness to exchange information, including performance information that would not normally be shared between organisations. However, beyond this, given that many alliances are about learning and experimentation, the acceptance of these as benefits of themselves by alliance members may be important. If one of the partners does not buy into such benefits and attempts to impose a 'static' strategy on the alliance this may well lead to problems.[21] There are also indications that alliances that develop knowledge-based products and services (as distinct from physical product) tend to bind alliance partners more closely together since they are likely to be mutually dependent on shared tacit knowledge in the development of such products and services.[22]

● *Managing alliance relationships*. Senior management support for an alliance is important since alliances require a wider range of relationships to be built and sustained. This can create cultural and political hurdles that senior managers must help to overcome. In turn strong interpersonal relationships to achieve *compatibility at the operational level* is also needed. In cross-country partnerships this includes the need to transcend national cultural differences. Consistently, however, research shows that *trust* is the most important ingredient of success and a major reason for failure if it is absent.[23] But trust has two separate elements. Trust can be *competence based* in the sense that each partner is confident that the other has the resources and competences to fulfil its part in the alliance. Trust is also *character based* and concerns whether partners trust each other's motives and are compatible in terms of attitudes to integrity, openness, discretion and consistency of behaviour. Overall the message is that it is the quality of the relationships in an alliance that are of prime importance; indeed to a greater extent than the physical resources in an alliance.[24]

A consistent message that recurs, then, is that whilst it may be very helpful to ensure that an alliance has clear *goals, governance and organisational arrangements* concerning activities that cross or connect the partners, it is also important to keep the alliance *flexible*, such that it can *evolve and change*.

10.3 STRATEGY EVALUATION

Part II of the book has now introduced an array of strategic choices as summarised in Exhibit 10.4. This section of the chapter turns to how these might be evaluated by asking why some strategies might succeed better than others. It does this in terms of three key success criteria which can be used to assess the viability of strategic options:

● *Suitability* is concerned with whether a strategy addresses the key issues relating to the *strategic position* of the organisation (as discussed in Part I).

Exhibit 10.4   Strategic options

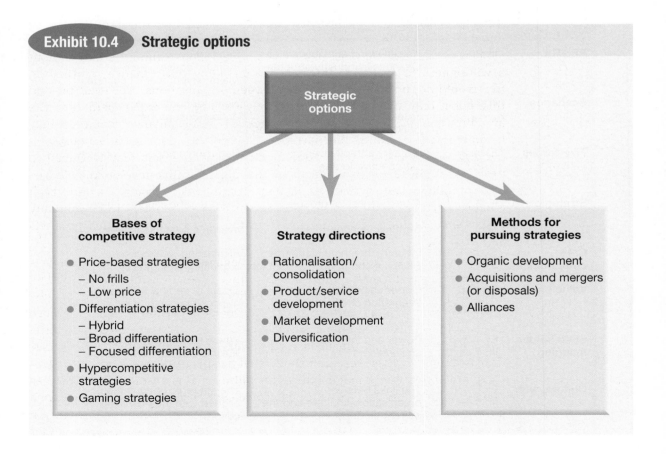

Strategic options

Bases of competitive strategy
● Price-based strategies
  – No frills
  – Low price
● Differentiation strategies
  – Hybrid
  – Broad differentiation
  – Focused differentiation
● Hypercompetitive strategies
● Gaming strategies

Strategy directions
● Rationalisation/ consolidation
● Product/service development
● Market development
● Diversification

Methods for pursuing strategies
● Organic development
● Acquisitions and mergers (or disposals)
● Alliances

● *Acceptability* is concerned with the expected *performance outcomes* (such as the *return* or *risk*) of a strategy and the extent to which these meet the *expectations* of stakeholders.

● *Feasibility* is concerned with whether a strategy could work in practice; therefore, whether it has the capabilities to deliver a strategy.

10.3.1 Suitability

Suitability is concerned with whether a strategy addresses the key issues relating to the strategic position of the organisation

Suitability is concerned with whether a strategy addresses the key issues that have been identified in understanding the strategic position of the organisation. It is therefore concerned with the overall *rationale* of a strategy. In particular this requires an assessment of the extent to which any strategic option would fit with key drivers and expected changes in the *environment*, exploit *strategic capabilities* and be appropriate in the context of *stakeholder expectations and influence* and *cultural influences*. So the concepts and frameworks already discussed in Chapters 2 to 4 can be especially helpful in understanding suitability. Some examples are shown in Exhibit 10.5. However, there is an important point to bear in mind. It is very likely that a great many issues will have been raised if the

---

Exhibit 10.5 **Suitability of strategic options in relation to strategic position**

Concept	Exhibit Illustrations	Helps with understanding	Suitable strategies must address (examples)
PESTEL	III. 2.1	Key environmental drivers Changes in industry structure	Industry cycles Industry convergence Major environmental changes
Scenarios	III. 2.2	Extent of uncertainty/risk Extent to which strategic options are mutually exclusive	Need for contingency plans or 'low-cost probes'
Five-forces	Ex. 2.2 III. 2.3	Industry attractiveness Competitive forces	Reducing competitive intensity Development of barriers to new entrants
Strategic groups	III. 2.5	Attractiveness of groups Mobility barriers Strategic spaces	Need to reposition to a more attractive group or to an available strategic space
Core competences	Exs 3.1, 3.6 3.8	Industry threshold standards Bases of competitive advantage	Eliminating weaknesses Exploiting strengths
Value chain	Exs 3.6, 3.7	Opportunities for vertical integration or outsourcing	Extent of vertical integration or possible outsourcing
Stakeholder mapping	Ex. 4.5 III. 4.4a, b	Power and interest of stakeholders	Which strategic options are likely to address the interests of which stakeholders
Cultural web	Ex. 5.7 III. 5.4	The links between organisational culture and the current strategy	The strategic options most aligned with the prevailing culture

concepts and tools discussed in Part I have been employed. It is therefore important that the really important issues are identified from amongst all these. Indeed a major skill of a strategist is to be able to discern these *key strategic issues*. Evaluating the suitability of a strategy is extremely difficult unless these have been identified.

The discussions about strategic directions in the preceding chapters in Part II and on strategy methods in section 10.2 above were concerned not only with understanding what directions and methods were 'available' to organisations, but also with providing reasons why each might be considered. So the examples in those sections also illustrate why strategies might be regarded as *suitable*. Exhibit 10.6 summarises these points from earlier sections and provides

Exhibit 10.6   Some examples of suitability

Strategic option	Why this option might be suitable in terms of:		
	Environment	Capability	Stakeholder and/or cultural influences
Directions			
Consolidation	Withdraw from declining markets Maintain market share	Build on strengths through continued investment and innovation	Stick to what the organisation and its stakeholders know best
Market penetration	Gain market share for advantage	Exploit superior resources and competences	
Product development	Exploit knowledge of customer needs	Exploit R&D	Minimise the risk of alienating stakeholders with interests in preserving the status quo or making counter cultural decisions
Market development	Current markets saturated New opportunities for: geographical spread, entering new segments or new uses	Exploit current products and capabilities	
Diversification	Current markets saturated or declining	Exploit core competences in new arenas	Meet the needs of stakeholders with expectations for more rapid growth But potential for culture clash
Methods			
Organic development	Partners or acquisitions not available or not suitable	Building on own capabilities Learning and competence development	Cultural/political ease
Merger/acquisition	Speed Supply/demand P/E ratios	Acquire competences Scale economies	Returns: growth or share value But potential for culture clash
Joint development	Speed Industry norm Required for market entry	Complementary competences Learning from partners	Dilutes risk Fashionable

examples of reasons why strategy directions or methods might be regarded as suitable.

Evaluation tools for assessing suitability

There are a number of tools that can be used to assess the suitability of strategic options. These include:

- *The TOWS matrix*.[25] This was introduced in the Introduction to Part II of the book (see Exhibit II.ii) as a method of identifying strategic options on the basis of a SWOT analysis. However, it can also be used to provide an assessment of suitability by 'justifying' options in terms of the extent to which they address the strengths, weaknesses, threats and opportunities relating to the strategic position of the organisation.

- The *relative suitability* of options that matters. There may be options 'available' to an organisation that are more or less suitable than others. There are useful frameworks that can assist in understanding better the relative suitability of different strategic options:

- *Ranking strategic options*. Options are assessed against key factors relating to the strategic position of the organisation and a score (or ranking) established for each option. See Illustration 10.2 for a detailed example

- *Decision trees* can also be used to assess strategic options against a list of key factors. Here options are 'eliminated' and preferred options emerge by progressively introducing requirements which must be met (such as growth, investment or diversity). See Illustration 10.3.

- *Scenarios*. Here strategic options are considered against a range of possible future situations. This is especially useful where a high degree of uncertainty exists (as discussed in section 2.2.2 – see Illustration 2.2). Suitable options are ones that are sensible in terms of the various scenarios so several need to be 'kept open', or perhaps in the form of contingency plans. Or it could be that an option being considered is found to be suitable in different scenarios.

10.3.2 Acceptability

Acceptability is concerned with the expected performance outcomes of a strategy and the extent to which these meet the expectations of stakeholders

Acceptability is concerned with the expected performance outcomes of a strategy. These can be of three types: *return*, *risk* and *stakeholder reactions*. Exhibit 10.7 summarises some frameworks that can be useful in understanding the acceptability of strategies, together with some of their limitations. It is probably sensible to use more than one approach in assessing the acceptability of a strategy.

Return

Returns are the benefits which stakeholders are expected to receive from a strategy

Returns are the benefits which stakeholders are expected to receive from a strategy. Measures of return are a common way of assessing proposed new ventures or major projects by managers within businesses. So an assessment of financial and non-financial returns likely to accrue from specific strategic options could be a key criterion of acceptability of a strategy – at least to some stakeholders.

Illustration 10.2

Ranking options: Churchill Pottery

Ranking can usefully build on a SWOT analysis by comparing strategic options against the key strategic factors from the SWOT analysis.

In the 1990s Churchill Pottery, based in Stoke-on-Trent, UK, was one of the subjects of a BBC series entitled *Troubleshooter*, where the management teams of a number of companies were invited to discuss their organisation's strategic development with Sir John Harvey-Jones (ex-Chairman of ICI). Like many traditional manufacturing companies at the time, Churchill found itself under increasing pressure from cheaper imports in its traditional markets, and was considering whether to move 'up market' by launching a new range aimed at the design-conscious end of the market. The ranking exercise below was done by a group of participants on a management programme having seen the Churchill Pottery video.

The results of the ranking are interesting. First, they highlight the need to do *something*. Second, the radical departures in strategy – such as moves into retailing or diversification – are regarded as unsuitable. They do not address the problems of the core business, do not fit the capabilities of Churchill and would not fit culturally. This leaves related developments as the front runners – as might be expected in a traditional manufacturing firm like Churchill. The choice boils down to significant investments in cost reduction to support an essentially 'commodity' approach to the market (options 2 and 5) or an 'added value' attack on the growing 'up-market' segments. The company chose the latter and with some success – presumably helped by its wide television exposure through the *Troubleshooter* series.

Source: Based on the BBC *Troubleshooter* series.

Questions

1　Has option 4 been ranked above the others because:
   (a) It has the most ticks?
   (b) It has the least crosses?
   (c) A combination of these?
   (d) Other reasons?
   Justify your answer.

2　List the main strengths and limitations of ranking analysis.

Ranking exercise

Strategic options	Key strategic factors						Ranking
	Family ownership	Investment funds	Low-price imports	Lack of marketing/ design skills	Automation low	Consumer taste (design)	
1. Do nothing	✓	?	✗	?	✗	✗	C
2. Consolidate in current segments (investment/automation)	✓	✗	✓	?	✓	?	B
3. Expand overseas sales (Europe)	✗	✗	✗	✗	✗	?	C
4. Launch 'up-market' range	✓	✓	✓	✗	?	✓	A
5. Expand 'own-label' production (to hotel/ catering industry)	✓	✓	✓	?	✗	?	B
6. Open retail outlets	✗	✗	?	✗	?	?	C
7. Diversify	✗	✗	?	?	?	✓	C

✓ = favourable; ✗ = unfavourable; ? = uncertain or irrelevant.
A = most suitable; B = possible; C = unsuitable.

Illustration 10.3

A strategic decision tree for a law firm

Decision trees evaluate future options by progressively eliminating others as additional criteria are introduced to the evaluation.

A law firm had most of its work related to house conveyancing where profits had been significantly squeezed. Therefore, it wanted to consider a range of new strategies for the future. Using a strategic decision tree it was able to eliminate certain options by identifying a few key criteria which future developments would incorporate, such as growth, investment (in premises, IT systems or acquisitions), and diversification (for example, into matrimonial law which, in turn, often brings house conveyancing work as families 'reshape').

Analysis of the decision tree reveals that if the partners of the firm wish growth to be an important aspect of future strategies, options 1–4 are ranked more highly than options 5–8. At the second step, the need for low-investment strategies would rank options 3 and 4 above 1 and 2, and so on.

The partners were aware that this technique has limitations in that the choice at each branch of the tree can tend to be simplistic. Answering 'yes' or 'no' to diversification does not allow for the wide variety of alternatives which might exist between these two extremes, for example *adapting the 'style' of the conveyancing service* (this could be an important variant of options 6 or 8). Nevertheless, as a starting point for evaluation, the decision tree provides a useful framework.

Questions

1 Try reversing the sequence of the three parameters (to diversification, investment and growth) and redraw the decision tree. Do the same eight options still emerge?

2 Add a fourth parameter to the decision tree. This new parameter is development by *internal methods* or by *acquisition*. List your 16 options in the right-hand column.

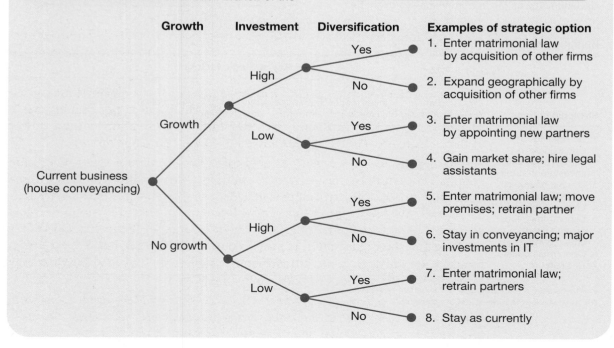

| Growth | Investment | Diversification | Examples of strategic option |

1. Enter matrimonial law by acquisition of other firms
2. Expand geographically by acquisition of other firms
3. Enter matrimonial law by appointing new partners
4. Gain market share; hire legal assistants
5. Enter matrimonial law; move premises; retrain partner
6. Stay in conveyancing; major investments in IT
7. Enter matrimonial law; retrain partners
8. Stay as currently

Exhibit 10.7	Some criteria for assessing the acceptability of strategic options

Criteria	Used to understand	Examples	Limitations
Return			
Profitability	Financial return on investments in major projects	Return on capital Payback period Discounted cash flow (DCF)	Apply to discrete projects Only tangible costs/ benefits
Cost–benefit	Wider costs/benefits (including intangibles)	Major infrastructure projects	Difficulties of quantification
Real options	Sequence of decisions	Real options analysis	Quantification
Shareholder value analysis (SVA)	Impact of new strategies on shareholder value	Mergers/acquisitions Assessment of new ventures	Technical detail often difficult
Risk			
Financial ratio projections	Robustness of strategy	Break-even analysis Impact on gearing and liquidity	
Sensitivity analysis	Test assumptions/robustness	'What if?' analysis	Tests factors separately
Stakeholder reactions	Political dimension of strategy	Stakeholder mapping	Largely qualitative

There are different approaches to understanding return. This section looks briefly at three of these. It is important to remember that there are no absolute standards as to what constitutes good or poor return. It will differ between industries, countries and between different stakeholders. Views also differ as to which measures give the best assessment of return, as will be seen below.

Financial analysis[26]

Traditional financial analyses are used extensively in assessing the acceptability of different strategic options. Three commonly used approaches are (see Exhibit 10.8):

- Forecasting the *return on capital employed (ROCE)* for a specific time period after a new strategy is in place. For example, an ROCE of 15 per cent by year 3. This is shown in Exhibit 10.8(a). The ROCE is a measure of the earning power of the resources used in implementing a particular strategic option.

- Estimating the *payback period*. This is the length of time it takes before the cumulative cash flows for a strategic option become positive. In the example in Exhibit 10.8(b) the payback period is $3\frac{1}{2}$ years. Payback is used as a financial criterion when a significant capital injection is needed to support a new venture. The judgement that has to be made is whether the payback period is too long and the organisation is prepared to wait. Payback periods vary from industry to industry. Public infrastructure projects such as road building may be assessed over payback periods exceeding 50 years.

- Calculating *discounted cash flows (DCFs)*. This is a widely used investment appraisal technique. It is an extension of payback analysis. Once the cash inflows and outflows have been assessed for each of the years of a strategic

Exhibit 10.8 **Assessing profitability**

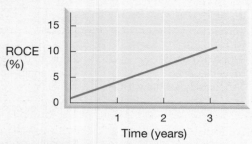

(a) Return on capital employed

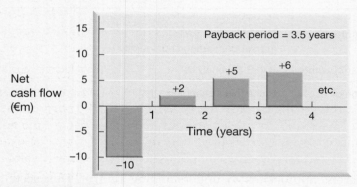

(b) Payback period

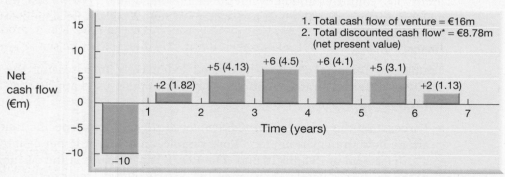

* Using a discounting rate of 10%.
Figures in brackets are discounted by 10% annually.

(c) Discounted cash flow (DCF)

option (see Exhibit 10.8(c)) they are discounted. This reflects the fact that cash generated early is more valuable than cash generated later. In the example, the cost of capital or discounting rate of 10 per cent (after tax) reflects the rate of return required by those providing finance for the venture – shareholders and/or lenders. The 10 per cent cost of capital *includes* an allowance for inflation of about 3–4 per cent. It is referred to as the 'money cost of capital'.

By contrast, the 'real' cost of capital is 6–7 per cent *after* allowing for or *excluding* inflation.

The projected after-tax cash flow of £2m at the start of year 2 is equivalent to receiving £1.82m now (£2m multiplied by 0.91 or 1/1.10); £1.82m is called the *present value* of receiving £2m at the end of year 1/start of year 2 at a cost of capital of 10 per cent. Similarly, the after-tax cash flow of £5m at the end of year 2/start of year 3 has a present value of £4.13m (£5m multiplied by 1/1.10 squared). The *net present value (NPV)* of the venture, as a whole, is calculated by adding up all the annual present values over the venture's anticipated life. In the example, this is 7 years. The NPV works out at £8.78m. Allowing for the time value of money, the £8.78m is the extra cash flow that a strategic option will generate during its entire lifetime. It is important to remember that DCF analysis is only as good as the assumptions on which it is based. For example, if sales volume increases of 3 per cent a year turn out to be unrealistic then the NPV calculation will be too optimistic. The *internal rate of return (IRR)* is that rate of return producing a zero NPV. For example, in Exhibit 10.8(c) a cost of capital or discounting rate of about 32 per cent would produce a zero NPV.

There are also other considerations to be borne in mind when carrying out a financial analysis. In particular, do not be misguided by the apparent thoroughness of the various approaches. Most were developed for the purposes of investment appraisal. Therefore, they focus on discrete projects where the additional cash inflows and outflows can be predicted relatively easily. For example, a retailer opening a new store. Such assumptions are not necessarily valid in many strategic contexts. The precise way in which a strategy develops (and the associated cash flow consequences) tend to become clearer as the implementation proceeds rather than at the outset. Nor are strategic developments and the relevant cash flows easy to isolate from ongoing business activities.

Additionally, financial appraisals tend to focus on the direct *tangible* costs and benefits rather than the strategy more broadly. For example, a new product may look unprofitable as a single project. But it may make strategic sense by enhancing the market acceptability of other products in a company's portfolio. In an attempt to overcome some of these shortcomings, other approaches have been developed in an assessment of return.

Cost–benefit[27]

In many situations, profit is too narrow an interpretation of return, particularly where intangible benefits are an important consideration. This is usually so for major public infrastructure projects, for example, such as the siting of an airport or a sewer construction project, as shown in Illustration 10.4, or in organisations with long-term programmes of innovation (for example, pharmaceuticals or aerospace). The *cost–benefit* concept suggests that a money value can be put on all the costs and benefits of a strategy, including tangible and intangible returns to people and organisations other than the one 'sponsoring' the project or strategy.

Although in practice monetary valuation is often difficult, it can be done and, despite the difficulties, cost–benefit analysis is useful provided its limitations are understood. Its major benefit is in forcing managers to be explicit about the various factors that influence strategic choice. So, even if people disagree on

Illustration 10.4

Sewerage construction project

Investment in items of infrastructure – such as sewers – often requires a careful consideration of the wider costs and benefits of the project.

The UK's privatised water companies were monopolies supplying water and disposing of sewage. One of their priorities was investment in new sewerage systems to meet the increasing standards required by law. They frequently used cost–benefit analysis to assess projects. The figures below are from an actual analysis.

Cost/Benefit	£m	£m
Benefits		
Multiplier/linkage benefits		0.9
Flood prevention		2.5
Reduced traffic disruption		7.2
Amenity benefits		4.6
Investment benefit		23.6
Encouragement of visitors		4.0
Total benefits		42.8
Costs		
Construction cost	18.2	
Less: Unskilled labour cost	(4.7)	
Opportunity cost of construction	(13.5)	
Present value of net benefits (NPV)	29.3	
Real internal rate of return (IRR)	15%	

Note: Figures discounted at a *real* discount rate of 5% over 40 years.

Benefits

Benefits result mainly from reduced use of rivers as overflow sewers. There are also economic benefits resulting from construction. The following benefits are quantified in the table:

- The multiplier benefit to the local economy of increased spending by those employed on the project.

- The linkage benefit to the local economy of purchases from local firms, including the multiplier effect of such spending.

- Reduced risk of flooding from overflows or old sewers collapsing – flood probabilities can be quantified using historical records, and the cost of flood damage by detailed assessment of the property vulnerable to damage.

- Reduced traffic disruption from flooding and road closures for repairs to old sewers – statistics on the costs of delays to users, traffic flows on roads affected and past closure frequency can be used to quantify savings.

- Increased amenity value of rivers (for example, for boating and fishing) can be measured by surveys asking visitors what the value is to them or by looking at the effect on demand of charges imposed elsewhere.

- Increased rental values and take-up of space can be measured by consultation with developers and observed effects elsewhere.

- Increased visitor numbers to riverside facilities resulting from reduced pollution.

Construction cost

This is net of the cost of unskilled labour. Use of unskilled labour is not a burden on the economy, and its cost must be deducted to arrive at opportunity cost.

Net benefits

Once the difficult task of quantifying costs and benefits is complete, standard discounting techniques can be used to calculate net present value and internal rate of return, and analysis can then proceed as for conventional projects.

Source: G. Owen, formerly of Sheffield Business School.

Questions

1 What do you feel about the appropriateness of the listed benefits?

2 How easy or difficult is it to assign money values to these benefits?

the value that should be assigned to particular costs or benefits, at least they can argue their case on common ground and compare the merits of the various arguments.

Real options[28]

The previous approaches assume a reasonable degree of clarity about the outcomes of a strategic option. There are, however, situations where precise costs and benefits of strategies only become clear as implementation proceeds. In these circumstances the traditional DCF approach discussed above will tend to undervalue a 'project' because it does not take into account the value of options that could be opened up by the particular project. Luehrman[29] argues that this extra value arises because

> executing a strategy almost always involves making a sequence of decisions. Some actions are taken immediately, while others are deliberately deferred. . . . The strategy sets the framework within which future decisions will be made, but . . . leaves space for learning from ongoing developments and for discretion to act based on what is learnt.

So the flexibility can be used to expand, extend, contract, defer or close down a project. So a strategy should be seen as a *series* of 'real' options (that is, choices of direction at particular points in time as the strategy takes shape). There are three main benefits of this approach:

● *Bringing strategic and financial evaluation closer together*. Arguably it provides a clearer understanding of both strategic and financial return and risk of a strategy by examining each step (option) separately. For example, the value that will accrue from investing in a technology that creates a 'platform' from which several products or process improvements may spring is not clear at the outset. However, as the project develops learning occurs as to which directions the development should progress or even if it should be terminated early.

● *Valuing emerging options*. In taking such an approach, it then allows a value to be placed on options that might be opened up by an initial strategic decision.

● *Coping with uncertainty*. Advocates of a real options approach argue it overcomes, or provides an alternative to, profitability analyses that require managers to make assumptions about future conditions that may well not be realistic. As such it can be linked into ways of analysing uncertain futures such as scenario analysis (see section 2.2.2). For example, applying a real options approach, as in Exhibit 10.9, shows that high levels of volatility should have two effects. First, to defer decisions as far as possible because (second) the passage of time will clarify expected returns – even to the extent that apparently unfavourable strategies might prove viable at a later date (the category 'maybe invest later' in the exhibit).

Shareholder value analysis[30]

There has been a growing interest in shareholder value analysis (SVA) and 'managing for value' (MFV) (see section 13.4.1). In the main this is because of the growing concern about the need for company directors to pay more attention to providing value for shareholders (see sections 4.2.1 and 4.2.2). A major limitation of traditional accounting measures such as operating profit (profit

Real options framework

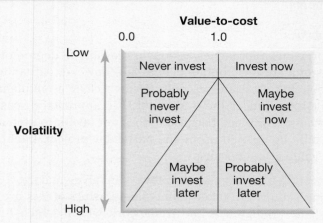

before interest and taxation) is that they ignore the cost of capital. Misleading signals are given, therefore, about whether value is created or destroyed. In turn, this can give misleading views about the acceptability of specific strategic options. In this context there have been increasing questions raised about the extent to which the waves of mergers and acquisitions generate shareholder value (see section 10.2.2).

There are two measures of shareholder value. One is external to the company. The other is internal:

● The external measure is referred to as *total shareholder return (TSR)*. In any financial year, it is equal to the increase in the price of a share plus the dividends received per share actually received in that year. This is then divided by the share price at the start of the financial year. A simple example is given as Exhibit 10.10(a).

● The internal measure is called *economic profit* or *economic value added (EVA)*. If the operating profit (after tax) is greater than the cost of the capital required to produce that profit then EVA is positive. An example is given as Exhibit 10.10(b). Evidence suggests that a positive EVA will lead to positive share price performance. For this reason, EVA is a good internal proxy for shareholder return.

Used effectively, both EVA and the subsequent improvement in TSR performance align the interests of owners and managers. Although shareholder value analysis has helped address the shortcomings of traditional financial analyses, it cannot remove all the inherent uncertainties surrounding strategic choices. It has also been criticised for overemphasising short-term returns.[31] Nevertheless, the idea of valuing a strategy may serve to give greater realism and clarity to otherwise vague claims for strategic benefits. Perhaps the major lesson, however, is that firms that most successfully employ SVA do so within an over-

Exhibit 10.10   **Measures of shareholder value**

(a) Total shareholder return (TSR)

Given
- Opening share price, £1
- Closing share price, £1.20
- Dividend per share received during financial year, 5p

Then
- Increase in share price (20p) plus dividend received (5p) = 25p

TSR is
- 25p divided by opening share price of £1 expressed as a percentage = 25%

(b) Economic profit or economic value added (EVA)

Given
- Operating profit after tax, £10m
- Capital employed, £100m
- Cost of capital, 8%

Then
- The capital or financing charge required to produce the operating profit after tax is the capital employed of £100m × the cost of capital of 8% = (£8m)

EVA is
- Operating profit (after tax) of £10m less the cost of the capital, £8m = £2m

all approach to managing for value throughout the firm rather than merely as a technique for purposes of analysis.[32] SVA is discussed further in section 13.4.1.

Risk

Another aspect of acceptability is the *risk* that an organisation faces in pursuing a strategy. **Risk** concerns the probability and consequences of the failure of a strategy. This risk can be high for organisations with major long-term programmes of innovation, where high levels of uncertainty exist about key issues in the environment or where there are high levels of public concern about new developments – such as genetically modified Crops.[33] Formal risk assessments are often incorporated into business plans as well as the investment appraisals of major projects. Importantly, risks other than ones with immediate financial impact are included such as 'risk to corporate or brand image' or 'risk of missing an opportunity'. Developing a good understanding of an organisation's strategic position (Part I of this book) is at the core of good risk assessment. However, some of the concepts below can also be used to establish the detail within a risk assessment.

Risk concerns the probability and consequences of the failure of a strategy

Financial ratios[34]

The projection of how key financial ratios might change if a strategy were adopted can provide useful insights into risk. At the broadest level, an assessment of how the *capital structure* of the company would change is a good general measure of risk. For example, strategies that would require an increase in long-term debt will increase the gearing (or 'leverage') of the company and, hence, its financial risk.

A consideration of the likely impact on an organisation's *liquidity* (cash position) is also important in assessing risk. For example, a small retailer eager to grow quickly may be tempted to fund the required shop-fitting costs by delaying payments to suppliers and increasing bank overdraft. The extent to which this increased risk of reduced liquidity threatens survival depends on the likelihood of either creditors or the bank demanding payments from the company – an issue that clearly requires judgement.

Sensitivity analysis[35]

Sometimes referred to as *'what if'* analysis, sensitivity analysis allows each of the important assumptions underlying a particular strategy to be questioned and challenged. In particular, it tests how sensitive the predicted performance or

Illustration 10.5

Sensitivity analysis

Sensitivity analysis is a useful technique for assessing the extent to which the success of a preferred strategy is dependent on the key assumptions which underlie that strategy.

In 2007 the Dunsmore Chemical Company was a single-product company trading in a mature and relatively stable market. It was intended to use this established situation as a 'cash cow' to generate funds for a new venture with a related product. Estimates had shown that the company would need to generate some £4m (≈ €6m) cash (at 2007 values) between 2008 and 2013 for this new venture to be possible.

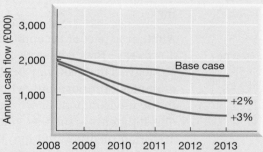

(a) Sensitivity of cash flow to changes in real production costs

Although the expected performance of the company was for a cash flow of £9.5m over that period (the *base case*), management were concerned to assess the likely impact of three key factors:

- Possible increases in *production costs* (labour, overheads and materials), which might be as much as 3 per cent p.a. in real terms.
- *Capacity-fill*, which might be reduced by as much as 25 per cent due to ageing plant and uncertain labour relations.
- *Price levels*, which might be affected by the threatened entry of a new major competitor. This

could squeeze prices by as much as 3 per cent p.a. in real terms.

It was decided to use sensitivity analysis to assess the possible impact of each of these factors on the company's ability to generate £4m. The results are shown in the graphs.

From this analysis, management concluded that their target of £4m would be achieved with *capacity utilisation* as low as 60 per cent, which was certainly

outcome (for example, profit) is to each of these assumptions. For example, the key assumptions underlying a strategy might be that market demand will grow by 5 per cent per annum, or that the company will stay strike-free, or that certain expensive machines will operate at 90 per cent loading. Sensitivity analysis asks what would be the effect on performance (in this case, profitability) of variations on these assumptions. For example, if market demand grew at only 1 per cent, or by as much as 10 per cent, would either of these extremes alter the decision to pursue that strategy? This can help develop a clearer picture of the risks of making particular strategic decisions and the degree of confidence managers might have in a given decision. Illustration 10.5 shows how sensitivity analysis can be used.

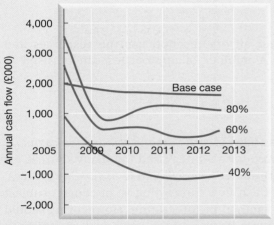

(b) Sensitivity of cash flow to changes in plant utilisation

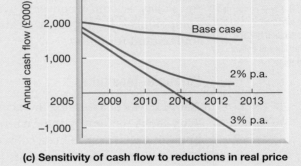

(c) Sensitivity of cash flow to reductions in real price

going to be achieved. Increased *production costs* of 3 per cent p.a. would still allow the company to achieve the £4m target over the period. In contrast, *price* squeezes of 3 per cent p.a. would result in a shortfall of £2m.

Management concluded from this analysis that the key factor which should affect their thinking on this matter was the likely impact of new competition and the extent to which they could protect price levels if such competition emerged. They therefore developed an aggressive marketing strategy to deter potential entrants.

Source: The calculations for the sensitivity test utilise computer programs employed in the Doman case study by Peter Jones (Sheffield Business School).

Question

What should the company do if its marketing campaigns fail to stop real price erosion:

(a) Push to achieve more sales volume/capacity fill?

(b) Reduce unit costs of production?

(c) Something else?

Stakeholder reactions

The discussion of *stakeholder mapping* in Chapter 4 (section 4.4.1) showed how it can be used to understand the political context and consider the political agenda in an organisation. However, stakeholder mapping can also be useful in understanding the likely reactions of stakeholders to new strategies, the ability to manage these reactions, and hence the acceptability of a strategy.

There are many situations where stakeholder reactions could be crucial. For example:

- *Financial restructuring*. A new strategy might require the financial restructuring of a business, for example an issue of new shares, which could be unacceptable to powerful groups of shareholders, since it dilutes their voting power.

- *An acquisition or merger* could be unacceptable to unions, government or some customers.

- A *new business model* might cut out channels (such as retailers), hence running the risk of a backlash, which could jeopardise the success of the strategy.

- *Outsourcing* is likely to result in job losses and could be opposed by unions.

10.3.3 Feasibility

> Feasibility is concerned with whether an organisation has the capabilities to deliver a strategy

Feasibility is concerned with whether an organisation has the resources and competences to deliver a strategy. A number of approaches can be used to understand feasibility.

Financial feasibility

A useful way of assessing financial feasibility is *cash flow analysis and forecasting*.[36] This seeks to identify the cash required for a strategy and the likely sources for obtaining that cash. These sources are sometimes referred to as *funding sources*. They are shown in Illustration 10.6. Cash flow forecasting is, of course, subject to the difficulties and errors of any method of forecasting. However, it should highlight whether a proposed strategy is likely to be feasible in terms of both cash generation and the availability and timing of new funding requirements. This issue of funding strategic developments is an important interface between business and financial strategies and is discussed more fully in section 13.4.2.

Financial feasibility can also be assessed through break-even analysis.[37] This is a simple and widely used approach for judging the feasibility of meeting financial targets such as the ROCE and operating profit. In addition, it provides an assessment of the risks of various strategies particularly where different strategic options require markedly different cost structures.

Resource deployment

Although financial feasibility is important, a wider understanding of feasibility can be achieved by identifying the resources and competences needed for a specific strategy. Indeed the effectiveness of a strategy is likely to be dependent on whether such capabilities are available or can be developed or obtained. For example, geographical expansion in a market might be critically dependent on

Illustration 10.6

Cash flow analysis: a worked example

A cash flow analysis can be used to assess whether a proposed strategy is likely to be feasible in financial terms. It does so, first, by forecasting the cash that would be needed for the strategy and, second, identifying the likely sources of funding that cash requirement.

Kentex plc (a UK electrical goods retailer) was considering pursuing a strategy of expansion. In the immediate future, this would involve opening new stores in the Irish Republic. To evaluate the financial feasibility of this proposal and to establish the cash requirements and funding sources, the company decided to undertake a cash flow analysis.

Stage 1: Estimation of cash inflows

The opening of the new stores was estimated to increase revenues or sales from the current £30m (≈ €45m) to £31.65m over the following three years. In turn, this was expected to generate operating cash flows of £15m during the same time period.

Stage 2: Estimation of cash outflows

There would be a number of costs associated with the new stores. First, Kentex decided to purchase rather than lease property so capital investment would be required to purchase and then fit out the stores. The forecast was £13.25m. Also there would be additional working capital costs to cover extra stock etc. Forecasts for these were based on a simple pro rata estimate. On the previous sales level of £30m, a working capital level of £10m was required, so pro rata, additional sales of £1.65m would require an additional £0.55m in working capital. Tax liability and expected dividend payments were estimated at £1.2m and £0.5m respectively.

Stage 3: Estimation and funding of the cash shortfall

The calculations show a cash shortfall of £0.5m. The issue facing Kentex was how to finance this deficit. It could raise cash through the issue of new share capital but the company decided to seek a short-term loan of £0.65m. In turn, this would incur interest payments of £0.15m over the three-year period assuming simple interest at 7.5 per cent annually. Therefore, the net amount of cash raised would be £0.5m.

The overall cash flow analysis is summarised below:

Cash inflows	Cash outflows
Operating cash flows, £15m	Capital expenditure, £13.25m
	Further working capital, £0.55m
	Tax, £1.2m
	Subtotal of cash outflows, £15m
	Dividends, £0.5m
	Total cash outflows, £15.5m

Note: The shortfall between the cash inflows and the cash outflows is £500,000.

Questions

1 Which parts of this assessment are likely to have the greatest probability of error?

2 What are the implications of your answer to question 1 on how the analysis should be presented to the decision makers?

3 How might this uncertainty influence the management of the implementation phase if approval is given?

marketing and distribution expertise, together with the availability of cash to fund increased stocks. Or a strategy of developing new products to sell to current customers may depend on engineering skills, the capability of machinery and the company's reputation for quality in new products.

A resource deployment assessment can be used to judge (i) the extent to which an organisation's current capabilities need to change to reach or maintain the *threshold* requirements for a strategy; and (ii) if and how unique resources and/or core competences can be developed to sustain competitive advantage. The issue is whether these changes are *feasible* in terms of scale, quality of resource or time-scale of change.

10.3.4 Evaluation criteria: three qualifications

There are three qualifications that need to be made to this discussion of evaluation criteria:

- *Conflicting conclusions and management judgement*. Conflicting conclusions can arise from the application of the criteria of suitability, acceptability and feasibility. A proposed strategy might look eminently suitable but not be acceptable to major stakeholders, for example. It is therefore important to remember that the criteria discussed here are useful in helping think through strategic options but are not a replacement for management judgement. Managers faced with a strategy they see as suitable, but which key stakeholders object to, have to rely on their own judgement on the best course of action, but this should be better informed through the analysis and evaluation they have undertaken.

- There needs to be *consistency between the different elements of a strategy*. It should be clear from the chapters in Part II that there are several elements of a strategy, so an important question is whether the component parts work together as a 'package'. So *competitive strategy* (such as low price or differentiation), strategy *direction* (such as product development or diversification) and strategic *method* (internal, acquisition or alliances) need to be consistent. They need to be considered as a whole and make sense as a whole. There are dangers that they do not. For example, suppose an organisation wishes to develop a strategy built on its inherent competences developed over many years as a basis of differentiation that competitors will find difficult to imitate. It may believe it can do this by using those competences to develop new products or services within a market it knows well. If so there may be dangers in looking to develop those new products through acquiring other businesses which might have very different competences and capabilities that are incompatible with the strengths of the business.

- *The implementation and development of strategies* may throw up issues that might make organisations reconsider whether particular strategic options are, in fact, feasible or uncover factors that change views on the suitability or acceptability of a strategy. This may lead to a reshaping, or even abandonment, of strategic options. It therefore needs to be recognised that, in practice, strategy evaluation may take place through implementation, or at least partial implementation. This is another reason why experimentation and low-cost probes may make sense. The next section of the book (Chapters 11 to 15) will look at the practical issues of translating strategy into action. More generally, care should also be taken in assuming that the careful and systematic evaluation of strategy is necessarily the norm in organisations. Chapters 11 and 15 explain more how strategies actually develop in organisations and what managers actually do in managing strategic issues.

SUMMARY

- There are three broad *methods* of strategy development:
  - *Organic development* has the major benefit of building on the strategic capabilities of an organisation. However, it can result in overstretched resources and is likely to require the development of those capabilities.
  - *Mergers and acquisitions* may have advantages of speed and the ability to acquire competences not already held 'in-house'. However, the track record of acquisitions is not good. (See the key debate in Illustration 10.7).
  - Successful *alliances* appear to be those where partners have a positive attitude to the evolving nature of the alliance and where there is trust between partners.

- The success or failure of strategies will be related to three main *success criteria*:
  - *Suitability* is concerned with whether a strategy addresses the strategic position of the organisation as discussed in Part II of this book. It is about the *rationale* of a strategy.
  - The *acceptability* of a strategy relates to three issues: the expected *return* from a strategy, the level of *risk* and the likely *reaction of stakeholders*.
  - *Feasibility* is concerned with whether an organisation has or can obtain the capabilities to deliver a strategy.

- Since a strategy comprises the broad *competitive strategy*, the *strategy direction* and the *method* of pursuing them, these three elements need to be consistent with each other.

Illustration 10.7   **key debate**

Merger madness?

Mergers and acquisitions involve huge sums of money, but how wisely is it being spent?

This chapter has introduced the importance of mergers and acquisitions as a method of development, but also pointed to some challenges. There have been some spectacular failures. When in 2001 media company Time Warner merged with Internet company AOL, Time Warner shares were worth a total of $90bn (£50bn; €78bn). Just under three years later, Time Warner investors' holdings in the merged company were worth only $36bn, a loss of over $50bn (in the same period, media companies' valuations had fallen on average 16 per cent).

Harvard Business School professor Michael Porter has been a prominent sceptic of mergers and acquisitions, noting that half of all acquired companies are sold off again within a few years.[1] The figure shows the aggregate dollar return (that is, the change in stock price associated with the acquisition announcement) of acquiring companies in the USA between 1996 and 2001.[2] In 2000, acquiring firms' shareholders lost, in all, more than $150bn. The authors of this study calculate that in the whole period of 1991 to 2001, acquiring firms' shareholders lost more than $7 for every $100 spent on acquisitions.

One interpretation of these large losses is that mergers and acquisitions represent a reckless waste of money by managers who are careless of investors' interests. Indeed there is evidence that CEOs suffer the consequences, over half being replaced within a relatively short time period.[3] It might be appropriate therefore to make mergers and acquisitions more difficult by legislating to help target companies resist or refuse hostile bids. If the law restricted hostile bids, wasteful acquisitions could be cut.

There are drawbacks to restricting mergers and acquisitions, however.[4] Even if acquiring companies often fail to make money for their shareholders, they can improve the profitability of the system as a whole in at least two ways:

- The threat of being taken over if they do not satisfy their shareholders helps keep managers focused on performance. The financial press report just such threats regularly.

- Mergers and acquisitions can be an effective way of restructuring stagnant firms and industries. The absence of hostile takeovers in Japan is often blamed for the slow restructuring of Japanese industry since the early 1990s.

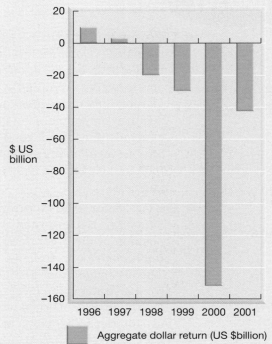

$ US billion

Aggregate dollar return (US $billion)

Sources:
1. M. Porter, 'From competitive advantage to corporate strategy', *Harvard Business Review*, May–June (1987), pp. 43–60.
2. S.B. Moeller, F.P. Schlingemann and R.M. Stulz, 'Wealth destruction on a massive scale? A study of acquiring firm returns in the recent merger wave', *Journal of Finance*, vol. 60, no. 2 (2005), pp. 757–782.
3. K.M. Lehn and M. Zhao, 'CEO turnover after acquisitions: are bad bidders fired?', *Journal of Finance*, vol. LXI, no. 4 (2006), pp. 1759–1810.
4. 'Hostile bids are back again: who should rejoice?', *The Economist*, 21 February (2004).

Questions

1 For a recent large merger or acquisition, track the share prices of the companies involved (using www.bigcharts.com, for instance), for several weeks both before and after the announcement. What do the share price movements suggest about the merits of the deal?

2 Identify a hostile takeover threat from press reports. What action did the company's managemnt do to resist the takeover?

Work assignments

*✱ Denotes more advanced work assignments.   * Refers to a case study in the Text and Cases edition.*

10.1   Write a short (one-paragraph) statement to a chief executive who has asked you to advise whether or not the company should develop through mergers/acquisitions. Write a similar statement to the chief executive of a hospital who is considering possible mergers with other hospitals.

10.2 ✱ 'Strategic alliances will not survive in the long term if they are simply seen as ways of "blocking gaps" in an organisation's resource base or competences.' Discuss this in relation to alliances which have recently featured in the business or public sector press.

10.3   Undertake a ranking analysis of the choices available to Numico*, Wimm Bill Dann* or an organisation of your choice similar to that shown in Illustration 10.2.

10.4 ✱ Bearing in mind your answers to the questions in Illustration 10.4:

(a) What is your feeling about the overall 'validity' of cost–benefit analysis?
(b) How could it be improved?

10.5   Using the criteria of suitability, acceptability and feasibility, undertake an evaluation of the strategic options that might exist for Tesco, Wimm Bill Dann* or an organisation of your choice.

10.6 ✱ Using examples from your answer to previous assignments, make a critical appraisal of the statement that 'Strategic choice is, in the end, a highly subjective matter. It is dangerous to believe that, in reality, analytical techniques will ever change this situation.' Refer to the Commentary at the end of Part II of the book.

Integrative assignment

10.7 ✱ Explain how the success criteria (see section 10.3) might differ between public and private sector organisations. Show how this relates to both the nature of the business environment (Chapter 2) and the expectations of stakeholders (Chapter 4).

An extensive range of additional materials, including audio summaries, weblinks to organisations featured in the text, definitions of key concepts and self-assessment questions, can be found on the *Exploring Corporate Strategy* Companion Website at **www.pearsoned.co.uk/ecs**

Recommended key readings

- A comprehensive book on mergers and acquisitions is P. Gaughan, *Mergers, Acquisitions and Corporate Restructurings*, 4th edition, Wiley, 2007.

- A useful book on strategic alliances is J. Child, *Cooperative strategy*, Oxford University Press, 2005.

- A companion book which explores techniques of strategy evaluation more fully is V. Ambrosini with G. Johnson and K. Scholes (eds), *Exploring Techniques of Analysis and Evaluation in Strategic Management*, Prentice Hall, 1998.

- Readers can gain useful insights into P/E ratios, financial motives and financial performance of acquisitions and associated financial material on acceptability and feasibility in G. Arnold, *Corporate Financial Management*, 3rd edition, FT/Prentice Hall, 2005.

References

1. See J.F. Mognetti, *Organic Growth: Cost-Effective Business Expansion from Within*, Wiley, 2002.
2. There are many publications on mergers and acquisitions: see P. Gaughan, *Mergers, Acquisitions and Corporate Restructurings*, 4th edition, Wiley, 2007. A practical guide for managers is T. Galpin and M. Herndon, *The Complete Guide to Mergers and Acquisitions*, Jossey-Bass, 2000; also D.M. DePamphilis, *Mergers, acquisitions, and other restructuring activities: An integrated approach to process, tools, cases, and solutions*, Elsevier, 2005. For a briefer discussion see R. Schoenberg, 'Mergers and acquisitions: motives, value creation and implementation', *The Oxford Handbook of Corporate Strategy*, Oxford University Press, 2003, chapter 21.
3. G. Muller-Stewens, 'Catching the right wave', *European Business Forum*, issue 4, Winter (2000), pp. 6–7, illustrates the major waves of mergers over the last 100 years.
4. Data from 'All aboard the M&A express', *Sunday Times Business Focus*, 31 December (2006), p. 5.
5. For example, see M. Zey and T. Swenson, 'The transformation and survival of Fortune 500 industrial corporations through mergers and acquisitions, 1981–1995', *Sociological Quarterly*, vol. 42, no. 3 (2001), pp. 461–486; and A. Gregory, 'An examination of the long term performance of UK acquiring firms', *Journal of Business Finance and Accounting*, vol. 24 (1997), pp. 971–1002.
6. There is a great deal published on the reasons for the success and failure of acquisitions. For example, a good discussion of the practicalities can be found in D. Carey, 'Making mergers succeed', *Harvard Business Review*, vol. 78, no. 3 (2000), pp. 145–154. Also see B. Savill and P. Wright, 'Success factors in acquisitions', *European Business Forum*, issue 4, Winter (2000), pp. 29–33; R. Larsson and S. Finkelstein, 'Integrating strategic, organisational and human resource perspectives on mergers and acquisitions: a case study survey of synergy realisation', *Organisation Science*, vol. 10, no. 1 (1999), pp. 1–26; J. Birkinshaw, H. Bresman and L. Hakanson, 'Managing the post-acquisition integration process: how the human integration and task integration processes interact to foster value creation', *Journal of Management Studies*, vol. 37, no. 3 (2000), pp. 395–425; R. Schoenberg, 'The influence of cultural compatibility within cross-border acquisitions: a review', *Advances in Mergers and Acquisitions*, vol. 1 (2000), pp. 43–59; D. Fubini, C. Price and M. Zollo: *Mergers: Leadership, Performance and Corporate Health*, Palgrave, 2007; P. Haspeslagh, 'Maintaining momentum in mergers', *European Business Forum*, issue 4, Winter (2000), pp. 53–56; D.N. Angwin *Implementing successful post-acquisition integration*, FT/Prentice Hall, 2000.
7. J. Bower, 'Not all M&As are alike', *Harvard Business Review*, vol. 79, no. 3 (2001), pp. 93–101.
8. See J. Child, D. Faulkner and R. Pitkethly, *The Management of International Acquisitions*, Oxford University Press, 2003.
9. Useful publications on strategic alliances are Y. Doz and G. Hamel, *Alliance Advantage: The art of creating value through partnering*, Harvard Business School Press, 1998; J. Child, *Cooperative strategy*, Oxford University Press, 2005; and R. ul-Haq, *Alliances and Co-Evolution: Insights from the Banking Sector*, Palgrave, 2005. For a detailed theoretical insight see Y. Doz, D. Faulkner and M. de Rond, *Co-operative Strategies: Economic, Business and Organisational Issues*, Oxford University Press, 2001. A practical guide for managers is E. Rigsbee, *Developing Strategic Alliances*, Crisp, 2000.
10. More specifically ul-Haq (reference 9) defines 'The "strategic alliance" is typically one which displays high levels of resource commitment, is of long or open ended duration and whose purposes represent a core activity of a strategic nature for one or more of the partners' (p. 6).
11. D. Ernst and T. Halevy, 'Give alliances their due', *McKinsey Quarterly*, no. 3 (2002), pp. 4–5.
12. For a consideration of the special issues of global strategic alliances see G. Yip, *Total Global Strategy II*, 2nd edition, FT/Prentice Hall, 2003, pp. 82–85.
13. But see J. Dyer, P. Kale and H. Singh, 'How to make strategic alliances work', *Sloan Management Review*, vol. 42, no. 4 (2001), pp. 37–43.
14. See Doz and Hamel, reference 9, chapters 1 and 2; Ernst and Halevy, reference 11; ul-Haq, reference 9; M. Koza and A. Lewin, 'The co-evolution of strategic alliances', *Organisation Science*, vol. 9, no. 3 (1998), pp. 255–264.
15. This definition is based on ul-Haq's explanation of infrastructure alliances (see reference 9, pp. 6–9).
16. For a fuller discussion of the role of alliances and joint ventures in exploration versus exploitation see

W. Kummerle, 'Home base and knowledge management in international ventures', *Journal of Business Venturing*, vol. 17, no. 2 (2002), pp. 99–122.

17. These characteristics are based on J. Carlos Jarillo, 'On strategic networks', *Strategic Management Journal*, vol. 9, no. 1 (1988), pp. 31–41.

18. See M. Jenkins, K. Pasternak and R. West, *Performance at the Limit: Business Lessons from Formula 1 Motor Racing*, Cambridge University Press, 2005.

19. See Doz and Hamel, reference 9; T. Pietras and C. Stormer, 'Making strategic alliances work', *Business and Economic Review*, vol. 47, no. 4 (2001), pp. 9–12; N. Kaplan and J. Hurd, 'Realising the promise of partnerships', *Journal of Business Strategy*, vol. 23, no. 3 (2002), pp. 38–42; A. Parkhe, 'Interfirm diversity in global alliances', *Business Horizons*, vol. 44, no. 6 (2001), pp. 2–4; ul-Haq, reference 9; I. Hipkin and P. Naude, 'Developing effective alliance partnerships', *Long Range Planning*, vol. 39 (2006), pp. 51–69; A. Inkpen, 'Learning and knowledge acquisition through international strategic alliances', *Academy of Management Executive*, vol. 2, no. 4 (1998), pp. 69–80; and 'Learning through joint ventures: a framework of knowledge acquisition, *Journal of Management Studies*, vol. 37, no. 7 (2000), pp. 1019–1045.

20. ul-Haq (reference 9) identifies different patterns of co-evolution he refers to as parallel, divergent and convergent.

21. See Hipkin and Naude, reference 19.

22. Inkpen in the *Academy of Management Executive*, reference 19.

23. See L. Abrams, R. Cross, E. Lesser and D. Levin, 'Nurturing interpersonal trust in knowledge sharing networks', *Academy of Management Executive*, vol. 17, no. 4 (2003), pp. 64–77. Also C. Huxham and S. Vangen, *Managing to Collaborate: The Theory and Practice of Collaborative Advantage*, Routledge, 2005; or their article, S. Vangen, and C. Huxham, 'Nurturing collaborative relations: building trust in interorganizational relationships', *Journal of Applied Behavioural Science*, vol. 39, no. 1 (2003), pp. 5–31.

24. This point is made by D. Lavie, 'The competitive advantage of interconnected firms: an extension of the resource based view', *Academy of Management Review*, vol. 21, no. 3 (2006), pp. 638–658.

25. H. Weihrich, 'The TOWS matrix – a tool for situational analysis', *Long Range Planning*, April (1982), pp. 54–66.

26. Most standard finance and accounting texts explain in more detail the financial analyses summarised here. For example, see G. Arnold, *Corporate Financial Management*, 3rd edition, FT/Prentice Hall, 2005, chapter 4.

27. A 'classic' explanation of cost–benefit analysis is J.L. King, 'Cost-benefit analysis for decision-making', *Journal of Systems Management*, vol. 31, no. 5 (1980), pp. 24–39. A detailed example in the water industry can be found in

N. Poew, 'Water companies' service performance and environmental trade-off', *Journal of Environmental Planning and Management*, vol. 45, no. 3 (2002), pp. 363–379.

28. Real options evaluation can get lost in the mathematics so readers wishing to gain more detail of how real options analysis works can consult one of the following: T. Copeland, 'The real options approach to capital allocation', *Strategic Finance*, vol. 83, no. 4 (2001), pp. 33–37; T. Copeland, T. Koller and J. Murrin, *Valuation: Measuring and managing the value of companies*, 3rd edition, Wiley, 2000; T. Copeland and V. Antikarov, *Real Options: A practitioner's guide*, Texere Publishing, 2001; L. Trigeorgis, *Managerial Flexibility and Strategy in Resource Allocation*, MIT Press, 2002; P. Boer, *The Real Options Solution: Finding total value in a high risk world*, Wiley, 2002. Also see M.M. Kayali. 'Real options as a tool for making strategic investment decisions' *Journal of the American Academy of Business*, vol. 8, no. 1 (2006), pp. 282–287.

29. T. Luehrman, 'Strategy as a portfolio of real options', *Harvard Business Review*, vol. 76, no. 5 (1998), pp. 89–99.

30. The main proponent of shareholder value analysis is A. Rappaport, *Creating Shareholder Value: The new standard for business performance*, 2nd edition, Free Press, 1998. See also R. Mill's chapter, 'Understanding and using shareholder value analysis', in V. Ambrosini with G. Johnson and K. Scholes (eds), *Exploring Techniques of Analysis and Evaluation in Strategic Management*, Prentice Hall, 1998.

31. A. Kennedy, *The End of Shareholder Value*, Perseus Publishing, 2000.

32. This point is made clear in a research study reported by P. Haspeslagh, T. Noda and F. Boulos, 'Its not just about the numbers', *Harvard Business Review*, July–August (2001), pp. 65–73.

33. L. Levidow and S. Carr, 'UK: precautionary commercialisation', *Journal of Risk Research*, vol. 3, no. 3 (2000), pp. 261–270.

34. See C. Walsh, *Master the Management Metrics That Drive and Control Your Business*, 4th rev. edition, FT/Prentice Hall, 2005.

35. A brief description of sensitivity analysis can be found in Arnold, reference 26, p. 218. For those readers interested in the details of sensitivity analysis see A. Satelli, K. Chan and M. Scott (eds), *Sensitivity Analysis*, Wiley, 2000. For a more detailed exploration of different approaches see A.G. Hadigheh and T. Terlaky. 'Sensitivity analysis in linear optimization: invariant support set intervals' *European Journal of Operational Research*, vol. 169, no. 3 (2006), pp. 1158–1176.

36. See Arnold, reference 26, chapter 3, p. 108.

37. Break-even analysis is covered in most standard accountancy texts. See, for example, Arnold, reference 26, p. 223.

Tesco conquers the world?

In 2006 Tesco, the UK's most successful grocery retailer (with about 30 per cent market share), again reported a record-breaking year. Over the previous four years it had almost doubled group sales (excluding VAT) and profits to £39bn (≈ €57bn) and £2.28bn respectively. The 'group statistics' painted a picture of what this growth meant on the ground: the number of stores had tripled to 2,672 and employee numbers had grown by about 60 per cent to 273,000. Significantly, sales to the rest of Europe had grown from 9 to 13 per cent of group sales and Asian sales were 11 per cent of group sales (up from 6 per cent in 2002). The company had also extended its product range significantly since 2002 – moving into non-food sectors and retailing services.

Not surprisingly the 2006 annual report was very 'upbeat' and the Chairman, David Reid, summarised the company achievements and prospects for the future:

UK Our sales performance in the UK core business has been strong, as we have invested in all parts of the customer offer.

International has delivered good growth in like-for-like sales, profits and returns. Our largest ever new store development programme delivered 5.4 million sq ft [500,000 m²] of sales area, with a further 6.6 million sq ft planned in the current year.

Non-food has again made strong progress, with UK sales up by over 13%, against the background of cautious consumer spending. Our established areas such as health and beauty (up 10%) have done well and newer departments such as consumer electronics (34% growth) and clothing (16% growth) have performed particularly strongly.

Retailing services have also had a good year with tesco.com delivering record results, Tesco Personal Finance (TPF) performing well in a challenging personal finance sector and good growth in telecoms.

The report went on to explain in more detail exactly how each of the main parts of the business were changing and developing:

Photo: Richard Jones/Rex Features

Core UK business

'giving customers what they want 24/7'

Ranges

Because everyone is welcome at Tesco, we appreciate that our customers have different tastes and requirements. We work hard to give our customers a broad assortment of leading brands, a really good range of Tesco products – from *Finest* to *Value* lines – and lots of new ideas for feeding the family.

Instead of offering a standard product range everywhere, we have put a lot of effort into tailoring our offer for local customers. For example, our new *Extra* store in Slough, Berkshire features over 900 speciality Asian products, from new vegetarian and Halal ready meals to extensive ranges of bulk-pack rice, and even Bollywood DVDs.

Formats

Our store formats are a way of meeting the different needs of our customers wherever they live and however they want to shop – in large stores, in small stores or on-line. Tesco *Express* brings great food and low prices into the heart of neighbourhoods. . . . *Metro* offers the convenience of Tesco in town and city centres where people live and work. At Tesco *Superstores*, customers can find everything they need for their weekly shopping and at our *Extra* stores customers can not only find our full range of food and convenience lines, but also a comprehensive range of non-foods. *Homeplus* non-food only store was trialed in 2005.

NON-FOOD

'offering great quality, range, price and service'

More and more people are choosing to buy not just their household essentials but also bigger ticket items at Tesco, from clothing to TVs and fridges and from sports equipment to toys. They appreciate the convenience of being able to do all their shopping under one roof in our Extra stores.

We will be sourcing products that are common in all countries (UK, Ireland and Central Europe) together as a group. Each country will retain the responsibility of identifying the local needs of their customers and sourcing those products from the appropriate suppliers within their respected country.

RETAILING SERVICES

'making on-line shopping simple'

Tesco.com is the most successful on-line grocery shopping service in the world. What is remarkable about our on-line business is the diversity of customers using it, from busy urban families to people in rural communities. It has also allowed many house-bound people to shop properly for the first time.

DVDs to your door 60,000 customers have now signed up to our DVDs to rent service, giving them access to the 30,000 titles that are available through our on-line DVD service.

Energy We have enabled tens of thousands of customers to save money on their gas and electricity bills (by comparing prices of different suppliers). This service is fully comprehensive, fully independent and fully impartial.

Getting healthy on-line E–diets help customers to tailor their eating plans to what's right for them, taking into account lifestyles, food preferences and health recommendations.

'financial services that are simple'

Tesco Personal Finance now offers 21 financial products and services from loans and savings accounts to credit cards and insurance. We are Britain's third largest on-line car insurer with over 1.4 million active car insurance policies.

We are continually trying to improve our offer for customers and now offer the opportunity to purchase travel money in-store, by providing kiosks in seven stores. We have also made the purchase of premium bonds much more convenient for customers [through] the partnership with National Savings & Investments (NS&I).

Tesco Mobile is a virtual network formed as a joint venture with [the mobile network operator] O2.

International

With the exception of Ireland (91 stores) the company's international expansion had been in Eastern Europe (272 stores) and Asia (450 stores). The company planned to enter the US market in 2007 with a completely new local format for the American consumer modelled on *Express*. What was most interesting was the way that each development reflected local market conditions rather than working to a standard entry model. Some of the details from the 2006 annual report are shown in the box.

Where next from here?

Despite this rosy picture not everyone was convinced that Tesco was yet a major world player. The obvious comparison was with the world's biggest retailer, the US company Wal-Mart, whose turnover of US$312 (≈ €250bn) was more than four times that of Tesco. Although Wal-Mart's US sales were flattening out it had a presence in some 70 countries with 2,285 stores outside the USA – this was almost three times Tesco's international 'footprint'. Importantly Wal-Mart won the race to enter India in the autumn of 2006 leaving Tesco with difficulties in finding a suitable local partner – crucial in that market.

Market research with UK consumers also highlighted issues for the company to think about. In particular, although Tesco had attracted a broad range of customers across demographics and age groups, there was evidence that the market was fragmenting. Tesco customers' loyalty seemed to be declining and in an analysis of people's favourite brands by age,[1] Tesco and other high street retailers did well among the over 55s, but did not feature at all in the top 10 brands of 16 to 24 year olds.

But the Tesco Chief Executive, Sir Terry Leahy, was clear about the Tesco 'formula' for success:

Tesco is about making the shopping experience better for customers and we've built our success and our growth by listening to them.

Note

1. Milward Brown research reported by Carlos Grande, *Financial Times*, 19 December (2006).

Source: Tesco Annual Report 2006 at www.tesco.com/InvestorRelations.

Tesco's international stores in 2006

China (39 stores)
We have begun to accelerate our expansion programme beyond the Yangtse delta and have teams working to develop our network in Beijing, Shenzhen and Guangzhou. We have also invested in capability, bringing Tesco systems and know-how into the business, focusing particularly on improving store design, the supply chain and store replenishment.

Japan (111 stores)
In Japan, we operate discount convenience supermarkets, typically 3,000 sq ft in size. We opened our first trial *Express* store in April 2006.

Malaysia (13 stores)
We are trialling our *Express* format in Malaysia with three stores, situated mainly in the area around Kuala Lumpur. We also opened our first *Value* store, a 3,000 sq m store in Banting. By offering a tailored hypermarket range in a smaller store which is cheaper to build, we have been able to bring a modern retail offer to a community which would not have been able to sustain a larger hypermarket.

South Korea (62 stores)
We opened eight new hypermarkets in South Korea this year, including three compact hypers. We have further adapted our *Express* model in South Korea, enabling us to focus on the key products which customers want to be able to buy, close to where they live and work.

Taiwan (6 stores)
[We have agreed an] asset swap deal with Carrefour . . . [which] will enable us to exit from Taiwan with minimal financial impact, allowing us to focus on investment in Central Europe and our other Asian businesses.

Thailand (219 stores)
[Through] the launch of our *Talad* format we have tailored our offer to customers who are used to shopping in local markets. We now have ten of these stores, which carry between 4,500 and 7,500 product lines in around 10,000 sq ft of selling space.

Czech Republic (35 stores)
We have accelerated our new store development programme, adding 20% to our sales area during the year, with eight new compact hypermarkets. (Also) we opened the Group's first 1,000 sq m, or '1K' store . . . [which] enables us to bring the Tesco offer to smaller towns, carrying a locally-tailored range of around 2,700 products.

Hungary (87 stores)
Customers are facing a more challenging economic and retail environment in Hungary, which has held back our growth but we have still made solid progress. Our customers have benefited from lower prices in store and from the roll-out of petrol stations, making it significantly cheaper to fill-up.

Poland (105 stores)
Customers love the convenience of our small format stores which bring many of the advantages of our larger hypermarkets closer to where they live and work.

Republic of Ireland (91 stores)
We continue to invest in bringing prices down for our Irish customers. . . . We are also focusing on extending our product ranges. With *Finest* growing in popularity, we have increased the number of lines in areas such as cheese, ready meals and wine.

Slovakia (37 stores)
In line with our other Central European businesses, Tesco Slovakia has introduced a price promise on 50 everyday items, guaranteeing that we won't be beaten by any local competitor. Our new store programme is now supported by the growth of our compact hypermarket format.

Turkey (8 stores)
In Turkey, Kipa delivered a very strong performance. . . . We successfully launched the *Kipa Value* brand in Turkey, with over 400 products so far and we plan to extend this in the coming year.

Questions

1 Using Exhibit 7.2 in Chapter 7 identify the strategic directions that Tesco had followed from its origins as a UK-based grocery retailer.

2 Identify the strategic directions 'available' to the company in the future and assess the relative suitability of each of these options by ranking them (using Illustration 10.2 as an example).

3 For each of the top four development directions in your ranking compare the relative merits of organic development, acquisition or strategic alliance.

4 Complete your evaluation of the options that now appear most suitable by applying the criteria of acceptability and feasibility (see sections 10.3.2 and 10.3.3 respectively).

In Part II of the book the central issue posed is how strategic choices are to be made. The chapters have offered a range of such strategic choices, evidence as to why some seem more effective than others and criteria by which managers may make judgements about them. But this raises two linked questions on which the four lenses provide differing insights:

1 How do managers actually make such choices?

2 How should managers conceive of strategic choice?

Note that:

● There is no suggestion here that one of these lenses is better than another, but they do provide different insights into the problems faced and the ways managers cope with the challenge.

● If you have *not* read the Commentary following Chapter 1 that explains the four lenses, you should now do so.

Design lens

Strategic choice can be made logically and objectively on the basis of linear, analytic, evaluative procedures driven by top managers or other managers working with them. This involves:

● Establishing clear objectives developed to reflect stakeholder expectations and used as a basis for evaluating options.

● Making argued cases for explicit options on the basis of a clear understanding of the strategic position of the organisation arrived at analytically.

● Evaluating options by systematically examining their relative merits in terms of (i) their suitability in addressing the strategic issues the organisation faces; (ii) the feasibility of implementing the strategic option and (iii) the acceptability of the strategic option to key stakeholders.

Demonstrating this approach to strategic choice is likely to be important in gaining the support for a strategy from some key stakeholders (for example, financial institutions).

Experience lens

There are different but complementary explanations here:

● Strategy develops incrementally based on past strategy, past experience and the culture of the organisation within a political context. So choices made are heavily influenced by that past experience.

● Indeed management experience and 'strong cultures' may militate against innovation or constrain innovation to that which is generated in terms of or acceptable to prevailing experience/culture.

● An extension of this is the 'garbage can' view: managers have ready-made solutions on the basis of their experience and search for opportunities and circumstances to put them into effect.

● Strategies emerge on the basis of experimentation and learning by doing (a logical incremental view).

● Political processes of bargaining and negotiation play an important role in strategic choice.

● The strategies of successful organisations are mimicked by others.

In any of the above, analytic tools may be used as a way of checking *why* a strategy might be worth following or developing. Or they might be used to post-rationalise strategic choice.

Commentary on Part II

Strategic choices

Ideas lens

The emphasis here is on the emergence of 'strategic ideas' as the source of strategic options from within the organisation rather than planned strategy from the top. This is characterised by:

- New ideas arising in conditions of instability or 'adaptive tension' rather than through formal plans.
- Experimentation and trial and error behaviour.
- The importance of imperfect copying: even if successful strategies are imitated, they will not be imitated perfectly; differences emerge.
- Internal and external networking giving rise to new ideas.

Managers cannot determine what these new ideas will be but can create a context where they will emerge and discern patterns of ideas as this happens.

Managers are one, but not the only, mechanism by which such selection takes place.

New ideas also get selected for by:

- attracting 'positive feedback' from inside and outside the organisation (for example, from managers in the organisation or customers in the market);
- winning out in competition with other new ideas;
- becoming embedded in organisational routines.

Discourse lens

What appears to be choice is very constrained by the discourse of which managers are part. For example:

- Managers are likely to be comparing their organisation to competitors delimited by who is talked about as being competitors rather than by objective analysis.
- Similarly, strategic options that prevail are likely to be those that fit within a 'dominant narrative' that prevails inside an organisation or in its organisational field/industry.
- There are also 'strategy fads' – commonly followed strategies popular at particular times.

In whatever way a strategy is selected, it is likely to be explained such as to:

- Achieve legitimacy of the strategy in the eyes of stakeholders; for example, 'achieving competitive advantage' is the sort of term likely to be used by managers to justify a strategy, whether or not there is substance to the claim.
- Signal its inevitable success.
- Or post-rationalise its failure.

Understanding *how* a strategy is talked about therefore needs to be seen as an important influence on what strategies are likely to be favoured in an organisation and which are not.

Part III

STRATEGY IN ACTION

This part explains:

→ How strategies develop in organisations; in particular, the organisational processes that may give rise to intended strategies or to emergent strategies.

→ The way in which organisational structures, organisational processes and the management of relationships is important in organising for strategic success.

→ The relationship between an organisation's overall strategy and the resource areas of people, information, finance and technology.

→ How strategic change might be managed and the importance of understanding organisational context and in managing change.

→ Who strategists are and what they do in practice.

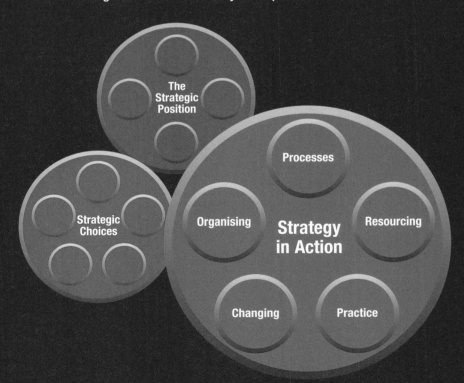

Introduction to Part III

This part of the book is concerned with strategy in action. A continuing question throughout the book has been the extent to which strategy can be seen as pre-planned intent. If this is so, strategy in action is to do with strategy implementation, with 'making strategy happen'. An alternative view is that strategy is more emergent, for example on the basis of people's experience or as a result of responses to competitive action. Here there is less of a separation of intent and action; it is more about 'strategy happening'. In fact elements of both explanations are likely to be evident in organisations and this part of the book reflects that.

The next chapter quite specifically addresses the distinction between intended and emergent explanations of strategy development by reviewing the different organisational processes that can explain how strategies come about. The two chapters that follow consider the relationship between a strategy and how an organisation functions: first in terms of how people work with each other within formal structures but also more informal relationships; second in relation to key resource areas of an organisation. The development of a new strategy may also require significant change for the organisation. Strategic change and how this might be managed is the theme of the penultimate chapter. This part of the book then concludes by discussing what strategists themselves actually do. In so doing it asks the question of the extent to which and how much of what is discussed in this book is put into practice.

More specifically the issues raised in the chapters are as follows:

- Chapter 11 explains how strategies develop in organisations. How intended strategy may be the outcome of the *vision, leadership or 'command'* of individuals, formal *planning systems* or the deliberate *imposition* of strategy from outside an organisation. Also how strategies might emerge out of more routine and day-by-day activities in organisations and through *cultural processes* and *political processes*. The chapter also discusses the implications of these various processes for strategists.

- Chapter 12 is about *organising* for success. It looks at three separate strands of organising: organisational structures, organisational processes and the management of relationships. The chapter highlights the importance for successful organising of making these various elements work together in order to create mutually reinforcing configurations that are well matched to an organisation's strategies.

- Chapter 13 looks at the relationship between an organisation's overall strategy and the strategies in four key resource areas: people, information, finance and technology. The two questions that are pursued through the chapter are these.

First, whether the separate resource areas of an organisation are capable of enabling strategies to be executed successfully. The second question is whether the strategies of an organisation are being shaped to capitalise on the expertise in a particular resource area.

● Chapter 14 examines more specifically how *strategic change* might be managed. This is done in several ways. First, by acknowledging that the challenge of managing change is not the same in all organisations; that the change context matters. Second, by looking at different approaches to managing change, including the roles that managers and others play and the styles of managing change they adopt. Next, by considering a range of levers that might be employed to help manage change in organisations, including changes to organisational routines, the management of political and symbolic processes and other specific tactics for managing change. Finally the chapter considers how these various levers might be employed in different change contexts.

● Chapter 15 examines three issues in the practice of strategy: first, who to include in strategy-making activities, often not just top management but middle managers, consultants and planners as well; second, the kinds of activities that strategists do, from selling strategic issues to communicating chosen strategies; third, the kinds of methodologies that strategists use, including away-days, projects, hypothesis testing and business plans.

Strategy Development Processes

LEARNING OUTCOMES

After reading this chapter you should be able to:

→ Explain what is meant by *intended* and *emergent* strategy development.

→ Identify intended processes of strategy development in organisations including the role of vision and command, strategic planning systems and externally imposed strategy.

→ Identify emergent processes of strategy development such as logical incrementalism, resource allocation processes, cultural processes and organisational politics.

→ Consider how different processes of strategy development may be found in *multiple forms* and in *different contexts*.

→ Explain some of the issues managers face in strategy development including the challenge of managing *intended and realised strategy*, the development of the *learning organisation* and strategy development in *uncertain and complex conditions*.

Photo: DIOMEDIA/Alamy Images

11.1 INTRODUCTION

www.pearsoned.co.uk/ecs

KEY CONCEPT

Intended and emergent strategy

Parts I and II of the book have so far addressed how strategists might understand the strategic position of their organisation and what strategic choices are available. This chapter raises the question as to *how strategies develop*; or more specifically, what overall processes give rise to organisational strategies. (Chapter 15 then examines in more detail which people get involved in these processes, what they actually do in developing strategies, and the methodologies they use.)

There are two broad explanations of strategy development, though they are not mutually exclusive. The first is associated with the idea of *intended strategy*: that strategies come about as a result of careful deliberation typically associated with top management decisions. This is also linked to the idea that strategies are developed using the sorts of concepts and tools so far discussed in the book. This is sometimes known as the *rational/analytic view* of strategy development, or, as in the commentary sections of this book, *a design view* of strategy development. The second view is that of *emergent strategy*: that strategies do not develop on the basis of some grand plan but tend to emerge in organisations over time. The discussion in the commentaries of the experience, ideas and discourse lenses relates to this explanation. This chapter is organised around these two views:

Exhibit 11.1 **Strategy development processes**

Processes of intended strategy development
- Strategic vision, leadership and command
- Strategic planning
- Externally imposed strategies

Processes of emergent strategy development
- Logical incrementalism
- Resource allocation routines
- Cultural processes
- Political processes

Challenges and implications
- Intended and realised strategy
- The learning organisation
- Uncertain and complex conditions

strategy as intended and strategy as emergent. Exhibit 11.1 explains the structure of the chapter:

● The first section (11.2) of the chapter discusses intended strategy. First there is an explanation of how strategies may be the outcome of the *vision, leadership or 'command'* of individuals. This is followed by a discussion of what formal *planning systems* in organisations might look like and the role they play. The section concludes with a discussion of how strategies might be deliberately *imposed* on organisations from the outside.

● The second section of the chapter (11.3) then switches to explanations of how strategies might emerge in organisations. The common feature of the different explanations here is that they do not see strategy making as a distinct and separate organisational activity, but rather see strategies developing out of more day-to-day and routine aspects of organisations. The section begins by considering what has become known as *logical incrementalism*. It then explains how strategies could be the outcome of *resource allocation processes* in organisations. The influence of *cultural processes* in organisations and their *political processes* are then discussed.

● Section 11.4 shows that these different explanations of strategy development should not be seen as independent or mutually exclusive. Indeed that they may all be seen within organisations to different degrees or at different times and in different contexts. However there is evidence that there are *patterns of strategy development* and these are explained in this section.

● The final section of the chapter (11.5) raises some *implications for managing strategy development* including:
  – The distinction between *intended strategy and realised strategy* and the implications for managing strategy development.
  – The challenge of developing what has become known as the *learning organisation*.
  – How different approaches to strategy development may be more or less well suited to *stable, dynamic or complex* environments.

11.2   INTENDED STRATEGY DEVELOPMENT

Intended strategy is an expression of a desired strategy as deliberately formulated or planned by managers

Intended strategy is an expression of a desired strategy as deliberately formulated or planned by managers. Its development may also be associated with the use of the sort of tools, techniques and frameworks for strategic analysis and evaluation explained in this book. These may be used in strategic planning systems, in the thinking of individual strategic leaders or groups of managers about the strategy of their organisation (see Chapter 15).

11.2.1   Strategy development through strategic leadership: the role of vision and command

Strategy development may be strongly associated with a strategic leader, an individual (or perhaps a small group of individuals) upon whom strategy is seen to be dependent. They are individuals whose personality, position or reputation may result in others willingly deferring to them and seeing strategy development as their province. They are therefore personally identified with and central to the strategy of their organisation. That individual may be central because he or she is the owner or founder of the organisation. This is often the case in small businesses and family businesses, some of which may be very large and successful. It may also be that an individual still remains central after a business is publicly quoted: such is the case with Charles Dunstone at Carphone Warehouse, or Rupert Murdoch at NewsCorp. Or it could be that an individual chief executive has turned round a business in times of difficulty and, as such, personifies the success of the organisation's strategy, as is the case with Michael O'Leary at Ryanair. Or perhaps an individual's network of contacts in an industry or organisational field are perceived as especially significant.[1]

In any of these circumstances, strategy may be – or may be seen to be – the deliberate intention of that leader. How such an intention comes about can, however, be explained in different ways:

- *Strategy leadership as design.* It could be that the strategic leader has thought through the strategy analytically. This might be by using the sort of techniques associated with strategic analysis and evaluation, or it might simply be that the individual has consciously, systematically and on the basis of his or her own logic worked through issues the organisation faces and come to his or her own conclusions.

- *Strategy leadership as vision.* It could be that a strategic leader determines or is associated with an overall vision, mission or strategic intent (see section 4.5.2) that motivates others, helps create the shared beliefs within which people can work together effectively and shapes more detailed strategy developed by others in an organisation. Some writers see this as *the* role of the strategic leader.[2]

- *Strategy leadership as command.* The strategy of an organisation might also be dictated by an individual. This is, perhaps, most evident in owner-managed small firms, where that individual is in direct control of all aspects of the business. Danny Miller and Isabel Le-Breton suggest there are advantages and disadvantages here. On the plus side it can mean speed of strategy adaptation and 'sharp, innovative, unorthodox strategies that are difficult for other companies to imitate'. The downside can, however, be 'hubris, excessive risk taking, quirky, irrelevant strategies'.[3]

11.2.2 Strategic planning systems

Strategic planning may take the form of systematised, step-by-step, chronological procedures to develop or coordinate an organisation's strategy

Often, strategy development is equated with formalised **strategic planning** systems.[4] These may take the form of systematised, step-by-step, chronological procedures involving different parts of the organisation. For example, in a study of strategic planning systems of major oil companies, Rob Grant[5] noted the following stages in the cycle for a large corporation:

- *Initial guidelines.* The cycle's starting point is usually a set of guidelines or assumptions about the external environment (for example, price levels and supply and demand conditions) and the overall priorities, guidelines and expectations of the corporate centre.

- *Business-level planning.* Business units or divisions then draw up strategic plans to present to the corporate centre. Corporate centre executives then discuss those plans with the business managers usually in face-to-face meetings. On the basis of these discussions the businesses revise their plans for further discussion.

- *Corporate-level planning.* The corporate plan results from the aggregation of the business plans. This coordination may be undertaken by a corporate planning department that, in effect, has a coordination role. The corporate board then has to approve the corporate plan.

- *Financial and strategic targets* are then likely to be extracted to provide a basis for performance monitoring of businesses and key strategic priorities on the basis of the plan.

Illustration 11.1 is a schematic representation of two different strategic planning systems Robert Grant found in his study of oil companies. Some companies were much more formal and regularised than others (for example, the French Elf Aquitaine and Italian ENI), with greater reliance on written reports and formal presentations, more fixed planning cycles, less flexibility and more specific objectives and targets relating to the formal plans. Where there was more informality/flexibility (for example, BP, Texaco and Exxon), companies placed greater emphasis on more general financial targets. Central corporate planning departments also played different roles. In some organisations they acted primarily as coordinators of business plans. In others they were more like internal consultants.

It is important to note that major strategic decisions may not, themselves, be made within or as a direct result of such planning processes. For example, the decisions about competitive strategy in a business-level strategic plan will quite likely be taken in management meetings in that business. There the processes associated with strategy development may correspond to any of those explained in this chapter and elsewhere in the book (see Chapter 15 and the commentaries). However, such decisions may *then* be built into the formal plan.

None the less a strategic planning system may have many uses. First, it may indeed play a role in how the future organisational *strategy is determined.* For example, it might:

- *Help structure analysis and thinking* about complex strategic problems.

- *Encourage questioning and challenge* of received wisdom taken for granted in an organisation.

- *Encourage a longer-term view* of strategy than might otherwise occur. Planning horizons vary, of course. In a fast-moving consumer goods company, 3–5-year plans may be appropriate. In companies which have to take very long-term views on capital investment, such as those in the oil industry, planning horizons can be as long as 15 years (in Exxon) or 20 years (in Shell).[6]

- *Enhance coordination of business-level strategies* within an overall corporate strategy.

It could be that in any of this planning systems could employ the tools and techniques of strategic analysis and decision making discussed in Parts I and II of this book.

Illustration 11.1

Strategic planning in Shell and ENI

The role of strategic planning systems may differ between firms.

Shell

Shell's strategic planning is based on (i) 20-year plans every 4–5 years on the basis of its scenario planning process and (ii) annual business plans with 5–10-year time horizons. The purpose is to enhance business unit strategies and coordinate strategy across the multinational operation.

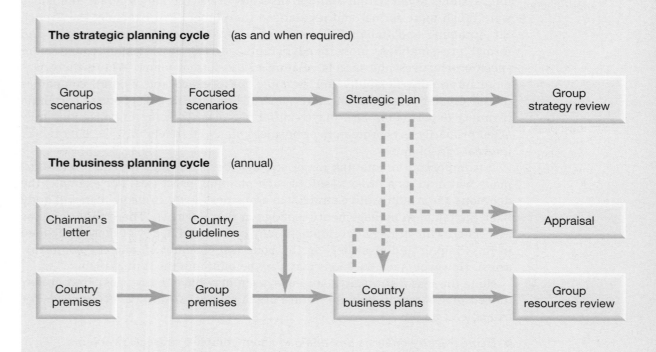

The strategic planning cycle (as and when required)

The business planning cycle (annual)

A planning system may also facilitate *converting an intended strategy into organisational action* by:

- *Communicating* intended strategy from the centre to operating units.
- *Providing agreed objectives or strategic milestones* against which performance and progress can be reviewed.
- *Coordinating resources* required to put strategy into effect.

A planning system may also have a *psychological role* by:

- *Involving people* in strategy development, therefore perhaps helping to create *ownership* of the strategy.

ENI

ENI has an annual planning cycle with a four-year time horizon embracing each business unit, sector and the whole group. The first year of the plan forms the basis of the annual budget and performance objectives. The emphasis is on central corporate control of business units and pressure on them to achieve greater efficiencies.

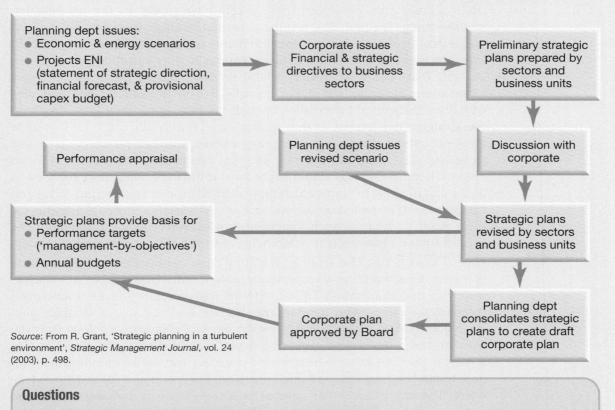

Source: From R. Grant, 'Strategic planning in a turbulent environment', *Strategic Management Journal*, vol. 24 (2003), p. 498.

Questions

1 Explain the main differences between the two planning systems.
2 What other processes of strategy development are likely to be found in a major oil company?

● Providing a *sense of security* and logic for the organisation, not least senior management who believe they *should* be proactively determining the future strategy and exercising control over the destiny of the organisation.

Henry Mintzberg has, however, challenged the extent to which planning provides such benefits.[7] Arguably there are four main dangers in the way in which formal systems of strategic planning have been employed:

● *Confusing strategy with the plan*. Managers may see themselves as managing strategy when what they are doing is going through the processes of planning. Strategy is, of course, not the same as 'the plan': strategy is the long-term direction that the organisation is following, not just a written document.

Linked to this may be a confusion between *budgetary processes* and strategic planning processes; the two may come to be seen as the same. The result is that planning gets reduced to the production of financial forecasts rather than the thinking through of the sort of issues discussed in this book. Of course it may be important to build the output of strategic planning into the budgetary process, but they are not the same.

- *Detachment from reality*. The managers responsible for the implementation of strategies, usually line managers, may be so busy with the day-to-day operations of the business that they cede responsibility for strategic issues to specialists or consultants. However, these rarely have power in the organisation to make things happen. The result can be that strategic planning becomes an intellectual exercise removed from the reality of operation. Strategic planning can also become over-detailed in its approach, concentrating on extensive analysis that, whilst technically sound in itself, misses the major strategic issues facing the organisation. For example, it is not unusual to find companies with huge amounts of information on their markets, but with little clarity about the strategic importance of that information. The result can be *information overload* with no clear outcome. At the extreme, strategic planners may come to believe that centrally planned strategy determines what goes on in an organisation. In fact it is what people do and the experience they draw on to do it that are likely to play a much more significant role (see section 11.5.1 and Chapter 15). If formal planning systems are to be useful, those responsible for them need to draw on such experience and involve people throughout the organisation if planning is to avoid being removed from organisational reality.

- *Lack of ownership*. The strategy resulting from deliberations of a corporate planning department, or a senior management team, may not be owned more widely in the organisation. In one extreme instance, a colleague discussing a company's strategy with its planning director was told that a strategic plan existed, but found it was locked in the drawer of the executive's desk. Only the planner and a few senior executives were permitted to see it! There is also a danger that the process of strategic planning may be so cumbersome that individuals or groups might contribute to only part of it and *not understand the whole*. The result can be that the business-level strategy does not correspond to the intended corporate strategy. This is particularly problematic in very large firms.

- *Dampening of innovation*. Highly formalised and rigid systems of planning, especially if linked to very tight and detailed mechanisms of control, can result in an inflexible, hierarchical organisation with a resultant stifling of ideas and dampening of innovative capacity.

The evidence of the extent to which the pursuit of such a systemised approach results in organisations performing better than others is equivocal[8] – not least because it is difficult to isolate formal planning as the dominant or determining effect on performance. However, there is some evidence that it may be especially beneficial in dynamic environments, where decentralised authority for strategic decisions is required (see Chapter 12) but where there is a need for coordination of strategies arising from such decentralisation.[9]

Certainly there has been a decline in the use of formal corporate planning departments[10] and a shift to line managers taking responsibility for strategy development and planning (see Chapter 15). Strategic planning is becoming more project based and flexible.[11] In this respect, strategic planning ceases to be a vehicle for the top-down development of intended strategy and more of a vehicle for the coordination of strategy emerging from below (see section 11.4.1 on resource allocation).

11.2.3 Externally imposed strategy

There may be situations in which managers face what they see as the imposition of strategy by powerful external stakeholders. Strategies being imposed in such ways may have been determined using the tools of analysis and evaluation associated with a rational/analytic approach, or perhaps through systematic strategic planning; or they may have developed in a more emergent fashion (see section 11.3). However, to the managers of the organisation having it imposed on them, it is certainly experienced as an 'intended strategy'.

For example, the government may dictate a particular strategic direction as in the public sector, or where it exercises extensive regulation over an industry. Or it may choose to deregulate or privatise a sector or organisation currently in the public sector. Indeed, in the UK public sector a more direct interventionist approach began to be used in the early 2000s. So-called 'special measures' were employed for schools or hospitals deemed to be underperforming badly, with specialist managers being sent in to turn round the ailing organisations and impose a new strategic direction. Businesses in the private sector may also be subject to such imposed strategic direction, or significant constraints on their choices. A multinational corporation seeking to develop businesses in some parts of the world may be subject to governmental requirements to do this in certain ways, perhaps through joint ventures or local alliances. An operating business within a multidivisional organisation may also regard the overall corporate strategic direction of its parent as akin to imposed strategy.

11.3 EMERGENT STRATEGY DEVELOPMENT

Although strategy development is typically associated with intentionality, this may not be so. Research on historical patterns of strategy development in organisations shows a pattern of what has become known as incremental strategy development. Strategies do not typically change in major shifts of direction. They typically change by building on and amending what has gone before. Prior decisions tend to affect future directions giving rise to the sort of pattern described in Exhibit 11.2. An apparently coherent strategy of an organisation may develop on the basis of a series of strategic moves each of which makes sense in terms of previous moves. Perhaps a product launch, or a significant investment decision, establishes a strategic direction which, itself, guides decisions on the next strategic move – an acquisition perhaps. This in turn helps consolidate the strategic direction, and over time the overall strategic approach of the organisation becomes more established. As time goes on, each move is informed by this developing pattern of strategy and, in turn, reinforces it.

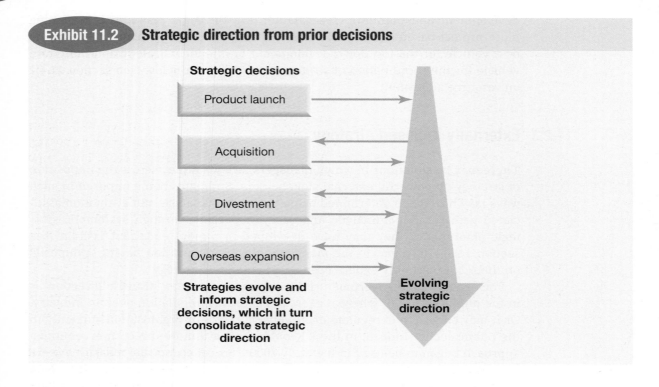

Exhibit 11.2 **Strategic direction from prior decisions**

In many ways this is to be expected. It would be strange and, arguably, dysfunctional for an organisation to change its strategy fundamentally very often. Moreover, if it has embarked on an overall strategic direction, it is to be expected that strategic decisions would be taken in line with that. So such a pattern is consistent with a view of strategy development as an intentional, considered and deliberate process. However, it is also possible to account for the same pattern as a persistent application of the familiar – organisations repeatedly taking decisions based on where they have come from, rather than a considered view of their future[12] or as the outcome of routines, activities and processes within an organisation leading to decisions that become the long-term direction – the strategy – of an organisation.[13] These cumulative decisions may then subsequently be more formally described, for example in annual reports and strategic plans, as the strategy of the organisation. This section explains the organisational processes that might account for such **emergent strategy** development.

Emergent strategy comes about through everyday routines, activities and processes in organisations leading to decisions that become the long-term direction of an organisation

11.3.1 Logical incrementalism

In a study of major multinational businesses, James Quinn[14] concluded that the strategy development processes he observed could best be described as logical incrementalism. **Logical incrementalism** is the development of strategy by experimentation and 'learning from partial commitments rather than through global formulations of total strategies'.[15] There are a number of reasons this is likely to be so:

Logical incrementalism is the deliberate development of strategy by experimentation and learning from partial commitments

● *Environmental uncertainty*. Managers realise that they cannot do away with the uncertainty of their environment by relying on analyses of historical data or predicting how it will change. Rather, they try to be sensitive to environmental signals by encouraging constant environmental scanning throughout the organisation.

● *Generalised views of strategy*. Managers have a generalised rather than specific view of where they want the organisation to be in the future and try to move towards this position incrementally. There is also a reluctance to specify precise objectives too early, as this might stifle ideas and prevent innovation and experimentation. Objectives may therefore be fairly general in nature.

● *Experimentation*. Managers may seek to develop a strong, secure, but flexible core business. They will then build on the experience gained in that business to inform decisions both about its development and experimentation with 'side bet' ventures. Commitment to strategic options may therefore be tentative in the early stages of strategy development. Such experiments are not the sole responsibility of top management. They emerge from what Quinn describes as 'subsystems', in the organisation. By this he means the groups of people involved in, for example, product development, product positioning, diversification, external relations, and so on.

● *Coordinating emergent strategies*. Top managers may then utilise a mix of *formal and informal* social and political processes (see section 11.3.4) to draw together an emerging pattern of strategies from these subsystems. These may then be formed into coherent statements of strategy for stakeholders (for example, shareholders, financial commentators, the media) that need to understand the organisation's strategy.

Quinn argues that, despite its emergent nature, logical incrementalism can be 'a conscious, purposeful, proactive, executive practice' to improve information available for decisions and build people's psychological identification with the development of strategy. In a sense, then, logical incrementalism encapsulates processes that bridge intention and emergence, in that they are deliberate and intended but rely on social processes within the organisation to sense the environment and experiments in subsystems to try out ideas.

This view of strategy making is similar to the descriptions that managers themselves often give of how strategies come about in their organisation. Illustration 11.2 provides some examples of managers explaining the strategy development process in their organisation as they see it. They see their job as 'strategists' as continually, proactively pursuing a strategic goal, countering competitive moves and adapting to their environment, whilst not 'rocking the boat' too much, so as to maintain efficiency and performance.

Arguably, developing strategies in such a way has considerable benefits. Continual testing and gradual strategy implementation provides improved quality of information for decision making, and enables the better sequencing of the elements of major decisions. Since change will be gradual, the possibility of creating and developing a commitment to change throughout the organisation is increased. Because the different parts, or 'subsystems', of the organisation are in a continual state of interplay, the managers of each can learn from each other about the feasibility of a course of action. Such processes also take account of the

Illustration 11.2

An incrementalist view of strategic management

Managers often see their job as managing adaptively: continually changing strategy to keep in line with the environment, whilst maintaining efficiency and keeping stakeholders happy.

- 'You know there is a simple analogy you can make. To move forward when you walk, you create an imbalance, you lean forward and you don't know what is going to happen. Fortunately, you put a foot ahead of you and you recover your balance. Well, that's what we're doing all the time, so it is never comfortable.'[1]

- 'I begin wide-ranging discussions with people inside and outside the corporation. From these a pattern eventually emerges. It's like fitting together a jigsaw puzzle. At first the vague outline of an approach appears like the sail of a ship in a puzzle. Then suddenly the rest of the puzzle becomes quite clear. You wonder why you didn't see it all along.'[2]

- 'We haven't stood still in the past and I can't see with our present set-up that we shall stand still in the future; but what I really mean is that it is a path of evolution rather than revolution. Some companies get a successful formula and stick to that rigidly because that is what they know – for example, [Company X] did not really adapt to change, so they had to take what was a revolution. We hopefully have changed gradually and that's what I think we should do. We are always looking for fresh openings without going off at a tangent.'[3]

- 'In our business you cannot know the future; it's changing so fast. That's why I employ some of the best brains in the industry. Their job is to keep at the forefront of what's happening and, through what they are working on, to help create that future. I don't give them a strategic plan to work to; my job is to discern a strategy from what they tell me and what they are doing. Of course they don't always agree – why would they, they can't *know* the future either – which means there's a good deal of debate, a good deal of trial and error and a good deal of judgement involved.'[4]

- 'The analogy of a chess game is useful in this context. The objective of chess is clear: to gain victory by capturing your opponent's king. Most players begin with a strategic move, that assumes a countermove by the opponent. If the countermove materialises, then the next move follows automatically, based on a previous winning strategy. However, the beauty of chess is the unpredictability of one's opponent's moves. To attempt to predict the outcome of chess is impossible, and therefore players limit themselves to working on possibilities and probabilities of moves that are not too far ahead.'[5]

Sources:
1. Quotes from interviews conducted by A. Bailey as part of a research project sponsored by the Economic and Social Research Council (Grant No.: R000235100).
2. Extract from J.B. Quinn, *Strategies for Change*, Irwin, 1980.
3. Extracts from G. Johnson, *Strategic Change and the Management Process*, Blackwell, 1987.
4. CEO of a hi-tech business in an interview with a co-author.
5. From a manager on an MBA course.

Questions

1 With reference to these explanations of strategy development, what are the main advantages of developing strategies incrementally?

2 Is incremental strategy development bound to result in strategic drift (see section 11.6.1)? How might this be avoided?

political nature of organisational life, since smaller changes are less likely to face the same degree of resistance as major changes. Moreover, the formulation of strategy in this way means that the implications of the strategy are continually being tested out. This continual readjustment makes sense if the environment is considered as a continually changing influence on the organisation.

11.3.2 Resource allocation processes

The **resource allocation process** (RAP) explanation of strategy development is that realised strategies emerge as a result of the way resources are allocated in organisations.[16] This is sometimes known as the Bower–Burgelman explanation of strategy development after two American professors – Joe Bower and Robert Burgelman[17] – who identified similar processes in their different studies, as have others later.[18]

As with the logical incremental view of strategy development, the RAP explanation acknowledges that it is unrealistic to determine strategy in a top-down, prescriptive, detailed manner across an organisation, especially a large, complex organisation. A changing and uncertain environment together with the cognitive limits of managers to cope with this (see pages 33–39 in the Commentary) mean that strategy is better explained as the outcome of problems or issues being addressed as they arise. The RAP explanation then emphasises the formal and informal processes by which this is done, particularly:

- *Negotiation across organisational levels.* The nature of problems and their resolutions are typically the outcome of negotiation across levels of an organisation. Most obviously this could be between a corporate centre and business units but it might also be between a business and its operating units or functions. Such problems or issues usually start with a discrepancy. For example, this could be a discrepancy between where top management wish a corporation to be in terms of its share price; or at a business level a decline in market share or competitive position; or perhaps a shortfall in profits below corporate expectations. In any of these cases there is then likely to be a need to make sense of the significance of that discrepancy from one level (for example, the business level) to another (for example, corporate) and align expectations as to what needs to be resolved. The problem will then, most likely, be worked on at the level most appropriate to the problem. For example, if it is a market-related issue, by the marketing department in a business or a project team in that business. It is unlikely it would be dealt with in any detail by the chief executive or strategic planner in the business, let alone at corporate level. The point that needs emphasising here again is that a good deal of choice as to what to focus on and what choices to make may lie far down in an organisation's subsystems.

- The *influence of RAP* on the nature of the resolution of the problem. All organisations have within them systems, routines and standards for deciding upon proposed new ventures, products and services. These play a significant part on what sort of solutions to problems are advocated and those to which resources are allocated. To take a common example, many businesses have criteria for acceptability of new venture proposals based on measures of

The **resource allocation process** (RAP) explanation of strategy development is that realised strategies emerge as a result of the way resources are allocated in organisations

Exhibit 11.3 **Strategy development through resource allocation processes**

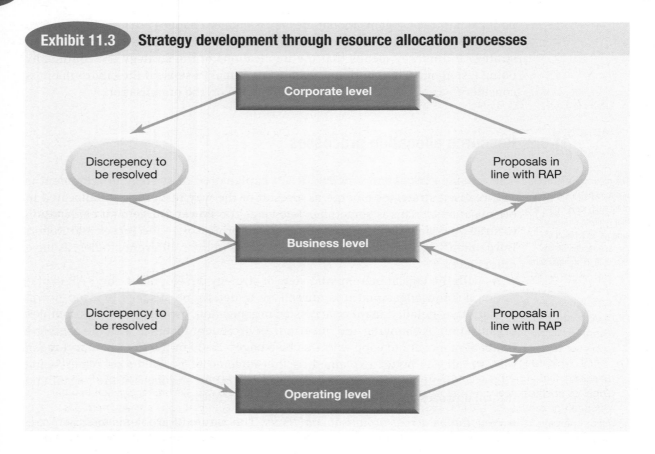

return (for example, return on capital employed). The level at which such returns are pitched will undoubtedly influence which new ideas are proposed; some will be seen as involving less capital resource or having the potential for greater returns than others. The same criterion will similarly affect which solutions are adopted. If different resource allocation criteria were to be used, different solutions would likely be advocated and different ones selected.

This RAP explanation of how strategies develop is summarised in Exhibit 11.3. The case example at the end of this chapter shows how this helps explain the major strategic changes at Intel in the 1980s. The top management of the firm were wedded to Intel as a memory company in the business of DRAMs – Dynamic Random Access Memories. Its major strategic switch to becoming a microprocessing company at that time did not come about because of top management direction, but because the internal resource allocation routines within the firm favoured projects with greater profit margins. This resulted in the emerging microprocessor business being allocated more resources and therefore a basis for future investment and growth greater than DRAMs.[19] However, as Illustration 11.3 shows, whilst localised processes may explain strategy development, they can lead to significant problems.

Finally it is worth noting that the explanations of RAP here bear a good deal of similarity to the developing role of strategic planning (see section 11.2.2) and

Illustration 11.3

European strategy at Viacom in the 1990s

Strategy processes at the business level may not be able to cope with corporate-wide issues.

After his takeover of the company in 1987, Sumner Redstone, as Chairman of Viacom, the US international media conglomerate, enlisted Frank Biondi as CEO. Under Biondi, Viacom grew steadily until the mid-1990s.

Biondi's corporate management approach was to cultivate a high-performance culture by providing divisions of the company with high levels of operating autonomy, reinforced by financial incentives linked to divisional results. This included them having responsibility for their strategy and the control of resources at the divisional level.

In the mid-1990s Viacom faced the task of rethinking its European strategy due to increasing global competition. Viacom's European divisions included Paramount and MTV/Nickelodeon and their major competitors in many of their markets at that time were businesses which were part of Rupert Murdoch's NewsCorp. NewsCorp was centrally run with a global vision. Murdoch, the central figure, employed a much more centralised management and interventionist style – he would take over temporary leadership of a division personally on occasions.

By late 1995, two separate strategic issues requiring major investment were being considered at Paramount and at MTV/Nickelodeon. Paramount wanted to move into what was then next-generation satellite-delivered programming services. Its preferred strategic option was to do this through a long-term partnership with the Kirch Group, which had such a service in place.

On the other hand, MTV/Nickelodeon was considering pursuing a wider market opening in Europe by creating locally tailored broadcasting channels. It believed this could allow it to build on its existing brand, but also accommodate the limited foreign language proficiency of young children in local markets. So the preferred strategy was to acquire localised content through equity-based partnerships with several companies wanting to launch satellite TV, rather than have an exclusive partnership with the Kirch Group.

These strategic issues were negotiated between the management teams of the two European divisions.

Although they wanted to collaborate to utilise the synergies they believed they had, they could not agree on the strategy to adopt. It was therefore decided that Paramount should take the lead in any negotiations with prospective media partners in Europe, while MTV/Nickelodeon would make clear its strategic preferences to Paramount. Biondi did not actively take part in these negotiations. The internal negotiations about the preferred strategy dragged on for the rest of that year, but no consensus was reached. This meant that the desired market developments in Europe were delayed, allowing competition to increase. This led to ever shorter time spans in which strategic issues had to be dealt with and the ultimate recognition that the devolved approach to corporate management was not working. Ultimately, in January 1996 Redstone released Biondi as CEO, assumed control himself and introduced a more centralised corporate strategic management style to improve the speed and efficiency of strategic decision making.

(Viacom later merged with CBS but by 2007 had demerged and was operating again as a separate company under the chairmanship of Sumner Redstone.)

Source: Based on T.R. Eisenmann and J.L. Bower 'The entrepreneurial M-form: a case study of strategic integration in a global media company', in J.L. Bower and C.G. Gilbert (eds), *From Resource Allocation to Strategy*, Oxford University Press, 2005, pp. 307–329.

Prepared by Michael Ubben, Lancaster University Management School.

Questions

1 How did Viacom's strategy development processes differ from the strategic planning approaches explained in Illustration 11.1?

2 Which of the corporate parenting approaches explained in Chapter 7 was being adopted by Biondi?

3 How might the problems that occurred at Viacom in 1995 have been avoided?

the way in which business or operating units within an organisation relate to the corporate centre. However, the RAP emphasis is much more on the processes within the subsystems driving an emergent strategy.

11.3.3 Organisational politics

The RAP explanation highlights the role of negotiation between organisational levels in strategy development. This signals the importance of organisational politics. Managers often suggest that the strategy being followed by their organisation is really the outcome of the bargaining and power politics that go on between important executives or between coalitions within the organisation and major stakeholders. These executives or coalitions are continually trying to position themselves such that their views prevail or that they control the resources in the organisation necessary for future success. For example, Motorola's inability to move fast enough from analogue to digital technology for mobile phones and its consequent loss of market dominance (see Illustration 5.1) was substantially the result of divisional 'warring tribes' across the company seeking to preserve their own interests.[20] The **political view**[21] of strategy development is, then, that strategies develop as the outcome of processes of bargaining and negotiation among powerful internal or external interest groups (or stakeholders). This is the world of boardroom battles often portrayed in film and TV dramas. Illustration 11.4 shows how the interests of different executive and non-executive directors of Vodafone in concert with various stakeholders hit the headlines as the company wrestled with its strategy development in 2006.

The political view of strategy development is that strategies develop as the outcome of processes of bargaining and negotiation among powerful internal or external interest groups (or stakeholders)

Political activity is often seen as an inevitable but negative influence on strategy development, getting in the way of thorough analysis and rational thinking. A political perspective on strategic management suggests that the rational and analytic processes often associated with developing strategy (see section 11.2.1) may not be as objective and dispassionate as they appear. Objectives that are set may reflect the ambitions of powerful people. Information used in strategic debate is not always politically neutral. Rather, information and data that are emphasised or de-emphasised can be a source of power for those who control what is seen to be important. Indeed one manager or coalition may exercise power over another because they control important sources of information. Powerful individuals and groups may also strongly influence the identification of key issues and the strategies eventually selected or the way they are selected.[22] Differing views may be pursued, not only on the basis of the extent to which they reflect environmental or competitive pressures, for example, but also because they have implications for the status or influence of different stakeholders.

None of this should be surprising. In approaching strategic problems, people may be operating within an overall organisational culture (see Chapter 4) but within this, they are likely to be differently influenced by at least:

● *Personal experience* from people's roles within the organisation.

● *Competition for resources and influence* between the different subsystems in the organisation and powerful people within them who are likely to be interested in preserving or enhancing the power of their positions.[23]

● *The relative influence of stakeholders* on different parts of the organisation. For example, a finance department may be especially sensitive to the influence of

Illustration 11.4

Boardroom battles at Vodafone

Political processes in organisations can influence the development of strategy.

Vodafone became a global player in the telecommunications industry under the guidance of Sir Christopher Gent, who had become the company's 'Life President'. However, following the takeover of the German company Mannesmann in 2000, Vodafone had seemed to lose its way. Some of the overseas acquisitions had not worked out, investors were calling for greater returns and commentators argued that the 'old guard' wedded to Gent's strategy had not embraced the convergence of technologies – broadband, information technology, TV and the Internet.

By mid-2006, Chief Executive Arun Sarin was known to be in discussions about the sale of Vodafone's controlling interest in its Japanese operation. There was talk that in the USA Verizon was interested in buying out Vodafone's 45 per cent share of Verizon Wireless. Sarin was also reported to be considering the sale of Arcor, Vodaphone's German fixed-line unit. In all this Sarin was portrayed as the 'shareholders' friend', trying to liquidate assets to improve dividends and fund expansion into broadband.

However, this had given rise to a major boardroom split between the supporters of Sarin and the old guard who supported the global development strategy of the Gent era. The *Financial Times* (6 March 2006) reported that Lord Maclaurin, Vodafone's Chairman, was 'losing patience with Mr Sarin'. The *Observer* (12 March 2006) reported that Maclaurin had sought to 'put the issue of Sarin's tenure . . . to a vote of the full board but after consultations with his non-executives it became clear that he could not carry a vote on this'.

Supporters of Sarin argued that he was trying to deal with strategic issues that should have been dealt with earlier.

It was also reported that there was pressure from investors for supporters of the old guard, including Lord Maclaurin, to retire earlier than planned and make way for a new chairman, Sir John Bond. One major investor was quoted in the *Observer* as saying that he was hoping that the arrival of Sir John Bond might help sort things out. He also added: 'I don't

know what Gent is still doing around. These positions always cause trouble. Do I think he should be there? No.' Indeed in March 2006 Sir Christopher resigned as Group Life President.

Investors also lobbied for the departure from the board of non-executive directors who were insufficiently independent, seen to be in either the Sarin or the old guard camp.

In all this, the *Observer* reported that Sarin had removed Peter Bamford, Chief Marketing Officer, who was seen as 'too pro-Gent and pro-Maclaurin' and added 'Sarin has tightened his grip; he has replaced 90% of the people at the top of the company over the last 12 months'.

In July 2006 when Sir John Bond arrived as the new Chairman he expressed support for Sarin but cautioned that his performance would be 'under constant review'. None the less, as Lord Maclaurin handed over to Sir John at the AGM, whilst admitting that the past six months had not been easy, he insisted that there had been 'no – repeat – no dissension on the board'.

By mid-2007 the reports of boardroom dissent were far less. What had emerged in the context of a flattening profit picture were reports of potential takeover or even the break-up of the group. The bases of such reports were, however, being dismissed by Sarin.

Sources: Daily Telegraph, 7 March (2006); *Financial Times*, 6, 8 March, 26 July (2006), 29 May, 1 June (2007); *Observer*, 12 March (2006).

Questions

1 Identify the key stakeholders, their views and their influence in the events of 2006.

2 Do you consider the reported events at Vodafone exceptional?

3 What strategy has Vodafone pursued since 2006? Does this suggest one or other of the rival camps prevailed?

financial institutions whilst a sales or marketing department will be strongly influenced by customers.[24]

● *Different access to information* or the salience of that information given their roles and functional affiliations.

In such circumstances emergent and incremental patterns of strategy development are likely. Emergent in the sense that it is this bargaining and negotiation that gives rise to strategy rather than carefully analysed, deliberate intent. Incremental for two reasons. First, if different views prevail in the organisation and different parties exercise their political muscle, compromise may be inevitable. Second, it is quite possible that it is from the pursuit of the current strategy that power has been gained by those wielding it. Indeed it might be very threatening to their power if significant changes in strategy were to occur. In such circumstances it is likely that a search for a compromise solution which accommodates different power bases may end up with a strategy which is an adaptation of what has gone before.

There are, however, alternative ways of considering the influence of political processes. Arguably, the conflict and tensions that manifest themselves in political activity, arising as they do from different expectations or interests, can be the source of new ideas (see the discussion on the 'ideas lens' in the commentaries) or challenges to old ways of doing things.[25] New ideas may be supported or opposed by different 'champions' who will battle over what is the best idea or the best way forward. Arguably, if such conflict and tensions did not exist, neither would innovation. The productive management of such tensions may be a learned competence or dynamic capability (see section 3.4.5) in some organisations that provides them with a basis for competitive advantage. Further, as Chapter 14 (section 14.4.5) shows, the exercise of power may be important in the management of strategic change.

All of this suggests that political activity has to be taken seriously as an influence on strategy development. Whatever thinking goes into a strategy will need to go hand in hand with activity to address the political processes at work. This is addressed in other parts of this book, in particular sections 4.4.1–4.4.2 and 14.4.5 as well as in the commentaries.

11.3.4 Cultural processes

Elsewhere in the book (see Chapter 5 in particular) the importance of culture has been discussed. Organisational culture is to do with the taken for granted in an organisation. That includes the basic assumptions and beliefs that are shared by members of an organisation (in this book termed the paradigm) and the taken-for-granted ways of doing things and structures that are encapsulated in the outer rings of the cultural web (see sections 5.4.5 and 5.4.6 and Exhibit 5.7). So a **cultural explanation of strategy development** is that it occurs as the outcome of the taken-for-granted assumptions and behaviours in organisations. The important thing to stress here is that this taken-for-grantedness works to define, or at least guide, how the people in an organisation view that organisation and its environment. It also tends to constrain what is seen as appropriate behaviour and activity. Some examples of this are given in Chapter 5 and in section 14.2. It

A cultural explanation of strategy development is that it occurs as the outcome of the taken-for-granted assumptions and behaviours in organisations

is important to realise the impact of this on the emergent and incremental development of strategy, and the potential consequences.

In some respects this provides an underlying dimension to previous explanations of strategy development. The observed pattern of incremental strategy development can be explained in terms of, for example, deliberate logical incrementalism (see section 11.3.1). However, it can also be explained in terms of the outcome of the influence of organisational culture.[26] Similarly, the cultural web emphasises the strong influence of taken-for-granted organisational routines and power structures. Routines include the RAPs central to the RAP explanation of strategy development – and power structures are central to the political processes discussed above.

11.4   PATTERNS OF STRATEGY DEVELOPMENT

The discussion of different strategy development processes in sections 11.2 and 11.3 raises some further important general points:

- *Multiple strategy development processes*. There is a danger that the descriptions of processes above suggest that they are somehow discrete or mutually exclusive. They are not. Indeed, it is likely that there will be multiple processes at work in any organisation. As has already been suggested, the different processes explained here can be seen to exist within each other. For example, in practical terms, if a planning system exists in a large organisation, that organisation will also have RAP. Within these there will undoubtedly be some level of political activity; indeed the planning system itself may be used for negotiating purposes. Moreover, if there is a dominant mode of strategy development in an organisation, it is most likely that other processes will be evident too. Indeed, there is evidence that those organisations that employ multiple processes of strategy development may perform better than those that take more singular approaches.[27] It has to be recognised, therefore, that there is *no one right way* in which strategies are developed. The challenge is for managers to recognise the potential benefits of different processes of strategy development so as to build organisations capable of adapting and innovating within a changing environment, yet achieving the benefits of more formal processes of planning and analysis to help this where necessary.[28]

- *Contextual differences*. Processes of strategy development are likely to *differ over time* and in *different contexts*. An organisation that is going through rapid change, perhaps the result of environmental turbulence or the need for internal strategic change, will very likely have different strategy development processes from an organisation in a more steady state. The chapter-end case study for this chapter shows this for Intel from the 1980s through to the turn of the century. Different strategy development processes tended to be more pronounced at one stage in its development than another and, apparently, beneficially for the organisation.

Drawing together these two observations, Exhibit 11.4 shows some typical patterns of strategy development processes in different organisational contexts.[29]

Exhibit 11.4 **Some configurations of strategy development processes**

Dominant dimensions	Characteristics	Rather than	Typical contexts
Planning Incrementalism (Logical incrementalism)	Standardised planning procedures Systematic data collection and analyses Constant environmental scanning Ongoing adjustment of strategy Tentative commitment to strategy Step-by-step, small-scale change	Intrusive external environment Dominant individuals Political processes Power groups	Manufacturing and service sector organisations Stable or growing markets Mature markets Benign environments
Incremental Cultural Political	Bargaining, negotiation and compromise amongst conflicting interests of groups Groups with control over critical resources more likely to influence strategy Standardised 'ways of doing things' Routines and procedures embedded in organisational history Gradual adjustments to strategy	Deliberate, intentional process Well-defined procedures Analytical evaluation and planning Deliberate managerial intent	Professional service firms (e.g. consultancy or law firms) Unstable, turbulent environment New and growing markets
Imposed Political	Strategy is imposed by external forces (e.g. legislation, parent organisation) Freedom of choice severely restricted Political activity likely within organisation and between external agencies	Strategy determined within the organisation Planning systems impact on strategy development Influence on strategic direction mainly by managers within the organisation	Public sector organisations, larger manufacturing and financial service subsidiaries Threatening, declining, unstable and hostile environments

The findings above are based on a survey of perceptions of strategy development processes undertaken at Cranfield School of Management in the 1990s.

- *Perceptions of how strategies develop* will be seen differently by different people. For example, as Exhibit 11.5 shows, senior executives tend to see strategy development more in terms of intended, rational, analytic planned processes whereas middle managers see strategy development more as the result of cultural and political processes. Managers in public sector organisations tend to see strategy as externally imposed more than managers in commercial businesses, largely because their organisations are answerable to government bodies.[30] People who work in family businesses tend to see more evidence of the influence of powerful individuals, who may be the owners of the businesses. Illustration 11.6, the chapter's key debate, shows very different accounts of the strategy development for a highly successful strategy.

Exhibit 11.5	Managers' perceptions of strategy development processes

Perceptions that there exists:	Level in organisation		Environmental stability	
	CEO	**Middle management**	**Higher**	**Lower**
Precision of objectives	Yes	No	Yes	No
Detailed planning	Yes	No	Yes	No
Systematic analysis of environment	Yes	No	Yes	–
Careful evaluation of strategic options	Yes	No	–	–

These findings are based on a survey of perceptions of strategy development processes undertaken at Cranfield School of Management in the 1990s. The findings indicate statistically significant differences.

11.5 CHALLENGES FOR MANAGING STRATEGY DEVELOPMENT

The discussion in this chapter raises some important challenges and has implications for how managers manage the strategy development process.

11.5.1 Managing intended and realised strategy

The discussion so far in this chapter has drawn a distinction between intended and emergent strategy. It has also made the point that the different processes of strategy development are not mutually exclusive; organisations have multiple processes. A problem that managers face, then, is that it is not unusual for organisations to have an intended strategy, perhaps the result of a strategic planning process, but to be following a different strategy in reality, perhaps the outcome of political and cultural processes. We all experience this as customers of organisations that have stated strategies quite different from what we experience: government agencies that are there purportedly to serve our interests but act as bureaucratic officialdom; companies that claim they offer excellent customer service but operate call centres that frustrate customers and fail to solve problems, universities that claim excellence of teaching but are more concerned with their staff's research, or vice versa. Exhibit 11.6 shows this. There may well be an *intended strategy*, agreed by senior executives, based on careful analysis and expressed in a formal document explaining the intended strategy in a systematic way with the intention that this will be implemented (see route 1). However, much of what is intended follows route 2 and is *unrealised*; it does not come about in practice, or only partially so. There may be all sorts of reasons for this. The plans are unworkable; the environment changes after the plan has been drawn up and managers decide that the strategy, as planned, should not be put into effect; or people in the organisation or influential stakeholders do not go along

Exhibit 11.6 **Strategy development routes**

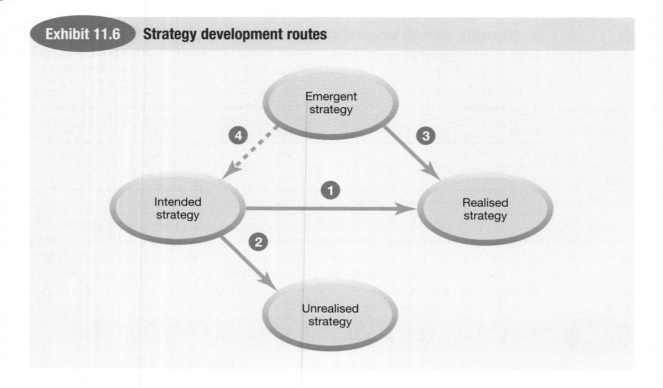

---

with the plan. (Also see the discussion of the drawbacks of planning systems in section 11.2.2) However, it could also be that the processes that give rise to emergent strategy give rise to a **realised strategy**: that is, the strategy actually being followed by an organisation in practice (route 3) rather than planned up front. There are at least three major implications here for strategists:

Realised strategy: the strategy actually being followed by an organisation in practice

● *Awareness.* First, and most fundamental, have managers taken steps to check if the intended strategy and realised strategy are different? It should not be assumed that the top management of organisations are always close enough to customers or get sufficient feedback from those who are to understand the extent of difference between the intended and the realised.

● *The role of strategic planning.* It was pointed out in section 11.2.2 that strategic planning might not perform the role of formulating strategies so much as the useful role of coordinating the strategies that emerge within the organisation (route 4 in Exhibit 11.6). The danger is that this does little more than pull together the 'received wisdom' built up over time in the organisation such that the planning systems merely post-rationalise where the organisation has come from. If strategic planning systems are to be employed managers need to learn two key lessons:

  – They are not a substitute for other processes of strategy development. These other processes need to be managed too (see below).

  – There needs to be realistic expectations of the role of strategic planning. For example, is its primary role one of coordination of emergent strategies; or is the expectation that it will contribute proactively to the development of strategy by, for example, encouraging the challenge of received wisdom and ways of doing things? If it is the latter, then the role of the strategic planner becomes more to do with internal consultancy than specialist analyst and coordinator.

- *The challenge of strategic drift.* One of the major strategic challenges facing managers was identified in Chapter 5 as the tendency of incremental strategy development to give rise to strategic drift (see section 5.1). The discussion in section 11.3 shows that incremental strategy development processes leading to the emergence of strategy is the natural outcome of the influence of organisational culture, individual and collective experience, political processes and prior decisions. This further highlights that strategy development processes in organisations need to encourage people in organisations to have the capacity and willingness to challenge and change their core assumptions and ways of doing things. This leads to the idea of the 'learning organisation' discussed in the next section. Desirable as this may be, the evidence is that it does not occur easily. It also emphasises the delicate balance that an organisation faces in developing its strategy. For example, it has internal cultural forces for inertia that tend to constrain strategy development, yet behaviours and routines within its culture that might potentially provide the capabilities for competitive advantage (see section 3.4.3).

- *Managing emergent strategy.* The processes of strategy development that give rise to emergent strategy may be rooted in organisational routines and culture, but they are not unmanageable. Indeed this is as much about managing strategy as is strategic planning. RAPs can be changed; political processes can be analysed and managed (see section 4.4.1 on stakeholder analysis); the challenge of the norms and routines of organisational culture can be encouraged (see section 11.5.1). Not least here is the management role of creating a clear vision directing future strategy.

11.5.2   The learning organisation

The **learning organisation** is capable of continual regeneration from the variety of knowledge, experience and skills of individuals within a culture which encourages mutual questioning and challenge around a shared purpose or vision

Traditionally, organisations have been seen as hierarchies and bureaucracies set up to achieve order and maintain control, as structures built for stability rather than change. A **learning organisation**, however, is one capable of continual regeneration from the variety of knowledge, experience and skills of individuals within a culture that encourages mutual questioning and challenge around a shared purpose or vision. It emphasises the potential capacity and capability of an organisations to regenerate itself from within, and in this way for dynamic strategies to emerge naturally.

Advocates of the learning organisation[31] point out that the collective knowledge of all the individuals in an organisation usually exceeds what the organisation itself 'knows' and is capable of doing; the formal structures of organisations typically stifle organisational knowledge and creativity. They argue that the aim of management should be to encourage processes that unlock the knowledge of individuals, and encourage the sharing of information and knowledge, so that every individual becomes sensitive to changes occurring around them and contributes to the identification of opportunities and required changes. This emphasises the importance of seeing organisations as *social networks*,[32] where the emphasis is not so much on hierarchies as on different interest groups that need to cooperate with each other and potentially learn from each other. So as ideas bubble up from below, the risk of their fizzling out because of lack of interest from other parts of the organisation is reduced.

The central tenets of organisational learning are:

- *Managers facilitate* rather than direct.
- *Information flows and relationships between people are lateral* as well as vertical.
- *Organisations are pluralistic*, where conflicting ideas and views are welcomed, surfaced and become the basis of debate.
- *Experimentation* is the norm, so ideas are tried out in action and in turn become part of the learning process.

All this relates to other concepts discussed in the book. It is akin to aspects of logical incrementalism described in section 11.3.1 and to insights from the ideas lens discussed in the commentaries. It also corresponds to what Gary Hamel calls 'resilient' organisations that continually reinvent themselves by refusing to take their success for granted and building the capability to imagine new business models.[33]

11.5.3 Strategy development in uncertain and complex conditions

Not all organisations face similar environments. They differ in their form and complexity; therefore different ways of thinking about strategy development and different processes for managing strategy may make sense in different circumstances. Exhibit 11.7 shows how organisations may seek to cope with conditions that are more or less stable or dynamic, and simple or complex:[34]

- In *simple/static* conditions, the environment is relatively straightforward to understand and is not undergoing significant change. Raw material suppliers and some mass manufacturing companies are examples, at least from the past. Technical processes may be fairly simple, and competition and markets remain the same over time. In such circumstances, if environmental change does occur, it may be predictable, so it could make sense to analyse the environment extensively on an historical basis as a means of trying to forecast likely future conditions. In situations of relatively low complexity, it may also be possible to identify some predictors of environmental influences. For example, in public services, demographic data such as birth rates might be used as lead indicators to determine the required provision of schooling, health care or social services. So in simple/static conditions, seeing strategy development in formal planning terms may make sense. It might also be tempting to rely on past experience and prior decisions since little is changing. There are, however, two problems. First, competitors in the same sort of environment may all end up following the same strategies, and this could be a recipe for high degrees of competition and low profits (see Chapter 6). Second, environmental conditions may change. Many organisations have found increasingly dynamic and/or complex conditions. When this happens it could well be that

Exhibit 11.7   **Strategy development in environmental contexts**

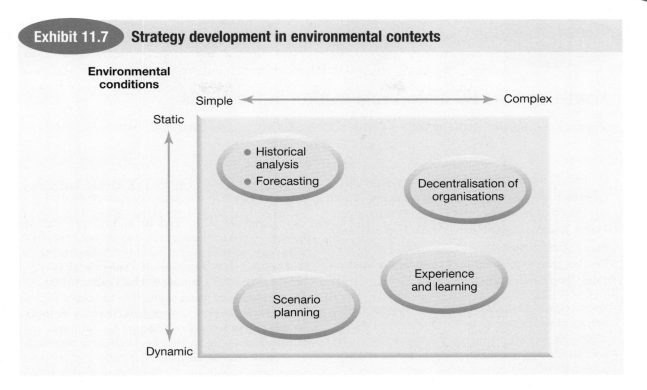

they find difficulties in adjusting to those changed conditions because their strategy development processes are not suited to them.

- In *dynamic* conditions, managers need to consider the environment of the future, not just of the past. The degree of uncertainty therefore increases. They may employ structured ways of making sense of the future, such as *scenario planning*, discussed in Chapter 2 (see section 2.2.2), or they may rely more on encouraging and creating the organisational conditions necessary to encourage individuals and groups to be forward thinking, intuitive and challenging in their thinking about possible futures, approximating to *organisational learning* described above.

- In *complex* situations managers face an environment that is difficult to comprehend. This may be because of the knowledge complexity of an industry. Or it may be because of organisational complexity. The corporate centre of a big multinational firm with multiple business units, or a major public service such as a local government authority with many services, may exhibit such complexity because of its diversity, for example. Such organisations, of course, face dynamic conditions too, and therefore a combination of complexity and uncertainty. The electronics industry is in this situation. In such circumstances top management's need to recognise that the possibility of planning detailed strategies from the top is limited, arguably dangerous since specialists lower down in the organisation know more about the environment in which the organisation operates than they do. Top management's role may be more to do with setting overall strategic direction and coordinating and shaping emerging strategy from below. Insights from the ideas lens (see the commentaries) and, again, of organisational learning may be helpful here too.

Illustration 11.5

Honda and the US motorcycle market in the 1960s

There are different explanations of how successful strategies develop.

In 1984, Richard Pascale published a paper which described the success Honda had experienced with the launch of its motorcycles in the US market in the 1960s. It was a paper that has generated discussion about strategy development processes ever since. First he gave explanations provided by the Boston Consulting Group (BCG):

The success of the Japanese manufacturers originated with the growth of their domestic market during the 1950s. This resulted in a highly competitive cost position which the Japanese used as a springboard for penetration of world markets with small motorcycles in the early 1960s. . . . The basic philosophy of the Japanese manufacturers is that high volumes per model provide the potential for high productivity as a result of using capital intensive and highly automated techniques. Their market strategies are therefore directed towards developing these high model volumes, hence the careful attention that we have observed them giving to growth and market share.

Thus the BCG's account is a rational one based upon the deliberate building of a cost advantage based on volume.

Pascale's second version of events was based on interviews with the Japanese executives who launched the motorcycles in the USA:

In truth, we had no strategy other than the idea of seeing if we could sell something in the United States. It was a new frontier, a new challenge, and it fitted the 'success against all odds' culture that Mr. Honda had cultivated. We did not discuss profits or deadlines for breakeven. . . . We knew our products . . . were good but not far superior. Mr. Honda was especially confident of the 250cc and 305cc machines. The shape of the handlebar on these larger machines looked like the eyebrow of Buddha, which he felt was a strong selling point. . . . We configured our start-up inventory with 25 per cent of each of our four products – the 50cc Supercub and the 125cc, 250cc and 305cc machines. In dollar value terms, of course, the inventory was heavily weighted toward the larger bikes. . . . We were entirely in the dark the first year. Following Mr. Honda's and our own instincts, we had not attempted to move the 50cc Supercubs. . . . They seemed wholly unsuitable for the US market where everything was bigger and more luxurious. . . . We used the Honda 50s ourselves to ride around Los Angeles on errands. They attracted a lot of attention. But we still hesitated to push the 50cc bikes out of fear they might harm our image in a heavily macho market. But when

SUMMARY

This chapter has dealt with different ways in which strategy development occurs in organisations (see also Illustration 11.5). The main lessons of the chapter are as follows:

- It is important to distinguish between *intended* strategy – the desired strategic direction deliberately planned by managers – and *emergent strategy*, which may develop in a less deliberate way from the behaviours and activities inherent within an organisation.

- Most often the process of strategy development is described in terms of intended strategy as a result through *planning systems* carried out objectively and dispassionately. There are benefits and disbenefits of formal strategic planning systems. However, there is evidence to show that such formal systems are not an adequate explanation of strategy development as it occurs in practice.

the larger bikes started breaking, we had no choice. And surprisingly, the retailers who wanted to sell them weren't motorcycle dealers, they were sporting goods stores.

Two very different accounts, yet they describe the same market success. Since the publication of the paper, many writers on strategy have hotly debated what these accounts actually represent. For example, Henry Mintzberg observed: 'the conception of a novel strategy is a creative process (of synthesis), to which there are no formal techniques (analysis)'. He argued any formal planning was in the implementation of the strategy: 'strategy had to be conceived informally before it could be programmed formally'. He went on to add, 'While we run around being "rational", they use their common sense . . . they came to America prepared to *learn*.'

Michael Goold, the author of the original BCG report, defended it on the grounds that

its purpose was to discern what lay behind and accounted for Honda's success, in a way that would help others to think through what strategies would be likely to work. It tries to discern patterns in Honda's strategic decisions and actions, and to use these patterns in identifying what works well and badly.

Richard Rumelt concluded that

the 'design school' is right about the reality of forces like scaled economies, accumulated experience and

accumulative development of core competences over time . . . but my own experience is that coherent strategy based upon analyses and understandings of these forces is much more often imputed than actually observed.

And Pascale himself concluded that the serendipitous nature of Honda's strategy showed the importance of learning; that the real lessons in developing strategies were the importance of an organisation's agility and that this resides in its culture, rather than its analyses.

Source: This case example is based on R.T. Pascale, 'Perspectives on strategy: the real story behind Honda's success', *California Management Review*, vol. 26, no. 3 (Spring 1984), pp. 47–72; and H. Mintzberg, R.T. Pascale, M. Goold and R.P. Rumelt, 'The Honda effect revisited', *California Management Review*, vol. 38, no. 4 (1996), pp. 78–116.

Questions

1 Are the different accounts mutually exclusive?

2 Which of the different explanations of strategy development explained in the chapter do you discern in the Honda story?

3 Do you think Honda would have been more or less successful if it had adopted a more formalised strategic planning approach to the launch?

- Intended strategy may also come about on the basis of the direction of central *command or the vision of strategic leaders* and the *imposition of strategies* by external stakeholders.
- Strategies may emerge from within organisations. This may be explained in terms of:
  - How organisations may proactively try to cope through processes of *logical incrementalism*.
  - The *resource allocation processes* employed in the organisation that may favour some strategy projects over others.
  - The outcome of the bargaining associated with *political activity* resulting in a negotiated strategy.
  - The taken-for-granted elements of *organisational culture* favouring certain strategies.
- *Multiple processes of strategy development* are likely to be needed if organisations wish to encourage and facilitate the *challenge of taken-for-granted* assumptions and ways of doing things, create a *learning organisation* and cope with *increasingly dynamic and complex environments*.

Work assignments

Denotes more advanced work assignments.   * *Refers to a case study in the Text and Cases edition.*

11.1   Read the annual report of a company with which you are familiar as a customer (for example, a retailer or transport company). Identify the main characteristics of the intended strategy as explained in the annual report, and the characteristics of the realised strategy as you perceive it as a customer.

11.2   Using the different explanations in sections 11.3 and 11.4 characterise how strategies have developed in different organisations (for example, Intel, Ericsson*, Direct and Care*).

11.3 ✷ Planning systems exist in many different organisations. What role should planning play in a public sector organisation such as local government or the National Health Service and a multinational corporation such as the News Corporation*?

11.4 ✷ Incremental patterns of strategy development are common in organisations, and managers see advantages in this. However, there are also risks of strategic drift. Using the different explanations in sections 11.2 and 11.3, suggest how such drift might be avoided.

11.5   Suggest why different approaches to strategy development might be appropriate in different organisations such as a university, a fashion retailer, a diversified multinational corporation and high-technology company.

Integrative assignment

11.6 ✷ How does the concept of the 'learning organisation' (section 11.5.2) relate, not only to strategy development, but also to (a) that of strategic capabilities, dynamic capabilities and organisational knowledge (Chapter 3), (b) organisation culture (Chapter 5) and (c) strategic change (Chapter 14)? Bearing this in mind, what would be the challenges of developing a 'learning organisation' in a large international corporation?

An extensive range of additional materials, including audio summaries, weblinks to organisations featured in the text, definitions of key concepts and self-assessment questions, can be found on the *Exploring Corporate Strategy* Companion Website at **www.pearsoned.co.uk/ecs**

Recommended key readings

- A much quoted paper that describes different patterns of strategy development is H. Mintzberg and J.A. Waters, 'Of strategies, deliberate and emergent', *Strategic Management Journal*, vol. 6, no. 3 (1985), pp. 257–272.

- The changing role of strategic planning in the oil industry is explained by Rob Grant; see 'Strategic planning in a turbulent environment: evidence from the oil majors', *Strategic Management Journal*, vol. 24 (2003), pp. 491–517. Also see M. Mankins, 'Stop making plans, start making decisions', *Harvard Business Review*, January (2006), pp. 77–84.

- For an explanation of logical incrementalism, see J.B. Quinn, *Strategies for Change: Logical incrementalism*, Irwin, 1980; also summarised in J.B. Quinn and H. Mintzberg, *The Strategy Process*, 4th edition, Prentice Hall, (2003). Compare this with the different explanations of incremental change and the explanation of strategic drift by G. Johnson, 'Rethinking incrementalism', *Strategic Management Journal*, vol. 9, no. 1 (1988), pp. 75–91.

- How resource allocation processes develop strategies is explained in J.L. Bower and C.G. Gilbert, 'A revised model of the resource allocation process', in J.L. Bower and C.G. Gilbert (eds), *From Resource Allocation to Strategy*, Oxford University Press, 2005, pp. 439–455. The book also includes many case studies. A fascinating case study of the effects of resource allocation routines on the developing strategy of Intel is provided by Robert Burgelman in 'Fading memories: a process theory of strategic business exit in dynamic environments', *Administrative Science Quarterly*, vol. 39 (1994), pp. 34–56.

- Insights into the importance of multiple processes of strategy development can be found in S.L. Hart, 'An integrative framework for strategy-making processes', *Academy of Management Review*, vol. 17, no. 2 (1992), pp. 327–351.

References

1. Indeed there is some evidence that the social networks of leaders are related both to higher performance and to their personal reputation; see A. Mehra, A.L. Dixon, D. Brass and B. Robertson, 'The social network ties of group leaders: implications for group performance and leader reputation, *Organization Science*, vol. 17, no. 1 (2006), pp. 64–79.

2. For example, see W. Bennis and B. Nanus, *The Strategies for taking Charge*, Harper & Row, 1985; and J. Collins and J. Porras, *Built to Last: Successful Habits of Visionary Companies*, Harper Business, 2002.

3. The role of a command style in small businesses is discussed in D. Miller and I. Le Breton-Miller, 'Management insights from great and struggling family businesses', *Long Range Planning*, vol. 38 (2005), pp. 517–530. The quotes here are from p. 519.

4. In the 1970s and 1980s there were many books written on formal strategic planning approaches to strategy development. They are less common now but, for example, see N. Lake, *The Strategic Planning Workbook*, 2nd edition, Kogan Page, 2006; J.M. Bryson, *Strategic Planning for Public and Nonprofit Organizations: a guide to strengthening and sustaining organizational achievement*, 3rd edition, Jossey-Bass, 2005; and S. Haines, *The Systems Thinking Approach to Strategic Planning and Management*, St Lucie Press, 2000.

5. 'Strategic planning in a turbulent environment: evidence from the oil majors' is a study carried out by Rob Grant. See the *Strategic Management Journal*, vol. 24 (2003), pp. 491–517.

6. Again from Grant's research; see reference 5.

7. Many of these dangers are drawn from H. Mintzberg, *The Rise and Fall of Strategic Planning*, Prentice Hall, 1994.

8. Studies on the relationship between formal planning and financial performance are largely inconclusive. For example, see P. McKiernan and C. Morris, 'Strategic planning and financial performance in the UK SMEs: does formality matter?', *Journal of Management*, vol. 5 (1994), pp. S31–S42. Some studies have shown benefits in particular contexts. For example, it is argued that there are benefits to entrepreneurs setting up new ventures; see F. Delmar and S. Shane, 'Does business planning facilitate the development of new ventures?', *Strategic Management Journal*, vol. 24 (2003), pp. 1165–1185. And other studies actually show the benefits of strategic analysis and strategic thinking, rather than the benefits of formal planning systems; see C.C. Miller and L.B. Cardinal, 'Strategic planning and firm performance: a synthesis of more than two decades of research', *Academy of Management Journal*, vol. 37, no. 6 (1994), pp. 1649–1665.

9. T.J. Andersen, 'Integrating decentralized strategy making and strategic planning processes in dynamic environments', *Journal of Management Studies*, vol. 41, no. 8 (2004), pp. 1271–1299.

10. See reference 5.

11. See M. Mankins. 'Stop making plans, start making decisions', *Harvard Business Review*, January (2006), pp. 77–84.

12. See S. Elbanna, 'Strategic decision making: process perspectives', *International Journal of Management Reviews*, vol. 8, no. 1 (2006), pp. 1–20, for a useful explanation of

differences between deliberate, intended strategy development and incremental explanations. Also for a fuller discussion of different explanations of incremental strategic change see G. Johnson, 'Re-thinking incrementalism', *Strategic Management Journal*, vol. 9 (1988), pp. 75–91.

13. Two of the early extensive case studies showing how cultural and political processes give rise to the emergence of strategies are A. Pettigrew, *The Awakening Giant*, Blackwell, 1985; and G. Johnson, *Strategic Change and the Management Process*, Blackwell, 1987.

14. J.B. Quinn's research involved the examination of strategic change in companies and was published in *Strategies for Change*, Irwin, 1980. See also J.B. Quinn, 'Strategic change: logical incrementalism', in J.B. Quinn and H. Mintzberg, *The Strategy Process*, 4th edition, Prentice Hall, 2003.

15. See J.B. Quinn, *Strategies for Change*, reference 14, p. 58.

16. This definition is based on that on p. 349 of J.L. Bower and C.G. Gilbert, 'A revised model of the resource allocation process', in J.L. Bower and C.G. Gilbert (eds), *From Resource Allocation to Strategy*, Oxford University Press, 2005, pp. 439–455.

17. The original studies are J.L. Bower, *Managing the Resource Allocation Process: a Study of Corporate Planning and Investment*, Irwin, 1972; and R.A. Burgelman, 'A model of the interaction of strategic behaviour, corporate context and the concept of strategy', *Academy of Management Review*, vol. 81, no. 1 (1983), pp. 61–70; and 'A process model of internal corporate venturing in the diversified major firm', *Administrative Science Quarterly*, vol. 28 (1983), pp. 223–244.

18. For example, see T. Noda and J. Bower, 'Strategy as iterated processes of resource allocation', *Strategic Management Journal*, vol. 17 (1996), pp. 159–192.

19. The Intel case is also written up by Robert Burgelman, see *Strategy as Destiny: How strategy making shapes a company's future*, Free Press, 2002. Also see by Burgelman, 'Fading memories: a process theory of strategic business exit in dynamic environments', *Administrative Science Quarterly*, vol. 39 (1994), pp. 34–56.

20. See S. Finkelstein, 'Why smart executives fail: four case histories of how people learn the wrong lessons from history', *Business History*, vol. 48, no. 2 (2006), pp. 153–170.

21. For political perspectives on management, see J.R. DeLuca. *Political Savvy: Systematic Approaches to Leadership Behind the Scenes*, 2nd edition, Evergreen Business Group, 1999; and G.J. Miller. *Managerial Dilemmas: The Political Economy of Hierarchy*, Cambridge University Press, 2006.

22. For a discussion and an explanatory model of this political perspective, see V.K. Narayanan and L. Fahey, 'The micro politics of strategy formulation', *Academy of Management Review*, vol. 7, no. 1 (1982), pp. 25–34.

23. For an example of how different political coalitions can influence, see S. Maitlis and T. Lawrence, 'Orchestral manoeuvres in the dark: understanding failure in organizational strategizing', *Journal of Management Studies*, vol. 40, no. 1 (2003), pp. 109–140.

24. This is sometimes referred to as a 'resource dependency view' of strategy development; for the original argument see J. Pfeffer and G.R. Salancik, *The External Control of Organisations: A Resource Dependence Perspective*, Harper & Row, 1978.

25. This is the argument advanced by J.M. Bartunek, D. Kolb and R. Lewicki, 'Bringing conflict out from behind the scenes: private informal, and nonrational dimensions of conflict in organizations', in D. Kolb and J. Bartunek (eds), *Hidden Conflict in Organizations: Uncovering Behind the Scenes Disputes*, Sage, 1992.

26. This is explained by Gerry Johnson more fully in 'Re-thinking incrementalism', reference 12.

27. See S. Hart and C. Banbury, 'How strategy making processes can make a difference', *Strategic management Journal*, vol. 15, no. 4 (1994), pp. 251–269.

28. This idea of a balance between analytic rigour and intuition and imagination is the theme of G. Szulanski and K. Amin, 'Learning to make strategy: balancing discipline and imagination', *Long Range Planning*, vol. 34 (2001), pp. 537–556.

29. For two approaches to analysing processes of strategy development see A. Bailey, K. Daniels and G. Johnson, 'Validation of a multi-dimensional measure of strategy development processes', *British Journal of Management*, vol. 11 (2000), pp. 151–162; and S.L. Hart, 'An integrative framework for strategy-making processes', *Academy of Management Review*, vol. 17, no. 2 (1992), pp. 327–351.

30. For a discussion of the differences between strategy development in the public and private sectors see N. Collier, F. Fishwick and G. Johnson, 'The processes of strategy development in the public sector', in G. Johnson and K. Scholes (eds), *Exploring Public Sector Strategy*, Pearson Education, 2001.

31. The concept of the learning organisation is explained in P. Senge, *The Fifth Discipline: The art and practice of the learning organisation*, Doubleday/Century, 1990. Also M. Crossan, H.W. Lane and R.E. White, 'An organizational learning framework; from intuition to institution', *Academy of Management Review*, vol. 24, no. 3 (1999), pp. 522–537. Also see J. Coopey, 'The learning organization, power, politics and ideology', *Management Learning*, vol. 26, no. 2 (1995), pp. 193–213.

32. The concept of the organisation as a set of social networks is discussed by, for example, M.S. Granovetter, 'The strength of weak ties', *American Journal of Sociology*, vol. 78, no. 6 (1973), pp. 1360–1380; and G.R. Carroll and A.C. Teo, 'On the social networks of managers', *Academy of Management Journal*, vol. 39, no. 2 (1996), pp. 421–440.

33. See G. Hamel and L. Valikangas, 'The quest for resilience', *Harvard Business Review*, September (2003), pp. 52–63.

34. R. Duncan's research, on which this classification is based, can be found in 'Characteristics of organisational environments and perceived environmental uncertainty', *Administrative Science Quarterly*, vol. 17, no. 3 (1972), pp. 313–327.

Strategy development at Intel*

Jill Shepherd, Segal Graduate School of Business
Simon Fraser University, Canada

Intel (an abbreviation of Integrated Electronics) is a digital company operating in, having arguably created, the semiconductor industry. Over 30 years the company has achieved strategic transformation twice.

Epoch I

Between 1968 and 1985, during which the CEO was mostly Gordon Moore, Intel was a memory company. Founded by Gordon Moore and Robert Noyce, Intel was the first company to specialise in integrated circuit memory products. Noyce co-invented the integrated circuit, whereas Moore, a physical chemist, saw the potential of metal–oxide–semiconductor (MOS) process technology as a way of mass producing semiconductors at low cost. Both managers left Fairchild Semiconductors, the subsidiary of Fairchild Camera and Instrument Corporation they had helped found. According to Noyce, senior management at Fairchild were unsupportive of innovation, perhaps because it had become too complex and big an organisation. In turn, Andy Grove joined Intel, thinking that the departure of Moore and Noyce left Fairchild fatally bereft of middle management. Their aim was not to transform the industry, but to make memory chips which did not compete directly with Fairchild and others because they were complex.

Two events were critical in these early days. First, the first Intel memory chip was static (SRAM), but was soon replaced by a dynamic (DRAM) chip. Second, the traditional strategic choice of second-sourcing manufacturing 'failed' as the chosen company could not deliver a new-generation manufacturing process. Intel was obliged to do all its own manufacturing, but also retained all the profits. This early success and

Photo: Courtesy of Intel Corporation

'luck', according to Gordon Moore, lasted nearly 20 years. Although this good fortune can be construed as luck, perhaps Intel was ahead of the silicon technology competence game – maybe without knowing it – and was expecting too much of its supplier.

Developing, manufacturing and marketing DRAM chips involved an approach to management which was structured, disciplined and controlled. Technical excellence was married with goals stipulated by senior management, which needed cross-functional discipline if they were to be reached on time. An ethos of top-down financial rigour was balanced by a culture in which those who knew what was needed to achieve the goals were never crowded out because they were junior. Knowledge was more powerful when associated with technical excellence than hierarchical position, creating an Intel ethos of constructive debate. Insofar as it existed, strategic

---

* Intel is one of the most researched companies, courtesy of a highly productive partnership between once CEO and subsequent Chairman of Intel, Andy Grove, and Robert Burgelman, a Professor of Management at Stanford University Graduate School of Business.

planning was fairly informal: ideas bubbled up from engineers and marketers which top management assessed and allocated funds to. Recruitment processes focused on hiring staff suited to the Intel culture, and rewards were associated with high performance.

Epoch II

Come the early 1980s, Intel moved towards a different era, courtesy of a more crowded marketplace. Over 10 years, the big earner, DRAM, lost market share from 83 per cent to 1.3 per cent and amounted to only 5 per cent of Intel's revenue, down from 90 per cent. Innovation moved towards the equipment manufacturers away from the chip suppliers and professional buyers sought much tougher deals. Competition had heated up with choices having to be made as to which technical areas to excel in.

At this time Intel made a decision to distance geographically its three main product development areas, DRAM, EPROM (its most profitable product in the mid-1980s) and microprocessors. In the case of microprocessors, the development of which had begun in Epoch I, the new basis of advantage increasingly became chip design rather than manufacturing process as it was in the other areas.

Over time DRAM lost manufacturing capacity within Intel to the unplanned microprocessor area. A rule, created by the first financial director and designed to maintain Intel as a technological leading-edge company, stipulated that manufacturing capacity was allocated in proportion to the profit margins achieved in the different product sectors. The emphasis within the DRAM group was on finding sophisticated technical solutions to DRAM's problems; it was, however, innovation in markets where innovation was no longer commercially viable. DRAM managers none the less fought to have manufacturing capacity assigned purely to DRAM, proposing that capacity be allocated on the basis of manufacturing cost. Senior management refused.

Once this decision was made to keep the resource allocation rule, the strategic freedom left to corporate managers to recover the founding businesses, SCRAM and DRAM, to which they were very attached, diminished as market share fell beyond what could be deemed worthwhile recovering. DRAM managers had to compete internally with the technological prowess of the other product areas where morale and excitement were at high levels and innovation was happening in an increasingly dynamic market. And as microprocessors gradually became more profitable, manufacturing capacity and investment were increasingly allocated away from memory towards them. Eventually corporate managers realised that Intel would never be a player in the 64K DRAM chip game, despite having been the creator of the business. In 1985, top management came to realise they had to withdraw from the DRAM market. In 1986, Intel made a net loss of $173m (≈ €150m; £103m) and lost nearly a third of its workforce.

However, lingering resistance to the exit continued. Manufacturing personnel ignored implications of exiting from DRAM by trying to show they could compete in the marketplace externally, by explaining failure in terms of the strong dollar against the Japanese yen and battling with poor morale. Eventually Andy Grove, CEO from 1987, took the executive decision to withdraw from EPROM, leaving no doubt that microprocessors now represented Intel's future strategic direction. The subsequent exit from EPROM was rapidly executed. Staff associated with EPROM left and set up their own start-up.

The period pre and post the exiting of DRAM was turbulent. Although seemingly messy, it gave rise to a great deal of new thinking. A new link was created between manufacturing and technology, trying to rid the company of the rivalries established in the era of internal competition between DRAM and other technology areas and return to the era of collaboration. The approach to technology was also rethought and moved away from being so product based. Product definition and design as well as sales and marketing became more important, manufacturing less so. Corporate strategy came into line with market developments and middle management priorities; and formal strategic planning processes and corporate management's statements of strategy began to champion microprocessors.

That said, the potential of the PC was not recognised immediately. Indeed, a presentation made by a newly recruited manager on that potential failed to grab the attention of managers. Later Intel managers reflected this was because the presenter, although enthusiastic, appeared to be 'an amateur'. Had that same analytical content been presented by a 'smooth-talker', perhaps the importance of the PC market would have been taken on board sooner by corporate management.

By the mid-1990s the relatively informal processes of strategy development were becoming difficult in what had become a huge corporation. More formal strategic long-range plans were introduced where each business unit had a subcommittee which on a yearly basis developed a business plan to be submitted for approval to corporate. Whilst this added discipline, the problem was that these plans became repetitive and lacked the innovation and renewal that had driven Intel's success.

Epoch III

Intel's performance as a microprocessor company was financially spectacular. In 1998 Andy Grove became Chairman and Craig Barrett took over as CEO. Both were aware that, once again, Intel was facing new challenges. After 10 years of 30 per cent per annum compound growth, 1998 saw a slow-down. The era of the Internet had arrived and the company needed to broaden its horizons. Not only did Intel need to maintain its competence in design and product development alongside continuing manufacturing competence, but also it needed to understand more the needs of the user and develop competences in corporate venturing, allowing part or full ownership of companies with strategically important technologies. After a period of adhering strongly to its focus on microprocessors, it needed ways of regaining the entrepreneurial flourish of its former days. In any case, the business had become more complex, requiring as many chips as possible to be put along the whole value chain of the Internet moving it towards wireless and the digital home.

Barrett launched a series of seminars for Intel top management aimed at getting them to dream up new businesses and a New Business Group (NBG), with different processes and values, was founded with the brief to kickstart new internal business ventures. A framework was created to handle the interface between the NBG and the rest of the company to establish whether any proposed new business was not only strategically important externally but also built on, or required, the development of new competences internally.

The early years under Barrett saw a flourish of activity and new ventures. In the first two years these

included: buying DEC's chip unit with rights to the zippy StrongARM processor, which Intel adopts for some mobile and networking products; dozens of new products in 1998, including routers and switches; the launch of the cheap Celeron chip; the establishment of a home-products group to develop web appliances and Internet-enabled TVs and set-top boxes; the acquisition of networking chipmaker Level One, specialising in chips that connect network cards to wiring; and of Dialogic, a maker of PC-based phone systems, giving Intel technology for the convergence of voice and data networks; and a home networking kit to send data over phone wiring in homes. The year of 1999 saw the launch of 13 networking chips and Intel's first web-hosting centre, with capacity for 10,000 servers and for serving hundreds of e-commerce companies; the acquisition of DSP Communications, a leader in wireless phone technology, and IPivot, a maker of gear for speeding up secure e-commerce transactions; and in 2000 the launch of seven server appliances, called the NetStructure family, to speed up and manage web traffic.

In 2002 efforts were directed at promoting wireless technology development through an investment fund which was extended in 2004 to fuel the advance of the Digital Age into people's homes making the transfer of photos, music, documents, films possible between various devices. The fund backed start-ups working in the area and was also aimed at expanding interest in the area, both technological and consumer oriented. Intel believed that PCs would be needed for storage in the digital home but saw its future in all kinds of semiconductors, not just those for PCs. For example, Intel invested in three companies: BridgeCo, which designs chips to link devices within the home; Entropic, which designed chips for networking over coaxial cable; and Musicmatch, selling software that records, organises and plays music. By how much digital appliances would complement or substitute for PCs remained to be seen, but by 2003 Intel had determined to establish itself as a leader in the design, marketing and selling of chips.

In 2004 it was announced that in 2005 Paul S. Otellini, who does not have the engineering background of Barrett, would take over from him as CEO, who would take over as Chairman, making Andy Grove Chairman Emeritus. *Business Week* commented:

In this new age of 'Think Intel Everywhere', not just inside the PC, Intel will face tough competition, as it enters the communication, entertainment and wireless sectors whilst also defending its flank from other microprocessor companies such as AMD. . . . Whilst remaining driven by innovation Barrett and Otellini have spent time trying to learn from past mistakes, to become more market savvy, forging closer relationship with customers to avoid designing products no one desires, becoming more cooperative and less arrogant whilst also investing in five new factories in 2005.

Sources:
R.A. Burgelman, *Strategy as Destiny: How strategy-making shapes a company's Future*, Free Press, 2002; R.A. Burgelman, 'Strategy as vector and the inertia of coevolutionary lock-in', *Administrative Science Quarterly*, vol. 47 (2002), pp. 325–358; *Business Week*, 13 March (2000), pp. 110–119.

Business Week, online (http://www.businessweek.com/technology/content/) (7 January 2004); O. Kharif, 'Intel bets big on the digital home', *Business Week*, 7 January (2004); *Business Week*, online (http://www.businessweek.com/technology/content/jan2004/tc2004017r7492rtc057.htm) (2 March 2004).

'What is CEO Craig Barrett up to? Hint: It's about much more than computers', *Business Week*, 8 March (2004), pp. 56–64.

Questions

1 Identify the different strategy development processes operating in Intel. How different/similar were these processes within and between the different epochs?

2 How effective were these different processes? What effect did these processes have on Intel's performance?

3 What were the tensions between processes within each epoch?

4 What proposals would you make as to the most appropriate strategy development processes that should exist as Intel moves into a more and more diversified business model?

Organising for Success

LEARNING OUTCOMES

After reading this chapter you should be able to:

→ Identify key challenges in organising for success, including ensuring control, managing knowledge, coping with change and responding to internationalisation.

→ Analyse main structural types of organisations in terms of their strengths and weaknesses.

→ Recognise how important organisational processes (such as planning systems and performance targets) need to be designed to fit their circumstances.

→ Appreciate how internal and external relationships can integrate knowledge and resources within and between organisations.

→ Recognise how the three strands of structure, processes and relationships should reinforce each other in organisational configurations and the managerial dilemmas involved.

12.1 INTRODUCTION

Perhaps the most important resource of an organisation is its *people*. So the structural roles people play, the processes through which they interact and the relationships that they build are crucial to the success of strategy. These are all issues of 'organisational design'. Recalling Yahoo!'s 'Peanut Butter Manifesto' from Chapter 1, organisational design can be a critical issue in the success and failure of organisations. Yahoo! was failing partly because the business unit structure created overlapping responsibilities, organisational 'silos' were fragmenting necessary internal relationships, and organisational processes were not working well to hold managers accountable for performance.

Views about designing organisations are changing in today's world. Traditionally management scientists have emphasised formal structures.[1] This formal approach suited a top-down, command-and-control view of strategy, where managers at the top made the decisions and the rest of the organisation simply implemented them. The key debate in Illustration 12.6 questions whether formal structures can really adapt to strategy in this simple way. In a world where key knowledge is held by employees at all levels in the organisation, and where change is constant, relying on formal top-down structures may no longer be enough.

A fast-moving, knowledge-intensive world raises two issues for organisations. First, a static concept of formal structure is less and less appropriate. Organisations are constantly having to reorganise themselves in response to changing conditions. For this reason some authors suggest that we should use the *verb* 'organising' more than the *noun* 'organisation'.[2] Second, harnessing the valuable knowledge that lies throughout the organisation requires more than top-down formal hierarchies. Informal relationships and processes are vital to generating and sharing the in-depth knowledge that is now often fundamental to competitive advantage.

This chapter takes on board new thinking about organisational design both by emphasising change and by including informal processes and relationships alongside the formal. An important idea here is that formal structures and processes need to be aligned with informal processes and relationships into coherent *configurations*. An organisation's **configuration** consists of the structures, processes and relationships through which the organisation operates[3] – as shown in Exhibit 12.1. Configuring the organisation so that all these elements fit both together and with key strategic challenges is crucial to organisational success.

> An organisation's **configuration** consists of the structures, processes and relationships through which the organisation operates

Exhibit 12.1 shows the three strands of an organisation's configuration, locking together into a coherent 'virtuous circle'. These three strands provide the structure for the first parts of the chapter, addressing in turn:

● The *structural design* (describing formal roles, responsibilities and lines of reporting) in organisations. Structural design can deeply influence the sources of an organisation's advantage, particularly with regard to knowledge management; failure to adjust structures appropriately can fatally undermine strategy implementation. But good structure alone is not enough for success.

Exhibit 12.1 Organisational configurations: structure, processes and relationships

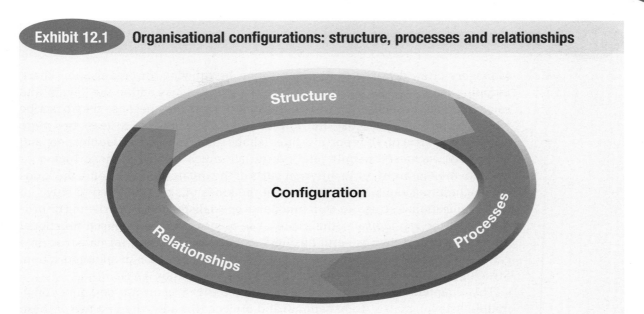

- The *processes* that drive and support people within and around an organisation. These processes too can have a major influence on success or failure, defining how strategies are made and controlled and the ways that managers and other employees interact and implement strategy in action.

- The *relationships* that connect people both within and outside the organisation, in particular:
  - relationships between organisational units and the centre (this relates to discussions in Chapter 7 about the role of corporate parents);
  - relationships outside the firm, including issues such as *outsourcing* (raised in Chapter 3) and *strategic alliances* (raised in Chapter 8).

The various structures, processes and relationships will be considered in the light of three key challenges for organisations in the twenty-first century:

- The *speed of change* and the increased levels of *uncertainty* in the business environment, as discussed in Chapter 2. As a result, organisations need to have flexible designs and be skilled at reorganising.

- The importance of *knowledge creation* and *knowledge sharing* as a fundamental ingredient of strategic success, as discussed in Chapter 3. Organisational designs should both foster concentrations of expertise and encourage people to share their knowledge.

- The rise of *internationalisation,* as discussed in Chapter 8. Organising for an international context has many challenges: communicating across wider geography, coordinating more diversity and building relationships across diverse cultures are some examples. Internationalisation also brings greater recognition of different kinds of organising around the world.

12.2 STRUCTURAL TYPES

Managers often describe their organisation by drawing an organisation chart, mapping out its formal structure. These structural charts define the 'levels' and roles in an organisation. They are important to managers because they describe who is responsible for what. But formal structures matter in at least two more ways. First, structural reporting lines shape patterns of communication and knowledge exchange: people tend not to talk much to people much higher or lower in the hierarchy, or in different parts of the organisation. Second, the kinds of structural positions at the top suggest the kinds of skills required to move up the organisation: a structure with functional specialists such as marketing or production at the top indicates the importance to success of specialised functional disciplines rather than general business experience. In short, formal structures can reveal a great deal about the role of knowledge and skills in an organisation. Structures can therefore be hotly debated (see Illustration 12.1).

This chapter begins with a review of five basic structural types: functional, multidivisional, matrix, transnational and project.[4] Broadly, the first two of these tend to emphasise one structural dimension over another, either functional specialisms or business units. The three that follow tend to mix structural dimensions more evenly, for instance trying to give product and geographical units equal weight. However, none of these structures is a universal solution to the challenges of organising. Rather, the right structure depends on the particular kinds of challenges each organisation faces.

Researchers propose a wide number of important challenges (sometimes called 'contingencies') shaping organisational structure, including organisational size, extent of diversification and type of technology.[5] This chapter will particularly focus on how the five structural types fit both the traditional challenge of control and the three new challenges of change, knowledge and internationalisation. This implies that the first step in organisational design is deciding what the key challenges facing the organisation actually are. As we shall see later, the configurational approach stresses that whatever structure is chosen should also be aligned with matching processes and relationships.

12.2.1 The functional structure

A **functional structure** is based on the primary activities that have to be undertaken by an organisation such as production, finance and accounting, marketing, human resources and research and development

KEY CONCEPT
www.pearsoned.co.uk/ecs

Structures

Once an organisation grows beyond a very basic level of size and complexity, it has to start dividing up responsibilities. One fundamental kind of structure is the **functional structure**, which divides responsibilities according to the organisation's primary roles such as production, research and sales. Exhibit 12.2 represents a typical organisation chart for such a business. This structure is usually found in smaller companies, or those with narrow, rather than diverse, product ranges. Also, within a multidivisional structure (see below), the divisions themselves may be split up into functional departments (as in Exhibit 12.3 below).

Exhibit 12.2 also summarises the potential advantages and disadvantages of a functional structure. There are advantages in that it gives senior managers direct hands-on involvement in operations and allows greater operational control from the top. The functional structure provides a clear definition of roles and tasks,

Illustration 12.1

Volkswagen: a case of centralisation

A new chief executive introduces a more centralised structure over this multi-brand giant.

In 2007, following the Porsche car company's building up of a controlling stake and the installation of a new chief executive, German car manufacturer Volkswagen announced a major reorganisation. For the previous few years, Volkswagen had been organised as two groups of brands under the main Volkswagen and Audi labels (see Figure 1), with technical and marketing expertise clustered around particular brands within these. Now the company was to be reorganised into two main groups, a mass market group (VW, Skoda, SEAT) and a more luxury market group (Audi, Bentley, Bugatti and Lamborghini). Volkswagen also had a large stake in truck company Scania. The company would be more centralised, with new corporate responsibilities for production, sales, distribution and R&D (see Figure 2). The new CEO, Martin Winterkorn, would also act as head of R&D and be directly responsible for the VW group of brands.

The stated aim of this more centralised structure was to increase synergies between the various brands. More centralised R&D would help ensure the sharing of engines and components, and

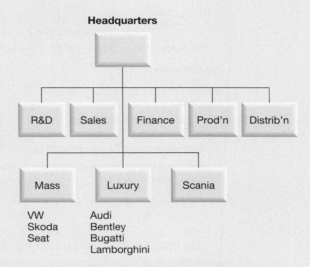

Figure 2 Volkswagen, January 2007 (simplifed)

centralisation of production would assist the optimisation of factory usage across the company. The departing head of the Volkswagen group took another view. He asserted that, in order to ensure cross-functional integration and motivation, expertise needed to identify closely with particular brands. According to him, the new structure mimicked the centralised Porsche structure, but Porsche was a much smaller company with just one main brand. Porsche's spokespersons responded by recalling that Porsche was the most profitable car company in the world, while Volkswagen was one of the least.

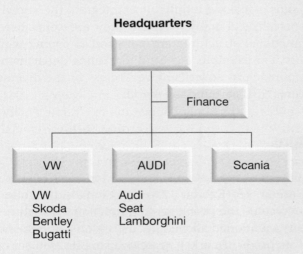

Figure 1 Volkswagen, November 2006 (simplified)

Questions

1 Which type of structure did the old decentralised structure resemble most and which type of structure is Volkswagen moving closer to?

2 What pros and cons can you see in the new Volkswagen structure?

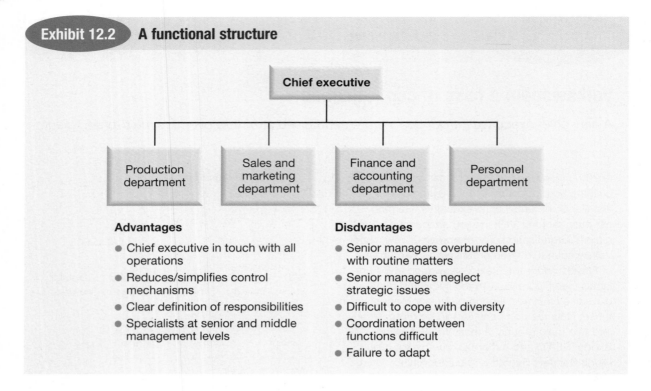

Exhibit 12.2 **A functional structure**

Chief executive

Production department | Sales and marketing department | Finance and accounting department | Personnel department

Advantages

- Chief executive in touch with all operations
- Reduces/simplifies control mechanisms
- Clear definition of responsibilities
- Specialists at senior and middle management levels

Disdvantages

- Senior managers overburdened with routine matters
- Senior managers neglect strategic issues
- Difficult to cope with diversity
- Coordination between functions difficult
- Failure to adapt

increasing accountability. Functional departments also provide concentrations of expertise, thus fostering knowledge development in areas of functional specialism.

However, there are disadvantages, particularly as organisations become larger or more diverse. Perhaps the major concern in a fast-moving world is that senior managers focus on their functional responsibilities, becoming overburdened with routine operations and too concerned with narrow functional interests. As a result, they find it hard either to take a strategic view of the organisation as a whole or to manage coordinated responses quickly. Thus functional organisations can be inflexible. Separate functional departments tend also to be inward looking – so-called 'functional silos' – making it difficult to integrate the knowledge of different functional specialists. Finally, because they are centralised around particular functions, functional structures are not good at coping with product or geographical diversity. For example, a central marketing department may try to impose a uniform approach to advertising regardless of the diverse needs of the organisation's various SBUs around the world.

12.2.2 The multidivisional structure

A multidivisional structure is built up of separate divisions on the basis of products, services or geographical areas

A **multidivisional structure** is built up of separate divisions on the basis of products, services or geographical areas (see Exhibit 12.3). Divisionalisation often comes about as an attempt to overcome the problems that functional structures have in dealing with the diversity mentioned above.[6] Each division can respond to the specific requirements of its product/market strategy, using its own set of functional departments. A similar situation exists in many public services, where the organisation is structured around *service departments* such as recreation, social services and education.

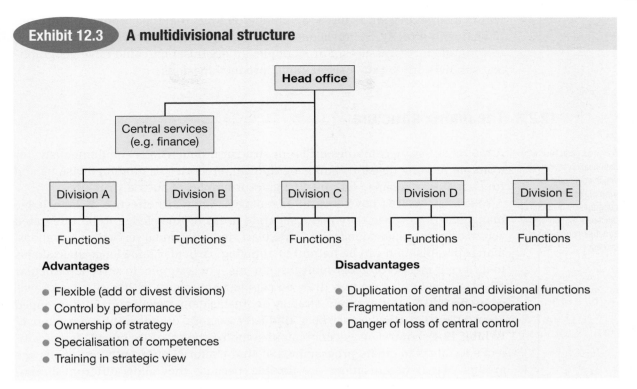

Exhibit 12.3 **A multidivisional structure**

Advantages

- Flexible (add or divest divisions)
- Control by performance
- Ownership of strategy
- Specialisation of competences
- Training in strategic view

Disadvantages

- Duplication of central and divisional functions
- Fragmentation and non-cooperation
- Danger of loss of central control

There are several potential advantages to divisional structures. They are flexible in the sense that organisations can add, close or merge divisions as circumstances change. As self-standing business units, it is possible to control divisions from a distance by monitoring business performance. Divisional managers have greater personal ownership for their own divisional strategies. Geographical divisions – for example, a European division or a North American division – offer a means of managing internationally. There can be benefits of specialisation within a division, allowing competences to develop with a clearer focus on a particular product group, technology or customer group. Management responsibility for a whole divisional business is good training in taking a strategic view for managers expecting to go on to a main board position.

However, divisional structures can also have disadvantages of three main types. First, divisions can become so self-sufficient that they are *de facto* independent businesses, but duplicating the functions and costs of the corporate centre of the company. So it may make more sense to split the company into independent businesses, and demergers of this type have been very common. Second, divisionalisation tends to get in the way of cooperation and knowledge sharing between business units: divisions can quite literally divide. Expertise is fragmented and divisional performance targets provide poor incentives to collaborate with other divisions. Finally, divisions may become too autonomous, especially where joint ventures and partnership dilute ownership. In these cases, multidivisionals degenerate into *holding companies*, where the corporate centre effectively 'holds' the various businesses in a largely financial sense, exercising little control and adding very little value. Exhibit 12.3 summarises these potential advantages and disadvantages of a multidivisional structure.

Large and complex multidivisional companies often have a second tier of *subdivisions* within their main divisions. Treating smaller SBUs as subdivisions within a large division reduces the number of units that the corporate centre has to deal with directly. Subdivisions can also help complex organisations respond to contradictory pressures. For example, an organisation could have geographical subdivisions within a set of global product divisions.

12.2.3 The matrix structure

A **matrix structure** is a combination of structures which could take the form of product and geographical divisions or functional and divisional structures operating in tandem

A **matrix structure** combines different structural dimensions simultaneously, for example product divisions and geographical territories or product divisions and functional specialisms.[7] Exhibit 12.4 gives examples of such a structure.

Matrix structures have several advantages. They are effective at knowledge management because they allow separate areas of knowledge to be integrated across organisational boundaries. Particularly in professional service organisations, matrix organisation can be helpful in applying particular knowledge specialisms to different market or geographical segments. For example, to serve a particular client, a consulting firm may draw on people from groups with particular knowledge specialisms (for example, strategy or organisation design) and others grouped according to particular markets (industry sectors or geographical regions).[8] Exhibit 12.4 shows how a school might combine the separate knowledge of subject specialists to create programmes of study tailored differently to various age groups. Matrix organisations are flexible, because they allow different dimensions of the organisation to be mixed together. They are particularly attractive to organisations operating globally, because of the possible mix between local and global dimensions. For example, a global company may prefer geographically defined divisions as the operating units for local marketing (because of their specialist local knowledge of customers). But at the same time it may still want global product divisions responsible for the worldwide coordination of product development and manufacturing, taking advantage of economies of scale and specialisation.

However, because a matrix structure replaces formal lines of authority with (cross-matrix) relationships, this often brings problems. In particular, it will typically take *longer to reach decisions* because of bargaining between the managers of different dimensions. There may also be *conflict* because staff find themselves responsible to managers from two structural dimensions. In short, matrix organisations are hard to control.

As with any structure, but particularly with the matrix structure, the critical issue in practice is the way it actually works (that is, the processes and relationships). The key ingredient in a successful matrix structure can be senior managers good at sustaining collaborative relationships (across the matrix) and coping with the messiness and ambiguity which that can bring. It is for this reason that Christopher Bartlett and Sumantra Ghoshal describe the matrix as involving a 'state of mind' as much as a formal structure.[9]

12.2.4 The transnational structure

The **transnational structure** is a means of managing internationally which is particularly effective in exploiting knowledge across borders. The transnational

Exhibit 12.4 Two examples of matrix structures

(a) Multinational organisation

(b) School

Advantages	Disadvantages
● Integrate knowledge	● Length of time to take decisions
● Flexible	● Unclear job and task responsibilities
● Allow dual dimensions	● Unclear cost and profit responsibilities
	● High degrees of conflict

A **transnational structure** combines the local responsiveness of the international subsidiary with the coordination advantages found in global product companies

structure seeks to obtain the best from the two extreme international strategies, the multidomestic strategy and the global strategy (see Chapter 8). As in Exhibit 12.5, a global strategy would typically be supported by global product divisions (for example, a worldwide cars division and a worldwide lorries division); a multidomestic strategy would be supported by local subsidiaries with a great deal of design, manufacturing and marketing autonomy for all products (for example, the local subsidiary responsible for both cars and lorries). In the exhibit, international divisions refer to stand-alone divisions tacked

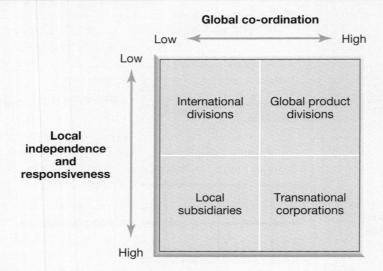

Exhibit 12.5 **Multinational structures**

alongside the structures of the major home-based business, as is often the case with American corporations as they start to internationalise (for example, in North America having car and lorry divisions, while overseas both businesses would be handled by the international division). The transnational structure, however, attempts to achieve both high local responsiveness and high global coordination.

As Bartlett and Ghoshal describe it, the transnational is like a matrix but has two specific features: first, it responds specifically to the challenge of internationalisation; second, it tends to have more fixed responsibilities within its cross-cutting dimensions.[9] The transnational has the following detailed characteristics:

● Each national unit operates independently, but is a *source of ideas and capabilities* for the whole corporation. For example, in Unilever, the centre for innovation in hair-care products worldwide is in France.[9]

● National units achieve greater scale economies through *specialisation* on behalf of the whole corporation, or at least large regions. Unilever in Europe has replaced its web of small national food manufacturing units with a few specialised larger factories that export its products to other European countries.

● The *corporate centre* manages this global network by first establishing the role of each business unit, then sustaining the systems, relationships and culture to make the network of business units operate effectively. Unilever has established a system of 'forums' bringing managers together internationally to help them swap experience and coordinate their needs.

The success of a transnational corporation is dependent on the ability *simultaneously* to achieve global competences, local responsiveness and organisation-wide innovation and learning. This requires clarity as to boundaries, relationships and the roles that the various managers need to perform. For example:

- *Global business managers* have the overriding responsibility to further the company's global competitiveness, which will cross both national and functional boundaries. They must be the *product/market strategist*, the *architect* of the business resources and competences, the *driver of product innovation* and the *coordinator* of transnational transactions.

- *Country or area managers* have potentially a dual responsibility to other parts of the transnational. First, they must act as a *sensor* of local needs and feed these back to those responsible internationally for new products or services. Second, they should seek to *build* unique competences: that is, become a centre of excellence which allows them to be a *contributor* to the company as a whole, in manufacturing or research and development, for instance.

- *Functional managers* such as finance or IT have a major responsibility for ensuring worldwide innovation and learning across the various parts of the organisation. This requires the skill to recognise and spread best practice across the organisation. So they must be able to *scan* the organisation for best practice, *cross-pollinate* this best practice and be the *champion* of innovations.

- *Corporate (head office) managers* integrate these other roles and responsibilities. Not only are they the *leaders*, but they are also the *talent spotters* among business, country and functional managers, facilitating the interplay between them. For example, they must foster the processes of innovation and knowledge creation. They are responsible for the *development* of a strong management centre in the organisation.

There are some disadvantages to a transnational structure. It is very demanding of managers in terms of willingness to work not just at their immediate responsibilities but for the good of the transnational as a whole. Diffuse responsibilities also make for similar complexities and control problems to those of the matrix organisation. The Swiss–Swedish engineering giant ABB was often used as a model for the transnational during the 1990s, but at the beginning of this century the company restructured along clearer product divisional lines.[10] Strengthening the product divisions over the country managers was intended to reduce internal politics and simplify international coordination.

12.2.5 Project-based structures[10]

A **project-based structure** is one where teams are created, undertake the work and are then dissolved

Many organisations rely heavily on project teams with a finite life span. A **project-based structure** is one where teams are created, undertake the work (for example, internal or external contracts) and are then dissolved.[11] This can be particularly appropriate for organisations that deliver large and expensive goods or services (civil engineering, information systems, films) or those delivering time-limited events (conferences, sporting events or consulting engagements). The organisation structure is a constantly changing collection of project teams created, steered and glued together loosely by a small corporate group. Many organisations use such teams in a more ad hoc way to complement the 'main' structure. For example, *taskforces* are set up to make progress on new elements of strategy or to provide momentum where the regular structure of the organisation is not effective.

The project-based structure can be highly flexible, with projects being set up and dissolved as required. Because project teams should have clear tasks to achieve within a defined life, accountability and control are good. As project team members will typically be drawn from different departments within the firm, projects can be effective at knowledge exchange. Projects can also draw members internationally and, because project life spans are typically short, project teams may be more willing to work temporarily around the world. There are disadvantages, however. Without strong programme management providing overarching strategic control, organisations are prone to proliferate projects in an ill-coordinated fashion. The constant breaking up of project teams can also hinder the accumulation of knowledge over time or within specialisms.

Overall, project-based structures have been growing in importance because of their inherent flexibility. Such flexibility can be vital in a fast-moving world where individual knowledge and competences need to be redeployed and integrated quickly and in novel ways.

12.2.6 Choosing structures

At the beginning of this chapter we stressed the challenges of control, change, knowledge and internationalisation for organisational design today. From our discussion so far, it should be clear that functional, multidivisional, matrix, transnational and project structures each have their own advantages and disadvantages with regard to these four challenges. Organisational designers, therefore, have to choose structures according to the particular strategic challenges (or 'contingencies') they face.

Exhibit 12.6 summarises how the five basic structures meet the challenges of control, change, knowledge and inernationalisation introduced at the beginning of the chapter. No structure scores high across all four challenges. Organisational designers face choices. If they seek control, but are less concerned for flexibility in response to change or global reach, then they might prefer a functional structure. If they want to foster knowledge and flexibility on a global scale,

Exhibit 12.6 **Comparison of structures**

Challenge	Functional	Multidivisional	Matrix	Transnational	Project
Control	★★★	★★	★	★★	★★
Change	★	★★	★★★	★★★	★★★
Knowledge	★★	★	★★★	★★★	★★
Internationalisation	★	★★	★★★	★★★	★★

★ Stars indicate typical capacities to cope with each challenge, with three stars indicating high, two indicating medium and one indicating poor.

then they might consider a matrix or transnational structure. Structural choice depends on the strategic challenges the organisation faces.

In reality, few organisations adopt a structure that is just like one of the pure structural types discussed above. Structures often blend different types (see section 12.5) and have to be tailor-made to the particular mix of challenges facing the organisation. Michael Goold and Andrew Campbell provide *nine design tests* against which to check specific tailor-made structural solutions.[12] The first four tests stress fit with the key objectives and constraints of the organisation:

- *The Market-Advantage Test.* This test of fit with market strategy is fundamental, following Alfred Chandler's classic principle that 'structure follows strategy'.[13] For example, if coordination between two steps in a production process is important to market advantage, then they should probably be placed in the same structural unit.

- *The Parenting Advantage Test.* The structural design should fit the 'parenting' role of the corporate centre (see Chapter 7). For example, if the corporate centre aims to add value as a synergy manager, then it should design a structure that places important integrative specialisms, such as marketing or research, at the centre.

- *The People Test.* The structural design must fit the people available. It is dangerous to switch completely from a functional structure to a multidivisional structure if, as is likely, the organisation lacks managers with competence in running decentralised business units.

- *The Feasibility Test.* This is a catch-all category, indicating that the structure must fit legal, stakeholder, trade union or similar constraints. For example, after scandals involving biased research, investment banks are now required by financial regulators to separate their research and analysis departments from their deal-making departments.

Goold and Campbell then propose five tests based on good general design principles, as follows:

- *The Specialised Cultures Test.* This test reflects the value of bringing together specialists so that they can develop their expertise in close collaboration with each other. A structure fails if it breaks up important specialist cultures.

- *The Difficult Links Test.* This test asks whether a proposed structure will set up links between parts of the organisations that are important but bound to be strained. For example, extreme decentralisation to profit-accountable business units is likely to strain relationships with a central research and development department. Unless compensating mechanisms are put in place, this kind of structure is likely to fail.

- *The Redundant Hierarchy Test.* Any structural design should be checked in case it has too many layers of management, causing undue blockages and expense. Delayering in response to redundant hierarchies has been an important structural trend in recent years.

- *The Accountability Test.* This test stresses the importance of clear lines of accountability, ensuring the control and commitment of managers throughout the structure. Because of their dual lines of reporting, matrix structures are often accused of lacking clear accountability.

● *The Flexibility Test*. In a fast-moving world, an important test is the extent to which a design will allow for change in the future. For instance, divisional domains should be specified broadly enough to allow divisional managers to follow new opportunities as they emerge. As Kathleen Eisenhardt puts it, structures should also have enough 'modularity' (that is, standardisation) to allow easy 'patching' of one part of the organisation onto another part of the organisation, as market needs change.[14]

Goold and Campbell's nine tests provide a rigorous screen for effective structures. But even if the structural design passes these tests, the structure still needs to be matched to the other strands of the organisation's configuration, its processes and relationships. Each strand will have to reinforce the others. The following two sections introduce processes and relationships in turn.

12.3 PROCESSES

Structure is a key ingredient of organising for success. But within any structure, what makes organisations work are the formal and informal organisational processes.[15] These processes can be thought of as controls on the organisation's operations and can therefore help or hinder the translation of strategy into action.

Control processes can be subdivided in two ways. First, they tend to emphasise either control over inputs or control over outputs. Input control processes concern themselves with the *resources* consumed in the strategy, especially financial resources and human commitment. Output control processes focus on ensuring satisfactory *results*, for example the meeting of targets or achieving market competitiveness. The second subdivision is between direct and indirect controls. Direct controls involve *close supervision* or monitoring. Indirect controls are more *hands-off*, setting up the conditions whereby desired behaviours are achieved semi-automatically. How the six processes we shall consider emphasise either input or output controls or direct or indirect controls is summarised in Exhibit 12.7.

Organisations normally use a blend of these control processes, but some will dominate over others according to the strategic challenges. Again, capacities to cope with change, knowledge and internationalisation are important. As we shall

Exhibit 12.7 **Types of control processes**

	Input	Output
Direct	Direct supervision Planning processes	Performance targeting
Indirect	Cultural processes Self-control	Internal markets

see, input measures tend to require that the controllers have high levels of knowledge of what the controlled are supposed to do. In many knowledge-intensive organisations, especially those generating innovation and change, controllers rarely have a good understanding of what their expert employees are doing, and tend to rely more on output controls. At least they can know when a unit has made its revenue or profitability targets. Direct control relies heavily on the physical presence of management, although now surveillance through IT can substitute. For this reason, international organisations may make use of indirect controls for their geographically dispersed subsidiaries. On the other hand, direct control processes can be very effective for small organisations on a single site.

12.3.1 Direct supervision

Direct supervision is the direct control of strategic decisions by one or a few individuals

Direct supervision is the direct control of strategic decisions by one or a few individuals, typically focused on the effort put into the business by employees. It is a dominant process in small organisations. It can also exist in larger organisations where little change is occurring and if the complexity of the business is not too great for a small number of managers to control the strategy *in detail* from the centre. This is often found in family businesses and in parts of the public sector with a history of 'hands-on' political involvement (often where a single political party has dominated for a long period).

Direct supervision requires that the controllers thoroughly understand what is entailed by the jobs they supervise. They must be able to correct errors, but not cramp innovative experiments. Direct supervision is easiest on a single site, although long-distance monitoring (for instance, of trading strategies in banking) is now possible through electronic means. Direct supervision can also be effective during a *crisis*, when autocratic control through direct supervision may be necessary to achieve quick results. Turnaround managers are often autocratic in style.

12.3.2 Planning processes

Planning processes plan and control the allocation of resources and monitor their utilisation

Planning processes are the archetypal administrative control, where the successful implementation of strategies is achieved through processes that plan and control the allocation of resources and monitor their utilisation (see also Chapter 11). The focus is on controlling the organisation's inputs, particularly financial. A plan would cover all parts of the organisation and show clearly, in financial terms, the level of resources allocated to each area (whether that be functions, divisions or business units). It would also show the detailed ways in which this resource was to be used. This would usually take the form of a *budget*. For example, the marketing function may be allocated €5m (£3.45m) but will need to show how this will be spent, for example the proportions spent on staff, advertising, exhibitions and so on. These cost items would then be monitored regularly to measure actual spend against plan.

One strength of this planned approach to strategic control is the ability to monitor the implementation of strategy. The detailed way in which planning can support strategy varies:

- Planning can be achieved by *standardisation of work processes (such as product or service features)*. Sometimes these work processes are subject to a rigorous framework of assessment and review – for example, to meet externally audited quality standards (such as ISO 9000). In many service organisations such 'routinisation' has been achieved through IT systems leading to de-skilling of service delivery and significant reductions in cost. This can give competitive advantage where organisations are positioning on low price with commodity-like products or services. For example, the cost of transactions in Internet banking is a fraction of that of transactions made through branches.

- *Enterprise resource planning (ERP) systems,*[16] supplied by software specialists such as SAP or Oracle, use sophisticated IT to achieve planning-type control. These systems aim to integrate the entire business operations, including personnel, finance, manufacturing operations, warehousing, etc. This started with the use of EPOS (Electronic Point Of Sale) systems in retail outlets, which linked back into stock control. Further advantage may be gained if these systems can stretch more widely in the value system beyond the boundaries of the organisation into the supply and distribution chains – for example, in automatic ordering of supplies to avoid 'stockout'. E-commerce operations are taking the integrative capability further (this is discussed more fully in Chapter 9). Illustration 12.2 shows an example of enterprise resource planning.

- Centralised planning approaches often use a *formula* for controlling resource allocation within an organisation. For example, in the public services, budgets might be allocated on a per capita basis (for example, number of patients for doctors).

Planning processes work best in simple and stable conditions, where a budget or a formula can apply equally well to all the units in the organisation and where assumptions are likely to hold good for the whole of the budget or formula period. Where there is diversity in the needs of business units, standard budgets or formulae are likely to advantage some units, while handicapping others. Thus in the UK some argue that the government should no longer treat all hospitals and universities the same way: each has its own challenges and opportunities. Also budgets and formulae can be inflexible where changing circumstances contradict original assumptions. Organisations can be penalised unfairly for adverse changes in circumstances, or denied the resources to respond to opportunities unforeseen in the original budget.

Because of the dangers of insensitivity to diverse needs in the organisation, it is often helpful to involve those most directly involved in *bottom-up* planning. In 'bottom-up' planning, local business units at the 'bottom' of the organisation propose initial plans 'up' to the corporate headquarters. The role of the corporate headquarters is to set guidelines for these initial plans and review them when they arrive. Initial proposed plans are often incompatible both with other units' plans and with headquarters' expectations and resourcing capabilities. Incompatibilities are resolved through processes of *reconciliation*, typically involving bargaining and some revisiting of some of headquarters' original guidelines. There are sometimes several iterations of this proposal and review process and so, while it can take into account business unit needs better than simple central planning, bottom-up planning can be very time consuming and political.

Illustration 12.2

Enterprise resource planning (ERP) at Bharat Petroleum

ERP systems were at the heart of Bharat Petroleum's strategic transformation as it prepared for deregulation in the Indian oil industry.

Bharat Petroleum is one of India's top three refining and distribution companies. It has 4,854 gas stations, some 1,000 kerosene dealers and 1,828 liquid petroleum gas (LPG) distributors scattered all over the vast country that is India. Facing deregulation of its markets, and possibly partial privatisation, Bharat Petroleum embarked upon enterprise integration through the implementation of an SAP R/3 ERP system. The aim was to gain control over the company's operations through improved information in areas such as inventory and product despatch, all working to support better customer service and satisfaction. The new system was to cover 200 sites and include a wide range of processes from financial accounting, to personnel administration, quality management, maintenance, plant management and sales. The finance director projected cost savings alone of £5m (€7.5m) per year.

The implementation of the ERP system was not conceived simply as an information systems project. It built upon a previous delayering and restructuring of the company around six new strategic business units. The ERP implementation itself was named project ENTRANS, short for Enterprise Transformation. The head of the project team was not an information systems specialist, but a human resource professional. Only 10 members of the 60-person project team were from information systems. A project steering group, meeting at least monthly, oversaw the whole process, with the heads of all six strategic business units, finance, human resources and IT represented. The head of IT at Bharat Petroleum commented himself: 'The unique thing about Bharat Petroleum's ERP implementation is that, right from its conception, it has been a business initiative. We (IT) just performed the necessary catalytic role.'

Implementation was carried out with assistance from PricewaterhouseCoopers, 24 SAP consultants, a team of 70 in-house SAP qualified consultants and six full-time change coaches. All users were involved in training, focused on improving 'organisational learning' and Visionary Leadership and Planning Programmes. Bharat Petroleum's chairman declared there would be no reduction in the workforce as a direct result of ERP, even though lower staff costs were included in the benefits case.

Implementation was scheduled over 24 months, with pilots selected carefully on the basis of proximity to the project team (based in Mumbai), salience of the processes involved, and business and IT-readiness. Many initial teething problems were encountered. Informal processes were not always fully incorporated into the new SAP system, with awkward consequences. However, plant managers felt that ERP's formalisation of processes did eventually contribute greatly to increasing discipline amongst staff. In the year after completion of the implementation, Bharat Petroleum achieved 24 per cent sales growth. SAP itself rated Bharat Petroleum as in the top quartile of SAP ERP implementations.

Source: A. Teltumbde, A. Tripathy and A. Sahu, 'Bharat Petrolem Corporation Limited', *Vikalpa*, vol. 27, no. 3 (2002), pp. 45–58.

Questions

1 What is the significance of the ERP implementation not being headed by an information systems expert?

2 What possible dangers might there be in the formalisation and embedding of detailed business processes in an ERP system?

3 What should a company like Bharat Petroleum do with the large team of specialised in-house consultants and coaches once the ERP implementation project is completed?

12.3.3 **Cultural processes**

With rapid change, increasing complexity and the need to exploit knowledge, employee motivation is increasingly important to performance. Under these pressures, promoting *self-control* and personal motivation can be an effective means of control, influencing the quality of employee input without direct intervention. Many workers have naturally a strong degree of self-control and motivation that can help ensure appropriate kinds of performance for the strategy: for instance, musicians or doctors, who have strong commitment to craft or professional standards. However, craft or professional standards can also deviate from what the organisation's strategy demands, and some workers will shirk in any case. Here managers can use cultural processes to achieve appropriate kinds of performance.[17]

Cultural processes are concerned with organisational culture and the *standardisation of norms* (as discussed in Chapter 5). Control is indirect, internalised as employees become part of the culture. Control is exerted on the input of employees, as the culture defines norms of appropriate effort and initiative. Three processes are particularly important in shaping appropriate cultures: *recruitment*, the selection of appropriate staff in the first place; *socialisation*, the integration of new staff through training, induction and mentoring programmes, for example, but also through informal influences such as role models; and *reward*, in other words, recognising appropriate behaviour through pay, promotion or symbolic processes (for example, public praise). These cultural processes often meet subtle kinds of resistance by employees, for example cynicism and 'going-through-the-motions', and once instituted become hard to change as strategies evolve. Organisations have many cultural processes that are not within formal management control, such as peer group pressure not to respond to organisational strategies.

None the less, cultural processes are particularly important in organisations facing complex and dynamic environments. Sometime these positive cultural processes happen without deliberate management intervention. Collaborative cultures can foster 'communities of practice', in which expert practitioners inside or even outside the organisation share their knowledge to generate innovative solutions to problems on their own initiative.[18] These informal, self-starting communities range from the Xerox photocopying engineers who would exchange information about problems and solutions over breakfast gatherings at the start of the day, to the programmer networks which support the development of Linux 'freeware' internationally over the Internet.

12.3.4 **Performance targeting processes**

Performance targets relate to the *outputs* of an organisation (or part of an organisation), such as product quality, prices or profit

Performance targets focus on the *outputs* of an organisation (or part of an organisation), such as product quality, revenues or profits. These targets are often known as key performance indicators (KPIs). The performance of an organisation is judged, either internally or externally, on its ability to meet these targets. However, within specified boundaries, the organisation remains free on how targets should be achieved. This approach can be particularly appropriate in certain situations:

- *Within large businesses*, corporate centres may choose performance targets to control their business units without getting involved in the details of how they achieve them. These targets are often cascaded down the organisation as specific targets for sub-units, functions and even individuals.

- In *regulated markets*, such as privatised utilities in the UK and elsewhere, government-appointed regulators increasingly exercise control through agreed *performance indicators* (PIs), such as service or quality levels, as a means of ensuring 'competitive' performance.[19]

- In *the public services*, where control of resource inputs was the dominant approach historically, governments are attempting to move control processes towards outputs (such as quality of service) and, more importantly, towards outcomes (for example, patient mortality rates in health care, as previously seen in Illustration 4.7).

KEY CONCEPT

Balanced scorecards

Balanced scorecards combine both qualitative and quantitative measures, acknowledge the expectations of different stakeholders and relate an assessment of performance to choice of strategy

Many managers find it difficult to develop a useful set of targets. One reason for this is that any particular set of indicators is liable to give only a partial view of the overall picture. Also, some important indicators (such as customer satisfaction) tend to get neglected because they are hard to measure, leaving the focus on easily available data such as financial ratios. In the last decade or so, *balanced scorecards* have been increasingly used as a way of widening the scope of performance indicators.[20] **Balanced scorecards** combine both qualitative and quantitative measures, acknowledge the expectations of different stakeholders and relate an assessment of performance to choice of strategy (as shown in Exhibit 12.8

Exhibit 12.8   **The balanced scorecard: an example**

Financial perspective		Customer perspective	
CSF*	**Measures**	**CSF***	**Measures**
Survival	Cash flow	Customer service (standard products)	● Delivery time ● Maintenance response time

Internal perspective		Innovation and learning perspective	
CSF*	**Measures**	**CSF***	**Measures**
IT systems development ● Features ● Cost	Performance per £ invested (vs. competitors)	Service leadership	● Speed to market (new standards) ● Speed of imitation (robustness)

* CSF = critical success factor

Illustration 12.3

The balanced scorecard: Philips Electronics

Balanced scorecards attempt to reflect the interdependence of different performance factors – which together will determine success or failure.

Philips Electronics, with more than 250,000 employees in 150 countries, uses the balanced scorecard to manage its diverse product lines and divisions around the world. The company has identified four critical success factors (CSFs) for the organisation as a whole:

- competence (knowledge, technology, leadership and teamwork);
- processes (drivers for performance);
- customers (value propositions);
- financial (value, growth and productivity).

Philips uses these scorecard criteria at four levels: the strategy review; operations review; business unit; and the individual employee. Criteria at one level are cascaded down to more detailed criteria appropriate at each level. This helps employees understand how their day-to-day activities link ultimately to the corporate goals. At a business unit level, for example, the management team determine the local critical success factors and agree indicators for each. Targets are then set for each indicator based on the gap between present performance and desired performance for the current year plus two to four years into the future. These targets are derived from an analysis of the market and world-class performance. Targets must be specific, measurable, ambitious, realistic and time phased.

Examples of indicators at the business unit level include:

Financial
Economic profit
Income from operations
Working capital
Operational cash flow
Inventory turns

Processes
Percentage reduction in process cycle time
Number of engineering changes
Capacity utilisation
Order response time
Process capability

Customers
Rank in customer survey
Market share
Repeat order rate
Complaints
Brand index

Competence
Leadership competence
Percentage of patent-protected turnover
Training days per employee
Quality improvement team participation

Source: A. Gumbus and B. Lyons, 'The balanced scorecard at Philips Electronics', *Strategic Finance*, November (2002), pp. 45–49.

Questions

1 Imagine yourself as the chief executive of Philips Electronics and draw up a table that shows the various ways that the balanced scorecard could be used in managing your organisation.

2 Imagine yourself as an ordinary employee of Philips Electronics and list possible pros and cons of the balanced scorecard as applied to you individually.

3 What possible disadvantages or dangers might the balanced scorecard technique have for organisations?

and Illustration 12.3). Importantly, performance is linked not only to short-term outputs but also to the way in which processes are managed – for example, the processes of innovation and learning which are crucial to long-term success.

Exhibit 12.8 is an example of a balanced scorecard for a small start-up company supplying standard tools and light equipment to the engineering industry. The owner–manager's financial perspective was simply one of survival during this start-up period, requiring a positive cash flow (after the initial investments in plant, stock and premises). The strategy was to compete on customer service for both initial delivery and maintenance backup. This required core competences in order processing and maintenance scheduling underpinned by the company's IT system. These core competences were open to imitation, so, in turn, the ability to improve these service standards continuously was critical to success.

12.3.5 Market processes

Market processes *involve some formalised system of 'contracting' for resources*

Market processes (or *internal markets*) can be brought inside organisations to control activities internally.[21] Here market processes typically involve some formalised system of 'contracting' for resources or inputs from other parts of an organisation and for supplying outputs to other parts of an organisation. Control focuses on outputs, for example revenues earned in successful competition for internal contracts. The control is indirect: rather than accepting detailed performance targets determined externally, units have simply to earn their keep in competitive internal markets.

Internal markets can be used in a variety of ways. There might be *competitive bidding*, perhaps through the creation of an internal investment bank at the corporate centre to support new initiatives. Also, a customer–supplier relationship may be established between a central service department, such as training or IT, and the operating units. Typically these internal markets are subject to considerable regulation. For example, the corporate centre might set rules for *transfer prices* between internal business units to prevent exploitative contract pricing, or insist on *service-level agreements* to ensure appropriate service by an essential internal supplier, such as IT, for the various units that depend on it.

Internal markets work well where complexity or rapid change makes impractical detailed direct or input controls. But internal markets can create problems as well. First, internal markets can increase bargaining between units, consuming important management time. Second, they may create a new bureaucracy monitoring all of the internal transfers of resources between units. Third, an overzealous use of market mechanisms can lead to dysfunctional competition and legalistic contracting, destroying cultures of collaboration and relationships. These have all been complaints made against the internal markets and semi-autonomous foundation hospitals introduced in the UK's National Health Service. On the other hand, their proponents claim that these market processes free a traditionally overcentralised health service to innovate and respond to local needs, while market disciplines maintain overall control. Illustration 12.4 shows internal markets being combined with other controls at successful investment bank Macquarie.

Illustration 12.4

Controlling investment bankers

Known as the 'Millionaire Factory', Macquarie's entrepreneurial bankers are pursuing deals all over the world.

Sydney-based Macquarie Bank is Australia's largest investment bank and its most successful division, the Infrastructure Group, is the largest operator of toll roads in the world. Its funds own Copenhagen Airport and Thames Water company and during 2006 it launched an audacious and ultimately unsuccessful bid for the London Stock Exchange. Despite this setback, 2006 was another record year for Macquarie. Its total staff has risen from under 5,000 in 2003 to just less than 10,000 in 2007; its international staff rose from less than a thousand to 3,200 in the same period.

The Chief Executive, Allan Moss, joined Macquarie in 1977, when it was still the subsidiary of British merchant bank Hill Samuel with about 50 employees. A Harvard MBA (he graduated in the top 5 per cent), Moss became chief executive in 1993 and listed the bank on the Australian Stock Exchange in 1995. According to the *Financial Times*, Moss has an image of a 'bumbling professor', spilling coffee and tripping over telephone cords. He does not travel overseas much, preferring to stay in Sydney, and he works short hours by investment banker standards, 8.30 a.m. to 7.30 p.m.

Moss describes the bank's culture as one of 'freedom within boundaries'. For him, Macquarie is a federation of businesses in which entrepreneurs can thrive: 'we provide the infrastructure, the capital, the brand and a controlled framework – and the staff provide the ideas'. The culture is very competitive internally, with colleagues pitching for 'mandates' (the responsibility for a bit of business) against each other. One former banker observed: 'Walking into Macquarie is like walking into a Turkish bazaar. Everyone has the same rug and they're all competing to sell the same rug.' In fact, though, the internal competition produces highly innovative ideas – for example, the proposal that the bank should provide financing for patients' operations, including cosmetic surgery such as breast implants. The rule of thumb guiding promotion to one of the coveted – and lucrative – 250 executive directorships has been generating an annual profit personally of A$5m (£2.1m; €3m). The company receives 70,000 unsolicited CVs from would-be Macquarie bankers every year. All hires go through the same distinctive and rigorous psychological testing process.

Of course, there are some who doubt whether Macquarie's successful run can go on for ever. The *Financial Times* quotes one close observer of Macquarie: 'I am starting to detect some hubris at the bank. It has done so well it is inevitable. Allan [Moss] is loyal to those he trusts and only time will tell whether he is trusting his lieutenants a bit too much'.

Key sources: Financial Times, 17 December (2005); Sydney Morning Herald, 19 August (2006).

Questions

1 What control processes in this account are particularly important to Macquarie?

2 What threats are there to these processes?

12.4 RELATIONSHIPS

A key aspect of an organisation's configuration is the ability to integrate the knowledge and activities of different parts of an organisation (both horizontally and vertically) and with other organisations (particularly within the value chain, as discussed in Chapter 3). Structures and processes are an important part of this, as discussed in the previous sections. However, there are basic issues too around how both internal and external *relationships* are built and maintained, especially in ways that are fluid enough to respond to an uncertain environment. This section looks at the following issues (see Exhibit 12.9):

- Relating internally, especially with regard to where responsibility and authority for operational and strategic decisions should be vested inside an organisation.
- Relating externally, for example through outsourcing, alliances, networks and virtuality.

12.4.1 Relating internally

Relating to the centre

Devolution concerns the extent to which the centre of an organisation delegates decision making to units and managers lower down in the hierarchy

One of the important continuing debates in both public[22] and private sector organisations has been concerned with devolution. **Devolution** concerns the extent to which the centre of an organisation delegates decision making to units and managers lower down in the hierarchy.

Devolution is particularly effective where important knowledge is dispersed throughout the organisation and where responsiveness to the changing needs of different customer segments is important. In these conditions, top managers can be too remote from the 'sharp end' really to understand the organisation's resources and opportunities. In fast-moving markets, it is often better to place

---

Exhibit 12.9 Relating internally and externally

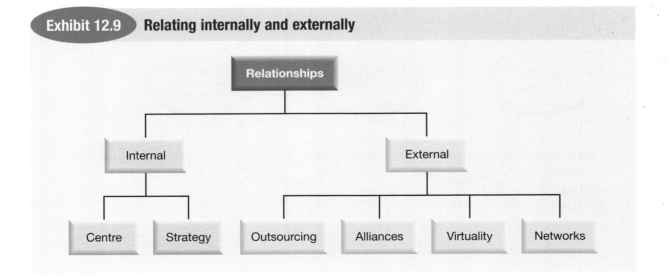

decision-making authority *close to the action* rather than force decisions up through slow and remote hierarchies.

Despite these reasons why increased devolution might make sense, it can become a 'fad' and simply a reaction to a previous era of overcentralisation. To avoid this risk the issue of centralisation vs. devolution needs to be seen as a *continuum* from highly centralised to highly devolved and not as a black or white choice.

Relating over strategy

Section 7.4 looked at the question of whether and in what ways a corporate parent can add value to its constituent business units or departments. An important determinant of organising for success is clarity around how responsibilities for strategic decision making are to be *divided* between the centre and the business units. Goold and Campbell[23] provide three *strategy styles* describing typical ways of dividing these responsibilities. The organisational processes and the way that relationships work are very different in each case.

Strategic planning style

In a **strategic planning** style of control, the relationship between the centre and the business units is one of a parent who is the *master planner* prescribing detailed roles for departments and business units

The **strategic planning style** (Exhibit 12.10) is the most centralised of the three styles. Here strategic planning refers not to planning in general but to a particular style of relationship between the centre and business units. The centre is the *master planner* prescribing detailed roles for departments and business units, whose role is confined to the operational delivery of the plan. In the extreme form of this style, the centre is expected to add value in most of the ways outlined in Exhibit 7.6. The centre orchestrates, coordinates and controls all of business unit activities through the extensive use of the formal planning and control

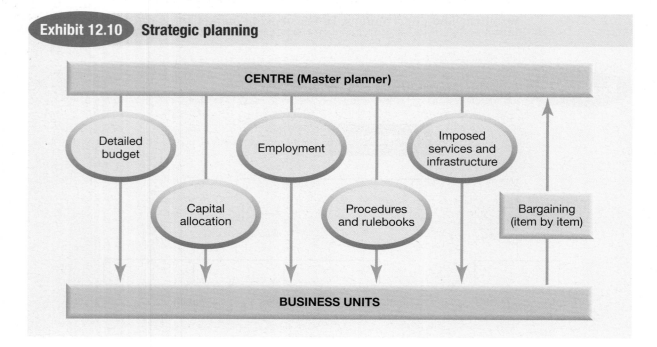

Exhibit 12.10 Strategic planning

CENTRE (Master planner)

Detailed budget

Employment

Imposed services and infrastructure

Capital allocation

Procedures and rulebooks

Bargaining (item by item)

BUSINESS UNITS

systems (as discussed in section 12.3.2) shown in Exhibit 12.10. The centre also directly manages the infrastructure and provides many corporate services. This is the classic bureaucracy familiar to many managers in large public sector organisations.

The strategic planning style is well suited to the synergy manager or parental developer roles adopted by corporate centres, as discussed in section 6.4. It is particularly appropriate where corporate managers have a detailed working knowledge of each business unit and where business unit strategies are of a size or sensitivity that can have major ramifications for the corporate whole. Where the corporate centre does not have detailed working knowledge, the strategic planning style can be dysfunctional. Corporate managers may hold back the development of business areas that they do not understand or steer them in inappropriate directions. There are also the bureaucratic costs of centralisation and demotivating effects on business unit managers who may feel little personal commitment to strategies handed down from the centre. Goold and Campbell and others have found many private sector organisations abandoning this style.[24]

Financial control style

In the financial control style, the role of the centre is confined to setting financial targets, allocating resources, appraising performance and intervening to avert or correct poor performance

Financial control (Exhibit 12.11) is the most extreme form of devolution, dissolving the organisation into highly autonomous business units. The relationship between the centre and the business units is as a parent who is a *shareholder or banker* for those units. As the name suggests, the relationship is financial and there is little concern for the detailed product/market strategy of business units – even to the extent that they can compete openly with each other provided they deliver the financial results. They might even have authority to raise funds from outside the company. This style is typically managed through a holding company structure, as discussed in section 12.2.2, and is suited to the portfolio manager or restructurer roles of a corporate centre, as discussed in section 7.4.

In financial control the role of the centre is confined to setting financial targets, allocating resources, appraising performance and intervening in the case

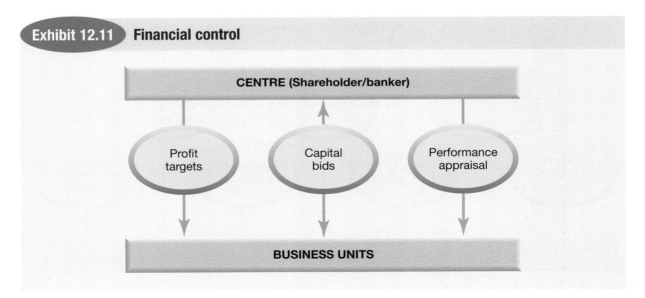

Exhibit 12.11 **Financial control**

of poor performance. Importantly, these interventions would usually be replacing business unit managers rather than dictating changes in strategy. So the dominant processes are performance targets as discussed in section 12.3.5. Business units managers are held strictly accountable for meeting these targets.

In the public sector, such extreme devolution is rarely found for reasons of political accountability: the minister is ultimately responsible. In the private sector, however, the style can be appropriate to organisations operating in stable markets with mature technologies and where there is only a short time lag between management decisions and the financial consequences: for example, organisations trading commodities or dealing with basic products. It is also appropriate where the diversity of business units is great – since the other two styles require some measure of relatedness between business units. A major concern with financial control can be the dominance of short-termism. No one has responsibility for fostering innovation and organisational learning. The business units are focused on meeting tough short-term targets set by a centre that does not have the resources or the competences to manage the knowledge creation and integration processes. So competence development can only really happen through acquisitions and alliances.

Strategic control style

The strategic control style is concerned with shaping the *behaviour* in business units and with shaping the *context* within which managers are operating

Strategic control (Exhibit 12.12) lies between the two extremes of the strategic planning and financial control styles and is the style most organisations operate. The relationship between the centre and the business units is one of a parent who behaves as a *strategic shaper*, influencing the *behaviour* in business units[25] and forming the *context* within which managers are operating. Like strategic planning, this is a style suited to the synergy manager or parental developer roles of a corporate centre as discussed in section 7.4. However, because it allows more

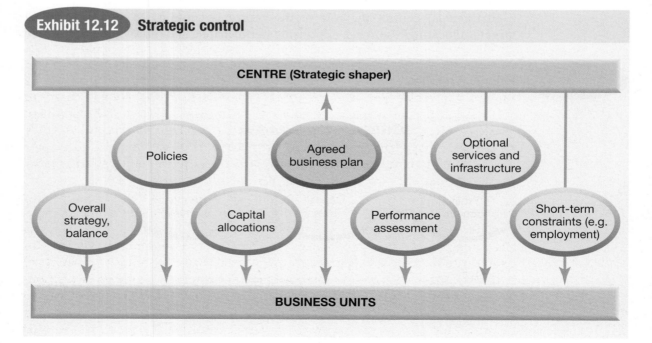

Exhibit 12.12 **Strategic control**

discretion lower down, it is more suitable where the centre has little knowledge about business unit operations and business unit strategies are unlikely to make major impacts on the corporation as a whole. The centre would expect to add value by:

- Defining and shaping the *overall* strategy of the organisation.
- Deciding the *balance* of activities and the role of each business unit.
- Defining and controlling organisational *policies* (on employment, market coverage, interaction between units, etc.).
- Fostering *organisational learning* between units.
- Defining standards and assessing the *performance* of the separate business units and intervening to improve performance (that is, the processes of performance targeting discussed in section 12.3.5).

However, the centre does not fulfil these roles through an imposed master plan. Rather, strategic control is built through the processes of agreeing strategies with business units (perhaps through their business plans) – but within central boundaries and guidelines. Perhaps the biggest risk with this style is that the centre tries to shape strategy in these ways without being clear about the 'corporate logic' or having the competences actually to add value in these ways.

12.4.2 Relating externally

Organisations have important relationships outside their boundaries as well, for example with customers, suppliers, subcontractors and partners. This section will look at four of the most important such relationships, all of which have seen a good deal of change in recent years.

Outsourcing

In Chapter 3, outsourcing was presented as an important issue about strategic capability that arises from the concept of the value chain. Outsourcing occurs where organisations decide to buy in services or products that were previously produced in-house. For example, payroll, component manufacture, IT services and training are all common examples of outsourced activities. Two important principles were established when searching for candidates for outsourcing: first, that an outside supplier can provide better value for money than in-house provision; second, that core competences should not normally be outsourced since these activities critically underpin competitive advantage.

Many managers take on board these principles of outsourcing but do not pay enough attention to the organisational implications of outsourcing. For example, outsourcing requires managers to be much more competent at maintaining performance through their management of supplier (or distributor) *relationships* rather than through management control systems within their own organisation. This may take some considerable attention. For example, suppliers or distributors will need to be educated about the organisation's strategies, priorities and standards and how their work influences the final performance of the product or service. They need to be motivated to perform consistently to these required standards. It should be clear from section 12.3 that there are different processes by which this might be achieved. At one extreme, suppliers might be 'tied in' through enterprise resource planning systems. This might be possible and desirable where the requirements of the supplier are clear and unlikely to change quickly. At the other extreme, the relationship may be maintained through cultural processes and norms – for example, working with suppliers who know the company well and are tuned into the cultural norms. This would be important where suppliers are adding creative input to the product or service (such as designers) where the two-way interaction needs to be much more fluid. Between these extremes, market mechanisms could be used if a contractual approach to the relationship is felt to be appropriate – for example, for one-off projects or where there is a range of potential suppliers.

Strategic alliances

This issue of managing relationships with other organisations (or other parts of the same organisation) surfaced in Chapter 8 in the discussion about strategic alliances. The organisational concerns are similar to those with outsourcing except that a strategic alliance may be much more overtly relational in the way the alliance is constructed (as against the contractual nature of many supplier–customer relationships). Readers are referred to Exhibit 10.3, which shows the spectrum of strategic alliance types from loose networks to joint ventures. The important organisational issue is finding the balance between the best sources of specialist knowledge (which would suggest many members of an alliance) and the competence to integrate these strands of specialist knowledge to create a best value product or service to customers. The more members of an alliance, the more complex this integration task becomes and the more effort that needs to be put into the ingredients of successful alliances, as discussed in section 10.2.3 – such as trust. This will be discussed further below when considering networks and the ability of some organisations to achieve a nodal position in a network of multiple partners.

Networks[26]

Outsourcing, alliances and virtuality are particular cases of a general trend to rely on network relationships outside the organisation's boundaries. Taken together, they mean that more organisations have become dependent on internal and external networks to ensure success (see Illustration 12.5 for a public sector example). So *cooperation* has become a key aspect of organising for success. Other important networks include:

● *Teleworking*, where people carry out their work *independently* but remain connected to key corporate resources (such as databases and specialist advice) and to colleagues, suppliers and clients through the telecommunications and computing infrastructure. Since the exploitation of the Internet remains a major strategic issue for many organisations (see Chapter 9), new ways of organising will be essential. The Internet allows many formal structures to be dismantled and replaced with well-functioning networks supported by this information infrastructure.

Illustration 12.5

Developing school leaders through networks

The UK's National College for School Leadership is using networks rather than traditional bureaucratic structures for developing school head teachers.

In the 2000s, British schools were facing a leadership crisis. The demands upon school head teachers were increasing, both because of greater decentralisation of responsibilities to schools and evermore stringent performance requirements. But there was an acute shortage of appropriately trained teachers prepared to take on the job of school head.

Traditionally, city and town local education authorities (LEAs) had taken primary responsibility for developing head teachers in their particular areas. They had often worked in regional consortia and with local universities to develop appropriate training mechanisms. Typically LEAs had a concentration of relevant expertise in a variety of professional areas, which provided the basis for advice and development for schools in their areas. LEAs were also under the control of their democratically elected councils, and so accountable to local electorates. For the last two decades, however, LEA budgets and roles had been under steady attack as too costly and too bureaucratic. Budgets were nearly wholly devolved to schools and some schools were allowed to opt out of LEA control altogether. Meanwhile, universities, under pressure to perform more research, were increasingly reluctant to get involved in post-experience teacher training.

The year of 2002 saw the launch of a new National College of School Leadership (NCL). Based on the campus of Nottingham University, it was explicitly concerned to use networks rather than traditional structures to deliver training and development assistance for head teachers and future leaders. The NCL launched a Networked Learning Communities programme, designed to bring teachers together to exhange experience and develop themselves. New information technologies were enrolled as platforms for initiatives such as 'TalkingHeads' and 'VirtualHeads'. David Jackson, Director of the Networked Learning Communities programme, commented: 'The twentieth century

was the century during which we built large organisations (with silos and hierarchies) to do things for people. The twenty-first century is the one in which we help people to help one another.'

LEAs now had a new role: network brokers. Their task was to use their knowledge of local schools, other services and communities to bring the right people together in the appropriate networks. As the NCL put it: 'Networks offer the possibility of new patterns of leadership – more lateral and more distributed – they offer new possibilities for Local Authorities and schools to engage in co-leadership.' One LEA was quoted as commenting:

We are learning – quickly – that we need to look outside education if we are really going to make a differerence for the children in our schools. Working with social services, the police and health service is difficult. But the Local Authority is the only place where that can happen, so we're persevering.

David Jackson, the Director, was clear about the challenges for LEAs:

A local authority might previously have had a hundred schools and they've now got ten networks – what opportunities that creates! But it requires a massive change within themselves, their own modes of thinking, the way in which they design policy, generate incentives, hold people accountable, deploy resources. Everything requires change.

Sources: 'What does a Local Authority broker do?', National College for School Leadership; 'Cracking the concrete: David Jackson, in conversation with Madeline Church, reflects on how networks work across, around and within standard structures', National College for School Leadership.

Questions

1 What are the advantages of a networked learning model in this context? Are there any disadvantages?

2 Why might LEAs find it difficult to take on this new role of network broker?

- *Federations* of experts who voluntarily come together to integrate their expertise to create products or services. In the entertainment business, musicians, actors and other creative artists sometimes come together in this way as well as through the more formal processes of agents and contracts. Some organisations make their living by maintaining databases of resources (people) in the network and possibly facilitating social contact through organising networking events.

- *One-stop shops* are a solution to the problem of coordinating diverse network members so that the customer experiences a coherent, joined-up service. The one-stop shop creates a physical presence through which all customer enquiries are channelled (see Exhibit 12.13). The function of the one-stop shop is to put together a complete package of products or services from various network members. A 'turnkey' contractor (say, in civil engineering) might operate in this way – using its own expertise in project management and managing a network of suppliers, but not actually undertaking any of the detailed work itself. With the growth of e-commerce, the one-stop shop may, in fact, be *virtual* in the sense that clients enter via a 'gateway' (say a website) but the physical services or products that are being integrated into the customer's product or service are actually dispersed (in physical terms). The critical issue is that it feels joined up to the customer whose needs can be satisfied through this one gateway.

- In a *service network* the client may access all of the services of the network through any of the constituent members of the network. A well-functioning

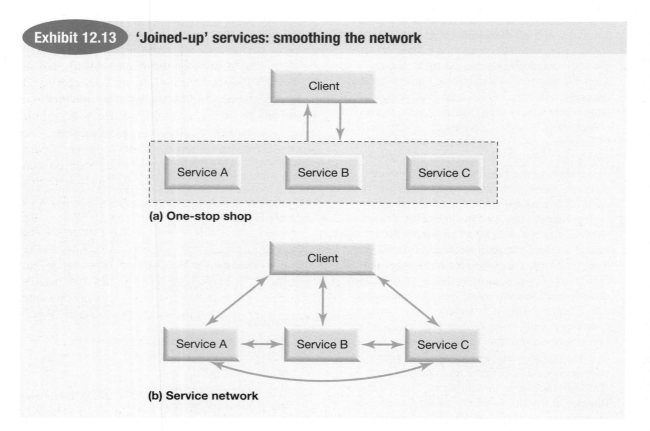

Exhibit 12.13 **'Joined-up' services: smoothing the network**

(a) One-stop shop

(b) Service network

service network may not be easy to achieve, since it requires all members of the network to be fully informed, capable and willing to 'cross-sell' other people's products and to act collaboratively. Above all else, it requires *trust and respect* between members of the network. Some service networks also have a one-start shop facility. For example, Best Western is an international network of independent hotels, where customers can receive information or make bookings at any hotel in the network or through central booking points. This facility has the clear advantage of encouraging travellers to 'book on' their next destination with Best Western.

It can be seen that coordination in a network is a crucial activity. It can also be well rewarded. Organisations that achieve a *nodal position* in the network, connecting many nodes in the network, are potentially highly valuable.[27] To achieve a nodal position, organisations should have three strengths:

- A *compelling vision* that legitimises the need for the network and entices in partners. In the public sector this may be a vision of politicians who then set up the network to deliver – for example, on drugs, crime and disorder, social exclusion, and so on.

- *Unique resources or core competences* to establish and hold the nodal position – such as a proprietary system as seen with technologies such as Apple's iTunes or the Windows computer operating system.

- *Networking skills* to sustain and develop the network.

Virtual organisation[28]

The logical extension of networking, outsourcing and alliances would be an organisation where in-house (owned) resources and activities are minimised and nearly all resources and activities reside outside the organisation. These so-called **virtual organisations** are held together not through formal structure and physical proximity of people, but by partnership, collaboration and networking. The important issue is that this organisation feels 'real' to clients and meets their needs at least as adequately as other organisations. It has been argued that such extreme forms of outsourcing are likely to result in serious strategic weakness in the long run, as the organisation becomes devoid of core competences and cut off from the learning which can exist through undertaking these activities in-house. This is now an important consideration in many industries such as civil engineering, publishing and specialist travel companies, all of which are highly dependent on outsourcing aspects of their business which hitherto were considered as core. The concern is whether short-term improvements are being achieved at the expense of securing a capacity for innovation. The danger of 'virtuality' is that knowledge creation and innovation only occur within the special-ist 'boxes' represented by the activities of separate partners. There is no one who has the competence or authority to integrate these pockets of knowledge.

Virtual organisations are held together not through formal structure and physical proximity of people, but by partnership, collaboration and networking

12.4.3 Configuration dilemmas

The beginning of this chapter stressed that successful organising requires fit-ting structure, processes and relationships to each other, all aligned to the key strategic challenges in a mutually reinforcing way. This mutual fit is described as an organisation's *configuration* (Exhibit 12.1). For example, the multidivisional structure lends itself to internal market processes (for example, divisions contracting with a central R&D function) and is compatible with certain strategy styles, particularly the financial control and strategic control styles. Project-based structures often rely on cultural processes to provide a common glue for fast-changing teams and can usually accommodate themselves to external relationships such as networks or virtual organising. Successful organisations thus tend to fall into a limited number of internally consistent patterns for integrating structures, processes and relationships.[29]

However, perfect fits across all three dimensions of the configuration can be hard to find. Sometimes, there are major trade-offs between optimising on one element and optimising on another. Managers face dilemmas in combining control with flexibility, for example. The chapter concludes by considering the most common practical dilemmas and the ways in which they can be addressed.[30]

Exhibit 12.14 summarises five key dilemmas in organising. Hierarchies are often necessary to ensure control and action, but they can sit uneasily with networks that foster knowledge exchange and innovation. Vertical accountability promotes maximum performance by subordinates, but can lead managers to maximise their own self-interest, at the expense of horizontal relationships. Empowerment of employees lower down the organisation gives scope for initiative, but over the long term can lead to incoherence. Centralisation might be needed for standardisation, but this can be at the cost of the initiative and flexibility fostered by devolution. Having the best practice on a particular element of the organisation, for instance financial controls, may actually be damaging if it does not fit with the needs of the organisation as a whole.

Exhibit 12.14 **Some dilemmas in organising for success**

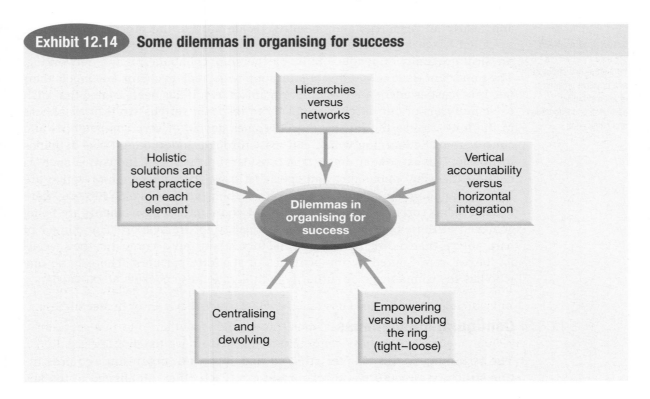

Managers should recognise that any organisational design is likely to face dilemmas of these kinds and is hard to optimise on all dimensions. However, they may be able to manage these dilemmas in three ways:

● By *subdividing* the organisation, so that the one part of the organisation is organised optimally according to one side of these dilemmas, while the rest responds to the other. Thus for example IBM created the PC in a specialised new venture division, kept separate from the traditional mainframe activities which were dominated by principles of hierarchy and vertical accountability highly antagonistic to radical innovation.[31]

● By *combining* different organising principles at the same time, for instance networks and traditional hierarchies. Managing simultaneously according to contradictory principles is obviously very demanding. However, it has been argued that organisations such as ABB and Unilever are now 'networked multidivisionals', combining network principles emphasising horizontal integration with divisional structures ensuring vertical accountability.[32]

● By *reorganising* frequently so that no one side of the dilemma can become too entrenched. The rate of major reorganisation for large UK companies increased from once every four years to once every three years in the last decade.[33] Given this pace of reorganising, many organisations are like pendulums, constantly swinging between centralisation and devolution, for example, without resting long on one side or another.[34]

A final dilemma arising from the interconnectedness of configurations is which element drives the others? The extent to which strategic elements drive structural elements is the subject of the key debate in Illustration 12.6.

SUMMARY

● Organising for success is about an organisation's configuration. This is built up of three related strands: structures, processes and relationships.

● Successful organising means responding to the key challenges facing the organisation. This chapter has stressed control, change, knowledge and internationalisation.

● There are many *structural types* (such as functional, divisional, matrix). Each structural type has its own strengths and weaknesses and responds differently to the challenges of control, change, knowledge and internationalisation.

● There are a range of different organisational *processes* to facilitate strategy. These processes can focus on either inputs or outputs and be direct or indirect.

● Relationships are also important to success. Internally, key issues are *centralisation versus devolution* and *strategy style*. Externally, there are choices around outsourcing, alliances, virtuality and networks which may help or hinder success.

● The separate organisational strands should come together to form a coherent *reinforcing cycle*. But these reinforcing cycles also raise tough dilemmas that can be managed by *subdividing*, *combining* and *reorganising*.

Illustration 12.6

Does structure follow strategy?

A key message of this chapter is that strategy and structure should fit together. But which determines which?

Alfred Chandler, Professor of Business History at Harvard Business School, proposes one of the fundamental rules of strategic management: 'unless structure follows strategy, inefficiency results'.[1] This logical sequence fits the 'design' lens for strategy, but does assume that structure is very much subordinate to strategy: structure can easily be fixed once the big strategic decisions are made. But some authors warn that this dangerously underestimates structure's role. Sometimes strategy follows structure.

Chandler's rule is based on the historical experience of companies like General Motors, Exxon and DuPont. DuPont, for example, was originally an explosives company. During the First World War, however, the company anticipated the peace by deliberately diversifying out of explosives into new civil markets such as plastics and paints. Yet the end of the war plunged DuPont into crisis. All its new businesses were loss making; only explosives still made money. The problem was not the diversification strategy, but the structure that DuPont used to manage the new civil businesses. DuPont had retained its old functional structure, so that responsibilities for the production and marketing of all the new businesses were still centralised on single functional heads. They could not cope with the increased diversity. The solution was not to abandon the diversification strategy; rather it was to adopt a new structure with decentralised divisions for each of the separate businesses. DuPont thrives today with a variant of this multidivisional structure.

D. Hall and M. Saias accept the importance of strategy for structure but warn that the causality can go the other way.[2] An organisation's existing structure very much determines the kinds of strategic opportunities that its management will see and want to grasp. For instance, it is easy for a company with a decentralised multidivisional structure to make acquisitions and divestments: all it has to do is add or subtract divisions, with few ramifications for the rest of the business. On the other hand, it can be very hard for the top managers of a decentralised multidivisional organisation to see opportunities for innovation and knowledge sharing within the operations of the divisions: they are too far away from the real

business. In other words, structures can shape strategies.

T. Amburgey and T. Dacin tested the relative impact of strategy and structure on each other by analysing the strategic and structural changes of more than 200 American corporations over nearly 30 years.[3] They found that moves towards decentralised structures were often followed by moves towards increasingly diversified strategies: here, structure was determining strategy. Overall, however, increased diversification was twice as likely to be followed by structural decentralisation as the other way round. In other words, structure does follow strategy, but only most of the time.

Henry Mintzberg concludes that 'structure follows strategy as the left foot follows the right'.[4] In other words, strategy and structure are related reciprocally rather than just one way. Mintzberg warns that a simple 'design' approach to strategy and structure can be misleading. Structure is not always easy to fix after the big strategic decisions have been made. Strategists should check to see that their existing structures are not constraining the kinds of strategies that they consider.

Notes

1. A. Chandler, *Strategy and Structure: Chapters in the History of American Enterprise*, MIT Press, 1962, p. 314.
2. D.J. Hall and M.A. Saias, 'Strategy follows structure!', *Strategic Management Journal*, vol. 1, no. 2 (1980), pp. 149–163.
3. T. Amburgey and T. Dacin, 'As the left foot follows the right? The dynamics of strategic and structural change', *Academy of Management Journal*, vol. 37, no. 6 (1994), pp. 1427–1452.
4. H. Mintzberg, 'The Design School: reconsidering the basic premises of strategic management', *Strategic Management Journal*, vol. 11 (1990), pp. 171–195.

Question

Hall and Saias suggest that organisational structures can influence the kinds of strategies that management teams will pursue. What kinds of organisations might be particularly susceptible to structural constraints on their strategies?

Work assignments

✳ Denotes more advanced work assignments.   * Refers to a case study in the Text and Cases edition.

12.1   Go to the website of a large organisation you are familiar with and find its organisational chart (not all organisations provide these). Why is the organisation structured in this way?

12.2   Referring to section 12.2.2, on the multidivisional structure, consider the advantages and disadvantages of creating divisions along different lines – such as product, geography or technology – with respect to a large organisation you are familiar with or a case organisation such as SABMiller*, CRH* or News Corporation*.

12.3 ✳   Referring to Exhibit 12.9 on the balanced scorecard, write a short executive brief explaining how balanced scorecards could be a useful management process to monitor and control the performance of organisational units. Be sure you present an analysis of both the advantages and possible pitfalls of this approach.

12.4   As a middle manager with responsibilities for a small business unit, which 'strategy style' (section 12.4.1) would you prefer to work within? In what sorts of circumstances or corporate organisation would this style not work so well for you?

12.5   Explain the statement: 'when the organisational structure isn't working, it is just as likely to be the fault of the strategy as the fault of the structure'.

Integrative assignment

12.6   Take a recent merger or acquisition (see Chapter 10), ideally one involving two organisations of roughly equal size, and analyse how the deal has changed the acquiring or merged company's organisational structure. What do you conclude from the extent or lack of structural change for the strategy of the company going forward?

An extensive range of additional materials, including audio summaries, weblinks to organisations featured in the text, definitions of key concepts and self-assessment questions, can be found on the *Exploring Corporate Strategy* Companion Website at **www.pearsoned.co.uk/ecs**

Recommended key readings

● The best single coverage of this chapter's issues is in R. Daft, *Organisation Theory and Design*, 9th edition, South-Western, 2006.

● M. Goold and A. Campbell, *Designing Effective Organizations*, Jossey-Bass, 2002, provides a practical guide to organisational design issues.

● A review of contemporary issues and cases in organising is A. Pettigrew, R. Whittington, L. Melin, C. Sanchez-Runde, F. van den Bosch, W. Ruigrok and T. Numagami (eds), *Innovative Forms of Organizing*, Sage, 2003. For a recent collection of relevant articles, see the special issue 'Learning to design organizations', ed. R. Dunbar and W. Starbuck, *Organization Science*, vol. 17 (2006), no. 2.

● Readers can gain useful insights into the financial aspects of strategy implementation, managing for value, expectation of stakeholders and strategic control in G. Arnold, *Corporate Financial Management*, 3rd edition, FT/Prentice Hall, 2005, Chapters 15 and 16.

References

1. Some of these early writings are to be found in D. Pugh, *Organisation Theory*, Penguin, 1984.
2. The point has been argued by R. Whittington and L. Melin, 'The challenge of organizing/strategizing', in A. Pettigrew, R. Whittington, L. Melin, C. Sanchez-Runde, F. van den Bosch, W. Ruigrok and T. Numagami (eds), *Innovative Forms of Organizing*, Sage, 2003; and also by R. Whittington, E. Molloy, M. Mayer and A. Smith, 'Practices of strategising/organising', *Long Range Planning*, vol. 39, no. 6 (2006), pp. 615–630.
3. This idea of configuration is similar to that of strategic architecture, as discussed by G. Hamel and C.K. Prahalad, *Competing for the Future*, Harvard Business School Press, 1994, chapter 10, and complementarities, as discussed by R. Whittington, A. Pettigrew, S. Peck, E. Fenton and M. Conyon, 'Change and complementarities in the new competitive landscape', *Organization Science*, vol. 10, no. 5 (1999), pp. 583–600.
4. A good review of new and old types can be found in G. Friesen, 'Organisation design for the 21st century', *Consulting to Management – C2M*, vol. 16, no. 3 (2005), pp. 32–51.
5. The view that organisations should fit their structures to key challenges ('contingencies') is associated with the long tradition of research on contingency theory: see L. Donaldson, *The Contingency Theory of Organizations*, Sage, 2001, or R. Whittington, 'Organisational structure', in *The Oxford Handbook of Strategy*, vol. II, Oxford University Press, 2003, chapter 28, for summaries.
6. This view of divisionalisation as a response to diversity was originally put forward by A.D. Chandler, *Strategy and Structure*, MIT Press, 1962. See R. Whittington and M. Mayer, *The European Corporation: Strategy, Structure and Social Science*, Oxford University Press, 2000, for a summary of Chandler's argument and the success of divisional organisations in contemporary Europe.
7. For a review of current experience with matrix structures, see S. Thomas and L. D'Annunzio, 'Challenges and strategies of matrix organisations: top-level and mid-level managers' perspectives', *Human Resource Planning*, vol. 28, no. 1 (2005), pp. 39–48.
8. For a discussion of matrix structures in knowledge-intensive R&D laboratory settings, see P. Rizova, 'Are you networked for successful innovation?', *Sloan Management Review*, vol. 47, no. 3 (2006), pp. 49–55.
9. Matrix structures are discussed by C. Bartlett and S. Ghoshal, 'Matrix management: not a structure, more a frame of mind', *Harvard Business Review*, vol. 68, no. 4 (1990), pp. 138–145.
10. The classic article on project-based organisations is by R. DeFillippi and M. Arthur, 'Paradox in project-based enterprise: the case of film-making', *California Management Review*, vol. 40, no. 2 (1998), pp. 125–145. For some difficulties, see M. Bresnen, A. Goussevskaia and J. Swann, 'Organizational routines, situated learning and processes of change in project-based organisations', *Project Management Journal*, vol. 36, no. 3 (2005), pp. 27–42.
11. For a discussion of more permanent team structures, see T. Mullern, 'Integrating the team-based structure in the business process: the case of Saab Training Systems', in A. Pettigrew and E. Fenton (eds), *The Innovating Organisation*, Sage, 2000.
12. M. Goold and A. Campbell, *Designing Effective Organisations*, Jossey-Bass, 2002. See also M. Goold and A. Campbell, 'Do you have a well-designed organisation?', *Harvard Business Review*, vol. 80, no. 3 (2002), pp. 117–224.
13. A.D. Chandler, *Strategy and Structure: Chapters in the History of American Enterprise*, MIT Press, 1962.
14. This practice of 'patching' parts of the organisation onto each other according to changing market needs is described in K. Eisenhardt and S. Brown, 'Patching: restitching business portfolios in dynamic markets', *Harvard Business Review*, vol. 25, no. 3 (1999), pp. 72–80.
15. The point has been argued by E. Fenton and A. Pettigrew, 'Theoretical perspectives on new forms of organising', in A. Pettigrew and E. Fenton (eds), *The Innovating Organisation*, Sage, 2000, chapter 1.
16. For readers who would like to read more about ERP the following are useful: P. Binngi, M. Sharma and J. Godia, 'Critical issues affecting an ERP implementation', *Information Systems Management*, vol. 16, no. 3 (1999), pp. 7–14; T. Grossman and J. Walsh, 'Avoiding the pitfalls of ERP system implementation', *Information Systems Management*, vol. 21, no. 2 (2004), pp. 38–42.
17. C. Casey, 'Come, join our family: discipline and integration in corporate organizational culture', *Human Relations*, vol. 52, no. 2 (1999), pp. 155–179; for an account of the socialisation of graduate trainees, see A.D. Brown and C. Coupland, 'Sounds of silence: graduate trainees, hegemony and resistance', *Organization Studies*, vol. 26, no. 7 (2005), pp. 1049–1070.
18. E.C. Wenger and W.M. Snyder, 'Communities of practice: the organized frontier', *Harvard Business Review*, vol. 78, no. 1 (2000), pp. 139–146.
19. D. Helm and T. Jenkinson, *Competition in Regulated Industries*, Clarendon Press, 1999, provides a number of in-depth case studies of competitive implications of deregulation. See also A. Lomi and E. Larsen, 'Learning without experience: strategic implications of deregulation and competition in the international electricity industry', *European Management Journal*, vol. 17, no. 2 (1999), pp. 151–164.
20. See R. Kaplan and D. Norton, 'The balanced scorecard: measures that drive performance', *Harvard Business Review*, vol. 70, no. 1 (1992), pp 71–79; for a recent development, see R. Kaplan and D. Norton, 'Having trouble with your strategy? Then map it', *Harvard Business Review*, vol. 78, no. 5 (2000), pp. 167–176; and R. Kaplan and D. Norton, *Alignment: How to Apply the Balanced Scorecard to Strategy*, Harvard Business School Press, 2006.
21. Companies like Royal Dutch Shell have been experimenting with internal markets to stimulate innovation. See G. Hamel, 'Bringing Silicon Valley inside', *Harvard Business Review*, vol. 77, no. 5 (1999), pp. 70–84. For a discussion of internal market challenges, see A. Vining, 'Internal market failure', *Journal of Management Studies*, vol. 40, no. 2 (2003), pp. 431–457.
22. For a discussion of these issues in the public sector context see K. Scholes, 'Strategy and structure in the public sector', in G. Johnson and K. Scholes (eds), *Exploring*

Public Sector Strategy, Financial Times/Prentice Hall, 2001, chapter 13; and T. Forbes, 'Devolution and control; within the UK public sector: National Health Service Trusts', ibid., chapter 16.

23. M. Goold and A. Campbell, *Strategies and Styles*, Blackwell, 1987.

24. See M. Goold, A. Campbell and K. Lucks, 'Strategics and styles revisited: strategic planning and financial control', *Long Range Planning*, vol. 26, no. 6 (1993), pp. 49–61; and R. Grant, 'Strategic planning in a turbulent environment: evidence from the oil majors', *Strategic Management Journal*, vol. 24, no. 6 (2003), pp. 491–517.

25. C. Bartlett and S. Ghoshal, 'Changing the role of top management: beyond strategy to purpose', *Harvard Business Review*, vol. 72, no. 6 (1994), pp. 79–88.

26. See W. Ruigrok, L. Achtenhagen, M. Wagner and J. Ruegg-Sturm, 'ABB: beyond the global matrix towards the network organisation', in A. Pettigrew and E. Fenton (eds), *The Innovating Organisation*, Sage, 2000, chapter 4. Also J.C. Jarillo, *Strategic Networks: Creating the borderless organisation*, Butterworth–Heinemann, 1993.

27. Y. Doz and G. Hamel, *Alliance Advantage*, Harvard Business School Press, 1998, p. 235.

28. Virtual organisations and the extensive use of subcontracting have been widely discussed. For example, W. Davidow and M. Malone, *The Virtual Corporation*, Harper Business, 1992. For a cautious view, see H. Chesborough and D. Teece, 'Organising for innovation: when is virtual virtuous?', *Harvard Business Review*, vol. 80, no. 2 (2002), pp. 127–136. See also Jarillo, reference 26.

29. H. Mintzberg describes common configurations in his classic *The Structuring of Organisations*, Prentice Hall, 1979.

30. A. Pettigrew and E. Fenton, 'Complexities and dualities in innovative forms of organising', in A. Pettigrew and E. Fenton (eds), *The Innovating Organisation*, Sage, 2000, chapter 10.

31. R.A. Burgelman, 'Managing the new venture division: implications for strategic management', *Strategic Management Journal*, vol. 6, no. 1 (1985), pp. 39–54.

32. R. Whittington and M. Mayer, *The European Corporation: Strategy, Structure and Social Science*, Oxford University Press, 2000; and Ruigrok *et al.*, reference 26.

33. R. Whittington and M. Mayer, *Organising for Success: A Report on Knowledge*, CIPD, 2002.

34. For an analysis of this process at a leading pharmaceutical firm, see S. Karim and W. Mitchell, 'Innovating through acquisition and internal development: a quarter-century of boundary evolution at Johnson & Johnson', *Long Range Planning*, vol. 37, no. 6 (2004), pp. 525–538.

Hurricane Katrina: human-made disaster?

Introduction

Early on Monday morning, 29 August 2005, Hurricane Katrina struck the southern American state of Louisiana, rushing quickly inland to the city of New Orleans. With wind speeds at 125 miles per hour (200 km/h), the levees (dykes) protecting the city collapsed in several places. Over the next few days, the world watched in horror as New Orleans and the surrounding areas struggled with chaos. Hurricane Katrina claimed 1,836 lives and left vivid images of bodies floating in the streets, families stranded on rooftops and 25,000 hungry and thirsty people trapped for days in the notorious Superdome. Six months after the hurricane, more than half of New Orleans' population had still not returned to the city.

Ultimately, of course, the destruction wrought by Hurricane Katrina had natural causes. But there is every sign that the damage and suffering were significantly increased by organisational failures. The disaster of Hurricane Katrina was partly a consequence of organisational design.

A new organisation

The government organisation ultimately responsible for coordinating the response to Katrina was the US Department of Homeland Security. This itself was a recent creation, a reaction to the terrorist attacks of September 11, 2001. One finding from investigations into the circumstances surrounding 9/11 was the difficulty of coordinating all the information regarding terrorist threats. For example, before the attacks, a flight training school had alerted local authorities about a student who only seemed interested in learning how to fly civil airliners, not about how to take off or land. But the information had not been passed on to the Federal Bureau of Investigations (FBI): the student went on to be one of the terrorist hijackers involved in 9/11.

Photo: Robert Galbraith/Reuters

The US government responded to 9/11 by placing terrorism as the highest priority. It believed that one way of improving coordination in response to potential terror threats was by centralising relevant government departments. Nine days after the 9/11 attack, President Bush appointed Pennsylvania Governor and decorated Vietnam veteran Tom Ridge to create and head a new department. The White House vetoed some of Tom Ridge's more radical proposals, so that both the Justice Department and the FBI remained independent. However, finally 22 departments were swept together in 2002 to create the new Department for Homeland Security (see Figure 1 for an organisational chart).

Involving more than 180,000 employees, this was the biggest reorganisation of the US government since the creation of the Pentagon in 1947. Amongst the major agencies that were gathered together under Tom Ridge's command were Customs, Immigration, Narcotics, the Coast Guard, the Secret Service and, most important here, the Federal Emergency Management Agency (FEMA). All were to unite in the fight against terrorism. As the head of the US Customs Service said: 'Terrorism is our highest priority, bar none. Ninety eight per cent of my attention . . . has been devoted to that one issue.' Tom Ridge anticipated turf battles between the

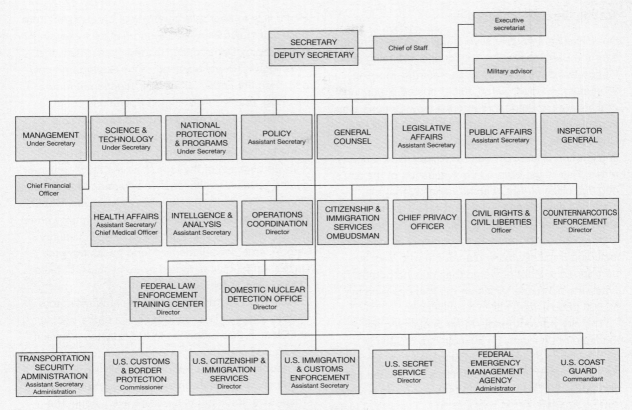

Figure 1 Department of Homeland Security organisation chart

Source: http://www.dhs.gov/xabout/structure/editorial_0644.shtm

newly amalgamated agencies but declared: 'The only turf we should be worried about protecting is the turf we stand on.'

FEMA, however, resisted the reorganisation. Responsible for responding to natural disasters such as hurricanes or earthquakes, FEMA had since 1993 been represented directly inside the President's Cabinet. Merger within the new Department of Homeland Security relegated FEMA to a mere internal division, with no direct Cabinet-level representation. FEMA's then head protested to the President's chief of staff: 'I told him it was a big mistake. The fact that FEMA could report to the President, any President – Democrat, Republican or independent – was what made the agency effective'. In the wake of 9/11, of course, this sounded like special pleading.

Within the new organisation, response to natural disasters had a low priority. In 2004, the Department drew up a list of 15 planning scenarios, doomsday events that could cause major fatalities. Twelve of these involved shadowy international terrorist groups, with plots involving mustard gas, sarin, nuclear weapons and anthrax, amongst other imaginative possibilities. One planning scenario did raise the threat of a hurricane flooding a nameless southern city and causing more than a thousand deaths. But terror attacks held the attention and these attracted the budgets.

Resources for protection against natural disasters began to get squeezed. Tom Ridge retired and was replaced by a new Secretary for Homeland Security, Michael Chertoff, a former judge. Various FEMA functions were stripped off and reallocated to other parts of the reorganisation. FEMA lost $80m (£44m; €64m) from its $550m operating budget. It struggled to get resources for rehearsing a response to a New Orleans hurricane scenario, and when it did do so, funds were denied for a follow-up. Between 2000 and 2005, the budget for the New Orleans Engineering Corps, responsible for the levees protecting the city, was cut by 44 per cent. Meanwhile, the Ohio Fire Service was able to get funds for bulletproof vests to protect their dogs in the event of terrorist attack.

Testing the new organisation

Hurricane Katrina gave several days' notice, forming over the Bahamas on 23 August and sweeping over Florida two days later. Early on Saturday morning, 27 August, a FEMA watch officer posted a warning of a severe hurricane threat to the New Orleans area, capable of causing thousands of fatalities. Michael Chertoff was at home that day, working on immigration issues. On Saturday night, New Orleans Mayor Ray Nagin ordered an evacuation of the city's 400,000 citizens. But, with no certainty that the hurricane would actually hit, and with what force, not everybody wanted to leave their homes for fear of looting. Moreover, many had no means of transport, including tragically many old people who were to be trapped without power in their nursing homes. When the hurricane struck on the Monday morning, 60,000 people were still in New Orleans.

The city was not ready. FEMA's planning for the state of Louisiana as a whole had called for 69 truckloads of water, 69 truckloads of ice and 34 truckloads of food to be in place. It planned for 400 buses and 800 drivers to ferry people to shelters. On the Sunday, FEMA had just 30 truckloads of water, 17 truckloads of ice and 15 truckloads of meals. FEMA had no buses in the state at all.

FEMA had got one officer into the city on the Sunday, but was otherwise not represented locally. When the flooding started, communications broke down. The various services had different communications systems, and the batteries on mobile devices soon ran down, with no power available to recharge. FEMA's high-tech communications wagon only reached New Orleans on the Friday (long after the world's journalists) and in the meantime Mayor Nagin's team had broken into an Office Depot store in order to steal functioning communications equipment. The sole FEMA officer on the ground had to bully his way onto one of the few helicopters available to confirm the broken levees on the first day. The Department of Homeland Security operations centre in Washington, guarding against panic responses, insisted on verification by a second source before passing the message up the chain, but no second source was available. Secretary Chertoff briefed President Bush about immigration issues on Monday morning, and made no mention of the hurricane.

The Department of Homeland Security struggled to cope over the following days. Michael Brown, FEMA's

Head, flew to nearby Baton Rouge, but suffered from poor communications and found himself increasingly bypassed by Department Head Michael Chertoff in Washington. The evacuation of the Superdome only began on the Friday, after the instigation of food rationing, and the Washington operations centre overlooked 20,000 refugees at the New Orleans Convention Center for several days, thinking it the same building as the Superdome. Aircraft were delayed because of the lack of air marshals required by anti-terrorist regulations. The Department of Homeland Security insisted that all evacuees would have to be security screened before being allowed on planes, and then took eight hours to fly in security staff. A large consignment of food packs from the United Kingdom was turned away because of fears of Mad Cow Disease.

At a Thursday press conference in Washington, Michael Chertoff praised 'the genius of the people at FEMA' in their response to the disaster. 'I think it is a source of tremendous pride to me to work with the people who've pulled off this really exceptional response'. But television reports direct from New Orleans contradicted this picture every hour. The failure of FEMA, and of local agencies, was becoming very apparent. Facing heavy criticism, FEMA's head, Michael Brown, resigned on 13 September. Michael Chertoff kept his job.

Sources: C. Cooper and R. Block, *Disaster: Hurricane Katrina and the Failure of Homeland Security*, Times Books, 2006; and I. Daaddler and I. Destler, 'Advisors, Czars and Councils', *The National Interest*, 1 July (2002).

Questions

1 What was the 'strategy' of the Department of Homeland Security in the period immediately before Hurricane Katrina?

2 In the light of this strategy, what, if any, changes should be made to the Department's organizational structure after Hurricane Katrina?

3 Who was responsible for the organizational failures surrounding the response to Hurricane Katrina?

13

Resourcing Strategies

LEARNING OUTCOMES

After reading this chapter you should be able to:

→ Analyse the resource management issues that are important to achieving strategic success in four key resource areas:
  - The management of *people*. This includes the development of people's competences, the management of their behaviour and the appropriate organisational structures and processes.
  - Access to and processing of *information* to build capabilities and change business models and/or management processes.
  - The management of *finance* to create financial value, fund strategic developments and address the differing financial expectations of stakeholders.
  - The management of *technology* to address changing competitive forces on an organisation and improve strategic capability.

→ Address the *integration* of resources and competences across resource areas to underpin the success of a strategy.

Photo: Horizon International Images Ltd/Alamy Images

13.1 INTRODUCTION

Most managers operate in a *part* of an organisation where their day-to-day work is dominated by issues that are specific to that function, department, division or project team. It should be clear from discussions earlier in this book that in all organisations, except the very smallest, this type of *specialisation* is usually a key factor underpinning success. Managers and individuals at this level will control resources, activities and business processes that are crucial to strategic success of the organisation as a whole. They are also likely to be the most knowledgeable about changes in parts of the business environment with which they interface. For example, HR specialists should understand the labour market, finance managers the money markets, R&D specialists the technological environment, and so on. So, many of the issues in the parts of an organisation have strategic implications. Therefore, these managers need to understand how the capabilities in 'their' resource area contributes to the overall success of organisational strategies and be capable of managing those resources (such as people, information, etc.) *strategically*.

This chapter will look at four key resource areas, people, information, finance and technology, and the ways in which they might underpin strategic success. In each case two related questions will be considered (see Exhibit 13.1):

● Are all of the different resource areas capable of *delivering* the organisation's business strategies? This will include the need for those managing resources to make sense of the business strategy and change capabilities and behaviours accordingly. For example, is the organisation using the appropriate mix of funding sources for the level of risk in its business strategies?

But also . . .

Exhibit 13.1 **Resourcing strategies**

● Are the business strategies of the organisation being shaped to *capitalise on the expertise* in each resource area? This requires senior managers to understand which business strategies might be made possible as a result of particular strengths in specific resource areas. For example, a particular expertise in IT can create better 'business models' than competitors. The resource-based view of strategy introduced in Chapter 3 is particularly concerned with this issue.

Resourcing strategies is concerned with the two-way relationship between overall business strategies and strategies in separate resource areas such as people, information, finance and technology

So, in summary, **resourcing strategies** is concerned with the two-way relationship between overall business strategies and strategies in separate resource areas such as people, information, finance and technology.

13.2   MANAGING PEOPLE[1]

The knowledge and experience of people can be the key factors influencing the success of strategies. So people-related issues should be a central concern and responsibility of most managers in organisations and are not confined to a specialist HR function. Creating a climate where people strive to achieve success is also a crucial role of any manager. Although formal HR systems and structures may be vitally important in supporting successful strategies, it is quite possible that they may hinder strategy if they are not tailored to the types of strategies being pursued. It is helpful to think about the people dimension of strategy as being concerned with three related issues (see Exhibit 13.2):

● people as a *resource* (which relates to Chapter 3);
● people and *behaviour* (which relates to Chapter 5);
● the need to *organise* people (which relates to Chapter 12).

13.2.1   People as a resource[2]

An important message from Chapter 3 of this book is that the possession of resources (including people) does not guarantee strategic success. Strategic capability is concerned with how these resources are deployed, managed, controlled and, in the case of people, motivated to create competences in those activities and business processes needed to run the business. This is a tough agenda in a rapidly changing world since the performance standards are constantly shifting in an upward direction. Much of this 'hard' side of HR management is concerned with these issues of performance management. So traditional HR activities can help underpin successful strategies in the following ways:

● *Audits* to assess HR requirements to support strategies and/or identify people-based core competences on which future strategies might be built.
● *Goal-setting and performance assessment* of individuals and teams. Most organisations will expect line managers to undertake these tasks, usually within a centrally designed appraisal scheme. This improves the chances of appraisals being linked to strategy. Also, there has been a move towards so-called 360° appraisals. These assess an individual's performance from multiple perspectives

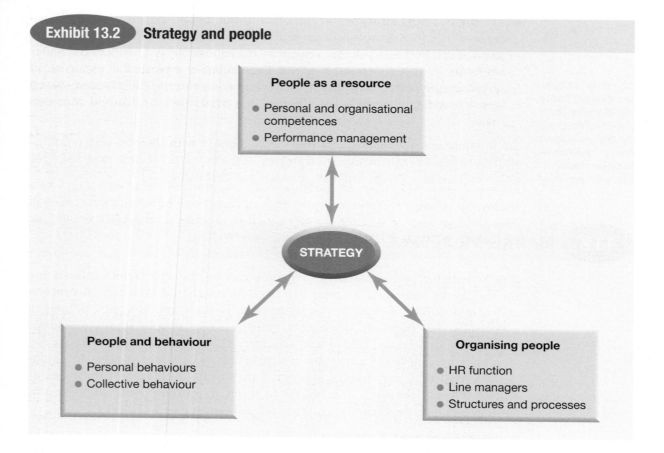

Exhibit 13.2 **Strategy and people**

- not just from the line manager but also from other parts of the organisation on which the work of the individual and/or his or her team impacts and even from external stakeholders. This is an attempt to assess the full impact of an employee's work on the success of strategy.

- In many organisations the planning of *rewards* has had to take on board the reality of more teamworking in delivering strategy. Highly geared individual incentives (often found in salesforces) may undermine this teamwork.

- *Recruitment and retention* are key ways of improving strategic capability. For example, many public sector organisations have needed to recruit and retain people with marketing and IT skills as they try to get closer to their customers and exploit IT. As organisations face faster changes, *succession planning* has had to be refocused away from preparing people for particular jobs to simply ensuring that a sufficiently large pool of talented individuals exists to meet future leadership requirements.[3] In some cases an organisation's strategy may require *uniquely competent individuals,* such as a top surgeon in a hospital, a criminal lawyer or a leading academic in a university. In contrast, some strategies might require *redeployment* and *redundancy* planning.

- Many *training and development* plans have reduced the use of formal programmes in favour of more coaching and mentoring to support self-development.

In order to put in place and execute HR strategies in all these areas, managers and HR professionals need to be familiar with the organisation's strategies, how these might be changing in the future and the implication to people's competences.[4] Many companies might attempt this alignment through formalised approaches to performance management – assisted by IT-based systems.[5]

However, it is not enough simply to adjust the performance management processes to support changing strategies. Managers need to be able and willing to envisage a future where the strategies and performance of the organisation are transformed by exploiting the performance management capabilities of the organisation better than their competitors. For example, a capability in mentoring and coaching could provide an environment that will attract creative people who like to be challenged and to learn. In turn, this creates a workforce that are much more able than competitors to 'think out of the box' and to produce innovative product features and new ways of competing in the market. This will require organisation structures and processes to support these behaviours, as explained in Chapter 12 and discussed further below.

13.2.2 People and behaviour[6]

People are not like other resources. They influence strategy both through their competence (section 13.2.1) and through their collective behaviour (culture) as discussed in Chapter 5. Chapter 14 will also emphasise that many of the problems of managing change result from a failure to understand, address and change culture. This 'soft' side of HR management is concerned with the behaviour of people – both individually and collectively. It is very often neglected in favour of the 'harder' issues discussed in the previous section. For example, these 'softer' issues might include:

- Understanding how they may need to change the *paradigm*[7] of the organisation as discussed in Chapter 5. This is particularly important when the business environment is changing quickly.

- Seeing their own role as people-oriented 'shapers of context'[8] and not just as 'business analysts'. This will require an understanding of how these 'softer' aspects of strategy help or hinder strategic success.

- Understanding *the relationship between behaviours and strategic choices*. This is crucial if managers are properly to prioritise their efforts in managing organisational behaviours. For example, there may be some strategies where an organisation's current culture gives unique advantage over other organisations. So culture is a core competence as discussed in Chapter 3.

- Being realistic about the *difficulty and time-scales* in achieving behaviour changes. Culture change is a long process of changing behaviours. The hard change tools (structures and systems) if used alone are unlikely to deliver, as seen in Chapter 14.

- Being able to vary their *style* of managing change with different circumstances, as will be discussed in Chapter 14. So a manager's relationship and leadership skills with both internal and external stakeholders are important. Also, *teams* in organisations must be capable of operating different styles simultaneously. Therefore, a manager's ability to build and maintain teams of different personality types is just as important as the mix of competences in those teams.[9]

Illustration 13.1 shows how important is the behaviour of front-line staff – particularly in service organisations. In this example their behaviour was clearly out of line with the stated business strategy of 'customer care'. So the intended strategy and the actual (realised) strategies were not the same. Fundamentally it is the day-to-day actions of managers that will shape and change the behaviour of front-line staff. But HR policies and frameworks can help with these softer-side issues. For example, in the high-technology sector the ability of staff and managers to build internal and external networks of personal contacts can be crucial in keeping at the leading edge of knowledge. These behaviours can be supported by 'hard-side' HR activities such as mentoring and rewards.[10]

13.2.3 Organising people[11]

Chapter 12 was concerned with the issues of organising for success with particular emphasis on how the balance of this agenda is changing in the twenty-first century. It is not the intention to repeat that detail here but to highlight some of the implications to how people might underpin strategic success.

The HR function

There are a number of important considerations concerning the HR function in organisations. The most challenging question is whether a specialist HR function is needed at all, or at least whether its traditional scale and functions are appropriate. In principle (and in practice in many organisations), people can be managed strategically without a specialist HR function. This may make sense for some HR issues – for example, the dismantling of across-company grades and pay scales as organisations globalise – to reflect the much greater diversity in the labour markets. But for other aspects the reverse might be true. For example, a major problem of highly devolved organisations is that managers at 'lower' levels are unfamiliar with corporate-level strategies, are extremely busy and may not have the professional HR knowledge.

If an HR function is felt to be valuable then the expectations as to its role must be clear and consistent with the discussion above. There are four broad roles that an HR function could fulfil in contributing to successful business strategies:[12]

- As a *service provider* (for example, undertaking recruitment or arranging training) to line managers who are carrying the strategic responsibility for the HR issues.
- As a *regulator* 'setting the rules' within which line managers operate, for example on pay and promotions.
- As an *advisor* on issues of HR strategy to line managers (ensuring that HR policies and practice are in line with the 'best practice').
- As a *change agent* moving the organisation forward.

The determinants of the most appropriate role for an HR function are the organisation's context.[13] The type of staff, the nature of the strategy and the broad structural arrangements in the organisation are all important. Of course it may prove difficult for the same HR specialists to operate in all of these roles

Illustration 13.1

Customer relations at KLM: The Reliable Airline

What people do in providing customer services needs to be aligned with an organisation's strategy.

Cityhopper Flight KL1481 was due to leave Amsterdam for Glasgow. As the time approached for boarding, passengers were informed that they would not be boarding that flight, though they were given no clear explanation as to why. They later found that it had been diverted to Leeds. They were, however, informed that there would be another aircraft departing at 21:30. It arrived at 21:00 and at 21:20 they began to board. This took 30 minutes. At 22:00 the pilot announced that this aircraft had a fault with the hydraulics. He went on to explain: 'We have had a bad day: five of our Cityhoppers have developed faults so we are short of planes.' Passengers wondered quite what this said about the maintenance standards of KLM. Some minutes later they were told that no replacement aircraft could be found and they would have to stay in Amsterdam that night. When they disembarked it became clear there would be further problems. Passengers were asked to move to a transfer desk where they would be informed of what would happen to them. When they arrived there were only five KLM ground staff and long queues developed. There was no announcement of what would happen the next day. One of the ground staff was heard to say that further of their colleagues would soon be arriving, so the back end of the queues moved to set up new lines. Additional staff did arrive but they could not deal with the passengers because their computer screens did not work. So whilst people queued, numerous ground staff stood around exchanging increasingly heated and acrimonious comments with passengers. One passenger was heard to say 'I'm being made to feel this is my fault!' Eventually a supervisor arrived. He also made no announcement to the passengers or engaged with them. After about 15 minutes he went away. It emerged, but was never announced, that KLM had

not laid on another flight to Glasgow, but was filling vacant seats on various other flights going to Scotland.

It was after midnight when the last passengers went on their way to hotels around the airport. Muttering passengers were heard to say they would never fly with KLM again.

The Director of Customer Relationship Management at KLM, commented:

We regret the problems encountered by our passengers on this particular flight. In this case, we certainly learnt that despite the fact that technical problems occur in our business, both to airplanes and computer systems, the number of ground handling staff was not sufficient to satisfy the needs of our customers at this particular moment. Consequently the attitude of our staff towards customers was not appropriate and communication was not managed properly.

We learn every day from our customers' negative travel experience by transforming this information into knowledge and action to prevent these things happening again to other passengers. Our product and services at all customer contact points, like for instance reservations, ground, transfer and inflight, is regularly monitored and measured by a set of standard survey and measurement tools. The process behind this information flow is organized in such a way that: the cause of the problem is notified; a correction is requested and implemented and the situation is monitored through regular surveys.

Questions

1 In what ways were KLM's HR policies and systems adequate or not to deliver the promise of The Reliable Airline?

2 How did the behaviour of front-line staff influence the actual service delivery?

3 What could be changed to improve the consistency of service delivery?

simultaneously. For example, they may feel a conflict between their role as a regulator whilst trying to advise or change a group of people in the organisation.

Middle (line) managers

It has been mentioned above that there has been a significant move towards line managers being centrally involved in managing people issues themselves. This has the clear advantage of more ownership and a better chance of blending people-related issues with business strategies. But there are also worries and research[14] confirms the concerns as to whether the circumstances in which line managers operate are conducive to their doing a good job on people management issues:

- Whether it is realistic to expect line managers to be *competent HR professionals*. Handled badly, this could be a formula for mediocrity. This same concern could equally be applied to other areas such as information management (discussed in section 13.3).
- The *short-term pressures* to meet targets do not help line managers in taking a more strategic view of people-related issues. Downsizing and de-layering have left the remaining managers too busy.
- Trade unions and professional associations have tended to *resist a dispersion of responsibility* for HR strategies. From a union's point of view it is much easier to deal with a single, centralised authority. Professional bodies may take a similar view.
- Managers may lack the *incentive* to take on more of the formal HR activities, either directly in their pay or grade or indirectly in their judgement as to which competences make them more marketable outside the company.

Despite these concerns it is important to recognise the crucial influence of middle managers on the day-to-day performance and behaviour of people in their organisation. The implication for top managers is not to bypass middle managers in the strategy development process, otherwise the changes may not stick with the people in the organisation.

Structures and processes

People may be held back from contributing to strategic success because the traditional structures and roles do not match future strategies. Also, as circumstances and strategies change, organisations may need to change the processes and relationships as discussed in Chapter 12.

Another challenge is whether some HR issues (for example, recruitment, training) should reside in the organisation or be bought in from specialist suppliers (for example, consultants). External agencies will have the advantage of a wider experience and knowledge of best practice but the disadvantage of being unfamiliar with the detailed circumstances of specific organisations.

13.2.4 Implications for managers

The various separate points about the relationship between business strategies and people have been brought together and summarised in the model shown in Exhibit 13.3:

| Exhibit 13.3 | **Competitive advantage through people** |

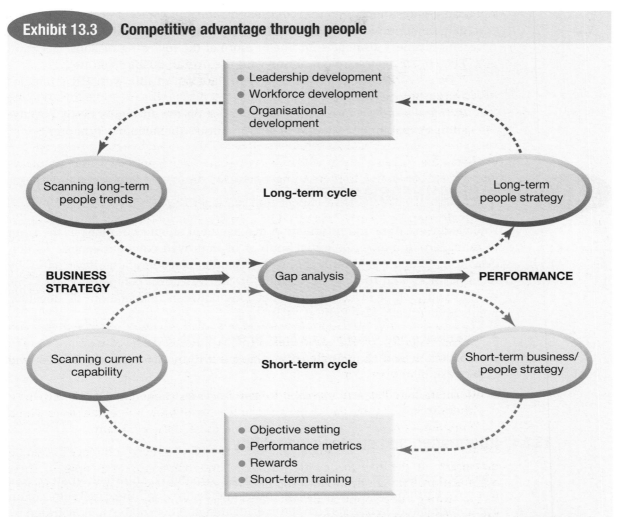

Source: Adapted from L. Gratton, V. Hope Hailey, P. Stiles and C. Truss, *Strategic Human Resource Management*, Oxford University Press, 1999, p. 185, Fig. 9.1. Copyright © 1999 Oxford University Press.

- There must be activities to ensure the *maintenance* of competitiveness. This is about ensuring that people are able to support the strategies of an organisation in the short term. For example, objective setting, performance appraisal, rewards and training.

- Simultaneously there must be activities to provide a *platform on which new strategies can be built* in the longer term. For example, leadership, culture, competences and organisation development. The management of these longer-term issues might create opportunities for significant *transformations* in strategy and competitiveness.

- These two 'cycles' of activities must be *linked*. Achieving short-term delivery goals must not be at the expense of longer-term capability. For example, using reward systems as the main tool to stimulate short-term success – say through individual bonus schemes – may compromise the ability to take more radical and strategic interventions, such as the creation of new roles and relationships to create a more innovative organisation.

- Those organisations that are *competent in managing these processes* are likely to gain competitive advantage.[15] Others run the risk of failing to deliver successful business strategies for one or more of the following reasons:
  - The *HR strategies* are out of line with the overall business strategy.
  - *People's competences and/or behaviours* are out of line with HR strategies and/or business strategies.
  - *Business strategies* are failing to capitalise on the strengths in an organisation's capabilities (Chapter 3) and/or culture (behaviours) (Chapter 5).

13.3 MANAGING INFORMATION[16]

Knowledge creation and information management should be issues at the front of managers' minds as potential sources of improved competitiveness, as discussed in Chapter 3. Within this wider agenda, considerations have naturally focused on IT and the extent to which it can transform competitiveness. This section will look at three main connections between information, IT developments and strategy (see Exhibit 13.4):

- information and *strategic capability* (linked to Chapter 3);
- information and changing *business models* within and across industries and sectors;
- information and *structures/management processes* (linked to Chapter 12).

13.3.1 Information and strategic capability

Chapter 3 explained the concept of strategic capability. Information strategies can have a profound influence on creating and destroying[17] the capabilities of an organisation and, hence, its competitive advantage. This will be demonstrated by

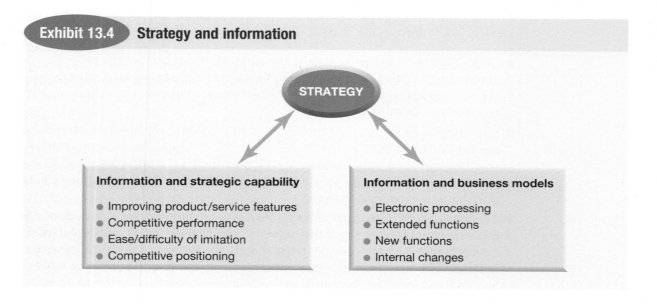

Exhibit 13.4 Strategy and information

STRATEGY

Information and strategic capability
- Improving product/service features
- Competitive performance
- Ease/difficulty of imitation
- Competitive positioning

Information and business models
- Electronic processing
- Extended functions
- New functions
- Internal changes

looking at examples of how information and IT might impact on three important 'elements' of a core capability as described in Chapter 3, namely: ensuring that products/services *are valued by customers*, *outperforming competitors* and making capabilities *difficult to imitate*. But wider availability of information will also accelerate the learning of competitors, so advantages gained through experience may be shorter-lived than hitherto. This will inevitably mean that organisations will need to revisit and redefine the basis on which they are competing more frequently, as discussed in Chapters 2 and 6.

Information and product/service features

The enhanced capabilities of IT already help organisations to provide product/service features that are valued by customers:

- *Lower prices* (through reduced costs) – particularly where the product is information, such as in financial services.
- Improved *pre-purchase information* (for example, website browsing, customer bulletin boards).
- *Easier and faster purchasing processes* (for example, online ordering) and delivery. This can allow customers to move closer to just-in-time with *their* business processes.
- *Shorter development times* for new features. These, in turn, might give purchasers advantage with *their* customers.
- *Product or service reliability* and diagnostics are being improved (for example, engine management systems in cars).
- *Personalised products* or services without price premium (for example, customising computer architecture for each purchaser).
- Improved *after-sales service*, for example automatic service reminders.

One of the most important implications for organisations producing or distributing physical products has been that competitive advantage is more likely to be achieved through service performance (for example, speed and reliability of delivery or maintenance) than in product features per se. So managers need to conceive of their business not as a product company with support services but as a service company which supplies a product. This has required a profound mindset shift for some managers when considering which competences are most crucial to competitive performance.

Information and competitive performance

If customers value some or all of these features listed above then competitors are likely to learn quickly how to provide those features. Therefore the threshold standards that need to be achieved to survive in a market will rise rapidly. So providers who are unable to deliver these higher standards will fall out of the market. Also Chapter 3 reminded readers that competitiveness and standards of performance are determined not just within a particular industry or sector. Customer expectations of service standards, for example on speed or reliability, become the universal benchmarks crossing all industries and public services.

The importance of market knowledge to competitiveness applies in all sectors of industry, commerce and the public services. This knowledge results from competences in analysing the subtle differences between customer needs in different parts of the market and building product or service features to meet these needs (as mentioned in Chapters 2 and 6). Most organisations have colossal amounts of raw data about these issues and the IT processing capacity to analyse the data (both of which are necessary). But they are not good at this data-mining process, which will convert data into market knowledge. **Data mining**[18] is the process of finding trends, patterns and connections in data in order to inform and improve competitive performance. For example, building up individual customer purchasing history as a basis for targeting promotional offers; identifying connected purchases (for instance, readers of particular newspapers or magazines have similar purchasing patterns for other goods and services); or simply finding underlying drivers of demand (such as demographic factors as discussed in Chapter 2). Data mining can also help with profitability analysis as a basis for creating priorities for customer retention. In financial services data mining can also help with credit risk assessment, customer attrition forecasts and detection of fraud.

> **Data mining** is the process of finding trends, patterns and connections in data in order to inform and improve competitive performance

Information and imitation

Chapter 3 considered several reasons why resources or competences might be difficult to imitate. Information processing capability can have an influence on any/all of these:

- First, a resource or competence might be *rare*. When IT infrastructure costs were high this was a reason why a few larger organisations gained advantage over others through their IT infrastructure. Others could not afford the capital costs. On the whole, this is no longer true. IT is now pervasive even in very small companies.

- Capabilities may also be difficult to imitate because they are *complex*. The mastery of the hardware and standard software needed to build information systems used to be complex – now it is not. The current areas of complexity are more in data-mining activities (discussed above) and the activities which underpin speed to market. Managing relationships in the value network (see section 3.6.1) is an area where 'e-relationship management'[19] with customers can be particularly important (such as joining up all the different routes through which customers interface with a company).

- Capabilities may be hard to imitate because of *causal ambiguity* – competitors find it hard to understand the reasons why an organisation is successful. This is because the competences are *culturally embedded* in the way the organisation works and are not explicit. Many IT developments – particularly intelligent systems – are attempting to codify the tacit knowledge in organisations to make it explicit. For example, helplines use every customer query and its solution to build up progressively knowledge as to what can go wrong with a product and how it is solved. This ability to codify previously tacit knowledge removes barriers to imitation and undermines core capabilities. There is a danger in becoming overdependent on information systems and ignoring tacit knowledge simply because it is difficult to codify and build into the system. But this is the very reason why it is difficult to imitate and may be crucial to competitive advantage.

Information and competitive positioning

The strategic role of information in organisations will need to be different depending on the way in which the organisation is positioning its products or services in the market (as described by the strategy clock from Chapter 6 – Exhibit 6.2):

● *Routinisation* (positions 1 and 2 on the strategy clock) – where the role of information (usually IT systems) is to reduce drastically the cost of transactions with customers, suppliers or channels. For example, by moving the customer towards self-service (such as websites replacing face-to-face selling).

● *Mass customisation* (position 3 on the strategy clock) – where information systems can create more product features that customers value (as discussed above) at the same or lower price. This is a major battleground in many sectors at the present time – such as consumer electronics.

● *Customisation* (positions 4 and 5 on the strategy clock) – where information can be provided to customers in advance of any face-to-face or telephone contact (for example, through websites). Personal contact is then reserved for advising a much more knowledgeable potential customer.

It should be remembered that significant parts of the market in most sectors consist of customers who do not value the features that IT-based systems can offer. So targeting these *IT laggards* provides a continuing opportunity for those providers who are especially good at providing information in more traditional ways, for example personal face-to-face service.

13.3.2 Information and changing business models

A business model describes the structure of product, service and information flows and the roles of the participating parties

Information processing capability has provided the opportunity to transform the way in which organisations build their relationships with others in their value network (as discussed in section 3.6.1). This is concerned with how business models[20] have changed in both the private and public sectors. A **business model** describes the structure of product, service and information flows and the roles of the participating parties. This includes potential benefits and sources of revenue to each of the parties. The value network framework discussed in section 3.6.1 can be used to identify many traditional business models. For example, the linear supply chain from component manufacturers, to finished product assemblers, primary distributors, retailers and finally the consumer. Even in this case – where the product 'flows' in a linear fashion through the chain – information and other services may exist in branches of the chain. For example, market research and after-sales service may be undertaken by other parties from outside this linear chain. In more complex e-commerce models a critical question is how each 'player' in the value network receives revenue. For example, this could be from sale of a product/service, 'commission' or providing advertising space. Exhibit 13.5 shows how e-commerce models have emerged out of traditional business models based on the degree of *innovation* from traditional approaches and the *complexity* (mainly the level of integration of activities). Three main changes have occurred:

| Exhibit 13.5 | **Changing business models** |

Degree of innovation

		Same as before	Extended	New
Degree of integration	**Single function**	E-shop E-procurement	E-auction Value chain services (e.g. payment systems, logistics) Trust services	Information brokerage (e.g. search engines)
	Integrated functions	E-mall	Third-party marketplace (e.g. web hosting)	Virtual communities Collaboration platforms Value chain integrator

Source: Adapted from P. Timmers, *Electronic Commerce*, Wiley, 2000, Chapter 3.

- *Electronic processes have replaced physical and paper-based processes*. For example, *e-shops* move marketing and 'display' to websites. *E-procurement* moves tendering, negotiation and purchasing processes to websites. In both cases the advantages are in reduced costs and wider choice. An *e-mall* takes the concept a little further by creating a collection of e-shops with a common umbrella – such as a brand. Nor is the public sector any different. Information gathering at scenes of crime is now aided by citizens and their digital camera/phones.

- Significant *extension of the functions* that traditional business models can offer. For example, sourcing or selling through *e-auctions* is both easy and cheap and can lead to significantly reduced purchasing costs or increased revenues. *Trust services* (such as supplier or customer certification or vetting) extend the types of information services available to members of trade associations. Other information functions in the value network can be provided more efficiently or effectively by *value chain service specialists* – such as payments or logistics. Some organisations see benefits in leaving a number of value activities to specialists who create *third-party marketplaces* and offer web-based marketing, branding, payment systems, logistics, and so on. This could be viewed as a complementary route to market rather than a complete replacement.

- Business models that are *transformational* in the sense that business can only be done this way electronically. Perhaps the most well-established example of transformational changes is the *information brokerage* role of companies like Yahoo! or Google with their search engines. *Virtual communities* can be sustained by IT – as Amazon tries to do in bringing authors, readers and publishers into dialogue on their website. Sometimes IT can provide a *collaboration platform*, for example, allowing customers and suppliers to work together on product design using specialist IT design tools. *Value chain integration* may be made possible through IT if separate activities can be knitted together by faster and more reliable information flows. For example, sales staff can discuss requirements with customers using both 'real-time' information about manufacturing capability, availability and production scheduling and also 'straight-through' information about the same issues in the supply chain. Frequently integration allows customers to change their specification and delivery schedules themselves – which then automatically reconfigures requirements back in the supply chain.

- In addition to these, there can also be important implications on how the internal 'business model' works. For example, better information can allow managers and external stakeholders to *bypass some of the traditional* **gatekeepers**, who gained power from their control of information. IT-based systems can create direct communication between the top and the bottom of an organisation and many chief executives use in-house websites for that purpose. The same issues also apply to the bypassing of unions as information conduits to employees. Also, externally, the salesforce are no longer the primary route through which customers gain their product knowledge or even place orders. Often their role has moved from 'closing deals' to relationship management and advice. In the public sector politicians are able to put in place two-way communication with their communities rather than relying on managers as the conduit and filter. There are already challenging implications for the whole way in which the political and service provision processes work.[21]

> **Gatekeepers** are individuals or groups who gain power from their control of information

From a strategic point of view the important considerations of any of these e-commerce business models is the extent to which they are able to create better value for money for customers and/or suppliers as shown in Illustration 13.2.

13.3.3 Implications for managers[22]

There are some important implications of these previous discussions for managers and those responsible for information strategy in organisations:

- Managers need to realise that information processing capability can *transform* the organisation, not just fine-tune current strategies and processes. They need to move away from seeing information management as a support function and place it on a par with other business functions.

- At the same time information managers[23] need to understand the *full potential of IT* from their professional knowledge and external networks (that is, be the company benchmarker). They need to understand the limitations of formal information systems, which cannot replace certain types of knowledge (such as intuition) or knowledge sharing that depends on social contact. Information managers need to be involved in and credible on business strategy as part of the corporate team (and not sit on the sidelines) and to see new business opportunities that IT could open up. They also need to have the influencing skills to educate and persuade senior colleagues about these opportunities.

Illustration 13.2

The DIY craze extends to loans

IT can support new business models which allow new intermediaries to displace established players – like banks. But is it a better deal for the customers and suppliers?

An article in the *Financial Times* in November 2005 outlined the activities of a new Internet-based financial intermediary:

Zopa (www.zopa.com) seeks to bring together borrowers and lenders without requiring them to go through a bank or other financial institution. Zopa was launched earlier this year. Its business model is relatively simple. If you are looking to borrow money you post your details on Zopa's website indicating how much you want to borrow and over what period you are looking to pay the money back. Zopa will then analyse your financial situation, giving you a credit rating according to your perceived ability to continue meeting the loan repayments. It claims that by using this model not only can it give most borrowers a much more competitive rate for loans than they could get off the high street but that people who lend money via Zopa will also get a much better return than had they stuck their cash in a bank account. Of course there are risks. . . .

Under the Zopa model, the rate charged by the lender is exactly the same as the rate incurred by the borrower. In short, Zopa does not take a cut as an intermediary. The average interest rate [were better] for [both] borrowers and lenders [than through traditional banks]. . . .

I can hear you asking: 'So how does Zopa make its money?' Well it is looking to two main revenue streams. One is by selling payment protection insurance (PPI) to some borrowers. In the event that the borrower is unable to meet repayments because of illness or redundancy, this insurance will cover the loan repayments. And from next year, it will also start charging borrowers an upfront fee of 1 per cent of the value of the loan. There will be no fee charged to lenders. . . .

But for lenders, the risks are less clear cut. As a lender to Zopa you are taking on all the default risks of the

borrower. So if the person you are lending to is unable to meet the loan repayments you risk losing out. Zopa seeks to minimise these risks in a number of ways. First, it conducts credit checks on its borrowers with three separate agencies. It also asks them an array of questions about their financial status.

Second, all loans are spread across 50 different borrowers with the same credit scores. So, in the event of one customer default, the maximum a lender could lose on a £5,000 [€7,250] loan is just £100. . . . In the event of a default, Zopa will also send out a debt collector on your behalf. The other risk is that Zopa itself goes under. Zopa insists that it has enough cash to see it through to profitability and, in the unlikely event that it did collapse, it has also set aside enough cash to continue acting as an intermediary.

This is of some comfort. But if you are lending via Zopa, you should be getting a much better return than you would from cash to compensate for these unknown risks.

Source: Robert Budden, *Financial Times*, 26 November 2005.

Questions

1 How has ZOPA changed the business model for both lending and borrowing compared with a traditional bank? (Refer to Exhibit 13.5.)

2 List the advantages and disadvantages for both lenders and borrowers of dealing with ZOPA instead of a bank.

3 How could the banks respond?

13.4   MANAGING FINANCE[24]

Finance and the way that it is managed can be a key determinant of strategic success. From a shareholder's point of view, what matters is the cash-generating capability of the business since this determines the ability to pay dividends in the short term and to reinvest for the future (which, in turn, should enable a future flow of dividend payments). In the public sector the equivalent issue is the need to deliver best value services within financial limits. There are three broad issues that organisations of all types face (see Exhibit 13.6):

● *Managing for value*, whether this is concerned with creating value for shareholders or ensuring the best use of public money, is an important consideration for, and responsibility of, all managers. However, the way in which finance is managed and controlled will have a major influence on this issue.

Exhibit 13.6   **Strategy and finance**

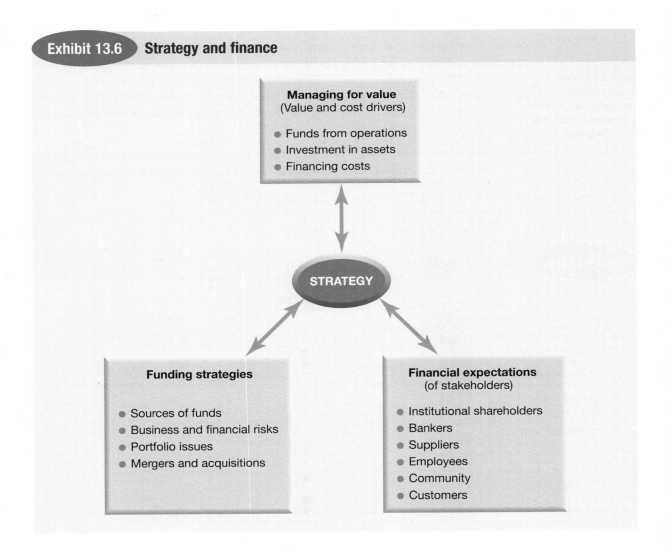

Managing for value
(Value and cost drivers)

● Funds from operations
● Investment in assets
● Financing costs

STRATEGY

Funding strategies

● Sources of funds
● Business and financial risks
● Portfolio issues
● Mergers and acquisitions

Financial expectations
(of stakeholders)

● Institutional shareholders
● Bankers
● Suppliers
● Employees
● Community
● Customers

- *Funding* strategic developments is clearly important too: in particular, that the nature of the funding is appropriate for the type of strategy – and vice versa. This is also concerned with balancing business and financial risks.

- The *financial expectations* of stakeholders will vary – both between different stakeholders and in relation to different strategies. This should influence managers in both strategy development and implementation.

13.4.1 Managing for value[25]

There has been a continuing theme through this book that the long-term success of strategies is determined by the extent to which they deliver best value in the eyes of major stakeholders. Two examples of this are competitiveness in the marketplace (that is, value to customers) and the ability to provide value to shareholders (through the returns they receive in dividends and share price movement). In competitive markets these two issues are likely to be closely linked in the long term since the returns to shareholders are driven by market success. However, this broad connection between competitiveness and shareholder value needs exploring further. It is important that managers understand what 'managing for value' means and how it might be achieved.[26] This is a crucial contribution which financial strategies should make to overall business success. **Managing for value** is concerned with maximising the long-term cash-generating capability of an organisation. As shown in Exhibit 13.7, value creation is determined by three main financial issues: funds from operations, investment in (or disposal of) assets, and financing costs.

> **Managing for value** is concerned with maximising the long-term cash-generating capability of an organisation

- *Funds from operations* are clearly a major contributor to value creation. In the long term, this concerns the extent to which the organisation is operating profitably. This is determined by:

Exhibit 13.7 **Financial aspects of value creation**

	DRIVERS	
	Value drivers (increase shareholder value)	**Cost drivers** (reduce shareholder value)
Operations	Revenue — Sales volume / Prices	Operational costs — Direct costs / Overheads
Investment	Disposal of fixed assets Reduction in current assets • stock • debtors	Capital investment (fixed assets) Reduction in current liabilities • creditors
Financing		Cost of capital — Equity / Loans

- Sales revenue – made up of sales volume and the prices that the organisation is able to maintain in its markets.
- 'Production' and selling costs – both made up of fixed and variable elements.
- Overhead or indirect costs.

● *Investment in assets* – the extent to which assets and working capital are being stretched is also a key consideration. This will affect value creation as follows:
  - The costs of capital investment or, in some cases, the disposal of redundant assets.
  - The management of the elements of working capital such as stock, debtors and creditors will increase or decrease shareholder value as indicated.

  Some organisations have developed competences in supporting much higher levels of business from the same asset base than others.

● *Financing costs* – the mix of capital in the business – between debt (requiring interest payments) and equity will determine the cost of capital (and also the financial risk as seen in the next section).

The issues in the public sector are very similar. The problem for most public sector managers is that their financial responsibilities are usually confined to managing their budget (that is, the cash outflows of operations). They will usually be doing this with little understanding of the other financial issues from the diagram, which will be managed by the corporate financial function. There is a real need for managers to be much more familiar with the impact of their day-to-day management decisions on the wider financial health of the organisation. For example, the use of fixed assets or the incurring of bad debts.

Key value and cost drivers

It is not the intention in this book to discuss the detailed issues concerning the management of each of the separate items shown in Exhibit 13.7. From a business strategy point of view, the critical issue is to understand what are the **key value and cost drivers**. These are the factors that have the most influence on the cash generation capability of an organisation or, in the public service, on the ability to provide best value services. The value network concept (section 3.6.1) is important in helping managers understand how and where value may be created within an organisation and in the wider value network. Importantly, it is likely that costs and value creation are spread *unevenly* across the activities in the value chain and value network. So some activities are more crucial to value (or cost) creation than others. However, this will vary with the type of business and with the circumstances in which it is operating, as will be seen below.

Some examples illustrate the importance of this identification of key cost and value drivers:[27]

● *Sources of capital* are usually a major cost driver and will vary with source. So the relative cash outflows which result from servicing loans as against equity would be an important strategic consideration.

● *Capital expenditure* (capex) can be a major cash outflow that can destroy shareholder value unless it contributes to improving the revenues or reducing the costs elsewhere in Exhibit 13.7. In principle, the business cases for capex

Key value and cost drivers are the factors that have most influence on the cash generation cabability of an organisation

items should address this issue before expenditure is approved. Commonly the case for expenditure would relate to *enhanced product features* leading to increased sales and/or better prices; or *reduced costs* (for example, through increased labour productivity) or *decreased working capital* (for example, through stock reduction by streamlining production or distribution).

- The detailed *cost structure* of businesses varies considerably from sector to sector and hence the relative importance of specific cost items. For example, service organisations are generally more labour intensive than manufacturing – underlining the importance of wage levels. Retailers are concerned with stock turnover and sales volume per square metre – reflecting two major cost drivers.

- Sometimes the crucial cost or value drivers are *outside the organisation* (in the supply or distribution chain). The strategic implication is that organisations need to be competent in maintaining the performance of key suppliers or distributors. This means the ability to select, motivate and 'control' suppliers and distributors. It may also mean reconsideration as to whether any of these activities should be taken 'in-house' if they are so critically important to cost and value creation. This was discussed in Chapters 3 and 12 (outsourcing).

- The key cost and value drivers may change *over time*. For example, during the introduction of a new product, the key factor may be establishing *sales volume*; once established, *prices and unit costs* might be most important; during decline, improving cash flow through *stock and debtor reduction* may be essential to support the introduction of the next generation of products.

Overall, the message is that managers can benefit considerably from a detailed understanding of the value creation processes within their organisation and the wider value network – it can help them be more strategic in how they prioritise their efforts for performance improvement.

13.4.2 Funding strategy development

Sources of funds

Managers need to be familiar with the advantages and drawbacks of different sources of funds, which are well explained in standard financial texts.[28] Decisions on which sources to use will be influenced by the current financial situation of the organisation such as ownership (for example, whether the business is privately held or publicly quoted) and by the overall corporate goals and strategic priorities of the organisation. For example, there will be different financial needs if a business is seeking rapid growth by acquisition compared with if it is seeking to consolidate its past performance. A critical issue is the way in which financial strategies address the financial and business risks of different types of funding. This will now be discussed.

Balancing financial and business risks[29]

This section uses the growth/share matrix (see Exhibit 7.7) to illustrate how financial strategies need to vary for the different 'phases' of development of a business – see Exhibit 13.8.

Exhibit 13.8   Balancing business and financial risk

GROWTH (Stars)		**LAUNCH** (Question marks)	
Business risk:	*High*	Business risk:	*Very high*
Financial risk needs to be:	*Low*	Financial risk needs to be:	*Very low*
Funding by:	*Equity* (growth investors)	Funding by:	*Equity* (venture capital)
Dividends:	*Nominal*	Dividends:	*Zero*
MATURITY (Cash cows)		**DECLINE** (Dogs)	
Business risk:	*Medium*	Business risk:	*Low*
Financial risk can be:	*Medium*	Financial risk can be:	*High*
Funding by:	*Debt and equity* (retaining earnings)	Funding by:	*Debt*
Dividends:	*High*	Dividends:	*Total*

Source: Adapted from K. Ward, *Corporate Financial Strategy*, Butterworth–Heinemann, 1993, Fig. 2.7, p. 33.

The greater the risk to shareholders or lenders, the greater the return these investors will require. Therefore, from an organisation's point of view, the important issue is how it should balance the business risk with the financial risk to the organisation. As a generalisation, the greater the business risk, the lower should be the financial risk taken by the organisation, and the growth/share matrix is a convenient way of illustrating this:

- *Question marks* (or *problem children*)[30] are clearly high business risk. They are at the beginning of their life cycle and are not yet established in their markets; moreover, they are likely to require substantial investment. A stand-alone business in this situation might, for example, seek to finance such growth from specialists in this kind of investment, such as venture capitalists who, themselves, seek to offset risk by having a portfolio of such investments. Schemes for private investors (so-called 'business angels') have also become popular.

- In the case of *stars* the degree of business risk remains high in these high-growth situations even though relatively high market shares are being achieved. The market position here remains volatile and probably highly competitive. Since the main attractions to investors here are the product or business concept and the prospect of future earnings, equity capital is likely to be appropriate, say by public flotation.

- Businesses that operate in mature markets with high shares (*cash cows*) should be generating regular and substantial surpluses. Here the business risk is lower and the opportunity for retained earnings is high. In these circumstances, it may make sense to raise finance through debt capital as well as equity, since reliable returns can be used to service such debt. Provided increased debt (*gearing* or *leverage*) does not lead to an unacceptable level of risk, this cheaper debt funding will in fact increase the residual profits achieved by a company in these circumstances.

- If a business is in decline, in effect a *dog*, then equity finance will be difficult to attract. However, borrowing may be possible if secured against residual assets in the business. At this stage, it is likely that the emphasis in the business will be on cost cutting, and it could well be that the cash flows from such businesses are quite strong. These businesses may provide relatively low-risk investments.

Illustration 13.3 shows how funding sources need to match circumstances.

Funding a portfolio of businesses

At the corporate level in *diversified* companies there can be a problem in developing a financial strategy for a portfolio with a mix of businesses growing at different rates and in high- or low-share positions. The organisation needs to consider its *overall* risk/return position. For example, a company seeking to develop *new and innovative businesses* on a regular basis might, in effect, be acting as its own venture capitalist, accepting high risk at the business level and seeking to offset such risk by 'cash cows' in its portfolio. Public sector managers know this too. They need a steady core to their service where budgets are certain to be met, hence reducing the financial risk of the more speculative aspects of their service. Some companies may need to sell off businesses as they mature to raise capital for further investment in new ventures.

Funding mergers and acquisitions[31]

Section 10.2.2 looked at the advantages and pitfalls of developing strategy through mergers or acquisitions (M&A). In particular it raised some warnings about potential conflicts between long-term strategic reasons and shorter-term financial reasons for M&A activity. One key decision relates to the way in which a merger will be funded. Again some general principles are useful in tying financial and business strategies together:

- Payment by *cash* is likely to be attractive to the target business's shareholders and the shareholder control of the bidding business is not diluted by new shares. However, it may prove difficult for most bidding companies to raise enough cash. Of course the danger for cash-rich bidders is that they spend unwisely and build empires that lack strategic logic and are difficult to manage without loss of value in some of the acquired businesses.

- The issuing of *shares* may be attractive to the target company shareholders as they exchange their old shares for shares in the bidding company. This needs to be handled carefully so as not to depress share price before the conclusion of the deal. From a strategic point of view this is the option that keeps the capital structure of the merged company least changed and so the financial risk may be the least.

- A bidding company may issue *loan capital* to the target company shareholders. This may be attractive to them if they have some doubts about future financial

Illustration 13.3

Renewable energy

Changes in the business environment create new market opportunities. But who will fund the development of capacity?

Energy is the lifeblood of any developed economy, but alternatives to oil, gas and coal – so-called renewable energy sources such as wind and tide – have long been treated as a feeble joke, ring fenced for well-meaning but naive hair shirts and ethical investors. . . .

Not any more. The London estuary venture (a planned £1.5 billion [€2.2bn] construction of 270 turbines off the Kent coast) is the latest sign that clean energy is coming of age as a serious business. Yes, it's an Anglo-Danish minnow, Core, that has submitted the plans, but the people stumping up the cash are energy giants Shell and E.On.

'We're approaching the point of no return', says Peter Shortt, director of innovation and investment at the Carbon Trust, a quango that is busy investing £1–2 million chunks of venture capital in renewable energy projects. 'Once building work begins on these massive offshore wind farms, we'll have reached the tipping point, the next step of very significant development.' . . .

Wind is just one element. Pioneers of a range of forward-looking renewable energy technologies have propelled the recent surge in Alternative Investment Market (AIM) flotations. . . . Only a couple of years ago, just a handful of ethical banks and funds would take calls from renewable energy start-ups. Now the City's bluest-chip banks, private equity houses and venture capitalists, such as Fidelity, Fleming, Nikko, New Star and Cazenove, have woken up to the market's promise.

Just how big is that potential? The government's target is 10% of electricity from renewable sources by 2010 [but] . . . critics also say the sector would fall flat without government subsidies . . . running at £700 million a year.

To a sceptical eye, the renewables market looks built to flip – irresistible only to investors and entrepreneurs seeking a quick killing. But there are mega trends driving investment in this sector over the long term: soaring demand for electricity, rising oil prices and concerted efforts to reduce carbon dioxide emissions. . . . These factors have made alternative power sources more attractive, just as engineering advances have made clean energy technologies more efficient. . . . Of course, the large energy companies can't afford to write off their existing infrastructures of pipelines, tankers, refineries and transmission lines. Some are waiting until the last moment to adopt new technology, wringing the last drop of revenue from existing assets. While they do so, smaller companies will continue to thrive: early innovators such as Vestas Wind Systems of Denmark and Iberdrola of Spain now have global reach.

But the energy business is full of big incumbents. In the UK electricity market, for example, the 'big six' – British Gas, Powergen, npower, Scottish Power, Scottish and Southern, and EDF – carve up all but 0.5% of the pie. Will there be a change in the balance of power? Unlikely, as the smarter players are already shifting their centres of gravity. Jeroen van der Veer, Shell's chief executive, says it is pouring resources into whichever renewable energy source looks promising. 'The philosophy is pots on the fire: try everything, and by 2015 we have to make up our mind,' he told journalists in June.

Who can predict which energy source will be the future of Britain? Only the entrepreneurs and investors who are inventing it.

Source: Ian Wylie, 'New Power Generation', *Management Today*, December 2005, pp. 48–53. Reproduced from *Management Today* magazine with the permission of the copyright owner, Haymarket Business Publications Limited.

Question

Referring to section 13.4.2 and Exhibit 13.8, describe how you would try to balance the business and financial risks if you were:

- a new start-up renewables company;
- one of the 'big six' energy companies;
- the British government.

performance of the merged company. The bidding company shareholders avoid dilution of their control but the gearing is increased and hence the financial risk.

- External *loans* are often used by bidders to offer cash to target company shareholders. This has been the subject of much controversy as aggressive bids from individuals have been successful in purchasing publicly quoted companies and taking them private – but with high gearing. The Manchester United case study (in the Text and Cases edition) is a high-profile example of this.

13.4.3 The financial expectations of stakeholders

Section 13.4.1 looked at how business strategies might create or destroy value for shareholders of a business. The public sector equivalent is the extent to which politicians (as the owners or guardians of public money) would regard public money to have been well spent. But it was seen in Chapter 4 that the owners are not the only ones who have a stake in organisations. Other stakeholders will have financial expectations of organisations. The question is to what extent business strategies should address these other financial expectations and how they can be squared with creating value for the owners. For example:

- Chapter 4 made the point that *institutional shareholders* (such as asset managers of pension funds) are the ones who usually represent the interests of the real beneficiaries of a company's performance. This is the concept of the governance chain. So strategy is strongly influenced by the financial expectations of these intermediaries who can become the key players in major strategic changes – such as mergers or acquisitions. There is a continuing concern that managers are distorting the long-term strategies of their companies as they respond to the shorter-term pressures on earnings exerted by stock market analysts and institutional shareholders.[32]

- *Bankers* and other providers of interest-bearing loans are concerned about the *risk* attached to their loans and the competence with which this is managed. A consistently good track record in managing that risk could be regarded (in itself) as a reason for bankers to invest further with some companies and not others. The risk would be influenced by the capital structure of the company – particularly the gearing ratio (of debt to equity), which determines how sensitive the solvency of the company is to changes in its profit position. Interest cover is a similar measure that relates interest payments to profit.

- *Suppliers* and *employees* are likely to be concerned with good prices and wages but also the *liquidity* of the company, which is a measure of its ability to meet short-term commitments to creditors and wages. Bankers will share this concern because a deteriorating liquidity position may require correction through additional loans and the increased risk profile discussed above. Again, a track record in this area could be a competence underpinning good supplier relationships, resulting in discounts or improved credit.

- The *community* will be concerned about jobs but also with the *social cost* of an organisation's strategies, such as pollution or marketing. This is rarely accounted for in traditional financial analyses, but it is an issue of growing concern. Matters of business ethics and social responsibility were discussed in Chapter 4 (section 4.3). Failure to pay proper attention to these issues could be a source of strategic weakness.

● *Customers* are concerned about best value products or services. This assessment is rarely made in traditional financial analyses, the implication being that companies that survive profitably in a competitive environment *must* be providing value for money.

Overall, managers need to be conscious of the financial impact on various stakeholders of the strategies they are pursuing or planning to pursue. They also need to understand how the capability to meet these varied expectations could enable the success of some strategies whilst limiting the ability of an organisation to succeed with other strategies.

13.5 MANAGING TECHNOLOGY[33]

This section is about the relationship between technology and strategic success. As mentioned in Chapter 3, the technology itself may be easy to acquire by competitors so is not necessarily a source of advantage. The way in which the technology is exploited is where advantage may be created. Indeed Chapter 7 gave examples of how many innovations come about through the novel exploitation of both established and new technologies. The chapter will look at the following issues about the relationship between business and technology strategies and how technology can underpin strategic success (see Exhibit 13.9):

● how technology changes the *competitive situation*;
● technology and *strategic capability*;
● *organising* technology to achieve advantage.

13.5.1 Technology and the competitive situation

Competitive forces

In Chapter 2, the five forces framework was used as a checklist for understanding the competitive forces within an industry and how they might determine the competitive position of different organisations. Before making decisions about the technology strategy of an individual organisation it is important to understand the ways in which technology can have a significant impact on these forces – particularly in industries that are globalising,[34] as the following examples illustrate:

● *Barriers to entry* for potential new entrants may be lowered by reducing the economies of scale, for example in publishing, or the capital requirements for set-up, for example in computing. In some cases, barriers may be raised as technologies become more difficult to master and products more complex, for example in the aerospace industry.

Exhibit 13.9 **Strategy and technology**

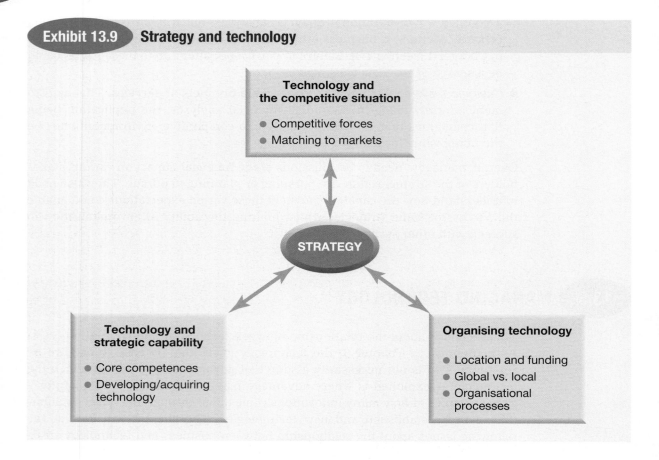

- *Substitution* may be made easier by technology at several levels. New products may displace old, for example DVDs for videotape. The need may be displaced, for example using video conferencing rather than travelling to meetings. Or technological developments in other sectors may 'steal' consumer demand through an array of exciting products, for example electronic goods displacing consumer spending on household durables such as kitchens and carpets. Sometimes technology can stop substitution, for example by tying the usage of one product to another – the 'debate' about Microsoft's success in tying software developments into the Windows operating system is an example.

- The *relative power of suppliers and buyers* can also be changed by technology. The Microsoft example applies here too since the issues raised in the court cases were about the extent to which Microsoft (as a supplier to most businesses and households) had unreasonably high levels of power over its customers. But technological developments can work in the favour of buyers by freeing them from a single source of supply. This often happens when international specifications and standards are agreed (say for steel).

- *Competitive rivalry* amongst organisations can be raised through this process of generic specifications or diminished if one firm develops a new product or process which it is able to patent. The level of competitive rivalry in generic pharmaceutical products as against ethical (proprietary) pharmaceutical products is markedly different.

The strategic issues raised for individual organisations through these examples are two-fold. First, some organisations may be technological leaders and trying to gain advantage in some of the ways outlined above. Second, other organisations may need to assess the likely impact on their competitive position of technological developments led by current or potential competitors.

Matching technology strategies to markets

The way in which technological developments can underpin competitiveness will vary depending on the nature of both the technology and the markets (see Exhibit 13.10):

- *Differentiated* strategies will be appropriate where both technologies and markets are mature. Product and service improvements are achieved by using existing technology to address a known customer requirement. Often this is concerned with improving quality – as the Japanese achieved with product reliability of automobiles. The danger is that this market looks attractive to imitators who might exploit technology to improve product features further or reduce cost.

- *Architectural* strategies work where existing technologies can be combined to create novel products or services or new applications. For example, glass and surface coating technologies have been used by glass companies to create a

Exhibit 13.10   **Matching technology strategies to markets**

Technological New solutions to existing problems	**Complex** Technology and markets co-evolve
Differentiated Compete on quality and features	**Architectural** Novel combinations of existing technologies

Novelty of technology (High / Low vertical axis)

Novelty of markets (Low / High horizontal axis)

Source: J. Tidd, J. Bessant and K. Pavitt, *Managing Innovation: Integrating technological, market and organisational change*, 3rd edition, Wiley, 2005, Figure 7.1, p. 243.

range of new properties such as energy saving, reflective and self-cleaning glasses.

- *Technological* strategies apply new technologies to known customer needs. Products and services compete on the basis of enhanced performance against current products. Some big prizes in this category are the development of new 'wonder drugs' or even electrical energy storage devices to outperform massively the traditional battery in capacity, weight and price. The dangers here are imitation and high development costs. So the strategy usually requires technology protection (patents).

- *Complex* strategies are needed where both technologies and markets are novel and need to co-evolve. At the outset there are no clearly defined uses for the technology. So the critical issues here are understanding the processes of new product diffusion (as discussed in section 9.3). For example, there is a need for developers to work with early adopters to create new applications. The development of multimedia products and services is an ongoing example.

Illustration 13.4 shows how the choices of strategy may need to change as both technologies and markets change over time.

13.5.2 Technology and strategic capability

Core capabilities

Chapter 3 underlined the importance of identifying core capabilities as the basis of an organisation's competitive advantage. From a strategic point of view the importance of technology lies in the potential both to create and to destroy core capabilities (as seen in the case of IT in section 13.3.1). So if technology is to underpin success there are some important implications for both business and technology strategies:

- To tie future developments to a *single technology* that an organisation has mastered can be both inappropriate and unduly risky. For example, stainless steel was the wonder material of the 1960s, substituting for other materials in many consumer and industrial applications. But, in turn, it has been substituted in some applications by developments in polymers, ceramics and composite materials.

- Core competences may be found in the processes of *linking technologies* together rather than the technologies per se. Indeed, many advances in manufacturing are concerned with how computerised process control can be grafted to the technologies of the plant and machinery – not in being excellent in just one or other technology.

- *Dynamic capabilities* (as discussed in Chapter 3) may be important in a rapidly changing and competitive world. The fruits of any particular development are likely to be shorter-lived than hitherto. So competitive advantage needs to be underpinned by the processes that ensure a constant flow of improvements and in the ability to bring improvements to market quickly. This can lead to first-mover advantages. However, there is also evidence that in some circumstances commercial advantages of technological developments may accrue to 'fast-follower' companies rather than the pioneers.[35]

Illustration 13.4

Psion chief's warning to tech wannabes

The market will be the judge of the value of products from any technological development. So companies and entrepreneurs ignore it at their peril.

In an interview with the *Financial Times*, Sir David Potter, Founder and Chairman of Psion, the UK handheld computer company, warned that technology start-ups need to become more market savvy to survive. Sir David, one of the UK earliest academics-turned-entrepreneurs, having resigned from his tenure at Imperial College to found Psion in 1980, also wants the UK government to step up its efforts to encourage the transfer of technology from university laboratories to the commercial sector.

'Science does not translate itself into business just like that, it is far more complicated. We have in Britain a rather kind of fey belief that you have a nice idea in a laboratory and you get a market out of that. It doesn't happen like that,' he says. 'We need to be much closer to the market and not imagine that Cambridge or Imperial College are by themselves going to be able to spin out companies that are going to become world beaters.'

He says 10 or 12 national institutes should be set up, which would help in the exploitation of technology such as semiconductors or nanotechnology. With or without them, however, Sir David stressed the need for UK technology start-ups to become more adept at understanding the market.

'My first advice is follow the market above all. Don't think about your technology. If you've got skills and advantage in a particular area, work in that area but use the technology for the market not the other way around. Don't try and create the market from the technology,' he says.

Psion itself is a case in point. The company has managed to survive the brutal technology markets for 25 years mainly by reinventing itself many times. Psion, founded with less than £100,000 ($173,000; €145,000) of Sir David's own savings, began as publishers of other people's software, and gradually moved to writing its own. By 1983 it was the UK's leading developer in the nascent computer games market, thanks to a popular flight simulator game.

In a parallel universe, Psion might have gone on to become an Eidos or an Electronic Arts. But Sir David quickly decided that games were not really the market he wanted to be in.

'It could have been fun,' he mused. 'I would have probably had pink hair and a ponytail, God knows. But it wasn't really the culture of the company.'

Spotting a market opportunity, Sir David and his team moved into hardware and developed the world's first handheld computer – the Organiser – which was launched in 1986. Several golden years followed, in which Psion's iconic handhelds had the run of the market and easily saw off challenges with their rapid pace of innovation.

In the mid-1990s the market changed with the arrival of US rivals Palm and Compaq. Suddenly, it was not differentiation but scale that mattered, and Psion could no longer compete. In 2001 it was time for a strategic retreat. Psion took wide-scale job cuts and exited the consumer market, opting to focus on its more niche enterprise business.

While Sir David admits he has some regrets about the way things turned out, he says the important thing is that Psion is still here when many other companies have fallen by the wayside.

Source: Maija Palmer, *Financial Times*, 26 December 2005.

Questions

1 Trace the positioning of Psion on the technology/markets matrix (Exhibit 13.10) through the phases of its development.

2 Suggest how Psion might have followed a more successful path.

| Exhibit 13.11 | Developing or acquiring technology |

Influencing factors

Method		Importance of the technology	Prior knowledge and reputation	Complexity	Willingness to take risk	Desire to lead or follow	Speed
	In-house	Key	High	Low/Medium	High	Lead	Slow
	Alliances	Threshold	Low	High	Medium	Follow	Medium
	Acquisition	Key or threshold	Very Low	High	Low	Follow	High

Source: Adapted from J. Tidd, J. Bessant and K. Pavitt, *Managing Innovation: Integrating technological, market and organisational change*, 2nd edition, Wiley, 2001, Table 8.6.

Developing or acquiring technology

Whether technology is developed 'in-house' or acquired externally can be a key determinant in the success or failure of strategies. This is a complex subject given that many different variables could influence these decisions.[36] However, for the purposes of illustrating the link between business and technology strategies a few general principles are useful (see Exhibit 13.11):

- *In-house development* may be favoured if the technology is key to competitive advantage and an organisation has expectations of gaining first-mover advantages. This will be feasible if the organisation already has a good knowledge of both the technology and the market opportunities and the complexity is not too great. This should be the case for *differentiated* strategies and possibly *architectural* strategies shown in Exhibit 13.10 above. It is also important that the organisation is willing to take commercial and financial risk.

- *Alliances* are likely to be appropriate for 'threshold' technologies rather than ones on which competitive advantage is to be built. For example, a manufacturer of branded drinks may seek a partner to improve bottling and distribution processes. These are both important activities but competitive advantage is concerned with the product itself and brand maintenance. Alliances might also be appropriate where there is an intention to follow and imitate rather than lead. This would be particularly the case where the complexity of product or market knowledge is beyond the current knowledge base – so organisational learning is an important objective (*complexity* strategies in Exhibit 13.10 above). Alliances also help to limit financial risk.

- *Acquisition of current players or rights* may be particularly appropriate if speed is important and there is no time for learning. It may also be essential if the level of complexity, in both technology and market application, is beyond current organisational knowledge (see *technological* and *complexity* strategies in Exhibit 13.10 above). It could be especially important where credibility of the technology is essential to business success – so the source of the technology matters. So production under licence of an established technology may be more successful than developing an alternative. Organisations acquiring technology need to have a good understanding of the technology needs of their product lines, an ability to identify and evaluate appropriate external technologies and the competence to negotiate an appropriate deal with the owners of the technology rights.[37]

The choice between in-house development, alliances and acquisition will also vary through the technology life cycle[38] as companies move from issues of product functionality and market share, through establishing industry-quality standards, to further developments in the technology. Long-term survivors may need to use all of these methods as they move through the life cycle.

13.5.3 Organising technology development

The location and funding of technology development

An important debate in many larger organisations is who within the organisation should be driving technology development and who should be funding it.[39] This is part of the wider strategic debate about how strategic responsibilities could be divided between the corporate centre and divisions/departments of an organisation as discussed above.

Exhibit 13.12 shows that different arrangements are likely to be suitable for different aspects of technology development. For example, at one extreme, new technologies are best assessed and funded corporately, whilst at the other, incremental product and process improvements are best undertaken and funded locally. Between these extremes, the commercialisation of new technologies is often best done locally but funded corporately since others will learn and benefit from the first moves. Experimentation with new technologies might

Exhibit 13.12 Funding and location of R&D

		Located at	
		Corporate	Divisional
Funded by	Corporate	Assessing new technologies	Commercialising new technologies
	Divisional	Exploratory development of new technologies	Incremental product or process improvements

Source: Adapted from J. Tidd, J. Bessant and K. Pavitt, *Managing Innovation: Integrating technological, market and organisation change*, 2nd edition, Wiley, 2001, Table 6.2.

remain corporate but be funded by divisions which see commercial potential in their arena.

These same principles might lead to conclusions that some technology development activities might be outsourced[40] where the technological expertise is inadequate in both divisions and the corporate centre but the particular technology development is crucial to securing current and future business. Also the different stages of development might be developed in different ways: for example, the ideas generation and early research might be undertaken internally whilst external organisations might be used to develop prototypes and/or undertake test marketing.[41]

Sometimes the technological expertise of an organisation might be greater than the current business can exploit – leading to considerations of spin-off of R&D (in whole or in part) to allow new commercial opportunities to be exploited (by licensing technology to third parties).

Global vs. local technology development

Another location decision for international organisations is where in the world it should locate R&D. The fact that major firms currently tend to locate smaller proportions of R&D overseas (compared with production) shows that this can be a difficult decision to make. The factors that managers need to consider when dispersing R&D away from the home base are:

- *Efficiency* losses – this includes slowness in dealing with problems.
- Loss of a *critical mass* of R&D staff at any location reducing the fostering of tacit knowledge by direct interaction. Also *proximity* to research and testing facilities may be lost.
- Increased difficulties in *integrating* R&D with production and marketing. Some large organisations also may have difficulties in integrating different technologies where they have created 'centres of excellence' in different locations for each technology.
- Dispersal may be needed because different *types of economy* require different technologies.[42]

These concerns tend to relate to an organisation's ability to launch major innovations – such as new products or processes. They are less problematic in terms of becoming or remaining part of a global knowledge network. Indeed scientists and technologists have always been good at this and IT developments are making the process easier.

Organisational processes

Chapter 12 underlined the importance of organisational processes in underpinning the success of strategies. This is particularly true in technology development where there are real dangers that an organisation's competence in technology fails to be exploited commercially. Since these processes are often difficult to manage, they may prove to be core competences that underpin competitive advantage, as mentioned above. Some of the following processes may be of crucial importance in achieving success through technology:

- *Scanning the business environment* (both technology and market developments) and spotting the opportunities for gaining advantage and the potential threats to current business. Related to this is the ability to select projects or developments that have a good strategic fit with the business. But this is not as easy as it sounds. It may mean giving preference to transformational technologies – which could be very challenging in terms of both competences and culture of the organisation.

- *Resourcing developments adequately*, but not over-generously, so as to ensure a good return for the investment. This is much easier to see in hindsight than in advance, but past experience, good benchmarking and a willingness to use appropriate approaches to investment appraisal[43] can help. This also includes the ability to monitor and review projects through their various stages – many organisations now use a **stage–gate process** to good effect.[44] This is a structured review process to assess progress on meeting product performance characteristics during the development process and ensuring that they are matched with market data. These processes must also include the ability to terminate and accelerate projects, to capture the learning from both successes and failures, and to disseminate results and best practice.

> A stage–gate process is a structured review process to assess progress on meeting product performance characteristics during the development process and ensuring that they are matched with market data

Of course, behind these processes is a set of much more detailed activities which will determine their success or failure. This would include activities ranging from forecasting, concept testing and option screening to communication, negotiation and motivation.

13.5.4 Implications to managers[45]

The preceding sections were intended to underline the importance of 'aligning' business and technology strategies in organisations as a way of achieving strategic success. Successful organisations will be those where there is a strong commitment from senior management to innovation through technology and a business acumen based on an understanding of the business strategy and technology relationship.

There needs to be a creative climate where innovation is fostered, communication is extensive and there is a culture of a learning organisation. Structures and processes must facilitate the creation of this environment and provide a commitment to individual and team development. In particular, it must support key individuals who will champion and facilitate the exploitation of technology for strategic success.

13.6 INTEGRATING RESOURCES

The sections above have looked at how separate resource areas need to support an organisation's strategies and/or provide the basis on which new strategies can be built. However, there is a third issue that has only partly emerged from the consideration of the separate resource areas above. As discussed in Chapter 3, most organisational strategies not only require capabilities in separate resource

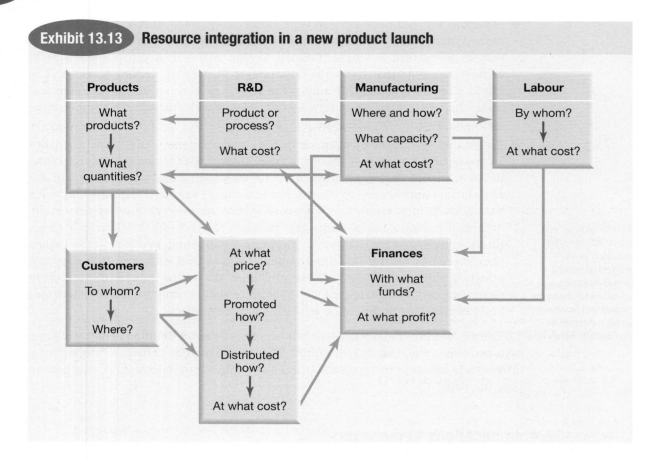

Exhibit 13.13 Resource integration in a new product launch

areas, but also require an ability to pull a range of resources and competences together – both inside the organisation and in the wider value network.[46] For example, Exhibit 13.13 shows some of the resources and activities that need to be integrated by an organisation hoping to gain competitive advantage through bringing new products to the market more quickly than competitors. Capability in new product launch requires an ability to integrate and coordinate the separate activities of R&D, manufacture, etc. – each of which, in turn, involves bringing together a complex mixture of resources. This can be a complex matter and, therefore, may be the basis of competitive advantage. Illustration 13.5 also shows how complex can be the resourcing and coordination for clearly prioritised strategies for governments and the public services – in that case, the reduction in anti-social behaviour. The key debate (Illustration 13.6) is a reminder of an important theme running through this chapter: that either too little or too much change of an organisation's resourcing strategies can create difficulties in delivering overall organisational strategic changes.

Illustration 13.5

Anti-social behaviour – nuisance neighbours

An important role of government is to improve the quality of life for its citizens. But this requires an ability to bring together and integrate many resources from both inside and outside government itself.

Together was a national campaign launched by the British government's Home Office in 2004. The focus of the campaign and subsequent action plans was anti-social behaviour (ASB). The government believed that

every citizen has a right to live their lives free from fear and distress and they, in turn, have a responsibility not to cause fear and distress to others . . . while it is a minority of people who persistently behave in a way that ruins the lives of those around them they have a disproportionate effect.

Commitments like this are easy for governments to make but notoriously difficult to deliver. The first step was a more detailed definition of what constituted ASB. The plan had four action areas: nuisance neighbours; begging; environmental crime; and putting victims and witnesses first. Government saw its role as bringing together resources and expertise from across government departments and external agencies to help 'practitioners' tackle these priority areas. For example, it developed and provided:

- The *Together Actionline* and website for help and advice.
- The *Together Academy* which ran training and conferences.
- New *money* to the already-established local *Crime and Disorder Partnerships* to help strengthen their response.
- *ASB Prosecutors* – a new national team in the Crown Prosecution Service.
- New *sentencing guidelines* for magistrates (courts) on ASB offences.

Of course a detailed action/resourcing plan had to be developed for each of the four priority areas (above). The plan to tackle *Nuisance Neighbours* centred round how families functioned and behaved:

At every stage in the development of a family this Government is committed to providing the help and intervention needed to make [families] strong. From improved ante-natal care, through 'Sure Start' and improved education, 'Parentline' and parenting classes the Government recognises the challenges of family life and the importance of support and help.

The plan then identified how government would contribute to sustaining stronger families:

- *Every Child Matters* – a commitment to ensuring that all children reach their potential. Resources to be increased for early years education, childcare, child poverty, supporting parents and raising school standards.
- *Behaviour Improvement Programme* – funds to improve behaviour and attendance at school in targeted areas.
- *Positive activities for young people* – a range of programmes to keep children off the streets.
- *Family and parenting policy* – including funding for the voluntary sector to support families in difficulty and direct help for 'perpetrators' to change their behaviour.
- *The Youth Justice Board* – including Youth Action Teams working to reduce the number of young people committing crimes and also preventing younger children being drawn into crime.
- *Nuisance noise and fireworks* – were to be tackled through advertising campaigns and new legislation about sale of fireworks.
- *Housing and benefits* – including licensing landlords and the withdrawal of state benefits for persistent offenders.

These initiatives were spread across several government departments (covering the key areas of: education, criminal justice, local government, environment, trade and industry, housing and benefits) which further raised the difficulties of a concerted government effort, not least because of the different priorities and cultures found in these separate departments.

Source: www.together.gov.uk. Reproduced under the terms of the Click-Use Licence.

Questions

1 Identify the key resources and activities that would contribute to a reduction in the 'nuisance neighbours' aspect of anti-social behaviour.

2 Show different ways in which these could be coordinated – giving the advantages and disadvantages of each approach.

Illustration 13.6

key debate

Resources or revolution

How far can an organisation go beyond its original resources in determining its strategy?

This chapter emphasises the importance of resources for supporting an organisation's strategy. For strategy guru Gary Hamel, Chairman of the international consulting firm Strategos, this reliance on resources can easily become too cautious. In the same way that Dorothy Leonard-Barton warns against 'core rigidities' (see Chapter 3), Hamel sees existing resources and markets as liable to trap organisations into a fatal conservatism. Incumbency, the sheer fact of already being in a market, is increasingly worthless. Hamel urges instead the importance of strategic 'revolutions', creating new markets and new business models.[1,2] We are now in an age when we need only be limited by our imaginations.

For Hamel, survival in the contemporary world of rapid technological change, shifting markets and global competition demands constant revolutionary innovation. Such innovation rarely comes from traditional strategy processes emphasising the 'fit' of resources to markets. As in his earlier work with C.K. Prahalad, Hamel emphasises 'stretch' over 'fit', and now 'revolutionaries' over 'planners'.

As an example, Hamel cites Pierre Omidyar, founder in 1995 of what rapidly became the world's premier Internet auction site, eBay. Omidyar's starting point was not the fit of resources to markets, but a desire to help his fiancée with her collection of Pez sweet dispensers. Starting on his own while retaining his day job, Omidyar had none of the resources of a traditional auction house. Far from fitting a market, he was creating a new kind of market. Traditional strategy processes would never have allowed eBay to happen.

A reminder of the importance of resources, however, comes from another of Hamel's exemplars of revolution, Enron. Enron is applauded by Hamel for its revolutionary capacity to create and trade in markets for gas, electricity, broadband and commodities. But it was inadequacies in unique and hard-to-imitate resources that contributed to Enron's ultimate failure. In the competitive markets that Enron created and traded in, Enron had few sources of sustainable advantage.[3] The result was losses that led to the largest bankruptcy in corporate history at that time. Here resources did matter.

Hamel points to an important truth about existing resources: they can constrain. At the same time,

however, building a strong resource base appears vital for sustained success. Even at eBay, Omidyar quickly brought in Harvard MBA Meg Whitman as Chief Executive Officer, who immediately invested in the managerial, measurement and infrastructural resources necessary to take it into the twenty-first century. It seems that David Teece's concept of 'dynamic capabilities',[4] the ability to develop and change competences (see Chapter 3), provides an essential bridge between the constraints of current resources and the unfettered but unsupported imagination of Gary Hamel's revolutionaries.

Notes

1. G. Hamel, *Leading the Revolution*, Harvard Business School Press, 2000.
2. G. Hamel and C.K. Prahalad, *Competing for the Future*, Harvard Business School Press, 1994.
3. S. Chatterjee, 'Enron's incremental descent into bankruptcy: a strategic and organisational analysis', *Long Range Planning*, vol. 36, no. 2 (2003), pp. 133–149.
4. D. Teece, G. Pisano and A. Shuen, 'Dynamic capabilities and strategic management', *Strategic Management Journal*, vol. 18, no. 7 (1997), pp. 509–533.

Questions

In his book *Leading the Revolution*, Gary Hamel notes that the current coffee bar fashion was created by Starbucks, a small Seattle coffee company founded in 1971, which only opened its first of more than 7,500 coffee bars in 1984. Hamel asks: why wasn't the coffee bar fashion launched by multi-billion-dollar multinational Nestlé, owner of Nescafé, the best-selling coffee in the world?

1 Compare the resources of Nestlé and Starbucks in the late 1980s and early 1990s (see www.nestle.com and www.starbucks.com). Why didn't Nestlé lead in the creation of the coffee bar fashion?

2 What implications does the failure of Nestlé have for other powerful incumbents in their present markets?

SUMMARY

- Understanding the relationship between resource management and strategic success is important. This is a two-way relationship. Resource management must support an organisation's business strategies. But the development of unique resources and core competences in parts of an organisation may provide the 'springboard' from which new business strategies are developed.

- The *'hard' side* of resource management – systems and procedures – is vitally important in enabling success. But in all resource areas the critical question is how these systems contribute to the creation and integration of knowledge. Only part of this knowledge can be captured in systems. Indeed, competitive advantage is more likely to be gained from knowledge that cannot be codified since it will be more difficult to imitate by competitors.

- Understanding the way in which *people* might underpin success concerns both the formal systems and procedures and the informal ways in which people behave. Also important are the ways in which people can be organised for success – the structures and processes discussed in Chapter 12.

- *Information* is a key resource which is of particular importance given the continuing advances in information technology. This increased ability to access and process information can build or destroy an organisation's core capabilities, so crucial to competitive advantage. IT has also spawned new business models – where traditional 'value networks' are reconfigured. This is a serious threat to some organisations and an opportunity for others.

- *Finance* is a resource of central importance in all organisations. It is particularly important to understand how business strategies might deliver financial value to shareholders or owners. Most strategic developments need funding which, in turn, creates risk. So the types of funding need to vary with strategy. Stakeholders other than owners have financial expectations that will also influence an organisation's business strategies.

- The final resource area considered in this chapter is *technology* development. This will affect the competitive forces on an organisation and also its strategic capability. So the ways that technology is developed, exploited, organised and funded will all influence the success or failure of strategy.

- Organisations need to be able to *integrate resources and competences across resource areas* to support current strategies or to develop new strategies. Capability in separate resource areas is not enough.

Work assignments

* *Denotes more advanced work assignments.*

13.1   Choose a strategic development for an organisation with which you are familiar and list the key human resource changes that will be needed to underpin success (refer to Exhibit 13.2 as a checklist).

13.2 * Write an executive report to your CEO advising on whether or not the HR function should be closed and the work devolved to middle (line) managers. Centre your arguments on the impact on the strategic performance of the organisation.

13.3 * (a) Choose an organisation which is shifting its generic competitive strategy from low price to differentiation (on the strategy clock). Describe how the information strategies will need to change to support this new strategy.
(b) Choose an organisation which is attempting the opposite shift (differentiation to low price) and undertake the same analysis.

13.4   Find examples of all of the business models outlined in Exhibit 13.5. Explain in which sectors you feel each business model is most likely to have particular impact. Why?

13.5   Referring to Exhibit 13.7, give as many reasons as you can why profitable companies might be destroying shareholder value (with examples). Now repeat the exercise for organisations with poor levels of profitability that are none the less creating shareholder value (with examples).

13.6 * Write an executive report on how sources of funding need to be related to the nature of an industry and the types of strategies that an organisation is pursuing.

13.7 * By referring to Exhibit 13.11, write a report advising your CEO how technology should be acquired by your organisation. Remember to justify your conclusions.

13.8   Refer to the new product launch example in Exhibit 13.13. If you were project managing this launch, identify the specific ways in which you would ensure integration between the various resource areas. Remember to identify both 'hard' and 'soft' ways in which you would achieve this integration.

Integrative assignments

13.9   Using examples, discuss the proposition that 'IT is seen as the servant of current strategies and business models rather than as a way of revolutionising the way an organisation does business and gains advantage'. Support your answer by references to both the value network (Chapter 3) and culture (Chapter 5).

13.10   The knowledge of an organisation is dispersed throughout the major resource areas discussed in this chapter. So how does an organisation manage to integrate and gain advantage from this knowledge? Refer to Chapters 3 and 5 to support your answer.

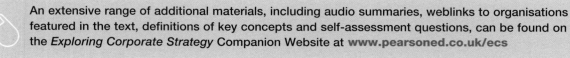

An extensive range of additional materials, including audio summaries, weblinks to organisations featured in the text, definitions of key concepts and self-assessment questions, can be found on the *Exploring Corporate Strategy* Companion Website at **www.pearsoned.co.uk/ecs**

Recommended Key Readings

- A good general reference book on human resource management is L. Mullins, *Management and Organisational Behaviour*, 7th edition, FT/Prentice Hall, 2005.

- Three general books on information management are: P. Bocij, D. Chaffey, A. Greasley and S. Hickie, *Business Information Systems: Technology, Development and Management for the E-Business*, 3rd edition, FT/Prentice Hall, 2006 (particularly chapters 13 and 14); J. Ward and J. Peppard, *Strategic Planning for Information Systems*, 3rd edition, Wiley, 2002; D. Chaffey and S. Wood, *Business Information Management*, FT/Prentice Hall, 2005.

- Readers may wish to consult one or more standard texts on finance. For example, G. Arnold, *Corporate Financial Management*, 3rd edition, FT/Prentice Hall, 2005; P. Atrill, *Financial Management for Decision Makers*, 4th edition, FT/Prentice Hall, 2006.

- The relationship between technology and strategy is extensively discussed in J. Tidd, J. Bessant and K. Pavitt, *Managing Innovation: Integrating technological, market and organisational change*, 3rd edition, Wiley, 2005.

References

1. A good general reference book on human resource management is L. Mullins, *Management and Organisational Behaviour*, 7th edition, FT/Prentice Hall, 2005. Two useful papers are: J. Pfeffer and J. Veiga, 'Putting people first for organisational success', *Academy of Management Executive*, vol. 13, no. 2 (1999), pp. 37–50; and B. Becker and M. Huselid, 'Overview: strategic human resource management in five leading firms', *Human Resource Management*, vol. 38, no. 4 (1999), pp. 287–301.

2. See Mullins (chapters 19, 20 and 21), reference 1.

3. Developing future talent internally may be less risky than recruitment. See B. Groysberg, A. Nanda and N. Nohria, 'The risky business of hiring stars', *Harvard Business Review*, vol. 82, no. 5 (2004), pp. 92–100.

4. The importance of HR professionals understanding business strategy is emphasised in D. Ulrich and W. Brockbank, 'Higher knowledge for higher aspirations', *Human Resource Management*, vol. 44, no. 4 (2005), pp. 489–504.

5. See also D.D. Van Fleet, T.O. Peterson and E.W. Van Fleet, 'Closing the performance feedback gap with expert systems', *Academy of Management Executive*, vol. 19, no. 3 (2005), pp. 9–12.

6. See Mullins (chapters 4, 13 and 14), reference 1.

7. In this book we use the term 'paradigm' but 'mental models' is a similar concept. See J. Pfeffer, 'Changing mental models: HR's most important task', *Human Resource Management*, vol. 44, no. 2 (2005), pp. 123–128.

8. C. Bartlett and S. Ghoshal, 'Building competitive advantage through people', *Sloan Management Review*, vol. 43, no. 2 (2002), pp. 34–41.

9. The seminal work on this issue of balanced teams was R. Belbin, *Management Teams: Why they succeed or fail*, Heinemann, 1981.

10. See C. Collins and K. Clark, 'Strategic human resource practices, top management team social networks and firm performance: the role of human resource practices in creating organisational competitive advantage', *Academy of Management Journal*, vol. 46, no. 6 (2003), pp. 740–751.

11. See Mullins (chapters 6, 15 and 16), reference 1.

12. J. Storey, *Developments in the Management of Human Resources*, Blackwell, 1992, used this categorisation of the roles of HR functions. D. Ulrich, *Human Resource Champion*, Harvard Business School Press, 1997, presents a slightly different categorisation based on the two dimensions of change vs. maintenance *and* people vs. processes.

13. The following articles from the same volume of *Human Resource Management* discuss this issue: W.F. Cascio, 'From business partner to driving business success: the next step in the evolution of HR', *Human Resource Management*, vol. 44, no. 2 (2005), pp. 159–163; G. Armstrong, 'Differentiation through people: how can HR move beyond business partner?', *Human Resource Management*, vol. 44, no. 2 (2005), pp. 195–200; E.E. Lawler III, 'From human resource management to organisational effectiveness', *Human Resource Management*, vol. 44, no. 2 (2005), pp. 165–169.

14. For example, downsizing creates problems in this respect. See R. Thomas and D. Dunkerley, 'Careering downwards? Middle managers' experience in the downsized organisation', *British Journal of Management*, vol. 10 (1999), pp. 157–169.

15. See also J.M. Hiltrop, 'Creating HR capability in high-performance organisations', *Strategic Change*, vol. 14, no. 3 (2005), pp. 121–131.

16. Three good general books on information management are: P. Bocij, D. Chaffey, A. Greasley and S. Hickie, *Business Information Systems: Technology, Development and Management for the E-Business*, 3rd edition, FT/Prentice Hall, 2006 (particularly chapters 13 and 14); J. Ward and J. Peppard, *Strategic Planning for Information Systems*, 3rd edition, Wiley, 2002; D. Chaffey and S. Wood, *Business Information Management*, FT/Prentice Hall, 2005. P. Timmers, *Electronic Commerce*, Wiley, 2000, has been used as background on the issues of information management and the power of IT. Readers might also find the following to be useful: C. Prahalad

and M. Krishnan, 'The dynamic synchronisation of strategy and information technology', *Sloan Management Review*, vol. 43, no. 4 (2002), pp. 24–31; M. Porter, 'Strategy and the Internet', *Harvard Business Review*, vol. 79, no. 2 (2001), pp. 63–78; J. Brown and J. Hagel, 'Does IT matter?', *Harvard Business Review*, vol. 81, no. 7 (2003), pp. 109–112; G. Carr, 'IT doesn't matter', *Harvard Business Review*, vol. 81, no. 5 (2003), pp. 41–50.

17. The dangers IT can bring in destroying competitive advantage are discussed by N. Carr, 'The corrosion of IT advantage: strategy makes a comeback', *Journal of Business Strategy*, vol. 25, no. 5 (2004), pp. 10–15.

18. The details of how data mining is done in various sectors are discussed in: C. Carmen and B. Lewis, 'A basic primer on data mining', *Information Systems Management*, vol. 19, no. 4 (2002), pp. 56–60; J. Firestone, 'Mining for information gold', *Information Management Journal*, vol. 39, no. 5 (2005), pp. 47–52; J. Xu and H. Chen, 'Criminal network analysis and visualization', *Communications of the ACM*, vol. 48, no. 6 (2005), pp. 101–107; A. Hormozi, Amir M. and S. Giles, 'Data mining: a competitive weapon for banking and retail industries', *Information Systems Management*, vol. 21, no. 2 (2004), pp. 62–71.

19. The need to join up the different customer interfaces (such as salesforce, websites, call centres) is discussed in *Customer Essentials*, CBR Special Report, 1999, pp. 7–20.

20. See Timmers, reference 16, chapter 3. Also useful as background is N. Sheehan, 'Why old tools won't work in the "new" knowledge economy', *Journal of Business Strategy*, vol. 26, no. 4 (2005), pp. 53–60.

21. Governments have invested heavily in 'e-government' information systems. For the UK see 'Two years on: realizing the benefits from our investment in e-government', *Office of the Deputy Prime Minister*, March (2005). For the USA see J. Young, 'Oracle solutions transform state and local governments', *IDC*, September (2003).

22. Readers should find the following article useful: G. Rifkin and J. Kurtzman, 'Is your e-business plan radical enough?', *Sloan Management Review*, vol. 43, no. 3 (2002), pp. 91–95.

23. M. Vernon, 'The smartest CIOs', *Management Today*, May (2006), discusses the strategic contribution that CIOs should make.

24. Readers may wish to consult one or more standard texts on finance. For example: G. Arnold, *Corporate Financial Management*, 3rd edition, FT/Prentice Hall, 2005; and P. Atrill, *Financial Management for Decision Makers*, 4th edition, FT/Prentice Hall, 2006.

25. The seminal work on managing for shareholder value has been updated: A. Rappaport, *Creating Shareholder Value*, 2nd edition, Free Press, 1998. See also J. Barlow, R. Burgman and M. Molna, 'Managing for shareholder value: intangibles, future value and investment decisions', *Journal of Business Strategy*, vol. 25, no. 3 (2004), pp. 26–34. T. Grundy (with G. Johnson and K. Scholes), *Exploring Strategic Financial Management*, Prentice Hall, 1998, chapter 2, is also a useful reference on managing for value.

26. See J. Martin and W. Petty, 'Value based management', *Baylor Business Review*, vol. 19, no. 1 (2001), pp. 2–3, review the arguments briefly.

27. S. Williams, 'Delivering strategic business value', *Strategic Finance*, vol. 86, no. 2 (2004), pp. 41–48.

28. See P. Atrill, *Financial Management for Decision Makers*, 4th edition, FT/Prentice Hall, 2006, chapters 6 and 7; G. Arnold, *Corporate Financial Management*, 3rd edition, FT/Prentice Hall, 2005, Part IV.

29. For readers who wish to follow up the discussion in this section, see K. Ward, *Corporate Financial Strategy*, Butterworth–Heinemann, 1993, and T. Grundy and K. Ward (eds), *Developing Financial Strategies: A comprehensive model in strategic business finance*, Kogan Page, 1996.

30. There have been a great deal of research and publications around the funding of this start-up phase. For example: D. Champion, 'A stealthier way to raise money', *Harvard Business Review*, vol. 78, no. 5 (2000), pp. 18–19; Q. Mills, 'Who's to blame for the bubble?', *Harvard Business Review*, vol. 79, no. 5 (2001), pp. 22–23; H. Van Auken, 'Financing small technology-based companies: the relationship between familiarity with capital and ability to price and negotiate investment', *Journal of Small Business Management*, vol. 39, no. 3 (2001), pp. 240–258; M. Van Osnabrugge and R. Robinson, 'The influence of a venture capitalist's source of funds', *Venture Capital*, vol. 3, no. 1 (2001), pp. 25–39.

31. See Atrill, reference 24, pp. 474–478.

32. See A. Kennedy, *The End of Shareholder Value: corporations at the crossroads*, Perseus Publishing, 2000; and H. Collingwood, 'The earnings game', *Harvard Business Review*, vol. 79, no. 6 (2001), pp. 65–72.

33. The major source for this section is J. Tidd, J. Bessant and K. Pavitt, *Managing Innovation: Integrating technological, market and organisational change*, 3rd edition, Wiley, 2005. See also P.H. Antiniou and H.I. Ansoff, 'Strategic management of technology', *Technology Analysis and Strategic Management*, vol. 16, no. 2 (2004), pp. 275–291.

34. A useful international comparison of R&D strategies can be found in E. Roberts, 'Benchmarking global strategic management of technology', *Research Technology Management*, vol. 44, no. 2 (2001), pp. 25–36.

35. W. Boulding and M. Christen, 'First mover disadvantage, *Harvard Business Review*, vol. 79, no. 9 (2001), pp. 20–21.

36. J. Tidd, J. Bessant and K. Pavitt, *Managing Innovation: Integrating technological, market and organisational change*, 2nd edition, Wiley, 2001, p. 222; and J. Tidd and M. Trewhella, 'Organisational and technological antecedents for knowledge acquisition', *R&D Management*, vol. 27, no. 4 (1997), pp. 359–375.

37. For example, see G. Slowinski, S. Stanton, J. Tao, W. Miller and D. McConnell, 'Acquiring external technology', *Research Technology Management*, vol. 43, no. 5 (2002), pp. 29–35.

38. E. Roberts and W. Lui, 'Ally or acquire? How technology leaders decide', *Sloan Management Review*, vol. 43, no. 1 (2001), pp. 26–34.

39. R. Buderi, 'Funding central research', *Research Technology Management*, vol. 43, no. 4 (2000), pp. 18–25, gives some useful examples including Siemens, NEC, Hewlett Packard and IBM.

40. See C. Kimzey and S. Kurokawa, 'Technology outsourcing in the US and Japan', *Research Technology Management*', vol. 45, no. 4 (2002), pp. 36–42.

41. E. Kessler and P. Bierly, 'Internal vs. external learning in product development', *R & D Management*, vol. 30, no. 3 (2000), pp. 213–223.

42. R. Grieve, 'Appropriate technology in a globalising world', *International Journal of Technology Management and Sustainable Development*, vol. 3, no. 3 (2004), pp. 173–187.

43. A. Lloyd, 'Technology, innovation and competitive advantage; making a business process perspective part of investment appraisal', *International Journal of Innovation Management*, vol. 5, no. 3 (2001), pp. 351–376.

44. The stage-gate process is discussed in R. Thomas, *New Product Development: Managing and forecasting for strategic success*, Wiley, 1993; and R. Cooper, S. Edgett, J. Kleinschmidt and J. Elko, 'Optimising the stage-gate process: what best practice companies do', *Research Technology Management*, vol. 45, no. 5 (2002), pp. 21–26 and vol. 45, no. 6 (2002), pp. 43–49.

45. See Tidd *et al.*, reference 33, Part V, p. 465.

46. L. Gratton, 'Managing integration through cooperation', *Human Resource Management*, vol. 44, no. 2 (2005), pp. 151–158, underlines the importance of working co-operatively across both internal and external boundaries.

Video games

By the mid–2000s the development of computer-based video games had become a major international industry – dominated by companies in the UK, North America and Japan. But at the beginning of the industry (in the late 1980s) it was largely driven by individual developers writing programs in their bedrooms – it was a cottage industry. Then games cost as little as €6,000 (£4,100; $6,250) to develop and required just a couple of people – a programmer and an artist. By the end of the 1990s there were more than 300 games companies in the UK alone. However, by the mid–2000s new titles were costing €3m to develop, needing teams of 30 or more programmers, artists, sound engineers and producers. Many expected development costs to rise to perhaps €15m per new title. This clearly had a major impact on the structure of the industry and how games companies were funded. Firms needed to be big to survive. Many of the company founders chose to sell out to corporate organisations or go public through a share flotation. Some companies, such as Rock Star, had been founded in the UK but moved to the USA.

The *Irish Times* commented on the funding situation in the mid–2000s:

Currently with very few exceptions, the money to create best-selling games comes from the games' publishers: a small group of multinationals such as Vivendi and Electronic Arts, whose strength in the market comes from negotiating licensing deals with existing media properties (movie tie-ins such as *Spiderman*, sports stars, and arcade game adaptations), close relationships with console manufactures like Sony and Microsoft, and, most importantly, strong control over the distribution of the games. Almost all games are sold the old-fashioned way: in shops, shrink-wrapped and distributed via the publishers' marketing infrastructure.

Orbiting around these publishers are the developers and designers. Sometimes employed by the publishers, sometimes working in small independent outfits, they are beholden to the publishers for almost all of the up-front cost of producing a video game. A game doesn't get the green

Photo: Superstock/Alamy Images

light without a publishing deal; a game can't make it to the shops without that publisher footing the bill. As the average cost of developing a game has grown, the publishers' control over the game development process has grown tighter. Independent outfits are vanishing and the publishers are growing more conservative. . . .

Why the explosion in costs? Partly, it's a product of the increasing complexity of the modern games platform. Whether written for a PC or a games console, the hardware and creative input that underlies the modern fast-moving, endlessly detailed, cinematically scored, 3D action film, requires a great deal of money and management. But partly it's a product of the system. Four out of five games, it is said, don't make money. Publishers invest heavily in marketing and support a surprisingly old-fashioned way of shifting product: putting those boxes on shelves. Often . . . it's not the coders who see the money and it's not the games that benefit.

Even those who have made millions from their successful games are growing tired. Valve, the creators of (the 2004) hit game Half-Life 2, created an internet distribution system, Steam, rather than rely on publishers to ship their product. The release of Half-Life was delayed while its publisher, Vivendi, sued to prevent Steam from operating its distribution network, claiming breach of contract. At the other end of the development process, the world-famous British games developer Peter Molyneux spurned investment from publishers and turned to venture capitalists (VCs) to raise funds for his latest games.

At the 2005 Games Developers Conference (GDC) in San Francisco, it seemed that such attempts to escape the video games industry's studio system had popular support. 'Can we do any worse if we just trusted the creative folks entirely instead of the publishers?' asked industry veteran Warren Spector. It's hard to say whether the atmosphere at GDC will lead to developers striking out against their masters and starting their own, innovative distribution and investment approaches. Even if this is more than just fighting talk among peers, it may be nothing more than part of a long repeating cycle – at least, if the parallels with Hollywood continue. After all, the games publishers were once scrappy small companies, just as studios such as United Artists and Dreamworks began as breakaway companies run by the 'talent'. Will the money from Steam, which allows Valve to charge a monthly subscription to play its games, corrupt its coders as completely as developers believe the publishers have been corrupted? Will the VCs who funded Molyneux be as forgiving as publishers if his games don't make their return first time around? Maybe the world of video games is different.

Like most things in both the computing and entertainment sectors, the pace of change created threats to many but opportunities for others. In 2005 the publisher Electronic Arts signed a deal with Steven Spielberg the director of *Schindler's List*, *Saving Private Ryan*, *War of the Worlds* and many other Hollywood blockbusters to make three video games. Meanwhile the Screen Actors Guild (the largest union representing actors in the USA) was bargaining hard for increased fees for actors who provided voices for video game characters. The huge development costs were forcing publishers and games developers to look to new sources of gaming software – spawning the growth of new entrepreneurial businesses in places such as India. The advantages of outsourcing some or all of the development to India lie in the abundant creative talent and programming skills with much lower wages. This could amount to as much as 40 per cent reductions in development costs. But perhaps the key factor which underlies the popularity of video games with consumers is the capability of the hardware – whether that be consoles, computers or even mobile phones. The year of 2005 was an important one in the battle for dominance of the hardware market as reported by the *Financial Times*:

Sony and Microsoft are to unleash products capable of the same ferocious speed. . . . Machines packed with processing power and the ability to display high-definition moving images will soon be on sale for a few hundred dollars, to drive video games. Yet this is about far more than shooting aliens. The games business long ago outgrew its roots in the toy industry, but that could be nothing compared with the transition it is now facing. These high-performance boxes are weapons in a much bigger war: the struggle for dominance of all forms of home digital entertainment. 'The stakes for next-generation hardware leadership are enormous,' says Warren Jenson, chief financial officer of Electronic Arts, the biggest video games publisher. 'It's about owning the set-top box that may ultimately connect the living room to the internet.' . . .

In video game hardware, such periodic transitions to new generations of technology have historically marked big shifts in industry leadership. Atari gave way to Sega, which in turn surrendered leadership to Nintendo, before Sony rose to prominence. This time it is Microsoft that is eager to force the pace. Microsoft certainly understands the cost of being late. Its first Xbox arrived 18 months after [Sony's] PlayStation 2 and, despite winning accolades for its technical prowess, never made up lost ground with consumers or the developers whose games are essential to selling the hardware. . . . Just as, in a previous era, the minicomputer took over from the mainframe as the source of innovation in computing, only to give way to the PC, the games console is becoming the focus of breakthrough technology. Not that the PC is about to give up its role as the digital brain of the home. Some 64m PCs were sold for home use last year, according to IDC, the technology monitoring company, compared with about 24m games consoles. Yet, with power pouring into the consoles, the PC's role is set to be reduced – and the box most likely to be connected to the family television set is the games console.

The companies leading this latest charge into digital entertainment are well aware of what is at stake. For Sony, video games have been a rare and much-needed bright spot. In the four years since the PlayStation 2 hit its stride, the games business has on average contributed nearly 60 per cent of the company's operating profits. The losses that Microsoft has amassed from video games are even bigger than Sony's profits. Over the four years, the games business has produced $2.6bn [€2.1bn; £1.4bn] in operating earnings for Sony. In roughly the same period, Microsoft's home and entertainment division – essentially, its Xbox business – has lost $3.7bn. Yet for the software group, this was the cost to get into the game that is about to begin. Bill Gates, its chairman, acknowledged as much last week when he said: 'What we got this round – at some significant financial cost – was the opportunity to play again.'

Despite their wider ambitions, Microsoft and Sony are both aware that console sales will depend mainly on how successful they are at harnessing the power of their new digital workhorses to produce more compelling game-playing. It is not just about the heightened visual images promised by high-definition television or the ability to render sophisticated graphics in real time: with more computing power at their disposal, the artificial intelligence algorithms in the machines will be able to produce far more complex and unexpected interactions.

As more forms of media and entertainment go digital, however, these machines will also take on a broader role. Whether through a direct connection to the internet or through a home network that links them to a PC, they are designed to become the gateway through which you delve into your store of family photographs, listen to digital music or tap a library of films. The internet connection will make it easier for family members or friends to look at each others' pictures, share music or play together.

Sony . . . suggested that the (cell) chip could break down the technological barriers that have separated games from films, where animation and special effects are created using different technology. With the ability to render more lifelike images, the cell chip could turn out images that could be slotted equally well into games or movies. 'There's huge potential for the convergence of movies and games – and for something new that comes out of it,' Sony says.

'We're thinking holistically about the platforms,' says Dean Lester, head of Microsoft's Games for Windows group.

'In the past, publishers had to redesign the control systems, now they can build the game across the platforms.'

It adds up to Microsoft strengthening its games platform to appeal to publishers and win game franchises that will power the success of the console'.

Sources: Sunday Times, 12 October 2003; 'Developers of video games feel disillusioned' by D. O'Brien, *Irish Times*, 18 March 2005; *Financial Times* (US edition), 11 May 2005.

Questions

1 Identify how the 'business model' for the industry changed as information technology capability improved. Where might the next changes of business model be?

2 What were the human resource implications of the changing 'shape' of the games industry to the different 'players'?

3 Use Exhibit 13.8 to undertake a critique of the extent to which the financial strategies are appropriate for the industry.

Strategy in Action

14

Managing Strategic Change

LEARNING OUTCOMES

After reading this chapter you should be able to:

→ Identify the scope of a required strategic change.

→ Analyse how organisational context might affect the design of strategic change programmes.

→ Undertake a forcefield analysis to identify forces blocking and facilitating change.

→ Assess the impact of the role and management styles of change agents.

→ Assess the value of different levers for strategic change, including the management of organisational routines, political and symbolic processes and other change tactics.

→ Identify the pitfalls and problems of managing change programmes.

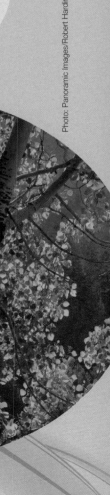

Photo: Panoramic Images/Robert Harding World Imagery

14.1 INTRODUCTION

This chapter is concerned with the management activities involved in changing strategies. Chapters 12 and 13 have addressed important issues to do with the structuring of organisations and the resourcing of strategies, both important in effecting strategic change. However, designing a structure and putting in place appropriate resources do not of themselves ensure that people will make a strategy happen. The major problem managers report in managing change is the tendency towards *inertia* and *resistance to change*;[1] people will tend to hold on to existing ways of doing things. As explained in Chapter 5 (section 5.1) this may lead to *strategic drift*. Discussion of the 'experience lens' in the Commentary at the end of the book and explanations of how strategies develop in Chapter 11 also emphasise the same tendency. Managing strategic change therefore poses a major challenge for managers. In addressing this challenge this chapter builds on three key premises:

● *Strategy matters*. It is important to remember that in managing strategic change much of what has been written in previous chapters should be seen as an essential precursor in identifying the need for and direction of strategic change. It will not be repeated in any detail here, but it is important to remember the need to understand:
  – Why strategic change is needed (discussed in Chapters 2, 3, 4 and 5).
  – The bases of the strategy in terms of strategic purpose, perhaps encapsulated in a statement of vision or mission (Chapter 4) and the basis of competitive advantage (Chapter 6).
  – The more specific strategy choices intended in terms of strategy directions and methods (Chapters 7 to 10).

● *Context matters*. The approach taken to managing strategic change needs to be *context dependent*. There is, therefore, no one 'right way' of managing strategic change. Managers need to consider how to balance different approaches according to the circumstances they face.

● *Multiple roles in managing strategic change*. Much of what is written on strategic change assumes that change happens in a *top-down* manner; that top managers put into effect the changes required. It is, of course, a major role of top managers to influence the strategic direction of the organisation. However, it is unrealistic to suppose they can control everything. There are many others in the organisation – middle managers and below – who play a major role in managing change. Indeed Chapter 11 (section 11.3) shows that strategies may emerge from lower down in the organisation.

Exhibit 14.1 provides a structure for the chapter. Section 14.2 begins by explaining important issues that need to be considered in *diagnosing the situation* an organisation faces when embarking on strategic change, in terms of the *types of change* required; the variety of *contextual and cultural factors* that need to be taken into account; and the *forces blocking or facilitating change*. Section 14.3 then discusses the management of strategic change in terms of the *styles of management* and the roles played by *strategic leaders* and other *change agents* in managing strategic change. Section 14.4 then goes on to review *levers for change*, including changes in *structure and control*, organisational *routines and systems*,

Exhibit 14.1 **Key elements in managing strategic change**

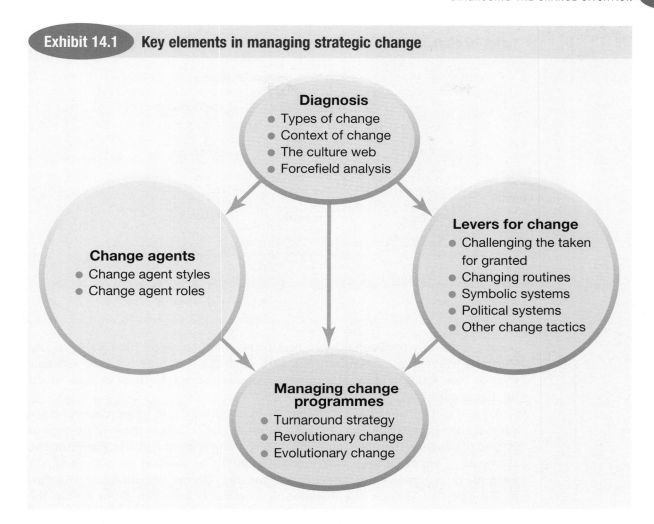

symbols, the role of *political activity*, and more specific *tactics*. Section 14. 5 draws all this together by considering how all this might take effect and what overall lessons can be drawn about *managing change programmes*.

14.2 DIAGNOSING THE CHANGE SITUATION

Types of strategic change

How change is managed will depend on the magnitude of the challenge faced in trying to effect strategic change. To understand this it is useful to consider the *type* of change required, the wider *context* in which change is to occur, the specific *blockages* to change that exist and forces that exist to *facilitate* the change process.

14.2.1 Types of strategic change

As was suggested in the discussion in Chapter 11, typically strategy development is *incremental* in nature. It builds on prior strategy; it is *adaptive* in the way it

Exhibit 14.2 **Types of change**

Extent of change

	Realignment	Transformation
Incremental	Adaptation	Evolution
Big Bang	Reconstruction	Revolution

Nature of change

Source: Adapted from J. Balogun and V. Hope Hailey, *Exploring Strategic Change*, 2nd Edn, Prentice Hall, Pearson Education Ltd, 1999.

occurs, with only occasional more *transformational* changes. Julia Balogun and Veronica Hope Hailey[2] develop this further to identify four types of strategic change (see Exhibit 14.2), and these have implications for how change might be managed.

Arguably, it is beneficial for change in an organisation to be *incremental* since such change should build on the skills, routines and beliefs of those in the organisation. Change is therefore more likely to be understood and win commitment. However, a *big bang* approach to change might be needed on occasions, for example if an organisation faces crisis or needs to change direction fast. In terms of the *extent* of change, the question is whether change can occur within the current culture as a *realignment* of strategy. Or does it require culture change? This is more *transformational* change. Combining these two axes suggests four types of strategic change:

- *Adaptation* is change that can be accommodated within the current culture and occur incrementally. It is the most common form of change in organisations.

- *Reconstruction* is change that may be rapid and involve a good deal of upheaval in an organisation, but which does not fundamentally change the culture. It could be a *turnaround* situation where there is need for major structural changes or a major cost-cutting programme to deal with a decline in financial performance or difficult or changing market conditions. How this might be managed is discussed further in section 14.5.1.

- *Revolution* is change that requires rapid and major strategic but also culture change. This could be in circumstances where the strategy has been so bounded by the existing culture that, even when environmental or competitive pressures might require fundamental change, the organisation has failed to respond. This might have occurred over many years (see the discussion of strategic drift in section 5.1) and resulted in circumstances where pressures for change are extreme – for example, a takeover threatens the continued existence of a firm. How this might be managed is discussed further in section 14.5.2.

- *Evolution* is change in strategy that requires culture change, but over time. It may be that managers anticipate the need for transformational change. They may then be in a position of planned evolutionary change, with time in which to achieve it. Another way in which evolution can be explained is in terms the idea of the *learning organisation* (see section 11.5.2) where an organisation continually adjusts its strategy as the environment changes. How this might be managed is discussed further in section 14.5.3.

The sort of cultural analysis explained in section 5.4.6 can be useful as a means of considering whether the change envisaged could be accommodated within the bounds of the culture as it is, or whether it would require a really significant cultural shift. For example, a business may launch new products without requiring fundamental changes in the assumptions and beliefs of the organisation. On the other hand, some changes in strategy, even if they do not take the form of dramatic product changes, may require fundamental changes in core assumptions in the organisation. For example, the shift from a production focus for a manufacturer to a customer-led, service ethos may not entail product changes, but will very likely require significant culture change.

14.2.2 The importance of context

Strategic change context

Managing change in a small entrepreneurial business, where a motivated team are driving change, would be quite different from trying to manage change in a major corporation, or perhaps a long-established public sector organisation, with set routines, formal structures and perhaps a great deal of resistance to change. Moreover, assuming that approaches to change are readily transferable between contexts is problematic. For example, many government departments in different parts of the world have sought to import change management practices from consultancies or by recruiting managers from commercial enterprises but with varying degrees of success.[3] Illustration 14.1 gives an example of the contextual issues faced in trying to manage change in the UK Ministry of Defence (MOD).[4]

Approaches to managing change therefore need to be differ according to context.[5] Balogun and Hope Hailey build on this point to highlight important contextual features that need to be taken into account in designing change programmes. Exhibit 14.3 summarises these.

Here are some examples of how the contextual features shown in Exhibit 14.3 might require different approaches to change:

- The *time* available for change could differ dramatically. A business facing immediate decline in turnover or profits from rapid changes in its markets has a quite different context for change compared with a business where the management may see the need for change coming in the future, perhaps years away, and have time to plan it carefully as a staged incremental process.

- The *scope* of change might differ in terms of either the *breadth* of change across an organisation or the *depth* of culture change required. The scope of change in an organisation such as the MOD in Illustration 14.1 is wholly different in terms of both breadth and depth and, in consequence, likely to be a much bigger challenge than, for example, adaptive change in a successful small business.

Illustration 14.1

The challenges of managing change in the UK Ministry of Defence

Understanding the challenge of managing strategic change requires an understanding of the context of change.

The UK Ministry of Defence (MOD) has found it difficult to make major changes. For example, in 2004, of the seven principles underpinning the recommendations of the Smart Procurement Initiative begun in 1998 only one was properly implemented and, of the other six, some hardly at all. Or, again, in 2000 the MOD established the Defence Logistics Organisation (DLO) to coordinate across the army, navy and air force. By 2005 it was accepted that this had stalled. Drawing on published studies and their own experience working with the MOD, Derrick Neal and Trevor Taylor, of the Defence Academy at Shrivenham, explain some of the reasons.

Size and complexity

The MOD comprises 300,000 people of whom 200,000 are military personnel. It also relies on a further 300,000 people in its supply chain. Moreover it comprises many parts so: 'Change initiated in one part of the system runs into resistance and difficulty from arrangements elsewhere, or has implications for other parts of the system that were not foreseen by the original change initiators.' It is also difficult to change all the systems simultaneously.

Empowerment

The MOD cannot decide overall defence strategy since that is decided by politicians. However, there is significant autonomy within the MOD. There are 13 top-level budget holders (TLBs), within each of which there is then further delegation of responsibility. The result is some 36 defence agencies and below them 120 'integrated project teams'. When the MOD centre tries to generate change, locally empowered leaders often produce their own version of change programmes. In 2003 it was found that there were 150 uncoordinated change initiatives under way within the DLO.

Personnel systems

The MOD employs both military staff and civilian staff. Military staff expect to move locations frequently.

Someone with 35 years of service is likely to have moved 20 times. Time horizons are therefore short within a 'can do' culture. Those who wish to make a quick impact do so by initiating change but moving on before initiatives are completed. However, follow-up is unlikely because 'you don't make your name by implementing another officer's change initiative'. The number of 'fast-track' civil servants who are likely to hold a series of jobs in quick succession is much more limited; most are not expected to move regularly. So time horizons are different for them.

The reluctance to invest for change

The MOD views change as a 'budget-neutral activity': that it is necessary to make savings in order to fund change, rather than fund change in order to make savings. For example, it was only after the stalled DLO initiative that the MOD recognised the need for investment in that change programme and obtained funding from the Treasury to try and address it.

The lack of urgency

There is no feeling of crisis. Paradoxically, for people who often find themselves at serious risk, they see the institutions that surround them as secure and fixed. The only signal of required change is from the Treasury's financial initiatives, which may be seen as a threat.

Source: Based on D. Neal and T. Taylor, 'Spinning on dimes: the challenges of introducing transformational change into the UK Ministry of Defence', *Strategic Change*, vol. 15 (2006), pp. 15–22.

Questions

1 Use the checklist of the change kaleidoscope in section 14.2.2 to identify the range of contextual issues that need to be taken into account in influencing change in the MOD.

2 What approach to change should be adopted to improve the MOD's ability to manage change?

Exhibit 14.3   **Contextual features of strategic change programmes**

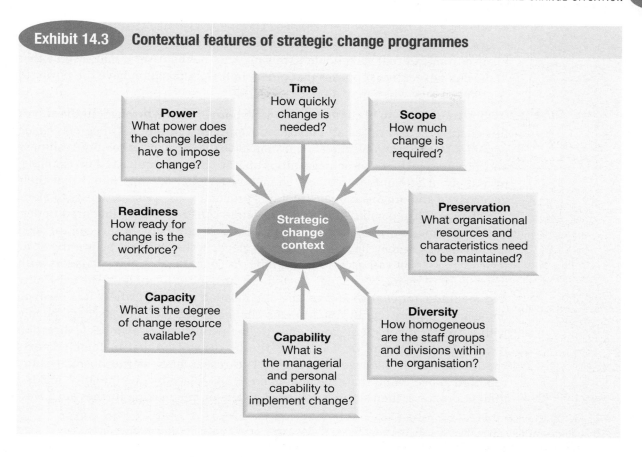

- *Preservation* of some aspects of an organisation may be needed: in particular, competences on which changes need to be based. Suppose, for example, that a computer software business needs to become more formally organised because of its successful growth. This could well upset technical experts who have been used to ready access to senior management, but it could be vital to preserve their expertise and motivation.

- A *diversity* of experience, views and opinions within an organisation may help the change process. However, if an organisation has followed a strategy for many decades, this may have led to a very homogeneous way of seeing the world. Change could be hampered by this. So gauging the nature and extent of diversity is important.

- Is there *capability* or experience of managing change in the organisation?[6] There may be managers who have managed change effectively in the past, or a workforce that have been used to and have accepted past changes, whilst another organisation may have little experience of change.

- *Capacity* for change in terms of available resources will also be significant. For example, change can be costly, not only in financial terms, but also in terms of management time.

- What is the *readiness* for change? Is there a felt need for change across the organisation, widespread resistance, or pockets or levels of resistance in some parts of the organisation and readiness in others?[7]

- Who has the *power* to effect change? Often it is assumed that the chief executive has such power, but in the face of resistance from below, or perhaps resistance from external stakeholders, this may not be the case. It may also be that the chief executive supposes that others in the organisation have the power to effect change when they do not.

This consideration of context needs to be borne in mind throughout the rest of this chapter. It also raises an important overarching question: *is one-off change possible?* Does the organisation in question have the capacity, capability, readiness and power structures to achieve the scope of change required? For example, in a study of attempts to manage change in hospitals[8] it was found that their governance and organisational structures prevented any clear authority to manage change. This, combined with the resource constraints they laboured under, meant that major one-off change initiatives were not likely to succeed. In such circumstances, it may be that the context needs to be changed before the strategic change itself can occur. For example, it could be that new managers with experience of managing change need to be introduced to enhance the capability and readiness for change and get the organisation to a point where it is ready to embark on a more significant strategic change programme. Or perhaps people with a greater diversity of experience in line with the future strategic direction need to be brought in. Or it may need to be recognised that in some contexts change has to be managed in stages. The researchers in the hospital study reported above found that change tended to take place by one initiative making limited progress, then stalling, followed by a later one making further advances.

14.2.3 Diagnosing the cultural context

Understanding the prevailing culture of an organisation can help inform the type of change needed, as well as an organisation's readiness for change. Chapter 5 introduced the cultural web (see section 5.4.6) as both a useful concept in explaining culture and a means of diagnosing the culture of an organisation. Illustration 5.4 showed the cultural web produced by managers and employees to analyse the prevailing culture for the Forestry Commission in the UK.[9] The collapse in world timber prices meant that alternative sources of income were needed. Additionally, the government's policy was to develop an emphasis on forestry for leisure and social inclusion, not just the production of timber. However, what emerged from the cultural web analysis was that the organisation's current culture (Illustration 5.4) raised problems over moving to such a future. Foresters saw themselves as *the* forestry experts, which translated into an attitude of 'FC knows best', a tendency to see the forests as 'theirs' and the public as a 'nuisance', getting in the way of efficient timber production. There was also an ingrained public sector ethos – a sense of contributing to society rather than working for commercial gain. The command and control style of management had led to a deference to senior management and there was the bureaucracy of a public sector organisation. It also took at least 50 years to grow trees: linked to this was a deep sense of tradition making the organisation conservative and slow to change.

As Illustration 14.2 shows, this analysis of the current culture can, however, be extended to consider changes that are needed if the desired future strategy is to

Illustration 14.2

The Forestry Commission of the future

The cultural web can be used to identify the desired culture of an organisation.

Stories
- Celebrating success – spreading good news about people and what they are doing
- Heroes who push boundaries
- Thanking and rewarding people
- Illustrating a sense of belonging
- The mistakes we learned from
- Success through empowerment and working in partnership

Symbols
- Diverse forest and people
- Of accessibility
- Accessible management
- Third-party endorsement
- Active sport and health symbols
- Icons of publications
- Open-plan working areas
- Two-tree logo on signs/clothing/vehicles

Rituals and routines
- People working inclusively
- Challenging the status quo
- Learning from mistakes
- Making time to talk
- Praise and recognition
- Resource and reward new ideas
- People regularly trying out new things
- Openness, honesty, mutual respect and trust in working relationships
- Flexible, adaptable, responsive

Paradigm
- **Inclusive**
- **Forests for the people**
- **Outward looking/forward thinking/innovative**
- **Strong work ethic, loyalty and commitment**
- **Focused on outcomes**
- **Valuing diversity**
- **Learning culture**

Power structures
- Less power distance between top/bottom of the hierarchy
- Greater autonomy and empowerment
- Internal networks – open, accessible, shared decision making
- External networks – partnerships and external funding
- Management encourage challenge of ideas

Control systems
- Communicating vision and plans, targets and milestones
- Measuring outcomes *not* processes
- Encourage debate/challenge rather than following the rules/allow for local action
- Two-way discussions about realistic forward job plans – expectations balanced with resources
- Common IT systems providing access to reliable and up-to-date guidance
- Improve rewards and recognition for innovation

Organisational structures
- Less hierarchical, networked organisation
- Flatter flexible, more organic structure
- Staff interchange across organisational boundaries
- Project working/working groups
- External partnerships
- Formal and informal networks
- Improved linkages at senior level
- Inclusive management style

Questions

1. How might the cultural web be used to help manage change?

2. What are likely problems in managing change indicated by the future web?

Source: Adapted from The Forestry Commission case study by Anne McCann.

be put into effect successfully. Together with an understanding of the context of the organisation, this can be used to inform discussions about what changes are required. If the Forestry Commission is to put more emphasis on social forestry or 'forests for the community', work with other organisations to do this and encourage its employees to embrace this mission, what would the culture be like? Illustration 14.2 shows the future cultural web envisaged by the same people in the Forestry Commission. Together with the understanding of the current culture (see Illustration 5.4) this helps identify what is problematic about the existing culture but also what might be added or introduced if change is to occur. It is useful in this respect, not least because it embraces the 'softer' aspects of culture, such as organisational symbols, but also political processes and the 'harder' aspects of organisations, such as operating routines, structures and control systems. What typically emerges from such an exercise is that all these aspects of an organisation's culture can be both important blockages and facilitators to change. In deciding which are blockages and which are facilitators a forcefield analysis can also help.

14.2.4 Forcefield analysis

A forcefield analysis provides a view of change problems that need to be tackled, by identifying forces for and against change

A **forcefield analysis** provides an initial view of change problems that need to be tackled, by identifying forces for and against change based on an understanding of the context of change – including the existing culture. It allows some key questions to be asked:

● What aspects of the current situation would block change, and how can these be overcome?
● What aspects of the current situation might aid change in the desired direction, and how might these be reinforced?
● What needs to be introduced or developed to aid change?

Exhibit 14.4 is a forcefield analysis for the Forestry Commission. Whilst the blockages identified constituted a significant problem, the forcefield analysis also identified aspects of the organisation and its culture that might facilitate change. The powerful support for change of the 'Director General', the commitment of employees to the organisation, the ethos of hard work and the potential flexibility, together with a desire from within the organisation to change the command and control culture, were all potentially positive. What was needed was to add to this: for example, widespread participation in the change programme could help achieve ownership of a clearly articulated future vision; and increased diversity of personnel together with a more organic management style could promote more innovation. It was, however, also clear that there were many blockages to be removed.

Changes in the structure, design and control systems of organisations have already been reviewed in Chapter 12. In the next two sections (14.3 and 14.4), different styles and roles in the change process and other levers for managing change are discussed.

Exhibit 14.4   **A forcefield analysis**

Pushing

- Hard work ethic that delivers results
- Commitment of employees
- Juggling priorities/potential flexibility
- Forestry know-how
- Encouragement/support of change from the top
- Feedback from staff survey – staff want changes in how they are treated

Additional

- Encouragement to work in new ways
- Increased diversity of staff
- Clear articulation of a vision for the future
- Participation in the change process
- Ownership of the future strategy
- Skills development

Resisting

- Traditional structure/ways of woking
- Bureaucracy
- Departmental silos
- Workloads/pressure of work
- Homogeneous workforce
- Conservative/risk averse/slow to change
- Blame culture
- Command and control management style
- Lack of ownership of the change – 'not invented here' syndrome
- Lack of local leadership/communication
- Deference to senior staff
- No past experience of change

14.3   CHANGE MANAGEMENT: STYLES AND ROLES

This section of the chapter is concerned with the role people play in managing strategic change and how they do it. It begins by considering the roles in strategic change played by *strategic leaders*, *middle managers*, *change teams* and the influence of *outsiders* such as consultants and external *stakeholders*. It then goes on to examine different *styles of managing change*.

14.3.1   Roles in managing change

> A change agent is the individual or group that effects strategic change in an organisation

When it comes to managing strategic change, there is too often an overemphasis on individuals at the top of an organisation. It is useful to think of *change agency* more broadly. A **change agent** is the individual or group that helps effect strategic change in an organisation. For example, the creator of a strategy may, or may not, be the change agent. He or she may need to rely on others to take a lead in effecting changes to strategy. It could be that a middle manager is a change agent in a particular context; or perhaps consultants, working together with managers from within the organisation.

> Leadership is the process of influencing an organisation (or group within an organisation) in its efforts towards achieving an aim or goal

Strategic leadership

The management of change is, however, often directly linked to the role of a strategic leader.[10] More generally, however, **leadership** is the process of influencing an organisation (or group within an organisation) in its efforts towards achieving an aim or goal.[11] So a leader is not necessarily someone at the top, but rather someone who is in a position to have influence in their organisation.

Leaders are often categorised in two ways:

● *Charismatic leaders*, who are mainly concerned with building a vision for the organisation and energising people to achieve it. The evidence suggests that these leaders have particularly beneficial impact on performance when the people who work for them see the organisation facing uncertainty.[12]

● *Instrumental or transactional leaders*,[13] who focus more on designing systems and controlling the organisation's activities.

However, ideally what is required is the ability to tailor the strategic leadership style to context and there is evidence[14] that the most successful strategic leaders are able to do just this. Indeed, with regard to the management of change, it would seem to be a problem if they cannot.[15] After all, some approaches are more to do with creating strategy or with control rather than the management of change, and might well lead to approaches to change not suited to the particular needs of the specific change context.

What is likely, however, is that those at the top of an organisation will be seen by others, not least those who work for them, but also other stakeholders and outside observers, as intimately associated with strategic change programmes when they occur. In this sense they are symbolically highly significant in the change process (see section 14.4.4 below on symbolic levers for change).

Middle managers

A top-down approach to managing strategy and strategic change sees middle managers as implementers of strategy. However, as chapter 15 (section 15.2.3) shows, they have multiple roles in relation to the management of strategy.[16] In the context of managing strategic change there are five roles they play:

● The *implementation and control* role. Here they are, indeed, the implementers of top management plans by making sure that resources are allocated and controlled appropriately, monitoring performance and behaviour of staff and, where necessary, explaining the strategy to those reporting to them.

● *'Sense making'* of strategy. Top management may set down a strategic direction, but how it is made sense of in specific contexts (for example, a region of a multinational or a functional department) may, intentionally or not, be left to middle managers. If misinterpretation of that intended strategy is to be avoided, it is therefore vital that middle managers understand and feel an ownership of it.

● *Reinterpretation and adjustment* of strategic responses as events unfold (for example, in terms of relationships with customers, suppliers, the workforce, and so on). This is a vital role for which middle managers are uniquely qualified because they are in day-to-day contact with such aspects of the organisation and its environment.

● A crucial *relevance bridge* between top management and members of the organisation at lower levels. They are in a position to translate change initiatives into a message that is locally relevant.

- *Advisors* to more senior management on what are likely to be blockages and requirements for change.

When it comes to strategic change, middle managers are therefore in a key 'mediating' role between those trying to direct from the top and the operating level. A number of researchers have made the point that, in this role, how they make sense of top-down strategy and how they talk about and explain it to others become critically important.[17] The key debate in Illustration 14.6 at the end of the chapter considers strategic change in relation to both a top-down perspective and some of the roles played by middle managers.

Outsiders

Whilst managers in the organisation have important roles to play, 'outsiders' can also be important. For example, these could include the following:

- A *new chief executive* from outside the organisation may be introduced into a business to enhance the capability for change. This is especially so in turnaround situations (see section 14.5.1). He or she changes the context for change by bringing a fresh perspective on the organisation, not bound by the constraints of the past, or the embedded routines that can prevent strategic change.
- *New management from outside the organisation* can also increase the diversity of ideas, help break down cultural barriers to change and increase the experience of and capability for change. However, their successful influence is likely to depend on how much explicit *visible backing* they have from the chief executive. Without such backing they may be seen as lacking authority and influence.
- *Consultants* are often used to help formulate strategy or to plan the change process. They are also increasingly used as facilitators of change processes: for example, in a coordinating capacity, as project planners for change programmes, as facilitators of project teams working on change, or of strategy workshops used to develop strategy and plan means of strategic change. The value of consultants is three-fold. First, they too do not inherit the cultural baggage of the organisation and can therefore bring a dispassionate view to the process. Second, as a result, they may ask questions and undertake analyses which challenge taken-for-granted ways of seeing or doing things. Third, they signal symbolically the importance of a change process, not least because their fees may be of a very high order.
- *Other stakeholders* may be key influencers of change. For example, government, investors, customers, suppliers and business analysts all have the potential to act as change agents on organisations.

14.3.2 Styles of managing change

Whoever the change agent is needs to consider the style of management they adopt. Different styles are likely to be more or less appropriate according to context. These styles are summarised in Exhibit 14.5.[18]

Exhibit 14.5	Styles of managing strategic change			
Style	**Means/context**	**Benefits**	**Problems**	**Circumstances of effectiveness**
Education	Group briefings assume internalisation of strategic logic and trust of top management	Overcoming lack of (or mis)information	Time consuming Direction or progress may be unclear	Incremental change or long-time horizontal transformational change
Participation	Involvement in setting the strategy agenda and/or resolving strategic issues by taskforces or groups	Increasing ownership of a decision or process May improve quality of decisions	Time consuming Solutions/outcome within existing paradigm	
Intervention	Change agent retains co-ordination/control: delegates elements of change	Process is guided/controlled but involvement takes place	Risk of perceived manipulation	Incremental or non-crisis transformational change
Direction	Use of authority to set direction and means of change	Clarity and speed	Risk of lack of acceptance and ill-conceived strategy	Transformational change
Coercion/edict	Explicit use of power through edict	May be successful in crises or state of confusion	Least successful unless crisis	Crisis, rapid transformational change or change in established autocratic cultures

Education involves the explanation of the reasons for and means of strategic change

● **Education** involves the explanation of the reasons for and means of strategic change. This might be appropriate when the problem in managing change is because of misinformation or lack of information and if there is adequate time to persuade people of the need for change. However, there are problems here. Assuming that reasoned argument in a top-down fashion will overcome perhaps years of embedded assumptions about what 'really matters' could be naive. Change may be more effective if those affected by it are involved in its development and planning.

Participation in the change process is the involvement of those who will be affected by strategic change in the change agenda

● **Participation** in the change process is the involvement of those affected by strategic change in the change agenda; for example, in the identification of strategic issues, the strategic decision-making process, the setting of priorities, the planning of strategic change or the drawing up of action plans. Such involvement can foster a more positive attitude to change; people see the constraints the organisation faces as less significant[19] and feel increased ownership of, and commitment to, a decision or change process. It may therefore be a way of building readiness and capability for change. However, there is the inevitable risk that solutions will be found from within the existing culture so anyone who takes this approach may need to retain the ability to intervene in the process.

Intervention is the coordination of and authority over processes of change by a change agent who delegates elements of the change process

Direction is the use of personal managerial authority to establish a clear strategy and how change will occur

Coercion is the imposition of change or the issuing of edicts about change

● **Intervention** is the coordination of and authority over processes of change by a change agent who delegates *elements* of the change process. For example, particular stages of change, such as ideas generation, data collection, detailed planning, the development of rationales for change or the identification of critical success factors, may be delegated to project teams or taskforces (see section 15.4.2). Such teams may not take full responsibility for the change process, but become involved in it and see their work building towards it. The change agent retains responsibility for the change, ensures the monitoring of progress and that change is seen to occur.[20] An advantage is that it involves members of the organisation, not only in originating ideas, but also in the *partial implementation* of solutions, giving rise to commitment to the change.

● **Direction** involves the use of personal managerial authority to establish a clear strategy and how change will occur. It is top-down management of strategic change associated with a clear vision or strategic intent and may also be accompanied by similar clarity about critical success factors and priorities.

● **Coercion** is direction in its most extreme form. It is the imposition of change or the issuing of edicts about change. This is the explicit use of power and may be necessary if the organisation is facing a crisis, for example.

There are some overall observations that can be made about the appropriateness of these different styles in different contexts:

● *Different styles for different stages*. Styles of managing change may need to differ according to stages in a change process. Clear direction may be vital to motivate a desire or create a *readiness* to change; participation or intervention can help in gaining wider commitment across the organisation and developing *capabilities* to identify blockages to change, plan and implement specific action programmes.

● *Time and scope*. Participative styles are most appropriate for incremental change within organisations, but where transformational change is required, directive approaches may be more appropriate. (It is worth noting that even where top management see themselves adopting participative styles, their subordinates may perceive this as directive and, indeed, may welcome such direction.)[21]

● *Power*. In organisations with *hierarchical power structures* a directive style may be common and it may be difficult to break away from it, not least because people expect it. On the other hand, in *'Flatter' power structures* (or an adhocracy, a more networked or learning organisation described elsewhere in this book), it is likely that collaboration and participation will be common and desirable.

● *Personality types*. Different styles suit different managers' personality types. However, those with the greatest *capability* to manage change may have the ability to adopt different styles in different circumstances (see section 14.3.2).

● *Styles of managing change are not mutually exclusive*. For example, clear direction on overall vision might aid a more collaborative approach to more detailed strategy development. Education and communication may be appropriate for some stakeholders, such as financial institutions; participation may be appropriate for groups in parts of the organisation where it is necessary to build *capability and readiness*; whereas if there are parts of the organisation where change has to happen fast, *timing* may demand a more directive style.

Illustration 14.3

Leadership styles for managing change

Successful top executives have different leadership styles.

Don't noodle

I have always been a pretty good listener, and I am quick to admit that I do not have all the answers. So I am going to listen. But shortly after I listen, the second piece is to pull the trigger. I have all the input, and here is what we are going to do. People need closure on a decision. If you listen and then noodle on it, people get confused, and that's not effective leadership.

Terry Lundgren, CEO of Federated Department Stores (Interviewed by Matthew Boyle, in *Fortune*, 12 December 2005, vol. 152, no. 12, pp. 126–127.)

Coach but don't coddle

My approach to leadership is to raise aspiration and then achieve great execution . . . communicate priorities clearly, simply and frequently . . . to a large degree our division leaders must define their own future. I play the role of coach; but coaching doesn't mean coddling. I expect our managers to make choices . . . to help managers make these strategic choices leaders must sometimes challenge deeply held assumptions. . . . Being a role model is vital . . . I know that I must be ready for moments of truth that alert the organisation to my commitment.

Allan G. Laffley, Chief Executive of Procter & Gamble (in *Leadership Excellence*, November 2006, vol. 23, no. 11, pp. 9–10)

Be dedicated

Sir Terry Leahy of Tesco has overseen one of the biggest retail transformations in the world. Yet he is 'disarmingly ordinary. . . . His speech is serious and straightforward. He's no showman . . . you are not confronted with some huge presence. . . . He talks only about Tesco; . . . it's like meeting a religious leader faithfully reciting a creed.' And strategically: 'He is a combination of the very smart – he's always seeing over the hill – and the very simple. . . . You give him a problem and he'll go off and work until he's solved it. His co-workers respect him for his decision-making but he doesn't make his moves on a whim. . . .

Everything is analysed, taken apart, discussed and put back together. . . . He's gathered around him senior managers who've been with him and the group for years. He's in charge but he's also collegiate.' He also likes to talk and listen to people in the stores: 'What makes Leahy different is the extraordinary degree to which he chats with junior staff and absorbs their views and the attention he pays to customers.'

Chris Blackhurst 'Sir Terry Leahy' *Management Today*, February 2004, p. 32. Reproduced from *Management Today* magazine with the permission of the copyright owner, Haymarket Business Publications Limited.

Build on the key influencers

William Bratton was the police commissioner of New York City responsible for the Zero Tolerance campaign that reduced crime in the city. Bratton's belief was that once 'the beliefs and energies of a critical mass of people are engaged, conversion to another idea will spread like an epidemic, bringing about fundamental change very quickly'. He put key managers face-to-face with detailed operational problems so that they could not evade reality and put them 'under a spotlight'. For example, he brought together senior policemen and required them to face questions from senior colleagues about the performance of their precinct and how it contributed to overall strategy. The aim was to introduce a 'culture of performance': to allow success to be applauded but to make it very clear that underperformance was not tolerated.

W.C. Kim and R. Mauborgne, 'Tipping point leadership', *Harvard Business Review*, April 2003, pp. 60–69.

Questions

1 What might be the benefits and problems of each of the leadership styles? In what circumstances?

2 Only some stakeholders are specifically mentioned in the examples. Does this mean that the style should be the same towards all stakehoders of the organisation?

Illustration 14.3 shows how chief executives may use different styles in different contexts.

14.4 LEVERS FOR MANAGING STRATEGIC CHANGE

The rest of the chapter examines different 'levers' for managing strategic change. Change agents need to consider which of these levers to emphasise according to the change context. On the basis of many years' study of corporate change programmes, Michael Beer and Nitin Nohria observe that, broadly, there are two approaches here that they describe as 'theory E and theory O':[22]

- *Theory E* is change based on the pursuit of economic value and is typically associated with the top-down, programmatic use of the 'hard' levers of change. The emphasis is on changes of structures and systems, financial incentives, often associated with portfolio changes, downsizing and consequent job layoffs.

- *Theory O* is change based on the development of organisational capability. The emphasis here is on culture change, learning and participation in change programmes and experimentation.

However, Beer and Nohria make the point that, stark as these alternatives seem to be, the use of change levers that combine both approaches may not only be required, but be beneficial. This might involve, for example:

- *Sequencing change* to start with theory E approaches and move on to theory O approaches.

- *Embracing both approaches* simultaneously and being explicit about it to people in the organisation and external stakeholders.

- *Combining direction from the top with participation from below.* By so doing the benefits of both clarity of overall strategic direction and potential upward spontaneity can be achieved.

- *Using incentives to reinforce change* rather than to drive change.

Some of the levers for change have already been discussed in Chapter 11 in relation to the effects of changes in structures and control systems of organisations. Here other possible change levers are discussed. In so doing it is worth noting that many of these correspond to the elements of the cultural web. The implication is that the forces that act to embed and protect current ways of doing things might also provide bases for change.

14.4.1 Challenging the taken for granted

One of the major challenges in achieving strategic change can be the need to change often long-standing mindsets or taken-for-granted assumptions – the paradigm (see section 5.4.6). There are different views on how this might be achieved.

One view is that sufficient evidence, perhaps in the form of careful strategic analysis, will itself serve to challenge and therefore change the paradigm.

However, where long-standing assumptions have persisted, they will be very resistant to change. People find ways of questioning, reconfiguring and reinterpreting such analysis to bring it in line with the existing paradigm. It may take much persistence to overcome this. Others argue that such taken-for-grantedness can be challenged by surfacing it analytically and encouraging people to question and challenge each other's assumptions and the received wisdom.[23] The idea is that making visible such assumptions means that they are more likely to be questioned. Scenario planning (see section 2.2.2) is similarly advocated as a way of overcoming individual biases and cultural assumptions by getting people to see possible different futures and the implications for their organisations.[24]

Others argue that senior managers in particular are often too far removed from the realities of their organisations and need to be brought face to face with them. They may rarely speak to customers directly or experience themselves the services offered by their own firms. A senior executive of a rail company explained that in the past senior executives in the organisation had always travelled first class or by chauffeur-driven car. Hardly any of them had ever travelled in a crowded railway carriage. He introduced a policy that all senior executives should travel economy class wherever possible.

14.4.2 Changing operational processes and routines

In the end, strategies are delivered through day-to-day processes and routines of the operations of the organisation. These might be formalised and codified or they might be less formal 'ways we do things around here'[25] which tend to persist over time and guide people's behaviour. As has been seen in the discussion in Chapters 3 and 6, it may be that such routines can be the basis of the organisation's core competences and therefore its competitive advantage. However, they can also be serious blockages to change; as Dorothy Leonard-Barton[26] points out, they can become 'core rigidities'. The relationship between strategic change and day-to-day processes and routines is therefore important to consider in a number of respects:

- *Planning operational change.* The planning of the implementation of an intended strategy requires the identification of the key changes in the routines of the organisation required to deliver that strategy. In effect, strategic change needs to be considered in terms of the re-engineering of organisational processes.[27] For example, in Shell Lubricants till 2002 seven people were involved in different aspects of order processing routines. In the search for improved efficiency and customer service, one person was given overall responsibility for an order, with the consequent reduction in order time of 75 per cent, reduction in order processing costs of 45 per cent and vastly improved customer satisfaction.[28]

- *Challenging operational assumptions.* Changing organisational processes and routines may also have the effect of challenging the often taken-for-granted assumptions underpinning them. This can be important because it may have the effect of getting people to question and challenge deep-rooted beliefs and assumptions in the organisation. Richard Pascale argues: 'It is easier to act your way into a better way of thinking than to think your way into a better way of acting';[29] in other words, that it is easier to change behaviour and by so doing change taken-for-granted assumptions than to try to change taken-for-granted assumptions as a way of changing behaviour. If this is so, the style of change employed (see section 14.3.2) needs to take this into account: it suggests that education and communication to persuade people to change may be less powerful than involving people in the activities of changing.

- *Operational-led change*. Operational change may not simply be the outcome of planned strategic change; it could be that opportunities for operational change can stimulate innovation and new strategic thinking. Michael Hammer[30] argues that managers do not consider changes at the operational level sufficiently radically. Typically they benchmark best practice against industry standards rather than looking for best practice wherever it can be found (see section 3.6.3). He gives the example of Taco Bell in the USA, which saved costs and improved the quality of its offering by re-examining its operational processes in terms of best practice in manufacturing instead of fast food operations.

- *Bottom-up changes to routines*. Even when changes in routines are not planned from the top, people do change them and this may result in wider strategic change. Martha Feldman[31] shows that, even where there are formalised (she calls them 'ostensive') routines in organisations, they themselves change as a result of how people actually carry them out (which she calls 'performative routines'). So, over time, the 'performative' can change the 'ostensive'. Other research shows that this may also occur more proactively through the bending of routines. Managers may deliberately *bend the rules of the game*. This could give rise to resistance, but persistent bending may eventually achieve enough support from different stakeholders such that new routines become acceptable. When sufficient questioning of the status quo is achieved, change agents may actively *subvert* existing ways of doing things so as to make clear a fundamental change from the past. This could, for example, be an approach adopted by middle managers in seeking to carry with them both more senior managers and people who work for them, both of whom may be resistant to change. It is an incremental, experimental process that is likely to suffer setbacks and require persistence and political acumen.

The overall lesson is that changes in routines may appear to be mundane, but they can have significant impact. Illustration 14.4 gives some examples of changes in routines linked to strategic change.

14.4.3 Symbolic processes[32]

Change levers are not always of an overt, formal nature: they may also be symbolic in nature. Chapter 5 (section 5.4.6) explained how the symbols of an organisation may help preserve the paradigm. Here the concern is their role in managing change. **Symbols** are objects, events, acts or people that convey, maintain or create meaning over and above their functional purpose. They may be everyday things which are nevertheless especially meaningful in the context of a particular situation or organisation. (In this sense the organisational processes and routines discussed above are also symbolic in nature.) Changing

Symbols are objects, events, acts or people that convey, maintain or creati meaning over and above their functional purpose

Illustration 14.4

Changes in routines and symbols

Changes in organisational routines and symbols can be a powerful signal of and stimulus for change.

Changes in routines

- A drug can only be promoted on launch on the basis of claims substantiated by clinical data, so how pharmaceutical firms conduct clinical trials is strategically important. The traditional approach has been to base extensive data collection on a scientific research protocol and then to write a report explaining why all this data had been collected: a highly time-consuming and costly process. Some firms changed their procedures to ensure that scientific tests addressed regulatory and medical need. They created ideal claims statements and drafted the report they would need. Only then did they create research protocols and data collection forms, specifying the data required from the trials to support the claims.

- In a retail business with an espoused strategy of customer care, the chief executive, on visiting stores, tended to ignore staff and customers alike: he seemed to be interested only in the financial information in the store manager's office. He was unaware of this until it was pointed out; his change in behaviour afterwards, insisting on talking to staff and customers on his visits, became a 'story' which spread around the company, substantially supporting the strategic direction of the firms.

Language that challenges and questions

- A chief executive facing a crisis addressed his board: 'I suggest we think of ourselves like bulls facing a choice: the abattoir or the bull ring. I've made up my mind: what about you?'

- When the new management team (Gordon Bethune as Chief Executive and Greg Brennemaan as Chief Operating Officer) took over ailing Continental Airlines they chose their language carefully. The future winning orientation was made clear consistently. The overall strategy was referred to as the 'Go forward plan', the marketing plan was 'Fly to win' and the financial plan 'Fund the future'. It was language reinforced in how Brennemaan explained the determination to succeed: 'Did you know there

are no rear view mirrors on an airplane? The runway behind is irrelevant.'

Source: J.M. Higgins and C. McCallaster, 'If you want strategic change don't forget your cultural artefacts', *Journal of Change Management*, vol. 4, no. 1 (2004), pp. 63–73.

Physical objects as symbols of change

- In a textile firm equipment associated with 'old ways of doing things' was taken into a yard at the rear of the factory and smashed up in front of the workforce.

- The head nurse of a recovery unit for patients who had been severely ill decided that, if nurses wore everyday clothes rather than nurses' uniforms, it would signal to patients that they were on the road to recovery and a normal life; and to nurses that they were concerned with rehabilitation. However, the decision had other implications for the nurses too. It blurred the status distinction between nurses and other non-professional members of staff. Nurses preferred to wear their uniforms. Whilst they recognised that uniforms signalled a medically fragile role of patients, they reinforced their separate and professional status as acute care workers.

Source: M.G. Pratt and E. Rafaeli, 'Organisational dress as a symbol of multi-layered social idealities', *Academy of Management Journal*, vol. 40, no. 4 (1997), pp. 862–898.

Questions

For an organisation with which you are familiar:

1 Identify at least five important routines, symbols or rituals in the organisation.

2 In what way could they be changed to support a different strategy? Be explicit as to how the symbols might relate to the new strategy.

3 Why are these potential levers for change often ignored by change agents?

symbols can help reshape beliefs and expectations because meaning becomes apparent in the day-to-day experiences people have of organisations, such as the symbols that surround them (for example, office layout and decor), the type of language and technology used and organisational rituals. Consider some examples:

- Many *rituals*[33] of organisations are concerned with effecting or consolidating change. Exhibit 14.6 identifies and gives examples of such rituals and suggests what role they might play in change processes.[34] New rituals can be introduced or old rituals done away with as ways of signalling or reinforcing change.

- Changes in *physical aspects* of the work environment are powerful symbols of change. Typical here is a change of location for the head office, relocation of personnel, changes in dress or uniforms, and alterations to offices or office space.

- The *behaviour of change agents*, particularly strategic leaders, is perhaps the most powerful symbol in relation to change. So having made pronouncements about the need for change, it is vital that the visible behaviour of change agents is in line with such change.

- The *language* used by change agents is also important. Either consciously or unconsciously, change agents may employ language and metaphor to galvanise change. Of course, there is also the danger that change agents do not realise this and, whilst espousing change, use language that signals adherence to the status quo, or personal reluctance to change.

Exhibit 14.6 **Organisational rituals and culture change**

Types of ritual	Role	Examples
Rites of passage	Consolidate and promote social roles and interaction	Induction programmes Training programmes
Rites of enhancement	Recognise effort benefiting organisation Similarly motivate others	Awards ceremonies Promotions
Rites of renewal	Reassure that something is being done Focus attention on issues	Appointment of consultants Project teams
Rites of integration	Encourage shared commitment Reassert rightness of norms	Christmas parties
Rites of conflict reduction	Reduce conflict and aggression	Negotiating committees
Rites of degradation	Publicly acknowledge problems Dissolve/weaken social or political roles	Firing top executives Demotion or 'passing over'
Rites of sense making	Sharing of interpretations and sense making	Rumours Surveys to evaluate new practices
Rites of challenge	'Throwing down the gauntlet'	New CEO's different behaviour
Rites of counter-challenge	Resistance to new ways of doing things	Grumbling Working to rule

Illustration 14.4 also gives some examples of such symbolic signalling of change. However, there is an important qualification to the idea that the manipulation of symbols can be a useful lever for managing change. The significance and meaning of symbols are dependent on how they are interpreted. So a change agent's intentions in the use of symbolic levers may not be interpreted as intended (see the nursing example in Illustration 14.4). So, whilst symbolic changes are important, their impact is difficult to predict.

14.4.4 Power and political processes[35]

Chapter 4 discussed the importance of understanding the political context in and around the organisation. There is also a need to consider the management of strategic change within this political context. This can be important because it may be necessary to build a political context for change (see section 14.2.2). It may also be important because, to effect change, powerful support may be required from individuals or groups. This may be the chief executive, a powerful member of the board or an influential outsider. Or, in managing strategic change, a reconfiguration of *power structures* may be necessary, especially if transformational change is required. Exhibit 14.7 shows some of the mechanisms associated with managing change from a political perspective:

- *Acquiring resources* or being identified with important resource areas or areas of expertise. In particular the ability to withdraw or allocate such resources can be a valuable tool in overcoming resistance or persuading others to accept change or build readiness for change.

- *Association with powerful stakeholder groups (elites)*, or their supporters, can help build a power base. Similarly, association with a change agent who is respected or visibly successful can help a manager overcome resistance to change. Or a change agent facing resistance to change may seek out and win over someone highly respected from within the very group resistant to change. It may also be necessary to *remove individuals or groups* resistant to change. Who these are can vary – from powerful individuals in senior positions to whole layers of resistance, perhaps in the form of senior executives in a threatened function or service.

- *Building alliances* and *networks* of contacts and sympathisers may be important in overcoming the resistance of more powerful groups. Attempting to convert the whole organisation to an acceptance of change is difficult, but there may be parts of the organisation, or individuals in it, more sympathetic to change than others, with whom a change agent might build support. He or she may also seek to marginalise those who are resistant to change. However, the danger is that powerful groups in the organisation may regard the building of such a team, or acts of marginalisation, as a threat to their own power, leading to further resistance to change. An analysis of power and interest using the stakeholder mapping (section 4.4.1) can, therefore, be useful to identify bases of alliance and likely resistance.

- *Symbolic change* is, again, potentially important. To build power, it may be necessary to identify initially with the very *symbols* which preserve and reinforce the paradigm – to work within the committee structures, become

Exhibit 14.7	Political mechanisms in organisations

| | Mechanisms | | | | |
Activity areas	Resources	Elites	Subsystems	Symbolic	Key problems
Building the power base	Control of resources Acquisition of/identification with expertise Acquisition of additional resources	Sponsorship by an elite Association with an elite	Alliance building Team building	Building on legitimation	Time required for building Perceived duality of ideals Perceived as threat by existing elites
Overcoming resistance	Withdrawal of resources Use of 'counter-intelligence'	Breakdown or division of elites Association with change agent Association with respected outsider	Foster momentum for change Sponsorship/ reward of change agents	Attack or remove legitimation Foster confusion, conflict and questioning	Striking from too low a power base Potentially destructive: need for rapid rebuilding
Achieving compliance	Giving resources	Removal of resistant elites Need for visible 'change hero'	Partial implementation and collaboration Implantation of 'disciples' Support for 'Young Turks'	Applause/reward Reassurance Symbolic confirmation	Converting the body of the organisation Slipping back

identified with the organisational rituals or stories that exist, and so on. On the other hand, in breaking resistance to change, removing, challenging or changing rituals and symbols may be a very powerful means of achieving the questioning of what is taken for granted.

However, the political aspects of change management are also potentially hazardous. Exhibit 14.7 also summarises some of the problems. In overcoming resistance, the major problem may simply be the lack of power to undertake such activity. Trying to break down the status quo may become so destructive and take so long that the organisation cannot recover from it. If the process needs to take place, its replacement by some new set of beliefs and the implementation of a new strategy is vital and needs to be speedy. Further, as already identified, in implementing change, gaining the commitment of a few senior executives at the top of an organisation is one thing; it is quite another to convert the body of the organisation to an acceptance of significant change.

14.4.5 Change tactics

There are also more specific tactics of change which might be employed to facilitate the change process.

Timing

The importance of timing is often neglected in thinking about strategic change. But choosing the right time tactically to promote change is vital. For example:

- *Building on actual or perceived crisis* is especially useful the greater the degree of change needed. If there is a higher perceived risk in maintaining the status quo than in changing it, people are more likely to change. Indeed, it is said that some chief executives seek to elevate problems to achieve perceived crisis in order to galvanise change. For example, a threatened takeover may be used as a catalyst for strategic change.

- *Windows of opportunity* in change processes may exist. The arrival of a new chief executive, the introduction of a new, highly successful product, or the arrival of a major competitive threat on the scene may provide opportunities to make more significant changes than might normally be possible. Since change will be regarded nervously, it may also be important to choose the time for promoting such change to avoid unnecessary fear and nervousness. For example, if there is a need for the removal of executives, this may be best done before rather than during the change programme. In such a way, the change programme can be seen as a potential improvement for the future rather than as the cause of such losses.

- *The symbolic signalling of time frames* may be important. Change agents should avoid conflicting messages about the timing of change. For example, if rapid change is required, they should avoid the maintenance of procedures and signals that suggest long time horizons, such as maintaining long-established control and reward procedures or routines.

Visible short-term wins

A strategic change programme will require many detailed actions and tasks. It is important that some are seen to be successful quickly. This could take the form, for example, of a retail chain quickly developing a new store concept and demonstrating its success in the market; the effective breaking down of old ways of working and the demonstration of better ways; the speeding up of decisions by doing away with committees and introducing clearly defined job responsibilities; and so on. In themselves, these may not be especially significant aspects of a new strategy, but they may be visible indicators of a new approach associated with that strategy. The demonstration of such wins will therefore galvanise commitment to the strategy.

One reason given for the inability to change is that resources are not available to do so. This may be overcome if it is possible to identify 'hot spots' on which to focus resources and effort. For example, William Bratton, famously responsible for the Zero Tolerance policy of the New York Police Department, began by focusing resource and effort on narcotics-related crimes. Though associated with 50–70 per cent of all crimes, he found they only had 5 per cent of the resources allocated by NYPD to tackle them. Success in this field led to the roll-out of his policies into other areas and to gaining the resources to do so.[36]

14.5   MANAGING STRATEGIC CHANGE PROGRAMMES

There are then a variety of change levers that change agents may choose. Choosing the appropriate levers, rather than following a set formula for managing strategic change, is critically important. This will depend on the change context and the skills and styles of those managing change. For example, to take the extremes, if the need is to overcome resistance to achieve fast results, then the emphasis may have to be on achieving behavioural compliance to a change programme. On the other hand, if there is a need and the time to 'win hearts and minds' then there will need to be a focus on changing people's values and a much greater emphasis on their involvement in changing the culture of the organisation as Illustration 14.5 shows. However, it is likely that there will be, none the less, elements of both 'theory E' and 'theory O' in most change initiatives. Indeed, most successful change initiatives rely on multiple levers for change,[37] again as shown in Illustration 14.5.

This section first revisits three types of change identified in section 14.2.1 to consider which levers managers use in which contexts. It then suggests some general lessons about managing change programmes.

14.5.1   Strategy reconstruction and turnaround strategy

In a **turnaround strategy** the emphasis is on speed of change and rapid cost reduction and/or revenue generation

There are circumstances where the emphasis has to be on rapid reconstruction, in the absence of which a business could face closure, enter terminal decline or be taken over. This is commonly referred to as a **turnaround strategy**, where the emphasis is on speed of change and rapid cost reduction and/or revenue generation, and managers need to prioritise the things that give quick and significant improvements. Typically it is a situation where a directive approach to change (see section 14.3.1) is required. Some of the main elements of turnaround strategies are as follows:[38]

- *Crisis stabilisation*. The aim here is to regain control over the deteriorating position. This requires a short-term focus on cost reduction and/or revenue increase, typically involving some of the steps identified in Exhibit 14.8. There is nothing novel about these steps: many of them are good management practice. The differences are the speed at which they are carried out and the focus of managerial attention on them. The most successful turnaround strategies also focus on reducing direct operational costs and on productivity gains. Less effective approaches pay less attention to these and more on the reduction of overheads.[39]

  However, too often turnarounds are seen as no more than cost-cutting exercises when a wider alignment between causes of decline and solutions may be important. For example, where the business decline is principally a result of changes in the external environment it may be folly to expect that cost cutting alone can lead to renewed growth. Other elements of turnaround strategies are therefore important.

- *Management changes*. Changes in management may be required, especially at the top. This usually includes the introduction of a new chairman/woman or chief executive, as well as changes in the board, especially in marketing, sales

Illustration 14.5

ValuesJam at IBM

Changing strategy by 'values-based management'.

Sam Palmisano took over as Chief Executive of IBM in 2002 as successor to Lou Gerstner who was credited with the turnaround of IBM in the 1990s. Palmisano's challenge was very different from the challenge that faced Gerstner. As he explained, then there was 'a burning platform; in fact the whole place was in flames'. Now there was a need for a continuation of change but no burning platform: 'instead of galvanising people through fear of failure, you have to galvanise them through hope and aspiration.' Palmisano's answer to this was 'values-based management'. He believed it was impossible to manage a company as complex as IBM operating in 170 countries with almost 70 major product lines and dozens of customer segments by relying on structures and control systems. It had to be through values. But how to identify the core values and get people not only to believe them but to live them?

Palmisano's answer was based on a bottom-up reinvention of the values of IBM. In July 2003 over a three-day period over 50,000 employees took part in an intranet discussion on company values: the 'ValuesJam' (see Illustration 15.2). Much of what was posted was highly critical. IBM talked a lot about trust but spent endless time auditing people; no one questioned the views of senior executives; mistakes were not tolerated or seen as part of learning. It was uncomfortable criticism and some senior executives wanted to pull the plug on the exercise. But Palmisano not only insisted it continue, he joined in, posting his personal views and acknowledging problems.

The comments from ValuesJam were analysed and values statements produced: 'dedication to every client's success', 'innovation that matters – for our company and the world', 'trust and personal responsibility in all relationships'. As Palmisano observed, in many respects these values extended what IBM had already espoused in the past. The important point was that they were not being enacted. So the next step was to charge people with identifying where the values were not being delivered. This started with top management but was quickly rolled out to an online jam (see Illustration 15.2 also) for employees again. They identified example after example of IBM processes and routines which were contrary to the values.

Palmisano then turned his attention to instigating changes in those routines to bring them in line with the values. He changed the incentive scheme for managing directors of IBM businesses. This was already based on how clients scored their performance, but within a single year. It was changed to be based on a mix of a project profitability, annual targets and client satisfaction over the long term, not just a single year. Other changes appeared to be small scale: for example, the allocation of $5,000 (£2,800; €4,000) annually to line managers to use at their own discretion to generate business or develop client relationships – but multiplied by 22,000 managers across IBM, a significant commitment. Another example was pricing. Price setting in IBM was not client-friendly, especially if it involved products and services crossing IBM businesses. Palmisano insisted that the process be changed so that prices were delivered to the client seamlessly. This involved significant reworking of the IBM pricing routines to deliver what the clients were looking for.

Source: Based on Paul Hemp, 'Leading change when business is good', *Harvard Business Review*, vol. 82, no. 12 (2004), pp. 60–70.

Questions

1 Which levers for change described in the chapter are evident? Which others might have been used?

2 Compare Palmisano's approach to that of John Howie's at Faslane (see the case example).

3 Compare this values-based approach to a programme of revolutionary change or reconstruction.

Exhibit 14.8   Turnaround: revenue generation and cost reduction steps

Increasing revenue	Reducing costs
● Ensure marketing mix tailored to key market segments	● Reduce labour costs and costs of senior management
● Review pricing strategy to maximise revenue	● Focus on productivity improvement
● Focus organisational activities on needs of target market sector customers	● Reduce marketing costs not focused on target market
● Exploit additional opportunities for revenue creation related to target market	● Tighten financial controls
● Invest funds from reduction of costs in new growth areas	● Tighten control on cash expenses
	● Establish competitive bidding for suppliers; defer creditor payments; speed up debtor payments
	● Reduce inventory
	● Eliminate non-profitable products/services

and finance, for three main reasons. First, because the old management may well be the ones that were in charge when the problems developed and be seen as the cause of them by key stakeholders. Second, because it may be necessary to bring in managers with experience of turnaround management. Third, because, if new managers come from outside the organisation, they may bring different approaches to the way the organisation has operated in the past.

● *Gaining stakeholder support.* Poor quality of information may have been provided to key stakeholders. In a turnaround situation it is vital that key stakeholders, perhaps the bank or key shareholder groups, and employees are kept clearly informed of the situation and improvements as they are being made.[40] It is also likely that a clear assessment of the power of different stakeholder groups (see section 4.4.1) will become vitally important in managing turnaround.

● *Clarifying the target market(s).* Central to turnaround success is ensuring clarity on the target market or market segments most likely to generate cash and grow profits. A successful turnaround strategy involves getting closer to customers and improving the flow of marketing information, especially to senior levels of management, so as to focus revenue-generating activities on key market segments. Indeed, a reason for the poor performance of the organisation could be because it had this wrong in the first place.

● *Refocusing.* Clarifying the target market also provides the opportunity to discontinue or outsource products and services that are not targeted on those markets, eating up management time for little return or not making sufficient financial contribution.

● *Financial restructuring.* The financial structure of the organisation may need to be changed. This typically involves changing the existing capital structure, raising additional finance or renegotiating agreements with creditors, especially banks.

● *Prioritisation of critical improvement areas*. All of this requires the ability of management to prioritise those things that give quick and significant improvements.

14.5.2 Managing revolutionary strategic change

Revolutionary change differs from reconstruction in two ways that make managing change especially challenging. First, the need is for not only fast change but also cultural change. Second, it may be that the need for change is not as evident to people in the organisation as in a turnaround situation, or that they see reasons to deny the need for change. This situation may have come about as a result of many years of relative decline in a market, with people wedded to products or processes no longer valued by customers – the problem of strategic drift. Or it could be that the problems of the organisation are visible and understood by its members, but that people cannot see a way forward. Managing such change is likely to involve:

● *Clear strategic direction*. In these circumstances the need for the articulation of a clear strategic direction and decisive action in line with that direction are critical. So this is the type of change where individual CEOs who are seen to provide such direction are often credited with making a major difference. They may well also become the symbol of such change, within an organisation and externally.

● *Combining economic and symbolic levers*. Very likely some of the hard decisions outlined above for reconstruction (or turnaround) will be taken: for example, portfolio changes, greater market focus, top management changes and perhaps financial restructuring. However, often these are also employed to send major symbolic messages of change. In the newspaper industry, for example, Rupert Murdoch's decision in the 1970s to close his newspapers' offices in Fleet Street and move to purpose-built modern premises in Wapping is still regarded as the single most significant event in modernising not only his business, but the industry.

● *An outside perspective*. The introduction of new managers, often at a senior level, with different perspectives is common. For example, the reform of public sector organisations has seen the introduction of managers with private sector experience. Consultants may also be used to provide a dispassionate analysis of the need for change or facilitate the change process.

● *Multiple styles of change management*. Whilst a *directive style* of change management is likely to be evident, this may need to be accompanied by other styles. It may be supported by determined efforts to *educate* about the need for change and the use of an *intervention style* to involve people in aspects of change in which they have specific expertise or to overcome their resistance to change.

● *Working with the existing culture*. It may be possible to work with elements of the existing culture rather than attempt wholesale culture change. This involves identifying those aspects of culture that can be built upon and developed and those that have to be changed – in effect a forcefield approach (see section 14.2.4). For example, when Ed Zander became CEO at the ailing

Motorola in 2004 he built a change programme that emphasised much more innovation and market refocusing around the long-established values of quality and reliability.[41]

● *Monitoring change*. Revolutionary change is likely to require the setting and monitoring of unambiguous targets that people have to achieve. Often these will be linked to overall financial targets and in turn to improved returns to shareholders.

14.5.3 Managing evolutionary strategic change

Managing change as evolution involves transformational change, but incrementally. It can be thought of in two ways. The first is in terms of the creation of an organisation capable of continual change: of a learning organisation. The characteristics of this were described in section 11.5.2 and insights into how this might be achieved are best described in the ideas lens in the commentaries. Trying to achieve this in practice is a significant challenge for management, not least because it requires:

● *Empowering the organisation*. Rather than top-down management, there is the need here for people throughout the organisation to accept the responsibility for contributing strategic ideas, for innovating, and for accepting change as inevitable and desirable. Clearly, then, there is a need for a high level of participation in the change agenda.

● *A clear strategic vision*. It is the responsibility of top management to create the context within which new ideas can bubble up from below around a coherent view of long-term goals. This requires them to provide very clear guidelines – vision, mission or 'simple rules' – around which those ideas can cohere. In so doing, they need to find the balance between the clarity of such vision that allows people to see how they can contribute to future strategy whilst avoiding specifying that strategy in such detail as to constrain people's enthusiasm to contribute and innovate. (See the discussion on the ideas lens in the commentaries.)

● *Continual change and a commitment to experimentation* with regard to organisational processes throughout the organisation.

The second way of conceiving of strategic change as evolution is in terms of the movement from one strategy to a changed strategy but over time, perhaps many years. Here the principles that might guide managers are these:

● *Stages of transition*. Identifying interim stages in the change process is important. For example, in terms of the change context (see section 14.2.2) there may be insufficient readiness or an insufficient capacity to make major changes initially. It will therefore be important to establish these conditions before other major moves are taken.

● *Irreversible changes*. It may be possible to identify changes that can be made that, whilst not necessarily having immediate major impact, will have long-term and irreversible impacts. For example, in the early 1990s when KPMG was conceiving of the sort of strategy it needed into the new millennium, it established new criteria for the recruitment of university graduates and appointment to partnership. The time horizons for the effects of such changes to take effect were five to ten years. However, once made, the effects could not be reversed.

● *Sustained top management commitment*. The danger is that the momentum for change falters because people do not perceive consistent commitment to it from the top.

● *Winning hearts and minds*. Culture change is likely to be required in any transformational change. This may be more problematic than for revolutionary change because people may simply not recognise that there are problems with regard to the status quo. The need is for multiple levers for change to be used consistently: education and participation as styles of managing change to allow people to see the need for change and contribute to what that change should be; the signalling of the meaning of change in ways that people throughout the organisation understand both rationally and emotionally; and levers that signal and achieve improved economic performance.

14.5.4 Some overall lessons on the management of change programmes

This section draws together some of the overall lessons about the management of change programmes. First, there are lessons from understanding what can go wrong:[42]

● *Programme overload*. Change agents may recognise that change is not a one-off process; that it might require an ongoing series of initiatives, maybe over years. However, the risk is that these initiatives are seen by others as 'change rituals' signifying very little. There is also the risk that the original intention of the change programme becomes eroded by other events taking place, for example a redundancy programme.

● *Hijacked processes*. Well-meaning change efforts can be hijacked by others for different purposes. For example, in an insurance firm, the introduction of computerised telephone systems to improve customer service became a vehicle for reducing the number of personnel dealing with customer enquiries. The result was no improvement in service and a workforce highly sceptical about that and future change initiatives.

● *Reinvention*. Here the attempted change becomes reinterpreted according to the old culture. For example, an engineering company's intended strategy of adding value in customer terms was interpreted by the engineers within the firm as providing high levels of technical specification.

● *Disconnectedness*. People affected by change may not see the change programme connecting to their reality. Senior executives, as proponents of the change, might not be seen to be credible in terms of understanding the realities of change on the ground. Or perhaps new systems and initiatives introduced are seen as out of line with the intentions of the intended change.

● *Behavioural compliance*. There is the danger that people appear to comply with the changes being pursued in the change programme without actually 'buying into' them. Change agents may think they see change occurring, when all they see is superficial compliance.

Since 1994 the Boston Consulting Group[43] has used four key factors in managing strategic change programmes and the change teams associated with them. It claims the likelihood of success of such programmes is greatly increased if the following is in place:

- *Milestones for reviewing progress*. Change programmes should be formally reviewed by senior management at least bi-monthly against key tasks that need to be completed. The criteria against which such reviews will take place also need to be explicit and widely known.[44]

- *A high-'integrity' change team*, by which it means a team that have the skills, checked through the regular reviews, to execute the change programme. The selection of such a team, with the required mix of skills, is a key responsibility of senior management.

- *Visible commitment to change* by top management and consistency in how the change is explained. This needs to be accompanied by 'straight talking' about change with those who will be affected.

- *Time and effort for managing change*, which are needed by the change team responsible. It is the responsibility of top management to make sure they have sufficient time and resource to carry out their tasks.

Many of the problems and challenges of managing strategic change are reflected in Illustration 14.6, the key debate for this chapter.

SUMMARY

www.pearsoned.co.uk/ecs
AUDIO SUMMARY

A recurrent theme in this chapter has been that approaches, styles and means of change need to be tailored to the context of that change. Bearing in mind this general point, this chapter has emphasised a number of key points:

- There are different *types of strategic change* which can be thought of in terms of the *extent* of culture change required and its *nature* – whether it can be achieved through incremental change or requires urgent action (the 'big bang' approach). Different approaches and means of managing change are likely to be required for different types of change.

- It is also important to diagnose wider aspects of organisational context such as *resources and skills that need to be preserved*, the degree of *homogeneity or diversity* in the organisation, the *capability, capacity and readiness* for change and the *power* to make change happen.

- The *cultural web* and *forcefield analysis* are useful as means of identifying blockages to change and potential levers for change.

- Change agents may need to adopt different *styles* of managing strategic change according to different contexts and in relation to the involvement and interest of different groups.

- *Levers for managing strategic change* need to be considered in terms of the type of change and context of change. Such levers include surfacing and *challenging the taken for granted*, the need to change *operational processes, routines* and *symbols*, the importance of *political processes*, and other change *tactics*.

Illustration 14.6

key debate

The management of change from top to bottom

Strategic change has always been seen as the responsibility of top management: but to what extent can top managers manage change?

John Kotter, one of the world's foremost authorities on leadership and change, argues that problems of strategic change arise because top executives fail to take the necessary steps to manage such changes. These include:

- Establishing a sense of urgency on the basis of market threats or opportunities.

- Forming a powerful coalition of stakeholders for change.

- Creating and communicating a clear vision and strategy to direct the change and ensuring that the behaviour of the guiding coalition is in line with the vision.

- Removing obstacles to change, changing systems that undermine the vision and encouraging non-traditional ideas and activities.

- Creating short-term wins.

- Consolidating improvements but also continuing the process of change.

However, Julia Balogun studied a top management change initiative from the point of view of how middle managers interpreted it. She found that, whilst top managers believed they were being clear about the intended strategy, change actually took place by middle managers making sense of change initiatives in terms of their own *mental models* in relation to their *local responsibilities and conditions*, through discussion with their peers and on the basis of rumour. Top managers were inevitably too far removed from these dynamics and could not be expected to understand them in detail or intervene in specific ways. She argues that 'Senior managers can initiate and influence direction of change but not direct change.' They can:

- Monitor how people respond to change initiatives.

- Engage as much as possible with how people make sense of change and work with their reality, responding to their issues and interpretations.

- Live the changes they want others to adopt, especially avoiding inconsistencies between their actions, words and deeds.

- Focus on creating the understanding of higher-level principles rather than the details.

Hari Tsoukas and Robert Chia go further. They argue that change is an inherent property of organisations. Hierarchy and management control dampen that inherent change.

Change programmes trigger ongoing change: they provide the discursive resources for making certain things possible, although what exactly will happen remains uncertain when a change programme is initiated. It must first be experienced before the possibilities it opens up are appreciated and taken up (if they are taken up). Change programmes are . . . locally adapted, improvised and elaborated. . . . If this is accepted what is, then, the meaning of 'planned change'? . . . Change has been taken to mean that which occurs as a consequence of deliberate managerial action. In the view put forward here such a definition is limited. Although managers certainly aim at achieving established ways of thinking and acting through implementing particular plans, nonetheless, change in organisations occurs without necessarily intentional managerial action as a result of individuals trying to accommodate new experience and realise new possibilities. In the view suggested here, an excessive preoccupation with planned change risks failing to recognise the always ready changing texture of organisations. (pp. 578–579)

Sources: J. Kotter, 'Leading change: why transformation efforts fail', *Harvard Business Review*, March–April (1995), pp. 59–67; J. Balogun and G. Johnson, 'Organizational restructuring and middle manager sensemaking', *Academy of Management Journal*, vol. 47, no. 4 (2004), pp. 523–549; J. Balogun, 'Managing change: steering a course between intended strategies and unanticipated outcomes', *Long Range Planning*, vol. 39 (2006), pp. 29–49; H. Tsoukas and R. Chia, 'On organizational becoming: rethinking organizational change', *Organization Science*, vol. 13, no. 5 (2002), pp. 567–582.

Questions

1 What are the problems associated with top-down or bottom-up views of change management?

2 If your were a senior executive which approach would you take and in what circumstances?

3 Are the different views irreconcilable?

(You will find the perspectives on the management of strategy in the commentaries useful background reading.)

Work assignments

*Denotes more advanced work assignments.   * Refers to a case study in the Text and Cases edition.*

14.1 Drawing on section 14.2.2 assess the key contextual dimensions of an organisation (such as for the case example on Faslane) and consider how they should influence the design of a programme of strategic change.

14.2 ✷ Draw up a cultural web and use forcefield analysis to identify blockages and facilitators of change for an organisation (such as one for which you have considered the need for a change in strategic direction in a previous assignment). Redraw the web to represent what the organisation should aspire to given the new strategy. Using the cultural webs and forcefield analysis, identify what aspects of the changes can be managed by a change agent and how.

14.3 Compare and contrast the different styles of managing change of executives you have read about in the press or in this book (for example, John Howie at Faslane, Fergus Chambers at Direct and Care* and Stuart Rose at M&S*).

14.4 ✷ Consider a process of strategic change that you have been involved in or have observed. Map out the steps in the change process in the following terms: new rituals introduced or old rituals done away with, and the impact of these changes.

14.5 ✷ In the context of managing strategic change in a large corporation or public sector organisation, to what extent, and why, do you agree with Richard Pascale's argument that it is easier to act ourselves into a better way of thinking than it is to think ourselves into a better way of acting? (References 29 to 34 will be useful here.)

14.6 ✷ There are a number of books by renowned senior executives who have managed major changes in their organisation. Read one of these and note the levers and mechanisms for change employed by the change agent, using the approaches outlined in this chapter as a checklist. How effective do you think these were in the context that the change agent faced, and could other mechanisms have been used?

Integrative assignments

14.7 ✷ What would be the key issues for the corporate parent of a diversified organisation with a multidomestic international strategy (see Chapter 8) wishing to change to a more related portfolio? Consider this in terms of (a) the strategic capabilities that the parent might require (Chapters 3 and 7), (b) the implications for organising and controlling its subsidiaries (Chapter 12), (c) the likely blockages to such change and (d) how these might be overcome (Chapter 14).

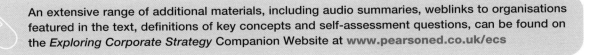

An extensive range of additional materials, including audio summaries, weblinks to organisations featured in the text, definitions of key concepts and self-assessment questions, can be found on the *Exploring Corporate Strategy* Companion Website at **www.pearsoned.co.uk/ecs**

Recommended key readings

- J. Balogun, V. Hope Hailey (with G. Johnson and K. Scholes), *Exploring Strategic Change*, 3rd edition, Prentice Hall, 2007, builds on and extends many of the ideas in this chapter. In particular, it emphasises the importance of tailoring change programmes to organisational context and discusses more fully many of the change levers reviewed in this chapter.

- The paper by John Kotter, 'Leading change: why transformation efforts fail', *Harvard Business Review*, March–April (1995), pp. 59–67 (also see Illustration 14.6), provides a useful view of what a change programme might look like. An alternative but complementary perspective is provided by Julia Balogun, 'Managing change: steering a course between intended strategies and unanticipated outcomes', *Long Range Planning*, vol. 39 (2006), pp. 29–49.

- For an understanding of different approaches to managing change: M. Beer and N. Nohria,

'Cracking the code of change', *Harvard Business Review*, vol. 78, no. 3 (May–June 2000), pp. 133–141.

- Martha Feldman has written about how organisational routines may play a role in creating organisational inertia, but may also help explain organisational change. See M. Feldman, 'Resources in emerging structures and processes of change', *Organization Science,* vol. 15, no. 3 (2004), pp. 295–309; and M. Feldman and B. Pentland, 'Reconceptualizing organizational routines as a source of flexibility and change, *Administrative Science Quarterly*, vol. 48, no. 1 (2003), pp. 94–118.

- The study of change programmes by L.C. Harris and E. Ogbonna, 'The unintended consequences of culture interventions: a study of unexpected outcomes', *British Journal of Management*, vol. 13, no. 1 (2002), pp. 31–49, provides a valuable insight into the problems of managing change in organisations.

References

1. Many books and papers on strategic change build on the idea that the current state of the organisation is likely to be one of inertia or resistance to change, and that there is, then, a need to 'unfreeze' this situation. The dominance of this idea can be traced back to the work of K. Lewin; see 'Group decision and social change', in E.E. Maccoby, T.M. Newcomb and E.I. Hartley (eds), *Readings in Social Psychology*, Holt, Reinhart and Winston, 1958, pp. 197–211.

2. *Exploring Strategic Change* by J. Balogun and V. Hope Hailey, 3rd edition, Prentice Hall, 2007, is a sister text to this book; this part of the chapter draws on their chapter 3 on the context of strategic change.

3. For a discussion of the problems of importing change programmes from the private sector to the public sector, see F. Ostroff, 'Change management in government', *Harvard Business Review*, vol. 84, no. 5 (May 2006), pp. 141–147.

4. Based on D. Neal and T. Taylor, 'Spinning on dimes: the challenges of introducing transformational change into the UK Ministry of Defence', *Strategic Change*, vol. 15 (2006), pp. 15–22.

5. For an interesting example of how different contexts affect receptivity to change, see J. Newton, J. Graham, K. McLoughlin and A. Moore, 'Receptivity to change in a general medical practice', *British Journal of Management*, vol. 14, no. 2 (2003), pp. 143–153.

6. Prior experience of change is one of the key success factors in change highlighted by S. Miller, D. Wilson and D. Hickson, 'Beyond planning strategies for successfully implementing strategic change', *Long Range Planning*, vol. 37, no. 3 (2004), pp. 201–218.

7. The extent of readiness for change is another factor highlighted by Miller *et al.*; see reference 6.

8. See J.-L. Denis, L. Lamothe and A. Langley, 'The dynamics of collective change leadership and strategic change in pluralistic organizations', *Academy of Management Journal*, vol. 44, no. 4 (2001), pp. 809–837.

9. Approaches to how to use the cultural web for the purposes outlined here are dealt with in detail in the chapter, 'Mapping and re-mapping organisational culture', in V. Ambrosini with G. Johnson and K. Scholes (eds), *Exploring Techniques of Analysis and Evaluation in Strategic Management*, Prentice Hall, 1998, and the similar chapter in G. Johnson and K. Scholes (eds), *Exploring Public Sector Strategy*, Prentice Hall, 2000.

10. Indeed John Kotter defines leadership as being about the management of change: see J. Kotter, 'What leaders really do', *Harvard Business Review*, December (2001), pp. 85–96.

11. This definition of leadership is based on that offered by R.M. Stodgill, 'Leadership, membership and organization', *Psychological Bulletin*, vol. 47 (1950), pp. 1–14. For a more recent and more comprehensive discussion of leadership, see G.A. Yukl, *Leadership in Organizations*, 6th edition, Prentice Hall, 2005.

12. For this evidence see D.A. Waldman, G.G. Ramirez, R.J. House and P. Puranam, 'Does leadership matter? CEO leadership attributes and profitability under conditions of perceived environmental uncertainty', *Academy of Management Journal*, vol. 44, no. 1 (2001), pp. 134–143.

13. For fuller explanations of the distinction between charismatic and instrumental and transactional leadership see M.F.R. Kets de Vries, 'The leadership mystique',

Academy of Management Executive, vol. 8, no. 3 (1994), pp. 73–89, and the paper by Waldman *et al.*, reference 12.

14. The discussion on different approaches of strategic leaders and evidence for the effectiveness of the adoption of different approaches can be found in D. Goleman, 'Leadership that gets results', *Harvard Business Review*, vol. 78, no. 2 (March–April 2000), pp. 78–90; and C.M. Farkas and S. Wetlaufer, 'The ways chief executive officers lead', *Harvard Business Review*, vol. 74, no. 3 (May–June 1996), pp. 110–112.

15. A study that tracked successful leaders from one company who took up leadership positions in other companies found that many did not readily transfer to the new context. See B. Groysberg, A.N. McLean and N. Nohria, 'Are leaders portable?', *Harvard Business Review*, May (2006), pp. 92–100.

16. See S. Floyd and W. Wooldridge, *The Strategic Middle Manager: How to create and sustain competitive advantage*, Jossey-Bass, 1996.

17. See for example J. Balogun and G. Johnson, 'Organizational restructuring and middle manager sensemaking', *Academy of Management Journal*, vol. 47, no. 4 (2004), pp. 523–549; J. Balogun, 'Managing change: steering a course between intended strategies and unanticipated outcomes', *Long Range Planning*, vol. 39 (2006), pp. 29–49; J. Sillence and F. Mueller, 'Switching strategic perspective: the reframing of accounts of responsibility', *Organization Studies*, vol. 28, no. 2 (2007), pp. 155–176.

18. Different authors explain change styles in different ways. This section is based on the typologies used by J. Balogun and V. Hope Haley (see reference 2, section 2.4, pp. 31–36) and D. Dunphy and D. Stace, 'The strategic management of corporate change', *Human Relations*, vol. 46, no. 8 (1993), pp. 905–920. For an alternative framework see R. Caldwell, 'Models of change agency: a fourfold classification', *British Journal of Management*, vol. 14, no. 2 (2003), pp. 131–142.

19. For evidence of the effects of involvement in the strategy development process see N. Collier, F. Fishwick and S.W. Floyd, 'Managerial involvement and perceptions of strategy process', *Long Range Planning*, vol. 37, no. 1 (2004), pp. 67–83.

20. The intervention style is discussed more fully in P.C. Nutt, 'Identifying and appraising how managers install strategy', *Strategic Management Journal*, vol. 8, no. 1 (1987), pp. 1–14.

21. Evidence for this is provided by Dunphy and Stace, reference 18; see also Collier *et al.*, reference 19.

22. See M. Beer and N. Nohria, 'Cracking the code of change', *Harvard Business Review*, vol. 78, no. 3 (May–June 2000), pp. 133–141.

23. For an example of this approach see J.M. Mezias, P. Grinyer and W.D. Guth, 'Changing collective cognition: a process model for strategic change', *Long Range Planning*, vol. 34, no. 1 (2001), pp. 71–95. Also, for a systematic approach to strategy making and change based on such surfacing, see F. Ackermann and C. Eden with I. Brown, *The Practice of Making Strategy*, Sage, 2005.

24. For a discussion of the psychological context, thinking flaws, and the impact that these have for managers as they consider the future, see K. van der Heijden, R. Bradfield, G. Burt, G. Cairns and G. Wright, *The Sixth Sense: Accelerating organisational learning with scenarios*, Wiley, 2002, chapter 2.

25. T. Deal and A. Kennedy refer to 'the way we do things around here', in *Corporate Cultures: The rights and rituals of corporate life*, Addison-Wesley, 1984. Routines have, however, also become the focus of much discussion by researchers who take a resource-based view (see Chapter 3) because they are, arguably, the bases of organisational competences. See, for example, A.M. Knott, 'The organizational routines factor market paradox', *Strategic Management Journal*, vol. 24, no. 10 (2003), pp. 929–943.

26. For a full explanation of 'core rigidities' see D. Leonard-Barton, 'Core capabilities and core rigidities: a paradox in managing new product development', *Strategic Management Journal*, vol. 13, no. 5 (Summer 1992), pp. 111–125.

27. See M. Hammer and J. Champy, *Reengineering the Corporation: A manifesto for business revolution*, Harper Collins, 2004.

28. This example is given by Michael Hammer in 'Deep change: how operational innovation can transform your company', *Harvard Business Review*, vol. 82, no. 4 (April 2004), pp. 84–93.

29. This quote is on p. 135 of R. Pascale, M. Millemann and L. Gioja, 'Changing the way we change', *Harvard Business Review*, vol. 75, no. 6 (November–December 1997), pp. 126–139.

30. See reference 27.

31. Martha Feldman has written a number of papers about the relationship between routines and change. For example, see M. Feldman, 'Resources in emerging structures and processes of change', *Organization Science*, vol. 15, no. 3 (2004), pp. 295–309; and M. Feldman, and B. Pentland, 'Reconceptualizing organizational routines as a source of flexibility and change', *Administrative Science Quarterly*, vol. 48, no. 1 (2003), pp. 94–118.

32. For a fuller discussion of this theme, see G. Johnson, 'Managing strategic change: the role of symbolic action', *British Journal of Management*, vol. 1, no. 4 (1990), pp. 183–200. Also see J.M. Higgins and C. McCallaster, 'If you want strategic change don't forget your cultural artefacts', *Journal of Change Management*, vol. 4, no. 1 (2004), pp. 63–73.

33. For a discussion of the role of rituals in change, see D. Sims, S. Fineman and Y. Gabriel, *Organizing and Organizations: An introduction*, Sage, 1993.

34. See H.M. Trice and J.M. Beyer, 'Studying organisational cultures through rites and ceremonials', *Academy of Management Review*, vol. 9, no. 4 (1984), pp. 653–669; H.M. Trice and J.M. Beyer, 'Using six organisational rites to change culture', in R.H. Kilman, M.J. Saxton, R. Serpa and associates (eds), *Gaining Control of the Corporate Culture*, Jossey-Bass, 1985.

35. This discussion is based on observations of the role of political activities in organisations by, in particular, H. Mintzberg, *Power in and around Organisations*, Prentice Hall, 1983, and J. Pfeffer, *Power in Organisations*, Pitman, 1981. However, perhaps the most interesting book on political management remains Niccolo Machiavelli's sixteenth-century work, *The Prince* (available in Penguin Books, 2003). It is also the basis of a management book by Gerald Griffin, *Machiavelli on Management: Playing and winning the corporate power game*, Praeger, 1991.

36. For a fuller discussion of this approach by Bratton and other change agents, see W.C. Kim and R. Mauborgne,

'Tipping point leadership', *Harvard Business Review*, vol. 81, no. 4 (April 2003), pp. 60–69.

37. For a review of research that makes this point see D. Buchanan, L. Fitzgerald, D. Ketley, R. Gallop, J.L. Jones, S.S. Lamont, A. Neath and E. Whitby, 'No going back: a review of the literature on sustaining organizational change', *International Journal of Management Reviews*, vol. 7, no. 3 (2005), pp. 189–205.

38. Turnaround strategy is more extensively explained in D. Lovett and S. Slatter, *Corporate Turnaround*, Penguin Books, 1999; and P. Grinyer, D. Mayes and P. McKiernan, 'The Sharpbenders: achieving a sustained improvement in performance', *Long Range Planning*, vol. 23, no. 1 (1990), pp. 116–125. Also see V.L. Barker and I.M. Duhaime, 'Strategic change in the turnaround process: theory and empirical evidence', *Strategic Management Journal*, vol. 18, no. 1 (1997), pp. 13–38.

39. See the 'Sharpbenders' study, reference 38.

40. See K. Pajunen, 'Stakeholder influences in organizational survival', *Journal of Management Studies*, vol. 43, no. 6 (2006), pp. 1261–1288.

41. The value of working with aspects of the existing culture is a finding from the research of S. Finkelstein, C. Harvey and T. Lawton, documented in *Breakout Strategy*, McGraw-Hill, 2007.

42. The observations and examples here are largely based on L.C. Harris and E. Ogbonna, 'The unintended consequences of culture interventions: a study of unexpected outcomes', *British Journal of Management*, vol. 13, no. 1 (2002), pp. 31–49.

43. See H.L. Sirkin, P. Keenan and A. Jackson, 'The hard side of change management', *Harvard Business Review*, vol. 83, no. 10 (October 2005), pp. 109–118.

44. The monitoring of change programmes is discussed more fully in L. Gratton, V. Hope Hailey, P. Stiles and C. Truss, *Strategic Human Resource Management*, Oxford University Press, 1999.

Managing change at Faslane

Just 30 miles (48 km) west of Glasgow is HM Naval Base Clyde (Faslane), the home of the UK's nuclear submarines that carry the Trident weapon system. It is a Ministry of Defence (MOD) installation, but managed by private sector Babcock Naval Services (BNS), part of Babcock International. In 2006 John Howie, the Managing Director, was interviewed about the BNS change programme at Faslane.

John Howie's office overlooks the Gareloch on which the naval base is situated and where the ships and submarines are maintained. To the right are the berths for the Trident submarines, each 148 metres long, and the huge shiplift, a covered facility capable of lifting the 16,000 tonne submarines out of the water for maintenance. To the left are the base's offices, installations and accommodation for the sailors when they are not at sea. To the back of the offices are the barbed wire and heavily guarded perimeter fence. Over the peninsular is Coulport, also part of the base, where nuclear warheads are processed and loaded onto submarines.

John, how did BNS get involved at Faslane?

Faslane had been run entirely by the MOD and the Royal Navy. However, by 2000 the MOD had decided they needed to significantly reduce the cost and improve operational effectiveness of their naval bases and that in-house MOD management would find that difficult given the restrictions they operated under as part of a wider civil service. So they established partnering arrangements with industrial firms. By May 2002 we had signed a contract for a five year period to deliver £76 million [€110m; $136m] of cost savings without affecting the service provided to the Navy. A percentage of that saving would come to us as profit; the bulk would go to the customer as a cost reduction. Our profit was entirely a share of the savings, so no cost reduction, no profit; but the contract made sure we couldn't do that by prejudicing service levels.

From September 2002 over 1,700 civil service posts and nearly 300 Royal Navy personnel and civil servants were seconded to us. Overnight BNS went from being a company with 20 employees to 2,000. In addition there remained 1,000 other civil servants on site, security personnel, police and the MOD Guard Service, Royal Marines, together with the sailors, ships and the submarines. The population of Faslane and Coulport is about 7,500 people.

What was it like when you arrived?

The customer support ethos didn't feel right. Despite being a naval base, the staff saw buildings and infrastructure facilities as more important than supporting the Navy. The focus was from the waterfront inward rather than looking outwards to the ships and submarines. I think that was because the people who looked after the site were often civilians who had been here much longer than the navy people, who looked after ships and submarines and generally moved on after 2–3 years. The civilians were here long enough for them to build up empires. So the challenge was to become focused on delivering services to the customer, the Navy.

Moreover a public sector manager who's got wide ranging responsibilities and a fairly large budget has no incentive to reduce costs. They don't share in any benefits and were brought up in a system where, if they hadn't spent their budget, next year their budget would be cut. So we believed that a big opportunity might come from changing the mindset: to see their job isn't to spend the money allocated, but deliver the job with the minimum possible spend.

Another difficulty is that civil servants carry political accountability; every significant decision they make could be questioned by an elected politician. That makes people naturally much more conservative. You also end up with lots of layers in the organization; lots of people with limited autonomy or empowerment who focus on doing things within their own control. It tends to be procedural; its a 'handle turning' exercise.

With political accountability it's also important to demonstrate an audit path for the decision you made. So speedy decision making can be secondary to being able to be accountable for the decision and being able to demonstrate why you made it. All fairly bureaucratic and cumbersome. Some of that is understandable because it's driven by having nuclear weapons and nuclear reactors on site, but some of it is a legacy of 'take a simple process and then start building things round it'.

What of the management here before BNS?

Commodore John Borley had overall responsibility. He was put in charge at the point when this whole process started and was willing to change in a way some of his predecessors hadn't been. He'd come to the same conclusion about the need to change from being infrastructure focused to being naval focused. He saw in partnering the opportunity to better manage the people. And then there was the commodore's management team. They were a mix of people who either believed change was necessary and were willing to give partnering a try or people who were likely to be personally disadvantaged by partnering and were less supportive.

What of the workforce?

There was a perception that because of the base's role supporting the nuclear deterrent, they were ring fenced from radical changes. Their view was also that the base was doing a really good job and therefore why would you want to change that? There was no

perception of financial pressure or need to save money. The base also has a 25–30 year role. There is no cliff edge. They'd been through a whole raft of MOD change, not least large scale outsourcing programmes. There was the feeling of flavour of the month change programmes. All very disruptive, not my day job, very much seen as negative. So the backdrop was a workforce forcibly transferred to a private company and fearful of what change by them would mean.

So how did you set about change?

We brought in people from Babcock who had lived through similar changes. What they didn't necessarily understand was how to run a naval base but the MOD transferred people to us who knew how to do that. Our job was to manage them differently.

The over-arching theme was to get visibility about how money was being spent whilst getting a focus back on things that matter to the customer. It meant looking carefully at structures and processes to figure out how they currently operated and ask how that could be done differently. For example, there was a process that required any change, such as a change of management structure, to be documented and passed through a series of review points. After all, in a nuclear naval base you have to be sure that changing something that's fundamental to safety can be done without unacceptable risk. At each stage of that process people were given a maximum of 14 days to review it; but of course everyone defaulted to looking at it on the thirteenth day. So the overall process took about 56 days. What became clear was a number of the review points weren't materially adding value; it was: 'I'm letting you look at this because you might be interested in it', not because involvement was critical. By taking those stages out you free up people's bureaucratic burden. You also don't give them 14 days to review it; you give them two days because they did it on the thirteenth and fourteenth day anyway. Now that 56 day process is six days. A simple example of process re-engineering.

All that sounds very mechanistic

It's not like that. We are an organisation that doesn't own any physical assets other than the people who walk through the gate every day. So change is very much about people. And with 2,000 people you get access to a whole raft of ideas and change initiatives that we would never have thought of because we had never worked in this environment. So part of it was about removing the shackles from people to come up with their own change ideas. But culturally that's a challenge when for many people there's no incentive to come up with a change when it might mean that people at the desk next to you get made redundant.

So how do you do it?

I'm not sure we entirely have yet. What became clear was that we had a management structure that wasn't right to deliver change. We had seven layers in it. It's now down to a maximum of four layers. We've reappointed all the jobs. We asked other companies who've been through large scale changes: 'what is the main lesson we should learn from what you did?' The answer was: 'Implement the management structural changes earlier than we did.' People tried to launch transformational change with the existing team, got two or three years into it, realised it wasn't working, and then changed the structure. We are doing it the other way round about. We implemented all the low level changes up front because they're easy. That allowed us to deliver £14 million of saving in the first year against a target of £3 million. But once you get into change which is more about transformation – about trying to deliver a strategy of being the best, most profitable organisation supporting the UK submarine fleet – we needed different skill sets. So we've changed the structure. The management team we had was about 250; it's now about half of that. Within 12 to 18 months that entire management team of 125 need to be change agents. At the moment it's about a dozen. However the signs are that the senior managers appointed will be better able to deal with the change challenge; they have enough knowledge of change in other environments.

The problem is that as we get away from the changes which are relatively mechanistic we get into changes that are much more complex in nature.

Such as?

Moving from 24 hour shifts to working day shift in some areas sounds like a simple thing to do, but when you've got a workforce and unions fearful of change, a management team without the skills to implement big change and people who just want the status quo maintained, it took far longer to deliver than it should have.

It also seems a difficult political situation

The first thing is to understand who you need to have as allies, such as the Naval Base Commander. Our success was intertwined. I have a parent company to satisfy, whilst Commodore Carolyn Stiat, the current Naval Base Commander, has to manage the relationships with the wider MOD and the Navy Board. Beyond that you have to look at the wider stakeholders. The commanding officers of the ships and submarines here: if they were saying 'we're getting a really bad service' we'd have struggled. Or if the security people thought we weren't interested in national security. And another key stakeholder was the local community. We did a lot of work up front with two local councils because the base represents 9.5% of all employment in the Dunbartonshire area and we've reduced by about 400 full time equivalent posts. Now some of those have been naval posts rather than people living locally. We've also been able to achieve about 98 reductions through voluntary redundancy, with attractive redundancy terms; so often people left without the need to be reliant on support from welfare services; even to set up businesses on their own. Fairly quickly the meetings with the council stopped because they became comfortable we were doing things the right way.

And are you on target in terms of the time frame you envisaged?

We discovered that getting through the evolutionary change took longer than we'd assumed, I suppose partly because we'd over-estimated the desire for change. It also took much more senior management involvement than we had assumed. Given that and a ten and a half year contract, there are two major milestones for me. One is getting to the end of the first five years having delivered against targets. We're now a year away from that but we will beat our target by some margin. The second is a more hazy 7–8 year time frame which is what the theorists say it takes to implement lasting cultural change: an organisation that's had the non-value-adding bureaucracy stripped away, team leaders managing people not paperwork, teams starting to get more responsibility to manage themselves. So instead of having somebody manage health and safety and training and the overtime allocation, people take responsibility in their own work teams to do that.

So, what has been achieved?

Year 1 the target was £3 million of savings, we delivered £14 million. Year 2 the target was £12 million, we delivered £16 million. By the end of Year 5 we had delivered around £100 million against our £76 million target. By the end of Year 10 we should have saved £280 million; that equates to a 38.2% reduction in annual running costs. By the end of Year 5 we had delivered over 20%. And the Navy's view was that the service they were receiving was better, attitude better, communication better, responsiveness better. So we have delivered cost reductions and service improvement.

Questions

1 In relation to sections 14.2.1 and 14.5, what is the type of change that is being pursued at Faslane?

2 Describe the change style of John Howie.

3 What levers for change are being used (see section 14.4)? What others might be used?

4 What problems of change may occur in the future?

5 Assess the effectiveness of the change programme.

The Practice of Strategy

LEARNING OUTCOMES

After reading this chapter you should be able to:

→ Identify key people involved in strategy making, including top management, strategy consultants, strategic planners and middle managers.

→ Assess which people should be included in strategy making for different kinds of issues.

→ Evaluate different approaches to strategising activity, including analysis, issue selling, decision-making and communications.

→ Recognise key elements in the various methodologies commonly used in strategising, including strategy workshops, projects, hypothesis testing and writing business cases and strategic plans.

Photo: Superstock/Alamy Images

15.1 INTRODUCTION

This final chapter is the place to examine how managers actually practice strategy, using the theoretical concepts, tools and techniques introduced earlier in the book. The concern here then is with the practicalities of strategy making – what managers do in making a strategy. Whereas Chapter 11 introduced the overall organisational process of strategy development, this chapter has a more detailed focus: it is about what gets done *inside* the process. The aim is to examine how people actually contribute to practical strategy making, whether as top managers, strategic planning specialists, strategy consultants or managers lower down the organisation. Strategic success is not simply about *having* a good strategy: that strategy has to be *made*, by the right people doing the right things in the right way.

The chapter has three core sections:

- *The strategists*. The chapter starts by looking at the various people involved in making strategy. It does not assume that strategy is made just by top management. As pointed out in Chapter 11, strategy is often emergent, and involves people from all over the organisation and often from outside. The key debate at the end of the chapter (Illustration 15.6) addresses the controversial involvement of external strategy consultants. Readers can ask themselves how they already fit into this set of strategists, or how they might in the future.

- *Strategising activities*. The chapter continues by considering the kinds of work and activity that strategists carry out in their strategy making. This includes not just the strategy analysis that has been central to a large part of this book, but also the managing of strategic issues over time, the realities of strategic decision making and the critical task of communicating strategic decisions throughout the organisation.

- *Strategising methodologies*. The final section covers some of the practical methodologies that managers use to carry out their strategising activities. This includes strategy workshops for formulating or communicating strategy; strategy projects and strategy consulting teams; hypothesis testing to guide strategy work; and the writing of strategic plans and business cases.

Exhibit 15.1 integrates these three sections in a *pyramid of practice*.[1] The pyramid highlights three questions that run through this chapter: *who* to include in strategy making; *what* to do in carrying out strategising activity; and *which* strategising methodologies to use in organising this strategising activity. The pyramid places strategists at the top. Placing strategists at the top in this way emphasises the role of managerial discretion and skill in strategy making. It is the strategists who choose and enact both the strategising activity and the strategy methodologies that are at the base of the pyramid. Strategists' choices and skill with regard to activity and methodologies can make a real difference to final outcomes. The rest of the chapter seeks to guide practising strategists through the key choices they may have to make in action.

Exhibit 15.1	The pyramid of strategy practice

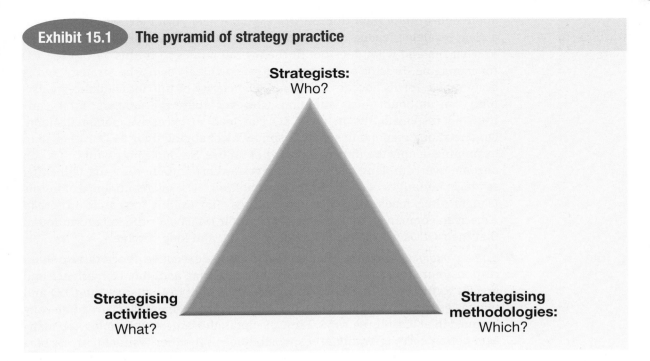

Strategists:
Who?

**Strategising
activities**
What?

**Strategising
methodologies:**
Which?

15.2 THE STRATEGISTS

This section introduces the different types of people involved in strategy. It starts at the top management level, but includes a much wider range of potential actors, from strategic planners and consultants to middle managers. One key issue is how middle managers can increase their influence in strategy making.[2]

15.2.1 Top managers and directors

The conventional view is that strategy is the business of top management. In this view, it is absolutely vital that top management are clearly separated from operational responsibilities, so that they can focus on overall strategy.[3] If top management are directly involved in operations such as sales or service delivery, they are liable to get distracted from long-term issues by day-to-day responsibilities and to represent the interests of their departments or business units rather than the interests of their organisation as a whole. In the private sector at least, top managers' job titles underline this strategic responsibility: company directors set direction; managers manage.

In reality, the top management role involves much more than setting direction. Also, different roles are played by different members of the top team, whether *chief executive officer*, the *top management team* or *non-executive directors*:

● The *chief executive officer* is often seen as the 'chief strategist', ultimately responsible for all strategic decisions. CEOs of large companies typically spend about one-third of their time on strategy.[4] Michael Porter stresses the value of a clear strategic leader, somebody capable of setting a disciplined approach to what fits and what does not fit the overall strategy.[5] In this view, the CEO (or managing director or equivalent top individual) owns the strategy and is accountable for its success or failure. The clarity of this individual responsibility can no doubt focus attention. However, there are dangers. First, centralising responsibility on the CEO can lead to excessive personalisation. Organisations respond to setbacks simply by changing their CEO, rather than examining deeply the internal sources of failure. Second, successful CEOs can become overconfident, seeing themselves as corporate heroes and launching strategic initiatives of ever-increasing ambition.[6] The overconfidence of heroic leaders often leads to spectacular failures. Jim Collins' research on 'great' American companies that outperformed their rivals over the long term found that their CEOs were typically modest, steady and long serving.[7]

● The *top management team*, often an organisation's executive directors, also share responsibility for strategy. Obviously they can bring additional experience and insight to the CEO. In theory, they should be able to challenge the CEO and increase strategic debate. In practice, the top management team are often constrained in at least three ways. First, except in the largest companies, top managers often carry operational responsibilities that either distract them or bias their strategic thinking: for example, the marketing director will have ongoing concerns about marketing, the production director about production, and so on. Second, top managers are also frequently appointed by the CEO: consequently, they may lack the independence for real challenge. Finally, top management teams, especially where their members have similar backgrounds and face strong leadership, often suffer from 'groupthink', the tendency to build strong consensus amongst team members and avoid internal conflict.[8] Top management teams can minimise groupthink by fostering diversity in membership (for example, differences in age, career tracks and gender) and by ensuring openness to outside views, for example those of non-executive directors.[9]

● *Non-executive directors* have no executive management responsibility within the organisation, and so in theory should be able to offer an external and objective view on strategy. Although this varies according to national corporate governance systems (see Chapter 4), in a public company the chairman/woman of the board is typically non-executive. He or she will normally be consulted closely by the CEO on strategy, as he or she will have a key role in liaising with investors. However, the ability of the chairman/woman and other non-executives in general to contribute substantially to strategy can be limited. Non-executives are typically part-time appointments. The predominant role for non-executive directors in strategy, therefore, is consultative, reviewing and challenging strategy proposals that come from the top management executive team. A key role for them also is to ensure that the organisation has a rigorous system in place for the making and renewing of strategy. It is therefore important that non-executives are authoritative and experienced individuals, that they have independence from the top management executive team and that they are properly briefed before board meetings.[10]

Top management capability in making strategy should not simply be assumed. Managers are often promoted to strategic roles for their success in dealing with operations or their professional skill in a particular functional specialism. These kinds of experience do not necessarily prepare them for the analytical and managerial tasks involved in making strategy. There are at least three important qualities senior managers need if they are to contribute effectively to high-level strategy making:

- *Mastery of analytical concepts and techniques*, as introduced in this book, is clearly important, and cannot be assumed, especially in arenas such as the public or not-for-profit sectors where strategy is still quite novel.[11] Sometimes an executive education course can help improve understanding of strategy concepts and techniques.

- *Social and influencing skills* are necessary if analysis is to be understood and accepted by senior colleagues. Again, senior managers are not equally effective in strategic discussions, but there are now many professional coaches who can help.[12]

- *Group acceptance as a player* in strategic discussions. Boards and senior executive teams are social groups like any other, where members have to win respect.[13] Clear and significant success in one's own particular sphere of responsibility is normally a precondition for being respected as a contributor to wider discussions of the organisation's strategy.

15.2.2 Strategic planners

Strategic planners, sometimes known as corporate development managers or similar, are managers with a formal responsibility for contributing to the strategy process

Strategic planners, sometimes known as corporate development managers or similar, are managers with a formal responsibility for contributing to the strategy process (see Chapter 11). Although small companies very rarely have full-time strategic planners, they are common in large companies and increasingly widespread in the public and not-for-profit sectors. As in Illustration 15.1, organisations frequently advertise for strategic planning jobs. As in Illustration 15.1, organisations frequently advertise for strategic planning jobs. For this UK government Strategy Unit post, the specifications give a clear picture of the skills a strategic planner might be expected to have. The strategist is not only making strategy, but helping other departments to develop their own capabilities in strategy. Strategic thinking and analytical skills are clearly very important, but so too are the ability to communicate clearly to various audiences and to work well with teams. The strategist's role here is much more than back-office analysis.

Although the job in Illustration 15.1 is being advertised externally, strategic planners are often drawn from inside their own organisations. Internal strategic planners are likely to have an advantage in the important non-analytical parts of the job. As internal recruits, they bring to the planning role intuitive understanding of the business, networks with key people in the organisation and credibility with internal audiences. Moreover, an internal appointment to a strategic planning role can serve as a developmental stage for managers on track for top management roles.[14] Participating in strategy provides promising managers with exposure to senior management and gives them an overview of the organisation as a whole.

Strategic planners do not take strategic decisions themselves. However, they typically do have at least three important tasks:[15]

Illustration 15.1

Wanted: Team member for strategy unit

The following advertisement appeared on the UK Cabinet Office website. It gives an insight into the kind of work such strategic planners do and the skills and background required.

Job Description for a Team Member: Band A

About the Strategy Unit

The PMSU has three main roles:

- to carry out strategy reviews and provide policy advice in accordance with the Prime Minister's policy priorities;
- to support Government Departments in developing effective strategies and policies – including helping them to build their strategic capability; and
- to identify and effectively disseminate thinking on emerging issues and challenges facing the UK e.g. through occasional strategic audits.

Post holders will be members of small teams set up to address issues where innovative approaches and fresh thinking are necessary to ensure the achievement of the Government's objectives. Teams will be drawn from both inside and outside the Civil Service and work intensively on an issue, for periods ranging from 3–4 weeks to 3–4 months or longer depending on the task.

Candidates will need to have first rate policy or strategy experience, strong interpersonal skills, and the ability to write clearly and compellingly. Outstanding analytical and problem solving skills are absolutely essential to the role.

Essential competences for the SU

Strategic Thinking
1. Knowledge and understanding of government priorities
2. Knowledge of the wider policy environment, including political or institutional restraints
3. Ability to derive clear goals and strategies from a complex brief

Analysis and Use of Evidence
1. Knows and deploys a range of analytical tools
2. Uses a variety of tools in collecting and analysing evidence
3. Works in partnership with a wide range of analytical experts to achieve project goals
4. Ability to understand complex statistical data
5. Understands what constitutes good evidence

People Management
1. Able to develop individuals for high performance
2. Champions equality and diversity, and promotes best practice
3. Able to give good feedback that people can act on

Programme and Project Management
1. Can work with a team to develop a project plan
2. Anticipates, manages and monitors programme/project risks
3. Ensures effective communications with stakeholders

Specialist Professional Skills

Essential
1. Good quality qualifications or training in economics, social policy, operational research or similar
2. Excellent quantitative and qualitative analytical skills
3. Sector knowledge – an understanding of social policy is an advantage

Desirable
1. Experience in working in a think-tank or high profile management consultancy role or policy or analytical arm of a government department.

Source: Extracts from Strategy Unit Job Description for a Team Member: Band A from http://www.cabinetoffice.gov.uk/strategy/jobs/band_a.asp. Reproduced under the terms of the Click-Use Licence.

Questions

1 What would be the attractions of this job for you? What would be the disadvantages?

2 What relevant skills and experience do you already have, and what skills and experience would you still need to acquire before you were to apply for this job?

- *Information and analysis*. Strategic planners have the time, skills and resources to provide information and analysis for key decision makers. This might be in response to some 'trigger' event – such as a possible merger – or as part of a regular planning cycle. A background of good information and analysis can leave an organisation much better prepared to respond quickly and confidently even to unexpected events as they occur. Strategic planners can also package this information and analysis in formats that ensure clear communication of strategic decisions.

- *Managers of the strategy process*. Both for the headquarters and for business units, strategic planners can assist and guide other managers through their strategic planning cycles. Strategic planners can provide templates, analytical techniques and strategy training to support managers at business unit level having to make strategy for themselves. They can help CEOs design strategy processes according to their particular needs.

- *Special projects*. Strategic planners can be a useful resource to support top management on special projects, such as acquisitions or organisational change. Here strategic planners will typically work on project teams with middle managers from within the organisation and often with external consultants. Project management skills are likely to be important (see section 15.4.4).

15.2.3 Middle managers

As in section 15.2.1, a good deal of conventional management theory excludes middle managers from strategy making. Middle managers are seen as lacking an appropriately objective and long-term perspective, being too involved in operations.[16] In this view, middle managers just implement. Yet involving middle managers in the strategy formulation itself can provide at least two benefits. In the first place, middle manager involvement can lead to better strategic decisions, because middle managers have direct, up-to-date experience of the realities of the organisation and its market, unlike many top managers. In the second place, including middle managers in the original strategy formulation can improve implementation. Middle managers who have been involved in the original formulation process will be better at interpreting strategic intentions into action, have a stronger personal commitment to strategic goals, and communicate the strategy more effectively to their teams.[17]

Three trends are leading to increasing middle management involvement in strategy making nowadays.[18] First, many organisations are decentralising their organisational structures to increase accountability and responsiveness in fast-moving and competitive environments. As a result, strategic responsibilities are being thrust down the organisational hierarchy. Second, the rise of business education means that middle managers are now better trained and more confident in the strategy domain than they used to be. These higher-calibre middle managers are both more able and more eager to participate in strategy. Third, the shift away from a traditional manufacturing economy to one based more on professional services (such as design, consulting or finance) means that often the key sources of competitive advantage are no longer resources such as capital, which can be handed out from the headquarters, but the knowledge of people actually involved in the operations of the business. Middle managers at operational level can understand and influence these knowledge-based sources of competitive advantage much more effectively than remote top managers. For these three reasons, middle managers are increasingly involved in strategy formulation (see also the key debate in Chapter 11).

Even where middle managers are not formally involved in making strategy, they can increase their informal influence when they have:

- *Key organisational positions.* Middle managers responsible for strategically important parts of the organisation are in a strong position to exercise informal influence, because they are likely to have critical knowledge and their full-hearted commitment to the strategy is important. Not surprisingly, middle managers who are responsible for larger departments or business units typically have greater influence on strategic decisions.[19] Also, managers with outward-facing roles (for example, marketing) tend to have greater strategic influence than managers with inward-facing roles (such as quality or operations).[20] Middle managers seeking influence on strategy need to position themselves in the right organisational roles.

- *Access to organisational networks.* Middle managers may not have hierarchical power, but they can increase their influence by using their internal organisational networks. Drawing together information from network members can help provide an integrated perspective on what is happening in the organisation as a whole, something that otherwise can be difficult to get when occupying a specialised position in the middle of an organisation. Mobilising networks to raise issues and support proposals can also give more influence than any single middle manager can achieve on his or her own.[21] Strategically influential middle managers are therefore typically good networkers.

- *Access to the organisation's 'strategic conversation'.* Strategy making does not just happen in isolated, formal episodes, but is part of an ongoing strategic conversation amongst respected managers.[22] An organisation seeking to involve middle managers in its strategic conversations should cultivate an open strategic culture, for example by including middle managers in strategy workshops (see section 15.4.1) or having top management discuss strategy at management training events. Middle managers wanting to participate in these strategic conversations should: maximise opportunities to mix formally and informally with top managers; become at ease with the particular language used to discuss strategy in their organisation; familiarise themselves carefully with the key strategic issues; and develop their own personal contribution to these strategic issues.

In the public sector, senior management–middle management have their parallel in the formal divide between politicians and public officials. Just as directors are formally concerned with strategic 'direction', elected politicians were traditionally responsible for policy. Public officials, meanwhile, were supposed to do the implementation. However, three trends are challenging this division of roles. First, the rising importance of *specialised expertise* has effectively shifted influence to public officials who may have made their careers in particular areas, while politicians are typically generalists. Second, public sector reform in many countries has led to increased *externalisation of functions* to quasi-independent 'agencies' or 'QUANGOs' (Quasi-Autonomous Non-Governmental Organisations), which, within certain constraints, can make decisions on their own. Third, the same reform processes have changed *internal structures* within public organisations, with decentralisation of units and more 'executive' responsibility granted to public officials. All this is supported by the discourse of 'New Public Management', which encourages officials to be more enterprising and accountable. In short, strategy is increasingly part of the work of public officials too.[23]

15.2.4 Strategy consultants

External consultants are often used in the development of strategy in organisations. Leading consultancy firms that focus on strategy include Bain, the Boston Consulting Group, Monitor and McKinsey & Co.[24] Most of the large general consultancy firms also have operations that provide services in strategy development and analysis. There are also smaller 'boutique' consultancy firms and individual consultants who specialise in strategy.[25]

Consultants may play different roles in strategy development in organisations:[26]

● *Analysing, prioritising and generating options.* Strategic issues may have been identified by the executives, but there may be so many of them, or so much disagreement about them, that the organisation faces a lack of clarity on how to go forward. Consultants may analyse such issues afresh and bring an external eye to help prioritise them or generate options for executives to consider. This may, of course, involve challenging executives' preconceptions about their views of strategic issues.

● *Transferring knowledge.* Consultants play a role in disseminating views, insights and the conclusions drawn from their analysis within organisations in meetings and discussions and in disseminating knowledge between organisations. In effect they are the carriers of knowledge and best practice within and between their clients.

● *Promoting strategic decisions.* In doing all this, consultants may themselves substantially influence the decisions that organisations eventually take. A number of major consultancies have been criticised in the past for undue influence on the decisions made by their client organisation, leading to major problems. For example, leading strategy consulting firm McKinsey & Co. was heavily associated with Enron's controversial 'asset-lite' business model, and was also the proponent of SwissAir's failed 'Hunter' strategy of strategic alliances.[27]

● *Implementing strategic change.* Consultants play a significant role in project planning, coaching and training often associated with strategic change. This is an area that has seen considerable growth, not least because consultants were criticised for leaving organisations with consultancy reports recommending strategies, but taking little responsibility for actually making these happen.

The real value of strategy consultants is often controversial (see Illustration 15.6, the key debate on page 584). Enron was paying McKinsey & Co. $10m (£5.6m; €8m) a year before it collapsed. But consultants are often blamed for failures when in fact it is the client's poor management of the consulting process that is ultimately at fault. Many organisations select their consultants unsystematically; give poor initial project briefs; and fail to act on and learn from projects at the end. There are three key measures that client organisations can undertake to improve outcomes in strategy consulting:[28]

● *Professionalised purchasing of consulting services*, using specialists in the organisation's purchasing function, for instance. Instead of hiring consulting firms on the basis of personal relationships with key executives, as is often the case, introducing consultants can be treated like any other purchasing decision, following standard purchasing procedures. Professionalised purchasing can help ensure clear project briefs, a wide search for consulting suppliers, appropriate pricing, complementarity between different consulting projects and proper review at project end. The German engineering company Siemens has professionalised its consultancy purchasing, for example establishing a shortlist of just 10 preferred management consulting suppliers.

● *Developing supervisory skills* in order to manage portfolios of consulting projects. The German railway company Deutsche Bahn and automobile giant DaimlerChrysler both have central project offices that control and coordinate all consulting projects throughout their companies. As well as being involved in the initial purchasing decision, these central offices can impose systematic governance structures on projects, with clear responsibilities and reporting processes, as well as review and formal assessment at project end.

● *Partnering effectively* with consultants can improve both effectiveness in carrying out the project and knowledge transfer at the end of it. Where possible, project teams should include a mix of consultants and managers from the client organisation. Client organisation managers can provide inside information, guide on internal politics and, sometimes, enhance credibility and receptiveness. As partners in the project, client managers retain knowledge and experience when the consultants have gone and can help in the implementation of recommendations. Client managers should be ready to work to the demanding standards and schedules of strategy consulting firms.

15.2.5 Who to include in strategy?

KEY
CONCEPT

Strategy
inclusion

There is, therefore, a potentially wide range of people to involve in any strategic issue: as well as the CEO and the top management team, non-executive directors, strategic planners, strategy consultants, middle managers and perhaps external stakeholders. This often raises practical dilemmas about who should be included on particular strategic issues. The paradox of strategy inclusion is that those with the most access to the CEO on strategy are often strategic planners and strategy consultants who have little responsibility for strategy implementation and little knowledge of business on the ground (see Exhibit 15.2). The middle managers who have both the knowledge and the implementation responsibility can have least access to the CEO in strategy discussions, either because they are too busy with operational realities or because they are seen as biased. Strategy is not necessarily being made by the right people.

However, there is no single correct answer about who should participate in strategy. McKinsey & Co research indicates that the people involved should vary according to the nature of the issue (see Exhibit 15.3).[29] Highly urgent issues, and those implying high strategic discontinuity (perhaps an acquisition opportunity), are often best approached by small special project teams, consisting of senior managers and perhaps planners and consultants. Issues which might imply

Exhibit 15.2   **The access/execution paradox**

High

Strategy consultants

Strategic planners

**CEO
access**

Middle managers

High

Execution responsibility

Exhibit 15.3   **Who to include in strategy making?**

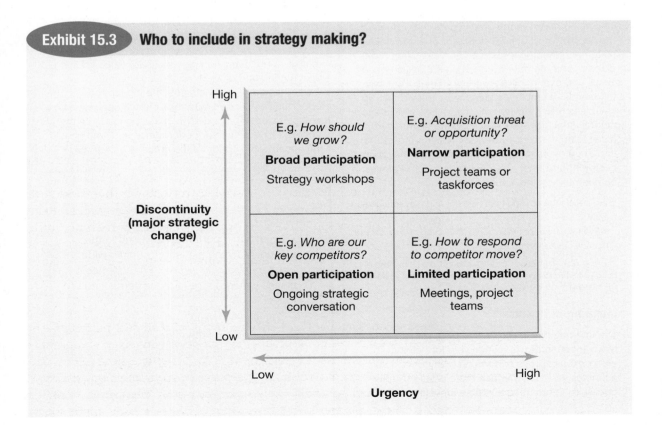

High

E.g. *How should
we grow?*

Broad participation

Strategy workshops

E.g. *Acquisition threat
or opportunity?*

Narrow participation

Project teams or
taskforces

**Discontinuity
(major strategic
change)**

E.g. *Who are our
key competitors?*

Open participation

Ongoing strategic
conversation

E.g. *How to respond
to competitor move?*

Limited participation

Meetings, project
teams

Low

Low   High

Urgency

Illustration 15.2

Jamming and mapping

Participation in strategy making can be important in global businesses and developing enterprises alike.

Jamming at IBM

IBM has developed a $3m information technology platform that allows its 300,000 employees to participate in global debates about strategic issues (see Illustration 14.5). These debates are called 'jams' after the structured improvisation ('jamming') used in jazz music. Jams typically combine off-site face-to-face brainstorming sessions with 'threaded' discussions, theme-based forums and electronic idea-ratings organised through the corporate intranet site. All IBM employees have equal access to the jam sessions. IBM manager Mike Malloney explains: 'It's like jazz collaboration, with people building on other people's ideas in a structured format. Jams are a blend of technology and a kind of grassroots discussion of ideas'.

IBM has used jams to address managerial roles, post-merger integration, organisational barriers to innovation and revenue growth (informally dubbed the 'logjam') and the development of a new values statement (the 'ValuesJam'). The ValuesJam took place over three days, generating 2.3 million page views and over a million words of input. Tens of thousands of employee ideas were refined into 65 key ideas, using online voting and IBM's proprietory natural language analytical software ('jamalyzer'). A small team then set to work on refining these further into three overarching values based on innovation, the customer and trust. Chief Executive Sam Palmisano commented on the ValuesJam:

'Yes, the electronic argument was hot and contentious and messy. . . . We had done three or four big online jams before . . . Even so, none of those could have prepared us for the emotions unleashed by this topic'.

Sources: S.J. Palmisano, 'Leading change when business is good', *Harvard Business Review*, December (2004), p. 60–70; PR Newswire, 30 November (2005).

Mapping in Uganda

The International Trade Centre (ITC) in Geneva (www.intracen.org) is responsible for helping enterprises improve exports. In many developing countries where it operates there is little reliable published information available, development

activities can be fragmented and people tend to be reticent unknown individuals. The Ugandan fish processing and exporting sector provides one example of how these difficulties can be overcome.

ITC worked alongside the Uganda Export Promotion Board to facilitate meetings of stakeholders from all stages of the fish value network on a strategy for export growth. Stakeholders included enterprise owners, community leaders, government and development agencies, services providers such as transport, inspections, customs, banks, freight forwarders and packagers. Meeting in Kampala, they collaborated on a series of exercises to identify market opportunities, diagnose sector performance issues and organise development activity implementation.

They mapped the core stages of their value chains on large wall sheets from target markets back to sources of supply. Sector-wide issues and market requirements were broken down into value chain stage components and illustrated on these maps. The process surfaced tacit information and 'market realities' and stimulated new ideas for value addition, cost cutting and diversification (see Illustration 3.4). It also helped participants see 'the big picture opportunities', understand their mutual dependency and participate in the design of solutions, agree on the priorities to raise sector performance and who should implement which parts of the strategy and how.

Source: Ian Sayers, Senior Advisor for the Private Sector, Division of Trade Support Services, the International Trade Centre, Geneva.

Questions

1. Why was it important at IBM and in the Ugandan fishing industry to obtain wide input on strategic issues? What strategic issues would not require the same kind of input?

2. If you were a smaller company, without the information technology resources of IBM or the help of government agencies as in Uganda, how might you be able to get employee input into strategy development?

equal discontinuity, but for which there is more time (such as growth options), can benefit from the participation of a broader group of managers, perhaps through a strategy workshop (see section 15.4.1). For issues that are more routine, but which still require speedy response (such as competitors' pricing moves), only limited participation is probably required, involving perhaps meetings between the relevant marketing and operations managers. The most open kind of participation would be in the on-going 'strategic conversation' of managers throughout the organisation, regarding for example key competitors or the long-run evolution of the market.

The point from the McKinsey & Co. research is that there is no general rule about inclusion or exclusion in strategy making, but that there are criteria that can guide managers about who to include according to the nature of the strategic issues in hand. Managers should think carefully about who to include and they should make skilled use of different strategy-making methods, whether project teams or strategy workshops to enrol people who might have valuable contributions to make but who might otherwise be excluded from the normal process. Managers can use a variety of techniques to generate a more inclusive approach, as for example IBM has done with its 'strategy jam' and the International Trade Centre did in Uganda (Illustration 15.2). The public sector often uses the internet for public consultations and discussion forums regarding controversial policy issues: see for example www.communities.gov.uk/.

15.3   STRATEGISING

The previous section introduced the key strategists; this section concentrates on what people have to do in strategising. The section proceeds logically through these activities, starting with the initial strategy analysis, then proceeding through issue selling and decision making and concluding with communications about the chosen strategy. In practice, of course, these activities rarely follow this logical sequence: decisions are often made without great analysis; they are often reinterpreted in subsequent communications. There are, however, key choices to be made in how these strategising activities are conducted, particularly with regard to which managers trust in formal, analytical rationality.

15.3.1   Strategy analysis

A good deal of this book is concerned with strategy analysis, and indeed analysis is an important input into strategy making. However, as suggested in Chapter 11, strategy is often not the outcome of simple rational analysis. Analysis is frequently done in an ad hoc and incomplete fashion and not always followed through. The analysis activity itself may serve other functions than a simple input into subsequent decisions.

First of all, analysis in practice tends to be rough and ready. SWOT (Strengths, Weaknesses, Opportunities and Threats) analysis is the most widely used tool in strategy,[30] but even this simple tool is typically used in a way far from the technical ideal (see Chapter 3). One study found frequent deviations from textbook recommendations, by both managers and consultants.[31] For example, in practice SWOT analyses tend to produce unmanageably long lists of factors (strengths, weaknesses, opportunities and threats), often well over 50 or so. The result is these factors are rarely probed or refined; little substantive analysis is done to investigate them; and they are often not followed up systematically in subsequent strategic discussions. Technically, SWOT analyses should be more focused, prompt further investigation and lead to concrete actions on prioritised factors. If this experience with SWOT is typical, managers can often add value by more rigorous use of strategy's analytical tools.

However, criticism of poor analysis may sometimes be misplaced. There are both *cost* and *purpose* issues to consider. First of all, analysis is costly in terms of both resources and time. There are of course the costs of gathering information, particularly if using consultants. But with regard to time there is also the risk of 'paralysis by analysis', whereby managers spend too long perfecting their analyses, not enough time taking decisions and then acting upon them.[32] Managers have to judge how much analysis they really need: 'quick and dirty' may be good enough. Second, with regard to purpose, analysis is not always simply about providing the necessary information for good strategic decisions anyway.[33] The purposes of analysis can be quite different. Setting up a project to analyse an issue thoroughly may even be a deliberate form of *procrastination*, aimed at putting off a decision. Analysis can also be *symbolic*, for example to rationalise a decision after it has already effectively been made. Managers may be asked to analyse an issue in order to get their *buy-in* to decisions that they might otherwise resist. Analyses can also be *political*, to forward the agenda of a particular manager or part of the organisation.

The different purposes of strategy analysis have two key implications for managers:

- *Design the analysis according to the real purpose.* The range and quality of people involved, the time and budget allowed, and the subsequent communication of analysis results should all depend on underlying purpose, whether informational, political or symbolic. Prestigious strategy consulting firms are often useful for political and symbolic analyses. Involving a wide group of middle managers in the analysis may help with subsequent buy-in.

- *Invest appropriately in technical quality.* For many projects, improving the quality of the technical analysis will make a valuable addition to subsequent strategic decisions. On other occasions, insisting on technical perfection can be counter-productive. For example, a SWOT analysis that raises lots of issues may be a useful means of allowing managers to vent their own personal frustrations, before getting on with the real strategy work. It may sometimes be better to leave these issues on the table, rather than probing, challenging or even deleting them in a way that could unnecessarily alienate these managers for the following stages.

15.3.2   Strategic issue selling

Organisations typically face many strategic issues at any point in time. But in complex organisations these issues may not be appreciated to the same extent by all senior managers, or may not even be recognised by them at all. Some issues will be filtered out in the organisational hierarchy; others will be sidelined by more urgent pressures. Moreover, senior managers will rarely have sufficient time and resources to deal with all the issues that do actually reach them. In effect, strategic issues compete for top management attention. What gets top management attention is not necessarily the most important issues.[34]

Managers therefore have to 'sell' their particular strategic issues to top management and other important stakeholders. They cannot assume that issues get automatic attention, or that they will necessarily win support, however important they might be to them in particular. Managers need to consider at least four aspects in seeking attention and support for their **strategic issue selling**:

> **Strategic issue selling** is the process of winning the attention and support of top management and other important stakeholders for strategic issues.

- *Issue packaging*. Care should be taken with how issues are packaged or framed. Clearly the strategic importance of the issue needs to be underlined, particularly by linking it to *critical strategic goals* or *performance metrics* for the organisation. The presentation of the issue should be consistent with the *cultural norms* of the organisation, but generally clarity and succinctness win over complexity and length. It usually helps if the issue is packaged with *potential solutions*. An issue can easily be parked as too difficult to address if no ways forward are offered at the same time.

- *Formal or informal channels*. Managers need to balance formal and informal channels of influence. Exhibit 15.4 indicates some *formal channels* for selling issues in a typical multidivisional organisation (based on General Electric).[35] Here formal channels are split between corporate, line and staff. On the corporate side, they include the annual business reviews that the CEO carries out with each divisional head, plus the annual strategy retreats (or workshops) of the top executive team. The line channel involves the regular line interaction of operational managers, divisional heads and the CEO and other executive directors. Finally, there are the various reporting systems to staff functions, including finance, human resources and strategic planning. Formal channels are of course not just for upward influence, but typically two-way: for example, strategic plans often iterate between divisions and corporate headquarters until a mutually satisfactory position is reached. Moreover, formal channels are rarely enough to sell strategic issues. *Informal channels* can be very important and often decisive in some organisational cultures. Informal channels might include ad hoc conversations with influential managers in corridors, on journeys or over meals or drinks.[36]

- *Sell alone or in coalitions*. Managers should consider whether to press their issue on their own or to assemble a *coalition of supporters*, preferably influential ones. A coalition adds credibility and weight to the issue. The ability to gather a coalition of supporters can be a good test of the issue's validity: if other managers are unpersuaded, then the CEO is unlikely to be persuaded either. But notice that enlisting supporters may involve compromises or reciprocal support of other issues, so blurring the clarity of the case being put forward.

- *Timing*. Managers should also time their issue selling carefully. A short-term performance crisis, or the period before the hand-over to a new top management team, are not good times to press long-term strategic issues.

| Exhibit 15.4 | Formal channels for issue selling |

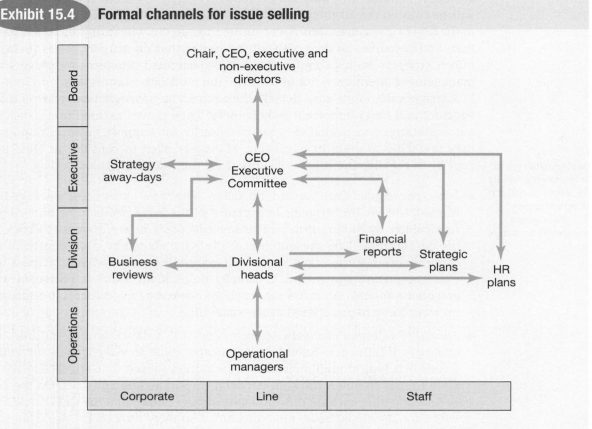

Source: Adapted from W. Ocasio and J. Joseph, 'An attention-based theory of strategy formulation: linking micro and macro perspectives in strategy processes', *Advances in Strategic Management*, vol. 22 (2005), pp. 39–62.

Selling an issue is only the start, of course. Even after an issue has been successfully sold, and actions and resources agreed, managers should make sure that attention is *sustained*.[37] Initial commitments in terms of top management attention and other resources need to be protected. As the strategic issue evolves over time, it may require more attention and resources than originally promised. Establishing at the outset a regular series of reviews and a set of relevant performance metrics will help keep top management attention focused on the issue and hopefully prepared to release more resources as required.

15.3.3 Strategic decision making

Strategic issues are ultimately decided upon in many ways. Success and failure are not always rational. Strategic decision making is also liable to several biases.[38] The notion of strategic issue selling points to the so-called *champion's bias*, the likelihood that people will exaggerate the case in favour of their particular proposal. Similarly, there is the *sunflower syndrome*, the tendency (like sunflowers following the sun) to follow the lead of the most senior person in the decision-making process, or to try to anticipate their view even before they have expressed it. Decision makers often hold exaggerated opinions of their competence, leading to over-optimistic decisions, especially where there is little data available. At the same time, they can be risk averse, being unduly deterred by substantial downsides, even when the chances of such downsides are very slight.

Just putting decisions in the hands of a team of managers, therefore, does not on its own guarantee rigorous and effective decision making. Katherine Eisenhardt's research on strategic decision making in fast-moving environments suggests four helpful guidelines for managers:[39]

- *Build multiple, simultaneous alternatives.* Having several alternatives on the table at the same time helps to encourage critical debate. This can help counter phenomena such as champion's bias and the sunflower syndrome. It is also faster than taking proposals sequentially, where alternatives are only sought out after a previous proposal has been examined and rejected. Examining multiple, simultaneous alternatives is a practice adopted by Barclays Bank, for example, where the rule is that proposals should never be presented in isolation, but always alongside at least two other alternatives.[40]

- *Track real-time information.* Eisenhardt's research found that fast decision makers do not cut back on the amount of information; they use a different type of information – real-time information. These managers prefer immediate information from current operations, rather than statistical trends and forecasts. They tend to spend a lot of time in face-to-face meetings, 'managing by wandering around' and reviewing the most up-to-date indicators, such as weekly and even daily measures of sales, cash, stocks or work-in-progress. In fast-moving environments especially, a quick decision may be better than a delayed decision, and trend data is liable to be rapidly outdated anyway.

- *Seek the views of trusted advisors.* Experienced managers in the organisation or sector can provide fast feedback on what is likely to work or not work based on their deep knowledge from the past. They can also ask tough questions given what they have seen before. The instincts of experienced managers are faster, and often both more reliable and more credible, than lengthy analysis undertaken by junior managers or consultants. Older middle managers whose careers have plateaued can be good people to listen to: not only do they have the experience, but they usually have less self-interest at stake.

- *Aim for consensus, but not at any cost.* Fast decision makers seek consensus amongst the decision-making team, but do not insist on it. Consensus can be too slow and often leads to mediocre choices based on the lowest common denominator. Fast decision makers recognise that debates cannot always be resolved to everybody's satisfaction. Eisenhardt's advice is that the CEO or other senior person should have the courage at a certain point simply to decide. Having had the chance to voice their position, the responsibility of other managers is to accept that decision as final and to get on with implementation.

However, it is easy to exaggerate both the importance and the effectiveness of decision making. Many decisions are not followed through with actions. Many strategies are emergent rather than consciously decided (see Chapter 11).[41]

Two widely held views about decision making are implicitly challenged so far. First, *intuition* is not always a bad thing.[42] Immersion in real-time information or the long experience of older middle managers can provide a strong 'gut-feel' for what should be done. This gut-feel can provide the basis for inspired hunches where there is little reliable data to be analysed anyway, for instance in the creation of radically new markets or products. Second, *conflict* in decision-making teams can be positively useful.[43] Conflict can expose champion's biases. It can challenge optimistic self-assessments of managerial competence. Conflict is fostered by having diverse managerial teams, with members prepared to be devil's advocates, challenging assumptions or easy consensus. But productive conflict needs careful management. Team members must accept decisions as final and share a fundamental mutual respect.

15.3.4 Communicating the strategy

Deciding strategy is only one step: strategic decisions need to be communicated. Managers have to consider which stakeholders to inform (see Chapter 4) and how they should tailor their messages to each. Shareholders, key customers and employees are likely to be particularly central, all with different needs. For every new strategy, there should be a communications strategy to match.

Employee communications are typically vital to ensure that the strategy is carried out in the first place. As in Chapter 5, strategies often drift away from original intentions. Unless people understand the strategy, then it is unlikely to be implemented. Everyday interactions of lower-level managers and ordinary staff can easily undermine an intended strategy. For instance, a new strategy of improved customer service will fail if managers do not hire, train and reward their staff consistently: old habits in the field will constantly spoil customer interactions. One example of an organisation seeking high understanding of strategy by all employees is the Volvo Group, where the target is that 90 per cent of employees will be aware of the company's strategic goals, tested by an annual attitude survey.[44]

In shaping a communications strategy for employees, four elements need to be considered in particular:[45]

- *Focus*. Communications should be focused on the key components of the strategy, avoiding unnecessary detail or complex language. CEO Jack Welch's famous statement that General Electric should be 'either Number One or Number Two' in all its markets is remembered precisely because of this clear focus on the importance of being a dominant player wherever the company competed.

- *Impact*. Communications should be impactful, with powerful and memorable words and visuals. For example, the United Kingdom's new community services strategy is powerfully titled 'Our health, our care, our say', in order to embody the inclusiveness and direct importance of the strategy for all citizens.[46] A strong 'story-line' can help by encapsulating the journey ahead and imagined new futures for the organisation and its customers. One struggling medical centre in New Mexico communicated its new strategy, and inspired its staff, with a story-line representing the organisation as 'The Raiders of the Lost Art', conveying a simultaneous sense of courage in adversity and recovery of old values.[47] Visual devices can be very important. Jeff Bezos at Amazon.com sketches a 'virtuous circle' to express how the growth strategy sets in motion a cycle in which lower costs produce improved customer experience, which in turn produces greater traffic, which would support a wider selection of goods, and so on.[48]

- *Media*. Choosing appropriate media to convey the new strategy is very important.[49] Mass media such as e-mails, voicemails, company newsletters, videos, intranets and senior manager blogs can ensure that all staff receive the same message promptly, helping to avoid damaging uncertainty and rumour mongering. However, face-to-face communications are important too in order to demonstrate the personal commitment of managers and allow for interaction with concerned staff. Thus senior managers may undertake *roadshows*, carrying their message directly to various groups of employees with conferences or workshops at different sites. They may also institute *cascades*, whereby each level of managers is tasked to convey the strategy message directly to the staff reporting to them, and these staff in turn are required to convey the message to their staff, and so on through the organisation.[50]

- *Employee engagement*. It is often helpful to engage employees directly in the strategy, so that they can see what it means for them personally and how their role will change. Interchanges through roadshows and cascades can help, but some organisations use imaginative means to create more active engagement. For example, one British public sector organisation invited all its staff to a day's conference introducing its new strategy, at which employees were invited to pin a photograph of themselves on a 'pledge wall', together with a hand-written promise to change at least one aspect of their work to fit the new strategy.[51] The same organisation also created a carpet depicting the strategic change journey, asking its employees to walk along the pathway to the envisioned future.

It is important to recognise that the process of communication is likely to change the strategy in various ways. Sense making by managers and staff typically involves reinterpretation; roadshows and cascades may raise new issues.[52] In a way, therefore, communications is not the end-point of a strategy-making process, but feeds into the identification of new strategic issues for the next round of strategising.

15.4 STRATEGY METHODOLOGIES

Strategists use a wide range of more or less standardised methodologies to organise and guide their strategising activity. The methodologies introduced here are not analytical concepts or techniques such as in most of the rest of the book, but approaches to managing the strategising process. This section, therefore, addresses which methodologies people might use in doing strategy activity. At the start of this process is often a strategy workshop. This can lead into a set of strategy projects. Projects are often driven by hypothesis testing techniques. Finally, strategising output typically has to fit the format of a business case or strategic plan. This section introduces key issues in each of these methodologies. While guidelines are offered, it should be clear that none of these methodologies offers an easy recipe for success.

15.4.1 Strategy workshops

Strategy workshops
(sometimes called
strategy retreats, away-
days or off-sites) usually
involve groups of
executives working
intensively for one or two
days, often away from the
office, on organisational
strategy

Strategy workshops (sometimes called strategy retreats, away-days or off-sites) are a common methodology for making strategy.[53] These workshops usually involve groups of executives working intensively for one or two days, often away from the office, on organisational strategy. These executives are typically senior managers in the organisation, although workshops can also be a valuable mechanism for involving a wider group of managers. Workshops are used typically to formulate or reconsider strategy, but are also used to address strategy implementation issues and to communicate strategic decisions to a larger audience. Workshops can be either ad hoc or part of the regular strategic planning process, and they may be stand-alone or designed as a series of events. As well as facilitating strategy making, workshops can have additional roles in team building and the personal development of individual participants. Illustration 15.3 demonstrates some of the purposes these strategy workshops can play.

Although strategy workshops can be a valuable part of an organisation's strategy-making activity, they are prone to at least two problems.[54] First, they are liable simply to reinforce managers' existing preconceptions. Especially when reduced to a routine part of the strategic planning cycle, and involving the usual group of senior managers, workshops may not be able to produce new ideas that radically challenge the status quo. Second, workshops can become detached from subsequent action. Precisely because they are separated from the ordinary routines of the organisation, it is difficult to translate workshop ideas and enthusiasm back into the workplace.

Strategy workshops need to be designed for the purpose they are intended to serve. Clarity of objectives is strongly correlated with perceived success.[55] Senior managers should discuss carefully what they want from the workshop, or workshop series beforehand, and design them accordingly. In designing workshops that seek to challenge existing strategy preconceptions, managers should consider:

- *Insisting on prior preparation.* Workshops are typically too short to allow much analysis during the workshop and data may be difficult and time consuming to access. It may be helpful to insist that participants bring key issues, analyses or data to the workshop, and present on them briefly as input to the workshop. Subsequent discussions are likely to be better grounded on firm facts, and awkward information is less easily dismissed.

- *Involving participants from outside the senior executive team.* It may be useful to invite non-executive directors who can be asked to bring an external and challenging view. Alternatively, promising middle managers can be included, as they may have a more direct understanding of issues on the ground and their participation could also be valuable for career development and management succession.

- *Involving outside consultants as facilitators.* Using consultants to chair and facilitate the workshop can free managers to concentrate on the discussion itself, help keep the discussion focused on the strategic issues and support all participants contributing equally to discussion. A consultant may be able to advise on workshop design, provide short stimulating exercises or analyses during the workshop and help with follow-up after the workshop. Such consultants need to be experienced, sensitive and not overbearing.

Illustration 15.3

Strategy workshops at ESB Power Generation

Strategy workshops may have a variety of purposes relating to strategy development and strategic change.

The managing director of ESB Power Generation, responsible for the running of power stations in Ireland, was concerned that impending deregulation and possible future privatisation would inevitably mean that the business would face a very different future. There would be pressure to reduce market share as well as costs, and the business could find itself in a competitive situation for the first time in its history. It was necessary to examine the future strategy of the business and he decided to do this through a series of strategy workshops involving different levels in the organisation.

Top team workshop

The process began with a two-day top team workshop which addressed a series of questions:

- What might be the key macro-environmental forces to affect the business in the next five years? Deregulation certainly, but that could take different forms. New technologies and raw material costs were also identified as major unknowns that could have significant impact.

- What form might future competition take? This was less likely to be local and more likely to be from the entry of power generators from other European Union countries.

- So what might the possible future scenarios be?

- What competitive advantage might the business have over possible new entrants and what strategic capabilities could these build on? Given the different types of power stations ESB had in Ireland, an advantage it should have was flexibility in its offering to the market compared with potential competitors.

- What were the strategic options to compete in a deregulated environment? The strategy would have to change significantly whichever scenario came about and more emphasis would have to be placed on the differential advantages ESB had and might further develop.

Workshops with middle managers

The next level of workshops spread the discussion to managers who reported to those in the top team,

together with specialists from other functions. These reviewed the deliberations of the top team, going through the same process in order to establish whether they would come to similar conclusions. The managing director confirmed that the process was also about ensuring that they saw the need for change themselves and checking that they would be 'on board' with a very different strategy from the past.

Two such workshops were held and they did, indeed, endorse the strategy of the top team. They also examined just what a strategy emphasising flexibility would mean in terms of operational priorities in the various business functions.

Involvement throughout the organisation in planning change

There remained the problem of strategic change. Changing from a public sector utility to a competitive strategy of differentiation built on flexibility would require changes in the organisation from top to bottom. It was decided that these should be considered by means of workshops to consider the culture change necessary. The aim was to ensure that, not just the physical resources, but the people in the organisation and the way they dealt with customers and each other could deliver the flexibility that would be required. Workshops were held at levels varying from senior executives to supervisors in the production units to examine just what a culture of flexibility meant, the changes needed in detail and the priorities for action.

Questions

1 What frameworks of analysis might the different workshops have used to tackle the issues?

2 If you were a consultant facilitating the workshops what potential problems might you foresee for each level of workshop?

3 What benefits (or disadvantages) might such workshops have in comparison with other approaches to strategy development for such an organisation?

● *Breaking organisational routines*. A distinctive off-site location can help detach participants from day-to-day operational issues and symbolically affirm the occasion is not subject to the usual norms of executive team discussion. Clear rules about restricting use of mobile communication devices can be important to minimise distraction by ordinary operations. Ice-breaking and other apparently playful exercises – sometimes called 'serious play' – at the beginning of a workshop can help generate creativity and a willingness to challenge orthodoxies.[56]

In designing workshops that will be closely connected to subsequent action, managers should consider:

● *Making an agreed list of actions*. Plenty of time should be set aside at the end of the workshop schedule for a review of workshop outputs, and agreement on necessary actions to follow up.

● *Establishing project groups*. Workshops can build on the cohesion built around particular issues by commissioning groups of managers to work together on them and report back either to a regular executive meeting or to subsequent workshops.

● *Circulating agreed actions*. Circulating agreed actions widely in the organisation will increase the commitment of participants to follow through, as well as appeasing the curiosity or anxiety of those who were not included.

● *Making visible commitment by the top management*. The CEO or other senior manager needs to signal complete commitment throughout the event and afterwards, by both statements and actual behaviours. Senior managers need to be present throughout, undistracted by matters external to the workshop, supportive of all participants, and clear leaders in post-workshop actions.

There is no formula for success with strategy workshops. They typically bring together powerful people to discuss issues of crucial personal importance. Just because a workshop is held off-site in deliberately casual style does not mean that the usual organisational politics are entirely suspended.[57]

15.4.2 Strategy projects

Strategy projects involve teams of people assigned to work on particular strategic issues over a defined period of time

Both strategy making and strategy implementation are often organised in the form of projects or taskforces.[58] **Strategy projects** involve teams of people assigned to work on particular strategic issues over a defined period of time. Projects can be instituted in order to explore problems or opportunities as part of the strategy development process: for example, they might be charged to explore new opportunities in overseas markets. Alternatively they might be instituted to implement agreed elements of a strategy, for example an organisational restructuring or the negotiation of a joint venture. Translating a strategic plan or workshop into a set of projects is a good means of ensuring that intentions are turned into action. The projects can also include a wider group of managers in strategy activity.

Strategy projects should be managed like any other project. In particular they need:[59]

- *A clear brief or mandate*. The project's objectives should be agreed and carefully managed. These objectives are the measure of the project's success. 'Scope creep', by which additional objectives are added as the project goes on, is a common danger.

- *Top management commitment*. The continuing commitment of top management, especially the top management 'client' or 'sponsor', needs to be maintained. Top management agendas are frequently shifting, so communications should be regular.

- *Milestones and reviews*. The project should have from the outset clear milestones with an agreed schedule of intermediate achievements. These allow project review and adjustment where necessary, as well as a measure of ongoing success.

- *Appropriate resources*. The key resource is usually people. The right mix of skills needs to be in place, including project management skills, and effort should be invested in 'team building' at the outset. Strategy projects are often part-time commitments for managers, who have to continue with their 'day jobs'. Attention needs to be paid to managing the balance between managers' ordinary responsibilities and project duties: the first can easily derail the second.

Strategy projects are often organised as *programmes* and as *portfolios*. A programme contains a group of projects that address interrelated issues: for example, a set of projects examining new growth opportunities. The portfolio is an organisation's total set of projects, perhaps including several distinct programmes of projects. It is important that both programmes and overall portfolios have clear systems for governance, reporting and review. Projects can easily proliferate and compete. Programme managers should manage overlaps and redundancies, merging or ending projects that no longer have a distinct purpose because of changing circumstances. Senior management should have careful oversight of the whole portfolio, and again be ready to merge and end projects or even programmes, in order to prevent the 'initiative fatigue' that is often the result of project proliferation.

15.4.3 Hypothesis testing

Hypothesis testing
is a methodology used
particularly in strategy
projects for setting
priorities in investigating
issues and options

KEY
CONCEPT

Hypothesis
testing

Strategy project teams are typically under pressure to deliver solutions to complex problems under tight time constraints. **Hypothesis testing** is an effective methodology for setting direction for a project, and is widely used by strategy consulting firms and members of strategy project teams.

Hypothesis testing in strategy is adapted from the hypothesis testing procedures of science.[60] It starts with a proposition about how things are (*the descriptive hypothesis*), and then seeks to test it with real-world data. For example, a descriptive hypothesis in strategy could be that being large scale in a particular industry is essential to profitability. To test it, a strategy project team would begin by gathering data on the size of organisations in the industry and correlate these with the organisations' profitability. Confirmation of this initial descriptive hypothesis (that small organisations are relatively unprofitable) would then lead

Illustration 15.4

Hypothesis testing at a bank

This outline of a consulting engagement for a large, diversified bank shows how the hypothesis testing process can shape a strategy project.

1 Defining the problem/question

The consultants' first step is to define the problem. As usual, the strategic problem has to do with the existence of a gap between what the client wants (here a certain level of profitability for a particular product) and what it has (declining profitability). In short, the consultants' problem is that the bank's profitability for this product is below target levels.

2 Develop a set of competing descriptive hypotheses about problem causes

The consultants gather some preliminary data and draw on their own experience to generate some possible descriptive hypotheses about the causes of the problem. Thus they know that some large national competitors are already exiting from this type of product; that profitability varies dramatically across competitors involved in this product; and that some specialised new entrants have taken significant market share. Three possible hypotheses emerge: that the industry structure is basically unattractive; that the bank lacks the right strategic capabilities; that the bank is targetting the wrong customer segments. The consultants use quick and dirty testing to reject the first two hypotheses: after all, some competitors are making profits and the bank has strong capabilities from long presence in this product area. Accordingly, the starting descriptive hypothesis is that the bank is targetting unprofitable customer segments.

3 Testing the starting descriptive hypothesis

The consultants next design a study to collect the data needed to support the descriptive hypothesis. They carry out a market segmentation analysis by customer group by doing interviews with customers across different geographies and income levels. They analyse the kinds of service different segments require and the fees they might pay. The consultants find that their data supports their starting hypothesis: the bank's branches are concentrated in locations which prosperous customers willing to pay higher fees for this product do not use. (Had they not been able to confirm their hypothesis, the consultants would have returned to the other two competing hypotheses, step 2.)

4 Develop prescriptive hypotheses

The consultants then develop prescriptive hypotheses about actions necessary to attract more profitable customer segments. One prescriptive hypothesis is that a better portfolio of branch locations will enhance profitability. The consultants carry out data gathering and analysis to support this hypothesis, for example comparing the profitability of branches in different kinds of locations. They find that the few branches that happen to be in the right locations do have higher profitability with this product.

5 Make recommendations to the client

The consultants prepare a set of preliminary recommendations based on the descriptive hypothesis and validated prescriptive hypotheses: one of these is that the branch locations need changing. These recommendations are checked for acceptability and feasability with key managers within the bank and adjusted according to feedback. Then the consultants make their formal presentation of final recommendations.

Source: Jeanne Liedtka, Darden School of Management, University of Virginia.

Questions

1 Select an important strategic issue facing an organisation that you are familiar with (or an organisation that is publicly in trouble or a case study organisation). Try generating a few descriptive hypotheses that address this issue. Use quick and dirty testing to select an initial descriptive hypothesis.

2 What data should you gather to confirm this descriptive hypothesis and how would you collect it? Should the descriptive hypothesis be confirmed, what possible prescriptive hypotheses follow?

to several *prescriptive hypotheses* about what a particular organisation should do. For a small-scale organisation in the industry, prescriptive hypotheses would centre on how to increase scale: one prescriptive hypothesis in this case would be that acquisitions were a good means to achieve the necessary scale; another would be that alliances were the right way. These prescriptive hypotheses might then become the subjects of further data testing.

This kind of hypothesis testing is ultimately about setting practical priorities in strategy work. Hypothesis testing in business (see Illustration 15.4) therefore differs from strict scientific procedure. The aim finally is to concentrate attention on a very limited set of promising hypotheses, not on the full set of all possibilities. Data is gathered in order to support favoured hypotheses, whereas in science the objective is formally to try to refute hypotheses. Business hypothesis testing aims to find a robust and satisfactory solution within time and resource constraints, not to find some ultimate scientific truth. Selecting the right hypotheses can be helped by applying *quick and dirty testing* (QDT). Quick and dirty testing relies on project teams' existing experience and easily accessed data in order to reject speedily unpromising hypotheses, before too much time is wasted on them.

15.4.4 Business cases and strategic plans

A business case provides the data and argument in support of a particular strategy proposal, for example investment in new equipment

A strategic plan provides the data and argument in support of a particular strategy for the whole organisation, over a substantial period of time

Strategising activities, such as workshops or projects, are typically orientated to creating an output in the form of a *business case* or *strategic plan*. Keeping this end goal in mind provides a structure for the strategising work: what needs to be produced shapes the strategising activities. A **business case** is usually focused around a particular proposal, perhaps an investment in new equipment. A **strategic plan**, of course, is more comprehensive, taking an overall view of the organisation's direction over a substantial period, usually three years and sometimes more (see Chapter 11). Many organisations have a standard template for making business cases or proposing a strategic plan, and where these exist, it is wise to work with that format. Where there is no standard template, it would be worth investigating recent successful business cases or plans within the organisation, and borrowing features from them. It is important that the business case or plan be consistent with the organisational culture, in terms of style, format and detail.

A project team intending to make a business case should aim to meet the following criteria:[61]

- *Focused on strategic needs*. The team should identify the organisation's overall strategy and relate its case closely to that, not just to any particular departmental needs. A business case should not look as if it is just an HR department or IT department project, for example. The focus should be on a few key issues, with clear priority normally given to those that are both strategically important and relatively easy to address.

- *Supported by key data*. The team will need to assemble appropriate data, with financial data demonstrating appropriate returns on any investment typically essential. However, qualitative data should not be neglected – for example, striking quotations from interviews with employees or key customers, or

Illustration 15.5

Planning to plan at the University Library of Notre Dame

A university library assesses its strategic planning process.

When the University of Notre Dame, Indiana, announced a campus-wide strategic planning initiative, the University's Library service launched its own strategic planning review. Specifically, the Library Director established a taskforce of four members to work for 10 weeks (alongside normal duties) in order to provide an initial assessment of the Library's own existing planning arrangements, which were thought to have been weak. This assessment would be the basis for the Library's own new strategic planning exercise.

The membership of the taskforce was as follows: the Director's own executive assistant, with 15 years' experience in the Library; the Library's budget officer; the business reference librarian, currently studying for a MBA; and the taskforce leader, a maths librarian who had joined the Library from a strategy consulting firm. The taskforce quickly established four stages to their work:

- Produce an operational definition of planning.

- Determine an appropriate planning framework for the Library and its existing materials.

- Evaluate the existing materials in the light of this framework and assess the coherence of the whole.

- Recommend a future planning process.

The taskforce soon arrived at an operational definition of strategic planning through a search of the business literature and professional resources. They then examined various published frameworks for planning, finally comparing five of them systematically on a blackboard. In the end, they settled on one of these frameworks, rather than trying to synthesise their own tailor-made variant. They next searched through the Library's own materials for anything relevant to planning, from presentations given by the Library Director

to formal vision and mission statements. Comparing against the chosen planning framework, the taskforce identified major gaps, such as the absence of any explicit statement about the Library's strategic planning process or anything that could be conceived of as an overall strategic plan. In evaluating these materials, the taskforce found that they were often inconsistent with each other, and light-weight with regard to implementation. In the end, the taskforce recommended that the Library create a completely new strategic plan, with library-wide input.

The last step for the taskforce was to present the findings and recommendations to the Library's senior management. The taskforce leader describes what went well and what went not so well in the presentation:

In a one hour session, we walked them through the four phases of work. We did well explaining . . . strategic planning and outlining a strategic planning framework. We should have taken more time to explain the definitions . . . this is a perpetual source of difficulty. Who can explain clearly the difference between a mission statement and a vision statement . . . ? Nevertheless we did well presenting our conclusions and recommendations and some in our audience were even enthusiastic about starting a thorough strategic planning process.

Within a year, the Library Director had developed a strategic plan, and won acceptance for it from the University's top management.

Source: J. Ladwig, 'Assess the state of your strategic plan', *Library Administration and Management*, vol. 19, no. 2 (2005), pp. 90–93.

Questions

1 What were the key strengths of the taskforce and the process they engaged in?

2 What could have gone wrong?

recent mini-cases of successes or failures in the organisation or at competitors. Some strategic benefits simply cannot be quantified, but are no less important for that: information on competitor moves can be persuasive here. The team should provide background information on the rigour and extent of the research behind the data.

● *Demonstrated solutions and actions*. As earlier, issues attached to solutions tend to get the most attention. The team should provide careful discussion of how proposals will be acted on, and who would be responsible. Possible barriers should be clearly identified. Also alternative scenarios should be recognised, especially downside risk. Implementation feasibility is critical.

● *Provide clear progress measures*. When seeking significant investments over time, it is reassuring to offer clear measures to allow regular progress monitoring. Proposing review mechanisms also adds credibility to the business case.

Many specific evaluation techniques for use in a business case are explained in Chapter 10.

Strategic plans have similar characteristics in terms of focus, data, actions and progress measures. Strategic plans are, however, more comprehensive, and they may be used for entrepreneurial start-ups, business units within a large organisation, or for an organisation as a whole (see also Illustration 15.5). Again formats vary, and it is important to follow one that fits the organisation's culture. However, a typical strategic plan has the following elements, which together should set a strategy team's working agenda:[62]

● *Mission, goals and objectives statement*. This is the point of the whole strategy, and the critical starting place. While it is the starting place, in practice a strategy team might iterate back to this in the light of other elements of the strategic plan. It is worth checking back with earlier statements that the organisation may have made to ensure consistency. See particularly Chapter 4.

● *Environmental analysis*. This should cover the whole of the environment, both macro trends and more focused issues to do with customers, suppliers and competitors. The team should not stop at the analysis, but draw clear strategic implications. See Chapter 2.

● *Organisational analysis*. This should include the strengths and weaknesses of the organisation and its products relative to its competitors and include a clear statement of competitive advantage. To avoid bias and reinforce credibility, the team might seek customer statements about organisational strengths and weaknesses. See Chapter 3.

● *Proposed strategy*. This should be clearly related to the environmental and organisational analyses and support the mission, goals and objectives. The team should offer a clear and realistic action timetable for implementation. Particularly useful here are Chapters 6 to 10.

● *Resources*. The team will need to provide a detailed analysis of the resources required, with options for acquiring them. Critical resources are financial, so the plan should include income statements, cash flows and balance sheets over the period of the plan. Other important resources might be human, particularly managers or people with particular skills. See particularly Chapter 13.

Illustration 15.6   **key debate**

What good are strategy consultants?

Strategy consultants are frequent participants in strategy making, and typically bring good analytical and project management skills. Why are they so controversial then?

There is no shortage of books criticising strategy consultants. Titles such as *Con Tricks*, *Dangerous Company* and *Rip Off!* provide the flavour. And there have been some spectacular failures. As in Section 15.2.4, McKinsey & Co. took a good deal of blame for the strategic mistakes of Enron and SwissAir.

The accusations made against strategy consultants are at least three-fold. First, they rely too much on inexperienced young staff fresh out of business school, who typically have the slimmest understanding of how client organisations and their markets really work. Second, they are accused of handing over strategy recommendations, and then walking away from implementation. Third, they are perceived as expensive, overpaid individually and always trying to sell on unnecessary extra projects. Clients end up paying for more advice than they really need, much of it unrealistic and unimplementable.

These accusations may be unfair. Most large strategy consulting firms are now organised on industry lines, so building up expertise in particular areas, and they increasingly recruit experienced managers from these industries. Most consultants also prefer to work in joint client–advisor teams, so that clients are involved in generating the recommendations that they will have to implement. Some consultanices, such as Bain, make a point of getting closely involved in implementation too. Finally, consultants are in a competitive market and their clients are typically sophisticated buyers, not easily fooled into buying advice they do not need: the fact that strategy consulting business increased in Europe from €3bn (£2.1bn; $3.8bn) in 1996 to €8bn in 2004 suggests there is plenty of real demand.

There are some successes too. Bain claims that, since 1980, its clients' stock prices have on average outperformed the Standard & Poors 500 large American companies index by four-to-one (www.bain.com). Some great corporate managers have originated in strategy consulting: Lou Gerstner, who turned around IBM, and Meg Whitman, leader of eBay, both started as McKinsey & Co. strategy consultants. And one of the world's most influential management books ever, *The Concept of the Corporation*, came from Peter Drucker's consulting assignment with General Motors during World War II.

There are clues to managing strategy consultants in the criticisms, however: for example, make sure to hire consultants with relevant experience; connect analysis to implementation; and keep a close eye on expenditure. James O'Shea and Charles Madigan close their book with a provocative quotation from Machiavelli's *The Prince*: 'Here is an infallible rule: a prince who is not himself wise cannot be wisely advised. . . . Good advice depends on the shrewdness of the prince who seeks it, and not the shrewdness of the prince on good advice.'

Sources: The European Federation of Management Consultancy Associations (www.feaco.org); J. O'Shea and C. Madigan, *Dangerous Company: Consulting Powerhouses and the Businesss they Save and Ruin*, Penguin, 1998; C.D. McKenna, *The World's Newest Profession: Management Consulting in the Twentieth Century*, Cambridge University Press, 2006.

Questions

1 What measures can a strategy consultant take to reassure a potential client of his or her effectiveness?

2 Are there any reasons to suspect that some people might want to exaggerate criticisms of strategy consultants' conduct?

SUMMARY

- The practice of strategy involves critical choices about *who to involve* in strategy, *what to do* in strategising activity, and *which strategising methodologies* to use in order to guide this activity.

- Chief executive officers, senior managers, non-executive directors, strategic planners, strategy consultants and middle managers are frequently all involved in strategising. Middle manager involvement in strategy can suffer from the *CEO access/implementation responsibility paradox*, but the degree of appropriate involvement none the less should depend on the nature of the issue.

- Strategising activity involves *analysing, issue selling, decision making* and *communicating*. Managers should not expect these activities to be fully rational or logical and can valuably appeal to the non-rational characteristics of the people they work with.

- Practical methodologies to guide strategising activity include *strategy workshops, strategy projects, hypothesis testing* and creating *business cases* and *strategic plans*.

Work assignments

*✱ Denotes more advanced work assignments.   * Refers to a case study in the Text and Cases edition.*

15.1 Go to the careers or recruitment web page of one of the big strategy consultants (such as www.bain.com, www.bcg.com, www.mckinsey.com). What does this tell you about the nature of strategy consulting work? Would you like this work?

15.2 Go to the website of a large organisation (private or public sector) and assess the way it communicates its strategy to its audiences. With reference to section 15.3.4, how focused is the communication; how impactful is it; and how likely is it to engage employees?

15.3 If you had to design a strategy workshop, suggest who the participants in the workshop should be and what roles they should play in (a) the case where an organisation has to re-examine its fundamental strategy in the face of crisis; (b) the case where an organisation needs to gain commitment to a long-term, comprehensive programme of strategic change.

15.4 ✱ For any case study in the book, imagine yourself in the position of a strategy consultant and propose an initial descriptive hypothesis (section 15.4.3) and define the kinds of data that you would need to test it. What kinds of people would you want in your strategy project team (see sections 15.2.4 and 15.4.2)?

15.5 ✱ Go to a business plan archive (such as the University of Maryland's www.businessplanarchive.org or use a Google search). Select a business plan of interest to you and, in the light of section 15.4.4, assess its good points and its bad points.

Integrative assignment

15.6 For an organisation with which you are familiar, or one of the case organisations, write a strategic plan (for simplicity, you might choose to focus on an undiversified business or a business unit within a larger corporation). Where data is missing, make reasonable assumptions or propose ways of filling the gaps. Comment on whether and how you would provide different versions of this strategic plan for (a) investors; (b) employees.

An extensive range of additional materials, including audio summaries, weblinks to organisations featured in the text, definitions of key concepts and self-assessment questions, can be found on the *Exploring Corporate Strategy* Companion Website at **www.pearsoned.co.uk/ecs**

Recommended key readings

- For an overview of top management involvement in strategy, see P. Stiles and B. Taylor, *Boards at Work: How Directors View their Roles and Responsibilities*, Oxford University Press, 2001. For an overview of the middle management role, see S. Floyd and B. Wooldridge, *Building Strategy from the Middle*, Sage, 2000.

- Three journal special issues offer academic studies of strategy practice: the 'Micro strategy and strategizing', *Journal of Management Studies*, vol. 40, no. 1 (2003); 'Strategizing: the challenges of a practice perspective', *Human Relations*, vol. 60, no. 1

(2007); and 'The crafts of strategy', *Long Range Planning* (2008, forthcoming).

- A practical guide to strategising methodologies is provided by E. Rasiel and P.N. Friga, *The McKinsey Mind*, McGraw-Hill, 2001, which has much more general relevance than that particular consulting firm.

- P. Walcoff, *The Fast-Forward MBA in Business Planning for Growth*, Wiley, 1999, is a practical guide to writing a business or strategic plan, with plenty of models and templates.

References

1. A theoretical basis for this pyramid can be found in R. Whittington, 'Completing the practice turn in strategy research', *Organization Studies*, vol. 27, no. 5 (2006), pp. 613–634; and P. Jarzabkowski, J. Balogun and D. Seidl, 'Strategizing: the challenges of a practice perspective', *Human Relations*, vol. 60, no. 1 (2007), pp. 5–27.

2. A good review of the role of different managers in strategy according to evolving notions of strategic management is in T. O'Shannassy, 'Modern strategic management: balancing strategic thinking and strategic planning for internal and external stakeholders', *Singapore Management Review*, vol. 25, no. 1 (2003), pp. 53–67.

3. The classic statement is A. Chandler, *Strategy and Structure: Chapters in the History of American Enterprise*, MIT Press, 1962.

4. S. Kaplan and E. Beinhocker, 'The real value of strategic planning', *MIT Sloan Management Review*, Winter (2003), pp. 71–76.

5. M.E. Porter, 'What is strategy?', *Harvard Business Review*, November–December (1996), pp. 61–78.

6. M. Haywood and D. Hambrick, 'Explaining the premium paid for large acquisitions: evidence of CEO hubris', *Administrative Science Quarterly*, vol. 42, no. 1 (1977), pp. 103–128.

7. J. Collins, *Good to Great*, Random House, 2001.

8. I. Janis, *Victims of Groupthink: A Psychological Study of Foreign-Policy Decisions and Fiascoes*, Houghton Mifflin, 1972; R.S. Baron, 'So right it's wrong: groupthink and the ubiquitous nature of polarized group decision making', in Mark P. Zanna (ed.), *Advances in experimental social psychology*, vol. 37. pp. 219–253, Elsevier Academic Press, 2005.

9. C. Boone, W. Von Olffen, A. Van Witteloostuijn and B. De Brabander, 'The genesis of top management team diversity: selective turnover among top management teams in Dutch newspaper publishing', *Academy of Management Journal*, vol. 47, no. 5 (2004), pp. 633–656.

10. T. McNulty and A. Pettigrew, 'Strategists on the board', *Organization Studies*, vol. 20, no. 1 (1999), pp. 47–74; P. Stiles and B. Taylor, *Boards at Work: How Directors view their roles and responsibilities*, Oxford University Press, 2001.

11. For an insightful case of an orchestra CEO inadequacy with regard to strategy techniques, see S. Maitlis, 'Taking it from the top: how CEOS influence (and fail to influence) their boards', *Organization Studies*, vol. 25, no. 8 (2004), pp. 1275–1313.

12. For an in-depth analysis of a director failing to persuade his colleagues, see D. Samra-Fredericks, 'Strategizing as lived experience and strategists' everyday efforts to shape strategic direction', *Journal of Management Studies*, vol. 42, no. 1 (2003), pp. 1413–1442.

13. For an analysis of senior management teams as 'communities of practice' in which practitioners have to win legitimacy for full participation, see R. Whittington, 'Learning to Strategise', SKOPE Working Paper no. 23, University of Oxford, 2002.

14. R.M. Grant, 'Strategic planning in a turbulent environment: evidence from the oil majors', *Strategic Management Journal*, vol. 24, no. 6 (2003), pp. 491–517.

15. E. Beinhocker and S. Kaplan, 'Tired of strategic planning?', *McKinsey Quarterly*, special edition on Risk and Resilience (2002), pp. 49–57; S. Kaplan and E. Beinhocker, 'The real value of strategic planning', *MIT Sloan Management Review*, Winter (2003), pp. 71–76.

16. A. Chandler, *Strategy and Structure: Chapters in the History of American Enterprise*, MIT Press, 1962.

17. S. Floyd and B. Wooldridge, *Building Strategy from the Middle*, Sage, 2000.

18. G. Johnson, L. Melin and R. Whittington, 'Micro-strategy and strategising: towards an activity-based view', *Journal of Management Studies*, vol. 40, no. 1 (2003), pp. 3–22.

19. A. Watson and B. Wooldridge, 'Business unit manager influence on corporate-level strategy formulation', *Journal of Managerial Issues*, vol. 18, no. 2 (2005), pp. 147–161.

20. S. Floyd and B. Wooldridge, 'Middle management's strategic influence and organizational performance', *Journal of Management Studies*, vol. 34, no. 3 (1997), pp. 465–485.

21. S. Mantere, 'Strategic practices as enablers and disablers of championing activity', *Strategic Organization*, vol. 3, no. 2 (2005), pp. 157–184.

22. F. Westley, 'Middle managers and strategy: microdynamics of inclusion', *Strategic Management Journal*, vol. 11 (1990), pp. 337–351.

23. See D. Moyniham, 'Ambiguity in policy lessons: the agentification experience', *Public Administration*, vol. 84, no. 4 (2006), pp. 1029–1050; and L.S. Oakes, B. Townley and D.J. Cooper, 'Business planning as pedagogy: language and control in a changing institutional field', *Administrative Science Quarterly*, vol. 43, no. 2 (1997), pp. 257–292.

24. The websites of the leading strategy consultants are useful sources of information on strategy consulting and strategy in general, as well as strategy consulting careers: see www.mckinsey.com; www.bcg.com; www.bain.com; www.monitor.com.

25. The European Federation of Management Consultancies Associations website www.feaco.org is a useful source of information on trends in the strategy consulting industry generally. P. May and F. Czeniawska, *Management Consulting in Practice*, Kogan Page, 2005, provides many cases of consulting interventions, including strategy.

26. For theoretical discussion of advisers in strategy, see L. Arendt, R. Priem and H. Ndofor, 'A CEO-adviser model of strategic decision-making', *Journal of Management*, vol. 31, no. 5 (2005), pp. 680–699; an empirically-based study is M. Schwarz, 'Knowing in practice: how consultants work with clients to create, share and apply knowledge', *Academy of Management Best Papers Proceedings*, 2004.

27. C.D. McKenna, *The World's Newest Profession*, Cambridge University Press, 2006; R. Whittington, P. Jarzabkowski, M. Mayer, E. Mounoud, J. Nahapiet and L. Rouleau, 'Taking strategy seriously: responsibility and reform for an important social practice', *Journal of Management Inquiry*, vol. 12, no. 4 (2003), pp. 396–409.

28. S. Appelbaum, 'Critical success factors in the client-consulting relationship', *Journal of the American Academy of Business*, March (2004), pp. 184–191; M. Mohe, 'Generic strategies for managing consultants: insights from client companies in Germany', *Journal of Change Management*, vol. 5, no. 3 (2005), pp. 357–365.

29. E. Beinhocker and S. Kaplan, 'Tired of strategic planning?', *McKinsey Quarterly*, special edition on Risk and Resilience (2002), pp. 49–57: figure 2, p. 56.

30. G. Hodgkinson, R. Whittington, G. Johnson and M. Schwarz, 'The role of strategy workshops in strategy development processes: formality, communication, co-ordination and inclusion', *Long Range Planning*, vol. 30 (2006), pp. 479–496.

31. T. Hill and R. Westbrook, 'SWOT analysis: it's time for a product recall', *Long Range Planning*, vol. 30, no. 1 (1997), pp. 46–52. For a practical example of better usage, see R.G. Dyson, 'Strategic development and SWOT analysis at the University of Warwick', *European Journal of Operational Research*, vol. 15, no. 2 (2004), pp. 631–640.

32. A. Langley, 'Between paralysis by analysis and extinction by instinct', *Sloan Management Review*, vol. 36, no. 3 (1995), pp. 63–76.

33. A. Langley, 'In search of rationality: the purposes behind the use of formal analysis in organisations', *Administrative Science Quarterly*, vol. 34 (1989), pp. 598–631.

34. This draws on the attention-based view of the firm: see W. Ocasio and J. Joseph, 'An attention-based theory of strategy formulation: linking micro and macro perspectives in strategy processes', *Advances in Strategic Management*, vol. 22 (2005), pp. 39–62.

35. Ibid.

36. For an insightful analysis of the role of mealtimes and other informal moments to influence strategy, see A. Sturdy, M. Schwarz and A. Spicer, 'Guess who's coming to dinner? Structures and the use of liminality in strategic management consultancy', *Human Relations*, vol. 10, no. 7 (2006), pp. 929–960.

37. B. Yakis and R. Whittington, 'Sustaining strategic issues: five longitudinal cases in human resource management', Paper presented to the *Academy of Management*, Philadelphia, 2007.

38. D. Lovallo and O. Siboney, 'Distortions and deceptions in strategic decisions', *McKinsey Quarterly*, no. 1 (2006). A good review of decision-making biases is in G. Hodgkinson and P. Sparrow, *The Competent Organization*, Open University Press, 2002.

39. K.M. Eisenhardt, 'Speed and strategic choice: how managers accelerate decision making', *California Management Review*, Spring (1990), pp. 39–54.

40. M. Mankins, 'Stop wasting valuable time', *Harvard Business Review*, September (2004), pp. 58–65.

41. S. Elbanna, 'Strategic decision-making: process perspectives', *International Journal of Management Reviews*, vol. 8, no. 1 (2006), pp. 1–20.

42. C. Miller and R.D. Ireland, 'Intuition in strategic decision-making: friend or foe in the fast-paced 21st century?', *Academy of Management Executive*, vol. 21, no. 1 (2005), pp. 19–30.

43. K.M. Eisenhardt, J. Kahwajy and L.J. Bourgeois, 'Conflict and strategic choice: how top teams disagree', *California Management Review*, vol. 39, no. 2 (1997), pp. 42–62.

44. C. Nordblom, 'Involving middle managers in strategy at Volvo Group', *Strategic Communication Management*, vol. 10, no. 2 (2006), pp. 24–28.

45. This builds on M. Thatcher, 'Breathing life into business strategy', *Strategic Communication Management*, vol. 10, no. 2 (2006), pp. 14–18.

46. See http://www.cabinetoffice.gov.uk/strategy/work_areas/index.asp.

47. G. Adamson, J. Pine, T. van Steenhoven and J. Kroupa, 'How story-telling can drive strategic change', *Strategy and Leadership*, vol. 34, no. 1 (2006), pp. 36–41.

48. R.W. Keidel, 'Strategize on a napkin', *Strategy and Leadership*, vol. 33, no. 4 (2005), pp. 58–59.

49. R.H. Lengel and R.L. Daft, 'The selection of communication media as an executive skill', *Academy of Management Executive*, vol. 2, no. 3 (1988), pp. 225–232.

50. For examples of roadshows and cascades, see M. Thatcher, 'Breathing life into business strategy', *Strategic Communication Management*, vol. 10, no. 2 (2006), pp. 14–18.

51. R. Whittington, E. Molloy, M. Mayer and A. Smith, 'Practices of strategizing/organizing: broadening strategy work and skills', *Long Range Planning*, vol. 39 (2006), pp. 615–629.

52. On middle manager sense making, see J. Balogun and G. Johnson, 'Organizational restructuring and middle manager sensemaking', *Academy of Management Journal*, vol. 47, no. 4 (2004), pp. 523–540.

53. For a recent survey of strategy workshops in practice, see G. Hodgkinson, R. Whittington, G. Johnson and M. Schwarz, 'The role of strategy workshops in strategy development processes: formality, communication, coordination and inclusion', *Long Range Planning*, vol. 30 (2006), pp. 479–496.

54. C. Bowman, 'Strategy workshops and top-team commitment to strategic change', *Journal of Managerial Psychology*, vol. 10, no. 8 (1995), pp. 4–12; B. Frisch and L. Chandler, 'Off-sites that work', *Harvard Business Review*, vol. 84, no. 6 (2006), pp. 117–126.

55. G. Hodgkinson, R. Whittington, G. Johnson and M. Schwarz, 'The role of strategy workshops in strategy development processes: formality, communication, coordination and inclusion', *Long Range Planning*, vol. 30 (2006), pp. 479–496.

56. L. Heracleous and C. Jacobs, 'The serious business of play', *MIT Quarterly*, Fall (2005), pp. 19–20.

57. For a discussion of a failed strategy workshop from different points of view, see G. Hodgkinson and G. Wright, 'Confronting strategic inertia in a top management team: learning from failure', *Organization Studies*, vol. 23, no. 6 (2002), pp. 949–978; and R. Whittington, 'Completing the practice turn in strategy research', *Organization Studies*, vol. 27, no. 5 (2006), pp. 613–634.

58. P. Morris and A. Jamieson, 'Moving from corporate strategy to project strategy', *Project Management Journal*, vol. 36, no. 4 (2005), pp. 5–18. A comparative study of strategy project development teams is in F. Blackler, N. Crump and S. McDonald, 'Organizing processes in complex activity networks', *Organization*, vol. 72, no. 2 (2000), pp. 277–300. See also S. Paroutis and A. Pettigrew, 'Strategizing in the multi-business firm: strategy teams at multiple levels and over time', *Human Relations*, vol. 60, no. 1 (2007), pp. 99–135.

59. H. Sirkin, P. Keenan and A. Jackson, 'The hard side of change management', *Harvard Business Review*, October (2005), pp. 109–118; J. Kenny, 'Effective project management for strategic innovation and change in an organizational context', *Project Management Journal*, vol. 34, no. 1 (2003), pp. 43–53.

60. This section draws on E. Rasiel and P.N. Friga, *The McKinsey Mind*, McGraw-Hill, 2001; H. Courtney, *20/20 Foresight: Crafting Strategy in an Uncertain World*, Harvard Business School Press, 2001; and unpublished material from J. Liedtka, University of Virginia.

61. J. Walker, 'Is your business case compelling?', *Human Resource Planning*, vol. 25, no. 1 (2002), pp. 12–15; M. Pratt, 'Seven steps to a business case', *Computer World*, 10 October (2005), pp. 35–36.

62. Two practical books on creating strategic or business plans are P. Tiffany and S. Peterson, *Business Plans for Dummies*, IDG Books, 2004; and P. Walcoff, *The Fast-Forward MBA in Business Planning for Growth*, Wiley, 1999.

Ray Ozzie, software strategist

During 2005 and 2006, Ray Ozzie took an increasingly important strategic role at the computer software giant Microsoft, finally emerging as the company's Chief Software Architect. At the centre of Ozzie's new strategy was the endeavour to 'webify' Microsoft, widely perceived to have fallen behind Internet upstarts such as Google and Yahoo!. Developing this new strategy involved more than formulating a bold and challenging new vision for Microsoft. Ozzie faced difficult decisions even in the sheer practicalities of strategy making. Thus Ozzie had to design a top management strategy retreat; he had to find a way of maintaining the momentum after that retreat; and finally, he had to decide how best to communicate the key themes of the emerging new strategy.

Bill Gates (left) and Ray Ozzie (right)

Ozzie was regarded by many experts as a software genius. In 1984 he had founded Iris Associates, which five years later launched, under contract for the Lotus Development Corporation, the first commercial e-mail and collaboration software for major corporations, Lotus Notes. Lotus Development Corporation bought Iris for $84m (£47m; €67m) in 1994, and the next year computer giant IBM in turn bought Lotus. Three years later, Ozzie left IBM to found Groove Networks, another collaboration software company. In March 2005, Microsoft bought Groove Networks in order to integrate its collaboration features into the next generation of its Office products. Ozzie joined Microsoft as a new employee.

What Microsoft paid for Groove Networks was undisclosed, but it certainly made Ozzie an even wealthier man. In other respects, however, Ozzie's position was not so comfortable. Ozzie's starting position was as only one of three chief technology officers at Microsoft, a company with 70,000 employees. Initially he would be commuting weekly from his home in Boston on the East Coast to the Microsoft headquarters in Redmond on the West Coast. Besides, Groove Networks had been Ozzie's own show, and much smaller, with just

200 employees. As Ozzie said in an interview with MSNBC: 'The great thing about a small company is that you can put a lot of effort into one thing – but you can have limited impact. In a larger role, I'll probably have less focused impact, across a broader range of things.'

The company that Ozzie was joining did indeed operate across a broad range of products. It was responsible for the near universal Microsoft Windows operating system; for the equally pervasive Microsoft Office range of products; for the Xbox games business; for the MSN Internet portal; and for MSNBC cable television. Total turnover was $40bn and the company had $35bn cash reserves. The company was still dominated by Bill Gates, who had founded it in 1975 and boasted in 2005 that he had worked every single day in the intervening 30 years. In 2005, Gates was still the company's Chief Software Architect.

But by 2005 the company was apparently stagnating. Turnover and profits were still climbing, but the stock price had been stuck for several years. From a peak of nearly $60 a share, Microsoft had been fluctuating around $25 (see the figure). Microsoft's core business model relied on selling

Microsoft corporation
Price history – MSFT (9/11/1996 – 9/8/2006)

Source: www.msnbc.com. MSNBC.com by MSNBC. Copyright 2006 by MSNBC Interactive News, LLC. Reproduced with permission of MSNBC Interactive News, LLC in the format Textbook via Copyright Clearance Center.

proprietary software direct either to users or to computer manufacturers for pre-installation on machines. This model was being challenged by free open-source software (such as Linux) and web-based companies whose software was free off the Internet and supported by advertising (such as Google or Yahoo!). Microsoft was widely perceived as yesterday's company.

Strategy Retreats

Ozzie was not going into Microsoft blind. As a Fortune article describes, even before being hired, Ozzie had attended the March retreat of the company's top 110 or so executives, including Bill Gates. The two-day retreat was organised by Microsoft's CEO, Steve Ballmer, and took place at the luxurious Semiahmoo Resort, overlooking the Pacific and with a spa and two golf courses. According to Fortune, the retreat kicked off with a team-building exercise in which the executives broke into groups of six or seven. Each group was given a bag of parts for a battery-powered Mars rover. The goal: build the rover quickly, but with the fewest parts. Bill Gates' team won. On the second

day, groups were assigned to breakout sessions in order to brainstorm various strategic issues. Gates, Ozzie and several other top technologists were put in a group tasked with defining Microsoft's 'core' – the set of things Microsoft does uniquely well that could be used across all Microsoft's product lines. Ozzie recalled the breakout session: 'It was the first time I had a chance as an insider to see how people within the company relate to Bill.' When the group went into its appointed conference room, he told Fortune, 'they tended to just naturally fall with Bill at one end and other people around the sides. In some ways they were being deferential, and in some ways he was just one of the gang in a really lively peer discussion.'

The nature of Microsoft's core emerged as the key strategic issue from Semiahmoo. Ballmer, however, seemed unable to push the issue forward. The group of executives he had asked to arrange a larger event to develop the issue refused to organise it. They argued it was premature and likely to cause undue alarm to involve more people at that stage. The momentum from Semiahmoo seemed to have evaporated, until Ballmer turned to Ozzie to ask him to take forward the concept of the strategic core. Soon after, Ballmer asked Ozzie to take the lead with another top management retreat, to take place in June. As Ozzie commented to Fortune: 'I had more than a bit of anxiety, given I had never worked with these folks before'.

Ozzie worked closely with Gates, Ballmer and some other senior executives to design this second retreat. It would take place over one day at Robinswood House, a small hotel based on a nineteenth-century pioneer lodge close to Microsoft's headquarters. Just 15 senior executives were to attend; Gates was not invited. The Robinswood facilities were cramped and somewhat basic, with everybody sitting elbow to elbow in a small room. The room was cold and the food attracted complaints. Everybody had been circulated before the meeting with a 51-page memo from Ozzie with his diagnosis of the strategic challenge facing Microsoft.

Ozzie kicked off the retreat by restating the strategic challenge to Microsoft. Fortune reports that Ozzie maintained his usual genial and non-confrontational style, but no punches were pulled about Microsoft's past mistakes. Ozzie recalled how the group of senior managers then went through a 'cathartic exercise of venting about every negative thing' in the company's technical and organisational strategy of recent years. 'It was story after story after story.' For 14 hours, the senior Microsoft executives worked continuously debating the future of the company. The group's conclusion was that Microsoft needed major change. At the end of the debate, Ballmer demanded of his colleagues: 'If there are any concerns, you've got to say them now.' There was no dissent.

This time Ballmer and Ozzie worked hard to ensure follow-through. A series of weekly half-day meetings were scheduled for the executives who had been at the retreat, with strong pressure for attendance. Ozzie set the agenda for the meetings and for eight weeks the executives debated specific aspects of the new strategy in a conference room right next door to Ballmer's office. There was a good deal of controversy still, but progress was made. In mid-September, Ballmer announced a set of major organisational changes and promotions. Most significant was the merger of Windows and MSN to create a new Platform Products and Services group within Microsoft, firmly based on the web. Significant too was Ozzie's promotion to chief technology officer for Microsoft as a whole, and the movement of his office and staff to the high-security top-floor suite where Gates and Ballmer had their offices too.

Communicating the Strategy

The web strategy moved forward. In late October Bill Gates and Ray Ozzie each released important internal memos (soon leaked to the Internet). The Gates memo was dated Sunday 30 October, subject Internet Services Software and e-mailed to all Microsoft Executive Staff and Direct Reports and the Distinguished Engineers group. Gates recalled his memo of 10 years earlier, entitled the Internet Tidal Wave, which had launched a revolution within Microsoft to catch up with the first-generation Internet challenge. He then introduced the new issue of Internet software (or web-based) services. He attached Ozzie's own memo on which he commented: 'I feel sure we will look back on [this] as being as critical as the Internet Tidal Wave. Ray outlines the great things we and our partners can do using the Internet Services approach. The next sea change is upon us.'

Ozzie's own attached memo dated from the Friday before and was addressed to Executive Staff and Direct Reports. It was 5,000 words long, with the subject line 'The Internet Services Disruption'. The memo started positively, by asserting that Microsoft was in the midst of its most important new product phase in its history, referring to the launch of the Xbox 360 and many other products. But it continued quickly to remind readers that the company was innovating at a time of great turbulence and change. This was not unprecedented, however. The memo continued by recalling that the company had needed to review its core strategy and direction roughly every five years throughout its history.

Ozzie recalled three previous changes, including the Internet Tidal Wave, on a five-year cycle going back to 1990. He then proposed the existence of a new business model, Internet-based software supported by advertising. He concluded the memo's introduction by insisting that everybody should reflect on the environmental change, on the company's strengths and weaknesses and on its leadership responsibilities. He warned that if his fellow employees did not reflect and respond quickly and decisively, the company as it stood was seriously at risk. He repeatedly used the word 'we' to underline the common challenge.

Ozzie's e-mail continued in detail. It contained criticism of Microsoft's past innovation leadership in the industry. It warned of more innovative competitors, specifically naming such companies as Google, Apple, Yahoo! and start-ups such as Flickr and Skype. The memo then proposed three key tenets driving fundamental shifts in the competitive landscape: the power of the advertising-supported economic model; the effectiveness of a new Internet download delivery model; and the demand for integrated user experiences that 'just work'. It developed new opportunities, in which the key repeated word was 'seamless', implying more integrated and user-friendly customer experiences across entertainment, communications and work applications. The memo also sketched key implications for all three Microsoft divisions.

The final parts of Ozzie's memo were particularly significant. In a section headed 'What's Different', Ozzie directly addressed possible sceptics amongst his audience. He acknowledged that many would just say that there was nothing very new in what he had said and that Microsoft had been trying similar things for many years, going back to the early 1990s. Some might say that this memo was no big deal.

Ozzie then specified four reasons why it would be different to last time. The first was simple. Invoking 'Bill' Gates and 'Steve' Ballmer by their first names, he insisted that the senior leadership was absolutely committed to the vision outlined in the memo. As evidence, he cited the recent reorganisation of the company into three divisions, including the creation of the new Platform Products and Services group.

The three other reasons highlighted the space opened up by the completion of the upcoming product launches, the technological opportunities now available and the competitive threat.

The memo continued with a final section headed 'Next Steps'. Here he specified a timetable by which division presidents would be assigning individual managers as 'scenario owners' to take forward various initiatives, to work together with Ozzie, to consult within Microsoft and finally to develop concrete new plans. Ozzie provided the address for an internal blog that he would keep, which would provide relevant documents and his own thoughts as they continued to develop. He also promised to experiment with various other ways to allow Microsoft employees to engage with him directly in the strategic conversation.

On 1 November, Bill Gates and Ray Ozzie jointly unveiled the new strategy to a press conference in San Francisco. In June 2006, Gates announced that he would be retiring from a full-time role in Microsoft, easing out over two years. Ozzie took over Gates' role as the company's Chief Software Architect. He had meanwhile bought himself an apartment near the Microsoft headquarters, overlooking Seattle harbour. His wife started commuting to him.

Main sources: D. Kirkpatrick and J.L. Yang, 'Microsoft's new brain', *Fortune*, 15 May (2006), pp. 52–63; 'Bill Gates: Internet Software Services', at http://blogs.zdnet.com/web2explorer/?page_id=53; 'Ray Ozzie: the Internet Services Disruption', at http://www.scripting.com/disruption/ozzie/TheInternetServicesDisruptio.htm; 'Microsoft to buy Groove Networks', MSNBC, 10 March (2005).

Questions

1 Why was the Semiahmoo retreat not successful in creating sustained momentum around the issue of Microsoft's 'core'?

2 Why was Ozzie more successful in creating follow-on action after the Robinswood retreat?

3 Comment on Ozzie's communications strategy with regard to the Internet Services Disruption.

Part III of the book has been concerned with strategy in action. Section 1.2 introduced the overall model to this book. The point that is made there is that strategic management should not necessarily be seen as a linear process: that, in effect, the activities and challenges raised in different parts of this book interact and inform each other. This is why the circles in Exhibit 1.3 overlap. However by necessity, the book is presented in a linear fashion and strategic management is often discussed in terms of strategy formulation followed by strategy implementation.

In this commentary the strategy lenses are used to explore this key issue further. Does it make sense to see strategic management as a process of formulating a strategy followed by a process of implementing a strategy?

Note that:

- There is no suggestion here that one of these lenses is better than another, but they do provide different insights into the problems faced and the ways managers cope with the challenge.
- If you have *not* read the Commentary following Chapter 1 that explans the four lenses, you should now do so.

Design lens

Building on the notion that thinking precedes organisational action, managing strategy is seen as a linear process. So, strategy is first formulated by top managers and then it is implemented through:

- Senior managers persuading people of the logic of the strategy.
- Project planning to ensure appropriate resourcing, timing and sequencing.
- Clear briefing of middle and junior managers.
- Establishing an appropriate organisational structure and control systems so that strategy implementation can be monitored. So 'structure follows strategy'.
- Senior managers as change agents identifying the style of change management required and the levers for managing change.

Experience lens

Strategies typically develop on the basis of experience and culture; current strategy informs and moulds future strategy. Moreover, control systems and resource allocation routines are likely to have become embedded and mould future strategy too. In effect 'strategy follows structure'. So the idea of implementation following formulation is misleading.

However, since it is likely that strategies will develop incrementally, strategic drift is likely over time and this may result in occasional periods of more top-down directed strategic change. At such times it is likely there will be a need to overcome cultural inertia and resistance to change (*unfreezing*). This may involve challenging the prevailing beliefs and assumptions of organisational culture.

Organisations are also political arenas so the management of change needs to be seen as a political process and managers need to be adept in such processes.

Commentary on Part III

Strategy in Action

Ideas lens

Strategies emerge as patterns of order from the ideas that bubble up from within and around an organisation. So, again, the division between strategy formulation and strategy implementation disappears.

It is top managers' role to identify the potential of new ideas and create the organisational context whereby these can be realised. In doing so, they need to bear in mind that:

- The greater the interaction within and across the boundaries of organisations, the more will new ideas and innovation come about. Formal structures and systems of control are unavoidable necessities, but can build barriers and boundaries.

- It may be helpful to change organisational structures in order to avoid relationships and routines becoming embedded and so as to encourage 'weak ties' which encourage new ideas.

- The need is not for cumbersome controls but a few key guiding principles or 'simple rules'.

- In dynamic environments there may be no need for *unfreezing* because the organisation is in a state of continual change.

Managers can usefully build structures and encourage organisational learning to promote all this, a role more important than trying to direct strategies in a top-down fashion.

Discourse lens

Strategy and its management are essentially about discourse – written and spoken. An implication is that the discourse of strategy is inevitably interpreted so the disconnect between intended strategy and how that is interpreted is likely to be higher than managers think.

A key lesson is that each stakeholder has their own identity and associated way of expressing that identity (their 'narrative'). The messages given to stakeholders about strategy may not be construed by them as intended; they will be 'rewritten' in terms of that narrative. It is important to manage strategic messages with stakeholders' identities and narratives in mind. So:

- The extent to which controls have the effect intended will depend on how congruent they are with the narratives of those affected. For example, challenging targets may work because people cannot afford not to comply, not because they like to be challenged.

- Managers need to consider carefully the nature of the discourse they employ, especially in managing the acceptance of the need for change and to ensure change initiatives, once under way, are not rejected.

- Discourse that is appropriate to the needs of stakeholders can have a powerful effect on getting strategies accepted and put into effect.

CASE STUDIES

Guide to using the case studies

The main text of this book includes 87 short *illustrations* and 15 *case examples* which have been chosen to enlarge specific issues in the text and/or provide practical examples of how business and public sector organisations are managing strategic issues. The *case studies* which follow allow the reader to extend this linking of theory and practice further by analysing the strategic issues of specific organisations in much greater depth – and often providing 'solutions' to some of the problems or difficulties identified in the case. There are also over 33 *classic cases* on the Companion Website. These are a selection of cases from recent editions of the book which remain relevant for teaching.

The case studies are intended to serve as a basis for class discussion and not as an illustration of either good or bad management practice. They are not intended to be a comprehensive collection of teaching material. They have been chosen (or specifically written) to provide readers with a core of cases which, together, cover most of the main issues in the text. As such, they should provide a useful backbone to a programme of study but could sensibly be supplemented by other material. We have provided a mixture of longer and shorter cases to increase the flexibility for teachers. Combined with the *illustrations* and the short *case examples* at the end of each chapter (in both versions of the book) this increases the reader's and tutor's choice. For example, when deciding on material for Chapter 2, the case example, *Global Forces and the European Brewing Industry*, tests a reader's understanding of the main issues influencing the competitive position of a number of organisations in the same industry with a relatively short case. For a case that permits a more comprehensive industry analysis *The Pharmaceutical Industry* could be used. However, if the purpose is more focused – illustrating the use of 'five forces' analysis – the *TUI* case study or Illustration 2.3 on *The Steel Industry* could be used.

Some cases are written entirely from published sources but most have been prepared in cooperation with and approval of the management of the organisation concerned. Case studies can never fully capture the richness and complexity of real-life management situations and we would also encourage readers and tutors to take every possible opportunity to explore the *live* strategic issues of organisations – both their own and others.

The following brief points of guidance should prove useful in selecting and using the case studies provided:

- The summary table that follows indicates the main focus of each of the chosen case studies – together with important subsidiary foci (where appropriate). In general, the sequence of cases is intended to mirror the chapter sequence. However, this should not be taken too literally because, of course, many of these cases cover a variety of issues. The 'classification' provided is therefore guidance only. We expect readers to seek their own lessons from cases, and tutors to use cases in whichever way and sequence best fits the purpose of their programmes.

- Where cases have been chosen to illustrate the issues of strategic choices and strategy in action covered later in the book, it will normally be a prerequisite that some type of analysis of the strategic position is undertaken, using the case material. When planning the use of these cases within programmes, care needs to be taken to balance the time taken on such strategic analysis so as to allow the time required to analyse the main issues for which the case has been chosen.

- Where the text and cases are being used as the framework for a strategy programme (as we hope they will), it is essential that students are required to undertake additional reading from other sources and that their 'practical' work is supplemented by other material as mentioned above.

Guide to the main focus of cases in the book

PAGE NUMBER IN THE BOOK / CASE	Introduction to strategy	Business environment: general	Five forces analysis	Capability analysis	Corporate governance	Stakeholder expectations	Social responsibility	Culture	Competitive strategy	Strategic options: directions	Corporate-level strategy	International strategy	Innovation and Entrepreneurship	Strategic options: methods	Strategy evaluation	Strategic management process	Organising	Resourcing	Managing change	Strategic leadership	Strategy in practice	Public sector/not-for-profit management	Small business strategy
605 **Ministry of Sound** – rapid growth but a questionable future in the music industry.	●●																						●
608 **Pharmaceutical Industry** – global forces at work in the ethical pharmaceutical industry.		●●					●					●											
619 **TUI** – competitive forces in the travel industry.			●●									●											
625 **HiFi** – how can small players survive changing markets?		●●		●					●														●
629 **Amazon (B)** – latest developments in a successful dot.com.						●●					●	●											
652 **Formula One** – developing the capabilities for competitive success in a hi-tech industry.				●●					●									●					
662 **Manchester United** – clash of expectations in the football world.					●●	●●																	
667 **Salvation Army** – strategic challenges for a global not-for-profit organisation with a mission.						●●						●●					●					●●	
677 **Bayer MS** – corporate social responsibility in the international development of a German company.							●●					●											
685 **Eurotunnel** – clash of cultures threatens to derail Anglo–French rail link.					●●			●●															
694 **Ryanair** – competitive challenge and strategic choice in the budget airline industry.			●	●					●●			●								●			
708 **IKEA** – quality and low prices at the Swedish furniture giant									●●			●											
712 **News Corporation** – corporate logic and corporate management in a worldwide media business.										●●	●●	●		●						●			
718 **CRH** – impressive international growth of an Irish company driven from a 'lean' corporate centre.										●●	●●	●		●									
727 **Numico** – difficulties with diversification for a Dutch nutritional products company.	●								●●			●											
733 **AIB** – competing in the global banking industry: the challenges for a mid-size bank.	●								●●														
740 **SABMiller** – an African brewer takes on the world: learning to thrive in difficult circumstances.	●								●	●		●●		●									
746 **MacPac** – from a New Zealand start-up to internationalisation in the outdoor equipment industry.												●●	●									●	●●

Key: ●● = major focus   ● = important subsidiary focus

PAGE NUMBER IN THE BOOK	CASE	Introduction to strategy	Business environment: general	Five forces analysis	Capability analysis	Corporate governance	Stakeholder expectations	Social responsibility	Culture	Competitive strategy	Strategic options: directions	Corporate-level strategy	International strategy	Innovation and Entrepreneurship	Strategic options: methods	Strategy evaluation	Strategic management process	Organising	Resourcing	Managing change	Strategic leadership	Strategy in practice	Public sector/not-for-profit management	Small business strategy
755	**Ekomate** – an Indian company uses networks and relationships to internationalise.												●●		●									●●
759	**Eden Project (B)** – latest developments in a successful tourist attraction.													●●			●							
766	**Brown Bag Films** – strategy development and strategic choice for a small business in an international market								●					●●										●●
770	**ACME** – innovation and entrepreneurship in the Indian mobile phone industry.													●●										●
773	**Wimm-Bill-Dann** – where from here for a high growth diversified Russian conglomerate?										●●	●			●●									
779	**Alliance Boots** – a major merger in the pharmaceutical distribution and retailing sector.														●●									
784	**Police Mergers** – are mergers the best way forward in tackling major crime?														●●								●●	
788	**Ericsson** – innovation from the periphery: the development of mobile telephone systems.									●							●●							
795	**Direct & Care** – strategy development in the multi-stakeholder context of public sector services.						●			●							●●						●●	
800	**BBC** – structural changes to deliver a better service.																	●●					●●	
805	**Sony (B)** – more structural changes at the high-tech multinational.																	●●			●			
811	**Web Reservations International** – growth of an Irish SME company through its online reservation system and business model.												●						●●					●●
817	**NHS Direct** – using communication and information technology to provide new 'gateways' to public services.																		●●				●	
823	**Doman Synthetic Fibres** – resource planning for new products in the synthetic fibres industry.																		●●					
831	**Marks & Spencer (B)** – turnaround at the high street legend.																			●●	●●			
840	**Haram** – managing change in a small Norwegian commune.										●	●								●●				●●
846	**RACC** – strategy development processes in Catalonia's automobile club.																●					●●		
849	**MacFarlane Solutions** – condition's for success and failure in strategy consulting.																					●●		

Key: ●● = major focus   ● = important subsidiary focus

Guide to the classic cases on the Companion Website www.pearsoned.co.uk/ecs

CASE	Introduction to strategy	Business environment: general	Five forces analysis	Capability analysis	Corporate governance	Stakeholder expectations	Social responsibility	Culture	Competitive strategy	Strategic options: directions	Corporate-level strategy	International strategy	Innovation and entrepreneurship	Strategic options: methods	Strategy evaluation	Strategic management process	Organising	Resourcing	Managing change	Strategic leadership	Strategy in practice	Public sector/not-for-profit management	Small business strategy
Airlines post-9/11 – reshaping strategies and planning for the future in the wake of a global shock.	●●		●							●													
Amazon (A) – long term planning of a successful dot.com.				●●						●	●												
Jordan – the challenge of building capabilities for success in Formula 1.				●●																●			
Sheffield Theatres – strategy formulation for a wide audience of public and commercial stakeholders.						●●		●														●●	
Fisons – disastrous consequences of stakeholder management.						●●																	
Iona – Mission-driven strategy and stakeholder management.						●●																●●	
HomeCo – wrestling with governance and strategy in the boardroom; a role play.					●●				●														●
BMW – driving organic growth through market development in the automotive industry.	●		●						●●														
VSM – the development of global competitive strategy in a declining market.									●●			●							●	●	●		
Thorntons – a variety box of strategies in the manufacture and retail of chocolates.			●						●●	●													
Burmah/BP – selling-off the company as a strategic choice.									●●														
Royal Bank of Scotland – corporate level strategy as seen by the company chairman.									●●														
Coopers Creek – developments in domestic and international collaboration for a New Zealand winery.			●									●●											●
KPMG (B) – building a global firm in professional services.												●●											
Eden Project (A) – inspiration, innovation and entrepreneurship to create a new 'wonder of the world'.													●●						●				
Chem Tech – innovative strategy development in the flavours and fragrances industry.													●●						●				

Key: ●● = major focus ● = important subsidiary focus

CASE	Introduction to strategy	Business environment: general	Five forces analysis	Capability analysis	Corporate governance	Stakeholder expectations	Social responsibility	Culture	Competitive strategy	Strategic options: directions	Corporate-level strategy	International strategy	Innovation and Entrepreneurship	Strategic options: methods	Strategy evaluation	Strategic management process	Organising	Resourcing	Managing change	Strategic leadership	Strategy in practice	Public sector/not-for-profit management	Small business strategy
Coors – an American brewer moves into the UK market.										●●		●											
Barclaycard – a market leader's strategic options for maintaining market dominance.										●●					●●								
GSK – the wisdom of mergers for a global pharmaceutical giant.														●●									
Brewery Group Denmark – how a small player survives in a globalising market.												●●		●●									
ST Electronics – total quality management for business excellence.																●●							
Sony (A) – a diverse hi-tech multinational responds to change with repeated reorganisations.																	●●		●				
Arts Council – changes in structure and responsibilities in funding the arts in the UK.																	●●					●●	
Tetra Pak – success through a project-based organisation structure.																	●●						
Fed-Ex – packaging new business models to deliver competitive advantage.																		●●					
Forestry Commission – from forestry management to service provider: the challenge of managing change.								●●											●●			●●	
Marks & Spencer (A) – can new initiatives and new management reverse a decline?																			●●	●			
KPMG (A) – managing change in professional services.																			●●	●●			
Xerox – difficulties with leadership at the global giant.						●														●●			
UNHCR – managing change in a global not-for-profit organisation.						●●													●●			●●	
Burtons (A,B,C) – three stages of a retailer's development under different leaders.																			●●	●●			

Key: ●● = major focus   ● = important subsidiary focus

Ministry of Sound

Richard Whittington

The Ministry of Sound went from start-up to maturity in little over a decade. The case raises issues concerning both business strategy, particularly regarding sustainable competitive advantage and resources, and corporate strategy, particularly regarding diversification and internationalisation. There are also issues of ownership and organisation. In the end, the fundamental question is: what future for the Ministry?

● ● ●

In 1991, 28-year-old James Palumbo invested £225,000 (≈€340,000) of his own capital into a new dance club located in an old South London bus depot. As an old Etonian (the UK's most elitist private school), a graduate of Oxford University and a former merchant banker, Palumbo was an unlikely entrant into a dance culture that was still raw and far from respectable. He actually preferred classical music. The club's name, the Ministry of Sound, ironically recalled Palumbo's father, a former Minister in the Conservative government of the day. Yet within just 10 years, Palumbo built the Ministry of Sound into a music and media empire worth nearly £150m. Two years later, Palumbo had quit as chief executive and the Ministry of Sound was looking for a new strategic direction.

The Ministry of Sound's start had been difficult. Dance music had its origins in 'acid house', itself with its roots in the futuristic, electronic music of the gay clubs of Chicago and New York. The new style had been picked up by British DJs in Ibiza, who combined it with the drug Ecstasy to create a new 'blissed-out' sound. Dance music arrived in the UK during 1988, the so-called 'Second Summer of Love', strongly associated with recreational drugs. By the early 1990s, drug-dealing in its most ugly sense had become part of the dance culture. Palumbo recalled:

> When I came into this business, with my bonuses and my nice City suits, I was completely naïve. Just a joke. I found that every Friday and Saturday night my door was taking £30,000 and the security team was making

Photo: S.I.N./Corbis

£40,000 on Ecstasy. It happens everywhere in the UK leisure business. There are all these fat bastards running chains of discos and bowling alleys, and none of them admits it. We went through a really traumatic time at the club.[1]

Palumbo changed his security team, bringing in security professionals from the North of England

---

[1] *New Statesman*, 5 September (1997).

with no links to the local drugs gangs. He even hired a psychoanalyst to cope with the gangland threats that followed his drugs crack-down:

> If they say 'we're going to kill you', you know what you're up against. But the threats [from London's East End drugs gangs] are much more sinister. The word is fed back that if the business is cut off, they will follow you home, go for your family, stab you or murder you.[2]

But Palumbo persisted in making his club a safer, cleaner environment. During the 1990s, he campaigned nationally against the use of drugs in youth venues.

Thus the Ministry of Sound led in the transformation of club culture from an underground movement associated with 'acid house' into a mainstream youth market activity. An illuminated sign on Palumbo's office wall read:

> We are building a global entertainment business based on a strong aspirational brand respected for its creativity and its quality. The Ministry of Sound team will be more professional, hard-working and innovative than any other on the planet.[3]

The Ministry established a distinctive logo and brand and invested heavily in club facilities and sound equipment. It was a leader in developing the new 'super-clubs', fronted by 'super-DJs' earning six-figure sums for playing other people's music. By 2001, over two and a half million clubbers had visited Ministry of Sound nightspots and that same year its first festival weekend attracted 55,000 people at Knebworth.

The business developed in many directions during this period. A magazine aimed at clubbers, *Ministry*, was launched in the mid-1990s and achieved a readership of 300,000. The Ministry of Sound radio show was broadcast in London and Central Scotland, besides being syndicated in 38 countries worldwide. The Ministry's Relentless joint venture became the largest independent record label in the UK, with its *Chill Out Sessions 1 and 2* reaching number one in the album charts and its *So Solid Crew* reaching the top of the singles charts. Large supermarket chain Asda was distributing the Ministry's albums to shoppers around the UK. The Ministry's distinctive logo had become the basis for a large merchandising business, mostly for clothing. By 2001, the Ministry's touring division was hosting 300 events worldwide, including China and India, and had regular summer

residencies in Ibiza, Ayia Napa and Benidorm. A Ministry of Sound super-club opened in Bangkok. By this point, the Ministry's original nightclub only accounted for about 3 per cent of a total turnover, reaching around £100m per annum.

As a mark of the Ministry's success, in the summer of 2001 venture capitalist company 3i acquired approaching 20 per cent of the Ministry's equity for £24m. Palumbo was quoted as saying: 'With 3i's support, we are now poised to spread the dance music gospel worldwide.' In its 'Rich List 2001', *The Sunday Times* estimated Palumbo's total fortune as £150m. A spokesman for 3i said:

> We had obviously heard a lot about the Ministry and James [Palumbo] has had a lot of good press. We were impressed by how successful the brand has become and by how fast it has grown. . . . Ministry has a phenomenal skill in helping new acts hit the big time. The more successful it became, the more people wanted to become associated with it. . . . When making an investment, you have to be totally comfortable and confident that you are backing an A1 team. With James we found the perfect deal. James is the sort of person VCs [venture capitalists] can make money out of.[4]

The Ministry of Sound was aiming for a stock market listing within a couple of years.

Then things started to go wrong. The dance music on which the Ministry was based was going out of fashion. Dance music (including house, trance, techno, breaks and drum'n'bass music) saw its share of the UK singles market fall to 15.4 per cent in 2002, down from 34 per cent in 1991. Dance clubs were closing or downsizing, while live music audiences were growing. Malik Meer, Deputy Editor of *New Musical Express*, commented in early 2004:

> The dance culture as a whole got lazy. It came to be perceived as one thing: this cheesy, superclub, larging-it lifestyle. . . . Dance music came from an underground culture and was about being edgy and anti-establishment. At the height of superclub-dom, a club would be £25 to get in and be full of slightly-older people, glammed up and wearing crap labels. If you are young and want to be cool, you are not going to buy into that.[5]

For many aficionados, the last straw was when the Sugababes got crowned the 'Best Dance Act' of 2003.

At the end of 2002, Palumbo was obliged to close down his flagship magazine, *Ministry*. The Ministry

---

[2] Ibid.
[3] *Marketing*, 4 December (1997), p. 3.

[4] *European Venture Capital Journal*, September (2001), p. 1.
[5] *Independent*, 2 January (2004), p. 10.

of Sound then worked with publishers Condé Nast to launch a new style magazine, *Trash*, which would be able to share expertise and economies of scale. *Trash* was closed after just one issue. The recording joint venture Relentless went out of business, owing £3m. Bangkok's Ministry of Sound closed after a change in local laws restricted late-night attractions. In February 2003, Palumbo quit as chief executive to become chairman of the company of which he was still the largest shareholder. Rumours that he was forced to stand down by venture capitalist investor 3i were dismissed.

Ministry's 36-year-old Marketing Director, Mark Rodol, took over as chief executive and launched a strategic review of the whole business. Rodol commented on Palumbo's exit:

> James is an entrepreneur – but what is going to make this business great is a focused, long-term brand strategy. To his credit James has had the foresight to step aside and let the people who understand and believe this run the company. It's about a difference in style.[6]

As to the strategic review, Rodol observed:

> Over the years, we've pursued a number of opportunities that we shouldn't have done. The intention we have over the next couple of months is to examine what the core of Ministry of Sound actually is.[7]

The Ministry of Sound was not, however, abandoning all initiatives. Rodol saw large potential in continued merchandising in areas such as branded clothing, specialist holidays and consumer hi-fi products, with turnover targeted to reach £5m by 2006. On top of this, Ministry was starting to sell branded DJ equipment and offering branded mobile phone games. A Ministry PlayStation game allowing gamers to mix their own dance music was being launched too. An advertising-supported online broadcast music channel was launched, with potential for streaming over mobile phones. As a spokesman put it, 'this will be just like MTV, only on the Web'.[8] A new super-club was also opened in Taipei, Taiwan, in the second half of 2003 and Rodol declared an ambition to have a Ministry of Sound club in every big city in the world.

Rodol also reorganised the Ministry, leading to several management departures. As well as the continuing record business and club activities, there would be three divisions: an international arm, encompassing radio, touring and record compilation; a brand division, focused on retail, product licensing and the Ministry website; and a marketing division, aiming to form long-term relationships with brands such as Philips and Bacardi. Rodol denied that the reorganisation was motivated by simple cost considerations, and underlined its importance for moving the brand forward towards long-term goals.

Central would be keeping the brand cool in the eyes of its customers. The Ministry of Sound was perceived by many as having lost its 'edginess'. Mark Rodol insisted:

> That's what we're working on. It is possible to be big and cutting edge – there are big mass market brands like Nike and PlayStation that manage to retain an edge despite their size. That's what we intend to do.[9]

---

[6] *Financial Times*, 30 April (2003), p. 13.
[7] *Financial Times*, 28 February (2003), p. 22.
[8] *New Media Age*, 13 November (2003), p. 24.
[9] *Financial Times*, 30 April (2003), p. 13.

The global pharmaceutical industry

Sarah Holland

The case looks at the development of the ethical pharmaceutical industry. The various forces affecting the discovery, development, production, distribution and marketing of prescription drugs and issues of corporate responsibility are discussed. The case also looks at the different types of strategies that are followed by pharmaceutical companies.

● ● ●

In late 2006, industry commentator IMS Health released its latest forecast, predicting pharmaceutical market growth at a 10-year low. IMS counselled that the industry was facing

> a new economic reality, one in which growth is shifting from mature markets to emerging ones; new product adoption is not keeping pace with the loss of patent protection . . . specialty and niche products are playing a larger role; and regulators, payers and consumers are more carefully weighing the risk/benefit factors of pharmaceuticals.[1]

This case explores some of the trends affecting the *ethical* (research-based) sector of the industry and invites readers to prepare their own analysis.

Photo: AstraZeneca UK Ltd

Industry evolution

As described in Box 1, the pharmaceutical industry is characterised by a highly risky and lengthy R&D process, intense competition for *intellectual property*, stringent government regulation and powerful purchaser pressures. How has this unusual picture come about?

The origins of the modern pharmaceutical industry can be traced to the late nineteenth century, when dyestuffs were found to have antiseptic properties. Penicillin was a major discovery, and during the 1940s and 1950s R&D became firmly established within the sector. The industry expanded rapidly in the 1960s, benefiting from new discoveries with permanent patent protection. Regulatory controls were light and health care spending boomed as economies prospered.

The pharmaceutical market developed some unusual characteristics. Decision making was in the hands of medical practitioners whereas patients (the final consumers) and payers (governments or insurance companies) had little knowledge or influence. As a result, medical practitioners were insensitive to price but susceptible to the efforts of sales representatives.

There were two important developments in the 1970s. First, the thalidomide tragedy (where an anti-emetic given for morning sickness caused birth defects) led to much tighter regulatory

---

[1] 'IMS Health forecasts 5 to 6 per cent growth for global pharmaceutical industry', IMS Health Press Release, 24 October 2006.

BOX 1   The drug development process

The pharmaceutical industry has long new product lead times, with period from discovery to marketing authorisation typically taking almost 12 years (Exhibit 1). New product development can be divided into distinct research and development phases. The research phase produces a *new chemical entity* (*NCE*) with the desired characteristics to be an effective drug. Development encompasses all of the formulation, toxicology and clinical trial work necessary to meet stringent regulatory requirements for marketing approval.

During all of these phases 'attrition' occurs, as promising agents fail particular hurdles, so most R&D projects never result in a marketed drug. Late-stage failures are particularly costly and not uncommon – in 2005–2006 AstraZeneca lost three Phase 3 drugs, Pfizer and BMS one each. Of those that reach the market, 80 per cent fail to recoup their R&D investment. The cost of developing and commercialising a new drug is estimated at over $800m (£440m; €640m). When the costs of all the projects that do not reach fruition are considered,

it becomes clear that pharmaceutical R&D is a very high-stakes game.

Given the enormous risks and considerable investment involved, it is not surprising that pharmaceutical companies compete fiercely to establish and retain *intellectual property* rights. Only by securing a patent that can be defended against imitators can the value of all this R&D be recouped. Once the patent application is made public, the race starts as other companies try to create improved, patentable versions.

The industry is subjected to rigorous regulatory scrutiny. Government agencies such as the *Food and Drug Administration* (*FDA*) in the USA thoroughly examine all of the data to support the purity, stability, safety, efficacy and tolerability of a new agent. The time taken is governed by legislation and averaged 12.5 months in 2005. Obtaining marketing approval is no longer the end of the road in many countries, as further hurdles must be overcome in demonstrating the value of the new drug to justify price and/or reimbursement to cost-conscious payers.

Exhibit 1   Creating new pharmaceuticals. It takes 10–15 years on average for an experimental drug to travel from the lab to patients

	Discovery/ preclinical testing		Clinical trials					
			Phase I	Phase II	Phase III		FDA	Phase IV
Years	6.5		1.5	2	3.5		1.5	
Test population	Laboratory and animal studies	File IND at FDA	20 to 100 healthy volunteers	100 to 500 patient volunteers	1,000 to 5,000 patient volunteers	File NDA/BLA at FDA	Review process/ approval	Additional post-marketing testing required by FDA
Purpose	Assess safety, biological activity and formulations		Determine safety and dosage	Evaluate effectiveness, look for side effects	Confirm effectiveness, monitor adverse reactions from long-lerm use			
Success rate	5,000 compounds evaluated		5 enter trials				1 approved	

Source: PhRMA, *Medicines in Development – Biotechnology – 2006 Report*, p. 51.

Exhibit 2 Methods used to control pharmaceutical spending

Controls on suppliers	Mixed effect	Controls to influence demand
Negotiated prices	Partial reimbursement at price negotiated with manufacturer	Patient co-payments*
Average pricing		Treatment guidelines
Reference pricing	Generic substitution	Indicative or fixed budgets
Positive and negative lists		Incentives to prescribe or dispense generics or parallel imports
Constraints on wholesalers and pharmacists		Transfer from prescription-only to OTC
Imposed price cuts		

* Where the patient pays some of the drug cost.

controls on clinical trials. Second, legislation was enacted to set a fixed period on patent protection – typically 20 years from initial filing. This led to the appearance of 'generic' medicines which have exactly the same active ingredients as the original brand, and compete on price. The dramatic impact of generic entry is illustrated by Allegra, a treatment for hay fever, which lost 84 per cent of US sales in just 12 weeks following patent expiry in 2006. Generics had a major impact on the industry, providing incentives for innovation and a race to market, since the time during which R&D costs could be recouped was drastically curtailed.

The pharmaceutical industry is unusual in that in many countries it is subject to a 'monopsony' – there is effectively only one powerful purchaser, the government. From the 1980s on, governments around the world focused on pharmaceuticals as a politically easy target in their efforts to control rising health care expenditure. Many introduced price or reimbursement controls. The industry lacked the public or political support to resist these changes.

Business environment

Ageing populations create pressure on health care funding systems, since 'over-65s' consume four times as much health care per head as those below 65. Combined with more expensive high-technology solutions and increasing patient expectations, this creates an unsustainable situation. Universal coverage systems (such as those in Spain and the UK) are slow or unable to introduce the latest treatments, while insurance-funded systems (such as in the USA) can afford the latest innovations but are unable to share the benefits with an increasing part of the population. In 2006 the number of US citizens without health insurance was 46.6 million, 15.9 per cent of the population, including 8.3 million children.

In response to these pressures, payers use a variety of methods to control pharmaceutical spending (see Exhibit 2). Some put the emphasis on the manufacturer and distributor, others on the prescriber and the patient. These controls are designed to reward genuine advances – price premiums and/or reimbursement levels are based on perceived innovativeness and superiority.

In countries with supply-side controls, negotiating price or reimbursement approval can take as long as a year. In those with demand-side controls, there are delays in market penetration while negotiating endorsement by bodies such as the *National Institute for Clinical Excellence* (*NICE*) in the UK. The impact of NICE decisions on cost-effectiveness reverberates well beyond the UK, as countries have begun to collaborate internationally in their value assessments.

Switching to generics is one way to save costs. Computers can print prescriptions in generic rather than branded form, enabling pharmacists to substitute the cheap generic version of the drug. Payers are increasingly effective in establishing generic drugs as a first-line treatment option, with patented drugs only used if those fail. For the top eight markets, annual growth in patented drug sales fell from 18 to 8 per cent from 2001 to 2005, reflecting underlying volume shifts – volume growth of 40 per cent for generics, but a volume decline of 4 per cent for patented drugs.

The industry has adopted a number of strategic responses to these challenges. Some companies introduced *'disease management' initiatives.*[2] Another common response was to conduct pharmacoeconomic evaluations to demonstrate the added value offered by a new drug as a result of improved efficacy, safety, tolerability or ease of use. For example, a study of the cost of diabetes – the fastest-growing chronic disease in the world – found that 60 per cent of the cost was for hospitalisations, 27 per cent was medicines, but correct outpatient treatment could avoid much of the hospital costs.

Government price controls create another challenge for the industry in the form of 'parallel trade'. The principle of free movement of goods across the Single European Market means that distributors are free to source drugs in low-price markets and ship them to high-price markets, pocketing the difference. EU parallel trade was estimated at €4.2bn in 2004, with the highest penetration in the UK where it accounted for 17 per cent of pharmacy sales.

Parallel trade is prevalent in Asia and there is a latent problem in the crucial US market due to price differentials with Canada. Canada has stringent and inflexible pricing and reimbursement criteria. In contrast, the USA has no formal price controls and price increases are customary. Over time, this has led to a wide disparity in prices (best-selling cholesterol-lowering drug Lipitor was $3.20 per pill in the USA in 2003, compared with just $1.89 in Canada) that exposes the industry to sensationalist newspaper headlines and consumer backlash.

Industry sectors

Prescription-only or *ethical* drugs comprise about 80 per cent of the global pharmaceutical market by value ($630bn; ~€500bn) and 50 per cent by volume. Ethical products divide into conventional pharmaceuticals and more complex 'biopharmaceutical' agents and vaccines. The other 20 per cent of the market comprises *'over the counter'* (OTC) medicines, which may be purchased without prescription. Both ethical and OTC medicines may be patented or 'generic'.

The typical cost structure at ethical pharmaceutical companies comprises manufacturing of goods (25 per cent), R&D (12 to 21 per cent), administration (10 per cent), and sales and marketing (25 per cent). The key strategic capabilities at these companies are R&D and sales and marketing. Pressure on margins created an incentive to restructure manufacturing, rationalising the number of production sites and placing them in strategic locations offering tax or cost advantages.

However, manufacturing and distribution efficiency was far more important for generics manufacturers. During the late 1990s, there was a collapse of generics prices in the USA and a shake-out to determine cost leadership. Economies of scale, including the finance to support complex legal patent disputes, proved decisive and the sector underwent consolidation. The speed and aggression of generic attacks on branded products increased sharply. Given the number of blockbuster brands facing patent expiry and markets with untapped potential (for example, Italy, Spain, France, Japan), it is not surprising that growth in generics outstripped overall market growth from 2002 to 2005.

A new type of industry player appeared in the 1980s – small biotechnology start-ups backed by venture capital to exploit the myriad opportunities created by molecular biology and genetic engineering. Initially, biotechs were associated with 'biopharmaceutical' agents, for example recombinant insulin, the industry's first product, launched in 1982. Biopharmaceuticals have very specific effects (with arguably greater safety) and, thanks to their complexity, are far less vulnerable to generic competition. As a result, biopharmaceuticals became mainstream – contributing a quarter of global sales by 2006 – and leading players developed or acquired biological capabilities. Biotechs meanwhile broadened to pursue a huge variety of core capabilities creating a global, extraordinarily diverse and innovative sector.

By 2005 there were nearly 700 publicly traded *biotechs* worldwide, generating over $63bn in revenues. Because of the very long product development cycle, biotechs take years to reach profitability, if at all. In 2005, the aggregate global

---

[2] These involved understanding the goals of the health care system in addressing a specific disease. The firm then aligned itself with the health care providers, offering a service to improve disease outcomes, positioning its drugs as one part of the solution.

industry loss was $4.4bn. That may seem low, but the profits are concentrated in a handful of outstanding success stories such as Amgen.

OTC medicines are bought by the consumer without a prescription. The US OTC market was estimated at $16bn in 2005 with growth of 3 per cent. The OTC sector has also undergone consolidation and the top 10 manufacturers account for more than half of volume. Switching medicines from prescription-only to OTC is costly both to secure approval and to undertake consumer-oriented marketing, so is only worthwhile for blockbusters. However, consumer brand loyalty may then provide defence against generic competition and prolong the product life cycle. Occasionally a brand which struggled as a prescription product can flourish in the OTC sector – for example, Xenical for obesity, which appeared to be a greater issue for consumers than health care professionals.

A final important category of medicine is vaccines. Prophylactic vaccines often provide lifelong protection against serious diseases, preventing at least 3 million deaths annually worldwide and saving an estimated $7–20 health care dollars for every dollar spent on vaccines. This $10bn market is highly concentrated, with just five global players accounting for around 85 per cent of market share. Entry barriers are high, with specialised skills required in manufacturing, conducting very large and complex clinical trials and managing surveillance programmes. Sales and marketing ability is generally less critical than the ability to negotiate with national governments and other major health care providers.

Thus there are five broad types of industry player: ethical, generic, biotech, OTC and vaccine companies. Each requires very different strategic capabilities. Producers of branded prescription drugs require strong R&D and global sales and marketing infrastructure. Generics companies focus on speed to market and manufacturing cost leadership. Biotechs need to create and defend intellectual property in specialised research fields, attract funding and make successful deals. Branded OTC drugs demand direct-to-consumer marketing capability. Because of the different skills and cost structures involved, multinationals which own generics, OTC and vaccine businesses usually operate them separately, even using another company name. Similarly, those that have acquired biotechs often leave them to operate fairly autonomously.

Key markets

The majority of global pharmaceutical sales originate in the USA, Japan, the EU, China and Mexico, with 10 key countries contributing over 80 per cent of the global market. Pharmaceutical market growth is aligned with GDP growth. The USA is by far the largest market by volume and value: $250bn in 2005 – nearly half of global sales (see Box 2). Historically the fastest-growing among key markets, the US contribution to global growth fell from 60 to 40 per cent in just three years from 2002 to 2005. Nevertheless, the USA will remain critical to success for the foreseeable future. In 2005, the US market accounted for two-thirds of sales of drugs launched since 2001, compared with just a quarter from the EU. This dominance is even more marked for biopharmaceuticals.

Following regulatory changes in 1997, *direct-to-consumer* (*DTC*) advertising transformed the US marketplace and fuelled rapid growth. However, managed care also changed market dynamics. Companies' costs for providing drug benefits to employees were increasing by up to 20 per cent annually, causing the CEO of General Motors to declare that 'the cost of health care in the U.S. is making American businesses extremely uncompetitive versus our global counterparts'.[3] *Managed Care Organisations* (*MCOs*) asked consumers for increasing co-pays on branded *versus* generic drugs and implemented other cost-control measures. Fortunately, litigious US consumers focused MCO attention on offering optimal rather than cheapest care, leaving the door open to genuine innovation. Medicare reforms in 2006 extended drug coverage for the elderly, but also made the government overnight the largest direct purchaser of medicines. (Powerful bulk purchasers such as the Veterans Administration had already negotiated prices even lower than those in Canada.) Concerns about high prices and drug safety risks provided fertile ground for resurgent Democrats to criticise the industry. With the potential for imposition of direct pricing controls, and legislation to determine the role and funding of the FDA up for renewal, the stage was set for further turbulence in the US operating environment.

Japan has the second largest market for pharmaceuticals, with sales of $60bn in 2005. The Japanese operating environment has historically

---

[3] *The Washington Post*, 11 February (2005).

BOX 2 Globalisation or US dominance?

A number of factors have contributed to industry globalisation. Chief is the international convergence of medical science and practice under the influence of modern communications technology and increased travel and information exchange. Well-funded US universities and hospitals generally lead their fields, while US congresses provide the most prestigious platforms for new discoveries.

Regulatory processes are also undergoing international harmonisation. In Europe the European Medicines Evaluation Agency (EMEA) was established to enable more rapid regulatory approvals through the 'centralised' procedure, which grants approval in all member states simultaneously. This offers great benefits in terms of reduced costs and accelerated time to market, but also increased risk as more is at stake on one decision. There is also a move towards global regulatory harmonisation through the International Conference on Harmonisation (ICH).

The doubling of the number of blockbuster brands between 1998 and 2004 provides further evidence of globalisation. Leading corporations have globalised, and are present in all significant markets. Production sites have a global mandate and are selected by worldwide screening. R&D is sourced from the best place worldwide, which often means the USA. Between 1990 and 2005, R&D investment in the USA grew 4.6 times; in Europe only 2.8 times. Investment in Japan actually declined from 2000 to 2004.

Biotechnology companies are 'born global': from their inception they draw upon a global pool of collaborators and investors, rather than growing from small domestic beginnings. Here once again the US dominates: publicly traded biotechs employ over four times more people in the USA than the EU, with a similar ratio for R&D spend.

In 2005, the leading global industry players originated predominantly from the USA and Europe, as Japanese companies lagged behind. Strong US market growth from 1994 to 2004 enabled US companies to grow faster than competitors and provided a springboard in achieving global ambitions. Of the top 30 brands in 2004, 21 originated from the USA, 8 from the EU and only 1 from Japan. Drugs first launched in the USA gain far greater global market share than those first launched elsewhere.

In the longer term, US dominance may be under threat from China and India. The Chinese government has declared its intention to become a leader in the field and is pouring money into new universities and science parks. Routine chemistry and toxicology are already often outsourced to China, but as US returnees (or 'turtles') seek more innovative projects, this will extend up the value chain. In 2005, India accounted for about 30 per cent of global generics, but has similar ambitions to become a major source of R&D and is already an important location for cost-effective clinical trials.

been very different from the USA or the EU. This divergence occurred at all levels, from medical practice, health care delivery and funding, to regulatory requirements, higher prices, the lack of generics, distribution, and the accepted approach to sales and marketing. Not surprisingly, domestic companies dominated the market. The industry experienced significant turbulence in the 1990s. Economic recession caused tax revenues to fall, while the cost of treating the world's most rapidly ageing population rose. This resulted in unprecedented price cuts, changes to health care funding and the introduction of stringent price controls, limiting market growth to an average below 3 per cent from 1994 to 2004, while in 2005 the population itself actually began to decline.

Europe makes up the third part of the triad, and is predicted to continue contributing around 30 per cent of global sales out to 2009. The European pharmaceutical market is highly fragmented and remains driven by governments' forever-changing cost containment plans, resulting in a lack of predictability for companies' operational planning. Combined with slowing economies, these pressures held average annual market growth below 8 per cent from 1994 to 2004. EU expansion provided opportunities for growth, but also new challenges from generics and low-priced imports.

Emerging markets accounted for 50 per cent of global GDP growth in 2005, and their enormous populations and high levels of unmet need offered significant long-term potential for pharmaceuticals. Many had strengthened patent protection and liberalised equity controls. Markets in Latin America had proved highly volatile, reflecting economic trends. Nevertheless they had large numbers of wealthy consumers who were able to afford branded drugs. Mexico became a top 10 market in 2005, while Brazilian sales grew by nearly 40 per cent. Turkey also posted very strong market growth of over 50 per cent.

Asian countries were rapidly becoming important. Copy products were traditionally an issue, but intellectual property reforms were beginning to take effect. Pharmaceutical companies focused particularly on China, the fastest-growing of the top 10 markets with $9bn sales in 2005. China, together with India, was becoming dominant in global manufacturing and attracting increasing R&D investment.

Although developing countries were not in a position to offer a significant market opportunity, they did present the industry with important choices in the area of corporate social responsibility.

Innovation

The ethical pharmaceutical companies' key contribution to medical progress is the ability to turn fundamental research findings into innovative treatments that are widely available and accessible. Companies with consistently high levels of R&D spending and productivity became industry leaders. For this reason, stock market valuations place as much importance on the R&D 'pipeline' (that is, the products in development) as on the currently marketed products.

The holy grail of pharmaceutical R&D used to be the 'blockbuster'. Like 'killer applications' in the software market, blockbuster drugs are genuine advances that achieve rapid, deep market penetration. Because of their superlative market performance, blockbusters determined the fortunes of individual companies. Glaxo went from being a small player at the beginning of the 1980s to a top-tier global company, on the strength of a single drug – Zantac for stomach ulcers. A blockbuster drug was typically a long-term therapy for a common disease that offered a step change in efficacy or tolerability, marketed globally with annual sales exceeding $1bn.

While blockbusters made immense contributions to company fortunes, they were few and far between. Focusing on blockbusters exposed an already high-stakes industry to even greater levels of risk. This was dramatically brought home in September 2004 when the cardiovascular safety risks of Vioxx became known, and Merck withdrew

the brand from the market, losing $2.5bn in annual sales. Merck lost a quarter of its stock market value and faced the prospect of numerous liability suits. Blockbusters also exacerbate the impact of patent expiries. Between 2006 and 2011, 20 blockbusters are due to lose patent protection and global exposure to generics is estimated at $125bn, with $55bn to be borne by Pfizer, GlaxoSmithKline and Merck.

Unfortunately, R&D productivity was in decline and development times were lengthening. The average number of trials and number of patients for each new drug application increased enormously, from 26 trials involving 1,500 patients in 1980, to more than 65 trials involving over 4,000 patients by 1995. As clinical trials became more complex and costly there was a sharp rise in R&D expenditure. The average fully capitalised resource cost to develop a new drug was estimated at $1.4bn in 2003.[4] The corresponding figure in 1987 was $231m and would have grown to under $500m by 2003 at the pace of general inflation. Industry R&D spending exceeded $60bn in 2006, but despite increasing average R&D spend from 11 to 12 per cent of annual sales to 16 or even 17 per cent, pharmaceutical companies had not much to show for it. The number of new product launches remained below 30 for 2005. Despite the attempt to find primary care blockbusters, most were for diseases treated by specialists.

Pharmaceutical companies endeavoured to be both creative and efficient. Some argued that the secret of successful R&D lay in organisational competences such as team working, knowledge management and close relationships with external opinion leaders. Others emphasised 'lean and flexible' operations and outsourcing of all but core competences. Some reorganised their R&D to create smaller and more nimble units – like internal biotechs. Others sought external innovation. Biotechs were contributing an increasing share of the industry's new products via licensing deals. Procter and Gamble actually closed internal Discovery efforts in 2006, with the declared intention of in-licensing its entire portfolio. The company argued that in-house efforts could not hope to keep pace with, nor offer the choice and impact of, external innovation.

Some questioned whether the levels of R&D investment could be sustained. For example, in 2005 there were nearly 650 cancer drugs in

---

[4] Including research on abandoned drugs.

development. With pressures on payers growing it seemed improbable that such enormous aggregate R&D investment could ever be recouped. The industry arguably had substantial R&D overcapacity.

Sales and marketing

Sales and marketing capability became an increasingly important source of competitive advantage. A company that developed a strong global franchise with its customers could maximise return on its in-house products and was in a good position to attract the best in-licensing candidates.

The traditional focus of drug marketing was the personal '*detail*' in which a sales representative (rep) discussed the merits of a drug in a face-to-face meeting with a doctor and often handed over free samples. Pharmaceutical promotion was subject to industry self-regulation. For example, in the UK, reps had to pass an examination testing medical knowledge. In some countries, government regulatory agencies checked that promotional claims were consistent with the data.

There are important differences in the marketing of 'primary care' and 'specialist' products. Office-based practitioners generally prescribe primary care products, whereas treatment with specialist products is typically initiated in hospitals. Sales volume, marketing spend and skills required differ for the two segments. Product-led muscle marketing is the name of the game in the primary care sector, while specialist products involve more cost-effective targeted relationship marketing. A small number of companies have built their strategies around under-served specialised customer groups, aiming to satisfy their needs on multiple dimensions. In other words, they have developed a franchise.

The term 'high-compression marketing' was coined to describe how leading companies launch global primary care brands. This involves near-simultaneous worldwide launches, global branding and heavy investment in promotion at time of launch. The aim is to create a rapid take-off curve that maximises return by creating higher peak year sales earlier in the product life cycle. An example was the launch of Celebrex in 1999, which netted $1bn sales in the first nine months. Truly global branding is vital, with consistent brand name, messages and visuals used around the world for maximum impact. Blockbusters launched between 1998 and 2003 typically reached $2bn in sales within 3.5 years, at least twice as fast as historical norms.

Another factor driving up sales and marketing costs was the growth in DTC advertising in the USA, where spending reached a colossal $4.5bn by 2006. Companies recognised that well-informed patients were prepared to ask for drugs by name, creating a powerful 'pull' strategy (see Box 3). DTC was costly because of the vast target audience and expensive television advertising. It also required new marketing skills – both Pfizer and Novartis employed consumer marketers. DTC rendered drug advertising much more visible and, combined with high-profile safety alerts, risked creating a backlash against the industry.

BOX 3 Health-conscious consumers

Increasingly vocal, well-informed and demanding consumers seem inevitable. Patients with Internet access can obtain information on new products directly themselves. Health is one of the top reasons for searches on the Internet. In the USA, up to 75 per cent of those that search for health-related information are likely to discuss that information with their health care providers.

This trend is likely to increase patient demand for new, effective, better-tolerated therapies, particularly in litigious countries such as the USA. However, the Internet also has the potential to raise awareness of international price disparities. Consumers are even beginning to purchase across borders, but with no guarantee that the drugs they receive have been stored and shipped correctly and are not adulterated, contaminated or counterfeit. The FDA estimates that fake drugs account for over 10 per cent of the global market, generating annual sales of more than $32bn, and this is on the increase as illegal drug cartels move into the less risky but equally lucrative business of fake pharmaceuticals. It is also easy to purchase addictive painkillers and other potentially harmful drugs over the Internet, and rogue websites even offer miracle cures for cancer and AIDS. The pace of change is outstripping the capabilities and powers of regulators.

Salesforce size, or 'share of voice', was a key competitive attribute. Companies that increased their salesforce size, such as Pfizer, found that the more sales reps they deployed, the higher their sales. As a result numbers in the USA tripled from 1995 to 2002, reaching around 90,000. However, doctors had less time to see sales reps, with the average call lasting less than five minutes. More reps selling fewer drugs cut returns from every dollar invested, and productivity declined sharply in 2004–2005. Eventually, in the wake of the Vioxx debacle which also affected their blockbuster Celebrex, Pfizer called a halt to the arms race, announcing a downsizing in 2005. With pipelines shifting to high unmet-need diseases treated by specialists, the era of lavish launches and massive salesforces appeared to be ending.

Corporate social responsibility

During the twentieth century average life expectancy in developed countries increased by over 20 years. Much of this improvement can be attributed to pharmaceutical innovation. Few other industries have done as much for the well-being of humankind. So how did an industry that has delivered such benefits acquire such a tarnished image and become an easy target for unpredictable government intervention?

One problem is that pharmaceuticals have the characteristics of what economists describe as a 'public good' – that is, expensive to produce but inexpensive to reproduce. The manufacturing cost of drugs is usually tiny compared with the amortised cost of R&D that led to the discovery. Setting prices that attempt to recoup R&D therefore looks like corporate greed in comparison with the very low prices that can be charged for generics.

Some companies damaged the industry's overall reputation. In the USA, pharmaceutical firms paid over $2bn in fines between 2000 and 2003 in cases brought by the US Justice Department, principally for pricing and marketing crimes. Even more seriously, companies were accused of putting profits before patient safety. After Vioxx was withdrawn from the market, Merck was accused of failing to pick up problems during product development, and of publishing misleading scientific results. The lack of trust from patients and politicians spilled over onto the FDA, which was perceived as too closely aligned with industry and paying too little attention to safety. The consequences for the industry were potentially severe, with the prospect of new onerous and costly safety data collection requirements being imposed, together with stringent prescribing controls.

The industry also faced condemnation of its response to the enormous unmet need in developing countries. Although for many diseases affecting millions of people, effective drugs and vaccines already existed, often their cost was beyond the means of the people who needed them. It was argued that companies could reallocate R&D efforts in favour of major tropical diseases, sell low-priced essential drugs and provide technology transfer.

Questions around the purpose and ethics of the global pharmaceutical industry gained a high public profile as disputes over access to modern AIDS therapies reached crisis point. When the South African government proposed legislation to allow generic imports of branded drugs, a coalition of 39 firms took legal action. Given the tragic AIDS epidemic and the saintly figure of Nelson Mandela, this was not the best example of industry public relations. The CEO of GlaxoSmithKline, Jean Paul Garnier, helped negotiate the industry out of the court case and established clear principles of operation, adopted by many companies. They would supply critical drugs to poor countries on a no-loss, no-profit basis. As for investing in research into 'not-for-profit' diseases, Garnier declared:

> We'll go after it. It's just that we've got to be street smart about the funding. . . . There's plenty of money . . . to fund those initiatives and we've never been turned down. I talk to Bill Gates all the time.[5]

Industry consolidation

While the pharmaceutical market remained relatively fragmented, with very large numbers of domestic and regional players, it was consolidating at the global level. The leading global corporation, Pfizer, held 8.4 per cent market share in 2005 while the top 10 players accounted for nearly half of global sales. A strong trend was for previously diversified conglomerates to divest their non-health-care businesses (for example, agrochemicals), to focus purely on high-margin pharmaceuticals.

---

[5] *Guardian*, 18 February (2003).

| Exhibit 3 | Leading global pharmaceutical companies, 2002 and 2005 |

2002		2005			
Company	Total sales ($bn)	Company	Total sales ($bn)	Share within global retail %	Sales growth, 2004– 2005 %
Pfizer[1] (USA)	29.5	Pfizer[3]	47.7	8.4	−7.4
GlaxoSmithKline[2] (UK)	27.9	GlaxoSmithKline	34.7	6.1	4.8
Merck (USA)	20.0	Sanofi-Aventis[4] (France)	30.1	5.3	8.2
Johnson & Johnson (USA)	18.6	Novartis	28.5	5.0	10.9
AstraZeneca (UK/Sweden)	18.1	Johnson & Johnson	25.3	4.5	0.2
Novartis (Switzerland)	16.6	AstraZeneca	24.1	4.3	9.0
Aventis (Germany/France)	14.3	Merck	23.5	4.2	−2.7
Bristol-Myers Squibb (USA)	14.3	Roche	19.8	3.5	16.3
Roche (Switzerland)	12.5	Abbott (USA)	15.9	2.8	8.4
Pharmacia (USA)	12.2	Bristol-Myers Squibb	14.7	2.6	−6.5

Notes:

No.	Created	Originating companies	
1.	2000	Warner-Lambert (USA)	Pfizer (USA)
2.	2000	Glaxo Wellcome (UK)	SmithKline Beecham (UK)
3.	2003	Pfizer (USA)	Pharmacia (USA)
4.	2004	Sanofi (France)	Aventis (France)

Exhibit 3 shows how the industry response to the need for critical mass was a wave of mergers and acquisitions. Mergers resulted in the formation of Novartis, Sanofi-Aventis, AstraZeneca and GlaxoSmithKline, while Pfizer acquired Monsanto (Warner-Lambert) and then Pharmacia. Pfizer overtook Merck, which followed an organic growth strategy.

A key rationale for mergers and acquisitions was to combine a company with a strong pipeline but weak sales and marketing with its converse. For example, the acquisition of Warner-Lambert gave Pfizer full marketing rights to the cholesterol-lowering agent Lipitor, which Pfizer then built into the world's best-selling drug with sales of $12bn in 2005. Another argument for increasing size was to leverage investment in 'technology platforms'. Companies had to invest in expensive new R&D capabilities to keep pace with industry leaders in speed to market. With a larger R&D programme, more projects could benefit from the new capability and help amortise its costs. Eliminating duplicated costs remained one sure-fire way to keep profits relatively healthy. But there was little conclusive evidence that mergers enhanced revenue or R&D productivity.

Some argued that mergers actually reduced R&D productivity: more management layers resulted in greater bureaucracy, less freedom to innovate and reduced research output. The success of biotechs in drug discovery suggested creativity was greater in small R&D organisations. Portfolio management was problematic in merged companies. Cutting too many projects in the search for blockbusters could exacerbate risk. Cutting too few meant under-resourcing potential winners and risked an over-stretched and unfocused organisation. In one analysis, the median number of projects at merged firms fell from 85 in both pre-merger companies, to 56 in three years post-merger. Companies were either removing duplication and focusing on winners, or becoming less productive. Definitive evidence was years away.

Another argument for increasing size was to secure greater 'share of voice' and to acquire global commercial reach. Pfizer's acquisition of Pharmacia took the new entity from fourth in Europe and third in Japan to first across the triad.

Companies which lacked presence in key markets were obliged to make use of licensing deals, sharing the profit with another company. A strong global or regional marketing capability was also vital in attracting the best in-licensing candidates to strengthen the product pipeline.

While the benefits of M&A at the global level might be under debate, there was no doubt that family-owned medium-sized European pharmas were in dire strategic straits and were forced to consider M&A as a survival strategy. Not surprisingly, in September 2006 the Altana/Nycomed, Schwarz Pharma/UCB and Merck KGaA/Serono tie-ups were all announced in the same month. The Japanese government was also calling for consolidation and globalisation of domestic companies, illustrated by the marriage of Yamanouchi and Fujisawa to form Astellas in 2005.

As global companies suffered declining R&D productivity, Phase 3 failures and product withdrawals, biotechs found themselves with the upper hand in terms of pipeline and innovation. Their investors stood to gain more from pursuing a revenue rather than royalty path, so biotechs increasingly strove to hold on to commercialisation rights, at least for the USA, and to use revenue from licensing deals to support in-house programmes. Whether they truly had the financial strength to take on the enormous risks involved remained to be seen, and mergers between biotechs became a way to marry revenue streams with promising but under-funded pipelines. As the cost of licensing deals spiralled upwards, outright acquisition of biotechs became a feasible alternative for cash-rich pharmas, driving further industry consolidation.

Where next?

At the end of 2006, global pharmas were pursuing a variety of strategies. A few were well positioned to benefit from the growth in generics through their generics divisions, such as Novartis (Sandoz) and Merck KGaA, but was this the right focus for a high-margin, innovation-based industry? A few owned vaccine businesses (GSK, Merck, Sanofi-Aventis, Novartis, Wyeth) or had just acquired them (Pfizer). Others had made belated moves into biopharmaceuticals (AstraZeneca). In the face of falling profits, problems with Celebrex, the looming Lipitor patent expiry and the late-stage

failure of a crucial product, Pfizer was undergoing a strategic overhaul with the loss of 10,000 jobs.

An intriguing response to environmental change was adopted by Roche, which positioned itself as operating an 'integrated health care' business model. Roche was the global leader in diagnostics and the strategic vision was to move from seller of instruments and reagents to a health information provider, offering value through better targeting of treatments. Linking diagnostics with therapeutics was still some way off, so this remained more vision than reality. However, it was hard to argue with the success of the overall Roche/Genentech strategy, which had been to focus on innovative medicines, particularly biopharmaceuticals, for areas of high unmet medical need, such as cancer. With the highest sales growth among the top 10 and industry-leading margins, Roche had benefited from the market shift to specialist-driven medicines and was the envy of its competitors, many of whom announced an identical strategic focus and rushed to invest in biopharmaceuticals and cancer R&D.

Summary

Pharmaceutical companies are facing their toughest outlook in a decade. The industry has made a tremendous contribution to human well-being, yet is vilified in the media and targeted by governments in their efforts to curb spiralling health care costs. R&D, in-licensing and sales and marketing costs have risen sharply, but productivity is down and the product life cycle has shortened. Product approval, pricing/reimbursement and promotion are subject to increasingly onerous regulation, yet free trade allows wholesalers to extract a large chunk from the value chain. Exciting opportunities do still exist – scientific advances, more educated consumers, large emerging markets and of course unmet medical need. Industry consolidation is still driven by the dominant belief that size is what counts, but the blockbuster paradigm is perceived to have failed. Companies now almost uniformly claim to focus on medicines that will deliver meaningful benefits for high unmet-need diseases. Niche areas are becoming crowded, which will create pricing pressures. The industry more than ever needs to get a handle on the slippery business of scientific creativity and provide its critics with indisputable evidence of its value.

TUI: achieving and maintaining leadership in the European tourism industry

Eric Viardot

TUI illustrates one of the most amazing and successful strategic changes of a firm, among the largest European companies. From 1997 to 2003, its management turned one of the oldest steel and mining conglomerates, known as Preussag, into TUI, the undisputed European leader in the tourism industry – a fast-growing but very volatile and competitive industry.

● ● ●

The tourism industry in the mid-2000s

In 2005, the tourism industry was a significant industry. Worldwide it generated US$6,201.49bn (≈€4,960bn) of economic activity, represented 10.6 per cent of total world GDP and provided 221,568,000 jobs or 8.3 per cent of total employment.[1]

In the previous 10 years, the tourism industry had been growing at an annual pace of 4.1 per cent as illustrated in Exhibit 1; 2005 was the best year ever for this industry: for the first time ever the number of international tourist arrivals recorded worldwide exceeded 800 million, according to the World Tourism Organization (WTO), a specialised agency of the United Nations (UN) for tourism policy issues.

This represented a 5.5 per cent growth rate, coming after the 10 per cent growth in 2004 which had seen a rebirth of the tourism industry after a plateau in 2001–2003 following the general insecurity created after the various terrorist attacks in New York (2001), Djerba (2002), Bali (2003) and Madrid (2004). The global economic downturn, and the health crisis, such as the outbreak of SARS in 2003, had also a traumatic effect on international travel from 2000 to 2004.

In 2005, Africa experienced 10 per cent growth, followed by Asia–Pacific (+7 per cent) which already had an exceptional recovery in 2004 (+24 per cent) and the Middle East (+7 per cent) cooling off after a swift expansion in the previous years. Then came the Americas (+6 per cent) where destinations in Central America (+14 per cent) and South America (+13 per cent) increased more than those in North America (+5 per cent).

Finally Europe had the lesser growth of +4 per cent, still one percentage point above its long-term trend. Northern Europe (+7 per cent) had benefited from the 10 per cent increase of arrivals in the UK, which was not really affected by the London bomb attacks in July 2005. In Southern and Mediterranean Europe (+6 per cent) Turkey had emerged as the champion growth with an expansion of 20 per cent reaching more than 20 million visitors. In Central and Eastern Europe, the Baltic states had registered a steady 12 per cent growth whereas in Western Europe the biggest increase was in west Germany (+6 per cent) and Switzerland (+6 per cent). More details can be found in Exhibit 2.

On a longer term, the expansion of tourism seemed to be a mega-trend shaping the future of the world economy and activity. The WTO forecasted that the 1 billion arrivals mark would be passed in 2010 and by 2020 there would be 1.6 billion international tourist arrivals.

---

[1] Tourism Satellite Accounting, http://www.wttc.org/frameset1.htm.

Exhibit 1   **World inbound tourism**

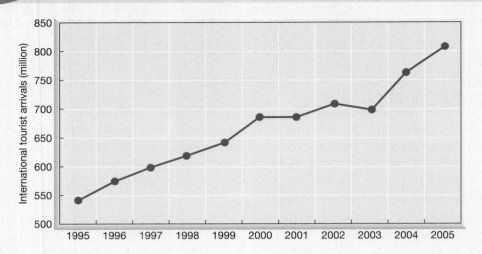

Source: WTO. © UNWTO, 2007, #92844/28/2007.

Exhibit 2   **International tourist arrivals by (sub)regions**

	Full year											Average	Share	
	2000	2001	2002	2003	2004	2005	03/02	04/03	05/04	05/04	05/00	2000–2005	2000	2005
	(million)						change (%)			(million)		change (%)	(%)	
World	639	633	709	697	788	808	−1.7	10.0	5.5	42.3	119.2	3.2	100	100
Europe	*398.2*	*385.8*	*407.4*	*408.8*	*425.8*	*443.8*	*0.3*	*4.2*	*4.3*	*18.3*	*47.7*	*2.3*	*57.5*	*54.8*
Northern Europe	44.6	42.3	43.8	44.5	48.4	51.8	1.8	0.6	7.1	3.4	7.2	3.0	6.5	6.4
Western Europe	139.7	135.8	138.0	136.1	138.7	141.1	−1.4	1.9	1.7	2.3	1.4	0.2	20.3	17.5
Central Eastern Europe	71.2	74.0	78.1	60.3	89.1	92.3	2.8	11.0	3.6	3.2	21.1	5.3	10.3	11.4
Southern Mediterranean Europe	140.0	143.7	147.6	147.7	149.5	158.8	0.1	1.2	6.2	9.3	18.0	2.4	20.4	19.6
Asia–Pacific	*111.4*	*116.6*	*128.1*	*114.2*	*145.4*	*156.2*	*−0.4*	*27.3*	*7.4*	*10.8*	*44.8*	*7.0*	*18.2*	*10.3*
North-East Asia	58.3	61.0	68.2	61.7	79.4	87.5	−9.6	20.6	10.2	8.1	29.2	0.5	8.5	10.0
South-East Asia	37.8	40.7	42.8	37.0	40.0	50.2	−13.6	30.3	4.1	2.0	12.5	5.9	5.5	6.2
Oceania	9.2	9.1	9.1	9.0	10.2	10.6	−0.9	12.4	3.9	0.4	1.3	2.7	1.3	1.3
South Asia	6.1	5.8	5.8	6.4	7.6	7.9	10.2	18.1	4.5	0.3	1.8	5.4	0.9	1.0
Americas	*128.2*	*122.2*	*118.7*	*113.1*	*125.8*	*133.1*	*−3.1*	*11.2*	*5.8*	*7.3*	*4.9*	*0.8*	*18.8*	*18.5*
North America	91.5	86.4	83.3	77.4	85.9	89.4	−7.1	10.9	4.1	3.5	−2.1	−0.5	13.3	11.1
Caribbean	17.1	16.8	16.0	17.0	18.2	19.2	6.5	6.7	5.4	1.0	2.1	2.3	2.5	2.4
Central America	4.3	4.4	4.7	4.9	5.8	6.6	4.2	17.0	13.6	0.6	2.2	0.6	0.6	0.8
South America	15.2	14.6	12.7	13.7	16.0	18.0	7.9	16.2	12.7	2.0	2.8	3.4	2.2	2.2
Africa	*25.2*	*23.9*	*28.5*	*30.7*	*33.3*	*38.7*	*4.1*	*8.4*	*10.1*	*3.4*	*8.5*	*5.4*	*4.1*	*4.5*
North Africa	10.2	10.7	10.4	11.1	12.8	13.6	6.6	15.5	6.1	0.8	3.4	5.9	1.5	1.7
Subsaharan Africa	18.0	18.2	19.1	19.6	20.5	23.1	2.8	4.5	12.6	2.6	5.1	5.2	2.6	2.9
Middle East	*25.2*	*25.0*	*28.2*	*30.0*	*35.0*	*38.4*	*2.8*	*18.8*	*8.8*	*2.5*	*13.2*	*8.8*	*3.7*	*4.8*

Source: WTO. January 2006. © UNWTO, 2007, #92844/28/2007.

History of TUI

In the mid-1990s, in a tough economic environment, Michael Frenzel and his team at Preussag made the decision to exit the smelting and mining industry, which was too cyclical, whose profitability was decreasing year on year, and which had no clear future with the closing of the last German coal mines and the growth of the aggressive competition of emergent countries. The top management team made a radical decision to enter the tourism business, a growth service business.

In order to become a European leader, the group embarked on a steady programme of major acquisitions while divesting the non-core businesses. This started at the end of 1997 when Preussag bought Hapag-Lloyd AG, a large German tour operator with its own travel agency chain, airline and logistic services. The same year, Preussag made the complete acquisition of TUI Deutschland, one of the leaders for package holidays, as well as the first German travel agency chain, and took significant equity share of Magic Life, a leading all-inclusive holiday club chain.

In 1998, Hapag Touristik Union, the tourism division of Preussag, purchased 24.9 per cent of Thomas Cook, one of the biggest British tourism and financial services group. In 1999, HTU acquired a majority stake in Thomas Cook.

On 1 January 2000 the Hapag Touristik Union was renamed 'TUI Group' and jumped into the European market. First it completed the takeover of the British Thomson Travel Group, then took a stake in the French leading tour operator Nouvelles Frontières (with an agreement for a future entire takeover), and finally the acquisition of Fritidsresor, one of the largest tour operators in Scandinavia. TUI was now a leading company in tourism with over 200 tourism brands around the world.

In August 2001, all these brands and firms were put under the global umbrella of 'World of TUI'. The group was then fully repositioned in the tourism industry. The vision was then visible and actionable. In April 2002, Preussag created TUI Air Management in order to manage the six group airlines centrally. In June 2002, at the general assembly, shareholders voted for 'Preussag AG' to be renamed 'TUI AG'. In October, TUI completed the 100 per cent takeover of Nouvelles Frontières.

In 2003, in order to adjust to the slump in tourism, the group started a new cost-cutting programme targeting yearly savings of around €260m in 2003 and €100m for 2004.

As for the other large tour operators, the binge of acquisitions, sometimes at very high prices, had increased the debt burden whilst all the operational synergies, the main reason for consolidation, had not yet been fully realised. Furthermore, no large tour operator had achieved a leading position in all key European markets at that time in order to realise significant economies of scale. The decrease on the revenues side added to the pressure on cash. Additionally, the tour operators appeared to be the most exposed to the economic downturn because they were handicapped by a high level of fixed assets and less able to manage their airline and hotel capacities.[2]

In April 2003, TUI also set up TUI China for Chinese tourists visiting Germany. One year later, in April 2004, TUI opened its first low-cost travel agency in Hamburg, Germany, with Touristik Express to sell low-cost holidays. There were no catalogues, no decorations and no seats; customers obtained information about the latest holiday offers by themselves and were able to book on the spot. In August 2004, TUI entered the Russian tour operator market and set up TMR (TUI Mostravel Russia) through a joint venture with the Russian tour operator Mostravel.

In March 2005 TUI launched the virtual tour operator Touropa.com, in Germany, selling travel tours not only online, but also through travel agencies, television and call centres. This bolstered TUI's position as the European leader in the direct sale of travel products with a turnover of €2.6bn in 2005, half of them made online (+73 per cent compared with 2004) and the other half bought via TV stations and call centres. In April 2005, TUI entered the Indian market with a 50 per cent holding in the incoming agency 'Le Passage to India'. In December 2005, TUI took the full control of CP ship, the leading Canadian container shipping line, and merged its container shipping division with it.

The TUI group in 2005

In 2005 TUI was the biggest tour operator in Europe. A tour operator (also named a tour wholesaler) offers packaged or 'all-inclusive' prepaid and preplanned holidays to its customers, usually through

---

[2] D. Schneiderbauer, P. Sweens, and F. Döring, 'Surviving the crisis in European tourism', Mercer on Travel and Transport, Issue Fall 2003/Winter 2004, at www.mercermc.com/Perspectives/Specialty/MOT_pdfs/MOTT_F03-W04-final.pdf.

travel agents. This was a pre-assembly of basic travel components sold for a fixed price. A standard package was composed of air transportation (outbound and return), hotel accommodation, transfers from the airport to the hotel and back, as well as optional items such as insurance, meals, excursions, etc.

The flights (usually charters) left and returned on given dates; the duration of the stay was fixed. This type of vacation offered security and good value for the vacationer as tour operators were able to get very good prices compared with a do-it-yourself holiday. Indeed, tour operators had managed to industrialise and standardise the process of holidaymaking, turning it into a mass market business.

With 18 million customers representing a turnover of more than €14bn, TUI in 2005 was the market leader in tourism in Europe. The group owned about 3,500 travel agencies in 17 countries with a very strong presence in Germany, the UK and The Netherlands as well as in Belgium (under the various brands of TUI ReiseCenter, FIRST Reisebüro, Hapag-Lloyd Reisebüro, TUI TravelCenter and Lunn Poly).

TUI also held 75 tour operators active in 18 European markets. Some of its most famous brands were TUI, Nouvelles Frontières 1-2-Fly, Gebeco, Robinson, Thomson, Fritidsresor, Star Tour, Jetair and Gulet. These tour operators were selling not only fully packaged tours but also individual travel components (flights, car rental, hotel accommodation, etc.).

TUI owned more than 100 aircraft with control of various airlines such as Arkefly, Britannia, Corsairfly, Hapagfly, Jetairfly and Thomsonfly. TUI was also present in the low-cost airline market with Hapag-Lloyd-Express in Germany and Thomsonfly.com in the UK. The airlines ran as independent entities with responsibility for results at a local level whilst the fleet operations, maintenance, and purchasing were centralised and managed by the TUI Airline Management team in Hanover.

In 2005, TUI was also the Europe's largest holiday hotelier with 285 hotels and some 163,000 beds. This made it number 13 in the ranking of the biggest hotel chains around the world. The group also owned 37 incoming agencies with more than 5,000 staff and tour guides who took care of the customers in more than 70 countries. They organised the transportation between airport and hotel, provided local excursions, offered assistance for car rentals, etc. TUI was also present in the cruise activity with four cruise liners belonging to Hapag-Lloyd Cruises.

TUI was also very active in the shipping business, mostly in logistics and containers. Its subsidiaries Hapag-Lloyd AG, located in Hamburg, and CP Ships, in Montreal, had a turnover of more than €3.4bn with 4,900 employees. It represented about 19 per cent of total TUI turnover. The rest of the activities were mostly related to international trading, an activity which represented 5 per cent of total TUI turnover and had grown by more than 50 per cent from the previous year.

In September 2005, TUI had 58,191 employees, of which 85.7 per cent were operating in tourism. Of the rest of the TUI employees, 7.8 per cent were in the logistics divisions, 2 per cent in trading and 4.5 per cent in sales operations.

Finally TUI enjoyed stable and management-friendly shareholders: the state-owned Westdeutsche Landesbank owned about a third of TUI; 14 per cent of TUI shares belonged to German institutional investors; while the Spanish RIU Group, the third biggest local hotel chain in Spain, had 5.1 per cent of the shares; the Caja de Ahorros del Mediterraneo, a Spanish savings bank, owned 5 per cent; and the rest of the shares were floating.

Competition

In 2005, TUI had a stronghold on the €60bn European tour operator market. With more than 32 per cent market share, TUI was the first player in a concentrated market where the four biggest companies were generating more than half the total revenues and the biggest 10 represented more than 80 per cent of the market (Exhibit 3). Its main competitors then were Thomas Cook, MyTravel Group, ReweTouristik and First Choice Holidays.

The German Thomas Cook was created in 2000 when German retailer Karstadt Quelle and Deutsche Lufthansa set up a joint venture for the purchase of Thomas Cook Holdings, the famous British tour company founded in 1841, with 900 travel agencies. It was selling travel tours and charter flights to more than 13 million customers and had about 26,000 employees. The main brands were Thomas Cook Holidays, Havas Voyages and Neilson.

With 17,500 employees, the British MyTravel Group was also an integrated international group. It was selling travel and tour services (including air travel, hotels, retail travel services, and tours, but

Exhibit 3   **Tour operator market share in Europe**

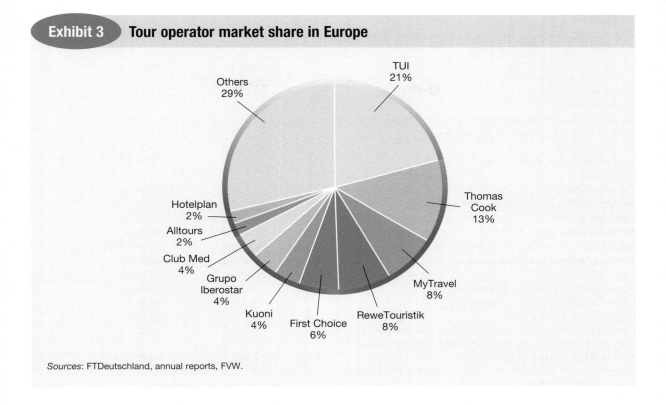

Sources: FTDeutschland, annual reports, FVW.

no longer cruises) from about 1,000 travel outlets in Europe, North America and the UK under more than 100 brands. MyTravel Group was very strong in the UK where it made more than 66 per cent of its revenues. The company was under reorganisation after several bad years, including 2005 when revenues decreased by 19 per cent, and under claims of accounting fraud and mismanagement.

ReweTouristik, Germany's third largest travel group, was offering package holidays under the brands ADAC Reisen, Dertour, ITS, Jahn Reisen, Meier's Weltreisen and Tjaereborg. It was operating more than 1,300 travel agencies, and was asserting to have the biggest managed travel dis-

tribution network in Germany. It was also running 54 hotel complexes, and had a stake in the LTU holiday airline.

First Choice Holidays, from the UK, was providing tour and travel services in 16 countries, mostly traditional packages, with its Mainstream Holidays Division, and destination and lifestyle offers, with its Specialist Holidays Division. For distribution, First Choice Holidays relied on its hundreds of First Choice and Holiday Hypermarkets retail travel stores, as well as third-party travel agents and Internet reservations. First Choice Holidays had 14,500 employees in 2005.

APPENDIX

TUI profit and loss statement for 2004 and 2005 (in €m)

	2004	2005
Turnover	16,293.3	18,201.3
Other income	655.0	602.5
Change in inventories and other own work capitalised	+12.0	−3.2
Cost of material and purchased services	11,216.6	12,900.3
Personnel costs	2,198.3	2,304.2
Depreciation and amortisation	438.5	505.1
Impairment	4.0	18.3
Other expenses	2,513.1	2,489.4
Result from the discontinuance of operations	–	–
Financial income	161.7	185.0
Financial expenses	370.6	421.9
Result from companies measured at equity	+39.7	+39.1
Earnings before taxes on income	**+420.6**	**+385.5**
Income taxes	+55.4	+86.9
Result from continuing operations	**+365.2**	**+298.6**
Result from discontinuing operations	+206.8	+196.2
Group profit for the year	**+572.0**	**+494.8**
Group profit for the year attributable to shareholders of TUI AG	+528.2	+456.7
Group profit for the year attributable to minority interests	+43.8	+38.1
Group profit for the year	**+572.0**	**+494.8**

Source: TUI Annual reports.

Industry dynamics in the hi-fi sector

Robert MacIntosh

This case explores the strategic issues facing specialist hi-fi manufacturers as the market around them changes, in particular the growth of online, digital and portable music sources. The case offers students the opportunity to reflect on a number of themes such as the segments of the market under consideration, the competences required to compete in new areas and the basis of competitive advantage. However, the primary focus of the case is around the barriers facing small players in global markets.

● ● ●

Music is spiritual. The music business is not.
(Van Morrison)

Introduction

Music has the power to change our mood, to mark the significant events in our lives, to shape our culture and to allow successive generations to delineate a sonic gap between them and their parents. In our increasingly wireless and digital world music can accompany you wherever you go. In the home, in the car, on your phone or on your PC; music is omnipresent.

As our music buying and listening habits change, so too the nature of the music business changes. Within the music business, our focus here is on those that manufacture high-quality sound reproduction equipment. This case study examines the strategic questions facing such firms and points to the difficulties these firms face in deciding how and where to compete.

As consumers we face a dizzying array of listening devices that might suit our needs. One obvious decision criterion might be the price we are willing to pay to hear music reproduced. Supermarkets will sell portable CD players for as little as £15 (€22). Electrical goods stores will offer greater choice, ranging from the cheap and cheerful to products that are more expensive from recognisable brand names such as Sony or Panasonic. They may also stock a limited number of 'hi-fi separates', that is individual components such as a CD players, turntables, amplifiers and speakers which can be used in conjunction to reproduce music. Then there are specialist hi-fi retailers who serve what is sometimes known as the 'audiophile' market. Audiophiles are those who demand exceptionally high levels of clarity and sonic performance from hi-fi equipment. A rule of thumb which is often quoted is that if your hi-fi is worth more than your car, then you qualify as an audiophile. Specialist manufacturers such as Linn, Meridian and Naim produce sound systems which can cost upwards of £40,000. Entry-level systems from such firms typically start between £1,000 and £2,000.

Finally, the last five years have seen rapid growth in the sales of digital music devices such as Apple's iPod or Creative's Zen players. These offer yet more choice to potential consumers. These small, portable, digital devices can be used in conjunction with PCs or attached to external speakers (often referred to as docking stations) to allow them to substitute for home hi-fi systems. Alongside greater portability, these devices (often known as MP3 players)[1] offer the ability to store

---

[1] The label MP3 refers to one particular technology for compressing and storing digital music. Despite the fact that the best-selling digital music device, the iPod, uses a different storage and compression technique developed by Apple, MP3 has become the most commonly used way of referring to such devices. An analogy might be the misattribution of the brand Hoover to describe the generic category of products that are vacuum cleaners.

---

huge volumes of data. A single iPod can contain up to 10,000 songs and more recent models also store digital pictures, video, web-casts, blogs, diary details and games. Prices for such digital systems vary enormously, but even the most expensive combinations in this category cost far less than an 'entry-level' audiophile system.

Specialist hi-fi manufacturers

A number of independent firms based in the UK produce some of the best hi-fi equipment in the world. We will consider three such firms: Linn, Naim and Meridian.

Linn Products was founded in 1972 by Ivor Tiefenbrun. As a music fan, Tiefenbrun felt that the mindset about good hi-fi was all wrong. The journey from recorded music to sound in your sitting room can be described as a chain with three main links: the source of the signal, the amplifier(s) and the speakers. The vogue in the early 1970s was for better sound systems to mean bigger and better speakers. The Linn Sondek LP12 turntable was a radical departure from that mindset. Using precision-engineered components and a suspended sub-chassis, the LP12 ensured that the first link in the chain (that is, the source) was of the highest quality.

The LP12 is still available today and is considered by many to be the definitive reference turntable. Although the original design concept persists, the LP12's sound quality has been improved through retrofittable upgrade kits. As the firm grew, it gradually turned its attention to the other links in the chain. In 1975, Linn patented its isobaric loading principle, and launched the Isobarik loudspeaker. Amplifiers and tuners (for FM radio) followed and the CD12 (Linn's flagship compact disc player) was launched in 1997.

Linn now has an extensive retailer network and exports to more than 50 countries from its custom-built factory on the outskirts of Glasgow. The product portfolio now covers a range of sources, amplifiers and speakers including surround systems and multi-room home installations. Linn established its own record label so that it covers the complete chain from the recording studio to the home and it is now possible to download tracks from the Linn catalogue.

Like other specialist hi-fi manufacturers, Linn sells its products in an unusual way. Potential customers are asked to audition the product at length before deciding that it is right for their needs. The bottom line is that if it does not sound better than the competition, it is not worth buying. This produces a passionate focus within Linn on producing equipment which is 'simply better'. The visibility of this performance criterion within the firm is extremely high. Many of the staff are audiophiles themselves and represent some of the most demanding critics. The technicians who assemble the products attach their name to each item shipped, producing a direct connection to the subsequent owner of the product.

The story of Naim bears striking similarities to that of Linn. Founded in 1969 by Julian Vereker, the firm displays a similarly single-minded and uncompromising approach to the quality of its products. The firm argues that Naim users across the globe are its most discerning critics. Current and past customers demand the very best and, from experience, they know that Naim will not release a product unless it has something genuinely new to offer. Like Linn, Naim offers an extended relationship with past customers who can upgrade their products to reflect improvements in specific components or technologies without starting from scratch again.

The service department at Naim reveals a lot about the firm's attitude to customers. Servicing and repair are run on a non-profit-making basis and instead are intended to support the experience of Naim ownership. An unusual sequence in the repair process means that first the repair is carried out, which means that a firm and accurate cost for the repair can be made known to the customer. If the customer is unhappy with the proposed charge for the work, the repair is undone and the product is returned in its original state to the customer.

Whilst Naim continues to develop new products, the vast majority of its production is still dedicated to two-channel audio. Given this relatively traditional stance, Naim argues that it will continue to support the vinyl format for as long as demand for this remains and will not rule out the development of new products in this area.

The final firm we shall consider is Meridian Audio, founded in 1977 by Bob Stuart and Allen Boothroyd. Meridian products have proved popular among audiophiles and more recently in the lifestyle technology/home theatre field. Of the three firms described here, Meridian was the first to embrace compact disc as a format. Meridian produced the first 'serious' CD player and has since developed a strong reputation for digital speakers and surround sound systems. Again, the founders of this business were themselves passionate about music and this has played a major part in their desire to ensure that the quality of original recordings is archived for lossless retrieval. As a result, Meridian Lossless Packing or MLP technology was developed by researchers at the firm and in 1999 these efforts were rewarded by having MLP mandated as the world's new DVD audio standard – a significant achievement for a small independent firm.

Bob Stuart, co-founder of Meridian, claims that traditional systems using separate amplifiers and 'passive speakers' represent very primitive approaches to reproducing sound. Meridian build speakers with one dedicated amplifier for each driver unit in the speaker and featuring sophisticated digital control of the speaker itself. He also says that he is 'amused by the claims for iPod docking stations that they can fill the room with natural sound' – despite the fact that the speakers themselves use drivers that are 1 inch (2.5cm) in diameter.

	Founded	Turnover	Profit/Loss
Meridian	1977	£9.1m	£1.3m
Linn	1972	£35.1m	£1.5m
Naim	1969	£8.1m	£0.4m

Source: Data Monitor, February (2006).

Market size

Quantifying the market size for specialist hi-fi equipment is not a straightforward exercise. A cursory examination of standard industry data and market reports shows that it is difficult to extract data on the specialist niche from the broader data set. In total, the market for audio and video products in Europe and North America is comfortably in excess of £35bn.[2] However, this data covers every type of platform, component and budget, though it is possible to extrapolate some realistic estimates from this broader data set.

If 1 per cent of all audio- and video-related sales represent the specialist hi-fi sector, the total market for such products in North America and Europe alone equates to £350m. The market for all audio and video products is growing slowly (annual growth rates of between 3 and 9 per cent have been recorded in recent years) but the sharpest growth has come in particular new technologies, for example home cinema systems, MP3 players, etc. The traditional, specialist hi-fi market is relatively stable in comparison and shows no signs of dramatic growth. Indeed, growth in one product area, for example home cinema systems, compensates for static or declining markets in older products like turntables and tuners.

Before going on to consider the challenges facing firms such as Linn, Naim or Meridian it is also worth noting the size of some of the other firms with which they compete. Philips has an annual turnover of almost £20bn; Sony's R&D spending has recently exceeded £2bn. To say that the three firms under consideration here are small in comparison is something of an understatement.

The challenge

Each of these businesses faces difficult competitive circumstances. Each of them has been established for a number of years and has established competences to service the needs of a particular group of customers. However, the very nature of the music industry is changing rapidly. CDs still account for about 85 per cent of all music sold but global sales of this format have fallen 23 per cent in value over the last five years.[3] The rapid growth of the Internet, online digital music stores and highly portable MP3 players are transforming the way in which music is sold and reproduced. Furthermore, the firms leading this musical revolution are different in almost every respect from those that the specialist hi-fi manufacturers have traditionally encountered. Strategic group analysis on the basis of company size, technological competences, product pricing, market segmentation or simply sound quality suggests that specialist firms (such as the three described here) do not currently reside within the same group as these new players.

None of the three firms described here would have listed Apple Computers as a player in their industry 10 years ago. Executives from the 'serious' end of the hi-fi world are often dismissive of the sound quality achieved by any of the portable devices or MP3 players on the market today. After all, MP3 or any of the other digital compression techniques fly in the face of Ivor Tiefenbrun's logic

---

[2] Source: Euromonitor statistics for 2006.

[3] The Business, no. 28, 28 April (2007), p. 18.

that the source is the most important link in the chain because they rely on further compressing the source signal in order to squeeze as many tunes as possible onto the miniature storage devices involved. Although Linn has now begun to make works from Linn Records available to download in digital format at a range of quality levels, formats such as MP3 have powerful advantages as the dominant technology.

The facts and figures associated with digital music are startling. The iPod was introduced in October 2001, and by 2005 the company had sold more than 10 million units (*source*: bbc.co.uk/news) and there are no signs of the pace slowing. Sales in the first quarter of 2006 saw an increase of 207 per cent compared with the same quarter in 2005 (*source*: MacWorld.co.uk). Apple now holds a dominant position in the digital music marketplace with 65 per cent of the hard-drive-based music market. A plethora of docking stations by brands such as Bose offer a means of turning a portable product into the basis for a home hi-fi system, thus nibbling away at the market for potential hi-fi sales. There are also USB turntables available now for around £100 which will transfer your old vinyl collection into digital format. Some are doing this and then selling their vinyl collection to specialist collectors via eBay.

The challenge, however, runs far deeper than simply the equipment on which we choose to play music. Apple is also leading the way in the online retailing of music. Its iTunes online store is now available in 19 different countries and has passed the landmark of selling its 400-millionth tune. iTunes offers registered users the chance to download songs direct to their computer using an Internet connection. Consumers no longer need to buy a complete album since individual tracks can be bought for 79 pence. As new versions of the iPod are released which can play video and store photos, the iTunes store is beginning to offer the chance to buy films and episodes of popular TV series online too. The recording industry is thinking carefully about the implications of iTunes and its equivalents for the consumers' preferred choice of format. Apple recently announced that it may offer higher-quality recordings for download at a premium price. Vinyl has moved from the dominant format to a specialist product. Although CD is by far the most commonly used format today there are signs that it could go the same way. One industry insider observed: 'ironically vinyl and streaming media may become the two dominant formats'.

Discussion

Specialist hi-fi manufacturers must respond to the competitive environment as it unfolds around them. They face difficult choices about whether to remain within a stable niche that has formed their core business to date. Change produces market opportunities and the potential for dramatic growth. Yet change may also involve competing with different firms and on different bases than in the past.

Amazon.com (B)* – from 2004 to 2006

Gary J. Stockport

This case is concerned with the roll-out of global strategy through the development of resources and strategic capabilities. It is about global dominance through the development and use of technology to offer an increasing array of products and services and continually enhancing customer experience. It continues to emphasise the focus upon customers as well as the trade-offs between increasing sales, profit margins, investment in technology and offers and discounts. The case shows Amazon continually adapting its business model through further movements towards a virtual one as well as added value technology development.

● ● ●

Introduction

Towards the end of 2006, Amazon.com's CEO Jeff Bezos took the opportunity to review his company's performance since start-up in 1995. He noted that increased sales year upon year had been generated. However, the growing profit generated since 2003, after eight years of negative income, had fallen in 2005 as Amazon continued to invest heavily in technology and shipping promotions. This led some investors to question whether Amazon was perhaps chasing unprofitable growth. Amazon's share price fell from around $50 (€40) during December 2005 to about $37 in February 2006 (see Exhibit 1). Exhibit 2 presents net sales growth and sales per segment, 1995–2005. Nevertheless, Jeff Bezos remained ruthless in his pursuit towards Amazon's longer-term perspective with regard to returns from its relentless customer-oriented initiatives.

A central tenet of Amazon's strategy had been customer-focused innovation designed to improve the convenience of the online shopping experience. This had included offering the world's biggest collection of goods and services where customers could find and buy anything they wanted online from financial services to diamonds. This strategy had been driven through technology development.

By 2006, Amazon was one of the most recognised brands in the world. The company had several retail websites and served customers in over 200 countries. It had a significant diversity of alliances through its associate programme and it also had unique patented software technology that drove its delivery of products and services. Furthermore, an increasing number of organisations were choosing Amazon's e-commerce platform to operate their websites. Exhibit 3 shows Amazon's strategy as hand drawn by Jeff Bezos in 2001.

At the end of 2006, Jeff Bezos had a number of key strategic issues to consider including:

● Is the Amazon business model the right model looking ahead five years or more?

● How can Amazon continue constantly to innovate and enhance the customer experience?

● What was the optimal trade-off between customer benefits and company profitability?

● Is Wal-Mart a threat?

This case was prepared by Professor Gary J. Stockport and MBA students Marnie Butson, Zohrab Ismail and Daniel van der Westhuizen, The University of Western Australia Business School (UWA). It is intended as a basis of class discussion and not as an illustration of good or bad practice. © Gary J. Stockport 2007. Not to be reproduced or quoted without permission. Professor Stockport would like to take this opportunity to thank MBA students David Street (The University of Cape Town) and Mark Ivory (UWA) for their work on earlier published Amazon.com case studies.

* Amazon.com (B) analyses the company from 2004 to 2006. It builds upon the previous case study, 'Amazon.com – from start-up to 2004', which was published in the seventh edition. The earlier case study is now available on the website within *Classic Collection*, if you would like to read the earlier story. It does provide useful background information before reading the new one.

Amazon.com stock prices: from start-up to March 2006

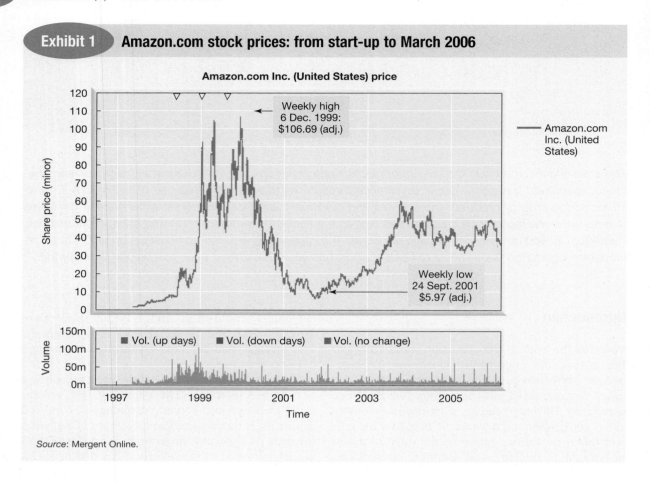

Amazon.com Inc. (United States) price

Source: Mergent Online.

Appendices A, B and C present Amazon's consolidated balance sheet, statement of operations and cash flows from 1996 to 2005. Appendix D shows net sales and net income as allocated to segments 2001–2005. Appendix E presents the timeline of company growth.

Soaring success, 2004

The year 2004 saw Amazon further expanding its product range to sell other items ranging from herbal remedies to outdoor equipment. Although the year was a success with a net profit of $588m, the effects of discounting and shipping were felt in the third quarter. During the year, Amazon tested greater discounts for books and books over $15 were discounted by 30 per cent. Customers were offered an additional 1.5 per cent discount when they used Amazon's A9 search engine. During the third quarter, customers using free shipping reached record levels. Despite the impact on the bottom line, Amazon continued to market free shipping.

During 2004, Amazon acquired *Joyo.com*, a British Virgin Islands company, which operated the www.joyo.com and www.joyo.com.cn websites in cooperation with Chinese subsidiaries and affiliates. The *Joyo.com* websites were China's largest online retailers of books, music and videos.

Amazon also launched A9.com Inc., which was a separately branded and operated subsidiary of Amazon. A9.com was created for building innovative search technologies that 'integrated' multiple sources and had access to most of Amazon's established search capability. It also incorporated user recognition and search activity 'memory'. Whilst Udi Manber, A9.com's CEO, extolled the practical aspects of the offering:

> Search has become an integral part of many people's work. We strive to extend current search tools by helping people not only to discover information easily, but also to remember and manage that information.

(Press release, 2004)

Exhibit 2   Net sales and sales by segment, 1996–2005

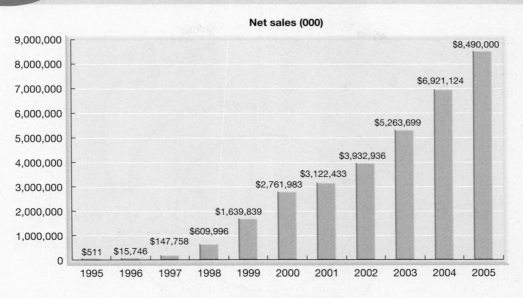

Net sales (000)

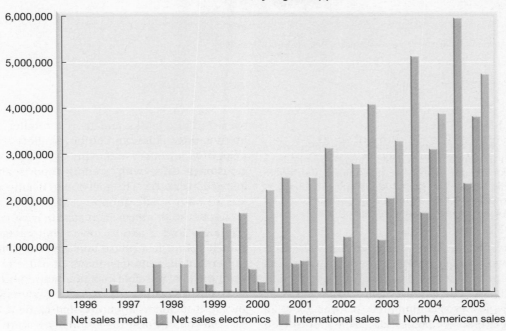

Sales by segment ($)

■ Net sales media   ■ Net sales electronics   ■ International sales   ■ North American sales

Source: Amazon.com Annual Reports, 1997 to 2005.

Exhibit 3   Amazon's strategy as drawn by Jeff Bezos in September 2001

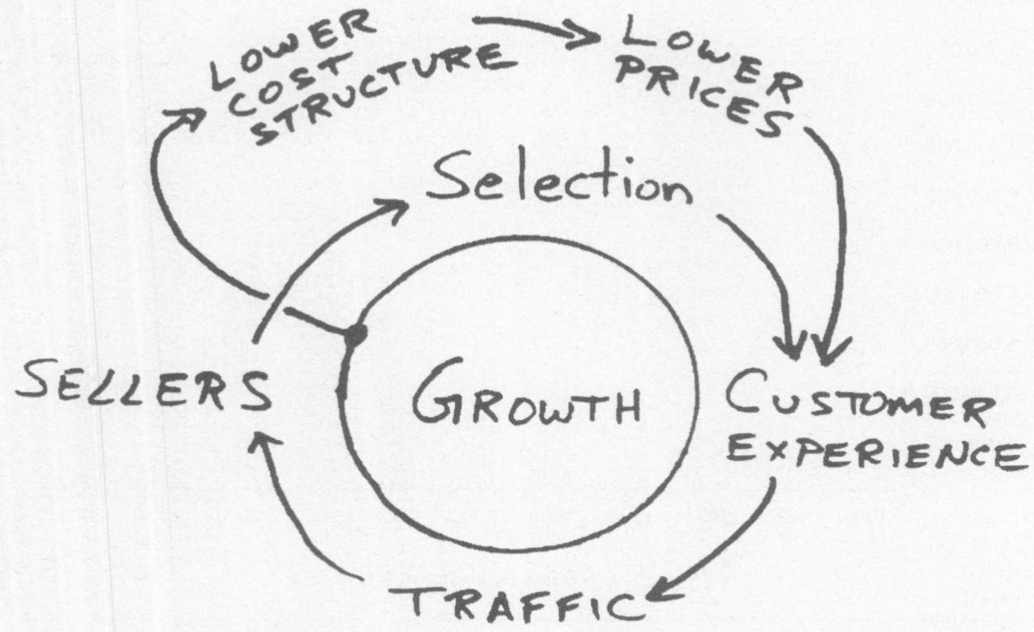

Source: Amazon.com Annual Shareholder Meeting Presentation, 17 May 2005.

Bezos added:

> A9.com gives people an incredible amount of power to discover information from diverse and comprehensive data sources and to manage that information effectively and easily. The search landscape is evolving at such a rapid pace that we must continue working hard to build innovative technologies that offer a great user experience.

'*Search inside the book*' debuted in 2004 with 120,000 books. Each book had to be scanned and indexed and this was both a huge logistical challenge and cost. The database took up 20 terabytes of 'space' and Bezos commented this was about 20 times larger than the biggest database that existed anywhere at the time Amazon was founded.

During 2004, Amazon launched two new product categories, 'Beauty' and 'Jewellery'. Amazon offered more than 75,000 jewellery items ranging from $15 earrings to a platinum diamond necklace for $93,000. The mark-up on jewellery items was about 13 per cent, which was significantly less than the mark-ups for retail jewellery stores. Amazon was able to do this because it did not have the high overhead of a bricks-and-mortar retailer. Amazon hired gemmologists and other jewellery experts to inspect its jewellery and many of its diamonds and gemstones came with grading reports and other inspection criteria. The goal of the 'Beauty' category was to be a single shopping destination offering thousands of products such as skin care, hair care, fragrance and make-up, etc. This category was launched in a test phase and Amazon continually gathered data from customers in order to try and build the best possible customer experience.

To ensure further that Amazon's prices were the lowest, it included a feature that made it easy for customers to inform the company if they found a lower price on a comparable product. When the lower price was verified, Amazon reduced its price on the website for all its customers. Exhibit 4 shows how the established product lines and newer offerings were deployed across Amazon throughout the globe.

During 2004, the company continued to nurture a culture of innovation. Chief Information Officer (CIO) Werner Vogels pointed out that staff were

Exhibit 4 **The 2004 chronology of functionality rolled out across global websites**

Selection

	Amazon.com	Amazon.co.uk	Amazon.de	Amazon.fr	Amazon.co.jp	Amazon.ca	Joyo.com
Books	'95	'98	'98	'00	'00	'02	'04
Music/Video	'98	'99	'99	'00	'01	'02	'04
DVD/Rental*	'98	'99/'04*	'99	'00	'01	'02	'04
Video Games & Software	'99	'00	'00	'01	'01	'03	'04
Electronics	'99	'01	'01		'03		
Toys & Baby	'99	'01	'04		'04		
Tools & Hardware	'99	'04	'04				
Kitchen & Housewares	'00	'04	'04		'03		
Magazines	'01		'02		'04		
Office Products	'02						
Apparel & Accessories	'02						
Sports & Outdoors	'03						
Gourmet Food	'03						
Jewelry & Watches	'03						
Health & Personal Care	'03						
Beauty	'04						
Musical Instruments	'04						
Third Party Sellers							
Marketplace	'00	'02	'02	'03	'02	'03	
Merchants@	'02						

Source: Amazon.com Annual Shareholder Meeting Presentation, 17 May 2005.

organised into small, loosely coupled groups which Bezos had dubbed 'two-pizza teams'. The 'two-pizza team' implied that if one cannot feed a team with two pizzas then the team were too large and their size should be limited from five to seven people depending on their 'appetites'. These 'pizza teams' created some of the site's most popular features. For example, they created the *Gold Box*, a little animated icon of a treasure chest that 'gleams' and 'wobbles' at the top of Amazon's home page. A click to 'open' the box revealed special offers that lasted for just an hour.

For the first time in the company's history, book sales were overtaken by consumer electronics for one weekend in 2004. Amazon had sought to 'harvest' a profit on the sale of electronics via the efficient procurement of inventory combined with strict controls in the amount of money spent picking, packing and shipping items. Frank Sadowski, Amazon's Vice President of Merchandising Consumer Electronics, pointed out:

> The company's electronics business is not of the order of a large big-box store retailer, but it has the buying power of a very large regional player. The company has relied on the support of suppliers to help make timely deliveries of the products. Amazon has hired experts in merchandising popular electronics, such as televisions and digital cameras.

During 2004, some technology problems hampered Amazon's customer service. For instance, during the Thanksgiving holiday shopping rush, Amazon experienced numerous breakdowns which effectively 'lost' thousands of customers. Many customers were unable to access the website at all or were 'turned away' at the home page by recurring error messages. Tests revealed that for 13 per cent of the time when customers attempted to buy goods, technology 'glitches' prevented the transaction.

During 2004, Amazon also found itself subject to a number of litigious actions including the following:

- *Cartier's* drive to stop counterfeit goods from being sold on the Internet led to its filing a federal lawsuit alleging that Amazon knowingly profited from selling 'knockoffs' of popular watches. Cartier was seeking to hold Amazon accountable for the 'contributory infringement' of its trademark based upon what the French luxury goods company alleged were Amazon's actions as a 'broker' for the sale of bogus Cartier watches.

- *Toys'R'Us* started litigation against Amazon over its partnership to sell toys online. In the lawsuit, ToysRUs.com blamed Amazon for violating its exclusivity agreement by allowing other retailers to compete for customers in some categories. Amazon denied the claim and countersued, citing what it called its partner's *chronic failure* to meet toy demand during the 2003 holiday season. In the countersuit, Amazon claimed that more than 20 per cent of the toy store's best-selling items were unavailable on the site during the peak of the season. (The ruling in March 2006 was in favour of Toys'R'Us and allowed it to operate an independent online retailing facility.)

There were a number of changes within Amazon's international operations during 2004. In the UK these included:

- Two new categories: 'DIY and Tools' and 'Garden and Outdoors'.
- DVD rental service for the UK, noting the intention of extending this to the US market.
- Amazon.co.uk and Borders (UK) Ltd, a leading UK bookseller and subsidiary of US-based Borders Group Inc., launched a new dedicated website (www.borders.co.uk) that was powered by Amazon's e-commerce platform.
- Amazon.co.uk and the bank HBOS created a co-branded credit card as part of a longer-term strategic alliance. The Amazon.co.uk MasterCard offered cardholders a loyalty programme in which customers were rewarded with Amazon.co.uk gift certificates.

In Germany, Amazon.de's offerings included:

- A new House and Garden shop with categories: 'DIY', 'Garden and Leisure Time', 'Body Care and Bath' and 'Kitchen and Household'.
- Free shipping for orders exceeding €20.
- 24-hour express shipping to a DHL distribution centre for customer collection.
- Other discounts and offers on calendars, computer and video games, some 3,000 CDs, DVDs below €10, DVDs over €39.95, and toys.

In Japan, Amazon.co.jp's offerings included:

- The launch of a new Computer Store which offered a wide selection of products from major

manufacturers such as Apple, Fujitsu, NEC and Sony.

- A new Toys and Hobby Store which offered more than 20,000 items in 21 product categories with discounts of up to 30 per cent. The website had a unique *'browse by age range'* function.

In Canada, Amazon.ca extended its aggressive discounting offer of 30 per cent off books over $30 to include books priced at $25 or more. This ongoing offer applied to more than 250,000 hardcover and paperback books.

Heavy investments squeeze profits – 2005

The year 2005 saw a continuation of the growing revenue and net sales grew by 24 per cent. However, profit margins were squeezed due to the increased investment in technology and shipping promotions. Many analysts were questioning whether Amazon was becoming 'too customer friendly'. However, Bezos continued to maintain his stance towards a longer-term perspective, noting that many customer oriented initiatives would not 'pay off for years' (Rivlin 2005). The new CIO, Tom Szkutak, added: 'We anticipate continuing to hire computer scientists and software engineers throughout 2005 to invest in further innovation for our customer' (*Evening Standard* 2005, p. 2).

One major success was that fourth-quarter jewellery sales increased by more than 100 per cent. This was attributed to the various enhancements to jewellery and watches including the addition of loose diamonds, more than 1,000 new watch styles, *Amazon Diamond Search* and *Create Your Own Ring*. Another success was The Beauty Store that was launched in May 2004 and generated $25m in its first year. In terms of market share, Amazon increased its dominance in online DVD sales to an estimated 90 per cent market share.

The assortment of acquisitions, strategic partnerships and innovations during the year included:

BookSurge. This was acquired, and was a global leader in inventory free book printing and fulfilment. BookSurge maintained a catalogue of thousands of titles that could be printed on demand. Greg Greeley, the Vice President of Media Products for Amazon, reported: 'Print-on-demand has changed the economics of small-quantity printing, making it possible for books with low and uncertain demand to be profitably produced' (Business Wire 2005, p. 1).

MobiPocket. This e-book retailer was also acquired and it provided virtual publishing by eliminating hard copies. Within this business model, the book distribution network consisted of nothing more than a writer, a reader and a server. Through BookSurge and MobiPocket, Amazon could forward orders to a printer to 'drop' books directly to the consumer. This innovation was particularly important when considering that Amazon owned millions of square feet of warehouse space and employed thousands of staff to process orders.

Marks & Spencer. Clothes, homewares and towels were planned to be available on the Amazon website sometime in the future. Marks & Spencer saw this as an innovative way to sell to more customers, particularly younger customers, who were used to buying books and CDs from Amazon.

Drugstore.com. During the year, Amazon and drugstore.com announced the end of their long-time and 'groundbreaking' partnership. Drugstore.com was the first Internet retailer to use Amazon's site in April 2000 and since then had paid a fee to have its products 'carried' on the site. However, Amazon had since built direct relationships with many major health and beauty brands such as Johnson and Johnson, Procter and Gamble and Unilever, which enabled it to offer customers a wider selection and lower prices. Consequently, it no longer needed the drugstore.com relationship. It was suggested this might signify to current and potential partners the risk that Amazon may 'partner with you today but compete against you tomorrow' (*The Seattle Times* 2005).

A9.com. This search site was upgraded with 'BlockView' technology to help users find information about businesses near them through building a vast collection of digital photographs. It enabled users 'virtually' to walk streets and businesses from street level as well as review, rate and provide information, create lists and get recommendations on more than 14 million US businesses.

Amazon Prime Membership Program. This consisted of a $79 annual fee for which members received unlimited two-day shipping on orders and overnight shipping for $3.99 per item. This membership programme was introduced to help to continue to build customer loyalty. Membership subscriptions more than doubled between November and December 2005.

Amazon Diamonds. Customers were able to find and buy loose diamonds at industry-leading prices in the Amazon Jewellery and Watches Store. *Amazon Diamond Search* introduced a propriety tool that allowed customers to search thousands of individual stones based on multiple diamond attributes. This provided customers with the 'ultimate flexibility in selecting loose diamonds and knowing they're getting a highly competitive price' (Russ Grandinetti, Vice President of Amazon.com Jewellery). Entering this market segment brought Amazon into direct competition with *Blue Nile*, an online jeweller that also offered diamond jewellery at prices well below industry averages.

'Amazon Pages' and 'Amazon Upgrade'. These two new programmes followed on from Amazon's BookSurge and MobiPocket acquisitions. They allowed customers access to any page, section or chapter of a book as well as the entire book in its Internet form.

Amazon Mechanical Turk. This was an innovative 'social experiment' based upon 'marketing' the spare time of Amazon's customers to businesses that needed small tasks performed online. The idea came from the need of A9.com to select thousands of photographs of shop-fronts for its mapping service. A typical human intelligence task (HIT) involved looking at 4 or 5 photographs and then selecting the one that best represented the shop in question. Each successfully completed HIT typically paid 3 cents and these payments could be used at Amazon or transferred into an external bank account. Amazon realised its huge customer base represented a massive pool of human intellect and it published a programming interface that allowed any developer to call on its service. Amazon then published these HITs for anyone to complete. The term, Amazon Mechanical Turk, made reference to the eighteenth-century hoax involving a chess-playing 'automation' that concealed a human chess master.

During the year, a number of companies turned to Amazon to power their websites:

- *Diane von Furstenberg (DVF) fashion label*, for its www.dvf.com website;
- *eHobbies.com site*, for its hobby and model products;
- *Sears Canada* (www.sears.ca), Canada's most popular retail website;
- *Shutterfly*, for its digital photo products and services.

A 2005 study of e-retail sites by FGI Research revealed that Amazon had continued to be a 'high flier' in customer satisfaction, ranking number 2 behind Netfix. However, results released for the American Customer Satisfaction Index (ACSI) revealed that the overall ACSI for e-commerce had fallen by about 2.7 per cent from the previous year. It was suggested that companies such as Amazon and eBay had struggled to maintain their high levels of customer satisfaction whilst also expanding product lines. Amazon was facing mounting pressure from traditional retailers expanding to the web who could offer more customer service options such as store pick-ups for online orders and store returns for online purchases.

Throughout 2005, Amazon restructured its multiple site locations with the closure and development of various facilities including the following:

- The Taocoma call centre closed as a consequence of its being too small to meet capacity. Some 20 customer service representatives were offered either a severance package or relocation to a job at one of the two other call centres in North Dakota and West Virginia.

- A newly expanded call centre was created with 60 higher-paying jobs at Grand Forks, in what was previously Amazon's power tool distribution centre. The inventory from Grand Forks was distributed among the other centres around the country, and this avoided customers having to pay multiple shipping charges due to the ordering of items stored at different locations;

- A new distribution centre in North Texas was opened in July 2005.

- Multiple software development centres were set up with the locations dependent on the degree of talented software professionals in that region. A second development centre was opened in India in Chennai (one in Bangalore was previously opened in July 2004). A centre in Cape Town, South Africa, was launched in July 2005 and Iasi in Romania became the site for the fifth international development centre. An existing one in Edinburgh, Scotland, was launched in July 2004 and all five complemented the main US development centre in Phoenix, Arizona. Appendix F shows Amazon's locations by 2006.

As 2005 was drawing to a close, Jeff Wilke, the company's Vice President of Worldwide Operations, stated that Prime membership had led members to buy more frequently and more broadly, beyond the 'flagship' categories of books, music, video and DVDs.

Technology, technology – 2006

Early in 2006, Amazon released its *Amazon S3 (Simple Storage Service):*

> Until now, a sophisticated and scalable data storage infrastructure like Amazon's has been beyond the reach of small developers. Amazon S3 enables any developer to leverage Amazon's own benefits of massive scale with no up-front investment or performance compromises. Developers are now free to innovate knowing that no matter how successful their businesses become, it will be inexpensive and simple to ensure their data is quickly accessible, always available, and secure.
>
> (Hof 2006, p. 1)

This was a web service which offered the latest ICT standards-based (REST[1] and SOAP[2]) web services interfaces for developers. Entire classes of companies could be built on S3 that would not have been possible before due to the high infrastructure costs for the developer.

New innovations during the year included:

Alexa Top Sites Web Service. Alexa Internet, a subsidiary of Amazon, launched the Alexa Top Sites Service which provided software and web developers with access to lists of websites, ordered by Alexa Traffic Rank. This Traffic Rank represented one of the largest and most up-to-date, global samples of Internet usage available.

Amazon Connect. The Amazon Connect program allowed authors to post messages directly to their readers via the Amazon home page. To ensure that the author's posts were relevant, they were only shown to customers who had purchased that author's works in the past, or those who had explicitly signed up to receive that author's posts

Moving into Apple's territory? It was reported in the press that Amazon was conducting talks with four record label giants to launch possibly a digital music service. This would directly compete with Apple Computers in the US digital music market which was dominated by Apple's iTunes service.

---

[1] REST: Representational State Transfer – an architectural style of networked systems.
[2] SOAP: Simple Object Access Protocol – a protocol for exchanging XML messages over a computer network and forming the foundation layer of web services.

Amazon appointed David Tennenhouse from Intel as the new CEO for A9.com. It believed this senior appointment helped further to build A9.com's reputation for developing unique and creative solutions for difficult search problems.

During 2006, Amazon continued to be seen as the 'gold standard' in customer satisfaction for online shopping. A survey by BIGresearch showed that Amazon led the race in attracting online shoppers. A study of 6,500 people over the 2005–2006 holiday season showed that 20 per cent used Amazon.

The lawsuit between ToysRUs.com and Amazon was finally settled. Amazon was found not to have honoured its contract as it had allowed other companies to sell toys through its website despite ToysRUs.com having an exclusive agreement with it. As mentioned earlier, this ruling allowed Toys'R'Us to operate an independent online retailing facility.

During the year, Amazon continued to focus upon global expansion. However, it announced that the 2006 results might be lower than analysts were expecting and this had a negative impact on the share price.

Defining the business

The vision behind Amazon had changed progressively since it started in 1995. What began as a goal to become the world's biggest and best online bookstore developed into a store where customers could buy *anything with a capital A*. It also wanted to become the world's most customer-centric company. Despite the progressive change in its vision, Bezos's answer in 2003 about the main difference between conventional retail and his business has remained relevant throughout Amazon's history:

> The three most important things in retail are location, location, location. The three most important things for our consumer business are technology, technology, technology. That's what takes the place of real estate in our business.
>
> (Quoted in BW Online, 25 August 2003)

The core of what defines the business has also remained constant, as reflected in the 1997 Letter to Shareholders. The letter contains a series of core commitments such as the emphasis on longer-term market leadership. Extracts from it are reproduced in Exhibit 5.

Exhibit 5   **Extract of 1997 Letter to Shareholders, reprinted in 2002 and subsequent annual reports**

1997 LETTER TO SHAREHOLDERS

(Reprinted from the 1997 Annual Report)

From the 6th Paragraph

Because of our emphasis on the long term, we may make decisions and weigh tradeoffs differently than some companies. Accordingly, we want to share with you our fundamental management and decision-making approach so that you, our shareholders, may confirm that it is consistent with your investment philosophy:

- We will continue to focus relentlessly on our customers
- We will continue to make investment decisions in light of long-term market leadership
- We will continue to measure our programs and the effectiveness of our investments analytically, to jettison those that do no provide acceptable returns, and to step up our investment in those that work best. We will continue to learn from both our success and our failures.
- We will make bold rather than timid investment decisions where we see a sufficient probability of gaining market leadership advantages. Some of these investments will pay off, others will not, and we will have learned another valuable lesson in either case.
- When forced to choose between optimising the appearance of our GAAP accounting and maximising the present value of future cash flows, we'll take the cash flows.

Source: Amazon.com 2002 Annual Report.

Amazon's retail offerings to customers purchasing its products have continued to include:

- browsing;
- searching;
- reviews and content;
- recommendations and personalisations;
- one-click technology;
- secure credit card payment;
- availability and fulfilment.

For operating purposes, Amazon's retail sites continued to be split into two principal divisions:

- The 'North American' division operated www.amazon.com and www.amazon.ca.
- The 'International' division operated www.amazon.co.uk, www.amazon.de, www.amazon.co.jp, www.amazon.fr, www.amazon.ca and www.joyo.com

Within these retail sites, there were three principal segments:

- *Media Sales Segment:* books, videos, DVDs and magazine subscriptions.
- *Electronics and Other Merchandise Segment:* electronics, photo items, software, cell phones, outdoor living items, kitchen and homeware products, toys and video games.
- *'Other' Segment:* co-branded credit card agreements and miscellaneous marketing and promotional activities.

It was also possible to divide the company into three (not necessarily equal) functional areas. These were:

- *Product development.* Departments within this area included editorial, marketing, product feasibility, pricing, as well as website design and site navigation, e-commerce solutions.
- *Technology content and development.* Software and technical production along with databases, information technology systems, engineering and computer science.
- *Supply chain and distribution.* Distribution centres, business-to-business client relationship management, supply chain management.

Amazon's strategic focus – the customer

Amazon had relentlessly followed through its strategy of focusing on the customer experience by offering low prices, convenience and a wide selection of merchandise. These three *'Customer Experience Pillars'*, supported by a foundation of innovation, have continued to be central to Amazon's operations. They are displayed in Exhibit 6.

The apparent 'tension' between offering both 'world leading customer experience (in terms of convenience and selection) and the lowest possible prices' was discussed by Bezos in his 2002 letter to shareholders:

Exhibit 6   **Amazon.com's Customer Experience Pillars**

Source: Amazon.com Annual Shareholder Meeting Presentation, 17 May 2005.

We transform much of customer experience – such as unmatched selection, extensive product information, personalized recommendations, and other new software features – into largely a fixed expense. With customer experience costs largely fixed, our costs as a percentage of sales can shrink rapidly as we grow our business.

Industry and market size

In the fourth quarter of 2003, the world Internet penetration was 10.7 per cent of an estimated 6.38 billion population. The fourth quarter of 2005 showed Internet penetration had grown to 15.7 per cent of an estimated world population of 6.5 billion. This represented a large increase in prospective customers for Amazon. Exhibit 7 shows world Internet usage and population statistics.

Competitors

Within the 2004 Annual Report, Amazon identified four different types of competitors:

1 Physical world retailers.

2 Other online e-commerce sites.

3 Indirect companies such as media companies and web search engines.

4 Companies that provided e-commerce services.

Exhibit 8 shows the revenues for Amazon's major competitors from 1999 to 2005.

Wal-Mart, whilst already the global giant in traditional retailing, with revenues of $288bn and around 1.8 million employees in 2006, had also progressively developed an online presence with www.walmart.com. It was now the third largest

---

Exhibit 7   **World internet usage and population statistics – updated 31 December 2005**

World regions	Population (2006 est.)	Population % of world	Internet usage latest data	% population (penetration)	Usage % of world	Usage growth 2000–2005
Africa	915,210,928	14.1	22,737,500	2.5	2.2	403.7%
Asia	3,667,774,066	56.4	364,270,713	9.9	35.7	218.7%
Europe	807,289,020	12.4	290,121,957	35.9	28.5	176.1%
Middle East	190,084,161	2.9	18,203,500	9.6	1.8	454.2%
North America	331,473,276	5.1	225,801,428	68.1	22.2	108.9%
Latin America/Caribbean	553,908,632	8.5	79,033,597	14.3	7.8	337.4%
Oceania/Australia	33,956,977	0.5	17,690,762	52.9	1.8	132.2%
World Total	6,499,697,060	100.0	1,018,057,389	15.7	100.0	182.0%

Source: http://www.internetworldstats.com/stats.htm. Copyright © 2005, Miniwatts Marketing Group. All rights reserved worldwide.

Exhibit 8   **Competitor revenue comparisons, 1999–2005**

Revenue (US$,000)	1999	2000	2001	2002	2003	2004	2005
Amazon	1,639,839	2,761,983	3,122,433	3,932,936	5,263,699	6,921,124	8,490,000
eBay	224,724	431,424	748,821	1,214,100	2,165,096	3,271,309	4,552,401
Barnes and Noble	3,005,608	3,468,043	4,375,804	4,870,390	5,269,335	5,951,015	4,873,595
Yahoo!	588,608	1,110,178	717,422	953,067	1,625,097	3,574,517	5,257,668
Apple	6,134,000	7,983,000	5,363,000	5,742,000	6,207,000	8,279,000	13,931,000
Wal-Mart	139,208,000	166,809,000	193,295,000	219,812,000	246,525,000	258,681,000	287,989,000
Google		86,426	439,508	1,465,934	3,189,223	6,138,560

Source: Mergent and Amazon annual reports.

online retailer with revenue of more than $1bn in 2005.

Beyond 2006 – the strategic issues

At the end of 2006, Jeff Bezos had a number of key strategic issues to consider including:

- Is the Amazon business model the right model looking ahead five years or more?
- How can Amazon continue constantly to innovate and enhance the customer experience?
- What was the optimal trade-off between customer benefits and company profitability?
- Is Wal-Mart a threat?

Selected sources

Alexa.com (1999) www.alexa.com.

Amazon.com Annual Reports 1997–2005.

Amazon.com (2003) Investor Relations Press Releases.

Amazon.com (2005) Annual Shareholder Meeting, 17 May.

Amazon.com (2005) Investor Relations. Available from: http://phx.corporate-ir.net/.

Banville, S. (2006) *Toys 'R' Us and Amazon.com part*, [Online] Breaking News English. Available from: http://www.breakingnewsenglish.com/.

BBC News (2006) *Toys R Us Wins Amazon Lawsuit*, [Online] BBC. Available from: http://newsvote.bbc.co.uk/.

Brandel, M. (2006) 'Views from three cutting-edge IT leaders: Amazon.com Inc.', *Computerworld Inc.*, 6 March.

Business Week (2003) *Speaking Out: Amazon.com's Jeff Bezos*, [Online]. Available from: http://www.businessweek.com/magazine.

Business Wire (2005) *'Alexa Top Sites' Web Service Now Available for Developers through Amazon. Web Services*, [Online], Business Wire. Available from: http://www.mergentonline.com.

Business Wire (2005) *Amazon Adds Loose Diamonds to Jewelry Store at Industry Leading Prices: Jewelry & Watches Sales Maintain Triple Digit Growth During the First Quarter*, [Online], Business Wire. Available from: http://www.mergentonline.com.

Business Wire (2005) *Amazon.com Acquires BookSurge LLC*, [Online], Business Wire. Available from: http://www.mergentonline.com.

Business Wire (2005) *Amazon.com Announces Plans for Innovative Digital Book Programs that Will Enable Customers to Purchase Online Access to Any Page, Section or Chapter of a Book as well as the book in its Entirety*, [Online], Business Wire. Available from: http://www.mergentonline.com.

Business Wire (2005) *Amazon.com Offers Harry Potter Fans Delivery of 'Harry Potter and the Half-Blood Prince' on the Day it is Released*, [Online], Business Wire. Available from: http://www.mergentonline.com.

Business Wire (2005) *A9.com Names David Tennenhouse Chief Executive Officer*, [Online], Business Wire. Available from: http://www.mergentonline.com.

Business Wire (2005) *Fast-Growing Specialty Apparel Retailer bebe Chooses Amazon Services for End-to-End E-Commerce Solution: Amazon Services to Provide Technology, Customer Service and Order Fulfillment for bebe.com*, [Online], Business Wire, Available from: http://www.mergentonline.com.

CNN Money (1998) *Discount retailer charges online bookseller with stealing trade secrets*, [Online], CNN Money Magazine. Available from: http://money.cnn.com/.

Corcoran, E. (1999) 'On-line: Amazoned', *Forbes*, March, p. 22.

Cox, J. (2003) *Amazon Dives Into Technology Services*, [Online], IDG News Service. Available from: http://www.arnnet.com.au.

DeMarco, A. (2004) *Amazon.com Enters the Jewelry Business*, [Online], JCK.

Dessauer, J. (1997) *Book Industry Trends*, Book Industry Study Group Inc. (Statistical Service Centre), New York.

Deutchmann, A. (2004) *The dotcom king*, [Online], Fairfax Digital. Available from: http://www.smh.com.au/.

Euromonitor (2003) *Amazon.com Inc./Books and publishing/ Company report*, [Online]. Available from: http://www.gmid.euromonitor.com.

Evening Standard (2005) *Discounting Strategy hits bottom line at Amazon*, [Online], Knight Ridder/Tribune. Available from: http://www.mergentonline.com.

Flynn, L.J. (2005) 'Rise in sales at Amazon lifts shares', *New York Times*, 27 July, p. C4.

Ganguli, P. (2001) *Leveraging Business/Trade Secrets for Competitive Advantage: Examples and Case Studies*, [Online], SJM School of Management, Indian Institute of Technology, World Intellectual Property Organization. Available from: www.wipo.org/.

Gibson, P. (1999) 'The sharp rise of e-commerce', *Information Today*, vol. 16, no. 7, pp. 28–33.

Haylock, C.F. and Muscarella, L. (1999) *Net Success: 24 Leaders in Web Commerce Show You How to Put the Web to Work for Your Business*, Adams Media Corporation.

Hines, M. (2005) *Amazon Nets Shutterfly for Photo Services*, [Online], CNET Networks. Available from: http://news.com.com/.

Hof, R.D. (1998) 'A new chapter for Amazon.com', *Business Week*, vol. 3591, pp. 39–41.

Hof, R.D. (2003) *Reprogramming Amazon*, [Online], Business Week Online. Available from: http://www.businessweek.net/.

Hof, R.D. (2004) *Jeff Bezos, Blind Alley Explorer*, [Online], Business Week Online. Available from: http://www.businessweek.com/.

Hof, R.D. (2006) *Amazon's newest product: Storage*, [Online], Business Week Online. Available from: http://www.businessweek.com/.

Klein, P. (2005) 'Amazon's not-so-secret-sauce: customers first', *Optimise*, vol. 4, no. 7, pp. 32–33.

Klein, P. (2005) 'Measuring e-commerce satisfaction', *Optimise*, vol. 4, no. 7, pp. 30–31.

Koselka, R. (1999) 'A real Amazon', *Forbes,* vol. 163, no. 7, pp. 50–53.

Marcial, G. (2006) 'Low tide for amazon?', *Business Week*, Issue 3975, 13 March, p. 96.

Massanari, A.L. (2003) '"Work hard. Have fun. Make history. [Make money.]": Narratives of Amazon.com', MA Dissertation, University of Washington.

Mergent Online, [Online], http://mergentonline.com.

Millot, J. (2004) *More Discounts from Amazon.com*, [Online], Publishers Weekly.

Nagal, A. (2005) 'Amazon beauty turns one', *WWD*, vol. 190, no. 75, pp. 18–19.

Netherby, J. (2005) 'Amazon.com: retailer of the year', *Video Business*, vol. 25, no. 51, pp. 4–6.

Nucifora, A. (1999) 'Despite the hype, marketing Internet's numbers adding up', *Business Press*, vol. 12, no. 8, pp. 13–14.

Pratt, M.K. (2004) 'Linux unchained', *Computerworld*, vol. 38, no. 47, pp. 37–38. [Proquest]

Rivlin, G. (2005) 'At Amazon.com, growth comes ahead of profit', *New York Times*, 2 May, p. C1.

Roth, D. (1999) 'Meg muscles Ebay uptown', *Fortune*, vol. 140, no. 1, pp. 81–87.

Sacharow, A. (1998) 'Amazon Calling', *Adweek*, vol. 48, no. 24, pp. 70–71.

San Jose Mercury News (2006) *Amazon music service rumoured*, [Online], Knight Ridder/Tribune. Available from: http://www.mergentonline.com.

Saunders, R. (1999) *Business the Amazon.Com Way: Secrets of the World's Most Astonishing Web Business*, Capstone.

Schwartz, N.D. (1999) 'The tech boom will keep on rocking', *Fortune*, vol. 139, no. 3, pp. 64–67.

Solotaroff, I. (2005) 'Amazon breaks loose and on-line diamond price war begins', *Modern Jeweller*, vol. 104, no. 6, pp. 15–16.

Soto, M.O. (2004) *Amazon.com Becoming Growing Force in Sales of Electronics Items*, [Online], Knight Ridder Tribune Business News.

Soto Ouchi, M. (2005) 'Amazon.com to stick with consumer strategy', *Knight-Ridder Tribune Business News*, 18 May, p. 1.

Spann, S. (2004) *E-commerce, Amazon and Corporate Culture*, [Online], Wall Street Journal. Available from http://wiki.media-culture.org.au/.

Stockport, G. (2002) 'Amazon.com: from start up to the New Millennium', in G. Johnson and K. Scholes, *Exploring Corporate Strategy – Text and Cases*, 6th edition, Prentice Hall, pp. 674–706.

Stockport, G. (2005) 'Amazon.com – from start up to 2004', in G. Johnson, K. Scholes and R. Whittington, *Exploring Corporate Strategy – Text and Cases*, 7th edition, Prentice Hall, pp. 647–672.

Stone, B. (1999) 'Amazon's pet projects', *Newsweek*, vol. 133, no. 25, pp. 56–57.

Sullivan, J.R. and Walstrom, K.A. (2001) 'Consumer perspectives on service quality of electronic commerce Web sites', *Journal of Computer Information Systems*, vol. 41, no. 3. pp. 8–14.

Tadjer, R. (1996) 'Redefining inventory', *Communications Week*, vol. 626, pp. 513–514.

TechWeb (2006) *Amazon. EBay Slip in Customer Satisfaction*, [Online], CMP Media.

The Seattle Times (2005) *Amazon, Drugstore.com to dissolve partnership*, [Online], Knight Ridder/Tribune.

The Seattle Times (2005) *A New Chapter for Amazon Selling Online Access to Books*, [Online], Knight Ridder/Tribune. Available from: http://www.mergentonline.com.

The Seattle Times (2005) *Online Retailers Blue Nile, Amazon.com hope all that glitters is sold*, [Online], Knight Ridder/Tribune. Available from: http://www.mergentonline.com.

The Seattle Times (2005) *Shipping Costs, Taxes depress Amazon results, raises concerns on Wall Street*, [Online], Knight Ridder/Tribune. Available from: http://www.mergentonline.com.

The Seattle Times (2005) *Street Slaps Amazon over Higher Costs, Missed Earnings*, [Online], Knight Ridder/Tribune. Available from: http://www.mergentonline.com.

Tri-City Herald (2005) *Amazon call centre in Kennewick, Wash. could employ 400*, [Online], Knight Ridder/Tribune. Available from: http://www.mergentonline.com.

United Nations (2002) E-commerce and Development Report.

United Nations (2002) World Population Data Sheet of the Population Reference Bureau.

US Census Bureau (2003) *Service Sector Statistics: Gateway to the Service Economy*, [Online], Available from: http://census.gov/mrts/www/current.html.

USA Securities and Exchange Commission (1999) Washington, DC.

Vanderkam, L. (2002) 'White collar sweatshops batter young workers', *USA Today*, 26 November, p. A13.

Wainewright, P. (2005) 'Amazon brokers customers' time', *Computer Trade Shopper*, 7 December, p. 7.

Webmergers.com (2003) *Internet Companies Three Years After the Height of the Bubble*, [Online], Available from: http://www.webmergers.com/data.

West, M. (2005) 'Amazon.com pursues customer satisfaction', *Chain Store Age*, July, p. 44A.

Wikipedia (2006) *Amazon.com*, [Online], Available from: http://en.wikipedia.org/.

Yahoo!Finance, [Online], http://finance.yahoo.com/.

APPENDIX A

Consolidated balance sheet

USA

As reported annual balance sheet	31/12/2005	31/12/2004	31/12/2003	31/12/2002	31/12/2001	31/12/2000	31/12/1999	31/12/1998	31/12/1997	31/12/1996
Currency	US$	US$	US$	US$	US$	US$	US$	US$	US$	US$
Auditor status	Not qualified	Not qualified	Not qualified	Not qualified	Not qualified	Not qualified	Not qualified	Not qualified	Not qualified	Not qualified
Consolidated	Yes	Yes	Yes	Yes	Yes	Yes	Yes	Yes	Yes	No
Scale	(000)	(000)	(000)	(000)	(000)	(000)	(000)	(000)	(000)	(000)
Cash	–	–	–	–	–	–	116,962	25,561	109,810	6,248
Cash & cash equivalents	1,013,000	1,302,600	1,102,273	738,254	540,282	822,435	–	–	–	–
Marketable securities	987,000	476,599	292,550	562,715	456,303	278,087	589,226	347,884	–	–
Cash, cash equivalents & marketable securs	2,000,000	1,779,199	–	–	–	–	–	–	–	–
Short-term investments	–	–	–	–	–	–	–	–	15,256	–
Inventories	566,000	479,709	293,917	202,425	143,722	174,563	220,646	29,501	8,971	571
Deferred tax assets, current portion	89,000	81,388	–	–	–	–	–	–	–	–
Accounts receivable, net & other current assets	317,000	–	–	–	–	–	–	–	–	–
Less: Allowance for doubtful accounts receivable	43,000	–	–	–	–	–	–	–	–	–
Accounts receivable, net & oth current assets	274,000	–	–	–	–	–	–	–	–	–
Accounts receivable, net & oth current assets	–	–	–	–	–	–	–	–	–	–
Prepaid expenses & other current assets	–	199,100	132,069	112,282	67,613	86,044	85,344	21,308	3,298	321
Total current assets	2,929,000	2,539,396	1,820,809	1,615,676	1,207,920	1,361,129	1,012,178	424,254	137,335	7,140
Computers, equipment & software	309,000	–	–	–	205,687	317,806	187,345	33,061	7,118	1,031
Leasehold improvements	69,000	–	–	–	102,412	107,367	43,968	5,535	914	130
Furniture, fixtures & leasehold improvements	–	–	–	112,943	–	–	–	–	–	–
Tech infrastructure & oth computer equipment	–	–	–	57,086	–	–	–	–	–	–
Software purchased or devel for internal use	–	–	–	94,561	–	–	–	4,547	4,505	134
Equip & oth fixed assets acq und cap leases	–	–	–	218,146	42,444	51,969	52,374	442	362	–
Construction in progress	–	–	25,592	–	24,846	4,122	83,290	–	–	–
Fulfillment & customer service	–	263,002	57,413	–	–	–	–	–	–	–
Technology infrastructure	–	38,408	241,497	–	–	–	–	–	–	–
Internal-use software, content & website deve	138,000	79,026	–	–	62,754	–	–	–	–	–
Other corporate assets	55,000	42,527	47,236	–	–	–	–	–	–	–
Fixed assets, gross	571,000	422,963	371,738	482,736	438,143	481,264	366,977	43,585	12,899	1,295
Less: accum depr-fulfillment & cust service	123,000	105,939	84,987	–	–	–	–	–	–	–
Less: accum depr-technology infrastructure	27,000	15,086	13,167	–	–	–	–	–	–	–
Internal-use software, content & website deve	51,000	31,866	24,530	–	–	–	–	–	–	–
Less: accum depr-other corporate assets	22,000	23,916	24,769	–	–	–	–	–	–	–
Less accumulated depreciation	223,000	176,807	147,453	222,731	152,443	99,244	–	–	–	–
Less accumulated amortization on leased asset	–	–	–	20,607	13,949	15,604	–	–	–	–
Less accumulated depreciation & amortization	–	–	–	–	–	–	49,364	13,794	3,634	310
Fixed assets, net	348,000	246,156	224,285	239,398	271,751	366,416	317,613	29,791	9,265	985
Goodwill & other purchased intangibles, net	–	–	–	–	–	–	–	186,377	–	–
Deferred tax assets, long-term portion	223,000	281,757	–	–	–	–	–	–	–	–
Goodwill	159,000	138,999	69,121	70,811	45,367	158,990	534,699	–	–	–

Other intangibles, gross	—	25,493	—	—	—	—	—	—	—	—
Less: Accumulated amort – other intangibles	—	24,975	—	—	—	—	—	—	—	—
Other intangibles, net	—	518	—	3,460	—	—	—	—	—	—
Investments in equity-method investees	—	—	—	—	34,382	96,335	195,445	—	—	—
Other equity investments	—	14,831	—	15,442	17,972	52,073	226,727	—	166	146
Deposits & other assets	—	—	—	—	10,387	40,177	144,735	7,412	—	2,240
Deferred charges	—	—	—	—	—	—	626	—	—	—
Deferred charges & other assets	—	—	—	—	—	—	40,154	—	—	—
Other assets	37,000	32,469	42,200	45,662	49,768	60,049	—	—	—	—
Total assets	3,696,000	3,248,508	2,162,033	1,990,449	1,637,547	2,135,169	2,471,551	648,460	149,006	8,271
Accounts payable	1,366,000	1,141,733	819,811	618,128	444,748	485,383	463,026	113,273	32,697	2,852
Accrued expenses & other current liabilities	563,000	361,128	317,730	—	—	—	—	—	—	—
Accrued advertising	—	—	—	314,935	305,064	272,683	126,017	13,071	3,454	598
Unearned revenue	—	41,099	37,844	47,916	87,978	131,117	55,892	—	—	—
Interest payable	—	74,059	73,100	71,661	68,632	69,196	54,790	—	—	—
Accrued product development	—	—	—	—	—	—	24,888	—	6,167	920
Other liabilities & accrued expenses	—	2,381	4,216	—	—	—	—	34,547	1,500	500
Current portion of long-term debt & other	—	—	—	13,318	14,992	16,577	14,322	684	—	—
Total current liabilities	1,929,000	1,620,400	1,252,701	1,065,958	921,414	974,956	738,935	161,575	43,818	4,870
Long-term debt & other	—	—	—	2,277,305	2,127,464	2,156,133	1,466,338	348,077	76,521	—
Long-term debt	900,000	899,760	1,049,760	—	—	—	—	—	—	—
Convertible subordinated notes	580,000	935,086	—	—	—	—	—	—	—	—
Premium adjustable convertible securities	—	7,922	869,711	—	—	—	—	—	—	—
Long-term restructuring liabilities	—	—	20,066	—	—	—	—	—	—	—
Capital lease obligations	—	1,744	2,717	—	—	—	—	—	—	—
Other long-term debt & capital lease obligation	44,000	—	—	—	—	—	—	—	—	—
Other long-term debt	—	13,188	7,401	—	—	—	—	—	—	—
Total long-term debt & other	1,524,000	1,857,700	1,949,655	—	—	—	—	—	—	—
Less current portion of cap lease obligations	—	1,229	1,558	—	—	—	—	—	—	—
Less current portion of other long-term debt	—	1,152	2,658	—	—	—	—	—	—	—
Less current portion of other long-term debt	-3,000	—	—	—	—	—	—	—	—	—
Long-term debt & other, net	1,521,000	1,855,319	1,945,439	—	—	—	—	—	—	—
Long-term portion of capital lease obligation	—	—	—	—	—	—	63	181	—	—
Preferred stock	—	—	—	—	—	—	—	—	—	6
Common stock	4,000	4,097	4,034	3,879	3,732	3,571	3,452	1,593	239	159
Advances received for common stock	—	—	—	—	—	—	—	—	—	—
Additional paid-in capital	2,263,000	2,124,598	1,899,398	1,649,946	1,462,769	1,338,303	1,195,540	300,130	63,792	9,873
Note receivable for common stock	—	—	—	—	—	—	-1,171	-1,099	—	—
Deferred stock-based compensation	—	2,038	2,850	6,591	9,853	13,448	47,806	1,625	1,930	612
Net unreal gains on fgn currency translation	15,000	29,948	30,450	—	—	—	—	—	—	—
Net unrealized gains (loss) on AFS securities	-5,000	9,341	20,327	—	—	—	—	—	—	—
Net unrealized losses on Euro currency swap,	-4,000	-7,180	-13,038	—	—	—	—	—	—	—
Accumulated other comprehensive income (loss)	6,000	32,109	37,739	9,662	-36,070	-2,376	-1,709	1,806	—	—
Retained earnings (accumulated deficit)	-2,027,000	-2,385,977	-2,974,428	-3,009,710	-2,860,578	-2,293,301	-882,028	-162,060	-33,615	-6,025
Total stockholders' equity (deficit)	246,000	-1,036,107	-1,352,814	-1,440,000	-967,251	266,278	138,745	28,486	-227,211	3,401

APPENDIX B

Consolidated statement of operations

USA

As reported annual income statement	31/12/2005	31/12/2004	31/12/2003	31/12/2002	31/12/2001	31/12/2000	31/12/1999	31/12/1998	31/12/1997	31/12/1996
Currency	US$	US$	US$	US$	US$	US$	US$	US$	US$	US$
Auditor status	Not qualified	Not qualified	Not qualified	Not qualified	Not qualified	Not qualified	Not qualified	Not qualified	Not qualified	Not qualified
Consolidated	Yes	Yes	Yes	Yes	Yes	Yes	Yes	Yes	Yes	No
Scale	(000)	(000)	(000)	(000)	(000)	(000)	(000)	(000)	(000)	(000)
Net sales	8,490,000	6,921,124	5,263,699	3,932,936	3,122,433	2,761,983	1,639,839	609,996	147,758	15,746
Cost of sales	6,451,000	5,319,127	4,006,531	2,940,318	2,323,875	2,106,206	1,349,194	476,155	118,945	12,287
Gross profit	2,039,000	1,601,997	1,257,168	992,618	798,558	655,777	290,645	133,841	28,813	3,459
Product development	–	–	–	–	–	–	–	–	–	–
Fulfillment expenses	745,000	590,397	477,032	392,467	374,250	–	–	46,807	12,485	2,313
Marketing expenses	198,000	158,022	122,787	125,383	138,283	–	–	–	–	–
Marketing & fulfilment expenses	–	–	–	–	–	594,489	413,150	133,023	38,964	6,090
Technology & content expenses	451,000	251,195	207,809	215,617	241,165	269,326	159,722	–	–	–
General & administrative expenses	166,000	112,220	88,302	79,049	89,862	108,962	70,144	15,799	6,573	1,035
Stock-based compensation expense	–	57,702	87,751	68,927	4,637	24,797	30,618	–	–	–
Amortization of goodwill & other intangibles	–	–	2,752	5,478	181,033	321,772	214,694	–	–	–
Continuing lease obligations	–	–	140	–	–	–	–	–	–	–
Restructuring-related & other	–	–	140	–	–	–	–	–	–	–
Restructuring-related & other	–	–	–	41,573	181,585	200,311	–	–	–	–
Merger & acquisition rel costs, incl amort	47,000	-7,964	–	–	–	–	–	50,172	–	–
Other operating (income) expense	–	–	–	–	–	–	8,072	–	–	–
Total operating expenses	1,607,000	1,161,572	986,573	928,494	1,210,815	1,519,657	896,400	245,801	58,022	9,438
Income (loss) from operations	432,000	440,425	270,595	64,124	-412,257	-863,880	-605,755	-111,960	-29,209	-5,979
Interest income	44,000	28,197	21,955	23,687	29,103	40,821	45,451	14,053	1,898	202
Interest expense	92,000	107,227	129,979	142,925	139,232	130,921	84,566	26,639	279	–
Gains on sales of marketable securities, net	–	586	9,598	–	–	–	–	–	–	–
Foreign-currency transaction losses, net	–	-5,214	-3,045	–	–	–	–	–	–	–
Miscellaneous state, foreign & other taxes	–	–	3,704	–	–	–	–	–	–	–
Other miscellaneous gains (losses), net	–	-73	-41	–	–	–	–	–	–	–
Other income (expense), net	–	-4,701	2,808	–	–	–	–	–	–	–
Other income (expense), net	2,000	–	–	5,623	-1,900	-10,058	1,671	–	–	–
Foreign-currency gain (loss) on remeasurement	90,000	–	–	–	–	–	–	–	–	–

Gain (loss) on sales of Euro-denominated inve	-2,000	—	—	—	—	—	—	—	—	—
Loss on redemption of long-term debt	6,000	—	—	—	—	—	—	—	—	—
Foreign-currency effect on intercompany balan	-47,000	—	—	—	—	—	—	—	—	—
Other remeasurements & other income (expenses)	7,000	—	—	—	—	—	—	—	—	—
Remeasurement & other	42,000	—	—	—	—	—	—	—	—	—
Remeasurement & other	—	-824	-129,661	-96,273	-2,141	-142,639	—	—	—	—
Non-cash gains & losses, net	—	—	—	—	—	—	-12,586	—	—	—
Total non-operating income (expenses), net	-4,000	-84,555	-234,877	-209,888	-114,170	-242,797	-37,444	—	—	—
Income (loss) bef income taxes – United States	601,000	359,268	—	—	—	—	—	—	—	—
Income (loss) before income taxes – Foreign	-173,000	-3,398	—	—	—	—	—	—	—	—
Income (loss) before income taxes	428,000	355,870	—	—	—	—	—	—	—	—
Current taxes: U.S. & state	16,000	12,148	—	—	—	—	—	—	—	—
Current taxes: international (benefit)	9,000	11,967	—	—	—	—	—	—	—	—
Total current taxes (benefit)	25,000	24,115	—	—	—	—	—	—	—	—
Deferred taxes (benefit)	70,000	-256,696	—	—	—	—	—	—	—	—
Provision (benefit) for income taxes	95,000	-232,581	—	—	—	—	—	—	—	—
Income (loss) before equity in losses	333,000	588,451	35,718	-145,764	-526,427	-1,106,677	-643,199	—	—	—
Equity in losses of equity-method investees	—	—	-436	-4,169	-30,327	-304,596	-76,769	—	—	—
Income (loss) bef change in acctg principle	333,000	588,451	35,282	-149,933	-556,754	-1,411,273	-719,968	—	—	—
Cumulative eff of change in acctg principle	26,000	—	—	801	-10,523	—	—	—	—	—
Net income (loss)	359,000	588,451	35,282	-149,132	-567,277	-1,411,273	-719,968	-124,546	-27,590	-5,777
Weighted average shares outstanding – basic	412,000	405,926	395,479	378,363	364,211	350,873	326,753	296,344	259,812	271,860
Weighted average shares outstanding – diluted	426,000	424,757	419,352	378,363	364,211	350,873	326,753	296,344	259,812	259,812
Year end shares outstanding	416,000	409,711	403,354	387,906	373,218	357,140	345,155	318,534	287,244	286,200
Income (loss) per share – cont operations – basic	1	1	0	-2	-2	-4	-2	0	0	—
Income (loss) per share – acctg change – basic	0	—	—	0	0	—	—	0	0	0
Net income (loss) per share – basic	1	1	0	-2	-2	-4	-2	0	0	0
Income (loss) per sh – cont operations – diluted	1	1	0	-2	-2	-2	-2	—	—	—
Income (loss) per share – acctg change – diluted	0	—	—	0	0	—	—	—	—	—
Net income (loss) per share – diluted	1	1	0	-2	-2	-4	-2	0	0	0
Total number of employees	12,000	9,000	7,800	7,500	7,800	9,000	7,600	2,100	614	256
Number of common stockholders	3,927	4,090	4,126	4,229	4,013	3,723	3,981	2,304	304	76
Depreciation & amortization	—	—	—	—	181,033	321,772	214,694	12,078	4,742	286

APPENDIX C

Consolidated statement of cash flows

USA

As reported annual cash flow	31/12/2005	31/12/2004	31/12/2003	31/12/2002	31/12/2001	31/12/2000	31/12/1999	31/12/1998	31/12/1997	31/12/1996
Currency	US$	US$	US$	US$	US$	US$	US$	US$	US$	US$
Auditor status	Not qualified	Not qualified	Not qualified	Not qualified	Not qualified	Not qualified	Not qualified	Not qualified	Not qualified	Not qualified
Consolidated	Yes	Yes	Yes	Yes	Yes	Yes	Yes	Yes	Yes	No
Scale	(000)	(000)	(000)	(000)	(000)	(000)	(000)	(000)	(000)	(000)
Cash & cash equivalents, beginning of period	1,303,000	1,102,273	738,254	540,282	822,435	133,309	25,561	1,876	6,248	996
Net income (loss)	359,000	588,451	35,282	–149,132	–567,277	–1,411,273	–719,968	–124,546	–27,590	–5,777
Depreciation of fixed assets, including inter	121,000	75,724	75,558	82,274	84,709	84,460	36,806	9,692	3,388	286
Amort of dfd stock-based compensation	–	–	–	68,927	4,637	24,797	30,618	2,386	–	–
Amortization of unearned compensation	–	–	–	–	–	–	–	–	1,354	–
Stock-based compensation	87,000	57,702	87,751	–	–	–	–	–	–	–
Eq in losses of equity-method investees, net	–	–	436	4,169	30,327	304,596	76,769	–	–	–
Amort of goodwill & other intangibles	–	–	2,752	5,478	181,033	321,772	214,694	–	–	–
Other operating expense (income)	7,000	–7,964	–	–	–	–	–	–	–	–
Impairment-related & other	–	–	–	3,470	73,293	200,311	–	–	–	–
Non-cash merger, acq & invest rel costs	–	–	–	–	–	–	8,072	47,065	–	–
Gains on sales of marketable securities, net	–1,000	–586	–9,598	–5,700	–1,335	–280	8,688	–	–	–
Non-cash investment gains & losses, net	–	–	–	96,273	2,141	142,639	–	–	–	–
Non-cash rev for advertise & promotion servs	–	–	–	–	–	–	–5,837	–	–	–
Non-cash interest expense	–	–	–	–	–	–	29,171	23,970	–	–
Remeasurements & other	–42,000	824	129,661	–	–	–	–	–	–	–
Non-cash interest expense & other	5,000	4,756	12,918	29,586	26,629	24,766	–	–	–	–
Deferred income taxes	70,000	–256,696	–	–	–	–	–	–	–	–
Cumulative eff of change in acctg principle	–26,000	–	–	–801	10,523	–	–320,987	–	–	–
Cash from operations	–	–	–	–	–	–	–	–	–	–
Inventories	–104,000	–168,896	–76,786	–51,303	30,628	46,083	–172,069	–20,513	–8,400	–554
Accounts receivable, net & other current asse	–84,000	–1,745	305	–32,948	20,732	–8,585	–60,628	–16,465	–2,977	–307
Prepaid expenses & other current assets	–	–	–	–	–	–	–	–	–	–
Deposits & other assets	–	–	–	–	–	–	–	–293	–20	–146
Accounts payable	274,000	286,091	167,732	156,542	–44,438	22,357	330,166	78,674	29,845	4,763
Accrued expenses & other current liabilities	60,000	–15,110	–25,740	4,491	50,031	93,967	65,121	21,448	5,066	–
Accrued advertising	–	–	–	–	–	–	42,382	9,617	2,856	–
Additions to unearned revenue	156,000	109,936	101,641	95,404	114,738	97,818	262	–	–	–
Amortization previously unearned revenue	–149,000	–106,886	–111,740	–135,466	–135,808	–108,211	24,878	–	–	–
Interest payable	–	959	1,850	3,027	–345	34,341	–	–	–	–
Net cash prov by chngs in oper assets, net	–	–	–	–	–	–	230,112	–	–	–
Net cash flows from operating activities	733,000	566,560	392,022	174,291	–119,782	–130,442	–90,875	31,035	3,522	–1,735

	(1)	(2)	(3)	(4)	(5)	(6)	(7)	(8)	(9)	(10)
Purchases of fixed asset, including internal-	–204,000	–89,133	–45,963	–39,163	–50,321	–134,758	–287,055	–28,333	–7,221	–1,214
Acquisition, net of cash acquired	–24,000	–71,195	–	–	–	–	–	–	–	–
Sales & maturities of marketable securities	–	–	813,184	553,289	370,377	545,724	4,024,551	332,084	5,198	–
Sales & maturities of marketable securs & oth	836,000	1,426,786	–	–	–	–	–	–	–	–
Purchases of marketable securities	–1,386,000	–1,584,089	–535,642	–635,810	–567,152	–184,455	–4,290,173	–546,509	–20,454	–
Invest in eq method investees & oth invest	–	–	–	–	–6,198	–62,533	–	–	–	–
Proceeds from sale of subsidiary	–	–	5,072	–	–	–	–	–	–	–
Acquisitions & investments in businesses, net	–	–	–	–	–	–	–369,607	–19,019	–	–
Net cash flows from investing activities	–778,000	–317,631	236,651	–121,684	–253,294	163,978	–922,284	–261,777	–22,477	–1,214
Proceeds from initial public offering	–	–	–	–	–	–	–	–	49,103	–
Proceeds from exercise of stk opts, sale of s	–	–	–	–	–	–	5,983	–	518	231
Proceeds fr iss of cap stk & exercise of sk o	–	–	–	–	–	–	8,383	–	–	–
Proceeds from sale of preferred stock	–	–	–	–	–	–	–	–	200	7,970
Proceeds from exercises of stock options	–	60,109	–	121,689	16,625	44,697	–	–	–	–
Proceeds from exercise of stock opts & other	66,000	–	163,322	–	–	–	–	–	–	–
Proceeds from issuance of common stock, net	–	–	–	–	99,831	681,499	1,263,639	325,987	–	–
Proceeds from long-term debt	–	–	–	–	10,000	–	–	–	75,000	–
Proceeds from long-term debt & other	11,000	–	–	–	–	–	64,469	–	–	–
Repayment of long-term debt	–270,000	–	–14,795	–	–19,575	–16,927	–188,886	–78,108	–	–
Repayments of long-term debt & capital lease	–	–157,401	–495,308	–	–	–	–	–	–2,304	–
Financing costs	–	–	–	–	–	–16,122	–35,151	–7,783	–	–
Net cash flows from financing activities	–193,000	–97,292	–331,986	106,894	106,881	693,147	1,104,071	254,462	122,517	8,201
Foreign-currency effect on cash & cash equivs	–52,000	67,332	38,471	–15,958	–37,557	489	–35	–	–	–
Net incr (decr) in cash & cash equivalents	–290,000	200,327	364,019	197,972	689,126	91,401	23,685	103,562	–	5,252
Cash & cash equivalents, end of year	1,013,000	1,102,273	738,254	540,282	822,435	116,962	25,561	109,810	–	6,248
Cash paid for interest expense	105,000	107,604	119,947	111,589	112,184	59,688	–	30	–	–
Cash paid for income taxes	12,000	4,051	1,825	–	92,253	–	–	–	–	–

APPENDIX D

Part 1: Net sales as allocated to segments, 2001–2005

Net sales ($m)	Calendar years ended 31 December				
	2005	2004	2003	2002	2001
North America:					
Media	3,046	2,589	2,270	1,995	1,811
Electronics and other general merchandise	1,443	1,128	879	681	578
Other	222	130	110	85	72
	4,711	3,847	3,259	2,761	2,461
International:					
Media	2,885	2,513	1,780	1,104	645
Electronics and other general merchandise	886	559	225	66	15
Other	8	2	–	2	2
	3,779	3,074	2,005	1,172	662
Consolidated:					
Media	5,931	5,102	4,050	3,099	2,456
Electronics and other general merchandise	2,329	1,687	1,104	747	593
Other	230	132	110	87	74
	8,490	6,921	5,264	3,933	3,123
Y/Y net sales growth					
North America:					
Media	18%	14%	14%	10%	1%
Electronics and other general merchandise	28	28	29	18	20
Other	71	18	29	18	(30)
International:					
Media	15%	41%	61%	71%	70%
Electronics and other general merchandise	59	149	241	308	1011
Other	234	98	(38)	280	249
Consolidated:					
Media	16%	26%	31%	26%	13%
Electronics and other general merchandise	38	53	48	26	23
Other	74	19	28	19	(30)
Consolidated net sales mix:					
Media	70%	74%	77%	79%	79%
Electronics and other general merchandise	27	24	21	19	19
Other	3	2	2	2	2

Source: Amazon.com Investor Relations.

APPENDIX D

Part 2: Net income as allocated to segments, 2001–2005

	Calendar years ended 31 December				
US ($m)	2005	2004	2003	2002	2001
North America:					
Net sales	4,711	3,847	3,259	2,761	2,461
Cost of sales	3,444	2,823	2,392	2,020	1,802
Gross profit	1,267	1,024	867	741	659
Direct segment operating expenses (1)	971	703	583	562	600
Segment operating income (loss)	296	321	284	179	59
International:					
Net sales	3,779	3,074	2,005	1,172	662
Cost of sales	3,007	2,496	1,614	921	522
Gross profit	772	578	391	251	140
Direct segment operating expenses (1)	502	409	313	250	243
Segment operating income (loss)	270	169	78	1	(103)
Consolidated:					
Net sales	8,490	6,921	5,264	3,933	3,123
Cost of sales	6,451	5,319	4,006	2,941	2,324
Gross profit	2,039	1,602	1,258	992	799
Direct segment operating expenses	1,473	1,112	896	812	843
Segment operating income (loss)	566	490	362	180	(44)
Stock-based compensation	(87)	(58)	(88)	(69)	(5)
Other operating income (expense)	(47)	8	(3)	(47)	(363)
Income (loss) from operations	432	440	271	64	(412)
Total non-operating income (expense), net	(4)	(85)	(232)	(215)	(144)
Benefit (provision) for income taxes	(95)	233	(4)	1	–
Cumulative effect of change in accounting principle	26	–	–	1	(11)
Net income (loss)	359	588	35	(149)	(567)
Segment highlights					
Y/Y net sales growth:					
North America	22%	18%	18%	12%	3%
International	23	53	71	77	74
Consolidated	23	31	34	26	13
Y/Y gross profit growth:					
North America	24%	18%	17%	13%	14%
International	33	48	55	78	83
Consolidated	27	27	27	24	22
Y/Y segment operating income growth:					
North America	(8%)	13%	58%	212%	N/A
International	59	116	N/A	N/A	(29)
Consolidated	16	36	101	N/A	(86)
Net sales mix:					
North America	55%	56%	62%	70%	79%
International	45	44	38	30	21

Source: Amazon.com Investor Relations.

APPENDIX E

Timeline of company growth

Categories	Launch	International categories	Launch	Distribution centres	Launch
Books	1995	UK & German Books	1998	Seattle, Washington	1996
Music	1998	UK & German Music	1998	New Castle, Delaware	1997
Video	1998	UK & German Auctions	1999	Bad Hersfeld, Germany	1999
Actions	1999	UK & German zShops	1999	Bedfordshire, UK	1999
Electronics	1999	France Books	2000	Campbellsville, Kentucky	1999
Software	1999	Japan Books	2000	Coffeyvill, Kansas	1999
Tools & Hardware	1999				
		UK & German DVD/Videos	2000	Fernley, Nevada	1999
Toys	1999	UK & German PC & Video Games	2000	Grand Forks, North Dakota	1999
Video Games	1999	France SW/PC & Video Games	2001	McDonough, Georgia	1999
zShops	1999	Japan Music, Video, CDs, DVDs	2001	Orleans, France	2000
Health & Beauty	2000	Canada Books, Music, DVDs	2002	Inverclyde, Scotland	2004
Kitchen	2000	Marketplace International	2002	Leipzig, Germany	2006
Lawn & Patio	2000	Japan Electronics	2003		
Photo Services	2000	UK & German Electronics	2003		
Jewellery	2004	UK & German Kitchens & Home	2003		
Beauty	2004	German House & Garden	2004		
		Japan Computer Store	2004		
Used@Amazon	2000	UK Home Improvement	2004		
Wireless	2000	Japan Toys & Hobby	2004		
Computers	2001	UK DVD Rental	2004		
Market Place	2001	Germany DVD Rental	2005		
Travel	2001	Japan Sports	2005		
Apparel and Acc	2002				
Web Services	2002				
Magazines	2003				
Sports Goods	2003				

Sources: Amazon.com Annual Reports 1997–2004 and Press Releases 1995–2006.

APPENDIX F

Amazon.com locations

Primary use	Operating segment	Geographical locations	Square footage
Corporate office facilities	North America	Palo Alto and San Francisco, California; Seattle, Washington	707,000
	International	Beijing and Shanghai, China; Luxembourg City, Luxembourg; Munich, Germany; Paris, France; Tokyo, Japan	185,000
Fulfillment and warehouse operations	North America	Phoenix, Arizona; New Castle, Delaware; Coffeyville, Kansas; Campbellsville, Hebron and Lexington, Kentucky; Fernley and Red Rock, Nevada; Chambersburg, Carlisle and Lewisberry, Pennsylvania; Dallas/Fort Worth, Texas (2005); Mississauga, Ontario, Canada	4,465,500
	International	Marston Gate, England; Gourock and Glenrothes, Scotland; Orleans, France; Bad Hersfeld, Germany; Tokyo, Japan; Beijing, Guangzhou and Shanghai, China (Joyo.com)	1,483,000
Customer service centres	North America	Grand Forks, North Dakota (2005); Huntington, West Virginia; Kennewick, Washington (2005)	440,000 total
	International	Slough, England; Regensburg, Germany; Sapporo, Japan and China; announcement in Mar. 2006 for new centre in Cork, Ireland	440,000 total
(Software) development centres	North America and International	Phoenix, Arizona; Edinburgh, Scotland (launched July 2004); Bangalore (launched July 2004) and Chennai (launched Oct. 2005), India; Cape Town, South Africa (launched July 2005); Iasi, Romania (launched Nov. 2005)	

Note: No real estate is owned.

Sources: Amazon.com 2004 Annual Report, Press Releases 2004–2006 and http://en.wikipedia.org/wiki/Amazon.com.

The Formula One constructors

Mark Jenkins

This case describes four periods of dominance by particular firms in a highly competitive technological context, Formula One (F1) motorsport. Highly specialised constructors design and build single-seat racecars (and sometimes engines) to compete for annual championships which bring huge financial and reputational rewards. These four eras explore the stories of three contrasting companies each within a different competitive time period in terms of how they both created and lost the basis for sustained competitive advantage.

● ● ●

Between two and four on a Sunday afternoon this is a sport. All the rest of the time it's commerce.
(Frank Williams, Managing Director, Williams F1)

In 1945 the Fédération Internationale de l'Automobile (FIA) established Formula A as the premier level of motorsport. In the years that followed Formula A became referred to as Formula One (F1) and a drivers' world championship was introduced in 1950. The first world champion was Giuseppe Farina of Italy driving an Alfa Romeo. At that time Alfa dominated the racing along with the other Italian marques of Ferrari and Maserati. By the mid-1960s F1 had moved from being a basis for car manufacturers to promote and test their products, to a specialist business where purpose-built cars were developed through leading-edge

technology to win a TV sporting event enjoying the third highest TV audience in the world, surpassed only by the Olympics and World Cup soccer.

Some 10–14 racecar manufacturers or constructors have competed in F1 at any one time. In 2006 the top three teams were Renault, Ferrari and McLaren, all medium-sized businesses turning over between $250 and $350 million (€200 and €280m) per annum. For the first three years of its entry into F1 in 2002, Toyota is estimated to have committed $1bn on capital and running costs of which only one-fifth will come from sponsorship. The top teams typically have their own testing and development equipment, including wind tunnels and other facilities. The larger teams employ between 450 and 800 people in their F1 operations, a quarter of whom travel around the world attending Grand Prix every two to three weeks throughout the F1 season (March to November). Labour costs account for around 25 per cent of the budget. All the teams have highly qualified technical staff including race engineers (who work with the drivers to set up the cars), designers, aerodynamicists, composite experts (to work with specialised carbon-composite materials) and systems specialists.

In addition to sponsorship, revenue is provided by prize money generated by winning championship points; in 2003 this was

Photo: Michael Kim/Corbis

allocated on a sliding scale for the first eight places. The prize money is a way of dividing up the royalties earned from media coverage and other revenues negotiated on behalf of the teams by Bernie Ecclestone's Formula One Administration (FOA). In 2003 Ferrari estimated that $30 million (9.7 per cent) of its revenues came from prize money.

The Formula One Constructors provide a unique context to consider the competitive advantage of different multi-million-pound organisations over time. The pace of change and the basis of advantage are constantly changing, shown by the fact that since the start of the world championships, only two constructors have won the championship consecutively more than four times (McLaren 1988–1991; Ferrari 1999–2004) and only Ferrari (1975–1977) and Williams (1992–1994) have also won for three consecutive years.

Ferrari and its renaissance in the mid-1970s

The period 1975–1977 saw a renaissance for the Ferrari team. Their previous F1 World Championship had been won in 1964, one of the few reminders of the glorious 1950s and early 1960s when the bright red cars of Ferrari dominated motor racing. Ferrari is the oldest of all the Grand Prix teams still racing. Its heritage gives it a special place in the hearts of all motor racing enthusiasts. Founded by Enzo Ferrari, an ex-driver and manager of the Alfa Romeo racing team in 1950, Ferrari and other Italian marques such as Maserati and Alfa dominated the sport during the 1950s. Ferraris have taken part in more than 740 Grand Prixs (the next highest is McLaren with 613) and, despite the variable nature of the team's performance, drivers continue to view a contract with Ferrari as something very special. Perhaps this is why world champions such as Alain Prost, Nigel Mansell and Michael Schumacher have been attracted to the team at times when their cars have been far from the fastest or most reliable.

In an era when the majority of constructors are British specialists who buy in components such as engines and gearboxes, Ferrari has always done everything itself. All the major components are made at its Maranello factory, which enjoys the most up-to-date facilities. While other constructors will paint their cars whatever colour required by their flagship sponsor, Ferraris have always been bright red, the national colour of Italy. The cars have, until recently, very little evidence of sponsorship; it has always been the Ferrari emblem – a black prancing horse – which has the most prominent position. The Italian public see Ferrari as a national icon as observed by Niki Lauda:

> The Italians love you when you win and hate you when you lose and whatever you do, win, lose or simply break wind everyone in Italy wants to know about it!

The influence of Enzo Ferrari, or *Il Commendatore* as he was known, was pervasive and the stories surrounding him still permeate the team. It was legendary that Ferrari himself hardly ever attended a race and very rarely left the Maranello factory where his beloved cars were made. He relied on the media and his advisors for information, which often created a highly political atmosphere. Ferrari's first love was motor racing despite having created a very successful range of road-going cars which he saw primarily as the source of funding for his racing. The merger between Fiat and Ferrari in 1969 provided Ferrari with a huge cash injection. Ferrari had sold 40 per cent of the company to Fiat and allowed Fiat to build the road cars. Enzo, who was then 71, would retain control of the racing operation, however, to concentrate on his first love, motor racing at the highest level: Formula One.

The resources the Ferrari team have at their disposal have always been the envy of other teams. They had always built their own engines and have a large technical team dedicated to engine design and development. In 1971 they opened their own test track at Fiorano, a few hundred metres from the Maranello factory. At the time it was the most advanced and sophisticated test circuit in the world, enabling cars to be constantly tested and developed between the track and the factory. This effectively gave Ferrari its own Grand Prix circuit. All other competitors were obliged to hire a circuit such as Silverstone in the UK and transport cars and equipment for a two- or three-day test. Ferrari himself attended most of the tests and made sure he was kept informed exactly what was being tested and why. Enzo had always declared his love for the distinctive sound and power of a Ferrari engine: Nigel Mansell said:

> Enzo Ferrari believed that the engine was the most important part of the race car. Colin [Chapman – head of Lotus] believed it was the chassis.

The early 1970s began shakily for Ferrari: the new ownership and influence from Fiat meant increased resources, but also increased pressure for results. At this time F1 was dominated by the Ford DFV engine. Built by Cosworth Engineering near Northampton and funded by the Ford Motor Company, the DFV was F1's first purpose-built engine; it was light, powerful and relatively inexpensive. In 1968 the engines were available for £7,500 (€10,500) each and were fully capable of winning a Grand Prix. This enabled the British constructors, who specialised in chassis design, to become increasingly competitive. In 1971 and 1973 every Grand Prix was won by a car using a DFV engine.

In 1971 the Ferraris were very fast, but not reliable. It got worse in 1972 and 1973 with cars only finishing every other race and rarely in the points. Enzo himself had been suffering poor health and the team seemed unable to turn things around despite having the huge resources of Fiat at their disposal. However, through 1974 things began to change. Mauro Forghieri had also been recalled to Ferrari in 1973 as Technical Director. Forghieri had been responsible for some of the more successful Ferraris of the 1960s, but had fallen from grace and spent the later part of the 1960s working on 'special projects'.

A new team boss was also appointed. At 25 years old, a qualified lawyer with connections to the Agnelli family who owned Fiat, Luca di Montezemolo was an unlikely right-hand man for *Il Commendatore*. However, he was given a relatively free hand by Ferrari and brought much needed management discipline to the team. Whilst there had always been a huge supply of talent at Ferrari, particularly in the design and development of engines, it had not always reached its collective potential. Enzo's autocratic style of 'divide and rule' had created confusion and rivalry within the team. Montezemolo defined strict areas of responsibility in order to reduce the amount of interference and internal politics. This created a situation where the various technical teams (chassis and suspension; engine; gearbox) concentrated on and were fully accountable for their own area. Montezemolo was also instrumental in the recruitment of driver Niki Lauda.

In 1974 Lauda and the design team had embarked upon an exhaustive testing and development programme at the Fiorano test track. The new car, the 312B, was very fast; however, there were still reliability problems and although Lauda was leading the championship at the British Grand Prix, the lead was lost through technical problems, with Emerson Fittipaldi in a McLaren taking the eventual honours.

In 1975 the fruits of Forghieri's creative ideas and the intensive testing at Fiorano were exemplified in the new 312T which featured a wide, low body with a powerful 'flat 12' 12-cylinder engine and a revolutionary transverse (sideways-mounted) gearbox which improved the balance of the car making it handle extremely well. Lauda, with the support of team-mate Regazzoni, was able to secure both the drivers and constructors world championships. The Ferraris dominated the 1975 season. With their elegant handling and the power advantage of the engine, they were in a class of their own. Because the majority of the competition all had the same engine gearbox combination (Ford DFV and Hewland gearbox), they were unable to respond to a chassis/gearbox/engine combination which was unique to Ferrari.

Things continued much the same in 1976, with Lauda and Regazzoni winning the early races. Montezemolo had been promoted to head up Fiat's entire motorsport operation. Daniele Audetto was moved from managing the rally team to Sporting Director at Ferrari. However, things were not to go as smoothly as in 1975. At the German Grand Prix Lauda lost control of the car in the wet and crashed in flames. He was rescued by four other drivers, but not before suffering severe burns and inhaling toxic fumes. His life was in the balance for some weeks whilst the Grand Prix series continued with James Hunt (McLaren) reducing Lauda's lead in the championship. Miraculously Lauda recovered from his injuries and although still badly scarred, he returned to race for Ferrari. He and Hunt went into the last Grand Prix of 1976 (Japan) with Lauda leading by three points. There was heavy rain and Lauda pulled out leaving the drivers' championship to Hunt, although Ferrari still collected the constructors' championship. On paper it was a good year, but Ferrari should have dominated 1976 as it had 1975. Audetto who, perhaps not surprisingly, had been unable to live up to the role created by Montezemolo and had failed to develop a strong relationship with Lauda, returned back to the world of rallying. Ferrari went into 1977 in a state of disarray.

In 1977 Ferrari was still the team to beat, although the testing and development lost through Lauda's six-week convalescence had undermined the crushing dominance which the team had earlier shown. The competition was beginning to find ways of catching up. The Brabham team moved away from the Ford DFV and used an Alfa Romeo 'flat 12' similar to the Ferrari engine. Tyrrell launched the revolutionary P34 six-wheeled car which seemed to be the only car able to stay with the Ferrari. Ferrari itself launched the 312T2 in 1976 which was a significant development of the original 312T. Ferrari won the 1977 drivers' and constructors' championships, but this was the end of the partnership with Niki Lauda; the relationship had never been the same since the Nurburgring accident. Lauda left to join Brabham. He was not perhaps the fastest racer on the track, but he was always able to develop a car and build relationships with the design team which enabled Ferrari to translate the driver's senses into reliable technical solutions.

The unprecedented run of Ferrari success continued in 1978 with the 312T3 car driven by two highly talented drivers: Argentinean Carlos Reutemann was joined by the flamboyant Gilles Villeneuve and whilst they were not able to win the constructors' championship they achieved a very strong second place. In 1979 Reutemann was replaced by South African Jody Scheckter whose consistency contrasted with Villeneuve's erratic speed. Scheckter won the drivers' championship, with Ferrari taking the constructors' championship. Ferrari's greatest moment was when Scheckter and Villeneuve finished first and second at the Italian Grand Prix at Monza.

However, 1979 was the last time that Ferrari was to win a drivers' world championship for 21 years; 1980 was a disaster for Ferrari. Scheckter and Villeneuve were totally uncompetitive in the 312T5 car which, although a significant development of the 312T4, was outclassed by competitors. New innovations in aerodynamics brought the 'ground effect' revolution, pioneered by Lotus and quickly adopted by Williams and Brabham. Here the underside of the car featured two 'venturi', or channels either side of the driver. These were aerodynamically designed to create a low-pressure area under the car which sucked the car to the track allowing faster cornering. Sliding strips of material or 'skirts' were used to create a seal for the air flowing under the car. Ferrari's engine was one of the most powerful, but it was a 'flat 12', meaning that the cylinders were horizontal to the ground creating a low and wide barrier which gave no opportunity to create the ground effect achieved with the slimmer V8 DFV engines. In 1978 Alfa Romeo had launched a V12 engine to replace the flat 12 for this very reason. No such initiative had been taken at Ferrari which was concentrating on a longer-term project to develop a V6 turbocharged engine. Autosport correspondent Nigel Roebuck commented on this change of fortune: 'Maranello's

flat-12, still a magnificent racing engine, is incompatible with modern chassis. Villeneuve and Scheckter were competing in yesterday's cars.' The lowest point came in the Canadian Grand Prix when the reigning world champion, Jody Scheckter, failed to qualify in his Ferrari for the race. The full wrath of the Italian press descended on the team.

McLaren and Honda domination in the late 1980s

The period from 1988 to 1991 was unusual in the hypercompetitive world of F1 because of the dominance of one constructor. In one year the McLaren team won 15 of the 16 races. Founded by New Zealander and F1 driver Bruce McLaren in 1966, the McLaren team had their first victory in the Belgian Grand Prix of 1968. Tragically McLaren himself was killed two years later while testing. Lawyer and family friend Teddy Mayer took over as team principal. In 1974 McLaren secured a long-term sponsorship from Philip Morris to promote the Marlboro brand of cigarettes. This was a partnership that was to last until 1996, probably the most enduring relationship between a constructor and a 'flagship' sponsor. However, in the late 1970s McLaren found itself left behind by some of the new aerodynamic advances. In September 1980 Ron Dennis became joint team principal with Mayer, a position which he took over solely in 1982, when Mayer was 'encouraged' by Philip Morris to take a less active role in the management of McLaren. In the previous year McLaren moved from its modest site in Colnbrook to a modern facility at Woking in Surrey, south of London.

Dennis had been a mechanic for the highly successful Cooper team in 1966, but left to set up his own Formula Two (a smaller, less expensive formula) team in 1971. By the end of the 1970s he had built up a reputation for professionalism and immaculate presentation. His Project Four company brought in designer John Barnard who had radical ideas about using carbon fibre, rather than metal, as the basis for a racecar chassis. These ideas were to provide the basis for the MP4 car. Both Dennis and Barnard were perfectionists; Dennis's obsession with immaculate presentation and attention to detail complemented by Barnard's quest for technical excellence.

Barnard was considered by many to be the reason for McLaren's developing dominance but in 1986 he left to join the struggling Ferrari team.

The partnership between Dennis and Barnard had been stormy, but a huge amount had been achieved through their energy, Dennis providing the managerial and commercial acumen and Barnard the highly innovative design skills. To replace Barnard, Brabham designer Gordon Murray was brought into the team, perhaps best known for developing the innovative 'fan car' for Brabham in 1978. Murray, like Barnard, was at the leading edge of F1 car design.

A further factor in McLaren's success had been the relationship with engine suppliers. In the mid-1980s turbocharging became the key technology and in 1983 McLaren used a Porsche turbo engine funded by the electronics company TAG, a sponsor previously with the Williams team. However, the emerging force in engine development was Honda, which had re-entered F1 in 1983 in partnership with Williams. Importantly the engines were supported by a significant commitment from Honda in both people and resources. Honda used the relationship as an opportunity to develop some of its most talented engineers and to transfer F1 design and development capabilities to its production car programme. In the mid-1980s the Williams/Honda partnership was very successful, but following Frank Williams' road accident in 1986, Honda began to have doubts about the future of the Williams team and agreed to move to supply both McLaren and Lotus for the 1987 season.

Halfway through 1987 McLaren announced that it had recruited two of the top drivers in F1 to the team for the 1988 season: Alain Prost and Ayrton Senna. This was unusual as most teams tended to have a clear hierarchy with a lead driver being supported by a 'number two' who was either regarded as less skilful and/or less experienced than the lead driver.

Prost and Senna were real contrasts. Senna, the young Brazilian, was fast, determined and ruthless; extremely talented, but very demanding to manage. Prost was fast too, but a great tactician and adept at team politics, making sure that the whole team were behind him. It was rumoured that a key reason for Honda moving to McLaren was that it now had Alain Prost.

In 1988 the Honda-powered MP4 car was without question the fastest and most reliable car on the circuit. This meant that effectively the only real competition for Prost and Senna was each other. This competition between two highly committed and talented drivers resulted in one of the most enduring and bitter feuds the sport has ever known. In 1990 the acrimony with Senna culminated in Prost moving to Ferrari.

Ron Dennis and his professional management style was synonymous with the success of McLaren, indicating that the era of the 'one-man band' F1 constructor was past. His record since taking over in 1982 had been impressive. Eddie Jordan, principal of the Jordan team, held him in high regard:

> He's won that many Grand Prix, he's won that many championships, he's been on pole that many times and he's got the best drivers. Everyone hates him; but they only hate him because he's the best.

Dennis's negotiating and marketing abilities were legendary throughout F1. McLaren also created its own marketing consultancy operation where the smaller teams engaged McLaren to find sponsors. In 1991 *Management Week* had Ron Dennis on the front cover with the question: 'Is Ron Dennis Britain's best manager?' Dennis likens the management of McLaren to that of a game of chess:

> you've got to get all the elements right, the overall package, the budget, the designer, the engine, the drivers, the organisation.

Dennis is renowned for being hypercompetitive and once chastised a driver who was delighted with finishing second with the comment – 'remember, you're only the first of the losers'.

The McLaren Honda combination had dominated F1 from 1988 through to 1991. However, in September 1992 Honda confirmed that it was pulling out of F1 racing. It had been hugely successful and achieved all of its objectives; it was now time to find new challenges. Dennis had been told about Honda's thinking in late 1991, but it appeared that he had not taken it seriously enough and the team had no real engine alternatives. This meant they lost valuable winter development time as they tried to find a new engine supplier. In 1993 they competed with 'off-the-shelf' Ford engines available to any team who had the cash to buy them. Senna's skills still gave McLaren five victories, despite having a less than competitive car. However, at the end of 1993 Senna left the McLaren team to move to Williams, whom he saw as having the superior car and engine combination. Former world champion and adviser to Ferrari, Niki Lauda, saw this as the terminal blow:

> Senna was a leader. He told them exactly what was wrong with the car. Hakkinen [Senna's replacement] is not in a position to do that, so the reaction time is much longer. Senna motivated the designers.

John Hogan, VP of European Marketing for Philip Morris and holder of the McLaren purse strings, saw the problem as design leadership and was advocating that Barnard be brought back to McLaren.

The mid-1990s were a difficult period for McLaren. Having tried Peugeot engines in 1994 it moved to Mercedes in 1995. However, 1995 was perhaps best remembered for the debacle at the start when neither Nigel Mansell nor Mika Hakinnen could fit into the new £50m MP4/10 and then Mansell's alleged £4.5m contract to race for the year fell apart when neither he nor the car came up to expectations. On a more positive note, 1995 was significant in that it heralded a new partnership between McLaren and Mercedes. Mercedes had been considering a major commitment to F1 and in 1995 it concluded a deal which involved taking equity stakes in McLaren (40 per cent) and also in specialist engine builder Ilmor engineering based near Northampton (25 per cent, increased in 2002 to 55 per cent) which was to build the Mercedes engines used in F1.

Williams and the technological revolution: the mid-1990s

If the McLaren MP4 was the dominant car in the late 1980s, the Williams FW15 and 16 powered by a Renault V10 was the car to beat in the early 1990s. From 1992 to 1994 Williams cars won 27 out of 48 races, they secured the F1 constructors' title for all three years and the world championship for drivers was won in a Williams in 1992 (Nigel Mansell) and 1993 (Alain Prost).

Like most of the founders of the F1 constructors, Frank Williams began as a driver. His desire to remain in the sport led him to develop a business buying and selling racing cars and spare parts and in 1968 Frank Williams (Racing Cars) Ltd was formed. A series of triumphs, tragedies and near bankruptcies led up to the establishment of Williams Grand Prix Engineering in 1977 when Frank Williams teamed up with Technical Director Patrick Head. Frank Williams' approach and style owed a lot to the difficult years in the 1970s when he survived on his wits and very little else, including at one time operating from a public telephone box near the workshop when the phones were disconnected as he had not paid the bill. His style was autocratic, entrepreneurial and frugal, despite the multi-million-pound funding he managed to extract from the likes of Canon, R.J. Reynolds and Rothmans. Williams saw his role as providing the resources for the best car to be built. His long-standing relationship with Head was pivotal to the team and brought together a blend of entrepreneurial energy and technical excellence needed to succeed in F1.

The first car from this new alliance was the FW06, designed by Patrick Head and with support from Saudi Airlines. The team enjoyed some success in 1980–1981 by winning the constructors' championship both years and with Alan Jones winning the drivers' title in 1980. Jones was a forthright Australian who knew what he wanted and was not afraid to voice his opinions. His approach to working with the team was very influential and coloured Frank Williams' view of drivers:

> I took a very masculine attitude towards drivers and assumed that they should behave – or should be treated – like Alan.

Further success occurred in 1986–1987 with Nelson Piquet winning the drivers' title in 1987 and Williams the constructors' title in both years. This was despite the road accident in 1986 which left Williams tetraplegic and confined to a wheelchair. However, 1988 was Williams' worst season, with Honda having switched to supplying McLaren he was forced to switch suddenly to an 'off-the-shelf' Judd V10. Williams did not win a single race, McLaren won 15 out of the 16 Grand Prixs of 1988 and a disillusioned Nigel Mansell left and went to Ferrari. Frank Williams had to search frantically for a new engine deal, which he found in 1990 with Renault. This relationship became a far-reaching and durable one, with Renault putting human and financial resources into the project with Williams. Williams also sought to develop the relationship further and extended its activities with Renault by running its team of saloon cars for the British Touring Car Championship, and providing engineering input and the Williams name for a special edition of the Renault Clio.

In 1990 a lack of driver talent meant that the team were only able to win two races. In 1991 Nigel Mansell was persuaded to return from retirement by Frank Williams and narrowly missed taking the 1991 title, but in 1992 the team dominated the circuits, effectively winning the championship by the middle of the season. Nigel Mansell went into the record books by winning the first five consecutive races of the season. However, deterioration in the relationship between Williams and Mansell led to the driver's retirement from F1 at the end of the year.

The Williams approach to design and development of a car was always the highest priority. In a sport where personnel change teams frequently, the stable relationship between Williams and Head provided enviable continuity compared with the rest of the field. Head's designs had often been functional rather than innovative, but he had always been able to take a good idea and develop it further. These included ground effect (originally developed by Lotus), carbon-composite monocoque (McLaren), semi-automatic gearbox (Ferrari) and active suspension (Lotus). The car development process was always a top priority at Williams and Head was supported by many junior designers who then went on to be highly influential in F1.

This focus on developing the car and engine combination sometimes meant that the driver took second place in the Williams philosophy, despite the fact that a good test driver, who could help the technicians define and solve problems, was essential to the development process. There had been a number of high-profile disputes which had, in part, been attributable to Frank Williams' 'masculine' approach to dealing with drivers. Controversy broke out when the relationship between Williams and two top British drivers broke down. In 1992 Nigel Mansell left when he felt his 'number one' driver position was threatened by the recruitment of Alain Prost for 1993 (although Prost himself left the following year for the same reason regarding the hiring of Ayrton Senna). A similar situation arose when the 1996 world champion, Damon Hill, was not retained for the 1997 season and was replaced with Heinz-Harald Frentzen. In an interview with the *Sunday Times*, Patrick Head explained the decision not to hold on to Hill:

> We are an engineering company and that is what we focus on. Ferrari are probably the only team where you can say the driver is of paramount importance and that is because [Michael] Schumacher is three-quarters of a second a lap quicker than anyone else.

This emphasis on the driver being only part of the equation was not lost on Paul Stewart who was concentrating on developing the Stewart Grand Prix entry to F1 in 1996:

> If you haven't got the money none of it is possible, so money is one key to success – but what makes a difference is how the money is used. It's not down to any one thing like a driver or a engine, but the interaction that matters. If you look at the Williams team, they rely

on a solid framework, their organisation, their engine, their car design is all amalgamated into something that gives a platform for everyone to work on. They don't believe putting millions into a driver is going to make all the difference.

Williams' dominance in the 1992 season was due to a number of factors: the development of the powerful and reliable Renault engine was perfectly complemented by the FW15 chassis which incorporated Patrick Head's development of some of the innovations of the early 1990s, namely semi-automatic gearboxes, drive-by-wire technology and Williams' own active suspension system. As summarised by a senior manager at Williams F1:

> I think we actually were better able to exploit the technology that was available and led that technology revolution. We were better able to exploit it to the full, before the others caught up . . . it wasn't just one thing but a combination of ten things, each one giving you another 200/300th of a second, if you add them up you a get a couple of seconds of advantage.

However, other teams were also able to use these innovations and in 1993 the Benetton team made great progress with both the gearbox and suspension innovations largely attributed to the development skills of their new driver, Michael Schumacher. Williams' technical lead coupled with the tactical race skills of Alain Prost, supported by promoted test driver Damon Hill (due to Mansell's sudden exit), secured the 1993 world championship and constructors' championship for Williams F1.

The year 1994 was a disastrous one, but not for reasons of performance as Williams won the constructors' championship for the third successive year (this was always its declared primary objective, with the drivers' championship very much a secondary aim). Frank Williams had, for some time, regarded Brazilian Ayrton Senna as the best driver around and, now with the obvious performance advantage of the FW15 chassis and the Renault V10 engine, Senna was keen to move to Williams. The problem was that a bitter and prolonged feud between Senna and Prost, originating from their time together at McLaren, meant that if Senna arrived Prost would leave. This was exactly what happened. Prost decided to retire (though he returned to run his own team) and Ayrton Senna was partnered by Damon Hill for the 1994 season. Tragically at the San Marino Grand Prix at Imola on 1 May 1994, Senna was killed in an accident, an event which devastated not only the Williams team but the sport as a whole.

In 1995 the Benetton team were eclipsing the Williams domination. Benetton had developed a car using many of the technological innovations used by Williams (with the help of ex-Williams designer Ross Brawn). In addition Renault's ambitions to match Honda's previous domination of the sport as an engine supplier from 1986 to 1991 led it to supply Benetton with its engines as well as Williams, a decision which incensed Head and Williams. The year 1995 was the year of Benetton and Michael Schumacher, breaking the three-year domination of the Williams team. However, in 1996 Schumacher moved to the then uncompetitive Ferrari team for £27 million, putting him in third place in the Forbes chart of sports top earners. This left the way clear for Williams to dominate the season, with Benetton failing to fill the gap left by Schumacher.

Ferrari: the return to glory: 1999–2004

Ferrari was struggling in the mid-1980s. A key problem was that new developments in aerodynamics and the use of composite materials had emerged from the UK's motorsport valley. Ferrari had traditionally focused on the engine as its competitive advantage, which made perfect sense given that, unlike most of the competition which outsourced their engines from suppliers such as Cosworth, Ferrari designed and manufactured its own engines. However, it appeared that these new technologies were effectively substituting superior engine power with enhanced grip due to aerodynamic downforce and improved chassis rigidity.

In 1984 British designer Harvey Postlethwaite became Ferrari's first non-Italian Technical Director and the first who was not an engine designer by background. In 1986 British designer John Barnard was recruited to the top technical role. However, Barnard was not prepared to move to Italy. Surprisingly Enzo Ferrari allowed him to establish a design and manufacturing facility near Guildford in Surrey that became known as the Ferrari 'GTO' or Guildford Technical Office. It seemed that rather than being a unique and distinctively Italian F1 team, Ferrari were now prepared to imitate the British constructors which Enzo had once, rather contemptuously, referred to as the *Garagistes*. The concept of the GTO was that it was concerned with longer-term research and development and would concentrate on the design

of the following year's car, whereas in Maranello, under Postlethwaite, Ferrari would focus on building and racing the current car. However, the fact that Barnard was defining the technical direction of Ferrari meant that he became increasingly involved in activities at both sites.

Enzo Ferrari's death in 1988 created a vacuum which was filled by executives from the Fiat organisation for a number of years. It was written into the contract that on Enzo's death Fiat's original stake would be increased to 90 per cent; this greater investment led to attempts to run Ferrari as a formal subsidiary of the Fiat group. Barnard became frustrated with the interference and politics of the situation and left to join Benetton in 1989. However, in 1992 Fiat reappointed Luca di Montezemolo as CEO with a mandate to do whatever was needed to take Ferrari back to the top. Montezemolo, who had been team manager for Ferrari during the successful period in the mid-1970s, had subsequently taken on a range of high-profile management roles including running Italy's hosting of the Soccer World Cup in 1990. One of his first actions was to reappoint Barnard as Technical Director and re-establish GTO. He was quoted in *The Times*: 'In Italy we are cut away from the Silicon Valley of Formula One that has sprung up in England.' With an Englishman heading up design he followed this up with the appointment of a Frenchman, Jean Todt, to handle the overall management of the team. Both appointments were clear signals to all involved in Ferrari that things were going to change. Todt had no experience in F1 but had been in motorsport management for many years and had recently led a successful rally and sportscar programme at Peugeot. A further indication of change was the new numbering system for the cars, which had previously been based on the engine specification: the model for 1992 was the F92A.

However, the physical separation between design and development in Guildford and the racing operation in Maranello led to problems and Barnard and Ferrari parted company in 1996, this time for good. This opened the way for Ferrari to recruit a number of the key individuals in the Benetton technical team which had helped their new driver, Michael Schumacher, to world titles in 1994 and 1995. Todt and Montezemolo also chose not to make a direct replacement for the role of technical supremo who would lead both the design of the car and the management of the technical activity. They split the role between a chief designer, Rory Byrne, who had overall responsibility for designing the car, and Ross Brawn, who managed the entire technical operation – roles which both had undertaken in working with Schumacher at Benetton. However, the new arrangement meant that Byrne and Brawn faced the task of building up from scratch a new design department – around 50 people, based in Italy. One of the most important tasks for the new team was to take advantage of the fact that Ferrari made its own engines by integrating the design of the engine, chassis and aerodynamics as early as possible in the process. Ferrari's historic emphasis on the engine was replaced by a focus on integration, summarised by Ross Brawn: 'it's not an engine, it's not an aero-package, it's not a chassis. It's a Ferrari.'

As part of its recruitment of Michael Schumacher in 1996 Ferrari entered into a commercial partnership with Phillip Morris to use the Marlboro brand on the Ferrari cars. In a novel arrangement Phillip Morris, rather than Ferrari, paid Schumacher's salary, and made a significant contribution to Ferrari's annual operating budget. In addition to Marlboro, Ferrari also entered into a long-term partnership with Shell to provide both financial and technical support to the team, a departure for Ferrari which had previously always worked with Italian petroleum giant Agip. In these kinds of arrangements Ferrari led a trend away from selling space on cars to long-term commercial and technological arrangements, with coordinated marketing strategies for commercial partners to maximise the benefits of their investments.

This rejuvenated team provided the basis for Schumacher's dominance of F1. In 1997 they raced the Barnard-developed Ferrari and finished second in the constructors' championship. Their competitiveness continued to improve and in 1999 they won their first constructors' championship for 12 years – although the drivers' championship went to Mika Hakkinen in a McLaren/Mercedes. However, in 2000 Ferrari secured both championships and felt it had truly returned to the glory of the mid-1970s. In 2002 Schumacher and Ferrari were so dominant that a series of regulation changes were introduced to try and make the racing more competitive.

Schumacher's talent as a driver and a motivator of the team (he learnt Japanese to converse with an engine technician recruited from Honda) was critical, but another key aspect in Ferrari's advantage for 2002 had been its relationship with Bridgestone tyres. In 2000 Bridgestone had been the sole supplier to all F1 teams and therefore tyres were no longer a source of advantage. However, in 2001 Michelin entered F1 and Ferrari's main rivals – Williams, McLaren and Renault – switched to Michelin. At the time the regulations stipulated that each manufacturer could create only two specific tyre compounds. For Bridgestone, which now only supplied Ferrari and a number of less competitive teams, the choice was clear: it had to design and develop its compounds specifically for Schumacher and Ferrari. Everyone else would have to make do with this specification. For Michelin the problem was more complex with many top teams and drivers vying for a compound that specifically suited their cars and driving style. Inevitably the Michelin solution was a compromise across many drivers and teams. However, in 2003 the regulations were relaxed and Michelin was able to develop specific compounds for each team/driver. Despite stronger competition from Williams, McLaren and Renault, in 2003 Ferrari won both drivers' and constructors' titles and repeated the feat again by a greater margin in 2004, giving it a record-breaking sixth consecutive constructors' title and Schumacher a seventh world championship.

However, for 2005 and 2006 the competition became much stronger and despite being competitive Ferrari lost the drivers' and constructors' titles to the Renault F1 team (formerly Benetton). Renault benefited from the rising talent of Fernando Alonso who proved himself a match for Schumacher in both driving and team motivation. In 2005 changes in the regulations meant that tyres were required to last for the whole race, which often benefited the Michelin technology used by Renault and left Ferrari struggling towards the end of the race on its Bridgestone tyres. In 2006 a more drastic change to the regulations meant that the constructors had to shift from 3.5 litre V10 engines to smaller V8s, with engine design to be frozen for three years from 2007. In many ways an engine change should have benefited Ferrari, which reverted to its old engine-based numbering system with the 2006 car, the F248 referring to the 2.4 litre eight-cylinder engine, but struggled to get the performance in the early part of the season. Towards the end of the 2006 season a series of major changes unfolded. Schumacher announced his intention to retire at the end of the year, Jean Todt was promoted to CEO, highly experienced engine director Paolo Martinelli moved to a job with Fiat and Ross Brawn announced he was taking a sabbatical in 2007.

APPENDIX
Summary of world champions

Year	Driver	Car/engine	Constructor's Cup
1950	Giuseppe Farina	Alfa Romeo	
1951	Juan Manuel Fangio	Alfa Romeo	
1952	Alberto Ascari	Ferrari	
1953	Alberto Ascari	Ferrari	
1954	Juan Manuel Fangio	Maserati	
1955	Juan Manuel Fangio	Mercedes-Benz	
1956	Juan Manuel Fangio	Lancia-Ferrari	
1957	Juan Manuel Fangio	Maserati	
1958	Mike Hawthorn	Ferrari	Vanwall
1959	Jack Brabham	Cooper/Climax	Cooper/Climax
1960	Jack Brabham	Cooper/Climax	Cooper/Climax
1961	Phil Hill	Ferrari	Ferrari
1962	Graham Hill	BRM	BRM
1963	Jim Clark	Lotus/Climax	Lotus/Climax
1964	John Surtees	Ferrari	Ferrari
1965	Jim Clark	Lotus/Climax	Lotus/Climax
1966	Jack Brabham	Brabham/Repco	Brabham/Repco
1967	Denny Hulme	Brabham/Repco	Brabham/Repco
1968	Graham Hill	Lotus/Ford	Lotus/Ford
1969	Jackie Stewart	Matra/Ford	Matra/Ford
1970	Jochen Rindt	Lotus/Ford	Lotus/Ford
1971	Jackie Stewart	Tyrrell/Ford	Tyrrell/Ford
1972	Emerson Fittipaldi	Lotus/Ford	Lotus/Ford
1973	Jackie Stewart	Tyrrell/Ford	Lotus/Ford
1974	Emerson Fittipaldi	McLaren/Ford	McLaren/Ford
1975	Niki Lauda	Ferrari	Ferrari
1976	James Hunt	McLaren/Ford	Ferrari
1977	Niki Lauda	Ferrari	Ferrari
1978	Mario Andretti	Lotus/Ford	Lotus/Ford
1979	Jody Scheckter	Ferrari	Ferrari
1980	Alan Jones	Williams/Ford	Williams/Ford
1981	Nelson Piquet	Brabham/Ford	Williams/Ford
1982	Keke Rosberg	Williams/Ford	Ferrari
1983	Nelson Piquet	Brabham/BMW	Ferrari
1984	Niki Lauda	McLaren/Porsche	McLaren/Porsche
1985	Alain Prost	McLaren/Porsche	McLaren/Porsche
1986	Alain Prost	McLaren/Porsche	Williams/Honda
1987	Nelson Piquet	Williams/Honda	Williams/Honda
1988	Ayrton Senna	McLaren/Honda	McLaren/Honda
1989	Alain Prost	McLaren/Honda	McLaren/Honda
1990	Ayrton Senna	McLaren/Honda	McLaren/Honda
1991	Ayrton Senna	McLaren/Honda	McLaren/Honda
1992	Nigel Mansell	Williams/Renault	Williams/Renault
1993	Alain Prost	Williams/Renault	Williams/Renault
1994	Michael Schumacher	Benetton/Ford	Williams/Renault
1995	Michael Schumacher	Benetton/Renault	Benetton/Renault
1996	Damon Hill	Williams/Renault	Williams/Renault
1997	Jacques Villeneuve	Williams/Renault	Williams/Renault
1998	Mika Hakkinen	McLaren/Mercedes	McLaren/Mercedes
1999	Mika Hakkinen	McLaren/Mercedes	Ferrari
2000	Michael Schumacher	Ferrari	Ferrari
2001	Michael Schumacher	Ferrari	Ferrari
2002	Michael Schumacher	Ferrari	Ferrari
2003	Michael Schumacher	Ferrari	Ferrari
2004	Michael Schumacher	Ferrari	Ferrari
2005	Fernando Alonso	Renault	Renault
2006	Fernando Alonso	Renault	Renault

Note: Constructors' championship is based on the cumulative points gained by a team during the season. Currently teams are limited to entering two cars and drivers per race.

Manchester United: a whole new ball game

Bob Perry

This case describes events before and after the hostile takeover of Manchester United in 2005. The case invites the reader to consider issues including organisational purpose, ownership, governance and stakeholder power.

● ● ●

Introduction

For football supporters the words *Manchester United* may conjure visions of European glory, triumph out of adversity and talented players of yesteryear. Those studying business may think instead of a brand, a corporate success story or a market leader. However, in early 2005 Manchester United took on the guise of a drama complete with villains, heroes and a storyline full of possibilities and tensions. The plot culminated in a further strategic era complete with new owners, plans, priorities and perspectives. This case explores these changes having briefly considered what the organisation once was.

In one poll,[1] 20 per cent of the UK population claimed to be Manchester United supporters. It would not be fanciful to speculate that a higher percentage loathe United, such is their capacity to polarise opinion. Aggressive marketing and the club's business aspirations appear at the root of much of this hostility, the very concerns felt by many genuine United supporters themselves. It is against this background that this case is set.

Manchester United: the growth of a brand

The basis of United's business success and position as a global brand is rooted in the club's history, both triumphal and tragic. Manchester United like many provincial English football clubs initially represented the locality their name suggested. One of the few converts to European as well as English competition, United took on the mantle of representing the country abroad in the mid-1950s. Disaster struck. In 1958 a plane crash in Munich resulted in death and injury to many of the club's (and country's) best players.

Photo: EMPICS Sports Photo Agency/PA Photos

_____
[1] Quoted by Mellor (2000).

This case was prepared by Bob Perry, University of Wolverhampton Business School. It is intended as a basis of class discussion and not as an illustration of good or bad practice. For a longitudinal view of strategic issues facing Manchester United refer to cases in previous editions of this text (6th edition, page 247; 7th edition, page 217). © Bob Perry 2006. Not to be reproduced or quoted without permission.

This could have broken the club's spirit but instead United showed determination to compete at the very highest level of domestic and international football with loaned players, youngsters and crash survivors. In so doing they attracted admirers far and wide so becoming one of the first to boast support beyond their area (even outside England). In addition successive United teams seemed to contain exciting flair players that helped build a brand.

In the boardroom the financial value of the brand was being explored. Louis Edwards became a director the same year as the air disaster and presided over a remarkable recovery to the pinnacle of winning the European Cup in 1968. In 1980, his son Martin inherited the club but nine years later he tried to sell his majority shareholding for £10m (€14.5m). Resistance from fellow directors and a failure by the proposed purchaser to raise enough finance frustrated the takeover.

Life as a listed company

Martin Edwards now turned his attention to the strategic problem of raising funds for ground improvements. In 1991 the club was floated on the stock exchange with a valuation of £40m. Further share issues followed in 1994 and 1997 and Edwards accumulated £71m in share sales. In December 2002 he stepped down as Chairman.

> When the plc started, [in 1991] there were grave doubts about it – I had them myself – but I think the supporters have come round to that.
> (Sir Alex Ferguson, manager)

> This is not just a football club. It consistently set itself apart from other clubs. . . . Manchester United will always attract huge speculation but what we have to get back to is that's its a well run business capable of giving our shareholders a return.
> (Peter Kenyon ex Chief Executive)

Peter Kenyon was appointed Chief Executive in May 1997 with a brief to broaden United's supporter base (and consequently the revenue potential). Having succeeded spectacularly in his task, Kenyon's resignation in September 2003 was a setback. (Kenyon had been lured away by a huge financial package from rivals Chelsea.)

Clean sheets or balance sheets?

Some supporters resented the way in which the traditionally working-class game had evolved. At the forefront of the change were United with their business attitude and growing list of commercial partners and corporate sponsors. United no longer represented Manchester in the same way, and the club was owned by businesses far and wide.

United had moved swiftly from a professional football club to a truly global enterprise. In the process, some genuine supporters felt alienated by the club's new values and aspirations to the extent that they 'loved the team but hated the club'. The nub of the issue was whether profit maximisation for shareholders was an appropriate purpose for a football club. Manchester United as a listed company had legal obligations to its shareholders. Inevitably the feelings of traditional supporters were overridden in meeting shareholder demands.

> Football clubs are marketing brands, not teams . . . it is no longer a case of doing well on the pitch; the more merchandise you sell, the better.
> (A Real Madrid spokesperson at the time of the Beckham transfer)

> We strive to ensure that shareholders, loyal supporters, customers and key commercial partners alike benefit from our performance.
> (Manchester United plc Annual Report 1999)

The battleground of strategic change

In the previous edition of this text,[2] the case closed by posing key questions, including:

> Would predators eye United's cash-rich position and seek to gain ownership possibly with the intention of diluting the current emphasis on investing on the playing side of the business?

It was no shock therefore that by early 2005 the media began reporting a hostile takeover battle.

United's financial report for 2003 had highlighted (the normal) increased performance. This time, however, the annual rise in turnover was particularly sharp (18 per cent to £173m) because of transfer dealings, most notably the sale of David Beckham to Real Madrid. At this time Malcolm Glazer, a reclusive American billionaire, had built a 3 per cent shareholding stake and talk of takeover was in the air. It was said that Glazer had never watched a football match in his life; he had, however, engineered the takeover of the American

---

[2] See page 217.

football outfit Tampa Bay Buccaneers in 1995. Once in control he operated it on an aggressive commercial basis but oversaw playing successes including victory in Super Bowl XXXVII.

Manchester United had operated as a publicly listed company with responsibilities to shareholders since 1991. Under stock exchange rules, for Glazer (or anyone else) to gain control, delist United from the London Stock Exchange and then move the club back into private ownership, 75 per cent of shares were needed. A further 15 per cent of shares would legally force any remaining shareholders to sell, giving a new owner absolute control.

As Glazer continued to build his stake the club's directors consistently opposed his advances for control.

As the battle lines became drawn a group calling itself *Shareholders United* rallied the support of small shareholders who were 'true' supporters. Together they argued they could become more powerful. By October 2004 and with a membership of 10,000 they planned to increase their combined stake to 25 per cent and block a takeover. Much media coverage was given to a public meeting in Manchester city centre that attracted 500 interested people. Meanwhile, Glazer had built his own stake to first 19.7 per cent, then 28.11 per cent and had once more unsuccessfully approached the board.

The 4,000 disillusioned supporters who hated the way in which their football club had changed decided enough was enough. With £100,000 pledged a new club called *FC United of Manchester* entered the football league 'pyramid' (some 10 divisions below Manchester United).

As Glazer tried to dampen opposition, manager Sir Alex Ferguson told the press 'we don't want the club to be in anyone else's hands'. Then Glazer's investment bank and public relations firm disassociated themselves from the manoeuvrings. Glazer's request to have access to the books was refused but in retaliation his vote was significant in denying three directors re-election at a November EGM.

The crucial block of shares was a 28.7 per cent holding by the club's biggest shareholders, J.P. McManus and John Magnier. When Glazer persuaded them to sell in March 2005 the battle was won.

Six years earlier, the board had wanted to accept an offer of £623m for the club from the broadcasting company BSkyB, but when news of negotiations 'leaked' there was stiff opposition from supporters and others concerned that media ownership would ruin the football club as they had known and loved it for generations. Part of the success in thwarting the bid involved enlisting the support of the British government who blocked the plan, ruling it 'against public interest'. Despite pressure from Members of Parliament, this time the government decided not to intervene, conceding that ultimately it was a matter for shareholders.

A revised proposal of £3 a share in February 2005 was at a level the board felt was 'fair'. Although declining to recommend the bid, the board had no alternative but to allow access to United's books. Chief Executive David Gill explained that the returns required by the Glazer business plan for the club would be unhealthy:

> The Board continues to believe that Glazer's business plan assumptions are aggressive and . . . could be damaging.

Those with knowledge of corporate governance must have been interested by the board's explanation that it had to decide between its commitment to shareholders or to a wider stakeholder group.

By now Shareholders United had grown to have in excess of 33,000 supporters and was backed by free legal representation. Will Rosen, a partner in Weil Gotshjal & Manges Legal advisors, explained:

> Many football fans are concerned with the trend towards big business buying clubs as commercial investments, with scant regard for the traditions and social functions of these clubs. By providing legal advice to this not for profit shareholders group we feel we're acting in the best interests of football supporters generally.

Shareholders United persuaded outlets like the supermarket chain Asda, Virgin Records, the book group WH Smiths, and JJB Sports to stock 'not for sale' charity-style wristbands at £3 each with profits going to a fighting fund. Combining with the *Independent Manchester United Supporters' Association* (IMUSA) it continued to lobby support (including Sepp Blatter, President of the world's football governing body, *FIFA*).

If Shareholders United and IMUSA represented 'respectable' opposition, others were more militant. A group called *Manchester Education Committee* claimed responsibility for (amongst other things) vandalising directors' cars, staging a pitch invasion and burning an American flag outside the ground. In one incident, merchandise in United's megastore was defaced and a mob burned an effigy of Glazer.

A new strategic era

In May 2005 with 76 per cent of shares secured Glazer was creeping towards the 90 per cent he craved. The Glazers claimed to be 'keen supporters and long-term owners of Manchester United shares', and attempted to dampen hostility by:

- pledging a yearly transfer fund of £20m for new players; and

- modifying the idea to generate £3m per annum for 'commercial naming rights' of the Old Trafford stadium, the club's ground since 1910.

Hugh McIlvanney, a respected sports journalist, commented that the takeover

> must be seen not as a sudden eruption of capitalist extremism in the national game but a logical consequence of football's progressive submission to the naked power of money.

United were taken back into private ownership in June with Glazer's three sons appointed to the board while Chairman Sir Roy Gardner resigned.[3] Shareholders United urged Chief Executive David Gill to do the same, but he chose to serve under the new regime (along with manager Sir Alex Ferguson).

The takeover had cost £812m, the majority financed by loans secured against future earnings and club assets (like Old Trafford). Later David Gill explained that the club's financial future was based on

> sensible levels we were following [before] ... the debt itself is serviceable because our cash generation will improve through expansion of the stadium and other things. We didn't have any debt before and now we do but I'm quite comfortable about the situation.

The financing deal	£m
Costs	
Bought shares	790
Advisors' fees	22
	812
Financed by	
Banks preference shares	265
Loans from US hedge funds	275
Personal contribution	272
	812

---

[3] Joel, Ave and Bryan, who were joined in June 2006 by siblings Kevin, Edward and Darcie.

Challenges and opportunities

Despite the debt financial signs remained promising. The club was the highest generator of match-day revenue in the world. Every home match was sold out and the ground capacity was increased to 76,000 (including 8,000 corporate seats) in August 2006.

The potential for further sponsorship and merchandising was also clear: globally over 75 million claimed to be supporters, including 40 million in Asia and 4.6 million in the USA. (In 2003 a four-match friendly tour of the USA produced an average attendance of 67,000 per game and matches were broadcast to 70m US homes producing a £4m profit.)

The *Sunday Times* published a list of the most powerful brands in 2006 with Manchester United ranking in the top 130 (above Ordnance Survey, Land Rover and Selfridges). The new regime clearly felt that future revenues could increase through further brand development, increased merchandising and levering improved television deals. Their business plan projected operating profits to triple in under five years (with season ticket prices rising 54 per cent) and projected annual revenues to reach over £245m.

Shareholders United complained that this blatant commercialisation was too much and urged 'fans to exercise their consumer choice and just not buy the products of the club or the products of the company and the products of the sponsors'. (Products under threat included Nike, Audi cars, Budweiser beer and Ladbrokes bookmakers.) Main sponsors Vodafone pulled out of a deal worth £9m but new sponsors formed a queue, unfazed by the threat.

Meanwhile, matters on the field were becoming problematic. Domestically, Chelsea (bankrolled by the personal fortune of Russian billionaire owner Roman Abramovich) dominated. Chelsea's spending power was now putting even United in the shade, and continued failure in European competition was also a source of frustration (and lost revenue). In addition, the *Deloitte Football Money League* reported in February 2006 that for the first time in nine years of publication United had been overtaken by Real Madrid as the world's biggest club (in terms of revenues generated). Based on the 2004–2005 season Real had generated £20m more than United due to commercial growth and (ironically) Beckham's earning potential. More encouragingly, Deloitte reported that 'football remains a growth sport, especially at the highest level'.

Some reflections

For all the downsides to United being a publicly listed company, an independent market research group indicated that 97 per cent of United supporters believed this was preferable to the Glazer takeover. The previous board doubtless felt that it had hit an appropriate balance between profits and principles. Despite sell-out crowds and a waiting list for season tickets, the club had tempered admission prices and few of the 20 Premiership clubs charged less. United paid their players what seemed obscene sums but refused to spend beyond their means. As a listed company Manchester United was debt free, well run and a source of employment for many.

The previous era (before 1991) when United were an English football club with limited sponsorship and modest income streams seemed light years away. Manchester United had after all become the successful business model that all other clubs aspired to. That model now seemed more business focused than anything witnessed before, but would it deliver success, however success is measured?

Sources

Anon (2003) 'United tighten purse strings', *Guardian*, 1 April.

Anon (2006) 'Gill plays down United debt burden', *Metro*, 24 January.

Deloitte (2006) *Deloitte Football Money League, Changing of the guard*, February.

McIlvanney, H. (2005) 'Hard truth for United martyrs', *Sunday Times*, 15 May.

Mellor, G. (2000) 'The rise of the Reds: an historical analysis of Manchester United as a super club', in *Singer and Friedlander Review, 1999–2000 Season*, Centre for Research into Sport & Society, University of Leicester/ Singer & Friedlander.

Northcroft, J. (2003) 'The American dream', *Sunday Times*, 16 November.

Northcroft, J. (2004) 'Fergie tells Glazer to back off', *Sunday Times*, 21 November.

Perry, B. (2001) 'Playing fair? Vision, values and ethics: a study of the co-existence of big business and football', in P. Murphy (ed.), *Singer and Friedlander Review, 2000–01 Season*, Centre for Research into Sport & Society, University of Leicester/Singer & Friedlander.

Perry, B. (2002) 'Playing the game?', in G. Johnson, and K. Scholes (eds), *Exploring Corporate Strategy: Text and Cases*, 6th edition, Pearson Education.

Perry, B. (2005) 'Manchester United, brand of hope and glory', in G. Johnson, K. Scholes and R. Whittington (eds), *Exploring Corporate Strategy: Text and Cases*, 7th edition, FT/Prentice Hall.

Other sources:
The excellent *Soccer Investor Weekly* (various issues)
Company annual financial reports
Other corporate data including www.manutd.com
Industry data, e.g. www.deloitte.co.uk
Financial and sports media

Belief in action: The Salvation Army, a global not-for-profit organisation

Alex Murdock

The Salvation Army is a global not-for-profit organisation which has a number of quite distinctive character-istics. It adopted almost from its inception the military form and this has continued to be a distinguishing factor in its work. Its Christian mission and UK origin have not prevented it from working successfully across religious, language, national and ethnic divides. The growth and range of activities of the organisation have been remark-able. The resulting size and complexity posed a challenge to the organisation in respect of both how it ac-knowledged and incorporated the range of stakeholders and also in terms of how it confronted future choices.

● ● ●

Introduction

In the year since Hurricane Katrina struck the Gulf Coast, The Salvation Army has undertaken the largest disaster response effort in its history, allocating do-nations of more than US$365 million [≈€292m] to serve more than 1.7 million people in nearly every American state. By way of comparison, the amount donated is more than three times greater than the US$86 million given after the events of September 11th – The Salvation Army's second largest mobilisation.[1]

In a world increasingly beset by both natural and humanmade disasters a global organisation like The Salvation Army has faced increasing pressures in terms of both scale and complexity.

The Salvation Army is an international Christian church working on a global basis. It is one of the largest, most diverse providers of social welfare in the world. Also it is a distinctive part of the univer-sal Christian Church. Its message and the lifestyle it advocates are based on the Bible's teaching. Its work is to make known the good news about Jesus Christ and to persuade people to become his followers. Alongside this primary aim, it shows practical concern and care for the needs of people regardless of race, creed, status, colour, sex or age.

It was founded in 1865 in London. A quasi-military structure was quickly adopted and subse-quently the organisation has become a worldwide movement which is to be found in 111 countries and operates in 175 different languages. This would be remarkable in any organisation whether in the private or not-for-profit sector. The long history of The Salvation Army and its associated steady growth also marked it out as an organisation which had stood the test of time whilst remaining close to its original mission.

However, the organisation is not static and Israel Gaither, one of the Commissioners, observed 'The twenty first century ministry requires a mission-centred Salvation Army in continuous renewal' and averred that it was time for more bold initiatives pushing beyond what he described as the 'comfortable patterns of missioning behaviour.[2] The actual mission statement of The Salvation Army in 2003–2004 read as follows:

---

[1] *Source*: The Salvation Army, 29 August 2006.

[2] Commissioner Israel L. Gaither quoted from *Salvation Army Yearbook*, 2004, p. 2.

The author gratefully acknowledges the assistance and advice of Major Ray Irving and David Rice of The Salvation Army in the preparation of this case study. However, the case study does not intend to present an official view of The Salvation Army. Any matters of fact, judgement or opinion in the case study are the responsibility of the author.

The Salvation Army, an international movement, is an evangelical part of the universal Christian Church. Its message is based on the Bible. Its ministry is motivated by love for God. Its mission is to preach the gospel of Jesus Christ and meet human need in his name without discrimination.

The range of activities undertaken by The Salvation Army

The Salvation Army provides a very wide range of programme-based services in the global context. The Salvation Army's social service function has become very significant. These services can be divided as follows (Appendix 1 gives the precise breakdown of the range of provision offered as of January 2004).

Social programmes

Residential services are widely provided in a range of forms. The single largest category is facilities for homeless people and there are altogether over 600 separate facilities with a total capacity of nearly 32,000. However, The Salvation Army provides residential accommodation for almost every conceivable need group ranging from mother and baby through children to the elderly and disabled. It also provides remand and probation facilities. Day care is similarly provided for a wide range of client groups and needs

Addiction dependency has long been a prime focus for the Army's work and this is reflected in the significant number of specifically targeted residential and day care resources. However, due to the nature of the client groups it is reasonable to assume that addiction problems are likely to be found extensively through much of the clientele in both the residential and day care provision.

The armed forces provision is very much a tradition from the long-established association of the Army with its 'armed counterpart'. The Salvation Army is, however, more akin to the Red Cross and has operated on both sides of conflicts. This apolitical approach is key to the ability of the Army to operate in a vast range of different countries.

Associated with this is the increased role the Army has come to play in disaster relief. This has often been undertaken in a similar manner to a range of other such organizations. The Salvation Army was a significant presence after September 11 in providing support and tangible sustenance to those affected and the rescuers.

The community services role has taken The Salvation Army into areas also peopled by probation and counselling services. There could have been potential areas of conflict here but The Salvation Army has traditionally been able to work in partnership with both statutory and voluntary agencies. These partnerships are often associated with the willingness of The Salvation Army to engage with clients whom other agencies are reluctant to assist, such as alcoholics and 'difficult clients'. The 'missing persons' service is very highly regarded and (in the UK) has acquired a well-deserved reputation for successfully tracing a very high proportion of referrals.

Health care and hospital provision

The Salvation Army has developed a significant number of programmes in this area particularly associated with its work in the developing world. The development of mobile clinics and outpatient services has been significant and the Army has been active in responding to HIV/AIDS.

Education

Missionary-based organisations often see educational services as an important part of their role and it is hardly surprising that The Salvation Army has been active here. However, the size of the provision is remarkable. The total number of pupils catered for globally is greater than the number of undergraduates in the whole of the UK.

The fundamental basis of The Salvation Army

As the name suggests, the basis of The Salvation Army which distinguishes it from other aspects of Christian (and for that matter other) religious organisations is the adoption of a quasi-military form of structure. The original structural concept was probably derived from the Indian Civil Service.[3] The military imagery evokes the concept of 'spiritual warfare'. It is reflected in the use of

---

[3] *Source*: Personal communication with David Rice, The Salvation Army, UK Territory.

ranks, uniforms and flags and indeed in the well-established publication *The War Cry*.

However, the actual work of The Salvation Army is not simply evangelistic but heavily focused upon the relief of poverty and the provision of practical, cost-effective and skilled services. In some ways The Salvation Army anticipated the changing role of the traditional military which has had to adapt to new 'peace-keeping' and disaster assistance roles. However, for The Salvation Army the service provision has long been a tradition. Previously the social service aspects were run in tandem with the missionary aspects, but the organisational structure has changed to bring the two together.

The charity is well known for the modest salaries paid to its officers (ministers). When Commissioner Alex Hughes took on the Territorial Commander role in the UK in 2002 the newspapers noted his salary with a degree of astonishment. He was a chief executive managing a £161m budget and 5,600 staff, yet he received a salary including benefits of £10,258. This represented a minute fraction (about 15 per cent) of what chief executives of similarly sized charitable organisations might expect. A person working in the lowest clerical capacity in a charity in the UK would probably have received more.

Growth of The Salvation Army

The Salvation Army draws much of its strength and vision from that of its founder, William Booth. Significantly for the Army, the role of Catherine Booth, his wife, is strongly acknowledged and the Army has had a long-established tradition of involving women in active and significant roles within the organisation.

The military form of the organisation does not mean that non-uniformed members are not important Appendix 2 indicates that there are a range of associations with The Salvation Army. Many non-officer employees hold a number of significant posts and responsibility throughout the organisation. The rank of lieutenant is regarded as appropriate for someone who wishes to become an officer on a temporary basis. It is somewhat akin to a 'short service commission' in the regular army.

The discipline associated with both the military mode of operation has been combined with a surprising degree of organisational flexibility. From its outset the organisation has been very practically orientated. The provision of relief services to the poor led naturally to the evolution of a strong social service function. The organisation became able to respond to crisis and disaster and increasingly became involved in international relief work.

The original focus upon poverty and the associated issues linked to alcohol and gambling has remained a strong part of the core of the organisation. The Salvation Army does not accept any donations or grants derived from these sources. Therefore it does not apply for monies from the UK National Lottery. However, in other respects The Salvation Army has been relatively flexible about accepting money from a range of sources. The pragmatic view has been expressed that money can be cleansed by being put to good use.

Nevertheless, there were some concerns expressed following the acceptance by the American Territory of a bequest from Joan Kroc, wife of the founder of McDonald's restaurants, in 2004. It was the world's largest single charity donation and had restrictions upon its use. A UK Salvation Army officer wrote in the *Guardian* in January 2004 referring to the US bequest:

> In the UK, where we run a vast array of services for vulnerable people, we rely on the support of the public and we would like to thank everyone who contributes. We don't need $1.5bn to make a difference to people's lives; £9 helps provide a homeless person with shelter for the night in a Salvation Army hostel, while £25 pays for one night's meal run, which can provide up to 60 people with soup and sandwiches.

The internationalisation and growth of The Salvation Army

From its beginnings in the UK, The Salvation Army has become a global organisation. The increase in countries has been matched by an increase in the number of 'soldiers' and in 2003 there were over 1,024,000 senior soldiers worldwide. The organisation employed that year nearly 110,000 people. Appendix 2 sets out the make-up of The Salvation Army as of January 2004.

This growth has been especially marked in developing countries and, as Exhibit 1 shows, the number of soldiers is particularly high in Africa.

The Salvation Army (unlike more conventional armies) prefers to work in countries where it is legally recognised by the law of the country. In the UK The Salvation Army enjoys its own specific legislative provision, The Salvation Army Act of 1980. This is somewhat unusual in the charitable

Exhibit 1	Geographical distribution of soldiers	

	Soldiers	% of total
Africa	438,483	43
Americas	127,460	12.5
Europe	71,888	7
South Asia	275,224	27
South Pacific and East Asia	107,082	10.5
		100

Source: Derived from Alan Read, 'The Salvation Army and government: marching in step into the 21st century', Masters thesis, South Bank University, London, 2002.

context. In part the legislation came about (in 1931) to deal with succession and to set a compulsory retirement age for the general.

The Army has sought to work alongside other faiths. On its website it states:

> In many countries The Salvation Army co-exists with non-Christian faiths such as Islam, Hinduism and Buddhism. It respects the sincerely-held beliefs of devout non-Christians, and does not regard conflict or bitter controversy as suitable means to making known the good news of Jesus.

However, the relationships with the governments of the countries in which it operates do not always run smoothly. The press made much of the attempts by the Moscow City Government to ban The Salvation Army in 2001, which led to a ban on The Salvation Army in Russia. The Salvation Army fought this through the Russian courts and was reinstated there as a charity in 2002. The Army has in fact been actively involved in Russia since 1913 and though banned by the communists had re-established itself in 1992 with the fall of communism.

One researcher commented on this aspect of The Salvation Army's work:

> That The Salvation Army relationship with governments varies so widely from country to country is a reflection not only of the internationalisation of The Salvation Army but also of the government frameworks, ideologies and policies within which it must work and it can also be conditioned by the work of The Salvation Army in the lives of government leaders in their childhood.[4]

_____
[4] Alan Read, 2002, op. cit.

The governance and change process

The Salvation Army differs in one important respect from its armed counterpart. There is no global high-command structure which determines local strategy and activities. The International HQ is in London but each territory has a high degree of autonomy. Indeed each territory is typically recognised through local legal provision in the country in which it operates. There are, however, several governance structures which affect the operation of The Salvation Army globally:

- The High Council is constituted of all the active commissioners and officers in charge of territories (some 63 in all). It is called to deal with succession or when the general is unfit to continue. The High Council can meet at any place in the UK, but normally meets at Sunbury Court (Sunbury on Thames) where there is a specific 'Conference Chamber' for the election of a new general.

- The Generals' Consultative Council comprises all the officers qualified to attend the High Council and advises on mission, strategy and policy. It meets more regularly (about four times a year) and operates electronically through the use of Lotus Notes.

- The International Management Council focuses on the efficiency and operation of the International HQ in London and meets monthly.

The Salvation Army has had some separation in its religious and social service functions with the latter being mainly run by professionals. There has been a move to integrate the social service provision into the religious part of Salvation Army activities. This has been greeted with a degree of apprehension by some of the professional staff.

The Salvation Army in the global context

The range and diversity of The Salvation Army's activities means that the global organisation confronts a very complex environment. The organisation primarily functions on a geographic basis through the territorial commissioners. However, there is a considerable amount of local autonomy and the commissioners are not to be compared in power and authority with their regular army counterparts.

Just as generals in the regular army have to deal with politicians so The Salvation Army has to deal with the individual governmental bodies which affect its work. This has presented an enormous degree of diversity.

In the UK political leaders of almost all persuasions are strongly supportive of The Salvation Army. In the USA it had been built into the official post-9/11 response to disaster and was praised by *Forbes* magazine as one of the top 10 US charities.

However, in Russia it encountered major problems and in areas of danger for Western charities (such as Iraq or Afghanistan) The Salvation Army's values may offer it only limited protection. As an avowedly Christian organisation with a missionary element to its work, the prospect of maintaining its global presence represents a major challenge. The development of disaster relief work places it in a strong position and its particular competence and presence make it one of the relatively few global charitable organisations.

The resourcing needs of The Salvation Army are likely to increase as the demands upon its services increase. The US bequest from the McDonald's heir raised some questions in the UK and it is possible that future fundraising strategies may test the limits of acceptability.

The apolitical stance of The Salvation Army may also be tested in the post-9/11 context. The Salvation Army's laudable desire to work in a non-conflictual way with other faiths may not sit easily with its involvement in homeland security in the USA.

The Salvation Army in the UK

The income and expenditure of The Salvation Army in the UK are shown in Exhibit 2. The size of the organisation is demonstrated and sector analysts will note the (relatively) low proportion of management and administrative costs. In part this is a product of the very low salaries paid to uniformed officer staff.

However, the recent years have been financially challenging for The Salvation Army. In October 2004 the *Guardian* reported that:

> The organisation has found that its fundraisers were overly optimistic about pledges of financial support, predicting income which did not materialise. To avoid cuts in frontline services for deprived communities, the army is targeting its administrative staff for redundancy and reviewing its property portfolio to establish whether assets can be sold.[5]

The Salvation Army confronted a hard choice because it felt a strong sense of loyalty towards its staff yet it was clear that the priority had to be to maintain services to its client group. The low proportion of management and administrative costs in the 2005 review demonstrates this.

In 2002 The Salvation Army in the UK had completed a major strategic review – the first such exercise undertaken by The Salvation Army anywhere. The strategic review identified a number of factors which were regarded as critical for the future of the organisation. The review had commenced in 1999 and had involved the use of external consultants. The Henley Centre had undertaken a number of studies which examined changes in society which were relevant for The Salvation Army.

The Henley studies identified some major societal changes. They highlighted problems arising from prosperity whereby the gaps between the haves and the have-nots were growing yet the long hours' working culture put those who had apparently benefited from prosperity under greater stress. This was associated with increased family breakdown and increased alcohol and drug abuse. There were issues associated with what the Henley Centre referred to as a 'responsibility gap' whereby there was a lack of both informal and formal care for those who needed it whether they were young or old. The increasing pressures and expectations which society placed upon young people were associated with increased mental health problems and substance abuse as well as, in some cases, significant exclusion from society.

---

[5] 'Salvation Army may cut jobs to plug £9.6m hole', *Guardian*, 30 October (2004).

Exhibit 2   **The Salvation Army in the UK**

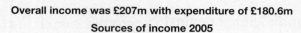

Overall income was £207m with expenditure of £180.6m

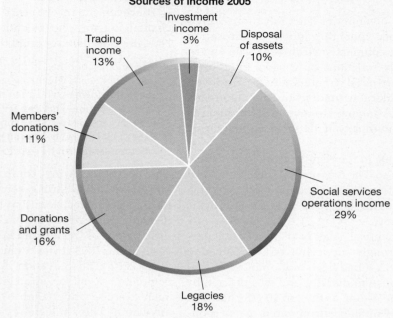

Sources of income 2005

Investment income 3%

Disposal of assets 10%

Trading income 13%

Members' donations 11%

Social services operations income 29%

Donations and grants 16%

Legacies 18%

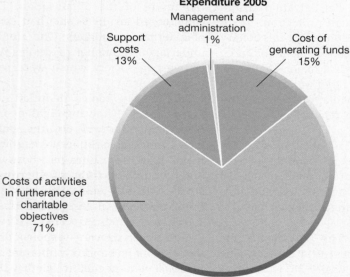

Expenditure 2005

Management and administration 1%

Support costs 13%

Cost of generating funds 15%

Costs of activities in furtherance of charitable objectives 71%

Source: The Salvation Army Annual Review, 2005.

The Salvation Army faced the following problems:

- A declining and ageing membership.
- A growing demand for the services it provided.
- Difficulties as an intergenerational organisation in relating to youth culture.
- Whilst there were pockets of local innovation, there was an inherited 'top-down' culture that made it difficult to resource innovation.
- A move in social policy from the institutional care that its social services had traditionally provided to more community-based provision.

However, the review identified the following strengths which The Salvation Army was seen to possess:

- A commitment to help the most needy.
- A willingness to undertake practical work as well as proclaim the gospel.
- Trustworthiness and sincerity, which made it an organisation people are comfortable to work with and contribute to.
- A strong caring ethos.
- An understanding of the needs of people today.[6]

The strategic framework stressed the need for The Salvation Army to focus upon the needs resulting from an increasingly fragmented society. The document did not set out the precise operational requirements of the analysis. Rather it exhorted the reader to consider the implications in terms of people, buildings and financial resources and to develop further plans at a local level.

The implication of the review and the Henley report were significant for the focus of The Salvation Army in the UK. As Commissioner Alex Hughes commented:

> When The Salvation Army was founded over 130 years ago, it focused on helping the poorer sections of society. Now it is not only the poor who need our help. All sectors of society are at risk of suffering from the modern social condition – loneliness, stress and a deteriorating quality of life.

It can be argued that The Salvation Army in the UK has taken the lead in both taking a strategic view of the future of the organisation and acknowledging that the circumstances that previously guided its work and directed it towards the poorest sectors of society have changed. In this respect the UK Territory may have broken the ground for those territories in other developed countries. If the strategic framework initiated by the UK Territory is rolled out in other territories then The Salvation Army may move away from its original focus upon the poorest parts of society. The long-established practice of paying officers extremely modest salaries has been part of the values of the Salvation Army, but will it be sustainable in the future if the Army extends its mission towards the wealthier sectors of society?

However, the needs of the developing world remain as pressing as ever and are acknowledged and recognised in the annual reports and literature of the UK Territory.

The Salvation Army has successfully grown over nearly 150 years to become one of the best known and widely respected organisations of its kind. It has been able to evolve and adapt its services whilst holding onto the core beliefs and practices associated with its founding. Peter Drucker, a well-respected authority on leadership, suggested that The Salvation Army has three challenges:

- To avoid losing its soul (in this case through being too successful).
- To concentrate on areas where it can set the standard.
- To maintain the crucial balance between being a religious organisation and a social organisation.[7]

However, it confronts an increasingly fragmented and uncertain world and as a global organisation it will need to negotiate its way. The pressure upon its services is likely to increase and it will be challenged to secure adequate resources to meet these demands within the constraints of its belief systems.

The Salvation Army in the UK, like its US counterpart, has responded to the emergency response agenda by engaging formally with the state sector. The most recent annual review observed in a positive vein:

---

[6] 'A strategic framework for the United Kingdom Territory with the Republic of Ireland', The Salvation Army, 2002.

[7] Source: Salvationist Magazine, 24 March (2001).

[The Salvation Army] emergency services work [is] to receive explicit inclusion in the Civil Contingencies Bill, which legislates on contingency planning and civil protection in handling emergencies. Major Bill Cochrane thanked parliamentarians, including Ruth Kelly MP then Minister of State for the Cabinet Office, for their support at a celebratory reception.[8]

The Civil Contingencies Act (2004), which was to a large extent a UK response to 9/11, came into force in November 2004. The Salvation Army played a major role and following the London bombings in a July 2005 press release noted:

The Salvation Army is part of the emergency response plan in London and teams were on hand at King's Cross and Russell Square over the weekend and into this week, helping the emergency services and supporting survivors. Teams are still in Russell Square to support the emergency services as they work tirelessly to retrieve the remaining bodies.[9]

After these bombings in London an official government report concluded that securing national preparedness for possible future attacks should be a 'continuous and essential activity' involving the public, private and voluntary sectors at all levels across the UK, and the community at large. The report also noted: 'The voluntary sector played a vital and significant role in the response providing a wide range of support services and assistance.'[10]

The future?

As the Salvation Army confronts new demands in changing stakeholder environments the comments of Peter Drucker remain as appropriate now as they were in 2001. Perhaps the additional need to balance work with governments with core values in order to continue to be a force for good globally is going to figure more prominently as the new general takes office. One of the two contenders, if appointed, would have been the first black occupant of the office. His own observation on his possible appointment was very much in keeping with The Salvation Army ethos:

I'm not here because of my color, and I wouldn't be here if I thought I was, I want to serve all men and women. I am aware I can serve as a model to African-Americans, as well as to whites and Hispanics.[11]

In the event The Salvation Army chose the other contender, Shaw Clifton. However, perhaps significant in his appointment was considerable experience of service in Africa. His strong academic credentials including a PhD and his numerous publications may suggest a particularly analytical and intellectual approach to the role. On taking office he noted:

I have inherited a strong Army. Today we are larger numerically around the world than at any time in our history.[12]

---

[8] *Source*: *The Salvation Army Annual Review*, 2005.
[9] *Source*: *The Salvation Army News*, 5 July (2005).
[10] 'Addressing lessons from the emergency response to the 7 July 2005 London bombings', UK Home Office, 22 September (2006).

[11] *Source*: *The Washington Post*, 8 April (2006).
[12] *Source*: Shaw Clifton's speech, 'Welcome and Dedication Meeting', Kensington, London, 8 April 2006.

APPENDIX 1

Salvation Army international activities, January 2006

Social programme

Residential

Hostels for homeless and transient	606
Capacity	34,681
Emergency lodges	185
Capacity	12,013
Children's homes	218
Capacity	9,320
Homes for the elderly	149
Capacity	8,655
Homes for the disabled	46
Capacity	1,667
Homes for the blind	8
Capacity	374
Remand and probation homes	61
Capacity	1,221
Homes for street children	37
Capacity	837
Mother and baby homes	48
Capacity	1,325
Training centres for families	19
Capacity	447
Care homes for vulnerable people	59
Capacity	1,071
Women's and men's refuge centres	87
Capacity	2,690
Other residential care homes/hostels	88
Capacity	4,748

Day care

Community centres	539
Early childhood education centres	114
Capacity	6,028
Day centres for the elderly	154
Capacity	9,100
Play groups	158
Capacity	4,664
Day centres for the hearing impaired	15
Capacity	122
Day centres for street children	11
Capacity	645
Day nurseries	196
Capacity	11,569
Drop-in centres for youth	276
Other day care centres	603
Capacity	14,886

Addiction dependency

Non-residential programmes	375
Capacity	29,452
Residential programmes	167
Capacity	9,235
Harbour Light programmes	35
Capacity	65,051
Other services for those with addictions	116
Capacity	6,785

Service to the armed forces

Clubs and canteens	24
Mobile units for service personnel	38
Chaplains	19

Emergency response

Disaster rehabilitation schemes (incl. civil unrest)	429
Participants	173,255

Refugee programmes – host country	16
Participants	7,523
Refugee rehabilitation programmes	12
Participants	6,470
Other response programmes	185
Participants	54,262

Services to the community

Prisoners visited	297,456
Prisoners helped on discharge	127,429
Police courts – people helped	329,727
Missing persons – applications	10,264
number traced	6,745
Night patrol/anti-suicide – number helped	351,064
Community youth programmes	764
Beneficiaries	49,075
Employment bureaux – applications	304,634
Initial referrals	91,262
Counselling – people helped	311,672
Feeding centres	612
General relief – people helped	13,686,003
Emergency relief	2,796,246
Emergency mobile units	1,333
Restaurants and cafés	226
Thrift stores/charity shops (social)	1,430
Apartments for elderly	629
Capacity	8,268
Hostels for students, workers, etc.	57
Capacity	2,977
Land settlements (SA villages)	13
Capacity	402

Health programme

General hospitals	20
Capacity	2,203
Maternity hospitals	13
Capacity	247
Other specialist hospitals	16
Capacity	1,906
General clinics	77
Specialist clinics	77
Capacity	387
Mobile clinics	37
Number of inpatients	260,509
Number of outpatients	1,030,748
Number of doctors/medics	920
Invalid/convalescent homes	27
Capacity	11,487
Health education programmes	419
Beneficiaries	450,894
Day care programmes	18

Education programme

Kindergarten/sub-primary	700
Primary schools	946
Upper primary and middle schools	201
Secondary and high schools	191
Number of pupils	482,870
Number of teachers	15,834
Vocational training schools	133
Schools for the blind	25
Schools for the disabled	10
Colleges, universities, staff training and distance learning centres	16

Source: The Year Book, The Salvation Army.

APPENDIX 2

International statistics (as at 1 January 2004)

Countries and other territories where SA serves	111	Other senior musical group members	66,257
Languages used in SA work	175	Senior and young people's local officers	119,160
Corps, outposts, societies, new plants and		Women's ministry members	505,586
recovery churches	14,966	League of mercy members	106,647
Goodwill centres	758	SAMF members	7,015
Officers	25,966	Over-60 clubs' members	109,295
Active	17,131	Men's fellowship members	58,507
Retired	8,835	Young people's band members	17,164
Auxiliary captains	134	Singing company members	90,562
Lieutenants	582	Other young people's music group members	61,249
Envoys/sergeants, full time	1,174	Sunday school members	616,946
Cadets	912	Junior youth group members	218,023
Employees	106,695	Senior youth group members	60,684
Senior soldiers	1,062,453	Corps-based community development	
Adherents	190,214	programmes	22,103
Junior soldiers	368,149	Beneficiaries	1,109,716
Corps cadets	43,488	Thrift stores/charity shops (corps)	1,583
Senior band musicians	23,273	Recycling centres	23
Senior songsters	97,677		

Source: *The Year Book*, The Salvation Army.

Bayer MaterialScience: responsible operations in Thailand and China

Lutz Kaufmann

This case study is based in the chemical industry and looks at the decisions of Germany's Bayer MaterialScience (BMS) when choosing appropriate measures of corporate social responsibility as part of setting up and running a plant in China.

• • •

Introduction

It was 21 March 2003 when Dr Dirk Van Meirvenne, Senior Vice President Production and Technology of Bayer MaterialScience (BMS), Polycarbonates Business Unit, and until recently responsible for the operations in Thailand, and his team were sitting at gate 15 of Frankfurt International Airport, waiting to board the plane to Bangkok. Then, 20 minutes before departure, Dr Frank Rövekamp, Head of Corporate Development at BMS, called:

> Mr. Meirvenne, you already know that BMS made its final decision to build a polycarbonate production plant in China some time ago. The Chinese government now asks us to provide them with a detailed investment and development plan for this undertaking. The required document should also include a chapter on our planned activities besides the core investment of erecting the production plant. We need to present and commit to certain activities that are more targeted at the surrounding community. That is the reason why I contact you as an expert from our operations and activities in Thailand. We count on your expertise and hope that we can transfer some of the gained knowledge to China. The deadline for this document is in one week and we really do not want to test the government's patience.

Mr Meirvenne quickly briefed his team since he wanted to use the flight to reflect on BMS's social activities in Thailand and to develop some initial thoughts for a holistic concept on how to implement Bayer's corporate social responsibility (CSR) policies in China. He knew that he would have to prioritise his suggested alternative fields of engagements due to economic restrictions. Another worry was to what extent the experiences from Thailand could be transferred to China.

Bayer AG

Bayer AG is the management holding company of the Bayer Group, which was founded in 1863. Today, Bayer is a research-based global enterprise with core competences in the fields of health care, nutrition and innovative high-tech materials. It is represented around the world by 350 companies, which market approximately 5,000 products. In fiscal year 2004, Bayer employed around 113,000 employees worldwide, spent €2.1bn (£1.5bn; $2.6bn) on research and development, generated net sales of €29.8bn and had a net profit of €603m.

With its global headquarters in Leverkusen, Gemany, Bayer's business is structured into three subgroups, Bayer HealthCare AG, Bayer CropScience AG and Bayer MaterialScience AG (BMS), which operate independently and have global responsibility for their businesses and management teams. They are supported by central service functions which are combined into the three service companies.

Bayer MaterialScience AG

BMS is one of the world's largest producers of polymers and high-tech plastics. In 2004, BMS employed around 17,900 employees, produced approximately 4 million tonnes of raw materials and generated sales of €8.6bn. Its main customers are the automotive and construction industries, the electrical/electronics segment and manufacturers of sports and leisure goods, packaging, and medical devices. BMS's roughly 40 production sites throughout the world ensure sufficient proximity to its major customers who demand flexible service and short delivery times. BMS does not neglect the importance of health, safety and the environment, which is reflected in the principles of its policy (see Appendix 1).

Corporate social responsibility of Bayer Group

Bayer believes that its technical and business expertise entails a responsibility to work for the benefit of society and to contribute to a sustained and environmentally-friendly development. The company states as its goal:

> 'to grow the value of our company over the long term and generate a high value added in the interests of our stockholders, employees and society at large in all the countries in which we operate'.

These objectives explain Bayer's commitment to CSR, which is believed to make a valuable contribution to the company's success.

Bayer started to invest in social activities soon after its foundation and has a long track record of welfare engagements. Its involvement in this area is part of the company's corporate culture and is not restricted only to meeting social needs in direct neighbourhoods of its production sites. In many cases, Bayer cooperates with non-governmental organisations (NGOs) to set up local or global initiatives that solve a wide variety of social problems.

Bayer derived its CSR objectives from the company's mission and strategy and is sure that its commitment to CSR contributes to the corporate success in various ways (see Appendix 2). Most activities are organised at the local level by Bayer's foreign subsidiaries, which can decide independently what instruments they prefer to use and which projects they want to support. At many sites,

Bayer also maintains public–private partnerships, which are cooperative projects with local and government organisations.

Bayer's CSR commitment covers a wide range of activities, which are supported by monetary and material donations or company foundations. Promoted activities include health education programmes and initiatives to improve child care, projects to combat child labour, education and vocational training, environmental protection, the promotion of culture and sports or projects to encourage cultural diversity and combat discrimination. Global projects are managed from Corporate Centre Communications in the Group's headquarters in Leverkusen. An example of such a project is the United Nations (UN) Global Compact Initiative (see Appendix 3 for Bayer's statement), which has the objective to pursue nine principles relating to human rights, labour standards and environmental protection on a global basis.

Sustainable development is a further aspect of Bayer's commitment to society and the environment. As partner to the United Nations Environment Programme (UNEP), Bayer supports and organises a number of projects, which aim to reinforce environmental awareness and advance knowledge about the environment among the young population.

Polycarbonates industry

Global polycarbonate market

In 1953, polycarbonate (PC) was invented by Dr Hermann Schnell of Bayer AG and shortly afterwards by Dr Daniel W. Fox at General Electric working independently. The global market for PC grew from 600,000 tonnes in 1990 to 1,800,000 tonnes in 2000. This strong growth continues as new developments and applications evolve. The market is served by a few big players (Bayer AG and General Electric Corp. have market shares of 28 per cent and 32 per cent respectively).

Generally PC is produced as resin, transported to appliance producers and further processed. It is naturally transparent, with the ability to transmit light nearly to the same degree as glass. It has high strength, toughness, heat resistance, and excellent dimensional and colour stability. The relatively high price of PC, however, restricts its use to mainly electronic and engineering applications such as CDs, DVDs, computer housings, sunglasses and automotive components.

BMS in Thailand

Bayer AG has been active in Thailand for more than four decades. In the late 1990s BMS decided to invest heavily in the newly acquired Map Ta Phut Industrial Estate in Rayong, about 150 kilometres east of Bangkok, following its strategy to expand in Asia. Production of its currently best-selling PC product Makrolon started at Map Ta Phut in September 1999.

Before production commenced, three challenges had to be met. First, the Thai government had to approve the investment. BMS had to find ways to convince the authorities. 'Development of the Kingdom' was the slogan chosen to achieve approval of the Map Ta Phut site. Arguments like modern, innovative technology transfer, creation of welfare and responsible development finally convinced the authorities. Since then, a close relationship with the king and the government has been established. Second, suppliers had to be developed, because there was no single supplier that could provide BMS with the required materials. Japanese, French and German companies were asked to start production of precursor products of PC close to the BMS Map Ta Phut plant. Third, the plant had to be built and tests had to be run. To run the plant, employees had to be recruited and educated to assure a smooth start in 1999. Therefore, the BMS crew learnt the Thai language and Thai employees were sent to Europe to be educated for one year. BMS has always been focused on the development and protection of its employees.

CSR in Thailand

'Responsible Care®' and 'Responsible Community Relations' are the two big CSR initiatives of Bayer and BMS in Thailand:

- *Responsible Care (RC)* is an international initiative adopted by chemical industries in more than 46 countries. Bayer companies across the world implemented RC including BMS Thailand. The goal of RC is to create a more positive public image that operations will have low risk with respect to health, safety and the environment. The strategy to achieve that goal can be divided into four parts which can be summarised by commitment, improvement, communication and reduction. In turn these have required the management practices shown in Appendix 4. These codes are an integral part of BMS's strategy in Thailand.

  The RC Codes of Management Practices affect not only BMS Thailand but also the upstream and downstream members of the value chain. For example, the Distribution Code requires suppliers to be aware of risks in distributing precursor products to BMS.

- *Responsible Community Relations (RCR)*. BMS has a range of activities within RCR. First, Bayer has always supported the king – for example, compiling a photographic book commemorating the 50th Anniversary of the King's Accession. In the same year, three scholarships were awarded to chemical engineering students to pursue their masters degrees at the University of Aachen, Germany. These measures resulted in a high reputation for all Bayer companies in Thailand. BMS integrates itself into the daily life of Thai society by weekly information visits to the Map Ta Phut site, by donating books and magazines to municipality school libraries, by educating pupils in subjects such as English or computer science and by a mobile health unit providing regular health care services for community members (see Appendix 5). Five students from Thailand were sent to Germany to learn how Thailand could improve environmental standards.

Despite all these activities Dirk Van Meirvenne wonders: 'Do those measures lead to achieving the CSR objectives? Are they effective? Can those measures be transferred to China?'

The People's Republic of China

Due to the immense growth of the Chinese market and the amount of PC delivered to customers across China, BMS started to plan the construction of a world-class plant in the new industrial park of Caojing near Shanghai in 2001.

Though not new to the market (Bayer has ties to China dating back as far as 1882 and has been serving the market with an independent trading entity that was established in Hong Kong in 1958), it became clear to Bayer that applying CSR measures was not only a question of reputation and building goodwill, but a strategic necessity that every company operating in China would have to face. In order to understand the specific situation of China, one has to know some basic facts about China and the Chinese society.

APPENDIX 4

Responsible Care Code of Management Practices, BMS Thailand

R C C O D E B M S T H A I L A N D	Process Safety	Prevent fires, explosions and accidental chemical releases with the expectation of continuous performance improvement. Exists of management leadership, technology, facilities and personnel.
	Employee Health/Safety	Protect and promote the health and safety of people working at or visiting member company work sites. Assess hazards, prevent unsafe acts and conditions, and foster communication on health and safety.
	Distribution	Reduce the risk of harm posed by the distribution of chemicals to the general public, to carrier, distributor, contractor, chemical industry employees and to the environment. Prevention by risk management.
	Emergency Response	Assure emergency preparedness and to foster community right-to-know. Community outreach program and an emergency response program helps to assure safety.
	Product Stewardship	Make health, safety, environmental protection an integral part of designing, manufacturing, marketing, distributing, using, recycling and disposing of products. Covers all stages of a product's life.
	Pollution Prevention	Achieve ongoing reductions in the amount of all contaminants and pollutants released to the air, water, and land from member company facilities. Broad waste management concept.

Source: Company information.

APPENDIX 5

Responsible community relations of Bayer and BMS in Thailand

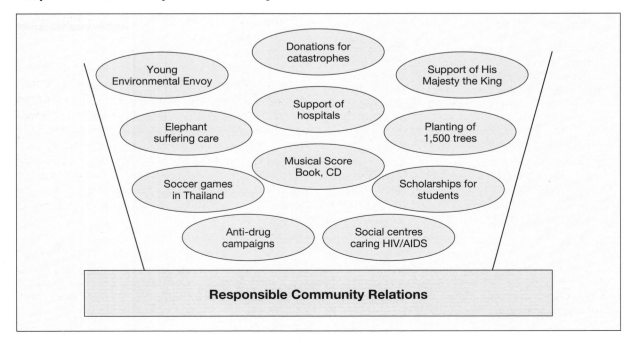

Source: Company information.

Eurotunnel's strategy journey: Anglo-Saxon creditors meet the French vision of capitalism

Geoff Goddin

This case investigates the key problems facing the managers of Eurotunnel, the cross-Channel tunnel and shuttle service operator, as it entered its 21st year of existence.

Eurotunnel's management had to negotiate a large debt write-off while retaining control and ownership for the shareholders, a task that UK commentators thought impossible. This case shows how contrasting stakeholder expectations, business cultures, and the differences in English and French legal and governance frameworks shaped the strategies followed by the management of this Anglo-French enterprise.

● ● ●

A significant announcement

On 2 August 2006 the Paris Commercial Court acceded to the Channel Tunnel operators' request of 13 July to place Eurotunnel and its constituent companies under 'judicial protection' while the company continued its commercial operations as normal.

Jacques Gounon, the Eurotunnel Chairman and Chief Executive, who is fluent in both English and French, remarked:

> In a difficult context, the Paris Commercial Court has made a positive decision which will protect the business and the public service it operates. The safeguard procedure decided upon today is the final stage of a consensual negotiation. I am convinced that we now have the conditions necessary to achieve a financial restructuring for Eurotunnel within the time allowed.
> *(Financial Times, 3 August 2006, p. 19)*

Why did Jacques Gounon welcome this move as good news for Eurotunnel's shareholders and the business?

The answer is found by examining Eurotunnel's unusual constitutional and legal position, its implausible financial position regarding debts and operational revenues, and the complex and conflicting stakeholder positions arising from its 'cross-cultural' structures of governance. These gave Eurotunnel's management negotiation opportunities not available to a UK or US company.

Eurotunnel: a cross-Channel and cross-cultural enterprise

Eurotunnel is a joint Anglo-French entity, Eurotunnel Plc and Eurotunnel SA, which under the 1986 Treaty of Canterbury, signed by President Mitterand and Prime Minister Margaret Thatcher, was granted the concession to build, maintain and operate the Channel Tunnel until 2086.

Eurotunnel operates shuttle trains between its terminals in Folkestone and Coquelles/Calais which carry cars, coaches and lorries. The revenues (see Exhibit 1) from these operations, together with handling utilities transmissions through the tunnel, account for roughly 60 per cent of total revenues. The remaining 40 per cent represents tolls paid by through rail services operated by Eurostar for passengers and EWS/SNCF for rail freight. That is, Eurostar is a major customer of Eurotunnel.

'Minimum Usage Charge' (MUC) paid each year.

The MUC came about because in 1994 Eurotunnel's railway customers, namely Eurostar and EWS/SNCF, signed a 12-year agreement to reserve 50 per cent of tunnel capacity for their trains. But by 2005 the actual traffic levels of 7.5 million passengers and 1.5 million tonnes of freight were well below original forecasts for 2005 of 23 million passengers and 11 million tonnes. In reality the rail customers are only using a third of tunnel capacity.

Thus the *Financial Times* talked of the tunnel facing a 'cash crunch'.

Eurotunnel's revenues and debts

In 2005 Eurotunnel had managed, by a voluntary staff redundancy programme, and by running less shuttles with higher load factors, to cut its operating expenses by 4 per cent from the previous year. Combined with a 2 per cent rise in transport revenues the tunnel enjoyed an operating margin (cash flow) of over 55 per cent of total revenue. (See below.)

But the tunnel carried a debt of £6.18bn (€8.96bn), the interest of which, £289m p.a., would be nearly twice the trading profit, clearly an unsustainable situation.

From 2007 this difficult situation would worsen for two reasons. First, Eurotunnel was scheduled to commence staged repayment of the debt principal; second, the company will lose about £72m in tunnel user tolls represented by the guaranteed

Eurotunnnel's stakeholder groups

Shareholders: mostly French individuals, mostly dissatisfied

From Exhibit 2 we can see that Eurotunnel has an unusual proportion of individual shareholders.

The 150,000 UK-based shareholders, who hold about 5 per cent of Eurotunnel's shares, enjoy substantial travel discounts when using the tunnel. 'Founder shareholders' pay £1 each way if they held 1000+ shares from 1987, others get a 30 per cent discount.

The 900,000 French shareholders are less keen about making cheap crossings to Folkestone, and are much more concerned to protect their investment and receive dividends. They had been encouraged by investment advisors to view

Exhibit 1	Eurotunnel: key financial data		
(Provisional unaudited 2005 figures)		**£m**	**Change 2004–2005**
Revenues shuttles		295	+4%
+ Revenues rail user tolls		235	
Revenues total transport activities		530	+2%
+ Revenues utilities		11	
Total revenues		541	+1%
Less operating expenses		242	−4%
Operating margin		299	+4%
Less indirect costs		146	
Trading profit		153	+19%

Source: *Eurotunnel Annual Review*, 2005.

Exhibit 2   **Shareholder analysis**

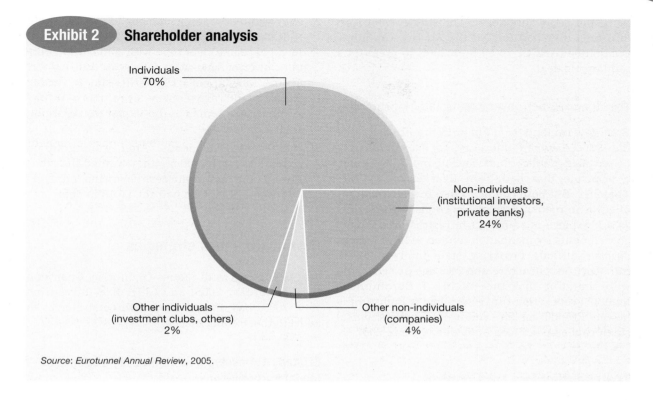

Individuals
70%

Non-individuals
(institutional investors,
private banks)
24%

Other individuals
(investment clubs, others)
2%

Other non-individuals
(companies)
4%

Source: Eurotunnel Annual Review, 2005.

Eurotunnel as a boring but profitable long-term infrastructure utility, spurred on by the share price nearly tripling in the late 1980s *before the tunnel opened*; these investors often had the shares in their pension funds.

Creditors: mostly American, mostly unsympathetic

Initially the tunnel's debt was held by the 174 project finance banks such as HSBC and the European Investment Bank (EIB). But in most cases the original holders had sold on the 'distressed' debt to financial intermediaries (such as hedge funds) as Eurotunnel began to promise less return and more risk. The sold-on debt would be bought at a discount to face value, sometimes for as little as 12p in the pound; this was particularly true for 'bondholders' who held £1.9bn of the lowest-ranked (highest-risk) 'bonds' and 'notes' in Eurotunnel's debt structure (see Exhibit 3).

The holders of £3.95bn of the higher-ranked (least-risky) Tier 1A and Junior debt were in a more powerful position to negotiate with the com-

Exhibit 3   **Eurotunnel debt structure, 2006**

£m	Debt	Interest p.a	Value as % face value 2006
Senior debt	366	21	
Tier 1A	740	51	Low risk 'secured'
Junior debt	3,212	157	60%
Resettable bonds	464	23	20%
Stabilisation notes	538	28	High risk 'unsecured'
Participating loan notes	862	9	
Total debt	6,182	289	

Source: Financial Times, 14 July (2006).

pany and could threaten to 'substitute' their own directors; they had formed the Ad Hoc Creditors' Committee (AHCC), in autumn 2005, to press for a refinancing deal.

The UK and French governments: differing priorities

Both governments stood behind the provisions of the 1986 Treaty of Canterbury, not least in refusing to advance public funds to bail out Eurotunnel, a principle that had been insisted on by Mrs Thatcher. But both countries had invested billions of euros in road and rail connections to the tunnel as a key piece of transport infrastructure. French governments by inclination tended to have a more *dirigiste* attitude favouring state intervention in transport infrastructure and prestige projects, and were mindful that the plight of Eurotunnel's million French retail investors had a high profile in the French media, and would have political significance in an election to take place in 2007.

The shareholders take control – 7 April 2004

French shareholders had become extremely dissatisfied with the mainly British-led board which in 2004 announced a continuing fall in revenues and shuttle traffic figures, a share price below 40p, and no sight of a dividend payment. They formed ADACTE, the *Association des Actionnaires d'Eurotunnel*, in 2002 to coordinate a shareholder campaign against the board and its strategy. They were led by Nicolas Miguet, a French financial journalist with political aspirations. At a stormy AGM in Paris on 7 April 2004 shareholders voted by over 60 per cent to eject the existing board and install a new and entirely French board, the first shareholder-led revolution in French corporate history!

Many of the lengthy and sometimes emotional speeches made by individuals at the 2004 AGM had three common themes:

1 They wanted the French board to be tougher on the mainly Anglo-Saxon creditors of Eurotunnel, whom Miguet had described as 'Banksters'. The 'British-led' board had appeared more concerned with repaying creditors than investing in the tunnel or rewarding shareholders, thus they had kept fares high, bringing about a worrying intensification in ferry competition.

2 They wanted strategy changes to achieve more profitable operation of the tunnel. Though it quickly became clear that, with some ferry operators offering one-way tickets as little as £25 against Eurotunnel's £98 tariff, simply raising prices would drive away even more traffic, so other means had to be explored, regarding pricing and costs.

3 They wanted dividends. After waiting up to 17 years as shareholders, they wanted the creditors to take less in interest payments, implying a write-off of at least half the £6.18bn debt.

New board – new strategies

The new board with Jaques Gounon as Chairman (since February 2005) and Chief Executive (from June 2005) has driven forward three strategies to address those concerns.

Strategy 1: Develop a more profitable business model for tunnel operations

A new commercial strategy for car, coach and lorry customers was implemented from summer 2005. Truck traffic was growing annually, but the overall cross-Channel car and coach market was static despite tunnel and ferry competition bringing about much lower fares. This contrasts with 'low-cost' airlines where competition and low fares brought about a rapid rise in passenger numbers.

Europe's major road hauliers, such as Norbet Dentressangle's distinctive red trucks, who alone make 100,000 crossings a year, are 60 per cent of Eurotunnel's lorry customers. A lorry strategy was introduced based on users supplying daily

Jacques Gounon

forecasts which were matched to priority crossings and guaranteed service. This caused truck traffic to grow by 3 per cent to 1,308,786 lorries in 2005. Non-booking hauliers are still carried on a 'turn-up' basis, but pay a higher toll and may have to wait for a slot.

On passenger (car, coach, motorcycle) shuttles Eurotunnel introduced a long-overdue dynamic pricing model using online pre-booking and 'yield management' pricing models common for many years in the airline business. Thus customers are encouraged to pre-book (now 70 per cent book online), and tolls take account of crossing time, direction (lowest fare £49 from UK, €55 from France), and available capacity.

This strategy has enabled Eurotunnel to hold car volumes at 2,047,166 yet run 30 per cent fewer shuttles, thus achieving higher shuttle capacity load factors of 59 per cent (45 per cent in 2004). With lorries Eurotunnel has been able to run 15 per cent fewer truck shuttles, but maintain service quality and achieve load factors of 71 per cent (59 per cent in 2004).

Online pre-booking and paying has been further encouraged by the installation of 24 touch-screen 'self-service' lanes from January 2006, which speed the transit from toll to embarkation, and further save call centre and check-in costs.

These new operational strategies enabled Euro-tunnel to reduce its 3,200 Anglo-French workforce by a quarter. Employment protection in France entitles French workers to more generous levels of voluntary redundancy compensation than for UK workers, but it was felt politic by the company to accept equal numbers of volunteers from each side of the Channel, and pay the more generous French levels of compensation to all.

The first year of operation of the new commercial strategy saw shuttle revenues grow for the first time since 2002, by +4 per cent, which together with cost savings associated with operational changes and the reduction of the workforce improved profits by 19 per cent (see Exhibit 1).

Higher profitability of course raises the enterprise value for creditors and shareholders, and would improve Eurotunnel's ability to pay debt, or dividends.

Strategy 2: Develop shareholder relations

Aware of its unusually high proportion of private shareholders, Eurotunnel had in 1996 set up UK and French shareholder committees which met quarterly with the board to 'advise on shareholder communication'. Clearly, however, despite exemplary shareholder consultation structures, communication at least with the French shareholders seemed to have totally broken down by 2004.

The new board launched monthly newsletters in April 2005, *Eurotunnel on Track* and *La voie de l'Avenir*; 20,000 shareholders also access them online together with e-mailed news flashes about major events affecting the group, which are archived on the www.eurotunnel.com website.

The composition of the board in particular reflects the interests of the French shareholders. The seven-member board includes Joseph Gouranton as representing the interest of ADACTE, and Mme Collette Neuville, co-opted in January 2006, who is President of 'ADAM', the Association for the Defence of Minority Shareholders. Both these board members had supported Jacques Gounon when he was elected as Chief Executive at the 17 June 2005 AGM.

Prior to that AGM, Gounon had argued that creditors would need to 'forgive' nearly two-thirds of the £6.18bn debt, based on his view that the company's cash flow would remain the same whether or not creditors seized control of the tunnel: 'I have never considered that I have a tough approach to the negotiations. I just remind them that we cannot invent profit.'

Jean-Louis Raymond, the previous Chief Executive since April 2004, had called for a more 'consensual' and less aggressive stance to be taken with creditors, and had argued for higher peak tunnel fares 'because ferry operators could not afford to cut prices much more'.

The creditors preferred Raymond's stance, but they thought both candidates' views 'unrealistic'. A London-based creditor source commented:

> If someone wins this election by raising unrealistic expectations, then they are deluding shareholders into thinking they will get something for nothing (i.e. less debt and no dilution of shareholder control) . . . if they think creditors will take a haircut on this, well, it just isn't going to happen.

Nicolas Miguet initially supported a campaign against Gounon's chairmanship, but at the June 2005 AGM the mercurial Miguet announced a volte-face and supported the reappointment of Gounon as Chair and Chief Executive with a solid majority.

Most financial observers commented that whatever positions taken to win shareholders' votes for their candidature at the June 2005 AGM, previously financial restructurings such as Marconi, British Energy, and Alstom had inevitably involved 'swapping' of debt for equity, that is 'dilution', leaving existing shareholders only 1 or 2 per cent of the company. But as at least 55 per cent of Eurotunnel shareholders would have to vote 'yes' to any restructuring plan, would French shareholders accept such a loss?

Strategy 3: The negotiation of a reduction of Eurotunnel's £6.18bn debt

New creditors – new cultures

When Eurotunnel embarked on its first financial restructuring in September 1995, it largely dealt with the 174 consortium banks that had financed the project alongside the shareholders. That creditor culture reflected an informal understanding that the lenders would support 'their' company through tough times and take a longer-term view of profitability. The Bank of England often stepped in to help broker agreement between lenders in what was known as the 'London Approach' to debt restructuring.

But by 2005 the *Financial Times* (23 June 2005, p. 22) noted that about 70 per cent of Eurotunnel's debt was held by US hedge funds which were likely to have no sympathy with French, and by implication Gounon's, visions of creditor capitalists having responsibilities to a wider set of stakeholders in the enterprise, and unlikely to agree to a carte blanche shareholder bailout.

The funds also traded the debt actively for profit, making it all but impossible for the Bank of England to broker an agreement between a stable set of creditors.

Unfortunately the French cultural view of such hedge funds echoed the German Vice Chancellor Franz Müntefering's 2005 description of them as '*Locusts . . . having no interest in the wider enterprise, its employees, customers, or shareholders*'. The *Financial Times* (17 June 2005, p. 22) noted: '[this] will undoubtedly make Eurotunnel a fascinating future business school case study of the clash between different visions of how capitalism should be done'.

Debt negotiations commence

Straight after the June 2005 AGM, Eurotunnel commenced negotiations with the 'Ad Hoc Creditors Committee' (AHCC) comprising MBIA (a US insurer), EIB, and Hedge Funds Franklin Mutual and Oaktree Capital Management. Eurotunnel insisted that AHCC members signed a memorandum of understanding with the company so that a restructuring agreement could be negotiated, so that sensitive company information could be disclosed under confidentiality and 'no-trading' rules. This they did on 31 January 2006.

The company needed a deal within 12 months. It became liable to pay all debt interest from July 2006, it would lose £72m p.a. of MUC revenues from November 2006, and was due to start debt capital repayments from January 2007.

The creditors had concern for Gounon's often-repeated view that the French courts, under whose jurisdiction the Anglo-French company fell, would not allow the '*substitution*' (of a creditor-appointed management) for such a politically sensitive company. In an interview with the *Financial Times* (15 June 2005, p. 23) he dismissed the creditors' position as 'Anglo-Saxon', saying: 'We have to take care that Eurotunnel is more a French company than a UK one.'

Under the provisions of the 1986 Treaty of Canterbury, AHCC senior debt holders held rights of '*substitution*', while the 'bondholders' lacked such rights. But both the UK and French governments had to approve any creditor business plan before '*substitution*' would be permitted. '*The French government, I think, would use that as a tool not to approve the idea of substitution*' commented a debt analyst (*Financial Times*, 13 April 2006, p. 23).

A missed opportunity to cut debt?

In 2005 Eurotunnel also had the option to convert or 'pay off' £538m of 'stabilisation notes' debt by the issue of new shares, at a fixed value of 114p per share, as against the then market share price of $16\frac{1}{2}$p, in effect a $14\frac{1}{2}$ per cent payback of this debt, which also saved £28m p.a. in interest. However, to secure conversion, even at such advantageous terms, the board would have had to secure shareholder approval at an AGM, just three months after its re-election on a platform of 'no shareholder equity dilution'.

On 28 September the board declined to take up the conversion option, to the delight of the bondholders.

Spring 2006 brinkmanship, Eurotunnel pressures for a deal

The alert procedure

In February 2006 an '*Alert*' had been initiated by the French Auditors *Commissaires aux Comptes*,

Exhibit 4	Eurotunnel restructuring proposals: two competing plans

	Eurotunnel/ AHCC plan (£bn)	Deutsche/ ARCO plan (£bn)
Senior debt	2.55	2.55
Mezzanine debt	0.35	0
'Hybrid' debt/equity convertible instrument	1.0	1.5
Rights issue	0	0.53
Debt written off (%)	3.3 (54%)	3.65 (59%)
Ongoing interest p.a. (Deutsche figures)	0.25	0.17
Future enterprise valuation	4.2	5.44
Minimum shareholder dilution	0%	0%
Maximum dilution for shareholders if hybrid		
Not redeemed or rights taken up	87%	84.5%

Sources: ARCO, Eurotunnel, *Financial Times*.

due to uncertainty as to whether Eurotunnel would be a 'going concern' beyond the year end. So in April the company decided to cancel publication of its 2005 accounts: 'An opportunity to put pressure on the negotiations . . . and conclude' commented Gounon (*Financial Times*, 13 April 2006, p. 23). Under the *Alert* procedure an AGM would have to be held by 27 July. Trading in Eurotunnel shares in London and Paris was suspended in May.

Restructuring agreements: two creditor groups compete for Eurotunnel

AHCC signed a restructuring agreement with Eurotunnel on 31 May. The headline terms were a 54 per cent write-off of the £6.18bn debt to £2.9bn (see Exhibit 4).

In this, £2.9bn of the senior debt would be refinanced or run on, and a £1bn 'hybrid' loan instrument would be used to redeem the remaining debt. This hybrid loan could be redeemed by company profits or a shareholders rights issue within five years at a cost of £1.6bn, or would be converted into shares whereby the creditors would control up to 87 per cent of Eurotunnel.

Thus (in a best case scenario) Gounon's insistence of 'no dilution' was delivered on; it was also a good deal for the AHCC creditors and their financiers.

But the plan needed support from 55 per cent of shareholders and 75 per cent of the holders of *each*

tier of debt; the 'bondholders' were only offered £75m compensation for their £1.9bn of debt, a 4 per cent payback, reflecting their limited legal powers and the low market value of their debt.

Unsurprisingly the 'bondholders' saw themselves as the losers in the AHCC plan, at the expense of the senior debt holders, financing banks and Eurotunnel shareholders. Led by Deutsche Bank, the 'Association of Eurotunnel's Secured Bondholders' (ARCO) now signed the required confidentiality and 'no-trading' agreements, and on 25 June they presented a rival restructuring plan (see Exhibit 4) appearing to offer lower debt, lower future interest payments (and hence more chance of dividend for Eurotunnel's shareholders).

With ARCO backing its own plan against the AHCC one, even at risk of an insolvency, Eurotunnel was faced with a conflict in creditor positions that needed to be resolved. Nicolas Miguet, who claimed to direct 19 per cent of the share vote, hoped both groups would compete to offer shareholders the best deal for their company.

July 2006: the deadline passes – a new era for Eurotunnel

Only on 12 July did the first three-way talks between Eurotunnel, AHCC and ARCO commence in Paris, less than 36 hours before the second waiver agreement expired.

With no firm creditor agreement in place for a successful vote at the 27 July AGM at Coquelles, Eurotunnel applied for a *'procédure de sauvegarde'* with the Paris Commercial Court, which was a new and untested French enterprise protection law.

This law allowed Eurotunnel to continue operations managed by the current directors for a six-month 'observation period' and to suspend paying debt interest. The Paris court appointed two creditor representatives, *mandataires judiciaires*, and two enterprise representatives, *administrateurs judiciaires*, to oversee negotiations between Eurotunnel and its creditors. Jacques Gounon saw this as the final stage to secure an agreed restructuring: 'I am convinced that we now have all the conditions necessary to achieve a financial restructuring for Eurotunnel within the time allowed'. Any proposed plan would then have to be approved by creditors and shareholders.

Eurotunnel was the largest and most financially complex company so far to be placed under *procédure de sauvegarde* protection, and the French court was thought likely to be sympathetic to the prestigious infrastructure project which was co-sponsored by the French government, also to its employees, shareholders and the French management team. The creditors meanwhile were obliged to hire French legal advisors and pursue their claims within an unfamiliar legal and business culture environment.

Eurotunnel regarded the *procédure de sauvegarde* as a pre-insolvency protection mechanism: 'There is one goal: the pursuit of the continuity of operations through negotiation with committees of the major creditors' (Eurotunnel on Track, September 2006).

By the end of October the *administrateurs judiciaires* – Maître Emmanuel Hess and Maître Laurent Le Guernevé – were able to state that Eurotunnel's 'proposed safeguard restructuring plan, constitutes a real point of equilibrium between many, often contradictory and sometimes antinomic demands'. Despite continuing rancour and division, the senior creditors voted 72 per cent in favour on 27 November, followed by a 69 per cent vote in favour by the bondholders on 14 December.

On 15 January the supervising judge, M Bernard Soutumier, gave the Paris court's approval to the restructuring plan, and at the same time dismissed 33 creditor petitions in less than 30 minutes. To add insult to injury each of the creditor litigants had to pay €10,000 towards Eurotunnel's costs.

Under the plan only £2.53bn of the most senior debt is transferred at face value to the new holding company, Groupe Eurotunnel SA. Holders of the remaining £3.66bn are offered £240m (a 6.5 per cent payback), or an opportunity to participate in the lucrative financing of a £1.17bn 'hybrid' loan. Eurotunnel made participation in this loan conditional on dropping any further litigation, and the two largest litigants, Oaktree Capital Management and Franklin, duly did so; having just seen £3bn of debt 'written off' the hedge funds were not about to throw good money after bad!

When shareholders move their shares into Groupe Eurotunnel SA, the company for the first time in its history will have a level of debt (£2.84bn) that can be serviced by conservative projections of revenue and cash flow (see Exhibit 5).

Depending on the proportion of the hybrid loan 'redeemed' by 2010, shareholder ownership of the company will be between 13 per cent and 67 per cent. This is in stark contrast to the situation had Eurotunnel been put into 'administration' under UK insolvency procedures, where control of the company is taken away from the shareholders and directors. It is not clear that the creditors would

Exhibit 5	The safeguard business plan		
£m	2007	2008	2009
Gross revenues	526	537	555
Operating profit	264	268	283
Interest on debt	139	139	140
Interest on hybrid loan	62	60	58
Thus positive cash flow	63	69	85

Source: Cash flow projections from 'Eurotunnel on Track', January (2007).

The Management and Shareholder Committee celebrating Eurotunnel's 20th anniversary

have fared any better as they had conflicting positions in the company's 'debt hierarchy', and the costs of legal battles as well as the costs of the administration process would have been enormous. It needs to be remembered that junior creditors had only paid a fraction of the 'face value' of the debt they held (revisit Exhibit 3), thus were mostly facing paper rather than real losses.

In September 2006 Gounon had proposed the 'nuclear option' of the two states withdrawing the concession to operate if Eurotunnel was put into administration. Had this happened the creditors would have been left with unusable assets of little value. More relevantly it is likely that in a creditor-led administration focused only on short-term payback, the consistency and effectiveness of Eurotunnel's commercial strategies would have suffered, and new investment initiatives would have been stifled.

Vive Le Groupe Eurotunnel: a conclusion

In addition to the usual conflict of interest between stakeholder groups found in all enterprises, Eurotunnel's difficulty (or opportunity?) was not only the clash of perspectives *between* Anglo-Saxon creditors and largely French shareholders, but also differences of perspective *within* each stakeholder group. The case highlights how 'European' perspectives on enterprise governance and the relative rights and responsibilities of the enterprise and its stakeholders differ from those prevalent in US and UK business cultures in the twenty-first century. Eurotunnel's management have used their understanding of key stakeholder power and expectations to try to negotiate an alternative strategy to insolvency, which was thought impossible by Anglo-Saxon business analysts. It will shortly be apparent whether the French legislative and governance frameworks they have exploited will enable Eurotunnel to do strategy differently as it continues to operate its business.

Provisional figures supplied by Eurotunnel in January 2007 suggest that revenues rose by 5 per cent in 2006 to £568m and operating margin improved to 59 per cent, even though actual vehicles carried fell by 1 per cent. Eurostar is at last growing rapidly at over 5 per cent yearly. When the new high-speed rail link from London, St Pancras, to the tunnel opens in November 2007, London and Paris will be just over two hours apart by rail, but still worlds apart in their business cultures, and in the legal and governance frameworks in which they operate!

Ryanair – the low-fares airline

Eleanor O'Higgins

Ryanair was the first budget airline in Europe, modelled after the successful US carrier, Southwest Airlines. The case offers students the opportunity to evaluate the strategy of Ryanair against the backdrop of the European airline industry and the burgeoning budget sector, in the response to the challenges facing the industry as a whole, and Ryanair in particular. The case also offers the opportunity to evaluate Ryanair's bid for fellow Irish carrier, Aer Lingus. The colourful personality of Ryanair CEO, Michael O'Leary, is an additional point of interest in the case.

● ● ●

Shock and awe

'He never fails to surprise, that man – it's incredible.' This was the reaction of a prominent Irish bookmaker to the shocking news that Ryanair, Europe's leading budget airline, led by its CEO Michael O'Leary, had launched a €1.48bn (£1.02bn) bid for its Irish rival, Aer Lingus, just a week after the flotation of the legacy national carrier.[1] Ryanair revealed that it had already procured 19.2 per cent of the shares through its stockbroker, Davy, and claimed that its all-cash offer of €2.80 a share represented a 27 per cent premium over the flotation price of €2.20. It intended to retain the Aer Lingus brand and

> up-grade their dated long-haul product, and reduce their short-haul fares by 2.5 per cent per year for a minimum of 4 years . . . the combination of Aer Lingus and Ryanair into one strong Irish airline group will be rewarding for consumers and will enable both to vigorously compete with the mega carriers in Europe . . . there are significant opportunities, by combining the purchasing power of Ryanair and Aer Lingus, to substantially reduce its operating costs, increase efficiencies, and pass these savings on in the form of lower fares to Aer Lingus' consumers.[2]

------

[1] Companies UK, 'Ryanair sets its cap at local rival Aer Lingus', *Financial Times*, 7 October (2006), p. 21.
[2] Statement from Ryanair's half-yearly results presentation, 6 November 2006.

Among those surprised by the bid were many Ryanair investors, who were concerned that it could distract the carrier from its heretofore successful ruthless approach to cost cutting, by taking on an airline with long-haul routes. In the past it had made a successful acquisition, but it was of a small (2 million passengers) Dutch budget, short-haul carrier, Buzz, which was easily absorbed. While perceived as a departure from its organic growth model, that deal had nevertheless been greeted as a coup for Ryanair. Apart from the bargain purchase price, it was a golden opportunity to pick up a ready-made bundle of take-off and landing slots at London Stansted Airport.

It had been quite an achievement by the Irish government finally to have floated Aer Lingus after many false starts and much agonising over a number of years. Once they recovered their collective breaths, Aer Lingus and its board firmly rejected the Ryanair approach. They said Ryanair had acted in 'a hostile, anticompetitive manner designed to eliminate a rival at a derisory price'. A combined Ryanair–Aer Lingus operation would account for 80 per cent of all flights between Ireland and other European countries. Aer Lingus Chief Executive Dermot Mannion said his company was fundamentally opposed to a merger with Ryanair, even if it raises its price. 'I cannot conceive of the circumstances where the Aer Lingus management and Ryanair would be able to work harmoniously

------

Photo: Yves Herman/Reuters/Corbis

although it would not have a seat on the Aer Lingus board. In fact, Michael O'Leary had previously admitted defeat for the bid when he realised it would not receive the necessary support, declaring that 'Aer Lingus has no long-term future', and that if the bid did not go through, Ryanair would not increase its price, but would continue to be a minority shareholder and exercise what influence it could to encourage Aer Lingus to reduce costs and offer lower fares.[4]

together', Mannion said in an interview. 'This is simply a reflection of the fact that these organisations have been competing head to head, without fear or favour, for 20 years. It would be like merging Manchester United and Liverpool football clubs. You just wouldn't do it.'[3]

In fact, the bid was opposed by a loose alliance representing almost 47 per cent of Aer Lingus shares. This included the Irish government, which still retained a 25.4 per cent holding, two investment funds operated on behalf of Aer Lingus pilots accounting for about 4 per cent of shares, and Irish telecom tycoon Denis O'Brien, who bought 2.1 per cent of shares explicitly to complicate Ryanair's move. A critical 12.6 per cent of the shareholding was controlled by members of the Aer Lingus employee share ownership trust (ESOT), whose members rejected the Ryanair offer by a 97 per cent majority vote, dismissing Ryanair's claim that each ESOT member stood to receive an average of €60,000 from the transaction, saying it would actually amount to only €32,000 after borrowing costs. The ESOT had the right to appoint two directors to the Aer Lingus board and a stake in future profits, under an agreement reached ahead of the flotation.

Although Ryanair had built its stake to 25.2 per cent, in December 2006, it pulled the Aer Lingus bid, in the face of serious misgivings about competition and lack of choice for passengers expressed by the European authorities, which announced the start of an in-depth investigation into the offer. However, Ryanair declared that it intended to make a further offer in the event of the deal eventually being cleared by the European Commission. In the meantime, it would retain its blocking stake,

Overview of Ryanair

Ryanair was founded in 1985 by the Ryan family, headed by Tony Ryan, to provide scheduled passenger airline services between Ireland and the UK, as an alternative to then state monopoly carrier, Aer Lingus. Initially, Ryanair was a full-service conventional airline, with two classes of seating, leasing three different types of aircraft. Despite a growth in passenger volumes, by the end of 1990, the company had flown through a great deal of turbulence, disposing of five chief executives, and accumulating losses of IR£20m. Its fight to survive in the early 1990s saw the airline successfully restyle itself to become Europe's first low-fares, no-frills carrier, built on the model of Southwest Airlines, the highly successful Texas-based operator. A new management team, led by Michael O'Leary, then a reluctant recruit, was appointed by Tony Ryan. Ryanair, first floated on the Dublin Stock Exchange in 1997, is quoted on the Dublin and London Stock Exchanges and on NASDAQ, where it was admitted to the NASDAQ-100 in 2002.

Ryanair in full flight

The world's most profitable airline

Up to Ryanair's announcement that it was bidding for Aer Lingus, it appeared to be business as usual for the company. It was continuing to outperform all other airlines, not only in its own European battleground, but also globally. In August 2006, an *Air Transport World* magazine announced that Ryanair

[3] S. Pogatchnik, 'Aer Lingus rejects Ryanair takeover offer', *Business Week* online, 3 November 2006. Manchester United and Liverpool have a long-standing legendary rivalry in English football.

[4] E. Oliver, 'Ryanair's profits rise 38% as Aer Lingus bid falters', *Irish Times*, 7 November (2006), p. 21.

was the most profitable airline in the world, on the basis of its operating and net profit margins, on a per-airplane and per-passenger basis.

In November 2006, the airline announced record half-year profits of €329m for the first half of fiscal 2007. Traffic grew by 23 per cent to 22.1 million passengers; yields increased by 9 per cent as total revenues rose by 33 per cent to €1.256bn. Ancillary revenues grew by 27 per cent. Unit costs increased by 7.5 per cent. Despite 42 per cent higher fuel costs of €337m, Ryanair's after-tax margin for the half-year rose by 1 point to 26 per cent. (Ryanair's

financial data is given in Exhibits 1a and 1b, and operating data is given in Exhibit 1c.)

Growth and expansion

At its 2006 Annual General Meeting on 21 September in Dublin and its Investor Briefing Day in New York on 26 September, Ryanair offered its investors good news. The airline had delivered a 12 per cent increase in net profit, despite a 74 per cent increase in fuel costs. Traffic had grown 26 per cent from 27.6 million passengers in 2005 to

---

Exhibit 1a Ryanair profit statement

	Half-year to 30 Sept. 2006 €000	Full year to 31 Mar. 2006 €000	Full year to 31 Mar. 2005 €000
Operating revenues			
Scheduled revenues	1,092,102	1,433,377	1,128,116
Ancillary revenues	164,321	259,153	190,921
Total operating revenues – continuing operations	*1,256,423*	*1,692,530*	*1,319,037*
Operating expenses			
Staff costs	(113,844)	(171,412)	(141,673)
Depreciation	(71,622)	(124,405)	(110,357)
Fuel and oil	(337,042)	(462,466)	(265,276)
Maintenance, materials and repairs	(21,313)	(37,417)	(26,280)
Marketing and distribution costs	(11,608)	(13,912)	(19,622)
Aircraft rentals	(25,394)	(47,376)	(21,546)
Route charges	(98,384)	(164,577)	(135,672)
Airport and handling charges	(139,097)	(216,301)	(178,384)
Other	(52,312)	(79,618)	(79,489)
Total operating expenses	*(870,616)*	*(1,317,484)*	*(978,299)*
Operating profit – continuing operations	*385,807*	*375,046*	*340,738*
Other (expenses)/income			
Foreign exchange (losses)	(1,229)	(1,234)	(2,302)
Gain on disposal of property, plant and equipment	–	815	47
Finance income	28,923	38,219	28,342
Finance expense	(41,311)	(73,958)	(57,629)
Total other (expenses)/income	*(13,617)*	*(36,158)*	*(31,542)*
Profit before taxation	*372,190*	*338,888*	*309,196*
Tax on profit on ordinary activities	(43,063)	(32,176)	(29,153)
Profit for the financial year	*329,127*	*306,712*	*280,043*
Earnings per ordinary share (in € cent)			
Basic	42.67	40.00	36.85
Diluted	42.39	39.74	36.65
Adjusted earnings per ordinary share (in € cent)			
Basic	42.67	39.32	35.28
Diluted	42.39	39.07	35.09
Weighted average number of ordinary shares (000)			
Basic	711,413	766,833	759,911
Diluted	776,456	771,781	764,003

Source: Ryanair Annual Report.

Exhibit 1b   Ryanair balance sheet

	Half-year to 30 Sept. 2006 €000	Full year to 31 Mar. 2006 €000	Full year to 31 Mar. 2005 €000
Non-current assets			
Property, plant and equipment	2,550,162	2,532,988	2,117,891
Intangible assets	46,841	46,841	46,841
Derivative financial instruments	3,888	763	
Available for sale financial asset	185,363		
Total non-current assets	*2,786,254*	*2,580,592*	*2,164,732*
Current assets			
Inventories	3,627	3,422	2,460
Other assets	48,842	29,453	24,612
Trade receivables	24,207	29,909	20,644
Derivative financial instruments	502	18,872	
Restricted cash	204,040	204,040	204,040
Financial assets: cash > 3 months	824,314	328,927	529,407
Cash and cash equivalents	1,064,692	1,439,004	872,258
Total current assets	*2,170,224*	*2,053,627*	*1,653,421*
Total assets	*4,956,478*	*4,634,219*	*3,818,153*
Current liabilities			
Trade payables	87,903	79,283	92,118
Accrued expenses and other liabilities	519,835	570,614	418,653
Current maturities of long-term debt	158,049	153,311	120,997
Derivative financial instruments	69,854	27,417	
Current tax	46,331	15,247	17,534
Total current liabilities	*881,972*	*845,872*	*649,302*
Non-current liabilities			
Provisions	22,723	16,722	7,236
Derivative financial instruments	74,864	81,897	
Deferred income tax liability	134,881	127,260	104,180
Other creditors	68,396	46,066	29,072
Long-term debt	1,476,874	1,524,417	1,293,860
Total non-current liabilities	*1,777,738*	*1,796,362*	*1,434,348*
Shareholders' equity			
Issued share capital	9,807	9,790	9,675
Share premium account	602,664	596,231	565,756
Retained earnings	1,796,750	1,467,623	1,158,584
Other reserves	(112,453)	(81,659)	488
Shareholders' equity	2,296,768	1,991,985	1,734,503
Total liabilities and shareholders' equity	*4,956,478*	*4,634,219*	*3,818,153*

Source: Ryanair Annual Report.

34.8 million in 2006, giving a 27 per cent increase in passenger revenues. Indeed, on the cover of its 2006 Annual Report, Ryanair designated itself as the 'World's Favourite Airline', on the basis that it predicted that it would be carrying 42 million passengers in 2007, surpassing even Lufthansa which carried over 39 million passengers on its intra-European routes in 2005. (However, Southwest Airlines, which had carried over 77 million passen-gers in 2005, was not mentioned as a comparator.) Ryanair reported that it flew out of 18 European bases with a fleet of over 100 new Boeing 737–800 aircraft and firm orders for a further 138 new air-craft to be delivered over the next six years. These additional aircraft would allow Ryanair to double in size to 80 million passengers per annum by 2012.

More immediate growth plans included the delivery of 30 aircraft between September 2006 and

Exhibit 1c	Ryanair operating statistics

	2006	2005	Change (%)
Total aircraft	103	87	18
Average aircraft age (years)	2.4	7	−65
Available seat miles (ASM, billion)	24.3	17.8	37
Average daily aircraft hours	9.6	9.3	3
Passengers (m)	34.8	27.6	26
Revenue passenger miles (RPM, bn)	18.8	13.9	35
Average length of haul	585	541	8
Average passenger fare	44.63	43.95	2
Revenue per RPM (€)	0.076	0.081	−6
Revenue per ASM (€)	0.058	0.063	−8
Operating costs per ASM (€)	0.052	0.053	−2
Break-even load factor (%)	68	65	5
Load factor (%)	77.6	77.8	−0.2
Average staff	3,063	2,604	18
Average staff per aircraft	29.7	29.9	−0.3
Passenger per employee	11,351	10,596	7
Average staff cost (€)	50,582	53,306	−5
Airport costs per passenger (€)	6.36	6.86	−7
Marketing costs/scheduled revenue (%)	1.70	2.00	−15
Airports served	111	95	17

Source: Ryanair 20F, September 2006.

April 2007 to dovetail with planned new capacity coming on stream in the winter season. As of January 2007, Ryanair was flying out of 127 destinations. The company was cautious in its outlook for the second half of fiscal 2007, since the capacity expansion would entail slightly lower load factors. However, yield stability was expected in a benign yield environment where some competitors were imposing fuel surcharges. As a result, it was expected that the increase in net profit after tax for fiscal 2007 would be approximately 16 per cent to €350m.

Ryanair affirmed that it would continue to offer the lowest fares in every market. In particular, Michael O'Leary declared that we 'guarantee our customers no fuel surcharges not today, not tomorrow, not ever'.[5] This was an allusion to a number of airlines which had added fuel surcharges to their fares when oil prices rose precipitously in 2005 and even further in 2006. Many of the surcharges were levied by carriers with long-haul routes, where the surcharge would not form a significant proportion of the overall fare. Examples were British Airways and Lufthansa.

[5] Ryanair Annual Report, 2006.

Ancillary revenues

Meanwhile, ancillary revenues had climbed by 36 per cent in 2006, considerably faster than passenger revenues, generating €7.70 per passenger, with very high margins. Ancillary revenues include non-flight scheduled services (hotels, travel insurance, excess baggage charges, flight change fees, car rental services, in-flight sales, rail and bus ground transport services, commission from Ryanair's credit card with MBNA and personal loans). It was claimed that Ryanair's website was the largest travel website in Europe and the fifth most recognised brand on Google, offering huge potential for Ryanair to convert this web traffic into e-commerce and advertising revenues.[6]

Ancillary revenue initiatives continued to be introduced, for example on-board and online gambling, and an in-flight mobile phone service. A poll of readers of the *Financial Times* produced a 72 per cent negative response to the question, 'Should mobile phones be allowed on aircraft?' Among the

[6] S. Furlong, *Ryanair as a Consumer Growth Company: Inside the 21st Century European Travel Phenomenon*, Davy Research, March 2006.

comments were that passengers do not wish to be disturbed and 'Just another reason not to fly Ryanair.'[7] However, Michael O'Leary declared 'If you want a quiet flight, use another airline. Ryanair is noisy, full and we are always trying to sell you something.'[8] Not all ancillary service initiatives were successful. In 2005, Ryanair pulled an in-flight entertainment system. Passengers had resisted paying €8 to rent a games and entertainment console, probably because they did not consider it a worthwhile investment for short flights.

Investor perspectives

Prior to its bid for Aer Lingus, Ryanair had come in for some criticism for sitting on a €2bn cash pile, instead of distributing it to investors, blaming uncertainty of demand in the second half of fiscal 2007 for its cautious approach.[9] However, announcing its excellent first half 2007 results in November 2006, the airline stated it was looking into a number of options for payouts to shareholders by the end of the 2007 calendar year, irrespective of the outcome of the Aer Lingus bid. The options included an annual dividend policy, share buyback and a one-off dividend. It also intended to seek shareholder approval for a 2-for-1 stock split, intended to improve the marketability and liquidity of the stock.

The shares rose by 3.6 per cent, to €9.28, a record high. The stock had gained 12 per cent during the year. Yet, despite its superior profit performance, historically, Ryanair was only mid-range or below average in its P/E multiple relative to peers like easyJet, whose shares had risen by 46 per cent during the year. However, this offered an upside potential for capital gains, and a low risk of derating, according to Davy, the company's stockbrokers.

Ryanair's operations in 2006

To quote Michael O'Leary:

> Any fool can sell low airfares and lose money. The difficult bit is to sell the lowest airfares and make profits. If you don't make profits, you can't lower your

air fares or reward your people or invest in new aircraft or take on the really big airlines like BA and Lufthansa.[10]

Certainly, Ryanair had stuck closely to the low-cost/low-fares model. Ever-decreasing costs was Ryanair's mantra, as it constantly adapted the model to the European arena and changing circumstances.

The Ryanair fleet

Ryanair continued its policy of fleet commonality to keep staff training and aircraft maintenance costs as low as possible, using Boeing 737 planes. Over the years, Ryanair replaced its fleet of old aircraft with new, more environmentally-friendly aircraft, reducing the average age of its fleet to 2.4 years, the youngest fleet of any major airline in Europe. The larger seat capacity of the new aircraft did not need more crew. The newer aircraft produced 50 per cent less emissions, 45 per cent less fuel burn and 45 per cent lower noise emissions per seat. Also, a winglet modification programme on the fleet was providing better aircraft performance and a 2 per cent reduction in fleet fuel consumption, a saving which the company believed could be improved over the next year.

Staff costs and productivity

In fiscal 2006, Ryanair's employee count rose by more than 700, to 3,500 people, comprising over 25 different nationalities. The new intake was almost entirely accounted for by flight and cabin crew to service the airline's expansion. Ryanair claimed in its 2006 Annual Report that its average pay, including commissions to cabin crew for on-board sales, was €49,612, a higher figure than any other major European airline. Also, by tailoring rosters, the carrier maximised productivity and time off for crew members, complying with EU regulations which impose a ceiling on pilot flying hours to prevent dangerous fatigue. The airline adhered to the general rule of a maximum of 900 hours flying time per annum, averaging 18 hours per week.

Passenger service costs

In 2006, Ryanair introduced cost-cutting/yield-enhancing measures for passenger check-in and

---

[7] *Financial Times*, 9 September (2006), p. 16.
[8] K. Done and T. Braithwaite, 'Ryanair to allow mobile phone calls next year', *Financial Times*, 31 August (2006), p. 1.
[9] Lex, 'Ryanair', *Financial Times*, 2 August (2006), p. 14.
[10] Ryanair Annual Report, 2001.

luggage handling. Estimates were that these tactics could save an average of more than €1 per passenger. One such measure was web-based check-in from March 2006, and priority boarding, with over half of passengers availing of this, thus saving Ryanair costs on check-in staff and airport facilities, as well as time. Another was charging for check-in bags, which encouraged passengers to travel with fewer and, if possible, zero check-in bags, again saving on costs and enhancing speed. Other rivals were also introducing charges for hold luggage, including Aer Lingus and FlyBE. After ruling out a similar move in February 2006, easyJet succumbed in September of the same year, charging passengers for any more than one item of hold luggage.

Airport charges and route policy

Consistent with the budget airline model, Ryanair's routes continued to be point to point only. Ryanair reduced airport charges by avoiding congested main airports, choosing secondary and regional airport destinations, anxious to increase passenger throughput. Most of these airports are significantly further from the city centres they serve than the main airports. For example, Ryanair uses Frankfurt Hahn, 123 kilometres from Frankfurt; Torp, 100 kilometres from Oslo; and Charleroi, 60 kilometres from Brussels. In December 2003, the Advertising Standards Authority rebuked Ryanair and upheld a misleading advertising complaint against it for attaching 'Lyon' to its advertisements for flights to St Etienne. A passenger had turned up at Lyon Airport, only to discover that her flight was leaving from St Etienne, 75 kilometres away.

In 2006, airport and handling charges increased by 21 per cent, slower than the growth in passenger numbers, reflecting a net reduction in costs from deals at new airports and bases, despite increased costs at certain existing airports, such as Stansted. Route charges also increased by 21 per cent because of an increase in the number of sectors flown and an 8 per cent increase in average sector length, as Ryanair ventured further afield into new EU member states, such as Poland, Hungary and Slovakia, as well as ex-EU destinations, such as Marrakesh in Morocco.

Ryanair continued to protest at charges and conditions at some airports, especially Stansted and Dublin, two of its main hubs. It vehemently opposed the British Airport Authority (BAA) airport monopoly plans to build a '£4bn gold plated Taj Mahal at Stansted which we believe could be built for £1bn'. The airline was

> deeply concerned by continued under staffing of security at Stansted which has led to repeated passenger and flight delays . . . management of Stansted security is inept, and BAA has again proven that it is incapable of providing adequate or appropriate security services at Stansted. This shambles again highlights that BAA is an inefficient, incompetent airport monopoly.[11]

Further, Ryanair continued:

> The tragedy at Dublin airport continues where the Dublin Airport Authority (DAA) monopoly recently obtained planning approval for a second terminal at a cost of €750 million, 4.5 times more than the €170 million cost it announced just 11 months earlier in September 2005. Only a government owned monopoly would seek a cost increase of over 4 fold – with no increase in passenger capacity . . . DAA has recently proposed an outrageous 60 per cent increase in charges at Dublin Airport to recoup the inflated cost of this facility which Ryanair passengers will never use. Ryanair will continue to oppose this waste and has appealed the planning decision.

Risks and challenges

Ryanair faced various challenges as it entered the second half of fiscal 2007. The airline itself predicted that its extra capacity building would create uncertainty about the success of new routes and locations and other difficulties. These were extra marketing and discounted fare costs incurred in launching new routes, as well as overcapacity leading to price cutting by rivals.

Fuel prices

Ryanair was especially vulnerable to rising fuel prices from 2005. Its low-fares policy limited its ability to pass on increased fuel costs to passengers through increased fares. Coupled with a guarantee that it would not impose any fuel surcharges on its customers, this placed extra pressure on the carrier to find cost savings in other spheres of its operations. Its fuel costs represented 35 per cent of operating costs in 2006, compared with 27 per cent the year before. Since jet fuel cost fluctuations are subject to unpredictable and volatile world events, Ryanair could neither predict nor control these costs, and was dependent on hedging, based on

---

[11] Ryanair 2007 half-yearly results.

educated guessing. Moreover, the fact that jet fuel prices are denominated in US dollars compounds the risk by introducing exchange rate exposure, also requiring hedging. Ryanair had not hedged early, so it was paying $70 per barrel of oil up to October 2006, and $73 to $74 up to March 2007 while better hedged competitors such as Lufthansa, Air France–KLM and Iberia had the bulk of their fuel needs hedged at an average of $50 to $60 a barrel until the end of calendar year 2006. Meanwhile, the price of oil stood at about $55 a barrel in late January 2007.

Compensation to passengers

On 17 February 2005, a new EU regulation came into effect, intended to reduce the inconvenience caused to air passengers by delays, cancellations and denied boarding. The regulation provides for standardised and immediate assistance for air passengers at EU airports where these events occur. It was expected that the compensation costs would amount to a sector-wide bill of €200m annually.

Passengers affected by cancellations must be offered a refund or rerouting and free care and assistance while waiting for their rerouted flight – specifically, meals, refreshments and hotel accommodation where an overnight stay is necessary. Financial compensation of up to €600 is also payable for flight cancellation, unless the airline can prove that it was caused by unavoidable extraordinary circumstances. Examples of circumstances which may fall within this exception are political instability, weather conditions incompatible with the operation of the flight, security and safety risks, and strikes. For Ryanair, the typical compensation cost would likely fall into the €250 category, based on the average distance of its flights. Passengers subject to long delays would also be entitled to similar assistance, including meals and hotel accommodation. However, two years after the new regulation, the EU had to recognise that it was being widely ignored.

Terrorism and security

Past terrorist attacks on airliners and in urban and holiday centres have inflicted added risks and costs to the airline industry worldwide. In August 2006, UK authorities imposed severe security measures at all airports in the face of an alleged imminent terrorist plot to attack up to 10 aircraft on transatlantic routes. These measures applied to all passengers, including short-haul ones, so they were to be body searched and banned from carrying liquids and gels in their carry-on luggage. Airports serving London were especially affected. Ryanair had to cancel 279 flights in the days immediately following the incident and refunded €2.7m in fares to approximately 40,000 passengers. In addition, Ryanair is estimated to have suffered a loss of €1.9m in reduced bookings.

While the restrictions were relaxed somewhat in November, they still limited severely the contents of carry-on luggage and made it more likely that passengers would have to bring check-in bags, thus impeding the efficiency of the budget airlines which relied on quick check-in and aircraft turnarounds, with a minimum of hold luggage. There was also a threat that passengers would choose other forms of transport, such as trains, rather than face the inconvenience and expense of checking in luggage, as well as the extra time spent in airport security queues.

In the past, Ryanair had recovered quickly from terrorist episodes and alerts, after initial dips in traffic, namely after the terrorist attacks on airliners in the USA on 9/11, and the aftermath of attacks on London transport on 7 July 2005, and abortive attempts two weeks later on 21 July. This had affected flight bookings to London for some weeks. Michael O'Leary's verdict on the new August 2006 security measures was that they were 'farcical' and that terrorists 'must be rolling around in their caves in Pakistan laughing at us'.[12] While various other airline executives protested too, Ryanair was on its own in launching two legal cases against the UK government. One was a claim for €4.6m to compensate the carrier for lost flights and bookings. In the other case, Ryanair was challenging the legality of the new security measures and sought to return to those in operation prior to August 2006. A lasting effect of the 9/11 attacks was significantly increased insurance costs for all commercial airlines. Ryanair has passed these costs on in its fares.

Environmental concerns

Environmental concerns about greenhouse gases from carbon emissions continue to climb up the public and political agenda worldwide, and especially in Europe, with an ever-greater focus on

---

[12] FT Reporters, 'Airlines in backlash over travel restrictions', *Financial Times*, 19/20 August (2006), p. 1.

the impact of aviation. Aviation represents 2.6 per cent of carbon emissions in the EU, but an Oxford University study predicted that carbon from aviation would accelerate, so that adverse climate impacts would far outweigh the positive commercial effects of aviation.[13] Another report warned that failure to curtail greenhouse gases would lead to catastrophic human and economic consequences. Hence, the airline industry should pay environmental taxes for the contributions they make to global warming.[14] Heretofore, aviation fuel was exempt from taxation, but there was mounting pressure to tax aviation fuel, and some plan to do so within the EU area seemed probable by 2010. In addition, aviation was likely to become part of some form of emissions trading scheme that could cost up to €9 for a return ticket within Europe.

Ryanair argued that aviation contributes only a small proportion of carbon emissions relative to the benefits of easily accessible cheap air travel. Moreover, taxes have proven ineffective as a means of reducing road vehicle use. None the less, the carrier has pledged to behave responsibly by deploying more efficient aircraft that use less fuel and produce less pollution. Ryanair has urged that any environmental taxation scheme should be to the benefit of more efficient carriers, so airlines with low load factors that generate high fuel consumption and emissions per passenger, and airlines that offer connecting rather then point-to-point flights, should be penalised. Ian Pearson, the UK Minister for Climate Change, reacted to Ryanair's protestations by branding the airline 'the irresponsible face of capitalism'. In turn, Michael O'Leary said the Minister was 'foolish and ill-informed . . . like most politicians, Minister Pearson talks a lot but does little. Being criticised by him was like being savaged by a dead sheep.'[15]

Industrial relations

Ryanair's industrial relations with staff, especially its pilots, are fraught. The company has come under fire for refusing to recognise unions and allegedly providing poor working conditions (for example, staff are banned from charging their own mobile phones at work to reduce the company's electricity bill). Ryanair's appeal to the Irish Supreme Court over a previous ruling allowing collective bargaining by its pilots through the Irish Airline Pilots' Association (IALPA), the largest pilots' union in Ireland, received a preliminary favourable ruling in February 2007, whereupon the company launched a claim for its legal expenses in the case. There is also pressure from the British Airline Pilots' Association to recruit Ryanair pilots based in the UK. In the absence of unions, Ryanair negotiates with all its employees through internally elected 'Employee Representation Committees'.

In July 2006, the Irish High Court found that Ryanair had bullied pilots to force them to agree to new contracts, where pilots would have to pay costs of €15,000 for retraining on new aircraft if they left the airline, or if the company was forced to negotiate with unions during the following five years. Moreover, some Ryanair managers were judged to have given false evidence in court. Meanwhile, Ryanair was contesting the claims of pilots comprising 3.5 per cent of the pilot workforce, for victimisation under the new contracts. It was conceded by the company that a ruling in favour of the pilots could incur damages of €100,000 per pilot. In another legal case, Ryanair was ordered to pay 'well in excess' of €1m in legal costs after a court refused the airline access to the names and addresses of pilots who posted critical comments about the company on a site hosted by the British and Irish pilots' unions. Ryanair, led by Michael O'Leary, had claimed anonymous pilots were using a website to intimidate and harass foreign-based pilots and dissuade them from working for the company. The pilots involved used codenames such as 'ihateryanair' and 'cant-fly-wontfly'.

Ryanair declared that its pilots were recognised as the best-paid short-haul pilots in Europe. Remuneration packages included a share option scheme. The company claimed that Ryanair pilots enjoy a stable roster pattern, offering a facility to plan time off, apparently unique in aviation. No overnights mean pilots are home every night. However, in the autumn of 2006, pilots in Ryanair lodged a pay claim with the Irish Labour Relations Commission on the basis that there were significant differences in take-home pay between Ryanair and Aer Lingus pilots. It also claimed that Ryanair training pilots were working for nothing. None the less, in effect, Ryanair appeared to have had

[13] S. Cairns and C. Newson, *Predict and decide: Aviation, climate change and UK policy*, ECI Research Report 33, Environmental Change Institute, University of Oxford, 2006.

[14] Sir Nicholas Stern, *Economics of climate change*, Review for UK government, 2006.

[15] B. Hall and K. Done, 'Pearson brought to earth in airline row', *Financial Times*, 6/7 January (2007), p. 2.

no problems recruiting cabin staff, including pilots, to meet its needs.

Sundry legal actions

In other disputes, Ryanair was in litigation with various airports over landing charges. A ruling in 2004 deemed that the carrier was in illegal receipt of state aid from publicly owned Charleroi Airport, its Brussels base. Ryanair was ordered to repay €4m, placed into an escrow account, pending an appeal in the European Court. The Walloon authorities were claiming back a further €2.3m in the Irish courts for their reimbursement to Ryanair of start-up costs at Charleroi. Sundry other legal challenges by competitors to Ryanair were also underway in 2006–2007. These were based on allegations of unfair discrimination favouring Ryanair over other airlines at various publicly owned airports, such as Lubeck and Frankfurt Hahn in Germany, and Shannon in Ireland, constituting illegal state aid. On another front Ryanair was vigorously defending French government attempts to protect Air France–KLM by forcing easyJet and Ryanair to move the staff they employ on French soil from British employment contracts to more expensive French ones.

Often, Ryanair took the initiative over illegal aid to rivals. For example, it filed a complaint with the European Commission accusing rival Air France–KLM of trying to block competition after the French airline filed a case, alleging that Marseille Airport was breaching the law by offering discount airlines cut-price fees at its second, no-frills terminal. Ryanair had planned to base two planes at Marseille, serving 13 routes. The latest complaint came a month after Ryanair called on the Commission to investigate allegations that Air France had received almost €1bn in illegal state aid, benefiting unfairly from up to 50 per cent discounted landing and passenger charges on flights within France, and should repay the cash.

Adverse rulings on these airport cases could have the effect of curtailing Ryanair's growth, if it was prevented from striking advantageous deals with publicly owned airports and confined to the smaller number of privately owned airports across Europe.

Other legal cases against Ryanair accused it of misleading passengers on its website by exaggerating the prices of its competitors in making comparisons. The carrier was also being sued by Sweden's prime minister and a former foreign minister over an advertising campaign that used their pictures alongside the tagline 'Time to leave the country?' The company's Scandinavian sales manager quipped, 'This must be the first time that a Swedish politician has objected to his image being used in a newspaper.'[16]

Safety issues

Safety is taken very seriously by Ryanair, with extensive safety training and protocols. A safety committee reports to the board at each board meeting. The airline is aware of the permanent damage to the company that could follow a serious accident to one of its aircraft. Indeed, a serious accident to any budget airliner could have knock-on effects on all the other budget carriers, and some industry experts have questioned the safety of the low-cost model on the basis of 'human factors'.

Ryanair's detractors have attempted to disparage its safety record, with reports of various incidents of 'near-miss' accidents, accusing the company of placing crew under such intensive pressurised work schedules that alertness levels are compromised. In February 2006, UK television Channel 4 broadcast a documentary 'Ryanair caught napping'. Two undercover reporters obtained jobs as Ryanair cabin crew based at London Stansted Airport, and secretly recorded Ryanair training and cabin crew procedures. The documentary criticised Ryanair's training policies, security procedures, aircraft hygiene, and highlighted poor staff morale. It filmed Ryanair cabin crew sleeping on the job; using aftershave to cover the smell of vomit in the aisle rather than cleaning it up; ignoring warning alerts on the emergency slide; encouraging staff to falsify references for airport security passes; and asking staff not to recheck passengers' passports before boarding.

Ryanair denied the allegations and published its correspondence with Channel 4 on its website. It claimed to have forwarded all 20 allegations to the UK and Irish aviation authorities, both of which agreed that there was no substance to them. It also alleged that the programme was misleading and that promotional materials, in particular a photograph of a stewardess sleeping, had been faked. Much of the subsequent coverage of the programme in the media considered that the

---

[16] P. Munter, 'Swedish premier and ex-minister sue Ryanair over adverts with their pictures', *Financial Times*, 7 April (2006), p. 9.

documentary was overblown and failed to make substantive claims against the airline, with some going so far as to label the attempted exposé as a vindication for Ryanair. Unfazed, Ryanair launched new services and a free flights offer following the documentary,

Customer services and perceptions

In 2003, Ryanair published a Passenger Charter, which embraces a number of doctrines, mainly dealing with low fares, redress and punctuality. However, in a poll of 4,000 travellers around the world by TripAdvisor in October 2006, Ryanair was voted the world's least favourite airline, with easyJet coming second worst. Unfriendly staff was cited as the worst part of the Ryanair experience, followed by delays and poor legroom. In fact, Ryanair scored badly in virtually all categories, which also included comfortable seats, safe/secure, never lose my luggage, best amenities (for example, snacks/food; TV/movies; magazines/newspapers). However, it scored well on 'best fares'. Ryanair's 'ultra-frugal approach to flying wins millions of customers but very few fans'.[17] Southwest Airlines, Ryanair's role model, emerged as the world's fifth most favourite airline in the survey.

There have been suggestions that Ryanair's 'obsessive focus on the bottom line may have dented its public image. In one infamous incident, it charged a man with cerebral palsy £18 (€25) to use a wheelchair.'[18] In response to protests over the charge, Ryanair imposed a 50 cent wheelchair levy on every passenger ticket. Campaigners for the disabled accused Ryanair of profiteering from its extra charges, declaring that the levy should be no more than 3 cents – the company would still have collected €1,000,000. Ryanair defended its position, saying that it costs €37 per person to transport disabled passengers at Stansted, and the airline carried 1.5 million such passengers every year. Ryanair was the only major airline in the UK to impose such wheelchair charges.

Further, the *Guardian* newspaper alleged that the insurance fee which Ryanair charges each passenger is unreasonably high. The insurance surcharge amounted to more than 10 per cent of Ryanair's average fare, the newspaper estimated. Rival easyJet claimed that 'Ryanair's insurance charges appear to be far higher than they actually incur. . . . Either this is poor cost management on Ryanair's behalf or it's a fuel surcharge in disguise.'[19]

Critics have accused Ryanair of poor treatment of customers whose flights have been cancelled. The airline formerly refused to provide accommodation or meal vouchers when flights were cancelled or delayed, until it became illegal to do so in 2005. Ryanair also refused to refund taxes and fees when passengers cancel their tickets, but revised this practice by introducing an 'administration' fee of €20 per ticket for handling refunds, a fee which often exceeds the amount for which passengers may be eligible. Norwegian consumer authorities have fined Ryanair €64,000 for this practice. However, it is not uncommon for airlines to charge an administration fee for changes or refunds.

In response to various complaints, Ryanair has declared that, in effect, customers vote with their feet by choosing Ryanair for its lowest fares. It also claims to be number one for punctuality among European airlines, with the lowest level of complaints, fewest cancellations and fewest lost bags. In March 2006, Davy, Ryanair's stockbrokers, reported on a quarterly customer survey conducted by Ryanair in 2005, with responses from about 20,000 passengers, with 'huge' repeat business.[20] Unlike external surveys, satisfaction with Ryanair was overwhelmingly 'excellent' or 'good' and certainly above average for airport check-in, boarding and departure, cabin cleanliness and cabin crew service. Seating space was regarded as largely average as was on-board catering. Davy concluded that the positive results were actually likely to improve with the new aircraft coming on stream. The only disappointing results pertained to on-board sales which, although improving, were not much above €1.30 per passenger.

Competitors and comparators

The potential of the budget sector in Europe was underlined by its growth, as low-cost carriers had 18 per cent of the market for all European flights in the three months ended 30 September 2006, compared with 15 per cent a year earlier. Davy saw the European market as healthy, with huge

---

[17] D. Milmo, 'Ryanair – the world's least favourite airline', *Guardian*, 26 October (2006).

[18] Milmo, ibid.

[19] A. Clark, 'Ryanair . . . the low-fare airline with the sky-high insurance levy', *Guardian*, 8 May (2006).

[20] See note 5.

Exhibit 2 European low-cost carriers overview**

Airline	Passengers (m)	% of total	Principal bases	Bases (no.)	Aircraft in Service (no.)	Skytrax star Rating*	Comment
Ryanair	34.9	29.90	Stansted, Dublin	16	107	2	Dominant lowest-cost producer: gross cash > €1.8bn
easyJet	30.3	25.90	Stansted, Luton	16	109	3	65% of passengers UK based, but becoming pan-European player
Air Berlin/Niki	13.8	11.80	Berlin	9	47	4	Founded in 1979 as charter operator, operates Majorca shuttle. Set up City Shuttle in October 2002. Partnership with Niki in Austria
FlyBE	5.5	4.70	Southampton	6	35	3	Independent regional UK LCC owned by the Walker Trust
Germanwings	5.5	4.70	Cologne–Bonn, Stuttgart, Hamburg	4	14	3	Majority owned by Lufthansa through its regional associate airline Eurowings; potentially expand fleet to 20 aircraft
Sterling/Maersk	3.8	3.30	Bilund, Copenhagen	2	29	3	Sterling merged with Maersk Air in 2005 but now owned by FL Group
bmibaby	3.5	3.00	Cardiff, East Midlands	5	16	2	Part of BMI British Midland Group
dba	3	2.60	Munich, Berlin	2	16	4	Largely domestic high-frequency German airline
Hapag Lloyd Express	2.7	2.30	Cologne–Bonn	5	15	3	Part of TUI Group, Europe's largest travel group
Vueling	2.5	2.10	Barcelona, Valencia	2	9	3	$30m start-up investment from Apax Partners and other investors, including JetBlue top managers
Norwegian Air Shuttle	2.1	1.80	Largely domestic Norway	1	14	3	Listed on the Oslo Stock Exchange in 2003
Virgin Express	2	1.70	Brussels	1	10	3	Merged with SN Brussels (formally Sabena)
SkyEurope	1.9	1.60	Bratislava	4	15	2	Floated on Vienna Exchange in late 2005
Wizz	1.9	1.60	Katowice, Budapest	3	6	3	Start-up funding of $34m from US private equity fund Indigo Partners. Focused on leased aircraft
Wind Jet	1	0.90	Sicily	2	8		Sicilian-based, largely Italian domestic carrier
Air Baltic	1	0.90	Riga	1	16	3	Majority-owned Latvian state; SAS has 47% stake
Fly Me	0.5	0.40	Gothenburg	1	4		Gothenburg-based LCC operating intra-Scandinavia
Jet2	0.5	0.40	Leeds, Manchester	3	9	3	Bases at Leeds, Manchester and Belfast
Monarch Scheduled	0.5	0.40	Luton, Manchester, Gatwick	3	10	3	Scheduled part of Monarch Group flying to Spain, Portugal and Cyprus
Totals	116.9				489		
Total Ryanair+easyJet		55.80					

* Skytrax survey scale: 1 star low to 5 star high.

** Table adapted from Furlong (see note 5). Reprinted by permission of Davy Research.

potential, and only incremental growth, even if many of the competitors were losing money. Some carriers were withdrawing from routes where they clashed with Ryanair, for example MyTravelLite from the Dublin–Birmingham route, or avoiding such routes altogether.

The attractiveness of the budget sector in Europe is signified by the large number of entrants and rivals, although as many as 50 have gone bankrupt, been taken over, disappeared or never got off the ground (www.etn.nl/lcostgra.htm – Low-Cost Graveyard website). Exhibit 2 gives an overview of the main budget carriers in Europe as of 2006.[21]

Learding Ryanair into the future

In November 2005, Michael O'Leary, aged 44, announced that he had set 2008 as his own departure date from Ryanair. At that stage he would have been with the airline for 20 years. He declared that he would sever all links with the airline, refusing to 'move upstairs' as Chairman. 'I think it is one of the worst things you can do; you have to get out, otherwise you will be like Banquo's ghost, hanging around the corridors,' he said. 'You don't need a doddery old bastard hanging around the place.'[22]

O'Leary bred horses at his Gigginstown Stud on a farm about 50 miles (80 kilometres) from Dublin. His horse, War of Attrition, won the Cheltenham Gold Cup, one of the most prestigious races in steeplechasing, in 2006.

In 2007, Michael O'Leary was Ryanair's largest shareholder with 4.53 per cent of the share capital. Although he consistently praised his management team, Ryanair was inextricably identified with its dynamic Chief Executive. He was credited with single-handedly transforming European air transport. The airline won various international awards, such as Best Managed Airline. In 2001, O'Leary was awarded the European Businessman of the Year Award by *Fortune* magazine; in 2004, the *Financial Times* named Michael O'Leary as one of 25 European 'business stars', who are expected

to make a difference. The newspaper described him as personifying 'the brash new Irish business elite' and possessing 'a head for numbers, a shrewd marketing brain and a ruthless competitive streak'.[23] In 2005, he was ranked 18th among the World's Most Respected Business Leaders in a *Financial Times/PricewaterhouseCoopers* poll.

Present and former staff have praised O'Leary's leadership style. According to Tim Jeans, a former Sales and Marketing Director of Ryanair, currently CEO of a small low-cost rival, MyTravelLite:

> Michael's genius is his ability to motivate and energise people. . . . There is an incredible energy in that place. People work incredibly hard and get a lot out of it. They operate a very lean operation for a company of its size. It is without peer.[24]

O'Leary's publicity-seeking antics have earned him a high profile. These included his declaration of war on easyJet when, wearing an army uniform, he drove up in a tank to easyJet's headquarters in Luton Airport. In similar vein, he flew to Milan Bergamo when Ryanair opened its hub there aboard a jet bearing the slogan 'Arrivederci Alitalia'. He has also dressed up as St Patrick and as the Pope to promote ticket offers.

It is O'Leary's outspokenness that has made him a figure of public debate. 'He is called everything from "arrogant pig" to "messiah"'.[25] He has certainly made investors very happy, and even detractors would credit Ryanair with opening up the era of inexpensive air travel. At the same time, he is a reviled figure among trade unionists, and he has antagonised Irish government circles with his continuous attacks on the state airport authority. He is very personally involved in Ryanair's battles with the EU, and some pundits believe that his abrasive style has only served to annoy the Commissioners. Indeed, the Belgian Commissioner, Philippe Busquin, denounced Michael O'Leary as 'irritating . . . and insists he is not the only Commissioner who is allergic to the mere mention of the name of Ryanair's arrogant chief'.[26]

An *Irish Times* columnist, John McManus, has suggested that 'maybe it's time for Ryanair to

[21] Details and comparisons of Ryanair's competitors as well as points of comparison with selected other carriers are provided in the supplement on the *Exploring Corporate Strategy* website www.pearsoned.co.uk/ecs.

[22] D. Dalby, 'I'm going for good, O'Leary tells Ryanair', *Sunday Times*, 20 November (2005), News, p. 3.

[23] B. Groom, 'Leaders of the new Europe: business stars chart a course for the profits of the future', *Financial Times*, 20 April (2004).

[24] G. Bowley, 'How low can you go?', *Financial Times Magazine*, no. 9, 21 June (2003).

[25] Ibid.

[26] S. Creaton, 'Turbulent times for Ryanair's high-flier', *Irish Times*, 31 January (2004).

jettison O'Leary'.[27] McManus claimed that O'Leary has become a caricature of himself, fulfilling all 15 warning signs of an executive about to fail. Professor Sydney Finklestein of the Tuck Business School at Dartmouth in the USA identified the 15 signs under five headings: ignoring change, the wrong vision, getting too close, arrogant attitudes and old formulae. After apparently demonstrating how well O'Leary fits the Finklestein criteria, McManus none the less concluded: 'So, is it time for Ryanair to dump Mr O'Leary? Depends whether you prefer the track record of one of the most successful businessmen in modern aviation, or the theories of a US academic from an Ivy League school.'

Perhaps the last words should go to Michael O'Leary himself: 'We could make a mistake and I could get hung', he said. He reiterated a point he had often made before: 'It is okay doing the cheeky chappie, running around Europe, thumbing your nose, but I am not Herb Kelleher (the legendary founder of the original budget airline, Southwest Airlines in the US). He was a genius and I am not.'[28]

In what could have been his darkest hour, O'Leary was irrepressible: 'This is the most fun you can have without taking your clothes off. It is much more fun when the world is falling apart than when things are boring and going well', he declared on the day he announced a shock profits warning in January 2004.[29]

So, how do these comments (and the Aer Lingus bid) fit with Michael O'Leary's declaration to part company with Ryanair? Would he really go in 2008, and, if so, what would happen to Ryanair and its ambitions? No one really knows the answer to these questions, but it would certainly lie in Michael O'Leary's propensity to surprise his admirers and detractors alike . . .

---

[27] J. McManus, 'Maybe it's time for Ryanair to jettison O'Leary', Irish Times, 11 August (2003).

[28] G. Bowley, 'How low can you go?', Financial Times Magazine, no. 9, 21 June (2003).

[29] S. Creaton, 'Turbulent times for Ryanair's high-flier', Irish Times, 31 January (2004).

IKEA: how the Swedish retailer became a global cult brand

A hybrid strategy (point 3 on the strategy clock – Exhibit 6.2) can be very successful and difficult for competitors to imitate. However, there is a danger that the organisation can drift into a 'stuck in the middle' position – being 'out-flanked' by both low-priced and differentiating competitors at the same time.

• • •

Since IKEA began in 1943 it has grown into a successful global network of stores with its unique retailing concept. An article in *Business Week* discussed the concept:

The Ikea concept has plenty of room to run: The retailer accounts for just 5–10% of the furniture market in each country in which it operates. More important, says CEO Anders Dahlvig, is that 'awareness of our brand is much bigger than the size of our company.' That's because Ikea is far more than a furniture merchant. It sells a lifestyle that customers around the world embrace as a signal that they've arrived, that they have good taste and recognize value. 'If it wasn't for Ikea,' writes British design magazine Icon, 'most people would have no access to affordable contemporary design.' The magazine even voted Ikea's founder Ingvar Kamprad the most influential tastemaker in the world today.

As long as consumers from Moscow to Beijing and beyond keep striving to enter the middle class, there will be a need for Ikea. Think about it: What mass-market retailer has had more success globally? Not Wal-Mart Stores Inc. (WMT), which despite vast strengths has stumbled in Brazil, Germany, and Japan. Not France's Carrefour, which has never made it in the U.S. Ikea has had its slip-ups, too. But right now its 226 stores in Europe, Asia, Australia, and the U.S. are thriving, hosting 410 million shoppers a year. The emotional response is unparalleled. The

Photo: Associated Press/PA Photos

promise of store vouchers for the first 50 shoppers drew thousands to an Ikea store in the Saudi Arabian city of Jeddah in September, 2004. In the ensuing melee, two people died and 16 were injured. A February 2005 opening in London attracted up to 6,000 before police were called in. . . .

Such buzz has kept Ikea's sales growing at a healthy clip: For the fiscal year ended 31 August 2005 revenues rose 15%, to $17.7bn (≈€14.2bn). And although privately held Ikea guards profit figures as jealously as its recipe for Swedish meatballs, analyst Mattias Karlkjell of Stockholm's ABG Sundal Collier conservatively estimates Ikea's pre-tax operating profits at $1.7bn (€1.36bn). Ikea maintains these profits even while it cuts prices steadily. 'Ikea's operating margins of approximately 10% are among the

This is an abridged version of an article from *Business Week online* (N. American edition) 14 November (2005).

best in home furnishing,' Karlkjell says. They also compare well with margins of 5% at Pier 1 Imports and 7.7% at Target, both competitors of Ikea in the U.S.

To keep growing at that pace, Ikea is accelerating store rollouts. Nineteen new outlets are set to open worldwide in the fiscal year ending Aug. 31, 2006, at a cost of $66m per store, on average. CEO Dahlvig is keen to boost Ikea's profile in three of its fastest-growing markets: the U.S., Russia (Ikea is already a huge hit in Moscow), and China (now worth $120m in sales). In the U.S. he figures the field is wide open: 'We have 25 stores in a market the size of Europe, where we have more than 160 stores.' The goal is 50 U.S. outlets by 2010: Five are opening this year, up from just one in 2000.

The key to these rollouts is to preserve the strong enthusiasm Ikea evokes, an enthusiasm that has inspired two case studies from Harvard Business School and endless shopper comment on the Net. Examples: 'Ikea makes me free to become what I want to be' (from Romania). Or this: 'Half my house is from Ikea – and the nearest store is six hours away' (the U.S.). Or this: 'Every time, it's trendy for less money' (Germany).

What enthrals shoppers and scholars alike is the store visit – a similar experience the world over. The blue-and-yellow buildings average 300,000 square feet in size [28,000m^2], about equal to five football fields. The sheer number of items – 7,000, from kitchen cabinets to candlesticks – is a decisive advantage. 'Others offer affordable furniture,' says Bryan Roberts, research manager at Planet Retail, a consultancy in London. 'But there's no one else who offers the whole concept in the big shed.'

The global middle class that Ikea targets shares buying habits. The $120 Billy bookcase, $13 Lack side table, and $190 Ivar storage system are best-sellers worldwide. (U.S. prices are used throughout this story.) Spending per customer is even similar. According to Ikea, the figure in Russia is $85 per store visit – exactly the same as in affluent Sweden.

Wherever they are, customers tend to think of the store visit as more of an outing than a chore. That's intentional: As one of the Harvard B-school studies states, Ikea practices a form of 'gentle coercion' to keep you as long as possible. Right at the entrance, for example, you can drop off your kids at the playroom, an amenity that encourages more leisurely shopping.

Then, clutching your dog-eared catalog (the print run for the 2006 edition was 160 million – more than the Bible, Ikea claims), you proceed along a marked path through the warren of showrooms. 'Because the store is designed as a circle, I can see everything as long as I keep walking in one direction,' says Krystyna Gavora, an architect who frequents Ikea in

Schaumburg, Ill. Wide aisles let you inspect merchandise without holding up traffic. The furniture itself is arranged in fully accessorized displays, down to the picture frames on the nightstand, to inspire customers and get them to spend more. The settings are so lifelike that one writer is staging a play at Ikea in Renton, Wash.

Along the way, one touch after another seduces the shopper, from the paper measuring tapes and pencils to strategically placed bins with items like pink plastic watering cans, scented candles, and picture frames. These are things you never knew you needed but at less than $2 each you load up on them anyway. You set out to buy a $40 coffee table but end up dropping $500 on everything from storage units to glassware. 'They have this way of making you believe nothing is expensive,' says Bertille Faroult, a shopper at Ikea on the outskirts of Paris. The bins and shelves constantly hold surprises: Ikea replaces a third of its product line every year.

Then there's the stop at the restaurant, usually placed at the center of the store, to provide shoppers a breather and encourage them to keep going. You proceed to the warehouse, where the full genius of founder Kamprad is on display. Nearly all the big items are flat-packed, which not only saves Ikea millions in shipping costs from suppliers but also enables shoppers to haul their own stuff home – another saving. Finally you have the fun (or agony) of assembling at home, equipped with nothing but an Allen wrench and those cryptic instructions.

A vocal minority rails at Ikea for its long lines, crowded parking lots, exasperating assembly experiences, and furniture that's hardly built for the ages (the running joke is that Ikea is Swedish for particle board). But the converts outnumber the critics. And for every fan who shops at Ikea, there seems to be one working at the store itself. The fanaticism stems from founder Kamprad, 79, a figure as important to global retailing as Wal-Mart's Sam Walton. Kamprad started the company in 1943 at the age of 17, selling pens, Christmas cards, and seeds from a shed on his family's farm in southern Sweden. In 1951, the first catalog appeared (Kamprad penned all the text himself until 1963). His credo of creating 'a better life for many' is enshrined in his almost evangelical 1976 tract, *A Furniture Dealer's Testament*. Peppered with folksy tidbits – 'divide your life into 10-minute units and sacrifice as few as possible in meaningless activity,' 'wasting resources is a mortal sin' (that's for sure: employees are the catalog models), or the more revealing 'it is our duty to expand' – the pamphlet is given to all employees the day they start.

Kamprad, though officially retired, is still the cheerleader for the practices that define Ikea culture.

One is egalitarianism. Ikea regularly stages Anti-bureaucracy Weeks, during which executives work on the shop floor or tend the registers. 'In February,' says CEO Dahlvig, 'I was unloading trucks and selling beds and mattresses.'

Another is a steely competitiveness. You get a sense of that at one of Ikea's main offices, in Helsingborg, Sweden. At the doorway, a massive bulletin board tracks weekly sales growth, names the best-performing country markets, and identifies the best-selling furniture. The other message that comes across loud and clear: Cut prices. At the far end of the Helsingborg foyer is a row of best-selling Klippan sofas, displaying models from 1999 to 2006 with their euro price tags. In 1999 the Klippan was $354. In 2006 it will be $202.

The montage vividly illustrates Ikea's relentless cost-cutting. The retailer aims to lower prices across its entire offering by an average of 2% to 3% each year. It goes deeper when it wants to hit rivals in certain segments. 'We look at the competition, take their price, and then slash it in half,' says Mark McCaslin, manager of Ikea Long Island, in Hicksville, N.Y.

It helps that frugality is as deeply ingrained in the corporate DNA as the obsession with design. Managers fly economy, even top brass. Steen Kanter, who left Ikea in 1994 and now heads his own retail consultancy in Philadelphia, Kanter International, recalls that while flying with Kamprad once, the boss handed him a coupon for a car rental he had ripped out from an in-flight magazine.

This cost obsession fuses with the design culture. 'Designing beautiful-but-expensive products is easy,' says Josephine Rydberg-Dumont, president of Ikea of Sweden. 'Designing beautiful products that are inexpensive and functional is a huge challenge.'

No design – no matter how inspired – finds its way into the showroom if it cannot be made affordable. To achieve that goal, the company's 12 full-time designers at Almhult, Sweden, along with 80 freelancers, work hand in hand with in-house production teams to identify the appropriate materials and least costly suppliers, a trial-and-error process that can take as long as three years. Example: For the PS Ellan, a $39.99 dining chair that can rock back on its hind legs without tipping over, designer Chris Martin worked with production staff for a year and a half to adapt a wood-fiber composite, an inexpensive blend of wood chips and plastic resin used in highway noise barriers, for use in furnishings. Martin also had to design the chair to break down into six pieces, so it could be flat-packed and snapped together without screws.

With a network of 1,300 suppliers in 53 countries, Ikea works overtime to find the right manufacturer for the right product. It once contracted with ski makers – experts in bent wood – to manufacture its Poang armchairs, and it has tapped makers of supermarket carts to turn out durable sofas. Simplicity, a tenet of Swedish design, helps keep costs down. The 50 cents Trofé mug comes only in blue and white, the least expensive pigments. Ikea's conservation drive extends naturally from this cost-cutting. For its new PS line, it challenged 28 designers to find innovative uses for discarded and unusual materials. The results: a table fashioned from reddish-brown birch heartwood (furniture makers prefer the pale exterior wood) and a storage system made from recycled milk cartons.

If sales keep growing at their historical average, by 2010 Ikea will need to source twice as much material as today. 'We can't increase by more than 20 stores a year because supply is the bottleneck,' says Lennart Dahlgren, country manager for Russia. Since Russia is a source of timber, Ikea aims to turn it into a major supplier of finished products.

Adding to the challenge, the suppliers and designers have to customize some Ikea products to make them sell better in local markets. In China, the 250,000 plastic placemats Ikea produced to commemorate the year of the rooster sold out in just three weeks. Julie Desrosiers, the bedroom-line manager at Ikea of Sweden, visited people's houses in the U.S. and Europe to peek into their closets, learning that 'Americans prefer to store most of their clothes folded, and Italians like to hang.' The result was a wardrobe that features deeper drawers for U.S. customers.

The American market poses special challenges for Ikea because of the huge differences inside the U.S. 'It's so easy to forget the reality of how people live,' says Ikea's U.S. interior design director, Mats Nilsson. In the spring of 2004, Ikea realized it might not be reaching California's Hispanics. So its designers visited the homes of Hispanic staff. They soon realized they had set up the store's displays all wrong. Large Hispanic families need dining tables and sofas that fit more than two people, the Swedish norm. They prefer bold colors to the more subdued Scandinavian palette and display tons of pictures in elaborate frames. Nilsson warmed up the showrooms' colors, adding more seating and throwing in numerous picture frames.

Ikea is particularly concerned about the U.S. since it's key to expansion – and since Ikea came close to blowing it. 'We got our clocks cleaned in the early 1990s because we really didn't listen to the consumer,' says Kanter. Stores weren't big enough to offer the full Ikea experience, and many were in poor locations. Prices were too high. Beds were measured in centimeters, not king, queen, and twin. Sofas weren't deep enough, curtains were too short, and kitchens didn't fit U.S.-size appliances. 'American customers were buying vases to drink from because the glasses were too small,' recalls Goran Carstedt, the former head of Ikea North America, who helped engineer a turnaround. Parts of the product line were adapted (no more metric measurements), new and bigger store locations chosen, prices slashed, and service improved. Now U.S. managers are paying close attention to the tiniest details. 'Americans want more comfortable sofas, higher-quality textiles, bigger glasses, more spacious entertainment units,' says Pernille Spiers-Lopez, head of Ikea North America.

Can the cult keep thriving? Ikea has stumbled badly before. A foray into Japan 30 years ago was a disaster (the Japanese wanted high quality and great materials, not low price and particle board). The company is just now gearing up for a return to Japan next year. Ikea is also seeing more competition than ever. In the U.S., Target Corp. (TGT) has recruited top designer Thomas O'Brien to develop a range of low-priced furnishings, which were launched in October 2005. Kmart has been collaborating with Martha Stewart on its own furniture line. An Ikea-like chain called Fly is popular in France. In Japan Nitori Co. has a lock on low-cost furniture.

Perhaps the bigger issue is what happens inside Ikea. 'The great challenge of any organization as it becomes larger and more diverse is how to keep the core founding values alive,' says Harvard Business School Professor Christopher A. Bartlett, author of a 1996 case study. Ikea is still run by managers who were trained and groomed by Kamprad himself – and who are personally devoted to the founder. As the direct links with Kamprad disappear, the culture may start to fade.

CASE STUDY

The News Corporation

Aidan McQuade

The case examines the shifting corporate logics and business strategies underpinning the development of The News Corporation, which at the beginning of the twenty-first century is one of the world's largest and most international media companies, in the main the creation of one man, Rupert Murdoch. The case shows how constant attention to changing business contexts is key to success, and how certain global businesses can sometimes influence in their favour the contextual environments in which they operate.

• • •

Introduction

Tony Blair and Gordon Brown, whenever I'm in town they say, 'Can't you come over for a cup of tea?' When you're invited by the Prime Minister to have a cup of tea, you have a cup of tea. It's sometimes very inconvenient – if you're only there two days and you have a month's work to do. And you have to be careful to have a cup of tea with them both, or they are very suspicious that you are lining up with the other one.

(Rupert Murdoch)[1]

Since its emergence from Australia onto the world market, the activities of The News Corporation (NewsCorp) have been intrinsically linked with the motivations, personality and perceptions of Rupert Murdoch. Writing in the 2006 annual report he noted: 'The News Corporation's mission has always been to provide as many consumers as possible with the highest quality content through the most convenient of distribution channels.' The year 2006, a year characterised by Murdoch as one where NewsCorp 'accelerated the transformation of our company from a traditional media company into a major digital player', also represented the fourth successive year of profits, stated at US$2.3bn (≈€1.85bn), since 2002.

---

[1] In an interview with John Cassidy for *The New Yorker*, reported in the *Observer*, 8 October (2006).

NewsCorp – corporate logic

In a speech to the International Institute of Communications in September 1988, Rupert Murdoch suggested that he did not have a very detailed strategic plan:

If in 1980 we had attempted to chart on paper the destiny of our company, we would never have anticipated the 30 very diverse acquisitions we made on four continents, almost all of which arose from unique and unanticipated events. Business situations and business opportunities simply change too quickly for there to be much point in loading ourselves down with piles of strategic speculation.

For some, however, such comments appear disingenuous. Writing in the 2003 annual report, perhaps with the benefit of hindsight and more reflection, Rupert Murdoch outlined a somewhat different vision of NewsCorp:

Throughout News Corporation's evolution our goal has been to create a Company as unified, as logical and as creative as possible. . . . We have worked to build a company with the agility to seize strategic opportunities when they arise, with the foresight to anticipate challenges and with little patience for conventional wisdom.

As noted above, Murdoch emphasised a consistency of approach in NewsCorp's strategy in 2006. However, it is perhaps this 'agility to seize strategic opportunities' provided by 'unique and unanticipated events' that is most striking about his strategic approach. One Australian financial analyst

---

also noted Murdoch's desire to retain control of that which he acquired. The nature of this control is indicated by Piers Morgan, a former Editor of the *News of the World*, a Murdoch-owned British tabloid. He describes weekly phone conversations with Murdoch in which Murdoch would dispense blunt editorial advice. Morgan acknowledges the value of the advice stating that Murdoch would make a great editor.[2] Another financial analyst noted: 'I think his biggest advantage is understanding the businesses that he's in. He can get down to the core of the business and has a lot of vision as to where that business ought to be going.'

In his 2006 annual report Murdoch notes the elements of NewsCorp's 'simple to understand [but] not always easy to implement' strategy:

> First, be willing to ignore or even take on conventional wisdom. Second, invest wisely and early in new business. Third, be patient as the new effort finds its footing. Fourth enjoy the growth and profitability as the business matures, but always be thinking about and building the next generation of new channel openings.

The extent of his influence is not exclusively restricted to the operation of the businesses of the corporation. Most governments believed that the media were an industry whose importance required regulation, particularly regarding foreign ownership, cross-ownership and concentration. As NewsCorp expanded globally, Murdoch consequently found himself affected by national regulatory systems. Many commentators have suggested that his political friendships have bought him influence in this area. For example, following Murdoch's newspapers support for Margaret Thatcher in the 1979 UK general election, in 1981 the British government called a 'three-line whip' to stop any referral of his acquisition of Times Newspapers to the Monopolies and Mergers Commission. One commentator has put it: 'his personal politics are right-wing . . . but he's opportunistic in his business dealings . . . he supports people who are going to promote his business interests'; hence his closeness to left-wing politicians such as Gordon Brown, the British Labour Chancellor from 1997.

Many have, however, doubted that Murdoch is guided by purely rational business motivations. In 1996 Ted Turner, a long time business rival of Murdoch, contrasted him with the executives of Time Warner: where Time Warner 'just wanted to make money', Murdoch wanted to 'rule the world'.[3]

Chenoweth also notes how often Murdoch has been prepared to gamble the entire company, and occasionally his own personal wealth, on the success of his business deals. Chenoweth styles Murdoch 'a crisis junkie', implying that Murdoch may have followed such an ambitious and risky strategy of expansion partly because he enjoyed the buzz from successfully competing.

Development of NewsCorp

The origins of NewsCorp lie with the establishment in 1923 of a local newspaper, *The News*, in Adelaide, Australia, by Rupert Murdoch's father. By 1980, along with other business interests, Rupert Murdoch and NewsCorp had created that country's only national newspaper, *The Australian*, two national magazines and over 20 provincial newspapers.

The profitability of this Australian base was the springboard to multinational status. It provided the financial backing for the 1968 purchase of the UK-based publishers of the *News of the World*. From 1973, with the purchase of the Express Publishing Company of San Antonio, Texas, NewsCorp also operated in the USA, expanding through the 1970s in the areas of local newspaper publishing. By 1980 the UK subsidiary was also publishing the large-circulation *Sun* in the UK and in 1981 acquired Times Newspapers Ltd. During the early 1980s, this UK subsidiary, with its newspaper and other interests, was the major contributor to NewsCorp profits.

The year 1984 saw the beginnings of a major geographical and product shift for NewsCorp. This expansion was US focused. In 1984, NewsCorp acquired the film company Twentieth Century Fox, and in 1985 it bought the six television stations of the Metromedia Broadcasting Group. These acquisitions provided the company with access to studios for making films and television programmes, to a 2,000 film library, and to a distribution platform for that content. This was the basis of the Fox Broadcasting Company, which with its affiliated local stations managed to establish in the late 1980s a fourth national television broadcaster in the USA.

This expansion into the USA had two significant implications for NewsCorp. Revenues and operating profits increased but so too did debt levels. Murdoch had to be careful not to breach private bank loan agreements. Furthermore, as US law prevented foreign citizens from holding more than

[2] P. Morgan, *The Insider: The Private Diaries of a Scandalous Decade*, Ebury Press, 2005.
[3] N. Chenoweth, *Virtual Murdoch*, Vintage, 2001.

25 per cent of any company with a broadcasting licence, in 1985 Rupert Murdoch became a US citizen.

Writing in the 2003 annual report Murdoch noted:

> One of the greatest advantages of a well-integrated worldwide company is our ability to respond to events with international strength: to share expertise, resources and personnel across platforms and across the globe.

Murdoch cited NewsCorp's coverage of the Iraq War (2003 onwards) as evidence of this, but such an approach has been characteristic of NewsCorp for years. For example, NewsCorp papers frequently promote NewsCorp satellite channels and vice versa. Murdoch himself has even obtained a much coveted cameo role in *The Simpsons*.

Entry into satellite broadcasting

On 5 February 1989 NewsCorp launched in the UK Sky Television, a direct-to-home satellite broadcasting television network. Satellite broadcasting represented a new approach to the distribution of programme material. Particularly, it provided the opportunity for any broadcaster to increase the 'footprint' (distribution) of any channel, allowing, for the first time, the distribution of programmes to more than one country.

Murdoch 'had chosen to launch a multi-million pound venture with a handful of Australian TV cronies he had known for years – and not much else' (Andrew Neil, *Full Disclosure*, 1996). Chenoweth commented that: 'It is difficult [now] to appreciate just how knuckleheaded this decision must have seemed at the time'[4] – given that all NewsCorp's experience in broadcasting thus far had been free to view and it did not appear to have appreciated the particular difficulties associated with a direct-to-subscriber operation. Furthermore the decision exacerbated an already parlous financial situation for NewsCorp.

Andrew Neil, editor of the *Sunday Times*, became Executive Chairman of Sky in November 1988 with the task of launching the channel ahead of its rivals. The launch target of 5 February 1989 was met, but it was a low-key affair – it had been a rush, no one was sure it would work on the day

and workers were still painting and fixing wires to the end.

Sky Television products were offered through both traditional cable channels and newly developed household satellite dishes. These and new encryption technology to restrict the content to only Sky subscribers opened up the possibility of viable business model.

UK media regulations barred national newspaper proprietors from owning more than 20 per cent of a television company. Even though Sky's programming was aimed mainly at a UK audience, Murdoch was able to evade this by beaming Sky's programmes from channels rented from a Luxembourg-controlled satellite, though this technicality might not have been sufficient were it not for the exceptionally close relationship that Murdoch maintained with the Thatcher government.

There were fewer subscribers than expected, resulting in lower revenues. Although stringent cost reductions were implemented (one of Murdoch's maxims being that it was easier to take a million off costs than add a million to revenues), the performance of Sky Television had marked financial consequences for NewsCorp. In the year to 30 June 1990, £134m (€188m) had been invested in the venture, yet losses of nearly £10m per month were being incurred.

Some respite was gained by November 1990, when Sky Television merged with its UK rival, British Satellite Broadcasting (BSB). The new company came to be dominated by Sky Television. Sky technology was adopted, redundancies following the merger occurred mainly among the BSB staff, and Sky executives came to dominate senior management, giving them operational and editorial control of the new company.

Financial chickens come home to roost

The financial risks that NewsCorp's radical expansion threatened finally overtook the company in 1990. There was a heavy cash drain at a time when there was a slowing of the economies in NewsCorp's main markets. These problems resulted in a gap in working capital financed by highly expensive short-term borrowing. At the same time, banks worldwide also experienced a liquidity crisis that resulted in NewsCorp facing difficulty in refinancing maturing bank debt and in

---

[4] Ibid.

meeting working capital requirements. NewsCorp's market value fell to less than one-fifth of its 1990 asset value, while borrowings rose to five times stock market capitalisation.

In October 1990, the financial strain on NewsCorp finally came to a head when it called in Citibank of New York and began negotiations for the refinancing of its debt. At the time it was the largest and geographically most diverse corporate restructuring sought from international banks. Agreement to the restructuring was not automatic and the negotiation process was complex. However, in February 1991, NewsCorp finally entered into a three-year, near A$9bn (€5bn) debt restructuring and A$700m bridging loan agreement.

Lessons from BSkyB

Sky was first marketed primarily to subscribers as movie channels. However, in September 1992, BSkyB launched Sky Sports channel, having secured exclusive rights to broadcast English football Premier League matches for five years. In less than six weeks, a million new subscribers were added. Rights to broadcast other sports followed. A gap in the market had been identified that was to revolutionise the nature of sport, the finances of BSkyB and the broadcasting strategy of NewsCorp.

A particular value of sport is that it is best viewed live. It is therefore ideal for subscription and pay-per-view-based programming. Moreover, it is ideal for advertising, as it attracts those 'with the fattest wallet: man in the prime of life' (*The Economist*, 10 February 1996). The success of BSkyB's sports strategy made the company the most profitable television broadcaster in the UK. By 2005 some commentators were asking whether BSkyB was a growth stock or whether it had become a utility.[5] The commentators were also noting that the changes in the business context, often wrought by BSkyB itself, were making the business more vulnerable to competition.

Developing the US market

The mid-1990s were a time of intense competition in the US media market. The prize was control of the '200-million-plus single-language media market in the US . . . whoever won the US mega media wars of the 1990s would create a juggernaut too big for anyone else in the world to handle'.[6] 'Indeed the economics of programme production meant that the only way to create a worldwide brand was to succeed first in the huge US market. It was the only way to achieve economies of scale.'

As a relative newcomer in the US media markets Murdoch was in the peculiar position of having access to some of the most critically and commercially acclaimed programming of the decade, a resource that other media players regarded as the key to commercial success, but with limited distribution channels of his own. Consequently the focus of NewsCorp's expansion in the mid-1990s was on obtaining such channels.

The strategy of sports-led programming was viewed by Murdoch as his 'battering ram' for entry into new markets. NewsCorp's Fox Group became a dominant player by accumulating stakes in numerous regional cable sports networks. Thus Fox built a national network by stitching together regional sports channels, often outbidding competitors in the process. Fox then wrapped its national programming around these local programmes. Where others had focused on national events, Fox was able to offer advertisers a unique alternative, a customised package of regional advertising that could in aggregate reach an audience larger than its principal competitor.

By 2000 through its combination of outright ownership of local television stations and its affiliated network, bound together by the quality of Fox's programming, Fox Broadcasting had the ability to deliver its programming service to 98 per cent of the existing US network.

NewsCorp's development in the USA was not all untrammelled success. In 1996 NewsCorp and MCI paid US$682m for the last unclaimed satellite frequency and set up a satellite television company, ASkyB. Murdoch let it be known that he intended to eliminate the much larger cable industry. This provoked a serious backlash by cable operators who threatened not to carry Fox's channels if NewsCorp began a satellite system in the USA. In any event, for Murdoch to carry out his threat would have required a change in the US copyright laws. When, by June 1997, it had become apparent that this would not be forthcoming, NewsCorp

[5] *Financial Times*, 12 October (2005).

[6] N. Chenoweth, *Virtual Murdoch*, Vintage, 2001.

backed out of an alliance with Echostar, a satellite company, and instead tried to forge an alliance with Primestar, a cable operator. When this deal was blocked by the Clinton administration as not being in the best interests of consumers, Murdoch was forced to sell ASkyB's assets to Echostar. However, the deal was structured by Echostar, bitter at what was perceived as a betrayal by Murdoch on their original agreement, so that as Echostar stock prices rose the proportion of stock that NewsCorp would receive would decline. In the end NewsCorp received only 1.7 per cent of voting rights instead of the 9 per cent it had anticipated at the outset, and a proportionate decline in other stocks.

By 2003 Murdoch had finally managed to establish a satellite foothold in the USA by acquiring 34 per cent of Hughes Electronics, including DirecTV with more than 11 million viewers. This deal was characterised by Murdoch in the 2003 annual report as a major strategic achievement. By June 2003, 81 per cent of NewsCorp's stated operating revenue and 76 per cent of its stated revenue was obtained from its US operations.

Harnessing the potential of the 'Juggernaut'

With its ultimate success in the US market NewsCorp has begun to maximise the potential of its production capabilities across its entire global operation. For example, the rising costs of producing content are offset somewhat by the fact that NewsCorp businesses, such as Twentieth Century Fox, now would provide commercially appealing television and film programming across the entire global operation. In 1996 Fox introduced the Fox News Channel to the USA (and later globally) to utilise better the 'journalistic' resources of NewsCorp as a whole. Despite its tagline of offering 'fair and balanced news', Murdoch was clear that it would stand in opposition to CNN's 'left-wing bias' and has consistently promoted an unapologetically right-wing position.[7] Writing in the British *Independent*, one journalist noted how 'Murdoch is a figure of hate in liberal Britain, accused of destroying media standards of decency'.[8]

---

[7] B.N. Hickey, 'Is Fox News Fair?', *Columbia Journalism Review*, vol. 36, no. 6 (1996), Mar./Apr.

[8] S. Sands, Comment & Debate, *Independent on Sunday*, 26 November (2006), p. 34.

In parallel with the expansion of the operation in the USA, NewsCorp moved into Asia with the acquisition, in 1993, of the satellite television company STAR TV. This broadcast free-to-air to approximately two-thirds of the world's population.

Initially, STAR was planned as a pan-Asian, English-language service. However, the diversity of the region indicated that such a pan-Asian approach was not viable. Regional programmes in local languages were needed to make any impact outside English-speaking elites. Murdoch's strategy therefore became a variant of the 'be global, act local' philosophy, or 'narrowcasting', customising the broadcast content to the different markets across Asia similar to the approach to developing Fox in the USA. To that effect, STAR acquired the world's largest contemporary Chinese movie, entered into exclusive agreements with prominent Hong Kong film companies, launched separate satellite services with costly local programming for India, the Philippines, Indonesia and China, and changed to become a subscriber service.

Other problems related to how to find a *modus vivendi* with Asia's political leaders. In September 1993, addressing an audience in London, Murdoch had claimed that 'advances in the technology of telecommunications have proved an unambiguous threat to totalitarian regimes everywhere'. A month after this speech the Chinese passed a law that virtually banned individual ownership of satellite dishes. In response, STAR removed the BBC World Service from its northern Asia channel and Murdoch offered Chinese authorities the opportunity of controlling satellite programming through NewsCorp's decoding technology, essentially allowing censors to filter programmes to be broadcast.

In 2003 NewsCorp reported that STAR posted its first full year of operating profitability. Much of the new success of STAR was attributed to Murdoch's younger son James, who had headed up the operation until late 2003.

Situation in 2006

In 2005 the changing conditions of the media market meant that BSkyB's position was challenged. Virgin announced the establishment of the world's first 'quadruple play' media company, offering television, broadband, fixed-line and mobile communications with 9 million direct customers, 1.5 million more than BSkyB. Following on from an extensive upgrading of the British cable system and challenges to BSkyB's dominance of British Premiership football by the European Commission, this company posed a very real threat, one that looked even more threatening with Virgin proposing a takeover of the principal British commercial channel ITV. This threat was quashed with BSkyB's purchase of a stake of nearly 18 per cent in ITV. BSkyB claimed it was purely a financial decision, but its strategic value in thwarting the growth of a dangerous rival was also apparent.

In July 2005 NewsCorp bought the business MySpace.com – described by *The Economist* as a 'left-leaning', social networking site. Writing in 2006, Murdoch noted that 'revenues from MySpace alone have nearly doubled every four months over the past year. . . . Our cable businesses are today where we hope and expect our Internet business to be in the near future.' Other recent activities by NewsCorp indicate that they see the Internet as a new distribution channel where different rules of operation apply. In 2005–2006 BSkyB offered free broadband to its customers. In all *The Economist* reported that in 2005 NewsCorp 'spent more than a billion dollars buying barely profitable internet companies' and had displayed interest in Now TV, a Hong Kong business that delivers television signals over broadband telephone lines. Already NewsCorp has made available through MySpace exclusive content to subscribers. In this may be discerned an extension of the 'narrowcasting' model, discussed above, where content is highly customised to suit the tastes of ever more precise segments of the market. Implicit in this is the ability of the company to provide advertisers with access to ever more precisely defined groups of consumers.

Technological developments continue to drive many of the competitive changes within the media industry as the shift from traditional terrestrial systems of television distribution via aerial found themselves in competition with satellite and cable systems, to digitisation and increasing importance of the Internet. NewsCorp has been involved in expansion at each stage of these technological developments, fighting and generally winning, albeit sometimes at great financial cost and risk to the company, increased distribution channels for the corporation's content. These technological changes went hand in hand with political changes in certain parts of the world that encouraged liberalisation and deregulation of national broadcasting monopolies or oligopolies. It may be that the devel-

opment of broadband Internet technology along with the rolling out of digital technology mean that the strategic focus of all media returns in the not too distant future to securing appealing content and the focus of competition of the major media corporations moves towards building brand loyalty in the sometimes anarchic and democratic medium of the Internet.

The future

NewsCorp's management structure has often been described as very informal, described by one aide as 'an emotionally driven and bonded company, where executives don't spend time guarding territories because nobody has one nailed down'.

In 1996, when aged 65, Murdoch was asked which of his two daughters and two sons he would like to succeed him. He was quoted as saying 'I hope we can work it out between us', adding, however, that he would probably make a judgement about his successor in about 20 years. In 2006, indicating that he was still intent on controlling the company for a large part of that 20 years, the NewsCorp annual general meeting passed a 'poison pill' vote that would make hostile bids for the company prohibitively expensive. This was seen as a response to Liberty Media building up an 18 per cent stake in the company.

In late 2003 Murdoch, despite loud shareholder criticism, imposed his younger son James as CEO of BSkyB. James attempted to quell some criticisms by stating 'I work for BSkyB's shareholders and they are my only concern'. However, given that the single largest shareholder is NewsCorp, many shareholders may have been concerned that when there is not a commonality of shareholder interests Murdoch junior may feel obliged to privilege some of Murdoch senior's more risky ventures. However, given James' success with STAR in Asia, with its strategy of 'narrowcasting', it could be argued that few have more relevant experience for leading the company into the Internet age. James Murdoch's credentials to lead NewsCorp were further enhanced by his coup in purchasing an 18 per cent stake in ITV from under the noses of Virgin. Rupert Murdoch on hearing of that purchase is reputed to have said, 'That's my boy!'

The predictions that NewsCorp will die with Rupert Murdoch may ultimately prove to be somewhat premature.

CRH plc: redefining corporate-level strategy

Mike Moroney

The pivotal role of corporate-level strategy is accepted widely. Less well understood are the mechanisms of this level of strategy, particularly the apparent conundrum of a small corporate centre generating substantial value added. These issues are explored in this case study on CRH, which is an exemplar of corporate management.

• • •

In March 2007, CRH announced financial results for 2006, celebrating 36 years of unrivalled growth and performance since the formation of the group in 1970. During that period, CRH had metamorphosed from a local player supplying the small, peripheral Irish construction market to one of the top five building materials companies in the world, with global operations and a market capitalisation of €16.6bn at end 2006. €100 invested in CRH shares in 1970 would have yielded more than €70,000 36 years later – a total annual shareholder return of over 20 per cent. Moreover, the group's performance was achieved in a notoriously hostile industry environment. CRH's accomplishments in no small way reflected the central role of its small corporate headquarters, in particular its strategy of acquisition-led expansion.

The building materials industry

The industry involves the manufacture and distribution ('merchanting' and DIY) of primary materials (such as cement, aggregates, asphalt, readymixed concrete, lime and magnesia), heavy-side building products (for example, concrete, bricks, insulation, glass and security products) and lightside building products (for example, plumbing, heating, electrical and lighting products). The sectors served are new construction work (residential, industrial, commercial and public works) and repair, maintenance and improvement (RMI).

In general, building materials and products are standard, similar across markets and largely stable over time. Production processes are also standard. Technology is non-proprietary and, for some products, relatively unsophisticated.

Characteristics

Building materials is a cyclical, commodity business, characterised in most markets by maturity and fragmentation. Cyclicality reflects the considerable capital investment involved, long lead times and 'lumpy' additions to capacity. Industry cycles are longer in duration and larger in amplitude than general economic cycles. However, their timing varies between countries. Building materials and products are largely commodities, with little differences between suppliers, which compete mainly on the basis of price. Construction is a mature sector in the Western world, reflecting stable economic activity and populations. Average growth in construction activity is less than half the rate of economic growth, while RMI accounts for upwards of half the total output. By contrast, in newly emerging areas of the world (Asia, Eastern Europe, Latin America) and in Western countries at an earlier stage of economic development (such as Ireland, Finland and Portugal), construction is buoyant. On the other hand, cyclicality in such markets is more pronounced.

Traditionally, the building materials industry has been highly fragmented. Production is often linked to the location of reserves, of varying value, leading to a proliferation of facilities and low barriers to entry. In addition, building materials and products are, by and large, characterised by a high weight to value ratio. As a result, high transport costs rapidly outweigh scale economies and determine the radius of economic activity and competition, which in many cases can be 150 kilometres or less. Furthermore, markets have tended to be local in nature due to differences in building regulations, construction practices and product standards. Finally, success was often determined by factors such as personal service, local contacts, close operational control and the ability to react to change. As a result, the industry had developed as a large number of small and medium-sized firms, often family owned and run.

Recent trends

Since the mid-1990s, a number of structural trends had emerged, in part prompted by sustained low levels of activity. In certain markets, supply-side concentration and significant corporate activity had occurred, resulting in the disappearance of a number of previously well-known industry names. This was most pronounced in UK markets for primary materials, 'heavyside' products and merchanting (Exhibit 1). At the same time, a number of large, international building materials companies had emerged over time, typically using the base of a strong local market position and/or product competence as a springboard to expand into other regions and areas of activity.

There was also evidence that local differences between geographic markets were eroding. Driven by institutional factors, such as at European Union (EU) level, a harmonisation of building regulations, product standards and tendering procedures was occurring. This was reinforced by convergence in building practices across markets, resulting from mobility of workers and the increasingly multinational character of contracting and of building materials firms. Relatedly, the industry's customer base was consolidating, customers' needs were homogenising and they were becoming more demanding. None the less, the underlying logic of fragmentation continued to prevail in many markets. In general, products and distribution were less concentrated than primary materials. Also, construction markets globally remained fragmented, in particular the large US market, with a value of $700bn (€550bn).

Profile of CRH

Headquartered in Dublin, Ireland, CRH employed 80,000 people in over 1,000 subsidiaries in more than 3,000 locations in 26 countries. The group enjoyed a major presence in mature markets in Europe and North America and a growing foothold in emerging regions, including Eastern Europe and Latin America. CRH's prominence was recognised by many industry awards over the years for financial reporting, investor relations, and excellence/ innovation in environmental and safety practices.

History, growth and development

CRH was formed in 1970 following the merger of Irish Cement and Roadstone/Wood, an Irish

---

Exhibit 1 UK building materials market concentration (2005)

	Largest player market share (%)	Top three market share (%)
Primary materials/heavyside products		
Cement	42	84
Aggregates	25	65
Asphalt	28	64
Readymixed concrete	23	62
Concrete blocks	32	81
Merchanting	20	65

Note: Merchanting concentration ratio is for top four producers.

Source: Data derived from Adding Value or Hot Air?: Sector M&A Trends, Themes, Prospects and Possibilities, pub Merrill Lynch, 25 October 2005, Chart 1, p. 17 and Chart 12, p. 31.

building materials company. Since then, the group has undergone major growth through three major phases of development (below). In general, change has been evolutionary, involving a managed, learning process of building, augmenting and layering competences.

Organic market penetration in Ireland (from 1970)

During the 1970s, Irish construction enjoyed a boom on the back of a modernising economy. The newly merged CRH capitalised on this favourable environment through its vertically integrated and leading positions in virtually all domestic markets for heavyside building materials and products.

Acquisition-led overseas expansion (from the late 1970s)

In the late 1970s, with a view to spreading risks and opportunities more broadly, CRH made a strategic decision to invest in familiar business sectors overseas, through add-on acquisitions of medium-sized, often family-owned, businesses. Early expansion in the UK and The Netherlands was followed by further acquisitions in mainland Europe. In 1977, Don Godson (later Chief Executive, 1994–2000) went to the USA with 'a telephone and a cheque book'. By 2006, the Americas accounted for more than half of group turnover and profits. CRH's presence in emerging regions gathered pace from the mid-1990s. The group also expanded in a limited, but highly rewarding, way into new product areas, including merchanting and DIY, security fencing, clay brick products and glass fabrication (in the USA).

Product focus, larger acquisitions (from the late 1990s)

During the 1990s, CRH's previous regional structure evolved to a more product-based organisation, to bring greater focus to business development and sharing best practice. At the same time, anticipating greater industry consolidation, the group began to supplement traditional mid-size deal flow with larger acquisitions.

Strategy

CRH's strategic vision is to 'be a responsible international leader in building materials delivering superior performance and growth'.[1] The group's strategy is 'to seek new geographic platforms in its

core businesses and to take advantage of complementary product opportunities in order to achieve strategic balance and to establish multiple platforms from which to deliver performance and growth'.[1] Growth is achieved:

- through investing in new capacity;
- from developing new products and markets;
- by acquiring and growing mid-sized companies, augmented from time to time with larger deals.[2]

Products and markets

CRH's core businesses included primary materials, heavyside building products and specialist distribution (through builders merchants and DIY stores). There were two notable characteristics of CRH's product/market portfolio. The first was leadership. Reflecting industry fragmentation, the group focused on securing and maintaining leading positions in local or regional markets and in product segments or niches. Also unique was CRH's deliberate geographic, product and segment balance (Exhibit 2), which smoothed the effects of varying economic conditions and provided greater opportunities for growth. (CRH outperformed peers in the industry downturns of the early 1980s, 1990s and 2000s.)

Two markets stood out in CRH's portfolio. The main driver of growth since the early 1990s, US operations earned above-average returns and demonstrated remarkably low volatility.[3] Analysts' estimates of 40 per cent return on net assets (RONA) for the group's Irish operations reflected CRH's 60 per cent share of the cement market on the total island of Ireland, buoyant Irish construction, a low rate of manufacturing corporation tax (12.5 per cent) and heavily depreciated assets.[4]

Management and organisation

Unlike its peers, CRH operated a federal structure, comprising a small central headquarters and four regionally focused product divisions (Exhibit 3). To capitalise on local market knowledge, a high degree of individual responsibility was devolved to operational managers, within group guidelines

[1] CRH Annual Report 2005, pp. 1, 2.

[2] http://www.crh.com/chrcorp/about/characteristics/.
[3] Goodbody Stockbrokers, 'CRH: The Foundation Stones of Value', July 2003, p. 41.
[4] Goodbody Stockbrokers, 'CRH: The Foundation Stones of Value', July 2003.

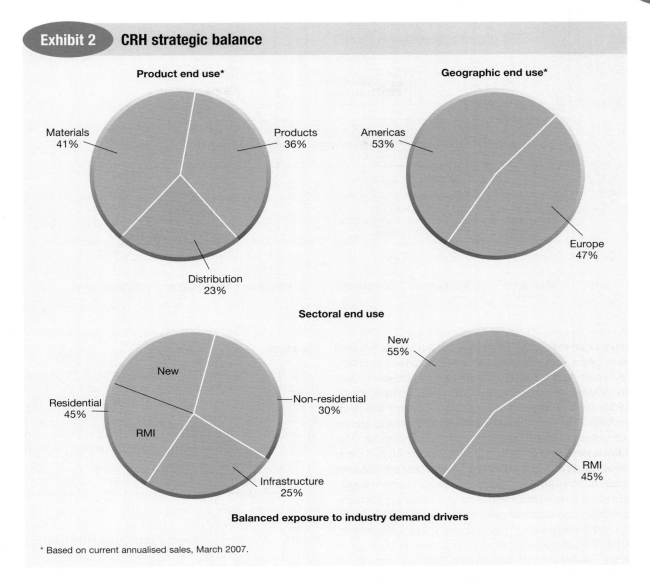

Exhibit 2   **CRH strategic balance**

Product end use*

Materials 41%
Products 36%
Distribution 23%

Geographic end use*

Americas 53%
Europe 47%

Sectoral end use

New
Residential 45%
RMI
Non-residential 30%
Infrastructure 25%

New 55%
RMI 45%

Balanced exposure to industry demand drivers

* Based on current annualised sales, March 2007.

and controls. According to Jack Golden, Human Resources (HR) Director, 'while the local operating units have operational autonomy, they do not have independence'.

CRH adopted a rigorous approach to project evaluation, approval and review. The twin requirements of performance and growth were continually reinforced, with entities having to earn the right to grow. Planning was formalised and interactive, centring on the rolling five-year strategic plan, year 1 of which constituted the budget. Stretch targets were established for financial and operational output measures. Performance measurement was timely, formal and rigorous. This allowed early critical review of underperformance, to identify reasons, provide assistance, put in place corrective

measures and enable senior management to draw broader lessons. However, ongoing cross-subsidisation was not contemplated. If necessary, CRH implemented a management change to support recovery of performance to satisfactory levels. This could include a strategic review to consider the most appropriate disposition for the business going forward.

Continuous improvement was relentless, as demonstrated by ongoing programmes of benchmarking and best practice. In addition, products and processes were continually re-engineered to yield greater returns, primarily through greater efficiencies (but also from selective expansion into related products and regional markets). Ongoing development investment (consistently well in

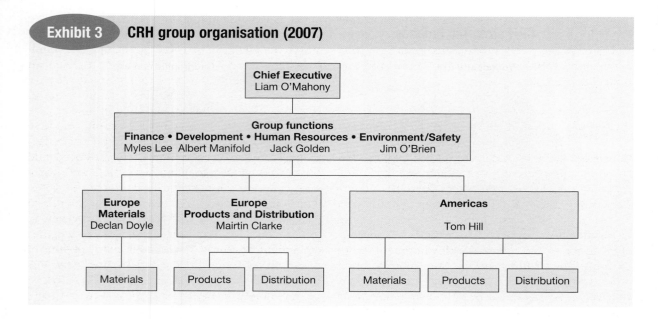

Exhibit 3 **CRH group organisation (2007)**

excess of the level of depreciation)[5] incorporated new plant, capacity extensions and major upgrades.

Over time, CRH's pool of managers had increased, as a result of continuing growth and a relentless stream of acquisitions. None the less, in 2006 the core group of key corporate, group and operational managers only numbered 350. Managers were drawn from internally developed operating managers, experienced finance and development professionals, and owner–entrepreneurs from acquired companies, providing a healthy mix and depth of skills.

Notwithstanding the strong pace of growth, CRH's management were characterised by experience, stability and continuity. In 36 years, there had been only five chief executives, all of whom (like a majority of senior managers) were Irish. Having joined the group, few managers left. There were several reasons for this constancy. Continuing success was clearly a factor, reinforced by CRH's market-driven, performance-related remuneration policy aimed at creating shareholder value. (This comprised variable compensation, share options for key managers, and employee share participation schemes.) In addition, a range of formal and informal mechanisms promoted integration (see below). Finally, low turnover, rotation and promotion from within resulted in a wealth of in-house industry knowledge and expertise.

Finances

CRH had a strong and consistent track record of financial performance: 2006 represented the 23rd consecutive year of dividend increase, while the group had experienced only two relatively short periods of declining EPS (in the early 1980s and early 1990s). Moreover, the group's peak to trough performance during industry downturns demonstrated an improving trend over time.[6] CRH's level and consistency of performance was also superior to its peers internationally. CRH enjoyed a premium of 2 per cent (one-sixth) in the bell-weather return on capital employed ratio (notwithstanding that the group's operating margin matched the industry average).

CRH was noted in financial markets for its finance function, which was characterised by extensive business knowledge and operational contribution, as well as diligence, conservatism and prudence. (The function frequently seconded in supplementary expertise.) Two hallmarks of CRH's financial management were a strong focus on return on capital and cash generation. Operations were required to earn 15 per cent RONA on an ongoing basis. Newly acquired businesses often found such financial rigour challenging. A cash generative mentality pervaded all operations and was central to the group's evaluation and control

---

[5] Goodbody Stockbrokers, 'CRH: Still to play its "Trump Card"', 13 July 2005, p. 18.

[6] Goodbody Stockbrokers, 'CRH: The Foundation Stones of Value', July 2003.

processes. Cash earnings were consistently around two-thirds higher than reported EPS, a major factor enabling CRH to fund its acquisition-led expansion overseas without compromising its financial principles.

Corporate-level strategy at CRH

Consistent with its federalist philosophy, CRH's corporate headquarters was small, with a limited range of central functions. Less than 100 people were employed in Dublin. Counting support staff in the four divisions, around 200 people were engaged in headquarters-type activities. Traditionally, finance and business development were the only central functions. Of late, internal audit had grown in line with external compliance requirements. Also, the group development team acted as a catalyst for renewal on cross-divisional deals, strategic planning and opportunities in emerging regions.

Notwithstanding small size and limited scope, headquarters drove the development and integration of CRH through a variety of formal and informal mechanisms.

Formal mechanisms

CRH's strategic stance was explicit, enduring and continually reinforced. Over time, the broad thrusts of the group's strategy had become progressively more articulated and refined under successive chief executives. Strategy was reinforced by rigorous measurement, evaluation and control processes, and by the value-added business contribution and advice of the finance function, ensuring early intervention and appropriate corrective measures.

CRH operated a group-wide management development system to develop the critical experience base of managers, particularly when they were mobile, in their twenties and thirties. Over time, this system had become more formal and structured because, unlike in the past, managers were unlikely to get the requisite exposure to a wide range of CRH's operations unsystematically. A key element was the management database, on which the core 350 managers in the group had recently been formally profiled.

There were a variety of formal development programmes for managers, many of which involved inputs and presentations on strategy from senior management, including the chief executive. The Management Seminar was held in Dublin in late March in advance of CRH plc's annual general meeting (AGM) in May. This event provided an opportunity for 130 senior managers to discuss strategy, based on a dedicated theme. Careful selection ensured that around 40 per cent of participating managers each year were first-time attendees. The Development Forum was run annually for a cross-section of experienced and relatively new development personnel, and was a very valuable training and best practice sharing/development activity. A Leadership Development Programme (LDP 1) was run in each division in the winter. (As building materials is weather dependent, winter is downtime in many regions of the group.) Aiming to give a periscope view, this programme covered strategy, personal development and networking. This was followed two years later by LDP 2, which was group-wide.

The Business Leadership Programme (BLP) involved the four divisions and corporate headquarters, with the aim of preparing experienced managers for senior leadership roles. (It was supplemented by other programmes for developing specific competences, for example negotiating skills for operating companies.) BLP involved four sessions over 12 months, with work-based assignments between sessions, and covered psychometric testing, mentor support and individually tailored development plans. The annual Euroforum with employees was initially established as a Section 13 agreement in response to the EU Information and Consultation Directive. Over time, an HR forum was established in conjunction with the Euroforum to tackle issues proactively, such as developing future HR competences for the group.

At division level, integrated product management had become progressively strengthened over time, especially in the USA. Coordinated divisionally, ongoing best practice activities involved meetings by small teams of experts at local, regional and international levels facilitated by technical advisors. These resulted in highly innovative ideas and exchanges of products, which 'push forward the frontiers of excellence and "sharing the learning" . . . we all have to continually get smarter in what we do, reducing costs and offering better quality and service to our customers'.[7] There were around seven best practice programmes in each of the

---

[7] CRH, *Contact*, issue 14 (2005), p. 7.

four product-based divisions. Best practice was supplemented by benchmarking exercises and the development of common systems platforms (the latter particularly in the USA).

Finally, communications and coaching opportunities were exploited to the full. CRH's excellence in external relations was mirrored internally, utilising communications technologies. The use of e-mail and bulletin boards was common, while regular editions of the internal news magazine *Contact* were read avidly by managers and employees alike. All formal integrative mechanisms involved *de facto* coaching, both team and individual. Such forums were used as opportunities to restate key messages, from reinforcing the 'right to grow' mantra at strategic level, to the minutiae of operational best practice.

Informal mechanisms

Notwithstanding the foregoing, 'the culture of performance and achievement which pervades CRH is its key strength'.[8] This restless culture was nurtured and sustained constantly. CRH continually reinforced its core values in formal statements of strategy, in external and internal communications and through corporate folklore. (Managers in Poland referred to 'RONA the bitch'!) More subtle mechanisms also existed, including leading by example and clear norms of acceptable behaviour (such as the ethos of 'owning up' in financial reporting).

Strong informal networks existed among managers, even between far-flung regions of the group's activities. These emerged from frequent manager rotation within and between divisions, and from management development programmes, benchmarking and best practice activities (which provided ready forums for interaction). In addition, a social dimension accompanied formal events (involving dinner and, occasionally, golf). This contributed to a family atmosphere, such as at the annual get-together of senior managers at CRH's AGM in Dublin each May. The AGM itself was an important ceremonial occasion, and served as an induction for new managers, all of whom attended in their first year in the group.

Other informal mechanisms underpinned integration. Hierarchy and job descriptions were highly flexible. Harry Sheridan, former long-

serving Finance Director, also held operational responsibility for the emerging region of Latin America in the 1990s. HR Director Jack Golden was involved in a wide range of group issues pertaining to France, based on his previous experience as country manager there for another multinational. At operational level, informal mentoring, hands-on assistance and individual coaching were common within and across entities.

Acquisitions

Acquisitions were the most visible aspect of corporate-level strategy. From 1978 to 2006, CRH completed around 620 deals, spending over €13.5bn, over 90 per cent in the period since 1995. The group's acquisition performance was extolled widely. A leading global investment bank commented: 'CRH has the best track record of its peer group . . . of growing returns through acquisitions'.[9] It was estimated that acquisitions accounted for 70 per cent of CRH's profit growth (with organic growth contributing one-quarter, and currency movements the remainder).[10]

Traditionally, CRH's acquisitions were add-on in nature. However, in the period since 1995, over half of expenditure had been on larger deals, of which materials businesses accounted for more than 70 per cent. By end 2006, the group had completed 22 such purchases, with no single deal amounting to more than 10 per cent of its capital base (Exhibit 4). In general, CRH acquired on very favourable terms: purchase prices represented a low 6.8 times operating profits[11] (although multiples for larger deals were somewhat higher). In part, this reflected 'the Group's commitment to completing transactions only at prices that will contribute to long-term value creation for its shareholders'.[12] Moreover, CRH was adept at generating superior returns from deals. From an estimated level of 10 per cent on purchase, in general RONA rose to 12 per cent within the first year and to the benchmark level of 15 per cent within two to three years.[13] Finally, as a result of its strong financial position, CRH had considerable

[8] CRH Annual Report 2005, Chairman's Statement, p. 7.

[9] Goldman Sachs, 'CRH', 18 October 2005, p. 3.
[10] Goodbody Stockbrokers, 'CRH: Still to play its "Trump Card"', 13 July 2005, p. 7.
[11] Goldman Sachs, 'CRH', 18 October 2005, p. 2.
[12] CRH Annual Report 2005, Chairman's Statement, p. 6.
[13] Goodbody Stockbrokers, 'CRH: Still to play its "Trump Card"', 13 July 2005, p. 10.

Exhibit 4   CRH acquisitions, 1991–2006

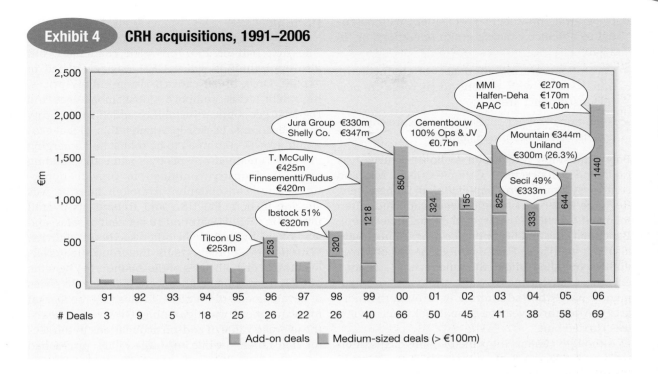

'fire-power'[14] to finance a continuing high level of acquisition spend.

The acquisition process

Rigorous, comprehensive and inclusive, CRH's acquisition strategy was singular in conception and execution and had 'proven very difficult to replicate'.[15] Much of the time of all levels of management was consumed in acquisitions. For the initial identification phase, CRH had 14 development teams spread across the group seeking opportunities and maintaining contact with an extensive database of potential targets accumulated over more than 25 years. At any one time, a considerable number of acquisitions were under active consideration, ensuring a steady deal flow. Each purchase gave rise to further opportunities, in other (occasionally new) product lines in other geographic areas.

Courtship involved a patient and often long approach of familiarisation and coaching. CRH took time to assess suitability and strategic fit, and to know management and their evolving needs. Much effort was spent appraising the target of CRH's strategy, management, values and expectations, including up-front clarity on post-acquisition priorities. It was not unusual for CRH to walk away from a deal, on grounds of timing, price or compatibility. Sometimes, acquisitions were completed at a later date.

To aid negotiation, CRH had codified in a classified, proprietary document the best practice, knowledge and processes involved in making an acquisition, gleaned from many years of experience. This was full of collected wisdom, including recommended letters of introduction, follow-up procedures and practical advice on deal making. An experienced operational manager guided each acquisition team. At the appropriate time, a senior level 'ambassador' was introduced to close the deal.

Before completion, each deal underwent rigorous evaluation, including qualitative operational review, due diligence, strict cash flow testing and board approval. Traditionally, CRH's acquisitions shared many common characteristics:

● Medium-sized, private, often family-run businesses.

[14] Ibid., p. 1.
[15] Merrill Lynch, 'Adding Value or Hot Air?', 25 October 2005, p. 12.

- Geographic/product market leaders, with potential to enhance existing group operations or fill a gap.
- Careful structuring of deals, often involving initial stakes with options to increase in new regions/product areas.
- Retention of owner–managers to ensure continuity and maintain human capital.

Post-acquisition integration to boost returns was rapid and well practised. Group financial, MIS and control systems were implemented immediately. Revenue and cost synergies were captured, often followed over time by targeted capital investment. Benchmarking and best practice programmes were also put in place. For a period, newly acquired entities operated under the guidance of a related existing CRH business, while the 'right to grow' mantra was exhorted informally through the hierarchy. After three years, a formal look-back review was carried out.

Although similar in principle, the acquisition process for larger deals was somewhat different. Higher-level (corporate/division) involvement and greater public availability of information on targets facilitated truncated courtship and rapid completion. While for the most part CRH engaged in negotiated deals, tendered bids were not uncommon and the group did not rule out hostile or disputed acquisitions. Integration was assessed on a case-by-case basis. In a new region or product area, experienced CRH managers might be brought in to run the business for a period, with the situation determining the skills and experience required.

Outlook

The first half of 2007 provided challenges, but also opportunities which CRH was positioned to exploit. On a broad canvas, rising energy prices, high debt levels, stubborn global imbalances and regional geopolitical instability added uncertainty to the economic backdrop. Against this, global economic growth continued to be robust and emerging markets remained prospective, while the building materials industry continued to provide opportunities for consolidation. Although housing was slowing in both the USA and Ireland, its overall impact on CRH was around 10 per cent of sales, and was offset by growth in other sectors of activity. With improved prospects for the group's materials businesses on both sides of the Atlantic, the benefits of CRH's strategic balance were manifest. In terms of development, there was evidence that the market for acquisitions was tightening. Over recent years, the average value of add-on acquisitions in the sector had fallen,[16] while for large deals, prices had risen and returns were lower. At the same time, the stock market looked to the group for a 'benchmark level' of acquisition spend of €1bn annually.[17]

As Liam O'Mahony and his management team celebrated 36 years of achievement, CRH could look to the future with the confidence borne of outstanding business success and robust financial health. But high shareholder expectations and the demands of a hostile industry environment bred constant vigilance. Specifically, could the corporate strategy and acquisition model that had served the group so well over the years be sustained?

---

[16] Goodbody Stockbrokers, 'CRH: Still to play its "Trump Card"', 13 July 2005, p. 16.
[17] Merrill Lynch, 'Adding Value or Hot Air?', 25 October 2005, p. 13.

Royal NUMICO NV: nutritional supplements – wrong entry or wrong/untimely exit?

D. Jan Eppink

NUMICO is one of largest companies in The Netherlands. Its traditional success was built on the manufacturing and sale of baby foods and specialist nutritional products in more than 100 countries. But in the late 1990s the company diversified into the market for nutritional supplements – from which it subsequently withdrew by 2003. The case looks at the reasons for these changes in the company's direction.

• • •

Background

In 1896, Martinus van der Hagen secured the exclusive rights to produce infant milk formula from cow's milk using the Backhaus method. He owned the Steam Dairy factory in a small village close to The Hague in The Netherlands. Around 1900 the company name was changed into Nutricia. In 1997 the company received the designation 'Royal' and changed its name into NUMICO NV to make a clear distinction between the company listed on the Amsterdam Stock Exchange since 1966 and the brands it had in its portfolio.

Photo: Koninklijke Numico N.V.

The infant milk formula was the beginning of a long line of food products for babies. Nutricia was a local Dutch player with limited exports. In 1946 the company introduced Olvarit vegetable-based baby meals into the Dutch market. In the 1960s Numico developed specialised nutritional products for hospitals and, for example, complete nutrition solutions for the chronically ill with feeding problems.

In its history Numico had made many acquisitions in many countries. As a result, by 2006 it controlled interests in more than 100 countries and sold its top-quality baby food under brands such as Cow & Gate, Milupa, Nutricia, Dumex, Mellin, Bambix and Olvarit. Clinical nutrition products

went under brands such as Nutrison, Peptisorb, Nutridrink, Fortimel and Diasip. Acquisitions and organic growth increased turnover from €676m in 1994 to €1,577m in 1998. Over the same period net profit increased from €61.8m (9.1 per cent of net turnover) to €153.9m (9.8 per cent). Numico had a manufacturing base of 21 supply points that were supported by an integrated worldwide procurement and supply chain.

Research and development had always been an important activity in Numico. It was closely aligned with the two core businesses, baby food and clinical nutrition, and focused on the relationship between nutrition, diseases and health. The laboratories were located in Wageningen, The

---

Netherlands; Friedrichdorf, Germany; Liverpool, United Kingdom; and Adelaide, Australia. Numico also had strategic alliances in research with several institutes, universities, hospitals, and participates in government projects. Patent protection was an important issue. The R&D organisation had become one of the largest industrial research organisations in the field of health-related nutritional products. Numico employs 250 scientists, half of whom have a PhD.

Strategy of the company in 1998

Numico's strategy was based on 'Medical Platform Marketing'. Products for vulnerable people were based on scientific data, and users were informed by practitioners in the medical and nutritional field. The company policy remained oriented towards disseminating the importance of its specialised foods and other products to the medical world, patients and society in general. Based on this strategic concept, which required high spend on both R&D and marketing, Numico had to internationalise further to recover these costs.

The 1998 annual report described the company profile as follows:

> Numico is a multinational company concentrating on the development, manufacturing and sales of specialised nutrition based upon medical scientific concepts with a high added value.
>
> (p. 6)

The strategy was described as follows:

> The strategy of Numico is focused on specialisation, continuing internationalisation and profitable growth, partly by acquisitions as well as by strategic alliances, and safeguarding the highest quality in all stages of production and services.
>
> (p. 6)

Numico's turnover in 1998 was as shown in Exhibit 1.

The data in the exhibit shows that almost half of the turnover came from infant nutrition. Moreover, some 60 per cent of total turnover was realised in Western Europe, a region with falling birth rates and an ageing population. Future growth could come from international expansion and from nutriceuticals for increasing health through better nutrition. Between 1994 and 1998, Numico bought a number of smaller European companies in the field of neutriceuticals.

Exhibit 1	Numico turnover, 1998 (€m)

Infant nutrition	
Infant formula	€538
Cereals	€95
Meals, drinks, and juices	€151
Total	€784 (49.7%)
Nutritional health care	
Enteral clinical nutrition and administration systems	€213
Dietary products	€99
Total	€312 (19.7%)
Nutriceuticals and health foods	€118 (7.5%)
Total specialised foods	€1,214 (76.9%)
Nutricia dairy and drinks	€309 (19.6%)
Skin and throat care	€54 (3.5%)
Total turnover	€1,577

The acquisition of General Nutrition Companies (GNC) in 1999

In July 1999 Numico announced the acquisition of General Nutrition Companies (GNC) of Pittsburgh (USA). GNC was the largest company in the world producing, marketing and selling nutritional supplements. GNC had more than 30 per cent of the sport-nutrition market. Its turnover in 1998 was approximately €1.4bn with an operating profit of around 13 per cent of turnover. GNC produced products under its own brands and for private labels. It had a nationwide distribution system selling through drugstore chains, its own stores, franchise stores and the Internet. GNC exported its products to some 25 countries.

The rationale behind the acquisition was twofold. For Numico it was a move to become a world leader in this field, but also GNC could make use of Numico's research outcomes to develop its product range further.

The press release on 5 July 1999 stated:

> Numico's scientific knowledge and research activities and GNC's brand, marketing know-how and leading market position in the US, will enable the combined entity to realise this strategy and to strengthen its global market position.

And:

> As a result of intensive active component research and development (Life Science), Numico has developed a range of specialised nutritional supplement products. The acquisition of GNC provides Numico with the world's leading brand and the largest distribution network in the US to sell these products without significant additional marketing expenses.

Both companies expected additional sales of €270m per year to be reached in three years after completion of the merger. Numico expected that the acquisition would immediately enhance earnings.

The Numico offer was US$2.5bn (€2bn), including US$760m GNC debt. The acquisition was financed by issuing new shares, a subordinated convertible bond, and debt.

The acquisitions of Enrich International and Rexall Sundown in 2000

On 4 November 1999 Numico announced the acquisition of Enrich International. This US-based company sold nutritional supplements and personal care products. Sales at the time of the announcement were approximately €170m. Enrich had its own in-house R&D which gave it an advantage in product development. Its products were sold in more than 10 countries outside North America, including Japan, Australia, New Zealand and Malaysia. Internationally, Enrich operated a network of some 250,000 distributors.

Numico announced on 5 June 2000 that it had completed the acquisition of Rexall Sundown Inc. of Boca Raton, Florida, USA. This company produced and marketed vitamins and other nutritional supplements as well as consumer health products. Sales for the year 2000 were expected to be US$820m. Its branded products were sold in the mass market, drugstores and food stores. Moreover, the company had a network of independent Rexall Showcase distributors that sold an exclusive line of products.

A press release stated:

> The acquisition reinforces Numico's leading position in the growing nutritional supplements market. Through intensive research and development, Numico has developed a range of specialised nutritional supplement products. These products will soon be launched through the specialty and multi-level channels of distribution in the U.S. where Numico already has a strong presence. The acquisition of Rexall Sundown, major supplier to the mass market, will provide Numico with leading nutritional supplements brands and the largest distribution network in the U.S. The acquisition will allow Rexall Sundown to enhance its strong market position in the U.S. mass market and provides access to the European market.

Numico expected that the acquisition would immediately increase earnings per share.

Total price of the acquisition was €1.9bn, including assumption of Rexall's net debt. It was financed by the issue of new shares (€518m), a subordinated convertible bond loan (€690m) and bank debt.

At a later stage Enrich was combined with the activities of Rexall Showcase International under the name Unicity.

Two comments on the entry into the nutriceuticals market

In an interview in October 2006 for this case, Hans van der Wielen, Numico's CEO from 1992 until 7 May 2002, commented on the background of the strategy of 1998 and the US acquisitions in later years:

> Numico was positioned between the pharmaceutical market and the food market. In the infant formula market it faced pharmaceutical companies such as American Home, Bristol Meyers, and Ross Abbott in the USA and Novartis in Europe. In the toddlers food market there are big companies such as Danone and Nestlé. It is difficult and unwise to compete head-on with them. . . . Many products in the pharmaceutical business end up on the shelf in the supermarket. . . . We bought the US companies and their distribution channels to be in a position to sell our clinical and diet foods on a large scale. We did not buy them just for selling vitamins. . . . More than half of the turnover in the USA was diet and sport nutrition.

Theo van Rooij, an industry expert, observed in an interview for this case in October 2006 that with the entry into the market for nutritional supplements, Numico faced market challenges that were quite different from its traditional businesses. First of all, this new market was one with much more influence from fashionable developments. Moreover, he considered these products to be much more income elastic and therefore more dependent on economic cycles. Finally, the competitors were often smaller companies with sometimes unpredictable and 'wild' behaviour.

Risks related to the strategy

In the annual report of 2000, the executive board of Numico recognised three kinds of risks connected to the strategy:

- First of all, Numico focused on the production of specialised nutritional products. 'This policy involves certain risks regarding the vulnerability of these products and of the target groups which these are aimed at, including babies, patients and people with specific nutritional needs.'

- The second risk was the increasing foreign exchange risk from the growth of the activities in the USA. Numico drew up its balance sheet in euros; a change in the rate of the dollar relative to the euro has a positive or negative impact on the sales reported. The same change would have the opposite effect on the value of debt if it was incurred in US dollar.

- Finally, the board recognised that 'sales of nutritional supplements were more sensitive to economic fluctuations than their traditional products. However this effect was somewhat reduced because consumers were becoming increasingly conscious of their health and the importance of balanced nutrition' (p. 26).

The report of the executive board of the same year contained the following observation:

> Numico is able to continue its growth even in less favourable economic circumstances. The weakening of the market in vitamins and herbal products has had only a limited impact on total sales of nutritional supplements of Numico.
>
> (p. 18)

Developments in 2001 and 2002

The year 2001 was a turbulent one with mixed results. The first half-year results were in line with the high expectations. The next six months were disappointing. Reasons were the economic slow-down in the USA, management problems and the delayed introduction of new product concepts. There was a notable decreasing trend in the market for vitamins and herbs for more than a year, which was magnified in 2001. Moreover, there was intense competition from manufacturers selling similar products at very low prices. The entire sector was facing negative publicity regarding the effectiveness of certain ingredients.

The annual report mentions that the dependence on the economic climate had been greater than expected. In its report the supervisory board observed that the economic slow-down of the US economy had a significant effect on the nutritional supplements business. This was discussed in detail with the executive board and measures had been taken to face up to the problems at Rexall Sundown in particular. Its Dairy and Drinks Group was sold in 2001 since it no longer fitted the strategy of high-value-added products based on medical and nutritional know-how. None the less, the same level of cash earnings was reached as in 2000, an extremely strong year.

In the summer of 2001 a conflict arose between the chairman of the supervisory board and CEO Hans van der Wielen. Some weeks later, van der Wielen handed in his resignation, which was initially not accepted by the supervisory board. It was agreed that the CEO would 'mind the store', but not take on any big projects. He could not address the management problems that arose in the US operations in 2001. Finally, he stepped down in the annual meeting of shareholders in May 2002.

2002 – a new CEO

Hans van der Wielen was succeeded by Jan Bennink. He described the strategy in a presentation at the annual meeting in 2002 as built on three businesses: infant nutrition, health care, and supplements, held together by medical endorsement of the products, research, brands, and supply synergy. Products would reach the customer through hospitals, pharmacies, specialty retail, mass market and the Internet.

In a presentation for analysts in November 2002, Numico stated the strategic objective of GNC to restore the company to its 'historical high growth/high margin levels' by fixing the fundamentals: pricing, product mix, new product development and marketing. Besides GNC, Numico would focus on its traditional businesses, Nutricia Clinical and Nutricia Babyfood.

The annual report for 2002 states that it was a dramatic year for Numico. Its turnover was almost 5 per cent less than in 2001. Net sales of GNC declined by 10.3 per cent and EBITA by almost 39 per cent. Net sales of Rexall Sundown fell by almost 22 per cent on a comparable basis. Unicity's sales were almost 20 per cent lower. Part of this decrease in sales is explained by the drop of the US dollar versus the euro: by year end the exchange rate was as follows: 2001, €1 = $0.8928; 2002, €1 = $0.9434; 2003, €1 = $1.1904. The sales volumes in the US market dropped less than the sales reported in euros suggest. The company took an extraordinary charge of some €1.7bn for its US activities.

Exit from the market for nutritional supplements in 2003

During the presentation of the financial results for 2002 in March 2003, Numico announced that the sale of Rexall Sundown was well under way. Rexall Sundown was characterised as a low-growth/low-margin business. Given the new strategy which focused on high-growth/high-margin businesses, Rexall Sundown no longer fitted both criteria. GNC was put on probation; it was a high-margin, but a low-growth business.

On 10 June 2003 Numico formally announced the sale of Rexall Sundown to NBTY Inc. for US$250m in cash. In 2002, Rexall Sundown had a turnover of €454m, and EBITA €23m. NBTY Inc. is a prominent vertically integrated US producer and distributor of a wide range of high-quality nutritional supplements in the USA and globally.

On 17 October 2003 the sale of GNC was made public. It was stated that there was no strategic fit with Numico. It was a retail brand, with little product overlap and synergies limited to research. Moreover, Numico's management could now focus their time and financial resources on its high-growth/high-margin businesses of baby food and clinical nutrition. GNC was sold to Apollo Management for US$750m in a deal completed on 5 December 2003. The estimated impairment was €450m. A press statement issued by GNC said that: 'Apollo . . . sees tremendous value in the power of the GNC brand'.

Some developments after the divestments

In the three years after the divestments, NBTY, which acquired Rexall Sundown, and GNC showed an increase in performance (see the Appendix).

The price of NBTY shares in New York almost doubled between June 2003 and October 2006, and reached its highest point in May 2004.

GNC's turnover decreased slightly in 2004 and 2005, but showed a large increase in the first six months of 2006. Operating income increased considerably after 2003.

Industry expert Theo van Rooij also observed in October 2006 that sales in the market for nutritional supplements had picked up remarkably in the second half of 2005!

APPENDIX

Some data on NUMICO,[1] NBTY and GNC

	2005	2004	2003	2002	2001	2000 pro forma[2]	2000	1999	1998
Turnover by division									
Baby food	1,314	1,115	1,058	1,060	1,068	n.a.	923	837	784
Clinical food	674	602	542	514	480	n.a.	426	370	312
Nutritional supplements						n.a.	2,333	650	118
Dairy and drinks							542	442	363
Other (including activities to be sold)	0	5	1,551	2,392	2,791	n.a.			
Total	1,988	1,722	3,151	3,966	4,339	3,807	4,224	2,299	1,577
Turnover by region									
Western Europe	1,317	1,160	1,151	1,225	1,207	1,121	1,121	1,024	958
Eastern Europe	323	257	223	208	216	180	180	158	158
North America			1,228	2,182	2,560	2,177	2,187	596	47
Asia	265	228	238						
Asia, Africa, America				351	356	329	336	155	105
ROW	83	77	311						
Dairy and drinks							400	366	309
Total	1,988	1,722	3,151	3,966	4,339	3,807		2,299	1,577
Other data									
Net profit	201	145	−504	−1,642	230	200	268	191	154
Total assets	3,536	1,514	1,616	3,607	6,415	6,920	6,920	4,031	935
Capital and reserves	680	−302	−469	173	2,166	1,875	1,875	955	222
Share price at year end: € per share	34.90	26.53	21.91	12.00	26.18	53.60	53.60	37.04	40.61
Number of employees[3]									
Employees in The Netherlands						1,362	1,462	1,475	1,439
Employees outside The Netherlands						26,498	30,061	17,378	9,138
Employees Europe	7,030	6,873	6,997	8,028	8,179				
Employees outside Europe	3,486	4,256	3,892	20,531	21,052				
Employees total	10,516	11,229	10,889	28,559	29,231	27,860	31,523	18,853	10,577

[1] Turnover and other financial data in €m.
[2] Adjusted for comparative purposes in 2001: sales and other revenue of discontinued activities excluded; included is €68m brand amortisation.
[3] Years 2001–2006, at year end; other years average per year.

NBTY

Share price:	1 June 2003	$15.50
	May 2004	$39.61
	1 October 2006	$29.31

GNC (% = compared with same period year before)

	Turnover	Operating profit
Q4, 2002	$301	
Q4, 2003	$347	
Q1+Q2, 2004	−1%	56%
FY 2005	−2%	27%
Q1+Q2, 2006	15%	50%

Source: Annual reports and company websites.

The internationalisation of Allied Irish Banks

Denis G. Harrington, Thomas C. Lawton and Chris O'Riordan

This case study explores the choices and challenges facing Allied Irish Banks (AIB) in its strategy for international market growth. It shows how the company diversified its revenue streams through international investment and acquisition and the limitations of international market expansion and management control for a bank with low brand recognition outside of its home market and limited experience of international operations. The case may be used to explore several strategic management issues: the competitive challenges faced by mid-sized companies in globally consolidating industries, the choice of foreign market entry strategies and the challenges of organisational control for internationalising companies.

● ● ●

The emergence of Allied Irish Banks

In 2006, Allied Irish Banks (AIB) celebrated its 40th birthday. Much had changed since the merger of three of Ireland's oldest and best known banks (The Provincial Bank, The Royal Bank and The Munster and Leinster) to form AIB. Today, AIB is the largest bank in Ireland, but also has a significant international presence.

In advance of most domestic competitors, AIB executives realised that internationalisation would be an effective strategy for market expansion. Limited growth potential in the home market – particularly acute prior to the economic boom of the 1990s – had necessitated a bold strategic move to ensure increased earnings and market competitiveness. The creation of a branch network in Great Britain in the 1970s was followed by an investment in the USA in the 1980s. The growth of the AIB Group escalated during the 1990s. The merger of its interests in Northern Ireland with those of TSB Northern Ireland created First Trust Bank. In 1995, AIB acquired UK-based investment management company John Govett. In addition, having done due diligence, AIB Capital Markets established twinning arrangements in Central Europe, primarily in Poland. Between 1995 and 1999, AIB enlarged its Polish presence, merging two banks in 2001 to form a top five national bank.

By the start of the new century, AIB had established itself as a dynamic and successful international banking and financial services organisation. At the time of its formation through merger in 1966, AIB's aggregate assets were €323.8m. By the end of 2005, the AIB Group had assets of €133bn and operated principally in Ireland, Great Britain and Poland. It employed over 24,000 people worldwide in more than 750 offices and operated through four main divisions:

● AIB Bank (Republic of Ireland) – focused on retail and commercial activities.

● AIB Bank (Great Britain and Northern Ireland) – offered retail and commercial banking services. Traded as First Trust in Northern Ireland.

● AIB Capital Markets – comprised the treasury and international, investment banking and corporate banking activities of the group. Based in Dublin, but also with offices in the USA.

● Poland – majority shareholding in BZWBK. The bank had more than 370 outlets.

Up until 2003, AIB had a stand-alone US division consisting of Allfirst Financial Inc., with 250

This case was prepared by Dr Denis Harrington, Head of Graduate Business at the School of Business, Waterford Institute of Technology, Dr Thomas Lawton, Associate Professor of Strategy at Tanaka Business School, Imperial College London and Mr Chris O'Riordan, Lecturer in Accounting at the School of Business, Waterford Institute of Technology. It is intended as a basis of class discussion and not as an illustration of good or bad practice. © Denis Harrington, Thomas Lawton and Chris O'Riordan, 2007. Not to be reproduced or quoted without permission.

branches in the mid-Atlantic region of the east coast. In 2006, AIB's presence in the USA consisted of a small number of AIB branches (under the Allied Irish America banner) in major US cities and a 22.5 per cent holding in M&T Bank – the top 20 US bank that acquired Allfirst.

AIB's position in the home market remained strong, with just under 50 per cent of its 2005 profits made in the Republic of Ireland. The company was widely recognised as Ireland's leading financial services organisation, slightly ahead of Bank of Ireland. Both banks reaped the benefits of a booming domestic economy and large increases in credit growth during the latter half of the 1990s and early/mid-2000s.

Competitive dynamics in retail banking

The Irish context

The nature of AIB's internationalisation strategy can be explained in part through an understanding of the bank's competitive context in both Ireland and internationally. Retail banking in Ireland is dominated by the main clearing banks, which provide a full range of financial services based on comprehensive nationwide accessibility and the integration of service provision across all sectors (small and large, business and personal, etc.). This contrasts with many countries where there is still a strong segmentation in the banking sector between retail and wholesale banks. In Ireland, a significant number of smaller banks and building societies also compete with the major banks for retail customers. The two largest Irish banks, AIB and Bank of Ireland, are both publicly quoted companies and have raised the bulk of their capital through the Irish Stock Exchange. In each case, ownership is widely diversified: 62 per cent of AIB's shares are held outside of Ireland, though 85 per cent of shareholders are within the country. In terms of market capitalisation, Anglo Irish Bank has leaped ahead of Irish Life and Permanent as Ireland's third largest bank on the back of considerable and rapid growth. Behind these key players lie Ulster Bank and its parent, Royal Bank of Scotland (the ninth largest bank in the world by market capitalisation), and National Irish Bank (owned by the Danske Bank Group). In recent years, non-traditional banking has come to Ireland in the form of Internet banks (such as Egg.com) and the diversification of other businesses (such as Tesco).

All of Ireland's leading banking institutions reported strong profits and growth in the late 1990s and early/mid-2000s and capitalised on the buoyant housing market, booming business banking profits and much lower write-offs than in previous years. Such profitability and growth have had a significant positive effect on the Irish economy. For instance, in 2004, banks spent more than €4.4bn within the domestic economy, paying over €1.5bn to the exchequer in taxes. The banking sector contributed 6 per cent to Ireland's GNP in 2004, up from 4.6 per cent in 2002. Banks are also one of the largest employers in Ireland, providing over 35,000 jobs in total.

The global context

These changes and developments in Ireland are in line with those occurring in the wider international banking environment. Across Europe and the USA, industry consolidation is ongoing and there is a scramble by many mid-sized banks to acquire other institutions in an effort to grow bigger and play at a different level. In the USA, for example, the 10 largest banks and thrift holding companies control over 60 per cent of all US banking assets. Many of these underwent merger or acquisition activity during the 1998–2001 period, including the top two banks (Citigroup's acquisition of Travelers and the merger of Chase Manhattan and J.P. Morgan).

In Europe the situation is slightly different in that regulatory barriers mean that large banking organisations – particularly retail banks – have difficulty in operating at a pan-European level. Few companies have been able to build strong competitive positions within the European market. In this sense many of the European banks have retained national status. However, change is under way across the EU, particularly in relation to cross-border mergers and alliances. In April 2006, the *Financial Times* reported that AIB itself could be a possible takeover target for the Spanish bank Santander. Liberalisation has freed financial institutions to increase the range of services they offer, thus removing barriers to competition and making it difficult to distinguish between institutions. In addition, technology advances have also facilitated entry into national banking markets, changing significantly the competitive environment in which banks operate. There has also been a trend towards the increasing international integration of trade and investment in recent years, facilitated by the strengthening of international trade agreements that in turn have implications for the ways in which banks can operate and compete.

AIB's internationalisation strategies

AIB in the UK

The depressed economic conditions of Ireland in the 1970s prompted AIB to consider alternative routes to growing its business. There was a general consensus that the bank would need to look abroad for growth opportunities, though some argued that AIB lacked the necessary resources and strategic vision. The group did lack the scale to compete directly with larger banks in markets such as the UK. Other strategic avenues would need to be explored if the group were to compete effectively in such a market. One such avenue was to exploit the Irish ethnic market in the UK. Through effective marketing and event sponsorship within the Irish expatriate community in Great Britain, AIB emerged as the bank of choice for many. In this way the group established a viable bridgehead within the UK banking market.

In considering the firm's options for further growth, AIB executives pointed to the value of pursuing a niche strategy and concentrating on particular markets where the bank might compete effectively, such as SMEs, professionals and not-for-profit organisations. In this sense, the bank's UK strategy would emphasise organic growth and market differentiation. AIB would work hard to prove itself as more customer oriented than any of its competitors. It would strive to work with the values of clients and to innovate in terms of service and product whenever possible.

The company specialises in the 'straightforward approach' to banking. Strategy in the UK market is therefore differentiation focused – AIB does not attempt to compete on cost or price. AIB (UK) emphasises relationship banking, focusing on providing personalised, tailored quality service to identified niches. This strategy has paid dividends for the company. Independent surveys of banking practices reinforce the success of the AIB formula. In Forum of Private Business (FPB) surveys,[1] AIB significantly outperforms all the main high street banks as a provider of banking services and ex-

pertise to business. In 2004, AIB (GB)[2] was voted 'Britain's Best Business Bank' for an unprecedented sixth time in succession. The FPB survey, produced in conjunction with the University of Nottingham, analysed the responses of more than 5,000 British business owners and is widely regarded as the UK's foremost benchmark of business banking. This was an important independent measure of the bank's strategic approach and provides the group with an opportunity to evaluate itself against key players in the market. Clearly, the differentiated, customer-focused approach has worked. According to Aidan McKeon (AIB (GB)'s Chief Executive at the time):

> We firmly believe that we have what every other UK bank would love to claim: experienced, dedicated and insightful bank managers who have the authority to make immediate decisions on behalf of their business customers; direct dial access to bank managers, customers even have their out of office numbers if needed, and staff who really understand the specific needs of our business customers and their industries.[3]

Through its relationship-oriented approach, the bank has earned a reputation for quality service that has proved difficult for others to imitate. AIB has invested heavily in developing its staff to meet the requirements of a more diverse and knowledgeable customer base. The key success factor is that each AIB branch operates as a full-service local bank and offers a full range of first-class banking products, predominantly catering for the SME market. The results show that the UK division is a significant profit earner for the wider group. For the year ended 31 December 2005, it turned a pre-tax profit of €322m, up 18 per cent on the previous year. This sum accounted for almost 19 per cent of total group profits.

In 2003, AIB disposed of Govett, its UK asset management business, to Gartmore Investment Management plc. AIB had been incurring losses in this business for some years and did not see a return to profitability in the near future. A loss of €152m was incurred on disposal.

AIB in the USA

The second stage in AIB's internationalisation strategy came in 1983, when the bank took a

---

[1] Established in 1977, the Forum of Private Business is a UK pressure group working on behalf of more than 25,000 private companies to influence laws and policies that affect businesses (www.fpb.co.uk).

[2] The award was given to AIB 'GB' and not AIB 'UK' as Northern Irish businesses are not included in the survey.
[3] AIB website (Press Office) 'Allied Irish Banks (GB) Gears Up', 21 May 2003.

minority stake (49 per cent) in the US regional bank First Maryland. This stake moved to 100 per cent in 1989. This wider and more ambitious entry into the large and highly competitive US market emerged from a willingness amongst AIB's senior management to extend their overseas market formula into selected parts of the US market. Although AIB had established a foothold in the US market during the 1970s with the opening of a New York branch (primarily serving the Irish expatriate community), US expansion began in earnest in the 1980s. It made further acquisitions before rebranding the entire US operations under the Allfirst banner in 1999, to become a top 50 US bank. Allfirst Financial Inc. became a regional bank headquartered in Baltimore, Maryland, offering a full range of financial services.

In the early 2000s, it appeared that AIB's investment had been a wise one. Allfirst was proving to be a profitable venture, with reasonable profit growth on the back of acquiring new customers as well as increased penetration of the existing customer base. Considerable growth was achieved in e-banking income, corporate deposit fees and deposits, so much so that by 2001, Allfirst had achieved the number one market position for deposits in the Greater Baltimore region. At the end of 2001, the company had financial assets of $18.8bn (€21.4bn).[4] According to Susan C. Keating, President and CEO of Allfirst at the time, the success of the company could be explained by its ability to anticipate and respond to changing customer demands and to keep abreast of non-traditional banking formats.

Despite these positive signs, some analysts questioned the rationale behind AIB's ownership of Allfirst, given its relatively listless revenue growth and high operating costs.[5] However, investors were willing to allow the bank time to consolidate its mainstream US market beachhead, seeing it as a key element in AIB's strategy to gain competitive advantage over its archrival, the Bank of Ireland. The strategy of focusing on building market share in specific regions seemed to be working.

AIB in Poland

The bank's entry to Poland was somewhat opportunistic. In the late 1980s, AIB had a surplus of senior managers and many were consequently 'hired out' to undertake consultancy projects – for example, for the World Bank in the newly opened economies of Central and Eastern Europe. These managers reported back to AIB Head Office on market opportunities in these countries. In 1993 the World Bank and the European Bank for Reconstruction and Development (EBRD) provided AIB with an opportunity, when they asked it to twin with a Polish bank to tutor it in free market principles and practices. AIB had done due diligence on the Polish market and therefore chose WBK in Poznan. This twinning led to AIB, in 1995, buying 16 per cent of the company. By 1997, AIB had increased its stake to 60 per cent. By 1999, AIB had bought the ninth largest bank in Poland, Bank Zachodni, based in the south-west of the country. This move further strengthened its 'local branding, local profile' approach. AIB subsequently acquired permission to merge Bank Zachodni with WBK. The new entity was called Bank Zachodni WBK, or 'BZ WBK'. To reinforce its strategy of 'local brands for local markets', AIB chose not to put its name on the newly merged organisation. The merged Bank Zachodni WBK is a top-tier bank in Polish financial services and the country's fifth largest.

Competition in Poland intensified as other companies recognised the potential of the Polish market – UniCredito, Bank Austria, ING and Citigroup all have Polish operations. In competition with these providers, the merger of WBK and BZ established a very strong business base for AIB in the west and south of Poland. However, a process of restructuring and rationalisation was needed at BZ WBK to achieve sought-after returns and to take account of the increased competitive activity in the marketplace. The programme included the introduction of a centralised branch-banking platform to streamline transaction processing to bring standards up to Western European levels. In order to reduce costs, jobs were also cut drastically. By December 2004, total employees were around 7,500, 3,500 fewer than when the firms merged in 2001.

As in other regions, the Polish acquisitions underscored the nature of the bank's internationalisation strategy: to be a top-tier niche or *regional* – not national – operator in overseas markets. Notwithstanding the company's ability to compete in this market, Poland has proven to be a challenge. In 2003, Polish profits fell by 17 per cent to €20m, before restructuring costs of €10m. The year 2004 showed a considerable improvement, thanks to higher revenues and strong cost management.

---

[4] Figures are prior to the 2002 fraud disclosure.
[5] Lina Saigol, 'AIB rules out any early disposal of Allfirst arm', *Financial Times*, 15 March (2002).

In 2005, the Polish division generated €132m of profit for the group, up 13 per cent on the previous year on a local currency basis. Eugene Sheehy, the Group CEO, commented in the 2005 annual report: 'There are early signs in Poland of an increase in demand for corporate loans – and BZ WBK is well placed to meet this demand while maintaining its risk profile.'

In May 2006, AIB introduced a new range of banking initiatives for the growing Polish community in Ireland, then numbering over 120,000 people. These initiatives consisted of:

- a Polish service desk in AIB Direct Banking's call centre;
- Polish-speaking staff in 12 branches;
- a dedicated Polish section on the AIB website;
- online international payments and marketing material made available in Polish.

This recognises the changing cultural landscape of Ireland, but also reflects the importance of AIB's presence in and relationship with BZWBK. Over the period 2003 to 2005, AIB customers had increased the number of payments sent back to Poland tenfold, to almost 60,000 transfers.

AIB in Singapore

While AIB placed considerable emphasis on developing its UK, US and Polish operations, management were also keen to establish a presence in East Asia. Market developments suggested that locations in East Asia represented strong growth opportunities and AIB was eager to capitalise on this opportunity. AIB has had treasury asset management and private banking operations in Singapore since the mid-1980s. The bank entered the Asian market in earnest in 1999 through a strategic alliance with Singapore-based Keppel Tat Lee Bank, acquiring 1 per cent of shares with an option to buy a further 25 per cent. The bank's holding company, Keppel Capital Holdings, was a financial services group offering a comprehensive range of services including consumer banking, corporate finance, international banking, treasury, asset management, capital market activities, stockbroking, bullion/futures trading and insurance.

In line with its strategic approach in other foreign markets, AIB was interested in Keppel Tat Lee due to its niche business in the mid/high-end consumer and SME markets. The Singaporean bank was also committed to providing innovative quality products and good customer service. These market positions and organisational competences coincided with those of AIB's operations in the UK, USA and Poland.

AIB's initial premise for taking a stake in Keppel Tat Lee was to investigate whether or not the AIB banking model would work in Singapore. Due to impending government-backed consolidation of the Singaporean financial services industry, AIB realised that it may have to withdraw from the market at a relatively early stage. Michael Buckley, Group CEO at the time, explained the reasons for withdrawing:

> In reaching our decision to accept the offer [from rival bank OCBC to buy AIB's stake in Keppel], we were mindful of the trend towards consolidation in the Singapore market and believe acceptance to be in the best interests of AIB's shareholders. We have enjoyed a very good relationship with KCH and look forward to continuing a strong commercial relationship with them and OCBC into the future.[6]

AIB withdrew from direct involvement in the Singapore banking market in mid-2001. In doing so, the company gained a substantial profit of €93m, from a minimal initial capital investment. The group maintained an investment presence until the disposal of Govett in 2003, which saw the closure of the Singapore operation.

The Rusnak affair

The Allfirst/John Rusnak affair was the most visible example of control problems in AIB. In February 2002, AIB uncovered fraudulent activities in the foreign exchange trading operations at the Baltimore headquarters of its US subsidiary, Allfirst. John Rusnak, an Allfirst trader, had accrued huge losses on currency options over a five-year period. The total pre-tax loss figure as of 8 February 2002, the end of the week the fraud was discovered, was $691.2m (€789m). That amount consisted of $291.6m in bogus assets and $397.3m in unrecognised liabilities, as well as $2.3m in legitimate trading losses incurred in 2002.[7] The crux of the problem was that the bank failed to detect very large sums passing through the books of a tiny foreign exchange trading business. Although

---

6 *Business Wire*, 14 July 2001.

7 These figures are derived from the report of the independent investigation (the so-called 'Ludwig Report') commissioned by the boards of AIB and Allfirst, March 2002.

definitive responsibility rested with Allfirst's treasury unit management, ultimate responsibility resided with AIB Group headquarters in Dublin.

The fraud dealt a severe blow to the bank's stakeholders. In and of itself, the financial damage was heavy, though absorbable. Unlike the Nick Leeson fraud that brought about the fall of Barings Bank in 1995, AIB was sufficiently large and financially robust to sustain the losses. More damaging was the way in which the episode preoccupied and undermined AIB's management for a considerable time afterwards. In particular, questions were asked both from within and outside the bank about how a mid-sized bank, not known as a major player in treasury markets, could have made losses of this order.[8] Furthermore, shareholders needed to be reassured of the bank's continued viability as an independent organisation. Speculation abounded during 2002 of a merger with archrival Bank of Ireland and even a possible takeover by non-Irish companies such as the Royal Bank of Scotland.

On 12 March 2002, the independent report commissioned by AIB's board was released.[9] Dubbed the 'Ludwig Report' after Eugene A. Ludwig, former US Comptroller of the Currency and the report's principal investigator, its findings exonerated the bank's senior management of any culpability but reproved them for failing to detect Mr Rusnak's fraudulent activities at an earlier stage. The report was critical of the control weaknesses that allowed the fraud to happen and go undetected for so long, as well as senior management's lack of attention to the operation itself. Ludwig's findings and recommendations were accepted and rapidly acted upon by the AIB Group board. Many questioned whether AIB's international presence was sustainable, particularly in the USA, or had the organisation over-stretched its resources and competences?

The *de facto* acquisition of Allfirst by US regional banking firm M&T Bank was approved by both M&T and AIB shareholders in December 2002. The US$3.1bn deal created a top 20 US bank with proforma combined assets of approximately $49bn. AIB management described this deal as an alliance allowing AIB to 'reposition and strengthen' its involvement in US regional banking. However, AIB emerged as very much the junior partner in the new combined company (controlling just over 22 per cent of the shares), indicating that AIB appeared in fact to be gradually withdrawing from large-scale US retail banking.

Since 2003, AIB has benefited from its investment in M&T, in which it is the largest single shareholder. Profits grew by 8 per cent in 2005, beating analysts' expectations and providing AIB with €148m of profits from a company generating a return on equity of over 13 per cent. AIB is also awaiting a court date (likely to be in 2007) for the case against Bank of America and Citigroup. The two largest US banks are being sued by AIB for $500m for their involvement in the Rusnak affair, alleging that they disguised Rusnak's losses and lent him $200m to keep him trading with them.[10]

AIB post-Rusnak

Since the downsizing of its presence in the USA, AIB has been quiet on the international stage. It has not established itself in any further locations in any significant way. Whether this is a strategic decision, in recognition of the difficulties it found with 'managing at a distance', or coincidental is difficult to tell. A factor in its relative inactivity may be the turmoil that the bank faced in 2004 and 2005 when revelations emerged of the overcharging of customers (to the tune of €34m) and the involvement of some senior managers in AIB with Faldor Limited, a BVI investment company, that was found to have benefited from 'inappropriate favourable deal allocations by way of artificial deals amounting to approximately €48,000 out of AIBIM's own funds'.[11] This period saw the departure of a number of senior personnel and the appointment of a new CEO, Eugene Sheehy, upon the scheduled retirement of Michael Buckley.

While AIB's profits continue to grow, one would speculate that further international moves will be made when the climate is right. The success of the Polish operation may prompt the bank to look at other Central and Eastern European locations, particularly those countries who joined the EU in 2004 and those expected to join in a short time.

---

[8] *Financial Times*, 'When Irish eyes are crying', 7 February (2002).
[9] *Report to the Boards of Directors of Allied Irish Banks, p.l.c., Allfirst Financial Inc., and Allfirst Bank Concerning Currency Trading Losses*, submitted by Promontory Financial Group and Wachtell, Lipton, Rosen and Katz, 12 March 2002.

[10] Sean O'Driscoll, 'Judge rejects US banks' view on AIB', *Irish Times*, 13 February (2006).
[11] *Irish Times*, 'Internal controls fail to rein in improper practices', 8 December (2004).

Whether AIB would contemplate a foray into the Chinese market at an early stage is hard to tell – the distance involved as well as the relative immaturity of the banking system there may cause concern. Beyond China, the turbulent nature of the Asian market would not fit well with a company that will surely steer clear of risky destinations. However, a low-risk strategy may result in stagnant growth and declining profits if the handful of economies that AIB is currently active in weaken. Certainly these are interesting times for AIB as the decisions regarding internationalisation that it makes now will have long-reaching consequences. One wonders, 40 years from now, what we will be saying about AIB!

SABMiller

Aidan McQuade

South African Breweries grew on the basis of its strength in developing markets, first in Africa and then in other parts of the world. Following pressure from investors to acquire a brewery in a developed market it acquired Miller in 2002 to become SABMiller and the second largest brewer by volume in the world. This case study explains the business's development. It shows how the strategy has changed with time and circumstances and provides the opportunity to consider its future at both the corporate and competitive strategy levels.

• • •

Introduction

In 2007 SABMiller, the renamed South African Breweries following its acquisition of the American brewer Miller in 2002, had become the second largest brewer by volume in the world. It still vied with Anheuser-Busch, its principal competitor; having dropped back to third place in 2005 it reclaimed the number two position following its conclusion of a US$7.8bn (≈€6.2bn) deal to take over Grupo Empresarial Bavaira, South America's second largest brewer.

In the 2006 annual report SABMiller outlined four strategic priorities upon which its success depended: 'Creating a balanced and attractive global spread of businesses. . . . Developing strong relevant brand portfolios in the relevant market. . . . Constantly raising the performance of the local businesses. . . . Leveraging our global scale.' This statement of strategy may be seen as a synthesis of the learning the company has developed over its history, first weathering the political crises of twentieth-century South African history, then building its operations in emerging and mature markets, where its

Photo: SABMiller plc

expertise as 'a turnaround specialist'[1] was further consolidated.

Background

As a company SABMiller is older than the state of South Africa itself and has faced the challenge of doing business amidst the upheaval that country experienced during the twentieth century. The most significant feature of this was the institution of the racist system of 'apartheid' in 1948 and the

---

[1] *The Economist*, 'The battle of big beer', 13 May (2004).

subsequent opposition to this. A central feature of the period was the campaign for economic sanctions on South Africa, aiming to restrict international business from investing in or trading with South Africa and restricting South African business from trading with international markets.

In 1950 SAB moved its head office and seat of control from London to Johannesburg. Southern Africa was the focus of the majority of its business expansion during the subsequent four decades. In 1970 SAB became fully incorporated in South Africa.

SAB responded to business restrictions by focusing on dominating domestic beer production through acquisition of competitors and rationalisation of production and distribution facilities. SAB also expanded its product portfolio, obtaining control of Stellenbosch Farmers' Winery in 1960 and in the course of the rest of that decade obtaining licences to brew locally Guinness, Amstel and Carling Black Label. Further expansions followed within the beverage sector, principally through acquisition leading, by 1979, to SAB controlling an estimated 99 per cent of the market in South Africa as well as commanding positions in Swaziland, Lesotho, Rhodesia and Botswana.

Subsequently SAB diversified surplus investment funds through joint ventures. In 1978 ground was broken on the Sun City casino resort, SAB's most high-profile development in hotels and gambling.

In the same year SAB published a code of non-discriminatory employment, one of the first industries in the country to do so. This did not immunise it against the growing pace of sanctions. In response it diversified further in South Africa. For example, in 1987 SAB became the leading safety match manufacturer in Africa, acquiring Lion Match Company from a disinvesting international investor.

By 1990 the process for the establishment of a multiracial democracy was irrevocably in train. SAB invested in the development of three mega-breweries across the country. The change in the political system also eased SAB's return and expansion through the rest of Africa. In 1994 it was invited to participate in a joint venture with the Tanzanian government to revitalise the brewing industry there. It was also invited back to Zambia, Mozambique and later Angola.

By 2000 SAB had weathered the economic travails caused by apartheid to such an extent that 49 out of every 50 beers consumed in the country were brewed by SAB. Such market dominance provided a serious deterrent to potential competitors. However, there remained little space for it to expand in southern Africa, particularly in the beverage sector. Hence the company looked for other opportunities to expand beyond its traditional region.

Emerging onto the global market

In 1993 SAB acquired Hungary's largest brewery, Dreher, in what it described as a 'beach-head move' into central Europe.

The 1998 annual report of SAB explained the group's strategy:

> SAB's international focus has been on countries in which it believes it could use its expertise, which has been gained over 100 years in South Africa, to develop beer markets in emerging economies. . . . Incremental growth, both organic and through acquisitions, is being pursued aggressively.

The rest of the decade saw it establish operations in China, Poland, Romania, Slovakia, Russia and the Czech Republic. In 1999 SAB moved its primary listing back to London in order to make it easier to raise capital for expansion through the purchase of new acquisitions.

SAB's strategy was more fully spelled out in 2000:

> In the less developed world, Africa and Asia and much of Europe, brewing remained highly fragmented, with beer drinkers supplied by breweries which were never more than small-scale and localised, often producing low-quality beer. . . . This fragmentation presented the opportunity for SAB from the mid-1990s to create a profitable and fast-expanding business in emerging markets with huge potential. This opportunity involves, generally, taking a share in a brewery with a local partner and, while retaining the brand because drinkers tend to have fierce attachments to their local brew, transforming the business. This starts with upgrading quality and consistency to create a beer for which people are prepared to pay more and which can give us a healthy profit margin. Then comes improvement to marketing and distribution. Next we improve productivity and capacity.
>
> In each country we have begun by acquiring an initial local stronghold from which we can advance into regions beyond the brewery's original catchment area. We then build critical mass in the region and progress, over time, to a national basis. This is often achieved by acquiring further brewing businesses and focusing the brand portfolio. An optimum brand portfolio gives us a better overall marketing proposition, increases total sales and delivers economies of scale in production and distribution.

This process demands, on one level, great political sensitivity in dealing with governments, partners, local communities and our workforce and, on another level, the deployment of expert operational management skills learnt in South Africa. At the same time we market and promote selected premium brands, either brewed locally or imported – often our own Castle Lager, which is the biggest selling beer in Africa. Our management structure is decentralised, reflecting the local nature of beer branding and distribution.

In most emerging markets, consumption of beer is directly related to the level of disposable income at consumer level. Attractive markets thus arise in developing economies as consumer spending increases. This is often accompanied by structural changes in society, such as increasing urbanisation and the development of more varied and sophisticated lifestyles, which also encourage beer consumption.

Our businesses do not all advance at the same speed, nor have the same potential. It is characteristic of emerging markets that growth can be variable, and we are accustomed to temporary setbacks. However, the spread of our international businesses provides a 'portfolio effect', thereby reducing the impact of setbacks in one or two individual countries.

The culture that this approach nurtured was illustrated in an interview in 2002 when Julie Corkish, SAB's UK Tax Manager, emphasised the point that 'Emerging markets is our forte'.[2] SAB managers have the reputation for resourcefulness in managing their operations in countries in turmoil or where there is poor infrastructure. To illustrate this *The Economist* magazine in 2000 reported an incident when the water supply to one of its breweries in Mozambique failed. Rather than shut down production, SAB paid the local fire brigade to fetch water and hose it into the beer vats. This focus on emerging markets led by 2001 to SAB becoming the world's fifth largest brewer by volume with breweries in 24 countries across the globe.

Analysts noted a problem with this portfolio in that it meant that SAB earned most of its profits in 'soft' currencies. Hence a loss of confidence in emerging markets could hurt it badly if there were a resultant devaluation of the currencies of those markets which would in turn lead to a loss of profits in hard currencies. This could result also in a dip in its share price that would make it vulnerable to takeover. The situation was exacerbated with a slump in the value of the rand in 2001 and there were fears it could be further effected by the devastating impact of the HIV/AIDS pandemic on the workforce, which, aside from the human cost, is causing a decrease in productivity through the chronic and debilitating effects of the illness, particularly in sub-Saharan Africa. Many commentators believed that for a brewery of its size SAB needed to have a major brand in the developed markets.

In 1999 SAB decided on listing on the London Stock Exchange (LSE). This was justified by SAB as follows:

> The Directors believed that the listing of the company on the LSE and the placing would put SAB in a strong position to pursue its strategy of growth by giving the group greater access to world capital markets and providing it with the financial resources and flexibility to pursue this strategy in an effective and competitive manner. This would enhance the ability of SAB to take advantage of increasing consolidation in the international brewing industry and to compete with other international brewers for development opportunities throughout the world. . . . Incremental growth, both organic and through acquisitions, is being pursued aggressively.

However, the listing had its problems. It was reported that SAB's share price lost 15.55 per cent relative to the FTSE 100 in the year to end November 2000 (in the same period it lost 2.68 per cent on the South African Stock Exchange). Analysts argued, again, that this was because of the failure to make a major acquisition of a first-world brand and its over-reliance on its developing markets.

The *Financial Times*[3] also believed that their reception in London had surprised SAB directors. They quoted John Clemmow, of the South African Investment Bank, Investec, as saying 'I think it came as a shock to them to come over here and discover how unimportant they were in the lives of the City.' The FT believed that, whilst in South Africa the firm was well known, it was necessary for SAB to spend a great deal more time explaining itself in London and that it was not sufficiently geared up to doing this. Indeed Graham Mackay, SAB's Chief Executive, was reported as being taken aback by the harshness of some of the comments: 'It's more picky, to the point of cynicism and hostility, than you encounter in South Africa.'

---

[2] *International Tax Review*, March (2002).

[3] 23 November 2000.

SABMiller

In 2002 SAB finally succeeded in acquiring a major brand in a developed market when it acquired 100 per cent of Miller Brewing Company, the second largest brewery in the USA, and becoming SABMiller in the process. SAB paid Philip Morris Co. US$3.6bn in stock of the merged company and assumed US$2bn of Miller's debt.

In the 2003 annual report the company explained this acquisition as follows:

> We acquired Miller Brewing Company in July 2002, giving the group access, through a national player, to a growing beer market with the world's largest profit pool, and at the same time diversifying the currency and geographic risk of the group.

This acquisition made SABMiller the second largest brewery by volume in the world. However, the acquisition brought with it its own problems. James Williamson, an analyst at SG Securities in London, commented: 'They didn't buy it because they thought it was a strong growth business. They bought it because they needed a mature cash cow. Unfortunately its been losing more market share than expected.'

Indeed following the first full year of SABMiller operating Miller, its market share had dropped from 19.6 to 18.7 per cent and by September 2003 the share price of the company had dropped from 530 pence (€7.9) on the day of acquisition of Miller, to 456.5 pence.

SABMiller appointed Norman Adami, previously Head of its Beer South Africa business, as Head of Miller, and introduced the traditional SAB system of employee performance rating, making clear that employees who consistently scored unsatisfactorily would be dismissed. This was a considerable change from Miller's previous system of performance rating which routinely rated all staff at the highest level. SABMiller also announced that there would be a rationalisation of Miller's product portfolio from 50 brands to 11 or 12, meaning that market share would go down before it could go up again.

The portfolio in 2006

Reviewing operations in the 2006 annual report, SABMiller noted that it had just 'completed a three-year turnaround plan, establishing a platform for future growth'. The CEO went on to note:

In *North America*, Miller has made further progress. The flagship Miller Lite brand has continued to grow while the company maintained firmer year-on-year pricing than its domestic competitors to protect its brand equity.

Miller's initial success has prompted a price-cutting response from the market leader, and this action by the market leader has limited the industry's ability to pass on rising costs such as energy and aluminium. Despite these tough conditions, the momentum remains strong and the business is benefiting from its three years of investment.

Miller Genuine Draft was relaunched in the final quarter of the year, with a new positioning at the upper end of the mainstream market. In the premium sector, Pilsner Urquell continued to grow – albeit from a small base – and Peroni Nastro Azzurro was well received in its launch year. Miller's emphasis, now, is on constantly improving its marketing, sales and distribution and on building a portfolio of brands capable of commanding premium prices.

In relation to Europe the CEO noted:

> *Europe* had another excellent year with the best performances from Poland, Russia and Romania. The Polish and Russian businesses increased their volumes well ahead of their markets and Russia and Romania are both expanding their capacity. The Czech business improved its productivity, increased its share and introduced new packaging. The Peroni brands in Italy began to grow for the first time in many years and we strengthened our position in Slovakia with the acquisition of the Topvar brewery.

Having established a substantial presence in developed economies, the focus of SABMiller's strategy seems to have shifted back to developing economies. The 2006 report notes that 'our ability to succeed in developing markets (a skill we owe to our African origins) has proven to be a competitive advantage on the world stage':

> The business in *South Africa* saw ongoing momentum in consumer spending with lager and soft drink sales continuing to rise. While the growth in volumes moderated in the second half, earnings continued to benefit as consumers traded up to the premium segment. To meet the demands of changing consumption patterns, we have introduced new sales and distribution systems and enhanced the flexibility of our production facilities.
>
> The licensing of more shebeens is bringing these previously unofficial outlets into the retail mainstream. This means they can operate more professionally and we can deliver to them direct – which in turn raises the performance of the business. During the year we trained over 6,000 newly-licensed taverners in business skills.

Our businesses in *Africa* continued to grow, helped by broader distribution and a clearer segmentation of our brands. Volumes in Botswana were affected by the devaluation of the currency, but results were good in Tanzania, Uganda and Mozambique. We see plenty of opportunity to keep improving efficiency in these relatively underdeveloped countries and the outlook for Africa as a whole is encouraging.

In 2004 SABMiller dropped its US$550m attempt at a hostile takeover of Harbin Brewery in China, in the face of an 'irrational' US$720m counter offer from Anheuser-Busch (*The Economist*, 13 May 2004). With the Chinese beer market growing at 6–8 per cent per year the Chinese market remains a highly attractive one. However *The Economist* (2005) notes that China is a costly market to operate in and currently the margins are 'tiny'. By 2006 the annual report described its operations in China thus:

Now in its twelfth year, our associate in *China* is well established as the country's second biggest brewer and sales are growing strongly. The business kept up its momentum with a particularly impressive performance by the Snow brand. Following improvements in marketing and distribution, Snow is now the country's top-selling beer. The year saw good progress in integrating recent acquisitions with several minor acquisitions completed during the year. The first phase of the greenfield brewery in Dongguan has now been completed and in May 2006 we announced that a second brewery in Heilongjiang province would be constructed in Harbin.

SABMiller also bought out its joint venture partner in India, though also with less immediate success in terms of profits given the high regulation of the Indian beer market:

India is included in our results for the first time following the purchase of our partner's interest in the company in May 2005. Volumes grew satisfactorily, though the business is still restricted in its volumes and pricing by the lack of regulatory reform. The focus now is on expanding capacity and improving our quality and productivity.

During the year we announced a new arrangement with a local distribution partner to build a brewery in *Vietnam*. The Vietnamese beer market is one of the fastest growing in the world and the move strengthens our presence in developing markets.

SABMiller merged in 2005 with Grupo Empresarial Bavaria, the second largest brewer in *South America*. This is noted as a deal which consolidates SABMiller's position as world number two producer by volume, making Latin America the second largest source of profits after South Africa. However, the debt incurred as part of the transaction with Bavaria led to an increase of the group's gearing from 25.2 to 52.1 per cent. Reviewing the Latin American operations the CEO noted:

since joining SABMiller just after the half-year, the businesses in Colombia, Peru, Ecuador and Panama have all performed well. Everything we've seen so far confirms our belief that these markets offer exciting prospects for growth.

Although the Bavaria businesses are well managed and profitable, we plan to create further value by applying SABMiller's operating practices and management skills. The best opportunities lie in brand portfolio development, creating good relationships with distributors and retailers, and improving merchandising at the point of sale. The coming year will see the start of considerable investment in these areas.

The results from Honduras and El Salvador, included for the first time in the Latin America region, were affected by hurricanes and severe flooding. Nevertheless, lager volumes continued to increase in Honduras, and both markets saw growth in soft drinks.

The 2006 annual report emphasised SABMiller's credentials as a brewery, downplaying the still significant stake (3 per cent of EBITA (Earnings Before Interest, Taxes and Amortisation) in 2006) that it gains from hotels and gaming in South Africa.

The report also noted that:

The worldwide trend towards *premium brands* makes this segment the fastest growing in the global beer market. Within the segment, it's the international brands that are growing most rapidly at nearly four times the rate of the beer market as a whole. To compete in this segment, we have a portfolio of international brands, each with its own distinct personality and attributes. While volumes are still small, they are growing rapidly. The largest brand, Miller Genuine Draft, has been particularly successful in Russia while Pilsner Urquell is growing in Europe and the USA. Peroni Nastro Azzurro was recently repackaged and relaunched with a major global campaign and is growing particularly strongly in the UK.

Compared to mainstream and economy brands, the premium segment requires greater nurturing and a specialised approach to marketing, sales and distribution. These capabilities are now being refined across the group – notably through a new programme to establish common techniques and disciplines for rolling out international premium brands in new markets. The programme was piloted during the year in Poland and the lessons learned are now being applied around the world.

The annual report emphasised the importance of the breadth of the portfolio in corporate success, noting, for example, how 'we benefited from having a broad enough portfolio to compensate for the ups and downs of individual countries. Botswana slipped as a result of difficult economic conditions, but Tanzania, Uganda and Mozambique continued to do well.'

Where from here?

The 2006 report shows a change in emphasis, stressing the need for consolidation rather than acquisition and emphasising the importance on a global portfolio to ensure 'that [it] is balanced geographically and exposes us to markets at different stages of development – one that offers long-term growth in the form of new, developing markets while generating cash from profitable developed markets'.

Having survived and grown for over 100 years, SABMiller had emerged onto the world market at a time when it appears that the twenty-first century may prove globally as turbulent as the twentieth century was in South Africa. The company notes that its operational productivity, which is already being benchmarked by competitors, cannot be a source of sustained competitive advantage. Its Africanist culture and fearlessness in tackling emerging markets is much less inimitable. However, as developed world tastes shift to wine and spirits (*The Economist*, 2005) SABMiller may find that the developing world is increasingly coveted by its competitors, with the battle with Anheuser-Busch over Harbin a foretaste of what is to come.

The company has also demonstrated an impressive record of appropriate strategic choices in the face of anticipated political developments. After a period when the company acquiesced to investor pressure to expand its business into developed economies, it seems to have reverted to a tried and tested approach from the earlier days of its post-apartheid global expansion. So far the results appear to bear out the value of this strategy. Whether this continues to be the case remains to be seen.

Main sources

N. Chaloner and D. Brotzen, 'How SABMiller protects its biggest asset – its reputation', *Strategic Communication Management*, vol. 6, no. 6 (2002), Oct./Nov., pp. 12–15.

Far Eastern Economic Review, 'The China brew', 11 June (2002).

Michael Skapinker, 'A whole world away from Johannesburg', *Financial Times*, 23 November (2000).

N. Hobday, 'Tapped out', *The Daily Deal*, 8 September (2003).

Hal Lux, 'Miller time (Mergers and Acquisitions). (South African Breweries acquires Miller Brewing Co.)', *Institutional Investor International Edition*, vol. 28, no. 1 (2002).

International Tax Review, 'Tax gets a look in as SAB goes global', vol. 13, no. 3 (2002).

Knight Ridder/Tribune Business News, 'Miller Brewing gets new CEO from new owner, South African Breweries', 15 January (2003).

Reports on SAB by HSBC and ING Barings.

South African Breweries annual reports and website.

The Economist, 'Special report on doing business in violent or chaotic countries', 18 May (2000).

The Economist, 'Big Lion, small cage', 10 August (2000).

The Economist, 'The worst way to lose talent', 8 February (2001).

The Economist, 'Lead boots', 13 December (2001).

The Economist, 'The battle of big beer', 13 May (2004).

The Economist, 'Andean thirst', 21 July (2005).

Macpac gears up and gets out there

Maureen Benson-Rea and Deborah Shepherd

This case tracks an entrepreneurial start-up company in the outdoor adventure equipment industry based in New Zealand. From a backyard operation making and repairing packs to a rapidly growing company with a strong niche brand, the founding entrepreneur, Bruce McIntyre, took the company through losses, retrenchment and offshoring its manufacturing production to the Philippines, Vietnam and China.

• • •

Introduction

By 2006 Bruce McIntyre, the entrepreneurial founder of Macpac, had built an iconic New Zealand company which had survived turbulent times in the late 1990s and early 2000s. After 30 years in the outdoor equipment manufacturing business, losses in 2001 and 2002 had forced the company to eliminate 11 management positions and 150 production jobs, reduce its 230 product lines, and outsource its manufacturing to Asia. Even with restructuring, the company lost money three out of the five years between 2001 and 2005. In 2006, the total staff at the company's Riccarton, Christchurch, headquarters was 65, with 12 manufacturing staff having been retained to produce prototypes and customised orders. The company had been rebuilt with a newly appointed CEO and strong sales, marketing and logistics teams, and reconfigured into a design and marketing company rather than a manufacturing company. Bruce McIntyre felt that Macpac could face the challenge of building a global high-quality outdoor equipment and clothing brand. Since Macpac was profitable again, he was thinking about easing himself out of the day-to-day running of his company to pursue new personal challenges. However, the changes also brought a whole new set of challenges for Macpac. How would it manage the critical relationships with the Asian manufacturers and the quality con-trol of stock going to its export markets? Would the Macpac culture and brand that had been built over 30 years survive in the new global marketplace?

New Zealand origins

At the age of 19, Bruce McIntyre dropped out of university in 1973 and borrowed NZ$2,000 (€1,000) from his father to buy a small Christchurch-based bag manufacturing and repair business. A keen tramper,[1] McIntyre began with the simple belief that he could make better and cheaper tramping packs than those available. For several years he worked out of his parents' garage, where his father also ran a bag-making business. After a cautious start making and selling packs to his friends, McIntyre learned how to sew from his father and started selling to the handful of specialist outdoor and sports retailers in his area.

By 1980, Macpac had grown to 20 staff with sales of NZ$300,000. One of Macpac's retailers at the time was Geoff Gabites, who had a shop in Dunedin, one of the few outdoor specialist stores in the country. Gabites and his wife Shelley also had a home-based business making clothing, sleeping

_____

[1] An Australasian term for hiking or hill walking.

This case was prepared by Dr Maureen Benson-Rea and Dr Deborah Shepherd, both Senior Lecturers, Dept of Management and International Business, University of Auckland Business School, New Zealand. It is intended as a basis for class discussion and not as an illustration of good or bad practice. The authors gratefully acknowledge the contribution of Dr Kevin Morris.

bags and a few tents, but in limited quantities and less profitably than McIntyre. Gabites proposed a merger of his company, Wilderness Products, with McIntyre's Macpac. They initially formed a marketing partnership and sold everything under the Macpac brand. The logistics between Christchurch and Dunedin were complicated and even the expense of phone calls became unmanageable. So the Gabites moved to Christchurch in 1981 and the merged company moved to a new 12,000 square foot (1,115m²) facility, increasing its staff to 30. McIntyre had a controlling interest and acted as Managing Director, and Geoff became a director and the Sales Manager. Shelley managed production planning.

The move ensured that the company was the first brand in the country offering a range of outdoor products. For McIntyre, however, the merger with Wilderness Products did not prove easy in the long term. He found it difficult to manage the merged operation while Geoff Gabites, an experienced entrepreneur with strong ideas about the direction of Macpac, was actively involved in the company. Geoff worked at the company on a daily basis until 1986 when he moved on to pursue other interests. Shelley Gabites has remained heavily involved in the company as a director and has continued to manage domestic and then later international production.

The 1980s: changes, exports and growth

After initially selling in Australia through an agent, McIntyre opened a Sydney office and warehouse and by 1983 exports there represented five per cent

of Macpac's total sales of NZ$1 million. Exporting to Australia and accounting for expenses there was demanding before the Closer Economic Relations (CER) agreement. Macpac's Australian operation was expensive and largely ineffective and McIntyre ultimately decided to run exports from the New Zealand headquarters. In the mid-1980s he began designing for the US market, and made three trips there to investigate the competition, taking prototypes and meeting with retailers, but with limited success. In 1984, with the company still growing, McIntyre asked the company's Production Manager, Doug, to run the business for a year. Doug had natural leadership skills, and he and Geoff Gabites had become close friends. It was an opportunity for McIntyre to take a step back from his business and operate solely as a director.

However, the performance of the company declined into a pre-tax loss in 1985, and McIntyre was unhappy with the hierarchical reporting structure that had been introduced in his absence. McIntyre appointed Doug to the role of Project Manager and again assumed leadership of the company. He explained:

> It was an absolutely major transition point in a business sense because it called on me to be the leader of the company. I couldn't stand making a loss and I couldn't stand seeing the business go down the tubes.

Internally, he knew he needed to build the Macpac culture with the intention of improving both the domestic and international success of the company. During the early years a family atmosphere was developed, and McIntyre worked hard to create good working conditions for his staff. It was an important time in terms of his developing management philosophy. He realised that, though he was the owner of the business, his staff also had a sense of ownership. In 1985 he employed a communications consultant to do a cultural audit of the business. She interviewed a third of the 100 staff and made recommendations, including introducing performance appraisal for all staff. Monthly meetings involving the whole company were introduced. McIntyre also brought in a productivity consultant in 1986, but not without some resentment from the staff, as he explained:

> I faced a bit of a battle to get him in the building because people in manufacturing obviously felt that they could do their job. But it led to fantastic changes

and people realised that they were probably behind in the way they were doing things. So we never ended up with any permanent problems in that area. People tended to always want to do the best thing.

The efficiency increased dramatically, and within three years the cost of labour reduced from 25 to 14 per cent.

The management team were continually reading about management ideas, and each developed particular interests. Early in his career McIntyre's financial knowledge was very limited, and many of his decisions had little foundation. 'It's amazing how far you can go in business without understanding finances,' he said in hindsight, 'but then it's amazing how much further you can go when you do understand them'. McIntyre was interested in 'sharp-bending', turnarounds and the concept of profit sharing (which he introduced in 1987). Others focused on quality circles (which Macpac introduced in 1988), team building and production refinements. McIntyre promoted the idea of creating a highly communicative culture. His philosophy was:

> I wanted to reward people for their sense of ownership, and I wanted something which would get all the energies of all the staff aligned in the same direction. I thought the profit sharing was the obvious thing that everyone in the organisation stood to benefit from.

The continual focus on internal culture and structures along with systems improvement were happening simultaneously with increasing international success. In 1987, Macpac began exporting to Europe via a Dutch marketing agent, and redesigned packs for that market. Two years later it had entered the UK, Switzerland, The Netherlands and Germany, and eventually appointed a distributor for Europe. Macpac also experimented with broadening its appeal and designing packs for travelling and school or university use. McIntyre looked at manufacturing in Korea in the late 1980s, but decided the infrastructure there was not ready.

Developing the brand and culture: the 1990s

An unwritten, internal philosophy had developed that encouraged staff to develop their specialist skills, but also to get involved and follow interests in other areas of the company. It was in this environment that McIntyre and Shelley Gabites

developed their belief and commitment to local manufacturing and all the expertise and efficiency they were developing internally. The team culture was also represented in the 'Macpac Quest', where teams of staff competed in orienteering, paddling, running and biking events. The head of sales and marketing described other benefits of the team structure:

> I always think one of the great Macpac attitudes is looking at the constraints of our ideas and deciding how we can turn them into positives rather than negatives. When we were edging into the UK market and supplying them directly, retailers there were saying, 'You're on the other side of the world, and there's a 12 hour time difference'. Well you can look at that as a big negative, or take advantage that we're actually 12 hours ahead and that we're working while they're asleep.

By 1990, sales had grown to NZ$8 million, with 35 per cent of sales overseas. In 1992, Macpac started selling directly to Australian retailers, which were carefully chosen. By that time, McIntyre found that many people saw Macpac as an iconic New Zealand brand, yet the company had never focused on marketing. 'We always kind of looked after the brand ourselves,' he said, 'and we simply believed that it had to remain true to its quality. We really just did a lot of talking about what the brand stood for.' In 1992, he established a marketing team.

As the years went by, the skills of various employees influenced the production and operations of the company, and the company developed internal accounting processes and computer systems. After visits to Toyota, Nissan, Fisher and Paykel and Interlock, Macpac introduced total quality management systems, and McIntyre also worked hard to ensure that management and staff never had an 'us and them' attitude. The company had always had a casual clothing policy for all, and no parking or privileges for management. 'We all got paid differently and we had different jobs,' he said, 'but it was just accepted as the way it was'. In 1994–1995 the company was restructured into teams. All performance reviews were changed to involve team performance. Shelley Gabites described the transition:

> When we went to a team-based environment, we wanted people to support each other . . . [asking] . . . 'How do we continue to support the values that we have?'

The company's leadership team typically initiated ideas, and each team appointed champions to embrace the concept and decide how it was going to be resourced. The team environment led to a lot of collaboration across the company.

By 1996 the selling strategy of working directly with retailers had evolved. As in Australia, Macpac eliminated agents and began selling directly to retailers in the UK, followed closely by a similar arrangement for the rest of Europe. With the strong New Zealand dollar, exports declined and McIntyre tested Vietnamese manufacturing, but found the quality to be unsuitable.

Global market trends

With 9/11, Macpac's sales dropped overnight by 30 per cent and dropped by another 10 per cent the following year. The outdoor industry experienced a massive shift from being hardcore, involving adventure travel, mountaineering, and multi-day tramping, to being softer and more focused on fashion. The fashion, soft end of the market continued to grow but the hardcore end collapsed. People stayed at home and stopped doing adventurous activities. The company did some market research and discovered that it was highly respected, especially by young people (which was good news), but was also seen to be quite elite and not taking a wider market perspective. When the market suddenly started crashing Macpac was forced to take note of the broader market. Macpac had a very high-quality product which many people said they did not need and were not prepared to pay for, preferring something less elite and at a much cheaper price.

So once again McIntyre came back into the company full time. Macpac waited to see what was going to happen with the market and, when it did not reverse, had to take some critical cost-cutting measures. The first round of cuts were not severe enough and Macpac continued to lose money. It concluded that it had to take almost all of the production offshore apart from small jobs and military contracts. So Macpac then found it was playing catch-up in that it was the last to go to Asia for its manufacturing. Macpac felt that closing down New Zealand manufacturing and going offshore did not make an ounce of difference to its customers, since they would not know whether the products were made in New Zealand or not, but the retailers certainly knew when Macpac dropped its prices. Macpac thought that it would get rapid growth when it dropped its prices, but whilst there

was growth it was far from massive and hard won against competition with already firmly established positions.

For McIntyre and his management team, 2003 was the lowest point. As a company, it had always promoted a family business atmosphere, and profit sharing with all staff had been an integral part of the culture. When the financial situation became worse it had tried to 'buy some time' and keep manufacturing in New Zealand. McIntyre did some financial modelling and realised that there was simply no way Macpac could return to profitability with the status quo. And as part of the company's communicative culture, management had always shared financial results with the staff. So when the job cutbacks were finally announced in July 2003, few employees were surprised. Over the next few months in the build-up to the layoffs, manufacturing productivity actually increased and absenteeism and turnover decreased – a phenomenon that truly surprised McIntyre and his leadership team. By early 2003 McIntyre had committed to offshore manufacturing production of some products in Asia, and by the end of the year had eliminated most of the in-house manufacturing and coped with the disappointment of staff layoffs. With the offshore production up and running, he started looking around for a CEO, to appoint someone who could come in and manage the changed company. This time, he was a bit wiser and looked for someone who could create strategy so that he would not have to come back in again in order to make it work.

The new business model

Staff

Macpac's recruitment policy had typically been to hire people who loved the outdoors and used its products. The expertise they brought to the company was invaluable, and this helped to build a consistent company culture. With the reduced workforce, the management team had to revisit some of the role agreements and change the focus of relevant functions. From around 250 staff in 2003, with some 200 in production and about 50 in sales and marketing, design and administration and IT, by 2006 Macpac had around 60 staff, with 10 in production, double the number on the sales team and 12 in the design team, and this was growing. Logistics, which managed the channels from the manufacturers to Macpac's markets and its off-shore warehouses, had gone from none to three people.

Finance

Some of the overheads Macpac saved in manufacturing were being spent on marketing and design, and this increased by 10 per cent in 2004–2005. The company's new global network created exchange rate complications, and the company tried to keep a long-term view of the strong New Zealand dollar. Two-thirds of Macpac's products were exported, so it had a lot of foreign currency receipts. The company used external consultants to help develop a strategy to manage foreign exchange. With the majority of raw materials purchased by the off-shore manufacturing partners, Macpac did not pay until the finished goods were supplied. With typically six to eight weeks before a product might be sold, depending on where it was going, this meant that Macpac did not have the financial burden of surplus stock kept as final goods. The new global workforce and increased travel needs required a new strategy for budgeting, and the company's bonus structure (which had previously been based on a sharing of 20 per cent of the profits) had also been revised.

Operations and logistics

Unlike the simplicity of the old system, with one manufacturing plant and one warehouse, the three warehouses and seven manufacturing sites required a new operations plan. Having stock in the right place at the right time required sales trends and stock levels to be continually monitored. Sending goods from the manufacturers in Asia directly to foreign warehouses raised questions about quality control and how quickly they could handle repairs and revisions. In addition to logistics planning, measures and assessment systems were required to scrutinise the performance of suppliers. Production and logistics were two separate areas, with logistics running the warehouses and ordering the products and their distribution. Shelley, who ran the production side of things, travelled extensively at critical times, evaluating the manufacturers' performance as well as ensuring that new runs were made to specifications. There was also a lot of Internet and e-mail communication and designs were often sent electronically.

Offshore partners

Macpac had seven manufacturing suppliers, in China, Vietnam and the Philippines. With the offshoring decision, the company had evolved from being a New Zealand company to a global one. Though the New Zealand factory had been shut down, the company was indirectly employing more people than ever. The overseas suppliers were specialist manufacturers who made to specification. McIntyre got on well with the Korean owner of the factory in the Philippines (who had been an engineer at Hyundai). He could see the local Filipino staff growing and moving through the ranks. In Vietnam, the factory was run by a Taiwanese, whom McIntyre identified as a 'real humanist' who cared about and wanted to educate his local staff. McIntyre felt that the Vietnamese were learning quite rapidly because of his influence. The manufacturers in China were more difficult to work with.

In researching potential manufacturers, McIntyre had amassed a pile of folders at trade fairs over the years. The Macpac team got supplier recommendations, and even sought the views of some of their competitors. In the outsourcing relationship, Macpac's business was of low importance to those manufacturers: no one was going to go under if Macpac pulled out, McIntyre thought. Whilst Macpac was quite significant in backpacks, its much smaller clothing contracts were split between four manufacturers, so none was getting very much business. It was useful, however, that Macpac's production cycle was in the opposite season from the northern hemisphere. In managing the offshore relationships, design, logistics and production had their own communication links. So there were a lot of people communicating with these factories and it was up to the partners to manage the complexity.

In terms of efficiency, the Macpac factory had been a highly efficient production unit, with fully automated machinery and a committed workforce. Faced with losses, Macpac had employed a world expert in production efficiency who had not been able to make more than a 1 or 2 per cent improvement and Macpac had needed 10, 15 or 20 per cent for production to be viable in Christchurch. So the cheap labour costs of Asia had been attractive, albeit on very antiquated machinery with variable quality control. McIntyre wondered how long this might last, before the cost of labour increased and/or the Chinese made their own cheaper sewing machines. It was difficult to manage quality offshore: everything had to be specified and it was easy to overlook something basic that could go wrong, meaning a good deal of travel and communication. Whereas Macpac had a system of quality assurance, where Macpac designed quality into the whole manufacturing process, the offshore manufacturers relied on quality control and the low cost of fixing errors.

On quality control, Macpac trusted the inspection processes of some of its manufacturers and allowed them to ship direct to Europe, Australia and New Zealand. For others, pre-inspections were done in New Zealand even when products arrived in Australia first (as Australia was only three weeks shipping time from Asia and New Zealand was four). The manufacturers were either visited by Macpac or air freighted random shipping samples to Christchurch before they could release the product. Another option for China was to employ someone in Hong Kong to do an inspection on Macpac's behalf, though the company had not done this as it was nervous about sending someone who did not know the product.

Sales

With 65 per cent of sales in overseas markets, Macpac's sales team (all young New Zealanders) were all based in Christchurch, though many of them spent 20 weeks per year on the road in Europe, North America or Australia. Having a home-based sales team was a critical decision for McIntyre, who believed that salespeople living in New Zealand were more effective as they were close to the product, close to the design and close to the innovation. The big disadvantage was the amount of air travel, which was expensive. A further challenge to growing international sales was competitors offering better margins each year, and more manufacturers in the market. Also, it was difficult aligning sales and manufacturing of the clothing ranges: compared with other product lines, the clothing market was much more volatile and less predictable. See Exhibit 1 for Macpac's sales. Exhibits 2 and 3 show Macpac's sales and financial performance, 1999–2005.

Design

Since its beginnings Macpac had constantly prided itself on being leading edge in design and innovation. Throughout the first years, McIntyre continually looked for new ideas in overseas catalogues and a defining moment occurred in the early 1970s when he was asked to make a copy of a pack purchased in the USA. The pack was crude, but had an internal frame and was the first McIntyre had seen of its kind. Compared with packs with wooden external frames the comfort of the internal frame was vastly superior. McIntyre made new models with internal frames and developed further

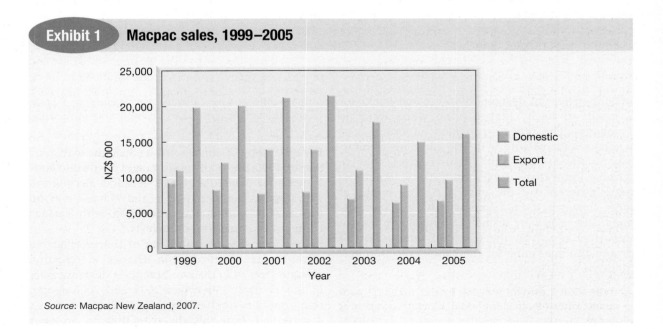

Exhibit 1   Macpac sales, 1999–2005

Source: Macpac New Zealand, 2007.

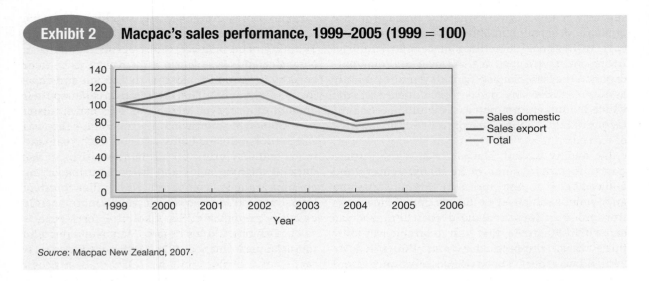

Exhibit 2 | Macpac's sales performance, 1999–2005 (1999 = 100)

Source: Macpac New Zealand, 2007.

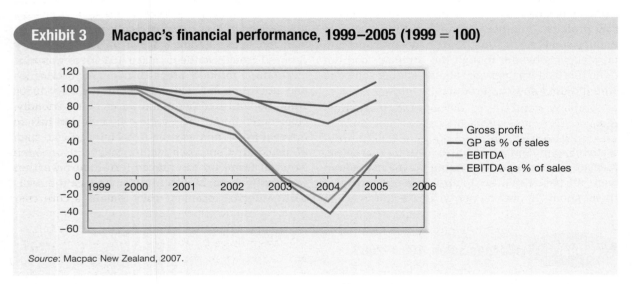

Exhibit 3 | Macpac's financial performance, 1999–2005 (1999 = 100)

Source: Macpac New Zealand, 2007.

insights when he designed and created packs for a group of local climbers who were going to Patagonia. The process provided important connections and insights with the climbing community. 'It was at that point,' McIntyre says, 'that we became innovative. It was the birth of something quite different for the outdoors.' The public at large, however, did not embrace his ideas immediately, and sales were dismal. In hindsight it was an important lesson in the essential intersection of design and marketing for the young entrepreneur. McIntyre explained:

> I had what I thought was the perfect tramping pack and hardly sold any. I realised that being very good at design was one thing, but that you've got to listen to

the public. It was a lesson in marketing, so I made alterations that the retailers were asking for and the products just suddenly took off.

His next step was developing a catalogue to display his products on retail counters and to educate consumers: it included a section entitled 'Packology'. The impact was astounding, and Macpac was on the road to building a reputation with serious climbers and outdoor enthusiasts.

Following the restructuring of the company to offshore manufacturing this change in direction brought new resources to Macpac's design group. In the two years between 2004 and 2006 design staff numbers doubled from 6 to 12, and felt less constrained, especially by cost, than in previous years. The new opportunity was to realise ideas and new products. The design goal was not to innovate with individual products, but to introduce ranges of products. In the heavily developed outdoor market, innovation was becoming elusive. McIntyre knew that the level of design talent needed to increase: 'What we're wanting are world class products.' He wanted an environment where people had the freedom to create, without bureaucratic and systemised tensions. To achieve these goals he employed a new design leader and Macpac became part of a pilot for a New Zealand government initiative 'Better by Design'. Through this process Macpac realised that although the company had grown based on its product innovation, it was more product led than design led. As such, Macpac has focused on becoming much more design orientated in its thinking, which was reflected in its marketing, branding, product development and strategy.

Marketing

As the move away from a manufacturing focus to a company centred on design and marketing, Macpac also employed a brand manager and increased its investment in promotions and improving the quality of communication about the brand. One of the challenges was capturing the company's New Zealand heritage in a meaningful way, and exploiting the country's image as a wilderness and 'untouched' paradise. McIntyre had seen a shift in the market for outdoor equipment, which posed a different marketing issue:

> The world's changed, so there aren't as many people travelling, and there aren't as many people going to the mountains as there used to be. They're not going as seriously as they used to, so we need to adjust to fit that new kind of modern, more urbanised form of outdoors, a less serious form of outdoors.

The company had to think more about its brand at a trade level, and learn more about what Macpac meant to its retailers.

Rebranding

In terms of the brand identity, Macpac's brand had historically been strongly associated with the hardcore, high-adventure, outdoor market segment. A newer challenge was more specifically to build a brand that was more mainstream in its appeal. Whilst Macpac was particularly strong in New Zealand, it was almost equally strong in Australia. Whilst the brand was quite strong in the UK, it had a much broader appeal in Australasia than outside. Macpac had to some extent created the outdoor market in Australasia and the brand had grown as the market grew. Whilst its products retained their quality and performance levels, the market itself was not so elite, so hardcore (that is, the segment that demanded high-performance outdoor gear). In the UK Macpac was strong, but again in the more specialist end of the market, and was also growing in the rest of Europe. The challenge was to break into broader sections of the mass market, for example the light travel market, child carriers.

Macpac realised it was going to have to put a lot more thought into the style and the cosmetic, aesthetic value of the products rather than just their performance. But the game was being played at a much more superficial level, and Macpac was slow in adapting to it: McIntyre thought that it was actually about 'the better looking mouse trap'. New Zealand had an outdoor image and there was a lot of potential in the New Zealand association which had not yet been realised in Macpac's products. New Zealand had a reputation of being friendly, clean and green and Macpac had to use this to create some uniqueness in the busy world marketplace. The specifications of Macpac's products were designed for the rugged terrain and weather in New Zealand. Materials and construction techniques were chosen for this. Macpac's core customers wanted to have the freedom to go anywhere and to know that they could forget about their gear: they were there for the adventure, for the people, with no question about the reliability of the gear. But in Continental Europe or Continental America, there was a different view of the world, McIntyre thought, and customers probably did not need that level of quality or performance, nor did they need to think about it unless one was at the extreme ends of those markets. Macpac had a diverse range of products all of which sold in relatively small volume, but McIntyre had no interest in making mass market products.

Leadership and succession

With an increasingly high dependence on teams to make decisions, McIntyre saw his role as the guardian of the company, questioning ideas and testing whether there was enough focus on its objectives. He had planned to look for a successor at the general management level, when the

in New Zealand and overseas, a new general manager had been hired in early 2006 with an option to buy in. Graeme Lord had a background with Boston Consulting Group and had held senior positions, including export marketing for a major wine company, so had strong strategic planning skills, which McIntyre saw as a powerful combination with his own more intuitive approach. He was now able to start stepping back as he felt strongly that the person who was leading the company had to own the strategy. McIntyre's personal goal was again to ease out of running the company, and by late 2006 he had achieved this by working at Macpac for one day a week. Graeme Lord, Shelley Gabites and Bruce McIntyre sat on the board and the intention was also to have some new non-executive directors join in the not too distant future. McIntyre was satisfied that Lord would lead Macpac successfully in the future as he had been attracted to Macpac because of its values as well as its opportunities. As the owner and founder of Macpac, McIntyre wanted to do all that was appropriate to support him to recreate the Macpac brand as a highly values-based brand. McIntyre had been looking for someone who would take over and be aligned with Macpac values and push it along further. He thought there was light at the end of the tunnel and was happy to support the company he founded. It continued to design outstanding products in an industry he was still passionate about, while maintaining the strong company values which had underpinned Macpac for over 20 years.

company returned to profitability. He wanted to ensure that the person had the right skills, and avoid the compromises he had made when he had previously relinquished the reins. After advertising

Ekomate Systems and the Indian software industry: leveraging network relationships for international growth

Shameen Prashantham

The case study looks at the importance of developing and maintaining a network of relationships in international markets and in the local milieu as a critically important capability for smaller firms seeking international growth. It also illustrates how the indirect benefit of acquiring new knowledge (learning) through network relationships is likely to be more sustainable than the direct benefits of gaining new business opportunities.

● ● ●

Origins of Ekomate

Ekomate Systems was founded in 1996 by Tom Thomas upon his return to his hometown of Bangalore after obtaining an MS in computer engineering at the University of Texas in Austin. The son of an entrepreneur, Thomas felt that starting a business would be considerably more remunerative in comparison with employment. Moreover, he had gained some work experience at Intel, while in the USA, and was acutely aware of the great potential of the Internet. He was therefore keen to start a company that would 'enable client companies to get on the Web'. According to him, when utilising Internet technology, companies 'not only have the public side [that is, a website] that any visitor would come in and see but also a private side where their customers, suppliers and vendors also interact through the Web'. His company, Ekomate, works in this area as a software services company. The Ekomate website describes its offering as follows:

> Ekomate uses the offshore development model to help its clients get their IT work done, maintaining international quality at reasonable costs, thereby resulting in tremendous cost advantages to its clients. Ekomate follows ISO compliant processes for software development.

The Bangalore software industry[1]

In founding Ekomate, Thomas was riding on the crest of what would prove to be a substantial wave, the ripples of which have since been felt throughout the world – the development of the Indian software industry. With Bangalore as its focal point, the Indian software industry has attracted several international companies from high-cost advanced economies to outsource, at least partially, their software development needs. The outsourcing of software development has been especially pronounced in the USA, although latterly European countries such as Germany and the UK have followed suit. Regional shares of Indian exports are approximately two-thirds to North America, a quarter to Europe and the rest to other markets including Asia–Pacific. It has been suggested that Bangalore's software industry emerged quite by accident, facilitated by historical factors. In the years following independence (1947), a strategic decision was taken by the Indian government to locate certain key defence laboratories away from

---

[1] For a more detailed discussion see S. Prashantham, 'Local network relationships and the internationalization of small knowledge-intensive firms', *Copenhagen Journal of Asian Studies*, vol. 19 (2004), pp. 5–26.

the nation's capital of New Delhi owing to its proximity to potentially hostile neighbours. Thus Bangalore, a city located in the South Indian peninsula and with an established military presence from the days of British rule, was chosen as the location of such vital public sector undertakings as Hindustan Aeronautical Limited. These organisations attracted technical personnel from around the country and from the prestigious Bangalore-based Indian Institute of Science. The resultant pool of talent was arguably the forerunner to the supply of software professionals now available in Bangalore. Numerous engineering colleges have since been established in India where over 150,000 English-speaking engineering and science graduates are produced every year. A parallel development that has latterly had an impact on the development of the Indian software industry was the steady emigration of engineers from India over the past three decades, many of whom have attained positions of importance in the US IT industry, notably in Silicon Valley.

Ekomate's 'emergent' phase (1996–2002)

For the first couple of years Ekomate's clientele was solely domestic. A notable success was the development of a website for the leading English daily in the city. However, it had always been Thomas's ambition to attract international business, especially from the USA. Not only was the USA without doubt the leading market for Indian software development outsourcing, but also Thomas had useful connections there through his Master's education in Texas and his stint at Intel. So he had been putting out feelers to former classmates and other contacts, seeking potential clients. These informal efforts paid off in 1998 when he secured his first US contract.

This breakthrough heralded a considerable change in Ekomate's geographic focus: the emphasis now clearly shifted to international business. Subsequent business deals followed from the USA, many of which were the consequence of connections with persons of Indian origin who are often referred to as non-resident Indians (NRIs). Thomas narrates various anecdotes that illustrate the benefits of information, advice and opportunities[2]

---

[2] S. Prashantham, 'Foreign network relationships and the internationalization of small knowledge-intensive firms', *International Journal of Entrepreneurship and Innovation Management*, vol. 6, no. 6 (2006), pp. 542–553.

obtained through these connections with fellow Indians working in the US IT industry. Often, it would be a case of a US-based former classmate or family friend referring Ekomate to prospective clients. Thomas notes of NRIs that:

> definitely for someone coming from India, or someone having an Indian perspective, it's very easy for them to talk to us. For example, the visitor we had from Chicago two days ago is a friend of my best friend at college. . . . For us NRIs have been a powerful source of business. They know our working conditions. If you say Republic Day is a holiday or some other day is a holiday, they'll know why [chuckles]. It is difficult to explain to an American client how many holidays we have in India or why we have to work on Saturdays . . . NRIs just need the trust factor [that] this guy will not screw up, they'll deliver when they say; otherwise it is their neck on the line there. So I think the NRIs definitely play a very important role and it's a role that we have consciously been cultivating.

Also around the same time, early 1998, Ekomate unexpectedly won a business contract to develop software for a client in another foreign market, namely the UK. This transpired when a British software entrepreneur learned of the emerging software industry in India through a documentary on television, and proceeded to identify prospective software firms in India via the Internet. He subsequently e-mailed these firms and visited in India those he had shortlisted. Ekomate ended up as the software outsourcing company of choice; apparently the British entrepreneur was particularly impressed by Thomas's speed of e-mail replies.

For a young, growing company, the string of business contracts signed provided sustenance and excitement. By 2002, fully 90 per cent of Ekomate's revenues were accounted for by international business. From a standing start in 1996, the company had grown to a size of about 20 employees. The USA remained the largest market. Ekomate wanted to maintain the strong focus on international markets. By that stage, Thomas saw international growth as being synonymous with the growth of his firm. In early 2002 he observed: 'If I have only Indian customers, then I cannot make payroll.' The international clients that Ekomate serves tend to be software SMEs that outsource some or all of their software programming to Ekomate. Thomas sought to continue his focus on working with software companies abroad rather than directly with end-users:

> Our clients are basically small to medium firms – IT firms, essentially. We have one of their tech people

interact with us and we develop software to their specifications. We have seen that working with the end-user is very difficult, as a small firm. We cannot afford to send people there and get specs.

Ekomate dabbled with a few other markets as well. For instance, in 1999 Thomas took advantage of a trade mission to New Zealand and sought business leads there. Also, he was able to get some business from Germany which prompted him to incorporate a German translation on his website at one stage. These initial inroads did not, however, lead to further success, in large part because Thomas did not have the same level of network relationships in these other markets compared with the USA. Consequently, Ekomate struggled to consolidate on the initial business obtained from or contacts made in these markets. Much more promising, however, was the British market and Thomas turned his attention there in the ensuing years. He talked of his targeted markets in the following way:

> Definitely the US market is key because they adopt technology very fast. And all the trends are being driven from there. Followed closely by Europe, I would say – especially the UK because it is English-speaking and easier to break into. We have done some work for Germany also. It has not been the level we wanted to achieve. We wanted to do much more . . . I think Japan is a lucrative market from what I've seen, but those I have seen who have succeeded in Bangalore are only people who are married to Japanese, or have lived there, or have some other connection. I think it is very hard for a company to just go in and break into Japan. It takes years.

In the light of the slowing US economy, compounded by the 9/11 terrorist attacks, by 2002 Thomas felt it imperative to diversify Ekomate's portfolio of markets so as not to be overly reliant on the USA, the most lucrative market for Indian software firms and also the market where he had the most network relationships.

Ekomate's 'deliberate' phase (2002 onwards)

Another related development at the time that strongly influenced Thomas's thinking was the mentoring he received from a seasoned Bangalore-based software entrepreneur. This individual had been part of the founding team of a highly respected Indian software company. He was a social acquaintance that Thomas's father had made

in a local tennis club. Thomas, in a manner not uncommon among (although by no means exclusive to) Indians, sought the guidance of this highly experienced person who agreed in November 2002 to play a mentoring role to Thomas and Ekomate. Thomas believes that much value has been added through this association. In his words:

> I think, as they say, providence brought us together. Basically we play tennis together at the Indiranagar Club. So he has seen me for many years and he's quite close to my dad also. I knew that he was a great person in the field of IT and I also knew when the downturn came that I needed guidance.

The mentor's influence on Ekomate was manifold. For instance, he emphasised the need to ensure the robust management of quality in the firm's processes; subsequent efforts culminated with Ekomate successfully applying for ISO accreditation of its software processes by mid-2005. One of the major areas in which the mentor influenced Thomas's thinking was Ekomate's internationalisation process. One strong recommendation that the mentor made was to seek *actively* additional international business with a view to achieving further growth and thereby stability for Ekomate. While this was consistent with Thomas's own views, hearing it from the mentor spurred him to a more urgent, yet also a more *deliberately strategic* approach than before.

Consequently, Thomas's attention shifted to the UK. However, this time he decided not to rely purely on happenchance or serendipity. Given that he lacked the same level of network relationships compared with the USA, Thomas decided to look for useful connections with the UK on his doorstep, as it were. He began to engage with the India-based representatives of British trade organisations. This brought him into contact with the India manager for Scottish Development International, which promotes trade to and from Scotland. As a result, he found himself on the guest list when a delegation of Scottish software firms visited Bangalore later that year. Thomas observed that:

> We definitely realised that just looking at the US alone is not a good strategy, so we're looking at parallel markets in Europe. So we've successfully built good relationships with trade organisation representatives of different countries. I have a good relationship with the Scotland country manager. . . . The point is just to get exposed so that whenever Scottish companies visit India we are invited for events, we know what they are looking for.

The interaction with the Scots made Ekomate aware of the relatively high concentration of software companies in that part of the UK. Moreover, virtually all of these firms were software SMEs – exactly the type of firm that Ekomate was interested in dealing with. Based on prior positive experiences in dealing with fellow Indians in the USA, Thomas's strategy for the UK in general and Scotland in particular was to partner with a non-resident Indian business based in Scotland. The local partner would provide the front-end interface with the client while Ekomate would provide the back-end software programming.

In the event, in the autumn of 2004, Thomas visited Scotland and an agreement was signed between Ekomate and a Scottish partner. Although the main individual involved at the Scottish end was not himself Indian, the connection had been made through a Scotland-based Indian contact that Thomas had cultivated in the interim. Thus, a strategy of tapping into ethnic ties overseas was continuing to be adopted. Thomas was very optimistic about the new relationship and business targets were agreed by the partners for the forthcoming quarter. The partnership was, however, short-lived. By early 2005 it became apparent that a personal crisis for the individual in Scotland made the relationship unsustainable. This was a setback for Ekomate, which had pinned great hopes on the additional growth that would accrue through new business in Scotland.

Thomas was nonetheless sufficiently convinced of Scotland's viability as a market for Ekomate that he went about building another partnership along a similar front-back-end principle. It took a further two years before this could be achieved. Once again, the Indian contact in Scotland played a part in identifying partners albeit this time in a more circuitous fashion. During the visit to Scotland in 2004, Thomas had been introduced to a software SME in Glasgow through the Indian contact. This company had, the following year, referred another Scottish firm to Thomas and it was eventually this firm that Ekomate signed up to do business with in November 2006. The outcome of this partnership remains to be seen.

Future directions

While the business development efforts in Scotland are at a nascent stage, Ekomate has continued to obtain repeat business from clients elsewhere in the UK and in the USA. The resultant growth has seen Ekomate's headcount almost double since 2002. Going forward, Ekomate is consciously targeting what Thomas describes as 'sustaining work', that is software projects that were likely to lead to continuous repeat business (such as maintenance service contracts) as opposed to merely one-off contracts to build some software for a client. One of Thomas's main dilemmas, however, has been the choice between focusing on a few core areas of competence and diversifying the portfolio of technologies on the basis of client needs. With a view to keeping customer loyalty, he has chosen the latter option. However, there is a continued focus on Internet-enabled technologies. Furthermore, Ekomate is in the process of diversifying into IT-enabled services commonly referred to as business process outsourcing, with a view to further augmenting international revenues.

Eden Project (B)

Roger Jones

This case continues the Eden Project story that explored Eden from its early beginning as an entrepreneurial idea in the mid-1990s, tracking and examining its early problems and incremental phases of formation as a new business start-up, and exiting the first case at the point of the official public opening on 17 March 2001. This date saw the fruition of the 'strategic dreams' of Eden's founders and the pioneering teams who brought a redundant china clay pit back to life in an economically deprived corner of South-West England. Eden Project (B) describes the key developments that have emerged since 2001 at the internationally acclaimed Eden Project, offering an extension to the first case.

● ● ●

From entrepreneur to business executive

Tim Smit is Chief Executive Officer of Eden Project Limited. Smit was undoubtedly the lead driving force and inspiration behind Eden's initial entrepreneurial idea, an idea that led to the Eden Project being acknowledged as an international business brand name by 2007. However, the transitions for Smit have not been easy, with his own strategic learning curve typifying those people who have to make the transfer from entrepreneur innovator to operational business executive – and in a short reaction time. Such transitions are necessary and influenced by strategic needs and corporate imperatives. These transitions almost always become obvious as soon as the 'initial entrepreneurial event' has been concluded and when governance and corporate accountabilities become increasingly transparent. Reflections of the official opening day on 17 March 2001 hint at Smit's position:

> Visitors had been queuing at our gates since 4.00am; travelling from all over the UK to see what we had been doing at Eden. Traffic congestion was a big problem and we had seriously underestimated volume. The Eden team had been brilliant, meeting the tight deadlines we had set, with the horticultural teams finishing their planting with less than twelve hours to opening. Together, we all worked through the night, and with little sleep were all ready to take on whatever job was necessary – some of us collecting entrance money – others acting as tour guides. Clearly, Eden was not finished completely on opening-day, but the response and patience from our first official visitors was fantastic.
>
> (Eden Project Video, 2001)

Smit reports 'a wonderful opening day' – but personally became overwhelmed by a sense of confusion and insecurity as the day drew to a close suggesting

> this is our baby, and together we have created Eden from nothing. Visitors can't really imagine what we have gone through to create this unique experience. I had the strange feeling that I didn't actually want any visitors to see Eden, feeling perhaps a sense of intrusion by the public on our creation.
>
> (Eden Project Video, 2001)

Up to the official opening day, the Eden Project had been built around an unstoppable flow of creative and innovative talent. Such talent, when harnessed together with entrepreneurial flair, imagination, inspiration and the will to succeed, had created a formidable business start-up culture.

Photo: Eden Project Ltd/Gendall Design. Photographer Bob Berry

But would it continue, and would Smit be able to make the necessary transfer from visionary entrepreneur into corporate CEO and leader of the management team – and ensure Eden's sustainability and strategic growth?

2001 to 2003

Beyond the opening-day euphoria

After the official opening Eden spent the remainder of 2001 concentrating on 'de-snagging' problems, improving visitor services, implementing its core aim of uniting the Eden site into a 'theatre of living plants and education' – whilst maintaining an eye on the regional economic impact Eden was making. Interest in the Eden experience was growing rapidly with a number of eminent horticultural scientists visiting, along with around 1.7 million paying visitors, all curious to see what was happening in Cornwall's high-technology jewel of human creativity.

Eden had been built with support and collaboration from the residents of its immediate location and the wider population throughout the county of Cornwall – but not without addressing public concerns and doubts. Moreover, Eden was a glowing example of public and private partnerships,

particularly with regard to the procurement of considerable financial investment. The residents of Cornwall (and funding investors) awaited evidence that the project that had received their backing was, in fact, delivering on its economic strategic intentions. In December 2001, Eden presented a first outline report of its economic impact called the 'Eden Effect':

£111 million 'Eden Effect' boosts South West economy

Cornwall's Eden Project has generated £111 million [€160m] of additional spend in the South West economy in the last eight months, according to the results of an economic impact study published today – Monday 17th December 2001. The study, conducted from April to November 2001, is the first time 'the Eden Effect' has been quantified, and confirms that the positive impact – both economic and in terms of the region's image – is being felt across the South West. Eden's phenomenal success will be further confirmed next month when new figures are expected to show the Millennium Commission Lottery funded project among the top five paid-for attractions in the UK, rubbing shoulders with the London Eye, Alton Towers, the Tower of London and Madame Tussauds. Between March and November, Eden attracted nearly 1.7 million visitors, smashing its own first year target of 750,000. It is now the region's most visited attraction, with no other attraction hitting the one million mark. By comparison, annual figures for the Roman

Baths at Bath, and Stonehenge, are 930,000 and 800,000 respectively. The economic impact survey included a visitor questionnaire filled-out by 1,395 respondents, a postal survey of 1,913 businesses in St. Austell, Penzance, Plymouth and Exeter, which attracted 530 responses, and a survey of Eden's top 60 local suppliers. The survey found that:

- Over 500,000 holiday visitors to Cornwall were influenced by the existence of Eden
- They spend an estimated £111 million in the region, staying an average of 5/6 nights
- Day trippers, of which there were 478,000 during the period, spent around £9.3 million
- 83% of businesses felt Eden had made a positive economic impact on the region
- 25% of businesses said their turnover had increased as a direct result of Eden
- The accommodation sector was most positively affected, followed by retail and catering
- Some 4% of business said they had taken on more staff – boosting local employment
- 94% said that Eden had made a positive impact on the region's image nationally
- Many respondents, especially in the accommodation sector, said Eden had extended the tourist season considerably, with trade up by between 14% and 21% across September and October, and by 11% to 13% in November

The survey also explored the direct economic impact Eden has had in terms of job creation, wages, and the amount of money it spends with suppliers, of which there are around 600. The survey found that:

- Eden directly employs around 400 people year-round
- 90% of employees live within a 20 mile [32 km] radius, and 95% are from Cornwall
- Eden's annual wage bill is £4 million, mostly spent locally
- Eden's positive 'buy local' policy spends £4.74 million (61%) of its purchasing budget in Cornwall, and 75% of its budget in the South West
- £1.46 million (81%) is spent with Cornish food and drink producers
- £1.1 million (61%) of the retail budget is spent with Cornish retailers
- £2.17 million (55%) of the general goods budget is spent with Cornish suppliers
- 47 of Eden's top 60 suppliers responded that they added 23 staff as a direct result of their Eden contracts which had boosted their turnover by £2.74 million
- Visitor spend at Eden during the period was £16.3 million. £7.8 million made up of admissions fees and Friends' subscriptions; £4.4 million was spent on buying goods and £4.1 million spent on buying refreshments

(*Economic Impact Report*, December 2001, cited in Eden Project Press Releases, 2002)

The economic impact survey and the 2001 report were warmly received, quantifying Eden's key strategic achievements, building confidence with all stakeholders – and all achieved within the first eight months of trading. But how sustainable is Eden's performance?

In January 2002 Eden's Marketing Director, Dave Meneer comments:

we've been learning every step of the way, and 2001 proved to be a very steep learning curve! We are dedicated to making the visitor experience at Eden as enjoyable as possible and therefore feel it is important to invest the money made last year on improvements throughout the site and on the entrance to Eden – particularly for those who come on our busiest days. These new developments will get our visitors through ticketing as quickly as possible, and allow them to enjoy a new space before they go down to the main site.

(Eden Project Press Releases, 2002)

Development plans included:

- Changes to the visitor centre into 'a stunning piazza', for visitors to sit, stroll and gather information about Eden.
- Expansion to Eden's on-site shop.
- Relocation of the café to the Gallery, giving stunning views of the biomes, with easy reversion flexibility for education and lectures.
- Transfer existing school and daytime education facilities to a new temporary educational structure, located next to the Warm Temperate Biome.

Whilst all these infrastructure changes are taking place, Dave Meneer wisely asks for visitor patience . . .

we hope our friends will bear with us whilst we are making these improvements, particularly as we may have to move things around a bit. . . . We are potentially looking at a few further changes in 2003 but feel it is best to do this one step at a time, so as to cause minimum disruption to our visitors.

(Eden Project Press Releases, 2002)

The first full-year trading and ambitious forecasts

In January 2002 Eden beat off strong competition from across the UK and won the Premier Award in the UK's longest-standing independent Environmental Awards Scheme. Commenting on the Business Commitment to the Environment (BCE) 2001 winners, the BCE president saluted the standard of entries and in particular Eden for 'the aim of educating and encouraging best practice in environment and conservation, both at a local and global level'. Was Eden, after such a short time, now being recognised on the global stage and as an exemplar to the world? Eden's Managing Director, Gaynor Coley, responded:

> When the Eden Team set out on this journey we wanted to demonstrate that good business is wholly compatible with environmental sustainability and that commercial viability does not have to be traded-off against social responsibility. We are thrilled to receive this award, as it is a visible marker that we must work with the grain of nature and not against it if we are to survive.
>
> (Eden Project Press Releases, 2002)

As the year progressed Eden continued introducing new initiatives, themes and exhibits all built around its core aims of communication and education, and all of which brought something new each month for visitors to enjoy. In addition to the stunning vista of the biomes and the stories they tell, Eden clearly had the lens of business diversification in its sights! However, during October 2002 three key initiatives were announced:

1 A reiteration of Eden's local and regional economic impact, published in 2001.

2 Key benchmarks for the future 10-year picture.

3 The unveiling of its strategic aims and ambitions.

With confidence growing and an unquestionable success story on which to build, Eden's management confirmed its regional economic impact and also made bold strategic forecasts:

> Our forward plan is predicated on 2 million visitors each year . . . and 3% inflation, and against a planning horizon that spans ten years of the 'Eden Effect'.
>
> (Eden Project Press Releases, 2002)

- 2001/2002's Eden Effect was £150m
- 2002/2003's Eden Effect forecast to be £162m
- Projected Eden Effect at first 10 years of full operation £1.8 to £2bn

Alongside these ambitious forecasts were the caveats:

> But only . . . if visitors keep coming!
> And only . . . if we look after visitors better and better!

To a packed audience of neighbours, suppliers, investors and industry leaders, Eden's management team presented facts from 2001 and their plans for the future. Alongside drawings and models of planned site developments, Gaynor Coley explained:

> Our aim is to maintain, not augment our two million visitors per year. We want to ensure that a visit to Eden is educationally enriching and entertaining. Only by implementing these development plans will we be able to look after our visitors in such a way that offers them the sort of experience that makes them want to keep coming back!
>
> (Eden Project Press Releases, 2002)

Dave Meneer offered the marketer's dimension: 'we hope this timely sharing of development plans and economic data should enable us all to guarantee the "Eden Effect" for years to come'; and in summarising, Tim Smit challenged those present to recognise that:

> Only once in a generation does something capture the public imagination in this way. It is imperative we complete what we began. Yes – it has had a sensational effect on our region's economy. Yes – people love it. But why? The answer is, we live in a cynical age and Eden is about the possibility of positive change. If we miss this opportunity we should all be ashamed.
>
> (Eden Project Press Releases, 2002)

The presentation revealed strategic intentions and details about:

- The third, 'dry tropics' biome.
- A new education building.
- Covered walkways and a field centre.
- New accommodation for horticultural staff.
- Student training facilities and further exhibition areas.
- An architectural review, commissioned as a Master Plan study for the whole site, aimed at ensuring that all developments maintained integrity.
- Exploring alternative modes of access and transport to the site, in close collaboration with the local community, railway services and coach operators.

During 2002 Eden had diversified its activities and introduced the first of a range of 'hugely successful and imaginative events' called Eden Sessions. By efficient site utilisation Eden launched a mixture of music, theatre and dance festivals that *The Times* described as 'half Glastonbury and half Glyndebourne'. Again, Eden's creativity and innovation had found an added-value niche!

Sticking to the knitting – but Big Build 2 is looming

The year 2003 was heralded by new developments for younger visitors with a range of new activities, and with Eden hosting an international conference of scientists to discuss ways of safeguarding world-wide banana crops – diversity in the extreme, and yet consistent with Eden's positioning across a broad business base. Recycling and 'waste-neutral' strategies came sharply into focus with Eden taking the lead on several domestic and inter-nationally important initiatives.

Eden confirmed 'the biggest ever line-up for 2003' of the successful Eden Sessions introduced in the previous year. Some of the biggest names in music were set to descend on Eden for the summer events, with the promotional hyperbole proclaim-ing Eden as 'the hottest venue around, and tickets are selling fast'. However, whilst this was attracting the attention of Eden's growing following of music lovers, the management team were busy drafting a new 'Eden Effect' statement reflecting the results of the 2003 Economic Impact Survey. This was reported on 1 October 2003.

The key features were as follows:

- The previous survey in 2001 provided strong evidence of the 'Eden Effect' and its outstanding achievements and benefits to the regional economy. The report demonstrated that such achievements had been consolidated in 2003.

- Profile raising of suppliers in the region.

- Extensions of business outside the traditional main tourist season.

- Developing extensive local supply chains and capacity building across diverse industries in the local community.

- Local businesses benefiting from Eden's show-case effect.

- Reversals of Cornwall's 'talent drain' by intro-ducing new practitioners into a wide and creative mix of regional businesses.

- Visitor numbers during 2003 echo those of 2002.

- New commercial projects on a national and international scale.

- Traffic queues have almost been eliminated, creating a more even spread of visitors.

- More younger visitors attracted with over 60% of those attending the sell-out summer concerts being the under 35s.

Dave Meneer commented:

> The continued economic effect of Eden is spectacular, as we are approaching our fourth year of trading next March. We anticipate a long term consolidation of the already impressive figures as plans for the next stage of our development move ahead. The results of this (second) survey prove that the 'Eden Effect' is here to stay. Thanks to the support of all our friends and visitors, we are now fully established as a 'must see' destination with robust, regular visitor numbers and a consistent economic impact. We are consolidating our partnerships with them, which will also benefit the Eden brand and the local economy.
>
> (Eden Project Press Releases, 2003)

Towards the end of 2003 came the long-awaited announcement of yet another of Eden's ground-breaking projects known as 'Big Build 2'. Eden planned to build a new state-of-the-art education building, with a design concept initiated by the architects of Eden's high-technology biomes, but based upon nature's perfect spiral. The design concept for the new education centre had been inspired by plant architecture – a design that has a track record going back some 400 million years. The principal design themes follow the Fibonacci mathematical sequence discovered by Leonardo da Pisa in the thirteenth century and echo the spirals at the centre of a sunflower or pine cone.

Estimated costs for Big Build 2 were forecast at around £15m with funding procured from some of Eden's established sources:

- Millennium Commission £10.5m
- South West Regional Development Agency £2.89m
- Objective One Partnership (Europe) £1.00m
- The balance from a number of smaller sponsors

Construction was planned to commence early in 2004 and would take around two years to complete. Tim Smit enthused:

> The response to our Eden Education Programme has overwhelmed us, so to finally be able to announce that we're beginning work is deeply satisfying – as is the knowledge that the 'hottest' design team in the world has dreamed up a building that I guarantee will be the most photographed and loved building of 2005. If it's possible, I'm more excited now than at anytime in the Project's history.
>
> (Eden Project Press Releases, 2003)

2004 to 2007

Investment flows in – with Eden at The Core and on The Edge

In March 2004 Eden announced a further investment of almost £20m. This consisted of:

- South West Regional Development Agency (SWRDA)   £6.78m
- Objective One Programme (Europe)   £12.9m

This new investment acknowledged Eden's economic impact on the region since start-up – a sum now calculated to be in excess of £462m. Gaynor Coley reflected:

> Supporting Eden's Big Build 2 developments with this new funding package is further recognition of our economic benefit to Cornwall and the region. The Objective One Partnership and the SWRDA worked with us at a strategic level to help ensure this 'Eden Effect' is not just a honeymoon but is captured and sustained.
>
> (Eden Project Press Releases, 2004)

Eden's management were delighted with the new cash injections, reflecting that the new investment of £20m completes Big Build 2 funding – a total of £33m including previous investment – and will be used towards the new Education Resource Building which is under construction. In addition, site developments will be commissioned, and strategies introduced for furthering Eden's commitment to sharing knowledge and science in an informative and entertaining way.

A summer season of Eden events again proved to be very successful, resulting at the end of 2004 with a new initiative aimed at increasing winter visitors. An ice skating rink was built over the existing lake and proved so popular that the skating period was extended to meet demand. Clearly, Eden was implementing a range of successful events during every month of the year, with appeal to much wider visitor audiences and age groups. Visitor sustainability was being shaped as a key strategic objective, with the winter season of 2004–2005 proving to be Eden's most successful to date.

Building on earlier successes Eden expanded its music and cultural programmes during 2005, engaging in several high-profile events such as the Live 8 concert, which received worldwide TV coverage, and continued to expand its international profile by winning multiple awards and accolades from around the world. However, what dominated Eden's management and staff during 2005 was the unveiling of the new £15m education centre on 19 September – aptly named 'The Core' to reflect education, learning and knowledge transfer being at the core of Eden's philosophy. The Core was heralded as 'the greatest moment in Eden Project's history since the opening of the world's biggest plant Biomes' – and the 'history' was only four and a half years old! But Eden is exceptionally good at hyping itself and has become expert at entrepreneurial self-marketing and promotion. Smit typifies marketing flair – and the entrepreneur enthusiasm still oozes:

> I hate exaggeration so I'll tell you the simple truth. This is the finest modern building in the world, and anyone who can show me a better looking one is either a liar or clairvoyant. I could give you a lot of guff about inspirational education and the success of the Eden Project; the genius of the architects and the artists involved, but it boils down to one thing. This building is a cathedral and it moves you and fills you with awe.
>
> (Eden Project Press Releases, 2005)

The year 2006 opened with two new milestones – and a management announcement:

> Eden Project has released its first annual report. The Trustees and Directors of the Eden Project have today issued the first of what they intend to be annual reports, setting out a range of charitable activities as well as full financial results.
>
> (Eden Project Press Releases, 2006)

The first annual report seemed to pass by unnoticed, but the first new milestone, announced on Thursday 1 June 2006, received international attention and wide media coverage – 'The Queen visits Eden for the first time and officially opens the iconic new education centre The Core' – which was now suddenly being hyped up as the Eden Project's 'Da Vinci Code Building' (apparently, the Fibonacci mathematical sequence at the heart of The Core's architectural design is also integral in the plot of Dan Brown's best-seller *The Da Vinci Code*).

The second new milestones revealed itself in the form of 'the next great chapter in the building of Eden, to be known as The Edge, comes closer with the news that Eden has been short-listed for a major new National Lottery award'. From August 2006, Eden has nine months to prepare its detailed bid for a staggering £50m Lottery award to build The Edge. Ultimately the winning venture will be chosen by the public in a nationwide TV vote. Tim Smit responded:

This is fantastic news and we are delighted to be on the shortlist. This is a great opportunity for Eden and Cornwall, but for us to be chosen as the Landmark Project we will have to win support from all around Britain. The Edge will explore what it is like to live with the grain of nature. It is a project for our time and is arguably the most challenging and essential call to arms for our generation. By exploring how great social transformations have happened in the past and how societies have at time failed to transform when need came, The Edge will tackle the great issues we need to face today – water supply and climate chaos. It will feature the arid and semi-arid areas of the world because it is in these regions where climate, energy and water-related tensions are experienced in their most acute forms; where the extremes of wealth and poverty, abundance and scarcity, live side by side on the edge. The Edge will define what skills, capacities and ambitions we need in order to resolve conflict and to foster and maintain healthy, adaptable and cohesive communities into the future. In the coming weeks, Eden will put together a sustainable strategic business plan and reach out to engage the community in the development process and the outcome. Cornwall played a vital role in the Industrial Revolution but subsequently experienced all the consequences of decline through resource depletion. It is the ideal place within Europe to pioneer the change for a post-industrial age.

(Eden Project Press Releases, 2006)

As Eden prepares its plans to compete and hopefully become the UK's leading agent for change and transformation, and to try and persuade the British public to get behind what Eden believes will be one of the most transformational projects in the world, 2006 closed and 2007 opened with an unusual silence from Eden. However, at January 2007, the Eden Project story continues!

Author's notes

1. Eden Project (A) was first published in the 7th edition of this text in 2005. The case tracks the Eden story from its first humble beginning in 1992, as an innovative new idea that stimulated the 'entrepreneurial event' – the physical creation of the Eden Project. Eden Project (A) addresses what Eden called the 'Big Build' and monitors not only the enormous civil engineering task undertaken, but also the pioneering way Eden combined public and private partnerships to raise the considerable financial investment needed for development. Eden Project (A) exited at the day Eden first opened its doors to public visitors. This case is now accessible to readers who may require detailed background information, and is located on the text website in the Classic Case Collection.

2. Eden Project (B) is presented as a continuation of the Eden story, and is set from the public opening day in March 2001 through to early January 2007. Thus far, Eden cases (A) and (B) build a history that spans 14 years of the company's emergence as a visitor attraction and its evolution as a corporate organisation. It is appropriately called the Eden Project – because it is defined as a project that is ongoing and without any predetermined end. As such . . . the story continues!

3. Eden Project Limited – senior managers featured in Eden Project (B):
   Tim Smit, Chief Executive Officer (entrepreneur and original co-founder of the Eden Project)
   Gaynor Coley, Managing Director
   Dave Meneer, Marketing Director

Sources

Sources of information consulted in support of this case study: Eden Project Video, Eden Project Books, 2001; Eden Project Press Releases, 2002–2006; www.edenproject.com.

Brown Bag Films

John Cullen

This case study explores the current strategic dilemma faced by a young, but highly successful animation company operating from Dublin, Ireland. The directors of this profitable and successful company are anxious not to rest on their considerable achievements (which include, amongst other awards, an Oscar nomination) and to continue growing and developing their enterprise. The international recognition that Brown Bag Films has won has not been easily attained and the case explores the current conditions in which it operates. Context is provided by outlining the unique social, cultural and economic environment at national and sectoral levels in which the company developed and grew. The key question suggested by the case is: what should the directors do now?

● ● ●

Background

We're very worried.

The business is running well and we make strong and consistent profits. We have an international reputation, and we've been told that every children's television station in the world know us. We've worked with and for national and commercial television stations, independent producers, advertising agencies. Since the Academy Award® nomination, we've had an opportunity to do some high-profile commercials with A-list clients such as Coca Cola, Danone, Cadburys, National Lottery and have produced TV series that have sold to broadcasters around the world.

But now that everything is going well, we've started to notice that we have started to finish each other's sentences, as if we've been married to each other! We know instinctively what each other thinks, or what the other would be thinking when they're not there.

And this can't be healthy. I mean, what are we missing? The fact that we've gotten to where we want to go is great, but now we're here we know that if we don't expand our perspective that we'll be flattened by change when it does happen.

What do people usually do with their business when they get to where we are? Brown Bag Films is twelve years old and as directors we're completely different people to when we started. What can we do to ensure that Brown Bag Films is still around in 12 years time?

Photo: Brown Bag Films

Darragh O'Connell and Cathal Gaffney formally started Brown Bag Films in 1994 following their successful production of a satirical series which lampooned *Peig*, an Irish-language classic which was required reading for secondary school students. Prior to this, they had both been in college together and collaborated on a number of low-budget short films.

They went to college in the backdrop of Sullivan-Bluth's animation studios in Dublin, which had

---

opened in Dublin in the mid-1980s in response to the Irish Industrial Development Agency's (IDA's) drive to attract large animation studios to Ireland (which promised large-scale employment in an industry that was non-existent in Ireland at the time). By the early 1990s the three main foreign studios attracted to Ireland in this particular drive, and which included Sullivan-Bluth, had withdrawn. Competitive pressures within the international animation industry and unfavourable global economic conditions had resulted in many of the American studios returning home. Many of the Irish staff employed in the largest studio, Don Bluth Entertainment, emigrated and several employees sought employment outside the Irish animation sector. However, following their departure, they left behind not only a well-developed training infrastructure, particularly in centres of excellence such as Ballyfermot College of Further Education and Dun Laoghaire Institute of Art, Design and Technology (National Film School), but also a cohort of young, highly-trained animators who had seen how successful, commercially oriented animation studios worked. More than anything, though, they had exposed young artists to the potential of a choice of animation as a career.

Bolstered by the critical acclaim they had received for *Peig* and by the experience of successfully completing a commercial project, the Brown Bag directors invested in high-spec animation technology and training. The directors were rapidly faced with a problem common to many entrepreneurs. During their start-up phase, as a result of their personal backgrounds, interests and training, they self-identified as *artists*, rather than *businesspeople*:

> At the start we knew little or nothing about the business-side. We were happy to be doing what we loved. We did like the fact that we were getting to meet important people in the entertainment industry and people with certain levels of celebrity attached to them. Whereas it was enjoyable to be working in animation and in television, the problem was that most of the business mentors we had at the time, were simply starstruck.
>
> One of the best lessons we had early on was when we came across a mentor who was able to disconnect with all that stuff. I remember telling him about a meeting with the BBC, and he said 'So what? Did you sign a deal?' It brought it home to us, that from a commercial point of view, it didn't matter whether we were making films or selling baked beans, securing arrangements which brought in profit was the only important thing. It's the key lesson for any

entrepreneur starting up a business: the ability to commercialize and not be precious about your creativity.

Focusing on the bottom line while still maintaining a creative edge has led to the development of a high level of commercial acumen in Brown Bag Films. During the 1990s, when television work was still hard to find, Brown Bag Films developed a strong competence in developing work for advertising agencies and in the area of digital media. The company had begun to expand its 'reach' and developed projects with broadcasting and advertising organisations in Europe, the USA and the Middle East. A key milestone for the company was a nomination for an Academy Award in the animated short-film category in 2001 for *Give Up Your Aul Sins* which resulted in huge international interest in the company. In 2002, the short series developed around the 'Sins' concept was the bestselling DVD in Ireland. Brown Bag continued to develop a range of innovative, award-winning commercials and TV series.

Economic and sectoral profile

The story of Ireland's economic recovery and boom period has been very well documented. At the time of the origin of the state, economic policies, driven by political and ideological concerns, were directed towards producing a state of self-sufficiency, but in reality led to Ireland being closed off from global markets. The small nation was predominantly dependent on agriculture and poverty and emigration became the norm. During the late 1950s economic policy changed and the economy was opened up to international forces. Dublin became the commercial capital of Ireland, and rural populations gradually depleted through migration to the east coast capital city. Ireland was highly susceptible to changes in global economic fortunes, and by the late 1980s high rates of inflation and employment resulted in many young people emigrating in large numbers.

An aggressive strategy of attracting foreign direct investment to Ireland was undertaken. High-tech companies such as Dell, Hewlett Packard and Intel invested heavily in Ireland and developed large presences. Attracted by a low rate of corporate taxation and a young, educated English-speaking population, many of whom were familiar with the US style of working, these companies had a massive impact on the Irish economy. Ireland underwent a period of massive social and economic change as the country rapidly modernised and caught up with levels of development which would be expected in a developed democratic state. The downside of this rapid turnaround, as might be expected, resulted in infrastructural inadequacies (particularly with regard to transport) and a high rate of inflation which has resulted in Ireland, particularly Dublin, now being a very costly place in which to live and do business.

Business growth and development

Having survived the initial evolutionary start-up period of development, Brown Bag Films has a very professional approach to sales and business development. Over time the company has learned how to pitch and present proposals effectively, and to budget its productions to ensure that they are profitable and of a high quality. Overall, though, Brown Bag Films recently split into two separate corporate entities. One focuses on the high-yield TV commercials area for domestic and international clients, and the other focuses on TV production work for international markets. The TV production wing of Brown Bag Films focuses mostly on developing animated series for children. The company invests in the R&D of original programme ideas which have the potential to achieve long-running success with exploitation possibilities beyond television, such as licensing, merchandise and consumer products. It has just sold a long-form series to the distributor HIT Entertainment (*Bob the Builder*, *Thomas the Tank Engine*) and broadcaster Nickelodeon. Gaffney and O'Connell remain as sole directors of the organisation, but they have employed a director of the commercials unit, a facilities and post-production manager and a financial manager. Brown Bag Films also employs a part-time financial director, who is an experienced finance professional and offers mentoring on commercial issues. O'Connell acts as Creative Director for both units, and Gaffney, as Producer, heads up the TV unit. At any given time, up to 5–10 projects are live within Brown Bag Films, employing around 30 individuals, so a professional management structure had to be put into place to ensure that work was delegated as effectively as possible.

The remainder of the staff are contracted freelance writers, animators, designers and directors who, in general, have an enduring relationship with the company. The freelance staff have proved themselves by producing high-quality work over the start-up years and their talent is a unique asset for the company. Brown Bag Films has invested heavily in training for all staff over its years in existence and this commitment to staff development remains a key value of the organisation. The directors, particularly Gaffney, have undertaken business and management training in a piecemeal fashion, but neither has completed a formal business degree.

This has enabled the directors to focus on developing the company, and large-scale international collaborative projects have been commissioned and completed with studios in the USA, Canada and the UK. They have gradually developed a solid financial base and reputation with an annual turnaround of approximately €3.5m per annum.

New issues

Brown Bag Films has a very good record on retaining staff, but acknowledges that strategic talent retention is something that it takes very seriously. The offices and studio in Dublin city centre are rented at capital city rates. Dublin's city centre is something of a spiritual home for the company as it is reasonably accessible by a sizeable proportion of the company's talent base and close to its advertising, marketing and media communities.

In the earlier stages of Brown Bag Films' development, the directors expressed concern about the cycles of work which might have blindsided them to potential opportunities. Animation is heavily time dependent and when a contract was secured, it would involve the full attention of all staff to the detriment of developing further business. Now that this issue is largely under control, the directors are faced with determining where it is that they want their company to go, how it will grow in the future, and where they would like it to be 12 years from now. The broadcast industry is in the throws of a complete renaissance with convergence of media platforms presenting many threats, opportunities and reasons for change. In developing this strategic plan, they are concerned with the fact that they have grown comfortable with their current operating model and organisational approach. They are self-aware to the extent that they appreciate the possibility that 'groupthink' is a very real phenomenon which might lead to the loss of opportunities in the future, or to the organisation's growth pattern becoming derailed.

APPENDIX 1
Key Brown Bag milestones

December 1994   Established by producers/directors Cathal Gaffney and Darragh O'Connell.

First production was *Peig* for RTE, Ireland's public broadcasting company.

1995–1997   Brown Bag Films worked on the production and co-production of television series in Ireland, the UK and Russia, and designed and directed the animation for video games.

1998–2000   Alongside other television and commercial work, produced a 52-part pre-school series *Why?*, which has sold to nearly 40 countries from China to the UK. Brown Bag Development Ltd established to develop state of television and cinema projects with an international outlook. Developed over 30 TV commercials for Ireland, the UK and the Middle East.

2001–2002   Produced *Give Up Your Aul Sins* based on real audio recordings of children in an inner-city Dublin school over 30 years ago. Shot as an animated documentary, it has won widespread acclaim and an Oscar nomination for its innovative approach. Best-selling Irish DVD in 2002.

2003–2006   Continued to grow staff and develop a range of television programmes for children and high-profile commercial clients (Coca-Cola, Danone, National Lottery). Brown Bag Films (www.brownbagfilms) and Brown Bag Commercials (www.weloveallthisstuff.com) separated and new organisational structure enacted (see Appendix 2). Growth continues in both fields.

APPENDIX 2
Organisational structure (2006)

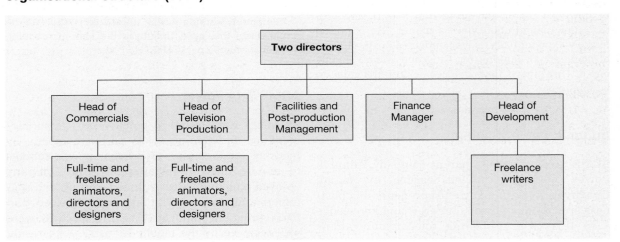

ACME Tele Power Ltd: leading through innovation

Kevan Scholes

Acme Tele Power is an innovative, entrepreneurial company serving the Indian mobile phone industry. But growth and successful products bring new challenges.

● ● ●

India's rise as an economic power is known the world over, thanks largely to the global ambitions of its biggest corporations. But names like Infosys, Tata and Reliance aren't necessarily as important to India's future as modest firms like Acme Tele Power Ltd. . . . ACME has a profit margin of 33 percent on 2006 revenues of $300 million [≈€240m], which have risen more than 3,000 percent in four years. ACME makes energy-efficient sheds that protect cell-phone relay stations, but its 32–year-old founder Manoj Upadhyay is plowing most of that profit into R & D, and files for a new patent about once a month. 'He is poised to grow exponentially,' says Sandeep Ghosh, director of commercial banking for Citigroup India. 'If only one of Upadhyay's new ideas comes off, it's going to be fabulous.'[1]

Adhunik Power Systems

ACME grew out of its parent company Adhunik Power Systems founded earlier by Manoj Upadhyay. As with many entrepreneurs this business grew from a personal interest and knowledge – in this case protecting telecommunications equipment from bad weather – particularly lightning. He explained this to the *Times Network*:[2]

> He turned his passion for studying lightning to start his first venture Adhunik Power System in 2000 to

manufacture lightning and surge protection systems. 'I borrowed Rs 2 lakh [≈€3,500] from friends and family to do that,' he says. He travelled once to Uttaranchal to install a lightning protection system to a telephone exchange and found the exchange switched off.

'I was appalled. Telephones are lifelines. Then the manager told me that if he let the exchange run it could easily get damaged in the lightning strike and then people would have to wait for months for replacement. I also saw how exchanges suffered because of lack of reliable power,' he says. Keeping the telecom equipment working during unreliable power was the challenge that gave Upadhyay the idea of founding another company, ACME Tele Power.

ACME Tele Power

So ACME was started in January 2003 to supplement the functioning of its parent company by focusing on the issue of reliable power sources to mobile telecom installations. The company enjoyed phenomenal growth, in terms of both customers and revenue. The organisation excelled in R&D, providing innovative solutions which were well received by the mobile industry. As a result, by 2006 almost all major private telecom operators in India were using ACME's innovations. The expanding customer base led to growth in revenue from Rs 3m (≈€52,000) in 2002–2003, to a projected Rs 10bn in 2005–2006. The company had 400 direct employees and 400–500 'associates'.

---

[1] *Times of India*, 20 September (2006). (Reported by Ron Moreau and Sudip Mazumdar, *Newsweek International*, 8 January 2007.)
[2] Shishir Prasad, *Times News Network*, 21 October (2006).
[3] Shishir Prasad, *Times News Network*, 21 October (2006).

The *Times Network*[3] explained ACME's operations further:

> Upadhyay's business model is simple. With millions of cell (mobile phone) sites coming up across the country, they have a unique problem. There are two parts of a cell site: electronic and the physical infrastructure. A cell site has an antenna tower (or antennae mounted on an elevated structure, such as a building), transmitter/receivers, control electronics, sometimes even a GPS receiver for timing, regular and backup electrical power sources.
>
> All [that] the electronic equipment on a cell site needs is power to run. The big problem a cell site faces here is fluctuations in power supply. Hence, each cell site has several boxes to control damage caused by power fluctuations. This is a very Indian problem and Upadhyay had an innovative solution for it. He has solved the power surge and power failure issue by compressing the equipment into a single box. ACME calls this box Power Interface Unit or PIU . . . [which] has been able to slash the maintenance cost at the cell sites by more than 50%. Now close to 70% of Bharti's cell-sites use the PIU. Almost 20–30% of Hutch's cell-sites run on PIU.

Breaking into established companies is always a challenge for entrepreneurs. 'Manoj was more concerned with delivering what we wanted. If we told him he would have to work on a pilot he wouldn't say "give me a trial order". He would just come back with a prototype,' says a senior official at Bharti Tele-Ventures. Upadhyay made sure that he was willing to eat his own food. 'When someone did not want to shell out money for buying PIUs we just went ahead and installed the equipment and asked them to pay us the cost savings as equal monthly installments to us. As power consumption is recorded inside the PIU and consumption prior to the installation of PIU is already known, those customers agreed,' he says.

With the power problem solved, Upadhyay then launched his concept of green shelters. These are completely collapsible shelters for cell sites which have a lining of a material called 'phase change material' that can absorb coolness from the night air and then releases it back during the day when temperatures rise. This further reduces the use of generators and air conditioners leading to further cost savings. Every site that uses a green shelter sees a reduction of operating expenditure by half. 'The best part about Upadhyay is that he is an engineer who actually spends more than 80% of his time on R&D and leaves management to other professionals he has hired. He has a fine brain and it is best used for R&D,' says an Hutch official.

Private equity investors who have been talking to him want to wait and see, how this transition takes place. 'Let us see if the team can work together when Manoj is busy driving the R&D programme,' says one private equity investor. The other concern is if the ACME model will become irrelevant as time goes by. 'That's a fair concern but there are large parts of India that will remain power deficient for a long time and then there are places like Africa and other emerging markets where his products should do well,' says an official in Bharti.

The threat is of course from China. 'Even though Manoj has filed for seven patents, it doesn't prevent a Chinese company from ripping off his designs and flooding the market with cheaper imitations,' says a potential investor. But as Manoj says, 'We will always be innovation-led. So when some copycat catches up we will already have developed two or three products that are new and which we will put out in the market.' That's risky but the only road for a man whose dream is to break the pattern of US and Europe as innovators, China as manufacturers and Indian as a place to service the manufactured product.

Research and Development – the key to success

It was clear from ACME's website[4] that the company saw its future as driven by its R&D investments:

> As a responsible Indian Organisation ACME has broadened its horizons with exclusive R&D bases in India, US, Canada & Australia. ACME always believes in creating and innovating comprehensive solutions rather than products. Instead of routine business practices, the company has always tried to demonstrate innovative ways to perform business, where the customer's exposure to risk can be minimized. ACME always believes in creating things that do not exist in the world.
>
> Equipped with the most modern infrastructure, [our R&D] facility encourages the process of thinking and nurtures innovation.
>
> Currently, we are . . . working on various projects in the areas of Power, Thermal Engineering, Agriculture and Biotechnology.
>
> We invest in excess of 5% of our revenues, annually, in the maintenance and upgrading of our R&D facility, ensuring that the think tank, which forms the crux of our innovations, is never short on necessary resources.
>
> We aim to set up an additional R&D facility . . . to conduct research related to alternate energy discovery and biotechnology, keeping pace with the growing demands of the 21st century.

ACME – part of a new wave of Indian entrepreneurs

ACME was not alone in India in terms of its entrepreneurial drive as reported by the *Times of India*:[5]

ACME is part of a new wave of small, entrepreneurial firms that are rising in the wake of the giants that first put India Inc. on the map. Whereas the first wave built global software-development and business-process outsourcing houses, the second is made of small and medium-size manufacturing companies in autos, pharmaceuticals and other sectors. Unlike the big conglomerates, these are not old family enterprises that can still capitalize on longstanding political connections. The newcomers are independent entrepreneurs who have learned to work around India's infamous bureaucracy. Many started out supplying larger Indian companies, and flourished as India's growth took off on the heels of free-market reforms over the last decade. 'It's an incredible segment that is really driving the Indian economy in a big way,' says Sanjay Nayar, Citigroup India's CEO.

To describe these smaller manufacturers as bullish hardly does justice to the energy they are bringing to their markets. While the national economy has been growing at 8 percent a year, manufacturing is growing at about 12 percent, small and medium-size manufacturers are growing at about 15 percent and the small-company stars like ACME are in the triple digits. Upadhyay says his ambition is 'to change the world'. He boasts that no company is keeping up with ACME in its specialty. He claims, for instance, to have invented a maintenance-free air-conditioning and refrigeration system that consumes one sixth as much power as a conventional unit because it does not have an energy-hungry compressor.

These second-wave firms are hard to define. Most of the hottest new companies seem to have at least several hundred employees, US$50m [≈€40m] in revenue, a position at or near the top in their section of the Indian market and a desire to expand globally. A few are already well established abroad. Everest Kanto Cylinder Ltd. has taken less than a decade to become the world's second largest maker of cylinders for high-pressure, compressed natural gas. Chairman P.K. Khurana says he can't expand fast enough, domestically or internationally, to keep pace with demand.

A salient characteristic of this industrial class is its lack of debt. Whereas bank loans and foreign credit have fueled much of Asia's national development, India's small firms are raising money from private banks and stock sales to the public. ACME has no debt, even though banks and venture-capital firms are now constantly plying its chairman with offers. To keep their independence, second-wave entrepreneurs are plowing money into design and R&D earlier than many young firms, which distinguishes them from their Asian forebears and current Chinese rivals.

Self-sufficiency has not always been a signal trait of small Indian companies. Mohandas K. Gandhi was sceptical of large firms, and made sure the nation's first prime minister after independence, Jawaharlal Nehru, championed the village loom and the individual shoemaker as a bulwark against corporate colonialism. New Delhi drew up lists of thousands of items, from pens to rubber stamps, that could be produced only by small manufacturers. Those uneconomical rules were gradually lifted, and then scrapped after free-market reform began in 1991. Since India has no bankruptcy laws, many of those defunct businessmen went into hiding from bill collectors. The lesson for many was to avoid entangling alliances with creditors.

Under the old regime, small companies that tried to grow big ran into the full force of the Indian bureaucracy. Survivors of that period tell horror stories of 180 percent tariffs and limits as low as $8 per day on what executives could take for foreign business trips. Arvind Kapur, the managing director of Rico Auto Industries Ltd., recalls that when he was a kid in the 1950s, New Delhi threatened to prosecute his father every time his small sewing-machine company produced too many machines. Sudhir Dhingra, founder and chairman of Orient Craft, a rising apparel exporter, recalls being summoned in the middle of the night by the export Enforcement Directorate to explain paperwork. 'Of course, all they wanted was to get their palms greased,' he says.

---

[5] *Times of India*, 20 September (2006). (Reported by Ron Moreau and Sudip Mazumdar, *Newsweek International*, 8 January 2007.)

Wimm-Bill-Dann: 15 years in business

Nadia Shchegrova

From a small-scale production of juices to become a national food conglomerate in just 15 years through diversification, acquisitions and vertical integration. The economic and political environment changes fast, so does the competition. What are the keys to sustainable market advantage in the long term?

• • •

History at a glance

Wimm-Bill-Dann (WBD) is perceived by many as a symbol of the Russian food industry of the new era. It was created in 1992, when a group of entrepreneurs launched the production of juices on a leased production line. By the end of 2006, the holding consisted of 36 production facilities in Russia and the Commonwealth of Independent States with more than a thousand types of dairy products, juices and soft drinks; its turnover exceeded $1.8bn (€1.1bn; £780m).

The company entered the Russian market with seven varieties of fruit juices and nectars under the brand 'J7', introducing new tastes and high quality to domestic consumers. The Tetra Pak technology was employed to pack juices, using bright colours and foreign-sounding labels to attract attention. The J7 juice series quickly became a benchmark for any domestically produced juice in Russia. With 25–40 per cent annual growth of the juice market over 2000–2003, WBD remained the absolute leader.

After two years of only making juices WBD expanded its product portfolio by including milk and other dairy products, which became possible after the takeover of the Lianozovo Dairy, one of the biggest dairies in Europe. In 1996 and 1997, WBD acquired majority stakes in the Baby Food Plant and in two more dairies in Moscow, which made WBD the leader in the dairy market in Moscow and the region and allowed it to add new types of products to its portfolio.

Seeking to replicate its success in Moscow, WBD started expansion into the regions, pursuing its objective to have a production base in every economically developed region in Russia. While dairy desserts and yoghurts were still a novelty in Russia, the company anticipated the vast capacity of high-added-value products and the potential of their local production. Between 1998 and 2003, WBD gained control of 12 enterprises in the Far East, Siberia, Central and Southern Russia. The selection of the acquisition targets was driven by several factors: the technical capacity and product specialisation of the dairies, access to local markets and the resource base. Prominent regional dairies had well-developed distribution systems, which helped to ensure that these plants, when modernised, maintained leading positions in their regions. Raw materials played another important role. WBD aimed to settle in the most resource-rich regions. For instance, about 15 per cent of all raw milk in Russia was produced in four regions where WBD had production facilities.

Availability of raw milk was one of the most important links in the supply chain. The growing demand for quality milk from domestic and international companies affected both the price of the finished product and the utilisation of production facilities. WBD was forced to secure future supplies of raw milk by spending on modernisation of several farms under lease agreements and then by investing directly in the acquisition of dairy farms.

Earlier than its competitors, WBD established its own distribution network. The company opened or acquired trade branches in 26 cities in those regions where it did not have production facilities and acquired distribution companies in more than 40 cities in Russia.

In 2000, WBD continued its expansion beyond Russia's boundaries by acquisition of majority stakes in dairies in Ukraine, Bashkortostan and Kyrgyzstan. The Ukrainian market of yoghurts grew by 25–30 per cent every year; and Kyrgyzstan has abundant natural resources, namely fruits (peaches, apricots and tomatoes) that can be processed into juice concentrates. The acquired dairy, Bishkeksut, produced hard cheeses – a capability that WBD had not had until then.

Product development in the dairy sector

Political changes in Russia in the 1990s opened the country to foreign companies attracted by the capacity of the emergent market. Having started with traditional products, such as milk, cottage cheese, soured cream and kefir in the late 1990s, WBD introduced new product lines, including yoghurts and dairy desserts, to match the assortment of Western rivals importing the goods. Market growth in food sectors in Russia was largely determined by changes in disposable income, therefore most of the products were positioned by price and not by distinctive qualities. WBD enjoyed obvious benefits of local production, so it was able to offer the same range of products in the same quality package at a lower price. While every city in Russia has a dairy plant, often local production and packaging technologies were not able to ensure a long shelf life, which led to very low-price products targeted on tight budgets. WBD occupied a niche of long-life goods that competed with imported analogues in the range and, due to lower transport and production costs, was price competitive.

The consequences of the financial crisis in 1998 had various implications for producers, processors and consumers. When the national currency lost 75 per cent of its value and consumers became extremely price conscious, the switch to cheap domestic goods was inevitable. Russian dairies faced a better situation than their Western competitors: access to local raw materials, low labour and production costs gave an edge that importers found difficult to achieve. WBD was one of the few companies that managed to increase sales at

the height of the crisis with a slight reduction in profitability.

Having recovered from the consequences of the 1998 financial crisis, consumers became wealthier, spending more money and changing their purchasing patterns. Yoghurt, for example, initially was perceived as a tasty product rather than a healthy one. Consumers preferred it creamy, with lots of fruit and a high fat content. The trend soon started changing. Customers were becoming increasingly interested in healthy diets and started buying more products with biologically active ingredients, vitamins and a lower fat content. Special product lines for children, with various supplements and multivitamins, became another rapidly expanding niche in the market.

In the juice market

The dynamics of the juice market resembled those of the dairy market. Between 2001 and 2005, the compound annual growth rate of the juice market was more than 50 per cent, which attracted new players who invested heavily in production, distribution and marketing. By the end of 2003, the juice market was dominated by four domestic producers: WBD, Multon, Lebedyansky and Nidan-Ecofruct. Together, they occupied more than 90 per cent of the national market (Exhibit 1).

High price sensitivity of customers in the regions resulted in the rapid growth of low- and medium-price juices. The target customer displayed little loyalty to any particular brand so producers had to find new marketing solutions, especially when the room for price wars was so limited.

Despite its overall leading position in the juice market and overall growth in consumption of juices by 20 per cent, WBD reported at the end of 2003 a reduction in produced juice by 0.6 per cent. By 2006, WBD's market share in the juice sector shrunk by a third (Exhibit 2).

Industry observers commented that WBD was too slow to react to the increased competitive pressure in the middle- and low-price segments. They also suggested that the delayed launch of new packaging, the protracted reformation of the distributing network, and the shift of the focus to new projects were some of the factors affecting the deteriorating performance. In September 2005, rumours that WBD was preparing to sell its juice division appeared in the press.

| Exhibit 1 | Market share in the juice sector, 2003 |

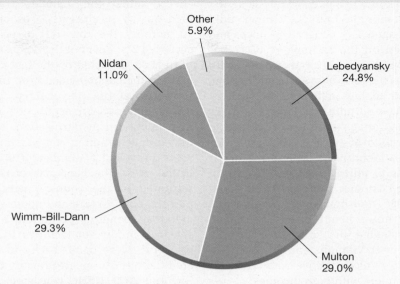

Source: Based on http:// prodresurs.gorod.ru/ru/press/news-agencies/smi/200402171437-3143.htm.

| Exhibit 2 | Market share in the juice sector, 2006 |

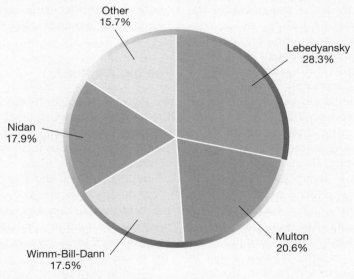

Source: Based on Wimm-Bill-Dan: results for 9 months. Issue 08.12.2006, www.bcs.ru.

Further product development and diversification

Production of drinks was one of the most dynamic industries in Russia in 2000–2003. Sales of beer were increasing by 16 per cent and bottled water by 23 per cent per annum. WBD saw this as a possibility for diversifying its product portfolio and for utilising the full potential of the existing distribution network. Further to the initial success of J7 juices, which by 2003 included 22 different flavours, other brands of juices, nectars and juice-based drinks were added to target customers in both premium and low–medium segments.

In 2001, WBD launched one of Russia's first juice and dairy umbrella brands, 'Ginger up!'. Aimed at children aged 5–9, Ginger Up! juices and nectars were based on the technology of J7 but priced 10 per cent higher than J7 and enriched with vitamins, which was the core message in advertising.

Products with a higher added value, such as mousses, fruit-flavoured milk and kefir, puddings and fruit-flavoured cottage cheese were added to the extensive portfolio of traditional dairy products. This area was identified as one of the major strategic directions to follow with the purpose of meeting changing customer preferences, keeping a competitive edge and improving operational efficiencies. A new line of health-oriented enriched products 'Neo' included drinks, fruit and milk cocktails enriched with vitamins and live bacteria. Neo was priced 25 per cent above retail average and targeted consumers with high incomes.

WBD also entered the mineral water and cheese markets. The decision to move into the water sector was prompted by the rapid growth of this sector and by the opportunity to level out revenues during summer when consumption of dairy products drops. The growth of the water market was attributed to the increasing income and gradual drift of consumers towards drinking bottled water instead of tap water and to the interest in the sports lifestyle. In spring 2003, WBD launched its own table mineral water 'Zapovednik', which became possible with the acquisition of a plant in the Novgorod region. In September 2003, the company acquired Healing Spring Ltd, a producer of 'Essentuki' brand mineral water, and Geyser Ltd, the owner of the Essentuki water wells. Industry observers were cautious about the chances of its becoming a leading producer as the Russian bottled mineral water market had long been divided among Coca-Cola (Bon-Aqua), Pepsi-Cola (Aqua-Minerale) and Nestlé (Saint Spring).

The cheese sector had long been occupied by imported products positioned in the premium and upper middle price segments (60 per cent of the national market) and domestically produced cheeses (40 per cent of the market, low-price segment). WBD identified a gap in the market for domestically produced high-quality cheese at reasonable prices. By targeting this segment WBD was intending to compete with imported analogues in the upper medium price segment that accounted for one-fifth of the total cheese market.

In mid-2003 WBD started production of processed cheese followed by the launch of hard cheese under the 'Lamber' trademark offering high-quality product at a reasonable price. Only 10 months after the start of production, Lamber occupied 2 per cent of the domestic cheese market.

In 2000, attracted by the fast growth of the beer market, the company acquired interests in several breweries across the country. The original plan was similar to that in acquisition of regional dairies: investments in modernisation, extensive marketing and distribution via existing channels. The move provoked a number of sceptical comments in the press: the beer market is one of the most saturated in the country, with well-established players, both foreign and domestic, abundant promotional spending, prominent brands and extensive local production facilities. In 2001 the acquired breweries were handed over to the specially created Central European Brewery Company (CEBC). By June 2003, CEBC consisted of four breweries and accounted for 2.6 per cent of the domestic bottled beer market.

Other projects in the food sector included production pickled vegetables (a joint venture agreement with the Hungarian cannery 'Globus') and ice cream (licensing agreements with various regional dairies) under WBD's brands.

Too big too fast?

By the end of 2003, the financial performance of the holding showed signs of deterioration: WBD's personnel, advertising, marketing costs and other commercial expenses increased by a quarter when compared with the same period in 2002, but net profit decreased by 40.6 per cent.

By the first quarter 2004 sales of juice fell by 13 per cent and, in terms of market share, the company moved to third position after Lebedyansky and Multon. The market, in the meantime, grew by 20 per cent.

Rapid growth through acquisitions – 10 production plants during the first two years after flotation followed by investments in modernisation, marketing, distribution and promotion – led to a reduction in profitability. WBD's operating profit margin fell from 8.9 per cent in 2001 to 6.25 per cent in 2005, whereas Lebedyansky, the leader of the domestic juice market, achieved 22 per cent and Danone 13 per cent. The company, however, saw acquisitions as a logical method of expanding business

| Exhibit 3 | Key operating and financial indicators in 2002–2006 ($m) |

	2002	2003	2004	2005	2006
Turnover	824.7	938.5	1,189.3	1,394.6	1,762.1
Gross profit	245.0	273.4	325.2	395.6	568.0
Selling and distribution expenses	(109.5)	(140.7)	(173.4)	(192.0)	(246.1)
General and administrative expenses	(63.0)	(76.0)	(92.8)	(109.6)	(134.5)
Operating income	66.0	49.2	52.9	87.5	155.6
Financial income and expenses, net	(14.1)	(15.3)	(14.6)	(22.9)	(15.5)
Net income	35.7	21.2	22.9	30.3	95.4

Source: WBD annual reports, www.wbd.com.

arguing that in the economy of saturating markets and increasing consolidation the potential for growth would soon be exhausted.

Misjudgement of consumer preferences resulted in a poor return on investment. The management had hoped that the success of high-tech products in the central part of the country would be replicated in the regions. By 2005, it became clear that the potential of the future demand was over-estimated and that regional consumers preferred traditional (and cheaper) products. Only 30–40 per cent of total capacity of the expensive production lines for premium products was utilised.

WBD had developed a huge portfolio of brands but the viability of the company's strategy to be present in all segments looked doubtful. The rapid growth and the focus on volumes also presented the problem of balancing long-term aspirations of the company and the necessity to manage short-term expectations of its shareholders. By mid-2005 the company's shares were selling at $18 per ADR,[1] which was $1.5 less than that at the time of flotation in 2002.

However, the situation was not completely hopeless. WBD still controlled the dairy market with a share of 34 per cent; its sales of baby food grew by 36 per cent in 2005, and the same rate was maintained in 2006. The owners were looking for new ideas and new people. Early in 2006, they appointed a new chief executive officer and later the same year a new head of marketing. More new people were brought in at the operations level.

The main areas identified for urgent restructuring were an in-depth review of all business units comprising the holding, marketing strategy, promotions, packaging, logistics, procurement, product portfolio and distribution functions. The company started shifting its focus from selling to independent distributors to direct delivery to shops and supermarkets. To improve profitability of the beverages branch of the business it was decided to close down the plant in Novgorod producing the mineral water Zapovednik. Special attention was devoted to cost reduction: now even the bonus system was linked to improvements in profitability.

First results did not take long to appear. During six months of 2006, market capitalisation grew by $700m and net profit increased six-fold when compared with the same period in the previous year (Exhibit 3).

Tony Maher, the new CEO, formerly Regional Director for Russia and Eastern Europe for Coca-Cola, commented:

> Wimm-Bill-Dann is a company that in 15 years grew from nothing to a business with a turnover of $1.5bn. The team created brands, new products and introduced juices as a mass and hugely popular product to the market. This is a story of success. However, there is a potential that is yet to be realised.

Sources

In the preparation of this case the following sources were used:

Isvestia, 19 June (2000), 5 December (2001), 24 April (2002).

Gazeta.Ru, 25 February (2004).

Financial Izvestia, 24 June (2003), 10 September (2003).

Financial Times, 31 May (1999).

---

[1] Rather than issuing shares directly in the USA, foreign companies generally issue American Depositary Receipts (ADRs). These are claims to the shares of the foreign company that are held by a bank on behalf of the ADR owners.

Kompania, 27 February (2003), 24 February (2004), 11 November (2005).

'Maher's Imperative', *Smart Money*, no. 25, 4 September (2006).

Moskovskie Novosti, 22 August (2000), 19 September (2000).

Vedomosti, 5 December (2001), 16 July (2003), 15 August (2003), 30 September (2003), 17 February (2004).

The Voice of Russia, 19 December (2003).

www.wbd.com.

www.tetrapak.su.

Russkii Gastronom, 19 August (2004).

http://www.wps.ru/ru/pp/food/2004/08/19.html.

Alliance Boots – a merger of equals?

Kevan Scholes

When companies plan to merge they must create a rationale that makes sense to investors. This is usually described in a merger prospectus. But how good a guide will this be to the future success of the merged company? The case looks at the merger of Boots and Alliance UniChem in the pharmaceutical distribution and retailing sector in 2006.

•   •   •

On 31 July 2006 the newly merged Alliance Boots plc issued a press release confirming the successful completion of the merger between Boots Group plc and Alliance UniChem plc to form a new international pharmacy-led health and beauty group. Richard Baker,[1] Chief Executive of Alliance Boots, commented:

> I am delighted that we are able to announce the completion of the merger between Alliance UniChem and Boots to create Europe's foremost international pharmacy-led health and beauty group. The union of these two great businesses also establishes a new market leader in UK pharmacy and provides exciting opportunities for international growth. . . . The merger will enable us to improve the offering for both our wholesale and retail customers. While there is a lot of hard work ahead and it will take time to deliver the full benefits of this merger . . . we have a firm foundation for our future success and we are determined to deliver the benefits of this to our enlarged group of shareholders in the years to come.

Background to the merged companies

Boots plc

The Boot family began trading in 1849, selling herbal remedies from a small store in Goose Gate,

Nottingham. In the 1870s the business began to develop under the management of Jesse Boot. He employed qualified pharmacists and opened a network of new stores, which, by 1900, had expanded to 181. This rapid rate of expansion was due to the success of Jesse's business philosophy of buying in bulk and passing the benefit of reduced prices on to his customers. His policy of superior goods at competitive prices delivered with expert care meant that the Boots name became synonymous with quality, value and service.

The retail business was supported by a burgeoning manufacturing capability, and diversification into pharmaceutical research and development. By the 1930s, there were over 1,000 Boots stores selling a wide range of products, including the new cosmetic range 'No7' and the suncare brand 'Soltan'. The first overseas store also opened – in New Zealand in 1936.

To support the stores, Boots commissioned the development of new factories at a site in Beeston, on the outskirts of Nottingham, which remains Boots' manufacturing and administrative centre. Following the Second World War the company continued to expand its manufacturing and research capabilities (which included an agricultural division), and the creation of the National Health Service in 1948 led to a vast increase in dispensing.

By 2005 The Boots Group was a health and beauty group with operations in retail and manufacturing. Its products were sold in 17 countries, it

---

[1] Richard Baker and Nigel Rudd (previously CEO and Chairman of Boots respectively) became CEO and Chairman of the merged company.

Photo: UK Retail Alan King/Alamy

employed approximately 63,000 people in total and operated approximately 1,500 health and beauty stores with an aggregate selling area of approximately 680,000 square metres. Boots sold a wide range of products under the 'Boots' brand and also owned a number of UK market leading brands by revenue such as 'No7' and 'Soltan'. Boots' international division, BRI, had 'Boots'-branded implants in host retailers' stores in 14 countries as well as approximately 95 owned stores in Asia. For the year 2005–2006 (ending 31 March 2006), the Boots Group generated trading profit from continuing operations of £335.9m (≈€487m) on revenue from continuing operations of £5.03bn.

Prior to the merger Boots had faced difficult trading conditions and in 2004–2005 issued three profit warnings as it suffered an 11 per cent fall in profits and the resignation of the financial director in March 2005. Appendix 1 shows the company share price movements compared with the average for food and drug retailers. The major contributing factor to the deteriorating competitiveness of the company was supermarkets starting to offer toiletries and pharmaceuticals at lower prices (particularly Tesco and Asda). Some commentators felt that this was the inevitable result of a poor strategic decision a few years earlier when Boots made significant increases in its prices – making market entry attractive to supermarkets. The company's attempts to broaden its retail offering in the previous 10 years by extending services into dentistry, chiropody and laser eye surgery had been largely unsuccessful.

Alliance UniChem plc

The UniChem Group was formed by a group of retail pharmacists in London in 1938, its initial business being the wholesaling of pharmaceutical products to independent pharmacists. UniChem subsequently converted to a public limited company and was listed on the London Stock Exchange in 1990. In 1991 UniChem established a significant presence in retail community pharmacy in the UK through the purchase of the Moss Chemists chain which at that time had 92 pharmacies. During the period up until the merger with Alliance Santé (in 1997), the UniChem group expanded the Moss UK retail chain to over 500 pharmacies alongside its original UK wholesale business and also merged its Portuguese wholesale business with the Portuguese business of Alliance Santé. At the time of the merger with UniChem, Alliance Santé was the second largest pharmaceutical wholesaling group in Europe in terms of turnover with owned businesses in France and Italy, the jointly owned wholesale business in Portugal and equity investments in similar wholesaling businesses in Spain, Greece and Morocco.

Following the merger the Alliance UniChem Group expanded rapidly through organic growth and acquisitions. During this period it acquired full control of Alliance Santé's business in Spain, acquired leading pharmaceutical wholesaling businesses in The Netherlands, Czech Republic, Norway and later in Russia, and acquired a leading European presence in pharmaceutical prewholesaling and contract logistics. In addition, it acquired a number of smaller regional wholesalers in existing geographical markets, which it integrated into its existing operations, and it acquired minority interests in businesses in Turkey, Germany and Switzerland and, through its Turkish interests, in Egypt. Since that merger, the Alliance UniChem Group had also rapidly expanded its retail division, increasing its total number of pharmacies to approximately 1,300 in five European countries. Of these, over 960 were located in the UK and over 120 were operated by associates. At the time of the merger The Alliance UniChem Group operated pharmacies in the UK, The Netherlands, Norway and Italy alongside its pharmaceutical wholesale businesses and its associate business in Switzerland. Alliance UniChem Group wholesalers distributed to over 125,000 pharmacies, hospitals and health centres in eight countries through a network of over 380 depots, its largest operations being in France and the UK. The company employed approximately 26,000 people (including directors and part-time staff). In addition, 15,000 people were employed by the group's associates.

At the time of the merger press comment about Alliance UniChem was broadly favourable. Although smaller than Boots the company had been growing profitably and was closing the gap on Boots and had become the third largest pharmacy chain in Europe. It was also the UK's biggest drug wholesaler and Europe's second biggest – supplying pharmacies direct from manufacturers.

Stated reasons for the merger

The intention to merge was announced jointly by the two companies on 3 October 2005. The *detailed* reasons for the merger stated at that time[2] were subsequently included in the merger prospectus:[3]

> The merger of equals between Boots and Alliance UniChem will create an international pharmacy-led health and beauty group. The merger is expected to build on the existing strategies of the Boots Group and the Alliance UniChem Group and combine their complementary skills and businesses to:
>
> - capitalise on growth in demand for healthcare and beauty products, which is expected to offer significant opportunities for the enlarged group;
> - create Europe's leading retail pharmacy business by revenue comprising approximately 3,000 retail outlets, including approximately 2,600 in the UK, with a wholesale and distribution network serving approximately 125,000 outlets;
> - enhance international growth opportunities in new markets by utilising the enlarged group's acquisition skills, management expertise, internationally-recognised brands, strong balance sheet and pipeline of existing acquisition opportunities in new geographical markets; and
> - deliver annual pre-tax cost savings of at least £100 million per annum by the fourth full year following completion by streamlining the enlarged group's purchasing, logistics and wholesale network and rationalising corporate costs.
>
> Alliance Boots also expects incremental revenue benefits from the increased availability of its leading brands, own label products and the Boots Advantage Card across the larger network. In addition, the Company is expected to benefit from the application of

retail pharmacy and wholesale skills across the broader enlarged group.

But did it make sense?

At the time of the announcement in October 2005 some of Boots' major shareholders were not happy with the stated reasons for the merger with Alliance UniChem. There was a feeling that the management had simply run out of ideas and the merger was a last ditch attempt to revive the business. Surely there were alternatives to having more shops (through the merger) such as: looking at ways of getting the most from their existing floor space, cutting costs and polishing up their brand name.

In order to persuade investors that the merger was, indeed, in their best interests the merger prospectus gave some detailed background about each company and its pre-merger strategies (see Appendix 2).

But even as the merger went 'live' both investors and journalists remained cautious about the benefits of mergers – which so often prove to be overstated. One journalist's view[4] the day after the merger is of interest:

> Richard Baker [Alliance Boots CEO] fulfilled his ambition of 'putting the chemist back into Boots' yesterday when the retailer pulled off its merger with Alliance UniChem to create Britain's biggest chemist chain and a new force in the European pharmacy sector.
>
> In a sign that the new group Alliance Boots means business, Mr Baker, the chief executive, said some of Boots' most popular products had gone on sale in 500 Alliance pharmacies yesterday morning. '*That bodes well for the future,*' he said.
>
> As tonics go, analysts believe that deciding to crunch the two companies together is a prescription for success when it comes to revitalising a flagging Boots, which is being squeezed by the supermarkets. In return, Alliance UniChem, which has a European-wide pharmaceutical wholesale business and retail chains across the UK, the Netherlands and Norway, will be better placed to benefit from likely regulatory changes in its main markets going forward. Being part of Alliance Boots will further diversify its earnings streams as well as bolstering its retailing credentials.
>
> As analysts at Morgan Stanley put in a recent research note: 'If the European pharmacy market deregulates, the opportunity to create the "Walgreen[5]

---

[2] Company websites, 3 October 2005.
[3] The merger prospectus was available on the company websites from 5 June 2006. It was subsequently available on the merged company website: www.allianceboots.com.

[4] Susie Mesure Retail Correspondent, *The Independent*, 1 August (2006). Copyright © The Independent, 1.8.06.
[5] Walgreen is a major US integrated pharmacy service company. See www.walgreenshealth.com.

of Europe" will emerge. We would argue that neither Boots nor Alliance UniChem was well placed to capitalise on such an opportunity. Alliance Boots, however, just might be.'

Task one for Mr Baker is to get started on delivering £100m of annual cost savings from combining the two groups. So far, all Mr Baker is promising is to cut cost from the enlarged group's buying bill and supply chain. He has yet to factor in the quantum of so-called 'sales synergies' from doing things like selling Boots'

suncream brand Soltan in Alliance's smaller Moss pharmacy stores. Other synergies will come from re-branding the group's entire UK estate as Boots and using Alliance's European wholesale network to sell Boots' products to independent chemist chains across Europe. Because of long lead times and the need to license products in different markets, this will be the 'third leg' of the group's combined strategy, Mr Baker said.

APPENDIX 1

Boots plc share price 2003–2006 (with food and drug retailers sector average for comparison)

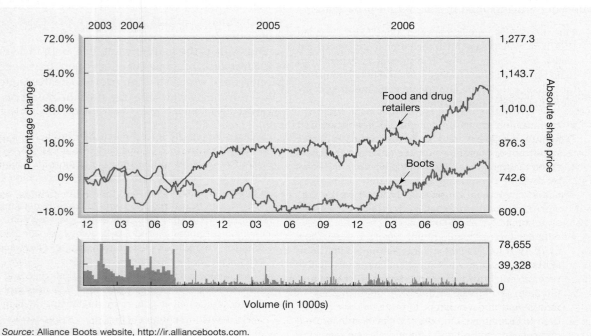

Source: Alliance Boots website, http://ir.allianceboots.com.

APPENDIX 2

Business overviews of the companies at the time of the merger – as presented in the merger prospectus[6]

Boots plc

The Boots Group is a leading health and beauty retailer in the UK.

It operates three principal businesses: Boots The Chemists ('BTC'), Boots Opticians ('BOL') and Boots Retail International ('BRI').

BTC comprises the Boots Group's health and beauty retail business in the UK and the Republic of Ireland. BOL comprises the Boots Group's optical and eye care business in the UK. BRI comprises the Boots Group's international business. These businesses are supported by (amongst others) the Boots Group's manufacturing functions.

Boots' strategy during the past three years has been to create shareholder value by investing to become a more modern, efficient and competitive health and beauty retail business.

To implement this strategy, Boots has sought to:

- refocus on its core health business by, in particular, investing in its dispensing category;
- reinforce its comprehensive beauty and toiletries offering and grow its own-brand and exclusive product ranges such as 'No7', 'Soltan' and '17', which Boots believes helps to differentiate its products from those of its competitors;
- offer better value for its customers by, in particular, reducing prices on its products (particularly in its toiletries category) and to grow its 'Advantage Card' membership;
- open new stores, mainly in edge-of-town locations, and modernise its stores to improve their convenience and accessibility;
- offer expert customer care including by investing in training of its pharmacists; and
- invest in its supply and information technology functions to make them more efficient.

Alliance UniChem plc

Alliance UniChem operates in a highly decentralised way, its business being grouped into two divisions, wholesale and retail. In addition, it has a number of associates operating similar businesses.

The wholesale division comprises businesses in eight European countries, each locally managed. In some countries local management operate a number of business units, each focused on particular segments of the pharmaceutical wholesaling market. Included within the wholesale division are Alliance UniChem's pre-wholesale and contract logistics operations.

The retail division, which excludes associates, comprises retail pharmacy chains in four European countries, each locally managed. Due to the nature of Alliance UniChem's businesses in Norway, The Netherlands and Italy, the local management teams have recently started to operate both the wholesale and retail businesses on a country basis.

Alliance UniChem's strategy has been to grow shareholder value consistently over an extended period of time by focusing on its key areas of expertise within the health care market, namely pharmaceutical wholesaling and retail pharmacies. In countries where regulations permit and it makes economic sense to do so, Alliance UniChem has sought to operate wholesale and retail pharmacy businesses alongside one another. Alliance UniChem seeks to grow its businesses organically through consistently delivering superior customer service, through utilising its expertise in margin management and through obtaining productivity savings and synergies from managing its businesses closely together. In addition to organic growth, Alliance UniChem's strategy has been to grow through the acquisition of businesses and associate interests, in both existing and new geographical markets, applying strict financial criteria for all investments.

---

[6] See note 3 above.

Will mergers improve police performance?

Kevan Scholes

Even when there is agreement about a chosen direction of development there may be fierce disagreement about which method of development will work best. This case study from the police service can be used to compare the arguments for mergers as against strategic alliances or organic development.

• • •

'*Axed police mergers cost millions*' read the headline on the BBC News website[1] on 11 September 2006. While the world was remembering the tragic terrorist attacks in New York exactly five years earlier and the important role that police play in democratic societies, the British government appeared to be quietly abandoning the work the Home Office[2] had put into reshaping the way that policing was organised in England and Wales. It was hoping to merge the 43 forces (which together employed about 224,000 people of whom 141,000 were police officers) into as few as 10 regional 'strategic forces'. Figures obtained under the Freedom of Information Act showed that by the summer of 2006, 27 of the 43 police forces collectively spent £6.1m (€8.9m) preparing for the move – only two-thirds of which was eventually reimbursed by the Home Office.

A Home Office spokesman said the work carried out in preparation for the mergers would stand forces in good stead. He said the process of preparing for mergers had caused police forces to work more closely together and build better working relationships. He said a number of forces and police authorities had told ministers they thought they could improve their performance through closer collaboration. 'The work already done will be essential to achieving such an outcome,' he added.

The impetus for change had come in an HMIC[3] report[4] in September 2005 entitled 'Closing the Gap'. The report argued that the current arrangement of 43 separate forces was not fit for purpose by concluding:

> The police service needs not only to deal effectively with volume crime . . . but also have demonstrable readiness to tackle complex, volatile threats to individuals, neighbourhoods and businesses. This implies a major development in capability [and] to achieve this changes must be made not only to structure, but [to] the whole configuration of policing at this level.

Charles Clarke, The Home Secretary at that time, concluded that the report provided 'unambiguous evidence to support the formation of strategic forces'. His opinions were probably also influenced by a parallel reduction that had taken place in the number of ambulance services (where 29 separate services had been merged into just 12).

---

[1] http://news.bbc.co.uk (11 September 2006).
[2] There is a 'tri-partite' responsibility for policing: (i) The *Home Office* is the government department responsible for 'home affairs' for England and Wales. It funds the police and has overall responsibility as overseer and coordinator. (ii) However, the direct responsibility for each of the 43 police forces rests with a local *police authority*. A police authority is an independent body made up of local people. The police authority sets the strategic direction for the force and holds the chief constable to account on behalf of the local community. (iii) The *chief constable* is responsible for the delivery of police services.

[3] Her Majesty's Inspectorate of Constabulary (HMIC) is the agency responsible for maintaining police standards. It is independent both of the Home Office and of the police service.
[4] *Closing the gap*, HMIC, September 2005.

Photo: Janine Wiedel Photography/Alamy

The term 'strategic force' was introduced to describe a force of sufficient size to achieve *simultaneously* the following:

- To better provide to national standards Level 2 policing such as murders or other serious incidents and cross-border issues (so called 'protective services').

- To better support front-line policing units (BCUs[5] in police jargon) in local and neighbourhood policing (so-called Level 1 policing).

- To provide a better flow of intelligence from the front line through to national level on serious and organised crime such as terrorist activities (so-called Level 3 policing).

- To strengthen relationships with key stakeholders in both the public and private sectors.

The Home Secretary also advised that:

> Proponents of alternative options should be able to demonstrate that they can deliver the same or better outcomes as the strategic force option in terms of enhanced capability and capacity in the provision of protective services, economies of scale, commensurate efficiency savings and clarity of responsibilities and governance.

This rather complicated language was essentially a strong vote for a significant reduction in the number of police forces through mergers.

A Home Office document was then sent to each of the 43 police forces in early October 2005 entitled 'Police Force Structures'. This document outlined a detailed timetable and methodology through which each force would identify and evaluate its options for mergers with other forces against nationally set criteria (see below). The intention was to achieve a full cost–benefit analysis of a shortlist of preferred merger options together with an initial implementation plan. The deadline was 23 December 2005.

Despite this very tight timetable there was little disagreement about the need to improve Level 2 and Level 3 policing. For example,[6] Association of Chief Police Officers' President Chris Fox said:

> The plans offered forces a 'great opportunity'. We are currently organised in a way that was designed to deal with Britain in the 1960s and Britain in the 21st century is slightly different. We've got to safeguard local policing but deal with the new world – very complicated, strategic crime, organised crime.

The Association of Police Authorities' Chairman Bob Jones said:

> They shared with Mr Clarke the need to 'raise our game' in terms of counter-terrorism, serious organised crime, major murder investigations. However, we have been given very little time to actually bring those plans together and we are also lacking in information, particularly about the financing and support for those particular plans, which means we don't feel that those plans are adequate and can guarantee improved performance in the near future.

Indeed by the 23 December deadline not a single force had completed its full submission and it was claimed that only 13 forces were actively interested in considering mergers and as many as 14 were opposed to *any* merger.[7] The Chairman of the Kent Police Federation (the 'union' for rank-and-file police officers), Ian Pointon, was reported as saying that:

> The county's force should remain independent as the majority of the public oppose the plans. I'm hopeful Kent Police will be left alone, I think the force has got a great reputation, the staff want it to be left alone as do 90% of the public – there's an overwhelming call.

Mr Pointon added that he was greatly concerned how the mergers would all be financed. He said the £58m it would cost to set up would pay for thousands of extra police officers:

---

[5] BCU stands for 'Basic Command Unit'. It is usually a geographical subdivision of a police force whose major responsibility is for day-to-day (Level 1) policing of its area. There were about 230 BCUs in England and Wales.

---

[6] http://news.bbc.co.uk (23 December 2005).
[7] http://news.bbc.co.uk (23 December 2005).

The government wants to fight serious organised crime and terrorism, so what better way to do that than have hundreds of extra police officers.

What had started to emerge as forces did their analyses were a set of assumptions or inferred guidelines as to what a strategic force would look like if it were to fulfil the roles outlined above. For example:

- It would need to be *big* enough: 4,000 police officers and about 6,000 total staff were discussed as a minimum size (only six forces were already that size).

- The local BCUs[8] would remain unchanged and simply be brought into a bigger grouping under a new strategic force.

- Mergers would only be made within the boundaries of the 10 *government regions* in England and Wales. Cross-regional mergers would not be approved even if they were adjacent (for example, South Yorkshire and Derbyshire). This was the basis on which many other public services were organised.

Perhaps inevitably some commentators started to suggest that the 'real' agenda was about creating stronger regions and wresting control of the police away from their local police authorities. The Home Secretary, Charles Clarke[9] vigorously denied this speculation. He said that the government had no secret regional agenda. Their only requirement was to ensure that all parts of the country had strategic forces of sufficient size to deliver both effective neighbourhood policing and to combat serious organised crime and terrorism (as HM Inspectorate of Constabulary had recommended). He also reaffirmed that local policing was an absolute cornerstone of the police reforms. The neighbourhood policing strategy would ensure that by 2008 every neighbourhood would have a dedicated team of officers and that every resident would know the name of their local police officer.

Over the first six months of 2006 the only merger approved by police authorities was that between Lancashire and the much smaller Cumbria force. Gradually other forces started to go cooler on mergers and started to emphasise the benefits of closer working between forces as an alternative way to achieving the desired results. The Liberal Democrat Home Affairs Spokesman (Nick Clegg)[10] emphasised this point:

> Government ministers should listen afresh to alternative ideas which meet the same objective of allowing our police forces to pool resources and tackle serious crime.

But perhaps the most crucial factor which slowed down the process was the replacement of Charles Clarke by John Reid as Home Secretary in early May 2006 following major difficulties with immigration issues and the prison service (other parts of the Home Office). The department's political priorities temporarily shifted to these other areas. In July 2006 Mr Reid announced that mergers would be delayed for further consultation although he said they remained the right way forward. This was just a few days after the Lancashire/Cumbria merger was called off for reasons of cost.

By this stage journalists and the public were following this 'drama' with interest as shown by some reactions from members of the public on a *BBC News Weblog*[11] on the day after the 'go slow' announcement:

> *Contributor 1*
> In my view England (certainly) and the UK (possibly) would benefit from a national Police Force. A united force could make the phrase 'joined-up working' a practical reality. National computer systems would allow all the existing disparate forces to use the same common intelligence and produce staff with transferable skills.
>
> My belief however is that (as usual) politics will dominate, and those Chief Constables & senior officers happy in their own 'empires' will fear and resist mergers that threaten their current positions. If mergers were introduced gradually I can't see why there would be any justification for significant additional funding.

> *Contributor 2*
> The very bedrock of policing in the UK is that it is locally delivered by locally accountable officers using citizens locally appointed and having their authority from the Crown. Without this local involvement in the setting and monitoring of policing priorities, the Police service would risk losing the support it has from the vast majority of the citizens.

---

[8] See note 5 above which explains the role of a BCU.
[9] Letter to the *Guardian* newspaper, 23 December (2005).

[10] http://news.bbc.co.uk (11 July 2006).
[11] Nick Robinson's weblog on: http://news.bbc.co.uk (12 July 2006).

One has to accept that the world is changing and the risk from terrorist and other major incidents is very real. Having said that, the service has both mutual aid arrangements in place to deal with such incidents as they arise. (The largest terrorist attack on this country was Lockerbie and Dumfries and Galloway – one of the smallest police forces in the UK – were able to deal with the matter thanks to the support of neighbouring forces).

In addition we now have the Serious Organised Crime Authority (SOCA) who transcend traditional boundaries.

Contributor 3

There is, of course, scope for the realignment of boundaries in line with changes in local political boundaries, just as there were in 1974, but moving away from the 'local' element of policing and, presumably abandoning the ethos of community service, is a disaster waiting to happen.

Contributor 4

Of course the police force mergers made sense. The Health Service just got on with theirs, and any large private company would not waste time worrying over a few pounds on the rates in one area (and a few pounds less to their neighbour). This government has lost its nerve, and the bleating of over-paid police authority members and clerks scared to lose their sinecures, along with a few chief constables (not the majority), means a sensible proposal long over due has been put on the back burner.

Contributor 5

Maybe we should have two types of police – local and national without any feeling within the police themselves that one is superior to the other. I am sure that the local police would be more appreciated by the populace.

This final contribution was a reminder that in many Continental European countries more than one type of police service was indeed the normal arrangement. Also at the 'other end' of police work the relatively newly created SOCA, as mentioned by contributor 2, was partly built on the FBI model from the USA.

So by 11 September 2006, almost a year after the process began, mergers appeared to be as far away as ever. But Prime Minister Tony Blair[12] still insisted that mergers were 'not off the agenda' and that greater strategic cooperation between forces was needed.

During the Autumn of 2006 the issue was largely dropped from news coverage except for an important contribution from the Chief Constable of Merseyside, Bernard Hogan-Howe, in November:[13]

> There are some police forces that are not big enough to do everything a police force needs to do. If there is that gap we need to do something and in my view a low-cost, low-tech solution would be to have some regional police commissioners.

He went on to say that there could be nine regional police commissioners – former chief constables – whose role would be to lead the forces to combine skills and resources across areas like the North-West. Regional units would deal with major incidents like a terrorist attack or a chemical explosion. He said it made sense for other services to be pan-regional, services like the police helicopters. If personnel and finance were centralised he said the savings could be enough to put an extra 10,000 officers on the beat.

However, the adjacent (and much smaller) Cheshire force was against these ideas as expressed by Peter Nurse, Chair of its Police Authority:

> I think a regional commissioner essentially would imply a regional force. It would be taking away [control] from local forces like Cheshire which have been around for a long time. They are cohesive. They have a loyalty. They do a lot for policing and . . . those forces would be undermined. We would have a regional force before you knew what had happened.

But Bernard Hogan-Howe was adamant that the current structure could not continue:

> There is no 'no risk' option. Standing still and staying where we are has risks . . . and there are threats. We have terrorism [and organised crime that] we need to deal with and terrorism is a growing concern. Not all forces can deal at the level . . . moving to a new world has risks . . . but I think that the world I have described would have a better chance of success and the benefits are worth the risks.

---

[12] http://news.bbc.co.uk (11 September 2006).
[13] Michelle Mayman, 'Politics show – North West', http://news.bbc.co.uk (16 November 2006).

Ericsson and the creation of the mobile telephony business

Patrick Regnér

The case describes the history of the Swedish telecommunications company Ericsson's entry into the mobile telephony market. It examines the characteristics of strategic change from a public telecommunication to a mobile telephony focus, and shows how strategic innovation may emerge from the periphery of an organisation. The case describes how a small and insignificant unit in Ericsson turned the company into becoming the world's largest supplier of mobile telephone systems. The focus is therefore on the dynamics of strategy innovation from the beginning of the 1980s to the turn of the century.

● ● ●

Ericsson delivered the first commercial mobile telephone system in the world to Saudi Arabia in 1981. The company sold the system despite Saudi Tel, Saudi Arabia's PTT (Post, Telephone and Telegraph),[1] not specifying it at all in its order of telecommunication networks and equipment. Furthermore, Ericsson did not actually have a mobile phone system to sell or the required products for its infrastructure. This was, however, the first step towards making Ericsson the largest mobile telephony company in the world.

SRA – an autonomous and self-reliant company with a vision

It was a small and autonomous subsidiary of Ericsson, SRA, that insisted on selling a mobile telephone system to Saudi Arabia. SRA led a rather languishing life as a radio communication supplier at the time and, basically, was an independent company. The company's focus had been on radio products for the military as well as civilian use (radio receivers, gramophones, TVs, radio systems for aviation and shipping, radar installations, etc.). Since the 1960s the company had consolidated into communication and military radio equipment, leaving consumer goods. Its major business was in the military market. SRA's independence from Ericsson not only was due to its small size, un-related technology and generally microscopic role in Ericsson, but reflected the fact that British GE-Marconi owned 29 per cent of the company at the time.

The President of SRA, Åke Lundqvist, was extremely enthusiastic about mobile telephony. He had joined SRA in the mid-1960s and had been in charge of the land–mobile radio division since 1970. He had been involved in mobile radio and mobile telephony since the end of the 1950s, when he worked for another company. He participated in the development of one of the early Swedish mobile telephone systems, MTB (which could only handle six telephone calls simultaneously in Stockholm). SRA also had a history in the system since it supplied the base stations and telephones.[2]

---

[1] PTT refers to Post, Telephone and Telegraph, which were the traditional government organisations or monopolies responsible for running a country's postal and telecommunications services.

[2] A base station is equipped with transmitters and receivers and covers a geographical area or a 'cell' with radio signals connecting to mobile telephones. Base stations are connected to mobile telephone switches, which in turn are linked to the fixed telephony network.

Lundqvist had an early vision of the importance of mobile telephony, a vision 'based on radio technology, to eliminate the wire from the regular telephony'. However, at Ericsson SRA's vision was derided, and the company was considered a 'garage outfit', a 'bicycle repair shop' represented by 'cowboys'. As one manager in Ericsson's largest division, the public telecommunications division, put it: 'They were not really a part of us. They looked different and behaved differently.'

Ericsson – a public telecommunications company with AXE as the flagship product

The main products of Ericsson had traditionally been switching and transmission equipment. A switch, or telephone exchange, controls and operates telephone calls in a telephone network. In the early days it consisted of a manual system where an operator used pairs of plugs to connect people on a switchboard. All major R&D was invested in switching and Ericsson introduced its digital switching technology, AXE, at an early stage. It became widely known and well respected and contracts all over the world had been signed by 1980. The PTTs had historically been the principal markets for these products. Roughly a dozen telecommunications companies dominated the world market (AT&T, Ericsson, CIT-Alcatel, Fujitsu, Hitachi, ITT, NEC, OKI, Plessey, Siemens, Strowger). They competed for orders from the PTTs where markets were open. The USA was still closed and the British PTT bought only from British companies. Similar arrangements prevailed in many other markets. Political considerations often played a larger role than commercial or technological ones. Once a relationship had been built with a PTT, it usually lasted for a long time with continuous follow-up contracts and competition was limited. As John Meurling, Director of Corporate Relations and Investor Relations at Ericsson, described at the time:

> The vendor-customer relationship could often be described as marriage-like: once a PTT had made its system choice – or often vendor choice, which might go back to the beginning of the century – the relationship was expected to continue for a long time. . . . Not many countries were supplied by one manufacturer only, but very few countries had more than two or three. For most companies it was cosy.[3]

Even if Ericsson had one of the least 'cosy' positions, because the Swedish PTT manufactured most of its own switches, the culture and way of doing business reflected the prevalent stable and semi-competitive environment. However, SRA, although quite remote in terms of both technology and products, had spent its whole 60-year history in a less protected and quite competitive business environment. Most managers at Ericsson did not know much about SRA; it was a minor, independent and pretty unglamorous business. AXE was the flagship of Ericsson and public telecommunications was its captain. As John Meurling described it:

> We [Public Telecom] were the biggest, the most important, and the most beautiful part of the Ericsson Group – and we knew it.[3]

The Nordic mobile telephone network

The Swedish and other Nordic PTTs were pivotal in developing and establishing mobile telephony in Sweden and the Nordic countries. They joined forces in order to develop the Nordic mobile telephone (NMT) network. Telecommunication equipment manufacturers were asked in 1977 to submit proposals to provide the NMT network. Ericsson and SRA and their competitors – among them NEC, Motorola, Mitsubishi and Fujitsu – were invited to bid. Ericsson, however, was not particularly enthusiastic about mobile phone systems. Its public telecommunications unit was not interested in providing switches for mobile systems. Ericsson finally offered switches, but it was more in order to preserve old relations with its long-term partner, the Swedish PTT, than enthusiastically to enter a new market. Ericsson did not offer its latest technology (AXE) at first. An adjusted AXE switch for mobile telecommunication was simply seen to have a limited future. The company, however, subsequently did offer AXE at the insistence of the Swedish PTT, which indicated that otherwise it might adopt the technology of NEC, the closest contestant.

Ericsson's lack of enthusiasm for mobile phone systems reflected its very small role compared with its other businesses and a belief that mobile telephony would continue to be of minor importance. Mobile telephony was seen as something more exclusive and directed towards professional use.

---

[3] J. Meurling, and R. Jeans, 'A switch in time: AXE – creating the foundation for the information age', *Communications Week International*, 1995.

Personal application was something not very serious – a service for the privileged. Ericsson was far from alone in its assessment of a limited mobile phone market. For example, the NMT network was initially thought to be complementary to manual mobile telephone systems. Bell Labs at AT&T, which originally invented mobile telephone networks, hired a major US management consultancy firm to study mobile telephony and its market potential around this time. The firm concluded that the potential was insignificant and firmly advised against involvement in mobile telephony. Another reason for Ericsson's resistance was that in radio the company's involvement was in closed radio systems and it was questionable if SRA had the right competences for mobile telephony. In fact, the rest of Ericsson did not think much of SRA personnel. As one SRA manager of the time explained: 'We were considered as lacking in knowledge, stupid and inexperienced.'

At SRA enthusiasm for the NMT venture was greater and they did have some radio technology competences. However, their mobile systems competences were limited. SRA did not yet have its own base stations, a central part of a mobile system. At first SRA was more focused on the mobile telephone itself than on the entire mobile system, but its technology in that area was inferior as well. It had succeeded in developing a mobile telephone, but it was not the latest technology. Instead, one of SRA's main resources at this time was its entrepreneurial spirit and, perhaps, insight compared with the rest of Ericsson and competitors. As Åke Lundqvist put it: 'We had a vision to eliminate the wire in telephony, everybody laughed at us!'

The first commercial cellular mobile system in the world

In the end, Ericsson got the order to deliver switches for the NMT network in the Nordic countries and SRA became a sub-supplier of a base station control unit for Magnetic, a local Swedish radio technology firm. SRA also supplied mobile telephones or stations for the system.[4] Since SRA needed competence in this area it acquired Sonab in 1978, a rival in radio technology and the leader in mobile stations in Sweden at that time.

That company had a land–mobile terminal that was upgraded to a mobile telephone. Despite winning the NMT order there was still limited interest in mobile telephone systems at Ericsson and consequently little integration of Ericsson's and SRA's products, mobile telephone switches and radio equipment.

The first commercial mobile telephony system in the world was delivered in 1981, not to the Nordic countries, but to Saudi Arabia. The NMT in the Nordic countries was not in operation until a couple of months after the Saudi premiere. In the late 1970s Ericsson won a major order to supply Saudi Arabia with a fixed telecommunication infrastructure. Åke Lundqvist enthusiastically took the initiative on a mobile telephony system in Saudi Arabia. He suggested to Ericsson's CEO, Björn Lundvall: 'Can't we try to sell a mobile telephone system to Saudi Arabia? They want the latest of everything else.' Lundqvist managed to convince both the CEO and the Head of Ericsson's Public Telecommunications Switching Division, Håkan Ledin, to offer the Saudis a mobile telephone system. They were prepared to go along with Lundqvist's ideas; after all, any mobile phone deal would only be small compared with the fixed network that represented the main order. Ledin actually believed a system already existed. However, SRA and Ericsson did not have a complete system at that time; even some of the core products did not exist.

The first cellular mobile systems were not without problems. The Saudi order included 8,000 mobile stations, which put pressure on production sources – there were no terminals left to sell in the Nordic home market. Competitors naturally exploited the situation. Furthermore, there were important quality problems. Among other things, the telephone station keypads melted in the hot Saudi sun, and the armour-plated limousines and cars caused installation problems. In addition, as SRA tried to get its first generation of mobile phones into production on the Nordic market, competitors were bringing out their second generation. Flemming Örneholm, SRA's Marketing Manager at the time, referred to the situation as a disaster:

> It was a mess. . . . Quality was certainly not up to expectations. . . . The competitors were beating the hell out of Ericsson [SRA].[5]

---

[4] The correct terminology here is mobile stations or terminals. At this time these were based on land–mobile products and were large and heavy units installed in vehicles.

[5] J. Meurling and R. Jeans, 'A switch in time: AXE – creating the foundation for the information age', *Communications Week International*, 1995.

Trying to sell integrated mobile telephony systems

At the end of the 1970s and beginning of 1980s more PTTs started to show an interest in mobile telephony. SRA began to see a sizeable potential market and started to penetrate more markets, 'shooting at everything they saw' as one manager put it. SRA wanted to provide a more coordinated and integrated mobile telephony *system* of Ericsson's switches and its own radio equipment to the operators. However, the initial orders were small, and the contracts were of modest size from the viewpoint of Ericsson's corporate management and the switching division. Switching merely regarded mobile telephony as another way among many others to sell switches. Attempting to exploit mobile telephony applications was more trouble than it was worth and it was out of the question that SRA, with not quite 4 per cent of total sales, would be in charge of Ericsson's flagship product AXE for mobile systems. Furthermore, it was far from obvious that mobile telephony was a promising future market. There were no indications in terms of market investigations or any other indicators and few thought that mobile telephony would grow into a mass market. Forecasts continuously underestimated the number of subscribers during the 1980s. Mobile phone network operators, governmental bodies, mobile phone infrastructure providers and mobile phone manufacturers all underestimated the tremendous growth of mobile telephony. During these early years of mobile phone networks, Ericsson and SRA continued to submit separate offers. And the different views on mobile system integration resulted in increased tension between the two units. However, even if there was no coherent arrangement for mobile phone systems, SRA was finally given at least the marketing responsibility for them.

A contract in The Netherlands

SRA continued to fight dual battles for a more complete system concept, both internally, versus the switching division and corporate management, and in the market. This was apparent in The Netherlands, where both the Dutch PTT and Ericsson's corporate management and the switching division had to be convinced of the advantage of the integrated system idea. From Ericsson there were separate offers as usual: the switching division offered switches, and SRA offered radio technology. The PTT wanted Ericsson's AXE switch since it had a high capacity. However, Motorola was involved in the discussion as well and suggested a combination of AXE switches and its own base stations. The Dutch PTT supported this concept. So did Ericsson at first. The arrangement could eventually lead to further AXE orders to be filled jointly with Motorola. However, Åke Lundqvist strongly disapproved. He argued that Ericsson should be a provider of integrated systems in mobile telephony, and should furnish the whole package – switches and base stations – or nothing. Lundqvist's position brought matters to a head, causing considerable distress among managers in the switching division. Ericsson might risk losing the entire order and would actually be declining an opportunity to sell its principal product. This was particularly frustrating since SRA was not ready either in terms of products – its base station was not fully developed – or in terms of competence. Since the switching division also supplied switches to the PTT's fixed network, relations with this customer had to be handled with care. As one manager of the time explained:

> That is a thriller, it was terrible. . . . They were absolutely lost. . . . They did not really understand, they made base stations and there was not much to it . . . I wondered: Can this be true?[6]

The Dutch PTT and Motorola considered that agreement had been reached on the arrangement, which would include Motorola's base stations and Ericsson's switch. However, Lundqvist did not give up, but tried to convince the parties involved. He managed to obtain the passive approval of Ericsson's new CEO, Björn Svedberg, and consent from some switching division managers. All in all, it was not a major AXE order; they were more concerned with the relationship with the Dutch PTT because of the supply of AXE to its fixed network which, naturally, was larger. Prompted by Motorola, the PTT now required a 'small-cell concept' (a technology where the cells – the geographical area covered by a base station – are particularly small) to suit the topography and the density of population in The Netherlands. SRA lacked knowledge of the small-cell technology

---

[6] M. McKelvey, F. Texier and H. Alm, *The Dynamics of High Tech Industry: Swedish Firms Developing Mobile Telecommunication System*, Working Paper No. 187, November, Linköping University, 1997.

required. Nevertheless, Lundqvist continued to fight. He happened to know, and managed to recruit, one of the best US consultants in the area, Chan Rypinski. SRA and Lundqvist were playing a tough game with high stakes. First, he obtained partial consent from the CEO. Second, he convinced the switching division. The PTT's purchasing department, however, showed no interest in the proposal. Unconventional methods were required. When the PTT did not listen, Lundqvist became furious, as he recalled: 'This was the only time I ever slammed my fist on the table while arguing with a customer.' With SRA playing the leading role, it and Ericsson finally managed to win the contract, which included a complete system of switches, base stations and cell planning services (the design and planning of number of cells, base stations, etc.), but it was a hard sell to the PTT. Thus, SRA and Ericsson had begun to sell a more integrated system and not just separate parts of mobile telephony.

Entering the USA

In 1983 Åke Lundqvist predicted that 'by the turn of the century, sales in Ericsson's mobile telephone business would pass those in public telecom'. John Meurling, Director of Corporate Relations and Investor Relations at Ericsson at the time, replied: 'God help us, that's ridiculous!' SRA, thus, continued its aggressive and ambitious ways of doing business. In order to acquire knowledge in mobile telephony, SRA had an active policy: 'We had a well-developed buying approach, we bought firms or consultancy services' (Åke Lundqvist). Through the consultant in The Netherlands case, Lundqvist happened to meet another US-based consultant, Jan Jubon, who urged SRA to enter the USA. Lundqvist was interested, and the consultant was hired to submit a market report. The SRA management made a decision to enter, initially as a trial and error expedition. SRA thought the risks were reasonable to justify making a try. The organisation set up was small, in temporary offices and with staff commuting to the USA. Its job was to get acquainted with the operators and the current products and services. Lundqvist regarded the pioneers in the US venture as heroes:

> There were two or three persons in the US, making calls for hours. They made a superhuman accomplishment. Ericsson did the opposite, they had hundreds of salesmen.

Continued international expansion – new markets and new standards

An opportunity in the UK for ERA (SRA had become a wholly owned company under the name Ericsson Radio System AB/Inc.) appeared at the same time as the US venture. Massive resources were required in the USA. An additional attempt in another market where Ericsson had limited and mostly unpleasant experience would put even more pressure on the organisation, but it entered nevertheless. As one ERA manager of the time explained: 'We had to choose between the US and UK markets, we decided to take them both on.' This step was a bold venture by ERA as it involved expansion from a small sales organisation to a large manufacturing and R&D company in the UK. In addition, it meant working with a new mobile telephony standard, TACS (Total Access Communications System). In 1983 Vodafone, one of two British operators, chose ERA as infrastructure supplier. The company won the contract in competition with AT&T and Motorola and it was fulfilled in 1985. As ERA entered more and more markets in Europe and North America, the company faced an increasingly complicated environment, including various uncertainties about technologies and standards, and deregulated markets involving more and more multifaceted customers. The market potential was highly unpredictable and competition intensified. ERA countered this complexity with a business and action-oriented culture, as one ERA manager of the time explained:

> We were independent entrepreneurs . . . hunting mobile telephone technology . . . fighting over markets . . . and firing at everything we saw.

The entrepreneurial and independent culture of ERA caused frequent friction with the more methodical and bureaucratically oriented corporate management and the switching division in the public telecommunications business area. 'It was two completely different worlds. Ericsson was ignorant, there was animosity and competition' explained an Ericsson manager of the time. Despite its market success and growth, ERA was still regarded as a minor business and was treated accordingly by corporate management and, in particular, by managers in the switching division, who 'considered us as something the cat dragged in' as one ERA manager put it. From corporate management's point of view ERA was not considered to have a strategy. The CEO of Ericsson criticised ERA's strategy for being 'completely absent'. One ERA manager of the time argued that there even seemed to be talk about getting rid of ERA altogether: 'It was most probably discussed . . . I am sure someone tried to strangle us.'

Recognition and success of mobile telephony

In 1986 Lars Ramqvist, former President of the Components Business Area, became one of three vice presidents, and part of the Ericsson Corporate Executive Committee. He was assigned to examine Ericsson's corporate strategy. Ramqvist identified several core businesses. Among them, mobile telephony was included, although the AXE switching system was clearly still the central product. As John Meurling put it:

> For the first time cellular [mobile telephony] was seen as a legitimate, worthwhile, even important, part of Ericsson's business. However, there was a great deal of lack of understanding and distrust left, even if more people saw its importance. They said 'those damn cowboys' and at ERA they said 'those damn bureaucrats'.

In 1988 ERA succeeded in its long-term internal battle and the mobile telephony business was almost fully integrated. Sales in the area had increased substantially and market growth continued to increase as well. ERA was given responsibility for the entire mobile telephone system, including switches. Nevertheless, the switching division within the public telecommunications business area controlled the R&D of digital switching. Other technological and development responsibilities for mobile system switches were shifted to ERA. Controversies continued between parts of the switching division and ERA, but more people now seemed to realise the impact of ERA and mobile telephony. In the same year the Swedish base station company Radiosystem was acquired. It considerably increased ERA's market share in base stations and together with strong market growth ERA gained almost a 40 per cent share of the world market for mobile telephone systems. Also in the same year Åke Lundqvist, who was considered 'too wild and unstructured' by corporate management and whose ERA still ran into conflict with the rest of the organisation, resigned. Lars Ramqvist became the President of ERA. He

came from the four-man Corporate Executive Management team and the change indicated the increasing importance of ERA in Ericsson. In addition, more structure and order in the organisation followed. As explained by one ERA manager:

> When Ramqvist arrived we got more freedom. There was a reorganization and some people disappeared then. But it is unclear if it was a strategic undertaking even at that time.

Lars Ramqvist was appointed new CEO of Ericsson in 1990. Kurt Hellström became the President of ERA. Some animosity continued between the radio and switching divisions, but it diminished after the entire responsibility for mobile telephony, including all switching development, including digital GSM, was transferred to radio communications and ERA in 1992. The two following years showed immense and sustained growth; 1993 was a turning point, since radio communications passed public telecommunications in sales with 40 per cent of total sales, compared with 32 per cent, respectively. Mobile telephony alone (apart from other product areas in radio communications) had achieved sales equal to the total for public telecommunications, 32 per cent. Now there was no doubt that mobile telephone systems were a strategic and important part of Ericsson as the 1994 annual report stated:

> Ericsson's success in mobile telephony is based on the very farsighted and advanced development work in the field of radio that was begun at an early stage within Ericsson Radio Systems [ERA].

Sales successes and expansion continued as ERA continued to enter into all standards as new digital ones were launched. Ericsson enjoyed repeated success when the digital standard was adopted in the USA. In addition, the Asian markets expanded rapidly for Ericsson during the end of the 1990s, especially Japan and China. By 1994, radio communications, including ERA, accounted for more than 50 per cent of Ericsson's sales and almost 30 per cent of its workforce. Radio communications was the main product area and mobile telephone systems were its flagship. Later mobile telephones and terminals would become another flagship. The tremendous growth of mobile systems continued and in 1997 total mobile telephony sales had reached 70 per cent of the corporate total, and the number of employees had almost quadrupled since 1992. In the same year the radio communications business area was divided into two new business areas, mobile systems, including mobile system infrastructure equipment, and mobile phones and terminals, with 44 and 26 per cent of total sales, respectively. Sales increased by another 10 per cent in 1998 to more than twice as much as four years earlier. The introduction to the strategy section, 'The new world of Telecom', in the 1998 annual report illustrates the importance of mobile telephony:

> Ericsson is a world leader in mobile telephony. The corporation is the largest supplier of mobile systems, with ca. 30% of the world market, in dollars. The corporation is also among the largest on the market for digital mobile telephones and public switches.

By the turn of the century Ericsson was completely dominated by the mobile telephony business. Meanwhile the public telecommunications business area, renamed Infocom, went through a restructuring process and some sections were outsourced and sold.

Other sources

Ericsson Annual Reports 1978–1998.

B. Mölleryd, 'Entrepreneurship in technological systems – the development of mobile telephony in Sweden', Dissertation, EFI, Stockholm School of Economics, 1999.

P. Regnér, 'Strategy creation and change in complexity – adaptive and creative learning dynamics in the firm', Doctoral Dissertation, Stockholm School of Economics, 1999.

Direct and Care Services

Gerry Johnson

This case study describes the development of the strategy of Direct and Care Services of Glasgow City Council. Recognised as one of the most innovative public sector service providers in the UK, its history and the approach to managing strategy are explained by Fergus Chambers, its Executive Director. The case provides a basis for considering strategy development in the multi-stakeholder context of public sector services.

• • •

Direct and Care Services is a department of Glasgow City Council. It provides school catering, home care services and facilities management to other departments of the council and more prestigious catering services to public and private sector customers through Encore Creative Catering. Over the years Direct and Care Services has established a reputation for innovation in the provision of public sector services.

Fergus Chambers is the Executive Director. His career had been in catering from the time he graduated from Glasgow College of Food Technology in the late 1970s. He then worked in the private sector, mainly for contract catering companies and in the later years with Douwe Egberts. However, not wanting to move to London, he joined what was then Strathclyde Regional Council in 1988 which was looking for someone with commercial, private sector experience at the time of the growth of competitive tendering in local government. There he developed Catering Direct, the first branded public sector caterer and the largest in Europe. He then became Director of Catering and Cleaning Services for the new Glasgow City Council. He describes how that organisation and its strategy developed into what became Direct and Care Services.

Getting started

As Fergus explains:

The business was formed out of the local government re-organisation in 1995/6, when we inherited four different businesses. The catering side of what had been Strathclyde Regional Council, which was predominantly school and welfare catering with a bit of staff catering thrown in and the cleaning business which was exclusively building and window cleaning. Also the catering arm and a small element of the cleaning services from Glasgow District Council, which had been a separate body.

In those circumstances we had to come up with a new structure, new processes, new systems, new policies and procedures. In effect we were starting a brand new business but with an inherited turnover of £46 million [€66m]. The first thing was to come up with a structure that merged the four operating units. That was relatively straightforward; but the major challenge was creating a new culture for the organisation because there were four different cultures inherited.

The catering arm of Glasgow District Council was in a highly competitive market environment and had been through two very severe rounds of competitive tendering. It was managed very aggressively. Though the businesses inherited from Strathclyde Region also faced competition, they didn't face such severe financial or commercial pressures. They also had much more money for investment, a predominantly female workforce who had been there for many years, with lots of loyalty, but also arguably an informal more relaxed style of management. The cleaning side of Strathclyde Region was a fairly aggressive business but that was because of who managed it.

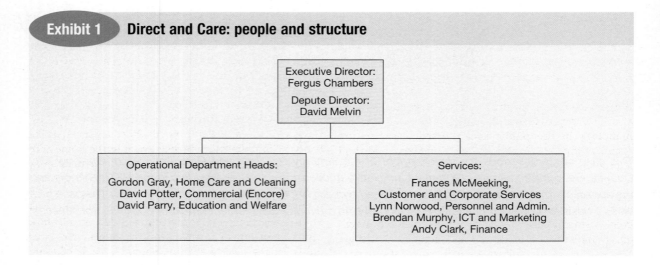

Exhibit 1 **Direct and Care: people and structure**

As director I had to decide on a management structure for the senior team. Some of them I inherited and some of them I recruited. I decided I wanted my number 2 to come from outside. It's always good to have new blood; new experiences; a fresh approach to management rather than an approach from one of the four businesses I inherited. It was of course a political committee decision; albeit I was in attendance and had a fairly major say. We decided to appoint somebody who came from Edinburgh with experience running catering and cleaning, but with a lot of private sector experience, similar to myself.

I then appointed three heads of service from the managers I inherited. One running the commercial business, most of which came from Glasgow District Council catering. That is now Encore. One running school and welfare catering. And one running building cleaning and other general services. I then needed a head of Personnel, a head of ICT and a head of Finance. I added Marketing at a later stage and then Corporate and Customer Services for all the services left over. [See Exhibit 1.]

Whilst the basic structure of the business, in particular the three operational areas, were fairly obvious based on my previous experience, the detail of how it would work was actually designed to suit some of the individuals. I had a fairly good idea who was going to end up with the top jobs, so I tried to design a structure partly influenced by who I felt was going to get the jobs to run it. For example Brendan Murphy is an ICT guru. He's not a conventional local government officer, but he's unbelievably creative. He has one of the most creative minds you can imagine. So I gave him marketing. Not the usual mix. But I designed the job to suit his particular skills. That worked out extremely well.

Getting established

Fergus explained the early priorities:

I was appointed in October 1995 and I had to take over on 1 April 1996. So I had a six month period to decide on structures, to recruit and appoint people to posts, to decide on how I was going to communicate and standardise processes, agree operating strategies, put budgets in place, merge the policies and procedures and make sure they were compatible with the new council's policies. I did that with the people who I thought were probably going to be appointed to the new jobs – people who weren't yet working for me. But let's be honest, they were in the process of having to secure a future for themselves, so there was a lot of co-operation. I suppose it was me selling my views, involving them in discussion, getting buy-in from them and trying to sell them on wanting to come and work for me.

Also at the political level there was a brand new council made up of former district councillors and former regional councillors. There was a huge power struggle there. There was also a good deal of jockeying for position at director level. In that context, the first thing we had to do was gain our credibility. For example the then Director of Building Services was very keen for me to locate my business in his office; an offer I gracefully declined. I wanted to be in charge of my own destiny, not on someone else's doorstep. I found my own premises. We also had to do an awful lot of data capture at that time. However we decided to build our systems from scratch. I wanted my own systems, my own accountants, my own computers and my own ICT experts.

The strategy

In the 10 years since it was established, turnover has grown from £46m (€66m) to £125m (€179m). Fergus explained how this was achieved:

We developed a reputation for delivering. We are a 'can do' organisation which is not necessarily commonplace in the public sector. Particularly in the period of time we're talking about. So if somebody had a problem, they would come to us because we had a reputation for solving problems. We also gained a reputation for quality in our markets. We invested money in training and development and we introduced good customer care practices; again things not inherently common within the public sector at that time. We also broke down barriers with some of our customer departments. Those barriers existed predominantly out of competitive tendering (CCT). If I go back to the early days of CCT, principal customers like the Department of Education were always suspicious that we were ripping them off because we were operating a contract we'd inherited years ago with lots of profit in it. There wasn't a bond of trust between Education and the former regional council Catering Department. We spent a lot of time developing open book accounting. If we made excessive profits we would give it back rather than keep it for our own good. We built trust with our customers that did not exist historically. The result was that if Education had something they wanted to address or we had a business idea, then we could have a decent discussion with them. Latterly the same has been the case with Social Work, which probably had an even smaller bond of trust before.

So originally we were seen as the catering and cleaning department; nothing really strategic or important. Technically it could be done by anybody or could even be outsourced. Now we're placed quite well strategically.

Home Care

Fergus continued:

In 2000 we then inherited Home Care; that is home help for the elderly and infirm. That was the result of a restructure. The council had 22 departments and there was a big drive to halve the number of departments to become more efficient and effective, reduce costs and overheads. Within a fairly short period of time we were able to make an impact. We brought a commercial edge to it but we kept the caring approach in terms of client delivery. We reduced absences and started to give the home helps in the field a feeling of

pride in their job; basic things like giving them the right uniform. We gave them a management structure so they had someone to talk to and developed a communications structure to get feedback on what we were doing. We then started investing in technology so that client information all became computerised.

When it transferred Home Care was £17m (€24.4m); now it's £44m (€63m) turnover. That's partly because Glasgow has a greater need than most areas of Scotland and therefore invests more in the home care service and partly because we've been able to demonstrate that by becoming more efficient it is worthwhile to broaden the range of services. It's no longer just a basic home care service 8–5; we're now running a 24 hour service seven days a week with 42% of the work undertaken out of normal working hours. We have an overnight service, turning people in their bed and toileting them in the middle of the night. We're taking over some of the work from the NHS. We've got direct ordering from hospitals which never existed before and that reduces bed blocking. We might get a hospital phoning us up saying 'Mrs Jones is leaving or being discharged from hospital at 4 o'clock this afternoon and she's going to need somebody to tuck her in at 7 o'clock tonight': we get that short notice. In the past we would never have been able to respond to that, but what we do now is to have a home help with a Blackberry. We email them the care plan that says Mrs Jones is coming out of hospital at 4 o'clock today and needs something at 7 o'clock tonight.

So we're seen as delivering and improving the efficiency and effectiveness of the service. In the most recent statistics Glasgow was way ahead in terms of benchmarking with any other local authority in Scotland.

When questioned as to how this innovative approach came about, Fergus explained:

These ideas usually come from the department heads. They might have heard of an idea somewhere else or they might have read about some technology development. Brendan Murphy promoted Blackberrys. I was the first person in Glasgow City Council to have a Blackberry. Then we gave the politicians some to pilot so they could start to see the benefits. We then piloted them in Home Care.

Encore

Encore, though part of Direct and Care, operates as a commercial business, often competing with private sector businesses. Fergus explained its development:

I've always liked branding. I started it in my days in Strathclyde Regional Council. We had what was known as Strathclyde Region Catering Services – not very exciting. We rebranded it Catering Direct. At that time it was the biggest public sector catering organisation in Europe with about 6,000 staff. Such branding was radical at that time. Then other divisions within the region also took on the Direct name. So Roads Direct was born; Parking Direct was born, and so on. By the time of the reorganisation people expected me to rebrand everything Catering Direct. But it became clear to me that we needed to do something to differentiate our catering operations. We actually had a very good product and a good team. We were also competing in some of our markets with the best of the private sector, particularly for banqueting, conferences coming to Glasgow, conventions, that type of thing. But we were seen as the council's catering arm and that was a problem. We therefore sought the approval of the politicians to create a separate identity for it. We came up with the Encore brand which has become highly successful. We've managed to expand the business with external contracts. Maybe not as many as we would like but we've developed quite a successful business.

Getting the politicians on board with this sort of thing is vital of course. That was helped by my training in sales in the catering contract world. That attunes your mind to determine what makes the customer, in this case the politicians, tick. What are they looking for? What are their objectives and motivations? Then you decide on whatever you're trying to sell to them and pitch it that way. They want the public catering aspect to be successful and make money because that allows them to reduce council tax. They also want to enhance the reputation of Glasgow as a visitor attraction. I convinced them that the way we were operating was not meeting the customer's expectations; it wasn't enhancing our reputation. I used comments from people like the Convention Bureau whose job is to attract international conferences to Glasgow. That helped convince them that international conventions didn't want to use council caterers, irrespective of how good they were; that there was a resistance to trading with us because of their experiences elsewhere.

The next stage in the development of Encore was a detailed Organisational Development Plan which set out a set of strategic goals, action plans along with a communications strategy. This was a crucial stage in the maturity of the business.

This plan was developed by David Potter who set up an initial planning team of six managers from his department. David explained that he based its work on what he had learned on his MBA:

We met fortnightly for a year. We undertook scenario planning, PEST, SWOT, Stakeholder and Five Forces Analysis to map out a strategic plan for a 3 year time period. Forty unit managers then attended a day's conference to work through the same techniques. They fully engaged in the process and then set about over a 3 month period developing unit plans with representatives from client groups, general staff and senior management. It made it OK for managers from craft and operational backgrounds to discuss strategy at a unit level and beyond. Service standards have improved and sales have increased. In some cases services have literally been transformed.

Managing strategy development

Fergus continued:

I think some of these elements of our strategy were planned and some just happened. The trust issue was planned, definitely. It partly arose out of discussions I had with Directors of Education and latterly with Social Work. The management team knew it was a problem and decided to try to build that bond of trust. And we deliberately developed strategies like open book accounting. Much of this comes initially from David Melvin and myself, but if we felt it appropriate we would take it to the wider management team. Or it might come from them picking the good ideas from within their departments and running with them. We also spent a whole day away a while ago talking about ideas. But also there are the regular coffee mornings where the top team meet regularly but informally and ideas get floated and developed.

As far as the reputation for solving problems, particularly with the introduction of technology, much of that was based on Brendan's ICT creativity. If someone had a problem we would develop a computer system to solve the problem whereas historically they would go to the head of ICT in the council and three years later might have something that didn't meet their needs.

I would say the majority of what we do doesn't originate in a structured way; it happens in a kind of creative moment. I don't see anything wrong in that. I push the managers to be creative. I will lay down a challenge if somebody comes up with a problem. I'll say: 'Well go and find a solution for it.' It is also helped by giving people a bit of freedom. I don't over-manage people and I'll encourage them to push themselves and to push their people; and to make mistakes. As long as the mistakes are not too big I'll carry the blame on my shoulders.

It's also important to learn from the best in your field. Thus far I've invested heavily in bespoke training including three senior managers travelling to the Disney Institute in Orlando to learn about International Customer Service.

Our success and reputation is largely down to my senior management team who I have relied upon over the last 11 years to create a high level of enthusiasm, positive team spirit and that 'can do' approach that is so much appreciated in our sector. I'm indebted to them for their support and I will fight for their futures as much as I would fight for my own.

I would also add that managing this sort of thing is much more complex in the public sector because you're influencing a much wider audience. You're not just accountable to shareholders: you're trying to influence personal and political agendas with a small and large 'P'. Glasgow is predominantly Labour, though with a vastly reduced majority following the May elections of 2007. Prior to then, Labour enjoyed a working majority of 59 out of a total 79 seats. Now, that majority has been reduced to 11. Therefore you're having to consider the political agendas of different parties and arguably influence that because you might need cross party support for a particular initiative. You're having to convince and sell things to officers like my boss, the Chief Executive, the director of finance, the head of personnel and so on. And ultimately you're accountable to the public. But my key stakeholder has got to be the politicians initially. If I cock it up they're the ones that are held accountable at the ballot box.

Building One BBC

Richard Whittington

A major reorganisation of the United Kingdom's state-owned broadcaster, the BBC, was welcomed by many of its employees. Four years later, however, this reorganisation contributed to a sequence of events including the suicide of a government scientist and the resignation of the BBC's popular chief, the Director-General.

● ● ●

In April 2000, Greg Dyke, the new Director-General of the BBC, announced a major reorganisation of one of the world's most famous broadcasters. His proposed management delayering was welcomed enthusiastically by many creative and journalistic staff in the organisation. Four years later, however, Greg Dyke was forced to resign, after a doubtful BBC news story set off a train of events that led to the suicide of government scientist Dr David Kelly. Although Dyke was still popular internally, his resignation prompted demonstrations of support inside the BBC, but some said that the earlier reorganisation was in part to blame for the events that led to his downfall.

The BBC had been founded in 1922 as a public service broadcaster of radio and, subsequently, television. It is independent of government and overseen by a board of governors. At the beginning of Greg Dyke's office, the BBC had an income of some £2bn (≈€3bn) derived from a licence fee paid by 22 million households in the UK. As such the BBC remained one of the few large broadcasters in the world which did not carry advertising, although it did derive commercial income of almost £100m from the sale of programme rights and branded products worldwide. In the UK, and to some extent in other parts of the world, the BBC was seen more as an institution than a company. Its broadcasts reached over 50 million people domestically each week and almost 300 million worldwide. It had a global reputation for the diversity, depth and quality of its programming – particularly in drama, documentaries and news.

Not surprisingly, such a prominent institution was constantly in the public eye – not only in terms of its broadcasting output but also in how it was financed and managed. The appointment of Greg Dyke as Director-General, combining the role of Chief Executive and Editor-in-Chief, was something of a shock to many people. He did not fit the 'establishment figure' image of most of his predecessors. He had a background in commercial television and was more flamboyant and 'streetwise'. Like many new leaders, his first steps in stamping his brand on the BBC was to review its structure and management processes and this is what was announced in April 2000 and published in the booklet *Building One BBC*.

Photo: BBC Photo Library

Exhibit 1 **John Birt's structure (pre-2000; simplified)**

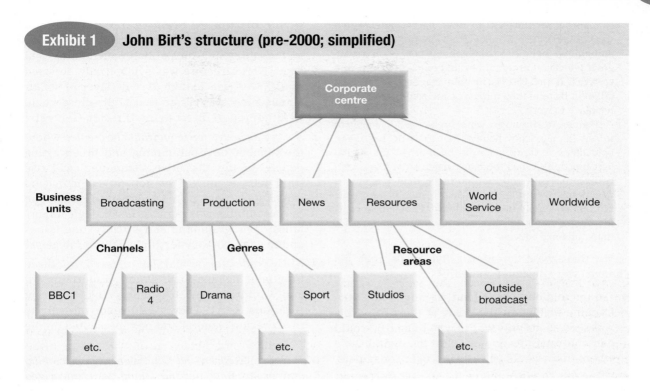

Structure prior to 2000

Dyke's, predecessor, John Birt, had established a structure for the BBC built on principles widely used in the public sector at the time. Birt created an internal market by separating the management responsibilities into divisions covering the three major aspects of broadcasting: Resources (such as studios, outside broadcast equipment, etc.), Programme Production and Programme Broadcasting (see Exhibit 1).

Each of these divisions had its own 'headquarters', several business units[1] and traded with each other in an internal market and also with third parties outside the BBC. For example, those broadcasting programmes would commission services both internally and from external production companies. The programme producers would hire infrastructure from BBC resources but also use external studios and equipment. They would sell their programmes both internally and to other broadcasters. BBC Resources would hire its facilities externally as well as to the BBC programme

producers. This structural arrangement was designed to bring some 'market discipline' to the organisation and to ensure that each of these three major areas was delivering value for money when tested against its competitors. In this BBC internal market John Birt saw the role of the centre as the regulator of the market – defining the 'rules' and setting up the systems and procedures to manage this internal market. This included targets and transfer prices between the 'customers' and 'suppliers'. But most things that might be centralised in other organisations were devolved and duplicated, such as financial management. Significantly, because of the very fast nature of news, that area of the BBC's activities was excluded from this internal market and both production and broadcast were managed as a single unit. Indeed, live news was broadcast as it was produced.

New goals for the future – Building One BBC

Greg Dyke wanted to change the old internal market structure. In his introduction to *Building One BBC*, he explained:

---

[1] For example, Programme Broadcasting included the various radio and television channels.

Our aim is for the BBC to be a place where people work collaboratively, enjoy their job and are inspired and united behind a common purpose – to create great television programmes and outstanding on-line services. If the BBC is to be a magnet for the best talent in Britain, then it must be an exciting and creative place to work. . . .

People are proud to work for the BBC, but want to see change. They believe that the BBC has taken bold steps towards a strong position in the digital age, but think it has too many managerial layers and costly processes, and that too much time is spent on negotiating within the BBC. As a result, as an organisation, we simply move too slowly. People also comment on a culture of division and of internal – rather than audience – focus.

He then went on to list five goals that his changes were designed to address:

- 'To put audiences first [and] creativity and programme making at the heart of the BBC.' This was seen as the only way in which the BBC could win and retain its audiences in the digital age – where there would be vast choice for consumers.

- 'Over time to raise the proportion of BBC funding that is spent on programmes from 76 per cent to 85 per cent.' Put another way, this meant reducing management overhead from 24 per cent to 15 per cent.

- 'To create a culture of collaboration, in which people work together to make great programmes.' The implication was that the current structure bred a divisive culture.

- 'To change the way the organisation works so that we can take decisions quickly and act decisively, while retaining sufficient checks and balances to avoid damaging mistakes.' This was contrasted with the way in which the digital world was spawning new entrants who acted decisively (such as Microsoft or AOL).

- 'To make sure that the BBC is properly equipped with the skills it needs to compete effectively in the digital world.' New skills were needed in things like cross-media brand building, distribution, gateway and rights management.

Greg Dyke's changes

Building One BBC went on to explain the nine changes that would help achieve these goals:

- *A flatter structure would be introduced* in which BBC Broadcast and BBC Production headquarters would disappear, bringing programme and channel interests closer to the centre of the BBC and resulting in a substantial reduction in overhead. This structure was symbolically depicted as a flower (see Exhibit 2). One layer of senior management was cut, so that 17 directors would in future report direct to the Director-General.

- *A more inclusive top team would be created* where the number of programming and broadcasting people on the Executive Committee[2] will rise from four to nine. The top 50–60 managers would join them in a Leadership Group. The purpose of this was to raise the strategic importance of programming and broadcasting issues and to gain more ownership of BBC strategies.

- *BBC Production would be replaced* by three programming divisions: Drama, Entertainment and Children (DEC); Factual and Learning (FL); and Sport. They would report directly to the Director-General and be represented on the Executive Committee.

- *In Sport, Children and Education[3] commissioning and programme making would be reintegrated to create a single BBC division for each area.* Previously it was only News that was integrated in this way. The reason for this change was that Sport was similar to News in having a high proportion of live coverage. Children and Education were felt to be two market segments where integrated management of all the products for that segment would be beneficial and give the managers 'cross-media capability'. For example, Sport would manage the online sports service as well as broadcasting of events.

- Similar arguments were used to justify *the reintegration of music commissioning and production in radio* (for Radios 1, 2, and 3).

- Over the whole corporation *a more collaborative commissioning process would be introduced, with programme guarantees in most areas*. This meant that broadcasters and programme makers would work more closely together in planning their activities over a sensible time period – such as a season or a year. It was an attempt to eliminate the worst of the internally competitive behaviour that the internal market had generated.

- *A* New Media *division would be set up*. BBC Online and Interactive TV would be brought

---

[2] The Executive Committee had 18 members.
[3] The latter two are units within DEC and FL respectively.

Exhibit 2 **Greg Dyke's new structure (2000)**

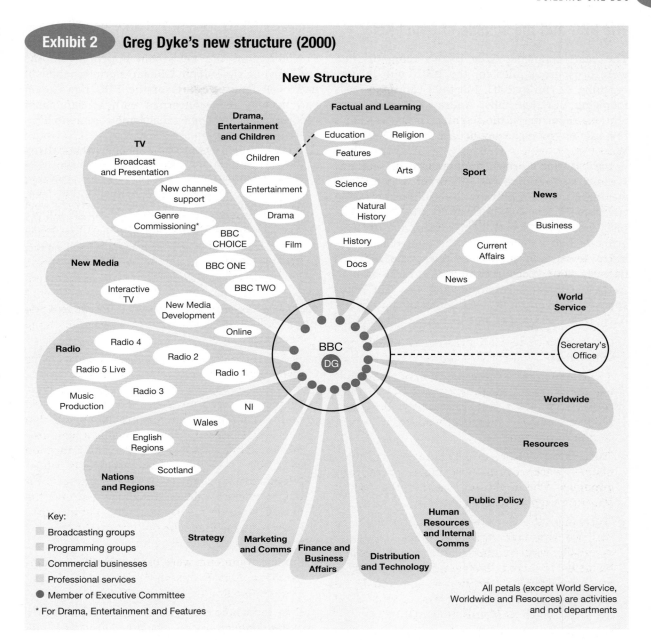

New Structure

Key:
- Broadcasting groups
- Programming groups
- Commercial businesses
- Professional services
- ● Member of Executive Committee
- * For Drama, Entertainment and Features

All petals (except World Service, Worldwide and Resources) are activities and not departments

together, as well as 'blue skies' developments. This was a response to merging technologies and a desire to ensure that the BBC had an integrated vision about new technologies and, more importantly, would develop and deliver a coherent rather than fragmented strategy.

- *Duplication of central and support functions would be eliminated (for example, Marketing, Strategy, Finance and Human Resources)*. If divisions needed support they would draw on resources provided centrally.

- *Internal trading would be simplified* with a reduction in business units from 190 to about 40. This would vastly simplify and reduce the cost of internal financial transactions between internal customers and suppliers in the internal market.

The BBC and the suicide of David Kelly

The years following Greg Dyke's reorganisation were prosperous ones for the BBC, with income reaching £2.7bn in 2003. But then came the crisis following BBC journalist Andrew Gilligan's contentious reporting of the scientist Dr David Kelly's remarks on the government case for the 2003 Iraq War.

Lord Hutton's official inquiry into the circumstances surrounding the death of David Kelly was prompted not only by the sad suicide of the government scientist, but also by the serious implications of Andrew Gilligan's claim that the government had knowingly led the United Kingdom into war on a false premise. When he reported in early 2004, Lord Hutton was critical of both Andrew Gilligan's reporting and the BBC's response to government accusations of inaccuracy. Greg Dyke was found not to have read Andrew Gilligan's report for a month after the broadcast, even while the BBC was vigorously defending it. Procedures in the newsroom appeared sloppy, and warning signs about Gilligan's professionalism had been ignored. Parts of the BBC news team had become over-concerned with sensationalist reporting. *The Economist* magazine commented:

> Mr Dyke cannot be expected to know about everything that happens in the BBC's sprawling 3,400 news empire. Furthermore, he is a television executive rather than an experienced journalist. But complacency followed by naivety was precisely not what the BBC needed at such a moment. . . . Ten times the size of a well-staffed broadsheet newspaper, the BBC's news team is too huge for hands-on editing from the top.

Sources
BBC Annual Reports; *Building One BBC* – April 2000; *The Economist*, 20 September (2003).

Sony Corporation (B) – more restructuring

Vivek Gupta and Indu Perepu

Between 1994 and 2003 Sony, the electronics and media giant, undertook several restructurings in attempts to turn round its poor financial performance. In March 2005 Howard Stringer became the company's first non-Japanese CEO and embarked on a further restructuring. But why should this one work?

● ● ●

On 27 October 2005, Japan-based Sony Corporation (Sony) announced its financial results for the second quarter ending 30 September 2005. The results showed that the trend of dismal financial performance at Sony was continuing. These results were announced after the declaration of the new restructuring plan in September 2005, under the new CEO Howard Stringer.

Sony had been subjected to a spate of restructuring programmes beginning in 1994, all of which had failed to revive its dwindling fortunes. Analysts attributed Sony's problems to the company's bloated cost structure, investments in non-core businesses and lack of new-age products.

Stringer's predecessor Nobuyuki Idei (Idei) became the CEO of Sony in June 1999. Idei stepped down from this position due to the failure of 'Transformation 60', a three-year restructuring plan through which he had proposed to improve significantly the financial performance of Sony. In September 2005, Stringer announced a restructuring plan for Sony. As part of the plan, Sony announced reduction of its global workforce by 6.6 per cent and sale of non-core assets valued at ¥120bn (≈€766m).

Background[1]

Sony was started in 1946 as Tokyo Tsuchin Kyogo by Masaru Ibuka and Akio Morita (Morita) in war-ravaged Japan. Initially, the company had 20 employees and capital of ¥190,000. Since its inception, Sony focused on product innovation and high quality.

Sony started off manufacturing telecommunications and measuring equipment and went on to manufacture transistor radios and tape recorders. In 1968, it introduced Trinitron Color TV, which was highly successful. Another highly successful product was the Walkman launched in 1979. Path-breaking products introduced by Sony included the world's first CD player (1982), Camcorder (1982), Discman portable CD player (1984), PlayStation (1994) and Digital Handycam (1995). Sony introduced several other products like home electronic equipment and 3.5 inch floppy disks.

From the beginning of the 1990s, in spite of a moderate increase in its operating revenues, the operating income and net income of Sony witnessed a decline. After the restructuring of electronics business in 1994 implemented by CEO Norio Ohga (Ohga), the company's performance deteriorated further and Sony reported a loss of ¥293.36bn in 1995. This led to another round of restructuring in 1996, in which Sony was organised into a 10-company structure. However, this restructuring did not lead to a sustainable improvement in the company's financial performance and for the financial year 1998–1999 the net income dropped by 19.4 per cent.

Another round of restructuring was proposed in 1999 in order to enable Sony to exploit the opportunities offered by the Internet. Though some of its products like the PlayStation were profitable, a

---

[1] Readers interested in more detail should look at the first Sony case study in the 7th edition of *Exploring Corporate Strategy* (pp. 924–936). Tutors can find this in the Classic Case Collection on the website.

This case was prepared by Professor Vivek Gupta, Senior Faculty Member, and Ms Indu Perepu, Senior Faculty Associate, at the ICFAI Centre for Management Research (ICMR), Hyderabad. It is intended as a basis of class discussion and not as an illustration of good or bad practice. © 2006, ICMR. Not to be reproduced or quoted without permission. Sony (A) case is held in the Classic Cases collection on the website and is accessible for reference.

majority of its other businesses like electronics, movies, mobile telecommunications and personal computers were not performing well. For fiscal 1999–2000, Sony's net income fell to ¥121.83bn, a decline of over ¥58bn compared with the previous year.

With none of the restructuring efforts proving fruitful, Sony decided to revamp its top management. In 1999, Idei became the Chairman and CEO of Sony and the Head of the company's PC division, while Kunitake Ando was made President. During 2000–2001, despite the increase in revenue due to higher sales of the PlayStation, net income dropped to ¥16.75bn from ¥121.83bn in the previous year. At this juncture, Idei came up with another round of organisational restructuring in 2001. This plan aimed at transforming Sony into a broadband network solutions company.

Sony's operating income declined by 40.3 per cent in 2001–2002, while revenues increased by 3.6 per cent. In April 2003, Sony presented its quarterly results, posting a quarterly loss of US$970m. In June 2003, Sony reported a net profit of ¥9.3m, which was 98 per cent lower than the profit reported in the corresponding quarter in 2002. In October 2003, Idei came up with yet another restructuring plan called 'Transformation 60'.

Transformation 60

Transformation 60 was a three-year restructuring plan, which required Sony to lay off 13 per cent of its workforce or about 20,000 people by March 2006. Sony planned to reduce costs by downsizing and consolidating manufacturing, distribution, customer service facilities and also by streamlining procurement. Through these efforts, Sony aimed to achieve cost savings of ¥300bn by March 2006. By Sony's 60th anniversary in 2006, the company aimed at achieving a profit margin of 10 per cent. The key underlying theme was the need to create convergence between separate products. For example, in the electronics business, converging television and games; in entertainment, converging movies, music and games; and so on. To enable convergence a new organisational structure was created (see Exhibit 1). The company was reorganised into seven business entities – four network companies and three business groups. Exhibit 2 shows the responsibilities of each of these business units.

The implications

The above plans were not successful mainly due to the significant drop in sales of conventional

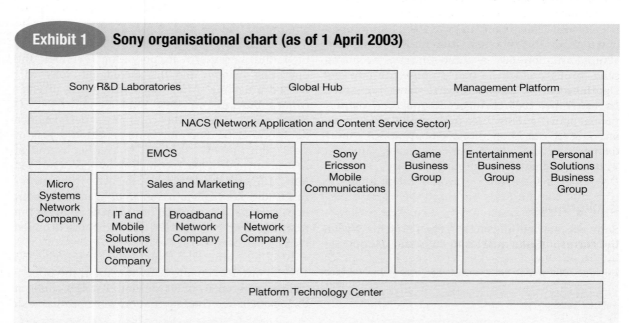

Exhibit 1 **Sony organisational chart (as of 1 April 2003)**

| Sony R&D Laboratories | Global Hub | Management Platform |

NACS (Network Application and Content Service Sector)

EMCS — Micro Systems Network Company — Sales and Marketing — IT and Mobile Solutions Network Company — Broadband Network Company — Home Network Company — Sony Ericsson Mobile Communications — Game Business Group — Entertainment Business Group — Personal Solutions Business Group

Platform Technology Center

Source: 'Sony announces executive appointments and organizational reforms effective as of April 01, 2003', www.sony.net, 31 March 2003.

| Exhibit 2 | Responsibilities of network companies and business groups (2003) |

No.	Network company/business group	Responsibility
1	Home Network Company	To create a new home environment with networked electronic devices centred on next-generation TV
2	Broadband Network Company	Development of next-generation electronics devices and linkages to game devices
3	IT and Mobile Solutions Network Company	To realise a connected world with PC and mobile devices and strengthen the B2B solutions business
4	Micro Systems Network Company	To enhance key devices and modules as core components of attractive set products
5	Game Business Group	To promote game businesses for the broadband era
6	Entertainment Business Group	To develop entertainment content businesses based on pictures and music and develop a new content business model for the network era
7	Personal Solutions Business Group	To integrate various business units providing services based on direct contact with customers (finance, retail, etc.). To strengthen synergies and develop attractive new business models for customers through the application of IT

Source: 'Sony announces executive appointments and organizational reforms effective as of April 1, 2003', www.sony.net, 31 March 2003.

televisions and portable audio products. Sony's electronics business witnessed losses for two consecutive years. The decline in sales of Sony's electronics products was prominent in Japan, where the demand for Vaio personal computers and cathode-ray-tube televisions fell significantly. The games division also did not fare well with sales of PlayStation 2 consoles falling rapidly. By December 2004, Sony's films division registered growth due to DVD and VHS sales of *Spiderman II* and *Seinfeld*. PlayStation Portable (PSP), which was released in December 2004, witnessed robust demand.

By the time Sony announced its October–December 2004 results, it was evident that the company was far from reaching the goals envisaged in its Transformation 60 plan. The revenues were 7.5 per cent lower than the revenues during the corresponding quarter in 2003 and the operating income had eroded by 13 per cent. Sony's profit margins for fiscal 2004–2005 were at 1.6 per cent, far lower than the 10 per cent that Sony planned to achieve by 2006.

Stringer becomes CEO

At this juncture, in March 2005, Stringer became the first non-Japanese CEO to lead Sony in its six-decade history. During the five years before he took charge as CEO and President, Sony's stock price had eroded by 75 per cent. Stringer was head of Sony's North American business and was known for drastic cost-cutting measures; he had reduced the workforce by 9,000 in Sony US. He played a major role in a group of private equity investors led by Sony acquiring MGM in September 2004.

Stringer brought with him a new leadership style. On the whole, he felt that being an outsider was an advantage. According to Stringer:

> In the end, there was an advantage to being an outsider. Sony is built up on a web of interpersonal relationships that go back to the dawn of history. The old boys never go away. But that also makes it very difficult for the insider who has to attack the problems of too much management, and turning that around.

There was overall optimism in Sony about Stringer's leadership, as one employee commented.

'We've been blasted the last couple of years for not having a Michael Dell in charge. Here is the face and voice of a powerful figure running a powerful company.'

Challenges for Sony

Stringer identified five main challenges for Sony. These were: getting rid of the 'silo' culture in Sony, obtaining profitability across businesses, making products in line with industry standard technologies, improving the competences in software and services, and divesting non-strategic assets.

Sony's movies, music and electronics businesses were facing internal conflicts. The content business wanted to protect its content, forcing device manufacturers to introduce products which prevented content from being pirated. The units operated with incompatible agendas. When the gadgets division wanted to manufacture digital music players that could play in the MP3 format, the music division did not agree. Sony's divisions were unable to work in tandem even when it was to their mutual advantage. For example, Sony was active in making movies and also in manufacturing devices that played the movies but was not able to integrate them, as Apple had done with the iPod and iTunes.

New strategies

On 22 September 2005, Sony announced a new strategy to revive its dwindling fortunes. The strategy concentrated mainly on three sectors – electronics, games and entertainment. The electronics business of Sony was to be revitalised through a series of structural reforms (see below) coupled with a growth strategy aimed at achieving group sales of ¥8,000bn by 2008. Sony aimed at achieving a profit margin of 5 per cent and cost reduction amounting to ¥200bn by the end of fiscal 2007–2008.

Products and markets

Sony aimed at regaining its leading position in the mobile audio devices market and also to establish itself in the portable video market. In the games business, Sony planned to introduce the PlayStation 3 and position it as the ultimate portable entertainment player, through which Sony aimed at increasing its market share in the computer entertainment market. Sony was increasingly opting for internally sourced games software. The company also aimed at achieving increased collaboration among different sectors like games, entertainment and software. According to Stringer, 'These products are a few of our weapons against commoditization.' Under the new strategy, Sony aimed at reviving the brand 'Sony'. With the new products that Sony was planning to introduce, a person with a Sony Walkman, mobile phone or portable PlayStation could watch movies, listen to music and play video games anywhere, anytime.

Sony Pictures Entertainment (SPE) was involved in theatrical releases, television licensing and DVD sales. The digital content assets of SPE were expected to grow with the introduction of new media like UMD and Blu-ray disc. SPE planned to digitise the MGM library. In the music division, the Sony BMG joint venture was going from strength to strength and digital distribution was being explored. Sony was also looking at developing short-form video content for mobile phones. In mobile phones, Sony Ericsson was developing products to help Sony put its entertainment assets to best use. One such product on the anvil was the Walkman phone. In 2005, the financial services division of Sony posted strong results.

Reducing costs

Sony planned to achieve cost reductions by reducing business categories and product models. It considered downsizing and initiating disposal of assets in 15 business categories. The number of product models was to be reduced by 20 per cent and the number of manufacturing sites from 65 to 54. Sony also planned to dispose of real estate, stock and non-core assets amounting to ¥120bn by the end of fiscal 2007. All these changes were expected to reduce the headcount by 10,000 globally, of which 4,000 would be in Japan. The company was expected to recover the cost of restructuring by 2008.

Focusing resources on high-growth businesses

Sony started focusing on high-growth businesses such as HD products, mobile products and semiconductor/key component devices, which were built around customer-driven technologies. It focused on semiconductors, specifically in gaming and imaging. In key components, innovative technologies for system LSIs, next-generation displays and Blu-ray-disc-related products were being developed. In order to maintain user interfaces, the software development business was strengthened by establishing a technology development group. By the end of fiscal 2005–2006, Sony aimed at establishing software development facilities in China and the USA.

New organisational structure (2005)

On 7 March 2005, Sony announced a new organisational structure (see Exhibit 3). Stringer assumed responsibility as Chairman, Group CEO and Representative Corporate Executive Officer, Sony Corporation, to run Sony's overall group business operations. He continued to be the Head of the Entertainment Business Group and Head of Sony Corporation of America. Ryoji Chubachi (Chubachi) was elected as Representative Corporate Executive Officer, President of Sony and CEO of the Electronics Business Group of the company. Katsumi Ihara assumed the role of Representative Corporate Executive Officer, Executive Deputy President and Group CFO, and would also oversee financial matters and support Stringer and Chubachi in corporate strategy and resource allocation.

When announcing the restructuring plans, Stringer said:

> We are battling on many fronts against many competitors, a number of whom have at times proved more agile and more nimble. We can and will compete vigorously. We are going to achieve our goals by breaking down the existing silo walls and eliminating the highly decentralized structure we've maintained in the past.

Sony adopted the new organisational structure from 1 October 2005. Sony was reorganised into five business groups, which included the Electronics Business, the Games Business Group, the Entertainment Business Group, the Personal Solutions Business Group and the Sony Financial Holdings

Exhibit 3   Sony organisational chart (as of October 2005)

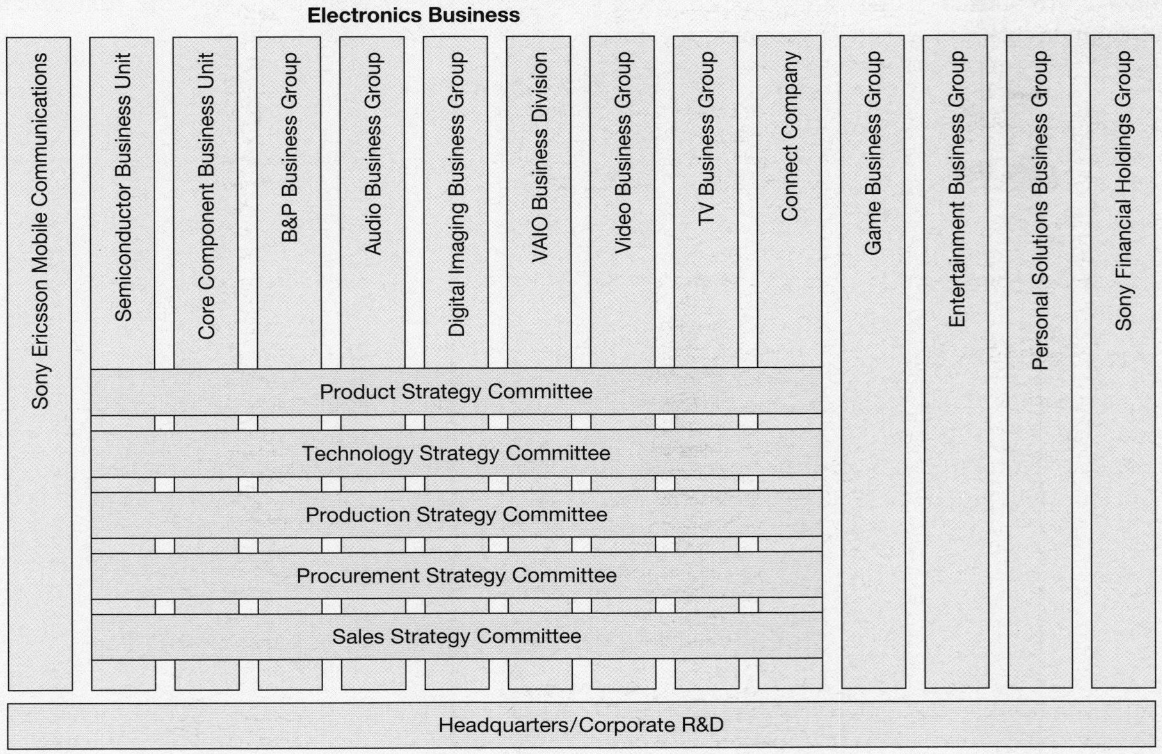

Source: www.sony.net.

Group. Through the new structure Sony expected to achieve coordination across different areas including planning, technology, procurement, manufacturing, sales and marketing.

Restructuring electronics

The Electronics Business was brought under the purview of Electronics CEO, Ryoji Chubachi. Exhibit 3 also shows various business units within the Electronics Business. On Sony's strategy for this business, Chubachi emphasised that the products, the technology and the organisation were all equally responsible for the downturn of Sony's electronics business.

The electronics division had a Product Strategy Committee headed by Nakagawa to look at things from the customer's viewpoint. The Sales Strategy Committee and Production Strategy Committee were headed by Chubachi while the Procurement Strategy Committee was led by Ihara. Matters of technology were looked after by Kimura, who controlled the Technology Strategy Committee.

To improve the technology, Sony planned to integrate internally sourced components with key products. It started using standardised design and components and aimed at reducing the time needed to come up with new designs. In the field of production materials, it concentrated on procuring from specific suppliers.

In the electronics division, television, digital imaging, DVD recorders and portable audio were the areas that Sony was looking into to establish itself as the leading player in the market. These efforts were expected to be helped by Sony's plans to develop a semiconductor and key components business. To turn around the television business, Sony planned to increase the number of internally sourced components, centralise engineering functions and reduce and consolidate the manufacturing sites. The company aimed at making the television business profitable by the second half of 2006.

Sony planned to invest around ¥340bn in the chip business over a span of two years. A new division, being developed in association with IBM and Toshiba Corporation, was created for the cell chip. Stringer was of the view that focusing on select products would help Sony regain its leading position in the consumer electronics industry. Cell chips were expected to be used in high-definition televisions, personal video recorders and other devices. The PlayStation 3 was the first product where cell chips were used.

Web Reservations International: executing a global footprint

James A. Cunningham and William Golden

The case describes the market growth of Web Reservations International, an Irish SME company, which is a market leader in the budget, youth and independent travel (BYIT) market through its online reservation system and business model. The case describes the development of the company from its inception through organic growth and recent acquisitions.

• • •

The world of independent travelling offers great expectations, new life experiences and opportunities to make new friends. For the independent traveller hostels provide low-cost accommodation and are used as key staging bases to explore new countries and continents. Hostels in addition to accommodation can provide a range of services including bar, bike hire, common room, free airport pick-up, guest kitchens, internal access, luggage storage and travel information desk.

Tom Kennedy owned the Avalon House Hostel in Dublin, Ireland. In the mid-1990s in an effort to make the business more efficient he contracted Ray Nolan, an IT specialist, a self-taught computer programmer and owner of Raven Computing, to develop a software program which would allow his hostel to manage the check-in and check-out processes. Following the successful installation of the software at Avalon House Hostel Nolan resold the reservations management system as *Backpack* to a number of hostels.

In 1999 Ray Nolan and Tom Kennedy founded privately owned Web Reservations International (WRI) and created an online reservation site for hostel bookings – www.hostelworld.com. By 2006 WRI employed over 75 people and was the biggest global provider of confirmed online reservations for the budget accommodation sector. The company's revenue grew by 1,436 per cent from 2000 to 2002 compared with the industry average of 269 per cent for the top 50 technology companies in Ireland. Turnover in 2003 was €7m with a profit of €1.8m on the basis of having handled bookings worth about €70m. By 2005, turnover reached €28.5m and pre-tax profit rose to €12.5m.

Budget, youth and independent travel (BYIT) market

Increasingly, the trend among travellers is to bypass traditional channels to organise holiday and business travel, particularly in the US market, where online travel booking revenue was worth $46bn (€37bn) in 2003 or 20 per cent of the total US travel revenue. Some industry analysts forecast this to grow to $91bn or 33 per cent of total US travel revenue by 2009 as more travellers use online booking systems and as direct suppliers and third-party organisations vie for customers.

The proportion of international tourists which are young travellers (15–24 year olds) grew from 14.6 per cent in 1980 to 20 per cent in 2001 and the

This case was prepared by Dr James A. Cunningham, Senior Lecturer in Strategy Management and Dr William Golden, Senior Lecturer in Information Systems at the J.E. Cairnes Graduate School of Business & Public Policy, National University of Ireland Galway, Ireland. It is intended as a basis of class discussion and not as an illustration of good or bad practice. © James A. Cunningham and William Golden 2007. Not to be reproduced or quoted without permission.

share was forecast to reach 25 per cent by 2005.[1] The BYIT market comprises students, youths, backpackers and independent travellers. They typically are web-savvy, value conscious, tend to take extended vacations and set the travel trends for the business travellers of the future.

Online travel companies, because of the low prices, low commission and margins and the high cost of traditional booking systems, have neglected the BYIT sector. These traditional booking systems, called Global Distribution Systems (GDS), provide pre-Internet travel booking systems. However, the high cost of installing and using GDS makes them unsuitable for both BYIT product providers and travel companies. In comparison, WRI's online booking system provides a web-only, low-cost booking system, effectively becoming the GDS of the BYIT sector.

Traditionally, the value of the market was vastly underestimated as hostel bookings' value ranged from €10 to €20 with a number of people sharing a room, but as Nolan points out: 'It's one of the hidden facts about the tourist industry. Hostels are a very profitable business.' The entire market has changed in many ways, making the Internet an obvious tool for reaching this global market. No longer is the BYIT market comprised of poor students checking out the cheapest possible holidays. Nowadays, hostellers and budget travellers are often older people or families, and hostels now offer single and family rooms to cater to this market, in addition to multi-bed dormitories. Hostellers and backpackers carry credit cards and typically go online daily in internet cafés, making online booking easy. Moreover, they demand a more structured travel experience, seeking outdoor adventure or cultural activities and tours. WRI's online reservation system and websites cater for this demand. In addition, hostellers spend plenty of money in restaurants rather than cook in a communal hostel kitchen. Reflecting on these market changes, Kennedy, the co-founder of WRI, notes:

> A few years ago, a hostel would have been full of people cooking their pasta or lentils, and they would all arrive by bike. Now everyone arrives by taxi from the ferry or airport and they all head into town for dinner.

The changes in the BYIT market coupled with the successful redevelopment of the *Backpack* software and the hostelworld.com and other related websites afforded WRI a dominant position in this

market. Both Nolan and Kennedy realised that, while it was time consuming and labour intensive for an individual hostel to deal with e-mails and booking software, an automated booking service for hundreds or thousands of hostels could be the basis of a solid business. As Nolan states: 'Budget tourism was totally bypassed by technology until we came along. . . . It was not serviced online before we existed. We created the industry.' In the early 1990s the 15,000 hostels worldwide generally ran their own individual websites, with no credit card booking facilities. Typically hostel users may spend less per night but go away for longer periods of time and therefore spend more money than average travellers. By 2003 WRI had built relationships with 5,000 hostels and was selling rooms on their behalf through an integrated Internet reservation system. This grew to over 12,000 hostels by 2006.

The product and websites

The core product offered to individual hostels is *Backpack* – a reservation management system for the youth hostels and budget accommodation. The software is designed to run on PCs running Microsoft Windows. Each hostel installs the software onto its PC and through a modem connection it integrates fully with WRI websites which allow hostel owners to upload availability and download bookings. In addition, the software provides a complete bed management system with functionality which includes the ability to browse for availability, search for guests, review pending arrivals and set room accommodation allocations. Financial functionality is also included, which allows the viewing and printing of invoices, letters and vouchers and the generation of over 40 different reports that assist in the management of the accommodation centre. These reports include end-of-shift payment analysis, bookings by booking source, income analysis, stock analysis and credit card pre-authorisation.

One example of the advanced functionality of the software is its ability to enable hostels to maintain accounts for different travel agents. Beds can be allocated to agents, and may not be booked by regular guests. That is, the agreed agent will override the hostel rack rate and cannot be changed. As guests arrive with agent vouchers, they are taken as a form of payment. At the same time an invoice is created to be sent to the travel agent, and the agents' debtors account is updated. Subsequently

___
[1] www.world-tourism.org.

Exhibit 1 — Hostelworld.com reservation details

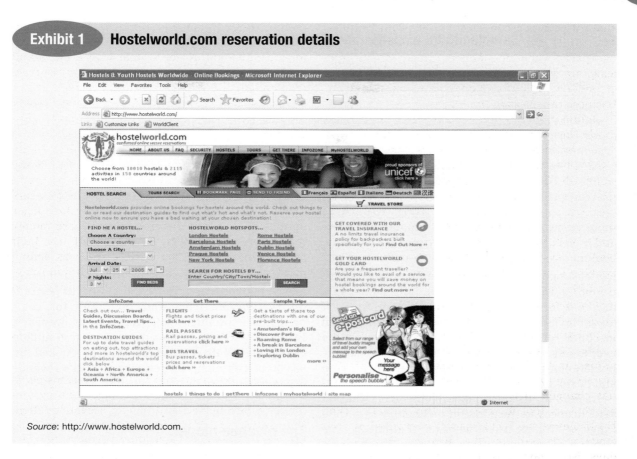

Source: http://www.hostelworld.com.

agent invoice reports, statements, payment history may be produced from the debtors ledger.

WRI's main site – www.hostelworld.com – allows visitors to choose a destination or hostel, select an arrival date and the duration of their stay, and quotes prices in whichever currency they wish to use, making the booking procedure extremely straightforward. Once a hostel has been selected, detailed information is available on the hostel's location, photographs of the exterior and interior, currency converter room reviews and all other relevant information for the chosen accommodation (see Exhibit 1). As well as the booking facility, WRI provides guides to the various continents, countries and cities where hostels are located. City guides provide lists of pubs, clubs, attractions and also an interactive map to locate each one and contain information on transport, weather, opening hours, public holidays, tourist offices, etc. In essence WRI websites provide all the necessary information travellers need to know before booking accommodation.

Hostelworld.com is aimed at the backpacker and student market and attracts over 12 million visitors annually. However, this is not the company's only site. It also operates and runs a number of hostel sites for city, country and continent sites, such as hosteldublin.com, hosteleurope.com. Another website is trav.com which offers budget accommodation, tours, activities, transport, travel insurance and ancillary products for the BYIT market. Things2do.com provides online booking and information for adventure activities, sightseeing tours, events and transport as well as accommodation including hostels, budget hotels and guesthouses. Linked to the BYIT market focus WRI runs www.insureandtravel.com which sells online insurance policies for backpackers and student travellers. WRI runs 500 websites targeted at the BYIT market (see Exhibit 2). The online service confirms online reservations for budget accommodation and other complementary travel products.

The purpose of having over 500 individual sites is to ensure that anybody searching for a hostel will ultimately land on a WRI site. The success of this strategy can be seen in the fact that sites controlled by WRI dominate any Google search for hostel accommodation in any major town or city in the world. This Internet-based marketing strategy is consistent with the emphasis of being a

Exhibit 2	Sample of WRI websites and affiliate licences

Flagship websites	Affiliate licences
www.hostelworld.com	www.studentuniverse.com
www.trav.com	www.lonelyplanet.com
www.things2do.com	www.ryanair.com
www.discounthotels-world.com	www.flybe.com
www.insureandtravel.com	www.letsgo.com
www.hostels.com	www.raileurope.com
	www.kasbah.com
	www.ebookers.com

Source: WRI.

low-cost operator. WRI uses search engine optimisation and it presents the same information in a different format depending on the website. So if an online user is looking for hostel accommodation in South Africa, a search engine might direct the user to any one of four sites that WRI own, namely hosteljohannesburg.com, hostelsouthafrica.com and hostelafrica.com

In pursing its dominance of the BYIT market WRI licences its reservation technology to a wide range of affiliate travel websites (Exhibit 2). The number of affiliates using WRI's online booking technology reached 1,000 by early 2006. WRI has targeted the travel agent market overlooked by many industry players in the dot.com rush. WRI has established a Travel Agent Extranet System for this market coupled with a loyalty card. This means that travel agents do not have to contract individual rates, invoice the providers and they have direct access to worldwide budget accommodation. As Kennedy stated in 2001: 'We have developed the software to benefit travel agents and affiliates such as Rough Guide and Time Out, which can offer a worldwide reach to accommodation and share in the commission we can generate.'[2]

WRI also provides a facility for tour/activity providers which allows them to advertise their offerings and allows customers to book them online. The WRI reservation system is being used by customers to book not just their hostel room, but also other elements of their holiday. Such activities may include museum tickets, exhibitions, city tours, bungee jumping, rafting, abseiling, skydiving, etc. WRI takes an annual fee ($500 per year for

one listing, $800 per year for two to four listings and $1,000 for five or more tours) and 10 per cent reservation fee from tour operators for complementary products sold through its websites. By 2006, WRI's websites attracted up to 6 million visitors a month and these visitors booked up 80,000 beds a night; 50 per cent of WRI's revenue is generated from its own websites.

The revenue model

As Nolan stated in 2004: 'WRI's model is simple: it handles hostel bookings through a huge network of websites, and makes its money by holding onto the deposit paid for the accommodation.'[3] When using WRI's websites travellers are told immediately if a hostel has space, which they can then book and reserve straight away by having a 10 per cent deposit and small booking fee charged to a credit card. WRI offers the rooms at the price the hostel charges, making its money by keeping the 10 per cent charge and the fee. The margins may be very small on a typical €10 hostel bed, but with 8,000 hostels in nearly 160 countries and 460 cities, WRI does very well on volume. WRI has not altered the revenue model for industry participants, but has provided a dominant electronic market forum for this international market. Coupled with international coverage, as Nolan described: 'When we sell a ticket, we are automatically out of the game and because we have hostels in both the southern and the northern hemispheres, we don't have a slow season.' Central to this is WRI's ability to keep

---

[2] *Travel Trade Gazette UK & Ireland*, 19 November, p. 41 (2001).

[3] Funding values Dublin tech firm at over $100 million, Gavin Daly, *Sunday Business Post*, 18 April (2004).

the cost base low and communications to a minimum. The business is entirely Internet based, and the premise is that if an employee has to lay a finger on a booking, WRI loses money. Given this premise and the increase in sales volume since 2000, the cost of making €1 revenue has fallen from €2.56 to 41 cents.

Competition

In April 2003, Nolan stated: 'We see Travelocity and Expedia as our peers. We are not afraid of them. They are huge billion dollar companies but our technology is every bit as good as theirs. In fact, our booking process is probably simpler.'[4] The competition for WRI breaks into two segments: competitors that compete in the accommodation booking market and online reservation competitors that offer hostel and budget accommodation.

General accommodation booking companies

Expedia, Travelocity and Orbitz were the top three online travel agencies ranked by US visitors in April 2005 (Nielsen/NetRatings Netview and Mega-View Travel, 2005). Expedia (www.expedia.com) is ranked as the fourth largest travel agency in the USA and is a wholly owned subsidiary of IAC/InterActiveCorp listed on the NASDAQ. Expedia continues to develop its Expert Searching and Pricing (ESP) technology which provides one of the most comprehensive flight options available online. ESP also allows customers to dynamically build complete trips that combine flights, special rate accommodation, transportation and destination activities. Expedia operates Classic Custom Vacations, a leading distributor of premiere vacation packages to destinations such as Hawaii, Mexico, Europe and the Caribbean. In addition, it operates a corporate travel agency and, through other subsidiaries such as Travelscape, it cross-sells to third parties on a private label basis. The gross bookings for Expedia in the first quarter for 2004 were $2,672m, and its unique visitors per month is in excess of 16 million with a visitor conversion rate of 5 per cent. The company has won many industry awards for its quality and user

experiences, marketing materials, PR, technology (an average transaction speed of 19.54 seconds), superior offers, service and security.

The Appendix gives similar details for Travelocity and Orbitz.

Hostel accommodation booking companies

Competitors that compete directly with WRI include hostelbookers, hostelmania and mobissimo. Hostelbookers (www.hostelbookers.com) is privately owned and was developed by FPL Webshows, which designs, builds and operates both simple and advanced websites as well as online interactive trade shows in a number of market sectors, and London Web Communications, which is also hosting the site as FPL's preferred ISP. Their marketing focus is centred on the theme 'Great Hostels, Free Booking, No Worries'. Unlike its competitors, hostelbookers does not charge a booking fee to use its services and it only debits customers the deposit required to guarantee bookings.

Hostelmania (www.hostelmania.com), founded by three backpackers in 2004, operates from offices in Spain, Gibraltar and the UK and employs 20 staff. Its marketing focus is centred on making worldwide hostel reservations easy. It operates a similar revenue model as WRI.

Market expansion and growth

Half of this is in the technology, and half of it is in the unbelievable brand we have. . . . It is outrageous what we have done.

(Ray Nolan in 2006)

Nolan and Kennedy since the foundation of the business were keen to become dominant players in the BYIT market through organic growth and acquisitions. Hostels.com has been in operation since 1994 and had a well-established brand name in the market, listing over 6,000 hostels worldwide. Hostels.com received numerous industry awards (Yahoo Internet Life, CNET EZ Connect) and had over 10 million page requests per month for a variety of services including hostel accommodation, rail and airline tickets, car hire and travel guidebooks.

In a bold strategic move WRI acquired hostels.com in January 2003. It was a key player in

---

[4] Hostels to Fortune, Gavin Daly, *Sunday Business Post*, 9 November (2003).

the BYIT market and was a good fit with WRI in relation to market and product fit. Further acquisitions followed which included WRI acquiring Hostels of Europe which provided marketing support and operated a website featuring 450 hostels throughout Europe in early 2004. In March 2005 it acquired WorldRes, a US booking business. In tandem with these acquisitions, Summit Partners (www.summitpartners.com), a leading private equity and venture capital firm, bought an equity stake in WRI for an undisclosed figure.

Future challenge

The main challenge is how WRI would continue to maintain its dominant position in the BYIT market and transfer its technology and business model to the low-cost hotels market or other sectors of the travel industry. The issue of trust and security in relation to its over 500 websites and affiliate programmes could become an issue in the future given the lack of an overall brand for WRI. The cost of making €1 of revenue had fallen from €2.56 in 1999 to 41 cents in 2003 and was forecasted to drop by another 20 cents in the next few years.

On the technology front backpackers are more technologically savvy according to a WRI survey, with 80 per cent carrying a mobile phone and an increasing number taking laptops on trips. Future investment in technology development is a must given the industry model software is moving towards a new revenue model. Software as a service is the new business model. In addition, trends in social networking pose challenges for all web service providers. MySpace, Bebo, Facebook have all seen dramatic rise in activities and market valuations. The ongoing risk of imitators continues to be a challenge but Nolan dismisses this challenge as:

> This is a sizable business that is doing great things – and we are about to do a lot more. This company is on fire with this new, new thing. There are other companies skirting around the edges of what we are doing, but there is only one company in the world that can do it – and that is us.

APPENDIX
Further details about Travelocity and Orbitz

Travelocity (www.travelocity.com) distributes travel-related products and services directly to business and leisure customers through its branded website, call centres and websites owned by its supplier and distribution partners, such as Yahoo!, Travel, America Online, American Express, US Airways. In 2003, Travelocity launched a new technology platform called *TotalTrip* which enables it to market higher-margin travel products, and in the third quarter of 2004 it launched the *Travelocity Business* platform, which integrates and automates the corporate travel reservation process from beginning to end. By year end 2003 revenues had increased by 16.5 per cent from $339m to $395m, while transaction revenue increased by $74m or 34.4 per cent. Its revenue mix consisted of stand-alone hotel revenue (50 per cent under own merchant model), package trip revenue, cruise and car revenue, in addition to advertising. Travelocity's unique audience is in excess of 11 million with a visitor conversion rate of 3 per cent. In the last quarter of 2004 Travelocity acquired direct control of *Travelocity Europe*, which it had partially owned, and the company intends to continue the joint venture with The Otto Group in the German market. The strategy for Travelocity going forward is to grow revenue from its merchant model hotel, last minute packaging, develop the appeal of *Travelocity Business*, to invest in new opportunities in European and Asian markets and develop the *TotalTrip* package.

Orbtiz (www.orbitz.com) was founded by American, Continental, Delta, Northwest and United airlines. In September 2004 Cendant Corporation acquired it in a $1.2bn deal. Cendant Corporation is a US-based conglomerate, which has a diversified portfolio of business in four main areas: real estate franchises and brokerage (Century 21 Coldwell Banker), hospitality services (Ramada, Days Inn, Travelodge), travel distribution services (Galileo, Orbitz, CheapTicket.com) and supplier services which operate and franchise Avis and Budget vehicle rental businesses. The strategic focus of Cendant is to simplify their business mix and focus solely on core travel and real estate businesses. Orbitz offers a wide selection of low airfares, as well as deals on lodging, car rentals, cruises, leisure packages and other travel. Orbitz's inventory includes more than 455 airlines, tens of thousands of accommodation properties worldwide and 22 rental car companies. To complement its product offering Orbitz has invested in technology such as its automated travel alerts via mobile phone, pager, PDA, or e-mail and through its customer care, which constantly monitors travel conditions for all its travellers and provides real-time information to its customers. Orbitz is estimated to have a unique audience in excess of 11 million with a visitor conversion rate of 4 per cent.

NHS Direct – a gateway to health

Alex Murdock

The National Health Service (NHS) in the United Kingdom is one of the largest public sector organisations of its kind in the world. It is the largest single employer in the United Kingdom. Making major change in such an organisation is challenging and often frustratingly slow. The case study is concerned with how resourcing issues can enable or frustrate the success of strategy.

NHS Direct has been a leading example of the new modernised NHS based around the needs of patients. In five years it has grown from a small pilot scheme to a unique national service.

(Recruitment Material for NHS Direct)

In May 2006 The *Guardian* Newspaper reported that NHS Direct, the nurse-led health helpline in England and Wales, planned to axe more than 1,000 staff in a comprehensive restructuring of branches and business objectives. It was to close 12 call centres across England and shed more than a quarter of the workforce to avert a forecast £15m [€22m] deficit for 2006–07.[1]

Scarcely a month or so later Audit Scotland, the body which audits NHS 24, the Scottish equivalent of NHS Direct, reported positively on the way in which NHS 24 in Scotland had opened up more local call centres and noted some concerns about whether the service would recruit more staff to operate them.

NHS Direct and its Scottish equivalent, NHS 24, provide people with help and advice on health issues over the telephone. It also offers Internet-based services and covers emergency out-of-hours services. The original model of a telephone helpline had thus been considerably extended.

Every month NHS Direct and NHS Direct Online each handle over 500,000 telephone calls and online visits respectively. This probably makes it the largest e-health service in the world. It had added Digital TV to its provision which already has about 500,000 contacts per month.[2] So the service had grown in both remit and complexity.

Although there were differences in operation and governance of NHS Direct and NHS 24 the service needed to function on a national level in respect of policies, networks, systems, performance and planning. The government regarded it as a national 'brand' which contributed to the development of the NHS.

The introduction of NHS Direct[3]

NHS Direct was the first step in a process that seeks to reconfigure radically the delivery of health care services and health care information. It provided both opportunities and challenges. The UK government hoped that NHS Direct would become a well-used and well-regarded '24×7' gateway to the NHS from people's own homes.

NHS Direct call centres recruited nurses with a range of experience in hospital and community settings. About 60 per cent of the nurses worked part time for the service – often combining it with work elsewhere in the NHS. The provision of flexible hours and, in one case, a workplace crèche

[1] NHS Direct dispute the *Guardian* figures.

[2] *Source*: NHS Direct Annual Report and Accounts 2006.
[3] The author acknowledges J.F. Munro *et al.*, 'Evaluation of NHS Direct first wave sites', 2nd Interim Report to Dept of Health, March 2000, as a background source.

---

also had a positive impact on staff recruitment. A national competency framework had been developed together with a planned rotation of staff between call centres and walk in centres.

NHS Direct was supported by considerable technology including extensive use of diagnostic software which prompted advisors to ask particular questions of callers and suggested possible diagnoses and recommended action.

The NHS and NHS Direct: size, finance and growth projections

The NHS is one of the largest public sector organisations in Europe. In September 2004 there were over 1.3 million staff in the NHS Hospital and Community Health Services The size and workforce trends are shown in the Appendix.

Chancellor Gordon Brown in his 2006 budget identified NHS expenditure as £96bn. This made it the second biggest area of government spending after social security. Furthermore NHS spending is planned to increase further to over £100bn in 2007–2008 (see Exhibit 1).

The proportion of GDP spent on the NHS will thus converge on the (higher) proportion of GDP spent on health by most other European countries.

In 2001 a university study assessed the cost of an NHS Direct call and calculated the impact on subsequent usage of other services. This suggested that NHS Direct saved about 45 per cent of its running costs through reduced usage of other services (see Exhibit 2).

Exhibit 1 **Projected NHS spending and share of gross domestic product (GDP)**

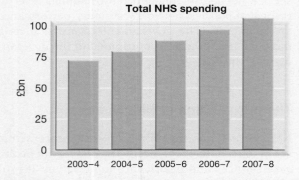 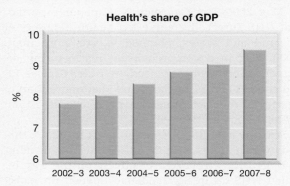

Source: Derived from HM Treasury sources, reported in 'NHS Five Year Spending Plans 2003–2008 in *The Guardian*, 26 April 2002 (and October 2003). Copyright Guardian News and Media Ltd, 2002.

Exhibit 2 **NHS Direct (England): costs and usage of various primary care services, 2001**

	Cost without calling NHS Direct (£)	Cost including call to NHS Direct (£)	Usage without NHS Direct advice (%)	Usage with NHS Direct advice (%)
Self-care		15.11	17	35
GP in-hours contact	15.70	30.81	29	19
GP out-of-hours (urgent) contact	22.66	37.77	22	15
Accident and Emergency Hospital attendance	64.96	80.77	3	3
Ambulance Journey	141.54	156.65	8	8

Source: Derived from National Audit Office Report, 'NHS Direct in England', January 2002, HC 505.

NHS Direct: implementation and service relationships

The implementation of NHS Direct has been regarded as successful. The Public Accounts Committee Report noted that:

> NHS Direct has quickly established itself as the world's largest provider of telephone healthcare advice, and is proving popular with the public. It has a good safety record, with very few recorded adverse events. Departments should consider what wider lessons they could learn from the successful introduction of this significant and innovative service on time.
>
> (40th Report of Public Accounts Committee of House of Commons, 'NHS Direct in England', 2002)

The importance of the relationship to other parts of the NHS and related services is shown by Exhibit 3 which illustrates how NHS Direct functioned as a gateway.

The original intention that NHS Direct would have a significant impact upon reducing the demands upon GP (Family Doctor), Accident and Emergency Hospital and Ambulance services has not been entirely fulfilled.

However, the Public Accounts Committee noted the challenge of integration with other NHS services. It cautioned the Department of Health to set a clear strategic direction for the service to avoid its trying to do too many things at once. Callers were waiting too long and the service needed to improve both its capacity and technical competence.

The NHS Direct Special Health Authority worked with Primary Care Health Trusts to ensure that locally relevant services were delivered.

Exhibit 3   The NHS gateway to services

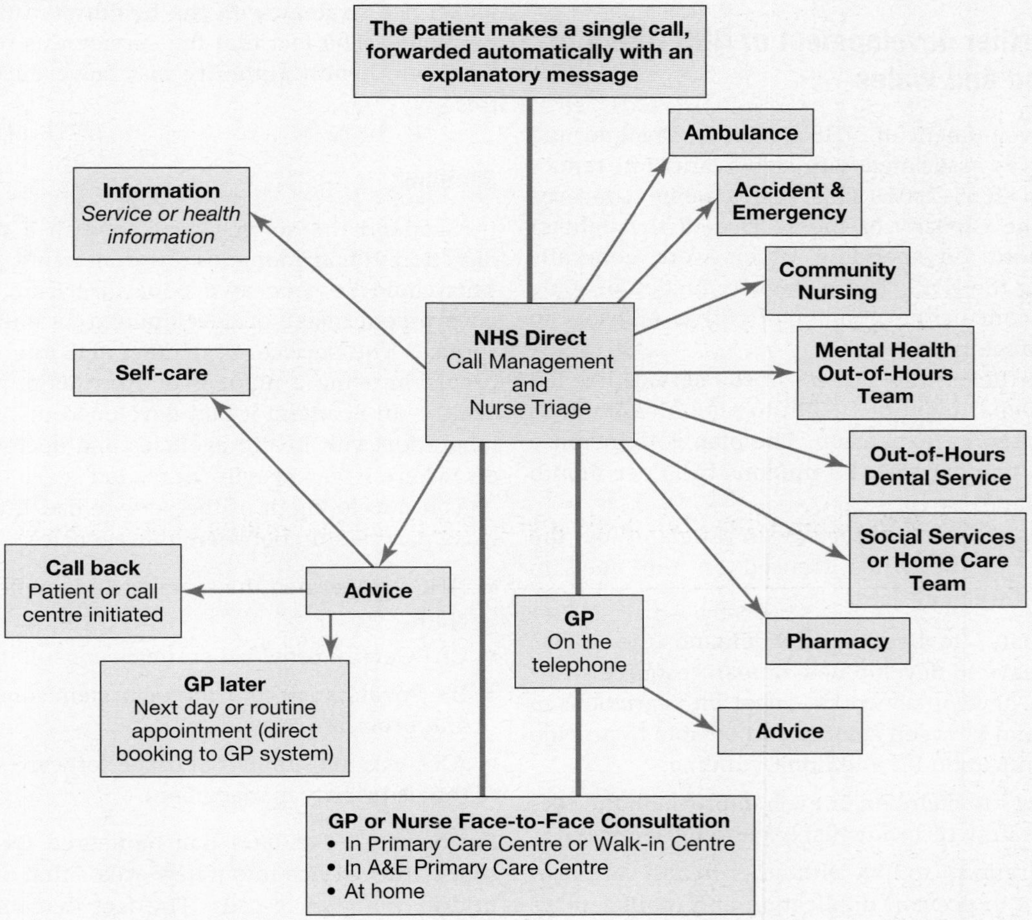

Source: 40th Report of Public Accounts Committee of House of Commons, 'NHS Direct in England', 2002.

NHS Direct Online

The growth of the Internet-based service has been particularly significant. This may be associated by the increased use of the Internet and growth of home-based broadband access in the UK.

NHS Direct Online forms one element of the NHS's new National Knowledge Service. It is aimed primarily at the public, whereas the National Electronic Library for Health is aimed at health professionals.

The users of the online service are not necessarily the same as the users of the telephone service. Quite naturally the online service may be reaching a more IT-literate user. It was quite likely (though NHS Direct does not provide any data) that the user group also includes health professionals.

NHS Direct has also developed a digital TV presence which is expected to reach over 6 million households. This was launched in December 2006.

The further development of NHS Direct in England and Wales

The development of NHS Direct in England and Wales was associated with significant staff reductions in 2005–2006. This raised some concerns about the capacity of the service in the light of restrictions on spending which were generally affecting the NHS. There was a reduction of some 13 per cent in the number of Nurse Advisors in NHS Direct in 2006.

Nevertheless the success of the service has led to the Department of Health to plan an ambitious programme for expansion. The plan is to increase capacity to deal with 1.3 millions calls per month (in England) by early 2007.

A review of the service in England by the National Audit Office focused on the need to address three key areas:

- Capacity – to meet the new demands the service will have to develop new human resource strategies, develop networks to deal with variations in demand between centres and be able to provide a justification for additional funding.

- Safety – to maintain or even improve on the current safety record whilst expanding services.

- Integration – to link with other health care providers to prevent duplication and inefficiencies and promote joint working. This will involve the need to develop further communication strategies and IT systems.

Variations in national development

The growth of devolution in the UK with a National Assembly in Wales and a separate Parliament in Scotland had created the potential for different service developments.

Wales

In Wales the service was managed by one health authority (Swansea) on behalf of all of Wales. The majority of the advice was for home care suggesting that the service was more likely to advise callers to pursue this option than in England. The service had also developed a significant role in the area of dental advice. The service had been used by over 10 per cent of the population of Wales in 2002. The service had also spearheaded relationships with voluntary organisations such as the Samaritans (suicide prevention) and Childline (child abuse). The service had sought to integrate its service strategy with the health plan priorities for Wales. The fact that the service was managed from one health authority may have encouraged this.

Scotland

In Scotland the service developed in a different direction. It had adopted a different name: NHS 24. This could be seen as a departure from the UK government image of developing a 'brand' for the service. The service was integrated into existing provision using a number of sites (as opposed to Wales). In Scotland it had developed in close collaboration with health agencies and doctors while elsewhere it was heavily 'nurse led'.

The development of the service had involved a close partnership between four agencies:

- NHS 24 operated the systems and employed the staff.

- CAPGemini provided strategic consultancy.

- BT Consultancy contributed system consultancy and provision.

- AXA was the supplier of triage software systems, that is priority management.

Furthermore, Scotland had pioneered the extension of the service into a new area – that of lower-priority ambulance calls. The fact that there was one ambulance service for the whole of Scotland had meant that this was easier to develop than elsewhere. The ambulance service in Scotland referred calls which were seen as neither life threatening nor serious (defined as Category C) to NHS 24. This had required close collaboration between the two services and a high level of trust and mutual understanding.

Other agencies in Scotland, such as the police, are closely monitoring the NHS 24 model and there is a possibility of further service integration taking place.

Scotland had undertaken evaluations of its services by independent academic and medical experts. A magazine was published to promote its evaluation activities.

The operation of the service was affected by other developments, in particular the new Family Doctor (GP) Contracts in 2004 which allowed doctors to opt out of providing services when their surgeries were closed (out-of-hours provision). There were long delays in accessing NHS 24 leading to 'dropped calls' (when callers simply gave up). The practice of call back (phoning callers back) was used to try to deal with the problems of long waits.

In 2005 following the death of a patient an Independent Report into NHS 24 was critical of the operation of the service.[4] In particular the report found the practice of 'calling people back' had led to situations where callers to the service had waited for three hours for a nurse advisor to phone them back. The report recommended that 'call back' be ended.

The report also advocated a 'radical overhaul' of the service. It suggested setting up new mini call centres around Scotland, that the roles of call handlers should be broadened and that they should work more flexibly.[5] Considerable concern was expressed about the need both to recruit more nurses to staff the service and to answer calls quickly, thus avoiding call backs and 'dropped calls'. The importance of this was perhaps highlighted by the use of a target measure of answering calls within 30 seconds (as opposed to the 60 seconds used in England and Wales). In June 2006 virtually all calls were answered within 30 seconds.

NHS 24 reported that through partnership with local health boards it had succeeded in setting up five local centres both to enable more locally responsive provision and to assist in nurse recruitment.

---

[4] *Source*: The Scotsman, 6 October (2005).
[5] See Audit Scotland: http://www.audit-scotland.gov.uk/publications/pdf/auditreports/05h12asg.pdf.

The extension of the service and ability to address challenge

The UK is a multicultural and multilingual society. NHS Direct (at least in England) has demonstrated an ability to reach users whose first language is not English through its non-English-language services focusing on most used languages. In Wales the service is provided in Welsh, though the actual usage of this facility was relatively limited accounting for some 1.5 per cent of total calls.

The experience in recent years of health scares has had an impact on NHS Direct locally and nationally. It regards its role to be a source of information, advice and reassurance. The service has a particular role in responding to health alerts and possible epidemics. If Avian flu becomes a problem in the UK, NHS Direct and NHS 24 might be key organisations in both identifying the problem and disseminating information to a worried population.

The future?

The continuing reorganisation of the health services in the UK will impact on NHS Direct and NHS 24. The technological bias in England and Wales with the development of more online provision is well established. However, Scotland has laid more emphasis upon locally focused provision and avoidance of delay in responding to telephone enquiries.

As the service expands into new areas such as dentistry, management of patient appointments and emergency service cover it is going to prove more complicated to deliver the prompt, safe and integrated service set for it by key government reports. The increasingly complex and fast-moving technological milieu within which it has chosen to move is not always conducive to consolidation and reflection. Possibly the Scottish context is driven by a different imperative to that of England and Wales. It is also possible that the plan for the electronic linking of patient records enabling wider access by medical (and some other) NHS staff may prove to be a stumbling point. In Scotland this may be less contentious than in the rest of the UK.

The warning note sounded by a manager quoted in an article in *Primary Care* in 2003 has proven to be prophetic:

NHS Direct has achieved a 20 per cent growth in capacity with the same number of staff. And there is more of that to come. But being a telephone service, the demand is there and then. When we've got the capacity we give a good service but if the capacity isn't there, then you can quickly cross the line, so it's going to be challenging.

(*Primary Care*, June 2003)

APPENDIX 1

Size and trends in NHS workforce: NHS staffing changes, 1999–2004

Increase in staff

	Sept. 1999	Sept. 2004	Increase since NHS plan[1]
Front-line staff of which:	926,200	1,119,600	193,400 (21%)
All doctors (excluding retainers)	94,000	117,000	23,100 (25%)
Nurses (including midwifery practice nurses and health visiting staff)	329,600	397,500	67,900 (21%)
Ambulance staff	14,800	17,300	2,500 (17%)
Scientific, therapeutic and technical staff	102,400	128,900	26,500 (26%)
Support to clinical staff	296,600	368,300	71,700 (24%)
Other frontline staff[2]	88,800	90,600	1,800 (2.1%)
NHS infrastructure support[3]	171,200	211,500	40,300 (24%)
Total NHS workforce	1,097,400	1,331,100	233,700 (21%)

Increase in training numbers

	In 1999/2000	In 2004/5	Increase since NHS plan[1]
Medical school intake	3,970	6,290[4]	2,320 (58%)
Nursing and midwifery training commissions	18,710	25,020	6,310 (34%)

1. Change since the NHS plan takes as a baseline the nearest annual figure before July 2000, compared with the latest annual position.
2. Includes practice staff (other than nurses) and other non-medical staff.
3. Includes central functions, properties and estates, and managers and senior managers.
4. Provisional Information as July 2005 student numbers have not yet been confirmed.

Source: Chief Executive's report to the NHS: December 2005.

Doman Synthetic Fibres plc (B)

Peter H. Jones

The case describes a company in the chemical/synthetic fibres industry that is in 'strategic drift'. The patent on its established product is about to expire but the company has a potential replacement. The case presents three strategic options for the future which can be evaluated in resource planning and profitability terms.

• • •

Over the past few years, as the results of major companies continue to show, textiles – and fibres in particular – have continued to be a difficult market and, although last year's results were up on the previous year, they were still very poor compared to other industries.

> (From an article in the textile trade press in July 2006)

It was against this gloomy scene that Doman Synthetic Fibres (DSF) had been trading. Appendices 1 and 2 give details of its financial results for 2004–2006. DSF was a small but technically successful company by the standards of the synthetic fibre industry. Founded in 1946 by Wilfred Doman, grandfather of the present Managing Director, Wendy Doman, the company was heavily dependent on the sales of Britlene which accounted in 2006 for some 95 per cent of total sales. This heavy dependence on a single product had been a familiar characteristic of the company for nearly 20 years, first with Aslene and then since the mid-1990s with Britlene. It was only the patent protection on Britlene which had enabled DSF to survive the turbulent and difficult situation of recent years.

Synthetic fibres as a whole represented some 40 per cent of the total UK textile production but, within that, Teklatite fibres, of which Britlene was the leading commercial type, accounted for only 3 per cent of total synthetic fibre production. Britlene was used mainly in the manufacture of heavy-duty clothing, although small quantities were used to produce industrial goods such as tyre cord and industrial belting.

In 2005, however, the R&D department had developed a new product, Crylon, which like Britlene was a Teklatite fibre. Crylon had all the properties of Britlene but was superior in its heat-resistant qualities. It was hoped that this additional property would open up new clothing uses (for example, a substitute for asbestos clothing, adding to night wear to improve its flame resistance) and new industrial uses in thermal and electrical insulation.

Wendy Doman expressed her attitude to Crylon:

> For too long we've relied on Britlene as our only product. It's been a faithful friend to us but with patent protection running out in 2008, we must expand into something else and Crylon is the obvious candidate. We've got the technical experience in this area; it'll use our existing sales outlets; we could even convert some Britlene capacity to cut down on our capital costs and our agent has drawn up a watertight patent.

By mid-2006 the major technical and engineering problems associated with bulk production of Crylon seemed to have been solved but two years of the patent had already expired. Wendy Doman had set up a Capital Investment Working Party to put forward proposals on how the new product should be phased into the company's activities.

Production

The basic production method of Britlene and Crylon is similar to that of most synthetic fibres. To make a synthetic fibre, an oil-based organic chemical is polymerised (a process of joining several molecules into a long chain) in conditions of intense pressure and heat, often by the addition of a suitable catalyst. This polymerisation takes place in large autoclaves (an industrial pressure-cooker). The polymer is then extruded (similar to being forced through the rose of a garden watering can), rapidly cooled and then either spun onto cones and bobbins or collected in bales. The spun material is known as filament yarn; the bales are called staple fibre.

For Britlene, DSF had bought the polymer, Polymutastine 15, as its raw material, which was chemically processed before the extrusion stage. However, for Crylon, DSF would be buying Hexa-titanone, and polymerising this organic chemical itself. The raw materials for Britlene and Crylon were produced at Teesside by Hunters Chemicals. For both raw materials DSF took a low percentage of Hunters' production and Hunters were not a direct competitor of DSF in its fibre market.

Britlene facilities

Britlene was produced at three factories: Teesside, Bradford and Dumfries. The largest site was Teesside with three plants; there was one plant at each of the other two sites. The Teesside plant was next door to the raw material supplier and was not too far from the main markets in Lancashire and Yorkshire. Bradford was close to the main customers and as such proved a help for sorting out customer liaison on matters such as quality and rush orders.

All five production plants, purchased over the last eight years, had a design capacity of 5.5 million kg per annum of Britlene, independent of whether filament or staple was produced. However, after allowing for maintenance and an annual shutdown, expected output was 5 million kg p.a. Each plant was still in excellent order. Production was done on a basis of 5 days per week, 24 hours per day (three shifts). There was no weekend production although Saturday had been worked occasionally in times of high demand and the trade unions had agreed to allow members to work one Saturday per month at overtime rates.

Each plant employed about 56 people on pro-duction and 11 on maintenance. There was no difference in plant labour levels for the three shifts, but maintenance workers were mainly attached to the day shift.

Proposed Crylon facilities

The distinctive features of Crylon were created in the new polymerisation process. When asked to explain the differences between the two products, the Research Director, Roger Tillotson, used to draw the diagrams in Exhibits 1 and 2.

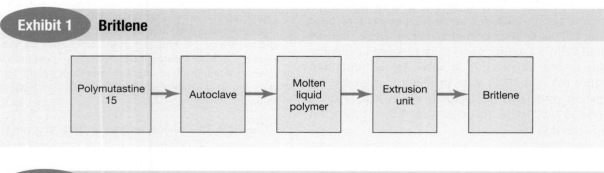

Exhibit 1 **Britlene**

Polymutastine 15 → Autoclave → Molten liquid polymer → Extrusion unit → Britlene

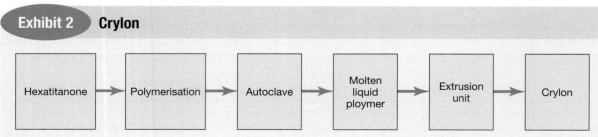

Exhibit 2 **Crylon**

Hexatitanone → Polymerisation → Autoclave → Molten liquid ploymer → Extrusion unit → Crylon

The key to Crylon is in the polymerisation. What we'll need is a new polymerisation-cum-autoclave unit to replace the old autoclave-only unit. The extrusion unit for Crylon is basically the same as we are using for Britlene. By the time we've reached the molten polymer state we've done the chemistry. Extrusion is just to get a storable and saleable product.

Together with a major construction company, DSF has produced an acceptable plant design. A pilot plant was working very satisfactorily. This had provided valuable cost information. Jim Lewis, the Operations Director, explained:

Our self-produced Crylon polymer should be about 10 per cent cheaper than Polymutastine 15, despite the extra costs of about 15 men on the new polymer plant and its extra depreciation. Of course these are only estimated from our pilot plant experience.

Acquiring Crylon capacity

There were two ways of acquiring Crylon capacity. DSF could convert a Britlene plant, or it could construct an entirely new plant.

For a *conversion* a new polymer unit would need to be constructed first; when complete it would be connected to the extrusion unit which would require minor conversion taking three months. Instrumentation and start-up checks would then be performed for a further three months, during which time there could be roughly half capacity. This meant that from completion of the new polymer unit the whole plant would not be at full capacity for about six months. At least six months' planning and technical work was required by Alpens, the suppliers of the plant and equipment, before construction could start.

Exhibit 3 sets out Alpens' estimated time-scale for conversion of a Britlene unit to make Crylon.

A *newly constructed* plant would mean building both a polymerisation and an extrusion unit. Although no conversion was involved such a plant could only operate at roughly half capacity for three months after start-up, while testing took place. Exhibit 4 shows Alpens' estimated time-scale for a newly constructed unit.

Preliminary market estimates for the new product made in 2006 indicated that an increase in the total number of plants might well be needed, especially if the predicted new industrial uses materialised. Wendy Doman, however, had gone on record saying:

The creation of an entirely new site for operations would increase the complexities of multi-site operation to an unacceptable level. Conversely, the complete closure of one of the three existing sites is, I consider, a waste of the human and physical resources that we have invested in that location. I believe expansion could take place at one, two or all of the existing sites.

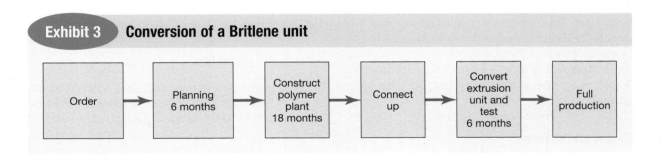

Exhibit 3 Conversion of a Britlene unit

Order → Planning 6 months → Construct polymer plant 18 months → Connect up → Convert extrusion unit and test 6 months → Full production

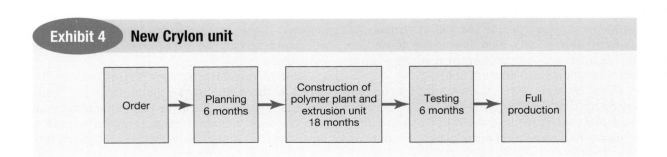

Exhibit 4 New Crylon unit

Order → Planning 6 months → Construction of polymer plant and extrusion unit 18 months → Testing 6 months → Full production

Estimated Crylon capital costs

The estimated costs and stage payments required by Alpens for Crylon polymer plant and extrusion unit construction were:

for a Crylon polymer plant	£3,000,000
for a new Crylon extrusion unit	£1,800,000
for a conversion of a Britlene extrusion unit to Crylon	£600,000

Thus the total cost of a new Crylon plant would be £4.8m and a conversion £3.6m. The cost of the polymer plant was payable in three six-monthly instalments of £1,000,000, the first being due one year after ordering. The cost of new extrusion units or conversions was due on completion.

Land for two more plants was already available at Teesside and for one more at Bradford, but any other developments would require an additional purchase.

Marketing

Since the mid-1980s DSF had been a one-product company. Prior to the introduction of Britlene in 1998 the company had relied on the patent-protected product Aslene before moving into Teklatite fibres with Britlene. Experience with Aslene suggested that the near monopoly position held by Britlene could be eroded fairly rapidly once patent rights were removed at the end of the year 2008. One other UK manufacturer was producing Teklatite fibres and was rumoured to have plans to produce Britlene after that date. There were also fears that international competitors would enter the market after the Britlene patent expired.

Supply and demand

Britlene had carved out a secure niche in the synthetic fibre market. Sluggish world trade in textiles and fibres had curtailed growth since 2003 but DSF had been able to produce and sell at virtually full capacity during 2003–2006. It had not needed nor had it tried to penetrate foreign markets with the exception of a small effort in 2001.

Peter Moore, DSF's Marketing Director, was confident that Crylon would enable DSF to regain a 90 per cent share in the UK of Teklatite fibres within three years of its introduction. He felt confident in the future of Crylon:

We've moved customers once from Aslene to Britlene. I see no reason why we can't do it again. Crylon is a better product than Britlene. Initial customer trials have been most encouraging. With the right kind of effort I believe we can also generate sales of 5–10 million kgs. of Crylon for use in thermal and electrical insulation. This is a mere flea-bite in comparison to sales of glass and mica for this purpose.

Pricing

Since 2004 prices for Britlene had only moved marginally. DSF had not attempted to pass on cost increases, as in the depressed textile market Peter Moore felt this would have been resisted by customers. In 2006 the list price for Britlene was 98 pence/kg.

There was considerable uncertainty about the price which could be obtained for Crylon. For textile uses it might command a premium (estimated at 10–20 per cent) over Britlene due to its improved qualities, but Peter Moore felt that this premium could well be used up in trying to shift customers to the new product. Additionally, the increased competition anticipated once Britlene patents expired was expected to depress Teklatite prices.

The industrial market was a great unknown. Rough and ready calculations suggested that a price between 100 and 120p/kg ought to put it on a competitive basis with existing materials. However, the conservative nature of manufacturers which would be taking a totally new material threw doubt on these estimates.

Selling and promotion

In 2006 promotion expenditure was £50,000, spent on sales literature (£13,000) and limited advertising in newspapers and trade journals (£7,000), and on the website (£30,000). This expenditure level was typical of the previous few years. For the launch of Britlene in 1998 the company had 'gone to town' by industry standards, spending £310,000 – on press advertising (£150,000) and a joint promotion with selected customers (£160,000). This had enabled the rapid acceptance of Britlene by the textile industry.

Peter Moore felt that once Crylon was established in the textile market its promotional needs would be similar to those for Britlene but to break into the new industrial markets would require a much greater promotional effort, and the media mix would need to be different.

Personnel

In December 2006 DSF employed 442 people. Of these, weekly payroll employees, concerned mainly with production and maintenance, numbered 336. There were approximately 67 payroll employees at each of the five plants. The remaining 106 employees were monthly paid staff. Apart from supervisory production staff and commercial staff at the sales offices, all staff worked at the Teesside headquarters. Most payroll employees in DSF were unionised and John Williams, HR Director, described the company's relationship with the union as 'good', although there was unease about possible plant closures. He was also concerned about labour relations in the construction industry which he feared could delay building programmes and increase costs.

Unemployment

At all locations the general unemployment rate was higher than the national average, but the rate for skilled workers was low at all sites. Supply of the particular skills DSF wanted was low and only at Teesside would extra demand for skilled labour be readily met.

Finance

Financial performance

The financial performance of the company during 2004–2006 had been a cause of real concern (see Appendix 1). Up to five years ago the profit figures had been steady and a return on capital employed before tax of around 20 per cent was considered to be most satisfactory. As Mr Greenhaugh, the Finance Director, put it:

> In the early part of this century this company was considered a good investment by most analysts. We have always been financed solely by the share capital and retained earnings and this, coupled with our patent protection, made us a safe bet. In the last 2 or 3 years, however, things haven't looked so good. Our share price has dropped to a disturbing level despite our continuing policy of maintaining the level of dividends. Our P/E ratio is now 7 and this is very disappointing. Investors are not sure where we are going as a company, but I believe the introduction of Crylon, if it comes through in time, will restore confidence.

Raising finance

Mr Greenhaugh compared the 2006 situation with the similar position in 1998 when Britlene had been introduced to the market. Then, the initial development costs had been financed internally out of the previous profits as had about half the capital investment. Another £2.5m had been required from external sources. This was a substantial quantity for a company the size of DSF but confidence had been high, and a one-for-one rights issue at 62.5p had been fully subscribed. (The share price at the time had been standing at 68p.) Mr Greenhaugh wished confidence in DSF was as buoyant in 2006 and the share price as strong.

The first working party meeting

In setting up the working party in early 2007 to consider the Crylon case, Wendy Doman had picked one obviously up-and-coming manager from each major function. It was clear that she considered this exercise as part of their development, and success could easily mean rapid advancement on the back of Crylon expansion. As they sat down for their first meeting, the members of the working party realised that they all had a personal as well as a professional interest in how the study progressed.

There was general, albeit reluctant, agreement among the team that trends in production techniques and locations would necessitate a hard look at whether all three sites should continue, this despite the MD's wish to preserve all three sites. However, there was considerably less consensus on the more strategic issue of whether to proceed with Crylon, and if so how fast and how much capacity to install.

Les Hill (from Finance) wondered whether DSF should develop it at all. He argued that Britlene was not yet a 'dog' in BCG terms. With suitable economies DSF could continue to make a profit from it, even if, as he acknowledged, the price might need to reduce in two years' time to deter new producers when the patent came off. He felt this was far less risky than significant capital investment which would stretch the company's resources and financial independence.

Chris Henson (from Sales and Marketing) viewed this as far too cautious, and favoured what she called a 'two-horse' strategy. She believed some existing customers would prefer to continue with Britlene while others would switch to Crylon. With a push on industrial users she believed DSF could achieve a total of 30 million kg of sales, split between the two products.

Trevor Bryant (from Operations) felt both approaches lacked ambition. He argued that Crylon had been well received by customers and that DSF should introduce it into both markets as soon as feasible: 'What is the point of being half-hearted and waiting?'

A simple Excel planning model had been produced to look at the financial consequences of various scenarios. Brief results of the three views above are given in Appendix 3. The Henson and Bryant views also include the two possibilities of achieving or not a 15 per cent premium on the Crylon price over Britlene.

APPENDIX 1

Profit and loss summary, 2004–2006

	2004 £000		2005 £000		2006 £000
Sales					
Products	23,602		23,840		24,042
Licences	951		976		1,050
		24,553		24,816	25,092
Cost of goods sold					
Raw materials	6,086		6,592		7,230
Direct labour	6,391		6,940		7,521
Prod. overheads	2,177		2,602		2,869
Depreciation	700		700		700
		15,354		16,834	18,320
Gross profit		9,199		7,982	6,772
Other overheads					
Promotion and sales	374		395		402
Distribution	905		986		1,030
General admin.	2,738		3,009		3,320
R&D	890		1,250		950
	4,907		5,640		5,702
Operating profit		4,292	2,342		1,070
Interest payable		(189)	(231)		(240)
Net profit before tax		4,481	2,573		1,310
Corporation Tax		1,814	1,146		704
Net profit after tax		2,667	1,427		606
Dividend declared		750	750		750
Retained earnings		1,917	677		(144)

Source: Company annual reports.

APPENDIX 2

Balance sheet at 31 December 2006

	£ 000	£ 000	£ 000
Fixed asset	Cost	Depn	Net
Freehold land and buildings	8,010	(150)	7,860
Teesside 5,210			
Bradford 1,605			
Dumfries 1,195			
Plant and machinery	8,790	(7,000)	1,790
Teesside 4,780			
Bradford 2,050			
Dumfries 1,960			
			9,650
Trade investments at cost			4,152
Working capital			
Current assets			
Work-in-progress and stock	2,720		
Debtors	2,980		
Cash	868		
		6,568	
Less current liabilities			
Creditors	2,307		
Taxation	436		
Dividend	510		
		3,253	
Net working capital			3,315
			17,117
Financed by:			
Share capital			5,000
Capital reserves			
Share premium		500	
Revaluation reserve		4,500	
			5,000
Retained earnings			
Balance at 31/12/05		7,261	
Retained profit 2006		(144)	
			7,117
			17,117

Source: Company annual report.

APPENDIX 3

Some results of possible future scenarios

Year	2007	2008	2009	2010	2011	2012
Option A – Hill						
Assumptions						
Price Britlene, p/kg	1	1	0.9	0.9	0.9	0.9
Sales vol. Britlene, m kg	25	25	25	25	25	25
Key results						
Net profit before tax, £m	2.0	2.2	0.6	0.6	0.6	0.6
Annual trading cash flow, £m	1.6	1.6	−0.7	0.2	0.2	0.2
Capital payments, £m	–	–	–	–	–	–
Net cash flow, £m	1.6	1.6	−0.7	0.2	0.2	0.2
Cumulative cash balance, £m (incl. trade investments at cost)	6.6	8.2	7.4	7.7	7.9	8.1
Option B1 – Henson (15% premium)						
Assumptions						
Price Britlene, p/kg	1	1	0.95	0.95	0.95	0.95
Price Crylon, p/kg			1.10	1.10	1.10	1.10
Sales vol. Britlene, m kg	25	25	20	15	10	10
Sales vol. Crylon, m kg			5	11	17	20
Key results						
Net profit before tax, £m	2.0	2.2	−1.1	0.2	1.3	3.8
Annual trading cash flow, £m	1.6	1.6	−1.8	0.5	2.1	4.3
Capital payments, £m	–	2.0	5.6	6.4	1.6	–
Net cash flow, £m	1.6	−0.4	−7.4	−5.9	0.5	4.3
Cumulative cash balance, £m (incl. trade investments at cost)*	6.6	6.2	−1.2	−7.1	−6.4	−2.0
Option B2 – Henson (no premium)						
Assumptions						
Price Britlene, p/kg	1	1	0.95	0.95	0.95	0.95
Price Crylon, p/kg			0.95	0.95	0.95	0.95
Sales vol. Britlene, m kg	25	25	20	15	10	10
Sales vol. Crylon, m kg			5	11	17	20
Key results						
Net profit before tax, £m	2.0	2.2	−1.5	−1.8	−1.3	0.5
Annual trading cash flow, £m	1.6	1.6	−2.2	−0.9	−0.2	1.9
Capital payments, £m	–	2.0	5.6	6.4	1.6	–
Net cash flow, £m	1.6	−0.4	−7.8	−7.3	−1.8	1.9
Cumulative cash balance, £m (incl. trade investments at cost)*	6.6	6.2	−1.6	−9.0	−10.8	−8.9
Option C1 – Bryant (15% premium)						
Assumptions						
Price Britlene, p/kg	1	1	0.95	0.95	–	–
Price Crylon, p/kg			1.10	1.10	1.10	1.10
Sales vol. Britlene, m kg	25	25	16	5	–	–
Sales vol. Crylon, m kg			9	22	33	40
Key results						
Net profit before tax, £m	2.0	2.2	−3.7	−0.8	3.6	6.9
Annual trading cash flow, £m	1.6	1.6	−1.0	0.2	6.0	8.8
Capital payments, £m	–	6.0	12.0	8.0	3.6	2.8
Net cash flow, £m	1.6	−4.4	−13.0	−7.8	2.4	6.0
Cumulative cash balance, £m (incl. trade investments at cost)*	6.6	2.2	−10.9	−18.7	−16.3	−10.3
Option C2 – Bryant (no premium)						
Assumptions						
Price Britlene, p/kg	1	1	0.95	0.95	–	–
Price Crylon, p/kg			0.95	0.95	0.95	0.95
Sales vol. Britlene, m kg	25	25	16	5	–	–
Sales vol. Crylon, m kg			9	22	33	40
Key results						
Net profit before tax, £m	2.0	2.2	−5.0	−4.1	−1.7	0.3
Annual trading cash flow, £m	1.6	1.6	−2.2	−3.0	1.0	4.1
Capital payments, £m	–	6.0	12.0	8.0	3.6	2.8
Net cash flow, £m	1.6	−4.4	−14.2	−11.0	−2.6	1.3
Cumulative cash balance, £m (incl. trade investments at cost)*	6.6	2.2	−12.0	−23.0	−25.6	−24.3

* The lowest negative figure in this row indicates the maximum cash injection needed by DSF to fund the strategy, in addition to selling the trade investments of £4.2m.

Marks & Spencer (B)

Nardine Collier

• • •

The case study continues the story of Marks & Spencer, the previously successful British retailer which had run into a series of strategic and financial problems in the late 1990s and early 2000s. This case examines the attempts of two CEOs, Roger Holmes and Stuart Rose, to turn around the company's fortunes with very different approaches.

Michael Marks began one of the world's most recognised brands by establishing a penny bazaar in 1884. The phenomenal success of the business led Marks to seek a partner; he chose Tom Spencer. From this partnership Marks & Spencer (M&S) steadily grew, but by the early twenty-first century its success was running out.

Hitch in the formula[1]

Until the late 1990s M&S was highly successful in terms of profit and market share. This was achieved by applying a fundamental formula to its operations, which included: simple pricing structures, offering customers high-quality, attractive merchandise under the brand name 'St Michael', working with suppliers to ensure quality control, and providing a friendly, helpful service. This was enhanced by a close-knit family atmosphere in the stores, which was compounded by employing staff whom M&S believed would 'fit in'.

Throughout most of the 1900s M&S was led by family members, who favoured close control and meticulous attention to detail. Central edict was given for purchasing, merchandising, layout, etc., hence every M&S was identical, resulting in a consistent image and guarantee of standards. M&S stocked generic 'essential' clothing, and priced its products at a 'reasonable' level, while emphasising their high quality, a claim based on its insistence of using British suppliers.

M&S's problems crescendoed in 1998 when it halted its European expansion programme, announced a 23 per cent decline in profits, and suffered decreasing customer satisfaction. Richard Greenbury (CEO) blamed this on a loss of market share to 'top-end' competitors such as Oasis, which offered more fashionable, but similarly priced goods, and at the bottom-end with competition from discount stores and supermarkets, which offered essential clothing, but at lower prices. Analysts felt M&S no longer understood its customers' needs, was preoccupied with its traditional risk-averse formula thus ignoring changes in the marketplace, focused on day-to-day operations rather than long-term strategy, and had an inward-looking culture, as executives were promoted internally, after immersion in M&S's routines and traditions.

To counter these problems successive CEOs implemented many strategies, including refurbishments, store acquisitions, restructuring, new ranges, overseas sourcing, European expansion followed by complete withdrawal, diversification into homeware, and moving from the corporate headquarters. However, these measures made little impact, and profits warnings and falling share prices (250³/₄p at its lowest) followed.

---

[1] For full details of M&S's success and problems throughout the 1990s to 2004 refer to Marks & Spencer (A).

Photo: Justin Kase/Alamy

New style

In 2001 Luc Vandevelde (CEO) head-hunted Roger Holmes, aged 40, to be Head of UK retailing. Holmes started his career as a consultant for McKinsey, moving to Financial Director of DIY chain B&Q, Managing Director of retailers Woolworths, and finally Chief of Electricals for the Kingfisher group. At M&S he began by implementing a store refurbishment, creating 'shops within shops', to show customers how different styles worked together. In implementing Vandevelde's plans to recapture core customers' confidence, Holmes employed Yasmin Yusuf (fashion buyer) as Creative Director, to target M&S's more traditional customers. He was then instrumental in brokering a collaboration with George Davies, founder of Next (womenswear retailer) and creator of supermarket clothing range 'George'. Davies' remit was to cater for M&S's fashion-conscious customers, aged 25–35. The new range, 'Per Una', attempted to compete with brands like Kookai. It had its own walled floor space to differentiate it from the rest of the store. Davies owned Per Una, and retained the profits from supplying M&S. One month after its launch, M&S reported its first sales increase for three years, and a rise in share price. Per Una was well received by customers, but as demand had outrun supply, roll-out was reduced.

M&S then delivered its 2002 end-of-year results: although there had been a rise in profits Vandevelde emphasised that it was not a recovery, but that M&S had 'turned the corner'. However, at the July 2002 AGM Vandevelde resigned as CEO to become part-time Chairman. Unsurprising to many, Holmes was promoted. Some analysts were worried Vandevelde was leaving too early in the recovery process, whereas others credited Holmes

with much of the responsibility for the recovery, and as the driving force behind the revitalisation of women's clothing. Heralded as 'the man behind the turnaround', in spite of having no previous experience of selling clothing, Holmes was described by the City as being 'very personable, bright, intelligent'. Holmes had spoken to customers, and was struck by how inwardly focused M&S had remained. His conclusion was to return to a 'passion for product'. He had also injected innovation into the food ranges, and was crucial in the overseas withdrawal.

As CEO Holmes started by leveraging financial services, as it was the most trusted, yet under-exploited part of M&S. Its profits had fallen £12.1m (€17.5m) and it was 'under review' following M&S's decision to accept credit cards, as this had minimised usage of its own charge card. To leverage its cardholders it launched a pilot scheme of a combined credit and loyalty card, named '&more'.

By October the jubilation surrounding M&S continued as it increased sales in a turbulent market. However, falling market share in childrenswear and overstocking in womenswear had spoilt M&S's performance, where Holmes admitted he was forced to discount heavily.

In December M&S achieved what many regarded as a coup, when it poached Vittorio Radice from Selfridges (department store) to head homeware. Analysts were impressed by M&S's ability to attract such renowned creative talent, feeling that it was a sign of recovery, and that its competitors should be worried.

Reporting on the Christmas trading, Holmes presented a like-for-like sales increase, which led M&S to outperform most of its competitors and beat the City's predictions:

> I think there is a building confidence among our customers. In the end, it all comes down to product and in clothing we have got the core fashionability right.
>
> (*Financial Times*, 16 January 2003)

In spite of this there were heavy mark-downs, at a cost 5 per cent higher than in 2001. Holmes blamed unseasonable weather for slow sales of winter coats and associated apparel.

Continuing the turnaround Holmes streamlined M&S's logistics by halving its contractors, and sourcing directly rather than through third parties. Further, following successful pilot trials, Holmes launched &more, which allowed cardholders to earn points for purchases they made, redeemable as M&S vouchers. M&S also won a Queen's Award for Enterprise for its washable suit, which Holmes hoped would instil a culture of innovation throughout the workforce.

The 2003 end-of-year figures showed an increase in profits. Holmes promised that M&S would soon recover from its recent sales slowdown, and win back market share and customers. To achieve this he vowed the top priority would remain clothing and food. In homeware he intended to build stand-alone 'Lifestores', which would showcase a functioning house, so that customers could see the homeware range *in situ*. It was hoped that customers would not buy one item, but instead purchase a way of life. Holmes also announced that M&S was to open its 'Simply Food' stores in motorway service stations. Although stressing that it would proceed cautiously with its new formula, he planned to open 150 stores by 2006, explaining that while operating smaller stores presented new challenges, they had delivered sales in excess of the average return for food.

Where from there?

By November 2003 there were concerns that M&S's recovery had seriously faltered. Senior and middle management were reported to be disappointed with the lack of progress. Holmes was seen as the problem: blamed for being too nice, taking too long to make decisions, and lacking relevant experience. M&S's complicated structure compounded these problems, where underneath the main board was an operating committee of 19 members. An insider commented:

> Everyone likes Roger, but he's really a management consultant, not a clothing retailer. Instead of taking a decision, there'll be another committee formed. . . . Decision making is so slow. The bureaucracy hasn't really changed. They had a go at it, but now it's gone back to the old ways. There's a general level of frustration and discontent.
>
> (*Daily Telegraph*, 3 November 2003)

In addition, employees described 'turf wars' between Davies and Yusuf. Further, commentators were shocked by unprecedented '20 per cent off' discounts, feeling M&S must have sold goods at less than cost price.

Yet in discussing M&S's performance, Holmes explained it had been solid, because of increasing profits. Countering the accusation that the recovery was running out of steam, Holmes stressed how much M&S had achieved, specifically regaining customer trust, and the success of &more, which had given it an opportunity to build relationships with, and understand, what Holmes called its 'most important customers'. Children's and womenswear continued to be a problem; to counter this Holmes was planning to segment M&S's offerings more attractively, with mix and match tailoring solutions.

Problems with food also returned, where, although market share was growing, it underperformed the market. In response Holmes increased the Simply Food stores, as they achieved significant performance. Homeware was also facing difficulties, which Holmes blamed on a dependence on promotions and under-exploiting opportunities. He continued to be confident for the future, explaining his intention to bring greater breadth and 'newness' to products.

However, by early 2004 total sales had fallen. The main concern was clothing, where Holmes described the womenswear ranges as 'not strong enough', with 'the wrong products in place'. As a result Holmes took a more direct interest in womenswear. He also reported that homeware had underperformed, and described food's performance simply as 'adequate'.

In presenting the 2004 end-of-year results Holmes admitted market share gains had not been delivered, after the initial surge in recovery of clothing and food had faltered. He also blamed market conditions, 'subdued customer spending' and increased investment from competitors for M&S's results. Commentators felt Holmes had an unrealistic understanding of events, when he stressed consumers' perception of clothing had improved, but admitted that this was mainly with Per Una. M&S also faced conversion issues as core customers were buying less and occasional shoppers declined, believed to be because customers were spending more at out-of-town supermarkets. Customers complained that trust had been damaged, and quality had fallen. To counter this Holmes promised fundamental action to improve products, supply chain, stores and operations:

> we face some significant structural and competitive issues, but I'm confident we can respond.
>
> (*Annual Report*, 2004)

Holmes created an executive committee to deliver the board's plans, and also commissioned 'Per Una Due', described as Per Una's 'funky younger sister' for those aged 15–30. He explained that customer demands had shifted; customers felt the clothes were uninspiring, their presentation confusing, and that M&S had not followed them regarding style or value. He planned to display the clothing more imaginatively to create well-signposted choice in terms of price and style. To appeal to the core older customers Holmes was developing new classic and contemporary sub-brands.

The food range had performed poorly at key celebration times, for example Easter and Mother's Day, periods at which M&S traditionally excelled. Holmes admitted this was due to 'insufficient product innovation'. Hence he planned to renew the food ranges, and promote them based on their 'unique qualities'.

Holmes acknowledged that customers liked the Lifestore, but it was too contemporary. He therefore opened two further stores, with a bigger range of better-priced products. Finally, he promised a tightening of logistics, store refurbishments, downsizing of headquarter staff, and to raise M&S's profile regarding corporate social responsibility (CSR).

Following this investors were shocked that M&S was underperforming the retail sector by 30 per cent, and the crisis was spreading from clothing to food. Papers reported that the board was concerned about Holmes, whom they saw as vulnerable, especially when justifying results to the City, as he explained that M&S had a lot to do, and that what it was doing was not enough.

Crisis point

M&S's problems pinnacled in May 2004, when Philip Green, retail entrepreneur, announced his intention to make a £7bn takeover bid. Although Green had previously made an offer for M&S (£6bn in 2000), this time it was considered far more seriously.

Green explained that he had made the bid for M&S because of its increasingly poor performance, but specifically when its shares fell to 290p, and following Holmes' announcement that recovery had faltered. This sparked a dramatic boardroom coup. Paul Myners, Non-executive Director, led the board in sacking Holmes and replacing him with Stuart Rose. Vandevelde stepped down and Myners became Chairman. In return for refusing Green's offer investors demanded M&S's turnaround.

Rose, aged 55, had many years of retailing experience, having worked for M&S as a trainee, progressing to senior executive over 17 years. He then became Head of Burtons menswear, and sub-

sequently women's retailers Evans and Principles. He was involved in the sale of Argos (catalogue chain), the merger of Booker (cash-and-carry), and transformed the Arcadia group before selling it to Green, while securing £25m for himself from the sale. Having made no secret that this was his dream job, Rose was well received by the board, as he enthusiastically discussed ideas for new ranges and competitive pricing. Rose brought with him colleagues Charles Wilson to run logistics and Steven Sharp to oversee operations. Rose explained that he would head clothing since it was the core of the business and the source of key problems; this resulted in Radice, who held the position, being dismissed.

The press believed that Rose, who characterised himself as a 'shopkeeper', was adept at building morale, comfortable with analysts and shareholders, and widely known for 'doing simple things well'. Colleagues described him as 'nice, quiet and ruthless'. These sentiments were echoed by investors who liked Rose's experience of re-energising fatigued retailers and record of delivering shareholder value.

Defending against the bid, Rose's top priority was tackling M&S's trading problems. He began by making culture changes, improving decision-making accountability, and revitalising clothing to get back in touch with the core customers. Rose's defence also hinged on dealing with Holmes' initiatives:

> They have got too many initiatives, there's a little bit of analysis-paralysis. There are too many decisions taken by committee.
>
> (*Financial Times*, 4 June 2004)

Rose felt his predecessors had focused on management processes instead of products and costs, and criticised them for not growing out of town.

Some directors, unhappy with the new regime, left, while the remaining non-executives from Greenbury's reign were persuaded to retire. Analysts complimented the board for a decisiveness that had hitherto been missing. Of M&S Rose said:

> People have forgotten their roots . . . there is a little bit of clinging to each other. But you can't hold hands. We live in a tough, commercial world. . . . The business definitely suffered a little from the A-word, arrogance, in the mid to late-90s. It looked out the window and found the world had passed it by.
>
> (*Irish Times*, 11 June 2004)

Shareholders were encouraged that Rose had begun addressing the weaknesses in quality and retail experience of the senior management.

In reversing Holmes' initiatives Rose closed the continuously underperforming Lifestores, which customers had branded as 'pricey' and 'too contemporary'. He also announced a deal with HSBC, which had acquired M&S's financial division for £762m, with M&S retaining 50 per cent of future profits until 2014.

Rose believed there was no coordination across departments, with product proliferation via sub-brands weakening the core proposition. He also thought the process from drawing board to shop floor was too slow, that there was a lack of innovation and, critically, no clear pricing strategy. M&S employees began to praise the combination of Rose and Myners:

> Holmes and Vandevelde let the business drift into a mire of inefficiency. Without Green knocking on the door, we would never have made these momentous changes.
>
> (*Financial Times*, 10 July 2004)

In mid-June Green returned with an £8.9bn offer (370p per share). This proposal was quickly rejected, as the board felt that it 'significantly undervalued the group and its prospects'. This led shareholders to pressure Rose to return capital to them. By July Green made a £9.1bn offer (400p per share). This time he received support from M&S's largest investor, Brandes. Shareholders seriously considered the offer, but again the board dismissed it for undervaluing prospects. Many investors were shocked by the rejection and, to justify the decision, wanted Rose to show that his plans would take shares to 450p.

In response Rose presented his strategic review:

> we have neglected, confused and disappointed our core customer. . . . This is not smoke, mirrors or magic tricks. Our objective is to rely on the founding principles of the past and modify them for today.
>
> (*Financial Times*, 13 July 2004)

He explained that M&S had been inward facing, failing to deliver what customers wanted. Rather than create short-term value, he intended to address the fundamentals of the business by:

- Shelving Per Una Due, as it was not targeted at natural M&S customers.
- Acquiring Per Una from Davies for £125m (with Davies remaining as CEO for two years to retain brand direction).
- Cancelling more than 500 food products.
- Developing supply chain and sourcing efficiency, to reduce the stock overhang.

- Stopping waste and unnecessary administration costs.
- Improving core services.
- Returning £2.3bn to shareholders (through buying back 635 million shares).
- Moving to out-of-town retail centres.
- Restructuring and redundancy.
- Changing employee mentality.
- Closing or upgrading stores, which he likened to hospitals.

Rose was confident that if he 'under-promised and over-delivered', he would achieve cost savings of £250m in a year, and sales growth. His conclusion was a return to five core values: quality, value, service, innovation and trust. Shareholders felt these values were a return to lost standards. Analysts believed that this would surpass Green's 400p, stating that Rose had done 'just enough to buy M&S some time'. However, investors were concerned that the plans did not focus on future sales growth, only the 'nuts and bolts' of recapturing the core customer, speculating that some would find Green's offer increasingly viable.

Meanwhile Green lobbied investors to pressure the board, finally contacting them to indicate that his bid was backed by 36 per cent of shareholders and that he wanted their support. M&S issued a statement that it would not accept Green's proposal. Green then issued a statement professing that he would 'fight them on the high street'. The share price fell sharply to 345p, with the press reporting that the pressure was on Rose to deliver.

Sharp then became Director of Marketing, launching M&S's highly popular 'Your M&S' ad-campaign, as part of its strategy to reposition the brand to give M&S back to the customers and employees. He explained that it was capturing M&S's heritage with modernity. M&S also rationalised its many sub-brands across food and clothing. However, sales and shares continued to fall as M&S admitted 'haemorrhaging market share', having continued clothing problems and a too contemporary homeware range. Rose explained that this was based on prior commitments (many of his visions would not be in store until Spring 2005), emphasising that M&S was merely 'troughing out' after being in a dip, and that it would take time for the results of his initiatives to emerge. Though stating that growth was likely to materialise over the next 18 months, investors were unhappy with the outlook.

By Christmas M&S began to receive some praise for its clothes, as it returned to delivering classics, with a fashionable edge. Kate Bostock joined to head womenswear; investors were delighted as she was the first woman in the position, although her initial collection would not reach stores until Autumn 2005. However, this was overshadowed by worsening performance in food, store-wide lost market share and a fall in half-year profits. Rose explained:

> It is fair to say that there is more to do than I had previously thought. . . . It is do-able.
>
> (*Financial Times*, 10 November 2004)

In reacting Rose halved the board, to himself, Wilson and Ian Dyson (replacing the ousted finance director), his aim being to move closer to the operating units, get more control and increase speed and flexibility, as he admitted turnaround was an uphill task.

As a first step Rose reduced stock commitments in clothing, cut lead times, simplified homeware's products and arranged new terms with suppliers. He conceded that M&S had failed its customers by not understanding their needs, and that more competitive pricing was needed. Hence he promised better range construction:

> We took a scattergun approach to our ranges rather than a rifle.
>
> (*Financial Times*, 10 November 2004)

Even with these aggressive tactics, M&S suffered a poor Christmas with its sixth consecutive quarter of falling sales, resulting in a profit warning. Investors were surprised, but said they would give Rose until December 2005 for recovery. Rose admitted feeling 'under the cosh', but was optimistic that he could deliver growth by 2006–2007, explaining that he had tackled underlying issues, and that the figures were improving.

In late May Rose presented M&S's results, which showed it was still more expensive in clothing and food than the UK average. Market share had been lost throughout clothing, and trading conditions were difficult. Commentators described clothing as 'drab, unappealing and confusing', compared with Per Una's vibrancy. Rose explained that recovery was on track, but there were no quick fixes.

Rose acknowledged there had been little communication with employees, as he had undertaken action without debate. Further, as they received customers' criticism, they had developed a trench mentality. He wanted them to understand M&S, so

implemented a £10m training initiative aimed at creating a 'can-do' attitude.

To complement Rose and Bostock's first collection Twiggy (1960s icon) and Erin O'Connor (supermodel) were used in ad-campaigns, which were well received, and evidenced by improved sales. A slick food ad-campaign, 'This is M&S', was also launched, and Amazon was commissioned to run its Internet operation, as Rose felt it was not up to date with technology, nor had the website been utilised to its full capacity, as it only sold a selection of items.

The 'R' word

In mid October, M&S reported its first sales increase since 2003. Analysts were pleased as this was in response to Rose's collection. The clothes were heralded as practical, stylish, with customer-friendly designer influences, and because new clothing was introduced fortnightly customers increasingly returned. Rose had also created a value range, and established a fabric pool for 'seasonal must haves'. A new pricing strategy was operationalised based on tiers: 'good', 'better', 'best', to indicate value and quality. The news made the shares rise above the psychological 400p barrier.

By November M&S's shares hit a six-year high at 428p after presenting increased profits:

> the changes are not rocket science or new to the industry . . . [but are] quite novel for M&S. This is the first sustained improvement in product and style of clothes for a long time . . . I'm not claiming perfection but we are beginning to deliver what customers want.
>
> (*Financial Times*, 9 November 2005)

Press headlines included 'Say it cautiously . . . M&S is on the up', praising Rose for 'achieving a turnaround in the worst consumer downturn for 15 years'. Yet Rose remained cautious:

> Let's put this into perspective. This is a fine business that needs some work on it. I think we're halfway there. I'm not going to say the 'R' word yet. We do need further work but we're on the right track.
>
> (*Observer*, 13 November 2005)

By late December the shares had risen to $504\frac{1}{4}$p, the highest price since 1998. The press heralded this as vindication for rejecting Green's offer. However, some commentators felt Rose had not delivered respectable sales growth.

Although Christmas 2005 trading was poor across the industry, M&S achieved its first underlying growth in clothing for more than two years. However, Rose was wary, explaining that it was not a rebound of fortunes. By February M&S was outperforming a falling market. Analysts were impressed, and deemed it a full recovery as M&S grew its market share in clothing, and was one of the best performers in the FTSE 100. This was predominantly credited to a refurbishment, rapid clothing turnover to match fashion trends, lowering of, and structure for, prices, and interesting ad-campaigns. By April 2006 M&S had delivered growth in clothing, home and food, which pleased investors as it followed the news that Next's sales had been hit by M&S's revival.

Rose issued bonuses to thank staff for their commitment. He admitted he was six months ahead in his three-year plan and felt M&S's position had stabilised. Shares were priced at 586p, and customers had reached 15 million per week. Yet Rose warned there was more to do before he would hang the recovery tag on M&S:

> we are pleased with the progress . . . but there remains much to do . . . I like to over-deliver and under-promise and recovery is a big word. Ask me in January 2007 and I'll probably be happy to use the R-word if we're still making progress. . . . It's like going into a garden that's not been tended for five years . . . you've got to do all the weeding, aerate the soil, re-landscape, plant, and it's not until you sit down a couple of years later you think 'Oh, its looking quite good!' And that's what we're doing, we're gardening.
>
> (*Financial Times*, 12 April 2006)

Analysts remarked that they feared for M&S's competitors, but warned that turning recovery into sustained growth and profitability would depend on Rose's strategic decisions.

APPENDIX 1

Marks & Spencer Group financial record, 2006–1997*

	2006	2005	2004	2003	2002	2001	2000	1999	1998	1997
Profit and loss account (£m)										
Turnover	7,797.7	7,942.3	8,301.5	8,077.2	8,135.4	8,075.7	8,195.5	8,224.0	8,243.3	7,841.9
Operating profit/loss before exceptional operating costs	850.1	709.4	866.0	761.8	643.8	467.0	543.0	600.5	1,050.5	1,700.2
Exceptional operating costs	–	–91.4	–42.1	–43.9	–	–26.5	–72.0	–88.5	53.2	–
Total operating profit/loss	850.1	618.0	823.9	717.9	643.8	440.5	471.0	512.0	1,103.7	1,037.9
Profit/loss on sale of property/fixed assets	–5.7	–0.4	18.7	1.6	41.2	–83.2	–22.3	6.2	–2.8	–1.8
Provision for loss on operations to be discontinued	–	–	–	–	–	224.0	–	–	–	–
Profit/loss on sale/termination of operations	2.5	218.6	–	–1.5	–366.7	–	–	–	–	–
Net interest (expense)/payable	–104.4	–102.3	–45.8	–40.5	17.6	13.9	14.2	27.9	54.1	65.9
Other charges/income	–	11.4	–15.2	–	–	–	–	–	–	–
Profit/loss on ordinary activities before taxation	742.5	745.3	781.6	677.5	335.9	145.5	417.2	546.1	1,155.0	1,102.0
Taxation	–225.1	–158.3	–229.3	–197.4	–182.5	–142.7	–158.2	–176.1	–338.7	–346.1
Profit/loss on ordinary activities after taxation	520.6	587.0	552.3	480.1	153.4	2.8	259.3	370.0	816.3	755.9
Minority interests	–	–	–	0.4	–0.4	–1.5	–0.6	2.1	–0.4	–1.3
Dividends	–204.1	–203.3	–263.2	–246.0	–238.9	–258.3	–258.6	–413.3	–409.1	–368.6
Retained profit/loss for the year	313.3	383.7	289.1	234.5	–85.9	–257.0	0.1	–41.2	406.8	386.0
Balance sheet (£m)										
Fixed assets	4,068.4	3,447.5	3,507.6	3,466.6	3,431.5	4,177.2	4,298.4	4,448.7	4,034.5	3,646.5
Net current assets	1,142.7	837.5	3,869.5	3,289.1	3,760.7	3,516.2	3,717.1	3,355.9	3,401.5	3,204.2
Short-term creditors	–2,007.8	–1,289.3	–1,884.7	–1,610.2	–1,750.8	–1,981.6	–2,162.8	–2,029.8	–2,345.0	–1,775.1
Long-term creditors	–1,224.2	–1,919.7	–2,519.6	–1,810.0	–2,156.3	–735.1	–804.3	–772.6	–187.2	–495.8
Provisions for liabilities and charges	–28.3	–80.4	–49.3	–228.4	–203.8	–315.7	–126.6	–105.0	–31.0	–31.8
Post-retirement liability	–794.9	–474.2	–469.5	–	–	–	–	–	–	–
Net assets	1,155.3	521.4	2,454.0	3,038.4	3,081.3	4,661.0	4,921.8	4,897.2	4,872.8	4,548.0
Statistics (p)										
Earnings per share	31.4	29.1	24.2	20.7	5.4	0	9.0	13.0	28.6	26.7
Adjusted earnings per share	31.4	21.9	24.7	22.2	16.3	11.4	13.2	15.8	27.3	26.7
Dividends per share	12.3	12.1	11.5	10.5	9.5	9.0	9.0	14.4	14.3	13.0

* M&S altered its accounting practices in 1998, 2004 and 2006.

Source: Annual Report 2006.

APPENDIX 2

Marks & Spencer share price (p), 1999–2006

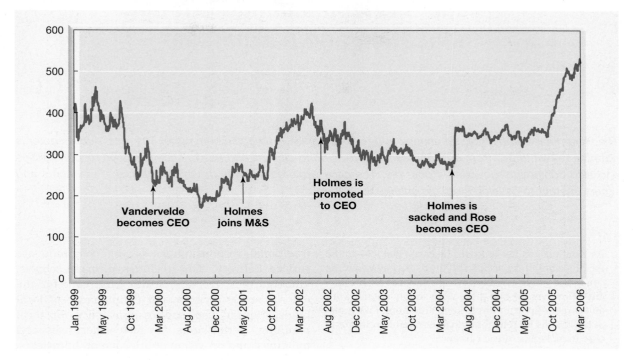

Haram: strategic change through education and partnership

Alex Murdock and Jan Ole Vanebo

The Haram case study looks at change in a relatively small Norwegian commune. The local public sector is not able to 'withdraw' from ensuring service provision to citizens and has to accept certain responsibilities and also constraints on what is possible. The case explores the way in which politicians, managers and others interact to develop strategic change for Haram.

● ● ●

As Knut packed his suitcases he cast a last look to the Islands where his parents still lived. He knew that the commune would provide day care services for his parents. However for him there were simply not the work and career opportunities to keep him there. Like many of his friends he reluctantly had decided to relocate to Oslo to make his future career.

Haram is an area on the coast of Norway. The basic level of local government in Norway is called the commune. Haram Commune has a population of 8,750 (2005) and is one of 36 communes in the county of Møre and Romsdal. The exact location is shown on the maps in the appendix.

In 2007 the commune employed 550 staff with a total budget of some 500m Norwegian krone (≈ €62m). Many of the staff were part time. The traditional responsibilities of the commune are service delivery. This includes primary schools, kindergartens, primary health care, care for the elderly, social security and maintenance of local roads. Haram also had responsibility for local planning, permissions for new enterprises and buildings, and provision of information libraries.

No single political party had a majority in the commune and party politics were perhaps less important at the local than at the national level. There was a higher than average proportion of women politicians in Haram and a general agreement on what were the challenges. The actual political make-up meant the largest party (Senterpartiet) was one that had traditionally represented rural and agricultural interests.

The demographic challenge

However, the commune of Haram faced a demographic challenge. The profile was changing as younger people left the area to seek work or because they preferred the life in the city. Some later returned but the numbers were sadly less than the commune hoped for. There was also a tendency for people with young families to leave once the children were in their teens. The

This case was prepared by Jan Ole Vanebo of Nord-Trøndelag University College and Alex Murdock of London South Bank University. It is intended as a basis of class discussion and not as an illustration of good or bad practice. The authors gratefully acknowledge the valuable assistance of Jan Petter Eide, the Chief Executive of Haram Commune, in the preparation of this case study. © Jan Ole Vanebo and Alex Murdock 2007. Not to be reproduced or quoted without permission.

commune needed more younger people of working age to move into the area.

Though Haram was seen as a good place to live and the local services were well regarded this was not enough to keep or attract younger people there. It was not like the municipalities in the far north of Norway which were able to use various government schemes and tax incentives to persuade people to move in – or stay. In Haram there was simply not sufficient diversity of attractive work and career opportunities for younger people.

Haram also included four large islands and this also was a challenge to public sector management. Communications were difficult and a degree of insularity and fragmentation was part of the lot of public managers and politicians. It was not a stop on the route of the main coastal shipping line – known as 'the hurtigrute' – so the tourism which other coastal areas have developed was not possible for Haram.

The educational challenge

The commune was confronting a mismatch between the future industry demands and the actual skills and education of the local workforce. Haram's adult population had significantly less higher education than the surrounding county. The county average was in turn lower than the Norwegian average (Exhibit 1).

Haram Commune has two shipyards and several manufacturers of maritime equipment. These enterprises are generally owned by big international companies such as Rolls-Royce and Aker RGI. There was a real concern that the traditional skilled work that these employers provided was likely to be outsourced elsewhere and that the future need of these employers was for a more highly educated workforce. The work at home in Norway would move to logistics, design and innovation. This move to a more knowledge-based economy would combine with the change in industrial jobs requiring a more highly educated workforce.

Engagement in local community and business development is not legally required of Haram Commune but it had become a priority policy area due to:

- the concerns about population demographics;
- the need to make the area attractive for younger workers;
- the need to improve the educational level of the workforce.

Confronting the challenge for Haram

What the managers and politicians confronted was not unique to Haram. Urbanisation and the loss of young workers and their families have confronted a number of local government areas in Norway and elsewhere.

The traditional 'public service' model which had served Haram well in the past was seen as an impediment to change. Some felt that Haram had become too 'inward looking'. 'You cannot eat the scenery' was a phrase that had come to have a philosophical ring to it.

There was a recognition that the problem would have to be confronted using different paradigms and finding new solutions. The key issues of outward migration and a potential change in the workforce requirements of the local industry were not amenable to solution through improvements – or even innovations – in public service delivery. Rather the key leaders of the commune would have to develop new ways of thinking. A key element in recognising this was first to accept that they needed to work together to find these new paradigms and solutions.

| Exhibit 1 | Haram Commune – education, 2002 |

	Haram Commune	County	Norway
People aged 16 and over with higher education (%)			
All	13.3	17.3	22.3
Men	13.5	16.5	22.1
Women	13.0	18.2	22.5

The response of Haram – early identification and initial response

In 2007 Jan Petter Eide was the Administrative Director of the commune (equivalent to Chief Executive). He is a long-serving manager having been there for 19 years.

In 1997 he had developed a close working relationship with the two largest maritime employers and developed a common vision with them:

> Haram shall be the leading maritime and industrial commune in Norway.

This led to a publicity campaign to stimulate recruitment of workers to the maritime industries in Haram, which included news coverage on Norwegian TV.

The CEO and many of the commune's political leaders saw that in the future the requirements of the industry sector would change. Some educational initiatives were launched. School pupils and industry managers exchanged visits. The commune and large companies had discussions on how to work together to improve education. This led to some innovations with IT in schools.

In 1999 the commune produced a strategic plan which was the first step in developing a concept of governance to promote community development as well as the provision of statutory services.

The commune had to develop a more strategy-focused organisation. Tougher competition, in terms of retaining inhabitants, recruiting highly skilled employees and more generally to develop economic activities, meant it was necessary to move away from a public service orientation.

The reorganisation of 2003

The CEO needed to replace the traditional public sector hierarchy with a flatter structure and a greater degree of autonomy. This was to enable a more empowered and responsive management team. This led to the new structure shown in Exhibit 2. The commune itself was reorganised on the basis of two levels with 11 autonomous service departments. The management team were internally recruited. Training for the team was commissioned from PricewaterhouseCoopers (PwC), a major consultancy firm. This external intervention fostered an interest in managers for further structured learning.

A university programme would enable the commune managers to develop the new commune plan. The academic team proposed the inclusion of

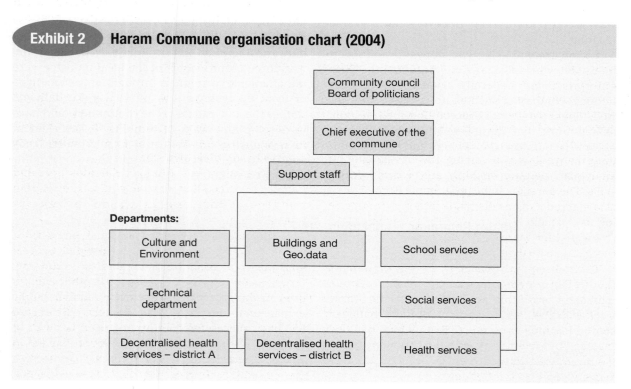

Exhibit 2   Haram Commune organisation chart (2004)

the commune's politicians – a radical innovation! The managers were enthusiastic about the potential synergies. They resolved to dismantle the usual barriers between top managers and politicians and to start to regard themselves as a collectivity. All would join in the search for a solution and it would not simply be a case of the politicians instructing the managers to go and find solutions. Political divisions between the elected representatives were to be buried and inclusivity would be the watchword. The restructuring was just the start of the process.

Change levers which impacted on the process

The reorganisation

The reorganisation was critical because it streamlined the hierarchy and empowered the managers in the new structure. It was associated with new planning and control systems. However, this restructuring in itself would not have been sufficient. Public sector managers are well used to regular reorganisations and there is a tendency to view such things as seasonal rather than as indicative of climate change.

The PwC input

The management training programme instituted with PwC had a critical impact. It was described as a 'Management Training School for Haram' and the fact that it was externally provided by a leading consultancy company was a significant factor which differentiated it from other training inputs. The actual delivery and content were in some respects quite conventional involving the development of analytical, decision-making and communication skills. The duration of the programme (some 2 years) also marked it out as distinctly different from training as normally experienced in the public sector. At the end the managers sought some form of continuation or further development.

The subsequent Master in Public Administration (MPA) programme with the senior commune managers was able to build upon the earlier work with PwC and in particular on the managers' shared learning experience. PwC, which had been involved in earlier work with the commune, joined the programme as a partner and its consultant was actively involved throughout.

The MPA programme

The university developed the Masters programme which was linked to meeting the objectives of the commune and in particular the need to develop the new-generation commune plan. Seminars were organised to involve key stakeholders and especially the politicians. In all five such seminars were held and proved to be a very effective means to foster a greater strategic awareness and commitment to the project. The actual work undertaken by the managers was closely aligned to the needs of the commune to develop a strategic plan for 2006–2016. Therefore the Masters programme was in the nature of a coordinated whole group project.

The political commitment

When the programme started in February 2005 the politicians made a commitment to remain involved in the learning process and to engage actively with managers in developing a strategic vision to work on the new commune plan.

Initially in the commune there had been a degree of scepticism about what was proposed. In particular – given the relatively small size of the commune – views were expressed that it was an inappropriate use of resources. However, when the politicians agreed to become actively engaged with the programme this changed. The local media reported on the strategic initiative and their comments were very positive.

The cascading down of learning and techniques

Managers were encouraged to use the approaches they had learned and were able also to bring these approaches to their own staff.

In particular, the Change Kaleidoscope and Balanced Scorecard were widely utilised by Haram managers to drive through a more strategic approach to their own work units.

In the Balanced Scorecard, the customer service and learning and growth aspects provided a useful and important focus for realigning the commune. Finance and internal processes (the other aspects used in the scorecard) were more familiar public management territory. The Balanced Scorecard has been successfully set up and used in all 12 of the units of the commune. Its adoption has led to a wider appreciation by staff of the need to realign the commune. It has increased the managers' focus on service quality and cost-effectiveness. Many indicators and benchmarks have been accomplished and compared with national data. Consequently, the focus has been targeting a better use of economic and human resources. Also for the managers the focal points have been to develop system-oriented solutions and to work optimally with resources. Through such measures the politicians were made aware of progress and achievement.

Style change and flexibility

Managers commented that an important lever of change was the increasing ability to adopt a range of styles to bring about change.

The involvement of politicians in the process enabled closer and more collaborative working relationships to emerge with a higher level of content in communication. More stakeholders were drawn into the strategic process of the commune – both internal and external. The mantra became:

Strategy is not simply the responsibility of the leader – it is part of everyone's job.

Common ownership and understanding of change

The planning envisaged that each of the commune managers would develop a project for the Masters programme which was linked to a key area for the new commune plan.

The managers and politicians grouped together went through a process of learning about understanding the concepts of strategic positioning, strategic development, implementation and managing strategic change.

Three overseas visits involving both managers and politicians took place – to Birmingham in the UK, Maastricht in Holland and Copenhagen in Denmark. They served as a valuable shared experience for participants of different ways of approaching public sector problems.

Conclusion

The evaluation of the programme showed that the managers had developed a keener sense of strategy. The projects undertaken had created a sense of purpose and urgency in completing the commune plan for 2006–2016.

The CEO of the commune observed:

> It's all about competitiveness and about making a new community in partnership with our main stakeholders who are from business and other organisations in the region and working with universities. In this way we will create an arena to develop competitiveness for the future.
>
> It is also about image and reputation – first of all we do the things which are required of us as a commune but it is important that people can rely on us when we are talking about a good life, a healthy life, We have started some programmes so young people can take their education linked to global business. We have made partnerships with institutions in the UK and in Holland. We are trying to build an education bridge which goes from Haram abroad and hopefully more people will return in the future.

The managers' Masters projects were highly relevant to the development of the commune. Examples included:

- How will the commune economy and the school reform affect the school structure in Haram?
- Haram community as an attractive place to live
- Strategic management in Haram – power base and strategic communication
- Common Assessment Framework (CAF) in Haram – as a tool for quality development
- What kind of strategic challenges is Haram community facing in terms of coordination of resources from public, private and idealistic organisations for use towards physical activity projects among inactive groups of people in the community?
- What kind of strategic challenges is Haram facing in terns of contribution to improved competitive abilities in the region of Ålesund?
- Which factors in Haram are most important for the improvement of regional competitive abilities?
- How should Haram be developed to ensure improved regional competitive abilities?

Looking back on how he might have handled things differently, Jan Petter Eide observed:

> I would have tried even harder – the most important thing for us is to be in some kind of dynamic development.

APPENDIX
Location of Haram in Norway

Haram Commune has a population of 8,750 and is one of the 36 communes in the county of Møre and Romsdal.

RACC's turning point

J. Ignacio Canales and Joaquim Vilà

This case study looks at the development of the strategy process over a 10-year period. The RACC process evolved by fostering managerial participation to achieve strategic goals. However, at the time of the case the strategic development department was puzzled as to whether the coming year's participation could be as helpful as it had been so far.

• • •

Santiago Llaquet had been running the strategy development exercise at RACC (Royal Automobile Club of Catalonia) at regular intervals over the last six years. Although the process had proved successful in the past, the 2006 process seemed to be more complex because it was being carried in a different way from the past.

Traditionally, the strategy development process had taken place once every three years. Previous planning exercises had been carried out promoting wide participation of managers at different levels following a bottom-up approach. The different businesses operated by RACC were stable enough at that time so the managers at different levels had a clear view of the goals which had to be achieved.

Nevertheless, during 2005 market conditions had changed. Competition had increased, forcing RACC to rethink its business model and making the executive committee review the strategic lines of action. A top-down approach had been suggested for the deployment of the strategy-making process. As a result, a broad list of projects, previously defined by the different business units, did not match with the new guiding principles.

It was April 2006 and Santiago Llaquet was preparing the basic recommendations of how the strategy-making process should proceed. The expected launch of the new process was July 2006, just about three months away.

Background

RACC had managed to expand its operations both geographically and financially from 1996 to 2006. Associated members, who in a traditional corporation would account as customers, have grown from 300,000, based only in Catalonia, to over 1,100,000 and spread across Spain. Turnover had grown from €70m to over €470m and employees from 600 to over 1,800.

Founded in 1906 as a sports association in Catalonia, RACC's original core business is similar to that of other automobile clubs, such as the AAA (USA), ANWB (The Netherlands), RAC or AA (UK) and ADAC (Germany). RACC offered a number of services to facilitate the daily use of the vehicle, such as road assistance. RACC had remained circumscribed to Catalonia, a wealthy region of Spain, until 1998, when the company decided to expand to the rest of Spain. Geographical expansion was the focus of the 2000 planning exercise. RACC had been simultaneously growing its service offerings around the car users' mobility concept. Yet, the next step in 2003 became to consolidate its growth by expanding the product offering within household customers. As openly claimed by CEO Josep Mateu, the key reason for this exponential growth and successful expansion had been the strategic planning process and the commitment of RACC people to contribute to the organisation.

This case was prepared by J. Ignacio Canales, Lecturer in Management, University of St Andrews, and Joaquim Vilà, Associate Professor, IESE Business School, Barcelona. It is intended as a basis of class discussion and not as an illustration of good or bad practice.

This commitment had been achieved mainly via a broad participation in the strategy process across the different stages that RACC had been through.

Stage I: 1996–2000

In October 1995, Josep Mateu was appointed as new CEO at RACC. From scratch, he stressed a desire to build a talented professional management team, proactive and well trained in strategic management. Immediately after his arrival he hired a number of top executives from multinational firms. He discarded the existing 1994 Strategic Plan for its lack of realism and practical usefulness, basically due to over-ambitious goals and non-existing measures. In 1997, Mateu and his management team invited a broader group of managers to come up with new ideas as a guide to assess what products or services RACC should keep and what should be eliminated. About 50 managers with business area or product line responsibilities participated (RACC had 700 employees and about 80 managers at that time). Opening up participation to the ranks in project generation proved useful in engaging organisational members in the development stage of strategy, yet as RACC top managers recognised, even more relevant to facilitate carrying out projects and plans in the implementation phase.

Stage II: 2000–2003

In 2000, a new strategic exercise was called for. With the aid of external consultants, the company again carried out a participative process. To start the strategy process, 21 managers from levels 1 (CEO) and 2 (divisional directors), during one month, and in small teams of about five people, first carried out an external analysis focused on assessing the impact of major external factors. The pursued output of this initial step was to develop an ideal for the company, a shared aspiration that was not constrained by the weakness of the company prevailing at that time ('writing a letter to Santa Claus' as some claimed ironically at the beginning). Subsequently, the same teams undertook an internal analysis to insert feasibility into the initial thinking. The result of this activity was the definition of five corporate strategic lines, where geographical expansion to the rest of Spain received the highest priority. Exhibit 1 shows the general approach of the process. The consultants provided guidance on how to put together tools of strategy analysis, organise the discussion within focus groups and make recommendations, which subsequently led to the adoption of a corporate Balanced Scorecard.

Then, 50 people from levels 1 to 4 (top and middle managers) developed the external and internal analysis at the level of each business unit. This analysis generated about 40 projects across business units. The executive committee, including the CEO and five top managers, was highly involved in the supervision of the process, and regularly met to judge the alignment of projects with corporate strategic lines. By late 2000, resource allocation to the different projects and plans took place. The emphasis on strategy implementation, throughout the years 2001–2002, was given to geographical expansion, which was deemed successful by early 2003.

Stage III: 2003–2006

In 2003, a strategic exercise was scheduled to tackle the issue of how to capitalise on the successful expansion. This time, even more of a specific emphasis was given to middle management participation. The first step was an assessment of the previous 2001–2003 strategic planning exercise, carried out by 25 people across the business units and support services. A hundred participants from levels 1 to 5 carried out the external analysis and derived an ideal for the company as a whole. Subsequently they focused on the internal analysis, to progress towards a feasible RACC corporate strategy. The strategic planning department carried out the internal organising of groups, timetables and group tutors over a three-month period. The executive committee, using the outcome of the external and internal analysis, devised the corporate strategy. The key organisational purpose was to balance two major objectives: first, consolidation of the successful geographic expansion; and second, the increase of customer loyalty. The new strategic line, to generate and develop loyalty from customers, received most attention in the steps of the process to come.

Next, each business unit was made responsible for developing new projects to achieve the corporate strategy. To do this they had to submit these projects to their division head and to the executive committee. By late 2005, RACC employed 1,800

Exhibit 1 Basic approach to strategy analysis in the 2000 Strategic Plan.

External analysis

- Market trends:
  - Current state
    - Opportunities
    - Threats
  - Future situation
    - Opportunities
    - Threats
- Supply analysis:
  - Best practices
  - Benchmarking
- Demand analysis:
  - Segmentation
  - Needs
  - Expectations
- Analysis of suppliers
  - Opportunities
  - Threats

- Opportunities and threats
- Strategic issues
- Key success factors
- Core competences 2003

Ideal strategy

Internal analysis

- Analysis of strengths and weaknesses in the operating model:
  - Processes
  - Structuring
  - Organisation
  - People
  - Technology
  - Financial resources
  - Alliances

- Position with respect to core competences and SWOT
- Strategic Alternatives
- Assessment of possible strategies
- Strategic choice

Possible strategy

- Mission
- Vision
- Goals
- Tactics
- Indicators

Source: Internal documents provided by RACC.

people, had a base of almost 1,100,000 members and revenues about €470m.

The turning point

However, during 2005 market conditions had changed. Increased competition had forced RACC to rethink its business model. Accordingly, these changing market conditions led the executive committee to review the current strategic lines of action. Business units had not expected significant change in strategic lines, when the process started by the end of 2005. This led business units and areas to propose projects and strategic initiatives. Besides, the business units and areas felt they had a strong understanding of the strategic analysis tools they had been using over the last six years. It

was April 2006 and Santiago Llaquet was preparing the basic recommendations on how the strategy-making process should proceed. The new process had to be launched in July 2006, just about three months away. A top-down approach had been suggested to him for the deployment of the strategy-making process, but how to run the process this time was puzzling him:

- On the one hand, a participative process had been previously carried out with each business unit having presented a list of projects.
- On the other hand, the executive committee had redefined the strategic lines of action, meaning that many of the projects previously defined by the business units would not be accepted.

What should he recommend?

Consulting in MacFarlane Solutions

Seonaidh McDonald

A small personally controlled company calls in a strategy consultant from a local business school. The consultant plans a series of strategy workshops based on scenario planning. After what seems like a successful initial workshop, the relationship is terminated and the consultant is left wondering why.

● ● ●

Twenty-seven years ago Bill MacFarlane left his job as an engineer in a major oil company to set up his own business. He saw an opportunity to set up a flexible, high-tech manufacturing facility which could produce and customise some of the very specialist components needed in the oil industry much more quickly than the larger manufacturers. He began by producing small batches of high-specification parts for firms with drilling operations in the North Sea. Today, MacFarlane Solutions is an established firm with around 100 employees and a management team of nine. Like all companies in this sector, MacFarlane Solutions has suffered from the cyclical boom and bust of the oil industry. However, Bill's perpetual innovation and foresight in investing in new production technology and researching new materials have meant that his firm has been able to continue to secure orders from customers. More recently, his timely diversifications into specialist training and consultancy services have created new income streams which have helped the company survive leaner times.

Bill's approach to strategy is strongly grounded in his own expertise as an engineer. He is passionate about new technology and is a personal authority on both production processes and materials science. He also has nearly 40 years of experience in the oil industry and knows its limitations and opportunities well. His ideas for new products, services and processes all spring from this knowledge base. He is driven by the challenge of producing remedies for specific technical problems or overcoming limitations in current practice:

we are like the AA[1] of the industry. People bring us their problems because we have a certain reputation for tackling anything, for delivering. I tell our customers, 'if my lot can't sort it out for you, it can't be done'.

The same strong leadership and intuitive strategy making that have for so long made MacFarlane Solutions a success now pose a major challenge: Bill is preparing to retire in 2 years' time. He has already decided which one of the managers will replace him as CEO. Although he has people on his management team who have expertise in all of the technical and management functions of the business, there is no one in the company who has any experience of making strategy. Bill decides that to prepare the company for his departure he is going to have to involve more people in making strategy. He believes that in order to do this, he will have to employ a more explicit and formal process than he has been used to.

With this in mind, he calls the local university business school and asks a professor he met at a Chamber of Commerce meeting to recommend someone who could help. The professor recommends a colleague, Dr Jane Robertson, who has done strategy research in a number of companies in the past. Bill calls Jane and invites her to meet with him at MacFarlane Solutions. Over a couple of meetings, Bill explains his situation to Jane and

---

[1] This stands for the Automobile Association. The AA is the UK's original roadside assistance service for motorists who have broken down. The AAA is the US equivalent.

Glossary

Acceptability is concerned with the expected performance outcomes of a strategy and the extent to which these meet the expectations of stakeholders (p. 368)

An **acquisition** is where an organisation takes ownership of another organisation (p. 357)

Backward integration is development into activities concerned with the inputs into the company's current business (p. 265)

Balanced scorecards combine both qualitative and quantitative measures, acknowledge the expectations of different stakeholders and relate an assessment of performance to choice of strategy (p. 451)

Barriers to entry are factors that need to be overcome by new entrants if they are to compete successfully (p. 61)

Black holes are subsidiaries located in countries that are crucial for competitive success but with low-level resources or capabilities (p. 316)

A **business case** provides the data and argument in support of a particular strategy proposal, for example investment in new equipment (p. 581)

Business-level strategy is about how to compete successfully in particular markets (p. 7)

A **business model** describes the structure of product, service and information flows and the roles of the participating parties (p. 329, 485)

Buyers are the organisation's immediate customers, not necessarily the ultimate consumers (p. 62)

A **cash cow** is a business unit with a high market share in a mature market (p. 279)

A **change agent** is the individual or group that effects strategic change in an organisation (p. 527)

Coercion is the imposition of change or the issuing of edicts about change (p. 531)

Competences are the skills and abilities by which resources are deployed effectively through an organisation's activities and processes (p. 96)

Competitive rivals are organisations with similar products and services aimed at the same customer group (p. 64)

Competitive strategy is concerned with the basis on which a business unit might achieve competitive advantage in its market (p. 224)

Complementors are products or services for which customers are prepared to pay more if together than if they stand alone (p. 67)

An organisation's **configuration** consists of the structures, processes and relationships through which the organisation operates (p. 434)

Consolidation is where organisations focus defensively on their current markets with current products (p. 260)

Contributors are subsidiaries of international businesses with valuable internal resources but located in countries of lesser strategic significance, which none the less play key roles in a multinational organisation's competitive success (p. 316)

Convergence is where previously separate industries begin to overlap in terms of activities, technologies, products and customers (p. 67)

Core competences are the skills and abilities by which resources are deployed through an organisation's activities and processes such as to achieve competitive advantage in ways that others cannot imitate or obtain (p. 97)

Core values are the underlying principles that guide an organisation's strategy (p. 163)

Corporate governance is concerned with the structures and systems of control by which managers are held accountable to those who have a legitimate stake in an organisation (p. 133)

Corporate-level strategy is concerned with the overall purpose and scope of an organisation and how value will be added to the different parts (business units) of the organisation (p. 7)

The **corporate parent** refers to the levels of management above that of the business units, and therefore without direct interaction with buyers and competitors (p. 256)

Corporate social responsibility is concerned with the ways in which an organisation exceeds its minimum obligations to stakeholders specified through regulation (p. 146)

Critical success factors (CSFs) are those product features that are particularly valued by a group of customers and, therefore, where the organisation must excel to outperform competition (p. 79)

A **cultural explanation of strategy development** is that it occurs as the outcome of the taken-for-granted assumptions and behaviours in organisations (p. 416)

The **cultural web** shows the behavioural, physical and symbolic manifestations of a culture that inform and are informed by the taken-for-granted assumptions, or paradigm (p. 197)

Data mining is the process of finding trends, patterns and connections in data in order to inform and improve competitive performance (p. 484)

The **design lens** views strategy development as a logical process in which the forces and constraints on the organisation are analysed and evaluated analytically to establish clear strategic direction and a basis for the planned implementation of strategy (p. 30)

Devolution concerns the extent to which the centre of an organisation delegates decision making to units and managers lower down in the hierarchy (p. 455)

A **differentiation strategy** seeks to provide products or services that offer benefits that are different from those of competitors and that are widely valued by buyers (p. 229)

Diffusion is the process by which innovations spread amongst users, varying in pace and extent (p. 331)

Direct supervision is the direct control of strategic decisions by one or a few individuals (p. 447)

Direction is the use of personal managerial authority to establish a clear strategy and how change will occur (p. 531)

The **directional policy matrix** positions SBUs according to (i) how attractive the relevant market is in which they are operating, and (ii) the competitive strength of the SBU in that market (p. 280)

A **disruptive innovation** creates substantial growth by offering a new performance trajectory that, even if initially inferior to the performance of existing technologies, has the potential to become markedly superior (p. 338)

Diversification is defined as a strategy that takes an organisation away from both its existing markets and its existing products (p. 262)

Dogs are business units with a low share in static or declining markets (p. 279)

A **dominant strategy** is one that outperforms other strategies whatever rivals choose (p. 244)

Dynamic capabilities are an organisation's abilities to renew and recreate its strategic capabilities to meet the needs of a changing environment (p. 107)

Education as a style of managing change involves the explanation of the reasons for and means of strategic change (p. 530)

Emergent strategy comes about through everyday routines, activities and processes in organisations leading to decisions that become the long-term direction of an organisation (p. 408)

The **experience lens** views strategy development as the outcome of individual and collective experience of individuals and their taken-for-granted assumptions (p. 33)

A **failure strategy** is one that does not provide perceived value for money in terms of product features, price or both (p. 231)

Feasibility is concerned with whether an organisation has the capabilities to deliver a strategy (p. 380)

In the **financial control** style, the role of the centre is confined to setting financial targets, allocating resources, appraising performance and intervening to avert or correct poor performance (p. 457)

A **first-mover advantage** exists where an organisation is better off than its competitors as a result of being first to market with a new product, process or service (p. 336)

The **five forces framework** helps identify the attractiveness of an industry or sector in terms of competitive forces (p. 59)

A **focused differentiation** strategy seeks to provide high perceived product/service benefits justifying a substantial price premium, usually to a selected market segment (niche) (p. 230)

A **forcefield analysis** provides a view of change problems that need to be tackled, by identifying forces for and against change (p. 526)

Forward integration is development into activities which are concerned with a company's outputs (p. 266)

A **functional structure** is based on the primary activities that have to be undertaken by an organisation such as production, finance and accounting, marketing, human resources and research and development (p. 436)

Game theory is concerned with the interrelationships between the competitive moves of a set of competitors (p. 241)

The **global–local dilemma** relates to the extent to which products and services may be standardised across national boundaries or need to be adapted to meet the requirements of specific national markets (p. 304)

Global sourcing: purchasing services and components from the most appropriate suppliers around the world regardless of their location (p. 302)

Horizontal integration is development into activities which are complementary to present activities (p. 266)

A **hybrid strategy** seeks simultaneously to achieve differentiation and a price lower than that of competitors (p. 230)

Hypercompetition occurs where the frequency, boldness and aggressiveness of dynamic movements by competitors accelerate to create a condition of constant disequilibrium and change (p. 71)

Hypothesis testing is a methodology used particularly in strategy projects for setting priorities in investigating issues and options (p. 579)

The **ideas lens** sees strategy as emergent from the ideas that bubble up from the variety and diversity in and around organisations (p. 36)

Implementers are subsidiaries of international businesses that simply execute strategies developed elsewhere and may generate surplus financial resources to help fund initiatives elsewhere (p. 316)

An **industry** is a group of firms producing the same principal product or service (p. 59)

Innovation involves the conversion of new knowledge into a new product, process or service and the putting of this new product, process or service into use, either via the marketplace or by other processes of delivery (p. 325)

Intangible resources are non-physical assets such as information, reputation and knowledge (p. 95)

Intended strategy is an expression of a desired strategy as deliberately formulated or planned by managers (p. 401)

Intervention is the coordination of and authority over processes of change by a change agent who delegates elements of the change process (p. 531)

The **key drivers for change** are environmental factors that are likely to have a high impact on the success or failure of strategy (p. 56)

Key value and cost drivers are the factors that have most influence on the cash generation cabability of an organisation (p. 491)

Leadership is the process of influencing an organisation (or group within an organisation) in its efforts towards achieving an aim or goal (p. 527)

The **learning organisation** is capable of continual regeneration from the variety of knowledge, experience and skills of individuals within a culture which encourages mutual questioning and challenge around a shared purpose or vision (p. 421)

Legitimacy is concerned with meeting the expectations within an organisational field in terms of assumptions, behaviours and strategies (p. 192)

Logical incrementalism is the deliberate development of strategy by experimentation and learning from partial commitments (p. 408)

A **low-price strategy** seeks to achieve a lower price than competitors whilst trying to maintain similar perceived product or service benefits to those offered by competitors (p. 227)

Managing for value is concerned with maximising the long-term cash-generating capability of an organisation (p. 490)

Market development is where existing products are offered in new markets (p. 261)

Market penetration is where an organisation gains market share (p. 258)

Market processes involve some formalised system of 'contracting' for resources (p. 453)

A **market segment** is a group of customers who have similar needs that are different from customer needs in other parts of the market (p. 77)

A **matrix structure** is a combination of structures which could take the form of product and geographical divisions or functional and divisional structures operating in tandem (p. 440)

A **merger** is a mutually agreed decision for joint ownership between organisations (p. 357)

A **mission statement** aims to provide employees and stakeholders with clarity about the overall purpose and *raison d'être* of the organisation. (p. 164)

A **multidivisional structure** is built up of separate divisions on the basis of products, services or geographical areas (p. 438)

A **'no frills' strategy** combines a low price, low perceived product/service benefits and a focus on a price-sensitive market segment (p. 227)

Objectives are statements of specific outcomes that are to be achieved (p. 164)

Operational strategies are concerned with how the component parts of an organisation deliver effectively the corporate- and business-level strategies in terms of resources, processes and people (p. 8)

Organic development is where strategies are developed by building on and developing an organisation's own capabilities (p. 357)

Organisational culture is the 'basic *assumptions and beliefs* that are shared by members of an organisation, that operate unconsciously and define in a basic taken-for-granted fashion an organisation's view of itself and its environment' (p. 189)

Organisational knowledge is the collective experience accumulated through systems, routines and activities of sharing across the organisation (p. 107)

An **organisational field** is a community of organisations that interact more frequently with one another than with those outside the field and that have developed a shared meaning system (p. 192)

A **paradigm** is the set of assumptions held relatively in common and taken for granted in an organisation (p. 195)

The **parental developer** is a corporate parent seeking to employ its own competences as a parent to add value to its businesses and build parenting skills that are appropriate for its portfolio of business units (p. 276)

Participation in the change process is the involvement of those who will be affected by strategic change in the change agenda (p. 530)

Path dependency is where early events and decisions establish policy paths that have lasting effects on subsequent events and decisions (p. 185)

Performance targets relate to the *outputs* of an organisation (or part of an organisation), such as product quality, prices or profit (p. 450)

The **PESTEL framework** categorises environmental influences into six main types: political, economic, social, technological, environmental and legal (p. 55)

Planning processes plan and control the allocation of resources and monitor their utilisation (p. 447)

The **political view** of strategy development is that strategies develop as the outcome of processes of bargaining and negotiation among powerful internal or external interest groups (or stake-holders) (p. 414)

Porter's Diamond suggests that there are inherent reasons why some nations are more competitive than others, and why some industries within nations are more competitive than others (p. 300)

A **portfolio manager** is a corporate parent acting as an agent on behalf of financial markets and shareholders (p. 274)

Power is the ability of individuals or groups to persuade, induce or coerce others into following certain courses of action (p. 160)

Primary activities are directly concerned with the creation or delivery of a product or service (p. 110)

Product development is where organisations deliver modified or new products to existing markets (p. 267)

Profit pools refer to the different levels of profit available at different parts of the value network (p. 113)

A **project-based structure** is one where teams are created, undertake the work and are then dissolved (p. 443)

A **question mark** (or problem child) is a business unit in a growing market, but without a high market share (p. 278)

Realised strategy: the strategy actually being followed by an organisation in practice (p. 430)

A **recipe** is a set of assumptions, norms and routines held in common within an organisational field about organisational purposes and a 'shared wisdom' on how to manage organisations (p. 192)

Related diversification is corporate development beyond current products and markets, but within the capabilities or value network of the organisation (p. 265)

The **resource allocation process** (RAP) explanation of strategy development is that realised strategies emerge as a result of the way resources are allocated in organisations (p. 411)

The **resource-based view** of strategy: the competitive advantage and superior performance of an

organisation is explained by the distinctiveness of its capabilities (p. 94)

Resourcing strategies is concerned with the two-way relationship between overall business strategies and strategies in separate resource areas such as people, information, finance and technology (p. 475)

Returns are the benefits which stakeholders are expected to receive from a strategy (p. 368)

Risk concerns the probability and consequences of the failure of a strategy (p. 387)

Rituals are activities or events that emphasise, highlight or reinforce what is especially important in a culture (p. 198)

Routines are 'the way we do things around here' on a day-to-day basis (p. 198)

Scenarios are detailed and plausible views of how the business environment of an organisation might develop in the future based on key drivers for change about which there is a high level of uncertainty (p. 57)

Social entrepreneurship involves individuals and groups who create independent organisations to mobilise ideas and resources to address social problems, typically earning revenues but on a not-for-profit basis (p. 346)

A **stage–gate process** is a structured review process to assess progress on meeting product performance characteristics during the development process and ensuring that they are matched with market data (p. 505)

Staged international expansion: firms initially use entry modes that allow them to maximise knowledge acquisition whilst minimising the exposure of their assets (p. 311)

Stakeholder mapping identifies stakeholder expectations and power and helps in understanding political priorities (p. 156)

Stakeholders are those individuals or groups who depend on an organisation to fulfil their own goals and on whom, in turn, the organisation depends (p. 134)

A **star** is a business unit which has a high market share in a growing market (p. 278)

A **strategic alliance** is where two or more organisations share resources and activities to pursue a strategy (p. 360)

A **strategic business unit** is a part of an organisation for which there is a distinct external market for goods or services that is different from another SBU (p. 7, 223)

Strategic capability is the resources and competences of an organisation needed for it to survive and prosper (p. 95)

Strategic choices involve understanding the underlying bases for future strategy at both the business unit and corporate levels and the options for developing strategy in terms of both the directions and methods of development (p. 14)

The **strategic control** style is concerned with shaping the *behaviour* in business units and with shaping the *context* within which managers are operating (p. 458)

The **strategic customer** is the person(s) at whom the strategy is primarily addressed because they have the most influence over which goods or services are purchased (p. 78)

Strategic drift is the tendency for strategies to develop incrementally on the basis of historical and cultural influences but fail to keep pace with a changing environment (p. 179)

A **strategic gap** is an opportunity in the competitive environment that is not being fully exploited by competitors (p. 81)

Strategic groups are organisations within an industry with similar strategic characteristics, following similar strategies or competing on similar bases (p. 73)

Strategic issue selling is the process of winning the attention and support of top management and other important stakeholders for strategic issues (p. 571)

Strategic leaders (in the context of international strategy) are subsidiaries that not only hold valuable resources and capabilities but are also located in countries that are crucial for competitive success (p. 316)

Strategic lock-in is where an organisation achieves a proprietary position in its industry; it becomes an industry standard (p. 235)

Strategic management includes understanding *the strategic position* of an organisation, *strategic choices* for the future and organising *strategy in action* (p. 12)

A **strategic method** is the *means* by which a strategy can be pursued (p. 356)

A **strategic plan** provides the data and argument in support of a particular strategy for the whole organisation, over a substantial period of time (p. 581)

Strategic planners, sometimes known as corporate development managers or similar, are managers with a formal responsibility for contributing to the strategy process (p. 561)

Strategic planning may take the form of systematised, step-by-step, chronological procedures to develop or coordinate an organisation's strategy (p. 402)

In a **strategic planning style** of control, the relationship between the centre and the business units is one of a parent who is the *master planner* prescribing detailed roles for departments and business units (p. 456)

The **strategic position** is concerned with the impact on strategy of the external environment, an organisation's strategic capability (resources and competences) and the expectations and influence of stakeholders (p. 13)

Strategy is the *direction* and *scope* of an organisation over the *long term*, which achieves *advantage* in a changing *environment* through its configuration of *resources and competences* with the aim of fulfilling *stakeholder expectations* (p. 3)

Strategy as discourse sees strategy development in terms of language as a 'resource' for managers by which strategy is communicated, explained and sustained and through which managers gain influence, power and establish their legitimacy and identity as strategists. (p. 42)

Strategy in action is concerned with ensuring that strategies are working in practice (p. 15)

The **strategy lenses** are four different ways of looking at the issues of strategy development for an organisation (p. 19)

Strategy projects involve teams of people assigned to work on particular strategic issues over a defined period of time (p. 578)

Strategy workshops (sometimes called strategy retreats, away-days or off-sites) usually involve groups of executives working intensively for one or two days, often away from the office, on organisational strategy (p. 576)

Substitutes can reduce demand for a particular 'class' of products as customers switch to the alternatives (p. 62)

Suitability is concerned with whether a strategy addresses the key issues relating to the strategic position of the organisation (p. 366)

Suppliers supply the organisation with what is required to produce the product or service, and include labour and sources of finance (p. 63)

Support activities help to improve the effectiveness or efficiency of primary activities (p. 111)

SWOT summarises the key issues from the business environment and the strategic capability of an organisation that are most likely to impact on strategy development (p. 119)

Symbols are objects, events, acts or people that convey, maintain or create meaning over and above their functional purpose (p. 199; 535)

Synergy refers to the benefits that are gained where activities or assets complement each other so that their combined effect is greater than the sum of the parts (p. 263)

The **synergy manager** is a corporate parent seeking to enhance value across business units by managing synergies across business units (p. 275)

Tangible resources are the physical assets of an organisation such as plant, labour and finance (p. 95)

Threshold capabilities are those capabilities needed for an organisation to meet the necessary requirements to compete in a given market (p. 97)

A **tipping point** is where demand for a product or service suddenly takes off, with explosive growth (p. 334)

A **transnational structure** combines the local responsiveness of the international subsidiary with the coordination advantages found in global product companies (p. 441)

In a **turnaround strategy** the emphasis is on speed of change and rapid cost reduction and/or revenue generation (p. 541)

Unique resources are those resources that critically underpin competitive advantage and that others cannot easily imitate or obtain (p. 97)

Unrelated diversification is the development of products or services beyond the current capabilities and value network (p. 267)

A **value chain** describes the categories of activities within and around an organisation, which together create a product or service (p. 110)

The **value network** is the set of interorganisational links and relationships that are necessary to create a product or service (p. 111)

Vertical integration is backward or forward integration into adjacent activities in the value network (p. 265)

Virtual organisations are held together not through formal structure and physical proximity of people, but by partnership, collaboration and networking (p. 463)

A **vision statement** is concerned with what the organisation aspires to be (p. 164)

Index of Names

General Index

Note: Page numbers in bold refer to definitions in the Glossary.